2013/14

THE GUIDE TO

GRANTS FOR
INDIVIDUALS
IN NEED

THIRTEENTH EDITION

Jude Doherty

Additional research by:
Jonny Morris & Lucy Lernelius-Tonks

Contributions from:
Ashley Wood

DIRECTORY OF SOCIAL CHANGE

D0300494

Published by the Directory of Social Change (registered Charity no. 80051)

Head office: 24 Stephenson Way, London NW1 2DP

Northern office: Federation House, Hope Street, Liverpool
L1 9BW
Tel: 08450 77 77 07

Visit www.dsc.org.uk to find out more about our books, subscription funding websites and training events. You can also sign up for e-newsletters so that you're always the first to hear about what's new.

The publisher welcomes suggestions and comments that will help to inform and improve future versions of this and all of our titles. Please give us your feedback by emailing publications@dsc.org.uk.

It should be understood that this publication is intended for guidance only and is not a substitute for professional or legal advice. No responsibility for loss occasioned as a result of any person acting or refraining from acting can be accepted by the authors or publisher.

First published 1987
Second edition 1990
Third edition 1992
Fourth edition 1994
Fifth edition 1996
Sixth edition 1998
Seventh edition 2000
Eighth edition 2002
Ninth edition 2004
Tenth edition 2006
Eleventh edition 2009
Twelfth edition 2011
Thirteenth edition 2013

ISBN 978 1 906294 67 0

British Library Cataloguing in Publication Data
A catalogue record for this book is available from the British Library

Cover and text design by Kate Bass
Typeset by Marlinzo Services, Frome
Printed and bound by Page Bros, Norwich

Contents

Foreword

R. L. Glasspool Charity Trust has been assisting people across the UK for over 70 years. We are one of the very few non-restricted individual grant-givers, meaning that the potential for us to be used as a 'back-stop' for those seeking financial support is massive. We only accept applications from approved referral agencies as a package of support and not from individuals directly.

We have been listed in DSC's *The Guide to Grants for Individuals in Need* for more than 15 years. We have found the Guide invaluable as it enables us to receive appropriate and cost-effective referrals from support workers. The scale and range of local and national charities and benevolent societies that provide financial assistance to individuals is captured brilliantly within the guide in an easy-to-use and logical format.

We constantly use the guide to signpost support workers to other complementary funds that may be able to assist where our limited resources are either inappropriate or insufficient on their own to provide the financial assistance required. By doing so we increase the impact we are able to make.

The charity sector is facing challenging times with reduced statutory funding available and benefits cuts facing many of the most vulnerable people in the UK which will only increase the demands upon us. This DSC guide is a cost-effective tool available to help us to meet these challenges.

Jason Tetley
Chief Executive, Glasspool Charity Trust

Introduction

Welcome to the thirteenth edition of *The Guide to Grants for Individuals in Need*. The main focus of the book is to list sources of non-statutory help for people in financial need. This edition details 2,043 trusts with £269 million available in grant awards, compared to 1,400 trusts giving £66 million in the first edition (1987).

Grants made by charities in this guide range from £10 food vouchers to larger contributions including grants for domestic items such as washing machines, wheelchairs and house adaptations, although few will cover the whole cost of these. This kind of help does not overcome long-term financial problems, but it can be extremely valuable in helping to meet immediate needs which the state does not currently cover.

This introduction looks at the trusts included in this guide and how to locate them, before discussing what help is available from them and how the trusts can improve their roles. It looks briefly at other funding sources for individuals, highlighting the need to explore all statutory sources available as well as surveying the relevant reforms in this area. Ashley Wood, formerly of the Gaddum Centre, has again provided a helpful section explaining how to make your application once the relevant trusts have been identified; see page xvii. We have also tried to highlight some of the key themes that have emerged from this research process in relation to the impact of the recession on grantmakers and how this may affect those wishing to apply.

About this guide

We aim to include all publicly registered charities (including those in Scotland and Northern Ireland) which give at least £500 a year to individuals in need, although most give considerably more than this.

With a few exceptions, we do not include:

- Organisations which give grants solely for educational purposes
- Organisations which give grants to members only and not to dependents
- Individual employer or company welfare funds
- Friendly Societies
- Local branches of national charities, although they may raise money locally for cases of need
- Organisations only providing services (such as home visiting) rather than cash (or in-kind) grants

Many of the trusts support individuals for educational causes as well. These are all included in the sister guide to this book, *The Guide to Educational Grants*, which includes details for funding opportunities for all forms of education and training up to the end of a first degree, including apprenticeships, personal development and expeditions. Some trusts support organisations such as community groups, others have large financial commitments (often providing housing). The entries in this guide concentrate solely on the trusts' social welfare grants to individuals in need.

How trusts are ordered in this guide

The trusts are separated into six sections: five UK-wide sections followed by a local section, broken down into nine countries/regions. The flow chart on page xvi shows how the guide works.

UK-wide trusts

The majority of the money in this book is given by the UK-wide trusts which are divided into five sections:

1. General charities (page 1)

This section includes charities which operate UK-wide (or at least in more than one country or more than two regions of England) and which are not tied to a particular trade, occupation or disability. These range from those which have very wide objectives, such as 'people in need', 'older people' or 'children and young people', to members of particular ethnic groups. General charities are among the best known and tend to be heavily oversubscribed.

2. Illness and disability charities (page 37)

These charities give grants to people with specific illnesses or disabilities. These trusts can help people (and often their families/carers) who are in financial need as a result of a particular illness or disability. Many of these also give advisory and other support, although for a fuller list of organisations providing these functions please see 'Advice organisations' starting on page 495.

3. Occupational charities (page 59)

This section contains trusts that benefit not only the people who worked in the particular trade but also, in many cases, their widows/widowers and dependent children. Membership or previous membership of the particular institute can be required, but many are open to non-members. Length of service can sometimes be taken into account. Many of these trusts are members of the Association of Charitable Organisations, an umbrella organisation which represents this area of the sector. There are some occupations which have a number of funds covering the industry, and others which have none.

4. Service and ex-service charities (page 135)

This section contains exceptionally thorough charitable provision for people who have served in the forces, whether as a regular or during national service. This funding is different to the other occupational funds as they support a large percentage of the male population over retirement age (many of them would have undertaken national service). Again, these usually also provide for the widows, widowers and dependent children of the core beneficiaries. Many of these funds have local voluntary workers who provide advice and practical help, and who in turn are backed up by professional staff and substantial resources. Soldiers, Sailors, Airmen and Families Association (SSAFA) Forces Help is an influential member of this sector, providing the well-used model, and often the initial contact and application form, for many of the regimental funds.

5. Religious charities (page 157)

This section deals with trusts that support religious workers, such as members of the clergy, missionaries and so on. Often this support extends to dependents of these workers. Support for people connected to particular faiths (Christian, Christian Science and Jewish) are also detailed.

Local charities (page 171)

Included in this section are those trusts which only support individuals in Northern Ireland, Scotland or Wales, or just one region of England. Trusts which are eligible for two of these chapters have generally been given a full entry in one chapter and a cross reference in the other; trusts relevant to three or more of the chapters have generally been included in the national section. Charitable help is unequally distributed across the UK, often with more money available in London and the south east of England than the rest of the UK. However, many of the main cities have at least one large trust able to give over £50,000 a year.

The local section starts with details on how to use this section.

Charities in Northern Ireland

Unfortunately the section for Northern Ireland is very limited, as very little information is available on charities based there at present. Consultation on public benefit and registration guidance began in February 2013 and the Charity Commission for Northern Ireland is expected to start registration in the autumn. There are believed to be between 7,000 and 12,000 charities in Northern Ireland, so we hope the process will be well underway by the time the next edition of this guide is researched. In the meantime, up-to-date information on the progress of registration can be found on the Charity Commission for Northern Ireland's website: www.charitycommissionni.org.uk.

How trusts can help

Some trusts lament the fact that the people whom they wish to support might refuse to accept charity because of a desire to maintain their independence. A charitable trust is public money being held for the benefit of a specific group of people. As such, just as people are encouraged to access any statutory funds they can, they should also be encouraged to accept all charitable money which has been set aside for them.

However, it is not just people who are classified as 'poor' who are eligible for support from trusts. Formerly known as the 'relief of sickness', this charitable purpose was re-defined under the provisions of the Charities Act 2006, and now comes under the purpose, 'the advancement of health or the saving of lives'.

The Charity Commission guidance 'The advancement of health or the saving of lives' broadened the scope of the previous guidance, 'Charities for the Relief of Sickness (CC6)', meaning a wider range of activities became charitable. The following extract is from the Charity Commission guidance:

> The advancement of health includes the prevention or relief of sickness, disease or human suffering, as well as the promotion of health. It includes conventional methods as well as complementary, alternative or holistic methods which are concerned with healing mind, body and spirit in the alleviation of symptoms and the cure of illness.

> The relief of sickness extends beyond the treatment or provision of care, such as a hospital, to the provision of items, services and facilities to ease the suffering or assist the recovery of people who are sick, convalescent, disabled or infirm or to provide comforts for patients.

> The saving of lives includes a range of charitable activity directed towards saving people whose lives are in danger and protecting life and property.

The guidance goes on to provide examples of the sorts of charities and charitable purposes which fall within this description, such as:

- *Charities that provide comforts, items, services and facilities for people who are sick, convalescent, disabled or infirm*
- *Charities that promote activities that have a proven beneficial effect on health*
- *Charities set up to assist the victims of natural disasters or war*

These examples focus mainly on the physical aspect of 'relief' rather than on the financial position of people who are living with an illness or disability. This is not because grants for the advancement of health are not means-tested, but simply because these trusts exist to relieve a physical need rather than a financial one. There are charitable trusts that exist to carry out either or both charitable purposes; they may either deal exclusively with the financial impact that an illness or disability can have on an individual's life or concentrate on the physical aspect of 'relief', or may address both.

Many trusts believe that people should not lose their life savings and standard of living to buy an essential item that they could afford, but would leave them financially vulnerable for the future. Charity Commission guidance differentiates between organisations which attempt to relieve sickness, and organisations for the relief of the sick-poor, which can only support people who are both sick and poor.

Although these are the areas trusts *may* support, it would be wrong to believe that any given trust will support all of these needs. Each trust in this guide has a governing document, stating in which circumstances people can and cannot be supported. As mentioned earlier, we have broken down the trusts in this guide to aid the reader in identifying those which might be of relevance to them, and we would strongly advise that individuals do not approach a trust for which they are not eligible.

Many trusts have complained to us that they receive applications outside their scope which they would like to support but their governing document prevents them from doing so. These applicants have no chance of being supported and only serve to be a drain on valuable resources. Please be aware that it is not the number of trusts you apply to which affects your chance of support but the relevance of them.

What types of help can be given?

Charity Commission guidance

The Charity Commission's guidance, *The Prevention or Relief of Poverty for the Public Benefit*, lists what type of help can be given. (Please note that this list should not be seen as comprehensive.) The list is given as follows:

Examples of ways in which charities might relieve poverty include:

Grants of money in the form of:

- *Weekly allowances for a limited period*
- *Payments to meet a particular need*

- *One-off payments in a crisis or disaster*
- *Payment of travelling expenses for visiting people, for example in a hospital, convalescent home, children's home, prison or other similar place, particularly where more frequent visits are desirable than payments from public funds will allow*
- *Payments to meet expenses associated with visiting people (as mentioned above) for example, child-minding, accommodation, refreshments etc.*
- *Payments to assist in meeting energy and water bills*

The provision of items (either outright or, if expensive but appropriate, on loan), such as:

- *Furniture, bedding, clothing, food, fuel, heating appliances*
- *Washing machines and fridges*
- *Payment for services, such as: essential house decorating; insulation and repairs; laundering; meals on wheels; outings and entertainment; child-minding; telephone line, rates and utilities*
- *The provision of facilities*
- *The supply of tools or books*
- *Payment of fees for instruction, examination or other expenses connected with vocational training, language, literacy, numerical or technical skills*
- *Travelling expenses to help recipients to earn their living*
- *Equipment and funds for recreational pursuits or training intended to bring the quality of life of the beneficiaries to a reasonable standard*

*Charities for the relief of financial hardship might give extra help to people in poverty who are also **sick, convalescent, infirm or with disabilities**, whether physical or mental. This might include:*

Grants of money in the form of:

- *Special payments to relieve sickness or infirmity*
- *Payment of travelling expenses on entering or leaving hospitals, convalescent homes, or similar institutions, or for out-patient consultations*
- *Payment towards the cost of adaptations to the homes of people with disabilities; or*
- *Payment of telephone installation charges and rentals*   *Charity Commission 2008*

One-off grants

Some trusts will only give one-off cash payments. This means that they will award a single lump sum (say £50) which is paid by cheque or postal order either direct to the applicant, to the welfare agency applying on the person's behalf, or to another suitable third party. No more help will be considered until the applicant has submitted a new application, and trusts are usually unwilling to give more than one such grant per person per year.

Recurrent grants

Other trusts will only pay recurrent grants. Recurrent payments or grants in kind are disregarded when entitlement to Income Support and Pension Credit are calculated. Although this is a long-standing principle please be aware that the rules may change with the introduction of Universal Credit, so please seek appropriate advice if in doubt.

Some trusts will give either one-off or recurrent payments according to what is more appropriate for the applicant, although some trusts which give small recurrent payments may also give one-off grants for irregular expenses

Grants in kind

Occasionally grants are given in the form of vouchers or are paid directly to a shop or store in the form of credit to enable the applicant to obtain food, clothing or other prearranged items. Some charities still deliver coal.

More commonly, especially with disability aids or other technical equipment, the charity will either give the equipment itself to the applicant (rather than the money) or loan it free of charge or at a low rental price for as long as the applicant needs it. More common items, such as telephones and televisions, can also be given as equipment because the charity can get better trade terms than the individual.

Statutory funding

Whilst there is a wide range of types of grants that can be given and a variety of reasons why they can be made, there is one area trusts that cannot support. No charitable trust is allowed to provide funds which replace statutory funding. The reason for this is that if a trust gives £100, say, to an individual who could have received those funds from statutory sources, then it is the state rather than the individual who is benefiting from the grant. This point is discussed further below in the context of social fund reform.

The effectiveness of grantmaking trusts

While some trusts, particularly national ones, produce clear guidelines, others (especially local trusts) do not. Based on our experience of researching this publication over the past 20 years, we would like to make some suggestions as to ways in which trusts giving grants to individuals, particularly local trusts, could seek to encourage greater fairness in funding:

▌ Local trusts could seek to expand their resources to meet new or more widespread needs. During 2013 the social fund will be abolished and replaced by localised provision. We would advise trusts to speak to their local authority as well as other local grantmakers in order to define what the local priorities are and see if they can adjust or develop an approach which will ensure that no groups will fall beneath the radar of statutory and voluntary bodies. Charities ought to guard their independence closely and should not unduly compromise on their principles in any collaborative enterprise, but they should also consider what can be gained from cooperation, including the sharing of expertise, and the potential to influence public services and reduce costs. For any trusts considering this route we would recommend the excellent reports produced by

Child Poverty Action Group as a starting point: cpag.org.uk/policy-publications.

▌ If trustees can only meet twice a year, they should aim to cover the peak periods. Although welfare needs arise throughout the year, there are obvious peak times; for example, for fuel needs this is around early winter.

▌ Trusts should also aim to ensure that needs can be met as rapidly as possible; for example by empowering the clerk or a small number of trustees to make payments up to a certain limit (such as £100).

▌ Trusts should ensure that they are very well known in their area of benefit. We recommend that each trust (depending on its eligibility restrictions) writes to at least the following places: all welfare agencies (especially Citizens Advice); all community centres and other public meeting points; and the offices of the relevant education authority.

▌ We would also recommend that trusts consider developing a website. A website is an accessible way of raising awareness of your work as well as outlining key information such as eligibility criteria, meeting dates and types of grants given. The website does not need to be overly technical and can be as simple as one page of text. There are also many free hosting sites such as Weebly (www.weebly.com) and BT Community Web Kit (www.btck.co.uk) which make expense and professional assistance unnecessary.

The Great Giving campaign and Ineligible Applications report

Over the years DSC has campaigned on a number of fronts for better grantmaking. We believe that grantmakers have a responsibility that extends far beyond providing funding. The way in which funders operate has a huge impact on the beneficiaries which their funding supports, as well as on the wider voluntary sector.

Our Great Giving campaign has grown out of these long established beliefs. The campaign encompasses four areas: (1) a clear picture of the funding environment; (2) accessible funding for campaigning; (3) an end to hidden small print; and (4) no ineligible applications.

Although the campaign relates mainly to grantmaking trusts that support organisations, the four principles of the campaign extend to the trusts covered in this guide. We believe that funders have a responsibility to understand the environment in which they are operating. At present there is little information about where money is going and what is being supported. Providing a clearer picture will enable better planning and decision-making from funders and policy makers, as well as contributing to the growing body of knowledge about the sector.

We know that most grantmakers receive more applications for funding than they can award. We also know that a significant proportion of those applications are ineligible. In some cases the fault lies with the information provided by the funder, and in some cases the fault lies with the interpretation of that information by the applicant. In our 2010 report on *Ineligible Applications* we made some recommendations on what grantmakers can do to try and avoid receiving large numbers of ineligible applications:

- Provide comprehensive and accessible information: state what you do and what you want to fund, preferably online if you have a website.
- Ensure your application guidance is clear, concise and as jargon-free as possible: encourage prospective applicants to read it.
- Explain the application procedure clearly: what information will be required, by when and in what form.
- Providing constructive feedback, especially if the application is rejected, this should make it less likely that the applicant submits the same ineligible bid again and again.
- Provide a clear contact point for any queries and instructions on how you prefer to be contacted.
- Keep track of ineligible applications and analyse them periodically to see if there are any patterns. Consider how the information you provide could be changed to reduce their number.

In the current financial climate (which we will touch upon more in the next section) where many grantmakers have experienced a rise in demand for their services, these recommendations are particularly important. Advertising clearly what you do and how you do it, will not only empower individuals to make informed decisions about their applications, it should also limit the number of ineligible applications received and free up vital resources, which will ensure more time can be spent on those individuals the trust exists to support.

Further information on our research into ineligible applications and the Great Giving campaign itself can be found on our website (www.dsc.org.uk/GreatGiving).

The impact of the recession

The recession has become something of a constant in our lives and is now is providing a context for a third time in this biennially published directory. Despite some tentative signs of growth in the tail end of 2012, the UK economy is still fragile. In the meantime unemployment has remained stubbornly high, wages have lagged behind inflation and benefits have been repeatedly slashed.

The research process for this guide has provided an opportunity, through analysis of annual reports and accounts and contact with grantmaking trusts and beneficiaries, to assess how grantmakers are dealing with the changes and the implications that this may have for individuals seeking funding.

Pressures in the funding environment

The last edition of this book noted three concerns for grantmaking charities: rising demand, financial difficulties and cuts to statutory funding. These challenges have not diminished and other challenges have also become apparent. Much has changed in the social welfare environment since the last edition of this guide was published. By the time the twelfth edition had gone to

print the global economic slump was continuing but we had little experience of what the coalition government's policies would entail for this branch of the sector. Now much has changed as policy has become law and law, in turn, has shaped practice.

Numerous pieces of legislation have sent shockwaves through the statutory social security landscape as existing systems were uprooted and new benefits have been installed in their place. 2013 will see seismic shifts in how out-of-work benefits, Housing Benefit and Council Tax Benefit are administered with the introduction of the all-encompassing Universal Credit.

In addition, below-inflation rises for jobseekers, Housing Benefit caps, the abolition of the discretionary elements of the Social Fund and the introduction of means-testing for, and freeze on, Child Benefit means that a real-terms fall in income for many families is on the cards. These transformations have also been awkwardly timed so that they coincide with cuts to advice services which are likely to exacerbate any difficulties. As Citizens Advice warned the select committee of the Department of Communities and Local Government in their written submission on the implementation of the Welfare Reform Act:

We consider that the advent of [Universal Credit], combined with increased recourse to local discretionary and cash-limited provision, will prove to be a major social policy issue in the coming years and a leading source of enquiries to bureaux.
Communities and Local Government 2012

The impact for individuals

The respected independent think-tank, the Institute for Fiscal Studies, has calculated that 2.5 million of 2.8 million workless households of working age will see their income fall by an average of around £215 per year in 2015 and 2016. Some 7 million of 14.1 million households with someone in work will lose up to £165 and this includes 3 million families who only lose out to child benefit freezes at a cost of £75 per year (IFS 2013). These income cuts will fall on those families with already low disposable incomes and thus will take up a larger proportion of their available income.

For many charities the impact of the reforms has been visible on their work already. One charity recognised that an increase in applications for support from November 2011 onwards was in part due to changes to housing benefit:

One support worker told me that her caseload had trebled as a result, so I think we were also seeing a fallout from that. One thing we are also seeing more of than we did two years ago is more people who are simply economically homeless, as opposed to being homeless due to problems with mental illness, substance dependency, etc.
Correspondence with Craig Norman, Charities Manager at St Martin-in-the-Fields (May 2012)

Looking at many of the comments in the annual reports of the charities in this book it appears as though 2010 and 2011 have been record-breaking years: record numbers of applicants, record numbers of grants and record levels of grant expenditure. The trend also appears to be for applications from younger and younger applicants with more complex cases. Older people appear to have been relatively well protected in the current economic storm thanks to the minimum income guaranteed by Pension Credit and the Government's 'triple-lock' pensions policy.

Working-age adults and families have continued to find it tough with the twin spectres of debt and falling incomes looming ever larger. In their 2010/11 accounts the Royal British Legion Women's Section noted an increase in requests for children's welfare grants (RBLWS 2011). Meanwhile, the Unison charity, There For You, noted that 94% of applicants during 2011 were in work, a 4% increase on the previous year; and that priority debts were the single biggest expense after short-term weekly support at £111,000. Applications to the charity for assistance with bankruptcy were up 50% in 2011 with grants totalling £48,000 (There For You 2011). We heard many similar responses in our Grants for Individuals in Need and Education survey with one commenting that in 2010 they had 14 applications for assistance with debt relief orders or bankruptcy deposits, 'whereas we had had no more than five such applications in total between the years 2003 and 2009'.

The R.L. Glasspool Charity Trust also noted a rise in requests for assistance with debt while also reflecting on how further debt is often masked:

> Many of our applicants are in debt but we allocate grants to the category which is the main immediate cause of the need we are meeting. As last year the highest number of grants (608, or 14.2%) went to people with mental health problems. The link between being unemployed/in debt and mental health problems is well documented.
>
> Glasspool Charity Trust 2011

The Veterinary Benevolent Fund has also noted a shift in giving patterns:

> There seems to be a move away from relatively small monthly grants, often to fairly elderly beneficiaries, to providing assistance to relatively younger members of the profession that have enormous health and/or financial problems. These cases often require urgent support and considerable financial input and expenditure may rise significantly in the future.
>
> VBF 2011

Similarly the Chartered Society of Physiotherapy's Members Benevolent Fund has noted the trend:

> [F]or younger members of the society to require assistance, the majority being in their 30's and 40's. The debts incurred by members are greater now with many relying on several credit cards or loans and they are encouraged to seek debt management advice.
>
> MBF 2011

Localisation of the social fund

Perhaps the most significant development since the last edition of this book has been the sweeping reform of the discretionary Social Fund. Responsibility for crisis loans and community care grants passes from the Department of Work and Pensions to local authorities in 2013. Real concerns have been raised as to whether councils will be able to meet demand given that the Social Fund financial package from central government for 2013/14 has been pegged back to 2005/06 levels and, crucially, the money has not been ring-fenced (CPAG 2012). The worry is that local authorities may be inclined to dip into these funds given the financial pressures they are under. Indeed, the scale of the cuts has prompted some local authorities to talk of the abolition rather than reform of the fund in order to 'manage expectations'.

Readers of this guide will find repeated warnings that applicants should approach statutory providers first to try and address their need before applying for charitable assistance. Applicants would be expected by trusts to have already applied for help, whether for a community care grant, disabled facilities grant or something else. Even where not stated this point is implicit: it is one of the primary planks of charity law that it is the individual beneficiary and not the state which should benefit from charitable assistance. However, early studies of the anticipated effects of social fund reforms have indicated that the line over who benefits will become a considerable grey area in the coming months and years as grantmaking trusts pick up the slack of local authorities that are unable or perhaps unwilling to meet local demand in the same way as the previous system had. For some, this will be an extension of practices with which they are already familiar. For example, the Burma Star Association reported that:

> The pressures being put on all service charitable funds continues as local authorities are still attempting to pass their responsibilities for the veterans in the service charities' direction.
>
> BSA 2011

There is also some anecdotal evidence that local authority disabled facilities grants have become increasingly difficult to obtain due to significant delays in processing applications and an increased rate of rejection which is placing further pressure on trusts. Legal and conceptual issues aside, these trusts will simply not be able to conjure funds equal to the sums extracted from the welfare system. For you, the applicant or referral agent, it is likely to mean increased competition at a time when grantmakers' incomes are static or even decreasing (see below). This underlines the need to make clear applications to relevant charities, which we advise on below.

Grantmaking – what the figures tell us

Our headline figures show that between the last edition of this book and this edition the total amount awarded has increased from £264 million to £269 million, despite there being three fewer charitable trusts in this edition. Once inflation is accounted for, however, the amount given suffers a fall in real terms by £12.3 million or around 4.4%. However, there are more encouraging signs if we dig deeper into these figures.

Our headline figures include the grant totals which we were able to obtain from charities' accounts as well as figures which we obtained by other means. This latter category of figures, which account for around one in five trusts, were not available from the Charity Commission, and this is mostly because the charities' incomes or expenditures fell below the threshold at which they were required to submit accounts. For these cases we obtained figures either by speaking directly with trusts or viewing their websites (if available). In the minority of instances in which we could not reach the trusts at all we relied on experience to give a best estimate of their charitable giving based on their income, total expenditure and past performance. In these cases we erred on the side of caution so as to not upwardly misrepresent the amount of grants available. This could have exerted something of a downward pressure on the headline figures.

For the remaining 80% of trusts, for which data was readily available, we were able to directly compare the grant total for each trust in this edition with their total from the previous edition. Here the results are more positive: showing a modest 1% real-terms rise in the grant total between editions of the book. This is to be welcomed given that the total had been falling in previous years.

So, the statistical evidence points to a rise in grantmaking. But only just. It should be asked why this figure was not higher when employment and earnings are down and applications for assistance are up. What else might explain the timid growth?

Firstly, the economy: since the stock market collapse in 2007, charity incomes have fallen, as a report for Elizabeth Finn Care found (Madden 2011). This finding is reinforced by the statistics that we have available for this book, which show a growth in real terms of less than 1% in the incomes of charities. (This is based on 59% of charities included in the book for which we had comparable data for both this and the last edition, with the totals adjusted for inflation.) Charities are also increasingly required to do more with less. The London Voluntary Service Council (2012) found that two thirds of voluntary organisations in London were reporting an increased demand for services, with a similar number reporting a decrease in funding in 2012. Doing more with less has now become business as usual.

Seemingly unconnected policy changes have also had implications for welfare charities. For the many old almshouse charities in this guide which make grants from the disposable balance available after meeting accommodation expenses, the reduction in local authority care grants for residents has left much less to distribute at the end of the month. The removal of VAT relief for work on listed buildings has also meant that small parish charities which divide their expenditure between welfare grants and repairing the Church roof are now spending more on the latter at the expense of individuals.

The quality of information which we are able to work with as researchers has undoubtedly improved in recent years as more trusts have begun to offer more detailed breakdowns of their annual activity in their accounts. The Charity Commission should be lauded for their work in promoting their statement of recommended practice. What this has meant for us is that we have been increasingly able to

retrieve more precise figures for grants to individuals from the accounts immediately rather than having a single, opaque figure for 'support', 'charitable activity' or 'grants', which could include a myriad of services beyond grants, as well as grants to organisations. So our information in turn has become more accurate, which may explain why the grant figure has not grown as much as might have been expected.

Unfortunately, however, some data has remained or become more opaque. For some charities, grantmaking is often lumped in along with a broad sweep of other care services and not distinguished in the accounts. Despite our requests in these instances for a grant total, we were frequently told that this was unavailable. We have continued to improve our listing criteria in this edition, which has meant that where an approximate value may have been listed in previous editions for larger charities we have chosen to list none this time. In the Blind Veterans UK (St Dunstan's) record, for example, we have chosen not to give a figure and instead explained their expenditure in the narrative section of the entry. Blind Veterans had a grant total of around £17 million in the previous edition of this book but it is listed as having no headline grant figure in this edition, nor have we included a figure for our background financial analysis. Omissions of large charities like these will have caused the headline figure to fall for this edition. However, these data collection policies will allow us to get an even clearer picture of the progress trusts are making in future.

The Grants for Individuals in Need and Education survey results

We sent an e-survey to 1,415 of the charities in this book and its sister publication, *The Guide to Educational Grants*, for which we held an email address. Of the 108 respondents we found that:

▪ 20% felt the recession and current economic environment has had little or no impact on their charity.

▪ Of those who have been affected 17% had a noticeable fall in income from investments which has impacted their capacity to help beneficiaries.

▪ Fluctuations in investment returns have also had an indirect impact, as a further 9% had commented that incomes were down from other sources of fundraising.

▪ One charity felt that the economic environment has had a 'substantial impact on fundraising (historically, all [our funds have been sourced] from charitable trusts who have less money to give as a result of the recession)'.

▪ Another respondent suggested that this was also partly due to increased competition for support from trusts and foundations as other charities increasingly turn to grants as other sources of income falter.

These comments correspond with our 2012 survey of major trusts and foundations, which found that less than

9% of trusts were receiving fewer applications in 2011 than in previous years, with around one third receiving more applications (Traynor et al. 2012). Other grantmakers in this volume anticipated increased competition from those who had once relied on government funding (Not Forgotten Association 2012). Meanwhile, benevolent funds have found their fortunes tied to that of the professional group they support, with the Builders' Benevolent Institution warning of the effects of the year-on-year decline in donations they have been experiencing at a time when their beneficiaries need their help more than ever (BBI 2011). Similarly, it will also be worth monitoring the fortunes of the armed forces charities in coming years. While these charities have proved themselves to be adept at raising funds from the public, (see the stellar rise of Help for Heroes, for example; launched in 2007, it had an income of almost £47 million in 2010/11) contributions from serving officers remains an important income stream. Given the defence redundancies proposed, it seems likely that not only will these charities' services be under further pressure but they are more than likely going to have to re-examine their fundraising models.

Almost one fifth of those affected were using their reserves to cope with the extra demand and decreasing income. This appears to be happening on an even larger scale: a 2012 survey of 488 charities carried out by the Charity Finance Group, the Institute of Fundraising and PriceWaterhouseCoopers found that 47% of charities expected to dip into their reserves in the short-term to help them survive (PwC 2012).

The majority of respondents (45%) had around the same number of applications in recent years with 39% noting an increase in applications and 15% noting a decrease. That a large proportion of charities reported an increase in applications is unsurprising given the squeeze on incomes across the UK. What is interesting, however, is the number of trusts noting a fall in the volume of applications as well as those remaining static. Some have reasoned that the fall is a result of cuts to statutory and voluntary advice services. Friends of the Elderly, a substantial grantmaker (giving £387,000 in 2010/11), had this to say in response to our Grants for Individuals in Need and Education survey:

We require applications to be submitted by a third party agency. The recession has reduced the number of such agencies and the staff time to support individuals to make applications. This has impacted negatively on application numbers.

Citizens Advice calculated that from April 2013 some 650,000 people across England and Wales will lose access to civil legal aid (CAB 2012). This will remove funding for cases which tend to have financial implications – from debt to employment to benefits – and part of the assistance given may be to apply for funds, such as those listed here, in order to help a client through a period of hardship. The report notes how around half of Citizens Advice bureaux may not be able to continue to offer advice at all, such is their reliance upon legal aid as an income stream. These cuts come at the same time as the benefit system is being overhauled and on top of steep cuts

from local authorities, which are likely to cause difficulties for readers seeking help from funds which will not accept direct applications but only through third parties. We offer some tips on making applications in our 'Advice for applicants' section below.

How are you reacting to increased demand from applicants?

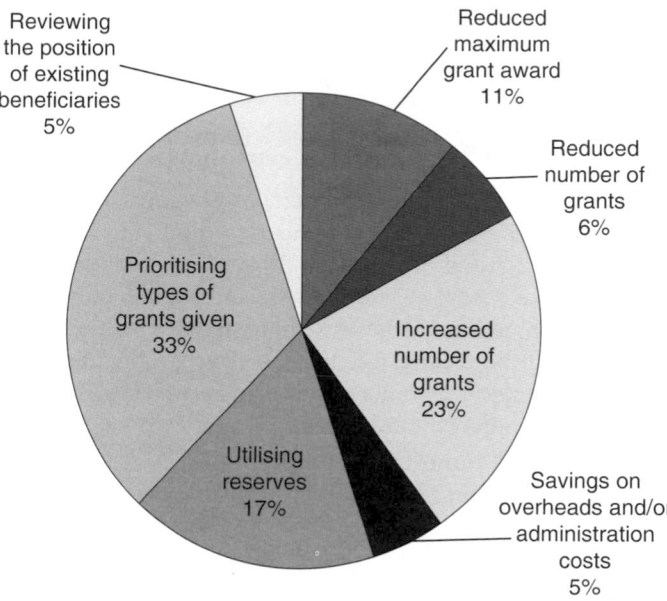

Of the 40 survey respondents who said that they were receiving more applications, 19 of them were pursuing more than one strategy to deal with the increase in applications, as the chart shows. By far the most popular strategy was to prioritise the types of grants given, with one in three opting for this route. Just under one quarter were increasing the number of grants made and, interestingly, four respondents were both prioritising the types of grant given while also increasing the number of grants made. This is suggestive of the real increase in demand for basic, everyday items which respondents also told us about in their comments.

An example of an organisation which has applied stricter criteria while expanding grantmaking is the Stroke Association. It gave 50% more in grants in this edition of the book than the last by doubling the value of available grants from £200 to £400 while also limiting the amount of savings an applicant could hold from £8,000 to £1,000 in order to help those in the severest need (Stroke Association 2012).

Overall, then, while expenditure is up slightly it seems that applications are increasing, but not perhaps by the amount that might have been expected. At a time of sweeping reforms to the welfare system, the increasing strain on advice services may in part explain why applications have not increased across the board and this could pose further problems down the line. One emerging trend has been for charities to increase their service provision or give grants to organisations such as food banks, thereby making scarce resources go further. This may be a model which grows in coming months and years.

Advice for applicants

While there is still a large amount of money available to help applicants, the competition seems likely to remain strong. It is difficult to say how grantmakers will fare in the coming years, but it is unlikely that those who are dipping into reserves can continue to do so indefinitely, and so trusts will be looking to ensure that they are making the maximum possible impact with their grants.

For those individuals applying for funding the same basic principles apply – see page xvii for Ashley Wood's excellent step-by-step guide. However, in the current climate it is worth bearing a few extra things in mind.

- **Check the latest criteria:** Financial pressures and rising applications have led many trusts to tighten up their eligibility criteria or limit the things for which they will give. Make sure that you have the latest guidelines and read them carefully to check that you are eligible to apply and the trust can help with your specific need. If in doubt, a quick phone call is usually welcomed and can save time in the long run.
- **Be open and honest when applying:** Take care to fill in any application form as fully as possible and try to be as clear and open as you can. The same applies if you need to write a letter of application. It will help grantmakers to assess your needs quickly and advise you on any other benefits or potential sources of funding for which you may be eligible.
- **Don't just apply to large, well-known trusts:** They are likely to be the most oversubscribed, leaving you with less chance of success. Take the time to look for others you may also be eligible to apply for.
- **Apply to all appropriate trusts:** Falling average grants may mean that one trust cannot offer enough to cover the full cost of the item or service you need. You may have to consider applying to several trusts and ask for a small contribution from each. If it has not been indicated already for any given trust in this guide whether calls are accepted or not, a quick phone call is usually enough to establish how much a trust is likely to give for an individual grant.
- **Seek advice:** Some applications require a third-party endorsement. With advice services under increasing pressure, you may find an alternative organisation to contact in this guide; these organisations are listed on page 495. Also consider other impartial professionals who may be able to assist with an application form; for example, a school teacher if the application is on behalf of a child or a medical practitioner such as a GP, consultant or therapist if the application is for a medical item or is related to a medical condition. Others who may be able to help include ministers of religion, social workers, local housing associations or probation officers. A quick telephone call to the trust can determine whether they can be flexible regarding who completes the application in exceptional circumstances.

Other sources of support

Whilst there are many situations in which approaching a trust might be the best option, there is, of course, a limit to the support that they can provide, individually or collectively. There are a number of alternative sources of support that should be considered in conjunction with looking at grantmaking trusts (note that these are beyond the scope of this publication).

Statutory sources

There are a lot of funding opportunities available to individuals from the state. The exact details of these sources vary in different countries in the UK, and in some instances among different local authorities. This area is likely to become ever more confusing in the light of further budget cuts and welfare reforms. Consequently, comprehensive details are beyond the scope of this guide.

However, full details should be available from government departments such as benefits agencies and social services, as well as many of the welfare agencies listed, starting on page 495. The government's website (www.gov.uk) and the Department for Work and Pensions' website (www.dwp.gov.uk) also have a wealth of information on what is available and how to apply.

There are a number of advice organisations that may also be able to offer advice and support to people who are unsure of their benefit entitlement or who are looking for extra support in the form of a grant. It may prove useful to visit websites such as Turn2Us (www.turn2us.org.uk) and Benevolence Today (www.benevolencetoday.org), which was a campaign set up by, and for, more than 35 coalition partners across the UK. These websites can offer advice on both statutory and non-statutory sources of funding to charities working on behalf of individuals and to individuals themselves. The Benevolence Today project has now come to an end, but there remains a wealth of useful resources on the website.

Citizens Advice provides an online Adviceguide (www.adviceguide.org.uk) also offers useful information on issues relating to statutory benefits and individual entitlement. Local branches of Citizens Advice can also offer people more assistance in this area.

Disaster appeals

If there has been a large unexpected hardship which is beyond the scope of being relieved from statutory or charitable sources, then one possibility is to establish a disaster appeal. These are commonly established as a public response to a well publicised disaster, such as the London Bombings in July 2005, or the South Yorkshire Floods in 2007, where the public wish to show their support. They can also be established in response to a personal misfortune. The Mark Davies Injured Riders Fund, for instance, was established by the parents of a talented rider killed during the Burghley Horse Trials to support injured riders. Appeals can also be established to aid a particular individual if they have needs which gain high levels of public sympathy and little time to apply for statutory or charitable sources. Disaster Appeals can be to relieve an epidemic rather than an individual case, or to leave a lasting legacy. The Charity Commission leaflet, *CC40 Disaster Appeals*, provides further information.

Companies

Many employers are unhappy to see former members of staff or their dependents living in need or distress. Few have formal arrangements but a letter or telephone call to the personnel manager should establish if help is possible.

Most large companies give charitable grants, although most have a policy of only funding organisations (possibly because charities have more ways of publicising this support than individuals do). Many that will support individuals have their own charitable trusts, and therefore are included in this guide.

There has been a growing trend for many prominent utility companies to establish charitable trusts which give to individuals who are struggling to pay their utility bills. These charitable companies have continued to grow and have for a number of years provided much relief to the individuals involved, lessening the financial burden upon them and ensuring that no legal action will be taken against them for non-payment. There are now nine such trusts in this volume with the addition of the Affinity Water Trust, Npower Energy Fund and South East Water's Helping Hand.

Community foundations

Over recent years, community foundations have established themselves as key community actors. According to UK Community Foundations' website, there are 55 community foundations throughout the UK which distribute around £50 million grants a year and they hold, as at March 2012, £309 million in endowed funds.

Community foundations aim to be cause-neutral and manage funds donated to them by both individuals and organisations, which are then distributed to the local communities in which they serve.

Whilst most community foundations only support organisations, many of them also have funds available for individuals and are therefore included in this guide. The UK Community Foundations website has a complete list and a map of community foundations (see ukcommunityfoundations.org).

Please note that, like most sources of financial support, funding for individuals is subject to frequent change. Even if your local community foundation is included in this guide it is worth checking the availability on your local community foundation website.

Vicars, priests and ministers of religion

There may be informal arrangements within a church, mosque, etc. to help people in need. Church of England vicars are often trustees of local charities which are too small to be included in the guide or which we have missed.

Hospitals

Most hospitals have patient welfare funds, but they are little-known, even within the hospitals and so are not used as frequently as other sources of funds. It may take some time to locate an appropriate contact. Start with the trust fund administrator or the treasurer's department of the health authority.

Local organisations

Rotary Clubs, Lions Clubs, Round Tables and so on are active in welfare provision. Usually they support groups rather than individuals and policies vary in different towns, but some welfare agencies (such as Citizens Advice) have a working relationship with these organisations and keep up-to-date lists of contacts. All enquiries should be made on behalf of the individual by a recognised agency.

Orders

Masonic and buffalo lodges and other organisations exist for the mutual benefit of their members and the wider community. Spouses and children of members (or deceased members) may also benefit, but people unconnected with these orders are unlikely to. Applications should be made to the lodge where the parent or spouse is or was a member.

Hobbies and interests

People with a particular hobby or interest should find out whether this offers any opportunities for funding. Included in this guide are a number of sporting associations which exist to relieve people who are in need, but there may be many more which are not registered with the Charity Commission, or have less than £500 a year to give, but are of great value to the people they can help. It is likely that other sports and interests have similar governing bodies wishing to help their members either through making a donation or organising a fundraising event.

Educational support

This guide only deals with grants for the relief of need, ignoring trusts which can support individuals for educational purposes. However, many educational trusts are prepared to give grants to school children for uniforms, for instance. Receiving financial support for the cost of uniforms would obviously enable parents to spend the money budgeted for that purpose on other needs, so people with children of school age should check for any educational grants available to them. For information on statutory funds, contact your local educational authority or enquire for information at the office of the individual's school. For charitable funding, this guide's sister publication, *The Guide to Educational Grants*, should provide the relevant information.

Charity shops

Some charity shops will provide clothing if the applicant has a letter of referral from a recognised welfare agency.

Getting help

Unfortunately, none of these methods can offer a quick fix. Applying for grants can be a daunting experience, especially if you are unfamiliar with the process; it is probably worth starting with the help of a sympathetic advisor. Most branches of Citizens Advice have money advice workers or volunteers trained in basic money advice work. If you find that you are in financial need try going to the nearest citizens advice bureau and talk to them about your financial difficulties. They may be able to help write an application to an appropriate charity, know of a welfare benefit you could claim or be able to re-negotiate some of your debt repayments on your behalf. They will certainly be able to help you minimise your expenditure and budget effectively.

Acknowledgements

Throughout this introduction, we have commented on the Charity Commission for England and Wales's guidelines and advice. Whilst we are aware that the Charity Commission only has rule over England and Wales, readers in Northern Ireland and Scotland (as well as the Isle of Man and the Channel Islands) should note that although the exact nature of charitable law differs in these countries, the spirit and guidance remains the same throughout the UK and the Charity Commission's advice should be seen as being just as relevant.

We are extremely grateful to the many people, trust officers and others who have helped compile this guide. To name them all would be impossible.

Request for further information

The research for this book was done as carefully as we were able, but there will be relevant charities that we have missed and some of the information is incomplete or will become out-of-date. If any reader comes across omissions or mistakes in this guide, please let us know so we can rectify them in future. A telephone call or e-mail to the Research Department of the Directory of Social Change (0151 708 0136; e-mail: research@dsc.org.uk) is all that is needed. We are also always looking for ways to improve our guides and would appreciate any comments, positive or negative, about this guide, or suggestions on what other information would be useful for inclusion when we research for the next edition.

References

BBI (2011), annual report and accounts 2011, Chestfield, Builders' Benevolent Institution

BSA (2011), annual report and accounts 2011, London, Burma Star Association

CAB (2012), *Out of Scope, Out of Mind: Who really loses from legal aid reform* [online publication], www.citizensadvice.org.uk, Citizens Advice, accessed 11 January 2013

Charity Commission (2008), *The Prevention or Relief of Poverty for the Public Benefit*, Liverpool, Charity Commission

Communities and Local Government (2012), 'Implementation of Welfare Reform: Written evidence received' [online pdf], www.parliament.uk, at point 1.3, p. 29, accessed 21 January 2013

CPAG (2012), 'Delivering the social fund at a local level' [online article], www.cpag.org.uk, issue 229, dated August 2012, accessed 9 January 2013

Glasspool Charity Trust (2011), annual report and accounts 2010/11, London, The R.L. Glasspool Charity Trust

IFS (2013), 'The Effects of the Welfare Benefits Up-rating Bill' [online article], www.ifs.org.uk, Institute for Fiscal Studies, accessed 8 January 2013

LVSC (2012), *The Big Squeeze 2012: Surviving not Thriving* [online publication], www.lvsc.org.uk, London Voluntary Service Council, dated July 2012, accessed 09 January 2013

Madden, Michele, Jennifer Shea, Mhairi Guild, Jonathan Baker and Clare Huxley (2011) *Understanding the Benevolent Sector*, London, Elizabeth Finn Care

Not Forgotten Association, annual report and accounts 2011/12, London, Not Forgotten Association

MBF (2011), annual report and accounts 2011, London, Members' Benevolent Fund, Chartered Society of Physiotherapy

RBLWS (2011), annual report and accounts 2010/11, www.rblws.org.uk, Royal British Legion Women's Section

Stroke Association (2012), annual report and accounts 2011/12, London, Stroke Association House

There For You (2011), annual report and accounts 2011, London, Unison

Traynor, Tom, Anna Adams, Jessica Carver, Catriona Chronnell, Jude Doherty, Susanne Hollywell, Sarah Johnston, Lucy Lernelius-Tonks, Denise Lillya, Jenny McIntyre, Emma Weston and Jonny Morris (2012), *Grant Making Trusts – Key Findings 2012* [downloadable publication], www.dsc.org.uk, Directory of Social Change

VBF (2011), annual report and accounts 2011, London, Veterinary Benevolent Fund

PwC (2012), *Managing Charities in the new normal – A perfect storm?* [online publication], www.cfg.org.uk, PwC, Charity Finance Group and the Institute of Fundraising, accessed 21 January 2013

How to use this guide

Below is a typical trust entry, showing the format we have used to present the information obtained from each of the trusts.

On the following page is a flowchart. We recommend that you follow the order indicated in the flowchart to look at each section of the guide and find trusts that are relevant to you. You can also use the information in the sections 'About this guide' and 'How to make an application' to help inform your applications.

The Fictitious Trust

£24,000 (120 grants)

Correspondent: Ms I M Helpful, Charities Administrator, 7 Pleasant Road, London SN0 0ZZ (020 7123 4567; email: admin@fictitious.org.uk; website: www.fictitious.org.uk).

Trustees: Annette Curtain; Felix Cited; Paige Turner; Russell Ingleaves.

CC Number: 112234

Eligibility
Children or young people up to 25 years of age who are in need. Preference is given to children of single parent families and/or those who come from a disadvantaged family background.

Types of grants
Small one-off grants of up to £250 for a wide range of needs, including school uniforms, books, equipment and educational trips in the UK and abroad. Grants are also available for childcare costs.

Annual grant total
In 2011 the trust had an income of £25,000 and an expenditure of £27,000. Grants to 120 individuals totaled £24,000.

Other information
The trust also gives relief-in-need grants to individuals.

Exclusions
No grants for private school or university fees.

Applications
On a form available from the correspondent, submitted either directly by the individual or by the parent or guardian for those under 18. Applications are considered in January, April, July and October.

Award and no. of grants
Total amount given in grants to individuals and how many individual grants were made, if this information was available.

Correspondent
The main person to contact, nominated by the trustees.

Trustees
Note: information on the trustees of Scottish trusts is often unavailable.

Charity Commission number
Note: occasionally some of the smallest Scottish organisations are not registered charities.

Eligibility
This states who is eligible to apply for a grant. This can include restrictions on age, family circumstances, occupation or parent's occupation, ethnic origin, or place of residence.

Types of grants
Specifies whether the trust gives one-off or recurrent grants, the size of grants given and for which items or costs grants are actually given. This section will also indicate if the trust runs various schemes.

Annual grant total
This shows the total amount of money given in grants to individuals in the last financial year for which there were figures available. Other financial information may be given where relevant.

Other information
This contains miscellaneous further information about the trust, including if they give grants to individuals for education, or to organisations.

Exclusions
This field gives information, where available, on what the trust will not fund.

Applications
Including how to apply, who should make the application (i.e. the individual or a third party) and when to submit an application.

How to identify sources of help - a quick reference flowchart

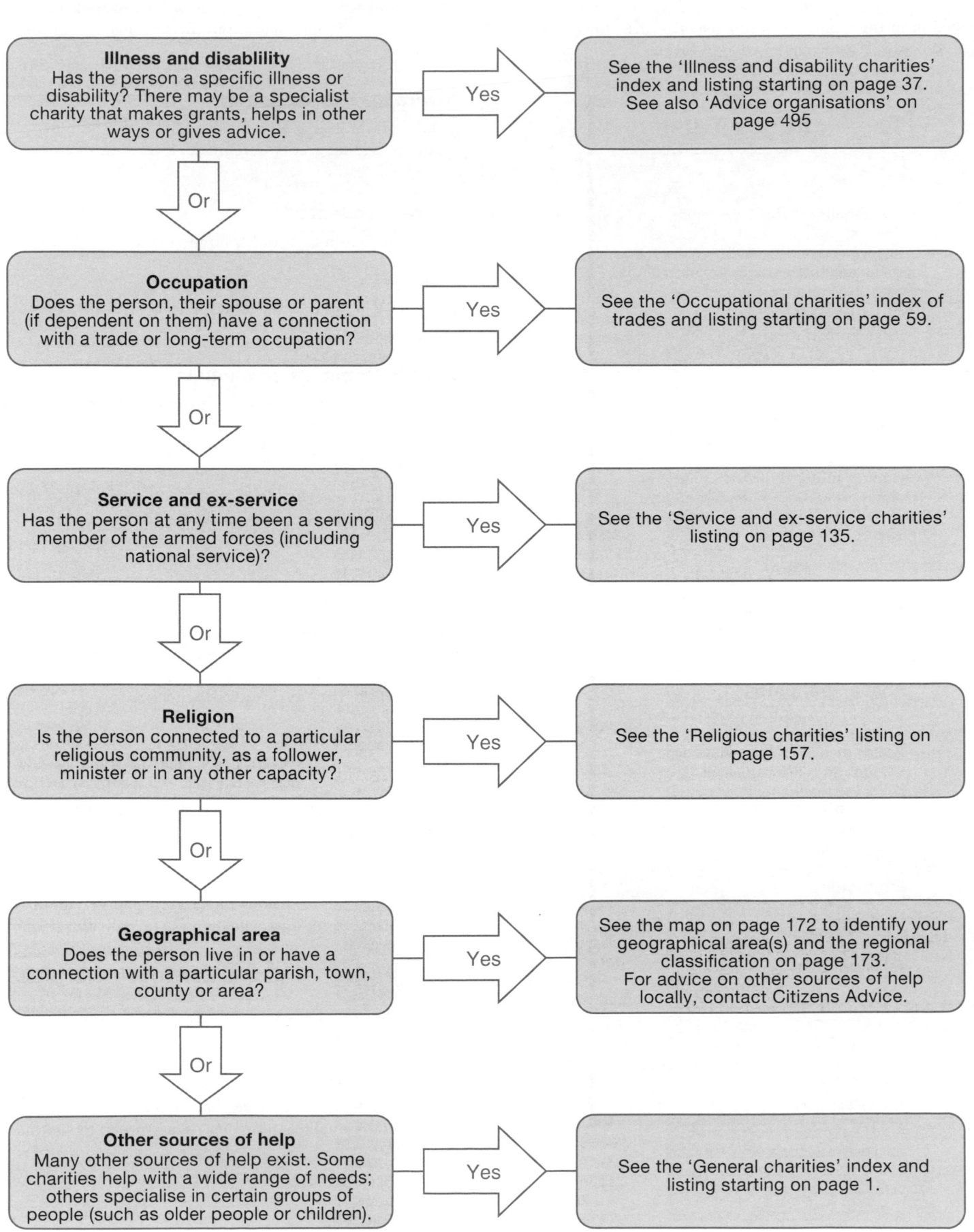

Illness and disablility
Has the person a specific illness or disability? There may be a specialist charity that makes grants, helps in other ways or gives advice.

Yes → See the 'Illness and disability charities' index and listing starting on page 37. See also 'Advice organisations' on page 495

Or

Occupation
Does the person, their spouse or parent (if dependent on them) have a connection with a trade or long-term occupation?

Yes → See the 'Occupational charities' index of trades and listing starting on page 59.

Or

Service and ex-service
Has the person at any time been a serving member of the armed forces (including national service)?

Yes → See the 'Service and ex-service charities' listing on page 135.

Or

Religion
Is the person connected to a particular religious community, as a follower, minister or in any other capacity?

Yes → See the 'Religious charities' listing on page 157.

Or

Geographical area
Does the person live in or have a connection with a particular parish, town, county or area?

Yes → See the map on page 172 to identify your geographical area(s) and the regional classification on page 173. For advice on other sources of help locally, contact Citizens Advice.

Or

Other sources of help
Many other sources of help exist. Some charities help with a wide range of needs; others specialise in certain groups of people (such as older people or children).

Yes → See the 'General charities' index and listing starting on page 1.

How to make an application

Once the appropriate charities have been identified, the next stage is the application itself. People often find making applications difficult and those who might benefit sometimes fail to do so because of the quality of the application submitted.

This article gives guidelines both to individuals applying directly and to welfare agencies applying on behalf of individuals on how to make good, clear and relevant applications.

The application form

The first stage in submitting an application is the question of application forms.

Applications on agency letter headings or personal letters direct from the applicant, no matter how well presented, are fairly pointless if the charity being approached has a specific application form which must be completed. This obvious point is often overlooked. It is frustrating when the application is returned with a blank form requesting substantially the same information as has already been submitted. The resulting delay may mean missing a committee meeting where the application would have been considered and a considerable wait until the next one.

Trust entries in this guide usually indicate when a particular application form is needed, but if there is any doubt the applicant should make a preliminary telephone call to the trust.

Who submits the application?

Again, it is important that an appropriate person sends the application. The guide usually indicates whether an individual in need can apply on his/her own behalf, or whether a third party (professional or otherwise) must apply for them.

In recognition of 'empowerment' of service users, advisory bodies sometimes simply advise families of funds they can approach themselves. However, many charities require applications and forms where appropriate to be completed by, for example, a professional person who is sponsoring the application. Therefore, the individual in need may have to press the agency to make an application on his/her behalf.

The questions

When application forms are used, the questions asked sometimes cause problems, often because they don't appear relevant. Applicants sometimes fail to realise all charities are governed by criteria laid down in their trust deeds and usually specific questions are designed to ensure these criteria are met.

For example, questions concerning date and place of birth are often answered very vaguely. 'Date of birth' is sometimes answered with 'late 50's' or, even worse, 'elderly'. Such a reply reflects the appearance of the person in question and not their age! If the charity can only consider applications for those below a pensionable age, and the request was on behalf of a woman, then the above answers would be too imprecise.

Equally 'Place of birth' is sometimes answered with 'Great Britain' which is not precise enough for funds whose area of benefit is regional or local. It is always better to state the place of birth as well as town and county, even if they are different from the current home address.

Where application forms are not requested, it is essential to prepare clear, concise applications that provide:

1. A description of the person or family and the need which exists

Although applications should be concise, they must provide sufficient detail, such as:

1   The applicant's name, address, place and date of birth

2   The applicant's family circumstances (i.e. married/ partners, separated/ divorced/single parent, widow/ widower, the number and ages of dependent children)

3   The applicant's financial position (i.e. breakdown of weekly income and expenditure and, where appropriate, DWP/housing benefit awarded/ refused, savings, credit debts, rent/gas/ electricity arrears, etc.)

4   Other relevant information, such as how the need arose (e.g. illness, loss of job, marital separation, etc.) and why other sources (especially DWP/housing departments) have not helped. If applying to a disability charity, applicants should include details of the nature and effects of the disability (although see Medical information below); if applying to a local charity, how long have they lived in the locality.

The application, which says 'this is a poor family who need their gas reconnecting', is unlikely to receive proper consideration. It is also worth mentioning that applications are dealt with in the strictest of confidence, so applicants should aim to provide as much information as is relevant. The form printed after this article may serve as a useful checklist to ensure that all relevant information is included for the particular application.

2. How much money is requested and what it will be used for

This second point appears to cause the most difficulty. Applications are often received without any indication of the amount required or without sufficient explanation as to the desired use of the money.

For example, an applicant may have multiple debts totalling over £1,000. A grant of £100 would clear one of the debts and free much-needed weekly income. So the applicant approaches a suitable charity for a grant of £100. If the applicant explains the situation clearly, trustees can see that a £100 grant in this instance would be an effective use of their charity's resources. However, if it is not made clear, trustees can only guess at the possible benefits of the grant. Because they are unwilling to take undue risks with charitable money, trustees may either turn down an incomplete application or refer it for more information, which inevitably means delays.

Charity and the State

Charities are not supposed to give grants for items that are covered by statutory sources. However, the Big Lottery and increasing reforms to the welfare state have made it much more difficult to say where statutory provision ends and charitable provision begins.

Similarly, means testing under some state provision such as Disabled Facilities Grants regulations can create shortfalls between the amount that statutory sources can and will pay, and the full costs of equipment and adaptations to properties. Sometimes, because of what can and cannot be taken into account, assessments of what families can pay appear unrealistic. Where this is the case it should be stated.

Changes arising from tightening of eligibility criteria and Community Care legislation are creating new areas of unmet need. If individuals are applying to charity because statutory provision is clearly no longer adequate, they should make it clear in the application that they have exhausted all possible statutory sources of funding but they are still left with a shortfall. A supporting reference from a knowledgeable agency may be helpful.

Where the identified need is not met, following any assessment process, applications for alternative or complementary finance should make the reasons clear.

The way that social and health care services are provided is changing. Traditionally, the state assessed an individual's need, and then provided, or arranged for those assessed services to be provided. The change gives those assessed as eligible for services, the money to purchase them themselves by way of an Individual Budget. The aim is to give more independence and choice of services purchased. It is accepted that this is a radical change for many people. Applications to charities, particularly those with social care needs may well have to reflect the services already being purchased from an individual budget, with a cogent argument as to how what is now being applied for is needed and improves quality of life.

Realism

It helps to be realistic. Sometimes families have contributed to their own situation. The applicant who admits this and seems not to expect miracles but rather seeks to plan afresh – even if with fingers crossed – will often be considered more positively than the applicant who philosophises about deprivation and the imperfections of the political regime of the day.

Likewise, the application, which tries to make the trustees feel guilty and responsible for the impending doom which is predicted for the most vulnerable members of the family unless money is given, is unlikely to impress experienced trustees, however sympathetic.

In general, be clear and factual, not moralising and emotional. In effect, a good application attempts to identify the need and promote possible resolutions.

Applications to more than one charity

Where large amounts are being sought, it can take months to send applications one at a time and wait for the outcome of each before applying to another. However, if a number of applications are being sent out together, a paragraph explaining that other charities are being approached should be included together with a commitment to return any surplus money raised. It is also worth saying if any other applications have been successful in contributing to the whole–nothing succeeds like success!

The same application should not be sent off indiscriminately. For example, if somebody is applying to a trade charity on behalf of a child whose deceased father had lengthy service in that particular trade, then a detailed description of the deceased father's service would be highly relevant. If an application for the same child was being made to a local charity, it would not.

Sometimes people who are trustees of more than one charity receive three or four identical letters, none tailored to that particular trust and none indicating that other trusts have been approached. The omission of such details and the neglect of explanations raise questions in the minds of trustees, which in the end can result in delays or even refusal.

Timing

When applying to charities, remember the time factor, particularly in cases of urgent need. Committees often sit monthly, or even quarterly. Without knowledge but with 'luck', an application can be received the day before the meeting – but if Murphy's Law operates it will always arrive the day after. For the lack of a little homework, applications may not be considered in time.

From experience, few organisations object to a telephone call being made to clarify criteria, dates of meetings or requests for application forms. So often it seems that applicants leave the whole process to chance, which leads to disillusionment, frustration and wasted time for all concerned.

Savings

When awarding a grant, most trustees take the applicant's savings into account. Some applicants may think this unnecessarily intrusive, but openness and honesty make for a better presented application and save time. However, sometimes savings may not need to affect trustees' calculations.

For example, if a woman has a motor accident in which she was not at fault but which leaves her permanently disabled, she will receive compensation (often a one-off lump sum) through the guilty party's insurance company based on medical prognoses at the time. If her condition deteriorates faster and further than anticipated, requiring her to obtain an expensive item of equipment, it could well be argued that this should not be paid for out of the compensation awarded. The compensation was paid to cover factors such as loss of earnings potential, a reduced quality of life, reduced ability to easily fulfil basic household tasks and a general loss of future security, not to pay for unexpected and expensive pieces of equipment.

In such circumstances, the applicant should include a paragraph in the application to explain why his/her savings are not relevant to grant calculations.

In conclusion

Two final points should be borne in mind.

1. Be clear

Firstly, social care & health care professionals often resort to the use of jargon when plain English would be more effective. There appears to be two extremes; one to present a report on the basis that the trustees are not very intelligent lay people who need to be educated, or alternatively that they are all psychotherapists who need to be impressed. Usually, this only causes confusion.

2. Medical information

Secondly, medical information should not be presented without an accurate medical diagnosis to support it. Applicants' or social workers' presumptions on medical matters are not relevant. Often what is necessary is to explain why a financial need arises from a particular condition. This may be because of the rarity of the condition or the fluctuating nature of it.

The medical information should be presented by a professional in that field. The task of the applicant or the sponsor is to explain the implications of the condition.

Using the model application form for financial assistance

Over the page is a general-purpose application form. It has been compiled with the help of Gaddum Centre. It can be photocopied and used whenever convenient and should enable applicants (and welfare agencies applying on behalf of individuals) to state clearly the basic information required by most trusts.

Alternatively, applicants can use it as a checklist of points to include in the letter. Applicants using this form should note the following things in particular:

1 It is worth sending a short letter setting out the request in brief, even when using this application form.

2 Because this form is designed to be useful to a wide range of people in need, not all the information asked for in the form will be relevant to every application. For example, not all applicants are in receipt of state benefits, nor do all applicants have HP commitments. In such cases, applicants should write N/A (not applicable) in the box or on the line in question.

3 Filling out the weekly income and expenditure parts of the form can be worrying or even distressing. Expenditure when itemised in this way is usually far higher than people expect. It is probably worth filling out this form with the help of a trained welfare rights worker.

4 You should always keep a copy of the completed form in case the trust has a specific query.

5 This form should not be used where the trust has its own form, which must be completed.

Ashley Wood
Former Assistant Chief Executive
Gaddum Centre

Application form template

Purpose for which grant is sought	Amount sought from this application £
Applicant (name)	Occupation/School
Address	
Telephone no.	
Date of birth Age	Place of birth
Nationality	Religion (if any)

☐ Single   ☐ Married   ☐ Divorced   ☐ Partnered   ☐ Separated   ☐ Widow/er

Family details: Name	Age	Occupation/School
Parents/ Partner	. . . . . .	. . . .
Brothers/Sisters/ Children	. . . . . .	. . . .
. . . .	. . . . . .	. . . .
. . . .	. . . . . .	. . . .
Others (specify)	. . . . . .	. . . .

Income (weekly)	£	p	Expenditure (weekly)	£	p
Father's/husband's wage	. . . . . .		Rent/mortgage	. . . . . .	
Mother's/wife's wage	. . . . . .		Council tax	. . . . . .	
Partner's wage	. . . . . .		Water rate	. . . . . .	
Income Support	. . . . . .		Electricity	. . . . . .	
Jobseeker's Allowance	. . . . . .		Gas	. . . . . .	
Employment and Support Allowance	. . . . . .		Other fuel	. . . . . .	
Pension Credit	. . . . . .		Insurance	. . . . . .	
Working Tax Credit	. . . . . .		Fares/travel	. . . . . .	
Child Tax Credit	. . . . . .		Household expenses (food, laundry etc.).	. . . . . .	
Child Benefit	. . . . . .		Clothing	. . . . . .	
Housing Benefit	. . . . . .		School dinners	. . . . . .	
Attendance Allowance	. . . . . .		Childcare fees	. . . . . .	
Disability Living Allowance	. . . . . .		HP commitments	. . . . . .	
Universal Credit	. . . . . .		Telephone	. . . . . .	
Personal Independence Payments	. . . . . .		TV rental	. . . . . .	
Maintenance payments	. . . . . .		TV licence	. . . . . .	
Pensions	. . . . . .		Other expenditure (specify)	. . . . . .	
Other income (specify)	. . . . . .		. . . .	. . . . . .	
. . . .	. . . . . .		. . . .	. . . . . .	
. . . .	. . . . . .		. . . .	. . . . . .	
. . . .	. . . . . .		. . . .	. . . . . .	

Total weekly income £   **Total weekly expenditure** £

Savings £ [   ]

Debts/arrears
Rent, fuels, loans, HP etc.

Has applicant received help from
any other source?   ☐ YES   ☐ NO
(If YES, please include details below)

Specify in detail	Amount owed	Sources of grant obtained	Amount
. . . .	£	. . . .	£. . . . .
. . . .	£	. . . .	£. . . . .
. . . .	£	Other sources approached	
. . . .	£	. . . .	
. . . .	£	. . . .	

Total £ [   ]   **Total still required** £ [   ]

Has applicant ever received previous financial help from this trust? ☐ YES ☐ NO   If so, when?

Reason for the application

Continue on a separate sheet if necessary

For applications being submitted through a welfare agency

Name of agency . . . .

Case worker . . . .

Address. . . . .

. . . .

Telephone. . . . .

How long has the applicant been known to your department/organisation?. . . . .

For all applications

Signature: **Date:**

Notes: application form template

1. Because this form is designed to be useful to the wide range of people who apply for grants, not all the information asked for will be relevant to every application. If, for example, you are not in receipt of state benefits, or do not have credit debts, you should write 'N/A' (not applicable) in the box or line in question.

2. If, similarly, you do not have answers for all the questions at the time of applying – for example, if you have applied to other trusts and are still waiting for a reply – you should write 'Pending' under the question: 'Have you written to any other trusts? What was the outcome of the application?'

3. Filling out the weekly income and expenditure parts of the form can be worrying or even distressing. Expenditure when itemised in this way is usually far higher than people expect. It is probably worth filling out this form with the help of a trained welfare rights worker.

4. You should always keep a copy of the completed form in case the trust has a specific query.

5. This form should not be used when the trust has its own form that must be completed.

About the Directory of Social Change

DSC has a vision of an independent voluntary sector at the heart of social change. The activities of independent charities, voluntary organisations and community groups are fundamental to achieve social change. We exist to help these organisations and the people who support them to achieve their goals.

We do this by:

- providing practical tools that organisations and activists need, including online and printed publications, training courses, and conferences on a huge range of topics
- acting as a 'concerned citizen' in public policy debates, often on behalf of smaller charities, voluntary organisations and community groups
- leading campaigns and stimulating debate on key policy issues that affect those groups
- carrying out research and providing information to influence policymakers.

DSC is the leading provider of information and training for the voluntary sector and publishes an extensive range of guides and handbooks covering subjects such as fundraising, management, communication, finance and law. We have a range of subscription-based websites containing a wealth of information on funding from trusts, companies and government sources. We run more than 300 training courses each year, including bespoke in-house training provided at the client's location. DSC conferences, many of which run on an annual basis, include the Charity Management Conference, the Charity Accountants' Conference and the Charity Law Conference. DSC's major annual event is Charityfair, which provides low-cost training on a wide variety of subjects.

For details of all our activities, and to order publications and book courses, go to www.dsc.org.uk, call 08450 777707 or email publications@dsc.org.uk

General charities

This section includes all the entries which could not be tied to a particular occupation, disability or locality. It starts with 'Index of general charities' (including, for example, 'Children and young people', and 'Older people') with a separate category for trusts that specifically give grants for holidays. 'Children and young people' contains trusts for people aged 25 or under while 'Older people' contains trusts for people aged 50 or over. This reflects the criteria of some of the trusts in the guide, although not every trust will use these exact limits. We have included refugees and asylum seekers under the 'Ethnic and national minorities in the UK' sections.

The entries under each category are arranged alphabetically, with those trusts which do not fit into any particular category listed at the start of the chapter under 'General'. These charities are listed under 'General' because they can give to a wide range of people, so if individuals are unable to find help from other sources in the guide then they should be able to approach one or more of these. However, note that most of these charities still have restrictions on who they can help. Applicants should not simply send off indiscriminate applications to any charity under the 'General' heading; rather, they should first consider carefully whether they are eligible.

Similarly, within the alphabetically arranged categories following 'General', older people should not apply to all the trusts in the 'Older people' section, for instance, as there may be criteria that will makes them ineligible for support.

Index of general charities

The ACT Foundation

£457,000 (411 grants)

Correspondent: James Kerr, Secretary, 61 Thames Street, Windsor SL4 1QW (01753 753900; fax: 01753 753901; email: info@theactfoundation.co.uk; website: www.theactfoundation.co.uk)

Trustees: John O'Sullivan; Michael Street; Paul Nield; Robert White; Denis Taylor; Christine Erwood.

CC Number: 1068617

Eligibility

At present the trust is focusing on helping people with mental or physical disabilities although the elderly, those in poverty, and those in danger of being excluded from society are also eligible.

Types of grants

Grants of up to £2,500 for equipment such as stair lifts, bathroom adaptations, mobility aids, specialist books and educational equipment, respite breaks, furniture and vehicle adaptations. The trust has stated that 'grantmaking now focuses more strongly on the transition that young physically and mentally disabled people make as they leave full time education and move into adulthood.'

Annual grant total

In 2010/11the foundation held assets of £42.5 million and had an income of £15.1 million. Grants to 411 individuals totalled £457,000.

Exclusions

No grants to replace statutory funding; for work, items or services already commenced, purchased or on order; for building alterations where a Disabled Facilities Grant has not been applied for.

Applications

Application forms are available to download from the website. Applicants may complete the form themselves or have it completed on their behalf by a third party. Medical reports may be attached to give evidence in support of the application. Trustees meet four times a year but applications are considered between these meetings. All applications will be acknowledged in writing. Decisions are usually made within one month and applicants may be visited. If the application is for an emergency you may request a faster timescale and the trust may be able to assist.

Other information
Grants are also made to organisations (£306,000 in 2010/11).

The Alchemy Foundation

£3,200

Correspondent: R Stilgoe, Trevereux Manor, Limpsfield Chart, Oxted, Surrey RH8 0TL (01883 730600; fax: 01883 730800)

Trustees: Dr Jemima Stilgoe; Holly Stilgoe; Jack Stilgoe; Rufus Stilgoe; Richard Stilgoe; Alexander Armitage; Andrew Murison; Annabel Stilgoe; Esther Rantzen; Joseph Stilgoe; Antoun Elias.

CC Number: 292500

Eligibility
Individuals in need in the UK.

Types of grants
One-off and recurrent grants according to need. Previously the trust has given grants for holidays for children and respite for carers.

Annual grant total
In 2010/11 the trust had assets of £2.4 million and an income of £335,000. Approximately £6,500 was given in grants to individuals for relief-in-need and educational purposes, distributed through other charities.

Applications
In writing to the correspondent.

Other information
The trust gives grants mostly to organisations, namely overseas development, social welfare and disability projects.

Al-Mizan Charitable Trust

£4,500

Correspondent: Mohammed Sadiq Mamdani, 2 Burlington Gardens, London W3 6BA (email: admin@almizantrust.org.uk; website: www.almizantrust.org.uk)

Trustees: Rukaiya Jeraj; Mohammad Musa; Ali Orr; Sanjana Deen; Sonia Malik; Karim Farrag; Fatema Bandali; Amir Rizwan; Afshaan Hena; Sarfaraz Hussein.

CC Number: 1135752

Eligibility
British citizens, those granted indefinite leave to remain in the UK and asylum seekers who are living in a condition of social or economic deprivation. Preference is given to the following groups:
- Orphans (a child who has lost either both parents or one parent who was the main bread-winner in the family)
- Children and young people under the age of 19 years (particularly those in care or who are carers themselves)
- Individuals who are disabled, incapacitated or terminally ill (particularly those who are severely mentally disabled)
- Single parents (particularly divorcees and widows/widowers with children)
- Estranged or isolated senior citizens
- Individuals with severe medical conditions or their families
- Ex-offenders or reformed drug addicts or alcoholics
- Victims of domestic violence and/or physical or sexual abuse
- Victims of crime, anti-social behaviour and/or terrorism

Types of grants
Mainly one-off grants ranging from £200–£250, though in some cases up to £500 may be awarded. Grants are available both for subsistence costs and those which help break the cycle of poverty by encouraging educational attainment and employability.

Annual grant total
In 2010/11 the trust had both an income and total charitable expenditure of £10,500.

Exclusions
No grants for: general appeals; applicants who are not claiming all available benefits; retrospective funding; expenses relating to the practice or promotion of religion; debt, including council tax arrears; fines or criminal penalties; university tuition fees; gap year trips; building work or construction projects; funeral expenses; gifts (including birthdays and festivals); vehicles; and, holidays or recreational outings, unless they serve a medical, social or educational need. No support is given to those who have received a grant in the last twelve months.

Applications
All applications for grant funding must be submitted using the trust's online application system.

Other information
The trust has an informative website.

Anglian Water Assistance Fund

£600,000

Correspondent: The Trustees, Anglian Water Assistance Fund, PO Box 42, Peterborough PE3 8XH (01733 421060; website: www.anglianwater.co.uk/awaf)

Eligibility
Customers of Anglian Water and Hartlepool Water who are in debt with their water and sewerage charges.

Types of grants
Gift vouchers ranging from £50 to £3,000 to clear or reduce arrears of domestic water/sewerage charges. On average, 1,700 grants are made each year.

Annual grant total
In 2010/11 the fund received a donation of £750,000 from its parent company and made assistance grants totalling £600,000.

Exclusions
No grants are given towards: fines for criminal offences; education or training needs; medical equipment, aids and adaptations; holidays; debts to central government departments such as tax and national insurance; business debts; overpayment of benefits; accommodation deposits; or catalogue, credit card, personal loan or other forms of unsecured lending. The trust cannot give loans, make payments towards bills, or make any grants in arrears.

Applications
The quickest way to apply is through the online application form on the trust's website. Alternatively applicants may download the form or call the trust to receive one in the post. The fund stresses that applicants should ensure that they have included the relevant information necessary to process the application. The fund will need to see evidence of income and water debts, if applicable. If there are arrears of water/sewerage charges, the fund will always look for a full explanation of how the arrears have arisen.

The fund will write to applicants to let them know whether they have been successful or not.

Individuals who receive an award from the trust can apply again after two years. Those who do not receive an award are eligible to re-apply after six months.

Other information
The Anglian Water Assistance Fund is administered by Charis Grants Ltd which also manages the British Gas Energy Trust, EDF Energy Trust, South East Water's Helping Hand and Affinity Water Trust.

The Attlee Foundation

£7,000

Correspondent: Tania Shaikh-McKenna, Centre Manager, c/o Attlee Youth and Community Centre, 5 Thrawl Street, London E1 6RT (020 7183 0093; email: info@attlee.org.uk; website: www.attlee. org.uk)

Trustees: Sandra Kabir; Mei Sim Lai; Christine Pointer; Thomas Roundell Greene; Alan Steele; Zakir Hussain; Richard Henchley; Martin Young.

CC Number: 1087259

Eligibility

People with disabilities or who are disadvantaged living anywhere in the UK. Priority will be given to applications involving children and young people when funds are low.

Types of grants

One-off grants up to £100 through the 'Tickets Please' programme towards travelling costs for therapeutic support. For example, to attend specialist treatment centres or to maintain family contacts with children or close relatives in hospital, prison or rehabilitation a long way from home within the UK.

Annual grant total

In 2010/11 the foundation had assets of £3.2 million and an income of £358,000. Grants made to individuals through the 'Tickets Please' programme totalled £7,000. At the time of writing (December 2012) the website stated that the programme was on hold until new funds were found. Check the website before applying.

Exclusions

No grants are given towards funerals, holidays, travel outside the UK, medical equipment, wheelchairs or mobility adaptations.

Applications

On a form available from the correspondent or to download from the website. Applications must be made through a social worker, Citizens Advice or other welfare agency, to which the cheque will be payable on behalf of the individual. A stamped addressed envelope must be enclosed. Covering letters should be kept to one page. There are no deadlines.

Other information

The foundation also manages a youth centre in the Spitalfields area of East London, which provides open access and inclusive facilities for children, young people and the local community.

The Bagri Foundation

£5,000

Correspondent: M C Thompson, 80 Cannon Street, London EC4N 6EJ (020 7280 0089; email: enquiries@ bagrifoundation.org; website: www. bagrifoundation.org)

Trustees: Lady Bagri; Hon Apurv Bagri; Lord Bagri.

CC Number: 1000219

Eligibility

People in need worldwide.

Types of grants

One-off and recurrent grants according to need.

Annual grant total

In 2010/11 the foundation had assets of £2.1 million and an income of £59,000. Grants were made totalling £54,000, the majority of which was given in institutional grants.

Applications

In writing to the correspondent.

Barony Charitable Trust

£2,500

Correspondent: Agnes H Cunningham, Secretary, Canal Court, 40 Craiglockhart Avenue, Edinburgh EH14 1LT (0845 140 7777)

SC Number: SC021091

Eligibility

People in need through age, ill health or disablement who live in Edinburgh and Central Scotland.

Types of grants

One-off grants of around £100, possibly up to £250 in exceptional circumstances. Recent grants have included support for people trying to make a fresh start, the purchase of disability aids such as wheelchairs or hoists and contributions towards the cost of a carer to accompany an individual on holiday.

Annual grant total

In 2010/11 the trust had an income of £2,700. No further information was available.

Applications

On a form available from the correspondent, submitted preferably through a recognised referral agency such as a GP, health visitor, priest or minister, social worker or care worker. Details of what the money is for, how it will help and any other funding applied for should also be included in the application.

Other information

Note, this trust is linked to the Barony Housing Association and applications from their area of activity receive priority.

British Gas Energy Trust

£2.7 million

Correspondent: Grants Officer, Freepost-RRZJ-XBSY-GYRG, British Gas Energy Trust, PO Box 42, Peterborough PE3 8XH (01733 421060; fax: 01733 421020; email: bget@charisgrants.com; website: www.britishgasenergytrust.org. uk)

Trustees: Stephen Harrap; Helen McLeod; Tom Wright; Gillian Tishler; Maria Wardrobe.

CC Number: 1106218

Eligibility

Domestic customers of British Gas or Scottish Gas.

Types of grants

Grants to cover arrears of domestic gas, electricity charges and other essential domestic bills, white goods, bankruptcy deposits/debt relief orders and funeral expenses.

Annual grant total

In 2010 the trust had assets of £390,000 and an income of £3.3 million. Payments for British Gas energy debts were made totalling £2.6 million. Further assistance grants totalled £162,000.

Exclusions

The trust cannot give loans or help with bills or items that have already been paid for. Nor can it help with the following: any household item that is not a 'white good'; fines for criminal offences; overpayments of benefits; educational or training needs; business debts; debts to central government departments, for example, tax and national insurance; catalogues, credit cards, personal loans and other forms of non-secured lending; medical equipment, aids and adaptations; deposits to secure accommodation; and holidays.

Applications

On a form available from the correspondent or to download from the website. The trust also has an online application facility. A local money advice centre such as a Citizens Advice may be able to provide help in completing the form. Applicants may receive letters, emails, telephone calls or a home visit as part of the assessment process.

Those in receipt of an award from the trust cannot reapply for two years.

Applicants who do not receive an award can apply again after six months.

Other information

Grants are also made to voluntary organisations working in the field of money advice, debt counselling or energy efficiency advice.

The Carnegie Hero Fund Trust

£81,000

Correspondent: Chief Executive, Andrew Carnegie House, Pittencrief Street, Dunfermline, Fife KY12 8AW (01383 723638; fax: 01383 749799; email: herofund@carnegietrust.com; website: www.carnegiehero.org.uk)

SC Number: SC000729

Eligibility

Heroes and their families (that is people who have suffered financial loss or have been injured – or the families of people who have been killed – in performing acts of heroism in saving human life in the UK, Eire, Channel Islands and territorial waters). About three to four new cases are recognised each year.

Types of grants

One-off and recurrent grants to help towards, for example, household bills and medical equipment.

Annual grant total

In 2011 the trust had an income of £156,000. Grants totalled £81,000.

Exclusions

Heroic acts performed in the saving of property are not recognised by the trust.

Applications

Attention to potential cases for consideration is brought to the trustees' notice by a press cutting agency. The trust's website also notes the following: 'Presentation of a potential case for consideration by the Trustees should be accompanied by a report/statement from a member of the emergency services confirming that the rescue/attempted rescue involved risk to the rescuer's life. Recognition of a case is at the sole discretion of the Trustees.'

Around a dozen cases are considered each year.

Other information

The trust was established in 1908 by Andrew Carnegie, who made a great fortune from steel. His Birthplace Museum in Dunfermline displays the Roll of Honour of the Hero Fund Trust, now containing the names of over 6,000 heroes and heroines.

Catholic Clothing Guild

£5,000

Correspondent: Mrs C Edwards, Hon Treasurer, 5 Dark Lane, Shrewsbury, Shropshire SY2 5LP (email: carmel. edwards@btinternet.com)

Trustees: Countess Charles De Salis; Countess of Balfour; Carmel Jacinta Edwards.

CC Number: 277952

Eligibility

People in need of clothing regardless of denomination in England.

Types of grants

The guild is a small charity which distributes new donated clothing (mainly to children). It may give small money grants when this is not possible, however this is in exceptional circumstances as funding is limited.

Annual grant total

In 2010 the trust had an income of £5,000 and total expenditure of £9,000.

Applications

Applications should be made by letter or email to their local branch. Telephone calls are not welcomed. Applications must be made through a welfare agency or social services who will also receive the grants. Under no circumstances will applications be accepted from individuals.

Other information

Note: the trust is only able to assist with up to six grants per month due to limited funding.

Coats Foundation Trust

£20,000

Correspondent: Mrs S MacNicol, Secretary, Coats Pensions Office, Pension Office, Pacific House, 70 Wellington Street, Glasgow G2 6UB (01412 076820; email: andrea.mccutcheon@coats.com)

Trustee: The Coats Trustee Company Ltd.

CC Number: 268735

Eligibility

Only applications where no statutory help or help from other charitable organisations is available.

Types of grants

One-off for essential items or services.

Annual grant total

In 2010/11 the trust had an income of £20,800 and total expenditure of £48,000.

Applications

In writing to the correspondent, giving full details of the reason for application, and provide copies of any documents which will back the claim, such as bank statements, payslips, benefit award letters, utility bills, etc. Applicants should also include details of what the extra money is needed for and the cost of the item(s).

Other information

This trust also makes grants for educational purposes.

The Coffey Charitable Trust

£1,000

Correspondent: Christopher Coffey, Oaktree House, Over the Melbourne Road, Denham, Uxbridge, Middlesex UB9 5DR (01895 831381)

Trustees: Christopher Coffey; Wendy Coffey; Christopher Green.

CC Number: 1043549

Eligibility

People in need in the UK.

Types of grants

Occasional one-off and recurrent grants according to need.

Annual grant total

In 2010/11 the trust had an income of £15,000 and a total expenditure of £21,000.

Applications

In writing to the correspondent.

Other information

This trust mainly provides grants to Christian organisations and events.

The Cordwainers' Company Common Investment Fund

£15,000 (80 grants)

Correspondent: The Clerk, Clothworkers Hall, Dunster Court, Mincing Lane, London EC3R 7AH (020 7929 1121; fax: 020 7929 1124; email: office@ cordwainers.org; website: www. cordwainers.org)

Trustees: Charles Philip Fairweather; Geoffrey Guy Trenchard Blanford; Glenn Appleyard Bridgman Shaw.

CC Number: 261891

Eligibility

The company administers a number of small trusts, the eligibility of which varies. Specific trusts exist for people who are blind, people who are deaf and dumb, widows of clergymen, unmarried women in the Church of England, ex-servicemen and widows of those who served in the merchant or armed forces.

Types of grants
Small annual grants depending on the trust and the circumstances.

Annual grant total
In 2010/11 the trust had assets of £1.6 million and an income of £49,000. Grants were made to around 80 individuals totalling £15,000.

Applications
In writing to the correspondent supported, if possible, by referrals from welfare or other charitable bodies.

Other information
The trust also makes grants to organisations (£68,000 in 2008/09).

The Dibs Charitable Trust

£23,000

Correspondent: The Administrator, Trustee Department, Coutts, 440 Strand, London WC2R 0QS

Trustees: David Isaacs; Patricia Bloch; Adrian M. W. Davis; Coutts and Co.

CC Number: 257709

Eligibility
People in need.

Types of grants
One-off grants for the relief of immediate distress only, ranging from £25 to £250. No pensions or annuities. Grants are not made directly to individuals.

Annual grant total
In 2010/11 the trust had an income and expenditure of £33,000. Grants totalled £23,000.

Exclusions
No grants for bankruptcy fees or associated costs, education, overseas travel, holidays, clothing, funeral expenses or group activities.

Applications
In writing to 212 Business Design Centre, 52 Upper Street, London N1 0QH. Applications should be made through a local social services department or Citizens Advice and are considered throughout the year.

East Africa Women's League (UK) Benevolent Fund

£15,000 (25 grants)

Correspondent: Mrs Joan Considine, Hon Secretary, 13 Benenden Green, Alresford, Hampshire SO24 9PE (email: honsec@eawl.org.uk; website: www. considine.eclipse.co.uk/eawl/eawl.html)

Trustees: Sheila Mary Heath; Ann Francis Narraway; Elfrida Margaret Murray; Joan Margaret Considine; Phyllida White Cockell; Eva White; Iris Isabel Scotchmer; Maggie Smith; Kate Honeywell; Pam Sparrow; Morag Owen-Burke.

CC Number: 294328

Eligibility
People of UK origin who have previously lived and worked in East Africa.

Types of grants
One-off and recurrent grants according to need. Grants range from around £100 to £800.

Annual grant total
In 2011 the fund had assets of £177,000 and an income of £62,000. There were 23 grants made in necessitous circumstances and two grants made as special one-off payments, totalling £15,000.

Applications
In writing to the correspondent. Members of a fund subcommittee may visit applicants. The trust does not accept any unsolicited applications.

EDF Energy Trust

£1.8 million (3,495 grants)

Correspondent: Grant Administrator, Freepost-RLXG-RBYJ-USXE, PO Box 42, Peterborough PE3 8XH (01733 421060; fax: 01733 421020; email: edfet@ charisgrants.com; website: www. edfenergytrust.org.uk)

Trustees: Denise Fennell; Steve Meakin; Tim Cole; Brian Cross; Bob Richardson; Richard Sykes.

CC Number: 1099446

Eligibility
Anyone in need in Britain.

Types of grants
Grants to cover the payment of energy bills and other essential household bills, items or costs.

Annual grant total
In 2011 the trust held assets of £925,000 and had an income of £2 million. Grants made to individuals totalled

£1.8 million. Of this total 2,855 grants were made to clear gas and electricity debts and 640 were made in further assistance payments. Overall there was an applicant success rate of 54% (of 6,435 applications received.)

The average energy grant was £565 while the average further assistance payment was £386.

Exclusions
The trust cannot help with the following: fines for criminal offences; overpayments of benefits; educational or training needs; debts to central government departments e.g. tax and national insurance; catalogues, credit cards, personal loans and other forms of non-secured lending; medical equipment, aids and adaptations; deposits to secure accommodation; or holidays.

Applications
Online via the website or by requesting an application form from the correspondent or downloading one from the site. Applicants must also submit relevant financial information: bank statements, wage slips or benefit letters showing income should be dated within the last three months. Annual benefit letters for works pensions, state pensions, child benefit and disability living allowance will also be accepted.

All applicants are advised to seek appropriate money or debt advice from an organisation like Citizens Advice before applying in order to maximise their chances of success. The trust's own statistics show that, 'an application submitted with the help of a funded organisation is twice as likely to succeed as an application submitted unaided.'

Those in receipt of an award from the trust cannot reapply for two years. Applicants who do not receive an award can apply again if their circumstances change. Payments for bills will be made directly to the supplier.

Other information
Grants are also made to support 16 voluntary organisations working in the field of money advice, debt counselling or energy efficiency advice (£600,000 in 2011).

Family Action

£648,000 (1,944 grants)

Correspondent: Grants Service, 501–505 Kingsland Road, Dalston, London E8 4AU (020 7241 7459 – Tuesday, Wednesday and Thursday ONLY between 2 pm and 4 pm; email: info@family-action.org.uk; website: www.family-action.org.uk)

Trustees: Ian Michael Harris; Peter Nigel Stoakley; Brent Thomas; Hilary Margaret

Seal; Lady Gillian Margaret Keene; Martin Michael Barnes; Sean O'Callaghan; Bryan Portman; John Rowlands; Sally Shire.

CC Number: 264713

Eligibility

Assistance from Family Action is primarily targeted at families and individuals living on low incomes, particularly those living on benefits.

Family Action's priority areas for funding are: (i) Mental health – adults with a clinical diagnosis of a mental health problem and parents and expectant parents (over the age of 18) with a drug or alcohol problem; (ii) Domestic abuse- support for six months for those leaving a violent relationship to help rebuild their lives; (iii) Older people – support to promote independence, improve the quality of life and reduce isolation for those aged 60 and over; (iv) Young people (aged 19 to 25) – support for vulnerable young people living alone; (v) Sickness/disability – grants to pay for treatment or disability aids; and (vi) Holidays for women living in Greater London – support to provide recuperative holidays.

Types of grants

Clothing, fuel bills, household needs such as beds and cookers and so on are most commonly requested. Help can also be given for more varied needs.

Annual grant total

In 2010/11 the charity held assets of £3.7 million and had an income of £22.1 million. During the year the charity disbursed grants to 1,944 (2010: 4,218) individuals totalling £648,000 (2010: £1.1 million).

Exclusions

Funds are not available for council tax arrears, debts (except utility bills), fines, funeral expenses, gifts, items already covered by statutory funds, private school fees, rent arrears or payments, repayment of Social Fund or other loans, bankruptcy or items already purchased.

Applications

Initial applications must be made by a professional person such a social worker, health visitor or by a voluntary agency using the association's application form which can be downloaded from the charity's website. Note that the application may require various supporting documentation, depending on which priority area the applicant meets.

The charity will write to the referral professional with the results of the application. Where a grant is made the cheque will be made payable to the referring agency or service/utility provider. Under no circumstances are cheques made to individuals. Grants cannot be made to applicants who have received a Family Action Welfare Grant or a Greater London Women's Holiday Grant within the previous 12 months.

The charity's website states that due to a lower return on investment income the amount available for welfare grants has been restricted. In consequence welfare grant applications are only accepted at specific times of the year, usually during nominated months. See the website for current dates.

Other information

The charity was formerly known as Family Welfare Association.

The Fielding Charitable Trust

£2,100

Correspondent: Richard Fielding, West Hall, Longburton, Sherborne, Dorset DT9 5PF

Trustees: Jacqueline Winifred Fielding; Jane Diana Auer; Richard Walter Fielding.

CC Number: 1091521

Eligibility

People in need in the UK. Preference is given to older people and people with disabilities.

Types of grants

One-off and recurrent grants according to need.

Annual grant total

Average expenditure is around £5,000 per year.

Applications

In writing to the correspondent.

Other information

Grants are also made to organisations.

Elizabeth Finn Care

£3.9 million (3,689 grants)

Correspondent: Director of Casework, Hythe House, 200 Shepherds Bush Road, London W6 7NL (020 8834 9200; email: enquiries.casework@elizabethfinn.org.uk; website: www.elizabethfinncare.org.uk)

Trustees: Richard John Halcrow; Francesca Quint; Richard Charles Alastair Down; Cllr Jeremy Nettle; Matthew Baker; Michael Pavia; Frederick Payne; William Colvin; Sally O'Sullivan; Bryan John Laxton; Catherine Hamp; Mark Guymer.

CC Number: 207812

Eligibility

People who are British or Irish and have a professional or similar background or connection, and their dependents. Applicants must have a low income and have less than £4,000 in savings.

Types of grants

Recurrent grants are made towards daily living expenses. One-off grants are also available towards needs such as car expenses, household items, house repairs and adaptations, specialist equipment and help with nursing/residential fees. All grants are means-tested.

Annual grant total

In 2010/11 the charity had assets of £45 million and an income of £23 million. Grants and allowances to over 3,600 individuals totalled £3.9 million.

Exclusions

The trust will not give grants for healthcare costs, computer equipment, holidays, educational costs, debts, legal fees or funeral expenses.

Applications

Applicants should contact the charity to enquire about whether they are eligible, either via telephone or the website. If eligible an application form will be issued. This may be submitted either directly by the individual, through a third party such as a social worker or through an organisation such as a Citizens Advice or other welfare agency.

Other information

The association also manages its own residential and nursing homes.

The David Fogwill Charitable Trust

£7,000

Correspondent: Alex Fogwill, 53 Brook Drive, Corsham, Wiltshire SN13 9AX (01249 713408)

Trustees: Lindsay Fogwill; Alex Fogwill; Matthew Shaw; Bob Lynn.

CC Number: 1062342

Eligibility

People in need who are involved in Christian outreach projects or ministry.

Types of grants

One-off and recurrent grants ranging from £50 to £1,000. Support costs are usually paid to the organisations for whom the Christian outreach worker is contracted to.

Annual grant total

In 2010/11 the trust had an income of £14,000 and a total expenditure of £16,500. Grants to individuals in need totalled around £7,000.

Applications

In writing to the correspondent. Applications can be submitted directly by the individual or family member and should include details of the Christian activity and the organisation involved. Applications are considered in January and July.

Other information

The trust also makes grants to organisations.

The Stanley Foster Charitable Trust

£1,000

Correspondent: The Trustees, 4 Meadowcroft, Bromley BR1 2JD (020 8402 1341)

Trustees: John Martin Graham Hamilton-Sharp; Linda Mary Hamilton-Sharp; Vicki Andrea Reckless.

CC Number: 1085985

Eligibility

People in need in south east England.

Types of grants

One-off grants up to £1,000 mainly for medical support.

Annual grant total

About £1,000.

Applications

Grants are only made to individuals known to the trustees. The majority of grants are made to organisations.

Other information

The trust also makes grants to organisations.

The Ernest and Marjorie Fudge Trust

£8,000 (19 grants)

Correspondent: Joan Biancoli, Clerk to the trustees, 12 Rock Lane, Warminster, Wiltshire BA12 7HD (email: jbiancoli@yahoo.co.uk; website: www.fudgetrust.co.uk)

Trustees: William Allen Charles Knowles; Francis Ann Pearson; Robert Charles Wright; Angela Mary May; Stephan Paul Godfrey.

CC Number: 298545

Eligibility

People in need who live in Warminster and surrounding areas, with a preference for people with learning difficulties.

Types of grants

One-off and recurrent grants according to need. Recent grants have been made for items like mobility scooters, stairlifts and winter fuel payments.

Annual grant total

In 2010/11 the trust had assets of £1.1 million and an income of £37,000. Grants were made to 19 individuals.

Applications

On an online application form or on an application form available to download from the website. Applications should be countersigned by a social worker, minister of religion, solicitor or some other professional person who is independent of the applicant.

Other information

Grants are also made to organisations.

Fund for Human Need

£13,000 (128 grants)

Correspondent: S H Platt, 50 Leeds Road, Selby, North Yorkshire YO8 4HX (01757 706040; fax: 07006 024004)

Trustees: Robin George David Holmes; Olabisi Warden; Priscilla Vivian; Revd Roger Cresswell; Revd David Andrew Woosley; Revd Lord Roger Roberts; Revd Robert Maginley; Stanley Hodson Platt.

CC Number: 208866

Eligibility

Grants are available to refugees, asylum seekers, people who are homeless and anybody attempting to get over a short-term hurdle.

Types of grants

One-off and recurrent grants of up to £100 each. Grants are generally distributed via other organisations and charities.

Annual grant total

In 2010/11 grants were made to 128 individuals totalling £13,000.

Applications

Applications may be made in writing to the correspondent, including details of financial circumstances, however, the majority of applications are made through intermediary organisations.

Other information

Grants are also made to organisations.

The R. L. Glasspool Charity Trust

£1 million (4,721 grants)

Correspondent: Grants team, Second Floor, Saxon House, 182 Hoe Street, Walthamstow, London EH17 4QH (020 8520 4354; fax: 020 8520 9040; email: application@glasspool.org.uk (for application requests only); website: www.glasspool.org.uk)

Trustees: Maureen Perkins; Kevin Connelley; Kevin Mansell; Dr Keith Nunn; Matt Luheshi; Robert Birmingham; Mary Stimson; Kerri Phillips.

CC Number: 214648

Eligibility

People in need who are on a low income.

Types of grants

One-off grants ranging from £50 to £5,000, though in practice they rarely exceed £750. Grants are available for white goods, other household goods, clothing, school uniform, flooring, vocational materials and training, baby needs (if not eligible for a sure start maternity grant), travel expenses for hospital visits, equipment and adaptations for people with disabilities.

In very exceptional circumstances grants may be given for holidays, outstanding bills, household repairs and driving lessons/tests.

Annual grant total

In 2010/11 the trust surpassed a long-held objective of exceeding the £1 million mark in grant spending. 4,721 grants were made to individuals. The average small grant award was £245.

Exclusions

No grants for loans, debts, bursaries, project funding, research, rent, funeral costs or equipment and adaptations that should be funded by statutory services.

Applications

On a form available electronically on the trust's website, to be submitted through an eligible agency such as social services, any Council-run service, Surestart, Connexions, youth offending teams, NHS agencies, prison/probation service, Citizens Advice, Family Service Units, hospices or a relevant welfare agency such as Age Concern, Shelter or Mind. Under no circumstances does the trust accept applications directly from individuals.

The Grant Team will contact you within two to three weeks from issue of the application reference number. Do not contact us during this time as it slows down the grantmaking process. During assessment you will receive emails that will explain the process in more detail.

The email application form is designed for applying by email only. It should not be printed off. Any applications received by post-on email forms will be rejected.

Other information

The trust is one of the few national charities that has no restrictions on the type of beneficiary it can support and as such it is usually heavily oversubscribed. It is also heavily involved in policy and campaigning work, pressing for change to improve the lives of their beneficiaries.

The Margaret Jeannie Hindley Charitable Trust

£5,000

Correspondent: The Trustees, Marshalls Solicitors, 102 High Street, Godalming, Surrey GU7 1DS (01483 416101)

Trustees: Barry Kilburn; Sara Caroline Coate; Lisa Gabrielle Rabinowitz.

CC Number: 272140

Eligibility
Relief of poverty and distress among people in 'reduced or destitute circumstances'. In practice priority is given to people living in the Godalming area.

Types of grants
Some recurrent grants of £40 to £50 each month are made. One-off grants up to £750 are more usual.

Annual grant total
In 2010/11 the trust had an income of £14,000 and a total expenditure of £17,000. Grants totalled around £15,000, most of which was given to organisations.

Applications
In writing to the correspondent. The trustees meet regularly throughout the year to consider applications.

The Hoper-Dixon Trust

£43,000 (60 grants)

Correspondent: The Provincial Bursar, The Dominican Council, Blackfriars, St Giles, Oxford OX1 3LY (01865 288231; email: enquiries@hoperdixon. org.uk; website: www.hoperdixon.org. uk)

Trustees: Revd Benjamin Earl; Elizabeth Robertson; The Dominican Council Trust Corporation.

CC Number: 231160

Eligibility
People in need connected with, or resident in or near, any house or pastoral centre under the direction of the Dominicans of the English Province Order of Preachers.

Types of grants
One-off and recurrent grants according to need ranging from £100 to £1,000. Recent grants have been made to assist: with medical expenses; those unable to work through illness or injury; with unexpected and unforeseen expenses; relocation costs; basic household goods; and funeral costs. Grants are also given to help pilgrims attend Lourdes.

Annual grant total
In 2010/11 the trust held assets of £350,000 and had an income of £16,000. Grants were made to 60 individuals or families totalling £43,000.

Applications
Applications are normally made by a Dominican Friar for the benefit of someone connected with the Order or living in the neighbourhood of a house of the Order. A list of Dominican houses and contact details is available from the English Province of the Order of Preachers website.

Third-party welfare organisations applying on behalf of an individual should contact the trust in writing or by email to enquire about possible eligibility.

Other information
Grants may also be made for educational purposes.

The Houston Charitable Trust

£4,300

Correspondent: G A Houston, Pednor Chase, Pednor, Chesham, Buckinghamshire HP5 2SY

Trustees: Geoffrey Alan Houston; Gina Grania Houston; James Alexander Houston.

CC Number: 1083552

Eligibility
People in need worldwide.

Types of grants
One-off and recurrent grants according to need.

Annual grant total
In 2010/11 the trust had assets of £507,000 and an income of £101,000. Grants were made totalling £119,000 and were broken down as follows:

Advancement of the Christian faith	£38,000
Charities for the relief in poverty and those in need	£81,000

Of the latter category £4,300 was made in grants to individuals, the rest went to organisations.

Applications
In writing to the correspondent, though the trust has previously stated: 'unsolicited applications are not supported as the funds are already committed for the foreseeable future.'

The Johnston Family Trust

£17,000

Correspondent: B J S Parsons-Smith, Aspen Cottage, Apse Manor Road, Shanklin PO37 7PN (01512 366666)

Trustee: Johnston Family Trust Ltd.

CC Number: 207512

Eligibility
'Members of the upper and middle classes (and widows and daughters of such people) who, through no fault of their own, have fallen into impoverished circumstances.' Assistance is limited to men over 50 and women over 40.

Types of grants
Recurrent grants of £650 a year and one-off grants of around £100 each for TV licences and birthday gifts.

Annual grant total
In 2010 the trust had an income of £14,000 and a total expenditure of £20,000.

Applications
In writing to the correspondent. Applications are considered throughout the year.

The William Johnston Trust Fund

£25,000

Correspondent: B J S Parsons-Smith, Aspen Cottage, Apse Manor Road, Shanklin PO37 7PN (01512 366666)

Trustee: Johnston Family Trust Ltd.

CC Number: 212495

Eligibility
Older people in need who live in the UK.

Types of grants
Recurrent grants ranging from £250 to £2,000 and one-off grants for TV licences and birthdays.

Annual grant total
In 2010 the fund had assets of £995,000 and an income of £30,000. Grants were made to 40 individuals totalling £25,000.

Applications
In writing to the correspondent. Applications can be submitted directly by the individual or family member and are considered throughout the year.

St Jude's Trust

£0

Correspondent: R G Millman, Arnold Fooks Chadwick, 15 Bolton Street, Piccadilly, London W1J 8AR (020 7499 3007)

Trustees: William George Duckett; Rosemary K. Duckett.

CC Number: 222883

Eligibility

People in need through disability or disadvantage.

Types of grants

One-off and recurrent grants according to need.

Annual grant total

In 2010/11 the trust had assets of £920,000 and an income of £31,000. Grants to organisations totalled £25,000. No grants were made to individuals during the year.

Applications

In writing to the correspondent. They are considered twice a year. Acknowledgements are not given.

Kilcreggan Trust

£5,500

Correspondent: The Secretary, Manton Grange, Preshute Lane, Manton, Marlborough, Wiltshire SN8 4HQ (01672 514050)

Trustees: Kenneth Alan Carter; Gillian Carter; Charles Kian Wookey.

CC Number: 1017264

Eligibility

People in need in England and Wales.

Types of grants

One-off and recurrent grants according to need.

Annual grant total

In 2010/11 the trust had an income of £10,700 and a total expenditure of £6,200.

Applications

In writing to the correspondent.

The McKenna Charitable Trust

£0

Correspondent: Mr John L Boyton, Ingenious Media plc, 15 Golden Square, London W1F 9JG (020 7319 4000)

Trustees: Howard Randell Jones; John Boyton Leonard; Margaret McKenna; Patrick Anthony McKenna.

CC Number: 1050672

Eligibility

People in need in England and Wales, with a preference for supporting the educational needs and support of people with disabilities.

Types of grants

One-off grants are occasionally made to individuals, according to need.

Annual grant total

In 2010/11 the trust had assets of £52,000 and an income of £146,000. Grants were made to five organisations totalling £116,000. There were no grants made to individuals during the year.

Applications

In writing to the correspondent although the charity has stated that it does not consider or respond to unsolicited applications.

Motability

£19,500,000

Correspondent: Grants Directorate, Warwick House, Roydon Road, Harlow, Essex CM19 5PX (01279 635999; fax: 01279 632000; website: www.motability. co.uk)

Trustees: Mr B. A. Carte; Prof. A. V. Stokes; Sir Bert Massie; Sir Gerald Acher; Lord Sterling of Plaistow; Mr R. Bennison; Mr P. Spencer; Joanna Lewis; Prof. Peter N. C. Cooke; Alan Dickinson; Jerome Church.

CC Number: 299745

Eligibility

People who receive one of the following benefits: Higher Rate Mobility Component of Disability Living Allowance; War Pensioners' Mobility Supplement (WPMS); or a government vehicle, trike or mini.

Types of grants

Grants can be given towards 'the best value suitable solution that meets basic mobility needs'. These are usually: vehicle advance payments; supplying and fitting adaptations, for instance hand controls to enable somebody with a lower body disability to drive an automatic car or hoists to load electric wheelchairs into estate cars; driving lessons for people who are disabled, or whose children or spouses are disabled, especially people aged 16 to 24; or wheelchair accessible vehicles for customers who wish to get in a car while seated in their wheelchair.

Annual grant total

In 2010/11 the trust had assets of £4.6 million, an income of £25 million and made grants totalling £19.5 million. The majority of the grant funding, over £17 million, was provided by the Department for Work and Pensions and administered by Motability. Around £2.2 million was raised independently by Motability for distribution. Grants were made towards the following:

Towards a vehicle and/or adaptations	1,869
Towards wheelchair accessible passenger vehicles	1,793
Towards driving lessons	951
Towards more complex adaptation vehicles	233

Applications

Potential applicants should contact the customer services team on 0845 456 4566 and have the following information to hand: national insurance number; details of current motability car (if applicable); make, model and dimensions of your wheelchair or scooter; and details of any benefits, allowance or pensions. Applicants may be asked to visit a centre for assessment of transfer ability, give permission for third parties such as doctors to be contacted, and may receive a home visit.

Note: all successful applicants are expected to contribute a minimum of £200 towards their vehicle and/or adaptations. This amount could increase depending on the applicant's individual circumstances.

At times there may be waiting lists for some of the schemes, check the website or contact the customer services team to check.

Municipal General Charities for the Poor

£5,800

Correspondent: Michael Gamage, Clerk, Payne and Gamage Solicitors, 48 Lombard Street, Newark, Nottinghamshire NG24 IXP (01636 640649; fax: 01636 640627)

Trustees: Joan Whicher; Valerie Picker; Revd Alistair Conn; Cllr Peter Foster; Jean Moore; Revd Vivian Enever; Cllr Leonard Wilkes; Max Cope; David Tingle; Doreen Westmoreland; Vincent Dobson; Cllr Marika Tribe; Anthony Charles Roberts; Thomas Bickley; Rita Crowe.

CC Number: 217437

Eligibility

People in need who live in the borough of Newark.

Types of grants

One-off grants up to £300 are mainly given towards household items such as cookers, washing machines and furniture. Christmas gifts of £150 are also made.

Annual grant total

In 2010 the trust had assets of £975,000 and an income of £28,000. Grants to individuals totalled £5,800.

Applications

On a form available from the correspondent submitted through a social worker, Citizens Advice or other welfare agency. Applications are considered in February, May, August and November and must include details of the particular need.

Other information

The trust also makes grants to organisations.

The Natlas Trust

£30,000

Correspondent: Joel Adler, 32 Brampton Grove, London NW4 4AQ (020 7427 6532)

Trustees: Sarah Adler; Joel Adler.

CC Number: 1019856

Eligibility

People in need living in the UK or the State of Israel.

Types of grants

One-off and recurrent grants according to need.

Annual grant total

In 2010/11 the trust had assets of £575,000 and an income of £131,000. Grants were made totalling £189,000, the majority of which was likely given in grants to organisations. A list of grants was requested but still not available at the time of writing (January 2013).

Applications

In writing to the correspondent.

Newby Trust Ltd

£56,000

Correspondent: Miss Annabel Grout, Hill Farm, Froxfield, Petersfield, Hampshire GU32 1BQ (01730 827557; email: info@newby-trust.org.uk; website: www.newby-trust.org.uk)

Trustees: Anna Lucinda Foxell; Anne Shirley Reed; Jean Margaret Gooder; Ben Gooder; Dr Richard Dennis Gooder; Susan Ann Charlton; Evelyn Frances Bentley; Nigel Callaghan.

CC Number: 227151

Eligibility

People in the UK with welfare or medical needs. Beneficiaries are generally in receipt of welfare benefits, such as Income Support and Disability Living Allowance or living on a low wage.

Types of grants

One-off grants of £10 to £200, for items such as mobility aids, household essentials, furnishings, clothing, school uniforms and footwear.

Annual grant total

In 2010/11 the trust had assets of £14 million and an income of £321,000. Grants were made to 380 individuals totalling £56,000, of which £51,000 was given for welfare purposes and £5,000 in medical grants.

Exclusions

The trust does not provide full funding for larger items, such as washing machines, but can make a contribution to the overall costs. No grants are given to pay debt arrears or bankruptcy fees.

Applications

Social Services, NHS Trusts or registered charities may apply online on behalf of individuals in need. Applications made directly by the individual are not accepted. Cheques are payable to the sponsoring organisation. Full guidelines are available on the website.

Other information

Grants are mostly given to organisations and for research purposes.

Npower Energy Fund

Correspondent: Charis Grants, Freepost-RSRX-JHTT-AZSG, PO Box 42, Peterborough PE3 8XH (01733 421060; email: npfef@charisgrants.com; website: www.npowerenergyfund.com)

Eligibility

Domestic customers of NPower who are in need, hardship or distress.

Types of grants

One-off grants to help customers clear household utility debts. Successful applicants will be notified that they have been awarded a provisional grant. An applicant must then prove that they can continue to make sustainable payments for three months and after successful completion of this period the award is confirmed. Grant recipients cannot re-apply for assistance for a period of two years. If you have been accepted onto the provisional scheme but your award is not confirmed you may re-apply six months after the date of the decision letter. If you do not make the provisional award stage you may apply again if your circumstances change.

Annual grant total

No figures were available and the administrators were not available for comment.

Exclusions

No grants to pay for: fines for criminal offences; overpayment of benefits; education or training needs; debts to central or local government; personal, non-priority debts; holidays; medical equipment, aids or adaptations; or accommodation deposits.

Applications

Online via the website or by downloading an application form or requesting one by calling the application request line. Applications must be made by the named account holder including all relevant supporting documentation. Applicants will be notified of the outcome of their application in writing. The fund recommends applicants seek money advice before applying in order to help them deal with any other creditors.

Other information

The fund was formed in November 2010 with a £2 million donation from NPower.

The Osborne Charitable Trust

£1,000

Correspondent: John Eaton, 57 Osborne Villas, Hove, East Sussex BN3 2RA (01273 732500; email: john@eaton207.fsnet.co.uk)

Trustees: John Head; David Goldin; John Eaton.

CC Number: 326363

Eligibility

People in need in the UK and overseas.

Annual grant total

In 2010/11 the trust had an income of £6,200 and a total expenditure of £13,000. Grants are made to organisations and individuals.

Exclusions

No grants for religious or political purposes.

Applications

This trust does not respond to unsolicited applications.

Professionals Aid Council

£80,000 (306 grants)

Correspondent: Fiona McNicholl, 10 St Christopher's Place, London W1U 1HZ (020 7935 0641; email: admin@professionalsaid.org.uk)

Trustees: Christopher Everett; Jennifer Anderson; Peter Dixon; Beryl Greenslade; Robert Caton; Mary

Springham; Lucy Carmichael; Astrid Lewis.

CC Number: 207292

Eligibility

Professionals with a strong educational background (degree level or equivalent). Applicants must be resident in the UK and have less than £10,000 in savings.

Types of grants

Grant recipients cannot re-apply for assistance for a period of two years. If you have been accepted onto the provisional scheme but your award is not confirmed you may re-apply six months after the date of the decision letter. If you do not make the provisional award stage you may apply again if your circumstances change.

Annual grant total

In 2011 the charity had assets of £2.1 million and an income of £108,000. During the year weekly grants were made to 103 beneficiaries and 203 one-off grants were also made, altogether totalling £80,000.

Exclusions

No grants for private medical fees, vet bills or pet insurance, debts, mortgage repayments or utility bills or electronic equipment.

Applications

By completing the initial enquiry form online or writing to the correspondent. Grants are means tested.

Other information

The organisation also offers advice and assistance. Grants are also made for educational purposes.

The J. C. Robinson Trust No. 3

£20,000

Correspondent: Christine Howe, Barnett Wood Bungalow, Blackboys, Uckfield, East Sussex TN22 5JL

Trustees: Christopher John Burns-Cox; Christine Howe.

CC Number: 207294

Eligibility

People in need in England, with a preference for the elderly, people with disabilities and those living in East Sussex, Bristol and south Gloucester.

Types of grants

Grants range from £50 to £1,000 according to need.

Annual grant total

In 2010/11 the trust had an income of £24,000. Grants to individuals totalled around £20,000.

Applications

In writing to the correspondent, including supporting documents giving evidence of need, such as a letter from a doctor or social worker. Applications should usually be made through an organisation such as Citizens Advice or through a third party such as a social worker.

Other information

A small number of grants are also made to organisations.

Mrs L. D. Rope's Second Charitable Settlement

£13,000 (16 grants)

Correspondent: Crispin Rope, Trustee, Crag Farm, Boyton, Near Woodbridge, Suffolk IP12 3LH

Trustees: Crispin Rope; Philip Hugh Jolly; Anne Folan; Anne Susan Ruffell.

CC Number: 275810

Eligibility

People in need, with a preference for people who are resident in Suffolk.

Types of grants

One-off and recurrent grants ranging from £50 to £10,000. Grants are given for the relief of poverty and for the support of religion and education. Almost all grants are made to charities or organisations with which the trust has long-term connections or at the recommendation of members of the late founders' families.

Annual grant total

In 2010/11 the trust made 39 grants totalling £87,000, 16 of which were made to individuals (around £13,000).

Applications

The trust does not invite unsolicited applications. The 2010/11 accounts note that grants were made to individuals 'known to the trustees.'

Mr William Saunders Charity for the Relief of Indigent Gentry and Others

£6,000

Correspondent: Richard Kirby, Speechly Bircham LLP, 6 St Andrew Street, London EC4A 3LX (020 7427 6400)

Trustees: Mark Musgrave; Richard Kirby; John Ward; Jeremy Hudson.

CC Number: 212012

Eligibility

'Indigent gentry, tutors, governesses, merchants and others'; and their dependents, who are in need.

Types of grants

One-off and recurrent grants according to need.

Annual grant total

In 2010/11 the trust had an income of £9,000 and a total expenditure of £11,000. In previous years grants have totalled about £6,000.

Applications

In writing to the correspondent.

Other information

Grants are also made to local organisations caring for people in need.

The Severn Trent Water Charitable Trust Fund

£3.4 million (4,291 grants)

Correspondent: Grants Officer, 12–14 Mill Street, Sutton Coldfield, West Midlands B72 1TJ (01213 557766; email: office@sttf.org.uk; website: www.sttf.org.uk)

Trustees: Derek Harris; Elizabeth Pusey; David Vaughan; Alexandra Gribbin; Lowri Williams; Mrs S. Hayman.

CC Number: 1108278

Eligibility

People with water or sewage services by Severn Trent Water or by companies or organisations which operate on behalf of Severn Trent, who are in financial difficulty and unable to pay their water charges.

Types of grants

One-off grants are given to clear or reduce water and/or sewage debt. Further assistance can be given through the purchase of essential household items or by the payment of other priority bills and debts. These grants are limited and will normally only be given if an application shows either that it will help the individual maintain a future sustainable weekly budget, or it will make an important and significant difference to the individual's quality of life.

Annual grant total

In 2010/11 the fund had assets of £1.4 million and an income of £5.6 million. During the year the fund received 10,000 applications for help. Grants were made to 4,291 individuals totalling £3.4 million and distributed as follows:

Water and sewage charges	£3,100,000
Council tax	£600
Rent	£2,000
Gas	£8,700
Electricity	£48,500
Telephone	£1,400
Other household needs	£136,500
Bankruptcy orders	£45,000

Exclusions

No grants are made for court fines, personal debts, social fund loans or benefit overpayments. No retrospective grants are given. Grants are usually one-off and applicants cannot reapply within two years of receipt.

Applications

On a form available from the correspondent or to download from the website. Applications can be submitted at any time by the individual or through a money advice centre, Citizens Advice or similar third party, to: Severn Trent Trust Fund, FREEPOST RLZE-EABT-SHSA, Sutton Coldfield B72 1TJ.

Applicants may receive a telephone call or visit as part of the application process. Unsuccessful applicants may reapply after six months.

Other information

The fund also makes grants to organisations which provide free debt advice and debt counselling services (£369,000 in 2010/11).

The Skinners' Benevolent Trust (formerly the Hunt and Almshouse Charities)

£20,000

Correspondent: Grants Administrator, Skinners Hall, 8 Dowgate Hill, London EC4R 2SP (020 7213 0562; fax: 020 7236 6590; email: charitiesadmin@skinners. org.uk; website: www.skinnershall.co.uk)

Trustee: Worshipful Company of Skinners.

CC Number: 1132640

Eligibility

The Skinners' Benevolent Trust aims to support individuals living on a very low income, who have been cut off in some way from society and who are trying to re-build their lives. It provides grants for essential household items that cannot be paid for from statutory funds.

Adults who fall into one (or more) of the following priority areas can apply: living with mental health issues; in recovery from substance/alcohol use; victims of domestic violence. Also, adults who are in receipt of a state retirement pension and/or have some kind of disability or chronic illness. Applicants must live in one of the designated

geographical areas. For a complete list of these (and all criteria and eligibility) refer to the website.

Types of grants

One-off grants of up to £250 towards essential household items.

Annual grant total

In 2010/11 grants and pensions were awarded to 168 individuals totalling £55,000.

Exclusions

The trust cannot help with applications made by individuals or organisations providing one-off support or advice; applicants who have received a grant from the charity in the previous two years; general financial assistance, including debt and utility costs; items that are available from the Social Fund (or Community Care Grant); mobility or computer equipment; building work; items that have already been purchased; applications on behalf of children; applications that fall outside its criteria.

Applications

On a form available from the correspondent. Applications must be supported by a medical professional or someone working within a recognised social care agency, such as Social Services, disability information and support organisations, housing support agencies or local charities. This person should have a personal and ongoing knowledge of the applicant's circumstances and the ability to receive and monitor any grant. Applications are normally processed within six weeks, though urgent cases can be considered more quickly.

Other information

The trust has an informative website.

The Henry Smith Charity (UK)
See entry on page 163

The St Martin-in-the-Fields' Christmas Appeal Charity

£377,000

Correspondent: Craig Norman, Clerk to the trustees, St Martin-in-the-Fields, 6 St Martin's Place, London WC2N 4JH (020 7766 1125; fax: 020 7839 0773; email: craig.norman@smitf.org; website: www.smitf.org/page/care/appeal.html)

Trustees: Simon Wethered; Veronica Fraser; Fred Pittock; Nigel Ray; Michael James Woolridge; Patricia Catahna.

CC Number: 261359

Eligibility

People in need or hardship. Priority is given to those who are in danger of becoming homeless, those who are currently homeless, destitute and/or vulnerable, and those attempting to establish or maintain a tenancy.

Types of grants

One-off grants of up to £250 to have a positive impact and help alleviate distress or avert a crisis. Grants have been given towards a range of needs, including furniture, child and adult clothing, domestic appliances, equipment for babies and toddlers, rent deposits, utility bills and household maintenance and repair.

Only one grant is usually made to an individual/family within 12 months.

Annual grant total

In 2010/11 the charity made over 2,000 grants totalling £377,000. The average grant was around £180.

Exclusions

No grants for holidays, course fees, recurring costs, holidays, respite breaks, school trips, IT equipment, medical treatment, TV's and TV licences, childcare expenses, toys, books and play equipment, administrative charges, fines and professional fees, structural renovations or specialist equipment such as wheelchairs.

Applications

On a form available from the administrator. Applications should not be made directly by the individual but through agencies such as social services, probation, Citizens Advice or other welfare agencies. If applying in writing, applicants are asked to print on letterhead. Applications should include the name and address of the individual/family in need, current circumstances, amount required and the name of the organisation the cheque will be payable to. When applying for repayment of arrears or for the cost of a bankruptcy petition, describe how the debts incurred. Requests for funds can usually be considered within four days.

Other information

The charity transfers 50% of its grants to The Connection at St Martin-in-the-Fields, a connected charity, each year.

The St Vincent de Paul Society (England and Wales)

£50,000

Correspondent: Elizabeth Palmer, 5th Floor, 291–299 Borough Hill Street, London SE1 1JG (020 7407 4644; fax:

020 7407 4634; email: info@svp.org.uk; website: www.svp.org.uk)

Trustees: Adrian Abel; Richard Edward Massey; Gregory Edward Pelham; Michael Anthony Worthington; Kevin Thomas McDermott; Joseph Gilfillan; Marie Atherton; Michael Walmsley; Michael Brady; Ingrid Phillips.

CC Number: 1053992

Eligibility

Anyone in need in England and Wales. Although predominantly a Catholic charity, it is completely non-denominational in its operation. Grants are only offered following a visit from a member of the society.

Types of grants

Material assistance is given in the provision of furniture, food, appliances, clothes, fuel and small financial disbursements. Friendship to anyone in need is a fundamental principle of the society; financial relief is incidental to this. During the year over 507,000 visits were made to 77,000 individuals and families across England and Wales. Approximately one in five visitations involved the provision of material assistance which the society notes 'is a significant increase on the previous year which reflects the increasing need in the current economic climate.'

Annual grant total

The trust is not primarily a grantmaking organisation, and will only make financial assistance through the family support and befriending schemes. In 2010/11 the total expenditure on these areas was £1.5 million, however, the trust does not publish separate grant figures. In previous years grants had amounted to around £50,000.

Exclusions

There are no grants available for education.

Applications

In writing to the correspondent at any time. Applications can be submitted directly by the individual or through any third party, such as advice centres or probation services. The application should detail the nature of the request and relevant background information. A contact address and telephone number for the person requiring assistance must be provided to enable staff to arrange a visit.

Other information

There are about 1,600 parish groups in England and Wales, with around 10,000 members. Most of the income is raised locally by members and distributed by them. The society runs several children's camps, holiday caravans and a number of hostels, shops and furniture stores. Prison visitations take place in some areas, and a 'Catholic Cassette' for the blind and partially sighted is available. Considerable support is given to the developing world and Romania.

Mary Strand Charitable Trust

£65,000

Correspondent: Lynda Walker, Universe Media Group Ltd, Landmark House, Station Road, Cheadle Hulme, Cheadle SK8 7JH (01614 881700; email: lynda. walker@totalcatholic.com)

Trustees: Anthony Murray; Joseph Kelly; Kevin Flaherty; Mary Concannon; Lynda Walker; Mark Wiggin.

CC Number: 800301

Eligibility

People who are in need due to poverty, sickness or old age.

Types of grants

One-off and recurrent grants, towards items like household goods, essential travel costs and clothing.

Annual grant total

In 2010 the trust had assets of £523,000 and an income of £70,000. Grants totalling £65,000 were made during the year.

Applications

In writing to the correspondent, to be submitted either directly by the individual or through a local priest, charity or welfare agency.

Other information

The trustees publish a column in each edition of The Universe, a weekly Catholic newspaper. The column contains details of deserving causes with names changed to preserve anonymity, and appeals are made for specific requirements. Donations from readers are received in answer to these appeals and then distributed.

Grants are also paid to organisations (£43,000 in 2010).

Sir John Sumner's Trust

£0

Correspondent: Ian Henderson, Secretary to the Trustees, 1 Colmore Square, Birmingham B4 6AA (0870 763 1490)

Trustees: J. Sumner; J. Fea; Lady J. Wellesley; Mrs V. McKie; A. Robson.

CC Number: 218620

Eligibility

People in need who are resident in the UK, with strong preference for the Midlands.

Types of grants

One-off grants ranging between £30 and £70. The trust will sometimes give an amount towards larger requests if other charities make up the rest.

Annual grant total

In 2010/11 the trust had assets of £765,000 and an income of £33,000. Grants made to institutions totalled £32,000; it appears that no grants were made to individuals during the year.

Exclusions

No grants towards religious or political causes.

Applications

On a form available from the correspondent, supported by an appropriate welfare agency. Applications can be considered at any time.

The Talisman Charitable Trust

£95,000 (117 grants)

Correspondent: Philip Denman, Lower Ground Floor Office, 354 Kennington Road, London SE11 4LD (020 7820 0254; website: www.talismancharity.org)

Trustees: Philip Denman; Dr Francesca Marie-Carola Denman; Nicholas Caine.

CC Number: 207173

Eligibility

People in the UK who are living on a very low income.

Types of grants

One-off and recurrent grants according to need.

Annual grant total

In 2010/11 the trust had assets of £8.6 million and an income of £155,000. Over 1,100 applications for assistance were received. Grants were made to 107 individuals totalling £95,000 and were distributed as follows:

Housing	73	£51,000
Disablement or disability	22	£33,000
Child poverty	6	£6,200
Small means or hardship	3	£3,200
Poverty	3	£1,500

Grants were also made to seven organisations totalling £50,000. The trust commonly distributes sums in the region of £130,000 – £150,000 each year and also makes grants for educational purposes.

Applications

In writing to the correspondent through a social worker, Citizens Advice or similar third party.

Applications should be on headed paper and include the individual's full name and address, a summary of their financial circumstances, what is needed and how much it will cost. A brief history of the case and a list of any other charities approached should be included as well. Supporting evidence such as medical documentation, a letter from the applicant's school and written quotations would also be helpful. Applications are considered throughout the year. Only successful applications will receive a reply.

Note: applications should not be sent by recorded delivery or any 'signed for' services. Original documentation should not be included as it cannot be returned.

Other information

This trust was previously called The Late Baron F A D'Erlanger's Charitable Trust.

The Three Oaks Trust

£68,000 (393 grants)

Correspondent: The Trustees, The Three Oaks Family Trust Co. Ltd, PO Box 893, Horsham, West Sussex RH12 9JD (email: contact@thethreeoakstrust.co.uk; website: www.thethreeoakstrust.co.uk)

Trustees: Carol Johnson; Pamela Anne Wilkinson; Dr Paul Kane; Sarah Anne Kane; Carol Vivian Foreman; Polly Elizabeth Hobbs; Dianne Margaret Ward; Giles Duncan Wilkinson; The Three Oaks Family Trust Company Ltd.

CC Number: 297079

Eligibility

People and families in need who live in West Sussex. There is a particular focus on people with a physical or mental disability (including learning difficulties), and on low-income families, single parents and the long-term sick.

Types of grants

One-off grants of up to £150 towards basic furnishings, clothing, washing machines, fridges, telephone connections and so on.

Annual grant total

In 2010/11 the trust held assets of £5.8 million and had an income of £212,000. 393 grants to individuals totalled £68,000.

Exclusions

No funding for gap year work or similar activities.

Applications

On a form available from the correspondent or to download from the website. Applications can only be made through Crawley and Horsham Social Services and Citizens Advicex and other invited local agencies. Details of the agency to which any cheque should be made payable should be included in the application. Unsuccessful applicants will not be contacted.

The trust has noted in its accounts that 'in the case of long-term difficulties, the trustees are more likely to be sympathetic to a request if the person or family on behalf of whom the request is being made, is able to reflect on whether there are any changes they could make to prevent the same problems reoccurring.' Further guidelines are offered on the trust website.

The Vardy Foundation

£59,000

Correspondent: The Chair of the Trustees, Venture House, Aykley Heads, Durham DH1 5TS (01913 744744; website: www.vardyfoundation.com)

Trustees: Lady Margaret Barr Vardy; Peter D. D. Vardy; Sir Peter Vardy; Victoria Helen Vardy.

CC Number: 328415

Eligibility

People in need in who live in the UK.

Types of grants

One-off and recurrent grants according to need.

Annual grant total

In 2008/09 the foundation had assets of £22 million and an income of £4 million. Grants were made to 41 individuals totalling £118,000, for both welfare and educational purposes.

Exclusions

The trust states that it 'does not accept unsolicited grants from individuals for educational or hardship grants. Grants are given to charitable organisations and individuals at the discretion of the trustees'.

Applications

In writing to the correspondent.

Other information

Grants are also made to organisations (£1.5 million in 2008/09).

Asylum seekers

Asylum Seeker Support Initiative – Short Term (ASSIST)

£62,000

Correspondent: Welfare Payments Team, c/o Victoria Hall Methodist Church, 60 Norfolk Street, Sheffield, South Yorkshire S1 2JB (01142 754960; email: admin@assistsheffield.org.uk; website: www.assistsheffield.org.uk)

Trustees: Mr P. Harvey; Mr R. T. Chessum; Mrs M. W. Davis; Ms J. McFarlane; P. Snell; G. Clayton; Mr T. Makwenha; Mr M. Magadzire.

CC Number: 1100894

Eligibility

Asylum seekers who live in Sheffield.

Types of grants

Small weekly grants for food and basic living expenses, usually £20 per person.

Annual grant total

In 2010/11 the charity had assets of £92,000 and an income of £171,000. Grants were made totalling £62,000. The normal grant for asylum seekers is £20 per week per person.

Applications

Preliminary contact should be made with the charity.

Other information

This charity is also provides advice and information and runs awareness-raising activities.

Carers and volunteers

The Andrew Anderson Trust

£5,500

Correspondent: Andrew Anderson, Trustee, 1 Cote House Lane, Bristol BS9 3UW (01179 621588)

SC Number: SC008507

Eligibility

People who are, or were, involved in charitable activities, and their dependents, who are in need.

Types of grants

One-off and recurrent grants according to need.

Annual grant total

In 2010/11 the trust had assets of £10 million and an income of £247,000. Grants to individuals for welfare and education totalled £39,000.

Applications

The trust states that it rarely gives to people who are not known to the trustees or who have not been personally recommended by people known to the trustees. Unsolicited applications are therefore unlikely to be successful.

Other information

Grants are also given to organisations.

The Care Professionals Benevolent Fund

£34,000 (19 grants)

Correspondent: Shaun Turner, 19 Bollin Grove, Prestbury, Macclesfield, Cheshire SK10 4JJ (0845 601 9055; email: info@ cpbenevolentfund.org.uk; website: www. cpbenevolentfund.org.uk)

Trustees: Martin Green; Dr Richard Hawkins; Avinsh Goyal; Davina Ludlow; Robin Cheesman; Janet Lloyd-Leech.

CC Number: 1132286

Eligibility

Current and former employees of the care profession and their dependents who are in need. Former employees must have worked one continuous year in the past five and have previously worked seven years in their lifetime in a registered domiciliary or residential care service in the UK. Applicants must have limited savings and income.

Types of grants

One-off grants of between £250 and £5,000. Recurrent grants are also given to top up low incomes and help people through short periods of crisis.

Annual grant total

In 2011 the fund held assets of £146,000 and had an income of £56,000. Grants to 19 individuals totalled £34,000.

Exclusions

No grants for education, most private medical treatments or care fees shortfalls.

Applications

On an application form available to download from the website. Applicants must complete an online entitlement check and send the results report along with their application. Detailed guidelines on completing the application form are also available on the website. Applications are usually considered within two weeks and decisions are confirmed in writing.

The Carers Trust

£46,000

Correspondent: The Clerk, Unit 14, Bourne Court, Southend Road, Woodford Green, Essex, IG8 8HD (0844 800 4361; email: grants@carers.org; website: www.carers.org)

Trustees: Dr Peter Mayer; Timothy Poole; Patrick Healy; Elin Fitzpatrick; Andrew Cozens; Mark Currie; Esrald Bennett; Tania Fitzgerald; Jo Barrett; Stuart Taylor; Dr Edward Wojakovski.

CC Number: 1145181

Eligibility

Unpaid carers in the UK, especially those who live near one of the trust's carers centres.

Types of grants

One-off grants. Carers can apply for grants of up to £400 from the Carers Relief Fund to purchase equipment that will have a direct and long-term impact, not only on their caring role, but also on their overall quality of life.

Annual grant total

In 2010/11 the Princess Royal Trust for Carers gave 399 grants to individuals totalling £92,000. Grants may also be made for educational purposes.

Applications

Applications are made via your local Carers Trust centre, a list of which is available on the website. Direct applications will not be considered.

Other information

The trust is a new charity formed by the merger of The Princess Royal Trust for Carers and Crossroads Care in April 2012. At the time of writing (March 2013) we were not able to confirm whether the trust was still continuing to make grants since the merger, therefore this information relates to the Princess Royal Trust as it was prior to the merger. Applicants are advised to contact their local centre to enquire about potential grants.

The Margaret Champney Rest and Holiday Fund

£15,000

Correspondent: Gillian Galvan, General Manager, The Gate House, 9 Burkitt Road, Woodbridge, Suffolk IP12 4JJ (01394 388746; email: ogilviecharities@ btconnect.com; website: theogilvietrust.org.uk)

Trustees: Patrick Grieve; Belinda Grant; Felicity Anne Lowe; Margaret Smith; Richard Aynsley-Smith; D. Allan Howell;

Jean Goyder; Jolyon Dean Sunderland Hall; Roger Brayshaw; Simon Gibbs; Edward Wright.

CC Number: 211646

Eligibility

Carers, particularly those caring for a severely disabled relative, who need a break away from the person they are caring for. Occasionally, grants may be made to couples or adult family members where one is the primary carer for the other and they wish to holiday together.

Types of grants

Generally one-off grants of between £200 and £300.

Annual grant total

In 2010 the trust had an income of £12,800 and a total expenditure of £17,000. Grants were made totalling around £15,000.

Exclusions

Grants are not available towards 'normal' family holidays.

Applications

In writing or via email to the correspondent, through a social worker, community nurse or similar professional agency. Applications can be considered at any time, and should include the professional's name, job title and name and address of the organisation they represent as well as the name of the applicant and a brief summary of their circumstances. They should also include full details of weekly income and expenditure, details of other agencies being approached for funding, who will care for the person while the break is being taken and the proposed holiday venue, date and likely costs.

An income and expenditure form may be downloaded from the trust's website.

Open Wing Trust

Correspondent: Jennifer Kavanagh, Clerk, 44 Langham Street, London W1W 7AU (email: Online contact form; website: www.openwing.org.uk)

Trustees: Jennifer Kavanagh; Penny Markell; Mirabai Swingler; Stephen Petter; Alexandra Porter; Maggie Waterworth.

CC Number: 1149779

Eligibility

Individuals in England and Wales at the beginning of their career and those contemplating a radical re-orientation of their life's work or the deepening of an existing vision. The trustees advise: 'we expect applicants to be in a process of inner change leading to a socially engaged commitment to working with those in need.'

Types of grants

One-off grants according to need. 'Trustees will consider funding specific living costs such as food and rent, training programmes, or offering support during voluntary work or an internship. We will not fund holidays or unspecified thinking time.'

Annual grant total

This newly established trust expects to fund up to three small grants each year, up to a total maximum of £4,000.

Exclusions

No re-applications for further funding will be considered within five years of an initial grant. No grants for organisations or to fund specific work.

Applications

On an application form available to download from the website. Applications should be accompanied by two supporting letters from referees who have known the applicant for at least five years. Applicants will need to demonstrate commitment to their purpose, and that they are in need of financial support to make it feasible. Consult the guidance notes on the trust website before applying to ensure that your application is in line with the aims and values of the trust.

Trustees meet twice a year to consider applications, but can make decisions between meetings. Suitable applicants will be invited to meet the trustees.

Children and young people

Active Foundation

£1,200

Correspondent: The Secretary, Unit G, 41 Warwick Road, Solihull B92 7HS (01217 074260)

Trustees: Ann Baddeley; Mark James Wilson; Robert Arthur Baddeley.

CC Number: 1076709

Eligibility

Children, people who are disadvantaged and people with disabilities.

Types of grants

One-off and recurrent grants according to need. Grants made have included those towards the purchase of equipment, wheelchairs, hoists and so on, activity holidays for children and adolescents being treated for various chronic illnesses and hospital

transportation costs for a girl who had a kidney transplant.

Annual grant total

In 2010/11 the foundation had an income and total expenditure of £1,300.

Applications

In writing to the correspondent.

Other information

Grants are also made to organisations.

Buttle UK – Small Grants Programme

£1.7 million (7,900 grants)

Correspondent: Alan Cox, Audley House, 13 Palace Street, London SW1E 5HX (020 7798 6227; email: info@buttleuk.org; website: www.buttleuk.org)

Trustees: David Anderson; Elizabeth Stearns; Keith Mullins; Richard Buttle; Stephen Fielding; Gordon Anderson; Clare Montagu; Trevor Reaney; Dominic Vallely; Julia Ogilvy.

CC Number: 313007

Eligibility

Children and young people with acute needs, including those living with any kind of disability; children suffering from illness, distress, abuse or neglect; children with behavioural or psychological problems; and, those living in severe poverty and deprivation.

The following groups are eligible to apply: adopted children; children cared for by grandparents, other relatives or friends; children and young people who are aged 18 years and under, cared for by single or two parents; and, estranged, orphaned and vulnerable young people under 21 who are living independently.

Types of grants

One-off grants for essential items or services which are critical to the well-being of the child. For example, beds, bedding, clothing (if there is very urgent need), essential items of furniture and household equipment, and, occasionally, short-term therapy costs.

Annual grant total

In 2010/11 the trust made 7,900 grants totalling £1.7 million under their small grants scheme.

Exclusions

The trust cannot help children and young people who are: in care, being rehabilitated home, subject to a Child Protection Plan, or where there is any other clear statutory responsibility; aged 19–20 and do not have full refugee status or exceptional or indefinite leave to remain in the UK, or who are normally resident abroad; living outside the UK. There are no grants towards payment of

debts, holiday and child care costs, flooring/carpeting, bedroom storage, specialist equipment, computers or adaptations to houses and cars. No repeat grants are made.

Applications

Register and apply online, or request a form from the correspondent. Applications must be made through a statutory agency or voluntary organisation that is capable of assessing the needs of the child and that can also administer a grant on behalf of the trust; where no such organisation exists, the trust will discuss alternative arrangements. For full details refer to the trust's website.

Contact details for applicants resident in:

England: Audley House, 13 Palace Street, London SW1E 5HX, infor@buttleuk.org, 020 7828 7311

Scotland: PO Box 5075, Glasgow G78 4WA, annmariep@buttleuk.org, 01505 850437

Wales: PO Box 224, Caerphilly CF83 9EE, wales@buttleuk.org, 01633 440052

Northern Ireland: PO Box 484, Belfast BT6 0YA, nireland@buttleuk.org, 02890 641164.

Other information

The trust was founded by the Rev W F Buttle in 1953.

Grants are also given for educational purposes to schoolchildren and university students.

Children Today Charitable Trust

£154,000 (104 grants)

Correspondent: A Dodd, The Moorings, Rowton Bridge, Christleton, Chester CH3 7AE (01244 335622; fax: 01244 335473; email: info@children-today.org.uk; website: www.children-today.org.uk)

Trustees: Nigel Rose; Paul Tranter; Peter Evans; David Allan; John Stitt.

CC Number: 1137436

Eligibility

Children and young people under 25 who have a disability.

Types of grants

Grants of up to £1,000 to provide vital, life-changing specialist equipment, such as wheelchairs, walking aids, trikes, educational toys, communication aids, lifting and posturepaedic sleep equipment and specially designed sensory equipment like fibre optic sprays.

Annual grant total

The trust incorporated in 2010, therefore, these figures are for the six month period between October 2010 and March 2011: during this time the trust held assets of £123,000 and had an income of £350,000. Money distributed for special aids and equipment totalled £154,000.

Applications

Application forms are available from the correspondent. Grants are only given for specialised pieces of equipment for individual children (not groups or schools), and applications must be made by the individual applying, their parent, or legal guardian. The charity aims to deal with all applications within 28 days of receipt.

Only one application in any 12 month period.

Other information

If you wish to apply for computer equipment, the charity works in partnership with the Aidis Trust, and encourages applicants to contact them directly.

The Family Fund

£30,600,000 (56,728 grants)

Correspondent: Claire White, Unit 4, Alpha Court, Monks Cross Drive, Huntington, York YO32 9WN (0844 974 4099; fax: 01904 652625; email: info@ familyfund.org.uk; website: www. familyfund.org.uk)

Trustees: Gareth Jones; Joe Leigh; Dr Patricia Jackson; Anthony Kemmer; Robin Hindle Fisher; Kate Eleanor Young; Paula De-Valle; Dr Christopher Peter Hanvey; Lady Karen Elizabeth Girvan.

CC Number: 1053866

Eligibility

Families who are caring at home for a child aged 17 or under who is severely disabled or seriously ill. Eligible families must show evidence of their entitlement to one of the following: child tax credit, working tax credit, income based job seekers allowance, income support, incapacity benefit, employment and support allowance, housing benefit and pension credit. If you do not receive any of the above, further information may be needed to complete your application. Applicants must have permanent legal residency in the UK and have lived in the UK for six months.

Types of grants

The help given must be related to the child's care needs. The top three types of grant in 2010/11 by total spend were:

Holidays and outings	£14.3 million
White goods	£4.8 million
Computers	£3.2 million

Grants were also given for clothing, bedding, hospital visiting expenses, driving lessons, recreation/entertainment, furniture and flooring.

Annual grant total

In 2010/11 the fund made grants to 56,728 individual families totalling £30.6 million.

The number of families helped was distributed across the UK as follows:

England	44,614
Scotland	4,816
Wales	4,465
Northern Ireland	2,833

Exclusions

The fund cannot provide items which are the responsibility of statutory agencies, such as medical or educational equipment or small items for daily living, such as bath aids, which are the responsibility of Social Services. No funding is given for general household bills, utility bills, mortgage or rent payments or household repairs. No grants for families receiving NASS payments. The fund cannot help foster carers.

Applications

Applications can be made by parents, carers or young people aged 16 and 17. Application forms and guidance notes are available to download from the fund's website or may be obtained by contacting the fund. Brief details about the child's disability and how this affects daily life are also needed. Tell the fund what kind of help is being requested, putting requests in order of importance to you and your family.

If you are making an application on behalf of more than one disabled child, complete an additional child form for each child you are applying for.

The fund tries to help families raising a disabled or seriously ill child or young person once every year. If you have been helped by the fund before the decision letter confirming the grant should state when you are eligible to re-apply, which is usually 12 months, but may be longer. If you have applied before you may be able to apply online using your Family Fund number. The fund may consider early applications in certain circumstances.

Receipt of applications is acknowledged by text message. If it is your first application the trust may arrange a home visit or a follow-up telephone call. Applications are typically assessed in 3–4 months.

Applicants are advised to always check the website before applying as an

increased demand has seen some funds close early in recent years.

Other information

The fund is funded entirely by the government administrations of England, Northern Ireland, Scotland and Wales, and works within guidelines agreed by the trustees. More information about the Family Fund and a publications list are available from the Information Officer at the above address. This includes 'Introducing the Family Fund Trust' which outlines how the trust works and the guidelines used.

The trust decides whether a child is 'severely disabled' by considering the child's age, how much his or her abilities are affected and how much care the child needs. The trust will ask for details of diagnosis, treatment and expected outcomes of the child's condition. However, it is the effects of these on the family rather than the actual diagnosis that is taken into account.

The Family Fund also produces a number of information sheets: adaptations to housing, bedding and clothing, benefits checklist, equipment for daily living, hearing impairment, holidays, behaviour and attention difficulties and transport and a guide to the opportunities available to young disabled people over sixteen called 'After 16 – What's New?' is available free to young disabled people and their carers (£10 to professional workers). 'Taking Care' is a book for parents and carers based on parents' own experiences of caring for a child with a disability. It is available free to parents and carers (£4 to professional workers) from the address above.

The fund maintains an excellent website which is full of information on its work and grantmaking.

Happy Days Children's Charity

£747,000 (16,680 grants)

Correspondent: Angela Dearmer, Clody house, 90–100 Collingdon Street, Luton, Bedfordshire LU1 1RX (01582 755999; email: enquiries@happydayscharity.org; website: www.happydayscharity.org)

Trustees: Peter Edward Nice; Iain Davidson; Diane May; Bernice Russell.

CC Number: 1010943

Eligibility

Children and young people aged 3 to 17 years (inclusive) who are disadvantaged, have ongoing chronic health conditions, have experienced trauma or abuse, have emotional behavioural difficulties or have special needs. The charity can only assist families that earn less than £25,000 a year. The charity wishes to see the children benefitting from the day trip activity to be more involved in the actual planning and evaluation of the trip activity.

Types of grants

One-off grants ranging from £25 to £1,250 for respite break family holidays in the UK (occasionally children who are terminally ill are funded for an overseas holiday). All funding is paid directly to the providers, such as venue/resort, transport provider and so on. All trips are organised and funded directly by the charity, therefore cheques are not normally given directly to the family. Essential key carers who are necessary to support the needs of the children on the holiday are also funded.

Annual grant total

In 2010/11 the charity had assets of £271,000 and an income of £1 million. Grants towards holidays and leisure activities amounted to £747,000, giving almost 17,000 children and their families access to a holiday or break.

Exclusions

No extra adults are funded.

Applications

On a form available from the correspondent or to download from the website. Applications are considered year round and should include a supporting letter from a doctor or healthcare professional to confirm the applicant meets the criteria. A telephone call is welcome for advice and guidance.

Note: the charity can take between 9–12 months to consider grant applications.

Other information

Grants are also made to groups of children and young people who have special needs for day trips and holidays.

Lifeline 4 Kids

£132,000

Correspondent: Roger Adelman, Appeals Team, 215 West End Lane, West Hampstead, London NW6 1XJ (020 7794 1661; fax: 020 8459 8826; email: appeals@lifeline4kids.org; website: www. lifeline4kids.org)

Trustees: Jeffrey Bonn; Paul Maurice; Beverley Emden; Roberta Harris; Roger Adelman; Irving Millman.

CC Number: 200050

Eligibility

Disabled people under the age of 19.

Types of grants

Cash grants are not given: rather, specific items are purchased and delivered on behalf of the individual in need.

The trust's website explains: 'For the individual child we provide the full spectrum of specialised equipment such as electric wheelchairs, mobility aids and varying items including specialised computers. We are also one of the only UK charities prepared to help a special needs child from a low-income family with essential smaller items such as shoes, clothing, bedding and specialist toys. We are able to give emergency and welfare appeals immediate approval within the authorised limits of our welfare subcommittee. No appeal is too large or too small for us to consider'.

Annual grant total

In 2010 the trust had assets of £659,000 and an income of £187,000. Charitable expenditure came to £132,000.

Applications

Initially, in writing (via email or post) to the correspondent, indicating any specific requirements and including brief factual information i.e. the child's name, date of birth and health condition as well as indicating specific requirements, cost of the help being sought and family contact details. If appropriate, an application form will then be sent out. The form contains questions relating to the child's medical condition and requires backup information from health professionals together with a financial statement of the applicant.

Applications are considered monthly, although urgent cases can be dealt with more quickly.

Other information

The trust also supplies equipment and so on for schools, hospitals and clubs for children who are disabled or underprivileged.

This trust was previously called *The Handicapped Children's Aid Committee*.

School Home Support

£18,000

Correspondent: Welfare Fund Coordinator, 40–42 Adler Street, Whitechapel, London E1 1EE (020 7426 5025 (Mondays and Fridays only); fax: 020 7426 5001; email: welfarefund@shs. org.uk; website: www. schoolhomesupport.org.uk)

Trustees: Douglas Blausten; Inigo Rodney Milman Woolf; Alexander John Scott-Barrett; Mike Simpkin; Liz Wolverson; Richard Evans; Rob Phillips; Andrew Dowell; Silke Scheiber.

CC Number: 1084696

Eligibility

Children and families working with SHS practitioners.

Types of grants

One-off payments for essential living costs and basic household items. Grants may be made for food, white goods, school uniforms, furniture, etc.

Annual grant total

In 2010/11 the charity held assets of £375,000 and had an income of £7.3 million. Around £18,000 is available for grants every year, although this is broken down into monthly budgets of £1,500.

Applications

Applications must be made on behalf of families by their SHS practitioner. For more information contact the welfare fund coordinator by telephone (Mondays and Fridays only) or by email.

Other information

SHS works with over 750 schools around the country helping to get children with complex needs and difficult backgrounds into school and ready to learn.

Eliza Shepherd Charitable Trust

£2,500

Correspondent: Carol Shepherd, Trustee, Southview Cottage, Islington Road, Islington, Alton, Hampshire GU34 4PR (01420 520375)

Trustees: Carol Presley; Jennifer Edbrooke; Carol Shepherd.

CC Number: 1064464

Eligibility

Children and young people who are in need.

Types of grants

Grants given according to need.

Annual grant total

In 2010/11 the trust had an income of £4,000 and a total expenditure of £3,000.

Applications

In writing to the correspondent.

Other information

Grants are also made to organisations.

S. C. Witting Trust

£5,000

Correspondent: Christopher Gregory, Secretary, Friends House, 173 Euston Road, London NW1 2BJ

Trustees: Ronald Barden; Richard Bloomfield; Mark Tod; David Stanton; Rod Usher; Philip Hills; Delia Suffling; Steven Pullan; Ian Watson; Colin Hulse.

CC Number: 237698

Eligibility

Individuals in need, ordinarily resident in England, and who are under 15 or over 60 years old, or students attending university.

Types of grants

One-off grants, on average of £110 for specific items such as electric appliances, furniture, clothing, toys pushchairs, bedding and so on.

Annual grant total

In 2011 the trust gave £15,000 to individuals in England, Germany and Poland for educational and welfare purposes. About £6,000 is available each year for distribution to individuals in England and grants are mostly made for welfare.

Exclusions

No grants towards debts or loans.

Applications

In writing to the correspondent, at any time, through a social worker, Citizens Advice or other welfare agency, including a short case history, reason for need and the amount required. Students can apply directly. Applications are considered monthly and unsuccessful applications are not acknowledged unless an sae is provided. Applications are considered monthly.

Other information

Grants are also made to individuals for educational purposes.

Divorced/ separated people

NCDS (National Council for the Divorced and Separated Trust)

£2,500

Correspondent: Joan Barbara Parnell-Raw, 68 Parkes Hall Road, Woodsetton, Dudley DY1 3SR (07041 478120; email: info@ncds.org.uk; website: www.ncds.org.uk)

Trustees: Cliff Glover; George Henry William Raw; Harry Taylor; Joan Barbara Parnell-Raw; John Leslie Rush; Martin Benson; Mally Trail; Anthony James Buckley; David Reginald Hamilton.

CC Number: 284710

Eligibility

People in need in the UK. All applications are considered regardless of marital status.

Types of grants

One-off grants according to need.

Annual grant total

In 2010 the trust had an income and total expenditure of £2,600.

Exclusions

No grants paid for bankruptcy fees, arrears of any kind, medical costs, educational fees, building works or holidays.

Applications

On a form available from the correspondent. Applications can be submitted directly by the individual or through a social worker, Citizens Advice or other welfare agency. Applications are considered every six to eight weeks, although urgent cases can be considered between meetings.

Ethnic and national minorities in the UK

Prisoners of Conscience Appeal Fund

£25,000

Correspondent: The Grants Officer, PO Box 61044, London SE1 1UP (020 7407 6644; fax: 020 7407 6655; email: info@prisonersofconscience.org; website: www.prisonersofconscience.org)

Trustee: Prisoner of Conscience Appeal Fund (Trustee) Ltd.

CC Number: 213766

Eligibility

Prisoners of conscience and/or their families, who have suffered persecution for their beliefs. The fact that the person is seeking asylum or has been a victim of civil war is not sufficient grounds in itself.

Types of grants

One-off grants ranging from £350 to £500 for the provision of food, clothing, toiletries, travel costs, basic furniture, counselling/therapy sessions, family reunion costs, medical needs which are not supplied by the NHS such as orthopaedic beds or repairs to wheelchairs and PLAB or some vocational conversion courses.

Family reunion grants are also available for costs involved with bringing close dependents to join prisoners of conscience in the UK such as flights and visa and DNA testing costs.

Annual grant total

In 2011 grants made in the UK totalled £52,000, distributed as follows:

- 17 family reunion grants totalling £17,000
- UK relief grants to asylum seekers totalling £7,300
- Refugees Liverpool grants totalling £800
- Bursaries totalling £27,000

Exclusions

No support is given to people who have used or advocated violence or supported a violent organisation.

Applications

Application forms are available from the correspondent and should be submitted by a third party such as human rights organisations, refugee groups, solicitors and organisations in the UK and overseas, from large NGOs to small refugee community organisations. Applicants who do not know of a third party organisation that they can submit an application through should contact the fund for advice. Applications should include evidence of identification of the applicant and of costs.

Family reunion grants are considered four times a year in January, April, July and October and applications should be submitted by the preceding month. Other grants are considered.

Other information

The fund was initially established in 1962 as the relief arm of Amnesty International, but is now a charity in its own right.

The Pusinelli Convalescent and Holiday Home

£3,000

Correspondent: David Leigh, Leigh Saxton Green, 4–7 Manchester Street, London W1U 3AE (020 7486 5553; email: enquiries@lsg-ca.co.uk)

Trustees: Gerda Thomas; David Heydorn; Ingeborg Asante; Ingeborg Smith; Phillip Todd; Margaret Spencer.

CC Number: 239734

Eligibility

People who are or were German citizens and their dependents. Applicants must live in Greater London, Essex, Hertfordshire, Kent or Surrey.

Types of grants

Grants of up to £500 for families who would not otherwise be able to have a holiday.

Annual grant total

In 2010/11 the home had an income of £5,800 and a total expenditure of £3,300.

Applications

Applications should be made to the correspondent directly from the individual or from any welfare agency on their behalf.

The Society of Friends of Foreigners in Distress

£12,000

Correspondent: Mrs Valerie Goodhart, 68 Burhill Road, Hersham, Walton-on-Thames, Surrey KT12 4JF (01932 244916)

Trustees: Brian Tew; Annmarie Schoor; Monica Slaughter; Valerie Goodhart; Peter Edwards; Sally Yates.

CC Number: 212593

Eligibility

People living in London or its surrounding area who are from countries not in the Commonwealth, the USA or which were once part of the British Empire.

Types of grants

Grants can be given for electrical goods, clothing, living costs, household bills, food, travel expenses, furniture and disabled equipment.

Annual grant total

In 2009/10 the trust had an income of £9,800 and a total expenditure of £21,000. Previously, grants were made totalling around £12,000.

Applications

In writing to the correspondent at any time. Applications should be submitted by a social worker, Citizens Advice or other welfare agency.

Tollard Trust

£21,000

Correspondent: Mrs J Carlyle-Clarke, Tollard Green Farm, Tollard Royal, Salisbury, Wiltshire SP5 5PX (01725 516323)

Trustee: Jacqueline Carlyle Clarke.

CC Number: 327369

Eligibility

▸ People living in Bournemouth, Poole and elsewhere in Dorset who are older or disabled, who live in their own

homes and are affected by hardship and sickness. Applicants should be, or have been: chemists; members of the clergy; ex-services and service people; farmers; legal professionals; masons; medical professionals; musicians; research workers; seafarers and fishermen; and textile workers and designers

▸ Older people from Asia and Africa who are disabled or in financial need

Types of grants

Recurrent grants of about £100, towards items, services or facilities.

Annual grant total

In 2010/11 the trust had a higher than usual income of £23,000 and a total expenditure of £24,000.

Exclusions

No grants are made for education and training, including expeditions or scholarships.

Applications

Grants are made once a year, usually in November. Most grants are in answer to requests from charities, for example, Salvation Army, Pramacare, RUKBA, Greenhill, McDougall and other local charities. Very occasionally grants are made directly to individuals in need who live locally.

Armenians

The Armenian Relief Society of Great Britain Trust

£250

Correspondent: The Secretary, 209 Syon Lane, Isleworth TW7 5PU

Trustees: Rubina Boghosian; Silva Beshirian; Mariette Nazloomian; Zovig Haladjian; Sonia Bablanian; Jaqueline Karanfilian; Jabet Kachatourian.

CC Number: 327389

Eligibility

Poor, sick or bereaved Armenians, worldwide.

Types of grants

One-off and recurrent grants of £150 are available.

Annual grant total

The majority of grants are usually made to organisations, although the trust does have the capacity to make grants to individuals.

Applications

In writing to the correspondent.

Assyrians

The Assyrian Charity and Relief Fund of UK

£450

Correspondent: Revd Henry Shaheen, 277 Rush Green Road, Romford RM7 0JL (01708 730122)

Trustees: Mr Andrious Mama Jotyar Mama; Emmanuel Samano.

CC Number: 1050419

Eligibility

People of Assyrian descent living in UK or worldwide who are in need, hardship or distress.

Types of grants

The fund offers food, medicine and temporary shelter to people in need. One-off and recurrent grants are made usually ranging between £10 and £400.

Annual grant total

In 2010/11 the trust had an income and expenditure of £450.

Exclusions

No grants are available for business people, political organisations, those already settled in Europe, America, Australia and Canada or those financially secure.

Applications

In writing to the correspondent, submitted through a social worker, Citizens Advice, welfare agency or other charity.

Belgians

The Royal Belgian Benevolent Society

£5,000

Correspondent: Patrick Bresnan, 5 Hartley Close, Bromley BR1 2TP (020 8467 8442)

Trustees: Mrs A. Verity; Mrs D. Massaux; Jean Francois-Dor; Mrs S. Ault; Patrick Bresnan; Baronne Van Havre.

CC Number: 233435

Eligibility

Belgians who live in Britain, and their close dependents, who are in need.

Types of grants

Regular grants of £300 to £2,000.

Annual grant total

In 2010 the society had an income of £620 and a total expenditure of £11,000.

Applications

On a form available from the correspondent, submitted either directly by the individual, or via a social worker, Citizens Advice or other welfare agency.

Dutch

The Netherlands' Benevolent Society

£42,000 (20 grants)

Correspondent: Loesje Roele-Van Hellenberg Hubar, PO Box 858, Bognor Regis PO21 9HS (01932 355885; fax: 01932 355885; email: info@ koningwillemfonds.org.uk; website: www.koningwillemfonds.org.uk)

Trustees: Ferdinand Folet Hooft Graafland; Leonard Victor Broese Van Groenou; Robert Rene Borgerhoff Mulder; Birte Patricia Roex-Geesink; Maria Melville Hadweij; Rosina Maria Heniette Renee; Cordula Waldeck Quarles Van Ufford; Louise Gerarda Roele-Van Hellenberg Hubar; Derk Hartman; Willem Van Arnhem; Maurits Le Poole; Daphne Thissen; Revd Johannes Hendricus Uytenbogaardt.

CC Number: 213032

Eligibility

People in need who are Dutch nationals or of Dutch extraction and living in the UK. Assistance may also be given to widows, widowers and dependents of Dutch nationals.

Types of grants

One-off grants ranging between £100 to £1,000 and regular allowances of £80 per month. In the past grants have included payments for: debts to allow someone to make a 'fresh start'; essential home repairs; clothing; basic living items; and the costs of a training course where they lead to employment.

Annual grant total

In 2011 the trust had assets of £822,000 and an income of £81,000. Grants were made to 20 individuals (of 39 applications received) totalling £42,000.

Exclusions

Beneficiaries must not have access to financial help from other sources.

Applications

On a form available from the society administrator. Applications are usually made through churches, the Netherlands Embassy, the Netherlands Consulates, the Department of Work and Pensions regional offices or welfare charities. They are considered every month, except in August, at the trustees' monthly meeting, although emergency cases may be considered sooner. Information on the individual's financial situation, including details of any social security benefits, should be included.

Egyptians

Egyptian Community Association in the United Kingdom

£250

Correspondent: Hosni El-Sherif, 100 Redcliffe Gardens, London SW10 9HH (020 7244 8925)

Trustee: Hosni El-Sherif.

CC Number: 289332

Eligibility

People in need who are Egyptian or of Egyptian origin and are living in or visiting the UK.

Types of grants

Grants towards a broad range of needs, for example, help with the costs of medical treatment and gas bills.

Annual grant total

Grants usually total around £500 per year.

Applications

In writing to the correspondent.

Other information

The association arranges seminars and national and religious celebrations, as well as offering other services. It also gives grants to individuals for educational purposes. Limited information was available due to no accounts being filed at the Charity Commission since 2007.

Germans

The German Society of Benevolence

£4,500

Correspondent: David Leigh, Leigh Saxton Green, 4–7 Manchester Street, London W1U 3AE (email: info@gwc-london.org.uk)

Trustees: Ingeborg Asante; Ingeborg Smith; David Heydorn; Geroa Thomas; William Todd.

CC Number: 247379

Eligibility

Older people in need who are, or were, citizens of Germany, and their dependents. Applicants must live in Greater London, Essex, Hertfordshire, Kent or Surrey.

Types of grants

Small one-off and recurrent grants for heating, clothing and other needs.

Annual grant total

In 2009/10 the society had an income of £7,100 and a total expenditure of £4,700.

Applications

Applications are considered from individuals or from agencies acting on their behalf.

Indians

India Welfare Society

£3,000

Correspondent: S K Gupta, President, 11 Middle Row, London W10 5AT (020 8969 9493; email: iwslondon@hotmail.com; website: www.indiawelfaresociety.org)

Trustees: Suresh Kumar Gupta; Saroj Gupta; Ashwin Pandya; Mr BK. Gupta; Asha Gupta.

CC Number: 286800

Eligibility

Members of the Indian community, who have membership with the society and are in need.

Types of grants

One-off and recurrent grants according to need for hardship and welfare purposes only.

Annual grant total

About £3,000.

Applications

In writing to the correspondent.

Swiss

The Swiss Benevolent Society

£17,000

Correspondent: Petra Kehr Cocks, Welfare Officer, 79 Endell Street, London WC2H 9DY (020 7836 9119; fax: 020 7379 1096; email: info@swissbenevolent.org.uk; website: www.swissbenevolent.org.uk)

Trustees: Elsbeth Baxter; Alan Martin; Erika Tan; Ursula Schoenenberger; Ursulina Talary; Jeannette Crossier; Jan Hofmann; Margrit Ledermann Prestofelippo; Dominique Thalmann.

CC Number: 1111348

Eligibility

Swiss citizens who are experiencing hardship and are temporarily or permanently resident in the consular district of London. In special cases, those living in other parts of the UK may also receive assistance.

Types of grants

One-off and recurrent grants towards holidays, heating costs, travel to and from day centres, therapies, household equipment, telephone and TV licences and so on.

Annual grant total

In 2011 the society had assets of £1.1 million and an income of £67,000. Grants were made totalling around £17,000.

Applications

In writing to the welfare officer including proof of nationality. Applications can be submitted directly by the individual, through an organisation such as Citizens Advice or via any third party. They are considered at any time.

Other information

The trust also provides emotional support and counselling where necessary.

Zimbabweans

The Rhodesians Worldwide Assistance Fund

£15,000

Correspondent: The Administrator, PO Box 213, Lingfield, Surrey RH7 6WW (email: ian@12buzz.com; website: zrwaf.com)

Trustees: Ian Dixon; Mary Miriam Sawyers; Ronald Lindsay Williams; Stuart R. T. Sawyers; Ian Dixon; Christopher John Tonge; Robert Bruce Knott.

CC Number: 802274

Eligibility

People formerly resident in Zimbabwe (previously Rhodesia) who are in need, and their widows and dependents.

Types of grants

One-off grants are given to meet short-term needs. Recent grants have paid for riser recliner chairs, stair lifts, specialised wheelchairs, furniture and rental deposits.

Annual grant total

In 2010/11 the fund had an income of £16,000 and a total expenditure of £35,000.

Exclusions

No grants are given for education, debts, business expenditure, house repairs, motor vehicles, legal expenses, foreign travel or medical expenses.

Applications

On a form available from the correspondent or to download from the website. Applicants will need to prove their former residence in Zimbabwe and their right to remain in the UK. Applications can be submitted directly by the individual or through another charity or close relative. Trustees meet four times a year to consider applications, though urgent cases can be dealt with between meetings.

Zimbabwe Rhodesia Relief Fund

£22,000

Correspondent: W D Walker, Secretary, PO Box 5307, Bishop's Stortford, Hertfordshire CM23 3DY (01279 466121)

Trustees: Peter Booth; Alexander George Broom; Anna Wathen; Frances Jane Tennant; Andrew Rosindell; Dr Ronald A. S. Black.

CC Number: 326922

Eligibility

Zimbabweans living worldwide who are distressed or sick.

Types of grants

One-off and recurrent grants of £70 to £300.

Annual grant total

In 2010/11 the fund had an income of £11,000 and total expenditure of £28,000.

Exclusions

Grants are not given for educational purposes or for travel.

Applications

In writing to the correspondent. Applications should be made through somebody known to the charity and include proof of past or present Zimbabwean citizenship.

Other information

In recent years the trust has also made grants to organisations operating in Zimbabwe.

Holidays

The Family Holiday Association

£796,000

Correspondent: Emma Rowland, Senior Grant and Project Officer, 3 Gainsford Street, London SE1 2NE (020 3117 0651; fax: 020 7323 7299; email: grantofficer@

familyholidayassociation.org.uk; website: www.fhaonline.org.uk)

Trustees: Keith Graham; Penny Cushing; Ian Reynolds; Alison Geldeard Rice; Anthony Lindsay Caplin; Martha Osamor; Pippa Ann Isbell; Kristina Anne Wallen; Felicity Clarkson; David John Burling; Richard Clegg.

CC Number: 800262

Eligibility

Families who are referred by social workers, health visitors or other caring agencies as desperate for a holiday break. Applicants must have a low income; not have had a holiday within the past four years, unless there are exceptional circumstances; and at least one child must be aged between 3 and 18.

Types of grants

Day trips, short breaks and week-long holidays. Either the family has an idea about where they want to go and the association decides how much to give towards the total cost, or the association funds the entire holiday at a holiday centre and gives money towards the costs of food, spending money and so on. Grants are generally from £250 upwards.

Occasionally, the association also receives offers of holidays at short notice, e.g. a half board holiday in the UK or an activity holiday abroad. If a family can travel with only a few days' notice their chance of receiving a break may increase.

Annual grant total

In 2010/11 the trust had assets of £768,000 and an income of £1.3 million. Holiday grants to over 2,000 families totalled £796,000.

Applications

Through the online application form or on a paper form available to download from the website. The association does advise that online applications are processed much faster. Applications should be submitted in November each year. The association usually has enough applications to commit all its funds by December. Applications must be referred by a welfare agency, voluntary organisation and so on. Those made directly by the individual are not accepted.

The Victoria Convalescent Trust

£86,000

Correspondent: Mrs A J Perkins, The Grants Co-ordinator, 11 Cavendish Avenue, Woodford Green, Essex IG8 9DA (020 8502 9339)

Trustees: Victoria Hipps; Hilary Hipps; Jean Morton; Nicholas Mark Heath; Solveig Karin Wilson; David Wells; Jean Dollimore; William Gibbs; Pouneh Bligaard.

CC Number: 1064585

Eligibility

People in medical need of convalescence, recuperative and respite care in England and Wales. Preference is given to people living in Surrey and Croydon.

Types of grants

Grants of up to £300 for services and equipment; and up to £600 for recuperative holidays and respite care.

Annual grant total

In 2011 the trust made grants totalling £86,000, £79,000 of which consisted of convalescence and respite grants and the remainder towards sundry grants.

Applications

On a form available from the correspondent. Applications must be submitted through a social worker, a health care worker or a welfare agency or another professional worker and will be considered every month. Medical and social reports supporting the need for a break must be provided.

Other information

Occasionally, support is given to women living in Greater London for vital equipment and services.

Vitalise
See entry on page 42

See entry on page 42

Homeless-ness

Housing the Homeless Central Fund

£22,500

Correspondent: The Clerk to the Trustees, 2A Orchard Road, Sidcup DA14 6RD (email: hhcfund@gmail.com)

Trustees: Colin Mason; Bob Roberts; Tony Zotti; Wendy Mead; My Jeremy Simons; Elizabeth Rogula.

CC Number: 233254

Eligibility

People who are either homeless or have serious accommodation problems. Priority may be given to expectant parents or those with children.

Types of grants

One-off grants of around £250 to £300 for household items and fuel bills.

Annual grant total

In 2010/11 the fund held assets of £325,000 and had an income of £42,000. Grants were made totalling £22,500.

Exclusions

No recurrent grants are given or grants for holidays, medical apparatus, funeral expenses, travel costs, vehicles, educational expenses, structural improvements to property, rent deposits, toys, computers or televisions.

Applications

Guidelines and application forms should be requested by a third party organisation, who will receive the information, on headed paper and enclosing an sae. Decisions are usually made within a week, although no grants are made in March or December. Note no telephone calls can be accepted and applications must be made through by a representative of a recognised third party organisation for example Citizens Advice, social services or other welfare organisation.

Other information

The trust cannot accept applications from individuals directly, they must apply through a relevant organisation.

Older people

Age Sentinel Trust

£3,000

Correspondent: Francesca Colverson, 2 Winchester Road, Bishops Waltham, Southampton SO32 1BE (020 8144 4774; email: agesentineltrust@googlemail.com; website: agesentinel.org.uk)

Trustees: Sarah Webb; Andrea Herriot; Paul Squire; Paulina Kadreeva.

CC Number: 1133624

Eligibility

People over 60, who are living on a low income. Priority is given to people with dementia, particularly Alzheimer's disease, and those with other debilitating illnesses.

Types of grants

One-off and recurrent grants to help people through a financial crisis or to pay for services, such as emergency home repairs, access improvements, maintenance and gardening costs.

Annual grant total

This trust was registered with the Charity Commission in January 2010. In 2010/11, its first full year operation the trust had an income of £34,000 and a total charitable expenditure of £10,000.

Applications

On a form available from the correspondent.

Other information

Grants are also made to organisations with similar aims.

Aid for the Aged in Distress (AFTAID)

£40,000

Correspondent: Susan Elson, Begbies Chettle Agar, Epworth House, 25 City Road, London EC1Y 1AR (0870 803 1950; fax: 0870 803 2128; email: info@aftaid.org.uk; website: www.aftaid.org.uk)

Trustees: Mrs Elson; Maj Brian Hudson; Alan Shooter; Malcolm Shaw.

CC Number: 299276

Eligibility

UK citizens of state pensionable age who reside in the UK and are living on a low income and have minimal savings.

The trust's accounts state that, 'an increasing number of applications that are received are having to be declined as they fall outside the Charity's remit and criteria. Unfortunately, this creates additional administration costs and a drain on resources.'

Types of grants

Emergency grants for essential items to facilitate the beneficiary to maintain their independence in the familiar surroundings of their home, for example heating appliances, bedding, cookers, washing machines or other white goods, essential furniture and carpets. Grants are also made towards more expensive items such as a stair lift, walk-in shower, motorised scooter and so on. Applications can sometimes be considered towards costs for an elderly carer to enjoy a respite break.

Grants are paid directly to the supplier of the goods or services.

Annual grant total

In 2010 the charity held assets of £309,000 and had an income of £67,000 (£101,000 in 2009). Grants and services for elderly people totalled £81,000.

Exclusions

Grants cannot be made for any ongoing payments, arrears or debts of any kind.

Applications

On a form available through the charity's website. Applicants will initially need to fill in an online form which will automatically issue the application form by return email.

Applications can be made directly by the individual or through a welfare organisation and should include written support from a social worker, doctor or similar professional of the official care services who are personally aware of the beneficiary's situation.

Barchester's Charitable Foundation

£128,000 (135 grants)

Correspondent: Grants Management Team, Suite 201, Second Floor, Design Centre East, Chelsea Harbour, London SW10 0XF (0800 328 3328; fax: 020 7352 2229; email: info@bhcfoundation.org.uk; website: www.bhcfoundation.org.uk)

Trustees: Prof. Malcolm Johnson; Elizabeth Mills; Chris Vellenoweth; Mike Parsons; Janice Robinson; Lesley Flory; Pauline Houchin.

CC Number: 1083272

Eligibility

Older people over the age of 65 and adults over the age of 18 with a physical or mental disability.

Each year the fund prioritises certain people or groups, in 2012 they were particularly interested in applications from those over the age of 65. Check the website for their latest priorities before applying.

Types of grants

One-off grants of between £100 and £5,000 according to need. Grants have previously been made for electric wheelchairs, riser/recliner chairs, mobility scooters, I.T. equipment, holidays, white goods, transportation, heating, home and vehicle adaptations, etc.

Annual grant total

In 2011 the foundation held assets totalling £60,000 and had an income of £132,000. Grant to 135 individuals totalled £128,000.

Exclusions

No retrospective grants. Successful applicants may not reapply for three years from the date of their award. Grants for white goods and home repairs or alterations will not be funded unless they relate to a disability or medical condition. No grants for daily living costs or repayment of debts.

Applications

Online via the foundation's website or by downloading an application form and submitting it to the correspondent. Applications must be completed and supported by a third party sponsor such as a health or social care professional, social worker or charity representative. Trustees meet quarterly, however, applications can be dealt with between meetings.

Other information

A smaller proportion of expenditure is made towards grants to organisations (£36,000 in 2011).

The Percy Bilton Charity

£176,000 (1,017 grants)

Correspondent: Tara Smith, Bilton House, 7 Culmington Road, Ealing, London W13 9NB (020 8579 2829; fax: 020 8579 3650; website: www.percybiltoncharity.org.uk)

Trustees: James Robert Lee; Mr Miles Andrew Graham Bilton; Stefan Jacek Paciorek; Kim Lansdown; Mayley Bilton.

CC Number: 1094720

Eligibility

People who are on a low income and are either:

- Over 65 years old
- Have a physical or learning disability
- Receiving hospital or other medical treatment for a long-term illness (including mental illness)

Types of grants

One-off grants of up to £200 for specific essential items only. For example, laundry equipment, cooking and heating appliances, basic furniture, beds and bedding, floor coverings, clothing and footwear and other essential household items.

Annual grant total

In 2010/11 the charity had assets of £19.6 million and an income of £723,000. Grants were made totalling £134,000 and were distributed as follows:

Household goods and furniture	572	£76,000
Home appliances	295	£45,000
Clothing and footwear	150	£13,000

A further £42,000 was given in Christmas hampers and £544,000 was awarded to organisations.

Exclusions

No payments are made towards items costing over £200; travel expenses, sponsorship, holidays or respite care; educational grants, computer equipment or software; house alterations and maintenance (including adaptations for disabled facilities); debts; dishwashers; reimbursement of cost for articles already purchased; garden fencing or clearance; motor vehicle purchase or expenses; nursing and residential home fees; funeral expenses; removal expenses; medical treatment of therapy; course fees including driving or IT lessons.

Applications

On a form available from the correspondent: to be submitted by a social worker, community psychiatric nurse or occupational therapist, including a covering letter on local or health authority headed paper. Full application guidelines are available on the website or on request. Applications can be made at any time.

The charity may be contacted by telephone or in writing for advice and guidance about submitting an application.

Note: the charity is unable to respond to applications made by anyone other than a social worker or occupation therapist or to requests which fall outside of the charity's funding criteria. Applicants should also ensure that they have applied to all statutory sources and any appropriate specialist charities (e.g. employment related funds and armed forces funds) before approaching the charity.

Other information

The trust also makes grants to organisations. 25% of total grant funding was paid to individuals in 2010/11.

Monica Eyre Memorial Foundation

£2,000

Correspondent: Michael Bidwell, 5 Clifton Road, Winchester, Hampshire SO22 5BN

Trustees: Barbara Miller; Michael Bidwell; Sheila Laxman.

CC Number: 1046645

Eligibility

People in need, particularly older people and people with disabilities/special needs in the UK.

Types of grants

Grants are made to enable people with low-mobility in residential care to get a holiday with essential carer support.

Annual grant total

In 2010/11 the trust had an income of £4,500 and a total expenditure of £6,000.

Applications

In writing to the correspondent.

Other information

The trust also makes grants to organisations and to individuals for educational purposes.

Friends of the Elderly

£387,000 (891 grants)

Correspondent: Supporting Friends Manager, 40–42 Ebury Street, London SW1W 0LZ (020 7730 8263; fax: 020 7259 0154; email: info@

supportingfriends.fote.org.uk; website: www.fote.org.uk)

Trustees: Mr K. Rubie; Mr S. Dawes; Mr D. Brazier; Mr M. Burdes; Mr M. Cardale; Viscount Devonport; Mrs S. Goodband; Mrs S. Hudson; Mrs V. Pendock; Mr P. C. Robinson; Mr M van der Schalk; Ms S. A. Taylor; Ms P. Wright; Mrs F. C de Zoete.

CC Number: 226064

Eligibility

Men and women who live in England and Wales aged 60 or over (over 50 for homeless people), with low income and with limited savings are eligible for support. The trust cannot help people living in residential care or those living in Scotland.

Types of grants

One-off grants are given for essential items such as mobility aids, basic furniture, electrical goods and appliances, household water, property repairs/adaptations and other expenses. A cheque will be made payable to the relevant organisation (or company providing the equipment or service).

The charity also distributes allowances, on a monthly or twice yearly basis, to support older people on low incomes in maintaining their independence.

Annual grant total

In 2010/11 grants were made to 891 older people totalling £387,000.

Exclusions

Unfortunately, the charity cannot help those living in residential care or those living in Scotland. Grants are not available for care home fees, rent arrears, none-UK respite breaks or council tax payments.

Applications

On a form available from the correspondent. Applications should be made through a third party organisation such as social services, Citizens Advice, Age UK or another welfare agency.

Other information

The charity offers a range of care and support options for their elderly beneficiaries through their residential homes, community nursing, befriending schemes and dementia support.

Home Warmth for the Aged

£18,000

Correspondent: W J Berentemfel, 19 Towers Wood, South Darenth, Dartford, Kent DA4 9BQ (01322 863836; email: w.berentemfel@btinternet.com)

Trustees: Brian Wagland; Eric Wilson; Leslie Williams; Melyvn Macdonald;

Melvyn May; Michael Homer; Ronald Hansell; Carol Batty; Graham Quincey.

CC Number: 271735

Eligibility

People of pensionable age, at risk from the cold in winter who have no resources other than their state pension/income support and have savings of less than £4,000.

Types of grants

Provision of heating appliances, bedding, clothing and solid fuel and to pay fuel debts where the supply has been disconnected. One-off grants only, ranging between £90 and £250.

Annual grant total

In 2010/11 the trust had an income of £21,000 and a total expenditure of £20,000.

Exclusions

No grants are made to people who have younger members of their family living with them.

Applications

On a form available from the correspondent and submitted through social workers, doctors, nurses etc. only, to whom grants are returned for disbursement. If there is an armed forces connection, applications should be made through SSAFA (see service section of this guide). Applications made directly by individuals are not considered. Applications are considered monthly.

Independent Age

£3.9 million (6,248 grants)

Correspondent: Care Services Department, 6 Avonmore Road, London W14 8RL (0845 262 1863; fax: 020 7605 4201; email: advice@independentage.org; website: www.independentage.org)

Trustees: Dame Diana Brittan; Ian Watson; Peter Mimpriss; Rodney Gritten; Thomas John Howe; Sarah Reed; Sue Douthwaite; Sue Collins; Richard Humphries; Nori Graham; Caroline Jacobs; Justine Frain; Nick Broadhead; Dr Helen Hanbury.

CC Number: 210729

Eligibility

People over 70 years old who are lonely or isolated and find themselves in financial need. Preference is given to individuals who will benefit most from long-term support.

Types of grants

Annuities of £750, which are granted for life (unless there is an unexpected and considerable improvement in the recipient's circumstances), are the main form of help. However, the trustees decided in December 2009 to take on no

new regular payment beneficiaries, while continuing to support existing recipients.

One-off grants are also made towards, for example, unexpected, emergency expenses and items which it is often difficult to budget for. The association states that 'there is no definitive list of what and how much is awarded, and each grant is considered individually, on the basis of need.' Grants may be made for things like household repairs and maintenance; white goods; convalescence and respite care; spectacles and dental treatment. The association also maintains a catalogue of mobility aids and appliances which are provided free of charge. Parcels of clothing and toiletries are also distributed to those entering hospital and warm packs are given to help older people through the cold winter months.

The average value of a one-off grant in the UK in 2011 was £184.

Annual grant total

In 2011 the association made regular payments totalling £3.5 million to 4,416 beneficiaries and one-off grants and loans totalling £334,000 to 1,832 people in the UK and Ireland.

776 older people also received items from IA's mobility equipment catalogue (this includes items like large button telephones and automatic can openers). 1,475 bedding packs and 604 warm packs were also distributed to individuals in need. This brought the total funds distributed to £3.9 million.

Exclusions

Grants are only available to existing beneficiaries.

Applications

Financial assistance is given as part of a holistic service whereby a caseworker will work with the individual to assess and help address their issues. Initial contact should be made through the advice line (0845 262 1863) or by emailing advice@independentage.org.

Other information

The association provides information, advice and practical help through its network of staff and dedicated volunteers across the UK. The website also offers a range of helpful publications relevant to older people. It also manages three residential and nursing homes.

The broader range of services now offered by the charity is in part due to the recent merger with two other older people's charities, Counsel and Care and Universal Beneficent Society.

The Heinz, Anna and Carol Kroch Foundation

£78,000 (679 grants)

Correspondent: Heather Astle, PO Box 5, Bentham, Lancaster LA2 7XA (01524 263001; fax: 01524 262721; email: hakf50@hotmail.com)

Trustees: John Seagrim; Margaret Cottam; Dr Amatsia Kashti; Daniel Lang; Xavier Lang; Christopher Rushbrook; Annabel Page.

CC Number: 207622

Eligibility

People who are older, have a chronic illness, have fled domestic situations or are homeless and are in financial hardship.

Types of grants

One-off grants usually ranging from £100 to £500 towards hospital travel costs, household bills, furniture, other hospital expenses, clothing, food, medical and disability equipment, living costs, home adaptations, help in the home and so on.

Annual grant total

In 2010/11 the foundation had assets of £4.5 million and an income of £133,000. Grants were made to 679 individuals totalling £78,000.

Exclusions

No grants for education or holidays.

Applications

In writing to the correspondent. Most applications are submitted through other charities and local authorities. Applications should include full financial information including income and expenditure, what the grant will be used for and a why it is needed. Applicants should also state if they have approached any other charities for financial assistance and how successful they have been to date. Applications are considered monthly.

Morden College

£201,000 (98 grants)

Correspondent: Sir Iain Mackay-Dick, Clerk to the Trustees, Clerk's House, 19 St German's Place, Blackheath, London SE3 0PW (020 8463 8330; fax: 020 8293 4887; email: amanda@mordencollege.org; website: www.mordencollege.org)

Trustees: Sir Alan Traill; Sir Christopher Walford; Sir David Brewer; Sir Alexander Graham; Sir Robert Finch; Sir Michael Oliver; Sir John Stuttard; David Wootton.

CC Number: 215551

Eligibility

People in need who are aged over 50, from a professional or managerial background, who have retired from paid employment either on medical grounds or because they have reached the statutory retirement age.

Types of grants

Quarterly allowances and one-off grants of between £200 and £1,000 towards household items, holidays and convalescence.

Annual grant total

In 2010/11 the trust had assets of £183 million and an income of £9.2 million. A total of £201,000 was paid out in donations and outpensions to 98 individuals during the year.

Exclusions

The trust does not give for nursing home top up fees or any services or products which should be funded by statutory authorities.

Applications

On a form available from the correspondent, for consideration throughout the year. Applications can be submitted either directly by the individual or through any third party.

Other information

Morden College is the general title used for the administration of Sir John Morden's Charity and Dame Susan Morden's Charity. Sir John Morden's Charity provides grants and accommodation for the elderly. Dame Susan Morden's Charity is primarily concerned with the advancement of religion by assisting the Church of England with the upkeep of their churches and associated activities.

The National Benevolent Charity

£192,000

Correspondent: Paul Rossi, Peter Herve House, Eccles Court, Tetbury, Gloucestershire GL8 8EH (01666 505500; fax: 01666 503111; email: office@thenbc.org.uk; website: www.thenbc.org.uk)

Trustees: Andrew Crawford; David McEuen; Air Com David Adams; Joanna Bradley; Chris Whitaker; Christopher Bell; John Baker; Fran Mahon; Philip Rosser.

CC Number: 212450

Eligibility

Older people in need who live in their own homes (rented or owned) and have reached state retirement age. Applications are also accepted from those under state retirement age in exceptional circumstances, for example those in receipt of Disability Living Allowance. Net income, after certain expenses have been disregarded (e.g. rent and council tax), should be less than £7,665 per year for a single person and £11,555 for a couple. Savings should not exceed £10,000 for individual applicants or £18,000 for couples.

Note that applications will not be considered unless the individual is claiming all the state benefits to which they are entitled.

Types of grants

Recurrent grants of up to £15 per week for single persons and £20 for couples in receipt of the state retirement pension (£20 and £25 respectively for those not in receipt of the state pension) to allow people to live in their own homes in comfort and warmth. They are paid quarterly in March, June, September and December. One-off grants are also available for unexpected household costs and other items.

Annual grant total

In 2011 the institution held assets of £11.5 million and had an income of £723,000. Grants were made totalling £192,000 of which £148,000 was paid in regular assistance grants to 206 people. A further £44,000 was paid in one-off grants.

Exclusions

No grants are available for nursing home top up fees.

Applications

On a form available to download from the website including full income and expenditure details. Applications can be submitted either directly by the individual or through a third party such as a social worker. Help is available from the welfare officer should there be any problems in completing the form.

Other information

The charity also operates residential properties in Tetbury, Westgate-on-Sea and Old Windsor, providing accommodation for people over 50 who are in financial need.

NBFA (National Benevolent Fund for the Aged)

£235,000

Correspondent: Julia Robinson, Chief Executive, 32 Buckingham Palace Road, London SW1W 0RE (020 7828 0200; email: info@nbfa.org.uk; website: www.nbfa.org.uk)

Trustees: Roger Pincham; Lord Anthony Newton of Braintree; David Brandon Griffiths; Sir John De Trafford; Joyce

Arram; Dame Marion Roe; Laura Jane Sandys.

CC Number: 243387

Eligibility

For away breaks applicants must be over 65, on a low income, not have been on holiday for three years or more, and to be mobile enough to get on and off a coach. Day trips are aimed at those over 65 years of age but people of all ages are welcome to attend.

For telephone alarms applicants must be over 60, on a low income and have no access to any other alarm system or provider.

For pain relief machines applicants must be over 65 and on a low income.

Types of grants

Short (five-day) breaks, pain relief equipment, subsidised day trips and low-cost emergency telephone alarms.

Annual grant total

In the period from July 2010 to March 2011 the fund spent £235,000 providing services and equipment to beneficiaries.

Applications

For away breaks, day trips and pain relief machines applicants should contact the trust by phone. Applications for pain relief units are usually completed after a trial arranged with a physiotherapist. Application forms for the telephone alarms are available from the website.

The Nottingham Aged Persons' Trust
See entry on page 320

The Roger Pilkington Young Trust

£54,000

Correspondent: Ben Dixon, Everys Solicitors, Magnolia House, Church Street, Exmouth, Devon EX8 1HQ (01395 264384; email: law@everys.co.uk)

Trustees: David Henry Smith; Ben Dixon.

CC Number: 251148

Eligibility

People over 60 years of age whose income has been reduced through no fault of their own, but prior to application was enough for them to live in a 'reasonable degree of comfort'.

Types of grants

Monthly pensions of about £45 for single people and £60 for married couples.

Annual grant total

In 2010/11 the trust had assets of £1.3 million and an income of £54,000.

Grants were made to around 100 individuals totalling £54,000.

Applications

On a form available from the correspondent, after the pensions are advertised.

The Florence Reiss Trust for Old People

£2,000

Correspondent: Dr Stephen Reiss, Trustee, 94 Tinwell Road, Stamford, Lincolnshire PE9 2SD (01780 762710)

Trustees: Dr Stephen Reiss; Dr Sarah Steed; Eunice Reiss.

CC Number: 236634

Eligibility

Women over 55 and men over 60 who are in need. Priority is given to those who live in the parishes of Streatley in Berkshire and Goring-on-Thames in Oxfordshire.

Types of grants

One-off and recurrent grants according to need.

Annual grant total

In 2010/11 the trust had an income of £11,000 and a total expenditure of £10,000.

Applications

In writing to the correspondent.

Other information

Grants are also given to organisations.

The Skerritt Trust

£400 (1 grants)

Correspondent: Anna Chandler, Freeth Cartwright LLP, Cumberland Court, 80 Mount Street, Nottingham NG1 6HH (01159 015562; email: anna.chandler@freethcartwright.co.uk)

Trustees: N. Cutts; C. Bonham; R. Costa; P. Davies; J. Le Mottee; D. Lowe; R. Taylor; D. Warzynska; K. Hemsley.

CC Number: 1016701

Eligibility

Older people who live within ten miles of the market square in Nottingham.

Types of grants

Funding is given for house repairs and improvements to assist older people so that they can remain in their homes as long as possible.

Annual grant total

In 2010/11 the trust had assets of £1.9 million and an income of £70,000. Grants were made totalling £57,000,

most of which was given to organisations. One grant of £400 was made to an individual.

Applications

In writing to the correspondent through a social worker, Age Concern, day centre or similar third party. Applications are considered all year round.

The Stanley Stein Charitable Trust

£20,000

Correspondent: Michael Lawson, Trustee, Burwood House, 14–16 Caxton Street, London SW1H 0GY (020 7873 1000)

CC Number: 1048873

Eligibility

People with a disability and those under 21 or over 75 who are in need.

Types of grants

One-off and recurrent grants according to need.

Annual grant total

The latest figures were for 2009/10 when the trust had an income of £20,000 and an expenditure of £44,000.

Applications

On a form available from the correspondent.

Other information

Grants are given for education.

The Straits Settlement and Malay States Benevolent Society

£11,000

Correspondent: Vince Cheshire, TMF Management (UK) Ltd, 400 Capability Green, Luton LU1 3AE (01582 439270; email: vince.cheshire@tmf-group.com)

Trustees: Michael Thesiger; Rory Roper Caldbeck; Peter Thring.

CC Number: 221599

Eligibility

People in need who have lived in the Straits Settlements or Malay States for at least two years, and their dependents.

Types of grants

One-off and recurrent grants according to need. The society tends to support Europeans and dependents of Europeans, although this is not exclusively so.

Annual grant total

In 2011 the trust had an income of £14,000 and a total expenditure of £12,000. The charity commission notes that payments were made to two individuals.

Applications

Applications should be sponsored by a subscriber.

Other information

The society has informed us that it is not currently accepting new beneficiaries and does not wish to incur further administration costs in replying to applications which cannot at present be considered.

Tancred's Charity for Pensioners

£23,000

Correspondent: Andrew Penny, Clerk, Forsters, 31 Hill Street, London W1J 5LS (020 7863 8522; email: andrew.penny@ forsters.co.uk)

Trustees: Sir Richard Thompson; Vice Admiral Sir Christopher Morgan; Sir Martin Nourse; Sir Christopher Hum; Prof. Kelly; Gen Sir Charles Redmond Watt; Brig Charles William Hobson.

CC Number: 229936

Eligibility

Men aged 50 or over who are UK citizens and clergy of the Church of England or Church in Wales, or officers in the armed forces.

Types of grants

Annual pensions of around £1,600 a year are paid quarterly to 13 to 15 beneficiaries.

Annual grant total

In 2011 the charity had an income of £21,000 and an expenditure of £25,000.

Applications

In writing to the correspondent. Individuals may apply at any time, but applications can only be considered when a vacancy occurs, which is approximately once a year.

WaveLength

£241,000

Correspondent: Anny Mills, Applications Officer, 159a High Street, Hornchurch, Essex RM11 3YB (Freephone: 0800 018 2137; fax: 01708 620816; email: info@w4b.org.uk; website: www.w4b.org.uk)

Trustees: Daniel Smith; Margaret Grainger; Steven Derrick; Anthony Judd; Chris Howell; Steven Turner; James Michael Buckland; Lindsey Mack.

CC Number: 207400

Eligibility

People who are confined to their bed, largely housebound, elderly or disabled and in financial need.

Types of grants

Radios are provided. Televisions are rented by the society on a full maintenance contract from a major rental company. The service is free to both recipient and sponsoring organisations. However, the sets remain the property of the society.

The society does not provide television licences unless the applicant is in receipt of, or is applying for, equipment.

Annual grant total

In 2010/11 the charity held assets of £3.2 million and had an income of £194,000. The charity spent £241,000 providing television rentals and licences to over 3,000 people.

Exclusions

No grants to: individuals applying on their own behalf; organisations; grantmaking bodies; statutory bodies; top up funding on under-priced contracts.

Applications

On a form available directly from the correspondent or to download from the website. Applications must be submitted through a third party such as a social worker, Citizens Advice, religious organisation or other welfare agency. Applicants must be UK residents and should provide evidence such as passport, birth certificate or citizenship document. The society aims to respond to applications within ten working days.

Other information

The charity was known as the Wireless for the Bedridden Society until 2010.

Williamson Memorial Trust

£4,000

Correspondent: Colin Williamson, 6 Windmill Close, Ashington, Pulborough, West Sussex RH20 3LG (01903 893649)

Trustees: Colin Williamson; Dr Roger Williamson; John Clark; Philip Cutts.

CC Number: 268782

Eligibility

People who are over 65 years of age.

Types of grants

One-off grants of between £20 and £100, given as gifts rather than maintenance. Grants are mainly given at Christmas.

Annual grant total

In 2010/11 the trust had both an income and total expenditure of £9,000. Grants are made for education and welfare purposes.

Applications

Due to a reduction of its funds and the instability of its income, the trust regrets that very few new applications will be considered to ensure it can meet its existing commitments. Support will generally only be given to cases known personally to the trustees and to those individuals the trust has existing commitments with.

Orders

Catenian Benevolent Association

£73,000

Correspondent: Michael Tudor, 2nd Floor, 1 Copthall House, Station Square, Coventry CV1 2FY (02476 224533; email: catena@btconnect.com; website: www.thecatenians.com)

Trustees: Dr M. O'Malley; Mr J. Fry; Mr P. Barnes; Mr R. M. Sutton Allanson; Mr E. F. Smith; Mr J. K. Jennings; Mr P. A. P. Astill; V. R de Cruz; Mr F. Hinds.

CC Number: 214244

Eligibility

Members of the association and their dependents who are in need.

Types of grants

One-off and recurrent grants according to need. Loans are also available.

Annual grant total

In 2010/11 the fund had assets of £7.6 million and an income of £286,000. Grants were made to 23 individuals totalling £73,000. Non-secured loans were also made amounting to £189,000.

Applications

In writing to the correspondent. Applications are considered four times a year.

Grand Charitable Trust of the Order of Women Freemasons

£4,000

Correspondent: Sylvia Joan Brown, Trustee, 27 Pembridge Gardens, London W2 4EF (020 7229 2368; website: www. owf.org.uk)

Trustees: Mrs H. I. Naldrett; Mrs Margaret Jean Pearn Masters; Beryl

Daniels; Zuzanka Daniella Penn; Dr Iris Monika Boggia-Black; Sylvia Hilary Major.

CC Number: 1059151

Eligibility

Women freemasons who are in need.

Types of grants

One-off and recurrent grants to help towards medical, household and living expenses.

Annual grant total

In 2010/11 the trust held assets of £770,000, had an income of £164,000 and made grants to individuals totalling £4,000 (2010: £10,000).

Applications

In writing to the correspondent, usually through the local lodge. The trustees meet regularly throughout the year to consider applications.

Other information

Grants are made primarily to organisations (£210,000 in 2010/11).

The Grand Charity (of Freemasons under the United Grand Lodge of England)

£4.2 million (1,787 grants)

Correspondent: Ms Laura Chapman, Freemasons Hall, 60 Great Queen Street, London WC2B 5AZ (020 7395 9261; fax: 020 7395 9295; email: info@the-grand-charity.org; website: www.grandcharity.org)

Trustees: Nigel James Cubitt Buchanan; Stuart Hampson; Peter Griffiths; Christopher John Grove; Rod Mitchell; Michael Daws; Michael David Patterson Turnbull; Grahame Elliott; Ian Johnson; Paul Stefan Richards; Raymond Lye; Ian MacBeth; Roy Frederick Skinner; Nigel Pett; Charles Assad Akle; Tom Hedderson; Dr Richard James Rowley Dunstan; Geoff Tuck; Terry Baker; Dr Kevin Rhydderch Williams; Roger Francis Richmond; Mr Simon D'Olier Duckworth; Anthony James Wood; Timothy David Dallas-Chapman; Judge Hone; Roger Anthony Needham; Alexander Ian Stewart; John Edward Hornblow; Ernest Roy Skidmore; Wayne Edward Smith; Masonic Charity Trustee Ltd.

CC Number: 281942

Eligibility

Any freemason, past or present (under the United Grand Lodge of England) in need, and their immediate dependents.

As a general guide, almost anyone in receipt of pension credit or another means-tested benefit is likely to be eligible; however, assets and capital (not including the home) will be taken into account.

Types of grants

One-off grants according to need, which can be renewed annually, to help with living expenses and unexpected needs. Emergency grants may also be paid within 48 hours for those experiencing temporary hardship.

Annual grant total

In 2010/11 the charity had assets of £61 million and an income of £18 million. Over 1,900 individuals received Masonic relief grants totalling £4.2 million. Approximately three quarters of the 2,450 applicants received were successful. A further £2.9 million was distributed to organisations.

Exclusions

There is no limit to the number of grants an individual may receive over their lifetime, although usually only one grant per year will be made.

Applications

Applicants should first contact their Lodge Almoner or Provincial Grand Almoner who will provide support throughout the application process. Applications can be submitted at any time and a decision is usually reached within 4–8 weeks of receipt. The charity has now adopted the use of a joint application form with the Royal Masonic Trust for Girls and Boys and the Masonic Samaritan Fund. The form is designed to make it easier for an applicant to seek support from more than one charity for different types of need at the same time.

For further information and questions on eligibility, applicants should contact Sandra Neary (020 7395 9391) or Mike Martin (020 7395 9293) at the charity's main office.

Current grant recipients will automatically receive an application form nine months after the date of the award of a grant to see if follow-on support is required.

Other information

The charity also manages the Relief Chest Scheme. Each 'relief chest' is used to accumulate funds collected by a Lodge, Chapter or Province for charitable purposes. These are then used by the individual Lodges to distribute grants to charities and individuals in need. Applications for these funds should be made through the relevant Lodge, Chapter or Province.

In 2002, the charity took over responsibility for the Transferred Beneficiaries Fund, which makes regular payments to former beneficiaries of the Royal Masonic Benevolent Institution Annuity Fund. This fund is not open to new applications for assistance.

Practical help and financial support for individuals in times personal distress and for local charities is also given independently of the Grand Charity by individual lodges and Provincial Grand Lodges. Addresses are available from the correspondent.

The separate entries for the Royal Masonic Benevolent Institution and the New Masonic Samaritan Fund in this *Guide* may be helpful. There is also the Masonic Trust for Girls and Boys, which helps children of any age (including adopted children and step-children) of Freemasons under the United Grand Lodge of England. (See entry in *The Guide to Educational Grants*, also published by DSC).

The Grand Lodge of Ancient, Free and Accepted Masons of Scotland

£155,000

Correspondent: D M Begg, Grand Secretary, Freemasons Hall, 96 George Street, Edinburgh EH2 3DH (01312 255304; website: www.grandlodgescotland.com)

SC Number: SC001996

Eligibility

Members and their dependents, and the widows and dependents of deceased members.

Types of grants

One-off and recurrent grants according to need.

Annual grant total

In 2010/11 the trust had an income of £1.9 million. About £155,000 is given in welfare grants each year and £25,000 in educational grants.

Applications

On a form available from the correspondent, or by direct approach to the local lodge. They are considered three times a year, although urgent requests can be dealt with between meetings.

Other information

The trust also runs care homes for older people.

Adelaide Litten Charitable Trust

£3,000

Correspondent: The Trustees, c/o Winckworth Sherwood, Minerva House,

5 Montague Close, London SE1 9BB (020 7593 5000; fax: 020 7593 5099)

Trustees: Brenda Irene Fleming-Taylor; Mrs H. I. Naldrett; Geraldene Mary Greenhalgh; Eva Whittam; Mary Shearn; Brenda Ann Jones; Zuznaka Daniella Penn.

CC Number: 219512

Eligibility

Women freemasons and their dependents who are in need.

Types of grants

One-off and recurrent grants according to need.

Annual grant total

In 2010/11 the trust had assets of £3.6 million and an income of £171,000. Grants to 'petitioners' totalled £2,500. A further £500 was paid in 'Christmas gratuities'.

Applications

In writing to the correspondent. Trustees meet to consider applications six times a year.

Other information

The trust also maintains two residential homes for members and former members.

The Masonic Province of Middlesex Charitable Trust

£0

Correspondent: Peter Gledhill, Secretary, 85 Fakenham Way, Sandhurst, Berkshire GU47 0YS (01344 777077)

Trustees: Peter Gledhill; Adrian John Howorth; Jonathan Markham Gollow; David Ridley Yeaman.

CC Number: 1064406

Eligibility

Freemasons or their families or dependents who are in need and live in the Middlesex area.

Types of grants

Grants are given according to need.

Annual grant total

In 2010/11 the trust had assets of £1.7 million and an income of £63,000. Grants totalled £43,000, all of which was given to organisations.

Applications

Requests should be made to the Provincial Grand Almoner and are considered on an ongoing basis.

The New Masonic Samaritan Fund

£4.5 million (1,036 grants)

Correspondent: The Secretary, 60 Great Queen Street, London WC2B 5AZ (020 7404 1550; email: mail@msfund.org.uk; website: www.msfund.org.uk)

Trustees: Michael Bernard Squires; Hugh William James Stubbs; John Clayton; Graham Malcolm Sisson; Malcolm David Childs; Michael Richard Heenan; David Nunn; John Graham Rudd; Richard William Killingbeck; Owen William Davison; Katherine Fender; Colin Leslie Kennedy; Oliver Bartholemew O'Toole; Norman Eric Heaviside; Dr Garth Ezekiel; Steven Adcott; Dr Simon Fellerman; James Dennison.

CC Number: 1130424

Eligibility

Freemasons, their families, dependents and widow or surviving partner who are in both financial and medical need.

Types of grants

One-off grants ranging between £1,500 and £15,000 towards medical, respite, mobility and dental care. Grants have previously been awarded for wheelchairs, stairlifts, bathroom adaptations, residential respite care, spinal surgery, chemotherapy, IVF treatment and cardiac surgery.

Annual grant total

In 2010/11 the trust had assets of £54 million and an income of £4.1 million. There were 1,036 grants made to individuals totalling £4.52 million.

Exclusions

No grants can be made towards treatment which has already been provided privately, or which can be made through the NHS without undue delay or hardship.

Applications

Potential applicants should initially contact the fund by phone. An Almoner or Visiting Brother will be appointed to assist with every application. Application forms will be sent to the Almoner/Visiting Brother. Once completed and returned a decision is usually made within four weeks.

The Royal Antediluvian Order of Buffaloes, Grand Lodge of England War Memorial Annuities

£25,000 (101 grants)

Correspondent: The Secretary, Grove House, Skipton Road, Harrogate, North Yorkshire HG1 4LA (01423 502438; fax: 01423 533979; email: hq@raobgle.org.uk; website: www.raobgle.org.uk)

Trustees: Derek Ernest Pryer; Arvind Jayantilal Patel; Eric Vivian Herbert.

CC Number: 220476

Eligibility

Members of the order who are elderly or who have disabilities, and their dependents.

Types of grants

Annuities, though the Grand Lodge may have other charitable funds available for one-off grants.

Annual grant total

In 2010/11 the trust held assets of £193,000 and an income of £37,000. 101 annuities were made totalling £25,000.

Applications

Applications should be made through the member's lodge. All assistance originates at the local lodge level; if its resources are inadequate, the lodge may then seek assistance at provincial or ultimately national level. For dependents of deceased members, it is necessary to give the lodge to which the member belonged. If its name and number is known, the correspondent will probably be able to identify a current local telephone number or address. If only the place is known, this may still be possible, but not in all cases, particularly when the lodge concerned does not belong to this Grand Lodge group.

Other information

The Grand Lodge of England is the largest of 15 separate and independent Buffalo groups in the country. They appear to exist for mutual sociability and support as well as the support of their local communities. There are over 3,500 local lodges, all of which may be concerned to help members, dependents and perhaps others in time of need or distress. This fund was established as a tribute to members of the order who died during the First World War.

The Royal Masonic Benevolent Institution

£64,000

Correspondent: David R Innes, 60 Great Queen Street, London WC2B 5AZ (020 7596 2400; fax: 020 7404 0724; email: enquries@rmbi.org.uk; website: www. rmbi.org.uk)

Trustees: Sushil Radia; Christopher James Caine; David Watson; James Newman; William Shackle; Dr John Reuther; Kenneth Edward Coatsworth Howe; Randal Marks; John Edgcumbe; Sylvia Quayle; Mark Smith.

CC Number: 207360

Eligibility
Freemasons (usually over 60 years of age, unless unemployed due to incapacity) of the English Constitution (England, Wales and certain areas overseas) and their dependents.

Types of grants
Christmas gifts and annuities.

Annual grant total
In 2010/11 annuities and grants amounted to £64,000.

Applications
On a form available from the correspondent, usually submitted through the lodge of the relevant freemason. Applications are considered every month.

Other information
The institution has a team of welfare visitors covering the whole of England and Wales and also runs 17 homes catering for around 1,000 older freemasons.

Politics

Conservative and Unionist Agents' Benevolent Association

£46,000

Correspondent: Sally Smith, Conservative Campaign Headquarters, Millbank Tower, 30 Millbank, London SW1P 4DP (020 7984 8172; email: sally. smith@conservatives.com)

Trustees: Sir David Kelly; Sir Anthony Garrett; Donald Porter.

CC Number: 216438

Eligibility
Individuals in need who are, or have been, Conservative and Unionist Agents, or Women Organisers, and their dependents. Support is also given to the dependents of deceased Conservative or Unionist Agents or Women Organisers.

Types of grants
Recurrent grants to help with living costs. One-off grants are given towards, for example, roof repairs, emergency plumbing, replacement kitchen equipment, stair-lifts, bathrooms suitable for those with disabilities, and new boilers. Support towards funeral costs, night nursing expenses and emergency medical care may also be given.

Annual grant total
In 2010/11 the association had assets of £2.5 million and an income of £101,000. Grants were made totalling £56,000.

Applications
Initial telephone calls are welcomed and application forms are available on request. Applications can be made either directly by the individual, or through a member of the management committee or local serving agent. All beneficiaries are allocated a 'visiting agent'.

Other information
The majority of the association's grants are made for relief-in-need purposes but some help is given to the children of deceased members for the costs of education.

Prisoners/ ex-offenders

The Aldo Trust

£4,750

Correspondent: c/o NACRO, Coast Cottage, 90 Coast Road, West Mersea, Colchester CO5 8LS (01206 383809; fax: 01206 383809; email: owenwheatley@ btinternet.com)

Trustees: Owen Wheatley; Anthony Heaton-Armstrong; Peter Ashman.

CC Number: 327414

Eligibility
People in need who are being held in detention pending their trial or after their conviction. The applicant must still be serving the sentence. Applicants must have less than £25 in private cash.

Types of grants
Grants up to a maximum of £10 a year towards any needs except toiletries and training shoes.

Annual grant total
In 2010 the trust had an income of £20,000. Previously 975 grants were made to individuals totalling £9,500.

Applications
On a form available from the correspondent. Applications must be made through prison service personnel (for example, probation, chaplaincy, education), and should include the name and number of the prisoner, age, length of sentence and expected date of release. No applications direct from prisoners will be considered. Applicants may apply once only in each twelve-month period, and applications are considered monthly.

Other information
NACRO also offers a fund for people on probation; see separate entry in this guide.

The Michael and Shirley Hunt Charitable Trust

£8,000 (71 grants)

Correspondent: Mrs D S Jenkins, Trustee, Ansty House, Henfield Road, Small Dole, West Sussex BN5 9XH (01903 817116)

Trustees: Chester John Hunt; Deborah Susan Jenkins; Kathy Doris Mayberry; Shirley Ethel Hunt; Wanda Jane Baker.

CC Number: 1063418

Eligibility
Prisoners and their relatives and dependents, such as their spouses and children.

Types of grants
One-off and recurrent grants for prisoners' families' welfare needs and for travel expenses for prisoners on care leave.

Annual grant total
In 2010/11 the trust had assets of £5.8 million, which generated an income of £322,000. Grants were made to 60 individuals totalling £8,000.

Applications
In writing to the correspondent. Applications can be made directly by the individual or through a third party such as Citizens Advice, probation service or a social worker.

Other information
Grants are also made to organisations (£54,000 in 2010/11).

The National Association for the Care and Resettlement of Offenders (NACRO)

£25,000

Correspondent: Finance Director, Unit 4, Park Place, 10–12 Lawn Lane, London

SW8 1UD (020 7840 6464; fax: 020 7840 6720; email: helpline@nacro.org.uk; website: www.nacro.org.uk)

Trustees: Waheed Saleem; Johnn Whitaker; Delbert Sandiford; Linda McHugh; Mary Whyham; Dominic McGonigal; John Darley; Matthew Litobarski; Teresa Mallabone; Jonathan William Aitken; Robert Booker.

CC Number: 226171

Eligibility

Ex-offenders and their partners and families.

Types of grants

One-off grants only, usually of around £50. Only one grant can ever be made to an individual.

Annual grant total

Grants usually total around £50,000 per year.

Applications

Either directly by the individual or through the Probation Service, social service department, Citizens Advice or registered charity. Applications are considered every two months.

SACRO Trust

£6,500

Correspondent: Trust Fund Administrator, 29 Albany Street, Edinburgh EH1 3QN (01316 247270; fax: 01316 247269; email: info@national. sacro.org.uk; website: www.sacro.org.uk)

SC Number: SC023031

Eligibility

People living in Scotland who are subject to a license/court order or who have been released from prison in the last two years.

Types of grants

Grants are usually to a maximum of £300, although applications for larger sums can be considered. Grants given include those for electrical goods, clothing, furniture, driving lessons and education and training.

Annual grant total

In 2010/11 the trust gave grants to 72 individuals totalling £13,000.

Exclusions

No grants are made where financial help from other sources is available.

Applications

On a form available from the correspondent. Applications can only be accepted if they are made through a local authority, voluntary sector worker, health visitor or so on. They are considered every two months. No payment can be made directly to an individual by the trust; payment will be made to the organisation making the application. Other sources of funding should be sought before applying to the trust.

The Paul Stephenson Memorial Trust

£500

Correspondent: Pauline Austin, The New Bridge, 27A Medway Street, London SW1P 2BD

Trustees: Tony Wise; Pauline Austin; Sir Peter Lloyd; Ben Owen; Donna King.

CC Number: 295924

Eligibility

People who have served at least two years of imprisonment and are near the end of their sentence or have been released recently.

Types of grants

One-off grants of up to £100. Grants can be in cash or in kind for a particular rehabilitative need of the applicant or their immediate family, e.g. home furnishings, clothing, tools for work or assistance with college expenses.

Annual grant total

Around £1,000.

Exclusions

Grants are not given for recreational activities, setting up small businesses or becoming self-employed, or for existing debts.

Applications

On a form available from the correspondent, which must be submitted via a probation officer, prison education officer or voluntary associate. Applicants should mention other trusts or organisations that have been applied to and other grants promised or received, including any statutory grants. Trustees usually meet twice a year.

Quakers

Open Wing Trust

See entry on page 15

The Westward Trust

£6,000

Correspondent: Alison Ironside, 17 Green Meadow Road, Birmingham B29 4DD (01214 751179)

Trustees: Alison Ironside; Bradley Dodd; John Ironside; Ruth Dodd.

CC Number: 260488

Eligibility

Quakers in need who live in the UK.

Types of grants

One-off and recurrent grants according to need.

Annual grant total

In 2010/11 the trust had an income of £11,500 and a total expenditure of £11,700.

Applications

In writing to the correspondent.

Other information

Grants are also made to organisations, particularly Quaker charities or projects in which members of the Religious Society of Friends are involved.

Vegetarian

The Vegetarian Charity

£10,000

Correspondent: Susan Lenihan, 56 Parliament Street, Chippenham, Wiltshire SN14 0DE (01249 443521; email: grantssecretary@vegetariancharity. org.uk)

Trustees: I. Allen; Ms C. George; J. Hickey; B. Harkison; Mrs S. Lenihan; Miss K. Lee; Mrs B. Holdsworth; Mrs K. Barker; Miss A. Pattenden; Mrs J. Hughes.

CC Number: 294767

Eligibility

Children and young people under the age of 26 who are vegetarian or vegan and are sick or in need.

Types of grants

One-off and recurrent grants to relieve poverty and sickness, usually ranging from £250 to £1,000.

Annual grant total

In 2010/11 the charity had assets of £987,000 and an income of £63,000. Grants paid during the year to individuals and organisations totalled £30,000; a further breakdown was not available.

Applications

On a form available from the correspondent, including details of any other grants received, a CV, covering letter and three references. Applications are considered throughout the year.

Other information

Grants are also made to organisations which promote vegetarianism among young people and to vegetarian children's homes.

Victims of crime or injustice

Caudwell Children

£3 million

Correspondent: Applications Manager, Minton Hollins Building, Shelton Old Road, Stoke-on-Trent, Staffordshire ST4 7RY (0845 300 1348; fax: 01782 600639; email: charity@caudwellchildren. com; website: www.caudwellchildren. com)

Trustees: Craig Bennett; Karl Roger Bamford; John David Caudwell; Jacqueline Griffiths; Richard Mark Weiler; Dale Melvyn Briscoe; Maurice Lindsay.

CC Number: 1079770

Eligibility
People under 18 with a disability or serious illness.

Types of grants
One-off and recurrent donations for mobility, sensory and sports equipment; therapy, treatment and family holidays.

Annual grant total
In 2011 the trust had assets of £6.5 million and an income of £7 million. Grants made directly to children in the community totalled £3 million.

Exclusions
No grants for: building works, fixtures and fittings; gardening and the making safe of gardens; respite care; dolphin therapy/faith healing; computers (unless specifically designed for people with special needs); motor vehicle purchase/ adaptations; equipment repair or maintenance; domestic appliances; non-specialist furniture, decoration, clothing or bedding; private education; speech or occupational therapy; or legal costs.

Applications
On a form available to download from the website or from the correspondent. The charity uses different application forms depending upon what is being applied for. Financial details must be included. The application process can, during busy periods, take up to six months and applicants may be visited by a trustee.

Other information
The trust also organises a holiday to Florida each year under the 'Destination Dreams' programme. There are approximately 25 fully-funded family places available. Applications for places should be made early in the year i.e. January to March. For further information contact the trust directly.

The Heinz, Anna and Carol Kroch Foundation
See entry on page 26

Women

Frederick Andrew Convalescent Trust

£35,000

Correspondent: Mrs Karen Armitage, Clerk to the Trustees, Andrew and Co., St Swithin's Court, 1 Flavian Road, Nettleham Road, Lincoln LN2 4GR (01522 512123; fax: 01522 546713; email: info@factonline.co.uk; website: www. factonline.co.uk)

Trustees: Miss C. Heppenstall; Mr G. Walter; Mrs J. Welch; Mrs R. Lamb; Peter Denby; Polly Clack; Wendy Gelder.

CC Number: 211029

Eligibility
Women who have been in paid employment at some time.

Types of grants
Grants of up to £1,000 for convalescence and domestic help, and up to £600 for therapy. Types of therapy covered include: physiotherapy, occupational therapy, speech therapy, chiropody and podiatry and counselling.

Annual grant total
In 2010 the trust held assets of £1.6 million and had an income of £62,000. Grants to individuals totalled £35,000.

Applications
An initial assessment form must be completed and returned to the correspondent. The form is available from the trust's website. The trust responds to every application.

Barley Women's Institute

£1,000

Correspondent: Mrs M Ashworth, Higher Whitehough Farm, Barley, Lancs BB12 9LF (01282 616063)

Trustees: Marlene Ashworth; Audrey Weatherill; Elizabeth Johnston; Nancy Cookson; Sylvia Broughton; Christine Clinch; Susan Statham; Rosemary Connor.

CC Number: 703125

Eligibility
Women in need living in rural areas in the UK.

Types of grants
One-off and recurrent according to need.

Annual grant total
In 2010/11 the institute had an income and total expenditure of £1,400.

Applications
In writing to the correspondent.

Bircham Dyson Bell Charitable Trust – The Crossley Fund

£3,700 (19 grants)

Correspondent: Helen Abbey, Bircham Dyson Bell, 50 Broadway, Westminster, London SW1H 0BL (020 7227 7000; fax: 020 7222 3480; email: helenabbey@bdb-law.co.uk)

Trustees: S. P. Weil; I. H. McCulloch; J. M. Stephenson.

CC Number: 803150

Eligibility
Single women, including widows, of at least 50 years of age, who are in need.

Types of grants
Grants of £4 per week towards rent, paid in quarterly instalments.

Annual grant total
In 2010/11 the trust had assets of £74,000 and an income of £49,000. Grants to individuals were made totalling £3,700.

Applications
Applications are usually made with the assistance of welfare organisations or third parties such as vicars. A form is sent to likely applicants on request. The trustees meet in June and December.

Note the following statement from the trust: 'The trustees have been affected by the current economic conditions and have decided reluctantly that as matters stand they must try to meet their existing commitments and have for the time being closed the fund to new applicants. They will review the position from time to time according to their resources and the number of beneficiaries.'

Other information
The trust has previously stated: 'We receive lots of inappropriate applications; we can only help older people with rent.'

The Eaton Fund for Artists, Nurses and Gentlewomen

£59,000 (341 grants)

Correspondent: Lorna Stagg, 33 St Annes Crescent, Lewes, East Sussex BN7 1SB (01273 480606; email: admin@ eatonfund.org.uk; website: www. eatonfund.org.uk)

Trustees: Marian Shaw; Charles Savin Stewart; Dr Harry Dawson; Nicola Brooker; Timothy P. Edwards.

CC Number: 236060

Eligibility

Artists, including painters, potters, sculptors and photographers but not performing artists; nurses, including SRN, SEN, medical carers and dental nurses who are in employment or retired; and women over 18, who are in need of financial assistance.

Types of grants

One-off grants for artist's materials and equipment; picture framing for an exhibition; wheelchairs; and the setting up of a new home due to disability, family breakdown or homelessness.

Annual grant total

In 2010/11 the fund had assets of £9.1 million and an income of £265,000. Grants were made to 341 individuals totalling £59,000.

Exclusions

Grants are not given for educational fees, recurring expenses such as mortgage repayments, rent, fuel or phone bills, special diets, care home fees, private treatments or to clear debt.

Applications

On a form available from the correspondent or to download from the website. Forms can be submitted directly by the individual but the trust also asks that a supporting letter from an appropriate third party, such as a doctor or social worker, be included. Any relevant documents like invoices or quotations should also be sent in with the form. They are considered six times a year and applicants will be notified of the decision within a month of the application deadline. For more information on specific application deadlines see the 'calendar' section of the trust's website.

The fund advises that an application is more likely to be successful where:

▶ Detailed background information is given about the applicant and their specific need

▶ Applicants have also applied to other charities for assistance when requesting sums of more than £400

The Arthur Hurst Will Trust

£20,000

Correspondent: The Public Trustee, Office of the Official Solicitor, 81 Chancery Lane, London WC2A 1DD (020 7911 7127; email: enquiries@offsol. gsi.gov.uk)

Trustee: The Public Trustee.

CC Number: 207991

Eligibility

Women and members of the clergy who are in need and who have been forced to give up their work because of ill health. The trust also supports widows and children of clergymen.

Types of grants

One-off grants according to need.

Annual grant total

In 2010/11 the trust had an income of £65,000 and gave approximately £20,000 in grants to individuals.

Applications

Applications can be submitted directly by the individual or through a social worker, Citizens Advice, a welfare agency or another third party. Applications can be considered at any time, although there is not always available funding to make payments.

Other information

The trust may also make awards to organisations.

The Morris Beneficent Fund

£25,000

Correspondent: Simon Jamison, No. 10 Evendons Centre, 171 Evendons Lane, Wokingham RG41 4EH (01189 798653)

Trustees: W. S. Morris; H. M. Shearing; M. H. Shearing; D. Pearson; A. Kinley.

CC Number: 256473

Eligibility

'Distressed gentlewomen' recommended by members of the fund. Grants generally go to older women.

Types of grants

Recurrent grants according to need.

Annual grant total

Grants and annuities usually total around £25,000 each year. In 2011 annuities were paid to nine ladies and one-off grants were paid in another two cases.

Applications

On an application form supplied by a member. No unsolicited applications will be considered.

Other information

The trustees decide each year how many annuitants can be supported, though this number rarely exceeds 20 as the trustees prefer to raise the level of grants rather than awarding a larger number of smaller annuities.

The Lilian Eveleigh Nash Foundation

£8,000 (6 grants)

Correspondent: The Committee, Natwest Trust Services, 5th Floor, Trinity Quay 2, Avon Street, Bristol BN2 0PT (01179 403283)

Trustee: Natwest Private Banking.

CC Number: 1043563

Eligibility

Women in need in the area comprising the Dioceses of London, Southwark and Chelmsford.

Types of grants

The provision of permanent accommodation, maintenance, holidays and so on.

Annual grant total

In 2010/11 the trust held assets of £170,000, had an income of £19,000 and a total expenditure of £73,000. Charitable payments to six individuals and nine organisations totalled £60,000.

Applications

In writing to the correspondent.

Other information

The trust committee is formed of the Anglican Bishops of the Dioceses of London, Chelmsford and Southwark.

The Perry Fund

£19,000

Correspondent: William Carter, Clerk to the Trustees, 7 Waterloo Road, Wolverhampton WV1 4DW

Trustees: Fiona Elizabeth Thompson; John Nicholas Richard Neville Bishop; Margaret Anne Gabb; Gillian Jane Williamson.

CC Number: 218829

Eligibility

For annuities: ladies who are struggling to manage on a low pension. For one-off grants any lady in need regardless of age or background.

Types of grants

Annuities of around £2,000 and one-off grants.

Annual grant total

In 2010 the fund held assets of £588,000 and had an income of £27,000. Annuities of £2,000 were paid to seven individuals and one-off grants were made totalling £4,500.

Applications

On a form available from the correspondent. Applications can be submitted directly by the individual or through a third party such as a social worker, nursing home manager or welfare organisation. The trustees usually meet twice a year to consider applications.

The Royal Society for the Relief of Indigent Gentlewomen of Scotland

£1.1 million

Correspondent: The Secretary and Cashier, 14 Rutland Square, Edinburgh EH1 2BD (01312 292308; fax: 01312 290956; email: info@igf.org; website: www.igf.org)

Trustees: John M. Chapman; Margaret M. F. Wilson; Dr Daphne Audsley; Adrian A. Johnston; Graeme A. Whyte; J. Allan Sturrock; Walter N. J. Thomson; Revd Dr Sheilagh Kesting; Maureen O'Neill; Elizabeth Dickson; Annemieke Cunningham; Dr Gillian Beattie; Walter M. Reid; Revd Ian Walker; David B. Wilson; Stewart Mackay; Catriona Reynolds.

SC Number: SC016095

Eligibility

Single women, widows or divorcees in need who are over 50 years of age, of Scottish birth, background or education, and have (or whose husband, ex-husband or father had) a professional or business background. Those prevented from pursuing a career by devoting their lives to the care of relatives may also be considered. Applicants need not live in Scotland.

Applicants must have a gross income of under £11,750 (April 2011) after deductions of council tax/rent/mortgage and the first £1,000 of factoring fees, but excluding Attendance Allowance or Disability Living Allowance. Where resident in a residential/nursing home an individual financial assessment is undertaken. Capital/savings must not exceed £23,500, excluding the value of house of residence.

Types of grants

Annuities, paid in quarterly instalments, of around £1,100 a year, or less if the beneficiary is under 60 years of age and receives help from DWP. Beneficiaries may also receive one-off grants for TV licences, telephone rental, holidays, nursing, property maintenance and so on.

Annual grant total

In 2010/11 the society had assets of £34 million and an income of £1.8 million. Grants were made totalling £1.1 million and were distributed as follows:

Annual annuities	£859,000
Supplementary grants	£149,000
Winter grants	£75,000
Initial grants	£15,000
Other grants	£11,000

812 annuitants were supported during the year.

Exclusions

The trust is unable to support ladies who are separated or currently in a civil partnership.

Applications

On a form available from the correspondent, to be submitted directly by the individual or through a social worker, Citizens Advice or other welfare agency or third party. Application deadlines are end of March and September for consideration in May and November. Details of applicant's age, current financial position, personal family background and a copy of the divorce document (if appropriate) are required.

Other information

The society also provides regular home visiting, counselling and assistance with application forms.

Sawyer Trust

£51,000

Correspondent: John Pooley, PO Box 797, Worcester WR4 4BU (email: info@sawyertrust.org; website: www.sawyertrust.org)

Trustees: Lt Col Brian Clarke; Dr David Albert Lees; John Pooley; Hilary Day; Jim Brown; David O'Dwyer; Nigel Stanley Wake; Ian Sonley; Richard Rogers.

CC Number: 511276

Eligibility

Women over 50 who are in need through financial hardship, sickness or poor health. If there are funds left over men over 50 in the same circumstances may also be helped.

Types of grants

One-off grants. Recent grants have paid for household items and fittings, removal costs, telephone bills, travel costs and rent arrears. The trust states that it will consider a wide range of assistance but it does not pay cash directly to applicants.

Annual grant total

In 2009/10 the trust held assets of £1.7 million and had an income of £60,000. Grants to individuals totalled £51,000.

Exclusions

Luxury goods or services, parties or outings, shortfall on insurance claims – except in certain circumstances, legal expenses, credit card debt or ongoing costs.

Applications

On an application form available to download from the trust website or by requesting one by writing to the correspondent. Applications may be completed by the applicant or someone else on their behalf. Applications must be posted. Trustees meet monthly to consider applications.

The Society for the Assistance of Ladies in Reduced Circumstances

£758,000

Correspondent: John Sands, Lancaster House, 25 Hornyold Road, Malvern, Worcestershire WR14 1QQ (0300 365 1886; email: info@salrc.org.uk; website: www.salrc.org.uk)

Trustees: Ravi Kumar; Catherine Connery; Ruth Christie; Paul Pasquill.

CC Number: 205798

Eligibility

Women who live completely alone, have savings less than £8,000, receive a means tested benefit, and are not eligible for help from any other charity.

Types of grants

Monthly payments towards day-to-day living expenses and one-off grants of up to £350 for TV licences, telephone rental charges, white goods and so on.

Annual grant total

In 2011 the society had assets of £23 million and an income of £888,000. A total of £758,000 was given in grants to individuals. Of these 162 were discretionary grants totalling £44,000 with £715,000 paid in recurrent monthly grants.

Exclusions

No grants for education, care or nursing home fees, holidays, repayment of debts or funeral expenses. The trust is unable to assist students or women who work 16 hours or more a week.

Applications

On a form available from the correspondent including information on employment history, financial situation and any other charities that have been approached. Applications can be submitted directly by the individual or through a third party such as Citizens Advice or a social worker.

Other information

Grants are also given to organisations (£83,000 in 2011).

St Andrew's Society for Ladies in Need

£43,000 (73 grants)

Correspondent: Mrs M Pope, 20 Denmark Gardens, Ipswich Road, Holbrook, Ipswich, Suffolk IP9 2BG (01473 327408; email: mpope@st-andrews.fsbusiness.co.uk; website: www.standrewssociety.ik.com)

Trustees: Bridget Clarke; Duncan Rabagliati; Patrick Desmond Scrivens; Marjorie Hallam; Alison Boreham; Peregrine Anthony Toft Bousfield; Lorna Baird; Sarah Shaw.

CC Number: 208541

Eligibility

Single women from a well-educated, professional or semi-professional background who are now living alone in reduced circumstances. Applicants must be retired or unable to work and of British nationality. Preference is given to elderly women who are over 80 years of age.

Types of grants

Recurrent grants, up to a maximum of £20 a week to help with daily living expenses, are paid each quarter. Priority is given to ladies who are trying to maintain their own homes but grants are also given to those struggling with nursing home fees. One-off special grants are also available for heating, the cost of moving house, domestic appliances, furniture, disability aids, holidays and convalescence.

Annual grant total

In 2010 the society held assets of £1.4 million and had an income of £57,000. Grants were made to 73 individuals totalling £43,000. The vast majority of this was given in regular grants and with just £200 awarded in one-off grants to meet particular short-term needs.

Exclusions

No grants to younger women and non-retired ladies who are able to work. No assistance with the discharge of debts.

Applications

On a form available from the correspondent, to be submitted either directly by the individual or through a social worker, Citizens Advice, other welfare agency or somebody with power of attorney. They should include as much background detail as possible, such as education, occupation and so on. Applications are considered at quarterly committee meetings, though urgent cases can be dealt with between meetings.

WRVS Benevolent Trust

£18,000 (13 grants)

Correspondent: Lynne Rawlings, Hon. Secretary, 26 Pound Lane, Isleham, Ely, Cambridgeshire CB7 5SF (07900 955070; email: wrvsbenevolenttrust@hotmail.co.uk; website: www.wrvs-benevolent-trust.co.uk)

Trustees: Ann Tribble; Shelagh Murray; Lynne Rawlings; Carol Ann Milford; Pauline Blyth; Gilli Galloway; John Fallon.

CC Number: 261931

Eligibility

Past or present members of the Women's Royal Voluntary Service (WRVS) who have given at least five years of service and are in need.

Types of grants

One-off grants ranging from £50 to £6,000. Recent grants have been made for washing machines, replacement windows, a new boiler, moving costs, a carbon monoxide alarm, car tax, nursing home top up fees and dry rot treatment.

Annual grant total

In 2011 grants were made to 13 people totalling £18,000.

Applications

On an application form available to download from the website. Applications can be considered year round.

Illness and disability charities

There are many charities for people with illnesses or disabilities. The entries in this section are only for those which give financial help from their own resources. There are many others that do not have a large enough income to do this but may be the starting point for getting financial help. For this reason we have a list of organisations which provide advice and support on page 495.

This section starts with an index of illness or disability. The entries are arranged alphabetically within each category, within those trusts which support more than one illness or disability listed at the start of the chapter.

Local disability charities are not included in this section but are listed in the relevant local section of the book. Northern Irish, Scottish and Welsh disability charities are also listed in the relevant locality rather than in this section.

Able kidz

£7,100

Correspondent: Grants Officer, 6th Floor, 456 – 458 Strand, London WC2R 0DZ (0845 123 3997; email: info@ablekidz.com; website: www.ablekidz.com)

Trustees: Theo Everett Kalogerides; Cathryn Walton; Andrew Turner.

CC Number: 1114955

Eligibility
Disabled children and young adults under the age of 18 in the UK.

Types of grants
One-off and recurrent grants according to need. Grants are typically made for specialist educational equipment and extra tuition.

Annual grant total
In 2010/11 the trust had an income of £43,000 and a total expenditure of £44,000. Donations paid amounted to £7,100.

Applications
In writing to the correspondent. Applications are not means tested. They should include the following:
- A summary of the child's circumstances
- What the child requires and how Able Kidz might be able to help
- An outline of the costs involved

The ACT Foundation
See entry on page 1

Active Foundation
See entry on page 16

ASPIRE (Association for Spinal Injury Research Rehabilitation and Reintegration) Human Needs Fund

£161,000

Correspondent: The Human Needs Manager, ASPIRE National Training Centre, Wood Lane, Stanmore, Middlesex HA7 4AP (020 8954 5759; fax: 020 8420 6352; email: info@aspire.org.uk; website: www.aspire.org.uk)

Trustees: Mr A. Lambert; Mrs F. Jerreat; Mr D. A. Edwards; Mr L. Hamill; Dr A. Gall; Mr M. King; Mr S. Roulstone; Ms E. Campbell; Dr S. Patel.

CC Number: 1075317

Eligibility
People in need with a spinal cord injury. Priority is given to re-establishing independent mobility.

Types of grants
One-off grants to help towards the purchase of specialist equipment such as wheelchairs and computers. The trust states that it will rarely offer full funding, but will offer part-funding and assistance with securing the remainder.

Annual grant total
In 2010/11 the association had assets of £1.9 million and an income £2.4 million. Human need grants totalled £161,000, which is the largest spend, helping the most people, in any one year of the charity's history.

Exclusions
Grants from the fund are solely for people with acquired non progressive spinal cord injury. The charity also states that it is unlikely to fund applications for holidays, standing wheelchairs, house adaptations, passive exercise equipment, vehicles or secondary functions on wheelchairs, including standing functions, for reasons that could be met by other means and cosmetic features.

Applications
On a form available from the charity's website. The assessment period is approximately 4–6 weeks and each application requires a supporting statement from an occupational therapist or medical consultant to explain why the specialist equipment is appropriate. A full list of application guidelines is available from the correspondent and on the website.

Other information
The charity also provides a range of services for eligible individuals. See the charity's website for further details.

Barchester's Charitable Foundation
See entry on page 24

The Birchington Convalescent Benefit Fund

£2,200 (11 grants)

Correspondent: Mr Michael Locke, Church Society, Dean Wace House, 16 Rosslyn Road, Watford WD18 0NY (01923 235111; fax: 01923 800362; email: admin@churchsociety.org; website: www.churchsociety.org)

Trustees: Revd Dr J. B. Hall; Revd George Curry; Revd Simon James Scott; Revd John Anthony Cheeseman; Revd Gordon Lenham Warren; Revd Richard Farr; Duncan Rodney Lecington Boyd; Revd Dr Michael John Ovey; Revd Stephen James Walton; Revd Gary Townsend; James Crabtree; Revd Rupert Mackay; Michael De Semlyen; Revd Andrew Price; Pavlos Karageorgi; Revd Timothy Mark Edwards; Peter Daniel Myers; Mark Stephen Smith; James Charles Taylor; John Anthony Telford.

CC Number: 249574

Eligibility
Children under the age of 18 who are chronically ill or recovering from surgery or long-term illness.

Types of grants
One-off grants of £200 towards part-payment of convalescent holidays for children.

Annual grant total
In 2011 grants were made to 11 individuals totalling £2,200.

Exclusions
Grants are rarely given for expensive or overseas holidays. Grants are not given for reasons other than holidays. This includes no grants to allow ill parents to have a break from their children.

Applications
On a form available from the correspondent or to download from the website. Applications should be made through a third party, for example, a doctor, social worker or hospital staff. Details of the sponsor of the application, type of illness or surgery, financial status and type and cost of the holiday needed should be included. Decisions on grant awards are made in February, April and June.

Other information
The fund is managed by the Church Society. Those awarded a grant also receive a complimentary children's bible.

Clevedon Forbes Fund

£34,000 (117 grants)

Correspondent: Wendy Robinson, Director, 4 Kenn Road, Clevedon BS21 6EL (01275 341777; fax: 01275 341777; email: wendy@clevedonforbes.org; website: www.clevedonforbes.org)

Trustees: Tim Simpson; Gillian Mantle; Joan Taffs; Neill Foster; Margaret Prudence Baker.

CC Number: 249313

Eligibility
People of limited means who are recovering from surgery or who are in need of a break due to illness or trauma. Grants are also available to those caring for someone who is sick or disabled. The majority of grants are given to

individuals living in the south west but those living further afield will be considered.

Types of grants

One-off grants to those in need.

Annual grant total

In 2010/11 the trust had assets of £1.5 million and an income of £76,000. 117 grants were made to individuals totalling £34,000.

Exclusions

Grants are not made for capital goods. Individuals cannot apply for another grant until a three year period has elapsed.

Applications

Applications need to be made through a professional in the statutory or voluntary sector, such as a social worker or welfare officer. Application forms are available on the trust website or directly from the correspondent.

Other information

A Christian gospel booklet is sent out to people receiving a grant unless there is a specific request to the contrary.

Equipment for Independent Living

£20,000

Correspondent: June Sutherland, Secretary, 10 Pembroke Walk, London W8 6PQ

Trustees: June Sutherland; Geoffrey Cox; Alistair Stoker; Heather Tarrant; Susan Herald; Trevor Watkins; Janet Hillman; Margaret Elliott; Helen Patterson; Eliot Charles Anthony Woolf.

CC Number: 228438

Eligibility

People over 16 who are disabled in the UK and overseas.

Types of grants

One-off grants towards disability equipment enabling people to obtain mobility, independence and earning power. Awards are usually in the range of £100 to £1,000.

Annual grant total

In 2010 the trust had an income of £21,000 and a total expenditure £22,000.

Exclusions

Normally grants are not made towards: medical equipment; course fees and materials; welfare expenditure of a non-capital nature, e.g. holiday or moving expenses; equipment which is supplied by the NHS or social services; equipment running costs; building adaptations and decorating; household equipment (unless specially adapted for the person's

disability); or private treatment, home care fees or computers (unless they are used as a speech aid or to enable the individual to earn their living).

Funds are not normally granted to cases submitted by other charities which have much larger resources than the trust.

Applications

Applicants must be referred in the first instance by a professional person involved with their welfare, for example, a social worker, occupational therapist or specialist nurse. The professional person should write to the Honorary Secretary describing the applicant's circumstances and saying what equipment is needed and why. If appropriate, a full application form will then be sent out.

Applications can be submitted at any time and are considered in January, April, July and October.

Monica Eyre Memorial Foundation
See entry on page 24

The Farrell Trust

£3,500

Correspondent: Reverend Mike Shaw, PO Box 531, Letchworth Garden City SG6 9ES (email: ftcharity@yahoo.co.uk; website: www.farrelltrust.org.uk)

Trustees: David Thompson; Angela Kinsbury Geal; Pamela Kingsbury Tredinnick; Michael Shaw; Sue Attwood.

CC Number: 257667

Eligibility

People who have physical or mental health problems, older people and those on low incomes.

Types of grants

Grants of between £50 and £200 are given towards holidays.

Annual grant total

In 2010/11 the trust had an income of £4,600 and a total expenditure of £3,900.

Exclusions

Successful applicants may not reapply for three years.

Applications

On an application form available from the trust website. Applications may be completed by the individual, a friend, family member or carer.

Evidence of income support and Disability Living Allowance or immediate and urgent need must be provided along with the application form. It is recommended that applicants attach a letter of support from a doctor,

social worker, occupational therapist or minister of religion.

Gardening for Disabled Trust

£25,000

Correspondent: The Secretary, PO Box 285, Tunbridge Wells, Kent TN2 9JD (email: info@gardeningfordisabledtrust. org.uk; website: www. gardeningfordisabledtrust.org.uk)

Trustees: Nigel Philips; Rosie Atkins; Hon Sarah Joiner; John Mankelow; Jilly Cholomondeley; Stephanie Donaldson.

CC Number: 255066

Eligibility

Members of the trust who wish to participate in gardening regardless of age or disability.

Types of grants

One-off grants according to need to help towards tools, raised beds, paving, labour and greenhouses.

Annual grant total

In 2010 the trust had assets of £199,000 and an income of £29,000. Grants were made totalling £25,000, some of which were paid through local organisations.

Exclusions

No grants to pay for a gardener for general maintenance or for clearing or fencing.

Applications

In writing to the correspondent detailing the work they would like done and an estimate of the cost of tools, materials and labour (if necessary). If labour is required the applicant should provide original copies of two quotes. Applicants should also include a note from their GP, social worker or occupational therapist describing their disability. Applications are considered monthly.

The Megan and Trevor Griffiths Trust

£800 (2 grants)

Correspondent: Janet Griffiths, Honorary Secretary, 46 Partridge Road, Roath, Cardiff CF24 3QX (email: mtgtrust@googlemail.com)

Trustees: Gerald Cheetham; Mererid Morgan; Gareth Wardell; Dr Carole Standley; Dr Roger Griffiths; Janet Griffiths; Paula Carpenter; Sally Davies; Revd Canon Aled Griffiths; Rod Belcher; Wyn Davies.

CC Number: 328684

Eligibility

People with physical or mental disabilities. Preference is given to people living in the former administrative county of Carmarthen (Carmarthenshire and parts of Ceredigion and Pembrokeshire).

Types of grants

Grants are provided for goods or services that cannot be obtained through statutory agencies, and specifically to promote independence. This can include IT equipment, electrical goods, hospital expenses, respite care, holidays, special toys/instruments, fees for training courses and disabled and therapeutic equipment. Grants are one-off and are usually limited to £100.

Annual grant total

In 2010/11 the fund had an income of £54,000, most of which came from a bequest, and made grants totalling £800.

In the year the trust considered 24 applications and made two grants.

Exclusions

Grants are very unlikely to be given for the payment of debt.

Applications

In writing to the correspondent from a third party such as a social worker or on a form available from the correspondent, which has to be supported by another person, preferably a professional, for verification. Application deadlines are in mid-October and at the end of May.

Other information

The trust has rarely supported applications from outside of Carmarthenshire and states that 'we always have more than enough worthy applicants from Carmarthenshire and surrounding counties'.

The N. and P. Hartley Memorial Trust

£2,000

Correspondent: Virginia Watson, Trustee, 24 Holywell Lane, Leeds LS17 8HA

Trustees: Gwendolyn Proctor; James Proctor; John Kirman; Virginia Watson.

CC Number: 327570

Eligibility

People who are disabled, older or terminally ill. Priority is firstly given to those living in West Yorkshire, secondly to individuals living in the north of England and thirdly to those elsewhere in the UK and overseas.

Types of grants

One-off grants towards, for example, specialist equipment for people with disabilities.

Annual grant total

Grants to individuals total between £3,000 and £4,000 each year.

Applications

In writing to the correspondent, preferably through a social worker, Citizens Advice or other welfare agency, for consideration twice yearly. Re-applications from previous beneficiaries are welcomed.

Other information

The trust also makes a number of grants to organisations and to individuals for educational purposes.

Independence at Home

£366,000 (1,296 grants)

Correspondent: Mary Rose, Chief Executive, 4th Floor, Congress House, 14 Lyon Road, Harrow HA1 2EN (020 8427 7929; fax: 020 8424 2937; email: iah@independenceathome.org.uk; website: www.independenceathome.org.uk)

Trustees: David Astor; Prof. Jennifer Rosemary Harrow; Richard Alan Opperman; William Francklin; Prof. Linda Luxon; Dr Ros Davies; Sue Douthwaite; Richard Wilson.

CC Number: 245259

Eligibility

People who are substantially disabled or severely ill and who live at home or who wish to do so. The trust cannot consider applications where more than £2,000 still needs to be raised.

Types of grants

Grants ranging between £100 and £750 towards specific additional costs associated with living at home with a disability, including equipment and adaptations. Grants can be made towards almost any expense which is not covered by statutory provision and which is related to a disabled person living at home.

Annual grant total

In 2010/11 the trust had assets of £3.4 million and an income of £570,000. Grants were made to 1,296 individuals totalling £366,000.

Exclusions

No grants are made to people living in residential care. Grants are not made towards medical treatment or therapies; funeral expenses; debts and arrears; leisure equipment such as televisions; motor vehicles (although the trust may be able to help towards the cost of adaptations); telephone rental or call charges; or TV licences. Only one grant can be held in any 12 month period.

Applications

Applicants must first be introduced by a referrer – this could be a social worker, occupational therapist, specialist nurse or other welfare body. The referrer must write to the trust describing the applicant's circumstances and what sort of help is required. Once the referred has done this they will receive an application form and guidance notes. The application form and guidance notes may also be downloaded from the website. Applications should be submitted by post. They are considered on an ongoing basis.

The trust accepts informal contact prior to applications being made.

The League of the Helping Hand (LHH)

£114,000

Correspondent: Moira Parrott, Secretary, LHH, P O Box 342, Burgess Hill RH15 5AQ (01444 236099; email: secretary@lhh.org.uk; website: www.lhh.org.uk)

Trustees: Julian Simmons Korn; Beatrice Ann Salter; David William Fellowes; Trot Lavelle; Joyce Helen Horley; Patricia Boucher; Oliver Haines.

CC Number: 208792

Eligibility

People who have a physical disability, learning difficulty or mental health problem and are in financial need. Those who care for somebody who is disabled, elderly or ill may also be eligible.

Types of grants

One-off grants ranging between £50 and £250 towards essential household items, specialist equipment and carers' breaks. Recurrent grants are also available to help with daily living costs.

Annual grant total

In 2010/11 the trust had assets of £2.3 million and an income of £138,000. Grants to individuals totalled £114,000 and can be broken down as follows:

One-off grants to (445) other beneficiaries	£65,000
Grants to regular beneficiaries	
Quarterly gifts	£41,000
Christmas gifts	£3,400
Holidays	£2,500
Visits	£2,000

Exclusions

No help is given for debts, business costs, holidays, tenancy deposits, building works, mobility scooters, wheelchairs, medical, dental or therapeutic treatments; or for education-related items.

Applications

On a form available from the correspondent or to download from trust's website. Applications must be submitted through a social worker, carers' support centre, Citizens Advice or other welfare body. An sae must be enclosed. Supportive letters accompanying completed forms are not required. The trustees meet every three weeks to consider applications, although emergency needs can be met more quickly. Telephone enquiries are welcome.

Mobility Trust

£95,000

Correspondent: Anne Munn, Chief Executive, 17b Reading Road, Pangbourne, Reading, Berkshire RG8 7LR (01189 842588; fax: 01189 842544; email: mobility@mobilitytrust. org.uk; website: www.mobilitytrust.org. uk)

Trustees: Thomas Loyd; Keith Davison; Janey Shephard; John Manning.

CC Number: 1070975

Eligibility

People with disabilities.

Types of grants

No grants are given. The trust provides powered wheelchairs or scooters for people who are unable to obtain such equipment through statutory sources or afford it themselves. If someone is unable to walk at all and requires a powered wheelchair they should apply to their local NHS Wheelchair Service before making an application to the trust.

Annual grant total

In 2010/11 the trust had assets of £258,000 and an income of £151,000. A total of £95,000 was spent on beneficiaries' equipment.

Applications

Applications must be submitted in the first instance by a letter directly by the individual or through a social worker, medical advisor or other welfare agency. The letter should explain why the person needs the equipment, detailing any disabilities and their cause. If there is a possibility of helping the person they will be sent a form to complete. On confirmation of acceptance of the application the trust will arrange for an independent occupational therapist to assess the person in order that they receive the right equipment to suit their clinical need.

The trust insures the equipment for the first year but expects the beneficiary to take over the payments in the second year. Servicing and repairs will be their responsibility following the expiry of the warranty period.

The Florence Nightingale Aid-in-Sickness Trust

£216,000 (293 grants)

Correspondent: Ann Griffiths, 6 Avonmore Road, London W14 8RL (020 7605 4244; email: fnaist@ independentage.org.uk or ann.griffiths@fnaist.org.uk; website: www.fnaist.org.uk)

Trustee: Independent Age.

CC Number: 211896

Eligibility

People who are in poor health, convalescent or who have disabilities. Preference will be given to people with professional, secretarial, or administrative qualifications or experience.

Types of grants

One-off grants are available for convalescence or respite care; medical equipment and other aids; sensory equipment; telephone installation (or mobile phones in rare cases); and hospital visiting expenses. Partial funding may be provided where a large grant is requested.

Annual grant total

In 2011 the trust had assets of £7.9 million and an income of £295,000. Grants were made to 293 individuals totalling £216,000.

Exclusions

Grants are not available for: house alterations, adaptations, improvements or maintenance; car purchase or adaptations; electrical wheelchairs, scooters or buggies; holidays, carers' breaks, exchange visits or nursing home fees; debts or repayments; general clothing; computers and software; stairlifts; or general house furnishing. Under normal circumstances, grants can only be given to any one household at intervals of three years.

Applications

On a form available from the correspondent or to download from the website. Applications should be submitted by a social worker, occupational therapist, doctor, health centre worker or a similar welfare professional. They should include a brief medical history of the applicant and proof of the need for assistance.

Applications are considered monthly, although urgent requests can be dealt with between meetings.

React (Rapid Effective Assistance for Children with Potentially Terminal Illnesses)

£414,000

Correspondent: Grants Administrator, St Luke's House, 270 Sandycombe Road, Richmond upon Thames, Surrey TW9 3NP (020 8940 2575; fax: 020 8940 2050; email: react@reactcharity.org; website: www.reactcharity.org)

Trustees: Rupert Anthony Wiles; Jacky Sales; Keith Richard Entwisle; Paul Graham Mellor.

CC Number: 802440

Eligibility

Financially disadvantaged families caring for a child under 18 years living with a potentially terminal illness.

Types of grants

Grants in kind and one-off grants ranging from £50 to £5,000. They can be made for domestic or medical equipment which may contribute towards the child's quality of life. A broad variety of items may be considered including carpets, furniture, kitchen appliances, clothing, bedding, toys, car seats, travel expenses, specialist chairs and beds, sensory equipment, wheelchairs and hoists, as well as mobile home holidays at one of six sites around the UK. The charity can also contribute towards hospital expenses such as food and travel and funeral and memorial expenses.

Annual grant total

In 2011/12 the trust held assets of £319,000 and had an income of £738,000. Grants to individuals totalled £414,000 and were broken down as follows:

Medical	242	£123,000
Domestic	311	£105,000
Mobile home holidays	270	£53,000
Travel and subsistence	222	£41,000
Home adaptations	45	£33,000
Funeral expenses	38	£33,000
Educational purchases	35	£15,000
Respite holidays	52	£9,700

Exclusions

No grants towards trips overseas, structural building works, private treatment or the purchase of vehicles.

Applications

On a form available from the correspondent or to download from the website. Forms must be completed and signed by a member of the family and endorsed by a medical or social care professional. Families are required to declare financial details and are asked to phone if in any doubt about eligibility. The charity aims to reply to every application within a few days, and the decision process in most cases takes less than a week.

Reuben Foundation

£38,000 (35 grants)

Correspondent: Malcolm Turner, Trustee, 4th Floor, Millbank Tower, 21–24 Millbank, London SW1P 4QP (020 7802 5014; email: contact@ reubenfoundation.com; website: www. reubenfoundation.com)

Trustees: Annie Benjamin; Michael Gubbay; Simon Reuben; Malcolm Turner; James Adam Reuben; Dana Lisa Reuben; Richard Anthony Stone; Patrick Colin O'Driscoll.

CC Number: 1094130

Eligibility

Persons who are in need, hardship or distress as a result of local, national or international disorder.

Types of grants

One-off grants according to need, generally for healthcare and educational purposes.

Annual grant total

In 2011 the foundation held assets totalling £65 million and had an income from investments of £3.6 million. Grants to 35 individuals totalled £76,000, some of which were made for educational purposes. The majority of grants were paid to organisations.

Applications

The foundation has stated that grants are made by invitation only and that suitable causes are identified 'through the existing trustees' contacts and by building new relationships with a range of charitable organisations and intermediaries.'

Contact the trust with inquiries about applications.

Other information

Grants are also made to individuals for educational costs as well as to organisations.

The foundation was established in 2002 as an outlet for the philanthropic giving of billionaire property investors David and Simon Reuben. The foundation was endowed by the brothers with a donation of $100 million (£54.1 million), with the income generated to be given to a range of charitable causes, particularly in the fields of healthcare and education.

The SF Group Charity

£34,000

Correspondent: Brenda Yong, Charitable Fund Manager, FREEPOST NAT13205, Nottingham NG8 6ZZ (email: brenda. yong@sfcharity.co.uk; website: www. sfcharity.co.uk)

Trustees: R. Warwick; R. Yong.

CC Number: NG8 6ZZ

Eligibility

Severely disabled people of all ages, primarily in the Midlands and North West. This can include people with significant sensory, physical and intellectual impairments and those with complex and challenging behavioural needs.

Payments for or towards specific items or services which will make a 'positive' difference to the quality of life of individuals or groups.

Types of grants

Applications are treated on their merit. Grants average around £1,000. There is no official upper limit to the amount offered, however grants of above £5,000 would be relatively rare.

Previously, grants have been given for special clothing, footwear, mattresses and beds, indoor/outdoor wheelchairs, mobility scooters, kitchen equipment, a Meywalker and structural amendments to houses and living areas. Grants may be given for ordinary household items if it can be shown that they will have an impact on alleviating the disability rather than improving general family circumstances. Grants for UK holidays may also be considered, but applications should be submitted 6–12 months in advance of proposed holiday dates.

Annual grant total

In 2011 the fund had assets of £244,000 and an income of £107,000. Direct charitable expenditure totalled £34,000.

Exclusions

No grants for: debts; education and course fees; debts; motor vehicle purchase or expenses; nursing and residential home fees; funeral expenses; removal expenses; driving lessons; items already purchased; therapies such as swimming with dolphins and hyperbaric therapy; alternative therapies such as reflexology, acupuncture and faith healing. Ipads and laptops are rarely funded.

Applications

Applications are welcomed from individuals, professional workers and representatives of organisations. Where the request is from a private individual, a detailed letter of support from a professional (e.g. family doctor, hospital consultant, social worker, teacher or a worker from a community or disability organisation) is essential. If applying for specialist seating, manual or powered wheelchairs, the letter must be from an occupational therapist or physiotherapist.

Applicants should first complete a short preliminary enquiry form. This can be done online at the sfgroup website, or by completing the form attached to the charity's information leaflet which can be requested by phone or email. The Fund Manager will make contact within two weeks of receiving the application to discuss the request in more detail.

Other information

Grants are also made to organisations.

Vitalise

£186,000 (438 grants)

Correspondent: Bookings Team, Shap Road Industrial Estate, Shap Road, Kendal LA9 6NZ (0303 3030145; fax: 01539 735567; email: bookings@vitalise. org.uk; website: www.vitalise.org.uk)

Trustees: George Duncan; Mindy Sawhney; Nick Buckland; Tim Prideaux; Kristie Galbraith; Linda Beaney; Philip Trevor White; Richard John Poxton; Rebecca Louise Mauger; Gavin David Wright.

CC Number: 295072

Eligibility

Adults with physical disabilities and carers who might not otherwise be able to afford a break. Applicants must not have been on a break for 18 months or more. Applicants must not have more than £23,000 in savings and must not qualify for full statutory funding.

Types of grants

Grants towards the cost of a Vitalise break. The grant allocated is dependent on individual circumstances.

Annual grant total

In 2010/11 the charity held assets totalling £9.1 million and had an income of £9 million. Grants totalling £186,000 from the Joan Brander Memorial Fund helped 438 people access breaks.

Exclusions

Grants do not cover associated costs, for example transport to and from the centre.

Applications

Both an online application form and a downloadable form are available on the website. Applications require a letter of support from a social worker or healthcare professional.

Provisional bookings must be made before completing the application form.

Other information

While the charity can only provide a limited number of grants they also fundraise and offer advice and assistance on accessing other funding for potential guests.

Bruce Wake Charity

£60,000

Correspondent: Mrs P D Wake, Trustee, PO Box 9335, Oakham, Rutland LE15 0ET (0844 879 3349; email: Online contact form; website: www. brucewaketrust.co.uk)

Trustees: Me Peter Kenneth Hems; Robert Rowley; Penny Wake; Thomas Adam Wake.

CC Number: 1018190

Eligibility

People who are disabled (predominantly wheelchair-users) in the UK.

Types of grants

The trustees will consider grant applications related to the provision of leisure activities for the disabled, but favour particularly applications whereby the potential beneficiaries meet one or all of the following criteria:

▶ The potential beneficiaries are physically disabled wheelchair users
▶ Improved access for wheelchair users is proposed
▶ A sporting or leisure activity involving disabled wheelchair users is proposed

Annual grant total

In 2010/11 the charity had assets of £8.3 million, which generated an income of £183,000. Grants were made to individuals totalling £60,000, of which £28,000 was paid through Leicester Charity Link and 61 grants totalling £32,000 were paid directly by the charity.

Applications

In writing through a charitable organisation or equivalent recognised body. Applications should include all appropriate financial information. They are considered quarterly.

Other information

Grants were made to 130 organisations totalling £300,000.

Aids/HIV

Eileen Trust

£45,000

Correspondent: Mr Martin Harvey, Alliance House, 12 Caxton Street, London SW1H 0QS (020 7808 1170)

Trustees: Patrick Spellman; Elizabeth Boyd; Peter Stevens; Sue Phipps; Russell Mishcon.

CC Number: 1028027

Eligibility

People who have become HIV positive because of NHS treatment, for example, following transfusions or a needlestick injury. It provides financial support in the form of small regular payments or one-off payments to affected individuals and their dependents.

Types of grants

Financial help is given in three ways: regular monthly payments to contribute to meeting the additional costs of living with HIV, or assist those who have been bereaved; single payments in response to specific requests for help; and winter payments (supplements to regular payments made in recognition of the additional costs of keeping healthy during the winter months).

Annual grant total

In 2010/11 the trust helped 19 individuals. Grants consisted of regular monthly payments to individuals and families, winter payments and single payments amounting to £45,000 overall. Of this total four single grants were made and seven people received regular payments at rates varying from £150 to £800 per month according to circumstances.

Total grantmaking has been down this year due to the establishment of a scheme of non-discretionary payments to beneficiaries from the Department of Health through a company called MFET Ltd. Consequently the beneficiaries' reliance on the trust has decreased substantially.

Applications

Applications for assistance are received in the main via the trust's case worker and from time to time by direct approach.

George House Trust

£30,000 (484 grants)

Correspondent: Ms Rosie Robinson, Chief Executive, 75–77 Ardwick Green North, Manchester M12 6FX (01612 744499; email: ght@ght.org.uk; website: www.ght.org.uk)

Trustees: Steven Ainscow; Paul Fairweather; David Joseph Teasdale; Joseph Phillips; Kotsani Stewart Murau; Damian Kelly; Adrian Walker; Kate Alcock; David Borrow; Gary Quinn; Jim Vann; Gary Bramwell.

CC Number: 1143138

Eligibility

People with HIV who live in the north west of England.

Types of grants

One-off grants ranging from £20 to £150 to help with essential items and household bills. Small emergency grants can be made to help with immediate hardship, for example, food.

Annual grant total

In 2011/12 the trust held assets totalling £1.2 million and had an income of £1.5 million. Welfare grants to 484 individuals totalled £30,000.

Exclusions

No grants are made to people without original proof of HIV diagnosis. Normally no more than one payment per person can be made each year.

Applications

Applications should be made in writing through the trust's website or on a form available from office (those living outside of Manchester can have one sent to their home). Evidence that the individual has been diagnosed HIV positive, such as a letter from the consultant at a HIV testing clinic, should be enclosed with the form. The letter must also include your date of birth. If funding is a matter of emergency (i.e. people with no money for food or gas) then it is worth contacting the trust as it may be able to make a small grant straight away.

The Terrence Higgins Trust Hardship Fund

£140,000

Correspondent: Hardship Fund Administrator, 314–320 Gray's Inn Road, London WC1X 8DP (020 7812 1682; email: hardshipfund@tht.org.uk; website: www.tht.org.uk)

Trustees: Nick Hulme; Mike Marchment; Sam De Silva; Paul Jenkins; Dr Karen Jochelson; Neil Beasley; Dr Evelyn King; Prof. Chris Bones; Revd Paul Flowers; Rt Hon Ben Bradshaw; Dr Helen Walters.

CC Number: 288527

Eligibility

People with HIV in the UK who are in financial need.

Types of grants

Grants are divided into three streams:

▶ Necessity Fund – up to £150 to those needing help with day-to-day essentials
▶ Transition Fund – up to £250 for one-off support drying a major life change

▶ Family Fund – up to £150 to families where a parent and/or child has HIV

Annual grant total

In 2011/12 the fund had incoming resources of £137,000 and a total expenditure of £163,000.

Exclusions

No grants for council tax, rent, holiday expenses, air fares or funeral costs.

Applications

Applications are made via the trust's network of offices and referral agencies, a list of which can be found on the THT website. Application enquiries to the correspondent can also be made by telephone and email.

Other information

The fund now incorporates the Crusaid Fund.

JAT

£5,000

Correspondent: Janine Clements, Fairacres, 164 East End Road, London N2 0RR (020 8952 5253; fax: 020 8952 8893; email: inmycloud@pinkruth.co.uk; website: www.jat-uk.org)

Trustees: Ruth Hilton; Dr Louise Morganstein; Laurence Lewis; David Cline.

CC Number: 327936

Eligibility

Jewish people with HIV/AIDS.

Types of grants

One-off grants of up to £500 a year are available from the trust, which may share the cost of major items with other agencies. Recent grants have been given towards Passover food, travel expenses for respite care, washing machines, cookers, moving costs and so on.

Annual grant total

In 2010/11 the trust had assets of £62,000 and an income of £103,000.

Exclusions

No grants are given towards rent, mortgage arrears, luxury items or repayments of loans, debts or credit cards.

Applications

On a form available from the correspondent. All referrals must be through a professional person such as a social worker, health visitor and so on. A referral must accompany every application and be on headed paper including client's name, date of birth, detailed breakdown of weekly income, details and nature of request, name, position and signature of referrer and details of whom the cheque should be made payable to. First applications

require symptomatic proof of HIV diagnosis from the applicant's doctor.

Other information

The trust was established to educate Jewish people about HIV and also provide support for those affected by it. The trust also carries out research into sex and relationships education in schools and manages sexual health information workshops in Jewish schools, clubs and in Jewish student unions in the UK.

The Macfarlane Trust

£1.7 million

Correspondent: Linda Haigh, Finance Manager, Alliance House, 12 Caxton Street, London SW1H 0QS (020 7233 0057; fax: 020 7808 1169; email: linda@macfarlane.org.uk; website: www.macfarlane.org.uk)

CC Number: 298863

Eligibility

People with haemophilia who as a result of receiving contaminated blood products are living with HIV, and their dependents. No other people are eligible. The trust is in contact with those known to have haemophilia and to be HIV positive through infected blood products and therefore any further eligibility to register with the trust seems unlikely. Assistance is also given to the bereaved spouses or partners of an infected beneficiary.

Types of grants

One-off and recurrent grants are available towards the additional costs associated in living with HIV. Grants can be given towards health-related needs such as convalescence, respite, travel, clothes, medical care, specialised equipment and so on. Grants are also given to ensure that widows and dependents of infected beneficiaries receive a minimum level of household income.

Annual grant total

In 2010/11 the trust had assets of £5.4 million and an income of £2.6 million. Grants totalled £1.7 million and were distributed as follows:

Discretionary payments	378	£846,000
Regular grants		£697,000
One-off grants	377	£197,000

Payments from the trust have fallen due to the Department of Health's decision to make non-discretionary payments to beneficiaries, which this trust had previously administered, through MFET Ltd. The 2010/11 accounts note that: 'This has led the Trustees to focus their discretionary support for infected beneficiaries on providing help for those with lower levels of income, while still

having particular regard to the additional cost of living with haemophilia and HIV.'

Applications

On an application form available from the correspondent, although requests by letter or telephone are also considered. A medical report and supporting letter from a doctor or similar medical professional are required. Applicants must be registered with the trust in order to apply.

Other information

The trust was established in 1988 to manage a £10 million fund given by the government to assist people with haemophilia who had contracted HIV through infected blood products administered by the NHS during their treatment.

The trust also offers benefits advice and organises social events.

Alzheimer's disease

The Margaret and Alick Potter Charitable Trust
See entry on page 214

Arthritis and rheumatism

The Arthritic Association

£11,000

Correspondent: B Hester, Consultant; G Weir, Company Secretary, One Upperton Gardens, Eastbourne, East Sussex BN21 2AA (0800 652 3188; fax: 01323 639793; email: info@arthriticassociation.org.uk; website: www.arthriticassociation.org.uk)

Trustees: D. R. Breakspear; S. J. Standell; Derk Edmund Piers Walter; Kathy Griffiths; Susan Mackenzie; Gillian Horwood; Graham Phillips; Kevin Michael Young; Robin Hendrie Nye.

CC Number: 292569

Eligibility

People who have arthritis or a related condition, and are in financial need. Grants are only available to: members of the Arthritic Association; those who are undertaking a dietary programme with the association; and, towards treatments associated with the programme.

Types of grants

One-off grants in kind for dietary supplements and remedial therapy.

Annual grant total

In 2010/11 the association had assets of £6.5 million and an income of £802,000. Grants totalled £11,000.

Applications

On a form available from the correspondent, for consideration in January, March, July and October. Applications can be submitted by the individual or through a social worker, Citizens Advice or other welfare agency.

Other information

The association works to promote natural dietary treatments for arthritis and grants are also made for research in this area.

Ataxia

Ataxia UK (formerly Friedreich's Ataxia Group)

£9,000 (5 grants)

Correspondent: Ms Susan Millman, Chief Executive, Ground Floor, Lincoln House, 1–3 Brixton Road, London SW9 6DE (020 7582 1444; email: office@ataxia.org.uk; website: www.ataxia.org.uk)

Trustees: Dr E. Harrison; Dr B. Hunt; Mr H. Marshall; Mr C. J. Bunton; Ms A. Gregg; Dr H. Bonney; Mr A. Thomas; Mr D. Winfield-Stanesby; Mr P. Reeves; Mr M. McCrudden; Mr S. Bonney; Mr R. Brown.

CC Number: 1102391

Eligibility

People who are in need and have Cerebellar Ataxia (Freidreich's Ataxia and spinocerebellar). The need for a wheelchair must have been properly assessed by a relevant qualified health professional or recognised agency.

People who are in receipt of welfare benefits or pension credit/working tax credit and are unable to pay for the wheelchair or computer without help from Ataxia UK.

Full eligibility criteria documents are available to download from the trust's helpful website.

Types of grants

One-off grants for things such as respite care, holidays, computers, equipment, aids and adapted furniture. A maximum award of £1,000 is available for wheelchairs. Only five applications will be awarded per year.

Annual grant total

In 2010/11 the charity had assets of £1.1 million and an income of £1.1 million. There were five grants made to individuals totalling £9,000. Funds are likely to be more limited than in previous years, the trust website states: 'this year we have had to reconsider our allocation of funds to welfare grants, in order to allow us to keep up our funding of vital research. We will still however be offering limited funding to help with purchasing wheelchairs and computers.'

Exclusions

People may apply only if they have not received a grant from the charity in the past three years.

Applications

Welfare grants: Applicants must be referred by the charity's advocacy service only after all other possible sources of funding have been exhausted. Applicants should first contact the helpline on 0845 644 0606 or helpline@ataxia.org.uk, who will advise and signpost you to alternative funding sources. If your applications to these other organisations are unsuccessful call the helpline again: they will refer you to the charity's advocacy service which will source other funding avenues and assist with applications if necessary.

Note the advocacy service will need to see the decision letters from other organisations to which you have applied and been unsuccessful.

Once all other sources of funding have been exhausted the advocacy team will apply to the welfare grants committee on your behalf during October and November only, once they have confirmed you meet the eligibility criteria. Decisions will be made 1 December.

Grants for computers are assessed differently. See the trust's website for details of how to apply for these and also for the Jerry Farr Travel Fellowship.

Blindness/ partial sight

Action for Blind People

£6,500 (19 grants)

Correspondent: Anita M South, 14–16 Verney Road, London SE16 3DZ (020 7635 4800; email: central@actionforblindpeople.org.uk; website: www.actionforblindpeople.org.uk)

Trustees: Dr Mike Nussbaum; Khalil Rehman; Lord Colin Low; Michael Dugeon; Rita Mary Kirkwood; Vidar Hjardeng; Alan Suttie; David Hewlett; Toby Davey; Louise Wright; Alistair Fielder; Waqas Hussain Chauhdry; Alan Tinger; Richard John Williams; Carol Hui.

CC Number: 205913

Eligibility

Registered blind or partially sighted people who are in need and live within the boundaries of the charity's action areas. Applicants will need to show that they have exhausted other funding options.

Types of grants

Grant assistance is available for holiday breaks (excluding travel costs) and assistive software technology, e.g. Supernova, Zoomtext, Hal and Jaws.

Annual grant total

In 2010/11 the charity had assets of £19.9 million and a consolidated income of £27 million. Grants were made to 19 individuals totalling £6,500 which was given in grants for assistive technology software. No awards were made for holidays in this period.

Exclusions

If applying for a holiday grant, the applicant must not have had a holiday in the last five years.

Applications

On a form available from the correspondent. Applications for assistance will only be accepted from people living within an action team area, supported by an action coordinator. A list of action areas can be found on the charity's website or by calling the national freephone helpline on 0800 915 4666.

Note: Grants are usually paid directly to the service or product supplier.

Other information

Following a review of its services in 2007, the charity has limited their grants programme to holiday and software grants and is only available to clients who live within the boundaries of the charity's 'action teams', which are all based in England (call 0303 123 9999 to check the boundaries). As a result it now gives far less in direct grants than it has done in previous years. However, the charity does provide help and advice on a wide range of issues including applying for benefits, housing, aids and adaptations, finding a job and accessing local services.

In 2009 the charity finalised an Association Agreement with the Royal National Institute for the Blind (RNIB), making it part of the RNIB Group. (*See the RNIB entry for further information on their activities*).

Gardner's Trust for the Blind

£41,000

Correspondent: Angela Stewart, 117 Charterhouse Street, London EC1M 6AA (020 7253 3757)

Trustees: Viscount Gough; D. R. Beardsley; R. Forster; J. W. Hawkins; S. C. Jones.

CC Number: 207233

Eligibility

Registered blind or partially-sighted people who live in the UK.

Types of grants

One-off grants for domestic household tools and for educational purposes. The trust also gives grants in the form of pensions.

Annual grant total

In 2010/11 the trust had assets of £2.8 million and an income of £87,000. General aid grants totalled £12,000 and pensions totalled £29,000.

Exclusions

No grants for holidays, residential or nursing home fees or for loan repayments.

Applications

In writing to the correspondent. Applications can be submitted either directly by the individual or by a third party, but they must also be supported by a third party who can confirm the disability and that the grant is needed. They are considered in March, June, September and December and should be submitted at least three weeks before the meeting.

Other information

Grants are also given for educational purposes.

National Blind Children Society

£20,000

Correspondent: Hazel Russell, Bradbury House, 33 Market Street, Highbridge, Somerset TA9 3BW (01278 764764; fax: 01278 764790; email: enquiries@nbcs. org.uk; website: www.nbcs.org.uk)

CC Number: 1051607

Eligibility

People aged up to 25 years in full-time education who are (or are eligible to be) registered blind or partially sighted and live in the UK.

Types of grants

One-off grants towards IT equipment or sensory/recreational equipment for use in the home to aid with the individual's learning and development.

Annual grant total

In 2010 the society had assets of £1.3 million and an income of £1.7 million. There were 19 small grants made to individuals totalling £20,000 for computers, sensory equipment, holidays and recreational activities including riding lessons, music lessons and for medical and legal fees.

Applications

On a form available from the correspondent, for consideration at monthly meetings. Applications can be submitted either by the individual with a supporting letter, or via a social worker, welfare agency or qualified teacher of people who are visually impaired. They are considered on a monthly basis.

Other information

Grants are also made to organisations in support of groups of children with visual impairments.

The Royal Blind Society for the UK

£1 million

Correspondent: Grants Co-ordinator, RBS House, 59–61 Sea Lane, Rustington, West Sussex BN16 2RQ (01903 857023; fax: 01903 859685; email: grants@ royalblindsociety.org; website: www. royalblindsociety.org.uk)

Trustees: John Heller; Richard Wood; Michael J. Smith; Eileen Howard; David Baxter; Colin Brown.

CC Number: 1131623

Eligibility

People who are registered blind or partially sighted and on a low income.

Types of grants

One-off grants of up to £200 (one per household) and annual grants of £208 per annum (one per household), running for three year periods. Grants can be made towards: household bills; specialist medical equipment such as thick-lens spectacles; daily living aids such as a washing machine with Braille controls; IT equipment, reading and literacy aids for young visually impaired people; holidays within the UK; and, other emergencies and unforeseen needs.

The society website notes that 'grants are not usually made where the household disposable income exceeds £104 per week for the first person, or £182 per week for the first two persons. For any other person in the household add an additional £47 per week.'

Applications are reviewed quarterly. Requests for one-off grants must include a quotation for the goods/services for which a donation is sought. The society offer informal advice on the application process and applicants should contact Derek Froud on 01903 857023 for assistance.

Annual grant total

In 2010/11 the trust had assets of £964,000 and an income of £1.2 million. Grants to almost 500 beneficiaries totalled £78,000, of which £16,700 was paid in annual grants. The society also provided holidays and breaks for more than 2,500 beneficiaries, with £963,000 spent providing breaks in 2010/11.

Applications

On a form available from the correspondent or to download from the website. Applications must be submitted through a professional welfare worker who knows the applicant well, for example, a social worker or similar welfare advisor. They are considered on a quarterly basis.

Other information

The society also provides holidays and breaks for beneficiaries, with £998,000 spent providing breaks in 2009/10.

The Royal National Institute of Blind People (RNIB)

£70,000

Correspondent: Grants Officer, Information Resource Team, RNIB, 105 Judd Street, London WC1H 9NE (Helpline: 0303 123 9999; email: helpline@rnib.org.uk; website: www.rnib. org.uk)

Trustees: Kevin Carey; Robert Silbermann; Terry Moody; Vidar Hjardeng; Derek Child; Michael Nussbaum; Tony Rucinski; Eleanor Southwood; Margaret Bennett; Richard Moore; Paul Ryb; Heather Giles; Paul Bryce; Lydia Harper; Linda Bancroft; Tanya Lawler; David Quigley; Ken Reid.

CC Number: 226227

Eligibility

Registered blind and partially-sighted people who receive a means-tested benefit (excluding tax credits). Applicants must have been rejected by their local Social Services Department or other statutory funding source (for example the Social Fund) before they approach RNIB.

Types of grants

One-off grants of up to £400, though the trust has strict guidelines on how much it will give for certain items.

  ▷ Essential household items: carpets and furniture; white goods; debts for

essential services (but not recurring debts); and other domestic equipment
▶ Essential adaptations, repairs or redecoration

Grant recipients cannot normally receive another grant for three years. Priority is given to items essential for day-to-day living.

The trustees emphasise that if the total amount applied for exceeds £400 the rest of the funding must be secured before applications are submitted.

Annual grant total
Grants were made totalling £70,000.

Exclusions
Emergency grants are not available. No grants for recreational needs, educational costs, nursing home fees, the costs of medical treatment, telephone installation, employment needs or repeatedly accruing debts.

Applications
Application forms are available from the correspondent or to download from the website. Applications must be supported by a social worker, rehabilitation officer or a voluntary organisation, such as Citizens Advice (applicants should not use a doctor as their support though). They are considered throughout the year.

Other information
The RNIB provides a number of services for blind and partially sighted people. Financial and other assistance is also available from the wide range of local charities for blind people, almost all of which work in close co-operation with the RNIB.

Bowel conditions

Crohn's and Colitis UK

£64,000

Correspondent: Julia Devereux, Personal Grants Fund Secretary, PO Box 334, St Albans, Herts AL1 2WA (01727 759654 or 01727 830038 (main switchboard); fax: 01727 759654; email: julia.devereux@nacc.org.uk; website: www.crohnsandcolitis.org.uk)

Trustees: John Stanley; Denise Cann; John Clarke; Martin Gay; Stuart Berliner; Tim Mutum; Kati Simpson; Michael Hilton; Peter Stewart; Deborah Hodges; Alan Thackrey.

CC Number: 1117148

Eligibility
People in need who have ulcerative colitis, Crohn's Disease or related inflammatory bowel diseases, who have been resident in the UK for at least six months and are on a low income, and their carers.

Types of grants
One-off grants of up to £300 to meet special needs which have arisen as a direct result of illness. For example, funding has been given for washing machines, refrigerators, telephone installation, clothing, beds and bedding and recuperative holidays.

Annual grant total
In 2011 the charity had assets of £2.3 million and an income of £2.8 million. There were five grants for education or training and 237 for welfare, altogether totalling £66,000.

Exclusions
Recurrant grants for needs such as heating and food are not usually made, nor are grants for repayment of debts.

Applications
On a form available from the correspondent or to download from the website, along with guidance notes. The form has two extra sections, one which should be completed by a doctor to confirm the individual's illness and one to be filled in by a social worker (or health visitor, district nurse or CAB advisor).

Other information
The association also operates a Young Persons' Assistance Scheme which helps to meet special vocational and educational needs arising from inflammatory bowel disease (IBD) and grants are also given to institutions for research. However, the association's main role is to provide information and advice to people living with IBD.

Brain tumours

Brain Tumour UK

£107,000 (232 grants)

Correspondent: Support Services, Tower House, Latimer Park, Chesham, Buckinghamshire HP5 1TU (0845 450 0386; email: enquiries@braintumouruk.org.uk; website: www.braintumouruk.org.uk)

Trustees: Angela Deacon; Elizabeth Preston; Jeremy Payne; Maryanne Roach; Richard Eaton; Robert Posner; David Hill; Graham Lindsay; Martina Murphy; Nigel McGinnity; Andy Foote; Tim Burchell.

CC Number: 1117538

Eligibility
Brain tumour patients, their carers, family and friends.

Types of grants
One-off grants of up to £300 to help increase independence and quality of life. Grants have been given for white goods, holidays and trips, clothing, computers, kindles and so on. Applications for wheelchairs and other mobility equipment will only be considered if you can demonstrate that you have exhausted all statutory options.

Annual grant total
In 2011 the fund held assets of £826,000 and had an income of £1.2 million. Denny care and relief grants were made to 232 individuals totalling £107,000.

Exclusions
No retrospective grants or grants for anything for which a Macmillan grant has already been awarded for. Funds will also not be provided for debts, household adaptations or medical treatment. Help with hospital discharge will only be funded in exceptional circumstances.

Applications
On an application form available to download from the website. Part of the form must be completed by a medical professional such as your GP or consultant. Applications are usually processed within 14 days.

Other information
Grants are also made to organisations.

Brittle bones

The Brittle Bone Society

£95,000

Correspondent: Patricia Osborne, Chief Executive, 30 Guthrie Street, Dundee DD1 5BS (01382 204446; email: bbs@brittlebone.org; website: www.brittlebone.org)

Trustees: Elaine Healey; Sheena Moreland; Catherine Potterton; Toni Potterton; Mark Ross; Harry Venet; Yvonne Grant; Simon McKeown; Samantha Renkie; James Sageman; John Phillips; Robert Gordon; Andrew Mills.

CC Number: 272100

Eligibility
Children and others with osteogenesis imperfecta (brittle bones) or similar disorders.

Types of grants
Grants in the range of £200 to £5,000 towards wheelchairs and other specialist

equipment. This could include home alterations, assistance with holiday costs and laptops for children who are unable to attend school for a prolonged period.

The Society note that they often will not be able fund the cost of whole items but will help raise the remaining funds on the applicant's behalf by applying to other trusts and grantmaking bodies.

Annual grant total

In 2010/11 the society had assets of £344,000 and an income of £331,000. Charitable expenditure totalled £95,000 and can be broken down as follows:

Wheelchair purchase and repair	£50,500
Welfare and equipment	£44,000
Holidays	£700

Applications

Contact the society by phone or email to make an initial enquiry and to receive an application via email or post. Health and social care professionals can request an application on a client's behalf. The application form should include formal quotes for cost and a supporting letter from an occupational therapist, social worker or other professional as appropriate. The letter of support should confirm you have osteogenesis imperfecta, and state the need and suitability of the item for which you are requesting financial assistance.

Other information

The society also provides advice and support for people affected by osteogenesis imperfecta.

Cancer and Leukaemia

Brad's Cancer Foundation

£12,000

Correspondent: Susan Bartlett, 14 Crosslands Meadow, Riverview Park, Colwick, Nottingham NG4 2DJ (01159 400313; email: mick@brads.org.uk; website: www.brads.org.uk)

Trustees: John Holecza; Mick Bartlett; Neville Utting; Brenda Cox; Holecza Michelle; Margaret Utting; Sue Bartlett; Tracy Caroline Shaw; Mark Shaw; Paul Utting; Nicola Utting.

CC Number: 1103797

Eligibility

Teenagers who have cancer and related illnesses throughout the East Midlands region.

Types of grants

The provision of financial assistance to teenagers and their families, including grants towards equipment.

Annual grant total

In 2010/11 the foundation had an income of £59,000 and a total expenditure of £62,000, around £12,000 was given in donations to families and children.

Applications

In writing to the correspondent.

Other information

Grants are also made to organisations, in particular, Teenage Cancer Trust.

CLIC Sargent

£818,000

Correspondent: Grants Department, Griffin House, 161 Hammersmith Road, London W6 8SG (020 8752 2800; website: www.clicsargent.org.uk)

Trustees: Daphne Pullen; Rachel Billsberry-Grass; Tim Holley; Meriel Jenney; Henry Kenyon; Jonathan Plumtree; Chris Wathen; Dr Hamish Wallace; Alison Arnfield; Keith Wexford.

CC Number: 1085616

Eligibility

Children and young people under the age of 24 living in the UK who have cancer or have been under treatment in the past six months.

Types of grants

Grants of up to £170 to alleviate crises or help with the quality of life of the child and/or family during treatment. Exceptional grants of up to £400 may be issued where no other support is available. Community Support Grants and Compassionate Grants are also available to some.

Annual grant total

The charity made nearly 5,000 care grants totalling £818,000. Grants are also made for educational purposes.

Applications

On a form, to be completed by the CLIC Sargent Care Professional working with the family.

Other information

The charity also provides respite holidays. Details of grants holidays and other services are available from the CLIC Sargent Care Professional.

The Leukaemia Care Society

£24,000 (106 grants)

Correspondent: Tony Gavin, One Birch Court, Blackpole East, Worcester WR3 8SG (0808 801 0444; email: care@leukaemiacare.org.uk; website: www.leukaemiacare.org.uk)

Trustees: Christopher Matthews-Maxwell; Roland Maturi; Rosalind Ann Ashley; Albert Podesta; Matthew Jackson.

CC Number: 259483

Eligibility

People with leukaemia and allied blood disorders. Financial support is open to all patients and carers who are no more than four years post-diagnosis or, if there has been bereavement, no more than two years after this.

Types of grants

The society gives limited financial assistance in the form one-off grants in kind and gift vouchers. The value of awards is usually in the range of £50 to £250. This can include help towards utility bills, holidays, supermarket vouchers which can be used for food, or petrol for travel to hospital or small necessary household items. Financial assistance is limited to £500 per year.

Annual grant total

In 2010/11 the society had assets of £1.2 million and an income of £683,000. Grants were made to 106 individuals totalling £24,000 towards general living costs. No grants were made during this period for holidays.

Applications

Applicants should first call the CARE Line on 0800 010 444 to discuss their case and request the necessary forms. Applications usually take 14–30 days to complete.

Other information

The society also provides a signposting service in respect of welfare rights and other charities and organisations that may be able to offer additional assistance.

Macmillan Grants

£10,600,000 (31,716 grants)

Correspondent: Grants Department, 89 Albert Embankment, London SE1 7UQ (0808 808 0000; fax: 020 7840 7841; website: www.macmillan.org.uk)

Trustees: Sue Kirk; Julia Palca; Dr Gareth Tuckwell; Simon Prior-Palmer; Tara Donnelly; Dr David Evered; Sir Joseph Pilling; Kenneth Lacey; Simon

Heale; Andrew Duff; Suki Thompson; Clare Hollingsworth; Sir Hugh Taylor; Prof. Timothy Eisen.

CC Number: 261017

Eligibility

People, of any age, who have cancer, or who are still affected by the illness, and are in financial need.

To qualify, applicants must not have capital savings of more than £8,000 per couple, or £6,000 for a single person. Household weekly disposable income (after housing costs) must not exceed: £170 for a single person, £289 for a couple, £85 for each child and £119 for each additional adult (when their income is relevant to the request). Certain benefits such as Disability Living Allowance and Attendance Allowance are not taken into account.

Types of grants

One-off grants of around £250 on average towards costs arising from cancer or its treatment: including travel to hospital, heating, clothing, furnishings, convalescence in the UK and so on.

Annual grant total

In 2011 the charity had assets of £60 million and an income of £145 million. Grants to almost 32,000 individuals totalled £10.6 million.

Exclusions

No grants for daily expenses, private medical care or holidays outside of the UK.

Applications

On a form available from the correspondent. No direct applications can be made; they must be made through a Macmillan or community nurse, health or social worker, hospital social worker or a health professional from another welfare charity and be supported by a short medical report from a second professional such as your doctor, consultant or Macmillan nurse. Welfare workers can receive more information about the scheme by calling Macmillan Support Line on 0808 808 0000. Applications are usually processed on the day they are received and if successful payments are sent out within three working days.

Macmillan advises that the grant request must demonstrate a clear link to the impact of cancer and its treatment. Comprehensive application guidance notes are available on the website.

Other information

Grants to patients are only one feature of the charity's work. Others include funding Macmillan Nurses (who are skilled in providing advice and support on symptom control and pain relief), Macmillan buildings for in-patient and day care, and financing an education programme for professionals in palliative care. The fund also gives grants to three associated charities.

The Ada Oliver Will Trust

£2,000

Correspondent: The Trustees, c/o Marshalls Solicitors, 102 High Street, Godalming, Surrey GU7 1DS (01483 416101)

Trustees: Barry Kilburn; Sara Caroline Coate; Lisa Gabrielle Rabinowitz.

CC Number: 234456

Eligibility

People who have cancer or rheumatism and are in financial need. Preference is given for people living in Surrey.

Types of grants

Monthly and one-off grants of up to £100 are given for a variety of needs. Recent grants have been given for settling rent arrears, nursing home fees and necessities.

Annual grant total

In 2010/11 the trust had an income of £3,600 and a total expenditure of £3,900. Grants are made to individuals and organisations.

Applications

In writing to the correspondent, including details of income and circumstances. Applications can be submitted throughout the year by a social worker, Citizens Advice or other welfare agency on behalf of the individual.

The Shona Smile Foundation

£8,000

Correspondent: Sue Gill, 18 The Combers, Grange Farm, Kesgrave, Ipswich IP5 2EY (email: sue_gill@sky.com)

Trustees: Adam Collacott; Sue Gill; John Murphy; Claire Murphy; Johanna Le Chalmers.

CC Number: 1110177

Eligibility

Children and young people under the age of 18 who have one of the forms of rhabdomyosarcoma.

Types of grants

Cash donations towards, for example, everyday items, something that the child/young person wants or needs, or helping to fulfil a dream of his/her choosing.

Annual grant total

About £8,000.

Applications

In writing to the correspondent.

Cerebral palsy

The Nihal Armstrong Trust

£9,500

Correspondent: Ms Rahil Gupta, 111 Chatsworth Road, London NW2 4BH (020 8459 6527; email: info@nihalarmstrongtrust.org.uk; website: www.nihalarmstrongtrust.org.uk)

Trustees: Anne Emerson; Rahila Gupta; Susan Gretton; Eui Sideri Logothetis; Sarah Ismail; Catherine Ford.

CC Number: 1107567

Eligibility

Children living in the UK, up to and including the age of 18, with cerebral palsy. Applicants must be in receipt of means tested benefits and be able to send evidence.

Types of grants

Grants up to £1,000 towards equipment, communication aids or a particular service that will benefit children with cerebral palsy. Items/services must not be available from the local authority.

Annual grant total

In 2010/11 the trust had an income and expenditure of £10,500.

Applications

Applications can be made via the trust's website and must be supported by a doctor, school, social worker, health visitor, speech, occupational therapist or physiotherapist. Trustees meet four times a year, with application deadlines falling one week before each quarterly meeting. See the trust's website for accurate dates.

The trustees prefer to receive applications via the website where possible. Individuals who are sending literature on equipment/services or suppliers' estimates, can forward any documents to the address provided in the 'contacts' section. A short list of supporting documents needed is given on the trust's website.

Other information

The trust is managed by a small group of trustees who between them, have a wealth of experience in relating to families who care for someone with cerebral palsy. The trust states it "is keen to make life easier for these families" and encourages individuals to apply.

Make A. Child Smile

£7,000 (12 grants)

Correspondent: John Somerset-How, Director, National Appeals Office, 1st Floor, 2 Woodberry Grove, North Finchley, London N12 0DR (020 7060 3003; email: enquiries@makeachildsmile. info; website: www.makeachildsmile. info)

Trustees: Cyn Masefield; Sarah Amanda Crowe; Charles Waters; Jane Waters.

CC Number: 1062275

Eligibility

Children with cerebral palsy.

Types of grants

One-off grants to support children with cerebral palsy through conductive education.

Annual grant total

In 2010/11 the charity had an income of £35,000 and a total expenditure of £22,000. 12 grants were made totalling £7,000.

Applications

On an application form available from the correspondent. Requests for applications should be made online, via email or in writing. Applicants are visited upon submission of the application form.

Other information

The charity is also known as the UK Network for Conductive Education.

Cystic fibrosis

The Cystic Fibrosis Holiday Fund

£124,000

Correspondent: Sue Nyfield, Secretary, 1 Bell Street, London NW1 5BY (020 7616 1300; email: info@cf-holidayfund. org.uk; website: www.cf-holidayfund.org. uk)

Trustees: Jane Jason; Daniel Ellison; James P. Jason; James Hall.

CC Number: 1088630

Eligibility

Children and young people up to the age of 25 who are diagnosed with cystic fibrosis.

Types of grants

Grants to enable children with cystic fibrosis to go on holidays or to go on short trips, this may also include the child's family.

Annual grant total

In 2011 the trust held assets of £74,000 and had an income of £118,000. Expenditure on holiday grants totalled £124,000.

Applications

On a form available to download from the fund's website. The child or young person's medical consultant must complete part of the form. Applications are assessed by the fund's medical advisory panel which meets three times a year (see the website for the date of the next deadline). Applicants should note that the approval procedure can take a few months so applicants should leave enough time before their proposed holiday when applying.

Cystic Fibrosis Trust

£196,000

Correspondent: Welfare Grants Officer, 11 London Road, Bromley, Kent BR1 1BY (0845 859 1020; fax: 020 8313 0472; email: enquiries@cftrust.org.uk; website: www.cftrust.org.uk)

Trustees: Prof. John Price; Ms Jenny Agutter; Sir Peter Creswell; Martyn Rose; Rupert Anthony Pearce Gould; Prof. Stuart Elborn; Brian Henderson; Ed Owen; Peter Sharp; Allan Gormly; Giorgia Arnold; Archie Norman; Katrina Dujardin.

CC Number: 1079049

Eligibility

People in need who have cystic fibrosis.

Types of grants

One-off grants ranging from around £100 to £300 for household items directly beneficial to those with cystic fibrosis, assistance to new homeowners, holidays (mainly for adults with cystic fibrosis∗), costs during hospital admissions, and help to fund a first annual prescription prepayment certificate. Up to £750 is also available towards funeral costs.

∗ The trust tends to refer families who have children with cystic fibrosis to the Cystic Fibrosis Holiday Fund and other charities (contact the welfare officer for more information).

Annual grant total

In 2010/11 the trust had assets of £4.5 million and an income of £8.8 million. Grants were made to individuals totalling £196,000.

Exclusions

Computers, cars, driving lessons, major home improvements, debts or to meet ongoing costs. Holiday grants are only awarded to people who have not had a holiday in the last two years (other than under exceptional circumstances).

Applications

Application forms are available from the correspondent or can be downloaded from the website. Applications must be supported by a social worker or other professional and should state whether the applicant has applied to other charities and the outcome, the general financial circumstances and the reason for the application. The trust strongly advises that individuals or their health professionals contact the welfare grants officer before submitting an application.

The trust has produced an application guideline document which is available on the website.

Other information

The trust also provides confidential advice, support and information on all aspects of cystic fibrosis in the form of factsheets and dedicated helplines for general and welfare benefits advice.

Deafblind

Sense, the National Deaf-Blind and Rubella Association

£30,000

Correspondent: Fiona Markey, Sense, 101 Pentonville Road, London N1 9LG (0845 127 0060, textphone: 0845 127 0062; fax: 0845 127 0061; email: info@ sense.org.uk; website: www.sense.org.uk)

Trustees: John Crabtree; Alan Jones; Richard Monaghan; Liz Booth; Hugh Gareth Jones; Ian Harley; Jim McManus; David Reeves; Dave Pearson; Roy Staines; Duncan Tannahill; Sue Turner; Oliver Walder; Gillian Wood.

CC Number: 289868

Eligibility

People who are deaf-blind or multi-sensory impaired, and their families.

Types of grants

One-off emergency grants only, in exceptional circumstances. Grants are generally £50. Grants have been given towards clothing and travel fares to hospitals.

Annual grant total

In 2010/11 the trust had assets of £35.5 million and an income of

£82 million. Grant totals vary from year to year.

Applications

In writing to the correspondent, to be considered as they arrive.

Other information

Sense provides a complete range of support and services for people with dual sensory impairments, or a sensory impairment and another disability (and their families) including holidays.

Dystonia

The Dystonia Society

£1,000 (6 grants)

Correspondent: Val Wells, Service Development Manager, The Dystonia Society, 1st Floor, 89 Albert Embankment, London SE1 7TP (0845 458 6211; fax: 0845 458 6311; email: info@dystonia.org.uk; website: www.dystonia.org.uk)

Trustees: Alan Tamlyn; Fiona Jean Ross; Michael Paul Newbigin; Roger John Edmonds; Penny Ritchie Calder; Joanna Atkin; Shona Baxandall; Nirmaljit Gill; Joy Bourne.

CC Number: 1068595

Eligibility

People living with Dystonia in the UK.

Types of grants

One-off and recurrent grants according to need.

Annual grant total

In 2010/11 the society had assets of £381,000 and an income of £454,000. During the year six grants were made to individuals totalling £1,000 (£8,000 in 2010).

Exclusions

No grants for medical treatment or other therapies, or for items or services available from the NHS.

Applications

On a form available from the correspondent. Application forms must be endorsed by a health or social care professional who has known the applicant for at least two years.

Grants do not usually exceed £300, except in special circumstances.

Haemato-logical disorders

Roald Dahl's Marvellous Children's Charity

£39,500 (128 grants)

Correspondent: Individual Grants Manager, 81A High Street, Great Missenden, Buckinghamshire HP16 0AL (01494 892170; fax: 01494 890459; email: individualgrants@roalddahlcharity.org; website: www.roalddahlcharity.org)

Trustees: Martin Andrew Forrest Goodwin; Felicity Ann Dahl; Roger Ernest Hills; Georgina Lyndsey Howson; Virginia Louise Fisher.

CC Number: 1137409

Eligibility

Children, and in exceptional circumstances young adults aged 18–25, who have a neurological or haematological condition and are from a low-income family. The only eligible cancer is benign brain tumour.

Families must be in receipt of Income Support, Working Tax Credit and/or Housing Benefit. Families who do not qualify for these benefits, but are on a low-income or whose income has been interrupted by the child's illness may also be considered.

Types of grants

One-off grants of up to £500. Grants can be given towards household appliances; clothing, beds and bedding; utility bills; respite care; medic alert bracelets; travel and subsistence payments whilst children are in hospital; and specialised equipment such as sensory toys, car seats, specialist tricycles, wheelchairs and motability vehicles.

Annual grant total

In 2010/11 the foundation had assets of £1.6 million and an income of £1.9 million. Grants were made to 128 families totalling £39,500.

Exclusions

Debts (except utility bills), funeral expenses (unless the child passes away whilst the application is being processed), computer equipment, educational fees or items that should be provided by statutory sources. Trips outside the UK for medical treatment or holiday are also excluded.

Applications

On a form available from the correspondent or to download from the website. Applications must be completed and submitted by a social worker or healthcare professional who is willing to see the application through to completion, supplying and confirming the information contained. There are no deadlines and applications are considered as and when they arrive.

Assistance may be available to those who do not qualify for state benefits but have an income lower than £22,000. Applicants should provide full details of family income and expenditure for consideration.

Other information

The foundation also makes grants to charities and NHS hospitals working in the fields of neurology and haematology (£135,000 in 2010/11) as well as remaining actively involved in policy and influencing work.

In November 2010 the charity succeeded the Roald Dahl Foundation.

Haemophilia

The Haemophilia Society (The Tanner Fund)

£3,600 (18 grants)

Correspondent: Rachel Goodkin, First Floor, Petersham House, 57A Hatton Garden, London EC1N 8JG (0800 018 6068 (freephone helpline) or 020 7831 1020; fax: 020 7405 4824; email: info@haemophilia.org.uk; website: www.haemophilia.org.uk)

Trustees: Lynne Kelly; Tim Metzgen; Jeremy Young; Bruce Norval; David Fielding; Sue Royal; Bernard Manson; Kate Khair; Matt Gregory; Barbara Scott.

CC Number: 288260

Eligibility

People with haemophilia and related bleeding disorders, and their families.

Types of grants

One-off grants for items relating to applicants' medical problems, such as fridges to store treatment, floor coverings, washing machines and bedding.

Annual grant total

In 2010/11 the society had assets of £402,000 and an income of £646,000. Individual grants made through the Tanner Fund totalled £3,600.

Exclusions

No grants are given for debts, holidays, motor vehicles or ongoing bills such as gas or electricity.

Applications

On a form available from the correspondent. Applications must be completed in conjunction with a health care professional affiliated to their local haemophilia centre. They are considered as received. Note each family may only make one application a year.

Other information

The society has centres across the UK and provides a wide range of support and advice to people affected by bleeding disorders.

Huntington's disease

The Huntington's Disease Association

£12,000

Correspondent: Karen Crowder and Mark Ford, Suite 24, Liverpool Science Park IC1, 131 Mount Pleasant, Liverpool L3 5TF (01513 315444; fax: 01512 989440; email: info@hda.org.uk; website: www.hda.org.uk)

Trustees: Nicholas Heath; Ken Taylor; Mary Howlett; Heather Thomas; Sally Phoenix; Peter Morse; Dr Elizabeth Mary Howard; Sandra Abbott; Matt Ellison.

CC Number: 296453

Eligibility

People with Huntington's disease, their immediate families and those at risk, who live in England or Wales.

Types of grants

One-off grants only, typically of up to £350, although each application is considered on merit. Recent grants have been for clothing, furniture, domestic equipment (e.g. washing machines and cookers) and flooring.

Annual grant total

In 2011/12 grants totalled £12,000. The annual grant budget for future years is expected to be around £20,000.

Exclusions

No grants towards equipment or services that should be provided by statutory services. Support will not be given for the payment of debts, loans, bills, funeral expenses, holidays or travel.

Applications

On a form available from the correspondent. Applications should be submitted through a Regional Care Adviser or other professional. Requests are processed monthly. Full guidance notes are available on request.

Liver

The Ben Hardwick Fund

£15,000

Correspondent: Anne Auber, 12 Nassau Road, Barnes, London SW13 9QE (020 8741 8499)

Trustees: Debra Joy Arnold; Mandy Hawkett; Michael Inkpen.

CC Number: 1062554

Eligibility

Children with primary liver disease, and their families, who are in need.

Types of grants

One-off and recurrent grants, usually ranging between £150 and £500, to help with costs which are the direct result of the child's illness, such as hospital travel costs, in-hospital expenses, telephone bills and childminding for other children left at home.

Annual grant total

In 2011/12 the fund had an income of £2,300 and a total expenditure of £16,500.

Applications

In writing to the correspondent, usually through a hospital social worker or other welfare professional. Applications are considered at any time.

Other information

The fund also makes grants to organisations.

Meningitis

Meningitis Trust

£104,000

Correspondent: Financial Grants Officer, Fern House, Bath Road, Stroud GL5 3TJ (01453 769043; fax: 01453 768001; email: info@meningitis-trust. org; website: www.meningitis-trust.org)

Trustees: Mr A. Irvine; Miss G. Noble; Mr M. Wolfe; Ms B. McGhie; Mr R. Johnson; Mr L. Green; Mr E. Wilson; Mr J. Kilmister; Mr R. Greenhalgh; Mr M. Hall; Mr P. Johnson; Prof. K. Cartwright.

CC Number: 803016

Eligibility

People in need who have meningitis or who are disabled as a result of meningitis.

Types of grants

One-off and recurrent grants towards respite care, sign language lessons, specialist aids and equipment, travel and accommodation costs, therapeutic activities, re-education and special training, and funeral expenses and headstones.

Annual grant total

In 2010/11 the trust had assets totalling £1.6 million and an income of £3.2 million. Grants for educational and welfare purposes were made to 151 families totalling £208,000.

Exclusions

Usually no grants will be given towards domestic bill arrears, clothing, bedding and furniture.

Applications

On a form available from the correspondent or downloaded from the website, where criteria is also posted. An initial telephone call to the grants financial officer on 01453 769043 or the 24-hour helpline on 0800 028 1828 to discuss the application process is welcomed. Applications should be submitted through a third party and are reviewed on a monthly basis.

Other information

The trust runs a 'family day' for children who have meningitis and their families. The day includes arts, crafts and music for children and gives parents an opportunity to meet the trust's staff and other families. The trust also supports a range of professional counselling, home visits, therapy and information services. The trust has an informative website.

Mental illness

The Matthew Trust

£39,000

Correspondent: Annabel Thompson, Director, PO Box 604, London SW6 3AG (020 7736 5976; fax: 020 7731 6961; email: amt@matthewtrust.org; website: www.matthewtrust.org)

Trustees: Patricia Priscilla; Revd Gary Piper; Sue Pierson; Patricia Still; Richard Oliver Wormell; Tania Butler; Priscilla Ladha.

CC Number: 294966

Eligibility

The trust is currently running four projects aimed at supporting:

- Children under 16 with mental health problems
- Providing breaks for child carers
- Young people aged 16–25 with mental health problems
- People over 60 with mental health projects with a view to promoting their inclusion in the wider community

The priorities of the charity may change so applicants are advised to consult the website before applying.

Types of grants

One-off grants of between £50 and £250 towards: counselling or medical bills; equipment and furniture to make a flat liveable; security equipment; clothing; second chance learning and skills training; taking up housing issues with local authorities; travel costs for prison visits; respite breaks; and debt support in special circumstances.

Annual grant total

In 2010/11 the trust had assets of £319,000 and an income of £81,000. Grants were made totalling £39,000.

Applications

In writing to the correspondent through a professional agency such as a social worker, probation officer, community care worker or GP. The professional representative should also include their name and contct details on the application. Applications should include the name, address, age and gender of the applicant; the health and age of other close family members; a summary of the mental health problem; the type of support required, including costs where applicable; if the applicant has received support from the trust previously; and details of any other organisations which have been approached for support. Applications may be posted or emailed.

Note: The Matthew Trust is a 'last-stop' agency and will only consider applications when all other avenues of statutory and voluntary funding have been exhausted and then only where a care programme has been established. The trust aims to provide a response within 14 days.

Motor neurone

The Motor Neurone Disease Association

£1.3 million

Correspondent: David Phillips, PO Box 246, Northampton NN1 2PR (01604 250505; fax: 01604 624726; email: enquiries@mndassociation.org; website: www.mndassociation.org)

Trustees: Dr Juliet Draper; Dr Jean Waters; Cynthia Hopkins; Dr Christina Lloyd; Prof. Victor Patterson; Dr Hilary Walklett; Prof. Brian Wilson; Barbara Howe; Alun Owen; Mark Todd; John Peter Bickley; Anne Christine Bulford; Richard John Coleman; Sandra Helen Smith.

CC Number: 294354

Eligibility

People with motor neurone disease, living in England, Wales and Northern Ireland.

Types of grants

i) Top-up of respite care (normally £500–£2,000).

ii) Equipment rental.

iii) Building adaptations.

Annual grant total

In 2010/11 the trust held assets of £7.2 million and had an income of £13 million. Grants to individuals totalled £1.3 million.

Of this grant total £923,000 was paid to 1,615 people to fund specialist equipment and respite care. The association also provided individuals with specialist equipment directly.

Applications

On a form available from the correspondent or a local regional care adviser. Applications must be submitted through a health or social care professional. In addition to stating what is requested, applications should include details of why the need is not met by statutory sources and where any payments should be made.

Other information

The trust has a network of association branches which can offer information about the grants available. Further information is available on the trust's website.

Multiple sclerosis

Multiple Sclerosis Society

£1.5 million

Correspondent: The Grants Team, MS National Centre, 372 Edgware Road, Cricklewood, London NW2 6ND (020 8438 0700; fax: 020 8438 0701; email: grants@mssociety.org.uk; website: www.mssociety.org.uk)

Trustees: Ian Douglas; Dave Denholm; Stuart Nixon; Clare Ball; Siobhan Gilmour; John Miller; Carolyn Heaney; Paul Pavia; John Litchfield; Dr Peter Mallaburn; Marsali Craig; Gideon Schulman; Martin Stevens.

CC Number: 1139257

Eligibility

People with multiple sclerosis and their families and carers, living in the UK. People living in Scotland or Northern Ireland may be subject to other conditions, contact MS Society Scotland (01313 354050) or MS Society Northern Ireland (02890 802803) for full details.

Types of grants

One-off grants towards: home adaptations or remedial work needed following adaptations; wheelchairs; mobility scooters; double profiling beds; riser-recliner chairs; car adaptations such as hoists or hand controls; motability advance payments (in certain circumstances); driving lessons; respite care; clinical and communication aids; bankruptcy and debt relief order fees; removal costs; and furnishings, flooring and domestic appliances. Other needs may also be considered.

The society now runs a new short breaks and respite care grant programme, with over 800 people benefitting from a break in 2011. Grants are considered for:

- Respite care, in the home or at a care centre or similar
- An activity, short break or holiday for someone with MS and/or their carer/ family
- Salary costs for a professional carer needed to help someone with MS, or their carer, have a break in the home or elsewhere
- Associated costs such as travel, accommodation and disability equipment hire
- Some alternative or complementary therapies

The society in England, Wales and Northern Ireland also has two specific funds for carers:

▶ Young Carers Fund – Grants of up to £300 are available for people aged 17 and under who help care for a parent or guardian with MS

▶ Carers Opportunities Fund – Grants of up to £400 for carers aged over 18 and those whose caring role has recently ended to develop an interest or undertake a course to get back into education or employment

In Scotland, carers can apply to the MS Society Scotland grants fund.

Annual grant total

In 2011 the society held assets totalling £20 million and had an income of £29 million. Grants to individuals totalled £1.5 million.

Exclusions

Applicants with more than £16,000 in savings are not eligible for regular grants and those with more than £8,000 in savings are expected to contribute towards the cost of the item. For a short break or activity grant you are not eligible if you have more than £23,000 in savings.

Grants cannot be made for purchases already made; long-term financial commitments (such as living costs and bills); loans, debt assistance or legal fees; or paying for treatments.

Applications

On a form available from the correspondent or a local MS Society branch. Application forms for the carers grant programmes may be downloaded from the website. Applications should include two quotes for the expenditure and a letter of support from a social worker, health professional or occupational therapist. Application forms for carers are available separately on the website.

Applicants in England, Wales or Northern Ireland should submit their form and supporting information to a local branch where the request will be considered confidentially by trained volunteers. If the branch is unable to award a grant for the full cost of the item, the form will be forwarded to the MS National Centre. Applicants in Scotland should submit their form to the Grants coordinator at the MS Society Scotland office.

Other information

The Society has a freephone helpline (0808 800 8000), free information booklets on all aspects of living with MS for people with, and affected by, MS and a network of branches, manned by volunteers, across the UK offering local support to people with MS.

Muscular dystrophy

The Joseph Patrick Trust

£52,000 (155 grants)

Correspondent: Mr D Jackson, Chair, c/o Muscular Dystrophy Group, 61 Southwark Street, London SE1 0HL (020 7803 4811; fax: 020 7401 3495; email: jptgrants@muscular-dystrophy. org; website: www.muscular-dystrophy. org/how_we_help_you)

Trustee: Muscular Dystrophy Group of Great Britain and Northern Ireland.

CC Number: 294475

Eligibility

People with muscular dystrophy or an allied neuromuscular condition.

Types of grants

On average about 200 one-off grants of between £200 and £1,250 are made each year to partially fund the purchase of wheelchairs (powered and manual), scooters, electric beds, trikes, computers, vehicle adaptations, riser chairs, mobile arm supports, portable aids, therapy equipment and so on. Discretionary payments can be made for funeral expenses and other emergencies.

Annual grant total

In 2010/11 the trust made grants totalling £52,000 to 155 individuals.

Exclusions

Grants are not given for: holidays, household adaptations, building works or domestic appliances; equipment which has already been bought; recurring costs (e.g. wheelchair repairs); the purchase or lease of vehicles, vehicle deposits, maintenance or repair of vehicles. No grants outside of the UK.

Applications

On a form available from the correspondent or to download from the website. Applciations can also be completed online but remember to send supporting documentation on by post-as well.

Completed forms can be submitted directly by the individual or via a third party and should be supported by an assessment and quotation for the equipment requested, confirming the need and suitability of the equipment. The assessment must be carried out by an approrpriately qualified professional, such as a physiotherapist, occupational therapist, social worker, etc. The assessment must be on headed paper.

For guidance on what to include in the assessment check the trust website. Applications are considered six times a year. Grants are only be made payable to the supplier.

Neurological disorders

Cerebra for Brain Injured Children and Young People

£509,000

Correspondent: Debbie Godsave, Grants Co-ordinator, Second Floor Offices, The Lyric Building, King Street, Carmarthen SA31 1BD (0800 328 1159; email: grants@cerebra.org.uk; website: www. cerebra.org.uk)

Trustees: Michael Imperato; Susan Hobbs; Dr Lillemor Jernqvist; Elizabeth Fleming; Prof. David Rose; Richard Peter Lumley; David John Beattie.

CC Number: 1089812

Eligibility

Children and young people aged 16 or under who have disabilities because of a brain related condition or injury. The condition may be of a physical nature, a learning disability or both.

Types of grants

One-off grants of up to a maximum of 80% of the cost or £400, whichever is the lowest amount, of equipment or resources that would improve quality of life and which are not available from statutory agencies like social services or the NHS. Examples of grants made include those towards touch screen computers, specialist car seats, power wheelchairs, therapies, trampolines, sensory toys, and tricycles and quadricycles.

For anything where there is a medical need the trust asks that potential applicants check with the trust as it may be able to help.

Annual grant total

In 2011 the charity had an income of £4.2 million and a total expenditure of £4.3 million. Grants totalled £509,000.

Exclusions

Grants are not given for: driving lessons; motorised vehicles such as quad bikes and motorbikes; anything that could be considered a home improvement e.g. paint for decorating, conservatories, carpet or other flooring; garden landscaping; household items e.g. vacuum cleaners, washing machines, wardrobes, standard beds (special beds may be considered); vehicle purchase or maintenance; assessments; general clothing; treatment centres outside of the UK; lycra suits; holidays; and educational items such as home tutors, standard teaching materials or the son-rise programme.

Applications

Application forms and guidance notes can be downloaded from the Cerebra website. Grants are all paid directly to the assistance provider. All applications must be accompanied by financial statements and two references: one from a medical professional and the other from someone who knows your child professionally, for example a teacher or social worker. Further guidelines on references are contained within the application form.

Other information

The trust also provides other support services such as telephone counselling and a wills and trust voucher scheme.

Parkinson's disease

Parkinson's UK

£95,000

Correspondent: Steve Ford, Chief Executive, 215 Vauxhall Bridge Road, London SW1V 1EJ (0808 800 0303; email: hello@parkinsons.org.uk; website: www.parkinsons.org.uk)

Trustees: Nadra Ahmed; Ralph Tingle; Melinda Letts; Elizabeth Ann Wolstenholme; Colin Cheesman; Paul Lister Boothman; Alun Morgan; Terence Kavanagh; Mark Goodridge; Dr Doug MacMahon; Teresa Watson.

CC Number: 258197

Eligibility

People with Parkinson's disease, with under £10,000 in individual savings or under £15,000 in joint savings.

Types of grants

One-off grants from the Mali Jenkins Fund of up to £1,500 for equipment or home adaptations, up to £1,000 for respite breaks for people with Parkinson's disease and their carer, and up to £500 for other items such as domestic appliances or household goods.

Annual grant total

Grants to individuals usually total around £95,000 per year.

Exclusions

No support for ongoing costs such as utility bills or care home fees; debt relief; legal costs, holidays, business costs,

funeral costs or for items which have already been paid for. No grants can be made for items for which statutory funding is available or for items which are the responsibility of the applicant's nursing home or care home.

Applications

Application forms and guidance notes can be obtained on the website or by calling the helpline. Applications should be accompanied by a supporting letter from an appropriate professional. If the application is for equipment or a home adaptation the letter must be from an occupational therapist, physiotherapist or speech and language therapist, as appropriate. Two price quotes should also be supplied. Forthcoming application deadlines will be advertised online.

Polio

The British Polio Fellowship

£60,000

Correspondent: Support Services Team, Unit A, Eagle Office Centre, The Runway, South Ruislip, Middlesex HA4 6SE (0800 018 0586; fax: 020 8842 0555; email: info@britishpolio.org.uk; website: www.britishpolio.org.uk)

Trustees: Robert Ernest Stephens; Aidan Thomas Linton-Smith; Michael Howard Egan; Pamela Susan Jones; Dorothy Crook; Archie Leyden; Bridget Flint; Linda Evers; Robert Howell.

CC Number: 1108335

Eligibility

People in need who have been disabled through poliomyelitis (polio) and live in the UK.

Types of grants

Welfare grants of up to £500 are given for scooters, electric or manual wheelchairs, riser/recliner chairs, specialist beds and mattresses; household aids and equipment to enable independence; and, home and car adaptations. Support may occasionally be given for essential home improvement and crisis prevention.

Grants of up to £100 are awarded each autumn to help with heating costs for those who are not eligible for state assistance.

The average holiday grant is £300, though it may not exceed £500. Call or email holidays@britishpolio.org.uk for more information and to request an application form.

Annual grant total

In 2010 the fellowship had assets of £3.5 million and an income of £975,000. Charitable activities totalled £838,000, of which £60,000 was given in grants to individuals.

Exclusions

No grants are given for hospital expenses, household bills or home carers. Statutory sources e.g. Social Services, Social Fund must be approached before approaching the fellowship.

Applications

Welfare and heating grant forms are available from the correspondent or a local branch welfare officer. Applications should be submitted by the individual or by an appropriate third party on their behalf and include a medical certificate or doctors note stating polio-disability. Welfare applications are considered throughout the year. Heating grants are awarded once a year in the autumn.

Holiday grant forms are available from the correspondent or by emailing holidays@britishpolio.org.uk. They are assessed every other month.

Other information

The fellowship has over 50 local branches and provides support and advice on a wide range of issues affecting people disabled through polio.

Renal

The British Kidney Patient Association

£321,000

Correspondent: Susan Lee, 3 The Windmills, St Mary's Close, Turk Street, Alton GU34 1EF (01420 541424; fax: 01420 89438; email: info@britishkidney-pa.co.uk; website: www.britishkidney-pa.co.uk)

Trustees: David Oliveira; Chris Rudge; Sally Taber; Robin Eady; Richard Chapman Jones; Marcelle De Sousa; Margaret Mitchell; Kathleen Shipton; David Sawyer; Lesley Rees; Sandra Verkuyten.

CC Number: 270288

Eligibility

Kidney patients and their families on low incomes, patients about to start dialysis, or within six months of having had a transplant and other patients whose renal condition is having a serious impact on their health and quality of life.

Types of grants

One-off grants can be given for all kinds of need caused by the condition, including clothing costs, gas/electric/ water bills, telephone installation, TV licences, and domestic goods such as washing machines and carpets. Grants can also be made to cover the costs of hospital visits, such as travel expenses, car tax and insurance. The charity may fund holidays, or part of the costs of a holiday including children's holiday organised by renal units.

Help may also be offered towards holidays at specialist centres equipped with dialysis treatment facilities. Applicants interested in such grants should refer to the BKPA website for more information.

Annual grant total

In 2011 the trust had an income of £2.6 million and an expenditure of £3.8 million, including £642,000 in patient grants for both welfare and educational purposes.

Exclusions

Grants are not made for: telephone bills; court fines; improvements to a patient's home e.g. showers, stair lifts, central heating; credit card and loan repayments; medical equipment such as wheel chairs; council tax payments; and reimbursement for loss of items due to theft.

Applications

Via a kidney unit social worker or a member of the kidney care team on a form available from the correspondent, or to download from the BKPA website. Applications are considered on an ongoing basis.

Other information

The trust also makes grants to hospitals and supports the Ronald McDonald Houses at the Alder Hey Children's Hospital, Liverpool, Bristol Royal Hospital for Children, Evelina Children's Hospital, London and the Royal Hospital for Sick Children, Yorkhill which provide support for the families of young renal patients attending the units at these hospitals.

They also fund non-laboratory research and provide support services, information and advice to kidney patients, amongst other projects.

Spinal muscular

The Jennifer Trust for Spinal Muscular Atrophy

£11,000

Correspondent: Heather Brown, General Manager, 40 Cygnet Court, Timothy's Bridge Road, Stratford Enterprise Park, Stratford upon Avon CV37 9NW (01789 267520; fax: 01789 268371; email: office@jtsma.org.uk; website: www.jtsma. org.uk)

Trustees: Steven Cocker; Maria Magdalena Sereda; Hilary Rattue; David Mateer; Jonathon Griffith; Richard Waltier; Neil Ashby.

CC Number: 1106815

Eligibility

People diagnosed as having the genetic condition spinal muscular atrophy. Note that the trust cannot give grants to people with any other condition.

Types of grants

One-off grants of up to around £300 for emergency items for babies and young children.

Annual grant total

In 2011/12 the trust had assets of £278,000 and an income of £636,000. Fast response grants totalled £11,000.

Exclusions

No grants towards vehicles or their adaptations.

Applications

Enquiries should be made with the trust's outreach workers.

Other information

Individual financial grants are only one way in which the trust provides support. For more information, contact the trust and request an information pack or visit the website.

Scoliosis

Strongbones Children's Charitable Trust

£86,000

Correspondent: April Fitzmaurice, Grants Officer, Unit B9 Seedbed Centre, Davidson Way, Romford RM7 0AZ (01708 750599; email: grantsofficer@ strongbones.org.uk; website: www. strongbones.org.uk)

Trustees: Hugh McDowell; Norman McNamara; Roger Stott.

CC Number: 1086173

Eligibility

Children under 21 with scoliosis, brittle bone disease, rheumatoid arthritis, bone cancer or any other condition of the bone.

Types of grants

One-off grants of around of £250 – £1,000 for medical equipment, mobility aids, sensory equipment, specially adapted wheelchairs and trikes, furniture, computers/software, clothes, social activities, hospital travel and toys. The trust also provides holiday homes for children and their families with each family receiving financial support along with any respite break.

Annual grant total

In 2011/12 the trust had assets of £52,000 and an income of £386,000. Grants to individuals totalled £86,000.

Exclusions

Holidays abroad, driving lessons, equipment where there has not been an assessment by an NHS physiotherapist, household appliances (excluding washing machines/dryers for incontinence).

Applications

Applicants may apply using the trust's online application form. Applications should include details of the child's condition and why a grant is needed. The trust also requires that forms are accompanied by a cover letter from the child's NHS consultant, physiotherapist, GP, school nurse or social worker. Grants of over £1,000 should be accompanied by a quote. Decisions can take up to three months. Families can only receive one grant in any 12 month period.

Sports injuries

RFU Injured Players Foundation

£376,000 (138 grants)

Correspondent: Tim Bonnett, Client Support Executive, Rugby House, Twickenham Stadium, 200 Whitton Road, Middlesex TW2 7BA (0800 783 1518; email: timbonnett@rfu.com; website: www.rfuipf.org.uk)

Trustees: Tony Nutt; Nigel Henderson; Peter Baines; Nigel Tarrant; Paul Murphy; Bob Udwin; Paul Smith; Dr Fred Middleton; Stephen Brown; John Owen.

CC Number: 1122139

Eligibility

People who are seriously injured playing sport under the auspices of the Rugby Football Union.

Types of grants

Small grants of up to £2,000 per year and large grants of up to £20,000 (or higher in exceptional circumstances) for a variety of needs.

Grants are commonly given for home improvements to provide disability access; medical equipment and mobility aids; exercise and therapy equipment; communication aids; respite care; and travel expenses.

Annual grant total

In 2010/11 the foundation had assets of £1.3 million and an income of £1.7 million. A total of £242,000 was given in large grants to 41 individuals and a further £134,000 was given in 97 small grants.

The largest single grant to an individual totalled £30,000 whereas small grants were all for £2,000 or less.

Exclusions

No grants for general household expenses such as food, clothing, utility bills or vehicle fuel costs.

Applications

Application forms for both small and large grants may be downloaded from the website although large grant applicants are advised to contact Tim Bonnett first. Applicants are advised to attach an estimate or invoice proving costs. Application forms may be returned by post-or email to the correspondent.

All applications will be acknowledged within five working days. Decisions on small grants are made within 14 working days. Decisions for large grants can take up to three months to process, although they tend to be quicker for amounts of less than £20,000.

Contact by applicants to discuss any aspect of the application process is welcomed by the foundation.

Other information

The foundation is usually notified of players who receive injuries through the RFU's Injury Reporting process. When someone is catastrophically injured, the RFU Injured Player Welfare Officer will contact the family of the person involved and offer initial help with travel and other expenses to visit the player in hospital and support them through their recovery and rehabilitation.

The Rosslyn Park Injury Trust Fund

£5,000

Correspondent: Brian Carr, Trustee, 8 Burbage Road, London SE24 9HJ (020 7733 9055; email: brian.carr@onetel.net)

Trustees: Peter James Thorley; Brian Carr; Dr John Gavin Bourdas Thurston; John Adair.

CC Number: 284089

Eligibility

Young people who have a disability or are in poor health as a result of an injury suffered while playing sports (amateur sports). Help may also be available to their dependents.

Types of grants

One-off grants for computers, special care, medical equipment, computers and disability aids.

Annual grant total

On average, about £4,000 is available each year to distribute in grants.

Applications

In writing to the correspondent. Applications can be submitted by either the individual or through social services and are considered as they are received.

Stroke

Stroke Association

£150,000

Correspondent: The Welfare Secretary, Stroke House, 240 City Road, London EC1V 2PR (020 7566 0300; fax: 020 7490 2686; email: grants@stroke.org.uk; website: www.stroke.org.uk)

Trustees: Sue Nyfield; Damian Jenkinson; Eric Frank Tracey; Dr John Bamford; Vivien Gould; Prof. Tony Rudd; Andrew Daws; Dr Anne Freeman; Jacqueline Fowler; Prof. Keith Muir; Prof. Sir Charles George; Peter Rawlinson; Michael Watts; Prof. Robert Stout; Prof. Marion Fraser Walker; Dr Michael Alan Cornbleet; Ian Black; Prof. Philippa Jane Tyrrell; Susan Mary Alison Duncan; Stuart Barron Fletcher; Rober James Empson; Sir David Robert Varney.

CC Number: 211015

Eligibility

People who have had a stroke and are in need. Applicants must have less than £1,000 in savings.

Types of grants

One-off grants of up to £400 to help improve the individual's quality of life. Recent grants have been given for hospital travel costs, extra heating, holidays, household items, clothing, phone installation, house adaptations, energy bills and so on.

Annual grant total

In 2011/12 the trust had assets of £13 million and an income of £31 million. Welfare grants were made totalling £150,000.

Exclusions

Private medical treatment; labour costs, including item removal and structural alterations; nursing home fees other than for respite care; computers and televisions; debt and rent arrears.

Applications

On a form available from the correspondent to be completed by a social worker, health professional or Stroke Association staff member on the individual's behalf. Applicants should ask their health or social care professional to contact the association by email using their professional email account to receive an application form. Awards are means-tested, taking into account the total household income.

Tuberous sclerosis

Tuberous Sclerosis Association Benevolent Funds

£11,000

Correspondent: Chris Johnson, Membership and Events Coordinator, PO Box 8001, Derby DE1 0YA (01214 456970; email: development-support@ tuberous-sclerosis.org; website: www. tuberous-sclerosis.org)

Trustees: Marie James; Christine Ann Naylor; Philip Goldenberg; Andra Campbell; Angela Huber; Dr Chris Kingswood; Perry James; Tom Carter; Janet Bower; Martin James Philip Balfour-Allen; Nicholas Peter Dale; Revd Martin Peter Short; David Robin Vaughan.

CC Number: 1039549

Eligibility

People in need who have tuberous sclerosis complex and their carers. The membership fee may be waived for non-members in cases of financial difficulty, send a membership form with the application form.

Types of grants

Grants can be made from one of three funds administered by the TSA:

- Support fund – grants of up to £200 to support people with TSC who need financial help
- Travel Bursaries – towards the costs of attending TSA events such as the AGM or regional gatherings
- Janet Medcalf Memorial Fund – three annual awards of £300 for anything you feel would make a difference to you as a carer or person living with TSC

Annual grant total

In 2011/12 the fund had assets of £3.2 million and an income of £408,000. Grants were made totalling £11,000, of which £6,800 was given in family days and weekends and £3,800 in benevolent grants.

Exclusions

There are no grants available for things which are the responsibility of a statutory service. No more than £800 can be given to one person in any five year period and only one application is allowed each year. No grants for car repairs or purchase or accommodation costs.

Applications

On a form available from the correspondent or to download from the website. Applications can be submitted either directly by the individual or through a parent or carer. For requests of more than £100 from the support fund a professional such as a social worker, therapist, doctor or teacher should fill in a professional reference form supporting the request.

Other information

The fund's main priority is to fund research into the causes and management of tuberous sclerosis. It also provides education and information about the condition.

Occupational charities

This section contains the following parts.

- An index of particular trades or professions. The categories of trades/professions are listed alphabetically.

- After the index, the charities themselves are arranged alphabetically within each trade/profession. Charities include both independent charities and benevolent funds associated with trade unions or professional bodies.

Trusts included are those that support both members of the occupation listed and their dependents. Individuals should also check for any trade unions listed that cover their area of work as unions will sometimes have resources available for workers in their sector who are not members. When a possible occupation has been identified, go to the relevant page and read the entries carefully. Being a member of a profession is not necessarily enough, there may well be other criteria that make individuals ineligible.

We have grouped together certain occupations to make relevant trusts easier to identify. For instance, dance, magic, music, painting, theatre and writing have all been placed under Arts, as there are some trusts that support arts generally (which would give to a number of these categories) and some that will give only to one specific branch. Paid work is not essential for all trusts: for instance, there are trusts for certain amateur sportspeople.

We have placed all medical and health workers in the same category, as again there are trusts that support these workers generally and some that will only support certain areas. The exceptions to this are the trusts that support carers, which have been included in the general section under the *Carers and volunteers* category (see page 14). The category *Food, drink and provision trade* (see page 89) contains many different individual roles within the industry. In this edition, trusts concerning clergy and missionaries have been listed in the *Religious charities* chapter (see page 157). Please also note that trusts such as the Hull Fishermen's Trust Fund, which support a particular occupation but only give in a particular locality, are included in the relevant local section of this guide.

Index of occupational charity funds

Accountancy

The AIA Educational and Benevolent Trust

£7,000

Correspondent: Mr T Pinkney, Staithes 3, The Watermark, Metro Riverside, Tyne And Wear NE11 9SN (01914 930277; fax: 01914 930278; email: trust.fund@aiaworldwide.com; website: www.aiaworldwide.com)

CC Number: 1118333

Eligibility

Fellows and associates of the institute, and their close dependents, who are in need.

Types of grants

One-off grants according to need.

Annual grant total

About £7,000.

Applications

On a form available from the trust's website which should be printed and posted to the correspondent.

Applications are considered on an ongoing basis.

Other information

Grants are also given to those wishing to undergo education and training in accountancy.

The Chartered Accountants' Benevolent Association

£800,000 (305 grants)

Correspondent: Donna Cooper, Grants Coordinator, 8 Mitchell Court, Castle Mound Way, Rugby CV23 0UY (0800 107 6163(24hr helpline); email: enquiries@caba.org.uk; website: www.caba.org.uk)

Trustees: Derek Hall; Nicholas Brooks; Tom Hughes-Parry; Revd Richard Wyber; Richard Wade; Hilary Lindsay; David Adams; John Heskett; Robin Fieth.

CC Number: 1116973

Eligibility

Members, former members and employees of the Institute of Chartered Accountants in England and Wales and the Society of Incorporated Accountants, and their dependents. Also those without full membership, who are registered as studying for examinations, with the expectation of becoming a full member. People who have been employed by the

Institute of Chartered Acoountants in England and Wales for five years.

Types of grants

One-off and recurrent grants towards daily living costs, respite care, household essentials and so on. The association also provides interest-free loans.

Annual grant total

In 2011 the association held assets of £80 million and had an income of £3 million. Financial assistance to 305 individuals totalled £800,000.

Applications

Initial contact can be made by calling the 24 hour helpline or by using the live chat feature on the association's website.

Other information

The association offers a wide range of support and advice on issues such as accessing state benefits, debt and financial problems and stress management.

The Chartered Certified Accountants' Benevolent Fund

£43,000 (20 grants)

Correspondent: Hugh McCash, Honorary Secretary, 2 Central Quay, 89 Hydepark Street, Glasgow G3 8BW (01415 344045; fax: 01415 344151; email: hugh.mccash@accaglobal.com; website: www.accaglobal.com)

Trustees: Alec Sandison; D. J. Argent; J. Beckerlegge; J. D. Moore; Dr M. J. M. Kedslie; J. Cole; Anthony Gordon Thorne; David Finch.

CC Number: 222595

Eligibility

Members, and former members, of the ACCA, and their dependents.

Types of grants

Grants range from £40 to £11,000. Recurrent grants are available to help with stairlifts, telephone bills, holidays, TV rental and so on; one-off grants in tragic circumstances to help beneficiaries get back on their feet; and low-interest or interest-free loans on property.

Annual grant total

In 2010/11 the association had assets of £2.6 million and an income of £152,000. Grants were made to 20 individuals totalling £43,000.

Exclusions

Grants are not available for the education of children.

Applications

On a form available from the correspondent or downloadable from the website (www.accaglobal.com/members/fund/apply). Applications can be submitted directly by the individual or through a social worker, Citizens Advice, welfare agency or other third party. They are considered at meetings held every two or three months.

The Chartered Institute of Management Accountants Benevolent Fund

£75,000

Correspondent: Caroline Aldred, Secretary, CIMA, 26 Chapter Street, London SW1P 4NP (020 8849 2221; email: benevolent.fund@cimaglobal.com; website: www.cimaglobal.com)

Trustee: The Chartered Institute of Management Accountants.

CC Number: 261114

Eligibility

Past and present CIMA members and their dependents anywhere in the world.

Types of grants

One-off grants for specific needs such as television licence/rental, telephone rental, motor insurance/tax, disability aids, some repairs and necessary household items such as fridges, cookers and so on. Grants are also made for medical bills for members outside the UK. Regular grants are also made to help meet basic living costs. Interest free loans may be provided in exceptional circumstances.

Annual grant total

In 2011 the fund had assets of £1.8 million and an income of £92,000. Grants to 53 individuals totalled £97,000, mostly for welfare purposes.

Exclusions

No grants to enhance property, for investment in business ventures, or for private medical care. Though, assistance may be given to members living outside the UK who do not have access to state-funded medical treatment or medical insurance and have large medical bills.

Applications

On a form available from the correspondent or to download from the website. Applications can be submitted directly by the individual or through a recognised referral agency (Citizens Advice, doctor, social worker and so on), or through a third party. They are considered monthly/as necessary.

Other information

Educational grants are also made for dependent children.

The charity can also signpost-people to relevant services and provide support from a welfare officer.

The Institute of Financial Accountants' and International Association of Book-Keepers' Benevolent Fund

£11,000

Correspondent: Christopher Brown, Burford House, 44 London Road, Sevenoaks, Kent TN13 1AS (01732 458080; email: mail@ifa.org.uk; website: www.ifa.org.uk)

Trustees: John Chapman; Christopher Morris; Christopher Brown; Beryl Shepherd.

CC Number: 234082

Eligibility

Past and present members of the institute or the association, and their dependents.

Types of grants

One-off grants according to need. Grants are normally only given in real cases of financial need, and usually range between £100 and £2,000.

Annual grant total

In 2010/11 grants were made totalling around £11,000.

Applications

On a form available from the correspondent. Applications can be submitted directly by the individual or on their behalf by a family member. Details of income and expenditure should also be included. Every application is considered on its merits.

Advertising and marketing

NABS

£369,000

Correspondent: Support Team, 47–50 Margaret Street, London W1W 8SB (0845 602 4497; email: support@nabs.org.uk; website: www.nabs.org.uk)

Trustees: Judith Salinson; Keith Fowler; James Murphy; Graham Duff; Marc Sydney Benjamin Mendoza; Tess Alps; Nick Bampton; Robin Mark Dodgson

Price; Pippa Glucklick Hughes; Ian Pearman; Mark Howe.

CC Number: 1070556

Eligibility

People who work or have worked in advertising, marketing, marketing services and related industries, and their dependents.

Types of grants

One-off and recurrent grants according to need. For one-off support the trust's 2010 accounts note that their aim is: 'to provide fast, critical, short-term financial support combined with practical help, e.g. debt advice, support from our careers department, access to other charities, etc, with the aim of getting people back on their feet and able to support themselves as quickly as possible.'

Annual grant total

In 2010 the trust had assets of £3.1 million and an income of £3.6 million. Grants were made to over 300 individuals totalling £369,000.

Applications

On a form available by calling the helpline or by emailing the correspondent. Completed forms, which should include a career history, financial information and references, are considered monthly.

Other information

The society also provides a wide range of services for members of the industry, including a telephone helpline, sheltered housing, residential care and nursing accommodation for older people, a flatshare scheme and a lonely-hearts service.

Agriculture and related rural issues

Forest Industries Education and Provident Fund

£400

Correspondent: Jane Karthaus, Woodland Place, Belford, Northumberland NE70 7QA (01668 213937; fax: 01668 213555; email: jane. karthaus@confor.org.uk; website: www. confor.org.uk)

Trustees: Jane Fraser Karthaus; Christopher Inglis; Gordon Little; Lord Hamilton; Michael Roy Box.

CC Number: 1061322

Eligibility

Members of the Forestry and Timber Association (or ConFor) and their dependents who are in need. Members must have been involved with the association for at least one year.

Types of grants

One-off grants are made towards expenses for those experiencing hardship.

Annual grant total

This fund has an average income of around £6,000 per year and an average expenditure of £800.

Applications

Application forms are available to download from the fund's website.

Other information

Anyone can join ConFor who has an interest in trees, woodlands or timber.

The Gamekeepers Welfare Trust

£5,000

Correspondent: Helen M J Benson, Keepers Cottage, Tanfield Lodge, West Tanfield, Ripon, North Yorkshire HG4 5LE (01677 470180; email: gamekeeperwtrust@binternet.com; website: thegamekeeperswelfaretrust.com)

Trustees: Ken Butler; Earl of Aylesford; Dave Clark; Ian Grindy; Mike Swan; Walter Cole; Lady Scott; Raymond Holt.

CC Number: 1008924

Eligibility

Gamekeepers and those in similar occupations who are in need, and their dependents.

Types of grants

One-off and recurrent grants according to need.

Annual grant total

The latest accounts available were for 2010. During the year the trust had assets of £168,000, an income of £53,000 and gave welfare grants totalling £5,000.

Applications

On a form available from the correspondent or the website. Applications can be made at any time.

Other information

The trust also makes grants for educational purposes.

Kent Farmers Benevolent Fund

£0

Correspondent: Simon Palmer, Trustee, Somerfield House, 59 London Road, Maidstone, Kent ME16 8JH (01622 690691)

Trustees: Robert Filmer; Robert Young; Robert Page.

CC Number: 254983

Eligibility

People who have been engaged in agriculture and their dependents who are in need. Beneficiaries must have a connection with Kent.

Types of grants

Grants given according to need.

Annual grant total

In 2009/10 the fund had an income of £1,500 and no expenditure. Total expenditure has averaged around £2,500 in previous years.

Applications

In writing to the correspondent.

The Royal Agricultural Benevolent Institution

£1.9 million (12,411 grants)

Correspondent: Welfare Team, Shaw House, 27 West Way, Oxford OX2 0QH (0300 3037373; fax: 01865 202025; email: grants@rabi.org.uk; website: www.rabi. org.uk)

Trustees: Julian Sayers; Christopher Riddle; William Cumber; Carol Rymer; Jeremy Lewis; Revd John Keith Oliver; Bob Forster; Pat Stanley; James Orme; Malcolm Thomas; Nicki Quayle; Stephen Miles.

CC Number: 208858

Eligibility

Farmers, farm managers, farm workers and their dependents who have less than £10,000 in savings. Retired applicants must normally be aged at least 65 and have worked full time in the industry for at least ten years. These qualifications may be waived if the applicant has been forced to give up work due to illness or disability.

There is an emergency fund available for working farmers and farm workers who are experiencing exceptionally difficult circumstances of a temporary nature.

Types of grants

One-off grants and regular financial assistance. Grants can be given towards white goods, disability equipment, TVs and licences, telephone rental, lifelines, help in the home, care home fees, replacement boilers and so on. Emergency relief is available for essential domestic expenses in times of financial difficulty. Emergency grants have also been made in the past to assist farmers who have struggled with flooding and the foot and mouth outbreak.

The institution can also pay for temporary help on the farm if the individual or an immediate dependent is seriously ill or has an accident. Grants may also be made through the Gateway Project which offers vocational training grants to enable farmers and their immediate family to gain qualifications to enable them to increase the farm income.

Annual grant total
In 2011 the institution had assets of over £47 million and an income of £5.1 million. Over 12,400 grants were made to individuals totalling £1.9 million.

Exclusions
No grants can be given towards business debts and expenses, medical expenses or private education costs.

Applications
Applications can be made by telephoning 01865 727888 or by letter or email to the correspondent either directly by the individual or through a social worker, Citizens Advice or other third party.

All new applicants for regular assistance will be visited by one of the institution's regional welfare officers. The grants committee meets every six weeks to consider applications, though emergency needs can be met immediately.

Other information
The institution also operates two residential homes, one in Bury St Edmunds and one in Burnham on Sea and also associated sheltered flats for older members of the farming community.

RSABI (Royal Scottish Agricultural Benevolent Institution)

£381,000 (505 grants)

Correspondent: Dr Maurice S Hankey, Chief Executive, The Rural Centre, West Mains of Ingliston, Newbridge, Edinburgh EH28 8LT (01314 724166; fax: 01314 724156; email: rsabi@rsabi. org.uk; website: www.rsabi.org.uk)

SC Number: SC009828

Eligibility
People who have worked for at least ten years, full-time in a land-based occupation in Scotland and their dependents. Applicants should be either retired or unable to work, on a low income and have limited savings (£12,000 for a single applicant, £16,000 for couples) or be facing a crisis due to ill-health, accident or bereavement, for example.

Qualifying occupations include agriculture, crofting, forestry, horticulture, fish-farming, gamekeeping, rural estate work and other jobs that depend on the provision of services directly to these industries.

Types of grants
Recurring (bi-annual) payments to those on limited incomes, or single grants to help individuals meet a particular crisis in their lives. One-off payments typically help with home repairs and modifications, essential transport costs, television licences or even respite breaks, and the charity also operates a fuel poverty fund to help those experiencing hardship heating their homes. TV licences and seasonal bonuses are also provided to older people and those who are unable to work. RSABI welfare staff ensure that individuals receive their full entitlements to any other benefits due them, and will help and advise with other difficulties such as care services, housing or other such matters.

Annual grant total
Grants to individuals totalled £381,000. Of this total £333,000 was made in recurrent annual grants and £48,000 was paid in single grants.

Exclusions
No grants can be made to help with business expenses or to cover loan, overdraft or debt repayments. Occupational, income and savings criteria apply to all applicants.

Applications
On a form available from the correspondent or to download from the website. Applications can be submitted directly by the individual or through a third party such as a social worker or an organisation such as Citizens Advice. They can be considered at any time. Applicants will be visited by a welfare officer to complete a more detailed form as part of the application process.

Other information
Grants are carefully tailored to match the needs of individual applicants.

RSABI operates GATEPOST – the listening and support service for Scotland's farming and land-based community. Call 0300 111 4166 – Monday-Friday, 9am-5pm.

The Rural, Agricultural and Allied Workers' Benevolent Fund

£5,000

Correspondent: Fund Administrator, Food and Agriculture, UNITE, 128 Theobald's Road, Holborn, London WC1X 8TN (020 7611 2500)

Eligibility
Rural and agricultural members of the organisation (now a trade group within Unite the Union).

Types of grants
One-off grants with an average value of £150. In some cases recurrent support may be given.

Annual grant total
The amount varies, but usually never more than £5,000 per year.

Exclusions
This fund does not award grants to individuals who are not current union members within the agricultural section.

Applications
Potential applicants should contact their local branch official.

The Timber Trades Benevolent Society

£103,000

Correspondent: Malcolm Job, General Manager, Masons Croft, 19 Church Lane, Oulton, Stone, Staffordshire ST15 8UL (0844 892 2205; email: info@ ttbs.org.uk)

Trustees: Ian North; Ian Menzies; David Edward Francis.

CC Number: 207734

Eligibility
People who have worked for a minimum of 10 (or five in exceptional circumstances) years for a firm selling timber commercially, such as timber merchants, importers or exporters or agents and their dependents. Note the society does not cover carpenters or joiners.

Types of grants
Grants have been awarded towards heating installation, adaptation of cars for disabled use, domestic appliances, phone rentals, TV rental or licences, hampers, funeral costs house repairs or essential car maintenance. Winter fuel grants (of £250 in 2011) are also made.

Annual grant total
In 2011 the society held assets of £2.3 million and had an income of

£226,000. Grants totalled £103,000 and can be broken down as follows:

Regular payments	£33,000
Winter fuel payments	£31,000
Telephone rental	£15,000
Christmas gifts	£13,000
TV rentals and licences	£4,300
One-off grants	£3,800
Spring gifts	£3,500

Exclusions

No grants are made towards care or nursing home fees. The society will not support furniture manufacturers and carpenters servicing the building trade.

Applications

On a form available from the correspondent. Applications can be submitted directly by the individual or through a social worker, Citizens Advice, welfare agency or other third party. They are considered on a regular basis.

Airline pilots

The British Airline Pilots' Association Benevolent Fund (BALPA)

£9,000

Correspondent: Carolyn Evans, BALPA House, 5 Heathrow Boulevard, 278 Bath Road, West Drayton UB7 0DQ (020 8476 4000; fax: 020 8476 4077; email: balpa@balpa.org)

Trustees: Andrew Gooch; Capt. Anthony Pell; Capt. David Marshall; Capt. Henry Hopkins; Capt. Dave Smith; David Hogg; Robin Keegan.

CC Number: 229957

Eligibility

Serving and retired commercial pilots, flight engineers and navigators who are or have been members of BALPA, and their dependents.

Types of grants

One-off and recurrent grants and interest-free loans. The fund prefers to give grants for specific needs such as electricity bills, school books for children and so on.

Annual grant total

In 2010/11 the trust had an income of £35,000 and a total expenditure of £69,000. The trust made grants of approximately £19,000 and gave about £39,000 in interest-free loans. Grants are also made for education.

Exclusions

Grants are not given for school fees.

Applications

In writing to the correspondent requesting an application form. Applications are considered quarterly.

The Guild of Air Pilots Benevolent Fund

£9,000

Correspondent: Chris Ford, Almoner, Cobham House, 9 Warwick Court, Gray's Inn, London WC1R 5DJ (020 7404 4032; fax: 020 7404 4035; email: gapan@gapan.org; website: www.gapan.org)

Trustees: Capt. J. Robinson; Squadron Leader J. Davy; Capt. C. Spurrier; Squadron Leader C. Ford; R. Bridge; Group Capt. T. Eeles; Capt. R. Felix; Capt. O. Epton; Air Marshal C. Spink; P. Tacon; D. Howard-Budd; Air Commodore Hughesdon; Capt. R. Keegan.

CC Number: 212952

Eligibility

Members of the guild and those who have been engaged professionally as air pilots or air navigators in commercial aviation and their dependents.

Types of grants

One-off and recurrent grants ranging between £250 and £2,000. Loans can also be made to assist in the rehabilitation of people after accidents or to enable them to regain licences. The guild does not grant money for the repayment of debts or long-term expenses such as school fees or prolonged medical care.

Annual grant total

In 2010/11 the guild had assets of £551,000 and an income of £76,000. Scholarships totalling approximately £45,000 were made to seven individuals and a further £9,000 was given in 'regular and occasional' welfare grants.

Exclusions

Training and higher education are not usually supported.

Applications

On a form available from the website, including details of the individual's financial situation and proof of an aviation career. Applications are considered in January, April, July and October. The fund has helpers and visitors who can assist applicants fill in the form. The trust attaches great importance to the comments and recommendations of helpers.

Other information

The fund works closely with the other aviation trusts for individuals (both military and civilian). If an applicant has approached another such trust, they should say so in their application to this fund.

Antiques

The British Antique Dealers' Association Benevolent Fund

£5,000

Correspondent: Mark Dodgson, 20 Rutland Gate, London SW7 1BD (020 7589 4128; fax: 020 7581 9083)

Trustee: David Pettifer.

CC Number: 238363

Eligibility

Members and former members of the association who are in need, and their dependents.

Types of grants

One-off or recurrent grants ranging from £100 to £2,000 for needs such as assistance with household bills.

Annual grant total

Grants usually total around £5,000 a year.

Applications

On a form available from the correspondent. Applicants should provide two references from members or former members of the association. Applications are considered on a regular basis.

Architecture

The Architects' Benevolent Society

£504,000 (303 grants)

Correspondent: Ken Bingham, Case Committee, 43 Portland Place, London W1B 1QH (020 7580 2823; fax: 020 7580 7075; email: help@absnet.org.uk; website: www.absnet.org.uk)

Trustees: Chris Cowen; Colin Morse; Freni Shroff; John Lane; Kenneth Bingham; Peter McKinley; Stella Saunders; Terence Hopegood; Ronnie McDaniel; Bill Evans; Dr Geoffrey Purves; Marjorie Smith; Brian Lingard; Malcolm Sinclair; John Assael; Lelia Dunlea-Jones; Chris Goodall; Hugh Woodeson; Christopher Warburton; Janet Dunsmore; Thomas M. Young; Anthony Clerici.

CC Number: 265139

Eligibility

People engaged or formerly engaged in the practice of architecture, and their dependents. This includes (but is not limited to) architects, assistants, technicians and technologists and landscape architects.

Types of grants

Recurrent grants, one-off grants and loans.

Annual grant total

In 2010/11 the society had assets of £18 million and an income of £1 million. 303 grants and gifts were made to individuals totalling £504,000.

Exclusions

No educational grants.

Applications

A short application form is available from the correspondent or to download from the website. Applications can be submitted directly by the individual or through a social worker, Citizens Advice or other welfare agency. Once received, the society will arrange a visit by one of their welfare officers. Applications are considered throughout the year.

Other information

The society also provides sheltered accommodation in Chester.

Arts

The Artists' General Benevolent Institution

£397,000 (130 grants)

Correspondent: Brad Feltham, Secretary, Burlington House, Piccadilly, London W1J 0BB (020 7734 1193; email: agbi1@ btconnect.com; website: www.agbi.org. uk)

Trustees: Charlotte Halliday; Laurie Bray; Sonia Lawson; David Gentleman; Eliza Bonham Carter; Dr Gerald Libby; Jacqueline Rizvi; Martin Bailey; Nichola Hicks; Philip Hicks; Richard Grasby; Ronald Maddox; William Pye; Bernard Dunstan; Prof. Brendan Neiland; Gus Cummins; Jonathan Horwich; Stephen Bartlett; William Packer; Frank Whitford; William Bowyer; Jennifer Durrant; Dudley Winterbottom; Prof. Ken Howard; Richard Gault; Susan Thomson; Bradley Faine.

CC Number: 212667

Eligibility

Professional artists, i.e. painters, sculptors, designers, who live in England, Wales and Northern Ireland whose work has been known to the public for some time. Artists widows/widowers and orphans are also supported.

Types of grants

One-off and recurrent grants to artists who through old age, illness or accident are unable to work and earn. Grants cover a wide range of items and uses, such as domestic and utility bills, repair of equipment or replacement of worn-out items, help to cover costs of car replacements, visits to family and friends and respite care.

Annual grant total

In 2010/11 the fund had assets of £10 million and an income of £598,000. Grants were made to 130 individuals totalling £397,000.

Exclusions

The fund cannot help with career or legal difficulties, or (except in exceptional circumstances) student fees.

Applications

Applications should initially be in writing, including a full CV listing all exhibitions in professional galleries and teaching experience (if any) at GCSE, A-level or above. They can be submitted directly by the individual, or through a recognised referral agency (Citizens Advice, doctor, social worker and so on). The trust visits most potential beneficiaries in order to carry out an assessment and to collect original works and letters from two referees and a doctor or consultant (if applicable) for examination by the trustees at their next meeting.

The council meets eight times a year to consider applications.

The Entertainment Artistes' Benevolent Fund

£125,000 (196 grants)

Correspondent: Roger Kitter, Executive Administrator, Brinsworth House, 72 Staines Road, Twickenham TW2 5AL (020 8898 8164; fax: 020 8894 0093; email: giles.copperl@eabf.org.uk; website: www.eabf.org.uk)

Trustees: Laurie Mansfield; Peter Richard; Philip Dale; Giles Cooper; Ray Greenwood; James Benet Jones.

CC Number: 206451

Eligibility

Entertainment artistes (that is professional performers in variety, pantomime, revue, circus, concert party, cabaret, clubs, television, radio, making of records and light entertainment in general), and their dependents.

Types of grants

Regular top-up pensions and one-off grants for gas, electricity and fuel bills, medical and nursing needs, television licences and rentals, household repairs and telephone bills. Help may also be given with funeral costs.

Annual grant total

In 2010 the fund had assets of £3.2 million, an income of £2.4 million and a total expenditure of £2.1 million. Grants were made totalling £125,000.

155 families were helped with top-up pensions and social grants and a further 41 individuals were awarded one-off grants.

Applications

On a form available from the correspondent. Applications can be made directly or through a social worker or welfare agency. They are considered on a regular basis.

Other information

The fund has its own home for older entertainment artistes in need of care.

Equity Trust Fund

£83,000 (77 grants)

Correspondent: Keith Carter, Secretary, Plouviez House, 19–20 Hatton Place, London EC1N 8RU (020 7831 1926; email: keith@equitycharitabletrust.org. uk; website: www.equitycharitabletrust. org.uk)

Trustees: James Bolam; Anne Bright; Glen Barnham; Robin Browne; David Cockayne; Oliver Ford Davies; Bryn Evans; Ryan Losco; Graham Hamilton; Frank Hitchman; Barbara Hyslop; Milton Johns; Ian McGarry; Harry Landis; Gillian Rayne; Frederick Pyne; Rosalind Shanks; John Rubinstein; Ian Talbot; Caroline Smith; Jeffrey Wickham; Josephine Tewson; Frank Williams; Johnny Worthy.

CC Number: 328103

Eligibility

Professional performers (under Equity or ITC contracts), stage managers and directors, and their dependents.

Types of grants

One-off grants for almost any welfare need.

Annual grant total

In 2010/11 the fund had assets of £8.1 million and an income of £367,000. Grants were made to 77 individuals, for welfare and benevolence needs, totalling £83,000.

Exclusions

No grants to amateur performers, musicians or drama students.

Applications

Download from the website or email Rosalind@equitycharitabletrust.org.uk Welfare grants are available at any time during the year, dependent upon the Trustees meetings.

Other information

The trust has an informative website.

Grand Order of Water Rats Charities Fund

£66,000

Correspondent: John Adrian, Secretary to the Trustees, 328 Gray's Inn Road, London WC1X 8BZ (020 7407 8007; fax: 020 7403 8610; email: charities@gowr. net; website: www.gowr.net)

Trustees: Wyn Calvin; Roy Hudd; Kaplan Kaye; Keith Simmons; Chas McDevitt.

CC Number: 292201

Eligibility

People, and their dependents, who have been involved in a theatrical profession for at least seven years and are in need.

Types of grants

One-off and recurrent grants according to need.

Annual grant total

In 2011 the fund had assets of £1.6 million and an income of £164,000. Grants totalled £66,000 and were distributed as follows:

| Monthly allowances, grants and gifts | £66,000 |
| Fruit and flowers | £900 |

Exclusions

No grants are given towards students' fees, education, taxes, overdrafts, credit card bills or bank loans.

Applications

In writing to the correspondent, including a CV of professional career. The trustees meet monthly to consider applications.

The Evelyn Norris Trust

£21,000 (29 grants)

Correspondent: Keith Carter, Plouviez House, 19–20 Hatton Place, London EC1N 8RU (020 7831 1926)

Trustees: Frederick Pyne; Barbara Whatley; Adam Knight; Michael Cashman; Nigel Gooch; Bryn Evans; Joanne Jones; John Webb.

CC Number: 260078

Eligibility

Members or ex-members of the concert or theatrical profession who are older, sick, disabled or in need.

Types of grants

One-off grants of up to £700 towards convalescence or recuperative holidays following illness, injury or surgery.

Annual grant total

In 2011 the trust had assets of £590,000 and an income of £30,000. Grants were made to 29 individuals totalling £21,000.

Exclusions

No grants for student/education course fees.

Applications

On a form available from the correspondent. Applications are considered monthly and can be submitted directly by the individual or through a social worker, Citizens Advice, welfare agency or any third party. Applications should include any relevant financial or personal information.

Other information

Grants may also be made to organisations.

The Royal Opera House Benevolent Fund

£150,000 (53 grants)

Correspondent: Cheng Loo, Secretary, Royal Opera House, Covent Garden, London WC2E 9DD (020 7212 9128; email: ben.fund@roh.org.uk; website: www.roh.org.uk/about/benevolent-fund)

Trustees: Sir Jeremy Isaacs; Herschel Post; Neil Dolby; John Rubinstein; Keith Haydon; Felicity Clark; Kenneth Tharp; John Mortlock.

CC Number: 200002

Eligibility

People who work, or have worked, for the Royal Opera House or Birmingham Royal Ballet, and their widows, widowers, partners or children. Applicants must have savings of less than £10,000 if single and £15,000 if married. Note: applicants do not have to have contributed to the fund in order to receive help.

Types of grants

Grants range from £50 per month to £3,000 as a one-off grant. Monthly allowances are towards food and clothing. One-off grants are towards essential home maintenance, domestic equipment, urgent medical costs, education, holidays and so on. Interest-free loans are also available.

Annual grant total

In 2010/11 the fund had assets of £6.9 million and an income of £140,000. 53 individuals received grants totalling £150,000; the majority of which (£136,000) was paid in monthly allowances to 36 beneficiaries.

Applications

On a form available from the correspondent, providing details of income and expenditure. They should be submitted directly by the individual for consideration on receipt.

Other information

Grants may occasionally be made to charities, for example the Royal Ballet Benevolent Fund. The fund continues to support counselling and legal advice services as well as an occupational health unit for ROH employees.

The Scottish Artists' Benevolent Association

£30,000

Correspondent: Leslie Nicholl, 2nd Floor, 5 Oswald Street, Glasgow G1 4QR (01412 487411)

SC Number: SC011823

Eligibility

Scottish artists in need and their dependents.

Types of grants

Regular or one-off grants according to need and single payments can also be made to cover emergency situations. Grants are mainly given to people who are older or in poor health.

Annual grant total

In 2010/11 the association had an income of £30,000. Grants usually total about £30,000.

Applications

On a form available from the correspondent to be submitted directly by the individual.

Other information

The association also administrates the Gertroude Annie Leuder Trust which distributes grants to female artists. Those interested in further information should contact the correspondent.

The Show Business Benevolent Fund

£50,000

Correspondent: T Davies Brock, Administrator, Royal Bank Buildings, 55 Main Street, Callander, Perthshire FK17 8DZ (01877 330033; fax: 01877 331248; email: info@ssbf.co.uk; website: www.ssbf.co.uk)

SC Number: SC009910

Eligibility

Members of The Show Business Association who are in need, and their dependents, including widows/widowers. Emergency help may also be given to non-members through the W F Frame Fund.

Types of grants

One-off and recurrent grants towards clothing, fuel, living expenses, funeral costs, TV rental and licences and holidays to Blackpool.

Annual grant total

In 2010/11 the fund had an income of £60,000. In previous years grants have totalled about £50,000.

Applications

In writing to the correspondent.

Other information

The fund administers two smaller funds: the Mozart Allan Benevolent Fund (SC004768) and the W. F. Frame Benevolent Fund (SC008402).

The Mozart Allan Fund makes grants to members of the Show Business Fund and their dependents for convalescence and home comforts.

The W F Frame Fund grants emergency relief to people who have been connected with the entertainment profession. A maximum of £250 per year is available.

Dance

The Dance Teachers' Benevolent Fund

£8,000

Correspondent: Mrs Elizabeth Claxton, Rostrons, Yare House, 62–64 Thorpe Road, Norwich NR1 1RY (01603 619166; email: info@dtbf.co.uk; website: www. dtbf.co.uk)

Trustees: Dr Wayne Sleep; Kathryn Wade; Marion Tait; John Travis; Peter Wilson; Janet Lupino; Sara Matthews; Lynn Wallis; Susan Handy; Val Aitken; Vernon Kemp; Dorothy Ind; Baroness Hooper; Peter Kyle; Elizabeth Claxton.

CC Number: 278899

Eligibility

Dance teachers or ex-dance teachers who are experiencing short or long-term hardship.

Types of grants

Grants of £100 to £1,000 for clothing, household items, medical treatment, and so on. Recurrent grants may be given to applicants living on a low income.

Annual grant total

In 2010/11 the fund had an income and a total expenditure of £20,000. Grants were made totalling £8,000.

Applications

On a form available from the correspondent. Forms can be submitted by the individual or any third party, and are considered all year.

The International Dance Teachers' Association Benevolent Fund

£10,500 (23 grants)

Correspondent: Keith Holmes, Chief Executive, International House, 76 Bennett Road, Brighton BN2 5JL (01273 685652; fax: 01273 674388; email: info@idta.co.uk; website: www.idta.co. uk)

Trustees: Yvonne Gout; George Coad; John Knight; Keith Austin Holmes; Pamela Jane Howard Hanson; Richard Arthur Hopkins; Judith Silvester; Philip Edward Diment; Michael Andrew Sandham.

CC Number: 297561

Eligibility

Members and former members of the association, other dancers, former dancers, teachers or former teachers of dance, employees or former employees of the association, and their dependents who are affected by hardship.

Types of grants

One-off grants ranging from £100 to £5,000. 'Grants are made of a benevolent nature for people in need during times of crisis or ill health. Grants are not for the purpose of developing career training or prospects'.

Annual grant total

In 2010 the fund held assets of £86,000 and had an income of £36,000. Grants were made to 23 individuals totalling £10,500.

Applications

In writing to the correspondent.

The Royal Ballet Benevolent Fund

£80,000

Correspondent: Clementine Cowl, Executive Secretary, Royal Opera House, Covent Garden, London WC2E 9DD (01273 626547; email: info@rbbf.org.uk; website: www.rbbf.org.uk)

Trustees: Richard Alston; Colin Gray Nears; Brenda Mary Last; Drummond Donald Alasdair Leslie; Ernest Patrick Colquhoun; John Edmond Anderson Morgan; Peter James Brownlee; David Butler; Julia Margaret Buckroyd; Dame Monica Mason; Andria Hall.

CC Number: 207477

Eligibility

Dancers, ex-dancers or people who have otherwise been employed on dance presentations, such as choreographers, who have been members of UK repertory ballet and contemporary dance companies for at least seven years, unless illness or injury has forced early withdrawal. In special cases, the dependents of such people after their death.

Types of grants

One-off grants and regular payments are available to relieve any form of hardship. This includes financial assistance to older people on a low income, aids for people with a disability, help with the transition from dance to another career, or specialist surgery/therapy for injured dancers. Typical grants cover items such as supplementary pensions; disability equipment and adaptations; medical treatment and care.

Annual grant total

In 2010/11 the fund had assets of £4.1 million and an income of £172,000. 13 beneficiaries received monthly allowances totalling £57,000 while 25 one-off grants were made totalling £24,000.

Exclusions

There are no grants available for students training to be dancers. The fund cannot help dancers whose careers have not been within ballet and contemporary dance companies, for example dancers whose main career has been in musical theatre.

Applications

On a form available from the correspondent or to download from the website. Applications should be submitted directly by the individual and include evidence of expenditure such as electricity and heating bills. The form may be completed by someone else on behalf of the applicant but the applicant must sign the form. The trustees meet to consider applications in March, June, September and December.

The trustees welcome informal enquiries to discuss an application prior to the submission of a formal application.

Other information

The Fund Welfare Officer also has a pastoral role and visits beneficiaries at home or in hospitals or care homes.

Magic

The Magic Circle Benevolent Fund

£8,000

Correspondent: Treasurer, The Magic Circle, 12 Stephenson Way, London NW1 2HD (020 7387 2222)

Trustees: Scott Penrose; James Freedman; Stephen Price.

CC Number: 222408

Eligibility

Members/former members of the Magic Circle and their dependents.

Types of grants

One-off grants according to need.

Annual grant total

In 2010/11 the fund had an income of £3,700 and a total expenditure of £8,900.

Applications

In writing to the correspondent either directly by the individual or by a third party. Applications may be considered at any time.

Music

The Concert Artistes' Association Benevolent Fund

£16,000

Correspondent: Pamela Cundell, Trustee, 13 Holmdene Avenue, London NW7 2LY (020 8959 3154)

Trustees: Larry Parker; Pamela Cundell; Barbara Daniels.

CC Number: 211012

Eligibility

Members of the association, and their dependents, who are in need. Applicants must have held their membership for at least two years (or five years if over 40 at the time of joining).

Types of grants

One-off and recurrent grants according to need. Recent grants have been given towards the payment of household bills, dentures, hearing aids, glasses, disability equipment and electrical goods. Monthly grants may also be made to pensioners.

Annual grant total

In 2010/11 the fund had an income of £29,000 and a total expenditure of £17,000.

Applications

On a form available from the correspondent to be submitted directly by the individual. Applications are considered on an ongoing basis.

The English National Opera Benevolent Fund

£24,000 (10 grants)

Correspondent: Humayun S Ahmed, ENO Benevolent Fund, London Coliseum, 38 St Martin's Lane, London WC2N 4ES (020 7845 9252; email: hahmed@eno.org)

Trustees: John Cooke; Jennifer Hassell; John Graham-Hall; Graeme Danby; Harriett Maunsell; Jane Livingstone; Roger W. Sanders.

CC Number: 211249

Eligibility

People who are or have been employed by the English National Opera and/or Sadlers Wells Companies.

Types of grants

Applicants for recurrent grants must be over 58 years old and grants '. . . would normally be to reimburse telephone, TV and insurance costs with small monthly cash payments or to reimburse such. One-off support is considered on a case by case basis.' Grants range between £150 and £3,000.

Medical/dental treatment is not normally supported, except where delay would affect a performing career. The fund will help with payments for treatment which is not generally available through the NHS.

Annual grant total

In 2010/11 the trust had assets of £318,000 and an income of £76,000. Grants were made to ten individuals totalling £24,000.

Applications

Submitted directly by the individual on a form available from the correspondent, to be considered in March, June, September and December.

The Incorporated Association of Organists' Benevolent Fund

£14,000

Correspondent: Michael Whitehall, 180 Lynn Road, Wisbech, Cambridgeshire PE13 3EB (01945 463826; email: michael@whitehalls.plus. com; website: www.iaobf.com)

Trustees: Dr Stephen Cleobury; Christopher Stokes; Richard Thomas Popple; Anthony Cooke; Graham Rock; John Stanley Perkins; James Parsons; Jeanne Cawley.

CC Number: 216533

Eligibility

Organists and/or choirmasters who are members/former members of any association or society affiliated to the Incorporated Association of Organists, and their dependents, who are in need.

Types of grants

One-off and recurrent grants according to need.

Annual grant total

In 2011 the trust had an income of £15,000 and a total expenditure of £16,000. Grants were around £14,000.

Applications

On a form available to download from the website or from the correspondent. Applications can be made by the individual or through the secretary of the local organists' association. They should be submitted by 31 March for consideration at the trustees' annual meeting in May. In urgent cases the secretary may obtain approval at other times.

ISM Members' Fund (The Benevolent Fund of The Incorporated Society of Musicians)

£77,000 (49 grants)

Correspondent: Deborah Annetts, 10 Stratford Place, London W1C 1AA (020 7629 4413; email: membership@ ism.org; website: www.ism.org)

Trustees: Margaret Lion; John Stephens; Prof. Paul Edlin; Jeremy Huw Williams; Peter Nickol; Reg Fletcher; Brenda Blewett; Trevor Ford; Suzi Digby; Jeremy Jackman; Graham Phillips; Walter Blair; Prof. George Pratt; Ivor Flint; Danielle Perrett; Richard Hallam; Param Vir; Virginia Rushton; Nicolas Chisolm.

CC Number: 206801

Eligibility

Members and former members of the society and their dependents who are in need.

Types of grants

One-off and recurrent grants according to need.

Annual grant total

In 2010/11 the society had assets of £2.9 million and an income of £162,000. Grants were made to 49 individuals totalling £77,000.

Exclusions

No grants towards professional training.

Applications

On a form available from the correspondent, to be submitted directly by the individual at any time.

The Musicians Benevolent Fund

£1.1 million

Correspondent: Susan Dolton, Director of Giving, 7–11 Britannia Street, London WC1X 9JS (020 7239 9100; fax: 020 7713 8942; email: info@helpmusicians.org.uk; website: www.helpmusicians.org.uk)

Trustees: William Parker; David Lester; Dr Jane Manning; Dr Martin Neary; Revd Ronald Corp; Thomas Sharpe; Kathryn Langridge; Hon Richard Lyttelton; Caragh Merrick; John Axon; Martin Campbell White; Felicity Osmond.

CC Number: 228089

Eligibility

Current and retired professional musicians which the fund defines as anyone who performs, creates or teaches music, has earned their living in this way or in a music related profession for at least three years, who are in need and their dependents. People who are just starting out in the music business may be helped. People such as piano tuners, orchestra managers, recording engineers, instrument makers, music librarians and critics are also helped.

Types of grants

Grants range from small single payments for items such as telephones and TV licences to more substantial sums to help with medical costs, re-training, motoring and holiday costs. Regular grants are also available to support, for example, individuals in residential care. The fund will occasionally offer loans to assist with paying off debts or house adaptations.

Annual grant total

In 2011 the fund had assets of £43 million and an income of £5.3 million. Benevolence grants were made totalling £1.1 million. Some of this was spent in the following categories:

Regular financial support	£258,000
Short-term crisis grants	£168,000
Care home top-up fees	£108,000

Applications

On a form available on request by calling the free helpline number: 0800 082 6700. Applications should be submitted directly by the individual and can be considered at any time. Potential beneficiaries are usually visited to discuss their circumstances and specific needs.

Other information

The fund also provides educational grants for outstanding young musicians towards the cost of their musical development.

Organists' Charitable Trust

£5,000

Correspondent: The Trustees, 10 Stratford Place, London W1C 1BA (020 8318 1471; email: secretary@ organistscharitabletrust.org; website: www.organistscharitabletrust.org)

Trustees: Dr Martin Gerard James Neary; Jonathan Rennert; Patrick Joseph Russill; Philip John Moore; Graham Keith Howell Jones; Dr Alan John Thurlow; Timothy Rogerson; John Wardle.

CC Number: 225326

Eligibility

Organists, and their dependents, who are in financial difficulties.

Types of grants

One-off grants ranging between £500 and £1,000.

Annual grant total

In 2011 the league had an income of £10,000 and a total expenditure of £5,600. Grants totalled around £5,000.

Applications

On a form available from the correspondent. Applications can be submitted directly by the individual or through a third party such as a social worker. They are considered at any time. Repeat applications are welcomed.

The Performing Right Society Members' Fund

£375,000

Correspondent: John Logan, General Secretary, 29–33 Berners Street, London W1T 3AB (020 7306 4067; email: fund@ prsformusic.com; website: www. prsformusicfund.com)

Trustees: Brian Willey; Megg Nicol; Ray Davies; Michael Leeson; Paul Patterson; David Vickerman Bedford; Lynsey de Paul; Michael Lindup; Nicky Graham; Peter Robin Callander; Sarah Louise Rodgers; Peter Glenister; Peter Knight; Muff Winwood.

CC Number: 208671

Eligibility

Songwriters and composers of music who are or were members of the Performing Right Society, and their

dependents. Members must have held membership for seven years or more.

Types of grants

The fund offers a variety of grants and loans:

- Special needs grants: one-off grants towards, for example, essential property repairs or the replacement of domestic equipment
- Regular grants: up to £20 per week to help members who are receiving benefits but still unable to maintain basic standards of living. Help may also be given towards telephone and TV rental, TV licences and holidays. Persons in receipt of regular grants also receive a Christmas hamper, and in some cases a Christmas bonus
- Winter heating grants
- Holiday grants: provide help to elderly members who would otherwise be unable to afford a holiday
- Short-term loans: to help with an unexpected financial crisis

Annual grant total

In 2011 the fund held assets totalling £8.6 million and had an income of £646,000. Recurrent grants totalled £152,000 and one-off payments totalled £223,000. During the year only five applications were declined because they failed to meet the eligibility criteria.

Exclusions

No grants towards: the cost of buying a home; the promotion costs of any commercial venture; supporting composers who don't have any other employment; payments as an advance against future royalties.

Applications

On a form available from the correspondent or to download from the website. Applications can be submitted by the individual, through a social worker, Citizens Advice or other welfare agency, or by next of kin or associate. In cases of claims based on illness, a medical or GP's report is required and new applicants will be visited.

Other information

As well as offering financial assistance the fund can make referrals for specialist financial advice as well as offering specialist health assessments in conjunction with their partners the British Association for Performing Arts Medicine.

The Royal Society of Musicians of Great Britain

£397,000

Correspondent: Maggie Gibb, Secretary, 10 Stratford Place, London W1C 1BA

(020 7629 6137; fax: 020 7629 6137; website: royalsocietyofmusicians.co.uk/)

Trustees: David Pettit; Francesca Carpos; Gillian Moira Cracknell; Linda McLaren; Ian Curror; Teresa Cahill; Rodney Slatford; Robert William Montgomery; David Richardson; Wilfred Gibson; John Alfred Stenhouse; Timothy Hewitt-Jones; Ian Partridge; Martin Elliott; John Victor Edney; Keith Geoffrey Stent; Lawrence Archer Wallington; Nicholas Justin Pearson; Hazel Patterson; Deirdre Dundas Grant; Donna Melodie Chapman; Colin Stark; Peter David Lewis; Tristan Frederick Allan Fry; Benjamin John Costello; Stephen Charles Henderson; Jane Lister; Margaret Elizabeth Ogonovsky; Allen Edwin Handy; Stuart Allen; Dr Terence James; Sally Wainwright; Anthony Sayer; Charles Fullbrook; Louis Halsey; Betty Roe; Colin Bradbury; John Herbert Leach; Paul Harvey; Robert Schuck; Roger Rostrom; Charles Beldom; Robert John Bourton; Margaret Ann Cable; Paul Frowde; Ian Thomas Haysted; Richard Thomas.

CC Number: 208879

Eligibility

Professional musicians and their families who are in need because of illness, accident or age. Membership of the society is not a requirement.

Types of grants

One-off grants from £50 to £5,000.

Annual grant total

In 2010/11 the society had assets of £14.9 million and an income of £716,000. Grants were made to individuals totalling £397,000.

Exclusions

No grants are given to students or people whose only claim for relief arises from unemployment.

Applications

On a form available from the correspondent. Enquiries from welfare organisations are welcomed as is the identification of need from any concerned individual. An application for financial assistance should have the support of a member, honorary member or officer of the society. A copy of the current membership list is supplied to applicants. Applications are considered monthly.

Other information

Specialist advice is also available from honorary officers, which include medical consultants.

Painting

The Eaton Fund for Artists, Nurses and Gentlewomen
See entry on page 34

Theatre

The Actors' Benevolent Fund

£436,000

Correspondent: Willie Bicket, 6 Adam Street, London WC2N 6AD (020 7836 6379; fax: 020 7836 8978; email: office@abf.org.uk; website: www.actorsbenevolentfund.co.uk)

Trustees: Mr W. J. A. Wickham; Philip Lowrie; Anny Tobin; Jemma Churchill Patricia Marmont; Sian Phillips; Milton Johns; Josephine Tewson; Rosalind Shanks; Alex Michael Jennings; Barbara Whatley; Brian Murphy.

CC Number: 206524

Eligibility

Professional actors who are unable to work because of an accident, sickness or old age.

If you are a dancer, a singer or a variety performer or if you are a member of the theatrical profession and have children under 19 there are other charities which may be able to help. Phone the office for advice.

Types of grants

Recurrent grants of up to £20 (or £30 in exceptional circumstances) per week (to be reviewed every 13 or 26 weeks). One-off grants are given for furniture, wheelchairs, convalescence, nursing home fees, household equipment, minor home adaptations, and funeral and holiday costs. Help is also available for T.V. licence bills, insurance costs, phone bills and transport costs.

Around 75% of the fund's beneficiaries are over 60, with the remainder as young as early 20s.

Annual grant total

In 2010 the fund had assets of £14 million and an income of £930,000. Grants were made to over 200 individuals totalling £436,000. Of this total 177 beneficiaries received regular financial help in the year amounting to £180,000. £256,000 was paid in one-off grants.

Exclusions

No grants are available to students. Grants are unlikely to be made for credit card debts, loans or private dental or

medical treatment, which should be covered by the NHS, although the trust will consider such applications.

Applications

On a form available from the correspondent or on the fund's website. Applications should be submitted directly by the individual and include a detailed CV. If applying due to ill health or an accident, a recent doctor's letter giving details of the individual's condition should be included. It may also be helpful to include any Benefit Agency letters which confirm the level of benefits received. Applications are considered on the last Thursday of each month and forms should be submitted by the Friday before a meeting.

In cases of emergency, where potential beneficiaries need their application to be considered before the next scheduled meeting contact the fund's office on 020 7836 6378 for advice.

Other information

The trust also provides welfare and debt advice services.

The Actors' Charitable Trust (TACT)

£117,000

Correspondent: Robert Ashby, The Actors Charitable Trust, 58 Bloomsbury Street, London WC1B 3QT (020 7636 7868; email: robert@tactactors.org; website: www.tactactors.org)

Trustees: Tim Denham; Lalla Ward; Geraldine James; Elizabeth Garvie.

CC Number: 206809

Eligibility

Children (aged under 21) of professional actors who are in financial need. Note: the trust cannot help those who have solely worked in variety, amateur dramatics or as an extra.

Types of grants

One-off and recurrent grants of up to £1,200 for help with essential furnishings, utility bills (where this will benefit the children), holidays, childcare costs, clothing and special equipment. Additional grants at Christmas and crisis grants are also available.

Annual grant total

In 2010/11 the trust had assets of £4.8 million and an income of £536,000. Grants for educational and welfare purposes were made to 125 families, with 196 children between them, totalling £256,000.

Exclusions

Grants are not usually given for private school fees; however, the trust may consider making a grant if private education would be beneficial to the child i.e. due to special educational needs or family situation.

Applications

On a form available from the correspondent or to download from the website. Applications can be considered at any time and can be submitted either by the individual or a parent. Telephone and email enquiries are welcomed.

Other information

The Actors' Charitable Trust also offer nursing, residential, dementia and palliative care to those over 70 from the acting profession in Denville Hall, which they have run since 1965.

The Royal Theatrical Fund

£202,000 (140 grants)

Correspondent: Mrs Sharon Lomas, Secretary, West Suite, 2nd Floor, 11 Garrick Street, London WC2E 9AR (020 7836 3322; fax: 020 7379 8273; email: admin@trtf.com; website: www. trtf.com)

Trustees: Brian Nicholson; Giles Watling; Jonathan Wicks; Paul Daniels; Paul Gane; Sir Donald Sinden; Stephanie Cole; Geoffrey Palmer; Barbara Whatley; Dr Keith McKee; David Michaels; John Nettles; Robert Noble; Matthew Mitchell; Janie Dee; Michael Ball; Paul Chapman; Robert Lindsay; Philip Talbot; Samantha Bond; Sir Stephen Waley-Cohen.

CC Number: 222080

Eligibility

People in need who have professionally practised or contributed to the theatrical arts (on stage, radio, film or television or any other medium) for a minimum of seven years, and the relief of families or dependents of such people.

Types of grants

One-off and recurrent grants of £250 to £3,000 are given towards domestic bills, monthly allowances, shortfall in nursing and residential fees, car tax, stairlifts, computers, insurance, TV licences and so on.

Annual grant total

In 2010/11 the fund had assets of £6.1 million and an income of £414,000. Welfare grants amounted to £202,000 and can be categorised as follows:

Monthly allowances	£78,000
One-off grants and special gifts	£71,000
Payments to people in care or convalescing	£41,000
Birthday and Christmas gifts	£12,000

During the year 269 applications were considered and 140 beneficiaries were helped.

Exclusions

No grants are made to students or towards courses or projects.

Applications

On an application form available from the correspondent. Alternatively by letter outlining your difficulties and how the fund might be able to help. You should include a letter of support from your GP, consultant or attach a current medical certificate if appropriate as well as a full CV or details of your theatrical career. Applications can be submitted at any time. The welfare committee meets on the first Wednesday of each month except August to consider applications. Telephone enquiries are welcome.

Other information

The fund works in collaboration with a number of sister organisations which they refer an applicant to if they cannot help themselves.

The Theatrical Guild

£23,000

Correspondent: Laura Hannon, Office Manager, The Theatrical Guild, 11 Garrick Street, London WC2E 9AR (020 7240 6062; email: admin@ttg.org. uk; website: www.ttg.org.uk)

Trustees: Barbara Penney; Bridget Hayward; Tilly Tremayne; Jane How; Brenda Edelstein; Jan Carey; Michael Carling; Elizabeth Robertson; Pandora Clifford; Beatrice Curnew; Claire Carrie; Hugh Sachs.

CC Number: 206669

Eligibility

People who work, or have retired from, either backstage or front-of-house in a professional theatre. Financial support may be given where accident, ill health or other circumstances have prevented the applicant from working. In special cases, support may be given to working members of the profession and to one-parent families who are prevented from accepting a job due to the cost of childcare.

Types of grants

One-off and recurring grants are typically given for bills, equipment, special medical needs and re-training costs. Applicants typically seek help when they are unable to work through accident, ill health, emergency or some other reason.

Annual grant total

In 2011 the trust had assets of £1.1 million and an income of £148,000. Grants totalled £46,000 to 58 beneficiaries for both welfare and educational purposes.

Exclusions

No grants are given for the repayment of credit card debt. Help cannot be given to help drama students, amateur performers or anyone who hasn't worked or doesn't currently work in professional theatre.

Applications

Application forms can be requested in writing or downloaded from the website. Applications can be submitted either directly by the individual, through a third party such as a social worker or through an organisation such as a Citizens Advice. They are considered monthly, with the exception of August and December. Those seeking emergency assistance should contact the office directly by email or phone.

Other information

The Guild also offers counselling, welfare support and educational sponsorship.

Writing

The Authors' Contingency Fund

£13,000

Correspondent: Sarah Baxter, The Society of Authors, 84 Drayton Gardens, London SW10 9SB (020 7373 6642; email: sbaxter@societyofauthors.org; website: www.societyofauthors.org)

Trustee: The Society of Authors.

CC Number: 212406

Eligibility

Professional authors in the UK and their dependents. Grants are also made to professional poets and their dependents and female journalists.

Types of grants

One-off grants of between £500 and £750 to relieve a temporary financial emergency.

Annual grant total

In 2011 the trust had an income of £20,000 and a total expenditure of £15,000.

Exclusions

The trust cannot help with the following:
▷ Grants to cover publication costs
▷ Grants to authors who are in financial difficulty through contributing towards publication costs
▷ Tuition fees
▷ General support whilst writing a book

Applications

On a form available from the correspondent or to download from the website, including information about the applicant's circumstances and career history. Applications can be submitted directly by the individual and are considered on receipt. The assessment process usually takes around three weeks.

Other information

The fund, in conjunction with the John Masefield Memorial Trust, makes grants to British poets and administers the Margaret Rhondda Awards to support women journalists.

Francis Head Award

£13,000 (6 grants)

Correspondent: Sarah Baxter, 84 Drayton Gardens, London SW10 9SB (020 7373 6642; fax: 020 7373 5768; email: sbaxter@societyofauthors.org; website: www.societyofauthors.org)

Trustee: The Society of Authors.

CC Number: 277018

Eligibility

Professional writers (writing in the English language) who were born in the UK and are over the age of 35. The focus of the trust is primarily on those who are temporarily unable to support themselves or their dependents due to illness or accident, although the trust's website does state that 'the terms of the trust are reasonably wide.'

Types of grants

Emergency grants ranging from £1,000 to £2,000.

Annual grant total

In 2010 charity had assets of £630,000 and an income of £25,000. Grants were made to six authors totalling £12,000.

Exclusions

No grants are given to cover publication costs, tuition fees or general maintenance whilst writing a book. Support is also unavailable to authors who are in financial difficulty because they have invested money in publication costs.

Applications

On a form available from the correspondent or to download from the trust's website. Applications can be submitted directly by the individual and should include a covering letter explaining the circumstances prompting the application. A decision is usually made within three weeks.

Peggy Ramsay Foundation

£72,000

Correspondent: G Laurence Harbottle, Trustee, Hanover House, 14 Hanover Square, London W1S 1HP (020 7667 5000; fax: 020 7667 5100; email: laurence.harbottle@harbottle.com; website: www.peggyramsayfoundation. org)

Trustees: Laurence Harbottle; John Tydeman; Michael Codron; Simon Callow; David Hare; Rupert Rhymes; Harriet Walter; Neil Adleman; Tamara Harvey.

CC Number: 1015427

Eligibility

Writers for the stage who have been produced publicly, are 'of promise' and are in need of time to write which they cannot afford, or are in need of other assistance. Applicants must live in the British Isles (including Republic of Ireland and the Channel Islands).

Types of grants

One-off grants. Individual awards rarely exceed £5,000 for writing time or £1,000 for computers.

Annual grant total

In 2011 the foundation had assets of £4.7 million and an income of £242,000. Grants to 70 individuals totalled £145,000. Grants are also made for education.

Exclusions

No grants towards production costs or to writers who have not been produced. Drama students or other artists learning their trade are not supported, just experienced writers who could not otherwise follow their career. No grants are made for writing not intended for the theatre.

Applications

Apply by writing a short letter to the correspondent, submitted with a CV directly by the individual. Applicants should also provide answers to the following questions:

- When and where was the first professional production of a play of yours
- Who produced the play which qualifies you for a grant
- When and where was your qualifying play produced, what was its run and approximate playing time and has it been revived
- For that production were the director and actors all professionals engaged with Equity contracts
- Did the audience pay to attend

Scripts and publicity material must not be included. Trustees meet quarterly although applications are dealt with between meetings. Applicants will usually receive a decision in six to eight weeks.

Other information

Grants were also made to organisations totalling £18,000.

The Royal Literary Fund

£1.5 million (229 grants)

Correspondent: Eileen Gunn, Chief Executive, 3 Johnson's Court, off Fleet Street, London EC4A 3EA (020 7353 7159; email: egunnrlf@globalnet.co.uk; website: www.rlf.org.uk)

Trustees: Douglas Matthews; John Tydeman; Anthony Simon Thwaite; Philippa Blake-Roberts; Euan Cameron; Bruce Hunter; Frances Fyfield; Hilary Hale; Nick Hern; Michael Ridpath; Mark Le Fanu; Sir Ronald Harwood; Maura Dooley; Gill Coleridge; Jeremy Lewis; Richard Davenport-Hines; Aminatta Forna; Prof. Richard Holmes; Philip Gwyn Jones; Colin Luke.

CC Number: 219952

Eligibility

Authors of published work of literary merit and their dependents. The work must be written in English. Books stemming from a parallel career as an academic or practitioner are not eligible.

Types of grants

Awards range between £3,000 and £10,000. Most grants are an outright grant which means that there can be no reapplication within three years. Pensions run for five years and are then renewable according to circumstances. In special circumstances the trust gives interim grants which allow reapplication after one year.

Recent examples of beneficiaries include: (a) a writer who could not relocate with her employer because of her caring commitments found herself-unemployed. Grant relief helped clear some of her debts; and (b) a writer diagnosed with anxiety and depression whose ability to write was affected received an annual grant for three years.

Annual grant total

In 2010/11 the fund held assets of £119 million and had an income of £2.7 million. Grants totalled £1.5 million.

Exclusions

No grants for projects or work in progress. The trust does not make loans. Books stemming from a previous academic or practitioner career do not count.

Applications

On a form available from the correspondent, including details of all income and expenditure. Applicants are asked to supply copies of their published work which is then read by two members of the committee who decide on the question of literary merit. When requesting an application form applicants are asked to provide a list of their publications, including names of publishers, dates and whether they were the sole author. If this is approved, a grant/pension may be made based on an assessment of need. A home visit may also be arranged.

Other information

One grant was paid to the Royal Society of Literature (£3,000).

The Society of Authors Pension Fund

£18,000 (10 grants)

Correspondent: The General Secretary, c/o The Society of Authors, 84 Drayton Gardens, London SW10 9SB (020 7373 6642; fax: 020 7373 5768; email: info@ societyofauthors.org; website: www. societyofauthors.org)

Trustees: Paula Johnson; Deborah Moggach; Rose Tremain.

CC Number: 212401

Eligibility

Authors over 65 who have been a member of the Society of Authors for at least ten years.

Types of grants

Annual grants of £1,800 which are paid in quarterly instalments.

Annual grant total

In 2011 the fund had an income of £26,000 and made grants totalling £18,000 to ten beneficiaries.

Applications

In writing to the correspondent when vacancies are announced in the society's journal.

Atomic energy

UBA Benevolent Fund

£40,000 (32 grants)

Correspondent: Elaine Price, Unit CU1, Warrington Business Park, Long Lane, Warrington WA2 8TX (01925 633005; fax: 01925 633455; email: info@ ubabenfund.com)

Trustees: Elizabeth Mansfield; Malcolm Andrew; Michael Turner; Paul Reilly; Peter Almond; Derek Williams; Gareth Benyon; Mrs L. Blakesley; Mr C. J. Manning; Jacqui Jackson.

CC Number: 208729

Eligibility

Past and present members of the non-industrial staff of UKAEA, Amersham International plc and British Nuclear Fuels plc (or any successor organisation) and their dependents, who are in need. (Where single status has been adopted, all employees are eligible.) People who left the company as industrial employees are not eligible. Applicants do not need to have been a subscriber to the fund.

Types of grants

Allowances of between £5 and £20 per week. One-off grants are given for most purposes, except where this would affect state benefits. Interest-free loans are possible. Grants are given towards furniture, disability aids (stair lifts, wheelchairs, alarms and so on), holidays, nursing home fees, Christmas grants, television licences and sets, repairs, fuel bills (to prevent disconnection), telephone bills, removal costs, debts (in some cases), minor repairs and child minding.

Annual grant total

In 2010/11 the fund had assets of £2.7 million and an income of £64,000. Grants were made totalling £40,000. Seven interest free loans were also made totalling £9,000.

During the year 65 cases were considered with financial assistance given in 32 of these.

Exclusions

Grants are not given for private health care (excluding convalescence and residential home fees) or private education.

Applications

On a form available from the correspondent. Applications may be channelled through the network of local representatives, located at or near the organisations' sites, direct to the fund's office, or through other charities or similar bodies. They are considered every two months from January onwards.

Other information

The fund relies on the services of 14 local representatives located throughout the country, primarily in the areas of participating organisations, to visit applicants and forward information to the cases committee.

Banking, finance and insurance

The Bank Workers Charity

£430,000

Correspondent: The Clerk, Pinners Hall, 105–108 Old Broad Street, London EC2N 1EX (0800 023 4834; email: info@ bwcharity.org.uk; website: www. bwcharity.org.uk)

Trustees: David Turton; Linda Lawrence; M. Locke; Ian Keynes; Jaqueline Hopgood; Paul Haynes; Tony Ramos; Douglas Belmore; Paul Szumilewicz; Christopher Beavan; Tariq Kazi; Lesley Davie; Lillian Boyle; Gary George; Shirley Hughes.

CC Number: 313080

Eligibility

Current and ex-employees of banks in the UK and their dependents.

Types of grants

Regular grant payments for those on limited incomes; limited help with residential and nursing home fees; contributions towards the cost of wheelchairs, scooters, mobility aids and domestic appliances; carer's respite breaks and some family holidays; in special cases, assistance with telephone bills and TV licences; grants towards house repairs and maintenance.

Annual grant total

In 2010/11 the charity had assets of £45 million and an income of £1.5 million. Grants to 553 beneficiaries totalled £616,000, broken down as follows:

▷ Regular grants – £327,000
▷ School fees and expenses – £158,000
▷ Support in crisis – £103,000
▷ Grants to students – £28,000

Exclusions

No grants for non-priority debts, private medical fees or home improvements, except when essential repairs are needed to ensure independent living, safety and security. People who have worked in the insurance or stock broking industries cannot be helped.

Applications

On a form available from the correspondent or to download from the website. Once the form has been received it will be reviewed by staff. Additional contact may be required to obtain further information or clarification. The trustees meet quarterly to consider new cases.

Other information

The charity also provides support in three main areas: home, money and wellbeing. They have client advisors who offer information, advice and guidance covering a range of issues as well as offering independent and confidential counselling.

The Chartered Institute of Loss Adjusters Benevolent Fund

£4,000

Correspondent: Executive Director, Warwick House, 65/66 Queen Street, London EC4R 1EB (020 7337 9960; fax: 020 7929 3082; email: info@cila.co.uk; website: www.cila.co.uk)

Trustees: Graham Cranford Smith; Mike Jones; Andy King; Simon Burley.

CC Number: 210559

Eligibility

Members of the institute and their dependents who are 'distressed through sickness or other misfortune'.

Types of grants

One-off and recurrent grants according to need. Recent grants have been given to people diagnosed with terminal illnesses.

Annual grant total

In 2010/11 the trust had an income of £10,000 and a total expenditure of £4,200.

Applications

In writing to the correspondent. If a member passes away, the fund notifies his/her partner of the financial assistance available.

The Alfred Foster Settlement

£20,000

Correspondent: Stephen Yoxall, Barclays Bank Trust Co. Ltd, Executorship and Trustee Service, Osborne Court, Gadbrook Park, Rudheath, Northwich CW9 7UE (01606 313426)

Trustee: Barclays Bank Trust Company Ltd.

CC Number: 229576

Eligibility

Employees and former employees of banks and their dependents who are in need.

Types of grants

One-off grants according to need.

Annual grant total

In 2010/11 the trust had an income of £30,000 and a total expenditure of £51,000. Grants were given to 37 individuals totalling £41,000.

Applications

By the employee's bank, to their local regional office or directly to the correspondent.

Other information

The trust also makes grants to individuals for educational purposes.

The Insurance Charities

£608,000

Correspondent: Mrs A J Thornicroft, Secretary, 20 Aldermanbury, London EC2V 7HY (020 7606 3763; fax: 020 7600 1170; email: info@ theinsurancecharities.org.uk; website: www.theinsurancecharities.org.uk)

Trustees: Roger Carr; Ron Iles; Ian James Templeton; Prof. David Bland; Tony Alderman; Ralph Bradshaw; Adrienne O'Sullivan; David Worsfold; Frank Harold Smith; Kirsten Watson; John Greenway; Allen Prior; Kenneth Muir Davidson; Andy Miller; Nick Starling; Peter Hutchinson; Graham Cave; Lindsay Williamson; Richard Wood; Mary Rogerson; Peter Staddon; Ray O'Doherty.

CC Number: 206860

Eligibility

Past and present employees of the insurance industry and their dependents experiencing financial hardship as a result of misfortune, who live in the UK or Eire. Applicants or dependent relatives must usually have spent five years in the insurance industry with service within the UK or Eire.

Types of grants

Grants or interest-free or low-interest loans towards day-to-day expenses or special needs such as domestic appliances, disability aids, property maintenance, therapy and holidays.

Annual grant total

In 2010/11 the charities had assets of £26.7 million and an income of £1.6 million. Grants were made totalling £608,000.

Applications

An initial form can be completed online or downloaded from the website.

Other information

The charities also assist the children of insurance employees through the Orphan Fund. The charities also provide financial advice and signpost-to other organisations where appropriate.

The Insurance Charities – The Orphans' Fund

£400,000

Correspondent: Mrs Annali-Joy Thornicroft, 20 Aldermanbury, London EC2V 7HY (020 7606 3763; fax: 020 7600 1170; email: info@ theinsurancecharities.org.uk; website: www.theinsurancecharities.org.uk)

Trustees: Kirsten Watson; Prof. David Bland; Graham Cave; Frank Smith; David Worsfold; Ralph Bradshaw; Anthony Alderman; Roger Carr; Julia Graham; John Greenaway; Peter Hutchinson; Andrew Miller; Ron Iles; Ray O'Doherty; Adrienne O'Sullivan; Allen Prior; Mary Rogerson; Nick Starling; Peter Staddon; Lindsay Williamson; Ian Templeton; Richard Wood.

CC Number: 206860

Eligibility

Children of people who have spent at least five years working in the insurance industry in UK or Eire. Adult children of insurance people can be considered where personal resources are insufficient to meet reasonable expenditure.

Types of grants

Ongoing grants and interest-free or low interest loans towards day-to-day expenses and one-off grants towards special needs such as domestic appliances, disability aids and property maintenance. Help is also given to students on first degree courses.

Annual grant total

In 2010/11 the charities had assets of £26.6 million and an income of £1.6 million. Grants were made to 231 individuals totalling £674,000. This includes £66,000 that was contributed through the Paul Golmick Fund.

Applications

An initial form can be completed online or downloaded from the website.

Other information

The charities also make grants to past and present employees of the insurance industry experiencing financial hardship.

The Paul Golmick Fund is administered by the charities and was set up to promote the maintenance and education of children and young people under the age of 24, but primarily under the age of 18, who reside in the UK or Republic of Ireland and who have at least one parent or guardian with service to the insurance industry.

The Lloyd's Benevolent Fund

£178,000 (27 grants)

Correspondent: Raymond G Blaber, c/o Lloyd's, 1 Lime Street, London EC3M 7HA (020 7327 6453; email: raymond.blaber@lloyds.com)

Trustees: Brian Wilkin; David William Higgins; Timothy Kemp; Nicholas Carl Marsh; Gordon David Gilchrist; Stephen Mark Wilcox; Christine Elaine Dandridge; Charles Peter Thrale Cantlay.

CC Number: 207231

Eligibility

People who work or have worked in the Lloyd's insurance market and their dependents, anywhere in the world.

Types of grants

One-off or recurrent grants can be given towards relieving general hardship.

Annual grant total

In 2010/11 the trust had assets of £7.4 million and an income of £257,000. There were 27 grants made totalling £178,000.

Exclusions

No assistance for underwriting members of Lloyd's. School fees or medical costs will not be covered.

Applications

On a form available from the correspondent. Applications can be submitted by the individual or through a social worker, Citizens Advice, other welfare agency or other third party. They are considered throughout the year.

UNITE the Union Benevolent Fund

£63,000

Correspondent: Nick Brown, Unite, 128 Theobald's Roadd, London WC1X 8TN (0844 880 1803; fax: 020 8315 8537; email: applications@unitebf. org; website: www.unitetheunion.org/ member_services/unite_the_union_ benevolent_fun.aspx)

Trustees: Margaret Hazell; Carolyn Taylor; Tim Harper; Stephen Skinner.

CC Number: 228567

Eligibility

Members, former members, employees or ex-employees of the union and their dependents.

Types of grants

One-off grants of between £100 and £1,000 to people who have fallen on hard times through being absent from work through prolonged sickness, retirement through ill-health, family bereavements or a change in domestic circumstances. Grants have included payment towards a riser/recliner for person with back problems, help to somebody dismissed while on sick leave, heating grants for older people, Christmas bonuses for people who are elderly or have young children, and general assistance with bills.

Annual grant total

In 2011 the fund had an income of £93,000 and total expenditure of £64,000. Grants to individuals totalled £63,000.

Exclusions

Help with legal fees, educational grants and credit card bills is not usually available.

Applications

On a form available from the correspondent or to download from the website. Relevant supporting documents such as doctors letters, bank statements, payslips, etc, should also be attached to the application. Applications are considered every other month.

Book retail

The Book Trade Charity

£100,000

Correspondent: David Hicks, Chief Executive, The Foyle Centre, The Retreat, Abbots Road, Kings Langley, Hertfordshire WD4 8LT (01329 848731; email: david@btbs.org; website: www. booktradecharity.org)

Trustees: Nigel Batt; Timothy Wright; Clare Harington; Marian Donne; Katie Fulford; Tony Mulliken; Lynette Owen; Timothy Lambert.

CC Number: 1128129

Eligibility

People in need who have worked in the book trade in the UK for at least one year (normally publishing/distribution/ book-selling), and their dependents. Priority will be given to people who are chronically sick, redundant, unemployed or over 50 years of age.

Types of grants

One-off grants of up to £1,000 and recurrent grants of around £1,300 a year. Grants are normally to supplement weekly/monthly income and for recuperative holidays. Other support is given in a variety of ways, for example, assistance with telephone and television rental, medical aid, aids for disabled people and house repairs/redecoration. Grants are also given to help retrain people from the book trade who have been made redundant.

Annual grant total

Grants for welfare and medical costs usually total around £100,000 a year. In 2010 grants were given to 92 individuals.

Applications

On a form available from the correspondent. Applications can be submitted by the individual or through a recognised referral agency (social worker, Citizens Advice, doctor and so on). They are considered as they arrive.

Brewing

E. F. Bulmer Benevolent Fund

£71,000 (279 grants)

Correspondent: James Greenfield, Welfare Manager, Fred Bulmer Centre, Wall Street, Hereford HR4 9HP (01432 271293; email: efbulmer@gmail.com; website: www.efbulmer.co.uk)

Trustees: Nigel Bulmer; Jocelyn Harvey Wood; Emma Bulmer; Hannah Lort-Phillips; Andrew Jeffries Maj. Patten.

CC Number: 214831

Eligibility

Former employees of H P Bulmer Holdings plc (before it was acquired by Scottish and Newcastle plc) or its subsidiary companies for a period of not less than one year, or their dependents, who are in need. Grants are occasionally made to other individuals in need in Herefordshire.

Types of grants

One-off grants according to need. Some top-up pensions are made from a historic list but the trust is not considering new pension applicants.

Annual grant total

In 2010/11 the trust held assets of £11.4 million and had an income of £292,000. Grants to individuals totalled £71,000 and can be broken down as follows:

Pension supplements	178	£35,000
One-off grants to H P Bulmer pensioners	77	£25,000
One-off grants to other individuals	24	£11,000

Applications

Initial enquiries should be made to the administrator, preferably by email. Applications should be made through a recognised organisation such as social services, Citizens Advice or other reputable organisations. The trust provides a guidance note on their website which applicants are encouraged to read before applying. Decisions are usually made within one week.

Other information

The fund maintains the Fred Bulmer centre which provides facilities and accommodation for other charities. Grants are also made to local organisations (£407,000 in 2010/11).

Building trade

Builders' Benevolent Institution

£57,000

Correspondent: The Secretary, 147 Trevor Drive, Maidstone, Kent ME16 0QL (01622 681997; email: bbi@fmb.org.uk)

Trustees: Dennis Williams; Mr S. G. Duxbury; Alan Baker; David Marriott; John Rawson-Smith; Roy Bates; Bill Lowry; Steve Litt; David James; John Davidson; Ken Head; James Harrison; Margaret Crowe.

CC Number: 212022

Eligibility

Those who are or who have been master builders (employers in the building industry), and their dependents. Applicants with less than ten years' experience are not eligible, nor are those who have been employees.

Types of grants

Mostly pensions and Christmas vouchers. Occasionally, the trust distributes one-off grants towards the cost of necessary items such as home alterations and urgent house repairs. The trust notes that the average length of time over which beneficiaries receive support is around 15 years.

Annual grant total

In 2011 the institution had assets of £908,000 and an income of £74,000. Grants were made totalling £57,000 and were distributed as follows:

Pensions	£52,000
Christmas gift vouchers	£4,400
Temporary relief	£500

Applications

On a form available from the correspondent, submitted directly by the individual, through a social worker, Citizens Advice, other welfare agency or third party. Applications are considered throughout the year.

The Chartered Institute of Building Benevolent Fund

£56,000

Correspondent: Franklin MacDonald, Secretary, Englemere, Kings Ride, Ascot, Berkshire SL5 7TB (01344 630780; fax: 01344 630777; email: fmacdonald@ciob.org.uk; website: www.ciob.org.uk)

Trustees: George Catnach; Chris Blythe; David Cheetham; Barry William Jones; Dr Brian John Smith; Malcolm Vere Lelliott; Norman Robert Cross; Peter Charles Watkins; Martin Tomlinson.

CC Number: 1013292

Eligibility

Members of the institute and their dependents who are in real need.

Types of grants

One-off and recurrent grants towards, for example, computer equipment for a housebound individual, help for a family in general financial hardship and continuing support for a member following redundancy and ill-health.

Note: The fund cannot allocate grants for academic study but it may be able to help members who are in circumstances of hardship to obtain specialised, skill-based training.

Annual grant total

In 2011 the fund had assets of £838,000 and an income of £143,000. Grants were made totalling £56,000.

Applications

In writing to the correspondent. Applications are considered as they arrive. Informal enquiries via email are welcomed.

Other information

A significant part of the charitable expenditure is spent on providing practical advice, information and advocacy. The fund also provides a guide called 'Fresh Start' which offers information for members coping with unemployment or redundancy and is available to download from the website.

The Lighthouse Club

£448,000 (345 grants)

Correspondent: Peter Burns, Armstrong House, Swallow Street, Stockport, Cheshire SK1 3LG (01614 290022; email: peterb@cooksonhardware.com; website: www.lighthouseclub.org)

Trustees: Donald Armstrong; John Mark Everett; Michael John Cummings; Leonard Smith.

CC Number: 205670

Eligibility

People, or dependents of people, who work or have recently worked in the construction industry, or in an industry associated with construction (e.g. civil engineering, demolition or design), in the UK or Republic of Ireland. Applicants should have worked in the industry for at least two years, although not necessarily consecutively.

Types of grants

Recurrent grants to help towards living costs for those in need through accident, disability or ill-health and for those in need because a member of their family (who was in the construction industry) has died or has a fatal illness. One-off grants are also available towards essential items or services, such as a new bed, a replacement washing machine, funeral costs and school uniforms.

Annual grant total

In 2011 the fund had assets of £544,000 and an income of £515,000. Grants were made to 345 individuals totalling £444,000 (2010: £493,000). Of those helped 185 received regular support while 162 received one-off support. Grants were also made for holidays for people with disabilities amounting to £4,000.

Exclusions

The maximum length of time for recurrent grants to be given is five years.

Applications

In the first instance contact the administrator or a branch welfare officer (a list of local branches is available on the fund's website) to receive a copy of the application form.

Other information

The fund works closely with Vitalise (see separate entry) to provide holidays for individuals with disabilities.

Scottish Building Federation Edinburgh and District Charitable Trust

£22,000 (23 grants)

Correspondent: The Trustees, Scott-Moncrieff, Exchange Place 3, Semple Street, Edinburgh EH3 8BL (01314 733500; email: charity@scott-moncrieff.com; website: www.scott-moncrieff.com/charitable_trusts/page7.html)

Trustees: A. R. Watson (Chair); D. R. Brown; A. P. Goudie; J. F. Dundas; A. Dundas; L. Hughes; J. McMenamin; I. Robb; F. Spratt; D. Stephen; Prof. A. C. Walker; E. M. Walker.

SC Number: SC029604

Eligibility

Persons in reduced circumstances who have been involved with the building trade in the City of Edinburgh or the Lothians.

Types of grants

One-off grants according to need.

Annual grant total

In 2011 the trust held assets of £1.2 million and had an income of £41,000. Grants were made to 23 individuals totalling £22,000.

Applications

On an application form available from the correspondent's website. Details of employment in the trade must be included.

Other information

Funding is also provided for educational opportunities (£14,500 in 2011).

Caravan

The National Caravan Council (NCC) Benevolent Fund

£3,200

Correspondent: Mrs S J Amey, PO Box 1421, Woking GU22 2ND (email: info@nccbf.org.uk; website: www.nccbf.org.uk)

Trustees: David Carver; Sara-Jane Amey; David Gale Hasleham; Mark Cheater; Glen Campbell.

CC Number: 271625

Eligibility

People in need who are, or have been, employed in the caravan industry, and their dependents.

Types of grants

Normally one-off grants ranging from £200 to £2,500, although occasionally recurrent grants may be given. Recent grants have been made towards redecoration, medical expenses, food, education or special equipment such as computers for people who are housebound or disabled.

Annual grant total

In 2010/11 the fund had an income of £6,900 and a total expenditure of £3,500.

Applications

On a form available from the correspondent including details of employment within the caravan industry. Applications can be submitted directly by the individual or through an appropriate third party.

Other information

The fund also helps people from outside the industry by providing caravan holidays in association with the Happy Days Children's Charity (1010943).

Ceramic

The Ceramic Industry Welfare Society

£3,500

Correspondent: The Secretary, Unity Trades Union, Hillcrest House, Garth Street, Stoke-on-Trent ST1 2AB (01782 272755; fax: 01782 284902)

Trustee: Mervin Stanyer.

CC Number: 261248

Eligibility

People in need who are or have been employed in the ceramics industry, or widows of former employees.

Types of grants

Recurrent grants are fixed at £45 per six week period depending on the circumstances of the applicant as confirmed by the visit of the society's representative.

Annual grant total

In 2010 the society had an unusually high income of £26,000 and total expenditure of £3,700.

Exclusions

No grants are payable beyond 12 months of the date of retirement.

Applications

In writing to the correspondent.

Chartered surveyors

Lionheart (The Royal Institution of Chartered Surveyors Benevolent Fund)

£1 million

Correspondent: Brin Corotana, Welfare Administrator, Surveyor Court, Westwood Way, Coventry CV4 8BF (02476 466696; fax: 020 7647 4701; email: info@lionheart.org.uk; website: www.lionheart.org.uk)

Trustees: Jennifer Ellis; Tony Jemmett; Barry Smyth; Michael Jeffreys; Patrick Hall; Caroline Pelham-Lane; Richard Lewis; Duncan White; Bryan Pickering; James Allan; William Jenkins; Charles Follows; Michael Greensmith.

CC Number: 261245

Eligibility

Members and former members of the Royal Institution of Chartered Surveyors or organisations it has merged with and their dependents. Applications are welcome from people in the UK and those living overseas.

Types of grants

One-off and recurrent grants and loans are given towards: essential domestic appliances, furnishings, re-decorations and property repairs; living expenses; care in the community, residential and nursing care; respite care and holidays; and, medical aids, adaptations and equipment for children with disabilities and the elderly. Additional financial help is also available for those most in need at Christmas.

Annual grant total

In 2010/11 the trust had assets of £14.4 million and an income of £1.6 million. Grants totalled just over £1 million.

Applications

On a form available from the correspondent or to download from the website. Evidence of RICS membership or details of the member of whom the applicant is a dependent should be provided. Applications are considered quarterly, although urgent cases can be considered between meetings.

Other information

The trust offers confidential advice, counselling, befriending, information and help in kind to members of the profession and their dependents on a range of social welfare, financial, employment and property-related matters. A helpline is operated on 0845 603 9057.

Chemical engineers

The Chemical Engineer's Benevolent Fund

£14,000

Correspondent: Jo Downham, Davis Building, 165–189 Railway Terrace, Rugby, Warwickshire CV21 3HQ (01788 578214; fax: 01788 560833; email: jdownham@icheme.org.uk; website: www.icheme.org.uk/about_us/benevolent_fund.aspx)

Trustees: Dr Philip Hawtin; Stephen Vranch; Ken Sutherland; Prof. Keith William Arthur Guy; Malcolm Peter Wilkinson; Professor Roland Clift; Professor Raymond William Kenneth Allen.

CC Number: 221601

Eligibility

Chemical engineers and their dependents. This includes all chemical engineers worldwide, not simply members or former members of the Institution of Chemical Engineers.

Types of grants

One-off and recurrent grants, and loans, for example, towards medical treatment, special equipment, nursing home fees, special education needs and general expenses.

Annual grant total

In 2010 the fund had assets of £258,000 and an income of £46,000. Grants were made totalling £14,000.

Exclusions

There are no grants available for students.

Applications

In writing to the correspondent, to be submitted either directly by the individual or through a third party such as a social worker, Citizens Advice or other welfare agency or another third party. Applications should include proof of employment as a chemical engineer, such as a passport descriptor or company document.

Civil service

Assist Fund (formerly known as the Century Benevolent Fund)

£56,000

Correspondent: The Administrator, PO Box 62849, London SE1P 5AE

CC Number: 251419

Eligibility

Employees and ex-employees of the Government Communications Bureau and its associated organisations, and their dependents.

Types of grants

One-off or recurrent grants and loans towards telephone bills, house repairs and so on.

Annual grant total

In 2010/11 the trust had assets of £1.1 million and an income of £137,000. Grants to individuals totalled £56,000 of

which £30,000 was made in regular grants and £26,000 in one-off grants.

Exclusions

No educational grants.

Applications

In writing to the correspondent, although applications are often made by word of mouth. Applications are generally considered four times a year, but exceptions can be made in urgent cases.

For You By You – The Charity for Civil Servants

£4 million (5,700 grants)

Correspondent: The Help and Advisory Team, Fund House, 5 Anne Boleyn's Walk, Cheam, Sutton, Surrey SM3 8DY (0800 056 2424; fax: 020 8240 2401; email: info@foryoubyyou.org.uk; website: www.foryoubyyou.org.uk)

Trustees: Brian Fox; Graeme Henderson; Peter Connor; Richard Hatfield; Stephen Laws; Dr Catherine Bell; Anna Southall; Richard Corden; Tim Flesher; Hilary Douglas; Patrick Hughes; Siobhan Benita.

CC Number: 1136870

Eligibility

Serving, former and retired staff of the Civil Service and associated organisations, and their dependents, who are in need.

Types of grants

Grants, loans and allowances according to need. Grants have been given towards daily living expenses, items of essential equipment, and in some cases towards household bills and funeral expenses. Allowances can be given towards the cost of community support services, nursing or residential home fees (by topping-up a local authority payment) or childcare.

Annual grant total

In 2011 the charity had assets of £37 million and an income of £8.1 million. They supported 5,700 individuals totalling £4 million, broken down as follows:

- Low/reduced income – £2 million
- Debt – £819,000
- Poor/inappropriate living arrangements – £501,000
- Bereavement – £236,000
- Illness – £185,000
- Immobility – £169,000
- Emergencies – £23,000
- Community projects – £9,000
- Education – £4,000

Exclusions

It does not help employees of the NHS or local/county councils. Funding is not

provided for house purchase, home improvements, strike action, legal costs, private medical treatment for infertility, private education, payment of fines or to those dismissed for gross misconduct.

Applications

Either using the online application process, by downloading an application form or requesting one to be sent in the post. The charity runs a freephone help service providing advice and information and assistance with an application.

Other information

The fund also helps people by providing an information service on a range of community-based services and a confidential visiting service to aid and advise on funding opportunities.

Overseas Service Pensioners' Benevolent Society

£125,000 (106 grants)

Correspondent: D F B Le Breton, Secretary, 138 High Street, Tonbridge, Kent TN9 1AX (01732 363836; fax: 01732 365070; email: bensoc@ospa.org.uk; website: www.ospa.org.uk)

Trustees: Peter Standley McLean; Peter Fullerton; Robin Mitchell; Darcy Terence Norman Payne; Keith Vernon Arrowsmith; Anne Clifford; Robert Wise; Satwant Singh Suman.

CC Number: 235989

Eligibility

Members of the Overseas Service Pensioners' Association or those with other relevant service in the Overseas Civil Service or in a former British dependent (colonial) territory, and their dependents, who are in need.

Types of grants

Grants of between £50 and £1,500 are usually paid quarterly to help with living expenses. Occasionally, single grants are given for special needs and recently a number of holiday grants have been made. All cases are reviewed annually.

Annual grant total

In 2011 the society had an income of £81,000 and helped 106 beneficiaries.

Exclusions

No grants are made for residential care or nursing home fees.

Applications

On a form available from the correspondent. Applications should normally be submitted directly by the individual or by a third party such as a close relative or a legal representative.

Prospect Benevolent Fund

£117,000 (112 grants)

Correspondent: Finance Officer, New Prospect House, 8 Leake Street, London SE1 7NN (020 7902 6600; fax: 020 7902 6667; email: enquiries@prospect.org.uk; website: www.prospect.org.uk)

Trustees: N. Titchen; A. Grey; C. Marshall; R. Arrowsmith; P. Kemball.

Eligibility

Members and retired members of the union (and the former Institution of Professional Civil Servants) and their dependents who are experiencing financial problems.

Types of grants

Generally one-off grants. Recurrent grants do not exceed £1,500. The trustees aim to relieve immediate problems and point applicants to other channels and agencies for long-term solutions. Grants are usually sent to the applicant, but for speed and/or reliability, some awards are sent direct to the utility/body owed money. Occasionally this is processed through an agency or second party (such as welfare officer, debt counsellor, branch officer or relative).

The union also makes death benefit grants to dependents of members or retired members which is equal to five times the higher national rate annual subscription.

Annual grant total

In 2011 the fund held assts of £420,000 and had an income of £15,000. Grants were made to 16 individuals totalling £34,000.

The death benefit scheme payment was worth £968 in 2011 with 86 members receiving payments totalling £83,000.

Exclusions

The trust does not make loans.

Applications

On a form available from the correspondent. Applications can be submitted directly by the individual or through employer's welfare officers or branch representatives. Applications are considered throughout the year and are processed quickly.

The Public and Commercial Services Union Benevolent Fund

£137,000

Correspondent: Benevolent Fund Secretary, 160 Falcon Road, London SW11 2LN (020 7801 2601, option 3; fax: 020 7801 2675; email: membenefits@pcs.org.uk; website: www.pcs.org.uk)

Eligibility

Members and Associate members of the Union who are suffering severe financial hardship, through sickness, family troubles or other problems. Applications will be rejected if the individual is not a fully paid-up member, or associate member, of the union.

Types of grants

One-off grants to a maximum of £500 in any 12 month period.

Annual grant total

In 2010 £137,000 was distributed by the benevolent fund.

Exclusions

No grants are given for help with private legal or medical expenses. No grants are given for credit card debts, overdrafts, loans, educational costs or strike action. Loans are not made.

Applications

On a form available from the correspondent or to download from the website. Completed applications should be submitted either directly by the individual or a family member, or through a third party such as a union representative and may be emailed or posted. They are reviewed weekly.

Clayworking

The Institute of Clayworkers Benevolent Fund

£2,000

Correspondent: Francis Morrall, Trustee, Federation House, Station Road, Stoke-on-Trent, Staffordshire ST4 2SA (01782 571846; email: francism@ceramfed.co.uk)

Trustees: David Graham; Dr Denzil Reginald Frank Spencer; Raymond William Doughty; Wayne Sheppard; Neale Perkin; Francis Morrall.

CC Number: 212300

Eligibility

People in need who had to retire early from the clay-working industry through accident or ill-health. Dependents of deceased clayworkers may also be eligible. The fund covers brick-making, roof tiles, clay drainage pipes and refractory industries, but not pottery workers.

Types of grants

One-off grants, usually of £250. In exceptional cases where applicants have been identified by other charitable bodies as being in extreme need, larger grants may be given.

Annual grant total

In 2010 the fund had an income of £2,500 and a total expenditure of £2,200.

Applications

In writing to the correspondent, including age, length of service, date of termination of employment (if applicable), brief description (two or three sentences) of circumstances leading to application, and brief testimonial (a sentence or two) from a supervisor/manager if appropriate. The fund only accepts applications made through a former employer and not usually those made directly by the individual. Applications may be made at any time.

Clothing and textiles

The Bespoke Tailors Benevolent Association

£66,000 (96 grants)

Correspondent: Susanne Smart, 20 Pinewoods, Bexhill on Sea, East Sussex TN39 3UD (01424 846614)

Trustees: Angus Howard Cundey; Brian Lishak; Cyril Fox; Eric Hart; Graham Lawless; Montague George Moss; Paul Frearson; Vincent Bulaitis; Alan Bennett; Rodney Benson; William Skinner.

CC Number: 212954

Eligibility

Journeyman tailors, tailoresses and their near relatives who were employed in the bespoke (made to measure) tailoring trade. Preference is given to past and present members of the institute but help can be given to other eligible applicants.

Types of grants

Small one-off grants and regular allowances. Previously, allowances have been in the region of £20 a week.

Annual grant total

In 2011 the institute (also known as the TBI) had assets of £1.8 million and an income of £38,000. Grants were made to 96 individuals totalling £66,000.

Applications

On a form available from the correspondent. Applications should preferably be submitted through a social worker. However, those submitted directly by the individual or through another third party will be considered.

Other information

In late 2012 the Tailors Benevolent Institute and the Master Tailors Benevolent Association merged to form the Bespoke Tailors Benevolent Association.

The City of London Linen and Furnishings Trades Association

£1,500

Correspondent: Geoffrey Blake, Trustee, 69a Langley Hill, Kings Langley, Hertfordshire WD4 9HQ (01923 262857)

Trustees: Earl Whitehead; Geoffrey Blake; Frederick Monger; Don Hanley; Ann Marie Ashwin-Kean.

CC Number: 211522

Eligibility

Members and former members of the association and their dependents.

Types of grants

One-off grants according to need. The trust can also contribute towards the cost of a holiday at one of the Textile Benevolent Association holiday homes.

Annual grant total

Grants usually total about £1,500 each year.

Applications

In writing to the correspondent.

The Cotton Industry War Memorial Trust

£141,000 (241 grants)

Correspondent: Hilda Ball, 42 Boot Lane, Heaton, Bolton BL1 5SS (01204 491810)

Trustees: Peter Booth; Christopher Robert Trotter; Prof. Albert Peter Lockett; Keith Lloyd; Keith Ronald Garbett; Peter Reid; Philip William Roberts; John Richard Reed.

CC Number: 242721

Eligibility

People in need who have worked in the cotton textile industry in the north west of England. This includes weaving, spinning and dyeing. Cotton industry workers who were badly injured while fighting for HM Forces in wartime may also be eligible.

Types of grants

Convalescence grants are available to people who are in poor health or who have suffered injury due to their work in the cotton textiles industry. One-off grants are also awarded for specific needs.

Annual grant total

In 2011 the trust had assets of £5.5 million, an income of £306,000 and a total expenditure of £568,000. Grants were made to 241 individuals under the convalescence scheme totalling £141,000. £150,000 was given to organisations.

Exclusions

People who have worked with clothing, footwear, hosiery and other man-made fabrics are not eligible.

Applications

On a form available from the correspondent. Note that the correspondent cannot send forms directly to applicants, just to employers, trade unions, SSAFA or similar welfare agencies for them to pass on to potential beneficiaries. Applicants must show that they have worked in the textile industry and provide medical evidence if claiming assistance due to employment injury or disability. Applications are considered quarterly.

Other information

The trust gives substantial grants to educational bodies to assist eligible students in furthering their textile studies, to other bodies which encourage recruitment into or efficiency in the industry and to organisations furthering the interests of the industry by research and so on.

The Fashion and Textile Children's Trust

£45,000

Correspondent: Anna Pangbourne, Director, Winchester House, 259-269 Old Marylebone Road, London NW1 5RA (020 7170 4117; email: anna@ftct.org.uk; website: www.ftct.org.uk)

Trustees: Kenneth Young; Colin Llewellyn Evans; David Carter-Johnson; Ian Thomson; Josephine Collins; Jill Butterworth; Anne Horton; Nikki Zamblera; David Shepherd; Jill Little; Nayna McIntosh; Sue Shipley; Jessica Brown; Amit Chowdhury; Mike Trotman.

CC Number: 257136

Eligibility

Children and young people under 18 years whose parents work or have worked in the UK fashion and textile retailing and manufacturing industry.

Types of grants

The trust concentrates its grant giving on 'the essential costs of education'. However, it also makes some welfare grants to children from particularly poor backgrounds for items such as, disability equipment, clothing, bedding and shoes.

Annual grant total

In 2010/11 the trust had assets of £7.2 million and an income of £461,000. Grants were made to individuals totalling £268,000, broken down as follows:

- Ongoing school fee cases: 56 grants
- New school fee cases: 27 grants
- Welfare grants: 42 grants
- Bursaries: 6 grants

Welfare and general assistance grants totalled £45,000.

Exclusions

No grants are given towards child care, study/travel abroad; overseas students studying in Britain; student exchange; or people starting work. No grants are available for those in higher education.

Applications

On a form available from the correspondent or an initial enquiry form from the trust's website. Applications can be submitted at any time either directly by the individual or through a third party such as a social worker, teacher or Citizens Advice. Applicants are encouraged to call the trust in the first instance to discuss an application.

The Feltmakers Charitable Foundation

£7,300

Correspondent: Maj. Jollyon Coombs, Post-Cottage, The Street, Greywell, Hook, Hampshire RG29 1DA (01256 703174; email: jcpartnership@btopenworld.com; website: www.feltmakers.co.uk)

Trustees: Cmdr J. M. D. Curteis; S. D. Curtis; Mrs J. George; R. C. Gray; W. Horsman; J. S. Ray.

CC Number: 259906

Eligibility

Employees or former employees of the hat trade who are in need.

Types of grants

Annual pensions.

Annual grant total

In 2010/11 the foundation had assets of £431,000 and an income of £41,000. Grants were made totalling £7,300.

Applications

Applicants must be nominated in the first place by their employer or former employer, or in exceptional circumstances by a welfare organisation.

Other information

The foundation also makes grants to organisations (£28,000 in 2010/11).

Footwear Friends

£71,000 (215 grants)

Correspondent: Gabi O'Sullivan, Secretary, 3 Queen Square, Bloomsbury, London WC1N 3AR (020 7843 9486; email: info@footwearfriends.org.uk; website: www.footwearfriends.org.uk)

Trustees: Peter Schweiger; Simon Goodman; Richard Kottler; Peter Lamble; John Barrett; Gordon Smart; David Lockyer; Justin Morgan; Adam Marsden; Matthew Eatough; Martyn Harvey; Tim Cooper; Harvey Jacobson; Gemma Treglia.

CC Number: 222117

Eligibility

People who are working or have worked in the boot trade and footwear industry, usually for a minimum of five years, and their dependents.

Types of grants

One-off grants to meet a particular need, for example, domestic appliances, furnishings or essential disability equipment. Regular grants are also made for those on low-incomes. Holiday grants may also be made.

Annual grant total

In 2011/12 the society had assets of £1 million and an income of £160,000. Grants were made to 215 individuals totalling £71,000 and can be analysed as follows:

Christmas grants	£20,000
Mid-year grants	£17,000
One-off grants	£15,000
December bonus grants	£8,500
Half-yearly allowances	£7,800
Cordwainers Christmas grants	£1,500
Holiday grants	£1,400

Applications

On a form available from the correspondent. Applications can be completed by the individual or a third party. If completed by the individual it must be verified by either someone who has known the applicant for some time, who works in a professional capacity and is not related to the applicant; or a third party acting on behalf of the applicant, for example a welfare adviser.

Other information

Also known as the Footwear Benevolent Society and formerly The Boot Trade Benevolent Society.

Johnson Charitable Trust

See entry on page 96

Sydney Simmons Pension Fund

£2,000

Correspondent: David Matanle, Homefield, Fortyfoot Road, Leatherfield, Surrey KT22 8RP (01372 370073; email: luchar@btinternet.com)

Trustees: David Matanle; Brian Simpson; Karen Milner.

CC Number: 252677

Eligibility

People in need who are or have been employed in the carpet trade.

Types of grants

One-off grants usually in the range of £300 to £500.

Annual grant total

Grants for individuals usually total about £2,000 a year.

Applications

On a form available from the correspondent.

Other information

The fund also makes grants to organisations.

The Textile Benevolent Association (1970)

£13,000

Correspondent: Mrs Sandra O'Hara, 72a Lee High Road, Lewisham, London SE13 5PT (020 8852 7239; fax: 020 8463 0303)

Trustees: David Butler; John Merlin; Helen Bull; Gordon Crerar.

CC Number: 261862

Eligibility

People in need who are employees and former employees of: wholesalers and retailers engaged in the textile trade; and of manufacturers in the trade which distribute to retailers as well as manufacture. The wives, widows, husbands and widowers of such people can also benefit.

Types of grants

Grants are towards holidays, winter fuel bills, clothing, cookers, washing machines and so on.

Annual grant total

In 2011 the association had an income of £2,200 and a total expenditure of £62,000. Grants were made totalling around £13,000.

Applications

On a form available from the correspondent, usually via employers, doctors or social services.

Coal industry

The Coal Industry Benevolent Trust

£691,000

Correspondent: Vernon Jones, Secretary, The Old Rectory, Rectory Drive, Whiston, Rotherham, South Yorkshire S60 4JG (01709 728115; fax: 01709 839164; email: mail@ciswo.org.uk; website: www.ciswo.org.uk)

Trustees: Richard John Budge; Wayne Thomas; Colin Ambler; Robert Henry George Young; George James Shearer; John Humble; Jon Hattersley; Ian Davies; Christine Kaye; J. Wood; Terence Leslie Fox.

CC Number: 1015581

Eligibility

Widows and families of miners who have died as a result of industrial accident or disease (mainly pneumoconiosis). Help is also available to mineworkers and their dependents who are experiencing financial difficulties.

Types of grants

- General hardship grants of up to £500 towards, for example, buying a motorised wheelchair, specialist equipment and home adaptations
- Grants of up to £1,500 to the dependents of miners who have died as a result of their work (made soon after the death) and £500 for the following three years, if his widow remains single, and £250 to the children (£350 if the child has a disability)
- Grants of £50 every four weeks are available to miners who are in hospital as a result of their work, up to £200 a year
- Grants of £5 per journey up to £200 for miners who have to travel to an outpatients centre as a result of an accident at work

Annual grant total

In 2011 the trust held assets of £31 million and an income of £3.4 million. Grants were made totalling £691,000 and were distributed as follows:

Hardship grants	£328,000
Regulation cases	£294,000
Special needs	£52,000
Social intervention fund	£12,000
Christmas voucher scheme	£4,000
Other grants	£1,200

Applications

In writing to the correspondent for consideration by the trustees. The trust usually sends one of its own social workers to visit the individual to assess their needs and assist with the application form.

Other information

The trust also operates a number of convalescence homes throughout the UK and a comprehensive social work service.

From January 2010 the Coal Industry Benevolent Trust merged with the Coal Industry Social Welfare Organisation who now administer the trust.

The Coal Trade Benevolent Association

£149,000 (318 grants)

Correspondent: Nicholas Maxwell Ross, Unit 6 Bridge Wharf, 156 Caledonian Road, London N1 9UU (020 7278 3239; email: coalbenev@btconnect.com; website: www. coaltradebenevolentassociation.org)

Trustees: John Boddy; Elizabeth Lockley; Jane Mary Heginbotham; John Douglas Cowcill; Dr Timothy Minett; Tomas John Allchurch.

CC Number: 212688

Eligibility

Non-manual workers of the coal industry in England and Wales who have worked in the production or distribution sectors and allied trades, and their dependents.

Types of grants

Weekly grants to supplement low income and one-off grants towards, for example, telephone costs, televisions, fuel payments, respite holidays and capital items. Special one-off payments have also been made to help beneficiaries with fuel bills during exceptionally cold periods.

Annual grant total

In 2011 the association had assets of £4.7 million and an income of £221,000. Grants were made to 318 individuals totalling £149,000.

Applications

On a form available from the correspondent for consideration throughout the year.

Commerce

The George Drexler Foundation

£60,000

Correspondent: Jonathan Fountain, 35–43 Lincolns Inn Fields, London WC2A 3PE (020 7869 6080; email: georgedrexler@rcseng.ac.uk)

Trustees: Alastair Collett; Tina Dresher; Leela Kapila; Michael Edgar.

CC Number: 313278

Eligibility

Former employees of the Ofrex Group and their dependents.

Types of grants

One-off and recurrent grants of £1,000 to £10,000.

Annual grant total

In 2010/11 the foundation had assets of £5.7 million and an income of £222,000. Grants for welfare totalled £60,000.

Exclusions

The foundation does not support funding for medical electives, volunteering or gap year projects.

Applications

On a form available from the correspondent, submitted directly by the individual, enclosing an sae. Applications should be submitted in May for consideration in June/July.

Other information

The foundation also provides educational grants to people in need who have a direct link with commerce, that is, who have owned and run their own commercial business. Applicants whose parents or grandparents have this link can also be supported. This does not include professional people such as doctors, lawyers, dentists, architects or accountants. No exceptions can be made.

The Ruby and Will George Trust

£10,000

Correspondent: Damien Slattery, 125 Cloverfield, West Allotment, Newcastle upon Tyne NE27 0BE (01912 664527; email: admin@rwgt.co.uk; website: www.rwgt.co.uk)

Trustees: David Waters; Jean Waters; Edward Ellis; Charles Ellis; William Ellis.

CC Number: 264042

Eligibility

People in need who have been or who are employed in commerce, and their dependents. Preference is given to people who live in the north east of England.

Types of grants

One-off or recurrent grants for items which are needed but cannot be afforded, usually related to sickness and disability, for example, wheelchairs, washing machines and clothes. Grants usually range from between £250 and £5,000.

Annual grant total

In 2010/11 the trust had an income of £102,000 and a total expenditure of £57,000. Previously grants were given to individuals mainly for the advancement of education.

Applications

The trust has an online application process, though those without access to the internet can still submit a paper-based application. Applicants will need to prove their commerce connection and their income and expenditure. Two references are required.

The trust considers applications four times a year, usually in January, May, July and October. Applications should be submitted two weeks in advance. Note: upcoming deadline dates can be found on the trust's website.

Other information

The trust also makes grants to institutions. Accounts were received by the Charity Commission but were unavailable to view.

H. J. Rawlings Trust

£7,500

Trustee: Liverpool Charity and Voluntary Services.

CC Number: 265690

Eligibility

People in need, with a preference for current and former employees of John Holt and Company.

Types of grants

One-off and recurrent according to need.

Annual grant total

In 2009/10 the trust held assets of £883,000 and had an income of £29,000 from investments. Grants totalled £37,000, with £7,500 going to individuals and the remainder to local organisations.

Applications

In writing to the correspondent.

Other information

Grants are also made to organisations that work with people in need, hardship or distress (£30,000 in 2009/10).

Commercial travellers

The CTBI – The Salespeople's Charity

£469,000 (254 grants)

Correspondent: Mandi Leonard, 2 Fletcher Road, Ottershaw, Chertsey, Surrey KT16 0JY (01932 429636; email: sec.ctbi@ntlworld.com; website: www. ctbi.org)

Trustees: Alister McGuire; Douglas Snoad; Jim McLellan; Michael Hill; Dennis Brian Underwood; Michael Eric Pickering; Neil Webster; Thomas Annett Cherry; Trevor Grant; Paul Martin George Gardner; Brian Riddell; Gillian Tate.

CC Number: 216538

Eligibility

People in the UK who are in need and have worked as a sales representative/agent promoting or selling to the trade for at least five years, and their dependents. Applicants must have been employed for a minimum of six months in each of these years. Sales must be business to business and involve the representative leaving their office and visiting client sites.

Types of grants

Recurrent grants and gifts in kind. One-off grants are also given towards respite breaks, disability aids, home adaptations, TV licences and for critical one-off payments.

Annual grant total

In 2011 the trust had assets of £5.2 million and an income of £555,000. Grants to 254 beneficaries totalled £460,000 and can be broken down as follows:

Quarterly benefit payments	£372,000
Hampers and food vouchers	£46,000
One-off grants	£28,000
TV licences, phones, etc	£12,000
Respite	£1,500
TV and aidcall hire	£150

Exclusions

No help is given to those engaged in 'van sales', retail, telesales or general selling to the public.

Applications

On a form available from the correspondent or to download from the website. Applications should include evidence of employment in commercial sales and be submitted either directly by the individual or through a third party. The trustees meet five times a year to consider applications, though emergency payments can be made quickly in cases of extreme hardship.

UCTA Samaritan Benefit Fund Society

£75,000

Correspondent: Peter Brennan, The Cottage, Dairyhouse Lane, Dunham Massey, Altrincham, Cheshire WA14 5RD (01612 653462; email: pjb@pbrennan.freeserve.co.uk)

Trustees: Edward Mason; Peter John Brennan; Albert Hayden Thornton;

David Picton Evans; Geoffrey Frederick Rollinson; John Southern; Simon Marks.

CC Number: 1071037

Eligibility

Commercial travellers and their dependents in the UK who are in need.

Types of grants

One-off and recurrent grants according to need.

Annual grant total

In 2011 the society had assets of £225,000, an income of £67,000 and made grants totalling £75,000.

Applications

On a form available from the correspondent.

Cooperative

The National Association of Cooperative Officials' Benevolent Fund

£12,000

Correspondent: Lynne Higginbottom, 6a Clarendon Place, Hyde, Cheshire SK14 2QZ (01613 517900; fax: 01613 666800; email: info@naco.coop; website: www.naco.coop)

Trustees: Jayne Webb; Karen Froggatt; Roger Myddelton; Jack Devers; Maria McGettigan; Ann Breen; Chris Morgan; Alan Tattler; Darren Leverington; Mark Alexander; Phil Barr; Colin Downes; Gary Chappell; Andrew North; Jas Sandhu; Paul Winstanley.

CC Number: 262269

Eligibility

Members and former members of the association and their families. Widows and children of deceased members are also eligible for assistance.

Types of grants

One-off grants up to a maximum of £1,000.

Annual grant total

In 2010 the association had an income of £24,000 and a total expenditure of £13,000.

Applications

On a form available to download from the website, to be submitted directly by the individual. Applications should include details of personal finance. They are usually considered quarterly.

Coopers

William Alexander Coopers Liverymen Fund

£2,000

Correspondent: A G Carroll, The Clerk, Coopers' Hall, 13 Devonshire Square, London EC2M 4TH (email: clerk@coopers-hall.co.uk; website: www.coopers-hall.co.uk/coopers)

Trustees: Mr P. J. Timms; Alderman Ian Luder; John Hughesdon; Keith Brown; Michael Andre Zuckerman; Judge Brian John Barker; George Andrew Prescott; Graham Sutton; John Anthony Newton; Mr John Wilfred Spencer Clark; Mr Thomas Paul Hicks Godfrey; Vivian Bairstow; Bryan Scott Pickering; Dr Ian James Macaulay Frood; Richard Sibley; Roy Edward Campbell; Richard Robin Wilmington; Andrew William Behrens; Julian Day; Peregrine Antony Guy Bousfield.

CC Number: 234614

Eligibility

Members of the Coopers' Company, their widows and other dependents, who are in need.

Types of grants

Money can be given to supplement relief or assistance provided out of public funds, in the form of one-off grants and Christmas grants.

Annual grant total

In 2010/11 the fund had an income of £4,500 and a total expenditure of £2,300.

Exclusions

No funds are available for education.

Applications

In writing to the correspondent.

Corn exchange

The Bristol Corn Trade Guild

£6,000

Correspondent: R Cooksley, Portbury House, Sheepway, Portbury, Bristol BS20 7TE (01275 373539; fax: 01275 374747; email: cooksleyandco@btconnect.com)

Trustees: Mr A. C. Gullard; Mr G. B. Coombes; Dr B. C. Cooke; Mr B. J. P. Nutter; Mr C. A. Platt; Mr G. C. Seymour; Mr D. B. J. Jenkins; Mr

M. A. Spencer; Mr S. L. Fear; Tom Hart; Bill Harper; Paul Boulton; John Townend.

CC Number: 202404

Eligibility

People who work in the corn and feed trade, and their dependents, who are in need.

Types of grants

One-off grants ranging from £200 to £840. Recent grants have been given towards utility bills, medical equipment, repairs and as food vouchers.

Annual grant total

In 2010 the guild had an income of £5,700 and a total expenditure of £8,700.

Applications

In writing to the correspondent. Applications can be submitted directly by the individual or through a social worker, Citizens Advice or other welfare agency.

The Corn Exchange Benevolent Society

£28,000 (31 grants)

Correspondent: Richard Butler, 20 St Dunstan's Hill, London EC3R 8HL (020 7283 6090; email: richard.butler@baltic-charities.co.uk or jane.boyd@baltic-charities.co.uk; website: www.baltic-charities.co.uk)

Trustees: Jeremy Savage; Barry Rose; Peter Rawlinson; Ray Hayes; Nick Hayley; John Stokoe; Richard David Cooksley; James Stafford; Julian Walker.

CC Number: 207733

Eligibility

Members of the society and their dependents who are in need. Limited funds are also available for non-members who work or have been engaged in any aspect of grain trading in England and Wales (corn, grain, seed, animal feed stuffs, pulses, malt, flour or granary-keeping trades) and their dependents.

Types of grants

Quarterly grants are available to help towards day-to-day living costs. One-off grants are given for general household expenses, repairs, decorating materials, mobility aids, TV licences, winter fuel, respite care and special therapy. Christmas gifts are also made to all beneficiaries.

Annual grant total

In 2011 the society had assets of £2.8 million and an income of £89,000. Grants were made to 31 individuals totalling £28,000.

Applications

On a form available to download from the website or from the correspondent. Applications can be submitted directly by the individual or through a social worker, Citizens Advice or other welfare agency.

Customs and excise

The North West Customs and Excise Benevolent Society

£2,000

Correspondent: Brian Roberts, Fifth Floor West, Commercial Directorate, Ralli Quays, Stanley Street, Manchester M60 9LA (01618 270399; email: brian.roberts@hmrc.gsi.gov.uk)

Trustee: Brian Roberts.

CC Number: 225008

Eligibility

Serving or retired members of HM Revenue and Customs within the Merseyside area who are in need, and their dependents.

Types of grants

One-off grants according to need.

Annual grant total

Around £2,500 is usually available for grantmaking.

Applications

Potential applicants should contact the correspondent either in writing or by telephone.

Driving instructors

The Driving Instructors' Accident and Disability Fund

£120

Correspondent: Dean Scott Mayer, Trustee, Leon House, 233 High Street, Croydon CR0 9XT (0206868010)

Trustees: Dean Scott Mayer; Carly Lisa Brookfield.

CC Number: 328419

Eligibility

Driving instructors, former driving instructors and members of the Driving Instructors' Association who have been injured or disabled and their dependents.

Types of grants

One-off grants ranging from £150 to £250.

Annual grant total

Grants have averaged around £450 a year, though the actual grant figure tends to fluctuate quite widely.

Applications

In writing to the correspondent.

Electrical

Electrical and Electronics Industries' Benevolent Association

£403,000

Correspondent: Val Austin, EEIB Office 012, Orega Wandsworth, 1–9 Hardwicks Way, London SW18 4AW (020 7198 8453; email: welfare@eeiba.org; website: www.eeiba.org)

Trustees: Pauline Cooke; James A. I. Clarke McArthur; Dave Elliott; Ray Hall; Stewart Gregory; Jim Speirs; Charles Gordon; Ian Humphreys; Stuart Mackenzie; Rafe Bateson; Catherine Connolly; Paul Loke.

CC Number: 1012131

Eligibility

Employees and former employees of the UK electrical and electronic industries and allied sciences, including mechanical engineering, and their dependents. There are no age limits.

Types of grants

Grants are: 'To provide practical help and support in any form most appropriate to each individual applicant including one-off grants, ongoing budget balancing grants, clothing, house repairs (specific criteria), aids for disabled people, holidays, wheelchairs (specific criteria), television and telephone rental and so on.'

Annual grant total

In 2010/11 the association had assets of £4.8 million and an income of £1.6 million. Grants totalled £403,000.

Exclusions

Grants are not normally given to cover the costs of private medical care, educational fees, bankruptcy fees, nursing/residential fees or for headstones or funeral plaques.

Applications

On a form available from the trust's website or by contacting the trust by phone. They can be submitted directly by the individual or through a social worker, Citizens Advice, other welfare agency or a human resources department. They are considered throughout the year.

Other information

The association also runs a sheltered housing scheme in Sellyoak, Birmingham and provides welfare advice.

The Institution of Engineering and Technology Benevolent Fund (IET Connect)

£351,000

Correspondent: Casework Manager, IET Connect, 2 Savoy Place, London WC2R 0BL (0845 685 0685; email: ietconnect@theiet.org; website: www. ietconnect.org)

Trustees: George O'Neill; Dorothy Giles; Colin Porter; Peter Weaver; Colin Cunningham; Graham Patterson; Alan Stubbs; Dr Hanna Sykulska-Lawrence; Don Brown; Arlene Elizabeth McConnell.

CC Number: 208925

Eligibility

Members and former members, including those of the Institution of Electrical Engineering and the Institution of Engineering and Technology and their dependents.

Types of grants

Grants given include those for living costs, counselling, emergency needs, assistive technology, independence at home, care and disability, respite for carers, counselling, family support, help following a change of circumstances such as bereavement, relationship breakdown or redundancy. The fund is moving away from giving recurrent grants, as the latest accounts note:

> The preference is now to give a larger initial sum, where appropriate, to get the person or family 'back on their feet' and into a good position to resolve their personal situation and move forward.

Annual grant total

In 2010/11 the fund had assets of £19.6 million and an income of £1.4 million. Grants were made totalling £351,000.

While the fund's priorities are changing, in recent years over half of total expenditure has still been used to make regular grants to beneficiaries.

Applications

On a form available from the correspondent.

Other information

The fund has reformulated its policies and now support is viewed in a more holistic manner, as the 2010/11 accounts note:

> Previously we divided the welfare work of the Charity into distinct areas but what we have learnt is that many cases do not comfortably fit into one category – they frequently involve a number of areas such as advice, personal contact, financial assistance, disability, care or carer support. We offer a bespoke service so that every person who contacts us is treated as unique and we discuss with them their individual needs and wishes and arrive at a tailored response to help with their specific circumstances... While IET Connect will always provide financial help to members who need it, the emphasis is increasingly directed at offering preventative support.

The RTRA Benevolent Fund

£900

Correspondent: Jan Bray, Retra Ltd, 1 Ampthill Street, Bedford MK42 9EY (01234 269110; email: retra@retra.co.uk)

Trustees: Joseph Moran; John Barry Pattison; Sydney Smith; Robert Hughes; Bryan Lovewell; Shaun Barrett; Stephen Anthony Norman.

CC Number: 1002444

Eligibility

People in need who are directly connected with the electronic and electrical retailing industry.

Types of grants

One-off grants in the range of £250 to £1,000 to give short-term support to individuals in need.

Annual grant total

In 2010/11 the fund had an income of £4,400 and a total expenditure of £900.

Applications

In writing to the correspondent at any time. Applications should be submitted either directly by the individual or a family member, through an organisation such as a Citizens Advice or other welfare agency, or via a member of RTRA.

Engineering

The Chartered Institution of Building Services Engineers' Benevolent Fund

£42,000 (53 grants)

Correspondent: Stephen Matthews, CIBSE, 222 Balham High Road, London SW12 9BS (020 8675 5211; fax: 020 8673 3302; email: benfund@cibse.org; website: www.cibse.org)

Trustees: Ronald George Farminer; David Wood; Graham Manly; Colin Howlett; Chris Sealy; Mike Simpson; Nick Mead; Andrew Ramsay; Andy Ford.

CC Number: 1115871

Eligibility

Members and former members of the institution and their dependents (on death of member), who are in need.

Types of grants

Regular payments to supplement pensions and other income sources. One-off grants towards the cost of special equipment such as stair lifts or equipment which will enable the individual to work from home and major one-off bills such as essential repairs to the home. Help may also be given in the form of waived CIBSE subscriptions.

Annual grant total

In 2010 the trust held assets of £431,000 and had an income of £54,000. Grants to 53 individuals totalled £42,000.

Exclusions

Private health care or education.

Applications

In writing or by contacting the helpline. Applications can be submitted at any time either directly by the individual or through a social worker, Citizens Advice or other welfare agency. An almoner will visit the applicant to obtain details. Applications are considered on receipt.

The Worshipful Company of Engineers Charitable Trust Fund

£7,000

Correspondent: A G Willenbruch, Clerk, The Worshipful Company of Engineers, Wax Chandlers Hall, 6 Gresham Street, London EC2V 7AD (020 7726 4830; email: clerk@engineerscompany.org.uk; website: www.engineerscompany.org.uk)

CC Number: 289819

Eligibility

Engineers who are in need. Applicants do not necessarily have to be members of the Worshipful Company.

Types of grants

Grants of up to £1,000 for welfare purposes.

Annual grant total

In 2010/11 the trust had assets of £564,000 and an income of £54,000. Grants totalled £14,000 with a further £3,000 being spent on medals, prizes and associated costs.

Applications

In writing to the correspondent at any time providing as much detail about your circumstances as possible. Applications are considered throughout the year.

Other information

Grants are also made to organisations and individuals for educational purposes.

The Guild of Benevolence of The Institute of Marine Engineering Science and Technology

£180,000 (86 grants)

Correspondent: A D Muncer, Hon. Chairman, 33 Aldgate Street, London EC3N 1EN (020 7382 2638; fax: 020 7382 2670; email: guild@imarest.org; website: www.imarest.org/guild)

CC Number: 208727

Eligibility

Past and present members of the Institute and Guild, certified marine engineers, past and present employees of the Institute or Guild; and the dependents of the above.

Types of grants

Regular weekly grants of around £25 are given to supplement a low income. One-off grants, to a maximum of £4,000, are also available for disability aids, debt relief, reasonable nursing home fees, funeral costs, home maintenance and respite care. All regular beneficiaries receive a Christmas gift of £100.

Annual grant total

In 2010/11 the trust held assets of £524,000 and had an income of £109,000. Grants were made to 86 individuals totalling £180,000.

Exclusions

There are no grants for educational costs.

Applications

On a form available from the correspondent or to download from the website. Evidence of service or qualifications as a marine engineer must be produced if not already a member of the Institute of Marine Engineers, as well as full disclosure of financial situation. Applicants should expect a visit by a guild representative who will assess their needs and assist in completing the application form. Applications are considered every two months.

Other information

This trust was launched as a response to the sinking of the Titanic in 1912, a disaster which no marine engineer aboard survived. Since 1989 the guild has administered the Marine Engineers' Benevolent Fund. The guild also gives a grant to the Royal Merchant Navy School Foundation, towards the education of eligible dependents. It has close links with many service charities.

The Benevolent Fund of the Institution of Civil Engineers Ltd

£520,000

Correspondent: Kris Barnett, Chief Executive, 30 Mill Hill Close, Haywards Heath, West Sussex RH16 1NY (01444 417979; fax: 01444 453307; email: benfund@ice.org.uk; website: www.bfice. org.uk)

CC Number: 1126595

Eligibility

Past and present members of the institution, and their dependents in the UK and overseas. The dependents of former members of the Institution of Municipal Engineers.

Types of grants

One-off grants and loans towards: essential domestic appliances, furnishings, re-decorating and repairs to property; residential and nursing home care; building and contents insurance; aids, adaptations and equipment to promote independence; respite care and holidays; and Christmas and Easter gifts. Monthly payments may be made to those on very low incomes.

A small number of grants are also available to student members of the fund to help with living costs and course materials.

Annual grant total

In 2011 the fund had assets of £13 million and an income of £904,000. Grants were made to 195 individuals totalling £532,000, most of which was for welfare purposes. 177 beneficiaries were in the UK and 18 overseas.

Applications

On a form available from the correspondent. Applications can be submitted directly by the individual or through a social worker, Citizens Advice or other welfare agency, or through a close relative, solicitor or similar third party. They should include information about the individual's income, expenditure and capital and can be submitted at any time. Most applicants will be visited by one of the fund's volunteer visitors.

Other information

The fund owns properties in West Sussex and has nomination rights to the Hanover Housing Association which it uses to help (ex-)members and their families who are facing difficult circumstances and need somewhere to live.

It also runs a 24-hour helpline (0800 587 3428) which offers support and advice on a wide range of issues including, stress management, debt problems, childcare and substance abuse.

The Benevolent Fund of the Institution of Mechanical Engineers (IMechE)

£350,000

Correspondent: Maureen Hayes, Casework and Support Officer, 3 Birdcage Walk, Westminster, London SW1H 9JJ (020 7304 6816; fax: 020 7973 1262; email: info@supportnetwork.org. uk; website: www.supportnetwork.org. uk)

CC Number: 209465

Eligibility

Past and present members of the institution, and their dependents, who are in need. Former members must have paid subscription fees for at least five years. Priority is given to those on low incomes who qualify for means-tested state benefits.

Types of grants

One-off grants and loans are available towards a variety of needs, including house repairs and adaptations, medical equipment, domestic appliances, beds and bedding, furniture, respite care, holidays and carer's breaks. Recurrent grants are also available to help with living expenses.

Annual grant total

In 2011 the fund had assets of £16 million and an income of £860,000. Grants to 224 individuals totalled £394,000, mostly for welfare purposes.

Exclusions

No grants are given for school fees, business ventures, private medical treatment or the payment of debts.

Applications

Applicants should first contact the fund, by phone, letter, email or fax. If they are eligible they will be asked to complete an application form and meet with one of the fund's volunteer visitors. Applications are considered by the grants committee every two months.

Other information

The support network offers a range of support and advice services which also includes student grants, sheltered housing and residential care, help with job seeking and telephone helplines. Visit the website to find out more.

The Institution of Plant Engineers Benevolent Fund

£13,000

Correspondent: Grants Administrator, 22 Greencoat Place, London SW1P 1DX (020 7630 1111)

Trustees: Ronald Henry Dunnett; John Collins; Malcolm James Studholme; Brian Cooke; Arthur Hills; Frances David Chapman; Ian Ling.

CC Number: 260934

Eligibility

Members/former members of the institution, and their dependents living in England, Scotland and Wales.

Types of grants

One-off grants according to need. Most grants are given to people who are financially stressed through serious illness, unemployment or bereavement. For example, support for a young member no longer able to work due to multiple sclerosis.

Annual grant total

In 2010 the fund had a total income and expenditure of £14,500.

Applications

In writing to the correspondent. Applications can be submitted directly by the individual or by a relative or close friend. They are considered in March, July and November.

The ISTRUCTE (Institution of Structural Engineers') Fund

£69,000 (23 grants)

Correspondent: Dr Susan Doran, Secretary, 11 Upper Belgrave Street, London SW1X 8BH (020 7235 4535; fax: 020 7235 4294; email: benfund@istructe.org; website: www.istructe.org)

Trustees: Dr J. M. Roberts; J. M. Allen; S. M. Craddy; A. L. Gilbertson; J. D. Parsons; D. Stevenson; G. Watts; I. G. Hill; M. Ryland.

CC Number: 1049171

Eligibility

Members of the institution and their dependents who are in financial difficulties due to circumstances such as: unemployment; illness, accident or disability; family problems; difficulties during retirement; or bereavement.

Types of grants

One-off and recurrent grants and loans up to a maximum of £10,000 per year towards, for example, home repairs, household equipment, property adaptations, disability equipment, carers' breaks and daily living costs for those on very modest incomes.

Annual grant total

In 2011 the fund had assets of £1.7 million and an income of £113,000. Grants were made to 23 individuals totalling £69,000.

Exclusions

No grants for private health care. If the fund settles debts for a beneficiary, it will not usually pay any subsequent debts. The fund will not normally help members' children over the age of 21.

Applications

On a form available by emailing the correspondent which can be submitted by the individual or an appropriate third party. The trust likes to visit applicants before any grant is made.

NB. In cases of genuine emergency, the fund can pay up to £500, as a loan, normally within days.

The Matthew Hall Staff Trust Fund

£164,000 (170 grants)

Correspondent: Mrs P R Pritchard, AMEC, Booths Hall, Chelford Road, Knutsford WA16 8QZ (01565 683281)

Trustees: Alan Brown; Anthony Frank Millen; David Philip Mardinor Harris; Grant Richmond Ling.

CC Number: 1019896

Eligibility

Former employees of Matthew Hall (1992) plc may apply for grants if they are in financial hardship and only when they have reached the age of 65. Applicants must have been employed by Matthew Hall (1992) plc for at least five years.

Types of grants

One-off and recurrent grants according to need.

Annual grant total

In 2010/11 the fund had assets of £2.3 million and an income of £57,000. Grants were made to 170 former employees totalling £164,000.

Applications

In writing to the correspondent. Trustees meet at least twice a year, normally in July and December to consider applications.

Royal Engineers' Association

£559,000

Correspondent: Lt Col John McLennan, Brompton Barracks, Dock Road, Chatham, Kent ME4 4UG (01634 822982; fax: 01634 822394; email: benevolence@reahq.org.uk; website: www.reahq.org.uk)

Trustees: Lt Cnl Nat Parmley; Lt Col Robert Murfin; Gen Sir Peter Wall; Maj. Gen John Moore-Bick; Brig Andy Craig; Roger Hunt; Thomas Hartley; Mike Barry; Bob Prosser; Col Sean Harris; Brig Steve Hodder; Gerry Walsh; Barry Heyes; Cnl Michael Gill; Freddie Ford; Roger Price; Maj Ron MacGregor; Cap Graham Littleford; Brig Ian James; Barry Owens; Jason Blaylock.

CC Number: 258322

Eligibility

Past or present members of the corps, and their dependents, who are in need.

Types of grants

One-off and recurrent grants. Grants are given for a wide range of purposes including mobility aids and walk-in showers. Regular weekly allowances are made to around 140 people and Christmas cards and monetary gifts are sent out in November to around 1,200 people who are resident in elderly people's homes, hospitals and homes for the mentally infirm and to those in receipt of weekly pensions. Annuities for top-up fees for nursing homes are given in exceptional circumstances.

Annual grant total

In 2010 the association had assets of £9.2 million and an income of £1 million. Grants were made to nearly 1,000 individuals totalling £559,000 and were distributed as follows:

Grants	£425,000
Christmas Grants	£31,000
Weekly Allowances	£104,000

Exclusions

No grants for private education, private medical fees, court or legal fees or debts.

Applications

On a form available from the correspondent, to be submitted through SSAFA or The Royal British Legion. Applications for less than £500 will be considered at any time, while cases requiring over £500 are considered at monthly committee meetings.

Other information

Grants are also made to other affiliated charities, for example in 2010 the Army Benevolent Fund (£35,000) and SSAFA Families Help (£7,500) received donations.

Environmental health

Environmental Health Officers Welfare Fund

£7,800

Correspondent: Andrew Gardner, Chadwick Court, 15 Hatfields, London SE1 8DJ (020 7827 5803; fax: 020 7827 5866; email: membership@cieh.org; website: www.cieh.org)

Trustees: John Bryson; Janet Szlamp; Mark Elliott; Alan Higgins; Peter Archer; Steven Bidwell; Steven Cooper; Kendal Davies; Tim Deveaux; John Freear; Steve Miller; Les Milne; Andy Statham; Rosemary Lee; Roger Wastnedge; David Purchon; David Williams; Bob Foster; Keith Moles; Dr Stephen Battersby; Peter Kemp; Michael Parkes; Stuart Taylor;

Tom Crossan; Roger Braithwaite; Stephen Browne; Patrick Mackie; Andrew Mathieson; Claire Turbutt.

CC Number: 224343

Eligibility

Past and present members of Chartered Institute of Environmental Health Officers, Association of Public Health Inspectors or The Guild of Public Health Inspection and their dependents, who are in need.

Types of grants

One-off and recurrent grants according to need.

Annual grant total

In 2010 the fund had an income of £20,000 and made grants totalling £7,800.

Applications

Initial enquiries should be made by telephone or through the contact form on the CIEH website. Applications should then be forwarded through the regional or branch secretary.

Estate workers

Midhurst Pensions Trust

£37,000

Correspondent: Laura Gosling, 4th Floor, Swan House, 17–19 Stratford Place, London W1C 1BQ (020 7907 2100; email: charity@mfs.co.uk)

Trustees: The Cowdray Trust Ltd; Rathbone Trust Company Ltd.

CC Number: 245230

Eligibility

People in need who have been employed by the Third Viscount Cowdray, Lady Anne Cowdray, any family company or on the Cowdray Estate, and their dependents.

Types of grants

One-off grants usually in the range of £25 to £2,000.

Annual grant total

In 2010/11 the trust held assets of £4.1 million and had an income of £74,000. Grants to pensioners totalled £37,000.

Applications

In writing to the correspondent.

Other information

Grants are also made to organisations with one payment of £103,000 made in 2010/11.

Farriers

The Worshipful Company of Farriers Charitable Trust

£2,400

Correspondent: The Clerk, 19 Queen Street, Chipperfield, Kings Langley, Hertfordshire WD4 9BT (01923 260747; fax: 01923 261677; email: theclerk@wcf.org.uk; website: www.wcf.org.uk/charity)

Trustee: The Worshipful Company of Farriers.

CC Number: 1044726

Eligibility

Registered farriers, their widows and dependents who are in need.

Types of grants

One-off and recurrent grants according to need. Grants are usually given to people who are unable to work through injury or sickness.

Annual grant total

In 2010/11 the trust had assets of £1.4 million and an income of £54,000. Grants were made to individuals totalling £2,400.

Applications

In writing to the correspondent. Applications are considered eight times a year.

Fire service

The British Fire Services Association Member's Fund

£14,000

Correspondent: David Stevens, Secretary and Treasurer, 9 Brooksfield, South Kirkby, Pontefract, West Yorkshire WF9 3DL (01977 650245; email: welfare.bfsa@btinternet.com)

Trustees: Mr G. Halstead; Mr Peter William Thomas Mills; Raymond Walter Leather; Brian Sidney Wood; Vernon Fisher.

CC Number: 216011

Eligibility

Fire-fighters and ex-fire-fighters who have held BFSA membership, and their dependents.

Types of grants

One-off grants according to need. It assists with one-off hardship grants, mobility aids, furniture, domestic appliances, emergency property repairs, convalescence and travel costs.

Annual grant total

In 2010 the fund had an income of £24,000 and total expenditure of £30,000.

Applications

In writing to the correspondent, including details of income and expenditure and a record of fire service employment. Applicants are usually visited at home by a representative of the fund to assess their needs.

The Fire Fighters Charity

£189,000 (660 grants)

Trustees: Kenneth Edward Seager; Michael Anthony Brown; Peter Craig; Michael James Rich; Andrew John Goves; Helen Victoria Hogg; Howard Robinson; Mark Stewart Jones; Ann Margaret Millington; Robert Dickson Scott; Lynne Marie Swift; Andrew Lynch; Paul Alexander Whelch.

CC Number: 1093387

Eligibility

Serving and retired fire service fire-fighters (having served five years, made redundant after two years or been medically discharged), non-uniformed fire service personnel, retained and works fire-fighters, current and former (with at least five years service, or retired on the grounds of illness or injury) employees of the charity and dependents of the above categories (including widows and widowers). The charity has defined eligibility criteria for each of these categories.

Types of grants

The charity looks to assist its beneficiaries by providing practical solutions to meet beneficiary need. The majority of these solutions are one-off and the type of solution can vary depending on the need, in some cases this may be a monetary solution in the form of a grant or the charity may assist practically by purchasing the solution (for example equipment or home adaptations that are required due to disability/ill health). Assessments are made under either a health or general category and the cost of the solution can vary according to the needs of the beneficiary.

Annual grant total

In 2010/11 the charity made 660 grants to individuals totalling £189,000. Of these, 348 were one-off payments and the remaining 312 were continuing support payments.

Exclusions

The charity cannot finance private medical care, pay off debts or cover funeral or repatriation costs. The charity does not provide loans to beneficiaries, pay university/educational fees or residential care nursing fees. Statutory provision must be exhausted in the first instance.

Applications

Initial contact should be through the helpline but requests for assistance can be made by email or in writing. Initial assessment is made on the helpline and if the beneficiary cannot be helped through advice then a referral is made to beneficiary support coordinator who may arrange a home visit. Home visits may be required to assess individual circumstances. A financial assessment may also need to be carried out as part of the application process.

Other information

The charity has been reformulating its approach to helping individuals. The 2010/11 accounts note: 'Over recent years the charity has sought to move away from making grants and the level of assistance in this manner has now substantially reduced. This has taken place alongside the introduction of the beneficiary support services. The grant application process has now ceased, however, a small number of beneficiaries will require ongoing support from grants, but this is now administered through the beneficiary support services.'

The charity also runs rehabilitation and recuperation programmes at various residential sites.

Food, drink and provision trades

The Bakers' Benevolent Society

£11,000

Correspondent: Suzanne Pitts, Clerk to the Society, The Mill House, 23 Bakers Lane, Epping, Essex CM16 5DQ (01992 575951; fax: 01992 561163; email: bbs@bakersbenevolent.co.uk; website: www.bakersbenevolent.co.uk)

Trustees: Andrew Manzie; Anthony Slingsby; Dennis Hume; Graham Harris; Jose Meehan; Marshall Pennington; Maureen Scott; Anthony Greenwood; Peter Meadows; Dee Cassey; Jackie

Springett; Christopher Beaney; Christopher Tomkins.

CC Number: 211307

Eligibility

People in need who have worked in the baking industry and its allied trades and are now retired, and their dependents.

Types of grants

Recurrent grants to top-up a low income. One-off grants are also available towards essential items such as, mobility aids, lifelines and telephone rental.

Annual grant total

In 2010/11 the society had assets of £1.4 million and an income of £369,000. Pensions and grants to individuals totalled £11,000.

Applications

On a form available from the correspondent to be submitted either directly by the individual or a family member or through an appropriate welfare agency. Applications should include details of occupational history, age and financial circumstances. Applications are considered upon receipt.

Other information

The society also manages almshouses and sheltered housing in Congleton and Epping.

Barham Benevolent Foundation

£20,500 (27 grants)

Correspondent: Michael Cook, Hobson and Arditti, 1st Floor Holborn Gate, 330 High Holborn, London WC1V 7QT (020 7203 8299)

Trustees: Michael Geoffrey Cook; Graham L. Flight.

CC Number: 249922

Eligibility

People who have been employed in the dairy business, and possibly their dependents, who are in need.

Types of grants

One-off grants according to need. In some circumstances the foundation will provide holiday accommodation in Southsea for employees, their close relations and former employees of the milk business.

Annual grant total

In 2010/11 the foundation held assets of £4.3 million and had an income of £128,000. Grants to 27 individuals totalled £20,500.

Applications

In writing to the correspondent.

Other information

Bursaries are also made available for the benefit of eligible students who study dairy related subjects.

The Butchers' and Drovers' Charitable Institution

£220,000 (90 grants)

Correspondent: The Clerk to the Trustees, Butchers' and Drovers' Charitable Institution, 105 St Peter's Street, St Albans, Hertfordshire AL1 3EJ (01727 896094; fax: 01727 896026; email: info@bdci.uk.com; website: www.bdci.uk.com)

Trustees: Graham Sharp; Ian Kelly; Hylton Christian Oberst; Andrew Richard Garvey; Colin Charles Lambert Taylor; Kenneth Frank Charles Wakelin; Peter Christopher Frederick Imison; Peter Frank Godfrey; Susan White; Graham Philip Yandell; Dennis Leslie Clark; Richard Cracknell; Derek Howard-Budd; Anne Haigh; Christine Taylor; Frederick William A'Court; Derek William Berry; Miles Ivor Levy; Edward Ernest Price; Edward Hoefling; Alan Jennings; Ed Bedington.

CC Number: 296990

Eligibility

People in the UK, who have worked in any aspect of the meat industry whether wholesale, retail or otherwise, and their close family members.

Types of grants

Pensions, one-off grants and loans. The average value of one-off grants in 2010 was £870, these are made towards heating bills, mobility aids, white goods, house repairs and clothing. Grants of up to £50 a week are made to top up nursing home fees.

Annual grant total

In 2010 the trust had assets of £9.2 million and an income of £817,000. Grants were made to individuals totalling £220,000, which included pensions, one-off grants and assistance towards the cost of nursing fees.

Applications

On a form available from the correspondent or to download from the website. Applications can be submitted directly by the individual or through a social worker, Citizens Advice, other welfare agency or third party and are considered on a regular basis.

Preference is given to applications which provide details of meat trade connections, verified in writing by existing meat traders or by production of other documentation.

The Fishmongers' and Poulterers' Institution

£26,000

Correspondent: Roy Sully, Secretary, Butchers' Hall, 87–88 Bartholomew Close, London EC1A 7EB (020 7600 4106; fax: 020 7606 4108; email: fpi@butchershall.com; website: www.butchershall.com)

Trustees: Charles Caisey; Tim Silverthorne; Mr F. M. Everard; David Butcher; Richard Link; Helen Leftwich.

CC Number: 209013

Eligibility

People in need who are, or have been, involved in the processing, wholesale and retail fish and poultry trades for at least ten years, and their dependents.

Types of grants

Pensions and one-off grants. Grants average about £250 and have been given for mobility aids, respite holidays, property repairs and heating systems.

Annual grant total

In 2010 the institution had assets of £534,000 and an income of £25,000. Grants were made totalling £26,000, of which £22,000 was given in pensions and the remaining £4,000 was distributed in one-off grants.

Applications

On a form available from the correspondent. Applications can be submitted directly by the individual or through a third party. They are considered three times a year.

Sir Percival Griffiths' Tea Planters Trust

£10,000

Correspondent: Stephen Buckland, Trustee, Duncan Lawrie Ltd, Wrotham Place, High Street, Wrotham, Sevenoaks, Kent TN15 7AE (020 7201 3065)

Trustees: Gillem Sandys-Lumsdaine; Donald Clive Roberson.

CC Number: 253904

Eligibility

People who live in the UK who are or have been involved in tea planting in India and their dependents.

Types of grants

One-off and recurrent grants of up to £3,000 to help with general living expenses. One-off grants include those for assistance with medical equipment, electrical goods and so on.

Annual grant total

In 2010 the charity had an income of £4,000 and a total expenditure of £11,000.

Applications

On a form available from the correspondent including details of career in India (dates, tea garden and so on). Applications can be submitted directly by the individual, through a social worker, Citizens Advice, welfare agency, or third party and are considered at any time.

GroceryAid

£2.1 million

Correspondent: Gillian Barker, Director General, Unit 2, Lakeside Business Park, Swan Lane, Sandhurst, Berkshire GU47 9DN (01252 875925; fax: 01252 890562; email: info@groceryaid.org.uk; website: www.groceryaid.org.uk)

Trustees: Tony Smith; Tony Paine; Nigel Matthews; Bart Dalla Mura; Judith Batchelar; David Hudson; John Black; Ruston Smith; Geraldine Huse; Zameer Choudrey.

CC Number: 1095897

Eligibility

To qualify for assistance applicants must:

▷ Have worked for a minimum of ten years in the UK grocery industry (including food manufacturing, wholesaling and retailing in all its aspects and the retail off-licence trade)

▷ Have no more than £12,000 in savings/capital (excluding property)

▷ Be able to demonstrate a degree of financial hardship

Full-time and part-time workers are eligible and the grant can transfer to spouses or long-term partners in the event of the beneficiary's death. The charity also note that: 'For those in the industry who have worked for some time but perhaps not quite long enough to qualify for our ongoing support, or who do not qualify within our financial parameters, we are sometimes able to provide one-off grants. These applications are judged on their own individual merit.'

Types of grants

Annual grants of £830, paid quarterly (roughly £16 per week). Grants are also provided for one-off items such as white goods, telephones, telephone response systems, televisions and mobility equipment. Emergency grants for specific financial problems such as house repairs, boiler replacement and household equipment are also available.

Annual grant total

In 2011/12 the charity had assets of £9 million and a consolidated income of £5 million. Quarterly grants were made totalling £1.6 million. A further £510,000 was spent on providing goods and services which can be broken down as follows:

Christmas 'virtual hampers'	£117,000
Emergency assistance	£111,000
Basic essentials	£106,000
One-off payments	£104,000
Mobility	£63,000
Telephone response systems	£8,500

Applications

On a form available from the correspondent or to download from the website. Applications can be submitted directly by the individual, through a social worker, Citizens Advice, other welfare agency, or via a third party such as a relative. Applications are considered throughout the year. Applicants will be visited if possible by a welfare assessor who will carry out a more detailed assessment of their needs.

Other information

In February 2012 Caravan and the Sweet Charity, the charity for the confectionary trade, merged to form GroceryAid.

A helpline is also operated for all staff from the grocery industry, whether or not they are eligible for financial help from the charity.

The Benevolent Society of the Licensed Trade of Scotland

£128,000

Correspondent: Chris Gardner, Chief Executive, 79 West Regent Street, Glasgow G2 2AW (01413 533596; fax: 01413 533597; email: chris@bensoc.org. uk; website: www.bensoc.org.uk)

SC Number: SC005604

Eligibility

Members of the society and people who have been employed full time in the licensed trade in Scotland for at least three years.

Types of grants

Annual pensions of up to £640. Each pensioner also receives a substantial Christmas and holiday gift. One-off grants are also available for temporary emergencies.

Annual grant total

In 2010/11 the society had an income of £533,000. Grants totalled £128,000.

Applications

On a form available from the correspondent or to download from the website. Applications can be made directly by the individual or through a social worker, Citizens Advice or other welfare agency. Volunteers can visit the applicant to assist with the application if necessary.

Licensed Trade Support and Care

£536,000

Correspondent: Head of Welfare, Heatherley, London Road, Ascot, Berkshire SL5 8DR (01344 898550; fax: 01344 884703; email: support@ supportandcare.org.uk; website: www. supportandcare.org.uk)

Trustees: Eric Morgan; Maureen Batty; Anita Adams; Bernard Brindley; John Andrews; Anita Law; Ray Batty; Ray Russell; A. King; Jeff Booth; Anthony Mears; Ian Inder; Sarah Marjason; Pauline Ross; William Boulter.

CC Number: 230011

Eligibility

People in need who are working, or have worked, in the licensed drinks industry, including their spouses/partners and dependent children. To qualify for assistance applicants should have worked in the trade for a minimum of five years continuously at some time in their working lives.

Types of grants

Recurrent grants are given to those on a very low income to help with utility bills, food costs and hospital travel expenses. One-off grants are also made towards: urgently needed equipment, such as household appliances and mobility aids; household improvements like door widening, stair-lifts and ramps; convalescent care and nursing costs for those recovering from illness; winter fuel grants and funeral expenses.

Annual grant total

In 2011 the charity had assets of £49 million and an income of £17 million. Welfare grants to individuals totalled £536,000.

Exclusions

No grants for: education related costs such as fees for educational courses, student maintenance, and student loan repayments; top up fees for residential care; or private medical treatments.

Applications

On a form available to download from the website, including proof of employment, personal details, personal history and full financial circumstances. Applications can be submitted either directly by the individual or through a social worker, Citizens Advice or other welfare agency. Enquiries about the application process are welcome and if necessary a volunteer may visit the applicant to help complete the application.

Other information

The charity also operates two schools in Brighton and Ascot and offers bursaries to students whose parents have worked in the licensed drinks industry amounting to around £719,000 in 2011.

The National Association of Master Bakers, Confectioners and Caterers Benevolent Fund

£10,000

Correspondent: The Secretary, 21 Baldock Street, Ware, Hertfordshire SG12 9DH (01920 468061; email: namb@masterbakers.co.uk; website: www.masterbakers.co.uk)

Trustees: Peter Jan Lonican; Graham Roy Nash; Mark Bernard Connor; Neil MacSymons; Michael Holling.

CC Number: 206691

Eligibility

Former master bakers and their families who are in need.

Types of grants

Quarterly grants to help towards living costs such as gas, electricity and telephone bills. One-off grants are also available for specific items such as wheelchairs and household adaptations.

Annual grant total

In 2011 the fund had an income of £17,000 and a total expenditure of £13,000.

Exclusions

No grants are given for business debt or towards nursing home fees.

Applications

On a form available from the correspondent, to be submitted by the individual or through a recognised referral agency such as a social worker, Citizens Advice or doctor. Applications are usually considered on a monthly basis.

The National Federation of Fish Friers Benevolent Fund

£2,500

Correspondent: The General Secretary, New Federation House, 4 Greenwood Mount, Meanwood, Leeds LS6 4LQ (01132 307044; fax: 01132 307010; email:

mail@federationoffishfriers.co.uk;
website: www.federationoffishfriers.co.
uk)

Trustees: Gregg Howard; Mark Gavin
Drummond; Andrew Stephen Crook.

CC Number: 229168

Eligibility

Members or former members of the
federation and their dependents
(whether subscribers to the fund or not).

Types of grants

One-off grants in the range of £150 to
£300 for necessities and convalescent
holidays in the UK.

Annual grant total

Grants average about £3,000 a year,
though the actual grant figure tends to
fluctuate quite widely.

Exclusions

No grants are available for debts due to
poor business practice or to
organisations.

Applications

On a form available from the
correspondent. Applications can be
submitted by the individual, through a
recognised referral agency (such as a
social worker, Citizens Advice or AFF
Associations/branches) or by the
individual's family, and are considered
throughout the year.

Other information

The fund maintains several convalescent
homes.

The Provision Trade Charity

£39,000

Correspondent: Mette Barwick,
Secretary, 17 Clerkenwell Green, London
EC1R 0DP (020 7253 2114; fax: 020 7608
1645; email: secretary@ptbi.org.uk;
website: www.ptbi.org.uk)

Trustees: Charles Richard Stephen Link;
David Edwards; Alex Knight; Derek
Mackay; Jozef Ashley Eilers; Mike
Donovan; Sarah Elizabeth Hubbard;
William Francis Bowes; Lin Adams;
Derek Mersh; Tony Staunton; John
Brooks.

CC Number: 209173

Eligibility

People in need in the provision and
allied trade, and their dependents.
Applicants are normally retired and must
have been employed in the trade for at
least ten years.

The provision trade covers the following
sectors: Bacon, pork, canned meat/fish
and dairy products.

Types of grants

Recurrent grants are issued quarterly.
Summer and winter gifts and one-off
grants can also be awarded where
appropriate. One-off grants may also be
issued to assist with special purchases or
home improvements.

Annual grant total

In 2010 the charity had assets of
£726,000 and an income of £65,000.
Grants totalled £39,000.

Exclusions

The charity does not provide loans.

Applications

On a form which can be downloaded
from the website. Applications may be
returned by email or post. Applications
are usually considered in February, May,
August and November. They can be
submitted directly by the individual or
through a social worker, Citizens Advice,
other welfare agency or through a
relation or friend. Prospective
beneficiaries are visited by the trust's
welfare visitor.

Other information

This trust was founded as the
Cheesemonger's Benevolent Institution
in 1835 'for pensionary relief of indigent
or incapacitated members of the
Provision Trade and their widows'. The
trust is also referred to as 'PTBI'.

The Wine and Spirits Trades' Benevolent Society

£340,000 (552 grants)

Correspondent: Paul Newman, Chief
Executive, 39–45 Bermondsey Street,
London SE1 3XF (020 7089 3888; fax:
020 7089 3889; email: paul.newman@
thebenevolent.org.uk; website: www.the
benevolent.org.uk)

Trustees: Andrew Laurence Reed;
Anthony Francis Dee; Christopher
Carson; Christopher Charles Porter;
Christopher Wesley Mason; Robert
Vivian Lawson Rishworth; Anthony
Christopher Mair; John Edward Dudley
Smith; Philip Duggan; Simon Thomas;
Edward Dove; James Rackham; Pam
Rowan.

CC Number: 1023376

Eligibility

People living in England, Northern
Ireland or Wales who have worked for
more than five years, directly or
indirectly, in the buying, selling,
producing or distributing of wines and
spirits, and their dependents.

Types of grants

Regular beneficial grants towards general
living expenses of up to £65 paid
monthly and one-off grants of up to
£250 for a variety of items, including
cookers, fridges, other household
furniture, structural repairs, respite
breaks, electric scooters and stairlifts.
The society also makes Christmas gift
donations and gives grants towards TV
licence fees.

Annual grant total

In 2011 the society had assets of
£4 million and an income of
£1.1 million. Grants to individuals
totalled £340,000 and were broken down
as follows:

Beneficial grants	375	£292,000
Discretionary grants	118	£39,000
TV License scheme	59	£8,500

Exclusions

No grants are given towards business
equipment.

Applications

On a form available from the
correspondent. Applications can be
submitted directly by the individual, or
through a social worker or welfare
agency. They are considered throughout
the year and should include history of
employment within the drinks industry.
All new beneficiaries are visited by the
society's welfare officer before a regular
donation is made.

Other information

The society, formerly known as 'The
Wine and Spirits Trades' Benevolent
Society', also has two residential estates
and a care home and offers personal
welfare support and advice.

The Wine Trade Foundation

£5,000

Correspondent: Michael Hasslacher,
Trustee, Broomwood, Kettlewell Hill,
Woking, Surrey GU21 4JJ (01483
761129)

Trustees: Simon Leschallas; Edward
Demery.

CC Number: 266121

Eligibility

People in need who are or were
employed in the wine and spirit and
ancillary trades in the UK and Republic
of Ireland, and their dependents.

Types of grants

One-off grants for the general relief of
poverty.

Annual grant total

In 2010 the trust had an income of £9,400 and a total expenditure of £11,000.

Applications

In writing to the correspondent, preferably submitted directly by the individual. Applications are considered throughout the year.

Other information

Grants are also made to the Wine and Spirits Trades' Benevolent Society.

Fur

Fur Trade Benevolent Society

£5,000

Correspondent: Mrs E Lockyer, Brookstone House, 6 Elthorne Road, London N19 4AG (email: info@ britishfur.co.uk)

Eligibility

People in need who have worked in the fur industry in the UK and their dependents.

Types of grants

One-off grants according to need.

Annual grant total

Around £5,000 a year.

Exclusions

No loans are made.

Applications

In writing to the correspondent directly by the individual, with information about the type of grant being requested and an outline of the applicant's employment in the fur trade. Applications are usually considered within a month.

Furnishing trade

The Furniture Makers

£148,000 (280 grants)

Correspondent: Welfare Officer, Furniture Makers' Hall, 12 Austin Friars, London EC2N 2HE (020 7256 5954; fax: 020 7256 5155; email: welfare@ furnituremakers.org.uk; website: www. ftba.co.uk)

Trustees: Peter Oldfield Murray; Clive Nicholson Thirkell; Edward Randolph Tadros; Penelope Janet Wendy Victoria Williams; Peter Douglas Spinks; Shaun

Lewis; Tony Attard; Andrew Richard Vaughan; Charles Patrick George Annable; Nigel Malcolm Anthony Blake; Margaret Mary Miller; Adrian Sell; Theresa Raymond; Lotta Sjoblom.

CC Number: 1015519

Eligibility

Current and former employees of the furnishing industry and their dependents who are in financial need. Applicants must have worked in the industry for a minimum of two years.

Types of grants

One-off grants averaging around £350 to help towards the purchase of scooters, recliner chairs, TV licences, the installation of walk-in showers, central heating and telephone lines. Help is also given towards the payment of rent arrears, interior decorating costs and holidays. Weekly grants given to those struggling to live on state pension benefits.

The Edenfield Holiday Scheme enables beneficiaries with ten years' experience in the industry to take respite breaks or holidays.

Annual grant total

In 2010, the most recent year for which accounts were available at the time of writing (winter 2012); the association had assets of £6.3 million and an income of £274,000. Grants were made totalling £148,000, with £114,000 paid in weekly grants, £30,000 paid in one-off grants and £4,000 paid towards the Edenfield Holiday Scheme.

Applications

Initial enquiries should be made by telephoning or emailing the grants and welfare team.

Other information

In February 2012 the Furnishing Industry Trust and the charity of the Furniture Makers Company merged to form the Furniture Makers.

Gas engineering

The Institution of Gas Engineers Benevolent Fund

£1,500

Correspondent: Lesley Ecob, IGEM Secretariat, IGEM House, High Street, Kegworth, Derbyshire DE74 2DA (01509 678167; email: lesley@igem.org.uk; website: www.igem.org.uk)

Trustees: D. Morgan; G. Davies; E. Swindells; C. Taylor; G. Davies; S. Course; D. Cummings; N. Dalley; L. Ecob; R. Murray; R. Armstrong; G. Ng; M. Tonry; P. Brown; S. Mistry; G. Judge; E. Muriithi; D. Wasson; D. Anderson.

CC Number: 214010

Eligibility

Members and ex-members of the Institution of Gas Engineers, and their dependents. Note that other people in the gas industry who have no such connection with the institution are not eligible.

Types of grants

One-off and recurrent grants according to need.

Annual grant total

In 2010 the trust had an income of £11,000 and a total expenditure of £6,000. Grants were made to individuals totalling £3,000.

Applications

In writing to the correspondent.

Hairdressing

The Barbers' Amalgamated Charity

£12,000

Correspondent: Colonel P J Durrant, The Worshipful Company of Barbers, Barber-Surgeons' Hall, 1A Monkwell Square, Wood Street, London EC2Y 5BL (020 7606 0741; fax: 020 7606 3857; email: clerk@barberscompany.org; website: www.barberscompany.org)

Trustees: Roger Pincham; Sir Barry Jackson; Sir John Chalstrey; Lord McColl; Francis Read; Mr J. T. Bach; Prof. John William Last; Adam Anthony Murless Lewis; Chris Sprague; George Grant MacDonald; Howell M. Harris Hughes; Prof. John C. Buckland-Wright; Robin R. C. Bloomfield; Ronald Simmons; William Stewart Shand; Jeremy S. Bolton; Bruce Winston Cope; Jonathan Neil Rounce; Lord Ribeiro of Achimota and Ovigton; Prof. James Patrick Carley; Roger Vickers; Geoffrey Robert Preston; Anthony E. Hoskinson; Dr Timothy Patrick Cutler.

CC Number: 213085

Eligibility

Poor, generally older, members of the medical, barber or hairdressing professions.

Types of grants

Annual pensions to those in need.

Annual grant total

In 2010/11 the charity had an income of £17,000 and a total expenditure of £14,000.

Applications

In writing to the correspondent directly by the individual or via a family member, or through an organisation such as a Citizens Advice or other welfare agency. Applications are considered throughout the year.

Hair and Beauty Benevolent

£100,000

Correspondent: Secretary, 11 The Leys, Chesham Bois, Amersham, Bucks HP6 5NP (01494 729358; email: info@ habb.org; website: www.habb.org)

Eligibility

Members and former members of the hairdressing and beauty industries and their dependents.

Types of grants

One-off and recurrent grants to those in need. Grants have been made for house adaptations, mobility aids, TV licences and holidays. In some cases regular financial assistance may be given.

The HABB children's welfare fund also provides one-off and recurrent grants. Grants have been made for monthly pocket money to children from low-income families as well as one-off grants for specialist equipment, holidays, school uniforms, bedding and Christmas/birthday payments.

Annual grant total

The fund is not registered with the Charity Commission and so limited financial information was available. The website notes that the fund needs '£150,000 a year to meet our existing commitments to beneficiaries and to take new requests for assistance on board.' Grants are likely, therefore, to total around £100,000.

Exclusions

No assistance with non-priority debts or bankruptcy fees. The trust cannot help those who have not worked in the profession since 1970.

Applications

In writing, by email or by telephoning the fund. In order to process your application HABB will need to know: what help you need, why you need the help, your length of involvement in the industry and when you last worked in the industry. If it was a partner of yours who worked in the industry, you should provide the same information on them. After this initial enquiry if you are eligible for assistance HABB will let you know and you can then download an application form from the website which should be returned along with copies of bank statements and proof of work in the industry.

Applications are decided on the second Tuesday of each month. All applicants will be informed of the decision in writing. Regular beneficiaries will have their cases reviewed annually.

Horticulture

The Horticultural Trades Association Benevolent Fund

£0

Correspondent: David Gwyther, 19 High Street, Theale, Reading, Berkshire RG7 5AH (01189 303132)

Trustees: Jeffrey Bernhard; Edward Topping.

CC Number: 271129

Eligibility

Nurserymen and seedsmen and their dependents who are in need.

Types of grants

Usually one-off grants.

Annual grant total

The fund has a fairly steady income, averaging around £5,000 each year, however, total expenditure fluctuates: in 2010 there was a nominal £1 expenditure and £1,000 the year before.

Applications

In writing to the correspondent.

Perennial

£250,000

Correspondent: Sheila Thomson, Director of Services, 115 – 117 Kingston Road, Leatherhead, Surrey KT22 7SU (0845 230 1839; fax: 01372 384055; email: info@perennial.org.uk; website: www.perennial.org.uk)

Trustees: Roger Singleton; Lisa Buckland; Jim Buttress; Christine Cohen; Ken Crowther; Geoff Dixon; Colin Ellis; Mike Fitt; Alan Kendall; Ian Maxwell-Scott; Charles Notcutt; Dougal Phillip; Lousie Robinson; Marie Seaton; Sue Tasker; Adrian Thompson.

SC Number: SC040180

Eligibility

People who are, or have been, employed in the horticultural industry and their spouses/partners. This includes qualified and unqualified gardeners, nursery workers, garden centre employees, arboriculturists and many more. Following the merger of Perennial and the Royal Fund for Gardeners Children in early 2011, Perennial can now help the dependent children of horticulturists.

Types of grants

One-off grants ranging from £20 to £2,000 towards a variety of needs, including support for mobility aids, property adaptations, property maintenance, domestic appliances, furniture and fittings, personal items, funeral expenses, travel and other costs linked to training, holidays and personal care. In certain circumstances grants may also be available for debt clearance. Regular weekly allowances and top up for care home fees are also paid to eligible clients

Annual grant total

In 2011 £175,000 was awarded in one-off grants for general welfare purposes and a similar figure in ongoing benefit and top up totalling £250,000.

Exclusions

No help is available for maintaining council or other rented property. Grants are not usually awarded where statutory provision is available.

Applications

Perennial has a regionally based caseworker team. Initial contact should be via the correspondent or direct to the relevant caseworker team (telephone numbers are on the website) and can be made directly by the individual or through any welfare organisation or other third party. All applicants are visited by a caseworker, usually within 14 days, who will make an initial assessment and fill in an application form with the prospective client (or their parent if the applicant is the child of a horticulturalist).

Other information

The charity provides advice, advocacy and support on welfare rights, entitlement to benefit, and accommodation issues. It also has a specialist debt advice team and a dedicated debt helpline (Tel: 0800 294 4244). Further details can be found on the website or by contacting the charity.

Perennial also gives grants to individuals for education and training purposes.

Hotel and catering

Hospitality Action

£451,000 (691 grants)

Correspondent: Grants and Advisory Team, 62 Britton Street, London EC1M 5UY (020 3004 5507; fax: 020 7253 2094; email: help@ hospitalityaction.org.uk; website: www. hospitalityaction.org.uk)

Trustees: Sue Harrison; William Baxter; Dick Turpin; Andrew Latham; Patrick Dempsey; Robert Cook; Andrew Guy; Peter Hazzard; Mark Lewis; Richard Ball; Jon Dee; Simon Dobson; Tracey Rogers; Robert Walton; Matt Johnson; Jonathan Raggett.

CC Number: 1101083

Eligibility

Former and current workers in the hospitality industry in the UK. The individuals or the company they work for would need to have been involved in the direct provision of food, drink and accommodation away from home. Individuals must have worked in the industry for one continuous year in the past five years or have worked for seven continuous years in their lifetime.

Types of grants

One-off grants for essential needs, including short-term crisis grants to the maximum amount of £5,000. Recurrent grants are also made to older people with a limited income.

Annual grant total

In 2011 the charity held assets of £8.1 million and had an income of £1.2 million. Grants to 691 individuals, the majority of which were under £1,000, totalled £451,000. Grants can be broken down as follows:

Essential needs grants	£252,000
Top up grants	£102,000
Short-term crisis grants	£55,000
Christmas grants	£20,000
TV licence and phone grants	£8,500
Family members' scheme	£8,300
Winter fuel grants	£4,700
Other grants	£600

Exclusions

Funding is not available towards the following: private school fees, fees for educational courses, student maintenance, student loan repayment, most private medical treatments, legal costs, residential care fee shortages. Grants for property repairs or adaptations may be refused if equity release is a considered a viable option.

Only one grant per applicant in any twelve month period.

Applications

On a form available from the website. If writing include the individual's work history, savings available, evidence of income and specific need. Applications should be supported by an independent third party such as a social worker, Citizens Advice or other welfare agency. They are considered weekly. Decisions will be confirmed in writing.

Other information

Hospitality Action runs The Ark Foundation Programme which offers seminars on drugs and alcohol misuse. The organisation has a membership scheme for retirees of the hospitality industry.

It also has a contact scheme for retirees of the hospitality industry which includes a bi-monthly newsletter and birthday card.

The Sir John Edwin and Arthur Mitchell Fund

£33,000

Correspondent: Anne E Holmes, Clerk, Cobbetts LLP, 1 Colemore Square, Birmingham B4 6AJ (0845 404 2505; website: www.mbtrusts.org.uk)

Trustees: Mitchells and Butlers Trust Funds Ltd; Mitchells and Butlers Welfare Funds Ltd.

CC Number: 528922

Eligibility

Employees and former employees of Mitchells and Butlers, Six Continents and Bass Companies, in brewing, licensed retailing or catering.

Types of grants

Recurrent and one-off grants to pay essential bills or buy essential household items, assistance with property deposits, home adaptations for people with disabilities, convalescent and respite breaks, wheelchairs and aids, counselling, etc.

Annual grant total

In 2010/11 the fund held assets of £1.2 million and had an income of £38,000. Grants totalled £33,000, of which the majority – £24,000 – was paid through the Licenced Trade Charity. However, a further seven grants were made to individuals directly from the fund totalling £9,000.

Exclusions

Top-up fees for residential care, private medical treatment or retrospective funding of items/services already purchased.

Applications

Applications are made through Licensed Trade Support and Care, part of the Licensed Trade Charity, who provide support to current and former brewery and licensed trade workers where it is needed. An application can be made by contacting the helpline on 01344 898550, by contacting the trust by email or downloading an application form and guidelines directly from the website.

Applicants may receive a visit by a member of the welfare team in order to assess their needs and also, if necessary, provide help with the application process.

Other information

The fund supplies money to beneficiaries through the umbrella welfare organisation Licenced Trade Support and Care (LTSC). LTSC provide a holistic support service offering benefit, housing and debt advice as well as financial assistance.

Jewellery

The British Jewellery, Giftware and Finishing Federation Benevolent Society

£45,000 (65 grants)

Correspondent: Lynn Snead, Secretary, Federation House, 10 Vyse Street, Hockley, Birmingham B18 6LT (01217 441046; email: lynn@teg.co.uk; website: www.batf.uk.com)

Trustees: Michael Ferraro; Mary Rose Gilbert; Barbara Deacon; The Earl of Aylesford Charles Heneage; David Harrison; David John Montague Simons; Geoffrey Oakley; Jeff Evans; Jerry Arkinstall; Marie Geraldine Brennan; Pat Ash; David Doyle; John William Easom; Wendy Webb; Tom Green; Andrew Ross.

CC Number: 208722

Eligibility

People in need who have worked in the industries covered by the federation, and their dependents. Eligible trades are jewellery manufacture and distribution, giftware, surface engineering and travel goods and fashion accessories industries.

Types of grants

One-off grants and loans are given towards the provision of essential items such as cookers, washing machines, fridges, freezers, bedding, telephone rental, television licence fees and household repairs. Recurrent grants are also paid to those on a low income.

Annual grant total

In 2011 the society had assets of £556,000 and an income of £76,000. Grants were made to 65 individuals totalling £45,000.

Applications

On a form available from the correspondent. Applications can be submitted either directly by the individual or through a social worker, Citizens Advice, welfare agency or other third party. Applications are considered quarterly.

The Silversmiths and Jewellers Charity

£62,000

Correspondent: Julie Griffin, PO Box 61660, London SE9 9AN (020 8265 9288; fax: 01582 599810; email: info@ thesjcharity.com; website: www. thesjcharity.com)

Trustees: G. G. MacDonald; Susan Bailey; Ian Morton; Ian Thomson; James Alexander Dallas; John Michael Bowles; Keith Grant-Peterkin; Victoria Elizabeth Cox; Zoe Caroline Simpson; David Anthony Marshall; Gordon Daniel Hamme; James Henry Riley; Richard Jarvis; Ian David Goodwin.

CC Number: 205785

Eligibility

People in need who are, or have been, employed in any sector of the gold and silver smithing trade or the jewellery trade, and their dependents.

Types of grants

Quarterly payments of £135, summer gifts of £50, Christmas gifts of £150 and Christmas hampers are given to regular grantees. One-off grants are also made for special needs such as domestic goods, furniture, bedding and hospital travel costs.

Annual grant total

In 2010 the society had assets of £1.5 million and an income of £156,000. Grants were made totalling £62,000.

Applications

On a form available from the correspondent. Applications can be submitted directly by the individual or through a social worker, Citizens Advice or other welfare agency.

Other information

This charity was previously known as the The Goldsmiths', Silversmiths' and Jewellers' Benevolent Society.

Laundry

Johnson Charitable Trust

£30,000

Correspondent: Yvonne May Monaghan, Company Secretary, Johnson Service Group plc, Johnson House, Abbots Park, Monks Way, Preston Brook WA7 3GH (01928 704600; fax: 01928 704620; email: enquiries@johnsonplc.com)

Trustees: Yvonne May Monaghan; Elizabeth Wade; Karen Gaynor Castle; Christopher Sander; Margo Green.

CC Number: 216974

Eligibility

Employees and ex-employees of the Johnson Group plc and their dependents.

Types of grants

One-off and recurrent grants according to need.

Annual grant total

In 2010/11 the trust held assets of £1.4 million and had an income of £47,000. Grants totalled £30,000 and can be broken down as follows:

Widows and widowers allowances/ gifts	£22,000
Christmas hampers	£7,600
Hardship grants	£250

Applications

In writing to the correspondent.

The Worshipful Company of Launderers Benevolent Trust

£6,400

Correspondent: Mrs Jacqueline Polek, Launderers' Hall, 9 Montague Close, London SE1 9DD (020 7378 1430; fax: 020 7378 9364; email: clerk.launderers@ btconnect.com; website: www.launderers. co.uk)

Trustees: Martyn Lewis; Colin Hill; Ivan Kerry; Roger Edward Salmon.

CC Number: 262750

Eligibility

Existing and retired members of the laundry industry and their dependents.

Types of grants

Grants can be paid annually (towards fuel bills); bi-annually (fuel bills and a summer grant), or monthly (towards general living expenses).

Annual grant total

In 2010/11 the trust had assets of £493,000 and an income of £46,000. Grants made to individuals totalled £6,400.

Applications

In writing to the correspondent.

Other information

Grants are also made to organisations.

Leather

The Leather and Hides Trades' Benevolent Institution

£77,000

Correspondent: Karen Harriman, Secretary, 143 Barkby Road, Leicester LE4 9LG (01162 741500; fax: 01162 741500; email: karenharriman@ btconnect.com; website: www.lhtbi.org. uk)

Trustees: J. W. Tusting; John Epstein; Christopher Scopes; John Buckley; Martin Pebody; Paul Pearson; Mr J. Jonathan Freeston; Jill Williams; David Santa-Olalla; Ian Michel; Roy Winnard.

CC Number: 206133

Eligibility

People who work or have worked in the leather trade (i.e. in the production of leather or in the handling of hide and skin) for ten years or more, and their dependents. Applicants are usually over 60, though people under 60 may also be considered.

Types of grants

Annuities of between £240 and £1,040 a year (paid quarterly). Also, one-off grants to annuitants and others for special needs, and help towards shortfalls in nursing home fees.

Annual grant total

In 2010 the charity had assets of £816,000 and an income of £53,000. Annuities (paid to 80 beneficiaries) and grants were made totalling £77,000.

Exclusions

No grants for funeral expenses.

Applications

On a form available from the correspondent or through the charity's website. Applications can be submitted directly by the individual or through a social worker, Citizens Advice or other welfare agency. Applications can be considered at any time.

Note: Recurrent grants are subject to annual review.

Legal

The Barristers' Benevolent Association

£139,000

Correspondent: Susan Eldridge, Secretary, 14 Gray's Inn Square, London WC1R 5JP (020 7242 4761; fax: 020 7831 5366; email: enquiries@the-baa.com; website: www.the-bba.com)

Trustees: Terence Mowschenson; David Phillips; Sara Hargreaves; Gillian Brasse; Mark Studer.

CC Number: 1106768

Eligibility

Past or present practising members of the Bar in England and Wales, and their spouses, former spouses and dependents. No grants to those who when qualified went straight into commerce.

Types of grants

One-off grants, maintenance allowances and loans. The correspondent states that some form of grant is given in most cases.

Annual grant total

In 2011 the charity had assets of £8.9 million and an income of £589,000. £239,000 was given in grants to individuals and £106,000 in loans.

Applications

On a form available from the correspondent. Applications can be submitted by the individual or through a social worker or other welfare agency. They are considered at monthly meetings of the management committee.

Other information

Grants are also made for educational purposes.

The Institute of Legal Executives' Benevolent Fund

£4,000

Correspondent: Valerie Robertson, The Institute Of Legal Executives, Kempston Manor, Kempston, Bedford MK42 7AB (01234 845763; email: vrobertson@ilex.org.uk; website: www.ilex.org.uk)

Trustees: Diane Burleigh; John Watkins; Sandra Barton.

CC Number: 295527

Eligibility

Members and former members of the institute (including associates, fellows and student members), and their dependents.

Types of grants

One-off grants ranging between £100 and £1,000 for specific purposes such as telephone/fuel bills, nursing/residential care, medical equipment and so on. Grants can also be made to members who are unable to pay their membership subscriptions through redundancy or illness and so on.

Annual grant total

In 2010 the fund had an income of £6,500 and a total expenditure of £4,200.

Applications

On a form available from the correspondent. Applications should be submitted directly by the individual or a dependent and can be considered at any time.

The United Law Clerks Society

£20,000

Correspondent: John Dungay, Innellan House, 109 Nutfield Road, Merstham, Surrey RH1 3HD (01737 643261; email: john_a_dungay@hotmail.com)

Trustees: T. P. Lester; Mark Norman Millin.

CC Number: 277276

Eligibility

People employed or who were employed by any person of the legal profession in England, Scotland and Wales, and their dependents.

Types of grants

One-off and recurrent grants according to need, mainly to pensioners and people who are sick. Recurrent grants are usually for £5 to £10 a week, but can be for up to £720 a year. One-off grants can be for up to £500 or £600 a year, for example, towards cookers, roof repairs, special chairs/beds and so on.

Annual grant total

In 2010/11 the trust had an income of £1,500 and a total expenditure of £23,000.

Exclusions

No grants for students.

Applications

On a form available from the correspondent at any time. Applications can be submitted either directly by the individual, through a third party such as a social worker, or through an organisation such as a Citizens Advice or other welfare agency.

Librarians

The Chartered Institute of Library and Information Professionals (CILIP) Benevolent Fund

£3,400

Correspondent: Eric Winter, Secretary, 7 Ridgmount Street, London WC1E 7AE (020 7255 0648; fax: 020 7255 0501; email: eric.winter@cilip.org.uk; website: www.cilip.org.uk)

Trustees: Michael Saich; Dr Bernard Naylor; Graham Peter Cornish; Mary Auckland; Gillian Pentelow; Jean Plaister; Terry Bell.

CC Number: 237352

Eligibility

Members and former members of the CILIP and their dependents. This includes former members of the Library Association and the Institute of Information Scientists who may not have chosen to become members of CILIP.

Types of grants

One-off grants only for 'unusual or unexpected expenses that may be causing anxiety and hardship'. For example, urgent house repairs, household equipment, unexpectedly large heating bills, debts which have accumulated due to illness and so on.

Annual grant total

In 2011 the fund held assets of £117,000 and had an income of £26,000. Grants were lower than usual due to the administrative problems encountered by the trust, at £3,400 (£9,100 in 2010).

Exclusions

No grants to students. The fund is not able to offer recurrent grants or pension top-ups.

Applications

Applicants should either write to or telephone the correspondent and outline their difficulties. A visit will then be arranged to discuss the circumstances in more detail. The trustees meet three or four times a year to consider applications, though urgent requests can be dealt with more quickly.

Market research

The Market Research Benevolent Association

£21,000

Correspondent: Danielle Scott, Secretary and Treasurer, 11 Tremayne Walk, Camberley, Surrey GU15 1AH (0845 652 0303; fax: 0845 652 0303; email: marketresearchba@yahoo.co.uk; website: www.mrba.org.uk)

Trustees: Nicolas Brian Palmer; Ian Brace; Marian Stringer; Linda Rosemary Henshall; Christopher Patrick Molloy; Claire Rebecca Harris; Sue Blyth; Margery Hancock; Justin Gutman.

CC Number: 274190

Eligibility
People who are or have been engaged in market research, and their dependents.

Types of grants
Generally one-off grants for people in need. Interest free loans are also made on occasions.

Annual grant total
In 2010/11 the association had assets of £496,000 and an income of £36,000. Grants to individuals totalled £21,000. In addition a further £7,400 was converted from loans to grants by the association.

Applications
On a form available from the correspondent, by phone or emailing marketresearchba@yahoo.co.uk. Applications can be submitted either directly by the individual or by a third party and are considered throughout the year. Most applicants are visited as part of the application process and will be offered support in completing the application from a MRBA regional manager.

Urgent cases can be fast-tracked.

Other information
The association also provides a confidential telephone helpline offering advice on personal, employment and financial matters.

Match manufacture

The Joint Industrial Council and the Match Manufacturing Industry Charitable Fund

£1,100

Correspondent: Rachel Perks, Republic Technologies Ltd, Sword House, Totteridge Road, High Wycombe, Buckinghamshire HP13 6DG (01494 533300)

Trustees: Gary Long; Liz Pawley.

CC Number: 260075

Eligibility
People who are or have been involved in the manufacture of matches, and their dependents.

Types of grants
One-off grants towards, for instance, medical expenses, dental and optical expenses, home security, removal costs (to sheltered accommodation) and winter fuel costs. Christmas grants are also available.

Annual grant total
This fund has been relatively inactive over the past number of years, with neither income or expenditure rising above £1,400 per year. In 2011 it had no income and a total expenditure of £1,300. No further information was available.

Applications
In writing to the correspondent, directly by the individual. Applications are considered throughout the year.

Media

The Chartered Institute of Journalists Orphan Fund

£14,000

Trustees: Harvey Thomas; Michael Moriarty; Charlie Harris; Cyril Bainbridge; Dominic Cooper; Doreen Grimwood; Ken Brookes; Mary Tomlinson; Norman Bartlett; Robin Morgan; Paul Leighton; Peter Brown; Barrie Welford; Joshua Aidoo; Jules Annan; Kenneth Russell; Daljit Sembai.

CC Number: 208176

Eligibility
Orphaned children of institute members who are in need, aged between 5 and 22 and in full-time education.

Types of grants
Monthly grants (plus birthday/ Christmas/summer holiday payments).

Annual grant total
In 2011 the fund had assets of £1.8 million and an income of £86,000. Grants to individuals totalled £28,000, for welfare and education.

Applications
In writing to the correspondent.

Other information
This fund also gives grants for educational purposes.

The Cinema and Television Benevolent Fund

£652,000

Correspondent: Welfare Team, 22 Golden Square, London W1F 9AD (0800 138 2522; email: charity@ctbf.co. uk; website: www.ctbf.co.uk)

Trustees: Ian Lewis; Stanley Fishman; David McCall; John Mahony; Barry Charles Jenkins; Anne Bennett; David Murrell; Deborah Chalet; Richard Wilson; Trevor Green; Steve Jaggs; Derek Cooper; Denise Parkinson; Alan Musa; David Willing.

CC Number: 1099660

Eligibility
People who have worked behind the scenes in the cinema, film and commercial television industries in the UK for two years in any capacity, i.e. production, exhibition, distribution, administration or transmission of film or commercial television. Help is also available to dependents.

Types of grants
One-off and recurrent grants towards the payment of television licences, medical equipment, bankruptcy fees, fuel bills, household essentials and so on. Loans are also available.

Annual grant total
In 2011/12 the fund had assets of £29 million and a consolidated income of £3.9 million. Grants to individuals totalled £652,000. The major grant categories were as follows:

Regular monthly grants	£264,000
Support to Glebelands and Broccoli Cloisters residents	£145,000
Other grants	£50,000
Christmas gifts and hampers	£38,000
Birthday grants (vouchers)	£30,000
Telephone rentals and payments	£28,000

Applications

On a form available from the website or welfare department. Applications are considered on an ongoing basis and should be submitted either directly by the individual or through a third party such as a social worker. Most applicants will be assessed by a visitor from the fund.

Other information

The fund owns and manages a home for the elderly at Glebelands, which gives priority to those who have worked in the world of film, cinema and television. For more information contact the fund or go to the Glebelands website (www.glebelands.org).

The Grace Wyndham Goldie (BBC) Trust Fund

£915 (1 grant)

Correspondent: The Trustees, BBC Pensions and Benefits Centre, Broadcasting House, Cardiff CF5 2YQ (02920 323772; fax: 02920 322408; website: www.bbc.co.uk/charityappeals/grant/gwg.shtml)

Trustees: Mark Scrimshaw; Sandra Phillips; Andy Baker; Liz Rylatt.

CC Number: 212146

Eligibility

Employees and ex-employees worldwide engaged in broadcasting or an associated activity, and their dependents.

Types of grants

One-off grants to help relieve continuing hardship not covered by aid from other sources.

Annual grant total

In 2011 the trust had assets of £1.1 million and an income of £49,000. They made 15 grants for education totalling £19,000, four of which are ongoing and one grant for hardship of £915.

Exclusions

Grants are not given for medical, nursing or care home fees, funeral expenses or holidays.

Applications

On a form available from the correspondent. The deadline for applications is 31 July and they are considered in September. As the income of the fund is limited, and to ensure help can be given where it is most needed, applicants must be prepared to give full information about their circumstances.

The Journalists' Charity

£298,000 (177 grants)

Correspondent: David Ilott, Director and Secretary, Dickens House, 35 Wathen Road, Dorking, Surrey RH4 1JY (01306 887511; fax: 01306 888212; email: enquiries@journalistscharity.org.uk; website: www.journalistscharity.org.uk)

Trustees: Stephen Somerville; B. G. Ager; Ricky Marsh; Gillian James; Jean Morgan; Michael Watson; Nicholas Jones; Robert Gibson; Sydney Young; William Newman; William Hagerty; Laurie Upshon; Ramsay Smith; Chris Boffey; Raymond Massey; Keith Beabey; Anna Botting; Paul Jones; Susan Ryan; Stephen Dann.

CC Number: 208215

Eligibility

British journalists and their dependents who are in need.

Types of grants

One-off grants, typically in the range of £250 and £500. Regular payments on a weekly and monthly basis.

Annual grant total

In 2011 the charity had assets of £12 million and an income of £1.7 million. Grants to 177 beneficiaries totalled £308,000, most of which was given for welfare purposes

Exclusions

No grants for holidays, although support may be given for convalescence or respite breaks.

Applications

On a form available from the correspondent, including details of the career in journalism. Applications are considered monthly.

Other information

The fund also runs residential and care homes in Dorking.

The Guild of Motoring Writers Benevolent Fund

£8,000

Correspondent: Elizabeth Aves, 23 Stockwell Park Crescent, London SW9 0DQ (020 7737 2377; email: benfundamin@gomw.co.uk; website: www.gomw.co.uk)

Trustees: Ray Hutton; John Blunsden; John Baluth; Matthew Carter; Janet Wilkinson.

CC Number: 259583

Eligibility

Motoring writers, photographers and historians who are in need and are, or have been, members of the guild. Their dependents may also be supported.

Types of grants

One-off and recurrent grants according to need. For example, to help with short-term financial difficulties following redundancy or injury. Grants are also available to retired members for stair lifts, orthopaedic beds, interim nursing costs and so on.

Annual grant total

In 2010 the fund had an income of £12,000.

Applications

In writing to the correspondent at any time. Applications can be made either directly by the individual through a third party.

NUJ Extra

£88,000

Correspondent: Lena Calvert, Headland House, 308–312 Gray's Inn Road, London WC1X 8DP (020 7278 7916; email: lenac@nuj.org.uk; website: www.nujextra.org.uk)

Trustees: Anita Halpin; Ann Coltart; Michelle Stanistreet; Christopher Wheal; Donald Harkness; Miles Barter; James Doherty; John Barsby; Debbie Smith.

CC Number: 1112489

Eligibility

Members and former members of the National Union of Journalists and the dependents of deceased members. Applicants must have paid at least one year's full subscription to the NUJ. Note: current members are only eligible for short-term assistance.

Types of grants

One-off grants are given for urgent bills (mainly rent and utilities), wheelchairs, beds, domestic goods, medical equipment and minor home adaptations. Bills or rent payments will generally be made directly to the supplier or landlord. Recurrent grants of up to £175 a week are also available to top up the income of those living on a state pension and/or other benefits. Christmas bonus grants are also made.

Annual grant total

In 2011 the fund had assets of £2.1 million and an income of £65,000. Grants were made totalling £88,000.

Exclusions

No grants for: legal expenses, private medical treatment or private education. Help is unlikely to be available for consumer debts. Members who left owing the union contributions are not eligible for help.

Applications

On a form available from the correspondent or to download from the website. Applications can be submitted by the individual or through an NUJ welfare officer or other third party. They are considered throughout the year.

Other information

NUJ Extra is an amalgamation of charities previously known as National Union of Journalists Members in Need Fund and National Union of Journalists Provident Fund.

Medicine and health

The 1930 Fund for District Nurses

£32,000

Correspondent: Mia Duddridge, The Trust Partnership, 6 Trull Farm Buildings, Tetbury, Gloucestershire GL8 8SQ (01285 841900; fax: 01285 841576; email: 1930fund@ thetrustpartnership.com; website: www. 1930fundfornurses.org)

Trustees: Paul Beard; Kieron Lynch; Jean Bailey; Denise Dennehy; Michael Leeson; Peter Goodwin; Lindsey Hayes; Judy Joseph.

CC Number: 208312

Eligibility

Qualified nurses who have worked in the community as a district nurse, community nurse, school nurse, health visitor, community midwife or community psychiatric nurse.

Types of grants

One-off grants usually ranging from £100 to £300 for a variety of needs, including bathroom and kitchen equipment, household essentials, mobility aids, spectacles, dentures and specialist equipment. The fund also provides recurrent grants to help with living expenses. Grants are paid monthly or quarterly.

Annual grant total

In 2010/11 the fund had assets of £1.7 million and an income of £98,000. Grants were made totalling £32,000.

Exclusions

No grants are given for care home fees, educational fees, private healthcare, payment of debt, payment of rent/ council tax.

Applications

On a form available from the correspondent or to download from the website. Applications can be submitted directly by the individual, through a social worker, a Citizens Advice, other welfare agency or third party. They are considered throughout the year and should include details of nursing experience and an invoice or quote for any work or item being applied for. A third party applying on the individual's behalf should also include a letter of endorsement.

The trust welcomes enquiries.

Ambulance Services Benevolent Fund

£14,000 (25 grants)

Correspondent: Simon Fermor, Secretary, Cherith, 150 Willingdon Road, Eastbourne, East Sussex BN21 1TS (01323 721150; email: enquiries@asbf.co. uk; website: www.asbf.co.uk)

Trustees: Simon Fermor; Cliff Randell; Gerry Brown; Paul Leopold; Roland Chesney; Roy Norris; Vic Holdsworth; Trevor Shelbourne; Goulding Harry; Mik Webb; Gordon Enstone; Stephen Evans.

CC Number: 800434

Eligibility

Present and former ambulance men/ women, who have been employed by the NHS ambulance services, and their dependents. If retired, it must be for age or medical reason. People who only served for a couple of years before seeking other employment for the rest of their working life are not considered.

Types of grants

One-off grants of £100 to £1,000 are awarded to relieve genuine hardship, poverty or distress, or to assist medically.

Annual grant total

In 2010/11 the fund had assets of £194,000 and an income of £54,000. Grants were made to 35 individuals totalling £14,000 and distributed as follows:

Long-term sickness	£4,400
Disability aid	£4,100
Financial hardship	£3,500
Bereavement	£2,000
Convalescence/Respite Care	£200

Exclusions

No grants for items which have already been purchased.

Applications

Applications should be made through a third party, although if it is a particularly confidential matter applications can be accepted directly from the individual. Third parties should write to the correspondent setting out the issue, how the need arose, the applicant's personal details, their length of service, any dependents they have and any other relevant information needed to complete the picture. Applicants applying directly can download an application form from the website.

BMA Charities Trust Fund

£7,900 (13 grants)

Correspondent: Marian Flint, BMA House, Tavistock Square, London WC1H 9JP (020 7383 6142; email: bmacharities@bma.org.uk; website: bma.org.uk/about-the-bma/who-we-are/ charities)

Trustees: Dr Jane Richards; Connie Fozzrd; Tony Bourne; Dr Mike Downes; Dr Michael Wilks; Dr Steven Hajioff; Dr Andrew John Mowat; Dr Andrew Richard Dearden.

CC Number: 219102

Eligibility

Medical doctors and their dependents who are in financial need due to illness or unemployment, whether or not they are BMA members.

Types of grants

One-off grants of up to £6,000 for specific items in times of crisis and the payment of debts. Support is also available for terminal and palliative care, including night sitter services, respite breaks for carers, personal care, domestic help or a holiday break for the patient and their family.

Annual grant total

In 2011 the fund held assets of £3.8 million and had an income of £295,000. Grants to 13 individuals totalled £7,900 (£26,000 in 2010).

Exclusions

The trust does not help with legal fees, private medical treatment or career enhancement projects. There are no general grants for 'living costs'.

Applications

On a form available from the correspondent, to be submitted at any time. Two personal references are required, one of which must be from a doctor.

Other information

The BMA Charities Trust Fund incorporates the Hastings Benevolent Fund and the BMA Educational Fund.

The British Dental Association Benevolent Fund

£166,000

Correspondent: Mrs Sally Atkinson, 63–64 Wimpole Street, London W1G 8YS (020 7486 4994; email: dentistshelp@btconnect.com; website: www.bdabenevolentfund.org.uk)

Trustees: Ann Rockey; Dianne Waller; John Turner; Bill Nichols; Pradeep Vohra; Isobel Green; Prof. Philip Sutcliffe; John Craig; Allan Franklin; Anne Fox Robinson; Martin Everett; Michelle Slater; Dr Peter Ward; Angela Ball; Stuart Robson; Philip Henderson; Dr Ros Keeton; Dr Alexander Matthewson; Dr Brian David Skinner; Dr Julie Angela Kirkby; Dr Stuart Brooke Johnston; Dr Arabella Yelland; Dr Austin Banner; Dr Michael Townsend.

CC Number: 208146

Eligibility

Dentists who are or have been on the UK dental register and their dependents.

Types of grants

One-off grants to help meet specific needs such as washing machines, TV licences, fridges, fuel costs, household repairs, funeral costs, holidays and respite care. Regular grants to supplement income are also available as are interest-free loans to relieve difficulties with a limited time span.

Annual grant total

In 2010 the fund had assets of £5.3 million and an income of £278,000. Grants were made totalling £166,000.

Exclusions

Help is not usually given for private medical fees or private school fees. The trust does not generally help people with a considerable amount of capital.

Applications

On a form available from the correspondent. Applications are considered as they are received. Enquiries can be made directly by the individual or through a social worker, Citizens Advice, welfare agency or other third party.

The Cameron Fund

£94,000 (156 grants)

Correspondent: Jane Cope, Services Manager, Tavistock House North, Tavistock Square, London WC1H 9HR (020 7388 0796; email: info@ cameronfund.org.uk; website: www. cameronfund.org.uk)

Trustees: Dr R. J. Givans; Dr G. M. Hearn; Dr M. F. Duffy; Dr A. D. Richardson; Dr G. I. Graham; Dr D. Jawahar; Dr R. Chapman; Dr D. Brownridge; Dr E. Scott; Dr F. Marshall; Dr S. Milne; Dr S. Linton; Dr Gary Dennis Calver; Dr Ian Stewart Winterton; Dr David Wrigley; Dr Eugene Deeny; Dr Richard Brown; Dr Andrew Thomson; Dr Andrew Francis Rodgett.

CC Number: 261993

Eligibility

General practitioners and their dependents who are in need.

Types of grants

One-off and recurrent grants towards general expenses, holidays, house repairs, replacement of household equipment, children's needs, nursing home fees and so on. Each application is considered on its own merits. Occasionally support may be offered in the form of an interest-free loan.

Annual grant total

In 2011 the trust had assets of £4.6 million and an income of £315,000. Grants were made totalling £127,000 of which around £94,000 was made for welfare purposes and the remainder was given as educational grants.

Exclusions

No grants can be made towards items which should be provided through statutory sources. Educational grants are only given to families previously supported by the trust.

Applications

On a form available from the correspondent or to download from the website. Applications can be submitted at any time, either directly by the individual or through a social worker, Citizens Advice, solicitor or other welfare agency. Applications are considered on a quarterly basis, though decisions can be made sooner in urgent cases. A trustee will usually visit the applicant before agreeing a grant and beneficiaries are reviewed annually.

Other information

The fund also offers financial and career advice as well as counselling.

Cavell Nurses' Trust

£477,000 (866 grants)

Correspondent: Kate Tompkins, Grosvenor House, Prospect Hill, Redditch, Worcestershire B97 4DL (01527 595999; email: admin@ cavellnursestrust.org; website: www. cavellnursestrust.org)

Trustees: Alison Holdsworth; Simon Knighton; Christina Edwards; Paul Jackson-Clark; Susan Gostick; Di Caulfield-Stoker; Susan Osborne; Jill Cox; Deborah Critchley; Stephen Charlton; Linda Thomas.

CC Number: 210571

Eligibility

Working and retired nurses, midwives and healthcare assistants together with student nurses suffering hardship, through illness, disability, accidents and family breakdowns. To qualify for assistance, registered nurses must have more than three years' post-qualification experience. Auxiliary nurses should have at least five years experience of working in a hospital or under the guidance of a registered nurse (e.g. Marie Curie community nursing). In exceptional circumstances, help may also be given to student nurses. Applicants should hold no more than £4,000 in savings.

Types of grants

One-off and recurrent grants towards, for example, household repairs and equipment, current utility and telephone bills, specialist aids, spectacles, dental work, convalescence and respite breaks. One-off grants usually range from £100 to £500, but are occasionally up to £1,000. Regular grants range from £10 to £30 per week.

Annual grant total

In 2011 the trust held assets of £3.4 million and had an income of £313,000. Grants to individuals totalled £477,000. In the year 364 individuals received regular support while a further 502 one-off grants were distributed.

Exclusions

No grants for debt repayment, holidays, bankruptcy fees, funeral expenses, educational costs or nursing home fees.

Applications

On a form available from the correspondent or to download from the website. The website also has a short online eligibility form which can be completed first to see if your application is likely to be eligible. Applications should include a letter of support from someone who is aware of the applicant's situation, for example, a senior nurse, GP, social worker, Citizens Advice worker or minister of religion. They can be submitted at any time.

The trust welcomes informal calls to discuss eligibility prior to application.

Other information

Previously known as Nurseaid.

Chartered Physiotherapists' Benevolent Fund

£86,000 (63 grants)

Correspondent: Jennifer Jeffcoat Carey, Chartered Society of Physiotherapy, 14 Bedford Row, London WC1R 4ED (020 7306 6666; fax: 020 7306 6643; email: enquiries@csp.org.uk; website: www.csp.org.uk)

Trustees: Ann Compton; Janet Bird; Alison Skinner; Bridget Catherine Davis; Dorothy Mary Frances Toyn; Natalie Prudence Tiddy; Lawrence Owers; Lesley Whiteley; Jacqueline Brown; Evangeline Rogers.

CC Number: 219568

Eligibility

Members, past members, assistant members and student members of the society.

Types of grants

One-off grants for specialist equipment to aid independent living, for emergency needs such as respite care or house repairs. Recurrent grants (of £150 per month in 2011) to help with living expenses, household repairs, heating bills and road tax (where car use is essential).

Annual grant total

In 2011 the society had assets of £1.6 million and an income of £134,000. Grants were made to 63 beneficiaries totalling £86,000.

Exclusions

No grants towards payment of debts or when statutory help is available. Grants cannot be made to those who hold capital exceeding the maximum figure used by the Department of Work and Pensions to decide on benefit eligibility.

Applications

On a form available from the correspondent. Applications should be submitted directly by the individual or by a third party such as a carer or partner. Applications are considered in January, April, July and October.

The Benevolent Fund of the College of Optometrists and the Association of Optometrists

£66,000

Correspondent: David Lacey, Administrative Secretary, PO Box 10, Swanley, Kent BR8 8ZF (01322 660388; email: davidflacey@aol.com)

Trustees: Jonathan Swan; Norbert Cohn; Robert Edward Hogan; Jonathan Kay; Michael Meadley; Richard Broughton; Richard Llewellyn; Ruth Cuthbert; Ian Shaw.

CC Number: 1003699

Eligibility

Current and retired members of the optical profession and their dependents.

Types of grants

Regular monthly payments to elderly or ill members towards bills and other living expenses. One-off grants are occasionally given towards costly items of expenditure such as house repairs, wheelchairs and holidays. Christmas grants are also given. For younger practitioners unable to work, the fund may assist with professional fees. Grants usually range from £20 to £200.

Annual grant total

In 2010/11 the fund held assets of £1 million and had an income of £151,000. Grants were made to individuals totalling £66,000.

Exclusions

No grants to students.

Applications

Application forms are available from the correspondent and a financial form must be completed. Applications are considered all year round and applicants are usually visited by a member of the profession.

The Eaton Fund for Artists, Nurses and Gentlewomen
See entry on page 34

Ethel Mary Fund For Nurses

£2,900

Correspondent: Miss H M Campbell, Vice President, Royal British Nurses Association, The TA Centre, London Road, Stonecot Hill, Sutton, Surrey SM3 9HG (020 8335 3691; email: enquiries@rbna.org.uk; website: www.rbna.org.uk)

Trustees: Grace Nwodili; Henrietta Millicent Campbell; Mary Patricia McCabe; Pamela Selfe; Patricia McQueen; Yolanda Johns; Coral Goodridge-Felce; Angela Searle.

CC Number: 209887

Eligibility

Registered, or retired, state nurses over 40 years of age who are sick and disabled and who live in the UK.

Types of grants

Pensions are given.

Annual grant total

Grants total just under £3,000 per year.

Applications

On a form available from the correspondent. Applications are considered quarterly.

The Institute of Healthcare Management Benevolent Fund

£12,000

Correspondent: Grants Administrator, c/o Institute of Healthcare Management Ltd, 18–21 Morley Street, London SE1 7QZ (020 7620 1030; fax: 020 7620 1040; email: enquiries@ihm.org.uk; website: www.ihm.org.uk)

Trustees: Susan Hodgetts; Stuart Bain; Malcolm Wright.

CC Number: 208225

Eligibility

Members and former members of the institute and their dependents.

Types of grants

Emergency one-off grants (usually around £200); monthly grants (variable according to circumstances, presently £40 to £100 a month); special Christmas and summer holiday grants usually paid to people receiving regular grants (variable but with emphasis on dependent children); and top-up nursing/residential home fees and similar.

Annual grant total

In 2010 the fund had an income and total expenditure of £12,300.

Exclusions

Generally no grants given to students but some educational grants may be given to members of the institute, not their children.

Applications

Should be submitted through a regional representative on the national council of the institute. Applications are considered on receipt.

The Junius S. Morgan Benevolent Fund

£259,000 (119 grants)

Correspondent: Shirley Baines, SG Hambros Trust Company Ltd, Norfolk House, 31 St James's Square, London SW1Y 4JR (0207597306; email:

grantadmin@juniusmorgan.org.uk; website: www.juniusmorgan.org.uk)

Trustees: Alan Gibbs; Andrew Everard Martin Smith; William John Gordon; The Burdett Trust for Nursing.

CC Number: 1131892

Eligibility

Registered nurses and auxiliaries who have practised in the UK for a minimum of five years.

Types of grants

One-off grants of up to £1,500 for a variety of purposes including electricity and fuel bills, telephone charges, household renewal costs (decorating, furniture, furnishings) and television rental and licence fees.

Annual grant total

In 2011 the fund had assets of £2.2 million and an income of £343,000. Grants were made to 119 individuals totalling £259,000.

Exclusions

Grants are not given towards educational fees, funeral costs, bankruptcy fees, residential/nursing home fees, holidays or respite care.

Applications

On a form available from the correspondent or to download from the website. Applications must be submitted through an independent third party (i.e. a social worker, care worker or Citizens Advice) who has reviewed the application and provided a letter of support. Applications should include: three months of recent bank statements and gas/electricity bills; a current mortgage statement or rental agreement; and a written quotation if a purchase or repair is required. They are considered on a weekly basis and applicants will be notified of a decision in writing.

The NHS Pensioners' Trust

£70,000 (288 grants)

Correspondent: Frank Jackson, Director, PO Box 456, Esher KT10 1DP (01372 805760; email: enquiries@nhspt.org.uk; website: www.nhspt.org.uk)

Trustees: Peter Griffiths; James Coles; Paula Forecast.

CC Number: 1002061

Eligibility

i) Any person who has retired from service in any capacity in the NHS in England, Wales or Scotland; ii) Any person who has retired from service in England, Wales or Scotland for any of the related health service organisations or caring professions prior to the creation of the NHS; and iii) Any person

who is the wife, husband, widow, widower or other dependent of those specified above.

Types of grants

Grants of up to £350, for general upkeep to ease financial difficulty in cases of hardship, including the cost of disabled living, aids and equipment, repairs to the home and fuel bills. Larger grants can be considered in particular circumstances. Grants are one-off, but individuals can reapply in the following year.

Annual grant total

In 2010/11 the fund had assets of £954,000 and an income of £33,000. Grants totalled £70,000 and were distributed in 288 individual grants.

Applications

On a form available from the correspondent following receipt of an sae. Applications containing supporting information and/or the backing of social work agencies will be processed more quickly. A trust representative may follow up applications to verify information.

Pharmacist Support

£177,000 (147 grants)

Correspondent: Grant Officer, 3rd Floor, The Pinnacle, 73–79 King Street, Manchester M2 4NG (0808 168 2233; email: info@pharmacistsupport.org; website: www.pharmacistsupport.org)

Trustees: David Thomson; Dr Leonard Brookes; Doreen Laity; Prof. David J. Johns; Arthur Williams; Steve Churton; Richard Fass; Prof. Peter Noyce; Prof. Denis Anthony.

CC Number: 221438

Eligibility

Pharmacists and their families, pre-registration trainees and those retired from the profession. Support also available to pharmacists no longer on the register of the RPSGB or General Pharmaceutical Council e.g. those taking a break from pharmacy, on maternity leave or those who have been removed from the register (for whatever reason). Not available in Northern Ireland.

Types of grants

Health and wellbeing grants, one-off and regular grants and interest free loans where appropriate. Typical funding examples include grants to support mental or physical quality of life (for counselling, convalescence after an illness or accident or for purchasing a particular disability aid); to support those who cannot meet a specific cost and require temporary assistance (perhaps due to an unforeseen loss of work); to support those on a very low

income who are finding it difficult to make ends meet without getting into debt.

Grants may also be made to support students facing particular hardship due to unforeseen circumstances such as family issues, ill-health or bereavement.

Those seeking addiction support should contact the Health Support Programme helpline on 0808 168 5132.

Annual grant total

In 2011 the charity's assets stood at £11 million and it had an income of £363,000. Grants were made to 147 individuals (39 recurrent grants and 108 one-off) totalling £177,000.

Interest free loans totalling £24,000 were made to 15 individuals.

Assistance is also given to pharmacists dealing with issues of addiction through the Health Support Programme. In 2011 £49,000 was distributed in grants and direct assistance through the charity's partner, Action on Addiction.

Exclusions

There are no grants available for pharmacy technicians or pharmacy assistants. Support is not available in Northern Ireland.

Applications

On a form available for download from the charity's website, or by contacting the correspondent. Applications will be considered year round and can be submitted either directly by the individual or through a social worker, Citizens Advice, other welfare agency, or other third party on behalf of an individual. The charity recommends that applicants make contact informally before applying in order to discuss eligibility and needs.

Other information

The charity, formerly known as the Royal Pharmaceutical Society's Benevolent Fund, also provides debt, benefits and employment advice through partner agencies, a Listening Friends stress helpline (run by trained volunteer pharmacists), addiction support and information and signposting services.

The Queen's Nursing Institute

£111,000 (114 grants)

Correspondent: Joanne Moorby, Welfare and Grants Officer, 3 Albemarle Way, Clerkenwell, London EC1V 4RQ (020 7549 1405; fax: 020 7490 1269; email: joanne.moorby@qni.org.uk; website: www.qni.org.uk)

Trustees: John Palmer; William Rathbone; Zahir Fazal; Rosalynde Lowe; Michael Cooper; Nicola Walsh; Vicky

Bailey; Katie Billingham; Cheryl Dorall; Prof. Elizabeth Perkins; Nicola Goulder; Dr John Unsworth; Sue Nutbrown; Dr David Colin-Thome; Bob Browne; Jane Salvage.

CC Number: 213128

Eligibility

Nursing and Midwifery Council registered nurses who work or have worked in the community (not hospitals) for a minimum of three years. Also health care assistants who work or have worked in the community (not hospitals) under the supervision of a qualified nurse for a minimum of five years. Help is available in times of sickness, disability or other life trauma which lead to financial difficulties.

Types of grants

One-off and recurrent grants such as help with household essentials, building repairs and adaptations, specialist aids and equipment.

Annual grant total

In 2011 the institute had assets of £7.5 million and an income of £639,000. Grants were made to 114 individuals totalling £111,000 in providing welfare support.

Exclusions

No grants for residential or nursing home fees, overdrafts/debt, education costs, private health care or funeral expenses.

Applications

On a form available from the correspondent or to download from the website. Applications can be submitted by the individual, or through a recognised referral agency (social worker, Citizens Advice or doctor) or other third party.

The RCN Foundation

£179,000 (412 grants)

Correspondent: Jane Clarke, Welfare Service, 20 Cavendish Square, London W1G 0RN (0345 408 4391; email: jane. clarke@rcn.org.uk; website: www. rcnfoundation.org.uk)

Trustees: Hon John Colyer; Carol Evans; Susan Fern; Robert Sowney; Gordon Peterkin; Helen Ann Carter; Sarah Coward; Tony Butterworth; Jane Wendy Miles; Nicholas Pearson; Claire Hicks; Christopher Piercy; Ian Norris.

CC Number: 1134606

Eligibility

Registered or retired nurses, midwives, HCAs and health visitors in the UK, who are experiencing financial difficulties for one of the following reasons:

- During a period of ill health when full contractual sick pay has ceased
- Following ill health retirement
- During retirement (60+)
- Following a relationship breakdown, if there are children
- During a dispute with an employer

Types of grants

The foundation's website states: 'Assistance can be given for 'essential' outgoings that are not covered by statutory benefits, and where it can be shown that these cannot be met by current income. Disabled or elderly applicants on a low income can also apply for one-off grants towards disability equipment, household repairs, adaptations or other essential household items that they would not otherwise be able to afford.' Grants range between £50 to £400.

Annual grant total

In 2010/11 the foundation held assets of over £25 million. Income totalled £24.4 million, most of which is represented by the transfer of assets from the old charitable organisations. Regular income aside from these transfers was £403,000. During the year 549 applications were received with 412 members receiving grants totalling £179,000.

Exclusions

No grants to repay consumer debts; for private medical treatment; for awards for family members; or for top-up fees for care homes.

Applications

Members may apply by contacting the Welfare Rights and Guidance service on 0345 408 4391 or 020 7647 3463.

Claims are processed with 15–20 days.

Other information

Previously known as: The Royal College of Nursing Benevolent Fund.

The foundation can offer advice and assistance on welfare benefit entitlement.

The Royal College of Midwives Trust

£74,000

Correspondent: Clifford Crisp, The Royal College of Midwives, 15 Mansfield Street, London W1G 9NH (020 7312 3535; fax: 020 7312 3536; email: info@ rcm.org.uk; website: www.rcm.org.uk)

Trustees: Prof. Paul Lewis; Barbara Christine Kuypers; Corina Anastasia Casey-Hardman; Rosemary Janet Exton; Carole Floreen Garrick; Dr Patricia Ann Gillen; Marie McDonald; Christine McKenzie; Donna Ockenden; Prof. Lesley Ann Page; Vanessa Gwendoline Shand; Anna Natalie Shasha.

CC Number: 275261

Eligibility

Midwives, former midwives and student midwives who are in need. Preference is given to those who are members of the RCM or who have served as members of staff with the RCM or RCM Trust Ltd for at least five years.

Types of grants

Usually one-off grants for emergency or other unexpected needs (typically £50 to £200). Grants are given, for instance, towards the cost of a wheelchair, dealing with urgent priority debts, removal expenses, furniture, disability chairs, personal items and household equipment.

The trust website notes that 'unfortunately, the fund is not large enough to provide regular financial support, nor can it act as a top-up for low salaries or student midwives' bursaries, although it is able to advise on other sources of help.' However, Christmas grants are routinely paid to long-standing elderly midwife members on low incomes.

Annual grant total

In 2010 the trust had assets of £5.5 million and an income of £3.2 million. Support to members amounted to £74,000.

Exclusions

Dependents of those eligible are unable to receive grants.

Applications

On a form available from the correspondent or to download from the website. Applications should be submitted either directly by the individual or through a third party such as a nursing organisation. They are considered every six to eight weeks.

Other information

The trust engages in a range of other activities such as providing information, advice and support to members as well as running educational programmes and conferences and undertaking campaigning work. Total charitable expenditure amounted to over £3 million in 2010.

The Royal Medical Benevolent Fund

£360,000

Correspondent: The Senior Case Manager, 24 King's Road, Wimbledon, London SW19 8QN (020 8540 9194; email: enquiries@rmbf.org; website: www.rmbf.org)

Trustees: Robin Macleod; Dr Joan Trowell; Jackie Angel; Peter Bowen-

Simpkins; Judith Bamber; Professor David Black; Mike Carter; John Farr; Dr Amit Malik; Dr Mary Pierce; Professor Bhupinder Sandhu; Andrew Robson; David Haldane; Dr Katie Petty-Saphon.

CC Number: 207275

Eligibility

Assists GMC-registered, UK resident doctors and their recognised dependents who, through illness or disability are in financial hardship, through the provision of grants, loans and advice services.

Types of grants

One-off gifts/loans and regular grants are only provided for the relief of poverty and are made entirely at the discretion of the fund's case committee.

Annual grant total

In 2010/11 the fund had assets of £20 million and an income of £1.8 million. Grants were made to individuals totalling £725,000 for educational and welfare purposes.

Exclusions

The following are excluded:
- Private medical insurance/fees
- School fees
- Legal fees
- Inland revenue payments
- Debts to relatives or friends
- Private education

Applications

On a form available from the correspondent, which can be submitted either directly by the individual or through a social worker, Citizens Advice, other welfare agency, medical colleague or other medical and general charities.

Two references are required (at least one of which should be from a medical practitioner). All applicants are visited before a report is submitted to the case committee. Income/capital and expenditure are fully investigated, with similar rules applying as for those receiving Income Support. Applications are considered bi-monthly.

Other information

Voluntary visitors liaise between beneficiaries and the office. The fund has an informative website.

The Royal Medical Foundation

£44,000

Correspondent: Helen Jones, RMF Office, Epsom College, College Road, Epsom, Surrey KT17 4JQ (01372 821010; email: rmf-caseworker@epsomcollege.org.uk; website: www.royalmedicalfoundation.org)

Trustees: Celia Berwick; Surgeon Vice-Admiral Tony Revell; Greg Andrews;

Richard Bruce; Dr Hywel Bowen-Perkins; Michael Cook; Brigadier Alan Eastburn; Peter Hakim; Alan Hagdrup; Dr Alistaire Wells; Dr Andrew Vallance-Owen; Chris Titman; Helen Jones.

CC Number: 312046

Eligibility

Medical practitioners (registered with the GMC) and their dependents who are in need.

Types of grants

One-off grants, monthly pensions and maintenance grants of £500 to £15,000. Previous applications have included support for doctors with debt problems, fall-out from divorce or suspension, re-training expenses, practical financial support during/after rehabilitation, help with essential domestic bills, respite breaks, home alterations for the elderly or people with disabilities and nursing home fees.

Annual grant total

In 2010/11 the foundation gave grants to individuals totalling £77,000, which were broken down as follows:

Regular payments to medical practitioners and their widows/widowers	6	£18,600
Short-term or one-off grants for urgent assistance	18	£25,000
Financial assistance with educational expenses	8	£19,500
Financial assistance with educational expenses at Epsom College	1	£13,000
Other grants	2	£650

Applications

On a form available from the correspondent, for consideration throughout the year. Applications can be submitted either by the individual or a family member, through a third party such as a social worker or teacher, or through an organisation such as Citizens Advice or a school. The trust advises applicants to be honest about their needs. All applicants are means tested.

Other information

The foundation has an informative website.

The Society for Relief of Widows and Orphans of Medical Men

£23,000

Correspondent: Lotte Farrar, Secretary, Medical Society of London, Lettsom House, 11 Chandos Street, Cavendish Square, London W1G 9EB (01837 83022; email: info@widowsandorphans.org.uk; website: www.widowsandorphans.org.uk)

Trustees: Gordon Hickish; Priya Singh; Celia Palmer; Cyril Nemeth; Anthony

Richards; Christopher Hutter; Frank Schweitzer; Geoffrey Rose; Patrick England; John Barker; Roy Palmer; Simon Payne; Stewart Kilpatrick; Emily MacDonald; Stephanie Brown; Rohit Malliwal.

CC Number: 207473

Eligibility

Widows, widowers, orphans or dependents of any doctor who was at the time of his/her death, and for the preceding two years, a member of the society. Any surplus income may be used to help medical practitioners and their dependents who are in need but are not members of the society.

Types of grants

One-off and recurrent grants of between £500 and £3,000 towards: helping family hardship at times of illness or loss of the 'bread-winner'; debt repayments; home alterations to accommodate wheelchairs; household repairs; retraining; and for medical students who are the children of doctors where the family is in need.

Annual grant total

In 2011 the society had assets of £4.8 million and an income of £136,000. Grants to 75 individuals totalled £46,000.

Exclusions

Grants are not normally made towards nursing home fees, loans, long-term assistance or second degrees.

Applications

On various forms available from the correspondent or to download from the website. Applications should be submitted directly by the individual and are considered in February, May, August and November.

Other information

In practice most grants go to doctors who are not members of the society and their dependents.

The Society of Chiropodists Benevolent Fund

£24,000

Correspondent: Honorary Secretary, 1 Fellmongers Path, Tower Bridge Road, London SE1 3LY (020 7234 8623; email: hb@scpod.org)

Trustees: Gwen French; Peter Graham; Christopher Hunt; Peter Bennett; Stuart Andrew Baird; David Goulds.

CC Number: 205684

Eligibility

Members/former members of the society or one of its constituent bodies and their dependents.

Types of grants

One-off grants according to need, ranging from £50 to £1,000.

Annual grant total

In 2011 the fund had an income of £22,000 and a total expenditure of £28,000.

Applications

On a form available from the correspondent, to be submitted directly by the individual or through a third party. Applications are considered monthly.

The Society of Radiographers Benevolent Fund

£9,000

Correspondent: Grants Officer, 207 Providence Square, Mill Street, London SE1 2EW (020 7740 7200; email: info@sor.org; website: www.sor.org)

Trustees: Ann Pollard; Gytha McBirney; Zena Nannette Mossman; Indira Bhansali; Phillip Edwards.

CC Number: 326398

Eligibility

Past and present members of the society and their dependents, with a possible preference for people who are in ill health, elderly or incapacitated.

Types of grants

One-off grants towards, for example, stairlifts, re-training, orthopaedic beds, house adaptations, car repairs, healthcare travel costs, long-term residential care, computer equipment and washing machines.

Annual grant total

In 2010/11 the fund had an income of £11,000 and a total expenditure of £9,300.

Exclusions

There are no grants available for further education.

Applications

Applicants must complete an application form and a financial circumstances form, both of which are available on request from the correspondent or to download directly from the fund's website. Applications can be submitted by the individual or through a third party such as a colleague or relative.

The Trained Nurses Annuity Fund

£16,000

Correspondent: Miss H M Campbell, The Princess Royal House T.A.C, Stonecot Hill, Sutton, Surrey SM3 9HG (020 8335 3691; email: enquires@rbna. org; website: www.rbna.org.uk)

Trustees: Grace Nwodili; Henrietta Millicent Campbell; Mary Patricia McCabe; Pamela Selfe; Patricia McQueen; Yolanda Johns; Coral Goodrige-Felce; Angela Searle.

CC Number: 209883

Eligibility

Nurses aged 40 or over who are disabled and have at least three years service.

Types of grants

Annuities and occasionally one-off grants. Each year beneficiaries of recurrent grants send a short report explaining whether their financial circumstances have changed and whether they are still in need of assistance. Annuities are paid twice-yearly in July and December.

Annual grant total

In 2011 the fund had an income of £15,000 and a total expenditure of £17,000.

Exclusions

No grants for education or house improvements.

Applications

On a form available from the correspondent. These should normally be submitted by doctors or social workers along with a doctor's certificate or by the individual. Referrals may also be made through a third party such as Citizens Advice, Age UK, SSAFA, etc. Applications are considered at quarterly executive meetings and payments are made in July and December.

Metal trades

The Institution of Materials, Minerals and Mining – Benevolent Fund

£41,000

Correspondent: The Honorary Secretary, c/o The Member's Benevolent Trust, 1 Carlton House Terrace, London SW1Y 5DB (020 8299 4905; email: gjbowyer@aol.com; website: www.iom3. org)

Trustees: Charles Rhodes; Barry Lye; Christopher Corti; David Elliot; Eric Dempster; Norman Riley; Sheila Wright; Alan Baxter; Anthony Brewis; David Oxley; Richard Chambers; John Northcott; Maureen Johnston; Jan Lewis; Julian Bennett; Gavin Bowyer; Stephen Dawe; John Kailofer.

CC Number: 207184

Eligibility

Members of the institute and former members and their dependents who are in need.

Types of grants

One-off and recurrent grants in the range of £250 and £3,500. One-off grants in kind are also made. Grants are for general household needs, furniture, security installations, medical aids and adaptations, clothing, respite breaks and school uniforms.

Annual grant total

In 2011 the trust had assets of £1.1 million, an income of £71,000 and made grants totalling £41,000.

Applications

On a form available from the correspondent for consideration at any time.

London Metal Exchange Benevolent Fund

£16,000

Correspondent: Philip Needham, The London Metal Exchange Ltd, 56 Leadenhall Street, London EC3A 2DX (020 7264 5555)

Trustees: Brian Sidney Dorkings; John Philip Anthony Wolff; Clement Paul Danin.

CC Number: 231001

Eligibility

People in need who are members of, or have been connected with, the London Metal Exchange, and their dependents.

Types of grants

One-off and recurrent grants according to need.

Annual grant total

In 2010/11 the fund had an income of £2,500 and a total expenditure of £17,000.

Applications

On a form available from the correspondent.

Rainy Day Trust

£103,000

Correspondent: Martina Farragher, Administration Manager, Federation House, 10 Vyse Street, Birmingham B18 6LT (01212 371130; fax: 01212 371133; email: rainyday@brookehouse. co.uk; website: www.rainydaytrust. co.uk)

Trustees: Colin Petty; David Hibbert; Alan Hawkins; Simon Bicknell; Avril Hicks; Andrew Weiss; Liam Hyland; Rob Rowe; Jim Hodkinson; Peter Stone; Philip Duncan; Paul Woolley; John Poore; Matthew Lightburn.

CC Number: 209170

Eligibility

People who are in need and have worked in any of the DIY, hardware, housewares, ironmongery, builders merchants and brushware industries – normally for at least ten years. The trust has stated that 'we use the product category listing from BHETA (British Home Enhancement Trade Association) – if company in question processed (i.e. manufactured, distributed or sold) these products it is highly likely that they would be qualifying.'

Types of grants

One-off grants towards, for example, mobility equipment and installations, travel expenses to see distant relatives, nursing home or residential fees, holidays, TV licences, funeral expenses, food hampers at Christmas, utility bills, household equipment and so on. Pensions are also given to those on a low income.

Annual grant total

In 2011 the trust had assets of £1.4 million and an income of £115,000. Grants were made to 112 individuals totalling £103,000, and were distributed as follows:

Quarterly pensions	£83,000
Other grants	£9,700
Christmas hampers/grants	£5,200
Telephone	£3,300
Holidays	£1,000
TV Licence grants	£600
Funeral grants	£400

Exclusions

No grants are given to children, or to people working in the steel and motor industries.

Applications

On a form available from the correspondent or the trust website. Applications can be submitted directly by the individual or through a social worker, Citizens Advice or other welfare agency. Applications are considered at any time.

Mining

Mining Institute of Scotland Trust

£12,500

Correspondent: The Secretary, 14/9 Burnbrae Drive, Edinburgh EH12 8AS

SC Number: SC024974

Eligibility

Members or former members of the Mining Institute of Scotland and their dependents.

Types of grants

One-off and recurrent hardship grants of up to £1,000 a year. Widows of members can receive Christmas and summer holiday grants.

Annual grant total

The trust has about £25,000 available to give in grants each year, for both education and hardship purposes. It has difficulty in finding enough eligible applicants to support.

Applications

In writing to the correspondent, in the first instance, to request an application form.

Other information

Schools are also supported.

Motor industry

Ben – The Automotive Industry Charity

£590,000 (2,074 grants)

Correspondent: Fiona Gorman, Head of Welfare, Lynwood, Sunninghill, Ascot, Berkshire SL5 0AJ (01344 876770; fax: 01344 622042; email: careservices@ben. org.uk; website: www.ben.org.uk)

Trustees: Christopher John Macgowan; Robin Shaw; Timothy Victor Holmes; Graham Smith; Steven Dewey; Michael A. Breitheam Judge; Graeme John Potts; Anthony Sackett; Robin A. J. Woolcock; Brian Philip Back; Joseph Greenwell; Leslie Ratcliffe; Daksh Gupta; Pauline Wiseman.

CC Number: 297877

Eligibility

People from the UK or Republic of Ireland employed or formerly employed in the motor, motorcycle, commercial vehicle, or agricultural engineering industries plus associated trades and industries. Dependents of employees can also apply. Applicants must hold less than £4,000 in savings and be in real financial need.

Types of grants

Over 90% of grants made are for under £500. Larger amounts are sometimes available for people with complex needs requiring costly disability equipment or adaptations. Grants made have included UK travel costs, white goods, one-off help with priority bills, disability equipment and adaptations.

Annual grant total

In 2011/12 the fund had assets of almost £18 million and an income of £12 million. There were 2,074 (2010/11: 1,933) grants made to individuals totalling £590,000 (2010/11: £544,000).

Of this total 1,948 grants were discretionary and 126 were regular grants. The fund also paid £44,000 in one-off grants to individuals on behalf of other organisations.

Exclusions

The trust cannot assist with top up fees for people in care homes, property repairs (except heating and adaptations for a disabled person), private education costs, private medical costs or costs associated with bankruptcy.

Applications

On a form available from the correspondent. Applications can be submitted directly by the individual or through a social worker, Citizens Advice or other welfare agency. An initial phone call is welcomed. The grant committee meets once a month and it may take up to six weeks for a decision.

Other information

The fund also manages an extensive range of residential and nursing accommodation for people who are older or living with a disability, including sheltered accommodation as well as providing advice, support and friendship to those suffering hardship and distress.

The Society of Motor Manufacturers and Traders Charitable Trust Fund

£12,000

Correspondent: Sefton Samuels, SMMT, Forbes House, Halkin Street, London SW1X 7DS (020 7344 9267; email: charitabletrust@smmt.co.uk)

Trustees: Nic Reilly; Sir Ian McAllister; John Neill; Lord George Simpson of Dunkeld; Mike Baunton; Peter Ward; Sir Ian Gibson; Trevor Bonner; Roger

Putnam; Davide Owen; Graham Smith; Joe Greenwell; Tod Evans; Nigel Stein; Bill Parfitt; Tim Abbott; Dr Ralph Speth; Robin Woolcock.

CC Number: 209852

Eligibility

People in need who held 'responsible positions' in the motor industry, and their dependents.

Types of grants

One-off and recurrent grants and loans according to need.

Annual grant total

In 2011 the society had an unusually high income of £134,000 and a total expenditure of £15,000.

Applications

In writing to the correspondent.

Vehicle Builders and Repairers Association Benevolent Fund

£2,000

Correspondent: David C Hudson, c/o Vehicle Builders' and Repairers' Association Ltd, Belmont House, Gildersome, Leeds LS27 7TW (01132 538333; fax: 01132 380496; email: vbra@vbra.co.uk; website: www.vbra.co.uk)

Trustees: Howard Charlesworth; Bill Neish; John Law; Doreen Hutton.

CC Number: 225924

Eligibility

Present and former members, and employees of members, of the Vehicle Builders and Repairers Association who are in need, and their dependents. Applicants must have been a member or employee of a member for at least five years.

Types of grants

One-off and recurrent grants according to need.

Annual grant total

In 2010 the fund had an income of £3,500 and a total expenditure of £2,000.

Applications

On a form available from the correspondent.

Naval architecture

Royal Institution of Naval Architects

£56,000

Correspondent: Trevor Blakeley, Chief Executive, 10 Upper Belgrave Street, London SW1X 8BQ (020 7235 4122; fax: 020 7259 5912; email: hq@rina.org.uk; website: www.rina.org.uk)

Trustees: Alex Marsh; Prof. Jeom Kee Paik; Robert Curry; Prof. Dracos Vassalos; Harry Karanassos; Stephen Payne; Prof. Simon Christopher Rusling; John Campbell Hudson; Peter Douglas French; Prof. Konstantinos Spyrou; Anna Grace Evangelidis; Gillian Smyth; Robert John Hindley; Dr Arun Dev; Nicholas Pattison; Prof. Richard Birmingham; Miguel Palomares; Dr David Aldwinckle; Kong Seng Tham; Jacqueline Buchan; Richard Buchan; Pierre Besse; Ian Grant; Christos Hadjichristou; David Asprey; Stephen Forster; Thomas Gunn; Rosalind Spink; Andrew David King; Ben Lau; Dr Abdullahel Bari; Alan William Stokes; Robin Charles Gehling; Alan Glen Gavin; Bruce Rosenblatt; Jeffrey Derrick Frier; William Kelly; Sarah Watts; Dr Thomas Allan.

CC Number: 211161

Eligibility

Members and their dependents who are in need.

Types of grants

One-off grants for a variety of needs.

Annual grant total

In 2010/11 the trust had assets of £2.7 million and an income of £2.5 million. Grants were made totalling £56,000.

Applications

In writing to the correspondent, to be considered as they arrive.

Other information

This trust also provides scholarships and training programmes.

Newsagents

The National Federation of Retail Newsagents Convalescence Fund

£11,000

Correspondent: Michael Jenkins, Yeoman House, Sekforde Street, Clerkenwell Green, London EC1R 0HF (020 7017 8855; email: info@nfrn.org.uk; website: www.nfrnonline.com)

Trustees: Barrie Taylor; Vyas Sharma; James Maitland.

CC Number: 209280

Eligibility

Members of the federation and their spouses. Other people in the retail newsagency trade who are not members of the federation are not eligible.

Types of grants

One-off grants for convalescent holidays.

Annual grant total

In 2010, the most recent year for which accounts were available from the Charity Commission, the fund had an income of £12,000 and a total expenditure of £13,000.

Applications

In writing to the correspondent or by contacting the NFRN helpline on 0845 601 5818. Applications can be submitted directly by the individual, through a third party such as a social worker or through a district office of the federation. They are considered at any time.

NewstrAid Benevolent Society

£552,000 (1,079 grants)

Correspondent: Sinead Flood, Welfare Manager, Barnetson Court, Braintree Road, Great Dunmow, Essex CM6 1HS (01371 874198; fax: 01371 873816; email: sinead@newstraid.org.uk; website: www.newstraid.org.uk)

Trustees: David Holliday; Ingrid Jones; Thomas Melvyn Lewis; Michael David Mirams; Frank Mustard; Simon Mark Prodger; Ronald William Rushbrook; Richard John Webb; Neil Hilton Jagger; John George Stranger; Stephen Hirst; Nigel Roderick Lomas.

CC Number: 1116824

Eligibility

People and their immediate dependents, who have been employed in newspaper and magazine distribution in the UK and who have fallen on hard times. Distribution means people who deal with newspapers and magazines from the time they leave the printing press until they reach the reader. All applications are assessed on their merits but the society states that applicants should have normally been connected with the trade for a minimum of ten years.

Types of grants

Annual payments and one-off grants for various items including household appliances, special chairs, mobility aids, small repairs and disability equipment. The charity offers interest free loans to home owners in respect of costly repairs, repayable on the sale of their property.

Annual grant total

In 2011 the charity had assets of £5.5 million and an income of £2.7 million. £552,000 was given in grants to 1,079 individuals for welfare purposes.

Exclusions

No grants for private medicine or school or college fees.

Applications

Initial contact should be made by calling the welfare team or by submitting an enquiry form available to download from the website. The application will then be followed up by a telephone call from the welfare team.

Patent agents

The Incorporated Benevolent Association of the Chartered Institute of Patent Attorneys

£31,000

Correspondent: Derek Chandler, 95 Chancery Lane, London WC2A 1DT

Trustees: T. W. Roberts; J. D. Brown; H. G. Hallybone; C. T. Eyles; H. M. Jones; M. A. Lynd; P. D. Eke; S. J. Mohun; D. R. Chandler.

CC Number: 219666

Eligibility

British members and former members of the institute, and their dependents.

Types of grants

One-off and recurrent grants or loans according to need.

Annual grant total

In 2010/11 the association had assets of £717,000 and an income of £47,000. Grants to individuals for 'general assistance' totalled £31,000.

Applications

In writing to the correspondent, marked 'Private and Confidential'. Applications can be submitted at any time. Where possible, grants are provided via a third party.

Other information

The association also makes grants for educational purposes.

Pawnbrokers

The Pawnbrokers' Charitable Institution

£77,000 (32 grants)

Correspondent: Mrs K Way, Secretary, 184 Crofton Lane, Orpington, Kent BR6 0BW (01689 811978)

Trustees: Philip Malcolm Diaper; Kathryn Elizabeth Lyons; Kevin Raper; Philip Patrick Murphy.

CC Number: 209993

Eligibility

Pawnbrokers in need who have been in the business for at least five years, and their dependents. Help is primarily given to people over 60 but assistance may also be available to younger people if there is sufficient need.

Types of grants

Regular payments for those on a low income and one-off grants to meet emergency needs. Recent grants have been given towards new furniture, a cooker and a reclining chair. Christmas and summer grants of about £250 each are also available to beneficiaries.

Annual grant total

In 2010/11 the institution had assets of £2.9 million and an income of £85,000. Grants were made to 32 individuals totalling £77,000.

Applications

On a form available from the correspondent. The trustees meet on the first Tuesday of every month to consider applications.

Petroleum

BP Benevolent Fund

£17,000 (23 grants)

Correspondent: Peter Darnell, BP Benevolent Fund Trustees Ltd, 4 Woodside Close, Shermanbury, Horsham RH13 8HH (01403 710437; email: peter.darnell@uk.bp.com)

Trustees: David Howard Price; Frances Blois; Leslie Rees; Ms R. Murray; John Graham Mumford; Ian Woodley.

CC Number: 803778

Eligibility

Former employees of BP plc or subsidiary or associated companies and the dependents of such persons.

Types of grants

One-off and recurrent according to need and vouchers. Occasional hardship grants up to a maximum of £750.

In 2010 grants were paid for bankruptcy costs; household white goods and furniture; wheelchairs; heating; loan/debt repayments; and home repairs.

Annual grant total

In 2010 the fund had assets of £1.2 million and an income of £32,000. Of 29 applications received, awards were made to help 16 individuals.

Of these 14 occasional hardship grants were paid totalling £6,300. Nine other grants totalled £10,600.

The fund also provides interest free loans. They approved four new loans totalling £12,600 in 2010.

Applications

In writing to the correspondent.

Police

The Metropolitan Police Benevolent Fund

£337,000

Correspondent: Janice Berry, Exchequer Services (Charities), Metropolitan Police Services, Empress State Building, Empress Approach, London SW6 1TR (020 7161 1909; email: janice.berry@met. police.uk)

Trustees: Chris Allison; Robert James Broadhurst; Simon Noel Ovens; Victor William Kirby; David Michael Bryant; Neil Martin Cratchley; Mark Robert Nurthen; Robert James Elder; Mary Lyons; Des McCarthy.

CC Number: 1125409

Eligibility

Metropolitan Police officers and ex-officers who are in need, and their widows/widowers and orphans.

Types of grants

Generally one-off grants according to need. Loans are also offered.

Annual grant total

In 2011 the fund had assets of £3.6 million and an income of £2.3 million. Charitable activities totalled £2 million and can be broken down as follows:

- Donations to the police rehabilitation centre: £1.4 million – enables injured and sick members of the Metropolitan Police to attend the centre for free
- Grants to individuals: £337,000
- Support for the Metropolitan and City Police Orphans Fund: £325,000

A further £234,000 was provided in interest-free loans to members.

Applications

In writing to the correspondent directly by the individual. Applications are considered throughout the year.

Other information

In 2008 the Metropolitan Police Combined Benevolent Fund and its constituent charities amalgamated into one major fund that would encompass all the objectives of the current charities (Metropolitan Police Convalescent Home Fund, Metropolitan and City Police Orphans Fund, Metropolitan Police Relief Fund and Metropolitan Police Widows and Widowers Fund). This new fund is known as the Metropolitan Police Benevolent Fund.

Metropolitan Police Civil Staff Welfare Fund

£28,000

Correspondent: Mrs Janice Berry, Metropolitan Police Service, 10th Floor (East), Empress State Building, Empress Approach, London SW6 1TR (020 7161 1909; email: welfarefunds@met.police. uk)

Trustees: Edward Solomons; Anne McMeel; Nicky Piper; Val Harris; Ann Middleton; Majella Myers.

CC Number: 282375

Eligibility

Members and past members of the Metropolitan Police Staff and the Metropolitan Police Authority and their families and dependents who, through poverty, hardship or distress, are in need.

Types of grants

One-off grants and loans, generally ranging between £200 and £3,000 according to need.

Annual grant total

In 2010/11 the fund had assets of £262,000 and an income of £33,000. Grants were made totalling £28,000.

Exclusions

Grants are unlikely to be made towards private healthcare, private education fees, legal costs, business debts or bills that have already been paid.

Applications

On a form available from the correspondent. Applications should be submitted directly by the individual or through a social worker, Citizens Advice or other welfare agency.

Northern Ireland Police Fund

£1.71 million

Correspondent: The Secretary, Maryfield Complex, 100 Belfast Road, Holywood BT18 9QY (02890 393556; fax: 02890 393555; email: admin@nipolicefund.org; website: www.nipolicefund.org)

Eligibility

Serving and retired police officers in Northern Ireland, and their dependents, who have been directly affected by terrorist violence whether on or off-duty. This includes those with serious physical and/or psychological injuries which would be considered sufficiently serious to warrant the award of an IOD Band 2 medical discharge, as determined by an occupational physician. The applicant must also be able to demonstrate that the IOD was a result of the individual being the directly intended target of terrorist attack. Applications are also considered from the families of officers who have committed suicide if a causal link can be established between a direct attack on the officer and their subsequent death.

Types of grants

Regular grants to those on a very low income (£11,273 or below in 2010/11) paid in two annual instalments, usually in April and September. The fund also administers a number of separate schemes for one-off grants including:

- Disability support scheme – to provide equipment or household items which would improve the applicant's quality of life
- Bereavement support scheme – to provide financial support to the dependents and parents of officers who have lost their lives as a direct result of terrorist violence
- Disability adaptations scheme – for those seriously injured who need specialist equipment or adaptations to their homes
- Prostheses/wheelchair grants
- Carers respite breaks – for the primary carers of officers, ex-officers, parents and the widows of murdered officers
- Chronic pain management scheme – for pain management programmes
- Psychological support scheme – to help with the costs of counselling and treatment

In general unless the applicant has no or a negative disposable income grants will not be awarded for items costing £150 or less. Grants from the disability or bereavement schemes are capped at a maximum of £7,000.

Annual grant total

According to the NIPF website: 'Its remit is to provide support to those police officers injured as a result of terrorist violence, and their families, and the widows, children and parents of officers killed in terrorist incidents. The Fund has an annual budget of £1.8m per year for the provision of these services.'

In 2011/12 grants totalled £1.7 million.

Exclusions

Once an application has been approved the applicant must wait 12 months before re-applying. Applicants cannot re-apply for the same item if their first request has been declined nor can applications be split into separate parts to avoid the capping of awards.

Applications

In the first instance applicants should contact the fund to discuss eligibility. Once this has been established an assessment will follow. The fund publishes detailed eligibility criteria, limits and application information on their website. Ensure you consult the criteria for the relevant fund before applying.

Other information

The fund was established in 2001 following the Patten Report into policing in Northern Ireland.

Police Dependants' Trust

£1.4 million

Correspondent: David French, Chief Executive, 3 Mount Mews, High Street, Hampton, Middlesex TW12 2SH (020 8941 6907; fax: 020 8979 4323; email: office@pdtrust.org; website: www. pdtrust.org)

Trustees: Martin Richards; Sandie Wilde; Don Ratcliffe; Terry Spence; Pat Stayt; Paul Barker; Paul McKeever; Les Gray; Bill Berry; Marty Whittle; Rod Jarman; David Pellatt; Stephen Gilligan; Sue Akers; Graham Cassidy; Dr Ian Lattimer; Tony Harper.

CC Number: 251021

Eligibility

(i.) Dependents of current police officers or former police officers who have died from injuries received in the execution of duty.
(ii.) Police officers or former police officers incapacitated as a result of injury received in the execution of duty, or their dependents.

Types of grants

One-off grants in the range of £280 to £21,000, averaging about £2,300 each. Grants are available for specialist equipment, disability aids, clothing, holidays (including support for accompanying professional carers) and funeral expenses. Residential care grants may also be considered to assist with incidental expenses. Annual maintenance grants are given to help incapacitated officers and police dependents enjoy a reasonable standard of living.

Annual grant total

In 2010/11 the trust had assets of £25.2 million and an income of £1.2 million. Grants to individuals totalled £2.8 million and were distributed as follows:

Maintenance Grants	311
Children's grants	61
Special Purpose Grants	215
Holiday Grants	690
Funeral Grants	4

Grants are also made for educational purposes.

Applications

On a form available from the correspondent, to be submitted through one of the force's welfare officers. Applications are generally considered every two months although urgent decisions can be made between meetings.

St George's Police Trust

£254,000

Correspondent: Michael Baxter, St Andrews, Harlow Moor Road, Harrogate, North Yorkshire HG2 0AD (01423 504448; email: enquiries@ stgeorgespolicetrust.org; website: www. thepolicetreatmentcentres.org)

Trustees: Stuart Hyde; Ian Poultney; Mark Botham; Gordon Dixon; Raymond Pratt.

CC Number: 1147445

Eligibility

Children in full time education with at least one parent who was a member of a police force covered by the trust (see 'Other Information'), and who is now deceased or incapacitated due to their work. Young people not in full time education who have lost a police officer parent, but who are unable to earn their own living as a result of having special needs, may also be eligible.

Normally, to be eligible the police officer parent must have donated to the trust whilst serving.

Types of grants

One-off and recurrent grants towards living costs, holidays, clothing, birthday and Christmas gifts and so on.

Annual grant total

In 2011 the trust had assets of £8.9 million and an income of £1 million. Grants to individuals totalled £254,000.

Applications

On an application form available to download from the website. Applications should be submitted via the police force in which the parent served. This is usually done through the police federation office, the occupational health and welfare department or occasionally the force benevolent fund. Applications are considered as they arrive.

Other information

The trust covers the following police forces: Central Scotland; Cheshire; Cleveland; Cumbria; Derbyshire; Dumfries and Galloway; Durham; Fife; Grampian; Greater Manchester Police; Humberside; Lancashire; Lincolnshire; Lothian and Borders; Merseyside; Northern; Northumbria; North Wales; North Yorkshire; Nottinghamshire; South Yorkshire; Staffordshire; Strathclyde; Tayside; West Mercia; West Yorkshire.

Post-office

The Rowland Hill Memorial And Benevolent Fund

£269,000

Correspondent: Mary Jeffery, Room 412, Royal Mail Mount Pleasant, Farringdon Road, London EC1A 1BB (0800 688 8777; fax: 020 7239 2265; email: rowland.hill.fund@royalmail.com; website: www.rowlandhillfund.org)

Trustees: Alan Wiltshire; Bryan Roberts; David Blake; Philip Bowerman; Richard Poole; Ernie Dudley; Pauline Vickers; Sue Higgins; Jonathan Evans; Graham Hadfield; Steve Weston; Chris Littlejohns; Dale Thomas Haddon.

CC Number: 207479

Eligibility

People in need who have been employed by the Royal Mail, Post-Office, Parcelforce Worldwide or General Logistics for at least six months (full or part-time, not casual); retired employees in receipt of an occupational pension; and people who have a deferred pension. The direct dependents of such people may also be eligible for assistance.

Types of grants

One-off grants of up to £5,000 but usually less than £1,000 for disability aids, house adaptations, hospital travel

costs, funeral expenses, medical equipment, essential household items and increasingly, personal debt. Beneficiaries must be experiencing financial hardship due to unforeseen circumstances. Recurrent cost of living grants and help with nursing home fees are also available to older people.

Loans are available to Royal Mail Group employees to help short-term crises and are repaid from salary.

Annual grant total

In 2010/11 the fund had assets of £3.3 million and an income of £477,000. Grants were made totalling £269,000, with £227,000 paid in one-off grants and £42,000 paid in regular grants.

Applications

Employees of the Royal mail group or people in receipt of an occupational pension or deferred pension should call the free 24 hour helpline operated by Royal Mail (0800 688 8777). A trained advisor will conduct a short telephone assessment and, with permission, forward a report of the case to the fund for consideration. Some medical and/or financial evidence of need may also be required.

People applying through a third party such as a social worker or Citizens Advice should apply in writing to the correspondent, including as much background information and supporting documentation as possible.

The National Federation of Sub-Postmasters Benevolent Fund

£119,000

Correspondent: George Thomson, Evelyn House, 22 Windlesham Gardens, Shoreham-by-Sea, West Sussex BN43 5AZ (01273 452324; fax: 01273 465403; email: admin@nfsp.org.uk; website: www.nfsp.org.uk)

Trustees: Mervyn Hendry Jones; Keith Richards; Paul Christopher Haines.

CC Number: 262704

Eligibility

People in need who fall into one of the following categories:

(i) Serving or retired sub-postmasters and sub-postmistresses;

(ii) Serving or retired full-time employees of the NFSP; and

(iii) The widows, widowers and children of the above in the event of a breakdown in health; the death of a husband, father, wife or mother; or domestic distress.

Types of grants

One-off and recurrent grants according to need. Recent examples include:

fencing; a second hand scooter; a downstairs shower for a person with disabilities; house and roof repairs; an adjustable bed; a reconditioned stair-lift; and a holiday for somebody with disabilities.

Annual grant total

In 2010 the fund had assets of £1.4 million, an income of £56,000. Grants totalled £119,000: including 26 one-off grants and 19 beneficiaries who received recurrent help.

Applications

On a form available from the correspondent, submitted directly by the individual or a welfare charity. Applications are usually considered quarterly, but emergency cases can be dealt with as they arise.

Other information

The fund also provides access to a one-on-one counselling service with qualified counsellors who offer counselling and emotional support on all issues to subpostmasters, their immediate family members and sub post-office staff.

Pottery and glass

The Pottery and Glass Trade Benevolent Fund (formerly the Pottery and Glass Trade Benevolent Institution)

£17,000

Correspondent: Audrey Smith, Flat 57, Witley Court, Coram Street, London WC1N 1HD (020 7837 2231; fax: 020 7837 2231)

Trustees: Philip John Willoughby; Paul Wood; Herbert Clarence Fordham; Andrew Stewart Cullen; Anthony Geoffrey Houldsworth; Fiona Jane Milne; Frances Fox; Leigh Baildham; Leslie Raymond Elks; Michael Trotter; Neville Singer; Josephine Hawkins; Raymond Frank Windsor; Barbara Beadman; Ann Moult; David Mackenzie.

CC Number: 208227

Eligibility

People who are or were employed in manufacturing, wholesale or retail aspects of china or glass.

Types of grants

One-off grants and pensions. Recent grants have been made towards priority debts, house adaptations, central heating repairs, mobility scooters, essential household items and car repairs.

Annual grant total

In 2009/10, the most recent year for which accounts were available at the time of writing (winter 2012), the fund had an income of £12,000 and a total expenditure of £19,000.

Applications

On a form available from the correspondent. Applications can be submitted directly by the individual or through a social worker, Citizens Advice or other welfare agency. They are considered quarterly in March, June, September and December and should be submitted by 1st March, June, September and December.

Printing

The GPM Charitable Trust

£5,000

Correspondent: Keith Keys, 43 Spriggs Close, Clapham, Bedford MK41 6GD (07733 262991; email: gpmcharitabletrust@tiscali.co.uk; website: www.gpmtrust.org)

Trustees: Charles Cherrill; Glyn Beaver; Joe Smith; Rose Mooney; Brian Willoughby; Leslie Miller; Vernon Robson.

CC Number: 227177

Eligibility

Workers, former workers and their dependents in the printing, graphical, papermaking and media industries.

Types of grants

Grants for household essentials, medical aids, respite or convalescent breaks, goods, services or facilities.

Annual grant total

In 2011/12 the trust had an income of £15,000 and an expenditure of £26,000.

Applications

On a form available to download from the website, or from the correspondent, to be returned by email or post.

Other information

The trust has also been funding a refurbishment project for people in sheltered housing with another charity. They also give grants for educational purposes.

The Printing Charity

£318,000 (423 grants)

Correspondent: Henry Smith, Grants Officer, Suite B Underwood House, 235 Three Bridges Road, Crawley, West Sussex RH10 1LS (01293 649368; fax: 01293 542826; email: info@ theprintingcharity.org.uk; website: www. theprintingcharity.org.uk)

Trustees: Brian John Skerritt; James Povey; Jon Wright; Michael Charles Offer; Fiona Morris; Steve Sibbald; David Turner; Richard Brewster; Stephanie Delaszlo; Gary Cullum; Alan Thorburn.

CC Number: 208882

Eligibility

Ex-printers, or people who have worked for five years in the printing profession, graphic arts or allied trades and their dependents.

Types of grants

One-off and recurrent grants ranging from £100 to £1,000 for help with mobility needs, household items, house repairs, convalescence, bankruptcy fees, top-up fees for nursing homes and emergency relief for people affected by flooding. Biannual financial assistance grants are also available to help with everyday living costs.

Annual grant total

In 2011 the charity held assets of £31 million and had an income of £1.3 million. Grants to 423 individuals totalled £318,000 and can be broken down as follows:

Regular financial assistance	£221,000
One-off grants	£84,000
Nursing home grants	£14,000

Applications

On a form available from the correspondent or to download from the website. Assistance is means tested so applicants should be prepared to make a full declaration of their finances, including state benefits and funding from other charitable sources. Application forms can be submitted either directly by the individual or through a social worker, Citizens Advice or other third party.

The trust advises potential applicants to contact them before submitting an application.

Other information

Formerly the Printers' Charitable Corporation, the trust provides sheltered homes for older people at Basildon and Bletchley. It also advises pensioners on their statutory entitlements.

Probation

The Edridge Fund

£36,000 (115 grants)

Correspondent: The Secretary, The Limes, Lynn Road, Gayton, King's Lynn, Norfolk PE32 1QJ (01553 636570; email: office@edridgefund.org; website: www. edridgefund.org)

Trustees: David Cox; Anne King; Alessandra Evans; Nick Paul; Lizzy Bywater.

CC Number: 803493

Eligibility

Members, and ex-members, of the probation service and CAFCASS who are (or were) eligible to be members of NAPO and their bereaved partners, spouses and dependents.

Types of grants

Financial and welfare support, generally in a one-off grant, to alleviate cases of distress and hardship such as debt, relationship breakdown, accident or ill health.

Annual grant total

In 2010 the fund had assets of £199,000 and an income of £53,000. Grants to 115 individuals (from 137 applications) totalled £36,000.

Applications

On a form available from the correspondent, a local representative or on the fund's website. Applications can be submitted either directly by the individual or through the local representative of the fund. A decision is usually made within three weeks, though emergency cases can be dealt with more quickly.

NB. If applicants do not wish their local representative to be aware of their application it should be stated clearly on their form.

Property and Facilities

Sears Group Trust

£109,000 (128 grants)

Correspondent: Mick Harvey, Secretary to the Trustees, Sunningdale Centre, Sunningdale Road, Leicester LE3 1UR (01162 012528; email: mick.j.harvey@ sgp.co.uk)

Trustees: Sears Group Trustees Ltd (Gary Branston; Joe Goff; Margaret Hannell; Peter Holder).

CC Number: 1022586

Eligibility

Employees, former employees and their dependents of any company that is, or has been, associated with Sears Ltd, who are in financial need.

Types of grants

One-off and recurrent grants according to need. Recurrent grants, averaging around £800 per year, are made to top up low incomes and paid in two instalments, usually in June and December. One-off grants average around £700 and have been made for items and services like central heating, decorating, window repairs, bedding and clothes. The trust also owns a number of pieces of mobility equipment which may be gifted or loaned to individuals. Entitlement to recurrent grants is normally reviewed every three years.

Annual grant total

In 2011/12 the trust held assets totalling £9 million, had an income from investments of £394,000 and made grants totalling £109,000. During the year 120 beneficiaries received regular grants and eight one-off grants were paid.

Exclusions

No grants for bankruptcy or funeral costs.

Applications

Initial contact should be made with the correspondent who will arrange for a visit from one of the trust's welfare visitors. The visitor will assess the applicant and make a recommendation to the trustees. Trustees meet to consider applications two to three times per year, however, applications can be processed between meetings.

Other information

One grant of £3,000 was made to a local organisation in the year.

Public relations

Iprovision (formerly The Institute of Public Relations Benevolent Fund)

£1,200 (3 grants)

Correspondent: Jane Wharam, Administrator, 9 Eyston Drive, Weybridge KT13 0XD (020 8144 5536; email: administrator@iprovision.org.uk; website: www.cipr.co.uk/iprovision)

Trustees: Stuart Render; John Brown; Marc Evans; Beryl Evans; Pat Gaudin; Keith Johnston; Gill Dandy; Lis Lewis Jones; Jane Wilson; Joanne Sweeney.

CC Number: 242674

Eligibility

Members of the institute and dependents of members or deceased members.

Types of grants

One-off and recurrent grants according to need as well as interest free loans. Grants can cover white goods, daily living expenses, unexpected one-off costs, respite breaks, etc.

Annual grant total

In 2011 the fund had an income of £63,000 and a total expenditure of £19,000. Grants were made to three individuals totalling £1,200.

Exclusions

No grants for CIPR annual subscriptions, business costs or debts.

Applications

Initially in writing to the correspondent outlining your need and how you think the fund can help. Applicants are contacted and will be asked to complete an application form. Applications are considered every two months, although urgent applications can be considered at any time.

Public sector

City of London Benevolent Association

£18,000

Correspondent: Matthew Pitt, City of London, PO Box 270, London EC2P 2EJ (020 7332 1432; email: matthew.pitt@ cityoflondon.gov.uk; website: www. cityoflondon.gov.uk)

Trustees: Robin Anthony Eve; Dennis Cotgrove; Sir David Howard; John Barker; Simon Walsh; William Fraser; Robert Finch; Michael Snyder; Michael Sherlock; Roger Gifford; Catherine Sidony McGuinness; Richard Regan; Alastair King; Julian Malins; Stella Currie; Lord Mayor David Wootton; Stanley Ginsburg; John Owen-Ward; Janet Owen; Michael Cassidy; Anthony Noel Eskezi; Gerald Pulman; Greg Lawrence; Joyce Nash; Pauline Halliday; Michael Welbank; John White; Douglas Barrow; Henry Jones; Neil Redcliffe; Stephen Haines; John Bennett; Giles Shilson; Ken Ayers; William Dove; Keith Knowles.

CC Number: 206643

Eligibility

People in need who are, or have been, members of the Court of Common Council, and their dependents.

Types of grants

One-off grants according to need.

Annual grant total

In 2010/11 the charity had an income of £8,000 and a total expenditure of £19,000.

Applications

On an application form available from the City of London website.

Other information

In recent years, the charity's investment income has exceeded its expenditure and the trustees are keen to ensure that all members, and particularly their families, are aware of the opportunity for financial assistance.

There For You (UNISON Welfare)

£751,000

Correspondent: Julie Grant, Head of UNISON Welfare, UNISON Centre, 130 Euston Road, London NW1 2AY (0845 355 0845; email: welfare@unison.co.uk; website: www.unison.org.uk/welfare)

Trustees: June Poole; Sue Highton; Mark Fisher; Maureen Le Marniel; Mary Locke; Andrew Douglas; Melanie Fender; Carol Sewell; Kathy Symonds; Michael Dougherty; Brian Gowrie; Gail Jones.

CC Number: 1023552

Eligibility

Members of UNISON and past members of NALGO, and their dependents, who are in need. UNISON staff may also be helped in some circumstances. Unemployed members are eligible for assistance up to two years from the date their employment terminated.

Types of grants

One-off grants for individuals experiencing unforeseen difficulties such as redundancy, illness, bereavement or relationship breakdown. Recent awards have been given to help with household bills, travel costs, childcare, school uniforms, winter fuel costs, furniture, domestic appliances, funeral expenses, disability aids and so on. Emergency grants of up to £150 are available when there is a crisis and money is needed quickly. For example, if an individual has been forced to leave their home and is in need of food and temporary shelter. Weekly grants for up to twelve weeks may be considered if the applicant is in a temporary period of reduced income, especially if they have considerable debt.

Funding is also available for holidays, convalescence and respite breaks under the trust's 'Wellbeing Breaks' scheme.

Annual grant total

In 2011 the trust had assets of £5.4 million, an income of £1.2 million and a total expenditure of £1.4 million. Grants were made totalling £751,000 and can be broken down as follows:

Debt and bankruptcy	£249,000
Other purposes	£135,000
Household	£124,000
Income subsidy	£123,000
Wellbeing breaks	£53,000
Funeral expenses	£47,000
Health	£20,000

Exclusions

Assistance will not normally be given where the applicant has savings of £3,000 or more. Grants are generally not given for educational costs, private medical treatment, legal fees, car purchase or income lost due to industrial action.

Applications

Individuals should first contact their branch welfare officer or secretary who will help them to fill in an application form. Applications are usually processed within two weeks, though urgent requests can be dealt with more quickly, sometimes within 48 hours. People who are having difficulty contacting their local branch may submit the form, available from the website, directly to the national office.

Note that there are separate application forms for welfare grants and wellbeing breaks.

Other information

The trust, previously known simply as UNISON Welfare, provides support and advice on a variety of issues including personal debt and state benefits.

Public transport

The Worshipful Company of Carmen Benevolent Trust

£500

Correspondent: Robin East, Hon. Secretary, 5 Kings House, Queen St Place, London EC4R 1QS (020 7489 8289; fax: 020 7236 3133; email: clerk@thecarmen.co.uk; website: www.thecarmen.co.uk)

Trustees: Brig. Mike Turner; Telfer Saywell; John Older; Michael Joseph Power; Robert Harold Russett; Mary Patricia Bonar; M. Simpkin.

CC Number: 1050893

Eligibility

People based in the UK and have worked in the transport industry (for example, HGV drivers or bus drivers).

Types of grants

One-off grants usually in the region of £50 to £500, where the grant will make an exceptional difference to the individual. A recent grant was given, for example, to a disabled person who needed computer equipment.

Annual grant total

In 2010/11 the trust had assets of £1.1 million and an income of £117,000. Grants totalled £80,000, however nearly all of this went to organisations during the year.

Exclusions

The trust cannot help with holidays or bankruptcy fees.

Applications

In writing to the correspondent. Note, this trust only occasionally makes grants to individuals. The trustees meet four times a year.

The Transport Benevolent Fund

£360,000 (2,754 grants)

Correspondent: Chris Godbold, Director, 22 Lovat Lane, London EC3R 8EB (0300 333 2000; email: help@tbf.org.uk; website: www.tbf.org.uk)

Trustees: Freddy Soper; Ray Jordan; Susan Gilbert; Ian Wilson; Peter Sloan; Christopher Sullivan; David Phillips; June Carroll; Ravi Kalsi; John Macdonald; Terry Sharpe; Daniela Spagnoli; Cheryl O'Brien; Tom Shoesmith; Ben Wakerley; Rob Jones; Chris Reilly; Steve Barker; Beverley Holt.

CC Number: 1058032

Eligibility

Employees and former employees of the public transport industry who are in need (often due to being sick, disabled or convalescent), their partners and dependents. Only members of the benevolent fund are supported.

Types of grants

Grants are to meet unexpected one-off situations, where help is not available from other sources. They can be given towards medical equipment, complementary medical treatments (up to a maximum of £250 per year) and other needs. Long-term financial support is not offered. Loans may be made to beneficiaries of the Transport for London Staff Welfare Fund.

Annual grant total

In 2010/11 the fund held assets of £3.5 million and had an income of £2.2 million. Grants were made to individuals totalling £360,000. Of this total £7,000 was paid from the Transport for London Staff Welfare Fund with the remainder paid from the main Transport Benevolent Fund. Grants may be broken down as follows:

Hardship	2,686	£344,000
Medical equipment and mobility aids	40	£11,000
Convalescence	67	£4,000
Medical treatment	1	£1,000

Exclusions

There is no funding towards dental or optical treatment and funerals, except in special circumstances.

Applications

By writing to or emailing the fund with a description of your claim outlining your need, how it arose and how much you are asking for. They are considered monthly or when required.

Other information

In 2006 the charity acquired the assets of the Transport for London Staff Welfare Fund, which had been established in 1948 to provide help for staff of the London Transport Executive. The assets are held separately and used only for the relief of persons specified by Transport for London in the Deed of Grant.

The fund also offers financial and legal advice.

Quarrying

The Institute of Quarrying Educational Development and Benevolent Fund

£17,000 (6 grants)

Correspondent: The Secretary, 7 Regent Street, Nottingham NG1 5BS (01159 453882; fax: 01159 484035; email: mail@quarrying.org; website: www.quarrying.org)

Trustees: John Kenneth Hopkins; Philip John Hutchins; Anthony Morgan; Kenneth John Bradley; Martin Kent Isles; Lyn Bryden; Kevin Norman Parker; Russell David Mason; Gordon Temple; Dudley Lloyd; Calladine Paul.

CC Number: 213586

Eligibility

Members or former members of the Institute of Quarrying, and/or their dependents. People who are involved in the quarrying industry but are not members of the institute cannot be considered.

Types of grants

One-off grants ranging from £100 to £2,500. No recurrent grants are made, although most beneficiaries successfully reapply each year.

Annual grant total

In 2009/10 the trust had assets of £858,000 and an income of £30,000. Welfare grants were made to six long-term beneficiaries totalling £17,000.

Applications

On a form available from the correspondent. Applications may be submitted at any time.

Other information

Projects which advance the education and research of quarrying are also supported.

Railways

Associated Society of Locomotive Engineers and Firemen (ASLEF) Hardship Fund

£11,500

Correspondent: The General Secretary, ASLEF, 9 Arkwright Road, Hampstead, London NW3 6AB (020 7317 8600; fax: 020 7794 6406; email: info@aslef.org.uk; website: www.aslef.org.uk)

Eligibility

Members of ASLEF, and their dependents, who are in need.

Types of grants

One-off grants according to need.

Annual grant total

During the year the fund held assets of £1.4 million and had an income of almost £83,000 in contributions from 16,500 members. Grants paid to members totalled £11,500.

Applications

In writing to the correspondent.

The Railway Benefit Fund

£359,000

Correspondent: Margaret Skerratt, Grants Officer, Electra Way, Crewe, Cheshire CW1 6HS (01270 251316; fax: 01270 503966; email: info@railwaybenefitfund.org.uk; website: www.railwaybenefitfund.org.uk)

Trustees: Simon Osborne; C. R. B. Goldson; David RedFern; Peter Trewin; Alan Marshall; Ken Watson; Richard Eccles; Dominic Booth; Deborah Gilshan; Steve Montgomery; Gregg Ryan.

CC Number: 206312

Eligibility

Active and retired members of the British Railway Board, its subsidiaries and related organisations, and their spouses and children.

Types of grants

One-off and recurrent grants of £100 to £1,500.

- Single benevolent grants include help for mobility aids, minor house repairs, funeral expenses, household equipment, clothing, debt relief, convalescence and household bills
- Annuities are paid quarterly and are available to people on a low income. They are reviewed periodically
- Residential care grants are paid monthly to 'top up' care home fees
- Grants from the Webb Fund are paid quarterly to parents to assist underprivileged children
- Child care grants are given towards clothing, footwear and educational necessities like books and equipment

Annual grant total

In 2011 grants to individuals totalled £359,000, broken down as follows:
- 186 annuities (recurrent) – £87,000
- 339 single benevolent grants – £251,000
- 2 residential care grants – £5,000
- 29 Webb fund grants – £12,000
- 9 childcare grants – £3,200
- 45 other (Christmas presents) – £1,100

The 339 single benevolent grants were broken down again into various needs:
- 46 funeral expenses – £70,000
- 50 minor house repairs – £59,000
- 45 equipment for disability – £50,000
- 49 household equipment – £25,000
- 37 debts and arrears – £24,000
- 98 other – £20,000
- 14 convalescence – £7,800

Applications

On a form available from the correspondent. Applications can be submitted either directly by the individual or a family member or through a third party such as a social worker, teacher or Citizens Advice. Applicants must be able to provide verification of railway service.

The Railway Housing Association and Benefit Fund

£37,000

Correspondent: Anne Rowlands, Railway Housing Association and Benefit Fund, Bank Top House, Garbutt Square, Darlington, County Durham DL1 4DR (01325 482125; fax: 01325 384641; email: info@railwayha.co.uk; website: www. railwayha.co.uk)

Trustees: John Hilton Mayfield; John Reginald Carter; Anne Denzie Mumford; Geoff Proudlock; Barrie Ward; Mary Stella Norrie; Carol Anne Bustard; John Moorley; John Smailes; Michael Tasker; Alistair Brown.

CC Number: 216825

Eligibility
People who are working or who have worked in the railway industry, and their dependents, in England, Scotland and Wales.

Types of grants
One-off grants towards house repairs, care attendants, respite care, essential household items, aids and adaptations and general financial assistance.

Annual grant total
In 2010/11 the association held over £20 million in assets and had an income of £5 million. Grants to beneficiaries amounted to £37,000.

Applications
The association has transferred the administration of its grants to the Railway Benefit Fund and potential applicants should contact them directly at: Electra Way, Crewe Business Park, Crewe, Cheshire CW1 6HS – 01270 251316. However, the association is happy to help and advise any individual who wishes to discuss their case prior to making an application.

Other information
The association's primary concern is the management of affordable accommodation for the benefit of older people in need.

RMT (National Union of Rail, Maritime and Transport Workers) Orphan Fund

£150,000

Correspondent: The Benefits Section, Unity House, 39 Chalton Street, London NW1 1JD (020 7387 4771; fax: 020 7387 4123; email: info@rmt.org.uk; website: www.rmt.org.uk)

Eligibility
Children (aged under 22) of deceased members of the union.

Types of grants
Grants are made of £10 per week per child up to 16 years of age and £12.75 per week per child continuing to receive full-time education from 16 up to 22 years of age, payable on member's death. Grants are paid quarterly in March, June, September and December.

Annual grant total
Around £150,000.

Applications
Application forms are available from the branch secretary or to download from the union's website. For children over 16 years of age an education certificate should also be attached. Applications should be made through the local union branch and endorsed by the branch secretary.

Other information
The union also provides accident, retirement, death and demotion benefits and grants for widows or widowers of members of the union.

Removal trade

The Removers Benevolent Association

£4,000

Correspondent: Grants Officer, British Association of Removers, Tangent House, 62 Exchange Road, Watford, Hertfordshire WD18 0TG (01923 699480; fax: 01923 699481; email: rba@bar.co.uk; website: www.bar.co.uk)

Trustees: John Southerington; Derek Payne; John Court; Matt Purdie.

CC Number: 284012

Eligibility
People in need who are, or have been, employed for a minimum of one year by a member or former member of the British Association of Removers Ltd, and their dependents.

Types of grants
One-off grants, usually in the range of £250 to £750, to help those experiencing a temporary period of financial difficulty. Occasionally, recurrent grants may be given.

Annual grant total
In 2010 the association had an income of £9,500 and a total expenditure of £4,200.

Applications
In writing to the correspondent, to be submitted by the member company the employee has worked for. Applications are considered as they arrive.

Retail trade

Retail Trust

£828,000

Correspondent: Grants Manager, Marshall Hall, Marshall Estate, Hammers Lane, London NW7 4DQ (0808 801 0808; email: helpline@retailtrust.org.uk; website: www.retailtrust.org.uk)

Trustees: Paul Clarke; Adrian James Wright; Edward George Bentley; John Dickson Wilson; Ayo Daramola-Martin; Katherine Payne; Jane Gurney-Read; Judith Pilkington; Christopher Tideman; Avis Darzins; Richard Newman; John Lovering.

CC Number: 1090136

Eligibility
People in need (and their dependents) who have worked in the retail, wholesale, manufacturing and distribution trades for at least:
- Two years if still in the trade
- Two continuous years if retired
- Ten years for former retail employees who have moved on to other trades

Applicants who are unsure if they qualify should contact the support line.

Types of grants
One-off and recurrent grants towards medical equipment, essential household items and so on. Grants are paid directly to suppliers or other responsible organisations (such as Social Services) on behalf of applicants. Grants are never paid directly to individuals.

Annual grant total
In 2010/11 the trust held assets of £30 million and had an income of £8.5 million. Grants totalled £828,000 from a total charitable expenditure of £5.2 million.

Exclusions
No grants are given for private medical treatment, legal fees, most personal debts or for items purchased prior to the application.

Applications
On a form available from the correspondent or to download from the website. Applications should be submitted either directly by the individual or through a social worker, Citizens Advice or other welfare agency. Applications may be posted or emailed to the correspondent. They are usually

considered in February, April, June, October and December.

Other information

This trust also runs a help and support line for its beneficiaries (0808 801 0808), offers sheltered and extra care accommodation throughout the UK and a residential care home in Scotland. The charity website also offers relevant and helpful information.

Road haulage

The Road Haulage Association Benevolent Fund

£10,000

Correspondent: Alistair Morrow, Road Haulage Association, Roadway House, The Rural Centre, Newbridge EH28 8NZ (01313 334900; email: a.morrow@rha.uk. net; website: www.rha.uk.net)

Trustees: Andy Boyle; James MacDonald Barclay; John Walter Frank Marshall; William Oliver; Richard James Fry; Steve Bowles; Clive Hampson.

CC Number: 1082820

Eligibility

Current and former members and employees/ex-employees of members, of the association, and their dependents.

Types of grants

One-off grants according to need.

Annual grant total

In 2010 the fund had an income of £24,000. Grants were made totalling around £10,000.

Exclusions

Grants are not usually awarded towards holidays (unless there are exceptional circumstances).

Applications

On a form available from the correspondent, to be submitted directly by the individual or through a social worker, Citizens Advice or other third party. Applications are considered throughout the year.

School inspectors

HM Inspectors of Schools' Benevolent Fund

£4,000

Correspondent: Clive Rowe, Hassocks House, 58 Main Street, Newtown Linford, Leicester LE6 0AD (01530 243989)

Trustees: Wilf Agnew; David Lewis; Kath Cross; Clive Rowe; John Hertrich; Meg Buckingham; Val Scott.

CC Number: 210181

Eligibility

Present and retired HM Inspectors of schools in England and Wales and their dependents who are in need or distress.

Types of grants

One-off grants of £500 to £5,000 and loans of up to £10,000.

Annual grant total

In 2011 the trust had an income of £18,000 and a total expenditure of £25,000. Grants totalled around £4,000.

Applications

In writing to the correspondent, either directly by the individual or through a third party such as a friend or colleague. Applications are considered as they arise, and should include the applicant's financial situation, and for example, arrangements for repaying loans.

Other information

The trust also provides information and support services.

Science

The Benevolent Fund administered by the Institute of Physics

£41,000

Correspondent: Mrs S McGoldrick, Secretary, Institute of Physics, 76–78 Portland Place, London W1B 1NT (020 7470 4830; email: suemcgoldrick@ yahoo.co.uk; website: www.iop.org)

Trustees: Prof. Roland Blackwell; Prof. Colin Latimer; Dr Tony Scott; Prof. John Beeby; Prof. John Briers; Revd Dr David Weaver; Susan May McGoldrick; Prof. Robert Chapman; Penelope Endersby; Dr Brian Manley; Howard Watson.

CC Number: 209746

Eligibility

Physicists and members of their family in need, whether members of the institute or not.

Types of grants

One-off and recurrent grants according to need.

Annual grant total

In 2010 the fund held assets of £1.3 million and had an income of £56,000. Grants to individuals totalled £41,000.

Applications

In writing to the correspondent, marked 'Private and confidential'. The committee meets periodically through the year although emergency cases can be considered more urgently.

Other information

The benevolent fund also provides free access to legal advice; see the Institute of Physics website for details.

The John Murdoch Trust

£4,000

Correspondent: Grant Administrator, c/o The Royal Bank of Scotland plc, Trust and Estate Services, Eden Lakeside, Chester Business Park, Wrexham Road, Chester CH4 9QT (01244 688292)

SC Number: SC004031

Eligibility

People in need who are over 50 and have pursued science, in any of its branches, either as amateurs or professionals.

Types of grants

Yearly allowances and one-off grants, on average of about £200 to £1,000. Grants are given for relief-in-need rather than scientific needs.

Annual grant total

In 2010/11 the trust had an income of £30,000. The grant total varies, but is usually in the range of about £4,000 a year.

Applications

On a form available from the correspondent. Applications are normally considered twice a year.

The Scientific Relief Fund of the Royal Society

£0

Correspondent: The Executive Secretary, The Royal Society, 6–9 Carlton House Terrace, London SW1Y 5AG (020 7451

2500; email: info@royalsociety.org; website: www.royalsociety.org)

Trustees: Prof. Andrew Blake; Dr Robin Lovell-Badge; Prof. John Collinge; Prof. Trevor Robbins; Sir Peter Williams; Dame Jean Thomas; Prof. Martyn Poliakoff; Prof. John Pethica; Prof. Kim Nasmyth; Prof. Alexander Halliday; Sir Paul Nurse; Prof. Peter Donnelly; Prof. John McWhirter; Prof. Wilson Sibbett; Dr Simon Campbell; Prof. Nicholas Tonks; Prof. Anthony Cheetham; Prof. Gillian Bates; Dame Linda Partridge; Prof. Judith Howard; Prof. Christopher Snowden.

CC Number: 207043

Eligibility

Scientists professionally involved in the natural sciences, or their families, in need of assistance, and retired scientists who need help to continue their research. Whilst there is no nationality requirement, the scientist concerned must have some connection with British or Irish science.

Types of grants

One-off grants of between £1,000 and £10,000. In the past grants have been made for travel to and from hospital, residential care costs, a sighted assistant to aid scientific research, computer equipment for scientific reasons, medical and surgical treatment and therapeutic drugs.

Annual grant total

In 2010/11 the society held assets of £236 million and had an income of £73 million. The fund itself-has been on hold for around two years while its value recovers. At the time of writing (May 2012) the society was still not sure when the fund might be operational again.

Exclusions

No grants are given towards scientist's salaries.

Applications

Applicants should contact the society to check if the fund is open for applications.

Royal Society of Chemistry Benevolent Fund

£20,000

Correspondent: Jennifer Tunbridge, Thomas Graham House, Science Park, Milton Road, Cambridge CB4 0WF (01223 432227; fax: 01223 426594; website: www.rsc.org)

Trustees: David Phillips; Keith Smith; Derek Stevenson; Peter Machin; Duncan Bruce; David Cole-Hamilton; Helen Fielding; Annie Powell; Annette Doherty;

Emma Raven; Gillian Reid; Lesley Yellowlees; Tina Overton; Dominic Tildesley; Jannette Waterhouse.

CC Number: 207890

Eligibility

People who have been members of the society for the last three years, or ex-members who were in the society for at least ten years, and their dependents, who are in need.

Types of grants

Regular allowances, one-off grants and loans. Recent grants have been towards essential home maintenance; help with transport costs, household equipment and furniture, school uniforms, care breaks, medical expenses, Christmas bonuses and funeral costs.

Annual grant total

In 2011 the fund had assets of £10 million, an income of £551,000 and gave grants totalling £39,000.

Exclusions

Anything which should be provided by the government or local authority is ineligible.

Applications

On a form available from the website or the correspondent. Applicants are advised to contact the society before making an application, to ensure all other possible routes have been taken.

Other information

The Society also provides advice and guidance services.

The Worshipful Company of Scientific Instrument Makers

£2,900

Correspondent: The Clerk, Glaziers Hall, 9 Montague Close, London SE1 9DD (020 7407 4832; email: theclerk@wcsim.co.uk; website: www. wcsim.co.uk)

Trustees: Cpt Guy Brocklebank; David Smith; Dr Ken Reay; Dr Derek Cornish; Harry Tee; Eur Ing David William Kent; Keith Francis Etherington.

CC Number: 221332

Eligibility

Members and past members of the company and their dependents.

Types of grants

One-off grants according to need. Grants have been used for bereavement and funeral costs.

Annual grant total

In 2010/11 the trust held assets of £1.4 million and had an income of

£71,000. Grants to individuals totalled £2,900.

Applications

In writing to the correspondent.

Other information

The majority of the trust's charitable work is concerned with educational scholarships.

Seafaring and fishing

The Baltic Exchange Charitable Society

£87,000 (34 grants)

Correspondent: Richard Butler, Nordic House, 20 St Dunstan's Hill, London EC3R 8HL (020 7283 6090; fax: 020 7283 6133; email: richard.butler@baltic-charities.co.uk)

Trustees: David McNally; Derek Walker; Paul Vogt; Peter Harding; Jeremy Penn; Richard Henry Bilton; Francis Crouch; Tony Ring; Catherine Bacon; Basil Mavroleon; Mark Jackson; Simon Findlay Trowell; John Hopkins; Simon Trowell; John Francis Wood.

CC Number: 277093

Eligibility

Employees and ex-employees and their dependents of member companies of the Baltic Exchange as well as companies in the oilseeds trade. Help is usually given to retired or elderly people and occasionally to younger people who find themselves in a difficult situation.

Types of grants

One-off grants usually in the range of £50 to £10,000. Recent grants have been made for household items, repairs to property, mobility aids, debt relief, therapy and respite care. Recurrent grants are also paid quarterly to help with living expenses. Loans may also be offered.

Annual grant total

In 2011 the society had assets of £4.4 million and an income of £179,000. Grants were made to 34 individuals totalling £87,000. Of this total, £59,000 was given in quarterly payments and £28,000 in one-off grants.

Applications

On a form available from the correspondent. Applications can be submitted at any time.

Other information

Help can also be given in the form of loans.

The Corporation of Trinity House, London

£33,000

Correspondent: Graham Hockley, Secretary, Trinity House, Tower Hill, London EC3N 4DH (020 7481 6914; email: graham.hockley@thls.org; website: www.trinityhouse.co.uk)

Trustees: Rear Admiral Sir Jeremy de Halpert; Capt. Duncan Glass; Simon Sherrard; The Viscount; Cobham; Capt. Nigel Pryke; Commodore David Squire; Capt. Richard Woodman; Commodore James Scorer; Capt. Roger Barker; Capt. Ian McNaught.

CC Number: 211869

Eligibility
Mariners and their dependents.

Types of grants
The charity operates 18 almshouses at Walmer, Kent and makes provision for regular payments to up to 60 annuitants. During the year annuitants received £624, paid in two instalments, and an extra £80 at Christmas. Other direct support is made through occasional one-off grants to former seafarers and their dependents.

Annual grant total
In 2010/11 the corporation had assets of £140 million and an income of £7.1 million. Grants were made to 40 annuitants totalling £28,000. A further £14,000 was awarded in grants to individuals, some of which was distributed for educational purposes. The majority of the corporation's funds are allocated to the maintenance of their almshouses.

Applications
Enquiries regarding welfare grants can be made via email to the secretary.

Other information
The corporation also makes grants to organisations and to individuals for educational purposes.

Fawcett Johnston Charity

£1,200

Correspondent: Mrs Lisa Douglas, The Town Hall, Senhouse Street, Maryport CA15 6BH (01900 813205; email: maryport.council@talk21.com)

Trustees: John Fisher; Thomas Anthony Johnstone; B. Cameron; William Denwood.

CC Number: 208326

Eligibility
Grants for poor and destitute sailors and ship carpenters and their dependents who live in Maryport, Cumbria.

Types of grants
One-off and recurrent according to need.

Annual grant total
In 2010/11 the trust had an income of £2,500 and a total expenditure of £1,200.

Applications
In writing to the correspondent.

Fishermens Mission

£52,000 (1,748 grants)

Correspondent: David Dickens, Secretary and Chief Executive, Fishermen's Mission Head Office, Mather House, 4400 Parkway, Fareham, Hampshire PO15 7FJ (01489 566910; email: enquiries@rnmdsf.org.uk; website: www.fishermensmission.org.uk)

Trustees: David Harris; Brian Miles; Derek Young; John Lang; Revd Brian Wilkinson; James Parker; Malcolm Neale Greenside Cooke; Simon Jefferies Golding; Jill Henderson; Alan McCulla; Prof. Glyn Tonge.

CC Number: 232822

Eligibility
Commercial fishermen, including retired fishermen, and their wives and widows who are experiencing unforeseen tragedy or hardship.

Types of grants
Immediate one-off payments to widows of fishermen lost at sea. There are also other individual grants to alleviate cases of hardship (e.g. provision of basic furniture for impoverished older fishermen). Grants are almost always one-off.

Annual grant total
In 2011 the mission held assets of £8.2 million and had an income of £3 million. Welfare payments were made totalling around £52,000.

Applications
In writing to the correspondent or the local superintendent, either directly by the individual or through a social worker, Citizens Advice or other welfare agency. Record of sea service and names of fishing vessels and/or owners is required.

Other information
The Mission has a team of welfare staff who provide advice and assistance to fishing communities throughout the UK.

Grimsby Sailors and Fishing Charity

£28,000

Correspondent: Duncan Watt, Charities Administrator, 1st Floor, 23 Bargate, Grimsby, South Humberside DN34 4SS (01472 347914; fax: 01472 347914; email: duncan.watt4@gmail.com)

Trustees: Neil Parkes; Timothy Michael Bennett; Derek Young; Byron James Miller; Andre J. Allard; David S. Chadwick; Michelle Lalor; Antony Jewitt; Stephen James Norton.

CC Number: 500816

Eligibility
Primarily the children of Grimsby fishermen lost at sea or dying ashore while still fishermen. However, help may also be available to other beneficiaries living in Grimsby and the surrounding area, at the trustees' discretion.

Types of grants
Weekly and quarterly grants to support children of deceased fishermen while they are still in full-time education. Weekly grants are usually around £13 and quarterly grants range from £100 to £250.

Annual grant total
In 2011 the charity had an income of £489,000 and a total expenditure of £400,000. The majority of the charity's expenditure is spent on providing and maintaining almshouses. Grants to individuals totalled £28,000.

Applications
On a form available from the correspondent or from the Port Missioner. Applications should be submitted directly by the individual or through an appropriate welfare agency. They are considered when received.

Other information
The Grimsby Fishermen's Dependents Fund has recently transferred its funds to this charity and is now a subsidiary.

The Honourable Company of Master Mariners

£27,000

Correspondent: The Clerk, HQS Wellington, Temple Stairs, Victoria Embankment, London WC2R 2PN (020 7836 8179; email: info@hcmm.org.uk; website: www.hcmm.org.uk)

Trustees: Iain Stitt; Terry Jewell; Simon Culshaw; Tony Davis; Anthony Speed; John Freestone; Neale Rodrigues; Tom Starr; Peter Aylott.

CC Number: 1127213

Eligibility

British Master Mariners, navigating officers of the merchant navy, and their wives, widows and dependents who are in need.

Types of grants

One-off and quarterly grants according to need.

Annual grant total

In 2011 the charity had assets of £2.9 million and an income of £106,000. Grants to individuals totalled £54,000.

Applications

In writing to the correspondent. Applications can be submitted directly by the individual, through a social worker, Citizens Advice, or other welfare agency, or by a friend or relative. They are considered quarterly.

Other information

This trust is an amalgamation of four separate funds: the Education Fund, the Benevolent Fund, the London Maritime Institution and the Howard Leopold Davis Fund.

The London Shipowners' and Shipbrokers' Benevolent Society

£26,000 (8 grants)

Correspondent: Richard Butler, Secretary, 20 St Dunstan's Hill, London EC3R 8HL (020 7283 6090; email: richard.butler@baltic-charities.co.uk)

Trustees: Christopher Ace; Colm Nolan; Dougal Graham; Ian Mylam; Michael Cornish; Roger Seymour; John White; David Cross; James Greenley; Neil Harper; John Flynn; Christopher Edward Mark Cox.

CC Number: 213348

Eligibility

Shipowners and shipbrokers and their dependents.

Types of grants

Annual cost of living grants, paid quarterly and special one-off grants at Christmas and during periods of cold weather.

Annual grant total

In 2011 the society had assets of £1.1 million and an income of £42,000. Grants were made to eight individuals totalling £26,000, of which £18,000 was given in quarterly grants and £8,000 was given in special grants.

Applications

On a form available from the correspondent. Applications can be submitted at any time either directly by the individual or a family member, through a third party such as a social worker, or through an organisation such as a Citizens Advice or other welfare agency.

Other information

The society also offers advice and counselling.

The Marine Society and Sea Cadets

£1 million

Correspondent: Claire E Barnett, 202 Lambeth Road, London SE1 7JW (020 7654 7011; fax: 020 7928 8914; email: info@ms-sc.org; website: www.ms-sc.org)

Trustees: Capt. Nigel Palmer; Mr A. F. Given; Dr Louise Bennett; Rear Admiral K. J. Borley; Mr M. J. Gladwyn; Dr Sheila Fitzpatrick; David Jeffcoat; Alan Marsh; Alex Marsh; Chris Ledger; Dame Mary Richardson; Colin Wilcox; Richard J. Sayer; Robin Woods; David Snelson; Sir Alan Massey; Commodore W. M (BILL) Walworth; Rear Admiral Chris Hockley.

CC Number: 313013

Eligibility

Professional seafarers, active and retired, who are in need.

Types of grants

Bursaries, scholarships, one-off grants and loans. Interest-free loans rather than grants are given where the need is short-term and the applicant expects to be earning again.

Annual grant total

In 2010/11 the trust had assets of £17.2 million and an income of £12.8 million. Grants to individuals totalled £1 million, although the trust states that 'individual grants given are small and not material within the overall total.'

Exclusions

Recurrent grants are not made.

Applications

In writing to the correspondent in the first instance, requesting an application form.

Other information

Grants are also made to sea cadet units and for educational purposes.

The Nautilus Welfare Fund (previously The NUMAST Welfare Fund)

£182,000

Correspondent: Mike Jess, Secretary, Nautilus House, Mariners' Park, Wallasey CH45 7PH (01516 398454; fax: 01513 468801; email: welfare@nautilusint.org; website: www.nautilusint.org)

Trustee: Nautilus International Council.

CC Number: 218742

Eligibility

Seafarers, former seafarers and their dependents.

Types of grants

Regular payments of up to £12 a week and one-off grants towards household items, medical expenses, home adaptations to aid independent living and electrically powered vehicles.

Annual grant total

In 2011 the fund had assets of £18.6 million and an income of £2.3 million. Grants were made totalling £182,000, of which £154,000 was given in regular awards and the remaining £28,000 was distributed in one-off grants.

Applications

On a form available from the correspondent: to be submitted directly by the individual or through a third party such as SSAFA. Proof of sea-service, medical and birth certificates and details of income and expenditure, bills and so on are required to support the application. Applications are usually processed within two weeks.

Other information

The fund also manages the Mariners Park welfare complex in Wallasey, which accommodates independent older seafarers and their dependents in bungalows and flats, and older seafarers and their dependents assessed for residential or nursing care in the NUMAST Mariners Park Care Home. The management and maintenance of this site takes up a large proportion of the fund's income.

The fund is continually developing its holistic welfare service offering advice and other services suited to each individual beneficiary's needs.

Royal Liverpool Seamen's Orphan Institution

£24,000

Correspondent: Linda Gidman, Secretary, 2nd Floor, Tower Building, 22 Water Street, Liverpool L3 1BA (01512 273417; fax: 01512 273417; email: enquiries@rlsoi-uk.org; website: www. rlsoi-uk.org)

Trustees: Ian Higby; Peter O. Copland; Trevor Hart; John Hulmes; Lynn Cook; David Barbour; Michael Finn.

CC Number: 526379

Eligibility

Children of deceased British merchant seafarers, who are of pre-school age or in full-time education (including further education) and their families. Help can also be given to seafarers who are at home caring for their family alone.

Types of grants

Monthly maintenance and annual clothing grants. Grants usually range from £80 to £300 a month for each child. They are reviewed annually.

Applications

On a form available from the correspondent or to download from the website, to be considered at any time. Applications can be submitted either directly by the individual, or by the parent or guardian. They need to include confirmation of the seafarer's death and the child's birth certificate.

Other information

It was not possible to obtain a grant total for direct education purposes. However, all grants are given to children and young people who are in attendance at school and further or higher education institutions.

Sailors' Society

£24,000

Correspondent: Welfare Fund Manager, 350 Shirley Road, Southampton SO15 3HY (02380 515950; fax: 02380 515951; email: welfare@sailors-society. org)

Trustees: Jake Watson; William Ward; Ross Sinclair; Peter Goldberg; Michael Burridge; Jonathan Stoneley; Shyam Sharma; Natalie Shaw; Norman Jones; Michael Drayton; Peter Swift.

CC Number: 237778

Eligibility

Merchant seafarers and their dependents who are in need.

Types of grants

Emergency grants to ease financial hardship.

Annual grant total

In 2011 the society had assets of £13 million and an income of £3.5 million. Grants for welfare totalled £24,000.

Applications

In the first instance a short application should be sent by email to welfare@sailors-society.org.

Other information

The society maintains a network of Chaplains at the various key ports around the world who carry out ship visiting routines and minister to seafarers. It also provides centres and clubs for seafarers and associated maritime workers at strategic seaports.

Sailors' Children's Society

£150,000

Correspondent: Ian Scott, Welfare Manager, Francis Reckitt House, Newland, Cottingham Road, Hull HU6 7RJ (01482 342331; fax: 01482 447868; email: info@sailorschildren.org. uk; website: www.sailorschildren.org.uk)

Trustees: Martin Needler; Neil Parkes; Com Geoff Noble; John Warburton; Christopher Towne; Greg Medici; Debbie Rosenberg; Richard Vernon.

CC Number: 224505

Eligibility

Seafarers children who are in full-time education and the families are in severe financial difficulties. Grants can also be given if the seafarer is in a two-parent family but is permanently disabled. Usually, the only source of income for the family is Income Support or Incapacity Benefit.

Types of grants

(i) Monthly child welfare grants designed to boost income and enable families to provide basic essentials. (ii) A clothing grant payable per child twice a year, in August and January, to help children start off the new school year and to buy a new winter coat. (iii) Christmas grants to help to buy a special Christmas present. (iv) Educational holiday grants. (v) Ad Hoc grants to help with the purchase of essential items such as children's beds, cookers etc. (vi) Holiday Caravan Scheme. The society provides a week's free holiday to families in one of the seven caravans it owns around the coast.

Annual grant total

In 2010/11 the society had assets of £1.7 million, an income of £429,000 and gave grants totalling £193,000.

Applications

On a form available from the correspondent, with details about children, income and expenditure, including copies of relevant certificates, for example, birth certificates and proof of seafaring service. Applications can be submitted directly by the individual or through a social worker, Citizens Advice, other welfare agency, or through seafaring organisations. Applications are considered every other month, beginning in February.

Other information

Previously known as Sailors' Families' Society.

The Society has an informative website.

The Seamen's Hospital Society

£124,000

Correspondent: Peter Coulson, General Secretary, 29 King William Walk, Greenwich, London SE10 9HX (020 8858 3696; fax: 020 8293 9630; email: admin@ seahospital.org.uk; website: www. seahospital.org.uk)

Trustees: Peter McEwen; Jeffrey Jenkinson; Capt. Duncan Glass; Mark Carden; Alexander Nairne; Cap Colin Stewart; Anthony Lydekker; Cap Anthony Speed; Surg Cmmd Frank Leonard; John Newton; Rupert Chichester; Dr Charlotte Mendes Da Costa; Max Gladwyn; Graham Lane.

CC Number: 231724

Eligibility

Current or retired merchant seafarers or fishermen who are in need, and their dependents. Applicants must be seafarers with a long service except where accident or illness has interrupted intended long-term service. They may have worked anywhere in the UK and be of any nationality.

Types of grants

One-off grants can be given towards medical treatment and items such as wheelchairs, riser recliner chairs, stair lifts and installation of disabled access; household items such as cookers, beds and decorating costs; holidays, convalescence and respite breaks; clothing; priority bills and funeral expenses.

Annual grant total

In 2011 the society had assets of £7.4 million, an income of £480,000 and a total expenditure of £725,000. Grants were made to 306 individuals totalling £124,000. A further £332,000 was given to organisations.

Exclusions

No grants are given towards study costs or re-training costs. Members and former members of the Royal Navy are not eligible. Otherwise, 'there are no rigid rules about what you can get a grant for. We look at each case individually and assess the overall situation.'

Applications

On a form available to download from the website or from the correspondent, including full details of sea service and need. Applications should be completed in conjunction with a caseworker such as representatives from SSAFA, Citizens Advice or the Fishermen's mission. If you are not already in contact with a caseworker contact the society to arrange assistance. The society welcome informal contact prior to submitting applications to discuss eligibility, need, etc.

Other information

The society supports Dreadnought patients at Guys and St Thomas' Hospital in London as well as running various regional health and fitness programmes for seafarers. It also helps to fund the Seafarers Advice and Information Line (SAIL) (0845 741 3318), which provides advice and information on a wide range of issues.

The Shipwrecked Fishermen and Mariners' Royal Benevolent Society

£1.5 million (2,644 grants)

Correspondent: Malcolm Williams, Chief Executive, 1 North Pallant, Chichester, West Sussex PO19 1TL (01243 787761; fax: 01243 530853; email: grants@shipwreckedmariners.org.uk; website: www.shipwreckedmariners.org.uk)

Trustees: Neil Parkes; Cathy Walker; Jane Clementson; Capt. John Hughes; Eamonn Delaney; George Greenwood; Com Laurie Hopkins; Capt. Nigel Palmer; Com Rosie Wilson; Anthony Fawcett; Capt. Roger Barker; Richard Coleman; Tim West; Capt. John Vercoe; Michael Seymour; Penny Salt; Capt. Graham Pepper.

CC Number: 212034

Eligibility

Fishermen, mariners and their widows and dependents, who are on a low income, especially those who are over 60 or in poor health. Priority is given to widows with young children. There is a minimum sea service of five years for one-off grants (10 for recurrent grants), although this is reviewed periodically to reflect employment patterns. Grants are available in the UK and Republic of Ireland only. Applicants must be receiving all the state benefits they are entitled to.

Types of grants

Mainly regular grants of £624 a year (usually to people aged over 60). One-off grants ranging from about £250 to £2,000 are available for those who do not qualify for regular support for help towards electrical appliances, household repairs, rent deposit, beds and bedding, rent deposits, debt relief, stair-lifts, scooters and so on. Immediate grants are given to widows and children left in need following the death of a serving fisherman or mariner. Death benefit grants are also given to the widows of life members of the society.

Annual grant total

In 2010/11 the society had assets of £24 million and an income of £1.4 million. Grants were made to 2,644 individuals totalling £1.5 million, of which £1.3 million was given in regular donations and the remaining £200,000 in one-off grants.

Applications

On a form available from the correspondent or to download from the website. Applications can be submitted by the individual or through a third party and are considered on a weekly basis.

Other information

The Royal Seamen's Pension Fund and the Hull Fishermen's Trust Fund have been integrated into this society.

The Society has an informative website.

Secretaries

The Institute of Chartered Secretaries and Administrators' Benevolent Fund

£68,000 (122 grants)

Correspondent: Elizabeth Howarth, Charities Officer, 16 Park Crescent, London W1B 1AH (020 7580 4741; fax: 020 7323 1132; email: icsacharities@icsaglobal.com; website: www.icsaglobal.com/charities)

Trustees: Mr D. J. Prescott; Mr J. P. Kinch; Mr R. J. C. Grigg; Mr F. E. Curtiss; Mr J. Burger; Mr M. P. Jacob.

CC Number: 213345

Eligibility

Members and former members of the institute and their dependents who are in need, living in UK, Eire and associated territories.

Types of grants

Weekly allowances and regular support according to need, for example towards telephone line rental, white goods, house repairs, rental for emergency alarm systems and TV rental and licences. One-off grants are given for specific items and services, often paid directly to the supplier, including those for clothing, clearance of debts, decorating, property repairs. Loans are also considered.

Annual grant total

In 2010/11 the fund had assets of £4.8 million and an income of £34,000. Welfare grants and allowances supported 122 beneficiaries throughout the year totalling £68,000.

Applications

On a form available from the correspondent or to download from the website, indicating full current income and expenditure details. Institute members (volunteers) visit beneficiaries where necessary. Applications can be made throughout the year. Contact the correspondent if assistance in making the application is required. Applicants may be visited by a volunteer.

Self-employed and small businesses

The Prime Charitable Trust

£500

Correspondent: Pauline Weller, Federation of Small Businesses, Sir Frank Whittle Way, Blackpool FY4 2FE (01253 336000; fax: 01253 348046; email: admin@prime-charitable-trust.co.uk; website: www.prime-charitable-trust.co.uk)

Trustees: Dr Bernard Juby; Brian Prime; David Dexter.

CC Number: 328441

Eligibility

Members or former members of the National Federation of Self-Employed and Small Businesses Ltd and their family and dependents, who due to illness or incapacity are unable to maintain themselves.

Types of grants

One-off and recurrent grants according to need.

Annual grant total

In 2010/11 the trust had an income of £10,000. Total annual expenditure tends to range quite widely, for example £11,700 in 2008/9 and just £500 in 2010/11.

Applications

In writing to the correspondent.

Social workers

The Social Workers' Benevolent Trust

£24,000 (97 grants)

Correspondent: Kate Slade, Honorary Applications Secretary, 16 Kent Street, Birmingham B5 6RD (01216 223911; email: swbt@basw.co.uk; website: www. basw.co.uk)

Trustees: Jean Lockley; Katherine Slade; Ann Gegg; Julian Levitt; Simon Cole; Jane Banning; Hilary Makepeace; Carol Dutton; Margaret Faulkner; Ru Gunawardana.

CC Number: 262889

Eligibility

Social workers who hold a professional social work qualification and are experiencing financial difficulties, and their dependents. Unqualified social workers may also be considered depending upon the nature and length of their employment.

Types of grants

One-off grants up to £500 are given for specific debts and other needs.

Annual grant total

In 2010/11 the trust had an income of £26,000 and made grants totalling £24,000. 97 applications were received with 63 successfully receiving grants.

Exclusions

No grants for: daily living costs; social work training; private health care; private education; or private social care.

Applications

On a form available from the correspondent or to download from the website. Applications should be submitted directly by the individual and are considered bi-monthly.

Solicitors

The Solicitors' Benevolent Association Ltd

£827,000

Correspondent: John Platt, 1 Jaggard Way, Wandsworth Common, London SW12 8SG (020 8675 6440; email: sec@sba.org.uk; website: www.sba.org.uk)

Trustee: The Trustees.

CC Number: 1124512

Eligibility

Solicitors who are or have been on the Roll for England and Wales and have practised, and their dependents, who are in need.

Types of grants

One-off and recurrent grants and interest-free loans (if sufficient equity is available). They can be made towards living expenses, nursing home fees, TV licences, telephone rental, essential travel, emergency repairs or replacement of household appliances, holidays and medical or special equipment not provided for by the state.

Annual grant total

In 2011 the charity had assets of £16 million and an income of £2.2 million. During the year grants and loans were made to 344 individuals. Grants totalled £1.1 million and loans advanced £612,000. Grants were broken down into:
- Cost of living allowances – £468,000
- Leisure, special and miscellaneous – £344,000
- Educational support – £224,000
- Nursing home fees – £15,000

Exclusions

Solicitors who have been considered to have brought the profession into disrepute are not eligible but assistance may be available to their dependents.

Applications

On a form available on the website or by contacting the fund. Applications are considered at board meetings held ten times a year.

Sport

The Mark Davies Injured Riders' Fund

£18,000

Correspondent: Rosemary Lang, Lancrow Farmhouse, Penpillick Hill,

Penpillick, Cornwall PL24 2SA (01726 813156; email: rosemary@mdirf.co.uk; website: www.mdirf.co.uk)

Trustees: Jane Davies; Sarah Bullen; Cathryn Bell; Paul Crago; Pippa Funnelll; Edmund O. Reilly Hyland; David Pease; Dane Rawlins.

CC Number: 1022281

Eligibility

People injured in horse-related accidents (excluding professional and amateur jockeys and those injured in the horse racing industry) and their carers.

Types of grants

One-off cash grants and grants in kind according to need; loans are also made. Recent grants have been given towards wheelchairs, special beds, house adaptations, stair lifts, physiotherapy, stable help and other living costs.

Annual grant total

In 2010 the trust held assets of £554,000 and had an income of £50,000. Grants totalled £18,000.

Applications

In writing to the correspondent at any time. All applicants are visited by a local fund volunteer to discuss their medical and financial needs. A report is then made to the trustees, who will consider whether or not to award a grant.

Other information

The fund also offer legal and medical advice as well as providing practical advice on rider safety issues and producing a number of help sheets on the subject. These are available to download from the website.

The Francis Drake Fellowship

£3,000

Correspondent: Joan Jupp, 24 Haldane Close, London N10 2PB (020 8883 8725)

Trustees: John Fox; Lillian Brett-Golding.

CC Number: 248302

Eligibility

Widows, dependents and orphans of members of the fellowship who have died.

Types of grants

One-off and recurrent grants according to need. There is a sliding scale of grants depending on surplus income. If after general household/living expenses (excluding food, clothing etc.) the applicant has a surplus of under £70 per week, grants are £550; if the surplus income is between £70 and £90, grants are £450; between £90 and £110, grants are £350; between £110 and £130, grants are £200; and for incomes over £130, grants are £50. Grants are also made for education.

Annual grant total
In 2011 the trust had an income of £2,700 and an expenditure of £6,500.

Applications
In writing to the correspondent, requesting an application form. Applications should be submitted through the bowling club's Francis Drake Fellowship delegate. Applications are accepted two years after the date of the member's death.

The Rugby Football League Benevolent Fund

£76,000

Correspondent: Steve Ball, Red Hall, Red Hall Lane, Leeds, West Yorkshire LS17 8NB (0844 477 7113; email: info@rflbenevolentfund.co.uk; website: www.rflbenevolentfund.co.uk)

Trustees: Philip Clarke; David Hinchliffe; Timothy Adams; Gary Hetherington; Emma Rosewarne; Geoffrey Burrow.

CC Number: 1109858

Eligibility
People who play or assist, or who have played or assisted, in the game of Rugby League in the UK or for a team affiliated to an association primarily based in the UK and their dependents. Beneficiaries should be in hardship or distress, in particular, as a result of injury through playing or training, or when travelling to or from a game or training session.

Types of grants
Hardship grants, also donations towards special vehicles and repairs, home improvements, furniture, wheelchairs, gym equipment, computers, hotel accommodation, travel, physiotherapy, home appliances, educational courses and Christmas presents.

Annual grant total
In 2011 the fund had assets of £398,000 and an income of £251,000. Grants to 99 beneficiaries totalled £87,000 including £11,000 for 'educational courses'.

Applications
In the case of serious injury applicants should notify the RFL Operations Department (Tel. 0844477713 Ext. 6), who will then contact Dave Phillips, the RFL Benevolent Fund Welfare Officer.

Cricket
The Cricketers Association Charity

£28,000

Correspondent: David Graveney, 6 Southover Close, Westbury On Trym, Bristol BS9 3NG

Trustee: David Graveney.

CC Number: 286742

Eligibility
Members and former members of the association and any person who has played cricket on at least one occasion for any county which at the relevant time was recognised by the English Cricket Board (formerly the Test and County Cricket Board), and their dependents.

Types of grants
One-off or recurrent grants according to need.

Annual grant total
In 2010/11 the association had an income of £8,700 and a total expenditure of £29,000.

Applications
In writing to the correspondent, to be considered as they arrive.

The Hornsby Professional Cricketers Fund Charity

£43,000 (22 grants)

Correspondent: The Revd Michael Vockins, Birchwood Lodge, Birchwood, Storridge, Malvern, Worcestershire WR13 5EZ (01886 884366)

Trustees: Anthony Hugh Bartlett; Donald Bryce Carr; Douglas John Insole; Geoffrey Gilbert; Robert Victor Charles Robins; Michael James Stewart; David Collier; John Barclay; Keith Bradshaw; Christopher Martin-Jenkins.

CC Number: 235561

Eligibility
Former professional cricketers and their dependents who are in need.

Types of grants
Recurrent grants and special payments at Christmas or in mid-summer. Help is also given towards winter fuel bills, medical costs and special equipment such as electric wheelchairs and stairlifts.

Annual grant total
In 2010/11 the charity held assets totalling £421,000 and had an income of £218,000. Grants to 22 individuals

totalled £43,000 and were distributed in the following categories:

Monthly allowances	£18,500
Summer allowances	£6,300
Winter allowances	£6,600
Heating allowances	£4,200
Walter Hammond allowances	£1,500
Special allowances	£6,100

Applications
In writing to the correspondent. Applications can be submitted either directly by the individual or by the county cricket club.

Football
The Football Association Benevolent Fund

£30,000 (51 grants)

Correspondent: Richard McDermott, Wembley Stadium, Wembley, PO BOX 1966, London SW1P 9EQ (0844 980 8200; email: richard.mcdermott@thefa.com)

Trustees: Geoff Thompson; Barry Bright; Raymond Berridge; Mervyn Leggett; Brian Adshead.

CC Number: 299012

Eligibility
People who have been involved in Association Football in any capacity, such as players and referees, and their dependents, who are in need. The fund interprets people involved in football as broadly as possible, although it tends not to support professional footballers, passing their details on to the occupational benevolent funds which they can apply to.

Types of grants
One-off and recurrent grants ranging from £250 to £2,000 are given to meet any need.

Annual grant total
In 2010 the fund had assets of £3.8 million and an income of £66,000. Grants were made to 51 individuals totalling £30,000.

Applications
On a form available from the correspondent. Applications should be made through the County Football Associations. They are considered on a regular basis.

The Institute of Football Management and Administration Charity Trust

£2,500

Correspondent: Graham Mackrell, The Camkin Suite, 1 Pegasus House, Tachbrook Park, Warwick CV34 6LW (01926 831556; fax: 01926 429781; email: ifma@lmasecure.com)

Trustees: Olaf Dixon; Graham Mackrell; Andy Daykin.

CC Number: 277200

Eligibility

Members or former members of the institute (formerly the Football League Executive Staffs Association) who have worked for a Football League or Premier League Club and who are in need, and their widows/widowers.

Types of grants

One-off grants in particular cases of need, and Christmas vouchers.

Annual grant total

In 2010/11 the trust had an unusually low income of just £12 and a total expenditure of £2,600.

Applications

In writing to the correspondent. Applications can be submitted directly by the individual or through a family member, friend or colleague.

The League Managers Benevolent Trust

£25,000

Correspondent: The Trustees, League Managers Association, Unit 1 Pegasus House, Pegasus Court, Tachbrook Park, Warwick CV34 6LW (01926 411884; email: ifma@lmasecure.com; website: www.leaguemanagers.com)

Trustees: Sir Alex Ferguson; Howard Wilkinson; Olaf Dixon; Richard Bevan.

CC Number: 1016248

Eligibility

Members of the League Managers Association who are in need and their wives, widows and children.

Types of grants

One-off and recurrent grants according to need.

Annual grant total

In 2011 the trust had an income of £1,300 and a total expenditure of £30,000.

Applications

In writing to the correspondent. Applications are considered throughout the year.

Professional Footballers' Association Accident Insurance Fund

£1.7 million

Correspondent: Darren Wilson, Director of Finance, 20 Oxford Court, Bishopsgate, Manchester M2 3WQ (01612 360575; fax: 01612 287229; email: info@thepfa.co.uk; website: www.givemefootball.com)

Eligibility

Members or former members of the association in England and Wales who require medical treatment as a result of a specific injury or illness which results in their permanent total disability to play professional football.

Types of grants

Grants are to provide private medical treatment for all members and for members unable to claim under the terms of the PFA accident insurance policy due to the nature/circumstances of the injury. Grants are also given to meet operation costs which may not be covered by the insurance and free places are available at Lilleshall Rehabilitation Centre. Grants are also available to former members for treatment on injuries received as a result of their playing career.

Annual grant total

Grants totalled around £1.7 million in 2010/11 and were broken down as follows:

Medical fees and grants	£650,000
Permanent total disability	£442,000
Insurance premiums	£406,000
Lilleshall costs	£156,000
Other costs	£16,000

Applications

On a form available from the correspondent. Completed applications should be returned directly by the individual or by a family member/social worker on their behalf. There are no deadlines and applications are considered as they are received.

Other information

Contributions are made to FAPL and FH Club to ensure all PFA members are covered by private medical insurance.

Professional Footballers' Association Benevolent Fund

£458,000 (483 grants)

Correspondent: Darren Wilson, Financial Controller, 20 Oxford Court, Bishopsgate, Manchester M2 3WQ (01612 360575; fax: 01612 287229; email: info@thepfa.co.uk; website: www.givemefootball.com)

Trustees: Garth Crooks; Darren Anthony Wilson; Gordon Taylor; David Weir; Brendon Batson; Christopher Powell; Paul Elliott; Gareth Griffiths.

CC Number: 1056012

Eligibility

Current and former members of the association and their dependents in England and Wales who are experiencing financial hardship and are on a low income.

Types of grants

One-off grants in the range of £50 to £2,000 to help relieve financial difficulties such as the threat of losing a home due to mortgage/rent arrears or threat of bailiffs in respect of debts. Where appropriate, general advice regarding financial management and options concerning further education may be offered as required. There is also funding available in the event of the death of any member whilst under contract, up to a maximum of £1 million.

Annual grant total

In 2010/11 the fund had assets of £17.5 million and an income of £1.2 million. There were 483 grants made to current and former members and their families totalling £458,000.

Exclusions

No grants are made for cars, holidays or to set up businesses. Loans are not available to former members and there are no recurrent grants.

Applications

On a form available from the correspondent. Completed applications should be returned directly by the individual or by a family member/social worker on their behalf. There are no deadlines and applications are considered as they are received.

The Referees' Association Members' Benevolent Fund

£17,000

Correspondent: The General Secretary, Unit 12, Ensign Business Centre, Westwood Way, Westwood Business Park, Coventry CV4 8JA (02476 420360; fax: 02476 677234; email: ra@footballreferee.org; website: www.footballreferee.org)

Trustees: John Maxson; John Harvey; Kenneth Anderton; Roland Croysdale; John Harden; Mr Genner.

CC Number: 800845

Eligibility
Members and former members of the association in England, and their dependents, who are in need.

Types of grants
One-off and recurrent grants to relieve an immediate financial need such as hospital expenses, convalescence, clothing, living costs, household bills, medical equipment and help in the home.

Annual grant total
In 2010/11 the fund had an income of £6,300 and a total expenditure of £19,000.

Applications
On a form available from the correspondent. Applications should be submitted directly by the individual for consideration at any time.

Golf

The PGA European Tour Benevolent Trust

£144,000 (12 grants)

Correspondent: Mr Jonathan Orr, PGA Building, Wentworth Drive, Virginia Water, Surrey GU25 4LX (01344 840400; email: cduffain@europeantour.com; website: www.europeantour.com/tourgroup/benevolenttrust/index.html)

Trustees: George O'Grady; John O'Leary; Neil Coles; Mark Roe; Robert Lee.

CC Number: 327207

Eligibility
Members and former members of the PGA European Tour and other people whose main livelihood is, or has been, earned by providing services to professional golf, and their dependents.

Types of grants
One-off or recurrent grants according to need. In 2010 grants ranged from £2,000 – £30,000.

Annual grant total
In 2010 the trust had assets of £1.7 million and an income of £1.2 million. There were 12 grants made to individuals totalling £144,000.

Applications
In writing to the correspondent at any time. Applications can be submitted directly by the individual or through a social worker, Citizens Advice, other welfare agency or another third party.

Other information
The trust does not give to organisations.

Horse racing

The Injured Jockeys Fund

£783,000 (377 grants)

Correspondent: Lisa Jeanette Hancock, Chief Executive, 1 Victoria Way, Newmarket, Suffolk CB8 7SH (01638 662246; fax: 01638 668988; email: Contact form on website; website: www.injuredjockeys.co.uk)

Trustees: John Fairley; Pam Deal; John Brough Scott; Jeff Smith; Jonathan Powell; Simon McNeill; William Norris; Lord Peter Gilbert Daresbury.

CC Number: 1107395

Eligibility
Jockeys who have suffered through injury, and their families. Applicants must hold (or have held) a licence to ride under the Rules of Racing.

Types of grants
One-off and recurrent grants to assist with medical care and to help alleviate financial problems and stress. Recent grants have included help with medical treatment and equipment, contributions to private medical insurance, wheelchairs, holidays, televisions and emergency cash. Assistance may also be given to help with the cost of education where children have special needs.

Annual grant total
In 2010/11 the fund had assets of £31 million, an income of £4.1 million and a total expenditure of £3.1 million. Grants were made to 377 injured jockeys totalling £783,000. A further £11,000 was distributed in grants to organisations.

Applications
On a form available from the correspondent. The fund has nine almoners who cover the whole of the UK and visit potential beneficiaries to assess their needs.

Other information
The fund also provides accommodation for families and individuals in need. A range of permanent family homes, single apartments and disabled accommodation is available.

Racing Welfare

£254,000

Correspondent: Brig. Cedric Burton, Robin McAlpine House, 20b Park Lane, Newmarket, Suffolk CB8 8QD (01638 560763; email: info@racingwelfare.co.uk; website: www.racingwelfare.co.uk)

Trustees: Roger Weatherby; Michael Iain Cattermole; Piers Pottinger; Gary Middlebrook; Samuel Rodd Morshead; Baroness Ann Mallalieu; John Maxse; Jacqueline Fanshawe; General Sir Sam Cowan; Raymond Henley; Joey Newton; Antonia Deuters; Simon Clarke.

CC Number: 1084042

Eligibility
People in need who are, or have been, employed in the thoroughbred horse-racing and breeding industry, and their dependents.

Types of grants
One-off and recurrent grants and loans according to need. The majority of funding is given in the form of quarterly benefits of about £1,000 to retired staff, although the 2010 accounts note that the charity is reducing the number of quarterly grants while concentrating support on more specific grants one-off grants in future.

One-off grants to help towards disability aids and equipment, house adaptations, clothing, food, medical expenses, car adaptations, drugs rehabilitation and bedding. One-off grants have also been given in response to sudden, unexpected events such as family deaths, disease diagnoses, assaults or loss of employment. In most cases the money will be paid directly to service providers.

Annual grant total
In 2010 the charity had assets of £12.7 million and an income of £1.6 million. Grants were made to 358 individuals totalling £254,000.

Applications
On a form available from the welfare officer at most racing centres or from the correspondent. Applicants are visited by a welfare officer before the application is considered by the trustees.

Other information
The trust has welfare officers based all over the country who offer support and

advice on financial issues, diet and nutrition and housing. It also runs a 24-hour helpline (0800 630 0443) offering the same advice. It also runs a holiday scheme for its elderly and disabled beneficiaries.

Grants are also made to organisations that offer services to people who work in, or are retired from, racing (£110,000 in 2010).

Motor sport

The Auto Cycle Union Benevolent Fund

£44,000 (63 grants)

Correspondent: Roy Hanks, Benevolent Fund Chair, ACU House, Wood Street, Rugby, Warwickshire CV21 2YX (01788 566400; fax: 01788 573585; email: royacu@btconnect.com; website: www.acu.org.uk)

Trustees: Roy Hanks; Roy Collins; Wyn Evans; Frederick James Henley; Margaret Carter; Julie MacPhee; Robert William Smith; Charles Pattison.

CC Number: 208567

Eligibility

Past and present members of the Auto Cycle Union, and their dependents, who are in need through accident, illness or hardship in England, Scotland or Wales.

Types of grants

One-off and recurrent grants to supplement low income.

Annual grant total

In 2011 the fund had assets of £1.8 million and an income of £136,000. Grants were made to 63 individuals totalling £44,000.

Applications

On a form available from the local ACU officer or centre. Applications should be made directly by the individual and include details on current income and expenses. They are considered monthly. In very special circumstances the committee has the power to make emergency payments pending full information.

Other information

A full list of ACU clubs and centres is available on the website.

British Motor Cycle Racing Club Benevolent Fund

£10,000

Correspondent: Mike Dommett, CEO, Unit D2, Seedbed Centre, Davidson

Way, Romford, Essex RM7 0AZ (01708 720305; website: www.bemsee.net/ben-fund)

Trustees: Trevor Stafford; Edward McDonald; Tracey Ringrow; Jeff Lennox; Lee Yeoman.

CC Number: 213308

Eligibility

Members of the club and their dependents, who are in need.

Types of grants

One-off grants towards subsistence, travel and medical care and equipment costs.

Annual grant total

In 2011 the trust had an income of £9,700 and a total expenditure of £11,000.

Applications

In writing to the correspondent. Applications can be submitted at any time, either directly by the individual, or through a third party such as a spouse or next of kin.

British Racing Drivers Club (BRDC) Benevolent Fund

£14,000 (6 grants)

Correspondent: The Trustees, c/o Rawlinson and Hunter, Eighth Floor, 6 New Street Square, London EC4A 3AQ (020 7842 2000; website: www.brdc.co.uk)

Trustees: Mr C. J. A. Bliss; Mr D. P. Richards; Mr G. H. Mac Dowell.

CC Number: 1084173

Eligibility

Members of the BRDC and their families and dependents or persons involved with motor racing generally and their families and dependents.

Types of grants

One-off and recurrent grants according to need.

Annual grant total

In 2010/11 the fund had assets of £492,000 and an income of £40,000. The accounts state that grants were made to six individuals and total charitable expenditure, including the costs of the administrator, totalled £16,700.

Applications

On a form available from the correspondent including details of income and expenditure, assets and liabilities. Applications can be submitted directly by the individual, by an organisation such as Citizens Advice or through a third party such as a social worker. There are no deadlines and

applications are considered at trustee meetings.

Other information

During 2008/09 the British Racing Drivers Club (BRDC) Benevolent Fund merged with the British Motoring Sport Relief Fund and the assets of the latter have been transferred under the control of the trustees of the BRDC Benevolent Fund.

The trust's website states that the trust administrator is 'fully conversant with the benefits available from statutory or voluntary bodies' which illustrates the trusts ability to help beyond the provision of financial assistance.

The Grand Prix Mechanics Charitable Trust

£2,000

Correspondent: Fiona Miller, Administrator, Rawlinson and Hunter, Eighth Floor, 6 New Street Square, New Fetter Lane, London EC4A 3AQ (01896 820263; fax: 01896 820264; email: enquiries@gpmechanicstrust.com; website: www.gpmechanicstrust.com)

Trustees: Sir Jackie Stewart; James Allen; Martin Brundle; Brian Clark; David Coulthard; Norbert Haug; Patrick Head; Peter Hetherington; John Hogan; Michael Jakeman; Jo Ramirez; David Ryan; Michael Tee; Prof. Sid Watkins.

CC Number: 327454

Eligibility

Past and present Grand Prix mechanics and their dependents who are in need.

Types of grants

One-off and recurrent grants towards medical costs, bills and living expenses and so on.

Annual grant total

In 2010/11 the trust had assets of £1.9 million and an income of £152,000. Around £2,000 was distributed to individuals for welfare purposes.

Applications

In writing to the correspondent or via the online contact form.

Other information

During 2010/11 a £25,000 grant was made to BEN, the automobile industry charity.

Snooker and billiards

The Professional Billiards and Snooker Players Benevolent Fund

£16,000

Correspondent: Simon Brownell, World Snooker Ltd, Suite 2.1, Albert House, 111–117 Victoria Street, Bristol BS1 6AX (01173 178216; email: simon.brownell@ worldsnooker.com; website: www. worldsnooker.com)

Trustees: Alan Chamberlain; Mark Pears; Patsy Fagan.

CC Number: 288352

Eligibility
Current or retired professional snooker or billiards players who are members of the World Professional Billiards and Snooker Association and their dependents, who are in need.

Types of grants
One-off grants and interest-free loans according to need. Current trustee priorities include payments on the death of players, caring for injured or ill players and providing loans for specific purposes over a limited time.

Annual grant total
In 2011/12 the trust held assets of £169,000 and had an income of £24,000. Total expenditure was £17,000.

Applications
On an application form available from the correspondent, including medical evidence where appropriate.

Stationery

The British Office Supplies and Services Federation Benevolent Fund

£50,000 (250 grants)

Correspondent: Benevolent Fund Secretary, 2 Villiers Court, Meriden Business Park, Copse Drive, Coventry CV5 9RN (01676 526048; fax: 020 7405 7784; email: info@bossfederation.co.uk; website: www.bossfederation.co.uk)

Trustees: Edward Cheshire; Geoff Making; Michael Gowen; Roger Murphy; Stanley Vaughan; Ernest Parbury; Laurie Sly; Frances Stephen; Graeme Chapman.

CC Number: 279029

Eligibility
Applications are welcome from those who work or have worked in the stationery, office products and office machines sector, and their dependents.

Types of grants
One-off grants according to need are given towards, for example, wheelchairs or property repair. Regular quarterly payments are also made.

Annual grant total
In 2010 the fund made 250 grants to individuals totalling £48,000.

Applications
On a form available from the correspondent. Applications can be submitted directly by the individual or through a relevant welfare agency or third party. Applicants will usually be visited by one of the fund's volunteers who will assess their needs and offer support.

Other information
This fund was previously known as The British Office Systems and Stationery Federation Benevolent Fund.

Stock Exchange

The Stock Exchange Benevolent Fund

£655,000

Correspondent: James Cox, Secretary, 1–5 Earl Street, London EC2A 2AL (020 7797 1092/3120; fax: 020 7374 4963; email: stockxbf@yahoo.co.uk; website: www.sebf.co.uk)

Trustees: Brian Winterflood; Robert George Chambers; Christopher Holdsworth Hunt; Andrew Scott; Gerald Mordaunt; Mark Powell; Paddy Burgess; Jamie Matheson; Michael Lilwall.

CC Number: 245430

Eligibility
Members and ex-members of the Stock Exchange and their dependents.

Types of grants
Annuities and one-off grants according to need. Recent grants have been made for medical equipment, motor repairs and household essentials.

Annual grant total
In 2011 the fund held assets of £18 million and had an income of £733,000. Grants were made totalling £655,000, of which £464,000 was given in pensions to 79 individuals and £191,000 in one-off grants to 17 beneficiaries.

Applications
On a form available from the correspondent or to download from the website. Applications are considered quarterly, on the first Tuesday of March, June, September and December, though emergency grants can be made between meetings. Forms should be submitted two months before the next meeting.

Other information
The fund tries to keep in regular contact with its beneficiaries and is there to offer advice and support if needed.

The Stock Exchange Clerks Fund

£103,000 (55 grants)

Correspondent: Alfred Barnard, 1–5 Earl Street, London EC2A 2AL (020 7797 4373 or 01245 322985)

Trustees: Michael Willmott; John Culliford; Anne McNally; Karen George; Ian Baines; John Dust; Steve Tame; Andrew Hackling; Jeremy Paulson-Ellis.

CC Number: 286055

Eligibility
Former members of the fund and former employees of the London Stock Exchange or member firms of the London Stock Exchange, who are in need, and their dependents.

Types of grants
Monthly payments to help with living costs. One-off grants are available for medical equipment, domestic appliances, mobility vehicles, driving lessons for specialised vehicles, moving costs and so on. Most beneficiaries also receive a Christmas food parcel.

Annual grant total
In 2011 the trust had assets of £1.1 million and an income of £45,000. Grants were made to 55 individuals totalling £103,000.

Applications
On a form available from the correspondent. Applications can be submitted at any time by the individual or through a third party. New applicants are visited by the Funds Liaison Officer who will then make a report to the trustees.

Any information concerning individuals who were previously employed in the industry and who may be in need of assistance can be given in complete confidence to either the correspondent or any of the trustees.

Tax inspectors

The Benevolent Fund of the Association of Her Majesty's Inspectors of Taxes

£1,900

Correspondent: Jim Ferguson, Room 1/72, HM Revenue and Customs, 100 Parliament Street, London SW1A 2BQ (020 7147 2807)

Trustees: Simon Peter Norris; Frances Pickering; Roy Warden; Jim Ferguson.

CC Number: 207206

Eligibility
Current and former tax inspectors and other senior officers in the Inland Revenue who are members of the association, and their dependents, who are ill or in other necessitous circumstances.

Types of grants
One-off and recurrent grants of up to £500 for people on sick leave to help towards the cost of medical equipment, hospital travel and medicines.

Annual grant total
Grants average around £1,900 a year, though the actual grant figure tends to fluctuate quite widely.

Exclusions
Clerical grade inspectors are not normally eligible.

Applications
In writing to the correspondent at any time. Applications can be submitted directly by the individual.

Teaching

Association of Principals of Colleges Benevolent Fund

£500

Correspondent: Mr N Otley, Havering College of Further and Higher Education, Ardleigh Green Road, Hornchurch, Essex RM11 2LL (01708 455011)

Trustees: Mr N. Otley; Mr G. Hall; Dr P. Phillips; Mr D. Lambert.

CC Number: 291477

Eligibility
Members and ex-members of the association, and their dependents, who are in need.

Types of grants
One-off and recurrent grants according to need. Grants have been given to widows and dependents of members who have died.

Annual grant total
Grants usually total around £1,000 per year, however, in 2011 the trust had a lower than usual income of £700 and a total expenditure of £500. No further information was available.

Applications
In writing to the correspondent.

Church School Masters and School Mistresses Benevolent Institution

£11,600

Correspondent: The Trustees, 3 Kings Court, Harwood Road, Horsham RH13 5UR (01403 250798; email: info@cssbi.org.uk; website: www.cssbi.org.uk)

Trustees: Diana Bell; Gillian Mary Cooper; Jennifer Rosemary Barker; Patricia Anne Castle; Janet Palmer; David Cozens; Karen Ind; Christine Sorensen; Kay Croll.

CC Number: 207236

Eligibility
Present, former or trainee teachers and their dependents throughout the UK who are in need.

Types of grants
One-off grants according to need.

Annual grant total
In 2010/11 the trust held assets of £2.2 million and had an income of £29,000. Grants of £11,600 were made during the year.

Applications
On a form available to download from the website to be submitted directly by the individual or a family member. Applications are considered upon receipt.

Other information
During 2011 the members of the charity resolved to update the charitable objectives which have largely modernised and widened the Charity's remit.

The Headmasters' Association Benevolent Fund

£7,500

Correspondent: Andrew Smetham, Trustee, The Water Barn, Water Meadow Lane, Wool, Wareham BH20 6HL (01929 463727)

Trustees: Mr A. J. Smetham; Philip Lane Clark; Geoffrey Goodall; John Sutton; Michael Harrison; P. F. Johnston.

CC Number: 260303

Eligibility
The widows and dependents of deceased secondary school headmasters who were members of the association. Help is also given to headmasters and ex-headmasters who are, or were members of the association and are in urgent need of assistance.

Types of grants
One-off and recurrent grants according to need.

Annual grant total
Grants usually average around £10,000 a year.

Applications
In writing to the correspondent. Applications are considered as they arrive.

The IAPS (Independent Association of Prep Schools) Charitable Trust

£500

Correspondent: Richard Flower, 11 Waterloo Place, Warwick Street, Leamington Spa CV32 5LA (01926 887833; email: rwf@iaps.org.uk; website: www.iaps.org.uk/about/our-charities)

Trustees: Richard Graham Tovey; Edward Hugh Bradby; Charles Norman Carrington Abram; Kevin John Douglas; Joanna Ruth Pardon; David Peter Hanson; Richard William Flower; Jane Crouch.

CC Number: 1143241

Eligibility
Members, retired members and the dependents of retired or deceased members of IAPS. Support may also be given to association employees or, with the consent of the directors, anyone connected with education.

Types of grants
One-off grants according to need. Grants may be given to teachers for training or to enable them to conduct research.

Support may also be given to relieve general hardship.

Annual grant total

In 2011/12, the first accounting year for this new trust, it had an income of £453,000 and an expenditure of £1,600.

Applications

Initial enquiries should be made with the correspondent by phone or email.

Other information

The trust is also known as the I Trust.

The Incorporated Association of Preparatory Schools' Benevolent Fund

£10,000

Correspondent: Richard Flower, Trustee, 11 Waterloo Place, Leamington Spa, Warwickshire CV32 5LA (01926 887833)

Trustees: Richard Graham Tovey; Hugh Bradby; Joanna Ruth Pardon; David Peter Hanson; Richard William Flower; Kevin John Gordon Douglas; Charles Norman C. Abram.

CC Number: 281935

Eligibility

Past and present members of the association, or their staff, and their dependents, who are in need.

Types of grants

One-off and recurrent grants according to need.

Annual grant total

In 2010/11 the fund had an income of £13,000 and a total expenditure of £11,000.

Applications

In writing to the correspondent.

The National Association of Schoolmasters Union of Women Teachers (NASUWT) Benevolent Fund

£202,000

Correspondent: Legal and Casework Team, NASUWT, Hillscourt Education Centre, Rose Hill, Rednal, Birmingham B45 8RS (01214 536150; fax: 01214 576210; email: legalandcasework@mail. nasuwt.org.uk; website: www.nasuwt.org. uk)

Trustees: Michael Grant; Pamela Milner; Hopkin Thomas; Celia Foote; Andrew Curtis; Chris Holland.

CC Number: 285793

Eligibility

Members, former members and the dependents of members, former members and deceased members, provided a subscription has been paid to the union. Applicants should have less than £5,000 in savings and investments (though this limit may be waived in extenuating circumstances).

Types of grants

One-off and recurrent grants and interest-free loans according to need. Recent grants have been given to people with terminal illnesses to visit relatives; to pay for the services of an occupational therapist to assess disability home conversion needs; to buy a converted vehicle for a member who is paralysed; and a monthly grant to a member's widow with no occupational pension.

Annual grant total

In 2010 the fund held assets of £2.1 million and had an income of £290,000. 787 individuals received grants totalling £202,000.

Exclusions

No grants/loans available for private health care or dental treatment, private school fees, student loans, legal fees, house purchase or to repay money owed to friends or family. Assistance is not given if it would affect the applicant's entitlement to means-tested state benefits.

Applications

Potential applicants should either contact their local association secretary or the correspondent to arrange a meeting with a benevolence visitor. The visitor will complete an application form with the individual and submit a recommendation to the benevolence committee. The committee meets monthly (except August) to consider new applications. However, emergency cases can be processed more quickly.

Other information

Grants totalling £11,000 were also made to 20 NASUWT Federations in the year.

The fund also provides members with access to a money advice service through Payplan, see the website for further details.

The Ogilvie Charities

£1,000 (5 grants)

Correspondent: Gillian Galvan, General Manager, The Gate House, 9 Burkitt Road, Woodbridge, Suffolk IP12 4JJ (01394 388746; fax: 01394 388746; email: ogilviecharities@btconnect.com; website: www.ogilviecharities.org.uk)

Trustees: Patrick Grieve; Belinda Grant; Felicity Anne Lowe; Margaret Smith; Richard Aynsley-Smith; D. Allan Howell; Jean Goyder; Jolyon Dean Sunderland Hall; Simon Gibbs; Edward Wright.

CC Number: 211778

Eligibility

People who are, or have been, teachers or governesses in England and Wales, and, children resident in any London borough who are in need, hardship or distress by assisting with the cost of holidays or days out in the country; accompanied by or unaccompanied by other family members.

Types of grants

One-off grants of £100 to £250.

Annual grant total

In 2011 the charities had assets of £1.7 million and an income of £54,000. Grants totalling £1,000 were made to five families for holidays.

Applications

In writing to the correspondent, to be submitted through a social worker, Citizens Advice or other welfare agency. The referring agency may telephone the trust if there are doubts about their client's eligibility. Applications can be considered at any time.

Other information

The charities also make grants to organisations.

Recourse

£64,000

Correspondent: Support Line, 40a Drayton Park, London N5 1EW (0808 802 0304; email: enquires@recousre.org. uk; website: recourse.org.uk/)

Trustees: Michael Crilly; Anthony Tonks; Edward Ritson; Hank Roberts; Su Gillespie; Winifred Brass; John Bills; Claire Price; Dennis Bates; Rod Ruffle; Angela Roger; Susan Lancaster.

CC Number: 1116382

Eligibility

People working in adult, further and higher education who have less than £6,000 in savings. Applicants must work or have worked in further or higher education for at least two days a week and for at least one term.

Types of grants

Grants for energy bills, mortgage repayments, food, council tax, childcare costs, house repairs, special needs equipment, care home fees, clothing, white goods, furniture and removal costs.

Annual grant total

In 2010 the charity had assets of £1.1 million and an income of £486,000. Grants totalling £64,000 were made during the year.

Exclusions

No grants for student teachers, student loans, private school fees, educational course fees, school trips, unsecured debts, house purchases or private medical treatment.

Applications

Applicants should contact the charity by phone or email in the first instance for an application form. The charity will also provide financial advice.

Other information

Recourse also offers information and advice, telephone counselling and online coaching.

The Association of School and College Leaders Benevolent Fund

£10,000

Correspondent: Carole Baldam, 130 Regent Road, Leicester LE1 7PG (01162 991122; fax: 01162 991123; email: carole.baldam@ascl.org.uk)

Trustees: Ann Mullins; Ian Bauckham; Christine Shellard; Florence Kirkby; John Sutton; Michael Harrison; Rod Wilson; John Fairhurst; Joan McVittie; Mike Griffiths; Anthony Richardson; Rachel Bertenshaw.

CC Number: 279628

Eligibility

The dependents of deceased members of the association; current and former members of the association and their dependents; and, retired employees of the association.

Types of grants

One-off and recurrent grants according to need.

Annual grant total

Grants usually total around £10,000 per year.

Applications

In writing to the correspondent.

Other information

The association was previously known as The Secondary Heads Association Benevolent Fund.

Schoolmistresses' and Governesses' Benevolent Institution

£134,000

Correspondent: Case Secretary, SGBI Office, Queen Mary House, Manor Park Road, Chislehurst, Kent BR7 5PY (020 8468 7997; email: sgbi@fsmail.net)

Trustees: Dr Norman Hamblyn; John Davison; Derek Lutyens; Diana Rayne; Frank Attwood; John Clark; Pamela Parsonson; Christopher Kennedy; Pamela Mathew; Dr Eleanor Relle; Janet Davies; Susan Whitfield; Susan Eccles.

CC Number: 205366

Eligibility

Women who work, or have worked, as a schoolmistress, matron, bursar, secretary or librarian in the private sector of education. Self-employed teachers may also be assisted.

Types of grants

All types of help including annuities and one-off grants towards telephone bills, TV licences, household items, clothing, medical needs, holidays and mobility equipment. Grants usually range from £50 to £500.

Annual grant total

In 2010/11 the institution had assets of £4 million and an income of £1.4 million. Grants were made to 163 individuals totalling £134,000.

Applications

On a form available from the correspondent, to be submitted at any time directly by the individual or family member. Applications are considered monthly.

Other information

The institution arranges annual visits to beneficiaries.

The Society of Schoolmasters and Schoolmistresses

£2,000

Correspondent: The Case Secretary, Queen Mary House, Manor Park Road, Chislehurst, Kent BR7 5PY (020 8468 7997; email: sgbi@fsmail.net; website: www.sossandsgbi.org.uk)

Trustees: Revd Canon Keith Wilkinson; John Davison; Frank Attwood; John Clark; John Wolters; Richard Steel; Andrew Nott; Mark Phillips; Yvonne Burne; Dr Michael Spurr.

CC Number: 206693

Eligibility

Schoolmasters or schoolmistresses (employed/retired) of any independent or maintained school who have ten years of continuous service, and their dependents.

Types of grants

One-off and recurrent grants up to a maximum of £600 per year. Grants are normally made to retired schoolmasters or schoolmistresses who have no adequate pension, but exceptions can sometimes be made for younger teachers.

Annual grant total

In 2010 the trust had an income of £6,000 and a total expenditure of £2,100.

Applications

On a form available from the correspondent. Applications can be submitted directly by the individual. They are considered quarterly.

Teacher Support Network

£227,000 (3,366 grants)

Correspondent: Grants Manager, 40a Drayton Park, London N5 1EW (England- 0800 056 2561 Wales- 0800 855 088; email: enquiries@ teachersupport.info; website: www. teachersupport.info)

Trustees: Claire Price; Michael Crilly; Anthony Tonks; Dennis Bates; Edward Ritson; John Bills; Hank Roberts; Su Gillespie; Winifred Brass; Rod Ruffle; Angela Roger; Susan Lancaster.

CC Number: 1072583

Eligibility

Serving, former and retired teachers and their dependents who have less than £4,000 in savings.

Types of grants

One-off grants of between £300 to £3,000 are given towards a range of needs, including low income, illness and injury. Grants are also given for special needs equipment, clothing, removal costs, rent, council tax, utility bills, and funeral costs. Assistance towards household repairs will be considered for those who have retired.

Annual grant total

In 2010 the charity had assets of £4.4 million and an income of £3.6 million. £227,000 was awarded to 3,366 beneficiaries.

The charities main focus continues to be help with mortgage repayments, council tax arrears or other items that are fundamentally important to the daily functioning of teachers and their families.

Exclusions

Student teachers are not eligible for financial support. No grants are given for private school fees, educational course fees, school trips, unsecured debts, house purchases, care home fees, holidays, white goods, furniture or private medical treatment. Student loans are not made.

Applications

On a form available from the correspondent. Applications are usually considered on a monthly basis and can be submitted directly by the individual. Applications are means-tested so financial information is needed, alongside other supporting information such as proof of need.

Other information

Grantmaking is just one aspect of the work of this trust. In 1999, it established Teacher Support Line (formerly Teacherline), 'providing day-to-day support for teachers in both their personal and professional lives'. Services include: coaching, counselling, advice, information and financial assistance.

Telecom-munications

The BT Benevolent Fund

£616,000

Correspondent: Phil Jennings/Steve Melhuish, Room 323, Reading Central Telephone Exchange, 41 Minister Street, Reading RG1 2JB (0845 602 9714; fax: 01189 590668; email: benevolent@bt.com; website: www.benevolent.bt.com)

Trustees: Allan Gore; John Holme; Jane Shipway; Kevin Charlesworth; Tom Keeney; Daniel Fitz; Clare Chapman.

CC Number: 212565

Eligibility

People who work, or have worked, for British Telecom or its predecessors (GPO/Post-Office Telephones), and their dependents.

Types of grants

One-off grants of up to £2,500 are given towards: household appliances, disability aids, home adaptations, convalescence, carer's breaks, funeral costs and debt arrears, especially when there is a risk of eviction and small children are involved. Weekly grants of up to £20 a week are also available to older former employees, and their dependents, who are living on a low income. Recipients of weekly

grants are also eligible to receive a £100 one-off Christmas grant.

Annual grant total

In 2010 the fund had assets of £2.8 million and an income of £842,000. Grants totalled £616,000, of which £430,000 was given in single grants and £186,000 in weekly grants.

Weekly grants were paid to 223 recipients, with a total annual value of £168,000. This averaged out to around £14 per person, per week.

Applications

On a form available from the correspondent. Applications are considered when received and can be submitted either directly by the individual or through a third party such as a welfare agency.

Other information

The fund also operates a 'contact scheme' to provide advice and support for BT pensioners who are over 75 years old.

Tobacco

The Tobacco Charity

£216,000 (200 grants)

Correspondent: Simon Orlik, Company Secretary, Suffolk House, George Street, Croydon CR0 0YN (020 8663 3050; fax: 020 8663 0949; email: info@tobaccocharity.org.uk; website: www.tobaccocharity.org.uk)

Trustees: Roger Lewis Harold Merton; Stephen Luing Preedy; Fiona Adler; David Lewis; George Lankester; Graham Blashill; Michael Richards; David Glynn-Jones; Nigel Mervyn Sutherland Rich.

CC Number: 1135646

Eligibility

People who have been engaged for a substantial period of time in the manufacture, wholesale or retail sections of the tobacco industry and their dependents, who are in need. Both full-time and part-time workers are eligible for assistance. Applicants should have no more than £12,000 in savings/capital (excluding property).

Types of grants

Monthly allowances and one-off grants for household items and house repairs. Grants are also given to help with winter fuel costs.

Annual grant total

In 2010/11 the charity had assets of £5.1 million and an income of £364,000. Around 200 people were helped with grants totalling £216,000, broken down as follows:

Pensions and general relief	£83,000
Maintenance grant	£44,000
One-off grants	£38,000
Welfare assistance	£21,000
Christmas gifts	£16,000
TV rentals and licences	£13,000
House insurance	£600

Applications

Application forms are available from the correspondent or to download from the website. They can be submitted directly by the individual or through a social worker, Citizens Advice, welfare agency or other third party. Applicants are asked to provide details of the length of their service in the tobacco trade, financial position and whether they own their own home. Applications are considered every two months.

Other information

The charity was formed in April 2010 as a result of a merger between the Tobacco Trade Benevolent Association, the Worshipful Company of Tobacco Pipe Makers and Tobacco Blenders Benevolent Fund.

Travel agents

Thomas Cook Pensioners' Benevolent Fund

£1,100

Correspondent: Stewart Grant, Thomas Cook Pensions Department, Unit 15/18, Thomas Cook Business Park, Coningsby Road, Peterborough PE3 8SB (01733 416437; fax: 01733 416780)

Trustees: Roy Harold Butcher; Valerie Joy Ward; Stephen Verrall; Julia Seary.

CC Number: 1030497

Eligibility

Retired former employees of Thomas Cook and their dependents and the dependents of deceased former employees who are in need.

Types of grants

One-off grants to alleviate hardship, for example, the replacement of worn out electrical equipment or modifications to property to accommodate disability or immobility.

Annual grant total

Grants average around £1,000 a year, however, the actual amount of expenditure fluctuates annually with £0 expenditure in 2010/11 and 2008/9.

Applications

In writing to the correspondent. If eligible the individual will be required to complete a claim form.

Other information

If eligibility is established for an individual, the fund would consider an application in conjunction with another charity or organisation.

The Guild of Registered Tourist Guides Benevolent Fund

£9,200

Correspondent: Elizabeth Keatinge, c/o GRTG, The Guild House, 52D Borough High Street, London SE1 1XN (01980 623463; fax: 01908 625597)

Trustees: Carol Ann Gundersen; Betty Makin; Elizabeth Keatinge; Carole Marie Claude Hiley.

CC Number: 211562

Eligibility

Institute registered (blue badge) guides who are in need and have been qualified for at least one year and former and retired guides who have been qualified for five years or more. The dependents of guides qualified for at least five years may also be eligible for support.

Types of grants

One-off grants to relieve need and enable a guide to work. Grants can be up to £700, but are normally between £300 and £400.

Annual grant total

In 2010 the fund had an income of £12,600 and a total expenditure of £9,500.

Exclusions

Grants are not given for debts or private hospital care.

Applications

In writing to the correspondent, including the tourist board with which the applicant was registered, whether any statutory bodies have been approached and details of the specific need. Applications can be made directly by the individual or through a third party. They can be considered at any time. Each trustee has a portfolio of clients and is responsible for checking how the beneficiaries are getting on, sometimes through home visits.

Lifeline The ABTA Charitable Trust

£19,000

Correspondent: Grants Administrator, 3rd Floor, 30 Park Street, London SE1 9EQ (020 3117 0547; fax: 020 3117 0581; email: lifeline@abtalifeline.org.uk; website: www.abtalifeline.org.uk)

Trustees: Sidney Perez; Jack Smith; Group Capt. Colin William Charles Heal; John De Vial; Graham Brooks; William Maxwell; John Albert McEwan; Samantha Clare O'Brien.

CC Number: 295819

Eligibility

People who are or have been employed by ABTA members, ABTA itself-or other organisations within the industry who are engaged in the sale of ABTA products, and their dependents. In exceptional circumstances the parent of someone working in travel may be helped. Both the parent and the person applying on behalf of the parent will have to be assessed.

Types of grants

One-off and recurrent grants and loans unrestricted in size. Recent grants have been given for holidays, disability aids, bills, redecorating costs, school uniforms, and so on.

The trust advise that 'whilst we do not help with paying off debts, in exceptional circumstances we may be able to help with priority debts (rent, mortgage, utility bills). But first you must seek guidance from the Citizens Advice. The CAB can help you plan and budget according to your needs, and provide advice on how to tackle the debts that you have.'

Annual grant total

In 2011 the fund had assets of £511,000 and an income of £79,000. Grants were made to 19 individuals totalling £19,000.

Exclusions

The fund generally does not have any restrictions in relation to their grant criteria, except it cannot help with costs arising from the failure of a company.

Applications

On a form available from the correspondent or to download from the website. Applications should be submitted either directly by the individual, through a third party such as a social worker, or through an organisation such as a Citizens Advice. They are considered every twelve weeks, although urgent applications can be considered between meetings. There are detailed guidelines available on the Lifeline website, read these carefully to ensure that you attach the correct supporting documentation with your application.

United Nations

British Association of Former United Nations Civil Servants Benevolent Fund

£2,500

Correspondent: Nanda Wijayatilake, Clerk and treasurer, 41 Riverine, Grosvenor Drive, Maidenhead, Berkshire SL6 8PF (01628 636000; website: www. bafuncs.org/benevolent.html)

Trustees: Alfred Beer; Brenda Suitters; Cyril Groom; Nanda Witayatilake; Susan Mary Idreos; Penny Ratcliffe; John Miller.

CC Number: 297524

Eligibility

Former employees of the United Nations organisation or its specialised agencies and their dependents who are in need. Applicants must be resident in the UK, but do not have to be UK nationals.

Types of grants

One-off grants, grants in kind and loans of between £100 and £500. Grants can be made towards a wide range of needs, including health and convalescence needs, help in the home, living costs, electrical goods, furniture, aids for older people or those who are disabled and assistance towards hospital visits. Loans include those to people who are recently widowed, prior to establishing their pension rights.

Annual grant total

Grants usually total around £3,000 per year.

Applications

On an application form available from the BAFUNCS website. Applications are normally referred to appropriate BAFUNCS registered welfare officer for immediate follow-up. Applications are considered throughout the year.

Other information

The fund is also known by its short title, 'BAFUNCS Benevolent Fund'.

Veterinary

Veterinary Benevolent Fund

£162,000

Correspondent: Vanessa Kearns, Administration Manager, British Veterinary Association, 7 Mansfield Street, London W1G 9NQ (020 7908 6385; fax: 020 7980 4890; email: info@ vetlife.org.uk; website: www.vetlife.org. uk)

Trustees: L. A. Brown; R. C. Young; J. M. Rutter; D. J. Bartram; D. J. Bee; K. M. Coumbe; W. K. B. Lewis; G. P. Little; J. A. Moffitt; N. J. Paull; N. R. M. Short; R. A. Wickham.

CC Number: 224776

Eligibility

Applicants must be on, or have been on, the register of the Royal College of Veterinary Surgeons or be the dependent of someone who is or has been on the register.

Types of grants

Regular monthly payments for people living on a low income. One-off grants up to a maximum of £1,000 are also made towards TV licences, telephone line rental, additional heating costs, car tax and insurance, holidays, medical equipment and disability aids. The fund has noted an increasing trend towards providing more one-off support with less demand for recurrent grants. Interest-free loans may also be made to tide beneficiaries over in times of crisis.

Annual grant total

In 2011 the fund had assets of £6 million, an income of £530,000 (2010: £458,000) and a total expenditure of £344,000 (2010: £327,000). Grants were made totalling £162,000 (2010: £155,000), of which £133,000 was given in regular payments to 51 beneficiaries and £30,000 was awarded in special gifts. A further five beneficiaries received interest-free loans.

During the year 36 new enquiries were received with financial help given in 11 cases. Of the remainder, 14 were ineligible or did not complete the application process and 11 were referred on to other organisations.

Exclusions

No grants towards: business or partnership debt; mandatory training courses; indemnity insurance; private education; private medical care; repaying loans to family and friends; improvements and repairs to rented property. Grants are not available to veterinary students. Financial support is not given simply because someone is unemployed.

Applications

An application form is available from the VBF office or can be downloaded from the Vetlife website and should be submitted with three months of recent bank statements. A decision may be made immediately or VBF may request that one of their representatives make a home visit before a decision is reached. In any case, a decision will usually be made within two weeks of receipt of the completed form.

Other information

Alongside the benevolent fund the charity also runs a helpline, health programme and the Vetlife website.

Watch and clock makers

The National Benevolent Society of Watch and Clock Makers

£115,000 (160 grants)

Correspondent: Anne Baker, Secretary, 18a Westbury Road, New Malden, Surrey KT3 5BE (020 8288 9559; email: sec@ nbswcm.org; website: www.nbswcm.org)

Trustees: Keith Angliss; Brian Eric Pestell; Dennis George Williams; Elizabeth Crandon Gill; Paul Frank Cradock; Raymond Lionel Mellor; Robert Andrew Ball; Valerie Adelle Leonard; Lionel Arthur Blowes; John Hatt; Brian Newman; Paul Roberson.

CC Number: 206750

Eligibility

Members of the UK watch and clock trade and their widows/widowers and dependents that are in need. Generally grants are given to those with an income below £12,000 although the trustees have the discretion to act outside of this guideline if the circumstances permit.

Types of grants

Help is usually offered in the form of quarterly grants (£125 per quarter in 2010/11), Christmas payments (£200) and occasional gifts.

Annual grant total

In 2010/11 the charity had assets of £2.6 million and an income of £101,000. Grants totalled £115,000 and were broken down as follows:

Grants in aid	£80,000
Heating and seasonal gifts	£32,000
Television licence fees	£2,000

Applications

Applications for grants should be made by contacting the secretary who will send out an application form. All applications are treated in strict confidence. Completed application forms should be submitted by individuals or, if they require assistance, through a family member, social worker, welfare agency or Citizens Advice.

Service and ex-service charities

Unlike other occupations, the service/ex-service charities have been given their own section in this guide as there are many more trusts available and they can support a large number of people. This branch of the sector is committed to helping anyone who has at least one day's paid service in any of the armed forces, including reserves and those who did National Service, and their husbands, wives, children, widows, widowers and other dependents. It is estimated that this covers a quarter of the UK's population.

These charities are exceptionally well organised. Much of this is due to the work of SSAFA Forces Help, which has an extensive network of trained caseworkers around the country who act on behalf of SSAFA Forces Help and other service charities. Many of the trusts in this section use the same application forms and procedures as SSAFA Forces Help and assist a specified group of people within the service/ex-service community, while others (such as Royal British Legion) have their own procedures and support the services as a whole.

There is a standard application form which is used by many service and ex-service charities. This form should not be filled in by the applicant, rather by a trained caseworker at the applicant's home. The completed form is sent to the appropriate service, regimental or corps benevolent fund (and where appropriate, copies may be sent to other relevant funds, both service and non-service).

Although many service benevolent funds rely on trained SSAFA Forces Help volunteer caseworkers to prepare application forms, some do have their own volunteers who can complete the form. However, these may not be spread so comprehensively around the country. Alternatively, some funds ask applicants to write to a central correspondent. In such cases, applicants may like to follow the guidelines in the article 'How to make an application' earlier in this guide. Most entries in this section state whether the applicant should apply directly to the trust or through a caseworker. If in doubt, the applicant should ring up the trust concerned or the local SSAFA Forces Help office.

Some people may prefer to approach their, or their former spouse's regimental or corps association. Each corps has its own entry in this guide and the regimental associations are listed at the end of this section. Many of them have their own charitable funds and volunteers, especially in their own recruiting areas. In other cases they will work through one of the volunteer networks mentioned above. Again, if in doubt or difficulty, the applicant should ring up the regimental/corps association or the local SSAFA Forces Help office.

SSAFA Forces Help is much more than just a provider of financial assistance, providing advice, support and training. It can assist members of the service and ex-service communities on many issues, ranging from how to replace lost medals to advice on adoption. Its website (www.ssafa.org.uk) is an excellent source of reference for the members of the community, giving a wide range of useful information and links. Local SSAFA Forces Help offices can generally be found in the local telephone directories (usually under Soldiers', Sailors' & Airmen's Families Association – Forces Help) or advertised in such places as Citizens Advice, doctor's waiting rooms or libraries. Alternatively, the central office is based at: 19 Queen Elizabeth Street, London SE1 2LP (0845 1300 975; e-mail: info@ssafa.org.uk; Website: www.ssafa.org.uk).

ABF The Soldiers' Charity (also known as The Army Benevolent Fund)

£3.6 million (3,963 grants)

Correspondent: The Director of Grants and Welfare, Mountbarrow House, 6–20 Elizabeth Street, London SW1W 9RB (0845 241 4820; fax: 0845 241 4821; email: info@soldierscharity. org; website: www.soldierscharity.org)

Trustees: Maj. General S. M. Andrews; Maj. General G. W. Berragan; Mr S. Clark; Mr G. C. Davies; Mr D. E. Francis; Brigadier (Retd) A. W. Freemantle; Mrs A. M. Gallico; Maj. General (Retd) A. I. G. Kennedy; R. A. Martin; Maj. (Retd) Sir Michael Parker; Ms S. Ryan; Maj. General (Retd) P. J. Sheppard.

CC Number: 211645

Eligibility

Members and ex-members of the British Regular Army and the Reserve Army (TA) and their dependents who are in need. Serving TA soldiers must have completed at least one year's satisfactory service, and former TA soldiers should have completed at least three years' satisfactory service.

Types of grants

Grants are made in the following areas: debt relief; mobility assistance and home modifications; annuities and care home fees; war widow and family financial support; and holidays.

Annual grant total

In 2010/11 the fund had assets of £45 million, an income of £16 million and a total expenditure of £15 million. Grants to individuals totalled £3.8 million, the majority of which (£3.6 million) was made in welfare grants.

Applications

The fund does not deal directly with individual cases. Soldiers who are still serving should contact their regimental or corps association, who will then approach the fund on their behalf. Former soldiers should first contact SSAFA Forces Help or the Royal British Legion. Applications are considered at any time, but all are reviewed annually in July.

Enquiries may be made directly to the fund to determine the appropriate corps or regimental association. See also, in particular, the entries for SSAFA Forces Help and the Royal British Legion.

Other information

The trust also gives grants to individuals for educational purposes and to organisations.

The Airborne Forces' Security Fund

£135,000 (197 grants)

Correspondent: Mrs Tracy Miller, Controller, Regimental Headquarters, The Parachute Regiment, Merville Barracks, Colchester, Essex CO2 7UT (01206 817079; email: tracy.miller904@mod.uk)

Trustees: Col John Crosland; Col Michael Russell; Gen Sir Mike Jackson; Gen Sir Rupert Smith; Maj Gen Dair Farrar-Hockley; John Power; Lt Col Simon Brewis; Lt Col Banks Middleton; Mike Collins; Maj Gen Jonathan Shaw; Col Bernard Cazenove; Col Ranald Munro; Brig Hamish McGregor; Maj Gen Jacko Page; Maj Gen Nigel Richards; Lt Col Martyn Wills; Jonathon Scivener; Chris Daniels; Maj Gen John Lorimer; Maj Gen James Bashall.

CC Number: 206552

Eligibility

Serving and former members of the Parachute Regiment, the Glider Regiment and other units of airborne forces, and their dependents.

Types of grants

One-off grants according to need.

Annual grant total

In 2011 the fund had assets of £5.1 million and an income of £372,000. Grants were made to 197 individuals totalling £135,000.

Applications

In writing to the correspondent, usually through the Army Benevolent Fund, SSAFA or the Royal British Legion.

AJEX Charitable Foundation

£44,000

Correspondent: Ronald Shelley, Shield House, Harmony Way, Hendon, London NW4 2BZ (020 8202 2323; fax: 020 8202 9900; email: headoffice@ajex.org.uk; website: www.ajex.org.uk)

Trustees: Alan Cass; Clive Isaac L. Boxer; Leonard Stern; Lillie Davies; Lt Col Mordaunt Cohen; Ronald C. Shelley; David Sherman; Ivan Sugarman; Dr Peter Henry Wagerman; Dr Arnold L. Phelops.

CC Number: 1082148

Eligibility

Jewish ex-servicemen and women, and their dependents, who are in need.

Types of grants

One-off and recurrent grants according to need. Special grants are also made to cover emergencies and exceptional circumstances.

Annual grant total

In 2010 the foundation held assets of £2.1 million and had an income of £345,000. Grants were made totaling £44,000.

Applications

On a form available from the correspondent, to be returned directly by the individual or through a third party. Evidence of service in the British army and of Jewish religious status is required.

ATS and WRAC Benevolent Fund

£204,000 (511 grants)

Correspondent: Maj G M Shanahan, Regimental Secretary, Gould House, Worthy Down, Winchester SO21 2RG (01962 887612; fax: 01962 887478; email: benfund@wracassociation.co.uk; website: www.wracassociation.co.uk)

Trustees: Audrey Jean Smith; Col Eleanor Jean Bowles; Brig Dame Joanna Kelleher; Margaret Bolton Seafield Purkis; Lt Col Mary Wesley Soames; Brig Shirley Patricia Nield; Lt Col Susan Jane Westlake; Col Frances Mary Cook; Kathleen Rita McGregor; Lt Col Nicky Murdoch; Jo Young; Maj Leona Barr-Jones; Dorothy Ryder; Lt Col Sue Donovan; Lt Col Gerry Fahy; Brig Nicola Patricia Moffat; Maj Ann Maskens-McIntyre; Wendy Lynn Hooton; Eileen Carter; Carole Motessori-Gorman; Christine Brenda Corker; Maj Rowena Charlotte Griffiths; Karen Loftus; Col Alison Kay Brown; Maj Jacqueline Ann Walton.

CC Number: 206184

Eligibility

Former members of the Auxiliary Territorial Service during the Second World War and the Women's Royal Army Corps between 1949–1992 who are in financial hardship or who are disabled or have mobility problems.

Types of grants

One-off grants to those in need. The fund can also help with making up the shortfall for nursing home fees and supports some annuitants who receive regular payments throughout the year. Some annuities (around £20 per week) continue to be paid through the Princess Royal Memorial Fund.

Annual grant total

In 2010/11 the trust had assets of £5.4 million and an income of £383,000. Grants were made to 511 individuals totalling £204,000. Of this total £53,000 was paid from the Princess Royal Memorial Fund to provide annuities and top-up contributions for nursing home fees to 45 individuals.

Applications

All applications for financial assistance should go through the Soldiers, Sailors, Airman and Families Association (SSAFA) or the Royal British Legion caseworkers who will visit the applicants and submit whatever forms are necessary.

Other information

If you feel that you might qualify for financial assistance, apply to your local Royal British Legion or SSAFA office in the first instance.

The Black Watch Association

£75,000

Correspondent: Maj. A R McKinnell, Balhousie Castle, Hay Street, Perth PH1 5HR (01738 623214; fax: 01738 643245; email: bwassociation@btconnect.com; website: www.theblackwatch.co.uk)

SC Number: SC016423

Eligibility

Serving and retired soldiers of the regiment, their wives, widows and families.

Types of grants

One-off grants towards rent arrears, clothing, household equipment, funeral expenses and mobility aids. Support is also given towards holidays for widows and dependent children and former members of the regiment in necessitous circumstances.

Annual grant total

In 2010 the trust had an income of £158,000.

Exclusions

No grants towards council tax arrears, loans or large debts.

Applications

On an application form to be completed by a caseworker from SSAFA Forces Help (19 Queen Elizabeth Street, London SE1 2LP; Tel: 0845 130 0975; Website: www.ssafa.org.uk). Applications are considered throughout the year.

Blind Veterans UK (St Dunstan's)

Correspondent: Admissions and Pensions Manager, 12–14 Harcourt Street, London W1H 4HD (020 7723 5021; fax: 020 7262 6199; email: enquiries@st-dunstans.org.uk; website: www.st-dunstans.org.uk)

Trustees: David Knowles; Maj Gen David Shrimpton Joliffe; Maj Gen Andrew Myles Keeling; John Varley; Raymond Hazan; Timothy Bacon; Air Vice Mshl Richard Henry Kyle; David Stuttard; Lady Walker; Andrew Ross; Ianin Lumsden; Timothy John Beed Davis; Cnl Mike Brooke; Maj Gen David Rutherford-Jones.

CC Number: 216227

Eligibility

Eligibility for membership takes into account both military service and sight loss:

▷ All applicants must have served at any time in the Regular or Reserve UK Armed Forces, or in the Merchant Navy during World War Two, or in the Polish/Indian Forces under British Command

▷ The trust uses its own criteria for the level of sight loss required to receive help and the trust's doctors will assess this. The website advises that 'it doesn't matter how or when your sight loss was caused, or whether you were on active service at the time.'

Types of grants

Grants are given to allow applicants to develop their independence by a combination of training, rehabilitation, holiday and respite care. An annual support grant is given to all beneficiaries and further assistance is available for specific needs such as, help in the garden, a domestic help allowance, healthcare needs, nursing home fees and assistance with mobility and employment. Grants and equipment are also provided according to need once an applicant has become a member of St Dunstan's.

Annual grant total

In 2010/11 the trust held assets of £143 million and had an income of £24 million. The trust had a total charitable expenditure of £18 million.

No figures were available to detail the exact amount given in grants as the trust has informed us that it does not record these figures separately. Grants may have been awarded out of any of the following categories of charitable expenditure:

Care centre costs	£3.2 million
Independent living assistance	£2.3 million
Welfare services	£1.1 million
Housing provision	£897,000
Recruitment of beneficiaries	£304,000
Total	£7.8 million

Note these figures denote total charitable expenditure less staff costs and depreciation.

Exclusions

The charity can only assist those with a severe level of sight loss.

Applications

On a form available to download from the website or obtainable from the admissions department. The application must include details of the applicant's service (including service number and dates of service) and details of their ophthalmic consultant. On receipt the trust will contact the respective service office and ophthalmic consultant for reports. The process should take about ten weeks.

Other information

St Dunstan's provides lifelong support and advice to its beneficiaries and dependents. It operates three centres in Brighton, Sheffield and Llandudno which provide rehabilitation and training to individuals learning to cope with blindness. The Brighton and Llandudno centres also serve as nursing, residential and respite care centres.

St Dunstan's administers the Diana Gubbay Trust which exists for the benefit of men and women in the Emergency Services (Police, Fire and Ambulance) who suffer severe loss of sight whilst on duty. The ophthalmic criteria is the same as for St Dunstan's.

British Limbless Ex-Service Men's Association (BLESMA)

£372,000

Correspondent: Jerome W Church, General Secretary, Frankland Moore House, 185–187 High Road, Chadwell Heath, Romford, Essex RM6 6NA (020 8590 1124; fax: 020 8599 2932; email: headquarters@blesma.org; website: www. blesma.org)

Trustees: Lt Col Simon Brewis; Andrew Kenneth Mudd; David Asdell; Ian Ritchie; Group Capt. Martyn Ward; Colin Rouse; Philip Monkhouse; Col Duncan Dewar; Lt Col James Keating; Lt Gen Sir Cedric Delves; Charles Bishop.

CC Number: 1084189

Eligibility

Serving and ex-serving members of HM or auxiliary forces who have lost a limb or eye or have a permanent loss of speech, hearing or sight, and their widows/widowers. Despite the association's name, it serves members of both sexes.

Types of grants

One-off and recurrent grants towards, for example, wheelchairs and Electric Propelled Vehicles, stair lifts, car adaptations and gardening costs.

Annual grant total

In 2010 the association had assets of £19.7 million and an income of £5.1 million. Welfare grants were made totalling £372,000.

Applications

On a form available from the correspondent. Applications can be submitted at any time, either directly by the individual or through their local BLESMA representative, SSAFA Forces Help, Citizens Advice or similar welfare agency.

Other information

The association provides permanent residential and respite accommodation through its two nursing and residential care homes at Blackpool and Crieff in Perthshire.

The Burma Star Association

£157,000 (278 grants)

Correspondent: Glynis Longhurst, 34 Grosvenor Gardens, London SW1W 0DH (020 7823 4273; email: burmastar@btconnect.com; website: www.burmastar.org.uk)

Trustees: Hon Mark Slim; Dr Hugo Slim; Sir John Day; Richard Nunneley; Rear Admiral Chris Clayton.

CC Number: 1043040

Eligibility

People who were awarded the Burma Star Campaign Medal (or the Pacific Star with Burma clasp) during the Second World War, and their immediate dependents, who live in the UK, Republic of Ireland or other Commonwealth country.

Types of grants

One-off grants usually in the range of £200 to £1,000 towards: top-up fees for nursing, care and residential homes; respite care and holidays; domestic goods; debts; disability aids; funeral expenses; repairs and adaptations; travel costs; mobility aids and so on.

Annual grant total

In 2011 the association held assets of £1.2 million and had an income of £267,000. Grants to 278 individuals (of 300 applications) totalled £157,000, and were distributed as follows:

Nursing and residential homes	£75,000
Repairs	£21,000
Stairlifts and riser-recliner chairs	£18,000
Debts	£13,000
Wheelchairs	£10,000
Communication aids	£4,100
Personal aids	£3,000
Household goods	£2,700
Respite care	£2,300

A further £8,300 was also distributed by local branches for benevolence work. The 2011 accounts note that 'all applications for assistance which satisfied the charity's criteria were met.'

Exclusions

No grants are available towards private medical treatment, headstones or plaques. The association does not give loans.

Applications

On an application form available from the correspondent or a local branch officer. Applications can be made by the individual or through a third party. They should either be sent directly to the correspondent or submitted via branches of the association or other ex-service organisations. Grants are made through the local branches, SSAFA, the Royal British Legion or other ex-service organisations after investigation and completion of an application form giving full particulars of circumstances and eligibility (including service particulars verifying the award of the Burma Star). Applications are considered throughout the year.

Other information

The association has 73 branches across the UK and seven overseas, which offer support and advice to their local members and make small grants where possible. The contact details for local branch officers can be obtained from the correspondent.

The Commandos' Benevolent Fund

£32,000

Correspondent: Michael Copland, Old Pinkneys, Lee Lane, Maidenhead, Berkshire SL6 6PE (01628 630375; email: mandlcopland@yahoo.co.uk; website: commandosbenevolentfund.org.uk/)

Trustees: Desiree Leilam Roderick; Angela Van Der Horst; Martin Pugh; Brig John Thomas; Michael Copland; Eric Buckmaster; Lt Col Steven Turnbull; Graham Dunning; Dorothy Jenkins.

CC Number: 229631

Eligibility

People who served with the Army Commandos during the Second World War, and their dependents. Unfortunately service with any other commando group does not make people eligible for help from this fund.

Types of grants

One-off grants towards, hospital transport, household bills, stair-lifts, flooding costs, holidays, respite breaks, removal expenses, home adaptations, medical costs, funeral expenses and so on. The fund states that it will consider all applications on a case by case basis.

Annual grant total

In 2011 the fund had an income of £36,000 and made grants totalling £32,000.

Applications

In writing, with service details, to the Assistant Secretary, PO Box 104, Selby, Yorkshire YO8 5YY: or on a form available from the website. Applications can be submitted directly by the individual or through a social worker, Citizens Advice or other welfare agency such as SSAFA Forces Help. Applications are considered as soon as possible after receipt.

W. J. and Mrs C. G. Dunnachie's Charitable Trust

£80,000

Correspondent: Trust Administrator, c/o Low Beaton Richmond, Sterling House, 20 Renfield Street, Glasgow G2 5AP (01412 218931; fax: 01412 484411; email: murdoch@lbr-city.demon.co.uk)

SC Number: SC015981

Eligibility

People who are in poor health or who have a disability as a result of their service during the Second World War.

Types of grants

One-off and recurrent grants according to need.

Annual grant total

Grants average about £80,000 a year.

Applications

In writing to the correspondent at any time. Most applications are submitted via SSAFA Forces Help or through a regimental association.

The Hampshire and Isle of Wight Military Aid Fund (1903)

£19,000 (66 grants)

Correspondent: Lt Col Colin Bulleid, Serle's House, Southgate Street, Winchester, Hampshire SO23 9EG (01962 852933; email: secretary@hantsMAF.org; website: www.hantsmaf.org)

Trustees: Richard Ashenden; Dame Mary Fagan; Brig D. A. Harrison; Lt Col J. D. Roberts; J. L. Jervoise; J. M. Curtis; Maj Peter Shepherd; Shelagh Orchard.

CC Number: 202363

Eligibility

Members, or former members, of the British Army (whether regular, territorial, militia, yeomanry or volunteer), and their dependents, who are in need, and who are, or were:
a) Members or former members of any Regiment or Corps raised in Hampshire.
b) Members or former members of The Princess of Wales's Royal Regiment (Queen's and Royal Hampshire's) who were resident in Hampshire at the time of their enlistment.

Territorial Army soldiers must have had at least four years service with a TA unit in Hampshire or operational service.

Types of grants

One-off grants of up to £400 for stair-lifts, recliner chairs, walk-in showers, electrically powered vehicles and so on.

Annual grant total

In 2011 the fund had assets of £455,000 and an income £54,000. Individual grants were made totalling £19,000.

Applications

Normally through the local branch of SSAFA or the Royal British Legion. Applications are considered as they are received.

Other information

The fund also distributes grants and monthly allowances on behalf of the Army Benevolent Fund for nursing home top up fees and support for individuals on a low income trying to stay in their own homes (£24,000 in 2011).

Lloyd's Patriotic Fund

£57,000

Correspondent: The Secretary, Lloyd's, One Lime Street, London EC3M 7HA (020 7327 5921; email: communityaffairs@lloyds.com; website: www.lloyds.com)

Trustees: Robert Finch; Fraser Newton; Max Taylor; John Nelson; Graham Findlay; Peter Levene; Chris Klein; Thomas Ashton; Michael Hardingham; Patrick Holcroft; Graham White; Tim Coles; James Kininmonth.

CC Number: 210173

Eligibility

Ex-servicemen and women who are in need, and their dependents.

Types of grants

One-off grants averaging about £300 are provided for essential domestic items, electric wheelchairs, home adaptations and 'exceptional' expenses. In deserving cases grants may also be given for debt relief and help with utility bills. Annuity payments are also made.

Annual grant total

In 2010/11 the fund had assets of £1.8 million and an income of £477,000. Grants to individuals for welfare purposes totalled £57,000 including £12,000 in 27 annuities.

Applications

Applications should be made through SSAFA, using their application form.

Other information

Grants are also given for educational purposes.

The Nash Charity

£15,000

Correspondent: P A Williamson, Peachey and Co., 95 Aldwych, London WC2B 4JF (020 7316 5200; fax: 020 7316 5222)

Trustees: Steven John Walbourne; David Alan Wilson; Peter Williamson.

CC Number: 229447

Eligibility

Ex-service personnel who have been wounded or disabled during wartime.

Types of grants

Grants are usually paid through social services, Citizens Advice or other welfare agencies to purchase specific items.

Annual grant total

In 2010/11 the charity had an income of £14,000 and a total expenditure of £18,000.

Applications

In writing to the correspondent at any time. Applications can be submitted directly by the individual or through an appropriate third party.

The Not Forgotten Association

£670,000

Correspondent: Col. S D Rowland-Jones, Chief Executive, 4th Floor, 2 Grosvenor Gardens, London SW1W 0DH (020 7730 2400; fax: 020 7730 0020; email: info@nfassociation. org; website: www.nfassociation.org)

Trustees: B. H. Hewton; Brig Richard John Heywood; Capt. Brian James Adams; David John Cowley; Dac Smyth; Lord Newall; Col Sir Geoffrey Frederick Errington; Mark Nicholls; Cmmd P. J. Tribe; Jeremy Archer.

CC Number: 229666

Eligibility

Service and ex-service men and women who are disabled or suffering from some form of ill health. Applicants must have served in the Armed Forces of the Crown (or Merchant Navy during hostilities). The association cannot help wives, widows or families (unless they are themselves ex-members of the forces or they are acting as carers).

Types of grants

The association does not give financial grants direct to applicants; rather it gives help in kind of between £150 and £250 in the following areas: televisions and licences for those with restricted mobility or who are otherwise largely housebound; holidays (accompanied by carers if required) and day outings to events and places of interest; entertainment at ex-service care homes.

The association does not give cash grants, but in certain cases cheques may be sent to individual applicants for holidays or to office holders of bona fide ex-service organisations. The association does not have the resources to undertake case work.

Annual grant total

In 2011/12 the association had assets of £2.9 million and an income of £882,000. Grants were made totalling £670,000 and can be broken down as follows:

Televisions	£221,000
Holidays	£168,000
Entertainment	£136,000
Outings	£63,000

These totals do not include the staff and administration costs involved in providing these items and services.

Applications

Applications should be submitted through SSAFA Forces Help, Royal British Legion, Combat Stress or the Welfare Service of the Service Personnel and Veterans' Agency. These agencies will complete the common application form on behalf of the applicant and then make the appropriate recommendation to the association, with the applicant's income and expenditure details and degree of disability. Applications are considered throughout the year. Successful applicants can reapply after a three-year gap.

Other information

The association holds a summer garden party and Christmas party for war pensioners or for those in receipt of compensation from the Armed Force Compensation Scheme in London each year.

The Officers' Association

£1.2 million

Correspondent: Benevolence Department, 1st Floor, Mountbarrow House, 6–20 Elizabeth Street, London SW1W 9RB (020 7808 4175/0845 873 7150; email: k.wallis@officersassociation. org.uk; website: www.officersassociation. org.uk)

Trustees: Admiral the Lord Boyce; Lt Gen. Sir Alistair Irwin; Air Chief Marshal Sir Clive Loader; Vice Admiral Sir Richard Ibbotson; Lt Col Richard Marriott; Capt. Patrick Mitford-Slade; Dominic Fisher; Frank Froud; Jonathan Holdsworth; Air Commodore Peter Johnson; Maj. Jo Killip; Jocelyn Lynch; Capt. Giles Peel; David Scott; Alastair Singleton; Alex Spofforth; Capt. Ian Sutherland; Air Vice Marshall the Hon David Murray; Robert Robson; Maj. Gen. Martin Rutledge; Air Marshal Chris Nickols.

CC Number: 201321

Eligibility

Officers who have held a commission in HM Forces, their widows and dependents. Officers on the active list will normally be helped only with resettlement and employment.

Types of grants

One-off and recurrent grants according to need. Cash grants are made for specific items such as disability equipment, property repairs, convalescence, holidays or to help set up a new home following a family crisis. Regular allowances are given mainly to older people who are living on a low income. Help is also given towards residential care and nursing home fees.

Limited assistance may be given for education or training needs in exceptional circumstances.

Annual grant total

In 2010/11 the association had assets of £12.2 million and an income of £3.6 million. Grants were made to 873 individuals totalling £1.4 million and were given mainly for relief-in-need purposes.

Applications

On a form available from the Benevolence Secretary or downloaded from the website. Applications can be submitted either directly by the individual or via a third party. The association has a network of honorary representatives throughout the UK who will normally visit the applicant to discuss their problems and offer advice.

Other information

The association has a residential home at Bishopsteignton, South Devon, for ex-officers (male and female) over the age of 65 who do not need special care. There is also a small estate of 12 bungalows in Leavesden specially designed for disabled officers and their families.

The association provides a series of advice leaflets on finding accommodation in residential care or nursing homes, how to get financial assistance and how to find short-term convalescence accommodation and sheltered accommodation for older people who are disabled. It also has an employment department to help ex-officers up to the age of 60 find suitable employment. This service is open to officers just leaving the services and to those who have lost their civilian jobs.

The association has an informative website.

For applicants in Scotland: See entry for the Officers' Association Scotland.

The Officers' Association Scotland

£169,000 (99 grants)

Correspondent: Gary Gray, Head of Welfare Services, New Haig House, Logie Green Road, Edinburgh EH7 4HR (01315 501593; email: g.gray@ poppyscotland.org.uk; website: www. oascotland.org.uk)

SC Number: SC010665

Eligibility

Those who have held a Sovereign's Commission with embodied service in the Navy, Military or Air Forces, and their dependents. Applicants must be resident in Scotland at the time of their

initial application or have been members of a Scottish regiment.

Types of grants

Recurrent grants of £380 per quarter. One-off grants are also made and in the past have been used to fund things such as home repairs, respite breaks, mobility aids, etc. However, this list is not exhaustive.

Annual grant total

In 2011/12 the association had an income of £293,000 and a total charitable expenditure of £289,000. Grants to individuals totalled £173,000.

Applications

Potential beneficiaries can contact the correspondent to discuss eligibility. Alternatively, applications can be initiated by sending your personal and service details to the association via the online contact form on the website, by email or in writing. Applications are passed to the local SSAFA branch who will contact you to progress the application.

Other information

The association runs a 'friendship visits programme' to provide company for retired officers and their dependents who are feeling isolated. It also provides support and advice to officers making the transition from service to civilian employment and for the rest of their working lives.

The REME Benevolent Fund

£414,000 (483 grants)

Correspondent: Corps Secretariat, RHQ REME, HQ DEME (A), Isaac Newton Road, Arborfield, Reading RG2 9NJ (01189 763220; email: deme-corpssecro1@mod.uk)

Trustees: Col Richard Bennett; Col Martin Court; Col Stuart Weatherall; Col Amanda Cran; Maj Gen Ian Dale; Brig Martin Boswell; Brig Robert Nitsch; Col Mike Pendlington; Col Ian Paul Gibson.

CC Number: 246967

Eligibility

Members and former members of the REME who are in need, and their immediate dependents.

Types of grants

One-off grants usually up to £1,000 for any need, however in exceptional circumstances larger grants may be made. For example, a recent grant was made to a REME staff sergeant who lost a leg in a traffic accident to help towards the cost of an automatic car. Annuities and help with nursing home fees are also available.

Annual grant total

In 2011 the fund had assets of £633,000 and an income of £657,000. Grants were made to individuals totalling £414,000 and were distributed as follows:

Grants in aid – Individuals	£378,000
Annuity allowances	£18,000
Nursing home fees	£10,400
Erskine and Queen Alexandra' Hospitals	£5,400
Grants to Royal Star and Garter Homes	£1,600

682 applications were received for grant in aid support, with 415 (61%) of applicants assisted. A further 68 individuals were given financial assistance in nursing homes.

Exclusions

No grants for medical expenses, funeral expenses, litigation costs or debts.

Applications

On a form available from the correspondent or a local branch of SSAFA or the Royal British Legion. Grants are only made through a third party (e.g. SSAFA/RBL), and applications made direct will be referred to a welfare agency for investigation. Applications are screened immediately on receipt and are either rejected on sight, referred back for more information or to a committee which meets every three weeks. Grants of under £500 can be paid immediately on receipt of a suitable application.

Other information

The fund also makes grant to other service organisations.

Royal Air Force Benevolent Fund

£19,000,000 (7,591 grants)

Correspondent: The Welfare Director, 67 Portland Place, London W1B 1AR (0800 169 2942; fax: 020 7636 7005; email: mail@rafbf.org.uk; website: www. rafbf.org)

Trustees: David Couzens; Simon Dougherty; Allan Vaughan; Lawrie Haynes; Victoria Raffe; Bridget Towle; Pamela Bagnall; Arabella Hastie; Anthony Lea; Nigel Beet.

CC Number: 1081009

Eligibility

Past and present members of the Royal Air Force or associated forces and their immediate dependents.

Types of grants

Almost all types of assistance can be considered in the form of grants or loans. Common types of awards cover house repairs or modifications, mobility aids, maintenance and immediate need grants, specialist equipment and, in some cases, education and housing including residential and nursing homes. One-off and recurring grants and loans are available.

Annual grant total

In 2011 the charity had assets of £144 million, an income of £18 million and gave grants for welfare purposes totalling £19 million.

Exclusions

No grants for private medical costs or for legal fees.

Applications

On a form available directly from the correspondent or on their website via an online application form. Applications can be submitted by the individual or through an ex-service welfare agency such as RAFA or SSAFA. The fund runs a free helpline which potential applicants are welcome to call for advice and support on the application process. Applications are considered on a continual basis.

Other information

The charity provides advice and assistance on a range of issues including benefits and debt advice and relationships. The fund maintains a short-term care home in Sussex and a further three homes in Northumberland, Avon and Lancashire which are operated jointly with the RAFA. It may also be able to help with purchasing a house. The charity has two holiday homes available at reduced rates for beneficiaries. During the year the charity also gave grants to organisations totalling £2.1 million.

The Royal Air Forces Association

£21,000

Correspondent: Welfare Director, 117.5 Loughborough Road, Leicester LE4 5ND (020 8286 6667; email: welfare@rafa.org. uk; website: www.rafa.org.uk)

Trustees: Brian Drake; Dr Bryan Pattison; Ian McEnnis; John Lee; Judith Boothman; Sgt Wayne Swiggs; Wing Cmd Chris Goss; Geoff Middleton; Sqn Ldr John Tisbury; Frank Barrett; William McCann; Robert Bertram; Sgt Gail Evans; Air Vice-Mshl Nigel Bairsto; Sydney Graham; Air Comm Nigel Beet; Sir Dusty Miller; Philip Tagg; Alan Poole; Robert Chandler; Air Comm Andrew Neal.

CC Number: 226686

Eligibility

Serving and former members of the Royal Air Force (including National Service), and their dependents. The widows and widowers and dependents of

those that have died in service, or subsequently, are also eligible for assistance.

Types of grants

Small, one-off grants when all other sources of funding have been exhausted. Recent grants have been awarded for gas and electricity bills, clothing, bedding, electrical goods, furniture and hospital travel costs. The trust may also assist with nursing, convalescent and respite care costs.

Annual grant total

In 2011 the association had assets of £19 million, an income of £8.5 million and a total expenditure of £8 million. Welfare grants were made totalling £21,000.

Exclusions

Credit card debts are not eligible, nor are medical fees.

Applications

On a form available from the relevant area welfare officer. They are contactable on the numbers below. Confirmation of RAF service is required. Applications may be submitted directly by the individual, or through SSAFA Forces Help, Royal British Legion or other welfare agency.

Northern Area	Michael Grell	01772 426930
North East	Karen Leahair	01347 847525
Eastern Area	Paul Davies	01162 688784
South West	Glenford Bishop	01392 462088
South East	Sue Smith	020 8286 6667
Midlands	Tracey Khan	01214 499356
Scotland and Overseas	Mike McCourt	01312 255221
Wales, Midland and South Western Area	Glenford Bishop	01392 462088
Wales	Barbara Howells	01495 249522
Northern Ireland	Sarah Waugh	02890 325718

Other information

The association provides support and advice on state benefits, including war pensions. It also manages two sheltered housing complexes, a residential home and three respite care homes.

Royal Artillery Charitable Fund

£700,000

Correspondent: The Welfare Officer, Royal Artillery Barracks, Larkill, Wiltshire SP4 8QT (01980 634309; fax: 01980 634020; email: artycen-rhqra-racf-WelfareAsst@mod.uk; website: www. theraa.co.uk/website)

Trustees: John Milne; Clive Fletcher-Wood; Alan Jolley; Anthony Richards; Andrew Dines; David Radcliffe.

CC Number: 210202

Eligibility

Serving and ex-serving members of the Royal Regiment of Artillery and their dependents.

Types of grants

One-off and recurrent grants of £250 to £700 for essential needs such as household bills, kitchen and domestic equipment, rent, water rates, nursing home fees, disability equipment, clothing, council tax and utility or power bills.

Annual grant total

In 2011 the fund gave grants to 1,672 individuals totalling £755,000. Most of which were probably made for welfare purposes.

Exclusions

No grants towards income tax, loans, credit card debts, telephone bills, legal fees or private medical treatment.

Applications

In writing to SSAFA Forces Help (details of local branches can be found in telephone directories or from Citizens Advice). Applications can also be made to the Royal British Legion in England and Wales or to PoppyScotland (Earl Haig Fund) in Scotland (see Scotland section of this guide). Applications can be considered at any time.

The Royal British Legion

£18,400,000 (22,829 grants)

Correspondent: Welfare Services, 199 Borough High Street, London SE1 1AA (Telephone Legionline on 0845 772 5725 Tel: 020 3207 2100; email: info@britishlegion.org.uk; website: www. britishlegion.org.uk)

Trustees: Eddie Dixon; Eddie Hefferman; John Farmer; Bill Parkin; Dr Diana Henderson; Brig Jim Drew; Keith Prichard; Jenny Rowe; Terry Whittles; Revd Mike Williams; Adrian Burn; John Jean Crisford; Ken Ed Draper; Cecilia Harper; Noel Duston; John Fisher; Dennis Compton; Ian Lindsey; Peter Twidle; Una Cleminson; Denise Edgar; Martyn Tighe; Anthony Macaulay; Wendy Bromwich.

CC Number: 219279

Eligibility

Serving and ex-serving members of the armed forces and their wives, partners, widows, children and other dependents in England, Wales, Ireland as well as any country overseas (for Scotland see the entry for the Earl Haig Fund Scotland in the Scotland section of the guide).

Types of grants

Following a standard assessment of the beneficiary's financial situation, the Legion makes grants to individuals, either financial or by the provision of goods or services. Grants can be given for any purpose within the scope of the Royal Charter, which governs the Legion, and includes an Immediate Needs Scheme, help for homelessness, and a Property Repair Loan Scheme.

Annual grant total

In 2011 the Legion had assets of £285 million, an income of £136 million and a total expenditure of £139 million. Welfare grants to almost 23,000 individuals totalled £18.4 million.

Exclusions

No assistance with business debts, legal expenses, loans or medical care.

Applications

Individual applications to any local branch or the county field officers. A local telephone number for an initial enquiry can usually be found in any telephone directory or by contacting the national Legionline. Extensive information and contact details can also be found on the website.

Note: Most charities for ex-servicemen and women co-operate together in their work and the British Legion may also be approached through other service organisations and vice versa.

Other information

The Royal British Legion is one of the largest providers of charitable help for individuals in the country and is financed mainly by gifts from individuals, especially through its annual Poppy Day collection.

The Legion provides a comprehensive service for advising and helping ex-servicemen and women and their dependents (though for ex-service women, wives, widows and dependents, see also the entry for Royal British Legion Women's Section). Direct financial assistance is but one aspect of this work. There are over 3,000 branches of the Legion, all of which can act as centres for organising whatever help the circumstances may require. The support of the Legion is available to all who served in the forces, whether in war or peace-time, as regulars or those who have done national service.

The Legion has seven care homes which are exclusively for ex-service people and their dependents. They also have four Welfare Break centres in the UK and a recovery facility in Germany designed to give a break to those who have been ill or bereaved or to relieve carers for two to three weeks of caring for ex-service people with severe disabilities.

There is a 'Poppy Calls' service, offering help with awkward jobs such as minor repairs or fitting essential devices such as smoke detectors and care phones, allowing ex-service members and their dependents to stay independent in their own homes.

The Legion also works with SSAFA Forces Help on a Prison In-Reach programme, which gives advice and practical support to ex-service people who are serving a prison sentence and their immediate dependents.

Royal British Legion Women's Section

Correspondent: Welfare Team, 199 Borough High Street, London SE1 1AA (020 3207 2183; email: wswelfare@britishlegion.org.uk; website: www.rblws.org.uk)

Trustees: Eddie Dixon; Eddie Hefferman; John Farmer; Bill Parkin; Dr Diana Henderson; Brig Jim Drew; Keith Prichard; Jenny Rowe; Terry Whittles; Revd Mike Williams; Adrian Burn; John Jean Crisford; Ken Ed Draper; Cecilia Harper; Noel Duston; John Fisher; Dennis Compton; Ian Lindsey; Peter Twidle; Una Cleminson; Denise Edgar; Martyn Tighe; Anthony Macaulay; Wendy Bromwich.

CC Number: 219279

Eligibility

Serving and ex-servicewomen, the wives, husbands, partners, widows and widowers of service personnel and the dependent children of serving and ex-service personnel who are in need.

Types of grants

Women's Section Allowance: a small means-tested allowance of around £20 per week, paid quarterly, intended to help pay for daily living expenses. To be eligible applicants must be over 60 and have served in the armed forces. Spouses, widows, widowers, surviving civil partners, partners and divorced spouses (who have never remarried or entered another long-term cohabitating relationship) are also eligible. Applicants must live alone, be in real financial need, in receipt of all appropriate benefits and not have savings of more than £10,000. WSA beneficiaries also receive small Christmas and birthday gifts, cold weather supplementary payments and those aged between 60 and 75 will have their tv licence paid.

Children's Welfare Scheme: grants are available to children for essential items such as winter clothing, bedroom furniture or school uniforms. To qualify the children must be dependents of serving or ex-service personnel and under the age of 16 unless they are in full-time education. Parents and guardians of eligible children must be in financial need i.e. being a subsistence wage earner and/or in receipt of means-tested benefits.

Family Welfare Breaks: respite breaks for serving and ex-service families in genuine need of a holiday following an illness within the family, bereavement, or other life affecting events. Breaks are awarded for a period of up to seven days at a range of break centres throughout the UK. Additional funds may also be available for travel expenses. The scheme is also available for individuals who are carers of parents and siblings. Applicants should be in receipt of a low-income and have savings of no more than £10,000.

Welfare Breaks Scheme: grants for respite breaks of up to seven days at hotels and guesthouses around the country. Welfare breaks are available to serving and ex-service personnel and their spouses following hospitalisation, bereavement or other life affecting events. Applicants should not hold more than £10,000 in savings.

Annual grant total

While a distinct organisation with clear aims the funds of Women's Section are accounted for within the Royal British Legion and not distinguised from them. For further details of the expenditure of the Legion see the separate entry in this guide.

Exclusions

Unable to assist individuals in receipt of Attendance Allowance or an annuity from another charitable organisation.

Applications

Initial enquiries by telephone or email in writing requesting a visit by a welfare visitor who will submit an application form, which includes a financial statement. Applications are considered on a regular basis, with the exception of applications to the family welfare breaks scheme which are assessed by a committee who meet three times a year.

Other information

Grants are made through the Women's Section, which is an autonomous organisation within the Royal British Legion concentrating on the needs of widows and ex-servicewomen and dependent children of ex-service personnel. It works in close association with the Legion but has its own funds and its own local welfare visitors.

Royal Commonwealth Ex-Services League

£1.6 million (2,645 grants)

Correspondent: Colonel Paul Davis, Secretary General, Haig House,

199 Borough High Street, London SE1 1AA (020 3207 2413; email: mgordon-roe@commonwealthveterans.org.uk; website: www.commonwealthveterans.org.uk)

Trustees: General Sir Sam Cowan; John Farmer; Brian Watkins; Viscount John Slim; Brigadier David Innes; John Doble; Dr Ros Eskell; Brigadier John King; Brigadier Tony Berry; Colonel Michael Winarick; Maj. General Mike Regan; Brigadier David Williams; Colonel Andrew Martin; Patrick Mitford-Slade; Dallas Roy.

CC Number: 231322

Eligibility

Ex-servicemen and women of the crown, their widows or dependents, who are living outside the UK. There are currently member organisations in over 40 countries throughout the world.

Types of grants

All types of help can be considered. Grants are one-off, usually ranging from £100 to £500 and renewable on application. Grants are generally for medically related costs such as hearing aids, wheelchairs, artificial limbs, food or repairs to homes wrecked by floods or hurricanes and so on.

Annual grant total

In 2010 the league held assets of £3.2 million and had an income of £1.7 million. Total welfare expenditure was £1.7 million. 2,645 individuals were helped, of which 703 were received grants directly from the charity's own funds, with the remainder receiving funds administered by the league but received from other charities.

This total also includes grants made to local member organisations for benevolence work. Including these local cases takes the total number of individuals helped both directly and indirectly up to 14,508.

Applications

Considered daily on receipt of applications from member organisations or British Embassies/High Commissions, but not directly from individuals. Applications should include proof of military service to the crown.

Other information

The league has members or representatives in most parts of the world through whom former servicemen or their dependents living abroad can seek help. The local British Embassy or High Commission can normally supply the relevant local contact. In a Commonwealth country the local ex-service association will probably be affiliated to the league. The league's annual report, available from the Charity Commission or from the league, gives an interesting breakdown and analysis of funds allocated according to location.

The Royal Logistics Corps Association Trust Fund

£475,000 (1,308 grants)

Correspondent: Regimental Treasurer, The RLC Association Trust, Dettingen House, The Princess Royal Barracks, Deepcut, Camberley, Surrey GU16 6RW (01252 833334; email: rgttreasurer@ rhqtherlc.org.uk; website: www. rascrctassociation.co.uk)

Trustees: Brig Richard Rook; David Burden' Gen Sir Kevin O'Donoghue; Philippe Rossiter; Maj Gen Chris Steirn; Col Mathew Limb; Maj Gen David Shouesmith; Maj Gen Shumas Kerr; Brig Alistair Deas; Maj Gen Malcolm Wood; Col Alex Barnes; Col Paul Vignaux; WO1 CRSM. Stephen Johnson; Brig Paul Evans.

CC Number: 1024036

Eligibility

People in need who have at any time served in or with the former RASC or the former RCT, including people who served and are now serving in the Royal Logistics Corp. Members of the women's services and the dependents of any of the above are also eligible.

Types of grants

One-off grants towards wheelchairs and other mobility aids, house repairs, utility bills, bathroom conversions, house adaptations and so on.

Annual grant total

In 2011 the fund had assets of £22 million and an income of £14 million. Grants were made to 1,308 individuals totalling £475,000.

Exclusions

No grants for repayment of general debts or loans.

Applications

Applications should be made through SSAFA Forces Help, the Royal British Legion, PoppyScotland or similar welfare organisation. Grants are made to the sponsoring organisation rather than directly to the individual. Applications can be made at any time, though requests for larger amounts need to be considered by the executive committee, making them longer to process.

Other information

Grants are also made to other service charities.

The Royal Army Services Corps (RASC) and Royal Corps of Transport (RCT) charities merged with the trust in 2011.

Royal Military Police Central Benevolent Fund

£110,000 (126 grants)

Correspondent: Col John H Baber, Defence Police College, Postal Point 38, Southwick, Fareham, Hampshire PO17 6EJ (02392 284406; email: rhqrmp@btconnect.com)

Trustees: Cnl John Howard Barber; Cnl Peter Hewlett Smith; Brig Raymond Bell; Lt Cnl Tex Pemberton; Brig Norman Allen; Elliot Thomson; Lt Cnl I. S. Warren; Edward Forester-Knight; Cnl I. E. Prosser; Janet Waring; Mariane Van Staaten; Stephen Reddington.

CC Number: 248713

Eligibility

People who are serving or have served in the Royal Military Police corps, or any of its predecessors, and their dependents.

Types of grants

One-off cash grants of £100 to £1,000 towards heating, funeral expenses, household furniture, debts, clothing and bedding, mobility aids, holidays, medical needs, special chairs, removals and other needs. Christmas grants of £85 are distributed to people who have received an individual benefit grant and are over 80 years of age.

Annual grant total

In 2010/11 the fund had assets of £2.9 million and an income of £305,000. 160 applications for grants were received with 126 approved. Grants totalled £110,000 and were distributed as follows:

Individual Grants	£60,000
Christmas Grants	£16,000
Nursing Home Fees	£4,400
Annuities	£9,500

A further £19,000 was given to the Army Benevolent Fund to distribute.

Applications

In writing to the correspondent. All applications are passed to the Royal British Legion or SSAFA Forces Help, who will visit applicants to verify eligibility and financial need.

Other information

Grants are also made to other organisations and charitable funds with similar purposes (£81,000 in 2010/11).

Royal Naval Benevolent Trust

£2.2 million

Correspondent: The Grants Administrator, Castaway House, 311 Twyford Avenue, Portsmouth

PO2 8RN (02392 690112; fax: 02392 660852; email: rnbt@rnbt.org.uk; website: www.rnbt.org.uk)

Trustees: Owen Shread; Philip Shuttleworth; Jacqueline McCafferty; Andrew Cameron; Jonathan Woodcock; Capt. Tim Martin; Carole Davis; Kenneth Lambert; Nicholas Gartside; Sarah Bryant; Ian Bailey; Steven Willett; Gary Harvey; Julian Holmes; Rear Admiral Anthony Rix.

CC Number: 206243

Eligibility

Serving and ex-serving men and women of the Royal Navy and Royal Marines (not officers) and their dependents.

Types of grants

The grants vary in amount from under £100 up to several thousand pounds with the average being about £550 and go towards a variety of needs, including rent and mortgage payments, food, clothing, fuel, childcare, medical treatment, disability aids, respite and recuperative holidays, household goods and repairs, removal expenses, debts and training for a second career.

Annual grant total

In 2010/11 the trust had assets of £31 million and an income of £4.6 million. Single grants amounted to £1.2 million and annuity payments to £930,000.

Applications

On a form available from the correspondent, to be submitted through a social worker, welfare agency, SSAFA Forces Help, Royal British Legion or any Royal Naval Association branch. Applications are considered twice a week.

Other information

The trust pays 1,300 annuities of up to £15 a week to older beneficiaries. They cost about £900,000 a year.

The trust also runs a residential and nursing home for older ex-naval men (not women) namely, Pembroke House, Oxford Road, Gillingham, Kent.

The trust has an informative website.

The Royal Naval Reserve (V) Benevolent Fund

£2,000

Correspondent: Commander J M D Curteis, Hon. Secretary and Treasurer, The Cottage, St Hilary, Cowbridge, Vale of Glamorgan CF71 7DP (01446 771108)

Trustee: Cdr John Curteis.

CC Number: 266380

Eligibility

Members or former members of the Royal Naval Volunteer Reserve, Women's Royal Naval Volunteer Reserve, Royal Naval Reserve and the Women's Royal Naval Reserve, who are serving or have served as non-commissioned rates. The fund also caters for wives, widows and young children of the above.

Types of grants

One-off grants only, ranging from £50 to £350. Grants have been given for gas, electricity, removal expenses (i.e. to be near children/following divorce); clothing; travel to visit sick relatives or for treatment; essential furniture and domestic equipment; help on bereavement. Schoolchildren from poor families may very occasionally receive help for clothes, books or necessary educational visits, and help can also go to eligible children with aptitudes or disabilities which need special provision.

Annual grant total

About £3,000.

Applications

In writing to the correspondent directly by the individual or through the local reserve division, Royal British Legion, SSAFA Forces Help or Royal Naval Benevolent Trust, which investigates applications.

The Royal Navy and Royal Marines Children's Fund

£300,000

Correspondent: Monique Bateman, Director, 311 Twyford Avenue, Stamshaw, Portsmouth PO2 8RN (02392 639534; fax: 02392 677574; email: rnchildren@btconnect.com; website: www.rnrmchildrensfund.org)

Trustees: Dr Miranda Whitehead; David Brazier; Sheila Owens-Cairns; Heather Rimmer; Dug Hickin; Lt Col Ian Grant; Com Malcolm Williams; Judge Anthony Thorpe; Com David Bridger; Paul Austin; Anne Binnie.

CC Number: 1075015

Eligibility

Young people under 25 who are in need and are the dependent of somebody who has served, or is serving, in the Royal Navy, Royal Marines, the Queen Alexandra's Royal Naval Nursing Service or the former Women's Royal Naval Service.

Types of grants

One-off and recurrent grants ranging between £20 and £20,000 for general welfare needs including help in the home, hospital travel expenses, respite care, specialist equipment, house adaptations and childcare. Assistance is also available to children who have been traumatised by death or family break-up.

Annual grant total

In 2010/11 the fund had assets of £8.3 million and an income of £1.1 million. The sum of £1.1 million was given in grants to individuals or families for educational and welfare purposes.

Applications

On a form available from the correspondent or to download from the website. Applications can be submitted directly by the individual or through the individual's school/college, SSAFA, Naval Personal, social services or other third party. They can be submitted at any time and are considered on a monthly basis, though urgent cases can be dealt with between meetings.

The Royal Navy Officers's Charity

£320,000 (283 grants)

Correspondent: Cdr Ken Ridley, Director, 70 Porchester Terrace, Bayswater, London W2 3TP (020 7402 5231; email: rnoc@arno.org.uk)

Trustees: Sir James Perowne; Cap Andrew Slater; Rear Adm Derek Anthony; Cmd Peter Moore; Cmd Robert Grainger; Lt Cmd Ben Hughes; Adrian Mezzetti; Martin Poll; Evelyn Strouts; Col Roger Williams; Surg Cdre James Sykes; Zoe Margaret Penny; The Royal Navy and Royal Marines Charity.

CC Number: 207405

Eligibility

Officers, both active service and retired, of the Royal Navy, Royal Marines, QARNNS and WRNS and their respective reserves, of the equivalent rank of Sub-Lieutenant RN and above, and their spouses, former spouses, families and dependents. There are no age limits.

Types of grants

One-off and recurrent grants to augment inadequate incomes or to meet specific, unforeseen expenses. Grants have been given to help with: house repairs; car maintenance; removal costs; mobility aids; retraining and nursing home fees. Education grants may be given to complete a particular stage of a child's education (not school fees). Recurrent grants currently stand at £1,500 per year and are paid in two instalments.

Annual grant total

In 2011 the society had assets of £10.6 million and an income of

£684,000. Grants were made to individuals (15 members and 268 non-members) totalling £320,000.

Exclusions

The society does not make grants for school fees or medical care, except in very exceptional circumstances.

Applications

On a form available from the correspondent. Applications can be submitted either directly by the individual, or through a third party such as a social worker or Citizens Advice. They are considered monthly.

Other information

The society was founded on 16 May 1739 by a group of naval officers suffering from unreasonable treatment by the Admiralty. The benevolent function of the society emerged later and became its sole purpose in 1791.

In 2008, the Association of Royal Navy Officers Charitable Trust transferred its assets to the society and the charity changed its name from the Royal Naval Benevolent Society for Officers.

The Royal Observer Corps Benevolent Fund

£50,000

Correspondent: The Secretary, 120 Perry Hall Road, Orpington, Kent BR6 0EF (email: info@rocbf.org.uk; website: www. rocbf.org.uk)

Trustees: Kath Little; Hilary Martin Daniel; Christopher Howard; Norman Greig; Terry Giles; Diana Mothersole; Jenny Major; Jenny Morris.

CC Number: 209640

Eligibility

All former members of the Royal Observer Corps who are in need, hardship or distress. Length of service is not a consideration, except that the person for whom the application has been made must have served long enough to have received their Royal Observer Corps official number.

Types of grants

Almost all types of grants can be considered. Typically the fund can provide financial help for mobility aids, debt relief, essential home repairs or modification and respite care.

Annual grant total

In 2010 the trust had an income of £24,000. Grants were made totalling around £50,000.

Exclusions

Grants are not given towards debts or arrears owed to government bodies.

Applications

By direct contact with the fund or through SSAFA, the Royal British Legion or the Royal Air Forces Association. Applications are considered on receipt and normally a decision is given within days.

The Royal Signals Benevolent Fund

£460,000 (1,004 grants)

Correspondent: Cnl. T W Canham, The Regimental Secretary, RHQ Royal Signals, Blandford Camp, Blandford Forum, Dorset DT11 8RH (01258 482081; email: SOINC-RHQ-RegtSec@ mod.uk)

Trustees: Maj Gen Ashley Truluck; Brig John Edward Thomas; Lt Gen Robert Baxter; Brig Nigel Freeman Wood; Brig Edward Michael Flint; Maj Gen Timothy Gordon Inshaw; Cnl Keith Bruce-Smith; Brig Tim Watts; Brig Jim Richardson; Brig Steve Vickery.

CC Number: 284923

Eligibility

Members and former members of the Royal Signals, regular or territorial volunteer reserve, and their widows and other dependents.

Types of grants

One-off and recurrent grants according to need. Grants are given towards fuel and lighting costs, funeral expenses, domestic and medical appliances, carpets, house repairs, convalescence, nursing home top-up fees, priority debts, supplementary and Christmas allowances. Applications for amounts up to £600 may be decided between the funding committee meetings.

Annual grant total

In 2010 the fund held assets of £8.4 million and had an income of £1.5 million. Benevolence grants were made totalling £460,000.

The fund also administers grants from the Army Benevolent Fund (£139,000). The 170 ABF grants took the total number of benevolent grants funded up to 1,004.

Exclusions

The fund does not distribute loans.

Applications

Applications should be made through SSAFA Forces Help or another charitable organisation and are considered as required.

Other information

The fund also gives funding to other service charities (£45,000 in 2010).

The Sister Agnes Benevolent Fund

£61,000

Correspondent: PA to the Chief Executive, Beaumont Street, London W1G 6AA (020 7486 4411; email: info@ kingedwardvii.co.uk; website: www. kingedwardvii.co.uk)

Trustees: Field Marshal The Rt Hon Lord Inge; Charles Irby; Ian Adamson; David Badenoch; Robin Boardhurst; Gilles Graham; Dr Charles Mackworth-Young; Olga Polizzi; Sir Alan Reid; Group Capt. Carol Smith.

CC Number: 208944

Eligibility

People who have served in the armed forces, regardless of rank or length of service, who are uninsured and are either inpatients or outpatients at King Edward VII's Hospital Sister Agnes, and their spouses, ex-spouses, widows and widowers.

Types of grants

Means tested grants for up to 100 per cent of hospital fees. In some cases, consultant fees may also be covered.

Annual grant total

In 2010/11 the fund had assets of £721,000 and an income of £67,000. Grants were made to 14 individuals totalling £61,000.

Applications

On a form available from the correspondent or to download from the website, including evidence of service and financial details.

NB. Uninsured service personnel, their spouses, ex-spouses, widows and widowers are all eligible for a 20 per cent subsidy on their hospital bill (this is not means-tested). To claim, eligible individuals need to notify the hospital when booking their procedure.

Other information

The Sister Agnes Benevolent Fund is a restricted fund of King Edward VII's Hospital Sister Agnes.

SSAFA Forces Help

£13,400,000

Correspondent: Director of Welfare and Housing, 19 Queen Elizabeth Street, London SE1 2LP (0800 731 4880; fax: 020 7403 8815; email: info@ssafa.org.uk; website: www.ssafa.org.uk)

Trustees: Robin Shedden Broadhurst; Gen Sir Kevin O'Donoghue; David James Ashman; Brig Willie Shackell; Jonathan Jelley; Graham McMellin; Julia Ridgway; Cnl John Royle; Colin Smith; James

Carleton; Wing Cmdr Ian Miskelly; David Rowe; Henrietta Marriott; Kirsty Bushell; Richard Gordon; Lt Cnl David Summers; John O'Brien; Revd Lt Cnl Nick Cook.

CC Number: 210760

Eligibility

Service and ex-service men and women and their immediate dependents who are in need.

Types of grants

One-off grants are available for a variety of needs, for example, electrically powered vehicles, white goods, household items, holidays and carers' breaks.

Annual grant total

In 2010 the trust held assets of £18 million and had an income of £48 million. Grants for welfare purposes totalled £13.4 million, of which £592,000 was paid from charity funds and £12.8 million was given on behalf of service funds and other charities.

Grants are disbursed by caseworkers who work throughout the SSAFA branch network. In 2010 caseworkers dealt with 45,203 cases of which 20,000 (44%) received financial assistance. The charity also estimates that a further £5.4 million was secured for and paid directly to individuals from other sources.

Exclusions

The trust does not assist with legal issues, private medical care costs, educational grants and anything the state has a statutory duty to provide.

Applications

Contact should normally be made by letter direct to the honorary secretary of the local branch. The appropriate address can usually be obtained from the SSAFA website, a Citizens Advice, the local telephone directory (under SSAFA Forces Help) and most main post-offices. In case of difficulty, the local address can be obtained from the correspondent.

Other information

SSAFA Forces Help operates throughout the UK and in garrisons and stations overseas. It is concerned with the welfare of service and ex-service men and women and their families and provides a wide range of advice and support services.

All SSAFA branches are empowered to give immediate help without reference to higher committees. Also, because of their extensive coverage of the UK, they act as agents for service and other associated funds. Indeed, SSAFA is much more of a caseworking organisation than a benevolent fund.

A residential home is maintained on the Isle of Wight for older ex-service personnel and their dependents. Eligible men and women can be accepted from any part of the UK. SSAFA also manages cottage homes for ex-service men and women and their spouses, some purpose-built for people with disabilities, for which residents pay no rent but make a modest maintenance payment.

Two SSAFA Norton Homes provide short-term accommodation so that families can stay nearby whilst visiting a loved one at Selly Oak Hospital in Birmingham or the Defence Medical Rehabilitation Centre at Headley Court, Surrey. The houses are designed as 'homes from home' and are both located in secure and peaceful environments.

Stepping Stone homes are provided for service families facing relationship difficulties or marital breakdown who need somewhere to live while they consider their future.

Support services for serving and ex-service prisoners, with the aim of reducing re-offending and helping prisoners resettle into society, are also available.

SSAFA provides a confidential telephone support line for serving personnel which is staffed all year round and is outside the chain of command (call 0800 731 4880 in UK, Germany and Cyprus; 800 91065 in Falklands or +44 (0)1980 630854 from elsewhere). It also continues to grow and develop its health and social care services for serving personnel around the world with specialist health centres in Luton, Leicester and Nottingham. It also provides family support groups and adoption services.

For further information on all of the services listed here, and more, go to the trust's website or visit a local branch.

St Andrew's Scottish Soldiers Club Fund

£0

Correspondent: The Grants Officer, The Royal Scottish Corporation, 22 City Road, London EC1Y 2AJ (020 7240 3718; fax: 020 7497 0184; email: info@scotscare.com; website: www.scotscare.com)

Trustees: Stuart James Steele; Mr P. J. M. Scott; Cnl John Alistair Clemence; Peter Hay; Robin Majdalany; William Tonar McMahon; Wylie Graham Crawford White; Angus Gilroy; Dr Graeme Struthers Wilson; Eddie Tait; Fred Gray; Dr John Drysdale Johnston; Brian Griffin; John Meikle; Amanda Currie Brock Duguid; Ken Donnolly.

CC Number: 233297

Eligibility

Serving and former Scottish soldiers, and their dependents, who are in need.

Types of grants

One-off grants according to need.

Annual grant total

In 2010/11 the fund had an income of £4,600 but no expenditure (£0 in 2009/10).

Applications

In writing to the correspondent usually through an ex-service body such as SSAFA Forces Help or the Royal British Legion.

The WRNS Benevolent Trust

£345,000

Correspondent: Sarah Ayton, General Secretary, Castaway House, 311 Twyford Avenue, Portsmouth, Hampshire PO2 8RN (02392 655301; fax: 02392 679040; email: generalsecretary@wrnsbt.org.uk; website: www.wrnsbt.org.uk)

Trustees: Janet Crabtree; Cdr Jackie Mulholland; Cdr Jane Walton; Cdr Maggie Robbins; Lt Cdr Jan Edwards; Lt Cdr Sally Prendergast; Mary Brittan; Commodore Annette Picton; Cdr A. Crook; J. Clink.

CC Number: 206529

Eligibility

Ex-Wrens and female serving members of the Royal Navy (officers and ratings) who joined the service between 3 September 1939 and 1 November 1993 who are in need. People who deserted from the service are not eligible.

Types of grants

Recurrent grants of £221 a quarter for people of pensionable age who are living on a low income. These grants may also be awarded to younger people in exceptional circumstances. Amenity grants totalling up to £480 per annum are made in June and December and Christmas bonuses depending on need, with an extra £45 per child being added to the Christmas bonus for parents of children of school age or below. One-off grants are also available towards needs such as debts and arrears, household goods, medical aids, household repairs, funeral expenses, convalescent care, medical expenses, travel fares, education, removal costs, clothing and food.

Annual grant total

In 2011 the trust had assets of £3.3 million and an income of £555,000. Welfare grants including pensions totalled £345,000 with a further £4,500 being given for educational purposes.

Applications

Applications can be made direct to the correspondent, or through SSAFA.

Service and regimental funds

Army

The Afghanistan Trust

£84,000 (85 grants)

Correspondent: Victoria Hall, Secretary, RHQ Para, Merville Barracks, Circular Road South, Colchester, Essex CO2 7UT (01206 817074; email: secretary@ paracharity.org; website: afghanistantrust.org/)

Trustees: Col Stuart Tootal; Lt Col John Boyd; Ben Huxley; Steven Mark Szczesnowicz; Lt Col Adam Dawson; Lt Col Ed Sandry; Lt Col Michael William Shervington; Lt Col Martyn Russell Wills.

CC Number: 1121647

Eligibility

Soldiers of the Parachute Regiment injured in Afghanistan and families and dependents of the Regiment's soldiers killed or injured in Afghanistan.

Types of grants

Three types of grant are available to meet immediate needs, medium-term and long-term needs:

- Immediate needs grants – where there is a need for an immediate provision of funds (less than 24 hours)
- Medium-term grants – where needs are not immediate but will require further consideration and support, for example Motability deposits or adaptations, specialist equipment, family support or assistance to the bereaved
- Long-term grants – in cases where soldiers require longer-term assistance and are unable to remain in the Regiment. Help may include mobility support, home adaptations, etc

Annual grant total

In 2011 the trust held assets totalling £828,000 and had an income of £663,000. Grants totalled £240,000, of which £84,000 was paid in grants to 85 individuals.

Applications

Applications can originate through the Battalion welfare network or through other service charities such as Help for Heroes or Combat Stress. Direct applications may also be made in writing to the correspondent.

Other information

Grants are also made to other service charities.

The Household Division Charity

£20,000

Correspondent: Major William Style, Household Division Funds, Horse Guards, Whitehall, London SW1A 2AX (email: londist-so3accounts@mod.uk)

Trustees: Simon Corbett; Maj Gen Commanding the Household Division; Cdr of the Household Division; Lt Col of the Foot Guards; Brig Maj Household Division.

CC Number: 1138248

Eligibility

Current and former members of the Household Division, and their dependents, who are in need.

Types of grants

One-off and recurring grants according to need.

Annual grant total

In 2010/11 the charity held assets of £4.9 million and had an income of £459,000. Charitable expenditure totalled £130,000.

Applications

In writing to the correspondent. Applications may be submitted by the individual or by a third party such as a representative from SSAFA, Citizens Advice or other welfare organisation.

Other information

Grants are also made to organisations.

Irish Guards Charitable Fund

£47,000 (61 grants)

Correspondent: Capt R J Wilmont, Regimental Headquarters, Irish Guards, Wellington Barracks, Birdcage Walk, London SW1E 6HQ (020 7414 3293; email: igwebmaster@btconnect.com; website: www.helpforirishguards.com)

Trustees: Lord Bruntisfield; Peter Nutting; Robin Boyd; Ashe Windham; Harry Parshall; Lt Col Edward Boanas; Maj Gen Carleton Smith.

CC Number: 247477

Eligibility

Serving and retired officers of the Irish Guards and their dependents who are in need.

Types of grants

One-off grants according to need

Annual grant total

In 2011 the fund held assets totalling £1.4 million and had an income of £529,000. Grants to 61 individuals totalled £47,000.

Applications

In writing to the correspondent.

Other information

Grants are also made to military organisations (£38,000 in 2011).

Service and regimental funds

Royal Navy and Royal Marines

Royal Marines Charitable Trust Fund
RM Corps Secretary, Building 32, HMS Excellent, Whale Island, Portsmouth PO2 8ER (tel: 02392 547225; fax: 02392 547207)

Royal Naval Association
General Secretary, Room 209, Semaphore Tower (PP70), HM Naval Base, Portsmouth, Hampshire PO1 3LT (tel: 02392 723747; fax: 02392 723371)

Women's Royal Naval Service Benevolent Trust
General Secretary, Castaway House, 311 Twyford Avenue, Portsmouth, Hampshire P02 8RN (tel: 02392 655301; fax: 02392 679040)

Merchant Navy

Merchant Navy Welfare Board
Welfare Officer, 8 Cumberland Place, Southampton SO15 2BH (tel: 02380 337799; fax: 02380 634444)

Royal Alfred Seafarers Society
Western Acres, Woodmansterne Lane, Banstead SM7 3HA (tel: 01737 353763; fax: 01737 362678)

Royal Air Force

Princess Mary's Royal Air Force Nursing Services Trust
RAF Naphill, High Wycombe, Buckinghamshire HP14 4UE (tel: 01494 497297)

Royal Air Force Disabled Holiday Trust
Administrator, 67 Portland Place, London W1B 1AR (tel: 020 7307 3303; email: admin@rafdht.org.uk)

Royal Air Forces Ex-POW Association Charitable Fund
Welfare Officer, Mill House, Great Bedwyn, Marlborough, Wiltshire SN8 3LY (tel: 01672 870529)

Royal Observer Corps Benevolent Fund
Secretary, 120 Perry Hall Lane, Orpington BR6 0EF (email: info@rocbf.org.uk)

Army

The Adjutant General's Corps Regiment Association
Gould House, Worthy Down, Winchester SO21 2RG (tel: 01962 887435; email: a-regtsec@rhqagc.mod.uk)

Afghan Trust, the Parachute Regiment
RHQ PARA, Merville Barracks, Colchester CO2 7UT (tel: 01235 847614)

Argyll and Sutherland Highlanders' Regimental Association
Secretary, The Castle, Stirling FK8 1EH (tel: 01786 475165; fax: 01786 446038)

Army Air Corps Fund (post Sept 1957)
Headquarters Army Air Corps, Middle Wallop, Stockbridge, Hampshire SO20 8DY (tel: 01264 784565; email: AACHQ-RHQ-AsstRegtSec@mod.uk)

Army Physical Training Corps Association
Regimental Secretary, HQ RAPTC, Fox Lines, Queen's Avenue, Aldershot GU11 2LB (tel: 01252 787161; fax: 01252 340785)

Ayrshire Yeomanry
(See Yeomanry Benevolent Fund)

Bedfordshire and Hertfordshire Regiment
(See Royal Anglian Regiment Benevolent Charity)

Berkshire Yeomanry
(See Yeomanry Benevolent Fund)

Berkshire and Westminster Dragoons
(See Yeomanry Benevolent Fund)

Blues and Royals Association
Honorary Secretary, Home HQ, Household Cavalry, Combermere Barracks, St Leonards Road, Windsor

SL4 3DN (tel: 01753 755132; fax: 01753 755161)

Border Regiment
(See Duke of Lancaster's Regiment)

Buckinghamshire, Berkshire & Oxfordshire Yeomanry
(See Yeomanry Benevolent Fund)

Cambridgeshire Regiment
(See Royal Anglian Regiment Benevolent Charity)

Cameronians (Scottish Rifles)
(See King's Own Scottish Borders Association)

Cheshire Regiment
(See Mercian Regiment Benevolent Fund)

Cheshire Yeomanry
(See Yeomanry Benevolent Fund)

Coldstream Guards Association
Assistant Regimental Adjutant, Wellington Barracks, Birdcage Walk, London SW1E 6HQ (tel: 020 7414 3263; fax: 020 7414 3444)

Connaught Rangers Association
Applications should be forwarded directly to the ABF The Soldiers' Charity, see page 135.

Corps of Army Music
Corps Secretary, Kneller Hall, Kneller Road, Twickenham TW2 7DU (tel: 020 8744 8652)

County of London Yeomanry (3rd)
(See Yeomanry Benevolent Fund)

Derbyshire Yeomanry
(See Yeomanry Benevolent Fund)

Devonshire and Dorset Regiment
(See the Rifles – Exeter)

Devonshire Regiment
(See the Rifles – Exeter)

Dorset Regiment
(See the Rifles – Exeter)

Dragoons:
1st King's Dragoon Guards
(See Queen's Dragoon Guards Benevolent Fund)

2nd (Queen's Bays)
(See Queen's Dragoon Guards Benevolent Fund)

3rd Carabiniers (Prince of Wales's Dragoon Guards)
(See Royal Scots Dragoon Guards Association)

4th/7th Royal Dragoon Guards
(See Royal Dragoon Guards Benevolent Fund)

5th Royal Inniskilling Dragoon Guards
(See Royal Dragoon Guards Benevolent Fund)

2nd Royal Scots Greys
(See Royal Scots Dragoon Guards Association)

3rd Dragoon Guards
(See Royal Scots Dragoon Guards Association)

6th Dragoon Guards
(See Royal Scots Dragoon Guards Association)

25th Dragoon Guards
(See Royal Scots Dragoon Guards Association)

Westminster Dragoons
(See Yeomanry Benevolent Fund)

Duke of Albany's Seaforth Highlanders
(See Queens Own Highlanders (Seaforth and Camerons) Regimental Association)

Duke of Cornwall's Light Infantry
(See the Rifles – Bodmin)

Duke of Edinburgh's Royal Regiment
(See the Rifles – Salisbury)

Duke of Lancaster's Regiment
Fulwood Barracks, Preston PR2 8AA (tel: 01772 260362; fax: 01772 260583; email: rhqlancs-ao@mod.uk)

Duke of Wellington's Regiment
(See Yorkshire Regiment)

Durham Light Infantry
(See the Rifles – Durham)

East Anglian Regiment
(See Royal Anglian Regiment Benevolent Charity)

East Lancashire Regiment
(See Duke of Lancaster's Regiment)

East Yorkshire Regiment
(See Yorkshire Regiment)

Essex Regiment
(See Royal Anglian Regiment Benevolent Charity)

Fife and Forfar Yeomanry
(See Yeomanry Benevolent Fund)

Fusiliers Aid Society (Fallen Fusiliers)
City of London Headquarters, HM Tower of London, London EC3N 4AB (tel: 020 3166 6906; email: DINF-RHQRRF-AsstRegtSec@mod.uk)

Glasgow Highlanders
(See Royal Highland Fusiliers Benevolent Association)

Glider Pilot Regimental Association Benevolent Fund
Membership Secretary, 27 Honeysuckle Gardens, Andover, Hants SP10 3DD (admin@gliderpilotregiment.org.uk)

Gloucestershire Regimental
(See the Rifles – Gloucester)

The Gordon Highlanders' Association
Home HQ The Highlanders, St Luke's, Viewfield Road, Aberdeen AB15 7XH (tel: 01224 318174; fax: 01224 208652)

Green Howards
(See Yorkshire Regiment)

Grenadier Guards Association
General Secretary, Wellington Barracks, Birdcage Walk, London SW1E 6HQ (tel: 020 7414 3285; assnnco@grengds.com)

The Gurkha Welfare Trust
PO Box 2170, 22 Queen Street, Salisbury, Wiltshire SP2 2EX (tel: 01722 323955; fax: 01722 343119; email: staffassistant@gwt.org.uk)

Hampshire and Isle of Wight Military Aid Fund

Secretary, Serles House, Southgate Street, Winchester SO23 9EG (tel: 01962 852933; email: secretary@hantsMAF.org)

Herefordshire Light Infantry Regiment

(See the Rifles – Shrewsbury)

Highland Light Infantry

(See Royal Highland Fusiliers Benevolent Association)

Highlanders (Seaforth, Gordons & Camerons) Regiment

(See Highlanders Regimental Association)

The Highlanders Association

Regimental Secretary, HHQ The Highlanders, Cameron Barracks, Inverness IV2 3XE (tel: 01463 224380; fax: 01313 108172)

Honourable Artillery Company Benevolent Fund

Armoury House, City Road, London EC1Y 2BQ (tel: 020 7382 1543; fax: 020 7382 1538)

Hussars:

3rd The King's Own
(See Queen's Royal Hussars)

7th Queen's Own
(See Queen's Royal Hussars)

8th King's Royal Irish
(See Queen's Royal Hussars)

10th Royal Hussars
(See King's Royal Hussars Welfare Fund)

11th Hussars
(as above)

14th King's Hussars
(as above)

14th/20th King's Hussars
(as above)

20th Hussars
(as above)

23rd Hussars
(as above)

26th Hussars
(as above)

13th/18th Royal (Queen Mary's Own)

(See Light Dragoons Charitable Trust)

15th/19th King's Royal Hussars Regiment
(See Light Dragoons Charitable Trust)

The Queen's Own Hussars
(See Queen's Royal Hussars)

Queen's Royal Irish Hussars
(See Queen's Royal Hussars)

Imperial Yeomanry

(See Yeomanry Benevolent Fund)

Indian Army Association

c/o Royal Commonwealth Ex-Services League, Haig House, 199 Borough High Street, London SE1 1AA (tel: 020 3207 2413)

Inns of Court and City Yeomanry

(See Yeomanry Benevolent Fund)

Intelligence Corps Association

Building 200, Chicksands, Shefford, Bedfordshire SG17 5PR (tel: 01462 752229; email: dint-corpssec@mod.uk)

Irish Guards Association

RHQ Irish Guards, Wellington Barracks, Birdcage Walk, London SW1E 6HQ (tel: 020 7414 3295; fax: 020 7414 3446)

King's Royal Hussars Welfare Fund

Unit Welfare Officer, KRH, Aliwal Barracks, Tidworth SP9 7BB (email: KRH-HQSQN-RWO@mod.uk)

King's Regiment Liverpool/ Manchester

(See Duke of Lancaster's Regiment)

King's Own Royal Border Regimental Association

(See Duke of Lancaster's Regiment)

King's Own Royal Regiment

(See Duke of Lancaster's Regiment)

King's Own Scottish Borderers Association

(See the Royal Regiment of Scotland)

King's Own Yorkshire Light Infantry Regiment

(See the Rifles – Pontefract)

King's Royal Rifle Corps

(See the Rifles – Winchester)

King's Shropshire Light Infantry

(See the Rifles – Shrewsbury)

Labour Corps

Applications should be forwarded directly to the ABF The Soldiers' Charity, see page 135.

Lancashire Fusiliers

(See Fusiliers Aid Society)

Lancashire Regiment (Prince of Wales's Royal Volunteers) Regiment

(See Duke of Lancaster's Regiment)

Lancers:

9th/12th/27th Royal Lancers
(See 9th/12th Royal Lancers (Prince of Wales) Charitable Association)

16th, 5th, 17th & 21st Lancers
(See Queen's Royal Lancers)

9th Queen's Royal Lancers
(See 9th/12th Royal Lancers (Prince of Wales) Charitable Association)

Leinster Regiment (for those resident in UK)

Applications should be forwarded directly to the ABF The Soldiers' Charity, see page 135.

The Life Guards Association

Honorary Secretary, Home HQ Household Cavalry, Combermere Barracks, St Leonards Road, Windsor SL4 3DN (tel: 01753 755229; email: homehq@householdcavalry.co.uk)

Light Dragoons Regimental Association Charitable Trust

Fenham Barracks, Newcastle upon Tyne NE2 4NP (tel: 01912 393138; fax: 01912 393139)

Light Infantry

(See the Rifles – appropriate local office)

London Irish Rifles Benevolent Fund

Connaught House, 4 Flodden Road, Camberwell, London SE5 9LL (tel: 020 7390 4466 ext. 2406)

London Regiment

Applications should be forwarded directly to the ABF The Soldiers' Charity, see page 135.

London Scottish Regiment Benevolent Fund

95 Horseferry Road, Westminster, London SW1P 2DX (tel: 020 7630 0411)

Lothian & Border Horse

(See Yeomanry Benevolent Fund)

Lovat Scouts

(See Yeomanry Benevolent Fund)

Loyal Regiment (North Lancashire)

(See Duke of Lancaster's Regiment)

Machine Gun Corps

Applications should be forwarded directly to the ABF The Soldiers' Charity, see page 135. (For Heavy Branch Machine Gun Corps see **Royal Tank Regiment Association and Benevolent Fund**)

Manchester Regiment Aid Society and Benevolent Fund

(See Duke of Lancaster's Regiment)

Mercian Benevolent Fund

Heath Avenue, Whittington Barracks, Lichfield, Staffordshire WS14 9TJ (tel: 01543 434392; email: RHQMERCIAN-AsstRegtlSecStaffords@mod.uk)

Middlesex Regiment (Duke of Cambridge's Own)

(See Princess of Wales's Royal Regiment)

Military Provost Staff Corps Association

(See Adjutant General's Corps Regimental Association)

North Staffordshire Regiment

(See Mercian Benevolent Fund)

Northamptonshire Regiment

(See Royal Anglian Regiment Benevolent Charity)

Northamptonshire Yeomanry Association (1st and 2nd Regiments)

(See Yeomanry Benevolent Fund)

Nottinghamshire and Derbyshire Regiment

(See Mercian Benevolent Fund)

'Old Contemptibles'

Applications should be forwarded directly to the ABF The Soldiers' Charity see page 135.

Oxfordshire and Buckinghamshire Light Infantry

(See the Rifles – Winchester)

Oxfordshire Yeomanry

(See Yeomanry Benevolent Fund)

Parachute Regiment

(See Airborne Forces Security Fund)

Post Office Rifles

Applications should be forwarded directly to the ABF The Soldiers' Charity see page 135.

Prince of Wales Leinster Regiment Association

7 Nethercombe House, Ruthin Road, Blackheath, London SE3 7SL

Prince of Wales's Own (West & East Yorkshire) Regiment

(See Yorkshire Regiment)

Princess of Wales's Royal Regiment

Benevolence Secretary, Howe Barracks, Canterbury, Kent CT1 1JY (tel: 01227 818050; email: rhq@123pwrr.co.uk)

Queen Alexandra's Royal Army Nursing Corps Association

Secretary, AMS Headquarters, Slim Road, Camberley, Surrey GU15 4NP (tel: 01276 412754; email: regtsecqaranc@hotmail.com)

Queen's Dragoon Guards

Regimental Secretary, Maindy Barracks, Whitechurch Road, Cardiff CF14 3YE (tel: 02920 781227; fax: 02920 781384)

Queen's Lancashire Regiment

(See Duke of Lancaster's Regiment)

Queen's Own Buffs, The Royal Kent Regiment

(See Princess of Wales's Royal Regiment)

Queen's Own Cameron Highlanders' Regiment

(See Queen's Own Highlanders (Seaforth and Camerons) Regimental Association)

Queen's Own Highlanders (Seaforth and Camerons) Regimental Association

RHQ HLDRS, Cameron Barracks, Inverness IV2 3XD (tel: 01463 224380)

Queen's Own Yorkshire Dragoons

(See Yeomanry Benevolent Fund)

Queen's Regiment

(See Princess of Wales's Royal Regiment)

Queen's Royal Hussars

Regimental Secretary, Regent Park Barracks, Albany Street, London NW1 4AL (tel: 020 7756 2273; fax: 020 7756 2273)

Queen's Royal Lancers

Regimental Secretary, HHQ, QRL Lancer House, Prince William of Gloucester Barracks, Grantham, Lincolnshire NG31 7TJ (tel: 01159 573252)

Queen's Royal Surrey Regiment

(See Princess of Wales's Royal Regiment)

Reconnaissance Corps

(See Royal Armoured Corps War Memorial Benevolent Fund)

Rifle Brigade

(See the Rifles – Winchester)

The Rifles

Main Office: Benevolence Secretary, Peninsula Barracks, Romsey Road, Winchester, Hampshire SO23 8TS (tel: 01962 828530; fax: 01962 828534)

Regional offices:

Bodmin – The Keep, Victoria Barracks, Bodmin, Cornwall PL31 1EG (tel: 01208 72810; email: bodmin@the-rifles.co.uk)

Durham – Elvet Waterside, Durham City, Durham DH1 3BW (tel: 01913 865496: email: durham@the-rifles.co.uk)

Exeter – Wyvern Barracks, Exeter, Devon EX2 6AR (tel: 01392 492434: exeter1@the-rifles.co.uk)

Gloucester – Custom House, 31 Commercial Road, Gloucester, Gloucestershire GL1 2HE (tel: 01452 522682; email: regimental-secretary@rgbw.army.mod.uk)

London – 52–56 Davies Street, London W1K 5HR (tel: 020 7491 4936; email: london@the-rifles.co.uk)

Oxford – Edward Brooks Barracks, Cholswell Road, Shippon, Abingdon, Oxon OX13 6JB (email: oxford@the-rifles.co.uk)

Salisbury – The Wardrobe, 58 The Close, Salisbury, Wiltshire SP1 2EX (tel: 01722 414536; email: salisbury@the-rifles.co.uk)

Shrewsbury – Copthorne Barracks, Shrewsbury, Shropshire SY3 8LZ (tel: 01743 262425; email: shrewsbury@the-rifles.co.uk)

Taunton – 14 Mount Street, Taunton, Somerset TA1 3QE (tel: 01823 333434; email: taunton@the-rifles.co.uk)

Yorkshire – Minden House, Wakefield Road, Pontefract, West Yorkshire WF8 4ES (tel: 01977 703181; email: yorkshire@the-rifles.co.uk)

Ross-Shire Buffs, Duke of Albany's Seaforth Highlanders

(See Queen's Own Highlanders (Seaforth and Camerons) Regimental Association)

Royal Anglian Regiment Benevolent Charity

RHQ Royal Anglian Regiment, The Keep, Gibraltar Barracks, Bury St Edmunds IP33 3RN (tel: 01284 752394; email: RHQRANGLIAN-ChfClk@mod.uk)

Royal Armoured Corps War Memorial Benevolent Fund

c/o RHQ Royal Tank Regiment, Stanley Barracks, Bovington Camp, Wareham, Dorset BH20 6JB (tel: 01929 403444; email: rhqrtr@btconnect.com)

Royal Army Chaplains' Department Association

Ramillies, Marlborough Lines, Monxton Road, Andover SP11 8HJ (email: LF-CHAPLAINS-Group@mod.uk)

Royal Army Dental Corps Association

RHQ RADC, HQ AMD, The Former Staff College, Slim Road, Camberley, Surrey GU15 4NP (tel: 01276 412753; fax: 01276 412793)

Royal Army Medical Corps Association

Secretary, RHQ RAMC, Slim Road, Camberley, Surrey GU15 4NP (tel: 01276 412791; fax: 01276 412793; ramc_assoc@hotmail.com)

Royal Army Ordnance Corps Charitable Trust

(See Royal Logistics Corps Association Trust)

Royal Army Pay Corps

Secretary, RHQ AGC Centre, Winchester, Hampshire SO21 2RG (tel: 01962 887436; fax: 01962 887074; email: regsec.rapc@virgin.net)

Royal Army Veterinary Corps Benevolent Fund

Secretary, RHQ RAVC, HQ AMD, The Former Army Staff College, Slim Road, Camberley, Surrey GU15 4NP (tel: 01276 412749; fax: 01276 412793; reg_sec_ravc@hotmail.com)

Royal Berkshire Regiment

(See the Rifles – Salisbury)

Royal Dragoon Guards Benevolent Fund

3 Tower Street, York YO1 9SB (tel. and fax: 01904 642036)

Royal Dublin Fusiliers

Applications should be forwarded directly to the ABF The Soldiers' Charity, see page 135.

Royal Electrical and Mechanical Engineers Association & Benevolent Fund

RHQ REME, Headquarters DEME (A), Isaac Newton Road, Arborfield, Reading RG2 9NJ (tel: 01189 763220; deme-corpssecro1@mod.uk)

Royal Engineers Association

Ravelin Building, Brompton Barracks, Chatham, Kent ME4 4UG (tel: 01634 822407; email: deputycontroller@reahg.org.uk)

Royal Fusiliers Aid Society (Fallen Fusiliers)

City of London Headquarters, HM Tower of London, London EC3N 4AB (tel: 020 3166 6906; email: DINF-RHQRRF-AsstRegtSec@mod.uk)

Royal Gloucestershire Hussars

(See Yeomanry Benevolent Fund)

Royal Gloucestershire, Berkshire & Wiltshire Regiment

(See the Rifles – Gloucester)

Royal Green Jackets

(See the Rifles – Winchester)

Royal Hampshire Regiment

(See Princess of Wales's Royal Regiment)

Royal Highland Fusiliers Benevolent Association

518 Sauchiehall Street, Glasgow G2 3LW (tel: 01413 325639; fax: 01413 531493)

Royal Inniskilling Fusiliers

(See Royal Irish Regiment Benevolent Fund)

Royal Irish Fusiliers
(See Royal Irish Regiment Benevolent Fund)

Royal Irish Rangers
(See Royal Irish Regiment Benevolent Fund)

Royal Irish Regiment Benevolent Fund
RHQ The Royal Irish Regiment, Palace Barracks, Holywood, BFPO 806, Northern Ireland (tel: 02891 420640)

Royal Irish Rifles
(See Royal Irish Regiment Benevolent Fund)

9th/12th Royal Lancers (Prince of Wales) Charitable Association
Regimental Secretary, TA Centre, Saffron Road, South Wigston, Leicestershire LE18 4UX (tel: 01162 759572)

Royal Lincolnshire Regiment
(See Royal Anglian Regiment Benevolent Charity)

Royal Logistic Corps Association Trust
RHQ The RLC, The Princess Royal Barracks, Deepcut, Camberley, Surrey GU16 6RW (tel: 01252 833376; fax: 01252 833390)

Royal Military Academy Sandhurst Band
Applications should be forwarded directly to the ABF The Soldiers' Charity, see page 135.

Royal Munster Fusiliers Charitable Fund
Applications should be forwarded to the ABF The Soldiers' Charity, see page 135.

Royal Norfolk Regimental Association
(See Royal Anglian Regiment Benevolent Charity)

Royal Northumberland Fusiliers
(See Fusiliers Aid Society)

Royal Regiment of Fusiliers (post 1968)
(See Fusiliers Aid Society)

Royal Regiment of Scotland
Regimental Secretary, Edinburgh Castle, Edinburgh EH1 2YT (tel: 01313 105090; fax: 01313 105075)

Royal Scots Benevolent Society
c/o HHQ RS, The Castle, Edinburgh EH1 2YT (tel: 01313 105016; fax: 01313 105019)

Royal Scots Dragoon Guards Association
The Castle, Edinburgh EH1 2YT (tel: 01313 105100; fax: 01313 105101)

Royal Scots Fusiliers
(See Royal Highland Fusiliers Benevolent Association)

Royal Sussex Regiment
(See Princess of Wales's Royal Regiment)

Royal Tank Regiment Association and Benevolent Fund
RHQ Royal Tank Regiment, Stanley Barracks, Bovington Camp, Dorset BH20 6JA (tel: 01929 403331; email: regtlsec@royaltankregiment.org)

Royal Ulster Rifles Benevolent Fund
(See Royal Irish Regiment Benevolent Fund)

Royal Warwickshire Regimental Association
Area Headquarters, St John's House, Warwick CV34 4NF (tel: 01926 491653; email rrfhqwark@btconnect.com:)

Royal Welch Fusilier Comrades' Association
RHQ The Royal Welsh, Hightown Barracks, Wrexham, Clwyd LL13 8RD (tel: 01978 316176; fax: 01978 316121)

Royal Welsh Benevolent Fund
RHQ, Maindy Barracks, Cardiff CF14 3YE (tel: 02920 781202; fax: 02920 641281; email: RHQRWELSH-RegtlSec@mod.uk)

Scots Guards Association
2 Clifton Terrace Haymarket, Edinburgh EH21 5DR (tel: 0845 230 1642; 01313 371084; email: sga@scotsguards.co.uk)

Seaforth Highlanders' Regiment
(See Queens Own Highlanders (Seaforth and Camerons) Regimental Association)

Sharpshooters Yeomanry
(See Yeomanry Benevolent Fund)

Sherwood Foresters
(See Mercian Regiment Benevolent Fund)

Sherwood Rangers Yeomanry
(See Yeomanry Benevolent Fund)

Small Arms School Corps Comrades' Association
HQ SASC, Land Warfare Centre, Imber Road, Warminster, Wiltshire BA12 0DJ (tel: 01985 222487; fax: 01985 222972)

Somerset Light Infantry
(See the Rifles – Taunton)

South Lancashire Regiment (Prince of Wales's Volunteers)
(See Duke of Lancaster's Regiment)

South Staffordshire Regiment
(See Mercian Regiment Benevolent Fund)

Special Air Service Association
PO Box 35051, London NW1 4WF (tel: 020 7756 2408; fax; 020 7756 2409)

Staffordshire Regiment
(See Mercian Regiment Benevolent Fund)

Staffordshire Yeomanry
(See Yeomanry Benevolent Fund)

Suffolk Regiment
(See Royal Anglian Regiment Benevolent Charity)

Sussex Regiment

(See Princess of Wales's Royal Regiment)

Ulster Defence Regiment Benevolent Fund

Applications should be submitted through one of four regional contact centres of Aftercare Service: www.aftercareservice.org

Welsh Guards Afghanistan Appeal

RHQ Welsh Guards, Wellington Barracks, Birdcage Walk, London SW1E 6HQ (tel: 020 4714 3291; email: DINF-FtGds-WG-OffMgr@mod.uk)

Welsh Guards Benevolent Fund

Assistant Regimental Adjutant, Maindy Barracks, Whitchurch Road, Cardiff CF14 3YE (tel: 02920 781219; welshguardsassociation@live.co.uk)

West Riding Regiment

(See Yorkshire Regiment)

West Yorkshire Regimental Association

(See Yorkshire Regiment)

Wiltshire Regiment

(See the Rifles – Salisbury)

Women's Royal Army Corps Benevolent Fund

Gould House, Worthy Down, Winchester SO21 2RG (tel: 01962 887612; fax: 01962 887478)

Worcestershire Regiment

(See the Mercian Regimental Benevolent Fund)

Worcestershire & Sherwood Foresters Regiment

(See the Mercian Regimental Benevolent Fund)

Yeoman of the Guard – Queen's Bodyguard

(See Yeomanry Benevolent Fund)

Yeoman Warders

(See Yeomanry Benevolent Fund)

Yeomanry Benevolent Fund

Honorary Secretary, 10 Stone Buildings, Lincolns Inn, London WC2A 3TG (tel: 01962 779227) This fund covers all Yeomanry Regiments.

York and Lancaster Regiment

(See Yorkshire Regiment)

Yorkshire Hussars

(See Yeomanry Benevolent Fund)

Yorkshire Regiment

RHQ, 3 Tower Street, York YO1 9SB (tel: 01904 461013; email: RHQYORKS-OffrRec@mod.uk)

All-service funds

Funds marked with a (*) also have an entry in the main Service and Ex-Service Charities section.

*Association of Jewish Ex-servicemen and Women (AJEX)

Shield House, Harmony Way, London NW4 2BZ (tel: 020 8208 2323; email: headoffice@ajex.org.uk)

Fund dedicated to the welfare of Jewish veterans and their dependents.

British Korean Veterans (1981) Relief Fund

c/o Royal British Legion, 199 Borough High Street, London SE1 1AA (tel: 020 3207 2133)

Fund for the relief of distress amongst men and women who served with the British Forces during the Korean Campaign between June 1950 and July 1954, who are holders of, or entitled to, the British Korean Medal or United Nations Medal, their widows and dependents. Applicants need not be members of the British Korean Veterans Association to qualify for assistance.

*British Limbless Ex-Service Men's Association (BLESMA)

General Secretary, Frankland Moore House, 185–187 High Road, Chadwell Heath, Romford RM6 6NA (tel: 020 8590 1124; fax: 020 8599 2932)

To promote the welfare of all those of either sex who have lost a limb or limbs, or one, or both eyes, whilst in service or as a result of service in any branch of her Majesty's Forces or auxiliary Forces and to assist needy dependents of such limbless ex-Servicemen and women. It will also help those ex-Servicemen and women who suffer amputation of a limb or limbs after service.

*Burma Star Association

Benevolence Secretary, 34 Grosvenor Gardens, London SW1W 0DH (tel: 020 7823 4273)

Grants for men and women who served with his Majesty's or Allied Forces or in the Nursing Services during the Burma campaign and are Burma Star medal holders.

Canadian Veterans' Affairs

Welfare Officer, Department of Veterans' Affairs, Canadian High Commission, MacDonald House, 1 Grosvenor Square, London W1K 4AB (tel: 020 7258 6339)

Support for Canadian veterans, and their widows and dependents, living in the UK.

Chindits Old Comrades Association

Capt B K Wilson, Secretary & Welfare Officer, c/o The TA Centre, Wolsley House, Park Lane, Fallings Park, Wolverhampton WV10 9QR (tel: 01902 731841)

The aim of the association is to provide advice and aid (including, in appropriate cases, financial aid) to people who served in Burma with the Chindit Forces in 1943 and 1944, and their widows.

Ex-Services Mental Welfare Society (Combat Stress)

Tyrwhitt House, Oaklawn Road, Leatherhead KT22 0BX (tel: 0800 138 1619; email: contactus@combatstress.org.uk; website: www.combatstress.org.uk)

The society is the only organisation specialising in helping those of all ranks of the armed services and merchant navy suffering from combat related psychological injury caused by the traumatic events they have experienced in service. Remedial treatment is offered at three centres in Surrey, Shropshire and Ayrshire. The society also has a network of welfare officers who visit at home or hospital, and can help with war pensions and appeals. Information packs on request.

The Far East Prisoners of War (FEPOW) Trust Funds

c/o Royal British Legion, 199 Borough High Street, London SE1 1AA (tel: 020 3207 2133)

Support for people who were FEPOW and their spouses, widows/widowers and dependents from the Far East Prisoner of War Fund and the FEPOW Central Welfare Fund.

Forces Pensions Society

68 South Lambeth Road, London SW8 1RL (tel: 020 7820 9988; email: memsec@forpen.co.uk; website: www. forcespensionsociety.org)

This society provides advice on all aspects of Armed Forces Pensions Schemes. No financial assistance is given.

Irish Ex-Service Trust

c/o Royal British Legion, 199 Borough High Street, London SE1 1AA (tel: 020 3207 2030)

This is a government fund for those ex-service persons of the British Armed Forces who are resident in Northern Ireland or the Republic of Ireland, and their dependents. The trust makes one-off and recurrent grants for a variety of needs, particularly in those cases that might not normally be considered by other trusts/welfare organisations.

Joint Committee of the Order of St John and British Red Cross

c/o Royal British Legion, 199 Borough High Street, London SE1 1AA (tel: 0845 772 5725)

Help is available mainly by grants administered through other voluntary organisations, for War Pensioners and their widows/widowers, primarily those disabled in the first and Second World wars and the subsequent recognised conflicts, but not including Falklands War, the Gulf War 1990/91 or service in Northern Ireland.

*Lloyd's Patriotic Fund

c/o Welfare Department, SSAFA Forces Help, 19 Queen Elizabeth Street, London SE1 2LP (tel: 0800 731 4880)

The fund aims to help former members of the armed forces and their dependents who are in need. Grants will be given to a limited number of cases for one-off single grants for those with chronic illness or living in poverty, or in need of respite holidays.

National Ex-Prisoners of War Association

99 Parlaunt Road, Langley, Slough SL3 8BE (tel and fax: 01753 818308)

To relieve poverty and sickness among members of all ranks of the forces or nursing services and who during such service were prisoners of war in any theatre of war, and their widows and dependents.

Normandy Veterans Association Benevolent/ Welfare Fund

General Secretary, 53 Normandy Road, Cleethorpes, South Humberside DN35 9JE, 01472 600867)

The purpose of the fund is to give practical help to members, and to dependents of veterans, whose circumstances require it.

*"Not Forgotten" Association

4th Floor, 2 Grosvenor Gardens, London SW1W 0DH (tel: 020 7730 2400; fax: 020 7730 0020; website: www.nfassociation.org)

Provides recreational facilities for wounded service and disabled ex-service men and women as follows: TV sets (applicants whose mobility is severely restricted), TV licences, holidays, day outings and, for those confined to care homes, in-house entertainments.

Please note: the Association is unable to make cash grants, undertake welfare casework or assist widows.

*Officers' Association

First Floor, Mountbarrow House, 6–20 Elizabeth Street, London SW1W 9RB (tel: 0845 873 7153; website: www.officersassociation.org. uk)

The association awards regular and one-off financial help and advice to those in distress at home. Help is also provided towards care home third party shortfalls. Advice papers are also available on Care in the Community Legislation, Pension Credit and associated benefits, and accommodation; e.g. Care Homes and sheltered accommodation.

*Officers' Association Scotland

New Haig House, Logie Green Road, Edinburgh EH7 4HR (tel: 01315 572782; fax: 01315 575819; website: www.poppyscotland.org.uk)

Benevolence Secretary: Gary Gray (tel: 01315 501593); Benevolence Administrator: Gail Beaton (tel: 01315 501557); Employment Services: Dot Pringle (tel: 01315 501568)

The association aims to relieve distress among all those who have at any time held a Sovereign's Commission with embodied service in HM Naval, Military, or Air Forces, and among their wives, widows, husbands, widowers, children and dependents. This includes ex-officers who were commissioned into the Reserve, Auxiliary, or Territorial Forces. Applicants must be resident in Scotland at the time of their initial application or have been members of a Scottish Regiment. Financial assistance is available through the Benevolence Service and help to ex-officers looking for employment is given through the Employment Service.

*Poppyscotland (Earl Haig Fund Scotland)

New Haig House, Logie Green Road, Edinburgh EH7 4HR (tel: 01315 572782; fax: 01315 575819)

Head of Charitable Services: Gary Gray; Benevolence Secretary: Capt. Jim Macfarlane.

To relieve financially all ex-servicemen and women in need residing in Scotland, and their dependents. Poppyscotland also assists Merchant Seamen who have served in a war environment and Polish ex-Servicemen provided, in both cases, they are resident in

Scotland. Grants may be given either following an annual review or as an individual one-off payment.

Prisoners Families Fund

c/o Welfare Department, SSAFA Forces Help, 19 Queen Elizabeth Street, London SE1 2LP (tel: 0800 731 4880)

This fund makes grants for essential household items and children's clothing where a prisoner's family is struggling as a result of imprisonment.

The corporation provides financial help to widows, children and other dependents of officers and men of the Armed Forces who are in need, in the form of continuing allowances and grants, including education grants or bursaries.

Special Forces Benevolent Fund

c/o Brig Roger Dillon, D Group, 23 Grafton Street, London W1S 4EY (tel: 020 7318 9200)

Grants and pastoral support to 1939–1945 members of Special Operations Executive and their dependents.

Veterans Aid

40 Buckingham Palace Road, London SW1W 0RE (tel: 0800 012 6867; fax: 020 7630 6784; website: www. veterans-aid.net)

This organisation provides advice and assistance to homeless or 'pending' homeless ex-service personnel and their families in the UK and overseas. Help can be given in the form of food, clothing and shelter. Assistance is also given with drug, alcohol and gambling addictions and issues around mental health.

War Widows Association of Great Britain

c/o Royal British Legion, 199 Borough High Street, London SE1 1AA (tel: 0845 241 2189; website: www.warwidowsassociation.org.uk)

The association, formed in 1971 to improve conditions for all service widows and their dependents, works with government departments and service and ex-service organisations to help with all matters of its

members' welfare. The association does not make grants.

Religious charities

Christian

The Acorn Foundation

£25,000

Correspondent: Michael Wood,
14 Jordans Way, Jordans, Beaconsfield,
Buckinghamshire HP9 2SP (01494
870171)

Trustees: Revd Stuart Reid; Revd
Timothy David Simpson.

CC Number: 1068004

Eligibility
'Needy individuals in the UK.' The trust
gives towards the promotion of the
Christian faith.

Types of grants
Grants are given according to need.

Annual grant total
In 2011/12 the foundation had assets of
£1.8 million and an income of £93,000.
Grants were made totalling £68,000, of
which £25,000 was given to individuals
and £43,000 to organisations.

Applications
Grants are made in partnership with a
number of local authorities.

The Alexis Trust

£2,900

Correspondent: Duncan Vere,
14 Broadfield Way, Buckhurst Hill, Essex
IG9 5AG (020 8504 6872)

Trustees: Vera Vere; Prof. Duncan Vere;
Elisabeth Harwood; Chris Harwood.

CC Number: 262861

Eligibility
Members of the Christian faith.

Types of grants
Grants of between £50 and £100 are
available, mostly for Christian-based
activities.

Annual grant total
In 2010/11 the trust had assets of
£466,000 and an income of £36,000.

Grants to individuals for 'short-term
missionary projects' totalled £7,100.

Applications
In writing to the correspondent.

Frances Ashton's Charity

£55,000 (82 grants)

Correspondent: Mrs Georgina Fowle,
Damsons, Plum Orchard, Nether
Compton, Sherborne, Dorset DT9 4RG
(fax: 01732 520159)

Trustees: Adam Vere Balfour Broke;
Larence Nicholls; Raymond Henley;
Edward Vigant Eardley Fremantle; Revd
Brian Harvey Gwinn.

CC Number: 200162

Eligibility
Serving and retired Church of England
clergy, or their widows/widowers, who
are in need.

Types of grants
One-off grants of between £150 and
£880. The trust has a number of areas of
priority including emergency, medical or
care needs.

Annual grant total
In 2010 the charity had assets of
£1.4 million and an income of £57,000.
Grants totalled £55,000.

Exclusions
Grants are not given towards property
purchase, school fees or higher education
costs (unless the child is disabled),
parochial expenses, credit card debts and
loans, general living expenses, sabbatical
expenses or office furniture/equipment.

Applications
On a form available from the
correspondent, to be submitted directly
by the individual by 1 June each year.
They are considered in September.

Archdeaconry of Bath Clerical Families Fund

£900

Correspondent: Archdeaconry of Bath
Clerical Families Fund, The Bath and
Wells, Diocesan Board of Finance, The
old Deanery, Wells, Somerset BA5 2UG,
The Bath and Wells Diocesan Board of
Finance, The Old Deanery, Wells,
Somerset BA5 2UG (01749 670777; fax:
01749 674240)

Trustees: Revd J. Knott; Revd
M. C. L. Williams; V. A. Piggott; Revd
N. A. Nector.

CC Number: 230676

Eligibility
Widows and children of clergymen who
have died and who last served in the
deaneries of Bath, Chew Magna and
Portishead.

Types of grants
One-off and recurrent grants according
to need.

Annual grant total
Grants are generally in the region of
£900.

Applications
In writing to the correspondent.

The Bible Preaching Trust

£2,200

Correspondent: Richard Mayers,
Secretary and Treasurer, 5 The Crescent,
Egham, Surrey TW20 9PQ (email:
richard.mayers@tesco.net)

Trustees: Victor Pool; Revd Gwynne
Evans; Richard Foster Mayers; Pastor
Gary Brady; Ronald van den Broek.

CC Number: 262160

Eligibility
Ministers of the Evangelical Christian
faith who are in need. Theological
students may occasionally benefit.

Types of grants

Usually one-off grants ranging from £250 to £2,000.

Annual grant total

In 2010–11 the trust had an income of £6,800 and a total expenditure of £2,500.

Exclusions

Funding is not given for social causes, group projects, or to any person who cannot agree to the trust's doctrinal statement.

Applications

Either by recommendation or by letter: application forms and trust deed extracts are then sent out. Trustees' meetings are held every four months at which applications will be considered. 'Mass-targeting' applications or those outside the terms of the trust may not be answered.

Buckingham Trust

£2,000

Correspondent: Richard Foot, Trustee, 17 Church Road, Tunbridge Wells, Kent TN1 1LG (01892 774774)

Trustees: Mr R. W. D. Foot; Mrs T. Clay.

CC Number: 237350

Eligibility

People in need who are missionaries or Christian workers, or people with some Christian connection. Applicants must be known to the trustees.

Types of grants

One-off and recurrent grants according to need.

Annual grant total

In 2009/10 the trust had assets of £892,000 and an income of £187,000. Grants were made totalling £202,000, of which £135,000 was given to charities, £65,000 to churches and the remaining £2,000 to individuals.

Applications

In writing to the correspondent. However, the trust has previously stated that its funds are fully committed each year and not given to new applicants.

Other information

This trust also makes grants to organisations and Churches.

The Chasah Trust

£11,000

Correspondent: Richard Collier-Keywood, Trustee, Glydwish Hall, Fontridge Lane, Etchingham, East Sussex TN19 7DG (01435 882768)

Trustees: Richard Collier-Keywood; Karen Ann Collier-Keywood.

CC Number: 294898

Eligibility

Missionaries who are known to the trustees, or are a contact of the trustees.

Types of grants

One-off and recurrent grants to support Christian work.

Annual grant total

In 2010/11 the trust had an income of £24,000 and a total expenditure of £22,000.

Applications

In writing to the correspondent.

Other information

Grants are also made to organisations.

Children of the Clergy Trust

£1,000

Correspondent: Trustee, 4 Kierhill Gardens, Westhill, Aberdeenshire AB32 6AX

SC Number: SC001845

Eligibility

Children of deceased ministers of the Church of Scotland.

Types of grants

One-off or recurrent grants according to need. Previously grants have ranged from £500 to £1,000 to relieve poverty, hardship or distress.

Annual grant total

About £2,000.

Applications

In writing to the correspondent. Applications should be submitted directly by the individual and should include information about the applicant's ministerial parent, general family circumstances and other relevant information.

Christadelphian Benevolent Fund

£71,000

Correspondent: Kenneth Smith, Westhaven House, Arleston Way, Shirley, Solihull, West Midlands B90 4LH (01217 137100)

Trustees: David Philip Ensell; William Neville Moss; Dr John Michael Hellawell; Kenneth Howard Avery Smith; John Mark Buckler; Roger David Miles.

CC Number: 222416

Eligibility

Members of the Christadelphian body who are experiencing difficult times.

Types of grants

One-off and recurrent grants according to need.

Annual grant total

In 2011 the trust had assets of £2 million and an income of £122,000. Grants to individuals totalled £71,000 and were broken down as follows:

Compassionate grants	£19,000
Fuel aid	£17,000
Regular grants	£15,000
Annual holiday scheme	£10,000
Water aid	£8,000
Christmas bounty	£2,600

Applications

In writing to the correspondent. Compassionate grants are given to individuals on the basis of representations made by the ecclesia of which those individuals are members.

Other information

Grants are also made to organisations (£79,000) in 2011.

The Church of England Pensions Board

£257,000

Correspondent: Peter Lowings, 29 Great Smith Street, London SW1P 3PS (020 7898 1802; email: cepb.enquiries@ churchofengland.org; website: www.cofe. anglican.org/about/cepb)

Trustees: Bishop of Dudley; Clive Hawkins; Revd Ian Gooding; Colin John Peters; Dr Graham Campbell; Canon David Colin Froude; Ian Clark; Alan Keith Fletcher; Brian Wilson; Dr Jonathan Spencer; Jeremy Clack; James Archer; Simon Baynes; Revd Paul Boughton; Revd Nigel Bourne; John Ferguson; Canon Sandra Newton; Fr Paul Benfield; Roger Mounford; Jane Bisson.

CC Number: 236627

Eligibility

Retired clergy and licensed layworkers of the Church of England, their widows, widowers and dependents.

Types of grants

Allowances for those participating in the retirement housing scheme and to clergy widow(er)s to supplement their low income. No new grants are made for assistance with private nursing or retirement care.

Annual grant total

In 2011 the board held assets of £102 million and had an income of £22 million. Grants totalled £257,000.

Applications

On a form available from the correspondent.

Other information

The trust's main concern is the administration of the pension scheme and the provision of supported housing and nursing care. It operates seven such complexes across the country. The trust also runs a retirement housing scheme which offers mortgages and loans to assist those vacating 'tied' housing.

The Clergy Rest Fund

£50,000 (42 grants)

Correspondent: Hugh MacDougald, Wickworth and Sherwood Solicitors, Minerva House, 5 Montague Close, London SE1 9BB (020 7593 5000; fax: 020 7593 5099; email: info@wslaw.co.uk; website: www.wslaw.co.uk)

Trustees: Dr Sheila Cameron; Dr Frank Robson; Aiden Richard Hargreaves-Smith; Paul Moris.

CC Number: 233436

Eligibility

Church of England clergy who are in need.

Types of grants

One-off grants ranging from £500 to £1,500 for a variety of needs.

Annual grant total

In 2011 the fund had assets of £909,000 and an income of £34,000. Grants were made to 42 individuals totalling £50,000.

Applications

In writing to the correspondent.

Other information

The fund also makes grants to institutions connected with the Church of England.

The Collier Charitable Trust

£10,000

Correspondent: M A Blagden, Secretary, Cherry Tree Cottage, Old Kiln Lane, Churt, Farnham, Surrey GU10 2HX (01428 717534)

CC Number: 251333

Eligibility

Retired Christian missionaries and teachers in the UK and overseas.

Types of grants

One-off and recurrent grants of around £300 each.

Annual grant total

In 2010 the trust had an income of £20,000 and total expenditure of £105,000. No further information was available, however, grants to individuals usually take up between 5–10% of total charitable expenditure, with grants to organisations taking priority.

Applications

In writing to the correspondent.

The Deakin and Withers Fund

£34,000 (65 grants)

Correspondent: Alison Wade, c/o South Yorkshire Community Foundation, Unit 3 – G1 Building, 6 Leeds Road, Sheffield S9 3TY (01142 424857; email: karen.alsop@sycf.org.uk)

Trustees: Alan William Sherriff; Jonathan Hunt; Lady Ruby Sykes; Christopher Jewitt; Frank Carter; Galden Ives; Isadora Aiken; Jackie Drayton; Maureen Shah; Jane Marshall; Jane Kemp; Allan Jackson; Timothy Henry Reed; Tim Greenacre; Giles Bloomer; Peter John Hollis; Susan M. Scholey; William Warrack.

CC Number: 221932

Eligibility

Single women in the UK, whether divorced, unmarried or widowed, who are in reduced circumstances and who are members of the Church of England or of a church having full membership of the Council of Churches for Britain and Ireland. Grants are not given to ladies under 40 years of age and beneficiaries are usually over 55 years.

Types of grants

Annuities of around £500 paid in December.

Annual grant total

In 2010/11 the fund had assets of £1.6 million and an income £48,000. Grants were made to 65 individuals totalling £34,000. The bulk of these were paid as annuities, although some one-off payments were also made.

The 2010/11 accounts note that: 'the level of applications is not sufficient to maintain the level of annuitants required and steps are being taken to advertise the fund through Churches Together with a view to increasing awareness of the fund.'

Applications

On a form available from the correspondent submitted directly by the individual, through a third party such as a social worker, or through an organisation such as a Citizens Advice or other welfare agency.

If there is a surplus of income, the trustees will consider any new applications that have been received. Of the applications reviewed in August 2011 only one was considered eligible for a one-off grant of £500.

Other information

In 2008 the Deakin Institute and the Withers Pension amalgamated and became the Deakin and Withers Fund.

The Four Winds Trust

£4,800

Correspondent: P A Charters, Trustee, Four Winds, Church Lane, Ashbury, Swindon, Wiltshire SN6 8LZ (01793 710431)

Trustees: Simon Vincent Charters; Frances Mary Charters; Philip Arthur Charters; Mary Edith Charters; Peter John Charters.

CC Number: 262524

Eligibility

Evangelists, missionaries and ministers, including those who have retired, and their widows, widowers and other dependents who are in need.

Types of grants

One-off and recurrent grants according to need.

Annual grant total

In 2010/11 the trust had assets of £812,000 and an income of £43,000. Grants were made totalling £43,000, of which £4,800 was paid to individuals. £27,000 was distributed to organisations and a further £11,000 was given in other gifts and donations.

Applications

In writing to the correspondent, although the trust states that it does not consider unsolicited applications. Applications without an sae will not receive a response.

The Fund for the Support of Presbyters and Deacons

£200,000

Correspondent: Benefits Section, Methodist Church House, 25 Marylebone Road, London NW1 5JR (email: stipends@methodistchurch.org.uk; website: www.methodist.org.uk)

CC Number: 1132208

Eligibility

Retired ministers and deacons of the Methodist church and their dependents. Grants can also be made to enable ministers and deacons to continue to work where otherwise they would have to retire.

Types of grants
One-off grants to meet all kinds of need including, unexpected household expenditure (e.g. replacement of boiler/cooker/washing machine), gardening, property maintenance and repairs, bills, recarpeting, redecorating and medical needs (e.g. stair lifts, mobility scooters, opticians and dental costs). Grants of up to £3,000 are also available for residential care fees.

Annual grant total
Grants usually total around £200,000 each year.

Applications
In writing to the correspondent at any time.

Other information
Grants are also made to the Methodist Ministers' Housing Society.

The I. W. Griffiths Trust

£67,000

Correspondent: Lord Brian Griffiths of Fforestfach, 18 Royal Avenue, London SW3 4QF (020 7774 4015)

Trustees: Lord Griffiths of Fforestfach; Dr Aerowen Jane Williams Nee Griffiths; Lady Griffiths of Fforesfach; Hon. Owenna Mary Ruth Griffiths; Hon. James Griffiths.

CC Number: 1090379

Eligibility
People who are, or have been, engaged in Christian mission and are in need.

Types of grants
One-off and recurrent grants according to need.

Annual grant total
In 2010 the trust had assets of £168,000 and an income of £53,000. Grants were made totalling £67,000.

Applications
In writing to the correspondent.

The Lady Hewley Trust

£75,000

Correspondent: Neil Blake, Clerk, Military House, 24 Castle Street, Chester CH1 2DS (01244 400315)

Trustees: Gordon Simmonds; Stephen Gorton; John Lumsden; Phillip Thake; Dr David Robinson; Sarah Dodds; Neil Mackenzie.

CC Number: 230043

Eligibility
Present or retired ministers of the United Reformed, Congregational and Baptist churches and their widows who are in need. This is a national trust, although preference is given to applicants whose ministry is in the northern counties of England.

Types of grants
Welfare grants to a maximum of about £1,000 (unless outside the scope of social security payments).

Annual grant total
In 2010/11 the trust had assets of £13.8 million and an income of £357,000. Grants to individuals totalled £129,000, of which £75,000 was for welfare needs.

Exclusions
No grants will be given when local authority funds are available.

Applications
On a form available from the correspondent. Applications should be submitted by 15 March for the June meeting of the trustees and by 15 July for the October meeting.

The Hounsfield Pension

£3,500

Correspondent: Godfrey Smallman, Wrigleys Solicitors, Fountain Precinct, Balm Green, Sheffield S1 2JA (01142 675594; fax: 01142 763176)

Trustees: Nicholas James Anthony Hutton; David Francis Booker; Prof. G. D. Sims; P. W. Lee; S. A. P. Hunter; Mr D. Stanley; Mr I. G. Walker; Mr J. F. W. Peters; Revd Peter E. Bradley; Mr M. R. Woffenden; Mrs J. P. Banham; Mrs B. R. Hickman; Mrs S. Bain.

CC Number: 221436

Eligibility
Unmarried women, widows and widowers who are over 50 years old, live in England or Wales, are members of the Church of England and have never received parochial relief or public assistance.

Types of grants
Grants are fixed annually and paid in two instalments.

Annual grant total
In 2010/11 the charity had an income of £3,700 and a total expenditure of £3,700.

Applications
In writing to the correspondent. Only a limited number of pensions are available, and places become available at irregular intervals.

The H. E. Knight Charitable Trust

£2,800

Correspondent: Aubrey Curry, 14 Bramley Gardens, Whimple, Exeter EX5 2SJ (01404 822295)

Trustees: Gavin Knight; Aubrey James Curry; Brenda Knight.

CC Number: 283549

Eligibility
Individuals involved in missionary Christian work and spiritual teaching in the UK.

Types of grants
Ongoing support for Christian workers. Grants of up to £500 are awarded.

Annual grant total
In 2010/11 the trust had a higher than usual income of £11,500 (£1,300 in 2009 and 2010) and a total expenditure of £3,000.

Applications
In writing to the correspondent. Note, the trust has stated that the majority of its funds go to missionaries known to the trustees and as such, other applicants are unlikely to be successful. The trust does not accept unsolicited applications.

The Leaders of Worship and Preachers Trust

£19,000

Correspondent: Adrian J Needham, Unit 35 First Floor Offices, Orbital 25 Business Park, Dwight Road, Watford, Hertfordshire WD18 9DA (01923 231811; email: lwptoffice@lwpt.org.uk; website: www.lwpt.org.uk)

Trustees: Pastor Paul Busby; David John Charles Greet; Philip Nuttall; Angela Rosemary Davis; Brian Thornton; Victor Winchcombe; Naana Jackson; John Witt; Deacon Myrtle Poxon.

CC Number: 1107967

Eligibility
Preachers and leaders of worship who are in need, and their dependents.

Types of grants
One-off and recurrent grants towards the cost of care, mobility equipment and other aids.

Annual grant total
In 2010/11 the trust had assets of £344,000 and an income of £2.6 million. Grants were made totalling £19,000.

Applications
The trust has a series of different application forms depending on the

applicant's need. These are available to download from the website.

The Lind Trust

£20,000

Correspondent: Gavin Wilcock, Tithe Barn, Attlebridge, Norwich NR9 5AA

Trustees: Gavin Croft Wilcock; Leslie Charles Brown; Dr Graham Martin Dacre; Samuel Edward Dacre.

CC Number: 803174

Eligibility

Individuals in full-time Christian ministry.

Types of grants

One-off and recurrent grants according to need.

Annual grant total

In 2010/11 the trust had assets of £22 million and an income of £1.9 million. Grants and donations were made totalling £460,000, the great majority of which were made to organisations.

Applications

In writing to the correspondent at any time. The trust commits most of its money early, giving the remaining funds to eligible applicants.

The Lyall Bequest

£1,000

Correspondent: Miss E L Calderwood, c/o Pagan Osborne, 106 South Street, St Andrews, Fife KY16 9QD (01334 475001; fax: 01334 476922; email: elcalderwood@pagan.co.uk)

SC Number: SC005542

Eligibility

Church of Scotland ministers who are in need.

Types of grants

One-off grants generally in the range of £100 to £200 are given towards convalescence and holidays.

Annual grant total

Grants usually total about £1,000 each year.

Applications

In writing to the correspondent to be submitted directly by the individual.

Ministers' Relief Society

£17,000

Correspondent: A Lathey, 8 Marston Avenue, Chessington, Surrey KT9 2HF (020 8397 2483)

Trustees: Mr F. M. J. Raynsford; Alan Lathey; Colin Frank Taylor; Jimmy Louis; Joyce Margaret Griffiths; Dr Felix Konotey-Ahulu; Robert John Revell; Rosemary Konotey-Ahulu; Barry William Harlin.

CC Number: 270314

Eligibility

Protestant ministers, their widows and dependents who are in need. Children of deceased ministers must be under 21 and of 'genuine evangelical and Protestant convictions' to be eligible.

Types of grants

One-off and recurrent grants according to need. Recent grants have been given to: ministers who are retired or disabled, and their widows, with inadequate income or savings; specific emergencies, such as serious illness, removal costs, enforced resignation or dismissal by congregation; and candidates and students seeking vocational training in the ministry.

Annual grant total

In 2010 the society had an income of £23,000 and a total expenditure of £18,000.

Applications

On a form available from the correspondent, to be submitted directly by the individual.

The George Müller Charitable Trust

£697,000 (158 grants)

Correspondent: Wendy Clacker, Müller House, 7 Cotham Park, Bristol BS6 6DA (01179 245001; email: admin@mullers. org; website: www.mullers.org)

Trustees: Quentin Elston; Robert Lawrence Scott-Cook; Roger Maurice Chilvers; Neil Summerton; Tony Davies; David Gilbert Maldwyn John; Adrian Reed; Kim Jeanette Conlan; Edward James Marsh; Joanna Thistlewaite Pritchett; Peter James Christopher Metcalfe; Stewart Douglas North.

CC Number: 1066832

Eligibility

Christian missionaries in the UK or abroad.

Types of grants

Grants are made to provide support and encouragement to those involved in Christian work and education in the UK and overseas. Preference is given to those working amongst children. Most grants are given to those not supported or employed by a large missionary organisation.

Annual grant total

In 2010/11 the trust held assets of £7.9 million and had an income of £3.2 million. Grants were made to 158 individual Christian workers totalling £697,000.

Applications

In writing to the correspondent giving details of the nature of your work as well as need.

Other information

The trust runs sheltered accommodation, a church partnership scheme and also makes grants to organisations (£362,000 in 2010/11).

The Mylne Trust

£20,000

Correspondent: Paul Jenkins, PO Box 530, Farnham GU9 1BP (email: admin@ mylnetrust.org.uk; website: www. mylnetrust.org.uk)

Trustees: Brian Daniels; Elizabeth Barnes; Revd Andrew Tuck; Ian Sargeant; Mrs A. Mansell; Roy Picken.

CC Number: 208074

Eligibility

Members of the Protestant faith who have been engaged in evangelistic work, including missionaries and retired missionaries, and Christian workers whose finances are inadequate. Married ordinands with children are also supported when all other sources of funding have failed to cover their needs.

Types of grants

Annual and one-off grants for living costs and training expenses.

Annual grant total

In 2010/11 grants were made to over 134 people totalling £55,000.

Applications

On a form available from the correspondent. Applications should be returned to: The Mylne Trust, PO Box 530, Farnham GU9 1BP. The trustees meet quarterly to consider applications.

Other information

Grants are also made for educational purposes.

The Trust's website currently states that applications are suspended until further notice.

Nazareth Trust Fund

£2,700

Correspondent: Mr R W G Hunt, Barrowpoint, 18 Millennium Close, Salisbury, Wiltshire SP2 8TB (01722 349322)

Trustees: Revd David Richard Gainer Hunt; Eileen Mary Hunt; Elma Ruth Lilburn Hunt; Nicola Mhairi Hunt; Philip Roger William Hunt; Dr Robert Wiilliam Gainer Hunt.

CC Number: 210503

Eligibility

The trust gives support to individuals known to the trustees who promote the Christian faith and/or are Christian missionaries.

Types of grants

One-off grants ranging between £100 and £750.

Annual grant total

Grants are made to individuals totalling between £2,000 and £3,000 per year.

Exclusions

No support for individuals not known to the trustees.

Applications

In writing to the correspondent, although the trust tends to only support individuals and organisations personally known to the trustees.

Other information

Grants are also made to organisations (£37,000 in 2010/11).

The Paton Trust

£1,600

Correspondent: Trust Administrator, c/o Alexander Sloan, Chartered Accountants, 38 Cadogan Street, Glasgow G2 7HF (01412 048989)

SC Number: SC012301

Eligibility

Ministers of the Established Church of Scotland who are elderly or in poor health.

Types of grants

One-off grants up to £100. Grants are given to ministers who are in need of a convalescence break and to ministers who are retiring to provide them with a holiday at the time of retirement.

Annual grant total

In previous years grants have totalled around £1,600 although the total figure does tend to fluctuate.

Applications

On a form available from the correspondent. Applications are considered throughout the year and should be submitted directly by the individual.

Lady Peel Legacy Trust

£2,500

Correspondent: Mrs Chris Ruge-Cope, 21 Chace Avenue, Potters Bar, Hertfordshire EN6 5LX

Trustees: Charles Pickstone; C. Ruge-Cope; Richard Chamberlin; Christopher Irvine; Andrew Davison.

CC Number: 204815

Eligibility

Priests in the Anglo-Catholic tradition who, due to ill health or age, have had to resign their work or livings.

Types of grants

One-off or recurrent grants according to need.

Annual grant total

About £5,000 a year towards both educational and welfare purposes.

Applications

In writing to the correspondent. The closing dates for applications are 1 April and 1 November each year. Telephone contact is not invited.

The Podde Trust

£5,000

Correspondent: Peter Godfrey, 68 Green Lane, Hucclecote, Gloucester GL3 3QX (01452 613563; email: podde@supanet. com)

Trustees: Mr P. B. Godfrey; Mrs P. E. Godfrey; Mr A. Gent; Dr D. Maxted.

CC Number: 1016322

Eligibility

Individuals involved in Christian work in the UK and overseas.

Types of grants

One-off and recurrent grants.

Annual grant total

In 2010/11 the trust had assets of £3,800 and an income of £43,000. There were 28 grants to individuals for education and relief-in-need purposes totalling £10,000.

Applications

In writing to the correspondent: note, the trust states that it has very limited resources, and those it does have are mostly already committed. Requests from new applicants therefore have very little chance of success.

Other information

Organisations involved in Christian work are also supported (£33,000 in 2010/11).

The Pyncombe Charity

£11,000

Correspondent: Rita Butterworth, Wingletye, Lawford, Crowcombe, Taunton TA4 4AL (01984 618388; email: joeandrita@waitrose.com)

Trustees: Anthony Henry Trollope-Bellew; Diana Mary Taylor; Julian Luttrell; Peter Alec Charles Moore; Revd Robin Ray; Revd Peter David Maurice; Annabel Claire Trollope-Bellew.

CC Number: 202255

Eligibility

Serving Anglican clergy under 70 years of age and their immediate families who are resident with them, who are in financial need resulting from a serious illness or accident or special circumstance.

Types of grants

Small one-off grants.

Annual grant total

In 2010/11 the charity had an income of £15,000 and a total expenditure of £12,000.

Exclusions

No grants towards educational expenses.

Applications

Applications must be made through the diocesan bishop on a form available from the correspondent. Applications are considered in April. No direct applications can be considered and the charity has told us the majority of the direct applications received are ineligible.

The Rehoboth Trust

£17,000

Correspondent: Shakti Sisodia, Trustee, 71 Rydal Gardens, Hounslow TW3 2JJ (020 8893 3700)

Trustees: Lyndon Bowring; Andrea Tracey Sisodia; Shakti Singh Sisodia; Jonathan Gwilt.

CC Number: 1114454

Eligibility

Christian ministers or retired ministers who are in need in the UK and abroad.

Types of grants

Grants given according to need.

Annual grant total

In 2010 the trust had an income of £35,000 and made grants to individuals totalling £17,000.

Applications

In writing to the correspondent.

Other information

Grants are also made to organisations (£24,000 in 2010).

The Retired Ministers' and Widows' Fund

£28,000

Correspondent: Bill Allen, 7 Wendover Lodge, Church Street, Welwyn AL6 9LR (01438 489171; email: willallen@ tinyonline.co.uk)

Trustees: Revd Ashley Hills; Revd Julian James Macro; Revd James McClelland; Dr Doreen Jane Williams; Kenneth Meekison; Revd Kenneth Chambers; David Ernest Nixon; William Ellington; Jill Mahala Strong; Revd Basil William Oliver Amey; Malcolm James Johnston; Ruth Manson.

CC Number: 233835

Eligibility

Retired ministers, and ministers' widows of Presbyterian, Independent (including Unitarian, Free Christian, Congregational and the United Reformed) and Baptist churches, who live in England and Wales and are on a low income. In 2010/11 this was defined as those with an income (not including state benefits) of less than £5,000 (£7,500 for married couples) and savings not exceeding £40,000. The savings limit for one-off grants is £10,000. The limits may be disregarded in exceptional circumstances, such as when an applicant is in a residential or nursing home.

Types of grants

Biannual payments totalling £500 a year for widows and single ministers and £700 a year for married ministers. One-off grants of up to £250 may also be given to help in an emergency.

A maximum of two one-off grants may be received in a four year period by any single beneficiary.

Annual grant total

In 2010/11 the fund had assets of £606,000 and an income of £33,000. Grants were made to 50 individuals totalling £28,000.

Applications

On a form available from the correspondent. Applications can be submitted by the individual but should be signed by a local minister.

Retired Missionary Aid Fund

£532,000

Correspondent: Roger Herbert, Secretary, 64 Callow Hill Road, Alvechurch, Birmingham B48 7LR (01214 452378; email: enquiries@rmaf. co.uk; website: www.rmaf.co.uk)

Trustees: Andrew James Street; James Lees Maclellan; John Lower; Eric Joseph Noble; George Arthur Wheeler; Jim Gompertz; Andrew Jessop; Philip Andrews; Andrew Griffiths; Brian Davies; Roger Herbert; Stewart Simmons; Dennis Wattt; Neil Turner; David Nelson Logan; Howard Newton.

CC Number: 211454

Eligibility

Retired missionaries from the Christian Brethren Assemblies who are in need. Help may also be given to their dependents.

Types of grants

Quarterly grants, birthday gifts and Christmas hampers are given.

Annual grant total

In 2010/11 the fund held assets of £1.2 million and had an income of £621,000. Grants were made totalling £532,000 and can be broken down as follows:

Gifts to retired missionaries	£504,000
Earmarked gifts for retired missionaries	£17,000
Gift vouchers and Christmas hampers	£11,000

The 2010/11 accounts note that fund had 233 members in that year, the majority of whom were in receipt of some form of regular financial support.

Applications

The fund only gives support to its members, who should make their circumstances known to the correspondent.

The Rev Dr George Richards' Charity

£16,000

Correspondent: Dr Paul Simmons, Flat 98, Thomas More House, Barbican, London EC2Y 8BU (020 7588 5583)

Trustees: Revd Nicholas Holtam; David Meara Archdeacon of London; Annette Cooper, Archdeacon of Colchester; Dr James Thomson; Stephen Welch, Archdeacon of Middlesex; Elwin Cockett, Archdeacon of West Ham; J. P. Smith, Archdeacon of St Albans.

CC Number: 246965

Eligibility

Church of England clergy who are in need and their widows and dependents. Preference is given to older people and those in poor health.

Types of grants

One-off and recurrent grants for heating expenses, household costs, travel, education, clothing, Christmas gifts and medical care. Pensions are available for those who have been forced to retire early from active ministry and are on a low income.

Annual grant total

In 2010 the charity had an income of £20,000 and a total expenditure of £18,000.

Exclusions

No grants for repaying debt.

Applications

On a form available from the correspondent, including details of all sources of income. Applications should be submitted directly by the individual. They are usually considered twice a year.

The Silverwood Trust

£9,000

Correspondent: John Shergold, Trustee, 35 Orchard Grove, New Milton, Hampshire BH25 6NZ

Trustees: Jean Shergold; John Shergold; Gary Bowes-Read; Diane Bowes-Read; J. Wentzel; Martyn Travers.

CC Number: 292372

Eligibility

Christian missionaries in need through illness or retirement.

Types of grants

One-off or small recurrent grants according to need. (Normally restricted to people known to the trustees.)

Annual grant total

In 2011 the trust had assets of £37,000 and an income of £50,000. Grants to individuals totalled £19,000 for welfare and education.

Exclusions

No grants for computers or school fees.

Applications

In writing to the correspondent, directly by the individual.

The Henry Smith Charity (UK)

£1.1 million

Correspondent: Genevieve Ford-Saville, Grants Officer, Poor Clergy, Sixth Floor, 65–68 Leadenhall Street, London

EC3A 2AD (020 7264 4970; fax: 020 7488 9097; website: www. henrysmithcharity.org.uk)

Trustees: Gracia McGrath; Carola Goodman-Law; Sir Richard Thompson; James Daryl Hambro; Anna McNair Scott; Merlyn Lowther; Noel Manns; Rt Hon Clare Amabel Margaret Countes; Diana Barran; Marilyn Gallyer; Mark Newton; Patrick Maxwell; Peter Smallridge; Tristan Millington Drake; Miko Giedroyc; Bridget Biddell; Vivian Hunt; James Hordern.

CC Number: 230102

Eligibility

Kindred grants are open to direct legitimate descendants of one of the kindred previously registered, or the spouse, widow or widower of a kindred member. The onus is on the individual to prove their descent.

Clergy grants are only made to ordained clergy of the Church of England. Preference is given to those who work in 'tough and demanding' parishes.

Types of grants

The charity manages two funds for the benefit of individuals:

Kindred grants: one-off and recurrent grants, for example, to help those on low incomes, provide training for young people and cover funeral costs.

Poor clergy fund: one-off grants to help clergy families take a break and fund emergency or exceptional costs which cannot be afforded from family incomes.

Annual grant total

In 2011 the charity had assets of £672 million and an income of almost £13 million. Grants were made to individuals totalling over £1.1 million, of which £522,000 was given in grants to clergy and £624,000 was given in grants to 'poor kindred.'

The 2011 accounts include the following analysis of expenditure: 'During the year the Charity awarded payments totalling £624,000 to Kindred, of which the largest amount (£377,000) was to support elderly kindred, and the remainder to support adults and students.... Total grants rose by 20% reflecting rising demand as a result of the increasingly difficult economic climate.'

Applications

Applications for kindred grants should be made in writing to the Kindred Administrator. Clergy must make applications directly to the Bishop of the diocese.

Other information

The charity also makes a large number of grants to organisations (£27 million in 2011), a lot of which is further distributed to individuals.

The Society for the Relief of Poor Clergymen

£25,000

Correspondent: Secretary, c/o CPAS, Athena Drive, Tachbrook Park, Warwickshire CV34 6NG (01926 458458)

Trustees: The Ven Judith Rose; The Ven Ian Russell; Anne Thompson; Revd Duncan Whyte; Revd George Young; The Ven Ian Watson; Revd Canon John Moore; Revd Pamela Harvey; Revd John Dunnett; Marion Powell; Revd Martin Hayward.

CC Number: 232634

Eligibility

Evangelical ordained ministers and accredited lay workers and their dependents or widows/widowers in the Church of England and the Church in Wales.

Types of grants

One-off grants for illness or financial support when it can be shown that it has caused distress and hardship to the individual or family.

Annual grant total

In 2010 the trust had an income of £22,000 and a total expenditure of £29,000.

Exclusions

Grants are not given towards educational costs or travel expenses.

Applications

On a form available from the correspondent. The committee meets twice yearly (normally in March and September). Applications can be submitted directly by the individual or through a third party without the knowledge of the individual and in confidence if the individual is not inclined to apply.

The Sons and Friends of the Clergy

£544,000

Correspondent: Robert Welsford, Registrar, 1 Dean Trench Street, Westminster, London SW1P 3HB (020 7799 3696; fax: 020 7222 3468; email: enquiries@clergycharities.org.uk; website: www.clergycharities.org.uk)

Trustees: Tom Hoffman; Terry Knight; Graeme Knowles; Archbishop of Canterbury; David Brewer; Bishop of London; John Morrison; David Rossdale; David Lowman; Rodney Whiteman; Richard Askwith; Christopher Davies; Jill Sandham; John Chadwick; Charles Richardson; Colin Menzies; David Meynell; Fiona Daley; Ann Joyce; Alex Brougham; Patrick Walker; Lady Mawer; Roxanne Hunte.

CC Number: 207736

Eligibility

Anglican clergy of the dioceses of the UK and Ireland and the diocese in Europe, their widows/widowers and dependents under 25, separated or divorced spouses of such clergy and mature unmarried daughters of such clergy.

Types of grants

The corporation provides a guide as to what it will give grants for, however this is by no means exhaustive. The secretary and their staff are happy to discuss individual cases for other areas of funding and will try and help with any problem.

Bereavement expenses

▷ Grants may be considered for clergy and their widows/widowers towards the costs of their spouse's funeral

Cars for individuals with disabilities

▷ Help cannot be provided towards the cost of acquiring a car, but grants can sometimes be considered towards the cost of converting a standard car to enable its use by a person with disabilities who needs the car for the purposes of mobility

Child maintenance

▷ Grants can be considered for widows/ widowers and divorced and separated clergy/spouses in respect of their children who are under the age of 25 and who are still in full-time education or are below school age

Clothing

▷ Grants can be given towards adult clothing (including clerical clothing) as well as towards necessities for infants

Counselling

▷ Grants can be considered towards the cost of professional counselling, including marriage guidance counselling. A supporting letter from the counsellor will usually be required

Debts

▷ Help towards debts can sometimes be considered. It should be noted that debt relief is a formal procedure involving both the charities and the applicant's diocese, and permission for consultation by the charities with the diocese will be required. Anyone seeking help towards debts is advised to discuss the matter with the Registrar/Secretary at an early stage

Heating expenses

▷ Normally for retired clergy, widows/widowers and unmarried daughters over pensionable age who find these expenses particularly difficult to meet. Help is sometimes given to serving clergy where family illness necessitates extra heating

Holidays

Applications can be considered from:
▷ Serving clergy, particularly those in parochial work
▷ Retired clergy
▷ Widows/widowers
▷ Separated or divorced spouses if still dependent on their clergy spouses

In addition, applicants who live in an area that is considered 'unsafe' may, with their archdeacon's support, apply for a grant to help with the cost of employing someone to look after their home while they are away.

House repairs and decoration

▷ For retired clergy, widows/widowers, unmarried daughters and separated or divorced spouses. Help can be considered for essential work only. No assistance can be given in respect of repairs or decorations to property that is not owned by the applicant, nor to property for which a third party is responsible for the work in question

Medical expenses

▷ Grants towards the costs of medical treatment and medical aids can be considered where the treatment/aids cannot be provided on the NHS. A supporting letter from the applicant's doctor or other specialist will be required. The possibility of using St Luke's Hospital for the Clergy at 14 Fitzroy Square, London W1T 6AH (telephone number 020 7388 4954) should be explored in appropriate cases

Nursing home fees

▷ Help can be considered towards the costs of nursing home care where the shortfall in fees cannot be met by the State, church pension authority, local authority or family

Ordinands

▷ Book grants can be considered for those training for the ordained ministry. Applications will need to be supported by the principal of the applicant's training establishment. A maximum of two grants can be considered during the period of training

Removals and resettlement

Grants can be considered for:
▷ Serving clergy on taking up a new appointment, where costs are not covered by diocesan and other grants

▷ Clergy moving to the UK or Ireland from an overseas appointment (but only from the point of entry into the UK/Ireland)
▷ Clergy at the time of retirement, although any lump sum payable on retirement will be taken into account
▷ Retired clergy, widows/widowers, elderly unmarried daughters and separated or divorced spouses

Sabbaticals

▷ Grants towards sabbatical costs can be considered provided that the sabbatical is supported financially by the Diocese

Financial management courses

▷ Grants can be considered towards the costs of financial management courses for clergy where the relevant course is approved by the applicant's bishop or archdeacon

Annual grant total

In 2011 the charity had assets of £27 million and an income of £1.7 million. Grants to individuals totalled £1.1 million, broken down as follows:
▷ General welfare: £296,000
▷ Resettlement and house expenses: £176,000
▷ School fees: £195,000
▷ University maintenance: £111,000
▷ School clothing: £59,000
▷ Other education expenses: £159,000
▷ Ordinand book grants: £30,000
▷ Christmas: £31,000
▷ Debt: £5,400
▷ Bereavement: £5,600

Exclusions

Grants for any one purpose will not normally be awarded more frequently than annually. Holiday grants, however, will not normally be awarded more frequently than once every two years.

Grants are not normally made:
▷ To augment stipends or pensions
▷ In connection with the purchase of a house or flat
▷ In connection with the purchase or maintenance of motor vehicles (save in limited circumstances for applicants with disabilities)
▷ For the cost of fares or freight in connection with removals to or from the United Kingdom
▷ To reimburse litigation costs or other legal costs

Help for separated or divorced spouses can only be considered if the ordained spouse is still in Holy Orders.

The corporation does not make loans.

Applications

Application forms can be requested from the corporation via email, through which applicants must provide details of their request for a grant. All applications are means-tested.

Applications from non-stipendiary clergy or their dependents must be supported by the applicant's bishop or archdeacon, with details of the role performed by the relevant clergy person in his or her parish or diocese.

Other information

The Sons of the Clergy and the Friends of the Clergy have traditionally worked in conjunction with each other in their grant work. Since January 2005 the two charities have been working even more closely together in their grant administration following the establishment of a single body of trustees common to both organisations and a combined staff. As a result, it no longer matters whether an applicant applies to the Sons or to the Friends as there is a common application form for both charities and all applications are automatically considered by both organisations. The charities also submit joint accounts.

Sons of the Clergy CC number:207736

Friends of the Clergy CC number:207736.

The Foundation of Edward Storey

£152,000 (265 grants)

Correspondent: Timothy Burgess, Clerk to the Trustees, Storey's House, Mount Pleasant, Cambridge CB3 0BZ (01223 364405; email: info@edwardstorey.org. uk; website: www.edwardstorey.org.uk)

Trustees: Elizabeth Walser; Sue Young; Mrs J. Womack; Dr Michael Peter Halstead; Dr David Rubenstein; Richard John Smith; Nicky Blanning; Patricia Gail Clyne; Shelley Gregory Jones.

CC Number: 203653

Eligibility

'Financially unsupported' (i.e. single, separated, divorced or widowed) women who fall into either of two qualifying categories:

a) Women over 40 living within the county of Cambridgeshire

b) Widows, ex-wives or dependents of Church of England clergy; women priests, deacons or deaconesses of the Church of England; clergywomen, missionaries, or other women with a close professional connection with the Church of England.

Types of grants

Recurrent grants and pensions (which are annually reviewable and renewable). Pensions are usually only available to those over 60.

Annual grant total

In 2010/11 the foundation had assets of £12.4 million and an income of £1.3 million. Grants (£105,000) and pensions (£47,000) were made totalling £152,000.

Applications

On an application form available from the correspondent. Applications can be submitted directly by the individual or a family member (if sponsored by a suitable third party), through a third party such as a social worker, Diocesan Widows' Officers, Diocesan Visitors, clergy and so on, or through an organisation such as a Citizens Advice or other welfare agency. Applicants may be interviewed by the foundation's case officer. Applications are considered on a regular basis.

Other information

The trust also manages residential accommodation for local people and one grant (£1,500) was made to an organisation during the year.

The Thornton Fund

£7,500

Correspondent: Dr Jane Williams, 93 Fitzjohn Avenue, Barnet, Hertfordshire EN5 2HR (020 8440 2211)

Trustees: Dr David Wykes; Dr Doreen Williams; Jeffrey Teagle; Prof. Richard Booth; Revd Clifford Reed.

CC Number: 226803

Eligibility

Ministers and ministerial students of the Unitarian church and their families who are in need.

Types of grants

One-off grants ranging from £250 to £1,500. Recent grants have been given towards convalescence, counselling, replacement of equipment not covered by insurance and taxis for somebody unable to drive for medical reasons.

Annual grant total

Grants usually total around £15,000 per year.

Applications

In writing to the correspondent through a third party such as a minister. They are considered on an ongoing basis.

Other information

The fund occasionally makes grants to the general assembly of Unitarian and Free Christian Churches for special projects.

Torchbearer Trust Fund

£26,000

Correspondent: The Secretary, Capernwray Hall, Carnforth, Lancashire LA6 1AG (01524 733908; fax: 01524 736681; email: info@capernwray.org.uk; website: www.capernwray.org.uk)

Trustees: Alexander Thomas; Eveline Thomas; Susan Gilmore.

CC Number: 253607

Eligibility

People engaged in full-time Christian missionary work. Preference is given to students and former students of Torchbearer Bible schools.

Types of grants

One-off and recurrent grants according to need.

Annual grant total

In 2010/11 the fund had assets of £168,000 and an income of £45,000. Grants totalled £53,000.

Applications

In writing to the correspondent.

Other information

Grants are also available for missionary work.

Arthur Townrow Pensions Fund

£121,000 (166 grants)

Correspondent: P I King, Secretary, PO Box 48, Chesterfield, Derbyshire S40 1XT (01246 560560; website: www.townrowfund.org.uk)

Trustee: Revd Barry North.

CC Number: 252256

Eligibility

Women in need who are unmarried or widows, over 40 years of age and live in the Chesterfield and North-East Derbyshire areas. The fund specifies that the applicant should be 'of good character' and be a member of the Church of England or a Protestant dissenting church that acknowledges the doctrine of the Holy Trinity.

Types of grants

Recurrent grants of £60 a month are made to women who have an income below £8,000. One half of the pensions granted must be paid to unmarried women and widows living in Chesterfield, Bolsover and north east Derbyshire. The remaining grants may be paid anywhere in England but only to eligible unmarried women over the age of 40.

Annual grant total

In 2010/11 the fund had assets of £3.2 million which generated an income of £114,000. Annuities were paid to 166 individuals totalling £121,000.

Applications

On a form available from the correspondent. Applications should be submitted either directly by the individual or through a third party.

The Widows Fund

£45,000

Correspondent: Diane Naylor, Jardine Lloyd Thompson, St James House, 7 Charlotte Street, Manchester M1 4DZ

Trustees: Revd J. A. Midgley; Revd P. B. Godfrey; Revd P. L. Hughes; Revd John D. Allerton.

CC Number: 248657

Eligibility

Protestant ministers over 60 and their widows, widowers and children who are in need. Ministers who have been prevented from continuing in their ministries due to poor health or disability may also qualify for assistance.

Types of grants

Recurrent grants to supplement a low income and one-off emergency grants for specific purposes.

Annual grant total

In 2010 the fund had assets of £713,000 and an income of £33,000. Grants were made totalling £45,000, of which £42,000 was given in annuities and £2,500 in benevolent grants.

Applications

In writing to the correspondent.

Christian Science

The Morval Foundation

£83,000

Correspondent: Tricia Cullimore, Meadow Brook, Send Marsh Road, Ripley GU23 6JR (01372 210106)

Trustees: Timothy Rider; John Miller; Lindsey Taylor; Anne Priscilla Smart.

CC Number: 207692

Eligibility

Older Christian Scientists living in the UK who are members of The Mother Church, The First Church of Christ, Scientist in Boston, USA.

Types of grants

Monthly grants to allow older Christian Scientists to continue living independently in their own homes and one-off grants according to need.

Annual grant total

In 2010/11 the foundation had assets of £1.6 million and an income of £77,000. Grants to individuals were made totalling £83,000. Of this total £45,000 was paid in monthly grants to 18 recipients and £38,000 was one-off grants.

The foundation also administers two subsidiary charities, the New Chickering Fund and the Ruston Bequest. In 2010/11 the two charities contributed £38,000 to the grant total.

Applications

On a form available from the correspondent, to be submitted directly by the individual for consideration at any time.

Jewish

The AJR Charitable Trust

£1 million

Correspondent: Social Services Department, Jubilee House, Merrion Avenue, Stanmore, Middlesex HA7 4RL (020 8385 3070; fax: 020 8385 3080; email: enquiries@ajr.org.uk; website: www.ajr.org.uk)

Trustees: David Rothenburg; Andrew Kaufman; Frank Harding; Anthony Spiro; Eleanor Angel; Philippa Strauss.

CC Number: 211239

Eligibility

Jewish refugees from Nazi oppression, their dependents and descendants, who are settled in the UK. Potential applicants must be members of the Association of Jewish Refugees (AJR) or be eligible to become members and be willing to join the association.

Specific conditions attached to each fund:

- Homecare: applicants must not have income exceeding £10,000 or assets (not including their home or vehicle) exceeding £50,000
- Emergency Fund and Hungarian Scheme: applicants must not have income exceeding £10,000, or £14,000 for a couple, with few or no assets, excluding a car
- Austrian Programme: Austrian survivors (or spouses of Austrian nationals) who live on low incomes, under £11,000 for one person or

£15,000 for a couple, with limited assets (up to a maximum of £31,250)

Types of grants

The association administers emergency social, welfare and care funds on behalf of the Conference on Jewish Material Claims Against Germany, which can be used to pay for a number of services and essential items including dental treatment and specialist clothing as well as urgent house repairs, recuperative convalescence, respite breaks and homecare packages. Specifically these funds are:

- Homecare: the objective of the scheme is to assist clients to live in their homes for as long as possible. Homecare is assessed according to the client's functional capacity by a social worker. Homecare is funded by the German government and is only available to first generation clients. In exceptional circumstances second generation clients may be funded from the association's own funds
- Emergency Fund: grants of up to £2,000 (or £2,500 in exceptional cases) for essential items or services such as urgent house repairs, medical consultations, dental treatment or specialist clothing
- Austrian Holocaust Survivors Emergency Assistance Programme: financial assistance (up to a maximum of £10,000 in any twelve month period) for Austrian holocaust survivors on low incomes who require urgent medical attention or essential welfare services. Grants can be made for wheelchairs, disability aids, dental care, hearing aids etc. Assistance to buy into the Austrian social security pension scheme can also be given
- Hungarian Government Scheme: grants for essential items or services for Hungarian survivors

Annual grant total

In 2011 the association had assets of £14 million and an income of £2.3 million. Social work and welfare activities amounted to £1.9 million, of which £1 million was given in direct payments to beneficiaries.

Applications

Applications may be made by contacting the social work team by telephone.

Other information

The association provides support and advice on welfare benefits, foreign pension entitlements and reparations. It also has a day centre in Hampstead which runs entertainment programmes and serves Kosher lunches.

Carlee Ltd

£0

Correspondent: Secretary, 32 Paget Road, London N16 5NQ

Trustees: Hershel Grunhut; Pearl Grunhut; Bernard Dor Stroh; Blima Stroh.

CC Number: 282873

Eligibility

Jewish people in need.

Types of grants

One-off and recurrent grants according to need.

Annual grant total

No grants were given to individuals in 2010/11. Previously grants to individuals have totalled around £10,000.

Applications

In writing to the correspondent.

Other information

The main area of activity is grantmaking to organisations.

Chasdei Tovim Me'oros

£10,000

Correspondent: Yoel Bleier, Trustee, 17 Durlston Road, London E5 8RP (020 8806 2406)

Trustees: Yoel Bleier; Menachem Salamon.

CC Number: 1110623

Eligibility

People of the Jewish faith who are in need.

Types of grants

Grants given according to need for individuals and organisations.

Annual grant total

In 2010/11 the trust had an income and total expenditure of £20,000.

Applications

In writing to the correspondent.

Closehelm Ltd

£94,000

Correspondent: A Van Praagh, Trustee, 30 Armitage Road, London NW11 8RD (020 8201 8688)

Trustees: Mr A. Van Praagh; Hanna Rebecca Grosberg; Henrietta Wilhelmina Van Praagh.

CC Number: 291296

Eligibility

People of who are in need, but particularly people of the Jewish faith.

Types of grants

Grants and loans are given to needy families for housing, medical and other costs.

Annual grant total

In 2010/11 the trust had assets of £3.5 million and an income of £300,000. Grants were made totalling £94,000.

Applications

In writing to the correspondent.

Other information

This trust also gives to organisations.

The Engler Family Charitable Trust

£5,000

Correspondent: J Engler, Trustee, Motley Bank, South Downs Road, Bowdon, Altrincham WA14 3HB (email: jengleruk@yahoo.co.uk)

Trustees: J. Engler; Lydia Jane Peters; David Lee Scorah.

CC Number: 1108518

Eligibility

Members of the Jewish faith living in England or Wales.

Types of grants

Grants given according to need.

Annual grant total

About £5,000 a year.

Applications

In writing to the correspondent.

Other information

The trust also makes grants to Jewish organisations.

Finnart House School Trust

£11,000

Correspondent: Peter Shaw, Clerk to the Trustees, PO Box 603, Edgware, Middlesex HA8 4EQ (020 3209 6006; email: info@finnart.org; website: www.finnart.org)

Trustees: Mark Sebba; Robert Cohen; Hilary Blume; Anthony Yadgaroff; Linda Paterson; Sue Leiffer; Gideon Lyons; Gil Cohen.

CC Number: 220917

Eligibility

Young people of the Jewish faith who are in need through sickness or disadvantage. Priority is given to people over 16, although all applicants are considered.

Types of grants

Grants of between £100 and £1,000 to provide care or education.

Annual grant total

Funding is given to secondary schools to provide bursaries to students from low income families. In 2010/11 funding was given to two secondary schools in the UK totalling £11,000.

Exclusions

Only members of the Jewish faith can be supported.

Applications

On a form available from the correspondent. Applications must be submitted through a social worker or social welfare organisation and are considered three or four times a year. For information about the School Hardship Fund contact by email, telephone or letter.

Other information

This trust also gives grants for educational purposes and to organisations which work with children and young people of the Jewish faith who are in need.

Friends of Boyan Trust

Correspondent: Jacob Getter, Trustee, 23 Durley Road, London N16 5JW (020 8809 6051)

Trustees: Jacob Getter; Mordechai Freund; Nathan Kuflik.

CC Number: 1114498

Eligibility

People in need in the orthodox Jewish community.

Types of grants

Grants given according to need.

Annual grant total

In 2011 the trust had an income of £290,000 and made 'general grants' totalling £296,000 to both organisations and individuals. It was not possible to acquire a grants breakdown.

Applications

In writing to the correspondent.

Gur Trust

£7,000

Correspondent: The Trustees, 206 High Road, London N15 4NP (020 8801 6038)

Trustees: Sheldon Morgenstern; Mier Mandel; David Cymerman.

CC Number: 283423

Eligibility

People connected to the Jewish faith in the UK.

Types of grants

One-off and recurrent grants according to need.

Annual grant total

In 2010/11 the trust had assets of £1.4 million and an income of £40,000. Charitable expenditure totalled £34,000, to organisations and individuals.

Applications

'Funds are raised by the trustees. All calls for help are carefully considered and help is given according to circumstances and funds then available.'

Other information

The trust also makes grants to organisations and to individuals for educational purposes.

The Jewish Aged Needy Pension Society

£20,000

Correspondent: Sheila Taylor, Secretary, 34 Dalkeith Grove, Stanmore, Middlesex HA7 4SG (020 8958 5390)

Trustees: George Rigal; Margaret Hilda Rigal; Deborah Simon; Saul David Taylor; David Nicholas Rigal.

CC Number: 206262

Eligibility

Members of the Jewish community aged 60 or over, who have known better circumstances and have lived in the UK for at least ten years or are of British nationality.

Types of grants

Up to 60 pensions of up to £10 per week for all kinds of need.

Annual grant total

In 2010 the society had an income of £15,000 and a total expenditure of £24,000.

Applications

In writing to the correspondent. Applications are considered quarterly.

Kupath Gemach Chaim Bechesed Viznitz Trust

£262,000

Correspondent: Saul Weiss, Trustee, 171 Kyverdale Road, London N16 6PS (020 8442 9604)

Trustees: Israel Kahan; Saul Weiss; Alexander Pifco.

CC Number: 1110323

Eligibility

Members of the Jewish faith who are in need.

Types of grants

One-off and recurrent grants according to need.

Annual grant total

In 2010/11 the trust held assets of £46,000 and an income of £373,000, mainly from donations. Grants were made totalling £320,000, of which £57,000 was given to organisations and £262,000 to 'poor and needy' individuals.

Applications

In writing to the correspondent.

Mercaz Torah Vechesed Ltd

Correspondent: Joseph Ostreicher, Trustee, 28 Braydon Road, London N16 6QB (020 8880 5366)

Trustees: Joseph Ostreicher; Jacob Moishe Grosskopf; Mordche David Rand.

CC Number: 1109212

Eligibility

Members of the orthodox Jewish community who are in need.

Types of grants

One-off grants.

Annual grant total

In 2011/12 the charity had an income of £491,000. The majority of grants are made to organisations but funding for individuals is also available. Despite a written request a breakdown of grants was not available.

Applications

In writing to the correspondent.

MYA Charitable Trust

£5,000

Correspondent: Myer Rothfeld, Trustee, Medcar House, 149a Stamford Hill, London N16 5LL (020 8800 3582)

Trustees: Joseph Daniel Pfeffer; Myer Rothfeld; Eve Rothfeld; Hannah Schraiber.

CC Number: 299642

Eligibility

Individuals in need who are Jewish, worldwide.

Types of grants

One-off and recurrent grants according to need.

Annual grant total

In 2010/11 the trust had assets of £975,000 and an income of £257,000. Grants to individuals totalled £5,000 (£22,000 in 2010).

Applications

In writing to the correspondent.

Other information

The trust also makes grants to organisations (£117,000 in 2010/11).

The Chevras Ezras Nitzrochim

£169,000

Correspondent: H Kahan, Trustee, 53 Heathland Road, London N16 5PQ

Trustees: Hertz Kahan; Kurt Stern; Moshe Shmuel Rottenberg.

CC Number: 275352

Eligibility

Jewish people who are in need, with a focus on those living in the Greater London area. Help can also be given to individuals living further away.

Types of grants

One-off and recurrent grants according to need.

Annual grant total

In 2010 the trust had assets of £3,000 and an income of £204,000. Grants were made totalling £169,000.

Applications

In writing to the correspondent. Applications can be made at any time.

Other information

Grants are also made to organisations (£29,000 in 2010).

NJD Charitable Trust

£10,000

Correspondent: The Trustees, 35 Frognal, Hampstead, London NW3 6YD (020 7842 7306; email: info@igpinvest.com)

Trustees: Nathalie Louise Dwek; Jean Phillipe Glaskie; Jacob Wolf; Alexander Dwek.

CC Number: 1109146

Eligibility

Members of the Jewish faith who are in need.

Types of grants

One-off and recurrent grants according to need.

Annual grant total

In 2010/11 the trust had assets of £142,000 and an income of £100,000. Grants were made totalling £72,000. Grants are made to organisations and individuals.

Applications

In writing to the correspondent.

Norwood (formerly Norwood Ravenswood)

£55,000

Correspondent: The Chief Executive, Broadway House, 80–82 The Broadway, Stanmore, Middlesex HA7 4HB (020 8809 8809; email: info@norwood.org.uk; website: www.norwood.org.uk)

Trustees: Bernard Ian Myers; Ronnie Harris; Neville Kahn; David Ereira; Linda Goldberg; Gary Hilton Sacks; Ian Fagelson; Andrew Viner; David Goldstone; Elliott Goldstein; Estelle Ann Doctor.

CC Number: 1059050

Eligibility

People with learning disabilities and children and families in need. Beneficiaries are mostly Jewish although one-quarter of their clients are of mixed faith. This is a national trust but concentrates on London and the south east of England.

Types of grants

According to need, but no regular allowances. Grants towards the celebration of Jewish religious festivals, social need and occasional holidays.

Annual grant total

In 2010/11 the trust had assets of £14 million and an income of £34 million. Grants total about £55,000 each year.

Applications

Grants are recommended by Norwood staff. Initial contact should be made by phone or emailing socialwork@norwood.org.uk.

Other information

Grants are made in conjunction with a comprehensive welfare service. Norwood provides a range of social services for Jewish children and families, including social work, day facilities, residential and foster care.

Toras Chesed (London) Trust

£206,000

Correspondent: A Langberg, Trustee, 14 Lampard Grove, London N16 6UZ (020 8806 9589; email: ari@toraschesed.co.uk)

Trustees: Aaron Langberg; Akiva Stern; Simon Stern.

CC Number: 1110653

Eligibility

Members of the Jewish faith who are in need.

Types of grants

One-off and recurrent grants according to need.

Annual grant total

In 2010/11 the trust had an income of £223,000. Grants totalling £210,000 were paid to organisations. No grants were made to individuals during the year.

Applications

In writing to the correspondent. 'Applications for grants are considered by the trustees and reviewed in depth for final approval.'

Other information

Grants are also made to organisations.

The Benjamin Winegarten Charitable Trust

£20,000 (7 grants)

Correspondent: Benjamin Winegarten, 25 St Andrew's Grove, London N16 5NF (020 8800 6669)

Trustees: Esther Winegarten; Benjamin Winegarten.

CC Number: 271442

Eligibility

People involved in the advancement of the Jewish religion and religious education who are in social need.

Types of grants

One-off and recurrent grants according to need.

Annual grant total

In 2010 the trust had assets of £881,000, an income of £185,000 and gave £20,000 in seven grants to individuals

Applications

In writing to the correspondent.

The ZSV Trust

£570,000 (600 grants)

Correspondent: Z V I Friedman, 12 Grange Court Road, London N16 5EG

Trustees: Alta Mordechai Fogel; Aba Weinberger; Mr Z. Friedman.

CC Number: 1063860

Eligibility

Jewish people in need, particularly older people, refugees, orphans and families in distress.

Types of grants

One-off and recurrent grants according to need. Most of the trust's funds are spent on providing food parcels. Other recent grants have been given towards medical assistance, clothing, shoes and weddings.

Annual grant total

In 2010 the trust had assets of £57,000 and an income of £584,000. Grants to around 600 families totalled £570,000 and were broken down as follows:

Food parcels	£391,000
Relief of poverty	£92,000
Endowments to poor brides	£40,000
Families undergoing stress	£24,000
House repairs and utilities	£13,000
Clothing and shoes	£4,700
Youth activities	£4,300
Assistance with healthcare	£500

Applications

In writing to the correspondent. Individuals need to apply through social services or are often recommended by Rabbis or other community leaders.

Local charities

This section lists local charities that give grants to individuals for welfare purposes. The information in the entries applies only to welfare grants and concentrates on what the charity actually does rather than on what its trust deed allows it to do.

All the charities listed have a grant-making potential of £500 a year for individuals, but most give considerably more than this.

Regional classification

We have divided the UK into nine geographical areas, as numbered on the map on page 172. Scotland, Wales and England have been separated into areas or counties in a similar way to previous editions of this guide. On page 173, we have included the 'Geographical areas' list which shows the unitary and local authorities within each such area or county. (Please note: not all of these unitary or local authorities have a trust included in this guide.)

The Northern Ireland section has not been subdivided into smaller areas. Within the other sections, the trusts are ordered as follows.

Scotland:

- Firstly, the charities which apply to the whole of Scotland, or at least two areas in Scotland.
- Secondly, Scotland is sub-divided into five areas. The entries which apply to the whole area, or to at least two unitary authorities within, appear first.
- The rest of the charities in the area are listed in alphabetical order of unitary authority.

Wales:

- Firstly, the charities which apply to the whole of Wales, or at least two areas in Wales.
- Secondly, Wales is sub-divided into three areas. The entries which apply to the whole area, or to at least two unitary authorities within, appear first.
- The rest of the charities in the area are listed in alphabetical order of unitary authority.

England:

- Firstly, the charities which apply to the whole area, or at least two counties in the area.
- Secondly, each area is sub-divided into counties. The entries which apply to the whole county, or to at least two towns within it, appear first.
- The rest of the charities in the county are listed in alphabetical order of parish, town or city.

London:

- Firstly, the charities which apply to the whole of Greater London, or to at least two boroughs.
- Secondly, London is sub-divided into the boroughs. The entries are listed in alphabetical order within each borough.

In summary, within each county or area section, the trusts in Scotland and Wales are arranged alphabetically by the unitary or local authority which they benefit, while in England they are listed by the city, town or parish and in London by borough.

To be sure of identifying every relevant local charity, look first at the entries under the heading for your:

- Unitary authority for people in Scotland and Wales
- City, town or parish under the relevant regional chapter heading for people living in England
- Borough for people living in London

People in London should then go straight to the start of the London chapter, where trusts which give to individuals in more than one borough in London are listed.

Other individuals should look at the sections for trusts which give to more than one unitary authority or town before finally considering those trusts at the start of the chapter that make grants across different areas or counties in your country or region.

For example, if you live in Liverpool, first establish which region Merseyside is in by looking at the map on page 172. Then having established that Merseyside is in region 5, look at the 'Geographical areas' list on page 173 and see on which page the entries for Merseyside start. Then look under the heading for Liverpool to see if there are any relevant charities. Next check the charities which apply to Merseyside generally. Finally, check under the heading for the North West generally.

Having found the trusts covering your area, please read any other eligibility requirements carefully. While some trusts can and do give for any need for people in their area of benefit, most have other criteria which potential applicants must meet.

Geographical areas

Portishead; South Gloucestershire; Stanton Prior; Thornbury

Cornwall 357

Gunwalloe; Gwennap; Helston

Devon 359

Barnstaple; Bratton Fleming; Brixham; Brixton; Broadhempston; Budleigh Salterton; Colyton; Cornwood; Crediton; Culmstock; Dartmouth; Exeter; Exminster; Exmouth; Gittisham; Great Torrington; Highweek; Holsworthy; Honiton; Litton Cheney; Ottery St Mary; Paignton; Plymouth; Sandford; Sheepwash; Sidmouth; Silverton; South Brent; Sowton; Teignbridge; Topsham; Torbay; Torquay

Dorset 371

Blandford Forum; Charmouth; Christchurch; Corfe Castle; Dorchester; Poole; Shaftesbury; Wimborne Minster

Gloucestershire 374

Bisley; Charlton Kings; Cirencester; Gloucester; Minchinhampton; Tewkesbury; Wotton-under-Edge

Somerset 377

Axbridge; Bridgwater; Cannington; Draycott; Ilchester; Pitminster; Porlock; Rimpton; Street; Taunton; Wells

Wiltshire 380

Aldbourne; Ashton Keynes; Chippenham; East Knoyle; Salisbury; Swindon; Trowbridge; Westbury

8. South East 385

Bedfordshire 388

Bedford; Clophill; Dunstable; Flitwick; Husborne Crawley; Kempston; Potton; Ravensden; Shefford

Berkshire 391

Binfield; Datchet; Hedgerley; Newbury; Reading; Sunninghill

Buckinghamshire 394

Aylesbury; Bletchley; Calverton; Cheddington; Emberton; Great Linford; High Wycombe; Hitcham; Radnage; Stoke Poges; Stony Stratford; Water Eaton; Wolverton

Cambridgeshire 398

Cambridge; Chatteris; Downham; Elsworth; Ely; Grantchester; Hilton; Ickleton; Landbeach; Little Wilbraham; Pampisford; Peterborough; Sawston; Soham;

Stetchworth; Swaffham Bulbeck; Swavesey; Walsoken; Whittlesey; Whittlesford; Wisbech

East Sussex 403

Battle; Brighton and Hove; Eastbourne; Hastings; Mayfield; Newick; Rotherfield; Rye; St Leonards-on-Sea; Warbleton

Essex 406

Braintree; Broomfield; Chigwell and Chigwell Row; Dovercourt; East Bergholt; East Tilbury; Halstead; Harlow; Hutton; Saffron Walden; Springfield; Thaxed

Hampshire 410

Brockenhurst; Fareham; Gosport; Hawley; Hordle; Isle of Wight; Lyndhurst; New Forest; Portsmouth; Ryde; Southampton

Hertfordshire 417

Buntingford; Dacorum; Harpenden; Hatfield; Letchworth Garden City; Watford; Wormley

Kent 420

Borden; Canterbury; Chatham; Dover; Folkstone; Fordwich; Gillingham; Godmersham; Gravesham; Hayes; Herne Bay; Hildenborough; Hothfield; Hythe; Leigh; Maidstone; Margate; Rochester; Sevenoaks; Tunbridge Wells; Wilmington

Norfolk 428

Banham; Barton Bendish; Beeston; Burnham Market; Buxton with Lammas; Diss; Downham Market and Downham West; East Dereham; East Tuddenham; Feltwell; Foulden; Garboldisham; Gayton; Gaywood; Harling; Hilgay; Horstead with Stanninghall; Little Dunham; Lyng; Marham Village; Northwold; Norwich; Old Buckenham; Pentney; Saham Toney; Saxlingham; Shipdham; South Creake; Swaffham; Swanton Morley; Walpole; Watton; Welney; West Walton; Wiveton; Woodton; Wretton

Oxfordshire 438

Bletchington; Eynsham; Great Rollright; Henley-on-Thames; Over Norton; Oxford; Sibford Gower; Souldern; Steventon; Wallingford; Wheatley

Suffolk 443

Aldeburgh; Brockley; Bungay; Carlton and Calton Colville; Chediston; Chelsworth; Corton; Dennington; Dunwich; Earl Stonham; Framlingham; Gisleham; Gislingham; Halesworth; Ipswich; Kirkley; Lakenheath; Lowestoft; Melton; Mendlesham; Mildenhall;

Pakenham; Reydon; Risby; Rushbrooke; Stanton; Stowmarket; Stutton; Sudbury; Walberswick

Surrey 450

Abinger; Ashford; Betchworth; Bisley; Bletchingley; Bramley; Byfleet; Capel; Charlwood; Cheam; Chertsey; Chessington; Chobham; Crowhurst; Dunsfold; East Horsley; Effingham; Egham; Epsom; Esher; Guildford; Hascombe; Headley; Horne; Kingston-upon-Thames; Leatherhead; Leigh; Newdigate; Nutfield; Ockley; Oxted; Pirbright; Shalford; Shottermill; Staines; Stoke D'Abernon; Thorpe; Thursley; West Clandon; West Horsley; West Molesey; Weybridge; Woking; Worplesdon; Wotton

West Sussex 464

Crawley; Horsham; Midhurst; Wisborough Green

9. London 467

Northern Ireland

The Belfast Association for the Blind

£16,000

Correspondent: R Gillespie, Hon. Secretary, 30 Glenwell Crescent, Newtownabbey, County Antrim BT36 7TF (02890 836407)

IR Number: XN45086

Eligibility
People who are registered blind in Northern Ireland. Consideration may also be given to those registered as partially sighted.

Types of grants
One-off grants of towards holidays, house repairs, visual aids and so on. Grants are also given for educational purposes.

Annual grant total
Previously around £16,000 was given in grants to individuals.

Applications
In writing to the correspondent through a social worker. Applications are considered throughout the year.

Other information
Grants are also made to organisations.

The Belfast Central Mission

£15,000

Correspondent: Janet Sewell, Community Services Manager, Grosvenor House, 5 Glengall Street, Belfast BT12 5AD (02890 241917; fax: 02890 240577; email: csm@ belfastcentralmission.org; website: www. belfastcentralmission.org)

Eligibility
Children and older people who are in need and live in Greater Belfast.

Types of grants
One-off gifts of food parcels and toys at Christmas. Around 1900 toy parcels and 1000 food parcels are distributed every Christmas.

Annual grant total
Approximately £15,000 worth of donations and gifts in kind.

Applications
On a form available from the correspondent. Applications are considered in October and November.

Other information
This charity also runs advice centres and residential homes.

The Belfast Sick Poor Fund

£5,000 (18 grants)

Correspondent: Grants Officer, c/o Bryson House, 28 Bedford Street, Belfast BT2 7FE (02890 325835; fax: 02890 439156)

Eligibility
Families in Northern Ireland with children aged under 18 who are in poor health or who have a disability and are in receipt of benefits or on a low income and who are in need.

Types of grants
One-off grants ranging from £50 to £200 for necessities and comforts.

Annual grant total
Grants usually total about £5,000 each year.

Applications
In writing to the correspondent by a social worker or other health professional. The fund cannot accept self-referrals. Applications should include: background information on the applicant with a breakdown of needs; why the request is being made; how a grant will benefit the applicant; details of income and expenditure on a weekly or monthly basis; and details of other sources of financial assistance and outcomes of any applications.

Other information
The fund derives its income from BBC Children in Need who have been a long-term sponsor.

The Community Foundation for Northern Ireland

£10,000

Trustees: Les Allamby; Maurna Crozier; Geraldine Donaghy; Brian Dougherty; Sammy Douglas; Dr Jeremy Harbison; Julie Knight; Dr Mike Morrissey; Stephanie Morrow; Tony McCusker; Conal McFeely; Tayra McKee; Anne McReynolds; Hilary Sidwell; Colin Stutt; John R. Healy; Kevin Kingston.

Eligibility
McKibbin Fund: grants to young people in Northern Ireland with physical or learning disabilities or who are affected by illness.

Types of grants
McKibbin Fund: grants for equipment, outings, residential breaks and tutoring.

Annual grant total
Grants from the McKibbin fund average around £10,000 per year.

Applications
Apply online on the foundation website. There is one standard application form used for all funds.

Like all Community Foundations, funds may open and close at short notice. Check the website before starting an application.

The Londonderry Methodist City Mission

£1,500

Correspondent: Fund Administrator, Mission Office, Clooney Hall Centre, 36 Clooney Terrace, Londonderry BT47 6AR (02871 348531; fax: 02871 348531; email: office@clooneyhall.org.uk; website: www.methodistcitymission.com)

Eligibility

People in need who live in Derry/ Londonderry and the surrounding area.

Types of grants

One-off grants according to need up to £500 per application.

Annual grant total

Grants usually total around £1,500.

Applications

In writing to the correspondent. Applications can be submitted directly by the individual or family member, through an organisation such as Citizens Advice or through a third party such as a social worker. References are required to support applications made directly by individuals.

Other information

The trust has a specific interest in the homeless and runs a hostel for homeless men.

The Newtownabbey Methodist Mission

£10,000

Correspondent: The Administrator, 35a Rathcoole Drive, Newtownabbey, County Antrim BT37 9AQ (02890 852546; fax: 02890 859956; email: nhamilton@ newtownabbeymethodist.org.uk; website: newtownabbeymethodist.org.uk/)

Eligibility

Socially disadvantaged children, adults, families and older people who live in Rathcoole and the surrounding area and Newtownabbey.

Types of grants

One-off grants for food, clothing and fuel bills throughout the year, and food/ toy parcels at Christmas.

Annual grant total

Grants usually total around £10,000 per year.

Applications

By personal application or through a referral by a minister of religion, social worker or Citizens Advice at any time.

Other information

The mission also has a playgroup, a charity shop and provides hot meals for older people.

The Presbyterian Old Age Fund, Women's Fund and Indigent Ladies Fund

£126,000 (105 grants)

Correspondent: The Secretary, Presbyterian Church in Ireland, Assembly Buildings, Fisherwick Place, Belfast BT1 6DW (02890 322284; email: bsw@presbyterianireland.org; website: www.pcibsw.org)

Eligibility

Needy, elderly or infirm members of the Presbyterian Church who live at home in any part of Ireland.

Types of grants

An annual grant of £1,100 was paid in quarterly instalments. Grants of £275 were sent to every beneficiary in the run up to Christmas. One-off grants are also made to help in cases of immediate financial need.

Annual grant total

In 2010 105 people received grants totalling £126,000.

Applications

In writing through a minister to the correspondent. Applications are considered in January, April, June and October.

Other information

The Women's Fund and Indigent Ladies Fund are administered with the Old Age Fund.

The Church's Board of Social Witness runs a full social care programme spanning family and child care, older people's services, criminal justice, learning difficulties, mental health and disability.

The Presbyterian Orphan and Children's Society

£250,000

Correspondent: Dr Paul Gray, Glengall Exchange, 3 Glengall Street, Belfast BT12 5AB (02890 323737; fax: 02890 434352; email: paul-gray@ presbyterianorphanandchildrenssociety. org; website: www. presbyterianorphanandchildrenssociety. org)

Trustees: His Honour J. McKee; Revd P. P. Campbell; Dr G. D. B. Harkness; Mr B. Corry; Revd T. R. Graham; Very Revd Dr S. Hutchinson; Mrs V. McGuffin; Revd P. A. McBride; Mr N. W. Todd; Judge J. A. H. Martin; Mrs L. Yates; Mrs W. R. Wilson; Mr R. Orr; Revd Dr.J. I. Thompson; Mrs H. Morrow.

IR Number: XN45522

Eligibility

Children aged 23 or under who are in full or part-time education, living in Northern Ireland and Republic of Ireland, usually in single parent families. One parent must be a Presbyterian.

Types of grants

Regular grants paid each quarter. Depending on financial resources, a summer grant and Christmas grant is paid to each family. Exceptional grants of up to £300 (very occasionally up to £500) are also available.

Annual grant total

Around £500,000 per year. Grants are also given for educational purposes.

Applications

Applications are made by Presbyterian clergy; forms are available from the correspondent or to download from the website. They are considered in April and October. As recurrent grants are means tested, applications should be submitted with details of the applicant's income and expenditure. Any application for an exceptional grant must be made on the 'Exceptional Grant' application form.

The Protestant Orphan Society for the Counties of Antrim and Down (Inc)

£70,000

Correspondent: Jane Butler, Secretary, Church of Ireland House, 61–67 Donegall Street, Belfast BT1 2QH (02890 322268; website: connor.anglican.org/)

Eligibility

Orphaned children who live in the counties of Antrim or Down and who are members of the Church of Ireland.

Types of grants

Annual grants of up to £500 and one-off bereavement grants of £1,000 to a family on the death of a parent.

Annual grant total

Around £70,000 is available each year.

Exclusions

No grants to applicants living outside the beneficial area.

Applications

Applications can be made at any time through the clergy of the parish in which the individual lives. Direct applications cannot be considered.

The Retired Ministers' House Fund

£150,000

Correspondent: Ian McElhinly, Secretary, Presbyterian Church in Ireland, Assembly Buildings, Fisherwick Place, Belfast BT1 6DW (02890 322284; website: www.presbyterianireland.org)

Eligibility
Retired full-time members and servants of the Presbyterian Church in Ireland, and those contemplating retirement.

Types of grants
Provision of rented accommodation, equity sharing arrangements and loans.

Annual grant total
About £150,000, although this varies each year.

Exclusions
The fund does not distribute one-off grants.

Applications
In writing to the correspondent. Applications are considered as they arrive.

The Royal Ulster Constabulary – Police Service of Northern Ireland Benevolent Fund

£800,000

Correspondent: The Secretary, Police Federation for Northern Ireland, 77–79 Garnerville Road, Belfast BT4 2NX (02890 764215; email: info@ rucbenevolentfund.org; website: www. rucgc-psnibenevolentfund.com)

IR Number: XN 48380

Eligibility
Members and ex-members of the Royal Ulster Constabulary and their dependents who are experiencing financial hardship. The main objectives being to look after widows and their dependents, injured and disabled officers, pensioners, parents of deceased officers and serving PSNI officers experiencing financial hardship or difficulty.

Types of grants
One-off and recurrent grants and loans according to need. The fund offers a wide range of assistance including adventure holidays for children, short breaks for widows, convalescence for injured officers and financial help when required.

Annual grant total
Around £800,000 per year.

Exclusions
No grants for NHS treatment. Loans will not be provided for cases of personal debt.

Applications
Initial contact should be made with the central point of contact who will advise the applicant on which of the police organisations is most appropriate to offer support in their circumstances. Contact may be made by calling 02890 768686 or emailing office@northernirelandpolicefamilyassist-ance.org.uk with a brief outline of your circumstances. All applicants will be visited by a fund representative in order to prepare a case to present to the committee at their monthly meeting.

Other information
The fund also owns and operates eighteen apartments in Portrush for the benefit of its ex-members, hosts organised outings and events throughout the year for widows and is actively involved in supporting local voluntary welfare groups. Eligibility and booking information on the holiday apartments can be found on the website.

The Society for the Orphans and Children of Ministers and Missionaries of the Presbyterian Church in Ireland

£15,000

Correspondent: Paul Gray, Church House, Fisherwick Place, Belfast BT1 6TW (02890 323737)

Eligibility
Children and young people aged under 26 who are orphaned and whose parents were ministers, missionaries or deaconesses of the Presbyterian Church in Ireland.

Types of grants
One-off grants of £300 to £2,000 for general welfare purposes.

Annual grant total
Grants to individuals for educational and welfare purposes total about £30,000.

Applications
On a form available from the correspondent. Applications should be submitted directly by the individual in March for consideration in April.

Other information
The trust also gives educational grants to the children of living ministers and missionaries.

The Sunshine Society Fund

£5,000

Correspondent: Grants Administrator, c/o Bryson House, 28 Bedford Street, Belfast BT2 7FE (02890 325835; fax: 02890 439156)

Eligibility
Families in Northern Ireland with children aged under 18 who are ill, disabled or facing financial hardship.

Types of grants
One-off grants for necessities and comforts. Only a small number of grants (no more than 20) are made each year.

Annual grant total
Around £5,000 is available each year for grants.

Applications
In writing to the correspondent by a social worker or other health care professional. Applications should include: background information on the applicant with a breakdown of needs; why the request is being made; how a grant will benefit the applicant; details of income and expenditure on a weekly or monthly basis; and details of other sources of financial assistance and outcomes of any applications.

Scotland

General

The Adamson Trust

£36,000 (80 grants)

Correspondent: Edward Elworthy, PO Box 26334, Creiff, Perthshire PH7 9AB (07770 842502; fax: 01764 682359; email: edward@elworthy.net)

SC Number: SC016517

Eligibility

Children aged 17 or under who have a physical or mental disability.

Types of grants

Grants range from £150 to £5,000 and are given to help with the cost of a holiday or respite break. Grant recipients must take the trip before their 18th birthday.

Annual grant total

In 2010/11 the trust had an income of £69,000. Grants to 80 individuals totalled £36,000 while a further £26,000 was made in grants to schools and organisations.

Exclusions

No grants can be given towards the costs of accompanying adults.

Applications

On a form available from the correspondent, to be returned with: details of the planned holiday; booking confirmations (if possible); and information about the child beneficiary. All applications are considered by the trustees four times a year in February, May, August and November with closing dates of 31 December, 31 March, June and 30 September respectively.

Other information

The trust also makes grants to schools and organisations.

The Aged Christian Friend Society of Scotland

£700

Correspondent: Allan Sim, Johnston Smillie Ltd, 2 Roseburn Terrace, Edinburgh EH12 6AW (01313 177377; website: www.acfsos.org.uk)

SC Number: SC016247

Eligibility

Christians in need living in Scotland who are over 60 years of age.

Types of grants

Pensions of about £200 a year.

Annual grant total

In 2011 the society had an income of £311,000 and a total expenditure of £302,000.

Applications

In writing to the correspondent outlining need.

Other information

The society is now a company limited by guarantee. Its principal activity is the provision of sheltered housing for older people in Scotland.

The Airth Benefaction Trust

£20,000

Correspondent: Douglas Hunter, HBJ Gateley Wareing, Exchange Tower, 19 Canning Street, Edinburgh EH3 8EH (01312 282400; fax: 01312 229800; email: info@gateleyuk.com)

SC Number: SC004441

Eligibility

People in need in Edinburgh.

Types of grants

Recurrent grants and pensions are available up to £120.

Annual grant total

In 2010 the trust had an income of £25,000 and a total expenditure of £26,000.

Applications

On a form available from the correspondent to be submitted either directly by the individual or through a third party such as a social worker. These should be returned not later than 30 September for consideration in December. Beneficiaries are invited to reapply each year.

The Avenel Trust

£5,000

Correspondent: Administrator, 23 West Ferryfield, Edinburgh EH5 2PT

SC Number: SC014080

Eligibility

Children in need under 18 and students of nursery nursing living in Scotland.

Types of grants

One-off grants of £10 to £500 are given for safety items such as fireguards and safety gates, shoes, clothing, bedding, cots and pushchairs, money for bus passes, recreational activities for young carers and washing machines.

Annual grant total

In 2010 the trust had an income of £11,000. Grants are made for welfare and education.

Exclusions

Grants are not given for holidays or household furnishings.

Applications

Applications are considered every two months and should be submitted through a tutor or third party such as a social worker, health visitor or teacher. Applicants are encouraged to provide as much information about their family or individual circumstances and needs as possible in their applications. Applications can only be accepted from people currently residing in Scotland.

The Benevolent Fund for Nurses in Scotland

£150,000

Correspondent: Mrs A Davidson, Liaison Officer, 1 Lufra Bank, Edinburgh EH5 1BS (07584 322257; email: annedavidson40@yahoo.com; website: www.bfns.org.uk)

SC Number: SC006384

Eligibility

Nurses who have worked or were trained in Scotland and are experiencing financial difficulties.

Types of grants

One-off and quarterly grants to applicants with limited income owing to illness or disability, or in the case of retired nurses, those with little or no superannuation pension. The fund can also help by buying furnishings or equipment.

Annual grant total

In 2010 the association had an income of £167,000. Grants usually total about £150,000 a year.

Applications

Application forms, available from the correspondent, can be submitted by the individual or through a recognised referral agency (social worker, Citizens Advice, doctor and so on) and are considered as they are received. The trust may decide to visit potential beneficiaries.

The Biggart Trust

£9,500

Correspondent: Andrew S Biggart, McClay Murray and Spens, 1 George Square, Glasgow G2 1AL (01412 485011; fax: 01412 485819)

SC Number: SC015806

Eligibility

People in need, with preference for people related to the founders and their descendants.

Types of grants

One-off and recurrent grants (half-yearly), ranging from £600 to £1,100.

Annual grant total

In 2010/11 the trust has an income of £9,800.

Applications

In writing to the correspondent, directly by the individual.

Other information

The trust also makes grants to organisations.

The Blyth Benevolent Trust

£10,500

Correspondent: Trust Administrator, Bowman Solicitors, 27 Bank Street, Dundee DD1 1RP (01382 322267; fax: 01382 225000)

SC Number: SC017188

Eligibility

Women aged over 60 and in need. Preference is given to people who are blind or partially-sighted with the surname Bell or Blyth, and who live in or are connected with Newport-on-Tay, Fife or Dundee.

Types of grants

Annuities paid twice a year of £65. A Christmas bonus may be paid, if funds permit.

Annual grant total

In 2010/11 the trust had an income of £11,200.

Applications

In writing to the correspondent to be submitted either directly by the individual, through a third party such as a social worker, or through an organisation such as a Citizens Advice or other welfare agency.

Boath and Milne Trust

£3,500

Correspondent: The Trustees, Wilkie and Dundas Solicitors, 28 Marywell Brae, Kirriemuir, Angus DD8 4BP (01575 572608; email: admin@wdws.co.uk)

SC Number: SC016861

Eligibility

Bakers and their dependents resident in Angus.

Types of grants

Grants of around £90 each.

Annual grant total

In 2011 the trust had an income of £7,200.

Applications

There is a local press advertisement each year and further information can be gained from the correspondent.

The Buchanan Society

£25,000

Correspondent: The Secretary, 1F Pollockshields Square, Glencairn Drive, Pollockshields, Glasgow G41 4QT

SC Number: SC013679

Eligibility

Only people with the following surnames: Buchanan, McAuslan (any spelling), McWattie or Risk.

Types of grants

Pensions for older people in need. One-off grants can also be given.

Annual grant total

In 2010 the society had an income of £51,000. Around 70 people are supported each year. Grants are also made for educational purposes.

Applications

On a form available from the correspondent, to be submitted either directly by the individual or a family member, or through a third party such as a social worker or teacher. Applications are considered throughout the year.

Other information

The Buchanan Society is the oldest Clan Society in Scotland having been founded in 1725. Grantmaking is its sole function.

Challenger Children's Fund

£73,000

Correspondent: John Ritchie, Barstow and Miller CA, Midlothian Innovation Centre, Pentlandfield, Roslin, Midlothian EH25 9RE (01313 128508; email: info@ccfscotland.org; website: www.ccfscotland.org)

SC Number: SC037375

Eligibility

The trust aims to help any child in Scotland under the age of 18 years living with a disability through a physical impairment of the musclo-skeletal, neurological or cardio-respiratory system of the body

The following conditions on their own however, are not accepted: psychiatric disorders, learning disabilities, behavioural disorders, development delay, Down's Syndrome, autism, visual or hearing impairment, cancer, diabetes, epilepsy, HIV, back pain and chronic fatigue syndrome.

Types of grants

One-off grants averaging £250 but consideration is given to grants as large as £500. More may be granted in some circumstances. Grants can be given towards anything which is not provided by statutory sources and have previously included holidays, specialised equipment, a washing machine, clothing, fridges, beds and so on. In case of a holiday grant, if it is essential that a child must be accompanied, consideration will be given to the cost.

Annual grant total

In 2010/11 the trust had an income of £76,000. Grants to individuals totalled around £73,000.

Exclusions

Grants cannot be made retrospectively. Only one application per year.

Applications

On a form which can be obtained from the correspondent or via the website. Applications should be sponsored by a social worker, GP, health visitor, district nurse or therapist. Trainee workers and community care assistants may also apply, but a qualified person must countersign the application. Grants are given to the agency sponsoring the application, or company the purchase(s) are being made from. They cannot be given direct to the child or child's family. Applications can be submitted once a year.

The Craigcrook Mortification

£30,000 (23 grants)

Correspondent: Fiona Watson, Scott-Moncrieff, Exchange Place, 3 Semple Street, Edinburgh EH3 8BL (01314 733500; fax: 01314 733535; website: www.scott-moncrieff.com)

SC Number: SC001648

Eligibility

People in need who are over 60 and were born in Scotland or have lived there for more than ten years.

Types of grants

Pensions of between £1,000 and £1,500 per annum payable in half-yearly instalments. One-off payments are not available.

Annual grant total

About £30,000 is available for distribution each year.

Exclusions

Assistance is not normally given to those living with relations or in nursing homes.

Applications

On a form available from the correspondent or to download from the website. Applications should be supported by a minister of religion, doctor, bank manager, lawyer or similar professional.

Other information

The trust has limited capacity to take on new applicants.

The Educational Institute of Scotland Benevolent Fund

£100,000

Correspondent: The General Secretary, Educational Institute of Scotland, 46 Moray Place, Edinburgh EH3 6BH (01312 256244; fax: 01312 203151; email: enquiries@eis.org.uk; website: www.eis.org.uk)

SC Number: SC007852

Eligibility

Members of the institute suffering from financial hardship due to unexpected illness, long-term health problems or a sudden change in financial circumstances and their widows/widowers and dependents. Applicants must have held a membership for at least one year prior to application.

Types of grants

One-off and recurrent grants towards, for example, daily living costs, television licences, telephone rental, hairdressing and holidays. Emergency grants may also be available to members who have had an arrestment on their salary, who face eviction, or who have had their gas or electricity cut off.

Annual grant total

In 2010/11 the fund had an income of £179,000 and a total charitable expenditure of £100,000.

Applications

On a form available from the correspondent or a local EIS association. More information is available on the members' section of the EIS website. Meetings are normally held in January, March, May, June, September and November. Applications should be received two weeks prior to a meeting.

The Faculty of Advocates 1985 Charitable Trust

£51,000

Correspondent: Gaynor Adam, Secretariat Officer, Advocate's Library, Parliament House, Edinburgh EH1 1RF (01312 265071)

SC Number: SC012486

Eligibility

1. Widows, widowers, children or former dependents of deceased members of the Faculty of Advocates.
2. Members of the faculty who are unable to practise by reason of permanent ill health.

Types of grants

Single grants, annuities or loans appropriate to the circumstances.

Annual grant total

In 2010/11 the trust had an income of £124,000 and a total expenditure of £93,000. Grants totalled £51,000.

Applications

The trust is regularly publicised among members and applications are often informal, by word of mouth via a trustee. Alternatively applications may be made in writing to the correspondent.

The Hugh Fraser Foundation (Emily Fraser Trust)

£30,000

Correspondent: Heather Thompson, Turcan Connell, Princes Exchange, 1 Earl Grey Street, Edinburgh EH3 9EE (01312 288111; fax: 01312 288118; email: ht@turcanconnell.com)

SC Number: SC009303

Eligibility

People in need who work or worked in the drapery, printing, publishing, bookselling, stationery and newspaper and allied trades and their dependents. The trustees consider applications particularly from individuals who are or were in the employment of House of Fraser Ltd, Scottish Universal Investments Ltd and Paisleys.

Types of grants

One-off grants of £100 to £4,000.

Annual grant total

In 2010/11 the trust had an income of £1.8 million. Grants to individuals usually total about £30,000 each year.

Applications

In writing to the correspondent. The trustees meet on a quarterly basis, normally in January, April, July and October. Applications should be received one month before the meeting.

Note the foundation's focus is on making grants to charitable organisations and only in exceptional circumstances will the trustees consider applications from individuals and their dependents.

Other information

The Emily Fraser Trust has recently merged with the Hugh Fraser Foundation and been removed from the Scottish Charity Register.

The Glasgow Society of the Sons and Daughters of Ministers of the Church of Scotland

£28,000

Correspondent: Janice Couper, Exchange Place, 3 Semple Street, Edinburgh EH3 8BL (website: www. scott-moncrieff.com/charitable_trusts)

SC Number: SC010281

Eligibility

Children of ministers of the Church of Scotland who are in need, particularly students and the children of deceased ministers.

Types of grants

One-off and recurrent grants according to need.

Annual grant total

About £55,000 a year is given in educational and welfare grants to individuals.

Applications

On a form available from the correspondent or downloaded from the website. Applications from children of deceased ministers may apply at any time.

Other information

In 2011 fourteen children of deceased Ministers were supported, each receiving between £1,350 and £2,950.

The Douglas Hay Trust

£45,000

Correspondent: John D Ritchie, Barstow and Millar, Midlothian Innovation Centre, Pentlandfield, Roslin, Midlothian EH25 9RE (01314 409030; fax: 01314 409872; email: enquiries@barstowmillar. com; website: www.douglashay.org.uk)

SC Number: SC014450

Eligibility

Children aged under 18 who are physically disabled and live in Scotland.

Types of grants

One-off grants ranging from £40 to £500 towards shoes, clothes, bedding, home improvements, holidays, computers, equipment and education.

Annual grant total

In 2010/11 the trust had an income of £45,000 and a total expenditure of £54,000.

Applications

On a form available from the website or by contacting the correspondent. To be submitted through a social worker, medical practitioner or other welfare agency. Applications are considered monthly.

The Anne Herd Memorial Trust

£12,000

Correspondent: The Trustees, Bowman Solicitors, 27 Bank Street, Dundee DD1 1RP (01382 322267; fax: 01382 225000)

SC Number: SC014198

Eligibility

People who are blind or partially sighted who live in Broughty Ferry (applicants from the city of Dundee, region of Tayside or those who have connections with these areas and reside in Scotland will also be considered).

Types of grants

Grants are usually given for educational equipment such as computers and books. Grants are usually at least £50.

Annual grant total

In 2010/11 the trust had an income of £29,000. The trust gives approximately £25,000 a year in grants for both welfare and education.

Applications

In writing to the correspondent, to be submitted directly by the individual in March/April for consideration in June.

June and Douglas Hume Memorial Fund

£8,500

Correspondent: Jennifer McPhail, Empire House, 131 West Nile Street, Glasgow G1 2RX (01413 414964; fax: 01413 414972; email: Online contact form; website: www.scottishcf.org)

SC Number: SC022910

Eligibility

Terminally ill patients who wish to spend their final days in their own home. Grants may be made throughout Scotland, however, priority is given to applications from the West Coast, Highlands and Islands.

Types of grants

One-off grants of up to £1,000 to assist patients with specialist equipment, as well as any house modifications necessary to accommodate such equipment. Grants may be used for bath and stair lifts, reclining beds and chairs, wheelchairs and zimmers, for example.

Annual grant total

In 2011/12 the fund had a total expenditure of £9,000.

Applications

Applicants should contact Jennifer McPhail on 01413 414964 in the first instance and an application form will be sent out to applicants where funds are available. Applications completed by the applicant must be accompanied by a reference from a GP or consultant. Alternatively the application may be filled out directly by a medical professional. Applications are considered as they are received.

Other information

The fund is administered by the Scottish Community Foundation.

William Hunter Old Men's Fund

£10,000

Correspondent: The Trustees, Edinburgh Chamber of Commerce, Ground Floor, Capital House, 2 Festival Square, Edinburgh EH3 9SU (01312 212999)

SC Number: SC010842

Eligibility

Older men in need who were born in Scotland and are of Scottish parentage and who are/were merchants, manufacturers or master tradesmen.

Types of grants

Recurrent grants paid twice a year of £370 for people under 80, and £385 for those over 80.

Annual grant total

In 2010/11 the fund had an income of £13,000.

Applications

In writing to the correspondent.

The George Jamieson Fund

£100

Correspondent: The Trustees, Wilsone and Duffus, 7 Golden Square, Aberdeen AB10 1EP (01224 651700; email: info@key-moves.co.uk; website: www.key-moves.co.uk)

SC Number: SC007537

Eligibility

Widows and single women who are in need and live in the city of Aberdeen or the counties of Aberdeen and Kincardine.

Types of grants

Recurrent grants.

Annual grant total

In 2010/11 the fund had an income of £9,200 and a total expenditure of £120.

Applications

In writing to the correspondent. Applications can be submitted directly by the individual or through a social worker, Citizens Advice or other welfare agency. Applications should include details of circumstances and are considered on a regular basis.

Jewish Care Scotland

£1,000

Correspondent: Irene Black, Office Manager, The Walton Community Care Centre, May Terrace, Giffnock, Glasgow G46 6LD (01416 201800; fax: 01416 202409; email: admin@jcarescot.org.uk; website: www.jcarescot.org.uk)

Trustees: Maureen Solomons; David Bishop; George Hecht; Trevor Schuster-Davis; Lesley Roles; Natalie Cahif; Sylvia Cohen; Angela Hecht; Paul Morron; Oli Norman; Vivian Strang; Albert Tankel.

SC Number: SC005267

Eligibility

Jewish people in need living in Scotland.

Types of grants

One-off grants of £50 to £750 towards clothing, food, household goods, rent, holidays, equipment, travel and education.

Annual grant total

Welfare grants total around £1,000 each year.

Applications

In writing to the correspondent.

Other information

The board also helps with educational costs and friendship clubs, housing requirements, clothing, meals-on-wheels, counselling and so on.

Key Trust

£400

Correspondent: The Trustees, c/o Key Housing, Savoy Tower, 77 Renfrew Street, Glasgow G2 3BZ (01413 421890; fax: 01413 327498; email: info@keyhousing.org)

SC Number: SC006093

Eligibility

People living in Scotland who are in need due to age, ill health or disability.

Types of grants

One-off grants according to need. Recent grants have been given to help people setting up home, for example, towards furnishings such as carpets and to enable people to gain independence and 'experience more out of life'.

Annual grant total

In 2010/11 the trust had an income of £400.

Applications

On a form available from the correspondent, submitted either directly by the individual or through a social worker, Citizens Advice or other welfare agency.

John A. Longmore's Trust

£18,000

Correspondent: Robin D Fulton, Trustee, Turcan Connell, Princes Exchange, 1 Earl Grey Street, Edinburgh EH3 9EE (01312 288111; fax: 01312 288118; email: rdf@turcanconnell.com)

SC Number: SC007336

Eligibility

People who live in Scotland and have an incurable disease.

Types of grants

Annuities of £330 in two instalments. One-off grants of up to £1,000 to improve the quality of life on a day-to-day basis. Equipment sought can be either fixed or moveable such as a wheelchair.

Annual grant total

Grants usually total around £18,000 per year.

Exclusions

No grants are given towards holidays or house decoration.

Applications

On a form available from the correspondent, to be returned with a covering letter detailing income and expenses of the household and a breakdown of how the grant will be used. Applications are considered in the third week of every month and should be submitted by the 16th of the month. However, the trustees have informed us that the trust is still suffering from an income deficit and trustees are therefore not in a position to consider applications at this time.

The Agnes Macleod Memorial Fund

£3,400

Correspondent: Linda Orr, Secretary, Nurses Cottage, Hallin, Waternish, Isle of Skye IV55 8GJ (email: linda@m-orr.freeserve.co.uk; website: www.clan-macleod-scotland.org.uk)

SC Number: SC014297

Eligibility

Women in need who are over 60, living in Scotland and were born with the name Macleod or whose mothers were born Macleod.

Types of grants

To provide monetary grants or donations of gift vouchers when benefits from the state are either not sufficient or not appropriate. Grants range from £100 to £250 and are one-off.

Annual grant total

In 2010/11 the fund had an income of £3,700.

Applications

In writing to the correspondent. Advertisements are also put in newspapers. Applications are considered in May and November. Doctors, social workers, Citizens Advice, other welfare agencies, health visitors, ministers and priests may also submit applications on behalf of an individual.

The McLaren Fund for Indigent Ladies

£73,000

Correspondent: Rosina M Dolan, BMK Wilson, Second Floor, 90 St Vincent Street, Glasgow G2 5UB (01412 218004; fax: 01412 218088; email: rmd@bmkwilson.co.uk)

Trustees: Robert C. Robinson; P. Maureen Reid; Alasdair Robinson; Revd I. Patricia Lang.

SC Number: SC004558

Eligibility

To benefit widows and unmarried women over 40. Priority is given to women who are:
i) widows and daughters of officers in the Highland Regiment;
ii) widows and daughters of Scotsmen.

Types of grants

Annual pensions, one-off grants, holiday grants and Christmas gifts according to need.

Annual grant total

In 2011 the trust held assets of £2.2 million and had an income of £100,000. Pensions of £400 were paid to 91 individuals during the year. Along with one-off, holiday and Christmas grants total grant expenditure came to £73,000.

Applications

On a form available from the correspondent. Applications to be made throughout the year for consideration when the trustees meet in March, July and December. Beneficiaries' payments are reviewed annually at the discretion of the trustees. All applicants will be visited.

The George McLean Trust

£5,000

Correspondent: Grants Administrator, Blackadders Solicitors, 30–34 Reform Street, Dundee DD1 1RJ (01382 229222; fax: 01382 342220; email: enquiries@blackadders.co.uk)

SC Number: SC020963

Eligibility

People in need who are living with a mental or physical disability and reside in Fife and Tayside. Older people may also qualify for assistance.

Types of grants

Grants are made towards convalescence, hospital expenses, electrical goods, clothing, holidays, travel expenses, medical equipment, nursing fees, furniture, disability aids and help in the home.

Annual grant total

In 2009/10 the trust had an income of £29,000. Grants are made annually totalling about £25,000.

Exclusions

No grants are made towards debts.

Applications

On a form available from the correspondent. Applications can be submitted directly by the individual or through any third party. They are considered monthly.

Other information

The trust also makes grants to organisation. In the past around 20% of total grant expenditure has gone to individuals, although this may change in the future as grants are made entirely at the discretion of trustees.

The Annie Ramsay McLean Trust for the Elderly

£3,000

Correspondent: The Trustees, Blackadders Solicitors, 30–34 Reform Street, Dundee DD1 1RJ (01382 229222; fax: 01382 342220; email: toni.mcnicoll@blackadders.co.uk)

SC Number: SC014238

Eligibility

People aged 60 or over who live in Fife and Tayside.

Types of grants

One-off and recurrent grants of £100 to £1,000 towards needs such as convalescence, travel expenses, furniture, clothing, medical and disability equipment, electrical goods, holidays, nursing home fees, help in the home, household items, electrically operated chairs, motorised scooters and so on.

Annual grant total

In 2010/11 the trust had an income of £41,000. Previously grants to individuals have totalled around £3,000.

Exclusions

No grants are given towards debts.

Applications

On a form available from the correspondent. Applications can be submitted directly by the individual or thorough any third party. They are considered monthly.

North of Scotland Quaker Trust

£4,000

Correspondent: Marion Strachan, Treasurer, Quaker Meeting House, 98 Crown Street, Aberdeen AB11 6HJ

SC Number: SC000784

Eligibility

People who are associated with the Religious Society of Friends in the North of Scotland Monthly Meeting area, namely Aberdeen City, Aberdeenshire, Moray, Highland, Orkney, Shetland, Western Isles and that part of Argyll and Bute from Oban northwards.

Types of grants

One-off and recurrent grants according to need.

Annual grant total

In 2011 the trust had an income of £15,000 and an expenditure of £9,500.

Exclusions

No grants are given to people studying above first degree level.

Applications

In writing to the correspondent.

Other information

Grants are also given for educational purposes.

The Nurses' Memorial to King Edward VII Edinburgh Scottish Committee

£60,000

Correspondent: Secretaries and Treasurers, Johnston Smillie Ltd, Chartered Accountants, 2 Roseburn Terrace, Edinburgh EH12 6AW (01313 177377)

SC Number: SC023963

Eligibility

Nurses with a strong connection to Scotland (including nurses who have worked in Scotland, or Scottish nurses working outside Scotland) who are retired, ill or otherwise in need. Retired nurses are given priority.

Types of grants

One-off and monthly grants towards accommodation charges, domestic bills and to supplement inadequate income.

Annual grant total

In 2011 the trust had an income of £115,000. Between 50 and 60 nurses are usually supported each year, with grants totalling around £60,000.

Applications

Details of present financial and other circumstances are required on a form available from the correspondent. The information given should be confirmed by a social worker, health visitor, doctor or similar professional.

The Mrs Jean Panton and Miss Anne Stirling Trust

£3,000

Correspondent: John Stuart, General Synod, 21 Grosvenor Crescent, Edinburgh EH12 5EE (01312 256357)

SC Number: SC016939

Eligibility

Ministers or pastors (not bishops) of the Scottish Episcopal Church who were born in Scotland and have small incomes.

Types of grants

One-off grants are given to supplement the individual's regular income.

Annual grant total

Grants usually total around £3,000 per year.

Applications

In writing via bishops of the dioceses, who are the trustees and recommend ministers in need. Ministers cannot apply directly.

Poppyscotland (The Earl Haig Fund Scotland)

£770,000

Correspondent: Charitable Services Department, New Haig House, Logie Green Road, Edinburgh EH7 4HR (01315 501557; email: GetHelp@ poppyscotland.org.uk; website: www. poppyscotland.org.uk)

SC Number: SC014096

Eligibility

People in Scotland who have served in the UK Armed Forces (regular or reserve) and their widows/widowers and dependents.

Types of grants

Annual and one-off grants towards household items, medicine, respite breaks, mobility aids, travel expenses, clothing, living costs, home repairs and so on.

Annual grant total

In 2010/11 the fund had an income of £4.2 million. Grants were made to 1,360 individuals totalling £799,000, mostly for welfare purposes.

Exclusions

Grants are not normally given towards non-priority debt, headstones or the replacement of medals. Loans are not available.

Applications

In the first instance applicants should contact the correspondent or complete a 'request for assistance' form (available to download from the website). A representative from SSAFA Forces Help will then visit the individual to assess the level of need and complete any further forms. Applications can be made at any time.

Other information

Poppyscotland is in many respects the Scottish equivalent of the benevolence department of the Royal British Legion in the rest of Britain. Like the legion, it runs the Poppy Appeal, which is a major source of income to help those in need. There is, however, a Royal British Legion Scotland, which has a separate entry in this guide. The two organisations share the same premises and work together.

In 2006 the Earl Haig Fund Scotland launched a new identity – 'Poppyscotland' – and is now generally known by this name.

Radio Forth Cash for Kids

£200,000

Correspondent: Wendy Pearson, Charity Coordinator, Forth House, Forth Street, Edinburgh EH1 3LE (01314 751332; website: www.forthonline.co.uk)

Eligibility

Children under the age of 18 who have a disability or are disadvantaged and live in Edinburgh, the Lothians and Fife.

Types of grants

Grants are given towards clothing, hospital expenses and medical and disability equipment.

Annual grant total

Grants have previously totalled around £200,000.

Exclusions

Generally holidays are not funded except for in exceptional circumstances.

Applications

Application forms are available from the correspondent or to download from the website. A letter of support is required from a GP, health visitor, social worker, occupational therapist or other professional involved with the child who can support the claim. Trustees meet four times a year to consider applications.

Radio Tay Cash for Kids

£75,000

Correspondent: Lynda Curran, Cash for Kids, 6 North Isla Street, Dundee DD3 7JQ (01382 423263 or 01382 423285; email: lynda.curran@radiotay.co. uk; website: www.tayfm.co.uk)

Eligibility

Children and young people aged under 18 who are in need and live within Radio Tay's transmission area (Dundee, Angus, Perth and North East Fife).

Types of grants

One-off grants of £50 to £5,000 towards needs such as clothing, beds, bedding, holidays, disability equipment and so on.

Annual grant total

Grants totalled £150,000. Grants are made to both organisations and individuals.

Exclusions

Grants are not made to pay salaries or rent.

Applications

On a form available from the correspondent or to download from the website. Applications must be submitted with a letter of reference from a social worker, doctor, minister or health visitor. Grants are awarded quarterly and applications are accepted as follows:
- January for grants allocated in February
- April for grants allocated in May
- July for grants allocated in August
- October for grants allocated during November

The Royal Society for Home Relief to Incurables, Edinburgh (General Fund)

£130,000 (224 grants)

Correspondent: Fiona Watson, Scott-Moncrieff, Exchange Place 4, Semple Street, Edinburgh EH3 8BL (01314 733500; fax: 01314 733535; website: www.scott-moncrieff.com/charitable_ trusts/page10.html)

SC Number: SC004365

Eligibility

Adult people throughout Scotland under retirement age, who have earned a livelihood (or been a housewife) and are no longer able to do so because of an incurable illness.

Types of grants

An annuity is given quarterly (totalling £540 per year) to help provide extra comforts.

Annual grant total

About £130,000 is available for distribution each year.

Exclusions

No one-off grants.

Applications

On a form available to download from the website. Trustees meet four times a year to consider applications.

Sailors' Orphan Society of Scotland

£50,000

Correspondent: Joyce Murdoch, 18 Woodside Crescent, Glasgow G3 7UL (01413 532090; fax: 01413 532190; website: www.sailorsorphansociety.co.uk)

SC Number: SC000242

Eligibility

Dependents of seafarers who are or may be in a position of need either through disadvantage or through death or incapacity of one or both of their parents and, to provide support to disadvantaged young people within seafaring communities in Scotland.

Children must be under 16 or in full-time education if over 16.

Types of grants

Monthly grants of around £80 per child as well as two additional payments in July and December. One-off grants may also be paid at the trustees' discretion.

Annual grant total

In 2010/11 the trust had an income of £95,000. Grants usually total about £50,000.

Applications

On an application form available to download from the website. Applications should include a reference from a third party who can confirm the disadvantage suffered or the death or incapacity of a parent.

Scotscare

£338,000

Correspondent: Isabel Dunlop, Team Leader- Caseworkers, 22 City Road, London EC1Y 2AJ (020 7240 3718; fax: 020 7256 6527; email: info@scotscare.com; website: www.scotscare.com)

Trustees: John Clemence; Staurt Steele; P. Scott; Peter Hay; Wylie Crawford White; Angus Gilroy; Fred Gray; Jock Meikle; Brian Griffin; David Couchtrie; Eben Hamilton; Etienne Duval; James Chestnut; Joyce Harvie; Graeme Wilson; Amanda Brock.

CC Number: 207326

Eligibility

Scottish people, and their children and widows, who are in need, hardship or distress and live within a 35-mile radius of Charing Cross. Beneficiaries are usually in receipt of state benefits.

Types of grants

The trust gives weekly allowances to older people, one-off grants to people unable to improve their circumstances, help with respite holidays, outings and social events, household essentials, sheltered housing and help to come off benefits.

Annual grant total

In 2010/11 the organisation had assets of £45 million and an income of £2.1 million. Grants to 1,346 individuals totalled £388,000, most of which was given for welfare purposes.

Exclusions

No grants are made for debts or for items that have already been purchased.

Applications

On a form available by contacting the organisation. After receiving the completed form, which should include copies of the birth/wedding certificates, the corporation decides whether to submit the application for consideration at the trustees' monthly meeting. They may also decide to visit or ask the applicant to visit the corporation's office to discuss their case.

Other information

The organisation also runs a helpline: 0800 652 2989.

The Scottish Artists' Benevolent Association

See entry on page 66

The Scottish Association of Master Bakers' Benevolent Fund

£8,000

Correspondent: Grants Administrator, Atholl House, 4 Torphichen Street, Edinburgh EH3 8JQ

SC Number: SC010444

Eligibility

Members or ex-members of the Scottish Association of Master Bakers and their families who are in need. Other members of the Scottish baking industry may also be supported.

Types of grants

One-off grants of up to £700 towards electrical goods, household repairs, repayment of small debts and so on.

Annual grant total

In 2010 the association had an income of £9,000.

Applications

On a form available from the correspondent.

The Scottish Chartered Accountants' Benevolent Association

£60,000

Correspondent: Robert Linton, Secretary, Robert Linton and Co., Suite 30, 2nd Floor, 53 Bothwell Street, Glasgow G2 6TS (01415 728465; fax: 01412 487456; email: mail@robertlinton.co.uk)

SC Number: SC008365

Eligibility

Members of the Institute of Chartered Accountants of Scotland who are in need, and their dependents.

Types of grants

One-off and recurrent grants for a variety of needs. Recent grants have been given for hospital travel costs, house repairs, general living expenses, mobility aids, retraining and home help.

Annual grant total

Grants usually total about £120,000 each year.

Applications

An initial letter or telephone call should be made to the correspondent. A member of the fund will then make contact and arrange a visit if appropriate. Following this, an application, report and recommendation will be made to the fund's council for approval.

Other information

Grants are also given for educational purposes.

The Scottish Cinematograph Trade Benevolent Fund

£15,000

Correspondent: The Secretary, c/o Grant Thornton, Scottish Legal Life Building, 95 Bothwell Street, Glasgow G2 7JZ (01412 230000; email: info@sctbf.co.uk; website: www.sctbf.co.uk)

SC Number: SC001786

Eligibility

People in need who are, or have been, working in the cinema industry in Scotland for at least two years.

Types of grants

One-off and recurrent grants for living costs, household essentials, 'Aid Call' systems and convalescence.

Annual grant total

In 2010 the fund had an income of £6,000. Previously grants were made totalling about £15,000.

Applications

In writing to the correspondent. Applications can be submitted either directly by the individual, or through a social worker, Citizens Advice or other welfare agency or third party.

Other information

The fund also offers advice on state benefits and pensions and employs a welfare visitor.

Scottish Grocers' Federation Benevolent Fund

£14,000

Correspondent: John Drummond, Federation House, 222–224 Queensferry Road, Edinburgh EH4 2BN (01313 433300; fax: 01313 436147; email: info@scottishshop.org.uk)

SC Number: SC014216

Eligibility

Past members or employees of the grocery trade in Scotland who are in need.

Types of grants

One-off grants or recurrent grants distributed quarterly totalling £900 a year.

Annual grant total

In 2010 the fund had an income of £18,000. Grants have previously totalled about £14,000.

Applications

On a form available from the correspondent. Applicants are then visited to assess the most appropriate form of help.

The Scottish Hide and Leather Trades' Provident and Benevolent Society

£10,000

Correspondent: David Ballantine, c/o Mitchells Roberton Solicitors, George House, 36 North Hanover Street, Glasgow G1 2AD (01415 523422; fax: 01415 522935; email: info@mitchells-roberton.co.uk)

SC Number: SC004504

Eligibility

People of retirement age who have worked in the Scottish hide and leather trades.

Types of grants

The society exists principally to provide pensions to its members. It also pays pensions to the widows and widowers of members who have survived their pensionable spouse. Donations equivalent to the annual pensions are also paid to people who have been employed in the trades but who are not members. Very occasionally one-off payments of about £100 to £200 are made for specific purposes, usually for the replacement of household equipment, such as a washing machine, fridge and so on.

Annual grant total

Grants usually total about £10,000 each year.

Applications

Most applicants have been recommended by other members of the society or local organisations.

Scottish Hydro Electric Community Trust

£0

Correspondent: The Trust Secretary, 200 Dunkeld Road, Inveralmond House, Perth PH1 3AQ (01738 455154; fax: 01738 455281; website: www.scottish-southern.co.uk)

SC Number: SC027243

Eligibility

People living in the Scottish Hydro Electric supply area. Grants can be given for domestic properties and properties used for not-for-profit community projects. Domestic properties must be the sole residence of the applicant.

Types of grants

Grants are given towards the costs of domestic electricity connections. Grants are awarded at the trustees' discretion and range from a few hundred pounds to a few thousand, however the usual level is 30% of the connection cost.

Annual grant total

In 2010/11 the trust had an income of £93,000. No further information was available concerning grants total.

Exclusions

Applications for holiday homes or second homes will not be considered.

Applications

On a form available from the correspondent or to download from the website. Applications should be submitted directly by the individual and are considered about three times a year.

Other information

Grants are also given to community ventures for electricity connections.

The Scottish National Institution for the War-Blinded

£1.4 million

Correspondent: Richard Hellewell, Chief Executive and Secretary, PO Box 500, Gillespie Crescent, Edinburgh EH10 4HZ (01312 291456; email: enquiries.warblinded@royalblind.org; website: www.royalblind.org/warblinded)

Trustees: Douglas A. Osler; David C. Dunn; Iain C. Lumsden; Gordon W. Banks; James Cook; Margery M. Browning; Dr Brian Fleck; Lorraine Grady; David Johnston; Gwenn McCreath; Alex Scott; Kenneth D. Reid; Margaret M. Sibbald; Cllr Conor Snowden; Peter Stephenson; Janice Sugden; Glen Waddell.

SC Number: SC002652

Eligibility
Visually impaired ex-service personnel who live in Scotland.

Types of grants
Mainly regular monthly grants for aftercare and workshop allowances. Occasional hardship grants are also given.

Annual grant total
In 2010/11 the trust had assets of £54 million and an income of £2.8 million. Approximately £1.4 million was given in veterans' grants.

Applications
Through the Workshops and After-Care Department (Tel: 01313 331369). Applications are considered as required.

The Scottish Nautical Welfare Society

£56,000

Correspondent: Mrs Gail Haldane, Administrator, 937 Dumbarton Road, Glasgow G14 9UF (01413 372632; fax: 01413 372632; email: gvsa@hotmail.com)

SC Number: SC032892

Eligibility
Active, retired and disabled seafarers with ten years in service who are in need and their widows.

Types of grants
Recurrent quarterly grants of £156.

Annual grant total
In 2010/11 the trust had an income of £127,000. Grants have previously totalled £56,000.

Applications
In writing to the correspondent.

Other information
This society was established in April 2002 as an amalgamation of Glasgow Aged Seaman Relief Fund, Glasgow Seaman's Friend Society and Glasgow Veteran Seafarers' Association.

Scottish Prison Service Benevolent Fund

£15,000

Correspondent: The Governor, H M Prison, South Road, Peterhead AB42 2YY

SC Number: SC021603

Eligibility
Scottish prison officers, both serving and retired, and their families who are in need.

Types of grants
One-off and recurrent grants according to need.

Annual grant total
In 2010/11 the trust had an income of £23,000. About £15,000 is distributed in grants annually.

Applications
In writing to the correspondent.

Scottish Secondary Teachers' Association Benevolent Fund

£0

Correspondent: General Secretary, West End House, 14 West End Place, Edinburgh EH11 2ED (01313 137300; fax: 01313 468057; email: info@ssta.org.uk; website: www.ssta.org.uk)

SC Number: SC011074

Eligibility
Members and retired members of the association and in certain circumstances their dependents who are in need.

Types of grants
Recurrent grants, generally limited to a period of six months, to help members through a period of long-term illness or other difficulty. One-off grants may also be given.

Annual grant total
No financial information was available.

Applications
In writing to the correspondent, submitted directly by the individual or through a third party. Applicants are asked to provide details of their financial circumstances.

The Scottish Solicitors' Benevolent Fund (incorporating The Scottish Law Agents' Society Benevolent Fund)

£20,000

Correspondent: The Secretary, c/o Sheridans Solicitors, 166 Buchanan Street, Glasgow G1 2LW (01413 323536; fax: 01413 533819; email: secretary@slas.co.uk; website: www.slas.co.uk)

SC Number: SC000258

Eligibility
People in need who are or were members of the solicitor profession in Scotland and their dependents. Grants are generally awarded to minor dependent children, widows and widowers of solicitors who practised in Scotland and have died. Help is given to practising solicitors who are in need.

Types of grants
One-off and recurrent grants according to need.

Annual grant total
In 2009/10 the fund had an income of £21,000. Grants were made totalling around £20,000.

Applications
On a form available to download from the fund's website, including financial details and two referees.

Dr J. R. Sibbald's Trust

£4,000

Correspondent: Carol Gourlay, Brodies, 15 Atholl Crescent, Edinburgh EH3 8HA (01312 283777; fax: 01312 283878)

SC Number: SC001055

Eligibility
Adults living in Scotland who have an incurable disease and who are in financial need.

Types of grants
Usually £140 a year payable in two instalments in May and November. Occasional one-off grants are given in exceptional circumstances.

Annual grant total
Grants to individuals usually total about £4,000 per year.

Applications
On a form available from the correspondent. Applications should be accompanied by a certificate from a surgeon or physician giving full details of the disease and certify that in their opinion it is incurable. As much background information about the applicant as possible is also required which can be in the form of a letter from a social worker or friend describing the family circumstances and giving other personal information. Applications should be submitted by 15 November for consideration in late November/early December.

The Miss M. O. Taylor and Alexander Nasmyth Funds

£9,000

Correspondent: Bruce Laidlaw, Administrative Secretary, Royal Scottish Academy, The Mound, Edinburgh EH2 2EL (01312 256671; fax: 01312 206016; email: info@ royalscottishacademy.org; website: www. royalscottishacademy.org)

SC Number: SC007352/SC004198

Eligibility

Scottish artists of established reputation in painting, sculpture, architecture or engraving who are in need. To be eligible you must have had some previous experience of success in the profession, e.g. have exhibited and sold work with a recognised gallery or institution.

Types of grants

One-off payments of up to £1,000.

Annual grant total

The Nasmyth Fund is registered separately from the Taylor Fund which is held as fund within the Royal Scottish Academy. Despite requests a full, combined grant total was unavailable at the time of writing (Winter 2012). The Nasmyth Fund had an income of £10,000 and expenditure of £9,000 in 2010/11 and the RSA had a total grant expenditure of £152,000 in the same period, although this covers other funding programmes.

Applications

Application forms are available from the correspondent. The deadline is usually early June, check the website for the exact date.

Mrs S. H. Troughton Charitable Trust

£6,000

Correspondent: Laura Gosling, 4th Floor, Swan House, 17–19 Stratford Place, London W1C 1BQ (020 7907 2100; email: charity@mfs.co.uk)

Trustee: The Dickinson Trust Ltd.

CC Number: 265957

Eligibility

People in need who receive a pension and live on the estates of Ardchatten in Argyll, and Blair Atholl.

Types of grants

One-off and recurrent grants ranging from £400 to £600.

Annual grant total

In 2010/11 the trust had an income of £10,400 and a total expenditure of £13,000.

Exclusions

Grants are not given to people whose income is £1,000 above their personal allowance for income tax.

Applications

In writing to the correspondent at any time by the individual or via a third party such as a social worker or through an organisation such as a Citizens Advice or other welfare agency. Unsuccessful applications will not be acknowledged. The trust has stated that funds are fully committed until the end of 2014 and so it will not be in a position to consider any new applications until after this point.

Other information

The trust also makes grants to organisations.

The Eliza Haldane Wylie Fund

£10,000

Correspondent: Shona Brown, Trust Administrator, Balfour and Manson LLP, 54–66 Frederick Street, Edinburgh EH2 1LS (01312 001200; fax: 01312 001300)

SC Number: SC011882

Eligibility

People in need who are related to or associated with Eliza Haldane Wylie or her family and 'gentlefolk of the middle class' in need.

Types of grants

Small one-off payments.

Annual grant total

In 2010/11 the fund had an income of £14,000 and no reported expenditure. In previous years grant expenditure has averaged around £10,000.

Applications

In writing to the correspondent.

Aberdeen and Perthshire

The Neil Gow Charitable Trust

£10,000

Correspondent: A G Dorward, Miller Hendry, 10 Blackfriars Street, Perth PH1 5NS (01738 637311; fax: 01738 638685)

SC Number: SC012915

Eligibility

People in need who live in the district of Perth and Kinross or the immediate neighbourhood.

Types of grants

Annuities of around £90 each, paid quarterly.

Annual grant total

In 2010/11 the trust had an income of £11,400.

Applications

In writing to the correspondent.

Grampian Police Diced Cap Charitable Fund

£20,000

Correspondent: The Secretary, Grampian Police, Queen Street, Aberdeen AB10 1ZX (email: dicedcap@ grampian.pnn.police.uk; website: www. dicedcap.org)

SC Number: SC017901

Eligibility

People in need who live in the Grampian police force area.

Types of grants

One-off and recurrent grants to improve the health and well being of any deserving persons.

Annual grant total

In 2010/11 the fund had an income of £102,000. Grants usually total about £50,000, although most of this is given to organisations.

Applications

In writing to the correspondent.

Other information

This trust also gives grants to organisations.

The Gertrude Muriel Pattullo Trust for Handicapped Boys

£4,000

Correspondent: Toni McNicoll, Blackadders Solicitors, 30–34 Reform Street, Dundee DD1 1RJ (01382 229222; fax: 01382 342220; email: toni.mcnicoll@ blackadders.co.uk)

SC Number: SC015505

Eligibility

Boys aged 18 or under who are living with a physical disability and have resided in the city of Dundee or the county of Angus.

Types of grants

Gifts in kind and one-off cash grants. Recent grants have been given for electrical goods, clothing, hospital expenses, holidays, medical and disability equipment, travel expenses, furniture, nursing fees, help in the home and so on.

Annual grant total

Grants usually total about £4,000 each year.

Exclusions

No grants are given towards repayment of debts.

Applications

On a form available from the correspondent at any time. Applications can be submitted directly by the individual or through a social worker, Citizens Advice or other welfare agency.

Other information

Grants are also made to organisations.

The Gertrude Muriel Pattullo Trust for Handicapped Girls

£5,000

Correspondent: Mrs Beth Anderson, Blackadders Solicitors, 30–34 Reform Street, Dundee DD1 1RJ (01382 229222; fax: 01382 342220; email: toni.mcnicoll@ blackadders.co.uk)

SC Number: SC011829

Eligibility

Girls aged 18 years or under who have physical disabilities and live in the city of Dundee or the county of Angus.

Types of grants

One-off grants ranging from £100 to £500 for electrical goods, clothing, hospital expenses, holidays, medical and disabled equipment, travel expenses, furniture, nursing fees, help in the home and so on.

Annual grant total

In 2010/11 the trust had an income of £6,100. No further information was available.

Exclusions

No grants are given for the repayment of debts.

Applications

On a form available from the correspondent at any time. Applications can be submitted directly by the individual or through a social worker, Citizens Advice, or other welfare agency. Applications are considered monthly.

Other information

Grants are also made to organisations.

The Gertrude Muriel Pattullo Trust for the Elderly

£4,000

Correspondent: Toni McNicoll, Blackadders Solicitors, 30–34 Reform Street, Dundee DD1 1RJ (01382 229222; fax: 01382 342220; email: toni.mcnicoll@ blackadders.co.uk)

SC Number: SC004966

Eligibility

Older people (i.e. generally those of state pensionable age), especially those living with a disability, resident in the city of Dundee and county of Angus.

Types of grants

One-off grants for general welfare purposes. Recent grants have included help towards house adaptation and a grant to purchase a portable cylinder.

Annual grant total

Grants usually total about £4,000 each year.

Exclusions

No grants are given for debt repayment.

Applications

On a form available from the correspondent at any time. Applications can be submitted either directly by the individual or through a third party such as a social worker.

Other information

Grants are also given to organisations.

Shepherd Trust

£2,000

Correspondent: The Trustees, Wilsone and Duffus, 7 Golden Square, Aberdeen AB10 1EP (01224 651700)

SC Number: SC000112

Eligibility

Widows and daughters (aged over 25) of deceased merchants, shopkeepers or other businessmen who have lived in Aberdeen for at least 25 years.

Types of grants

One-off and recurrent grants according to need.

Annual grant total

Grants usually total about £2,000 each year.

Applications

In writing to the correspondent through a social worker, Citizens Advice or other third party.

Aberdeen and Aberdeenshire

Aberdeen Indigent Mental Patients' Fund

£4,000

Correspondent: Alan Innes, Peterkins Solicitors, 100 Union Street, Aberdeen AB10 1QR (01224 428000)

SC Number: SC003069

Eligibility

People who live in Aberdeen and are, or have been, mentally ill on their discharge from hospital.

Types of grants

One-off and recurrent grants according to need.

Annual grant total

In 2011 the fund had an income of £4,500. No further information was available

Applications

In writing to the correspondent.

The Aberdeen Widows' and Spinsters' Benevolent Fund

£40,000

Correspondent: Trust Administrator, c/o Raeburn Christie Clark and Wallace, 12–16 Albyn Place, Aberdeen AB10 1PS (01224 332400; fax: 01224 332401)

SC Number: SC002057

Eligibility

Widows and unmarried women over 60 years of age who live in the city or county of Aberdeen; in cases of special need and where surplus income is available, those between 40 and 60 are considered.

Types of grants

Generally yearly allowances of up to £360 paid in two instalments in June and December.

Annual grant total

In 2010/11 the fund had an income of £44,000 and a total expenditure of £45,000. Grants usually total around £40,000.

Applications

On a form available from the correspondent.

The James Allan of Midbeltie Trust

£55,000

Correspondent: Michael D McMillan, Burnett and Reid, 15 Golden Square, Aberdeen AB10 1WF (01224 644333; fax: 01224 632173; email: mdcmillan@ burnett-reid.co.uk)

SC Number: SC003865

Eligibility

Widows who live in Aberdeen and are in need.

Types of grants

Recurrent yearly allowances of around £300 a year payable in two instalments in May and November.

Annual grant total

In 2010/11 the trust had an income of £50,000 and a total expenditure of £65,000.

Applications

On a form available from the correspondent. Applications can be submitted either directly by the individual, through a third party such as a social worker or through an organisation such as Citizens Advice or another welfare agency. Applications are usually considered in April and October.

The Braemar Charitable Trust

£2,000

Correspondent: The Trustees, Coilacriech, Ballater, Aberdeenshire AB35 5UH (01339 755377)

SC Number: SC007892

Eligibility

People in need who live in the parish of Braemar.

Types of grants

Grants of about £25 each are given for a variety of purposes, including medical equipment.

Annual grant total

Grants usually total about £2,000 each year.

Applications

In writing to the correspondent: normally in November for consideration in December. The trust requires information about the applicant detailing their personal circumstances, age etc.

Dr John Calder Trust

£2,000

Correspondent: Clive Phillips, 21 Ferryhill Place, Aberdeen AB11 7SE

SC Number: SC004299

Eligibility

People in need who live in the parish of Machar, or within the city of Aberdeen.

Types of grants

This trust deals primarily with educational grants, although relief-in-need grants can be considered.

Annual grant total

Around £2,000 is available for individuals. A further £8,000 is given in grants towards educational projects or organisations.

Applications

The trust stated in January 2006 that funds were fully committed and that this situation was likely to remain so for the medium to long-term.

Other information

This trust also gives grants for educational purposes and to organisations.

The George, James and Alexander Chalmers Trust

£50,000

Correspondent: Grant Administrator, 2 Bon Accord Crescent, Aberdeen AB11 6DH (01224 587261)

SC Number: SC008818

Eligibility

Women living in Aberdeen who have fallen on hard times as a result of misfortune and not through any fault of their own.

Types of grants

Recurrent grants of about £450 a year, payable in half-yearly instalments.

Annual grant total

In 2010/11 the trust had an income of £113,000. Grants usually total about £50,000.

Applications

On a form available from the correspondent.

Other information

Regular grants are also made to organisations.

The Gordon Cheyne Trust Fund

£16,000

Correspondent: Grant Administrator, 12–16 Albyn Place, Aberdeen AB10 1PS (01224 332400; fax: 01224 332401)

SC Number: SC012841

Eligibility

Widows and daughters of deceased merchants, shopkeepers and other businessmen who are elderly natives of Aberdeen or who have lived there for at least 25 years.

Types of grants

Annual allowances of about £400, paid twice yearly.

Annual grant total

In 2010/11 the trust had an income of £17,000.

Applications

On a form available from the correspondent via a social worker, Citizens Advice or other welfare agency.

The Crisis Fund of Voluntary Service Aberdeen

£40,000

Correspondent: Crisis Fund Administrator, Voluntary Service Aberdeen, 38 Castle Street, Aberdeen AB11 5YU (01224 212021; fax: 01224 580722; email: info@vsa.org.uk; website: www.vsa.org.uk)

SC Number: SC012950

Eligibility

People in Aberdeen who are facing extreme hardship.

Types of grants

Immediate grants ranging from about £50 to £150 for emergency needs such as food, beds and bedding, clothing and essential household items.

Annual grant total

Grants usually total about £40,000 each year.

Applications

On an application form available from the correspondent. Applications should be submitted through a social worker or other professional welfare agency.

The Elisabeth Davidson Memorial Benevolent Trust

£500

Correspondent: Miss F M Whyte, 10 Croftlands, St Cyrus, Montrose DD10 0AX (01674 850374)

SC Number: SC005988

Eligibility

Sick, elderly, people who have physical or mental disabilities resident in the parish of Bervie which includes the burgh of Inverbervie and the town of Gourdon.

Types of grants

Grants ranging from £20 to £150 towards nursing care, medicines and medical equipment.

Annual grant total

This trust generally has an income of around £500. No further information was available.

Applications

In writing to the correspondent or via a committee member.

The Donald Trust

£23,000

Correspondent: Anne Henderson, 12–16 Albyn Place, 52–54 Rose Street, Aberdeen AB10 1PS (01224 332400; fax: 01224 332401; email: anne.henderson@ raeburns.co.uk)

SC Number: SC0158844

Eligibility

People in need who 'belong to' the city of Aberdeen and former county of Aberdeen. 'Advanced age, lack of health, inability to work, high character and former industry are strong recommendations.'

Types of grants

An annuity of £400 a year, paid in two instalments.

Annual grant total

In 2011 the trust had an income and total expenditure of £27,000.

Exclusions

Generally, people under the age of 60 are not eligible.

Applications

On a form available from the correspondent. Applications should be submitted through a third party such as a social worker. They are considered twice a year.

Garden Nicol Benevolent Fund

£6,000

Correspondent: Alan J Innes, c/o Peterkins, 100 Union Street, Aberdeen AB10 1QR (01224 428000)

SC Number: SC007140

Eligibility

Women in need who live in Aberdeen.

Types of grants

One-off and recurrent grants according to need.

Annual grant total

In 2010/11 the fund had an income of £6,800 and a total expenditure of £8,100. Grants usually total about £6,000 a year.

Applications

In writing to the correspondent.

Gilcomston South Church Benevolent Fund

£7,000

Trustee: D. Dominic Smart.

SC Number: SC013916

Eligibility

People in need who live in the parish of Gilcomston.

Types of grants

One-off and recurrent grants according to need.

Annual grant total

In 2011 the benevolent fund had an income of £5,200 and a total expenditure of £7,800.

Applications

In writing to the correspondent.

John Harrow's Mortification

£1,600

Correspondent: Alan J Innes, Peterkins Solicitors, 100 Union Street, Aberdeen AB10 1QR (01224 428250; email: aji@ peterkinns.com)

SC Number: SC003617

Eligibility

People in need who live in the parishes of Old Machar and Denburn, Aberdeen and attend the church in Denburn or St Machar Cathedral.

Types of grants

About £800 is given to the ministers of each parish at Christmas for distribution to older people.

Annual grant total

Grants total around £1,600 each year.

Applications

Applications are made via the ministers of the parishes of Old Machar and Denburn, not directly to the trust.

The Jopp Thomson Fund

£16,000

Correspondent: Peter M Robertson, Adam Cochran Solicitors, 6 Bon-Accord Square, Aberdeen AB11 6XU (01224 588913; fax: 01224 581149; email: mgrant@adamcochran.co.uk)

SC Number: SC009106

Eligibility

People in need through age, ill health or disability with a preference for widowed and single women living in Aberdeenshire and those whose name or maiden name is Thomson or Middleton.

Types of grants

Annuities of around £500 paid in two instalments to each beneficiary to be used at their discretion.

Annual grant total

In 2010/11 the trust distributed around £16,000 in grants.

Applications

On a form available from the correspondent. Applications can be submitted directly by the individual or through a third party. They are considered in April each year.

Other information

This fund is an amalgamation of the Henry John Jopp Fund and the Jessie Ann Thomson Fund.

The Mary Morrison Cox Fund

£10,000

Correspondent: The Trustees, 18 Bon-Accord Crescent, Aberdeen AB11 6XY (01224 573321)

SC Number: SC007881

Eligibility

People in need who live in the parish of Dyce, Aberdeen. Preference is given to older people and people living with disabilities.

Types of grants

One-off grants ranging from £100 to £400 to help with general living expenses.

Annual grant total

Grants usually total around £10,000 a year.

Applications

The trust has a list of potential beneficiaries to whom it sends application forms each year, usually in November. Applicants can contact the trust at any time to ask to be added to the list.

Simpson Trust

£10,000

Correspondent: Trustees of the Simpson Trust, c/o Alexander George and Co. Solicitors, 25 High Street, Banff AB45 1AN

SC Number: SC014008

Eligibility

Older people in need who are in poor health and live in the burgh of Macduff.

Types of grants

Annual payments of around £75 to £200, usually made in two instalments.

Annual grant total

Grants average around £10,000 a year.

Applications

On a form available from the correspondent. When there are vacancies on the list of annuitants, applications are invited through the local press.

Miss Caroline Jane Spence's Fund

£25,000

Correspondent: Charles Scott, c/o Mackinnons, 14 Carden Place, Aberdeen AB10 1UR (01224 632464)

SC Number: SC006434

Eligibility

Widows or unmarried females living within the city or county of Aberdeen who are in need.

Types of grants

Recurrent grants are made.

Annual grant total

In 2009/10 the trust had an income of £119,000 and a total charitable

expenditure of £55,000. Grants to individuals totalled around £25,000.

Exclusions

No grants are made where statutory funding is available.

Applications

On a form available from the correspondent. Applications can be submitted either directly by the individual, or through a social worker, Citizens Advice or other welfare agency or other third party. Applications are considered in November, January and April.

Other information

Grants are also made to organisations.

The Fuel Fund of Voluntary Service Aberdeen

£500

Correspondent: Gail Chandler, Administration Coordinator, 38 Castle Street, Aberdeen AB11 5YU (01224 358566; fax: 01224 580722; email: info@vsa.org.uk; website: www.vsa.org.uk)

SC Number: SC012950

Eligibility

People living in Aberdeen who need help in maintaining a warm home, particularly older people, people with a disability and families with young children.

Types of grants

One-off grants of about £30.

Annual grant total

Around £500 each year.

Applications

On an application form available from the correspondent. Applications should be submitted through a social worker or other professional welfare agency.

Angus

Charities Administered by Angus Council

£40,000

Correspondent: Sarah Forsyth, Angus Council, Angus House, Orchardbank Business Park, Angus DD8 2AL (01307 476269)

SC Number: SC025065

Eligibility

Residents of Arbroath, Brechin, Carnoustie, Forfar, Kirnemuir, Montrose, Kettins, Carmyllie and

Arbirlot (particularly older people and people who are in need).

Types of grants

One-off grants generally of £30 or more.

Annual grant total

The council administers over 100 charitable trusts – the largest of which is Strangs Mortification. Each year income from investments total around £40,000 which is used to pay grants to individuals in need in the Forfar area.

Applications

On a form available from the correspondent, any social work or housing office or Forfar Resource Store.

Other information

Over 100 charitable trusts are administered by Angus Council including: Brechin Charitable Funds, Arbroath Charitable Funds, Forfar Charitable Funds, Forfar Landward Charities, Carnoustie Charitable Funds and Kirniemuir Charitable Funds.

The Boyack Fund

£4,500

Correspondent: S J Cumming, Hodge Solicitors, 28 Wellmeadow, Blairgowrie, Perthshire PH10 6AX (01250 874441; fax: 01250 873998; email: info@hodgesolicitors.co.uk)

SC Number: SC004998

Eligibility

Pensioners in need who live in Monifieth by Dundee.

Types of grants

Grants of £50 a year.

Annual grant total

In 2010 the trust had a total expenditure of £5,000.

Applications

On a form available from the correspondent, to be submitted directly by the individual or a family member. Applicants must state how long they have lived in Monifieth and will be means tested. Anyone with significant assets/income will be excluded.

The Colvill Charity

£8,000

Correspondent: Grants Administrator, Thorntons WS, Brothockbank House, Arbroath, Angus DD11 1NJ (01241 872683; fax: 01241 871541; email: arbroath@thorntons-law.co.uk)

SC Number: SC003913

Eligibility

People who are in need and live in the town of Arbroath and the parish of St Vigeans and the surrounding area.

Types of grants

Annual grants of up to about £100 are given to older people. Special one-off grants of up to about £250 are also available for specific medical or household needs.

Annual grant total

In 2010/11 the charity had an income of £18,000. Grants usually total about £8,000 each year.

Applications

On a form available from the correspondent to be submitted directly by the individual or through a social worker, Citizens Advice or other welfare agency. Applications can be made at any time, though requests for regular grants are usually assessed once a year.

The Mrs Marie Dargie Trust

£8,000

Correspondent: David H Will, Trustee, Ferguson and Will, 28 Clerk Street, Brechin, Angus DD9 6AY (01356 622289)

SC Number: SC002408

Eligibility

People of pensionable age living within the city boundaries of Brechin.

Types of grants

Small one-off grants are given for a range of purposes, including television licences.

Annual grant total

In the past grants have totalled around £8,000. Accounts have not been submitted to the Office of the Scottish Charity Regulator since 2009 so more recent information was not available.

Applications

In writing to the correspondent including documentation proving the age of the applicant. Applications can be submitted either directly by the individual or a family member or through an organisation such as a Citizens Advice or other welfare agency. Applications can be considered at any time.

The St Cyrus Benevolent Fund

£1,000

Correspondent: The Secretary, Scotston of Kirkside, St Cyrus, Montrose, Angus DD10 0DA

SC Number: SC004237

Eligibility

People who are sick, infirm and in need and live in the parish of St Cyrus, Montrose only.

Types of grants

One-off grants of £25 to £100 are given as well as gift vouchers and grants in kind. Grants given include those towards clothing, food, travel expenses, medical equipment and disability equipment. Parcels are distributed at Christmas time.

Annual grant total

Grants usually total around £1,000 a year.

Applications

In writing to the correspondent. Recommendation by social worker, minister, doctor, nurse or similar is essential. The trust stated: 'An individual may make a direct application in the first instance but it will be thoroughly checked through the usual type of referee.' Applications are considered at any time.

Other information

The trust also makes grants to organisations for medical equipment and welfare.

The Angus Walker Benevolent Fund

£6,000

Correspondent: T Duncan and Co., Solicitors, 192 High Street, Montrose DD10 8NA (01674 672533)

SC Number: SC008129

Eligibility

People in need who live in Montrose.

Types of grants

One-off grants.

Annual grant total

In 2010/11 the trust had an income of £8,000. About £6,000 is given each year in grants.

Applications

By formal application through a trustee, local district councillors, the minister of Montrose Old Church or the rector of St Mary's and St Peter's Episcopal Church, Montrose.

Dundee

The Broughty Ferry Benevolent Fund

£60,000

Correspondent: The Trustees, 12 Tircarra Gardens, Broughty Ferry, Dundee DD5 2QF

SC Number: SC010644

Eligibility

People in need living in Broughty Ferry, Dundee, who are not in residential care.

Types of grants

One-off grants according to need.

Annual grant total

In 2010/11 the trust had an exceptionally large income of £70,000.

Applications

On a form available from the correspondent. Applications can be submitted either directly by the individual or through a social worker, Citizens Advice or other welfare agency.

The Dundee Indigent Sick Society

£2,000

Correspondent: Donald Gordon, Blackadders, 30–34 Reform Street, Dundee DD1 1RJ (01382 229222; fax: 01382 342220; email: toni.mcnicoll@ blackadders.co.uk)

SC Number: SC000287

Eligibility

People in need, who are in poor health or who have a disability and live in Dundee.

Types of grants

One-off grants of up to £100, although more can be given in exceptional circumstances.

Annual grant total

Grants usually total about £2,000 each year.

Applications

In writing to the correspondent either directly by the individual or a family member, or through a third party such as a social worker. Potential applicants are normally visited by the trust.

Johnston Charity

£100

Correspondent: Director of Finance, Dundee City Council, Floor 4, Tayside House, 28 Crichton Street, Dundee DD1 3RF (01382 434000)

SC Number: SC018893

Eligibility

Older people who are infirm and in need who live in the old City of Dundee boundary.

Types of grants

Yearly pensions of £50.

Annual grant total

In 2010/11 the trust had an income of £100.

Applications

Individuals should first contact their councillor who will submit an application form on the individual's behalf to the Director of Finance of Dundee City Council.

The Mair Robertson Benevolent Fund

£4,000

Correspondent: The Trustees, 144 Nethergate, Dundee DD1 4RB

SC Number: SC007435

Eligibility

Older women living in Dundee and Blairgowrie who are suffering from financial difficulties or are on a low income.

Types of grants

One-off grants of up to about £300.

Annual grant total

Grants usually total about £4,000 each year.

Applications

On a form available from the correspondent. Applications can be submitted directly by the individual or through a social worker, Citizens Advice, other welfare agency or other third party.

Other information

Grants are also made to local organisations.

Mrs Margaret T. Petrie's Mortification

£2,000

Correspondent: Administrator, Thorntons Solicitors, Whitehall House, 33 Yeaman Shore, Dundee DD1 4BJ (01382 229111; fax: 01382 202288)

SC Number: SC003464

Eligibility

Aged, infirm and indigent individuals over 55 years of age belonging to, or settled in, Dundee.

Types of grants

One-off and recurrent according to need.

Annual grant total

Grants to individuals usually total about £2,000 per year.

Applications

In writing to the correspondent. Applications can be submitted either directly by the individual, or through a social worker, Citizens Advice or other welfare agency, or another third party.

The Margaret and Hannah Thomson Trusts

£8,000

Correspondent: Graeme Fulton, Trust Manager, Thorntons Solicitors, Whitehall House, 33 Yeaman Shore, Dundee DD1 4BJ (01382 229111; fax: 01382 202288; email: dundee@ thorntons-law.co.uk)

SC Number: SC000276

Eligibility

Firstly, people in need who live in Dundee and were wounded during the Second World War, and their spouses. Secondly, ex-employees (or their dependents) of the carpet making industry in Dundee who were employed for at least 20 years and are in need of financial assistance for whatever reason.

Types of grants

Recurrent grants of £360 per year.

Annual grant total

In 2009/10 the trust had an income of £64,000. Grants were previously made totalling about £8,000; however this amount may have risen in line with the trust's sharp increase in income during recent years.

Applications

In writing to the correspondent. Applications can be submitted either directly by the individual or through a social worker, Citizens Advice or other welfare agency.

Moray

The Auchray Trust

£2,000

Correspondent: Grants Administrator, Finance and Information Technology Services, Moray Council, District Headquarters, High Street, Elgin IV30 1BX (01343 543451)

SC Number: SC019016

Eligibility

Older people or people who are infirm and were in business in the burgh of Elgin and who are now in financial need.

Types of grants

Help with council house rent.

Annual grant total

This trust's annual income is around £4,000.

Applications

On an application form available from the correspondent to be submitted by the individual or family member. There are no deadlines for applications.

Other information

The council also administers various small charities (under £500 grant total) for residents of the following areas: Kirkmichael, Inveravon, Mortlach, Keith and Aberlour (Keith/Dufftown Poor Funds and Keith Nursing Fund); Dufftown (Watt Bequest); Lossiemouth; the parishes of Boharm, Deskford, Dibble, Knockando, Rothes and Speymouth; and the burgh of Cullen. Further details are available from the correspondent.

Perth and Kinross

The Anderson Trust

£5,500

Correspondent: A G Dorward, Miler Hendry, 10 Blackfriars Street, Perth PH1 5NS (01738 637311)

SC Number: SC008507

Eligibility

Women in need who live in the parish of Kinnoull or Perth and who belong to the established Church of Scotland.

Types of grants

Grants are limited to a maximum of £500 per person each year.

Annual grant total

In 2010/11 the trust had an income of £5,600. About £5,500 is available each year for grant distribution.

Applications

On a form available from the correspondent at any time.

Mrs Agnes W. Carmichael's Trust (incorporating Ferguson and West Charitable Trust)

£2,000

Correspondent: Alison Hodge, Watson Lyall Bowie, Union Bank Building, Coupar Angus, Blairgowrie PH13 9AJ (01828 628395)

SC Number: SC004415

Eligibility

The relief of poverty, sickness and distress of people who are older, disabled and needy resident in Coupar Angus.

Types of grants

Grants of £50 to £250.

Annual grant total

In 2010/11 the trust had an income of £4,500.

Applications

On a form available from the correspondent. Applications should give details of the individual's financial circumstances. Deadlines are in November and applications are considered in December.

Other information

The trust also supports older people's organisations.

The Guildry Incorporation of Perth

£31,000

Correspondent: Lorna Peacock, Secretary, 42 George Street, Perth PH1 5JL (01738 623195)

SC Number: SC008072

Eligibility

People in need who live in Perth.

Types of grants

One-off and recurrent grants usually ranging between £100 and £500.

Annual grant total

In 2010/11 the guild had an income of £206,000. In previous years around £80,000 was given in grants to individuals, of which approximately £31,000 was given for welfare purposes, namely weekly pensions (£18,000); quarterly pensions (£8,500); and coal allowances (£4,800).

Applications

Application forms can be requested from the correspondent. They are considered at the trustees' meetings on the last Tuesday of every month.

Dr William Henderson's Mortification

£100

Correspondent: Douglas Lamond, c/o Kippen Campbell, 48 Tay Street, Perth PH1 5TR (01738 635353; fax: 01738 643773)

SC Number: SC001906

Eligibility

Men over 60 years of age who live in Perth or Perthshire and require financial assistance.

Types of grants

Recurrent grants are paid half-yearly in May and November. Usually £100 is awarded per person per year.

Annual grant total

This trust's income has declined from £1,000 to just over £130 since 2008.

Applications

On a form available from the correspondent directly by the individual or family member, for consideration throughout the year. The application must contain details of assets, income and any dependents.

Scones Lethendy Mortifications

£6,000

Correspondent: Graham MacKenzie, Treasurer, King James VI Hospital, Hospital Street, Perth PH2 8HP (01738 624660)

SC Number: SC015545

Eligibility

People in need who live in the burgh of Perth and are poor descendents of Alexander Jackson, or with the surname Jackson and other people who are in need (Jackson Mortifications)

Types of grants

Grants of about £65 a quarter.

Annual grant total

Grants usually total about £6,000 per year.

Applications

On a form available from correspondent. Both trusts have a waiting list to which applications would be added, although successful applicants are judged on need rather than when they applied.

Other information

A third trust is the Cairnie Mortification: Recurrent grants lasting for ten years can be given to two young men, starting when they are near the age of 14. Priority is given to those who are direct descendants of Charles Cairnie or any of his five brothers, otherwise grants can be given to people with the surname Cairnie.

Central

Clackmannanshire

The Clackmannan District Charitable Trust

£1,000

Correspondent: Trusts Administrator, Trusts Administrator, Legal and Administration, Clackmannanshire Council, Greenfield House, Alloa FK10 2AD (01259 452108; email: adminservices@clacks.gov.uk; website: www.clacksweb.org.uk)

SC Number: SC011479

Eligibility

People in need who have lived in Clackmannanshire for 12 consecutive months preceding the application being considered or who have lived in Clackmannanshire for three years at some time in the past and continuously for the six consecutive months preceding the application being considered.

Types of grants

Assistance is mainly given for essential household goods such as, electric cookers, washing machines, beds and bedding.

Annual grant total

Grants usually total about £1,000 each year.

Applications

On a form available either directly from the correspondent, at community access points or to download from the website. Applications can be submitted at any time but are only considered in March and September.

The Spittal Trust

£8,000

Correspondent: Ann Lomax, Administration Officer, Finance and Corporate Services, Clackmannanshire Council, Greenfield, Alloa FK10 2AD (01259 452108)

SC Number: SC018529

Eligibility

People in need who have lived in Alloa for at least ten years immediately before applying to the trust.

Types of grants

Small, one-off grants for essential household goods, for example, electric cookers, washing machines, beds and bedding.

Annual grant total

In recent years total grantmaking has averaged around £8,000 per year; however, the figure tends to fluctuate on an annual basis.

Applications

On a form available to download from the from the Clackmannanshire council website, by contacting the correspondent or from reception at the Council office. The trust also requires proof of income and, if necessary, evidence of any medical conditions. Application deadlines are at the end of February, May, August and November for consideration in March, June, September and December. Exact dates of trustee meetings are advertised on the website.

Falkirk

The Anderson Bequest

£7,500

Correspondent: J W Johnston, 13 Register Street, Bo'ness, West Lothian EH51 9AE (01506 822112)

SC Number: SC011755

Eligibility

People in need who live in Bo'ness.

Types of grants

Annual grants of about £150 per year.

Annual grant total

In 2010/11 the fund had an income of £18,000. About £7,500 is given a year in grants to individuals.

Applications

In writing to the correspondent.

Falkirk Temperance Trust

£1,000

Correspondent: Hazel Jones Director of Finance Dept, Falkirk Council, Municipal Buildings, Falkirk FK1 5RS (01324 506070; fax: 01324 506363; email: contact.centre@falkirk.gov.uk)

SC Number: SC001904

Eligibility

Individuals who have alcohol, drug or other substance abuse problems and live in the former burgh of Falkirk.

Types of grants

One-off grants according to need ranging from £1,000 to £2,000.

Annual grant total

In 2010/11 the trust had an income of £1,100.

Applications

In writing to the correspondent at any time giving details of the specific funding required and what it is for. Applications can be made directly by the individual or family member or by a third party such as Citizens Advice or a social worker.

The Shanks Bequest

£1,000

Correspondent: Hillary McArthur, Finance Services, Falkirk Council, Municipal Buildings, West Bridge Street, Falkirk FK1 5RS (01324 506354)

Eligibility

People in need who live in Denny.

Types of grants

There is a list of beneficiaries, which is updated each year, who receive a share of the income (about £40) as a Christmas gift.

Annual grant total

Grants usually total around £1,000 per year.

Applications

In writing to the correspondent.

Other information

Falkirk Council also administers other small trusts for individuals in need who live in the Falkirk area. Further details from the correspondent above.

Fife

The Bruce Charitable Trust

£5,000

Correspondent: Elizabeth Calderwood, Secretary, c/o Pagan Osborne, 106 South Street, St Andrews KY16 9QD (01334 475001; fax: 01334 476322)

SC Number: SC014927

Eligibility

People who are older, in need, infirm or distressed who live in the burgh of Cupar.

Types of grants

One-off grants of up to £400.

Annual grant total

In 2009/10 the trust had an income of £14,500.

Applications

In writing to the correspondent including the applicant's date of birth,

postal address and reason for request. Applications should be made by an organisation such as Citizens Advice or through a third party such as a social worker.

Other information

The trust also makes grants to assist youth groups, organisations providing holidays or convalescing facilities and projects considered of benefit to the community.

Charities Administered by Fife Council (West Fife Area)

£4,000

Correspondent: Linda Purdie, Team Leader, Fife Council, Fife House, North Street, Glenrothes, Fife KY7 5LT (0845 155 5555)

Eligibility

The beneficial area differs from charity to charity, the largest of which are the McGregor Bequest and the Wildridge Memorial Fund. The majority refer only to Dunfermline, but smaller ones exist for Aberdour, Culross, Lochgelly, Limekilns, Kincardine, Ballingry and Tulliallan.

Types of grants

Generally one-off grants to people in need. Grants may be made in cases of emergency, for fuel payments, groceries and so on.

Annual grant total

Grants usually total around £4,000 per year.

Applications

Applications should be made to one of the eight local panels in the communities. A list of local service centres can be found on the council website (www.fifedirect.org.uk).

Other information

At the time of writing (winter 2012) the administrators of the charities at Fife Council were working in conjunction with the Office of the Scottish Charity Regulator to rationalise and merge the charities.

The Fleming Bequest

£75,000

Correspondent: Elizabeth Calderwood, Pagan Osborne, 106 South Street, St Andrews, Fife KY16 9QD (01334 475001; fax: 01334 476322; email: webenquiry@pagan.co.uk)

SC Number: SC016126

Eligibility

People living in the parish of St Andrews and St Leonards in the town of St Andrews who are older, in poor health or in financial difficulty.

Types of grants

One-off grants, of up to around £300 each, for a specific household need such as clothing, carpets, fridge/freezers, special chairs and so on.

Annual grant total

The trust has an average yearly income of around £18,000, however, in 2010/11 it had an exceptionally high income of £83,000.

Applications

In writing to the correspondent preferably through a social worker, Citizens Advice or similar welfare agency. Applications are considered at any time and should include details of the applicant's postal address, date of birth and reason for request.

The Kirkcaldy Charitable Trust

£1,700

Correspondent: Trust Administrator, Fife Council, Finance and Procurement, Fife House, Glenrothes, Fife KY7 5LT (0845 155 5555)

SC Number: SC017193

Eligibility

People in need who live in Kirkcaldy.

Types of grants

One-off grants to those in urgent need. Recent grants have ranged from £10 to £250 for heating, fuel, clothing, aids, appliances and food.

Annual grant total

In 2010/11 the trust had an income of £1,900.

Applications

In writing to the correspondent either directly by the individual or through a social worker, Citizens Advice or other welfare agency. The trust requires evidence of Social Fund refusal before considering giving a grant.

Macdonald Bequest

£400

Correspondent: Elizabeth Calderwood, Pagan Osborne, 106 South Street, St Andrews, Fife KY16 9QD (01334 475001; email: elcalderwood@pagan.co.uk)

SC Number: SC011092

Eligibility

Young people in need who live in the city of St Andrews or in the parish of St Andrews and St Leonards.

Types of grants

One-off and recurrent grants according to need. Recent grants have been given towards living costs, holidays and disability equipment.

Annual grant total

Grants usually total about £400 each year.

Applications

In writing to the correspondent to be submitted either through a third party such as a social worker, or through an organisation such as a Citizens Advice or other welfare agency. Applications are considered throughout the year and should include details of the individual's financial position (which will be treated in confidence).

Other information

The trust also gives grants to organisations in the area of benefit.

The St Andrews Welfare Trust

£10,000

Correspondent: Elizabeth Calderwood, Pagan Osborne, 106 South Street, St Andrews, Fife KY16 9QD (0845 278 0005; fax: 01334 476332)

SC Number: SC008660

Eligibility

People in need who live within a four mile radius of St Andrews.

Types of grants

One-off grants of up to £400 are given towards carpeting, cookers, clothing, fireguards and so on.

Annual grant total

About £10,000 is given to individuals and about £4,000 to organisations each year.

Exclusions

No grants for educational purposes, such as gap year projects.

Applications

In writing to the correspondent through a social worker, Citizens Advice or other welfare agency. Applications should include applicant's date of birth, postal address and reason for request and are considered throughout the year.

Other information

Grants are also given to playgroups and senior citizen Christmas teas.

Stirling

The George Hogg Trust

£15,000

Correspondent: Secretary, Tayview, Main Street, Killin, Perthshire FK21 8UT

SC Number: SC001890

Eligibility

People who live in Killin and are in need.

Types of grants

One-off and recurrent grants according to need. For example, a recent grant of £200 was given towards an electric wheelchair.

Annual grant total

Grants usually total about £15,000 each year.

Applications

In writing to the correspondent via a third party such as a local doctor or minister. There are no deadlines and applications are normally considered at the Annual General Meeting.

Edinburgh, the Lothians and Scottish Borders

The Blackstock Trust

£18,000

Correspondent: William Windram, Secretary, Pike and Chapman, 36 Bank Street, Galashiels TD1 1ER (01896 752379)

SC Number: SC014309

Eligibility

People who are elderly or sick and live in the counties of Roxburgh, Berwick and Selkirk.

Serving and retired British police officers and their dependents who have been injured or incapacitated while serving as a police officer

Types of grants

Financial assistance (usually up to £500) for accommodation, maintenance or welfare, short holiday breaks, respite care and the provision of amenities.

Annual grant total

Around £18,000.

Applications

In writing to the correspondent. Applicants must provide details of financial position (income and capital).

The Capital Charitable Trust

£16,000

Correspondent: Yvonne Rafferty, 7 Abercromby Place, Edinburgh EH3 6LA (01315 566644)

SC Number: SC004332

Eligibility

People in need who live in the Edinburgh and Lothians area.

Types of grants

Small one-off grants of about £10 to £20 for clothes, decorating, household goods and so on.

Annual grant total

In 2010/11 the trust had an income of £16,000. Grants were made totalling around £16,000.

Applications

Application forms are available from the Lothian Regional Council Social Work Departments and other responsible bodies who will forward them to the correspondent. Applications are not accepted directly from the individual.

The Robert Christie Bequest Fund

£40,000

Correspondent: Trust Administrator, Gibson McKerrell Brown, 14 Rutland Square, Edinburgh EH1 2BD (01312 288319; email: enquiries@g-m-b.co.uk)

SC Number: SC000465

Eligibility

People over 60 who are in need, live in Edinburgh or Midlothian and have an acutely painful disease.

Types of grants

Annual allowances are given according to need.

Annual grant total

In 2010/11 the fund had an income of £167,000 and a total expenditure of £111,000. Grants to individuals totalled around £40,000.

Applications

On a form available from the correspondent. Applications can be submitted directly by the individual or through a social worker, Citizens Advice or other welfare agency. Applications are usually considered twice a year.

The ECAS (Access/ Holiday Fund)

£25,000

Correspondent: Grants Administrator, ECAS, Norton Park, 57 Albion Road, Edinburgh EH7 5QY (01314 752344; fax: 01314 752341; website: www.ecas-edinburgh.org)

SC Number: SC014929

Eligibility

People who are long-term and significantly disabled through impairment of the musculo-skeletal, neurological or cardio-respiratory systems of the body.

Unfortunately, people with the following conditions do not fall within the fund's eligibility criteria: psychiatric disorders, learning difficulties, behavioural disorders, developmental delay, Down's syndrome, autism, visual or hearing impairment, cancer, diabetes, epilepsy, HIV, back pain and chronic fatigue syndrome.

Types of grants

One-off grants of up to £500 for special equipment, white goods, special furniture, household equipment and so on. The fund also awards grants towards holidays and may contribute towards the cost of an accompanying carer or partner.

Applications requesting computer equipment will be asked to contact Ecas for assessment.

Annual grant total

In 2010/11 the trust had an income of £192,000. Around £25,000 is available for grantmaking each year.

Exclusions

There are no grants available for: bills, debts, wheelchairs or scooters. Funding is not given to pay for items which have already been bought.

The fund regret that the following conditions on their own do not meet the criteria for participation in Ecas activities: psychiatric disorders, learning difficulties, behavioural disorders, developmental delay, Down's syndrome, autism, visual or hearing impairment, cancer, diabetes, epilepsy, HIV and back pain.

Applications

On a form available from the correspondent or to download from the website. Applications must be supported by a social worker or health care professional. A short GP report is also required unless the applicant can provide a recent DLA (Care or Mobility) or Attendance Allowance award letter. Applications can be made at any time but individuals should allow around four weeks (12 weeks for holiday applications) for the administration of any grant.

Any application for funds for maintenance or repair for battery-packs, power-chairs or scooters must be accompanied by evidence of third party insurance.

The Edinburgh Merchant Company Endowment Trust

£105,000 (172 grants)

Correspondent: The Secretary, The Merchants Hall, 22 Hanover Street, Edinburgh EH2 2EP (01312 257202; fax: 01312 204842; email: info@mcoe.org.uk; website: www.mcoe.org.uk)

Trustee: Masters of the Company of Merchants of the City of Edinburgh.

SC Number: SC002002

Eligibility

'Decent, indigent men and women' who are over the age of 55 and have lived or worked in the city of Edinburgh or in Midlothian. Help may also be given to younger individuals who are certified on medical grounds as unable to earn their living.

Types of grants

The majority of funding is given in bi-annual pensions of about £500 per person. However, one-off cash grants and gifts in kind for household goods are also available.

Annual grant total

In 2010/11 the trust had assets of £14 million and an income of £752,000. Grants were made to 172 people totalling £105,000.

Applications

On a form available from the correspondent. Applications can be submitted at any time either directly by the individual, through a third party such as a social worker, or through an organisation such as Citizens Advice. The trust employs an almoner who assesses need and reports to the trust prior to any grant being made.

Other information

The trust also provides almshouse accommodation.

The Edinburgh Voluntary Organisations' Trusts

£61,000 (1,145 grants)

Correspondent: Janette Scappaticcio, Trust Fund Administrator, 14 Ashley Place, Edinburgh EH6 5PX (01315 559100; fax: 01315 559101; email: janette.scappaticcio@evoc.org.uk; website: www.evoc.org.uk)

Trustees: David Bennett; Sandra Blake; Mike Gilbert; Geoffrey Lord; Madeleine Allen.

SC Number: SC031561

Eligibility

Individuals in need who live in the city of Edinburgh and the Lothians. Priority is given where there is a serious illness of the individual or in the family.

Types of grants

One-off grants of up to £150 where they will be of real benefit to the family or individual. For example, grants are given for a specific need such as clothing and household essentials.

Annual grant total

In 2010/11 the trust held assets of £3.8 million and had an income of £172,000. Grants were made totalling £127,000, of which £61,000 was given to individuals and £31,000 to organisations. The remainder was constituted by distributions made on behalf of Ponton House to the value of £9,400 and BBC Children in Need to the value of £25,000.

Exclusions

No grants for electrical equipment, white goods, holidays (except in special circumstances), students' fees/equipment or the repayment of debt.

Applications

On a form available from the website. Applications should be submitted through a local authority, hospital or voluntary sector agency. They are considered monthly.

Other information

The Edinburgh Voluntary Organisations' Council (EVOC) previously administered a number of small trust funds which have now been amalgamated into a new fund, EVOT.

John Watt's Trust

£400

Correspondent: Mrs Elspeth Williamson, Mowat Hall Dick, 45 Queen Charlotte Street, Leith, Edinburgh EH6 7HT (01315 550616; email: elspeth.williamson@mhdlaw.co.uk)

SC Number: SC011575

Eligibility

- People over 55 who have the name Watt and who live in the parish of South Leith or those who have done so for at least ten years prior to their application
- People in need who have lived or are living in the City of Edinburgh or any part of Midlothian may apply

Types of grants

Grants are given in quarterly instalments.

Annual grant total

Grants usually total around £400 each year.

Applications

Prospective applicants must respond to an advertisement in the local press or through the local Leith churches, but more information can be gained from the correspondent. Applications are generally requested in November for consideration in January.

Other information

The trust has a visitor who is a member of South Leith Parish Church. He visits the pensioners throughout the year and reports to the trustees on their state of health and needs.

Edinburgh

Alexander Darling Silk Mercer's Fund

£22,000 (43 grants)

Correspondent: Alistair Beattie, Secretary and Chamberlain, The Merchant Company, The Merchants' Hall, 22 Hanover Street, Edinburgh EH2 2EP (01312 257202; fax: 01312 204842; email: alistair.beattie@mcoe.org.uk; website: www.mcoe.org.uk)

Trustee: The Master's Court of the Company of Merchants of the City of Edinburgh.

SC Number: SC036724

Eligibility

Unmarried or widowed women, over 55, who live in Edinburgh or who have worked in Edinburgh in the manufacture or sale of textile garments for ladies and children. Preference is given to women bearing the surname Darling, Millar, Small or Scott and to women born in the town of Lanark. Unfortunately, women who have only been involved in the manufacture and sale of textiles for men do not qualify for these grants.

Types of grants

Recurrent grants of £250 every six months to support living costs. The fund also helps with the cost of 'white goods' to qualifying people over the age of 55.

Annual grant total

In 2010/11 the fund had assets of £1.4 million and an income of £41,000. 43 pensioners were supported totalling £22,000.

Applications

Applications should be made in writing to the secretary of the Merchant Company, either directly by the individual or through a third party such as a social worker or Citizens Advice. Every written application is followed up by a visit from the almoner, during which a declaration regarding the applicant's financial circumstances is required.

The Edinburgh Royal Infirmary Samaritan Society

£16,000

Correspondent: The Honorary Secretary, 6a Randolph Crescent, Edinburgh EH3 7TH

SC Number: SC004519

Eligibility

Patients of NHS hospitals in Edinburgh who are in need.

Types of grants

Specific sums of money for clothing, bills, travel expenses or other help for the families and dependents of patients while in these hospitals or on leaving (such as grants for travel expenses for members of families visiting or accompanying patients). Grants range from £5 to £150.

Annual grant total

In 2010/11 the fund had an income of £18,000. Grants were made totalling around £16,000.

Applications

Through a medical social worker (at Edinburgh Royal Infirmary Social Work Department) on an application form. Applications are considered fortnightly.

The Edinburgh Society for Relief of Indigent Old Men

£30,000

Correspondent: R J Elliot, Secretary, c/o Lindsays, Caledonian Exchange, 19A Canning Street, Edinburgh EH3 8HE (01312 291212; email: mail@lindsays.co.uk)

SC Number: SC005284

Eligibility

Older men of good character resident in Edinburgh, who usually have no pension apart from statutory sources, have capital of £3,000 or less and are experiencing hardship or disability. (Under exceptional circumstances, men under 65 will be considered.)

Types of grants

Monthly payments of £50.

Annual grant total

Grants usually total around £30,000 per year.

Applications

In writing to the correspondent.

The Edinburgh Trust

Correspondent: Elizabeth Finn Care, Thorn House, 5 Rose Street, Edinburgh EH2 2PR

Trustee: Elizabeth Finn Care.

Eligibility

Applicants must live within the boundaries of the City of Edinburgh Council local authority area; have less than £10,000 accessible savings; and received means tested welfare benefits or have an income which is below 60% of the average national wage (approximately £16,000).

The trust contains a number of funds which have additional criteria. To be considered for these an applicant must:

 ▶ Be over 55 years of age; or
 ▶ Be over 55 years of age and have some connection with the building trade; or
 ▶ Be a resident of Corstorphine, Leith or Cramond

Types of grants

Small recurring grants. One-off payments for children – for example for school uniforms, books or IT support.

Annual grant total

The trust holds approximately £12 million in assets. As it is a relatively new trust we do not yet have any information on grants already made.

Exclusions

No help for private medical or dental costs; glasses; university or school fees; funeral costs; legal costs; loans; business start-up costs or personal debts.

Applications

Applicants may apply online via the Elizabeth Finn Care website or by contacting the correspondent.

Other information

The trust came under the control of Elizabeth Finn Care in 2011. It consists of 33 poverty related charities previously administered by Edinburgh Council.

EMMS International-Hawthornbrae

£18,000 (35 grants)

Correspondent: Joe Cooney, Office Manager, 7 Washington Lane, Edinburgh EH11 2HA (01313 133828; fax: 01313 134662; email: info@emms.org; website: www.emms.org)

Trustees: John Andrew; Philip Brookes; Peter Brown; Carol Finlay; Manish Joshi; Crispin Longden; Angus McLeod; Christopher Mackay; Joan McDowell; Helen Paxton.

SC Number: SC032327

Eligibility

People resident within the Edinburgh City Boundary who are recovering from an illness and are of 'good character' who have insufficient funds to pay for a holiday for themselves.

Types of grants

Grants of up to £300 for adults and £150 for children (under 16) for recuperative holidays. Grants to one family will not exceed £900.

Annual grant total

The fund has an income of around £15,000 a year. In 2011 grants totalling £18,000 were made to 35 beneficiaries.

Exclusions

The trust cannot give grants towards spending money.

Applications

On a form available from the correspondent. Applications must be sponsored by a social worker, health visitor or minister and be supported by a medical reference from a GP. Applications are considered throughout the year on a first come first served basis and usually take up to six to eight weeks to process.

Other information

Grants are not paid to individuals but to sponsoring agencies or accredited guesthouses or travel agents.

Emms International also runs a bursary scheme for medical students undertaking electives in mission schools and hospitals.

Miss Jane Campbell Fraser's Trust

£3,500

Correspondent: The Trustees, Wallace and Menzies, 21 Westgate, North Berwick EH39 4AE (01620 892307)

SC Number: SC017290

Eligibility

People in need who are over 60 and live in Leith.

Types of grants

One-off and recurrent grants of about £250 normally paid at Christmas.

Annual grant total

In 2009/10, the most recent year for which accounts were available from the Scottish Charity Regulator, the trust had an income of £4,100.

Applications

In writing to the correspondent. Applications can be submitted either directly by the individual or through a social worker or other welfare agency. They are considered throughout the year.

Leith Benevolent Association Ltd

£500

Correspondent: C Thomson, Catchpell House, Carpet Lane, Bernard Street, Leith, Edinburgh EH6 6SP (fax: 01314 670099; email: applications@ leithbenevolentassociation.co.uk; website: www.leithbenevolentassociation. co.uk)

SC Number: SC011276

Eligibility

People in financial need who live in Leith.

Types of grants

One-off grants, usually of £10 to £15 per person.

Annual grant total

About £500 a year.

Applications

On an application form available to download from the website. Applications are considered in September and February and should be received no later than the end of July and December preceding each meeting.

Other information

Grants are mainly given to organisations.

The William Brown Nimmo Charitable Trust

£20,000

Correspondent: Grants Administrator, Mowat Hall Dick, 45 Queen Charlotte Street, Leith, Edinburgh EH6 7HT (01315 531523; fax: 01315 531523; email: edinburgh@mhdlaw.co.uk)

SC Number: SC001671

Eligibility

Older women living on a low income who were born, and permanently live, in Leith or Edinburgh.

Types of grants

Annual grants of around £80.

Annual grant total

Grants total about £20,000 each year. The trust usually accepts several new beneficiaries a year, but this is dependent on available income and existing beneficiaries failing to re-qualify for a grant.

Applications

On a form only available from 1 June from the correspondent. They should be returned by 31 July for consideration in September/October. Applicants are visited.

The Police Aided Clothing Scheme of Edinburgh

£11,000

Correspondent: Administrator, Lothian and Borders Police Headquarters, Fettes Avenue, Edinburgh EH4 1RB (01313 113131; fax: 01314 406889)

SC Number: SC011164

Eligibility

Children in need who live in the area administered by City of Edinburgh Council.

Types of grants

In kind gifts of socks, shoes, sweatshirts and a coat or jacket are given to children.

Annual grant total

In 2010/11 the scheme received 110 applications for assistance and helped 220 children. Of this total all received footwear, 200 also received a sweatshirt and 198 received a winter jacket.

Exclusions

No cash grants are made, or help towards school uniforms.

Applications

Initial enqiries should be made in writing or by phone to the Custodiers Department of the police service. All applicants are visited in their homes by a police officer in uniform to complete an application.

The Surplus Fire Fund

£30,000

Correspondent: Laura Brockie, Committee Services Section, The City of Edinburgh Council, City Chambers (Room 9/43), High Street, Edinburgh EH1 1YJ (01315 294101; fax: 01315 297607; email: laura.brockie@edinburgh. gov.uk; website: www.edinburgh.gov.uk/ info/677/council_and_government_ grants/1100/surplus_fire_fund/1)

SC Number: SC018967

Eligibility

Anyone involved in a fire which took place in the Edinburgh city area.

Types of grants

One-off payments. Grants fall into two categories:

▶ Personal injury or death – for people suffering serious injury, or the dependents of people who have lost their lives or suffered serious injury, in connection with fires in the area

▶ Deserving act – for people who have given 'meritorious' service in connection with fires in the area

Annual grant total

In 2010/11 the fund had an income of £34,000 and a total expenditure of £35,000.

Applications

On an application form available to download from the council website or by contacting the correspondent. Applications should be accompanied by a GP's letter detailing injuries and ongoing health problems sustained. You may apply on behalf of yourself-or a dependent who has suffered a physical or psychological injury, or has lost their home or job as a result of fire.

Other information

The fund was established in 1824 to help victims of a number of fires in the High Street, with the surplus held in trust since.

Grants are also made to organisations with similar purposes to the fund.

Galashiels

The MacWatt Bequest

£500

Correspondent: Trust Administrator, Scottish Borders Council, Newtown St Boswells, Melrose TD6 0SA (0300 100 1800)

SC Number: SC017680

Eligibility

People in need who live in the former burgh of Duns.

Types of grants

Grants for coal and food.

Annual grant total

About £500 a year.

Applications

In writing to the correspondent.

Midlothian

The Cockpen Lasswade and Falconer Bequest

£0

Correspondent: Director, Corporate Resources, Midlothian Council, Midlothian House, Buccleuch Street, Dalkeith, Midlothian EH22 1DN (01312 713161; email: enquiries@midlothian. gov.uk)

Eligibility

People in need who live in Cockpen, Bonnyrigg and Lasswade.

Types of grants

Grants can be given for medical or convalescent expenses which are not covered by the NHS.

Annual grant total

Grants usually total about £1,000 each year although the trust made no grants in the last financial year.

Applications

In writing to the correspondent at any time.

Charities Administered by Midlothian Council

£0

Correspondent: The Director, Corporate Resources, Midlothian Council, Midlothian House, Buccleuch Street, Dalkeith EH22 1DN (01312 707500)

Eligibility

There are various bequests administered by Midlothian Council. Most of them are small (under £500) and therefore do not warrant individual entries in this guide. The following entry gives basic details about the bequests; further information is available from the correspondent.

Types of grants

One-off grants according to need.

Applications

In writing to the correspondent. Applications can be submitted directly by the individual or family member.

Other information

(a) The Ainslie, Sir Samuel Chisholm and Fraser Hogg Bequests
Eligibility: Poor people who live in the parish of Dalkeith.
Types of grants: Individual disbursements

(b) The Cockpen, Lasswade and Falconer Bequest
Eligibility: People in need who live in the former burghal areas of Bonnyrigg and Lasswade, and in the immediate surrounding district.
Types of grants: Individual disbursements for medical or convalescent expenses not covered by the National Health Service.

(c) The John and Margaret Haig Bequest
Eligibility: People in need over 70 who live in the former burghal area of Bonnyrigg.
Types of grants: Individual disbursements.

(d) The Earl of Stair Bequest
Eligibility: People in need who live in the parish of Cranston.
Types of grants: Logs for the poor.

(e) The Tod Bequest
Eligibility: Poor people in need who live in Loanhead or Polton.
Types of grants: One-off payments.

(f) The Mrs E W Yorkston Bequest
Eligibility: Poor young people belonging to the former burghal area of Lasswade who have an infectious disease.
Types of grants: Grants to help with the cost of a suitable rest in the country or at a convalescent home.

Scottish Borders

Mrs Agnes Black Bequest for Poor

£0 (0 grants)

Correspondent: Anne Isles, Legal and Licensing Services Manager, Scottish Borders Council, Council Headquarters, Newtown St Boswells TD6 0SA (01835 825002; email: aisles@scotborders.gov. uk)

Trustees: Trevor Jones; Donald Moffat; Frances Renton.

SC Number: SC017675

Eligibility
People in need who live in Coldstream and Coldstream Newton.

Types of grants
One-off grants according to need.

Annual grant total
In the financial years ending 2010 and 2011 the trust had unusually low incomes of £23 and £82 respectively. No grants were made, although the trust continues to hold assets of £4,500.

Applications
In writing to the correspondent.

Other information
The charity also maintains burial grounds.

Christie Fund

£500

Correspondent: John Grant, Trustee, Iain Smith and Partners, 11 – 13 Murray Street, Duns TD11 3DF (01361 882733; fax: 01361 883517)

SC Number: SC000957

Eligibility
People in need in Duns Parish.

Types of grants
One-off grants to a usual maximum of £200. Funds are available to help with specific items where the applicant does not have access to other means of funding.

Annual grant total
The trust usually has an income of less than £1,000.

Applications
In writing to the correspondent at any time, through a social worker, Citizens Advice or other welfare agency. Applications should include full details of the assistance needed, stating why funding is unavailable from other sources.

The R. S. Hayward Trust

£20,000

Correspondent: Trust Administrator, c/o Pike and Chapman Solicitors, 36 Bank Street, Galashiels, Selkirkshire TD1 1ER (01896 752379)

SC Number: SC015427

Eligibility
People in need who have been employed in Galashiels for at least ten years, and have retired or become incapacitated, either permanently or temporarily, from work, and their wives or widows.

Types of grants
Recurrent grants of around £10 per week.

Annual grant total
Approximately £20,000 a year.

Applications
In writing to the correspondent.

The Elizabeth Hume Trust

£500

Correspondent: Revd D Murray, The Manse, The Glebe, Chirnside, Duns, Berwickshire TD11 3XL

SC Number: SC005995

Eligibility
People in need who live in the parish of Chirnside.

Types of grants
'Grants are made at the sole discretion of the minister.'

Annual grant total
In 2011 the trust had an expenditure of £10,000. Income and expenditure have been erratic in recent years.

Applications
Applications can be made either directly by an individual or family member, through a third party such as a social worker or teacher, through an organisation such as a Citizens Advice or school or through a church elder.

Roxburghshire Landward Benevolent Trust

£500

SC Number: SC008416

Eligibility
People in need who live in the Landward area of the former Roxburgh County Council.

Types of grants
One-off grants up to £500. Grants are normally given to assist people with health and social problems where government assistance is not available. Financial help can be towards travel to hospital, respite care, equipment such as wheelchairs, and the purchase of domestic equipment.

Annual grant total
Grants to individuals generally total around £500. The trust also makes grants to organisations.

Exclusions
No grants to settle debts or to duplicate state aid.

Applications
In writing to the correspondent. Applications can be submitted directly by the individual, through a social worker, Citizens Advice or other welfare agency, or through other third party on behalf of an individual. They are considered in April and October. Applicants will be visited by a trustee before any decision to make a payment is made.

Glasgow and West of Scotland

The Association for the Relief of Incurables in Glasgow and the West of Scotland

£163,000

Correspondent: BMK Wilson, Solicitors, BMK Wilson Solicitors, 90 St Vincent Street, Glasgow G2 5UB (01412 218004; fax: 01412 218088)

SC Number: SC014424

Eligibility

People over 18 years of age in financial need with long-term illnesses and are living at home. Applicants must be living in Glasgow or the West of Scotland.

Types of grants

Pensions of around £400 a year paid quarterly. One-off grants of up to £350 per person, for specific needs such as telephone installation, washing machines and cookers.

Annual grant total

In 2011 the charity had an income of £155,000. Grants totalled £163,000.

Exclusions

No grants given to clear debts or towards holidays.

Applications

Applications must be made through a social worker, Citizens Advice or another welfare agency on a form available from the correspondent. GP must confirm medical condition. Applications are considered quarterly with deadlines 14 days prior to each meeting.

Dr James Black's Trust

£750

Correspondent: The Trustees, Mitchells Roberton, George House, 36 North Hanover Street, Glasgow G1 2AD (01415 523422; fax: 01415 522935; email: info@ mitchells-robertson.co.uk)

SC Number: SC012697

Eligibility

'Faithful domestic servants' who have for ten years or upwards been in one situation in Glasgow or the immediate neighbourhood. Preference is given to applicants over 60 years old.

Types of grants

Recurrent grants of £150 each are given twice a year.

Annual grant total

This trust has an annual income of around £750.

Applications

In writing to the correspondent either directly by the individual or via another third party, for consideration at any time.

Merchants House of Glasgow

£1,000

Correspondent: David Ballantine, The Collector, 7 West George Street, Glasgow G2 1BA (01412 218272; fax: 01412 262275; email: theoffice@ merchantshouse.org.uk; website: www. merchantshouse.org.uk)

SC Number: SC008900

Eligibility

Pensioner members of the House who are in need and live in Glasgow and the West of Scotland.

Types of grants

Recurrent pensions are paid to help elderly people who are facing hardship.

Annual grant total

In 2011 the trust had an income of £1.3 million. Grants totalled £380,000, the majority of which are given to organisations. A very small amount is given as pensions to members of the Merchants House.

Applications

In writing to the correspondent at any time.

Other information

The Merchants House administers several funds in trust, including the Inverclyde Bequest Fund for Seamen, RNVR Club (Scotland) Memorial Trust and the Commercial Travellers of Scotland Benevolent Fund for Widows and Orphans.

James Paterson's Trust

£22,000

Correspondent: Alastair Campbell, Mitchells Roberton Solicitors, George House, 36 North Hanover Street, Glasgow G1 2AD (01415 523422; fax: 01415 522935; email: ajc@mitchells-roberton.co.uk)

SC Number: SC017645

Eligibility

Women who have worked in factories or mills in the Glasgow area, consisting of the district of the City of Glasgow and the contiguous districts of Dumbarton, Clydebank, Bearsden and Milngavie, Bishopbriggs and Kirkintilloch, East Kilbride, Eastwood and Renfrew.

Types of grants

Grants are given to pay primarily for short-term convalescent accommodation and occasionally for medical expenses and private accommodation in any private hospital. Grants are usually one-off payments of around £250.

Annual grant total

In 2011 the trust had an income of £27,000. Grants to individuals usually total about £22,000.

Applications

In writing to the correspondent. Applications can be submitted directly by the individual or through a social worker, Citizens Advice or other welfare agency. They are considered throughout the year.

Lord Provost's Children's Fund

£500

SC Number: SC042267

Eligibility

Children and young people under 18 years of age living in the Glasgow City Council area.

Types of grants

One-off grants according to need.

Annual grant total

No financial information was available as the fund has yet to file accounts with the Scottish Charity Regulator. In the past the previous Provost charities made grants totalling around £500 per year.

Applications

Applications are made via a social worker.

Other information

The fund is one of three funds created to rationalise a number of smaller funds administered by Glasgow City Council Social Services department. The other funds are the Lord Provost's Fund for Vulnerable Citizens and the Lord Provost's Fund for Older People, which can also be found in this guide.

Lord Provost's Fund for Elderly People

£500

SC Number: SC042269

Eligibility

Older people in the Glasgow district council area who are in financial need.

Types of grants

One-off grants according to need.

Annual grant total

No financial information was available as accounts have not been filed with the Scottish Charity Regulator. In the past the old Provost charities gave around £500 per year.

Applications

Applications are made through social workers to those already in contact with the department.

Other information

The fund is one of three funds created to rationalise a number of smaller funds administered by Glasgow City Council Social Services department. The other funds are the Lord Provost's Fund for Vulnerable Citizens and the Lord Provost's Children's Fund, which can also be found in this guide.

Radio Clyde – Cash for Kids

£200,000

Correspondent: Grants Officer, Radio Clyde Cash for Kids, 3 South Avenue, Clydebank Business Park, Glasgow G81 2RX (01412 041025; email: lesley. cashforkids@radioclyde.com; website: www.clydecashforkids.com)

Trustees: Lord Jack McConnell; Sir Tom Hunter; Ian Grabiner; Graham Bryce;.

SC Number: SC003334

Eligibility

Families with children under 16 who live in west central and south-west Scotland who are sick or underprivileged.

Applications are accepted from families in the following local authority areas: Glasgow, Argyll and Bute, North Ayrshire, South Ayrshire, East Ayrshire, East Dunbartonshire, North Lanarkshire, South Lanarkshire, West Dunbartonshire, Inverclyde, Renfrewshire, East Renfrewshire, Dumfries and Galloway.

Types of grants

Christmas grants of £25 per child.

Grants are paid to a third party supporter, usually a social work department, health centre, housing association, recognised voluntary organisation or a person in authority such as a headteacher, doctor or member of the clergy.

Annual grant total

In 2011 the charity had an income of £1.6 million. Grants totalled just over £1 million. According to the website, 'throughout 2011 Cash for Kids distributed 25,000 'family grants' 'and 520 'community support grants'', directly supporting 100,000 vulnerable children in the west of Scotland.' The majority of grants are paid to organisations, however, a final breakdown of grant expenditure was not available.

Applications

Online via the website. Once complete applicants should print the confirmation page and pass it to their referee for endorsement. All applications should be referred by a third party such as a Citizens Advice, housing association, social work department, headteacher, GP or member of the clergy. The referee must be willing to accept payment on behalf of the applicant. The applicant will be notified of the decision by email.

Applications tend to open for a month in early October, check the website for the exact dates.

Other information

Details of the scheme are broadcast on radio Clyde in the run up to Christmas. Grants are also awarded to organisations.

Mairi Semple Fund for Cancer Relief and Research

£10,000

Correspondent: Mrs Margaret S Semple, Secretary, 4 Barrhill, Glenbarr, Tarbert, Argyll PA29 6UT (01583 421234)

SC Number: SC000390

Eligibility

People with cancer who live in Kintyre or the Island of Gigha.

Types of grants

Provision of equipment and/or nursing help in the home and help with hospital travel costs for patients or relatives.

Annual grant total

In 2010/11 the fund had an income of £15,500. Grants usually total about £10,000 each year.

Exclusions

No grants are given to students for research.

Applications

In writing through the doctor, nurse or church minister of the patient, at the relevant address:
(i) Minister, Killean and Kilchenzie Church, Manse, Muasdale, Tarbert, Argyll.
(ii) Doctor, The Surgery, Muasdale, Tarbert, Argyll.
(iii) Nurse, The Surgery (same address as (ii)).

Strathclyde Police Benevolent Fund

£75,000

Correspondent: Grants Manager, Strathclyde Police Federation, 151 Merrylee Road, Glasgow G44 3DL (01416 332020; fax: 01416 330276; website: www.strathclydepolicefederation.org.uk)

SC Number: SC009899

Eligibility

Members and former members of the Strathclyde Police Force and former members of the constituent forces, their families and dependents.

Types of grants

One-off and recurrent grants according to need.

Annual grant total

In 2011 the fund had an income of £180,000 and a total expenditure of £84,000. Grants totalled around £75,000.

Applications

In writing to the correspondent. Applications are considered on a monthly basis.

Argyll and Bute

The G. M. Duncan Trust

£1,000

Correspondent: Mary McCallum, Senior Accountant Assistant, Argyll and Bute Council, Witchburn Road, Campbeltown, Argyll PA28 6JU (01586 555236)

Eligibility

People in need who live in the burgh of Campbeltown.

Types of grants

Vouchers to be exchanged for groceries or goods at a local shop.

Annual grant total

Grants usually total about £1,000 each year.

Applications

In November each year an advert is published in the local press inviting applications. Successful applicants receive their voucher in early December.

The Glasgow Bute Benevolent Society

£16,000

Correspondent: The Secretary, McLeish Carswell, 7 Admiral Street, Glasgow G41 1HP

SC Number: SC016182

Eligibility

People in need, particularly older people, who live in Bute. The length of time a person has lived in Bute and how long they have been connected with the area is taken into consideration.

Types of grants

The society does not award grants as such; suitable applicants are admitted to the Society's Roll of Pensioners and receive a pension payable half-yearly and a Christmas bonus payment. The half-yearly pension is about £50; the value and availability of the bonus depends on income available.

Annual grant total

In 2010 the society had an income of £19,000. Grants were made totalling around £16,000.

Applications

On a form available from the correspondent, with a supporting recommendation by a minister of religion, doctor, solicitor or other responsible person.

Dumfries and Galloway

Elizabeth Armstrong Charitable Trust

£400

Correspondent: Kenneth Hill, Senior Partner, 38 High Street, Langholm, Dumfries and Galloway DG13 0JH (01387 380428; fax: 01387 381144)

SC Number: SC002180

Eligibility

People in need living in Canonbie in Dumfriesshire.

Types of grants

One-off and recurrent grants according to need.

Annual grant total

The trust has had an average income of around £800 over the past seven years.

Applications

In writing to the correspondent.

Samuel Elliot Bequest

£500

Correspondent: Alex Haswell, Corporate Finance, Carruthers House, English Street, Dumfries DG1 2HP (01387 260031; fax: 01776 704819)

SC Number: SC004899

Eligibility

Older people who are in need and live in the burgh of Lockerbie and the parishes of Dryfesdale and Johnstone.

Types of grants

Recurrent grants according to need.

Annual grant total

Grants total around £500 each year.

Applications

In writing to the correspondent.

The Holywood Trust

£75,000

Correspondent: Richard Lye, Trust Administrator, Mount St Michael, Craigs Road, Dumfries DG1 4UT (01387 269176; fax: 01387 269175; email: funds@holywood-trust.org.uk; website: www.holywood-trust.org.uk)

Trustees: Clara Weatherall; Charles Jencks; Louise Jencks; Ben Weatherall; Valerie McElroy.

SC Number: SC009942

Eligibility

Young people aged 15 to 25 living in the Dumfries and Galloway region, with a preference for people who are mentally, physically or socially disadvantaged.

Types of grants

One-off and recurrent grants of £50 to £500. The trust supports a wide range of causes, however applications which contribute to their personal development are more likely to receive support. This could include financial or material assistance to participate in education or training, access to employment, establish a home or involvement in a project or activity which will help the individual or their community.

Annual grant total

Grants to individuals totall around £150,000 annually.

Exclusions

No grants are given towards carpets or accommodation deposits.

Applications

Forms are available from the correspondent, or can be downloaded from the trust's website. Applications are considered at least four times a year. The trust encourages applicants to provide additional information about any disadvantage which affects them where their application form has not given them an opportunity to do so. It also welcomes any supporting information from third party workers.

Other information

The trust also provides the HANDY (Holywood Assistance to Needy and Disadvantaged Youngsters) Fund, which has been established to provide for individual welfare payments to disadvantaged children and young people who are referred to us by third party professional staff who are aware of their family circumstances, (education officials, social workers, health visitors, staff of voluntary sector organisations). Awards of up to £100 per child per year will be considered. View the website for more information.

Lockerbie and District Sick Benevolent Assocation

£2,700

Correspondent: Mrs Rosemary V Scott, Henderland, Greenhill, Lockerbie, Dumfriesshire DG11 1JB

SC Number: SC001472

Eligibility

People in Lockerbie and the surrounding parishes who are in need, with a preference for older people.

Types of grants

Grants are given towards food, appliances, clothing, convalescence and so on.

Annual grant total

In 2010/11 the association had an income of £2,800.

Applications

In writing to the correspondent.

The Lockerbie Trust

£5,000

Correspondent: Alex Haswell, Service Director, Chief Executive Services, Dumfries and Galloway Council, Council Offices, English Street, Dumfries DG1 2DD (01387 260006; fax: 01387 260034)

SC Number: SC019796

Eligibility

People in need who live in Lockerbie.

Types of grants

One-off grants according to need up to £500. Occasionally annual payments will be considered but only in exceptional circumstances.

Annual grant total

In 2010/11 the trust had an income of £15,000. Grants totalled around £10,000 and were made to both individuals and organisations.

Exclusions

Education grants are not awarded where Scottish Office grants are available.

Applications

On a form available from the correspondent, to be submitted directly by the individual. Applicants should note that the availability of grants from other sources will be taken into account in assessing applications. Applications are considered quarterly in February, June, August and November.

The Henry McDonald Trust

£700

Correspondent: Mairi Copeland, Dumfries and Galloway Council, Council Headquarters, English Street, Dumfries DG1 2DD (030 3333 3000; fax: 01387 260034; email: cis@dumgal.gov.uk; website: www.dumgal.gov.uk)

Eligibility

Mothers and babies or young children who live in Stranraer and are in need. Assistance will only be given to people who have exhausted all other sources of funding.

Types of grants

One-off grants up to about £500. Recent grants have been given for furniture and hospital travel costs.

Annual grant total

In the 2012/13 financial year around £700 in grants will be available from the fund.

Applications

On a form available from the correspondent. Applications can be submitted directly by the individual or through a third party such as a social worker. Note that applications not submitted through a social worker will usually be asked to undertake an interview to help the fund assess the individual's level of need.

Other information

The fund has recently been absorbed into the Stranraer Common Good Fund but the criteria and income available has not changed. The Stranraer Common Good Fund makes grants for organisations and projects in the Stranraer area.

The James McKune Mortification

£500

Correspondent: The Trustees, Blawearie, Kirkbean, Dumfries DG2 8DW

SC Number: SC011893

Eligibility

People in need who are natives of the parish of Kirkbean and have lived there for 20 years.

Types of grants

Annual pensions of £30 a year.

Annual grant total

Grants usually total around £500 a year.

Applications

On a form available from the correspondent. Applications should be submitted directly by the individual before 31 January for consideration in March.

The Nivison Trust

£1,000

Correspondent: Alex Haswell, Service Director, Dumfries and Galloway District Council, Carruthers House, English Street, Dumfries DG1 2HP

SC Number: SC019380

Eligibility

People in need who live in Sanquhar.

Types of grants

Quarterly payments of £20.

Annual grant total

About £1,000.

Applications

In writing to the correspondent. At the time of going to publication the trust was not making grants, call before making an application.

John Primrose Trust

£7,000

Correspondent: The Trustees, 1 Newall Terrace, Dumfries DG1 1LN

SC Number: SC009173

Eligibility

People in need with a connection to Dumfries and Maxwelltown by parentage or by living there.

Types of grants

Grants of £100 to £150 are given twice a year to 10 to 20 older people.

Annual grant total

About £14,000, half of which is given to individuals for relief-in-need and educational purposes.

Applications

On an application form available from the correspondent, to be considered in June and December.

East Ayrshire

The Shearer Bequest

£1,500

Correspondent: Grants Administrator, 13 Central Avenue, Kilmarnock, Ayrshire KA1 4PT

SC Number: SC020331

Eligibility

Unmarried women and widows in need, who are native to Kilmarnock.

Types of grants

Grants are given for general relief-in-need purposes.

Annual grant total

Over the last six years the trust's annual income has ranged from £11 to £9,500.

Applications

In writing to the correspondent.

Miss Annie Smith Mair Bequest

£4,000

Correspondent: Gillian Hamilton, Administrative Officer, Democratic Services, East Ayrshire Council, Council Headquarters, London Road, Kilmarnock KA3 7BU (01563 576093; email: gillian.hamilton@east-ayrshire. gov.uk; website: www.east-ayrshire.gov. uk)

SC Number: SC021095

Eligibility

People in need who live, or were born in, Newmilns.

Types of grants

One-off grants usually in the range of £50 to £1,000, towards household essentials, minor house or garden maintenance work/adaptations, short breaks, mobility and personal aids, clothing, and small donations for living expenses.

Annual grant total

Grants average about £4,000 per year.

Applications

On a form available from the correspondent or from the East Ayrshire Council website. Applications can be made directly by the individual or through a GP, social worker, Citizens Advice or other welfare agency.

Note: if an application is being made on health grounds alone, a GP's certification of need will also be required.

The Archibald Taylor Fund

£5,100

Correspondent: Head of Democratic Services, East Ayrshire Council, Council Headquarters, London Road, Kilmarnock KA3 7BU (01563 576093; fax: 01563 576245; email: gillian. hamilton@east-ayrshire.gov.uk)

SC Number: SC019308

Eligibility

People in need of special nursing, convalescent treatment at the coast or in the country; or a holiday during convalescence. Applicants must be in financial need.

Types of grants

Grants are given for the provision of special nursing or convalescent treatment and convalescent holidays of up to three weeks. Previously, awards have ranged from £250 to £1,000.

Annual grant total

In 2011/12 £5,100 was distributed in grants.

Applications

On a form available from the correspondent or to download from the East Ayrshire website, for consideration throughout the year. Applications can be made either directly by the individual, or through a social worker, Citizens Advice or other third party such as a GP. The following should be submitted with the application: details of the proposed holiday and cost, household income, employer's certificate of earnings and/or a benefit award letter and a declaration by the applicant's GP.

East Renfrewshire

The Janet Hamilton Memorial Fund

£200

Correspondent: Finance Department, East Renfrewshire Council, Council Headquarters, Eastwood Park, Rouken Glen Road, Giffnock, Glasgow G46 6UG (01415 773000)

SC Number: SC019475

Eligibility

People who are chronically sick or infirm, who live in the former burgh of Barrhead and are of pensionable age.

Types of grants

Postal orders of £15, distributed at Christmas.

Annual grant total

In 2010/11 the trust had a total income of £300.

Applications

Directly by the individual on a form available from the correspondent. A signature from a doctor confirming the person's state of health is necessary, as well as a signed copy of his/her life certificate. Grants are distributed in early December.

Glasgow

The City of Glasgow Society of Social Service

£137,000 (655 grants)

Correspondent: Mary McLean, Secretary, Fifth Floor, 30 George Square, Glasgow G2 1EG (01412 483535)

Trustees: Ronald G. Fulton; Joyce Stevenson; Daniel J. Brewster; Graeme Whyte; Mirren Graham; Margaret Robertson; Ann Pert; Philomena Strachan; David A. Roser; J. Michael Low; Francis E. J. McCrossin; Thia S. Begg.

SC Number: SC000906

Eligibility

People living in Glasgow, who are in need by reason of age, ill-health, disability, financial hardship or other disadvantage.

Types of grants

Pensions, holidays, Christmas gifts and one-off grants for a variety of needs.

Annual grant total

In 2010/11 the society had assets of £5.5 million and an income of £293,000. Grants totalling £274,000 were distributed between individuals and organisations.

Help was given to 655 individual applicants including 230 one-parent families, 217 elderly and infirm people, 137 families and 71 single people.

Applications

In writing to the correspondent by the individual or through a third party such as a social worker. The society's welfare officers visit and investigate all cases.

Other information

The society has traditionally administered a number of charitable foundations benefitting the people of Glasgow, which have been listed separately in this *Guide*. However, in 2009 the society was given permission by the Office of the Scottish Charity Regulator to consolidate all the trust funds of the various charities under the City of Glasgow Society of Social Service. This now also includes the Frances Lipton Memorial Fund.

Incorporation of Bakers of Glasgow

£500

Correspondent: Iain Paterson, Clerk, Trades Hall, 85 Glassford Street, Glasgow G1 1UH (01415 531605; fax: 01413 322613; email: iain.paterson@ tradeshouse.org.uk; website: www. tradeshouse.org.uk)

SC Number: SC014018

Eligibility

People who are members of the incorporation and their dependents.

Types of grants

One-off and recurrent grants according to need.

Annual grant total

Grants to individuals total about £500 each year.

Applications

In writing to the correspondent.

Other information

The exact date on which the Incorporation of Bakers was founded is uncertain but it is known that the Incorporation existed long prior to its first official mention in 1556.

Today the incorporation is engaged in works of charity and benevolence. Christmas and holiday gifts are paid to numerous needy pensioners and the incorporation provides prizes for students of baking and allied subjects at Glasgow College of Food Technology. Grants are also made to organisations.

Lethbridge – Abell Charitable Bequest

£1,000

Correspondent: The Private Secretary to the Lord Provost, 266 George Street, Glasgow G1 1QX

SC Number: SC019203

Eligibility

People in Glasgow who are in need.

Types of grants

One-off grants, usually up to £300.

Annual grant total

Grants usually total around £1,000 per year.

Applications

In writing to the correspondent.

The Andrew and Mary Elizabeth Little Charitable Trust

£45,000

Correspondent: R Munton, Low Beaton Richmond Solicitors, 20 Renfield Street, Glasgow G2 5AP

SC Number: SC011185

Eligibility

People in need whose sole source of income is income support, disability benefit or pension, and who live in the city of Glasgow.

Types of grants

One-off and recurrent grants according to need.

Annual grant total

In 2010/11 the trust had an income of £45,000. Grants total about £56,000 a year, of which 80% is given to individuals and 20% to organisations.

Applications

In writing to the correspondent, to be submitted through Social Services. Applications should include financial details and are considered monthly.

Lord Provost's Fund for Vulnerable Citizens

£500

Correspondent: Fund Administrator, Glasgow City Council, Social Work Services, Wheatley House, 25 Cochrane Street, Glasgow G1 1HL (01412 870555)

SC Number: SC042268

Eligibility

People in need who live in Glasgow.

Types of grants

One-off and recurrent grants of up to £300.

Annual grant total

No financial information was available, but in the past grants totalled around £500 per year.

Applications

Applications are made through social workers working in the Glasgow City Council area.

Other information

The fund is one of three funds created to rationalise a number of smaller funds administered by Glasgow City Council Social Services department. The other funds are the Lord Provost's Children's Fund and the Lord Provost's Fund for Older People, which can also be found in this guide.

The Trades House of Glasgow

£100,000

Correspondent: The Clerk, Administration Centre, North Gallery – Trades Hall, 85 Glassford Street, Glasgow G1 1UH (01415 531605; website: www.tradeshouse.org.uk)

SC Number: SCO40548

Eligibility

People in need who live in Glasgow, especially those receiving only a pension.

Types of grants

One-off grants of between £5 and £5,000.

Annual grant total

About £100,000 in relief-in-need grants to individuals.

Applications

In writing to the correspondent.

Other information

The Trades House also operates the Drapers Fund which distributes £50,000 annually to children-in-need who are under the age of seventeen. To apply write supplying as much detail as possible highlighting the circumstances of the individual/organisation concerned to: The Manager, The Drapers Fund, The Trades House of Glasgow, Trades Hall, 85 Glassford Street, Glasgow G1 1UH.

The Ure Elder Trust

£11,000

Correspondent: Eleanor Kerr, Maclay Murray and Spens Solicitors, 1 George Square, Glasgow G2 1AL (01412 715347)

SC Number: SC003775

Eligibility

Widows in need who live in Glasgow, particularly Govan.

Types of grants

Annual grants paid twice a year plus a bonus at Christmas.

Annual grant total

In 2011 the trust had an income £9,000 and a total expenditure of £12,000.

Applications

On a form available from the correspondent. Applications can be submitted directly by the individual or through a third party. They are considered in April and October.

Inverclyde

The Gourock Coal and Benevolent Fund

£3,000

Correspondent: The Trustees, 4D Cragburn Gate, Albert Road, Gourock, Renfrewshire PA19 1NZ

SC Number: SC009881

Eligibility

People in need who live in the former burgh of Gourock. There is a preference for older people, especially people who live on their own.

Types of grants

Gas and electricity vouchers are available and coal deliveries can also be made.

Annual grant total

Grants usually total about £3,000 each year.

Applications

In writing to any minister or parish priest in the town, or the local branch of the WRVS (not to the correspondent). Applications are normally considered in December and can be submitted either directly by the individual or through a social worker, Citizens Advice or other welfare agency.

Seamans' Friend Charitable Society

£800

Correspondent: William G Mitchell, Patten and Prentice Solicitors, 2 Ardgowan Square, Greenock PA16 8PP (01475 720306; fax: 01475 888127)

SC Number: SC013428

Eligibility

Seafarers in need in Greenock and Port Glasgow.

Types of grants

One-off grants usually of about £150, distributed once a year at Christmas.

Annual grant total

About £800.

Applications

In writing to the correspondent.

The Lady Alice Shaw-Stewart Memorial Fund

£1,000

Correspondent: Director of Finance, Inverclyde Council, Municipal Buildings, Greenock, Inverclyde PA15 1JA (01475 717171)

SC Number: SC019228

Eligibility

Female ex-prisoners recommended by the probation officer in the Inverclyde Council area.

Types of grants

On average one-off grants total about £200 each and are given for general welfare purposes, such as electrical goods, holidays and driving lessons.

Annual grant total

Grants usually total about £1,000 each year

Applications

In writing to the correspondent. Applications should be submitted by a probation officer on behalf of the individual.

Other information

The council administers about 20 other small trusts for people living in Greenock, Gourock, Inverkip and Kilmalcolm.

Mrs Mary Sinclair's Trust

£500

Correspondent: D I Banner, Neill Clerk and Murray Solicitors, 3 Ardgowan Square, Greenock PA16 8NW (01475 724522)

SC Number: SC002535

Eligibility

Older seafarers who were born or sailed out of Greenock, their widows and children, who are in need.

Types of grants

A twice yearly pension to each beneficiary of £12.

Annual grant total

In 2010/11 the trust had an income of £3,700. Grants generally total around £500 a year.

Applications

Application forms can be obtained from the correspondent.

South Ayrshire

The James and Jane Knox Fund

£200

Correspondent: Head of Legal and Administration Services, South Ayrshire Council, County Buildings, Wellington Square, Ayr KA7 1DR (0300 123 0900)

SC Number: SC008856

Eligibility

Older men in need, preferably bachelors, in the parish of Monkton and Prestwick.

Types of grants

One-off and recurrent grants for the provision of comforts.

Annual grant total

About £200.

Applications

In writing to the correspondent directly by the individual with as much information as possible. Applications are considered as and when required.

Other information

South Ayrshire Council administers 93 smaller trusts, details of which can be obtained from the correspondent.

The Loudoun Bequest

£400

Correspondent: Valerie Andrews, Head of Legal and Administration, South Ayrshire Council, County Buildings, Wellington Square, Ayr KA7 1DR (0300 123 0900)

SC Number: SC017166

Eligibility

People in need who live in Monkton and Prestwick.

Types of grants

Gifts of coal to individuals who meet the criteria.

Annual grant total

Grants usually total about £400 each year.

Applications

In writing to the correspondent directly by the individual, providing detailed information.

West Dunbartonshire

Dumbarton Children's Trust

£15,000

Correspondent: Secretary, Bridgend House, 179 High Street, Dumbarton G82 1NP (01389 841333)

SC Number: SC021302

Eligibility

Children in Dumbarton and district up to the age of 18 who have physical, mental or sensory difficulties or are suffering the effects of deprivation.

Types of grants

On average 150 one-off grants are made a year of up to £100 per child according to need. Medical and disability equipment is only available where it is not provided by statutory services. Toys and educational aids/equipment are available.

Annual grant total

Grants usually total around £15,000 per year.

Exclusions

No grants are given for household equipment (unless specifically for children), debts or items which should be provided by statutory services.

Applications

On a form available from the correspondent. Applications should be submitted by a social worker, health visitor or other third party and are considered every six weeks to two months. Deadlines for applications are a week before each meeting.

Lennox Children's Trust

£4,100

Correspondent: Administrator, c/o Citizens Advice, 179 High Street, Dumbarton G82 1NW (01389 765345)

SC Number: SC023740

Eligibility

Children who are in need and live in the Dunbartonshire area.

Types of grants

One-off and recurrent grants according to need. Recent grants have been given for medical equipment, disability aids, toys and educational equipment.

Annual grant total

In 2011/12 the trust had an income of £2,000 and total expenditure of £4,100.

Applications

On a form available from the correspondent, to be submitted by a third party with a connection to the child.

Highlands and Islands

Lady McCorquodale's Charity Trust

£5,000

Correspondent: Laura Gosling, 4th Floor, Swan House, 17–19 Stratford Place, London W1C 1BQ (020 7907 2100; email: charity@mfs.co.uk)

Trustee: The Cowdray Trust Ltd.

CC Number: 268786

Eligibility

People who are in need, with a preference for older people.

Types of grants

One-off and recurrent grants are given for day-to-day needs, such as clothing and food.

Annual grant total

In 2010/11 the trust had an income of £8,900 and a total expenditure of £11,400.

Applications

In writing to the correspondent. Applications can be submitted either directly by the individual or via a social worker, Citizens Advice or other third party.

Other information

This trust also makes grants to organisations.

Dr Sutherland's Fund

£1,500

Correspondent: Secretary, Murdoch Stewarts, 7 West George Street, Glasgow G2 1BA

SC Number: SC006694

Eligibility

People in need who live in the parishes of Olrig – Caithness and Kirkwall and St Ola in the Orkney Isles.

Types of grants

Grants of around £50 each typically.

Annual grant total

Grants usually total around £1,500 per year.

Applications

No grants given on application. The fund's administrators write to the relevant social work departments and ask for a list of eligible beneficiaries, who the administrators then contact.

Highland

Dr Forbes Inverness Trust

£7,000

Correspondent: D J Hewitson, Secretary and Treasurer, Munro and Noble Solicitors, 26 Church Street, Inverness IV1 1HX (01463 221727; fax: 01463 225165; email: legal@munronoble.com)

SC Number: SC005573

Eligibility

People with a medical or similar need who live in the former burgh of Inverness or immediately surrounding areas to the south of the Beauly/Inverness Firth.

Types of grants

Generally one-off grants to help with the cost of medical treatment and equipment, convalescence, food, clothing and travel expenses to visit sick relatives. Help has also been given with holidays for people who, from a medical point of view, would benefit from it.

Annual grant total

In 2010/11 the trust had an income of £7,700. No further information was available.

Applications

On a form available from the correspondent, can be submitted by the individual or through a recognised referral agency (e.g. social worker, Citizens Advice or doctor) or other third party. Forms are considered throughout the year and must be signed by the applicant's doctor. Supporting letters can also help the application.

The Highland Children's Trust

£10,000

Correspondent: The Administrator, 105 Castle Street, Inverness IV2 3EA (01463 243872; fax: 01463 243872; email: info@hctrust.co.uk; website: www. hctrust.co.uk)

SC Number: SC006008

Eligibility

Children and young people in need who are under 25 and live in the Highlands.

Types of grants

One-off grants of £50 to £500 are available for the following purposes:
- Student hardship funding
- School or educational trips
- Family holidays
- Educational items for children with special educational needs

Annual grant total

Around £20,000 for both education and welfare.

Exclusions

Grants are not given for postgraduate study, to pay off debts, nor to purchase clothing, footwear, food, furniture or cars and so on.

Applications

On a form available from the correspondent or downloaded from the website, where criteria and guidelines are also posted. They can be submitted at any time either directly by the individual or through a social worker, Citizens Advice or other welfare agency. Applications must include details of income and savings.

Shetland Islands

Shetland Charitable Trust

£468,000

Correspondent: Mary Anderson, 22–24 North Road, Lerwick, Shetland ZE1 0NQ (01595 744992; fax: 01595 690206)

Trustee: The trustee board is comprised of 19 Shetland Island Councillors ex officio, plus two others. A full list is available on the website.

SC Number: SC027025

Eligibility

Christmas grants: pensioners in receipt of pension credit, housing benefit or council tax benefit. It is also paid to disabled adults and children in receipt of certain disability benefits. In order to qualify applicants must have lived permanently in Shetland since 30 November 2010.Social assistance grants: people in financial need who live in the Shetland Islands.

Types of grants

An annual payment of £300 per person is made at Christmas.

Annual grant total

In 2011/12 the trust had an income of £9.5 million. Grants to individuals totalled £468,000: £454,000 in Christmas grants and £15,000 in social assistance grants. £34,000 was also paid in grants from the Arts Grants Scheme which makes grants to both individuals and organisations; however, a breakdown was not available.

Applications

Applications for Christmas grants tend to open in September of each year; check the website before contacting the trust to ensure applications are being accepted. Applicants for the social assistance grants should contact the duty social worker by email: duty@shetland.gov.uk.

Other information

Grants are also given to organisations.

Western Isles

The William MacKenzie Trust

£25,000

Correspondent: Jack Kernahan, 26 Lewis Street, Stornoway, Isle of Lewis HS1 2JF (01851 702335; fax: 01851 706132; email: jack@mannjudd.co.uk)

SC Number: SC001598

Eligibility

People who are older or in poor health and live in Stornoway.

Types of grants

One-off grants to enable individuals to continue living in their own homes. Recent grants have been given for house adaptations, reclining chairs and domestic equipment such as washing machines.

Annual grant total

In 2010/11 the trust had an income of £32,000.

Applications

In writing to the correspondent. Applications can be submitted directly by the individual, or through a social worker, Citizens Advice or other welfare agency.

Other information

The trust also makes grants to organisations.

Wales

General

Children's Leukaemia Society

£36,000

Correspondent: Elain M Churchill, 384 Coed-Y-Gores, Llanedeyrn, Cardiff CF23 9NR (020920250132)

Trustees: Brian Powell; Keith Williams; Steve Monk; Elaine Churchill; Sarah Louise Churchill; Brian Stafford.

CC Number: 1008634

Eligibility

Children under 16 who are in need and have leukaemia. Grants are made to those living in south Wales and the West Country.

Types of grants

One-off gifts to those in need. Previously, a gift of the child's choice was made to them while they were in hospital for example, a TV or a games console.

Annual grant total

In 2010/11 the society had assets of £119,000 and an income of £87,000. Holidays and gifts made to children amounted to £36,000.

Applications

In writing to the correspondent.

Other information

The society also makes caravans available for the children and their families to have a free holiday when they are well enough.

LATCH Welsh Children's Cancer Charity

£214,000

Correspondent: Grants Manager, LATCH Office, Children's Hospital for Wales, Heath Park, Cardiff CF14 4XW (02920 748858/9; fax: 02920 748868;

email: info@latchwales.org; website: www.latchwales.org)

Trustees: Judge Philip Price; Paul Lyndon Edward Wilkins; Stephen Murray; Ian Rogers; Sian Howell; Ingrid Nutt.

CC Number: e1100949

Eligibility

Children who have cancer and leukaemia (including tumours) and have been referred to the Paediatric Oncology Unit at The Children's Hospital for Wales.

Types of grants

One-off and recurrent grants for children and the families of children who are in need of financial assistance. Recent grants have been given for travel expenses, living costs, car repairs, washing machines, holidays and outings.

Annual grant total

In 2011 the charity had assets of £3.2 million and an income of £589,000. Grants were made totalling £214,000.

Applications

Through one of the LATCH social workers, who submit applications for consideration by the trust.

Other information

The charity also supports the development of the specialist medical care the Unit provides for the children and their families.

The Welsh Rugby Charitable Trust

£155,000

Correspondent: Edward Jones, Hon. Secretary, 55 West Road, Bridgend, Mid-Glamorgan CF31 4HQ (01656 653042; email: ehjones100@googlemail.com; website: www.wrct.org.uk)

Trustees: Alun Thomas; Carolyn Hitt; Dennis Hughes; Brian Rees; Gareth Williams; Edward H. Jones; Dennis Gethin; Tony Gray; Dr Christopher Robert Williams; Rupert Moon.

CC Number: 502079

Eligibility

People who have been severely injured whilst playing rugby union football in Wales, and their dependents.

Types of grants

One-off grants to help injured players regain their independence. Grants can be made towards cars, wheelchairs, hoists, domestic aids, holidays and Christmas gifts.

Annual grant total

In 2010/11 the trust had an income of £522,000 and a total expenditure of £175,000. Grants totalled £155,000.

Applications

In writing to the correspondent, including the circumstances of the injury and the effect it has on the applicant's career. Information on the financial position before and after the accident should also be included. Applications are considered every two months (or sooner in emergency cases) and can be submitted either directly by the individual or by a club representative.

Players who have been seriously injured but not permanently disabled are usually visited by the trust to assess the degree of need before any grant is made.

The Widows, Orphans and Dependents Society of the Church in Wales (WODS)

£88,000 (74 grants)

Correspondent: Louise Davies, 39 Cathedral Road, Cardiff CF11 9XF (02920 348228; email: louisedavies@churchinwales.org.uk; website: www.churchinwales.org.uk)

Trustees: Frances Ann Jackson; Peter Jenkins; John Berry Thelwell; Ronald Glyndwr Hackett; Gillian Brenda Knight; Peter Evans; D. Llewellyn; Revd Deiniol Prys; Revd Kathleen Anne Rogers; Christine John; Revd Dorrien Paul Davies; Clive Myers.

CC Number: 503271

Eligibility

Widows, orphans and dependents of deceased clergy of the Church in Wales only, who are living on a low income. Each year the society sets minimum income levels which each diocesan committee should aim to achieve. In 2011 these levels were set at £13,150 for widows, £12,550 for dependents and £2,400 for orphans.

Types of grants

One-off grants in the form of birthday, Christmas and Easter bonuses.

Annual grant total

In 2011 the society had assets of £541,000 and an income of £107,000. Grants to 74 individuals totalling £88,000 were made across all six Welsh dioceses.

Applications

In writing to the correspondent, including details of the individual's income and their relationship to the relevant member of the clergy and the last parish they served in. Applications can be considered at any time. Grants should be made through one of the six diocesan committees of the Church in Wales.

Mid-Wales

Ceredigion

The Margaret and Alick Potter Charitable Trust

£550

Correspondent: Joan Miller, Y Nyth, Capel Bangor, Aberystwyth SY23 3LR (01970 880637)

Trustees: Beryl Thomas; Joan Miller; Geraldine Taylor; Mair Cave; James O'Neill; Janice Petche.

CC Number: 1088821

Eligibility

People with all types of dementia (as well as Alzheimer's disease) and their families who live in North Ceredigion.

Types of grants

Grants given according to need.

Annual grant total

The trust has an average annual income of around £5,000 although total expenditure varies more widely – for example from a high of £10,000 in 2008/9 to just £600 in 2010/11.

Applications

In writing to the correspondent.

Other information

The trust also makes grants to local organisations.

Powys

The Brecknock Welfare Trust

£1,000

Correspondent: Gail Rofe, Brecon Town Council, The Guildhall, High Street, Brecon, Powys LD3 7AL (01874 622884; email: brecon.guildhall@btinternet.com)

Trustees: A. Morgan; B. Williams; M. Gittins; A. Williams; R. Evans; D. Meredith; A. Weale; P. Ashton; M. Dorrance; N. Sandford; R. Lewis; M. Foster; C. Walsh; M. Phillips; I. Williams.

CC Number: 240671

Eligibility

People in need who live in the town of Brecon.

Types of grants

One-off grants in kind according to need, such as electrical goods, clothing, medical and disabled equipment and furniture.

Annual grant total

Over the last five years the trust's annual expenditure has ranged from £200 to £7,000. Grants are primarily made to organisations.

Exclusions

Grants are in kind and no cash awards are made.

Applications

In writing to the correspondent. Applications should be submitted through a recognised referral agency (such as a social worker, Citizens Advice or doctor and so on).

The Llanidloes Relief-in-Need Charity

£700

Correspondent: Mrs S J Jarman, Clerk, Llwynderw, Old Hall, Llanidloes, Powys SY18 6PW (01686 412636)

Trustees: Gwenda Trow; John Williams; Lynne Evans; Ann Hughes; Revd Michael Starkey.

CC Number: 259955

Eligibility

People in need who live in the communities of Llanidloes and Llanidloes Without only.

Types of grants

One-off grants for fuel, equipment for people who are disabled and to families and students in need.

Annual grant total

About £1,500.

Applications

In writing to the correspondent. Applications should be made through social service, doctors, Citizens Advice or churches.

The Montgomery Welfare Fund

£3,000

Correspondent: Wendy Anne Elizabeth Davies, 15 Lymore View, Montgomery, Powys SY15 6RJ (01686 668734)

Trustees: Margery Elizabeth Richards; Revd Roger Brignell; David Jones; Michael Mills; Revd Toni Bennett; Cerys Elizabeth Thomas.

CC Number: 214767

Eligibility

People in need who live permanently in the ecclesiastical parish of Montgomery (not the county).

Types of grants

One-off grants ranging from £25 to £100. Reapplications can be made. Grants cover a wide range of needs.

Annual grant total

Grants usually average around £3,000 per year.

Exclusions

No grants to pay rates, tax or other public funds.

Applications

In writing to the correspondent. Applications can be submitted directly by the individual or family member. Applications can be received all year round.

Other information

Grants can also be given to individuals for education, 'development in life' and so on.

The Visual Impairment Breconshire (Nam Gweledol Sir Brycheiniog)

£1,700

Correspondent: Edward Vince, Ken Dy Gwair, Aber Farm, Talybont-on-Usk, Brecon LD3 7YS (01874 676202)

Trustees: Michael Knee; Edward Jeffrey Vince; Terrence Ottewell; Eileen Bufton;

Margaret James; Margaret Seaman; John Cecil King; John Lloyd; Derek Stephens.

CC Number: 217377

Eligibility
Blind and partially-sighted people living in Brecknock.

Types of grants
One-off grants at Christmas and for special equipment/special needs, for example, cookers and talking books.

Annual grant total
Grants average around £1,700 a year, though the actual grant figure tends to fluctuate quite widely.

Applications
In writing to the correspondent, to be considered when received.

Other information
This charity also runs activities, provides resources and makes grants to organisations.

North Wales

The Corwen College Pension Charity

£1,200

Correspondent: Diane McCarthy, The Diocese of St Asaph, Diocesan Office, High Street, St Asaph, Denbighshire LL17 0RD (01745 582245; fax: 01745 530078; email: dianemccarthy@ churchinwales.org.uk)

Trustees: Revd Christopher Nicholas Lynden Potter; Ven John Berry Thelwell; Revd Bethan Scotford; Ven Bernard Thomas; Ven Malcolm Squires; Ven Shirley Thelma Griffiths.

CC Number: 248822

Eligibility
Needy widows or widowers of clergy of the Church in Wales who have held office in the district of Merionydd in Gwynedd or the communities of Betws Gwerfil Goch, Corwen Gwyddelddern, Llandrillo, Llangar and Llansantffraid Glyndyfrdwy (all in Clwyd).

Types of grants
Recurrent grants according to need.

Annual grant total
Grants generally total around £1,000 a year.

Applications
In writing to the correspondent, for consideration in February.

The North Wales Police Benevolent Fund

£3,500

Correspondent: Mel Jones, North Wales Police Federation, 311 Abergele Road, Old Colwyn, Colwyn Bay LL29 9YF (01492 805404)

Trustees: Ian Shannon; Gwyn Roberts; Mark Polin; Gareth Pritchard.

CC Number: 505321

Eligibility
Members of the North Wales Police Force and former members of this and previous forces amalgamated within constituent forces, and their families and immediate dependents who are in need.

Types of grants
One-off and recurrent grants according to need. Grants are also made at Christmas.

Annual grant total
In 2010/11 the trust had an income of £5,000 and a total expenditure of £3,800.

Applications
In writing to the correspondent. Applications are considered quarterly, although urgent applicants can be considered as they arrive.

The North Wales Psychiatric Fund

£6,500

Correspondent: Mr A Banks, Finance Department, Stanley Hospital, Upper Denbigh Road, St Asaph LL17 0RS (01745 589646)

Trustees: Clwyd Wynne; Richard Rowley-Williams; Dr Neil Sandon Davies.

CC Number: 235783

Eligibility
People in North Wales who are mentally ill and are under the care of a social worker or health professional.

Types of grants
One-off grants for clothes, furniture, holidays and learning courses.

Annual grant total
Both income and expenditure tend to fluctuate annually, with grants averaging around £8,000 a year over the past few years.

Exclusions
There are no grants available for the payment of debts.

Applications
In writing to the correspondent through a social worker or health professional, including details of income and other possible grant sources. Applications are considered throughout the year.

The Evan and Catherine Roberts Home

£4,000

Correspondent: Ken Owen, Ael Y Garth, 81 Bryn Avenue, Old Colwyn, Colwyn Bay LL29 8AH (01492 515209)

Trustees: Revd Philip Barnett; Ken Owen; John Jones; Arfon Williams; Ifor Jones.

CC Number: 244965

Eligibility
People who live within a 40-mile radius of the Bethesda Welsh Methodist Church in Old Colwyn, with preference for members of the Church.

Types of grants
One-off grants ranging from £50 to £150.

Annual grant total
In 2011 the trust had an income of £1,400 and a total expenditure of £4,100.

Applications
On a form available from the correspondent.

Elizabeth Williams Charities

£5,000

Correspondent: Mrs Alison R Alexander, Arfon Cottage, 19 Roe Parc, St Asaph, Denbighshire LL17 0LD (01745 583798; email: alison.alexander@btinternet.com)

Trustees: Revd Christopher Potter; Robert Lloyd Williams; Meirick Lloyd Davies; Barbara Rust; Ralph Graham Pierce; Ffion Mererid Lloyd-Williams; Helen Owens; Arfon Jones Hughes.

CC Number: 216903

Eligibility
People in need who live in the communities of St Asaph, Bodelwyddan, Cefn and Waen in Denbighshire.

Types of grants
One-off grants, generally between £50 and £100, are given as Christmas bonuses for people who are older, to families with parents suffering serious illnesses and for particular needs.

Annual grant total
Grants usually total around £7,000 per annum, although in 2010/11 the trust had a lower overall income and expenditure and so it seems likely that around £5,000 was made in grants.

Exclusions

Grants are not given for aid that can be met specifically by public funds, for private education or if the grant would affect a claimant's benefit from the DWP.

Applications

In writing to the correspondent, to be submitted either directly by the individual or through a social worker, Citizens Advice or other welfare agency. Applications can also be submitted via a trustee. They are generally considered in November, although specific cases can be considered at any time.

Anglesey

Anglesey Society for the Welfare of Handicapped People

£2,000

Correspondent: Mr R W Jones, 8 Gorwel Deg, Rhostrehwfa, Llangefni, Anglesey

CC Number: 218810

Eligibility

People living in Anglesey who have tuberculosis or any other disease, illness or disability.

Types of grants

One-off or recurrent grants according to need.

Annual grant total

Around £2,000 each year is given in grants to individuals.

Applications

In writing to the correspondent.

Other information

The trust also makes grants to organisations.

Conwy

Conwy Welsh Church Acts Fund

£5,000

Correspondent: Mrs Catherine Dowber, Conwy County Borough Council, Bodlondeb, Conwy LL32 8DU (01492 576201 – For Welsh Language Officer call 01492 576130; email: welshchurchactsfund@conwy.gov.uk)

Eligibility

People in need living in the County Borough of Conwy.

Types of grants

One-off grants ranging from £50 to £2,000, for relief of poverty and sickness, financial aid for older people, medical treatment, help for people on probation, assistance for the blind or visually impaired and to relieve emergencies and disasters.

Annual grant total

The fund generates approximately £10,000 per annum for distribution.

Exclusions

Grants are not made to individuals for sport or tuition fees.

Applications

On a form available from the correspondent, to be submitted directly by the individual or through a third party. The closing date for applications is the first week in October, for consideration in November/December.

Other information

The fund also supports organisations.

Denbighshire

The Freeman Evans St David's Day Denbigh Charity

£5,000

Correspondent: Medwyn Jones, Denbigh Town Council, Town Hall, Crown Square, Denbigh, Clwyd LL16 3TB (01745 815984; email: townclerk@ denbightowncouncil.gov.uk)

Trustees: Revd Jonathan Smith; Revd Wayne Roberts; Medwyn Jones; Ann Larson; Gwyrfai; Dr Chris Madoc-Jones; Alan Davies.

CC Number: 518033

Eligibility

People in need who are older, in poor health or who have a disability and live in Denbigh and Henllan.

Types of grants

One-off grants towards disability aids, furniture, travel costs, home adaptations, Christmas gifts and so on.

Annual grant total

In 2010/11 the charity had an income of £112,000 and made four grants to individuals totalling £6,000. The charity also gave grants totalling £30,000 to organisations.

Applications

In writing to the correspondent. Applications can be made either directly by the individual or through a third party such as a social worker, Citizens Advice or other welfare agency. The

trustees meet regularly throughout the year to consider applications.

Other information

Grants are also given for educational purposes.

Flintshire

Flintshire Welsh Church Acts Fund

£1,000

Correspondent: Philip Latham, Funds and Treasury, Flintshire County Council, County Hall, Mold CH7 6NA (01352 702264; fax: 01352 702279; email: philip. latham@flintshire.gov.uk)

Trustee: Kerry Ann Feather.

CC Number: 504476

Eligibility

People who are sick or who have disabilities and are living in Flintshire.

Types of grants

One-off and recurrent grants, ranging between £100 and £500.

Annual grant total

In 2010/11 the fund had an income of £22,000 and a total expenditure of £25,000. Grants to individuals have previously totalled around £1,000.

Applications

On a form available from the correspondent. Applications are considered quarterly.

Other information

This trust was previously listed as County Council of Clwyd Welsh Church Acts Fund.

It also makes grants to organisations.

The Owen Jones Charity

£1,500

Correspondent: Dr Jack Wolstenholme, Secretary, 18 St Peter's Park, Northop, Mold, Clwyd CH7 6DP (01352 840739)

Trustees: Revd Ray Billingsley; Dr Jack Wolstenholme; Muriel Patterson.

CC Number: 525453

Eligibility

People in need who live in Northop.

Types of grants

One-off and recurrent grants according to need.

Annual grant total

In 2010/11 the charity had an income of £4,500, a total expenditure of £7,300 and made grants to individuals totalling £3,000.

Applications

In writing to the correspondent. An application form for students to use is currently being drafted and should be used when available.

Other information

The charity also makes grants to local schools.

Gwynedd

The Freeman Evans St David's Day Ffestiniog Charity

£38,000

Correspondent: Maldwyn Evans, Natwest Bank plc, Merionnydd Business Centre, Bridge Street, Dolgellau, Gwynedd LL40 1AU (01341 421242)

Trustees: William Maldwyn Evans; Elwyn Hughes; Ann Coxon.

CC Number: 518034

Eligibility

People who are older, in poor health, or who have disabilities and live in the districts of Blaenau Ffestiniog and Llan Ffestiniog as they were prior to the 1974 reorganisation.

Types of grants

One-off and recurrent grants for home adaptations, specialist chairs, stair-lifts, electric wheelchairs and phone lifelines.

Annual grant total

In 2011/12 the charity had an income of £22,000. Grants were made totalling around £38,000.

Applications

Applications can be submitted in writing directly by the individual or through a recognised referral agency such as a social worker, minister of religion, councillor, Citizens Advice or doctor. Applications are considered by the trustees twice a year, though urgent cases can be dealt with between meetings.

Wrexham

The Jones Trust

£31,000

Correspondent: Mrs Melissa Thomas, 33 Deva Way, Wrexham LL13 9EU (01978 261684)

Trustees: Frank Newsome; Rowland Basil Cole; Margaretta Jones; Anthony Williams.

CC Number: 229956

Eligibility

People who are sick, convalescing, disabled or infirm in the county of Wrexham.

Types of grants

Grants for respite care in residential and nursing homes and convalescence. Grants for appliances and surgical aids not readily available through the health service are also considered.

Annual grant total

In 2011 the trust had an income of £34,000 and the accounts note that the trust 'experienced a higher level of grant applications in 2011 and agreed to a short-term increase in its grant allocation,' by distributing £31,000 to beneficiaries. However, in the future grants are likely to be capped at £20,000.

Applications

In writing to the correspondent.

The Ruabon and District Relief-in-Need Charity

£700

Correspondent: J R Fenner, Secretary, 65 Albert Grove, Ruabon, Wrexham LL14 6AF (01978 820102; email: jamesrfenner@tiscali.co.uk)

Trustees: Mair Mates; Vera Wainwright; John Griffiths; Joan Lowe; Jean Speare; Michael Edwards.

CC Number: 212817

Eligibility

All people who are considered to be in need who live in the county borough of Wrexham, which covers the community council districts of Cefn Mawr, Penycae, Rhosllanerchrugog (including Johnstown) and Ruabon.

Types of grants

One-off and occasionally recurrent grants of up to £200. Grants can be towards installation of a telephone, heating costs, children's clothing, cookers, furniture, musical instruments, electric wheelchairs, clothing for adults in hospital, travel costs for hospital visits and books and travel for university students. One-off grants in kind are also given. On average, 15 grants are given by the charity each year.

Annual grant total

About £1,400 in educational and relief-in-need grants.

Exclusions

Grants are not given for instigating bankruptcy proceedings. Loans are not given.

Applications

In writing to the correspondent either directly by the individual or a family member, through a third party such as a social worker or teacher, or through an organisation such as Citizens Advice or a school. Applications are considered on an ongoing basis.

The Wrexham and District Relief in Need Charity

£11,000

Correspondent: Mrs Frieda Leech, Clerk, Holly Chase, Pen Y Palmant Road, Minera, Wrexham LL11 3YW (01978 754152; email: clerk.wpef@gmail.com)

Trustees: Ida Turley; Revd Mike West; Roger Berry; Carol Ann Jones; Revd Noel Carter; Peter John Blore; John Kenworthy; Cllr Joan Lowe; Revd James Harris; Shirley Griffiths; Nicola Jayne Hulley.

CC Number: 236355

Eligibility

People in need who live in the former borough of Wrexham or the communities of Abenbury, Bersham, Bieston, Broughton, Brymbo, Esclusham Above, Esclusham Below, Gresford, Gwersyllt and Minera in Wrexham.

Types of grants

One-off or recurrent grants according to need ranging from £40 to £500. For example, grants have been given towards the cost of maternity necessities, household equipment, wheelchairs, clothing and a stairlift.

Annual grant total

In 2011 the charity had an income of £16,000 and a total expenditure of £12,000.

Applications

In writing to the correspondent. Applications should be submitted directly by the individual, or by a third party, and should include full details of the applicant's weekly income and expenditure together with the cost of the item required where applicable. Applications are considered throughout the year.

South Wales

Gwalia Housing Trust

£10,000

Correspondent: Tracey Healey, Trust Administrator, Grwp Gwalia Cyf, Ty Gwalia, 7–13 The Kingsway, Swansea

SA1 5JN (01792 460609; fax: 01792 466198; email: ght@gwalia.com; website: www.gwaliahousingtrust.com)

Trustees: George Valentine Kennedy; Edwina Olive Drew; Eileen Nielsen; Margaret Thorne; John Hadden Button; Colin Rabey Williams; John Frederick Morse; Revd Anthony Edward Pierce.

CC Number: 700822

Eligibility

People in need who live in areas where Grwp Gwalia Cyf owns properties (south Wales, including Newport, Haverfordwest, Newtown, Machynlleth, Carmarthenshire, Swansea and Neath Port Talbot).

Types of grants

One-off grants for housing related needs.

Annual grant total

In 2010/11 the trust had assets of £2.5 million and an income of £1.1 million. Grants totalled £38,000.

Applications

Via the online application form on the trust's website which may also be printed and sent to the correspondent. Applications can be submitted directly by the individual or through an appropriate third party and should include the relevant supporting information. They are considered on a quarterly basis.

Other information

The trust provides housing for people in necessitous circumstances, particularly older people, students and those living with disabilities. The trust also makes grants to organisations.

Local Aid for Children and Community Special Needs

£1,000

Correspondent: Ms D Inger, 89 Clase Road, Morriston, Swansea SA6 8DY (01792 405041; email: amanda.lervy@ swansea.gov.uk; website: www.localaid. co.uk)

Trustees: Linda Wellington; Maria Powell; Nigel Steven Williams; Terry Richardson; Ms D. Inger; James Price; Sandra Anne Hylan.

CC Number: 1104585

Eligibility

People with special needs/learning difficulties, between the ages of 3 and 30, who live in Swansea or Neath Port Talbot.

Types of grants

One-off grants or grants in kind ranging from £50 to £150 for specialist

equipment such as a specialist bed, chair or bike, or towards the costs of travel.

Annual grant total

In 2010/11 the charity had assets of £121,000 and an income of £249,000.

Exclusions

No grants are given for items which should be funded by statutory sources.

Applications

In writing to the correspondent, including confirmation that the amount requested is not available from statutory sources. Applications should be submitted through a social worker, Citizens Advice or other welfare agency or professional. They are considered quarterly.

Other information

Grants are occasionally made to individuals in need, however the majority of expenditure is allocated to funding the charity's own projects working with children with disabilities.

The South Wales Police Benevolent Fund

£21,000

Correspondent: Head of Performance Management, Communications Division, Cowbridge Road, Bridgend, Mid-Glamorgan CF31 3SU (01656 869342; website: www.south-wales.police.uk)

Trustees: Chief Supt Richard Lewis; Chief Insp Keith Prosser; Wyn Rowlands.

CC Number: 501454

Eligibility

Serving or retired members of the South Wales Police or constituent force pre-1968 and their dependents, who are in need.

Types of grants

One-off grants, usually up to a maximum of £200, and recurrent grants to meet relief in cases of financial need for those who are sick, convalescent, disabled, infirm, poor or aged. Recent grants have been made to assist with travel expenses to and from a police convalescent home; to assist in buying orthopaedic beds for older people with disabilities and specialist equipment for children with disabilities in hospitals; to assist in travel expenses for specialist treatment in hospitals; and to help for financial hardship 'not brought about by folly'.

Annual grant total

In 2009/10 the trust made welfare payments totalling £100, death benefits to 33 individuals totalling £12,000 and benevolence assistance to six individuals totalling £8,900.

Exclusions

Grants are not made for private medical treatment or for holidays of convalescence other than at a police home. Loans are not given.

Applications

On a form available from the correspondent or to download from the force intranet. Applications should be submitted either by the individual or by any committee member or member of the Force's Welfare Staff on behalf of the individual. Applications are considered quarterly, but emergency payments can be made more quickly.

Other information

At the time of writing (winter 2012) the charity's accounts for 2010/11 were overdue at the Charity Commission.

Cardiff

The Cardiff Caledonian Society

£3,500

Correspondent: Cathy Rogers, 2 Llandinam Crescent, Cardiff CF14 2RB (02920 623680)

Trustees: Iain Breckenridge; Len Richards; Douglas Gowans.

CC Number: 257665

Eligibility

People of Scottish nationality and their families, who live in Cardiff or the surrounding district and are in need.

Types of grants

One-off grants are given for clothing, food, household bills, travel expenses and furniture. Support may be given to people who are homeless, disabled or affected by hardship.

Annual grant total

Grants usually total around £7,000 each year, for both educational and welfare purposes.

Applications

In writing to the correspondent. Applications can be submitted directly by the individual or through a social worker, Citizens Advice or other welfare agency at any time. Applications are considered on a regular basis.

Cardiff Citizens Charity

£2,700

Correspondent: Ms Liza Kellett, The Community Foundation in Wales, Unit 9 Coopers Yard, Curran Road, Cardiff CF10 5NB (02920 536590; email: mail@ cfiw.org.uk; website: www.cfiw.org.uk)

Trustee: The Community Foundation in Wales.

CC Number: 206549

Eligibility
People in need who live in the city of Cardiff.

Types of grants
One-off grants in the range of £100 to £400 for funeral expenses, clothes, specialist computer software, household appliances and so on.

Annual grant total
In 2010/11 the fund had an income of £5,700 and paid grants totalling £2,700.

Exclusions
No grants are made for educational purposes.

Applications
On a form available from the correspondent, to be submitted through a recognised referral agency (such as a social worker, Citizens Advice or doctor) or other third party. Evidence of weekly/monthly expenditure must be submitted. Trustees meet twice yearly to consider applications.

Other information
This charity was formerly known as the Cardiff Charity for Special Relief. The charity is now administered by the Community Foundation in Wales.

The Duffryn Trust

£8,000

Correspondent: D C Williams, 89 Cyncoed Road, Cardiff CF23 5SD

Trustees: David Christopher Williams; Jane Elizabeth Williams.

CC Number: 1031718

Eligibility
People in need with a preference for those who live in Cardiff.

Types of grants
One-off and recurrent grants according to need.

Annual grant total
In 2010/11 the trust had an income of £6,700 and a total expenditure of £9,600.

Applications
In writing to the correspondent.

Other information
The trust also makes grants to organisations.

Merthyr Tydfil
Merthyr Mendicants

£9,000

Correspondent: A G Lane, 4 Georgetown Villas, Georgetown, Merthyr Tydfil, Mid-Glamorgan CF48 1BD (01685 373308)

Trustees: David Idwal James; John Wallbank; Leonard Aird Goodwin; Alan Gunter.

CC Number: 208105

Eligibility
People in need who live in the borough of Merthyr Tydfil.

Types of grants
One-off grants according to need. Recent grants have been given towards medical equipment not available from the National Health Service (providing it is recommended by a medical authority); Christmas parcels; holidays for children; telephone helplines for incapacitated people; and help with domestic equipment such as cookers, refrigerators, washing machines, bedding and beds.

Annual grant total
Grants average around £10,000 a year.

Applications
In writing to the correspondent, including information on any other sources of income. Applications can be submitted directly by the individual or through a social worker, Citizens Advice or other welfare agency.

Other information
Grants are also made to local organisations.

Monmouthshire
Llandenny Charities

£500

Correspondent: Dr Graham Russell, Forge Cottage, Llandenny, Usk, Monmouthshire NP15 1DL (01633 432536; email: gsrussell@btinternet.com)

Trustees: Dr Graham Russell; Noel Porter; Revd Joan Wakeling; Richard Moorby; Sue Russell.

CC Number: 223311

Eligibility
People over 65 and in need who are in receipt of a state pension, live in the parish of Llandenny and have lived there for more than one year.

Types of grants
Pensions to people receiving a state pension.

Annual grant total
About £1,000 for educational and welfare purposes.

Applications
In writing to the correspondent, to be submitted directly by the individual. Applications should be submitted by 15 January for consideration in February.

Monmouth Charity

£5,000

Correspondent: Andrew Pirie, Pen-y-Bryn, Oakfield Road, Monmouth NP25 3JJ (01600 716202)

Trustees: Andrew Pirie; George Griffiths; Heather Colls; Stephen Clarke.

CC Number: 700759

Eligibility
People in need who live within a ten-mile radius of Monmouth and neighbourhood.

Types of grants
One-off grants usually up to a maximum of £500.

Annual grant total
In 2010/11 the charity had an income of £12,000 and an expenditure of £11,000. Grants are made for both educational and welfare purposes.

Applications
The trust advertises in the local press each September/October and applications should be made in response to this advertisement for consideration in November. Emergency grants can be considered at any time. There is no application form. Applications can be submitted directly by the individual or through a social worker, Citizens Advice or other welfare agency.

Monmouth Support Fund

£850

Correspondent: Philip Henry Bly, Marshall House, 8 The Gardens, Monmouth, Monmouthshire NP25 3HF (01600 719787; email: philip.bly@dsl.pipex.com)

Trustees: Susan Chivers; Heather Colls; David McGladdery; Philip Henry Bly.

CC Number: 223790

Eligibility
People in need who live in Monmouth town.

Types of grants
One-off grants of up to £60 including those towards winter heating costs.

Annual grant total

Total expenditure for this charity averages around £850.

Applications

In writing to the correspondent by 1 January for consideration in the same month. Applications can be submitted directly by the individual, through a social worker, Citizens Advice, other welfare agency or a member of the clergy.

The Monmouthshire Welsh Church Acts Fund

£90,000

Correspondent: David Jarrett, Central Finance, Monmouthshire County Council, County Hall, Cwmbran, Monmouthshire NP44 2XH (01633 644657; website: www.monmouthshire. gov.uk)

Trustee: Monmouthshire County Council.

CC Number: 507094

Eligibility

People living in the boundaries of Monmouthshire County Council who are in need.

Types of grants

Grants of money or payment for items, services or facilities. Accommodation can be provided to older people who need it because of infirmities or disabilities. People who are blind may also be given access to charitable homes and holiday homes. Grants range from £50 to £500.

Annual grant total

In 2010/11 the fund had assets of £4.8 million and an income of £69,000. Grants totalled £186,000. The grants were made to the following administering Local Authorities for them to make to individuals on behalf of the fund: Monmouthshire County Council, Torfaen County Borough Council, Newport City Council, Blaenau Gwent County Borough Council and Caerphilly County Borough Council.

Applications

On a form available from the correspondent or downloaded from the website, which can be submitted at any time and must be signed by a County Councillor. Applications can be made either directly by the individual, or through a third party such as a social worker or Citizens Advice and are usually considered in June, September, December and March.

Pembrokeshire

Haverfordwest Freemen's Estate

£8,000

Correspondent: P K Lucas, R K Lucas and Son, The Tithe Exchange, 9 Victoria Place, Haverfordwest, Pembrokeshire SA61 2JX (01437 762538)

Trustees: Lionel Evans; Peter Higgon; Malcolm Thomas; George Green.

CC Number: 515111

Eligibility

Hereditary freemen of Haverfordwest aged 18 years and over.

Types of grants

One-off grants according to need.

Annual grant total

In 2010/11 the trust had an income of £17,000 and a total expenditure of £18,000.

Applications

Freemen must be enrolled by the chairman of the local authority. The honour is hereditary being passed down through the male or female line.

Other information

Grants are also made to organisations.

The William Sanders Charity

£5,500

Correspondent: Henry Johnston, St Johns Parish Office, St Johns Community Hall, Church Street, Pembroke Dock SA72 6AR (01646 680024)

Trustees: Henry Herbert Johnston; Bradley Eynon Perry.

CC Number: 229182

Eligibility

Widows and unmarried women in need who live within a five mile radius of the parish of St John's, Pembroke Dock.

Types of grants

Christmas grants ranging from £25 to £40.

Annual grant total

In 2010/11 the charity had an income of £9,000 and a total expenditure of £5,800.

Applications

In writing to the correspondent directly by the individual or family member.

The Tenby Relief-in-Need and Pensions Charity

£26,000 (130 grants)

Correspondent: Clive Mathias, Clerk to the Trustees, Lewis Lewis and Co., County Chambers, Pentre Road, St Clears, Carmarthen SA33 4AA (01994 231044)

Trustees: Eileen Hodgson; Trisha Putwain; Brian Clement Hilling; Revd Nanette Lewis-Head; Andrew Davies; Brian Hodder; Clive Webb; Ellie Craig; Roland Grigg; Philip Smith; Marilyn Cray; Sue Lane; Kerri Durham; Revd Andrew Davies.

CC Number: 231233

Eligibility

Older people in need who live in the community of Tenby.

Types of grants

Pensions of £17 a month to help relieve financial difficulties. Most beneficiaries will also receive a small Christmas bonus of £18. Usually, once a grant has been agreed it will be paid indefinitely.

Annual grant total

In 2011 the charity had assets of £666,000 and an income of £33,000. Grants were made to individuals totalling £26,000.

Applications

On a form available from the correspondent, to be submitted directly by the individual or a family member.

William Vawer's Charity

£2,000

Correspondent: R K Lucas, The Tithe Exchange, 9 Victoria Place, Haverfordwest, Pembrokeshire SA61 2JX (01437 762538; fax: 01437 765404)

Trustees: Mrs H. Richards; Capt. Henry Phillips; Maurice Hughes; Barbara Morgan; Peter Stock; Roy Thomas.

CC Number: 213880

Eligibility

People in need who live in the town of Haverfordwest.

Types of grants

Pensions to existing pensioners. Other grants to those in need, hardship or distress.

Annual grant total

Grants usually average around £2,000 per year.

Applications

In writing to the correspondent.

Swansea

The Swansea and District Friends of the Blind

£4,900

Correspondent: John Allan, Secretary, 3 De La Beche Street, Swansea SA1 3EY (01792 655424; email: allan.john@ btconnect.com)

Trustee: Mr R. O. Thomas.

CC Number: 211343

Eligibility

People who are registered blind and live in Swansea.

Types of grants

One-off grants towards talking watches, kitchen equipment, computers and so on. Gifts are also given out at Christmas and Easter.

Annual grant total

In 2010/11 the trust had assets of £258,000 and an income of £89,000. Christmas and Easter gifts totalled £4,400 and a further £500 was distributed in welfare grants

Applications

In writing to the correspondent. Applications are considered on a regular basis.

Other information

The majority of the trust's funds go towards organising events such as summer outings and Christmas dinners and generally providing advice, information and services for visually impaired people in the area.

Torfaen

The Cwmbran Trust

£11,000

Correspondent: Kenneth Maddox, Arvinheritor HVBS (UK) Ltd, Grange Road, Cwmbran, Gwent NP44 3XU (01633 834040; email: cwmbrantrust@ arvinmeritor.com)

Trustees: Ken Maddox; John Cunningham; Anthony Rippon; David Bassett; Anna Price; C. Thomas.

CC Number: 505855

Eligibility

People in need living in the town of Cwmbran, Gwent.

Types of grants

One-off and recurrent grants are awarded for a wide variety of educational and welfare purposes, such as stair-lifts, home-study courses, computer equipment, wheelchairs, holidays, debt clearance, removal costs, building renovation, funeral costs and respite care. Grants usually range between £125 to £2,500.

Annual grant total

In 2011 the trust had assets of £1.9 million and an income of £80,000. Grants were made to 34 individuals totalling £21,000 for educational and welfare purposes. One loan of £2,000 was also provided

Applications

In writing to the correspondent. Applications can be submitted directly by the individual or through a social worker, Citizens Advice, welfare agency or other third party. Applications are usually considered in March, May, July, October and December.

Vale of Glamorgan

The Cowbridge with Llanblethian United Charities

£23,000

Correspondent: Clerk to the Trustees, 66 Broadway, Llanblethian, Cowbridge, Vale of Glamorgan CF71 7EW (01446 773287; email: unitedcharities@aol.com)

Trustee: Jacqueline Thomas.

CC Number: 1014580

Eligibility

People in need who live in the town of Cowbridge with Llanblethian.

Types of grants

The provision of items, services or facilities that will reduce the person's need.

Annual grant total

In 2010/11 the charities had an income of £20,000 and a total expenditure of £25,000. Previously Christmas and summer grants totalled £23,000, with a further £300 given in general grants locally.

Applications

In writing to the correspondent. Applications can be submitted directly by the individual or through a welfare agency.

Other information

Grants are also made for educational purposes.

The Neale Trust Fund for Poor Children

£0

Correspondent: David Ward Jenkins, Trustee, Lanby, 16 White House, Barry CF62 6FB (01446 730204)

Trustees: Dr Anne Hughes; David Ward Jenkins.

CC Number: 225652

Eligibility

Schoolchildren in need who live in the district of Barry and are aged 16 or under.

Types of grants

One-off grants of up to £500 each for: clothes; shoes; educational, medical or disability equipment; and travel expenses.

Annual grant total

On average, about £1,000 is available each year to distribute in grants, although spending does tend to fluctuate.

Exclusions

No grants are given for video/computer equipment.

Applications

In writing to the correspondent, who will then send out a form to be completed. The need for support has to be shown by the applicant. Applications are considered in January and September according to availability of funds or in special cases by home visit of the secretary. Applications can be made through the social services, Citizens Advice or local childcare officer, or directly by the individual. The trust does not accept unsolicited applications.

North East

General

The Christina Aitchison Trust

£600

Correspondent: Revd Massingberd-Mundy, c/o The Old Post-Office, The Street, West Raynham, Fakenham, Norfolk NR21 7AD

Trustees: Allen Carding; Paul Mundy; Revd Roger Massinberd-Mundy.

CC Number: 1041578

Eligibility

People who are blind or have any ophthalmic disease or disability, and people who have a terminal illness, who are in need, and live in north east or south west England.

Types of grants

One-off and recurrent grants for up to £200 to relieve blindness, ophthalmic disease or disability, and terminal illness.

Annual grant total

In 2010/11 the trust had an income of £1,800 and a total expenditure of £2,400.

Applications

On a form available from the correspondent, to be submitted in March or September for consideration in April or November.

Other information

Grants are also given to individuals and organisations concerned with education, equitation, sailing and music.

Mrs E. L. Blakeley-Marillier Charitable Fund

£12,000

Correspondent: Sophia Honey, Wollen Michelmore, Carlton House, 30 The Terrace, Torquay, Devon TQ1 1BS (01803 213251; fax: 01803 296871; email: sophia.honey@wollenmichelmore.co.uk; website: www.wollenmichelmore.co.uk)

Trustees: Nigel James Wollen; Christopher Duncan Hart; Edward Michael John Richards.

CC Number: 207138

Eligibility

Ladies over 55 who are in need and are not of the Roman Catholic faith or members of the Salvation Army. Preference is given to women from the counties of Yorkshire and Devon and in particular the towns of Scarborough and Torquay.

Types of grants

Annuities of about £520 a year paid twice a year. Grants will not be given if the effect is to reduce income support or other benefits or to reduce debt.

Annual grant total

Grants average around £12,000 per year.

Applications

On a form available from the correspondent to be submitted directly by the individual including a general financial overview. Applications are usually considered in November and May.

Lord Crewe's Charity

£12,000

Correspondent: Philip Davies, Clerk, The Cathedral Office, The College, Durham DH1 3EH (01913 751226; email: philip.davies@durhamcathedral.co.uk)

Trustees: Harry Vane; Paul Langford; Ian Jagger; John Anderson; Stuart Bain; Geoffrey Miller; John Blackett-Ord.

CC Number: 230347

Eligibility

Necessitous clergy, their widows and dependents who live in the dioceses of Durham and Newcastle. Grants may also be given more generally to people in need who live in the area.

Types of grants

One-off and recurrent grants according to need.

Annual grant total

The latest accounts available were for 2012, when 'clergy support' totalled £12,000.

Applications

On a form available from the correspondent.

The Olive and Norman Field Charity

£11,500

Correspondent: John Pelter, Chairman, c/o British Red Cross, Red Cross House, Zetland Street, Northallerton, North Yorkshire DL6 1NB (01609 771554)

Trustees: Jean Slater; Eileen Brereton; Karl Podmore; Martin Huitson; Paddy Chapman; John Pelter; Angela Connor; Denise Davies; Andy Nuttall.

CC Number: 208760

Eligibility

People who are in poor health, convalescent or who have disabilities and live in the former North Riding of Yorkshire (now the counties of Durham and North Yorkshire and the unitary authorities of Darlington, Hartlepool, Middlesbrough, Redcar and Cleveland, Stockton-on-Tees and York).

Types of grants

One-off grants, usually in the range of £100 to £350, are given towards electric goods, convalescence, medical equipment, furniture and disability equipment.

Annual grant total

In 2010 the charity had an income of £26,000 and a total expenditure of £25,000. Grants to both individuals and organisations totalled £23,000.

Exclusions

The charity is unable to assist with debt, computer equipment (unless there is a specific medical need) or house renovations.

Applications

On a form available from the correspondent or social services.

Applications should be submitted either through a social worker, Citizens Advice or other welfare agency. Applications are considered in February, April, June, September and December.

The Greggs Foundation

£203,000

Correspondent: Foundation Manager, Fernwood House, Clayton Road, Jesmond, Newcastle upon Tyne NE2 1TL (01912 127626; fax: 01912 819536; email: greggsfoundation@greggs.co.uk; website: www.greggsfoundation.org.uk)

Trustees: Andrew John Davison; Kate Welch; AnneMarie Norman; Fiona Nicholson; Peter McKendrick; Richard Hutton; Melanie Nicholson.

CC Number: 296590

Eligibility

People in need who live in the north east of England (Northumberland, Tyne and Wear, Durham and Teesside). Priority is given to children and families.

Types of grants

Grants range from £50 to £150 and are given for essential items such as white goods, furniture, baby equipment, flooring, clothing and school uniforms.

Annual grant total

In 2011 the foundation had assets of £10.7 million and an income of £1.5 million. Grants totalled £1.7 million, of which £203,000 was given to individuals in hardship grants. Of this total 1,021 people received grants directly from the foundation, totalling £107,000. A further £96,000 was given in block grants directly to social organisations to make grants on the foundation's behalf.

Exclusions

Grants are not given to cover debts, bankruptcy fees, holidays, funeral expenses, medical equipment, overseas expeditions, computer equipment or sponsorship.

Applications

The foundation now uses an online application form. In exceptional circumstances, if you cannot use the online form contact the trust to make other arrangements. Applications should be made through a welfare agency, such as social services, probation service, Citizens Advice, victim support, health, disability and housing projects or other similar organisations. Applications submitted directly by the individual will not be considered.

Applications received by Friday at 4pm will be processed in the following week. The foundation asks that applicants do not send any additional information as this will not be considered.

Other information

Through the Hardship Fund, Greggs Trust administers funds on behalf of a number of other local charitable trusts, including The Brough Benevolent Association, The Hadrian Trust, The 1989 Willan Charitable Trust, The Sir James Knott Trust, The Joicey Trust and The Rothley Trust

Note, only one form from each applicant should be submitted to the joint trusts, as the payment will be made from joint funds.

Lady Elizabeth Hastings' Non-Educational Charity

£160,000 (117 grants)

Correspondent: E F V Waterson, Carter Jonas, 82 Micklegate, York YO1 6LF (01904 558201)

CC Number: 224098

Eligibility

Clergy working in the parish of Burton Salmon, in the county of north Yorkshire, the ecclesiastical parishes of Thorp Arch, Collingham with Harewood, Bardsey with East Keswick and Shadwell, in the county of west Yorkshire and the ecclesiastical parish of Ledsham with Fairburn in the counties of north and west Yorkshire, and their dependents.

Types of grants

One-off grants averaging about £700 per person are given for welfare purposes.

Annual grant total

In 2010/11 the non-educational branch of the charity made grants to 117 clergy and their dependents totalling £140,000.

A further £30,000 was paid from the non-educational fund in fixed yearly payments, grants to the Churches and grants to the poor.

Applications

In writing to the correspondent.

Other information

The trust is managed by and derives its income from the Lady Elizabeth Hastings Estate Charity. Grants from the non-educational charity are made to members of the clergy, with any residue paid as grants for the maintenance of specified churches, the maintenance of specified clergy residences or the relief of persons in need.

The John Routledge Hunter Memorial Fund

£13,000

Correspondent: Mary Waugh, Dickinson Dees (Solicitors), One Trinity, Newcastle upon Tyne NE1 2HF (01912 799000)

Trustee: Dickinson Dees (Trust corporation) Ltd.

CC Number: 225619

Eligibility

People who live in Northumberland and Tyne and Wear (north of River Tyne) who have (or recently have had) chest, lung or catarrhal complaints.

Types of grants

Grants of £200 to £500 towards a two or three week recuperative holiday in a hotel in Lytham St Annes or Southport (including rail travel expenses, bed, breakfast, evening meal and £25 in cash). Holidays are taken between Easter and September.

Annual grant total

Grants to individuals usually total around £13,000 each year.

Applications

On a form available from the correspondent, supported by a certificate signed by a doctor. Applications should be submitted directly by the individual and are considered from January to April.

Hylton House Fund

£4,000

Correspondent: Brenda Dye, Grants Manager, County Durham Community Foundation, Victoria House, St John's Road, Meadowfield Industrial Estate, Durham DH7 8XL (01917 806344; fax: 01917806344; email: brenda@cdcf.org.uk; website: www.cdcf.org.uk)

Trustee: County Durham Community Foundation.

CC Number: 1047625–2

Eligibility

People in the North East (County Durham, Darlington, Gateshead, South Shields, Sunderland and Cleveland) with cerebral palsy and related disabilities, and their families and carers. Applicants (or their family members, if the applicant is aged under 18) must be on income support or a low income or have a degree of disability in the family, which creates a heavy financial demand.

Types of grants

Grants of up to £500 towards: holidays and respite support for carers of up to two weeks in the UK or abroad;

education, training and therapy; training and support for carers and self-help groups (if there is no statutory support available); domestic equipment (maximum award £250); aids and equipment, particularly specialist clothing, communication and mobility aids; travel costs to allow applicants and their carers to attend a specific activity, specialist centre or hospital if no alternative transport is available; respite support to pay for an employed carer in the home or for visiting a specialist centre where care is provided; costs of setting up home (unless this is a SCOPE or Local Authority led move); debts, if it can be proved that they were incurred by the disability.

Annual grant total

Grants usually total around £4,000. Grants are given for both educational and welfare purposes.

Exclusions

No grants for: legal costs; ongoing education; medical treatment; decorating and/or refurbishment costs (unless the work is due to the nature of the applicant's disability); motor vehicle adaptations; motor insurance, deposits or running costs; televisions or DVD players; assessments, such as the costs involved in the Scope Living Options Schemes; or retrospective funding. Only one grant can be held in each financial year starting in April.

Applications

On a form available from the correspondent downloaded from the website. All applications must include a reference from a social worker or professional adviser in a related field, with a telephone number and the individual's permission for them to be contacted about an application. A full breakdown of costs should also be included. For specialist equipment and therapy, confirmation from an occupational therapist/doctor/physiotherapist or other professional advisor that the equipment is suitable, is also required.

Appeals are considered in January, April, July and October and should be received before the start of the month. They can be considered between these dates within a month of application if the need is urgent, but the applicant will need to request this and provide a reason why an exception to the usual policy needs to be made.

The Rose Joicey Fund

Correspondent: Grants team, The Community Foundation, Tyne and Wear and Northumberland, 156 Pilgrim Street, Newcastle upon Tyne NE1 6SU (01912 220945; fax: 01912 300689; email:

general@communityfoundation.org.uk; website: www.communityfoundation.org.uk)

CC Number: 226263

Eligibility

Families or individuals in need who live in the counties of Durham, Northumberland or Tyne and Wear.

Priority for grants is given to groups which organise holidays for people in need. Requests from individuals will only be considered if made through a proper social work agency. Preference will be given to people in poor health or who have a disability.

Types of grants

One-off grants usually ranging from £100 to £200 for holidays and short breaks.

Annual grant total

Reflecting the fact that the assets of the fund have been reallocated in 2010/11 the trust had a low income of just £3,400 (£1 million in 2009/10).

Exclusions

Grants are not given for furniture, clothing, building restoration or medical care and equipment.

Applications

Applications are administered by the Community Foundation for Tyne and Wear and Northumberland and applications are submitted online through the foundation's website.

Other information

The administration of the fund has been altered in recent years with the assets transferred to the Newcastle upon Tyne Council for Voluntary Services. The Rose Joicey endowment fund is now administered by the Community Foundation for Tyne and Wear and Northumberland.

The Kelly Charitable Trust

£9,000

Correspondent: Sir David Kelly, Stanton Fence, Stanton, Morpeth, Northumberland NE65 8PP (01670 772236; email: stantonfence@hotmail.com)

Trustees: Ralph Charlton; Lady Kelly; Sir David Kelly; Mrs Humphrey; Mrs Waddington; Mrs Allport.

CC Number: 1075895

Eligibility

People in need in England and Wales, primarily in the north east of England.

Types of grants

One-off and recurrent grants according to need, mainly for relief-in-need purposes.

Annual grant total

In 2010/11 the trust had an income of £4,200 and a total expenditure of £9,800.

Applications

In writing to the correspondent.

The Leeds Jewish Welfare Board

£4,000

Correspondent: Rebecca Weinberg, 311 Stonegate Road, Leeds LS17 6AZ (01132 684211; email: theboard@ljwb.co.uk; website: www.ljwb.co.uk)

Trustees: Arnold Reuben; Andrew Michael Lewis; Edward Ziff; Helen Rachel Lewis; James Stephen Denton; Martin Bernard Lee; Russell John Manning; Simon Walton; Michael Sandpearl; Nikki Ross; Jonathan Straight; Ronald Weiner.

CC Number: 1041257

Eligibility

Primarily people of the Jewish faith who live in Leeds or North and West Yorkshire.

Types of grants

Grants may be given as part of a 'support package'. They are rarely given as a one-off without a full assessment of the situation. Loans may also be given and depending on individual circumstances may be part-grant/part-loan. A flexible approach together with budgeting advice is offered. The majority of grants are given to families with children. These may be for clothes, bedding requirements and so on. Grants are also given at Jewish festivals such as Passover. Counselling and meals-on-wheels services along with a comprehensive range of services and resources are also offered to children, families and older people primarily, but not exclusively, of the Jewish faith.

Annual grant total

In 2010/11 the board had assets of £5.3 million and an income of £4.1 million. Each year a small amount is available to make grants; in 2011/12 the board distributed approximately £4,000 in grants.

Applications

Applications for help can be made at any time by individuals, welfare agencies, friends or relatives. The board can respond quickly in urgent cases. The applicant will be seen by a case worker who will assess the application and gather the relevant information.

Other information

The organisation's main area of activity is the provision of culturally appropriate social care and support.

The North East Area Miners Social Welfare Trust Fund

£0

Correspondent: Vincent B Clements, Coal Industry Social Welfare Organisation, 6 Bewick Road, Gateshead, Tyne and Wear NE8 4DP (01914 777242; email: vincent.clements@ciswo.org.uk; website: www.ciswo.org.uk)

Trustees: Denis Murphy; Ian Lavery; David Guy; David Hopper; William Etherington; Gerrard Huitson.

CC Number: 504178

Eligibility

People in need living in Durham, Northumberland and Tyne and Wear who are employed by the coal industry, or who have not been employed since retirement or redundancy from the coal industry.

Types of grants

One-off grants according to need.

Annual grant total

In 2010/11 the trust had assets of £3.5 million and an income of £126,000. No grants were made to individuals in the year.

The trust continued to help miners and people from former mining communities to afford convalescent holidays spending £159,000 to assist individuals in the year.

Applications

In writing to the correspondent. Applications can be submitted directly by the individual or through a social worker, Citizens Advice or other welfare agency. They are usually considered four times a year.

Other information

The trust also makes a number of grants to organisations (£160,000 in 2010/11).

The Northern Ladies Annuity Society

£159,000 (708 grants)

Correspondent: Jean Ferry, Secretary, MEA House, Ellison Place, Newcastle upon Tyne NE1 8XS (01912 321518)

Trustees: Susan Veronica Ridley; Elizabeth Etridge Inglis; Sarah Westcott Crone; April Freda Claire Stephenson; Diana Mary Barkes; Elspeth Alexia Chattan Melrose; Alice Louise Bryant; Annabel Jane Dickinson; Diana Mary Braithwaite; Jane Wood; Claire Morgan.

CC Number: 1097222

Eligibility

Single, unmarried and widowed ladies in need who live or have lived for a number of years in the northern counties of England. At present only those over the state retirement age are considered. The applicant should have an annual income of less than £8,000 and savings of no more than £10,000.

Types of grants

Annuities of £1,300/£975/£650/£325 (depending on circumstances) paid quarterly. One-off grants are also available for those in receipt of an annuity for expenses such as, holidays, domestic appliances, household items and other unexpected costs. Christmas hampers are also distributed to most annuitants. The society has also distributed fuel grants during recent spells of cold winter weather.

Note individuals not already in receipt of an annuity are ineligible for any other form of help from the society.

Annual grant total

In 2010/11 the society had assets of £6.9 million and an income of £248,000. Grants were made totalling £159,000, of which £138,000 was given in annuities to 450 ladies and £21,000 in special grants.

Exclusions

The trust does not give one-off grants to non-annuitants, nor support students, and will ignore any such requests for assistance.

Applications

Applications to become an annuitant should be made on a form available from the correspondent. Completed forms can be submitted directly by the individual or through a third party such as Citizens Advice or a social worker. Applications are considered monthly.

Other information

The society also owns a number of properties, which are available on a low rent to annuitants in need.

The Sir John Priestman Charity Trust

£400

Correspondent: McKenzie Bell, 19 John Street, Sunderland, Tyne and Wear SR1 1JG (01915 674857)

Trustees: Peter Taylor; Richard Farr; Timothy Norton; Anthony Coates; Thomas Greenwell.

CC Number: 209397

Eligibility

People in need who live in the historic counties of Durham and York (especially the county borough of Sunderland).

Types of grants

One-off and recurrent grants ranging from £50 to £1,000.

Annual grant total

In 2011 the charity gave £11,000 for young people to attend outward bound courses and one Christmas gift of £400.

Applications

In writing to the correspondent. Applications are considered quarterly.

Other information

The trust also assists charities serving County Durham (especially the Sunderland area) and helps maintain Church of England churches and buildings in the area.

The Rycroft Children's Fund

£29,000

Correspondent: J N Smith, 10 Heybridge Drive, Northernden, Manchester M22 4HB (01619 983127)

Trustees: Mr C.P. Lees-Jones; Miss M.R. Mason; Mr A. Maddocks; Miss I. Walton; Dr R. Briggs; Mr A. Greatbatch.

CC Number: 231771

Eligibility

Children in need who live in Cheshire, Derbyshire, Greater Manchester, Lancashire, Staffordshire, South and West Yorkshire. There is a preference for children living in the cities of Manchester and Salford and the borough of Trafford. Applicants should be aged 18 or under.

Types of grants

One-off grants according to need.

Annual grant total

In 2010/11 the fund had an income of £36,000 and a total expenditure of £34,000. Grants totalled £29,000.

Exclusions

Grants are not given to individuals for education, holidays or computers.

Applications

On a form available from the correspondent either directly by the individual or through a social worker, Citizens Advice or other welfare agency. Details of the applicant's available income and contributions from other sources must also be included. Applications can be made at any time.

The SF Group Charity

See entry on page 42

Sherburn House Charity

£790,000

Correspondent: Stephen Black, Administration Manager, Ramsey House, Sherburn Hospital, Durham DH1 2SE (01913 722551; fax: 01913 720035; email: admin@sherburnhouse.org; website: www.sherburnhouse.org)

Trustees: Ray Pye; Mary Hawgood; Lindsay Perks; William Brooks; Ian Stewart; Margaret Bozic; Tony Garland; Susan Davey; Susan Martin; Michael Laing; Mac Williams; Margaret Rushford; Neville Padgett; Dr Gillian Willmore.

CC Number: 217652

Eligibility

People in 'extreme social need' who live in the North East of England between the rivers Tweed and Tees.

Types of grants

One-off grants according to need.

Annual grant total

In 2010/11 the charity had assets of £27 million and an income of £2.3 million. Grants to individuals totalled £790,000.

Exclusions

No grants for central heating; driving licences; telephones and/or telephone arrears; specialist medical equipment; funeral expenses and holidays (unless there are exceptional circumstances). Applicants should wait two years before reapplying.

Applications

The charity prefers applicants to apply online via the website, though there is an option to download a hardcopy of the form to complete by hand. Applications must be made through a welfare agency such as social services, probation service, Citizens Advice and so on. They are normally assessed on a monthly basis.

Other information

The charity has an informative website.

Wright Funk Fund

£3,000

Correspondent: Brenda Dye, Grants Officer, County Durham Community Foundation, Victoria House, Whitfield Court, St John's Road, Meadowfield Industrial Estate, Durham DH7 8XL (01913 786340; fax: 01913 832969; email: brenda@cdcf.org.uk; website: www.cdcf.org.uk)

Trustee: County Durham Community Foundation.

CC Number: 1047625

Eligibility

Families in Darlington and County Durham.

Types of grants

Hardship grants averaging around £150 – £200 per applicant to help keep families together or to support families in crisis. Recent grants have been made for domestic equipment e.g. fridges, washing machines and cookers; carpets and bedding; support for carers; and, in exceptional circumstances, household bills.

Annual grant total

The fund awards between £2,500 and £3,000 each year.

Exclusions

The fund does not assist with bankruptcy fees or debt and will not make retrospective grants.

Applications

In writing to the correspondent, explaining what is needed and why it cannot be afforded without a grant. Applications should be completed by the individual, with help from a social worker or other relevant third party if necessary. A reference from a social worker or professional advisor in a related field should also be attached. Application forms, reference forms and guidance notes can be downloaded from the County Durham Foundation's website. Alternatively, a paper copy can be requested from the correspondent.

Yorkshire County Bowling Association Benevolent Fund

£900

Correspondent: David Oliver, 31 Redland Drive, Kirk Ella, Hull HU10 7UX (01482 656411)

Trustees: Ernest Roach Douglass; Ian R. D. Woodcock; Alan Price.

CC Number: 508927

Eligibility

Bowlers and their dependents from Yorkshire County EBA Clubs who are in need.

Types of grants

Christmas grants of £100.

Annual grant total

Grants have averaged around £900 over recent years.

Applications

On a form available from the correspondent submitted via club secretaries. Applications are usually considered in November.

Yorkshire Water Community Trust

£604,000 (1,325 grants)

Correspondent: Mark Lee, Trust Officer, Freepost-BD3074, Bradford BD3 7BR (0845 124 2426; fax: 01274 262265; email: info@ywct.org.uk; website: www.ywct.org.uk)

Trustees: David Robert Summers; Geraldine Penelope Pilling; Kenneth Jackson; Trevor Donald Eager; Elaine White; Dave Pickering; Phil Leadbetter; Glenn Snowley; Babul Miah.

CC Number: 1047923

Eligibility

People who are in arrears with Yorkshire Water and have at least one other priority debt. Council and housing association tenants whose water charges are included with their rent may also apply.

Types of grants

No cash grants are given. One-off payments of up to £750 are made to Yorkshire Water and credited to the applicant's account.

Annual grant total

In 2010/11 1,325 grants (of 1,656 applicants) were made totalling £604,000. The trust also noted in its accounts that 'during the year, every applicant who met the criteria received an award for the full amount to which they were entitled.' The average award was £450.

Applications

On a form available to download from the trust website or by contacting the trust. Although applications can be submitted directly by the individual or a friend or relative, the trust prefers them to be submitted by a social worker, Citizens Advice or other welfare agency. You must attach proof of household income in the form of wage slips or a confirmation of benefits, as well as proof of debts. Applications are considered quarterly. Successful applicants may not reapply within two years.

Other information

Small grants may also be available to advice agencies dealing with debt.

County Durham

Bull Piece Charity

£1,000

Correspondent: Mrs A Layfield, Secretary, New Row Farm, Hamsterley, Bishop Auckland, Co. Durham DL13 3QX (01388 488358)

Trustees: Valerie Balchin; Malcolm Maughan; Susan Heslop; David Wallace; Kenneth Robinson; Ann Layfield; Robert Collinson; Yvonne Wilkinson; Frank Johnson.

CC Number: 237477

Eligibility
People in need who live in Hamsterley, South Bedburn, Lynesack and Softley.

Types of grants
Recurrent gifts of £30, usually made at Christmas.

Annual grant total
Income and total expenditure average around £1,500 each year.

Applications
Applications by word of mouth (or in writing) to: K Robinson, 11 The Edge, Woodland, High Summer Hill, Bishop Auckland DL13 5RF. Applications are normally considered in June or December.

County Durham Community Foundation

£150,000

Correspondent: Barbara Gubbins, Chief Executive, Victoria House, Whitfield Court, St John's Road, Meadowfield Industrial Estate, Durham DH7 8XL (01913 830055; email: info@ countydurhamfoundation.co.uk; website: www.countydurhamfoundation.co.uk)

Trustees: Mark l'Anson; David Watson; Michele Armstrong; Ada Burns; George Garlick; John Hamilton; Christopher Lendrum; Andrew Martell; David Martin; Lady Nicholson; Gerry Osbourne; Kate Welch.

CC Number: 1047625

Eligibility
People in need who live in County Durham and Darlington.

Types of grants
Usually one-off grants of between £50 to £2,000. Visit the foundation's website for further details. Individuals can only hold one grant per each financial year starting in April.

Annual grant total
In 2010/11 the foundation had assets of £8.5 million and an income of £2 million. Grants were made totalling £1 million to 378 organisations and 258 individuals. The foundation administers eight funds that give for both educational and welfare purposes.

Exclusions
No grants are made towards medical treatment, nursing care or anything which is the responsibility of Social Services or the NHS. Grants are not made retrospectively.

Applications
Applicants can either: use a form available from the correspondent or the website; or write to the correspondent including their name, address, how they fit the criteria, what is needed and why, costs, when the grant is needed, details of income and savings, details of why the need can't be met, where any other money will be coming from (if not requesting the full amount), names of other organisations approached and details of how a cheque should be made payable to (unless directly to the provider, such as a residential home, rather than to the applicant).

In all cases, applications must include a reference from a professional third party, such as a GP, community nurse or social worker. The foundation will give a decision within one month, although this can be sooner if the request is particularly urgent. As with all community foundations, fund may open and close at short notice so check the website before beginning any application.

Other information
Grants are also made to organisations.

The Ferryhill Station, Mainsforth and Bishop Middleham Aid-in-Sickness Charity

£1,150

Correspondent: Zoe Whent, Dunelm, Mainsforth Village, Ferryhill, County Durham DL17 9AA (01740 652434)

Trustees: Andrew Steward Clements; Dorothy Evans; Lawrence Douglass Cockayne; Zoe Ann Whent; Tony Brimm; Carolyn Clark; Sue Patchett.

CC Number: 500190

Eligibility
People in need who are in poor health, convalescent or who have disabilities and live in the parishes of Ferryhill Station, Mainsforth and Bishop Middleham.

Types of grants
One-off grants ranging from £250 to £1,000 towards medical care and equipment, holidays for people with disabilities (and their carers) and for special needs arising from disability or illness.

Annual grant total
About £2,000 a year. Grants are given to both individuals and organisations.

Applications
In writing to the correspondent, either directly by the individual or via a third party such as a district nurse, social worker, Citizens Advice or other welfare agency. Applications are considered on a regular basis.

The Ropner Centenary Trust

£20,000 (39 grants)

Correspondent: Alan Theakston, 15 The Green, High Coniscliffe, Darlington, County Durham DL2 2LJ (01325 374249)

Trustees: Alan Theakston; Sir John Ropner; Robert Ropner.

CC Number: 269109

Eligibility
Present and former maritime employees who are in need, and their dependents. Preference is generally given to people living in the North East of England and particularly those who have worked for Ropner Shipping Company Ltd.

Types of grants
One-off and recurrent grants according to need.

Annual grant total
In 2010/11 the trust had assets of £951,000 and an income of £27,000. 39 individuals received grants totalling £20,000.

Applications
In writing to the correspondent. Applications are considered annually, although urgent requests can be dealt with between meetings.

Other information
Grants are also paid to organisations with similar aims (£8,000 in 2010/11).

The Sedgefield District Relief-in-Need Charity

£2,500

Correspondent: John Hannon, Clerk, East House, Mordon, Sedgefield, County Durham TS21 2EY (01740 622512; email: east.house@btinternet.com)

Trustees: Christine Hearmon; Edwin Lofthouse; John Robinson; Robert Elders; Shirli Traynor; Peter Brookes; Kenneth Threlfall; Susan Cook; Alan Thompson; Peter Terry; Patricia Little; Christine Luke; Michael Gobbett; Allan Blakemore.

CC Number: 230395

Eligibility

People in need who live in the parishes of Bishop Middleham, Bradbury, Cornforth, Fishburn, Mordon, Sedgefield and Trimdon in County Durham.

Types of grants

One-off grants, including those for furnishings, bedding, medical requisites, mobility aids, hospital travel costs, travel for the disabled, living expenses and respite care.

Annual grant total

About £5,000 to individuals for welfare and educational purposes.

Applications

In writing to the correspondent. Applications can be submitted directly by the individual or through a social worker, Citizens Advice, welfare agency or other third party such as a carer or relative. They are considered as they arise.

Other information

The trust also makes grants to local organisations.

East Yorkshire

The Joseph and Annie Cattle Trust

£12,500

Correspondent: Roger Waudby, Administrator, PO Box 23, Hull HU12 1OWF (01964 671742; fax: 01482 211198)

Trustees: Michael Gyte; Joan Collier; Stephen Jowers; Paul Edwards.

CC Number: 262011

Eligibility

Primarily people who live in the Hull or East Riding of Yorkshire area and are in need. Preference is given to people who are older, disabled or disadvantaged, particularly children who are dyslexic.

Types of grants

One-off grants of £200 to £500 for needs such as travel expenses, furniture, medical and disability equipment, electric goods and help in the home.

Annual grant total

In 2010/11 the trust had assets of £7.5 million and an income of £269,000. Grants for educational and welfare purposes were made to 41 individuals totalling £25,000.

Applications

In writing to the correspondent, only via a welfare organisation, for consideration on the third Monday of every month. Note, if applicants approach the trust directly they will be referred to an organisation, such as Disability Rights Advisory Service, or social services.

Other information

Grants are also made to organisations (£251,000 – 2010/11).

The Leonard Chamberlain Trust

£2,500

Correspondent: Avril Russell, Fieldside House, Hooks Lane, Thorngumbald, Hull HU12 9QA (07961 034643)

Trustees: Mavis Lake; Michael Tracey; John Williams; Barry Cundill.

CC Number: 1091018

Eligibility

Applicants must live within the area of benefit: East Riding of Yorkshire, particularly Hull and Selby.

Types of grants

One-off grants according to need.

Annual grant total

In 2011 the trust made hardship grants totalling £2,500.

Applications

In writing to the correspondent.

Other information

The trust also provides housing for the needy and makes grants for religious and educational purposes.

The Hesslewood Children's Trust (Hull Seamen's and General Orphanage)

£16,500

Correspondent: Mr Rex Booth, 1 Canada Drive, Cherry Burton, East Yorkshire HU17 7RQ

Trustees: Mr R. Allenby; Mr D. Moore; Mr C. Andrews; Mr P. Evans; Revd T. Boyns; Mrs Lidgett; Mr M. Mitchell; Mrs G. Munn; Dr D. Nicholas; Mr D. Turner; Capt; P. Watts; Dr C. Woodyatt.

CC Number: 529804

Eligibility

People under 25 and in need who are native to, or have family connections with, the former county of Humberside and North Lincolnshire. Students who have come to the area to study are not eligible.

Types of grants

One-off and recurrent grants, typically up to £1,000, according to need. Grants have been given for specified short periods of time at special schools, holiday funding for individuals and youth organisations in the UK and overseas, and for musical instruments and special equipment for children who are disabled.

Annual grant total

In 2010/11 the trust had assets of £2.5 million and an income of £82,500. Grants made to or on behalf of individuals totalled £34,500.

Exclusions

Loans are not made.

Applications

On a form available from the correspondent. Applications can be made either directly by the individual or through the individual's school/college/welfare agency or another third party on their behalf. Applicants must give their own or their parental financial details, the grant required, and why parents cannot provide the money. If possible, a contact telephone number should be quoted. Applications must be accompanied by a letter from the tutor or an educational welfare officer (or from medical and social services for a disability grant). The deadlines are 16 February, 16 June and 16 September.

Other information

Grants are also made to organisations (£39,000 in 2010/11).

The Hull Aid in Sickness Trust

£17,000 (35 grants)

Correspondent: Dawn Singleton, 34 Thurstan Road, Beverley, Hull HU17 8LP (01482 860133; email: haist@thesingletons.karoo.co.uk)

Trustees: Pat Ellis; Revd John Allen Bagshawe; Mr J. Douglas Stones; Cllr Karen Woods; Val Horspool; Peter J. D. Brewer; Heather Todd.

CC Number: 224193

Eligibility

People in need, on a low income, who live in the city and county of Kingston upon Hull and are sick, disabled, infirm or convalescent.

Types of grants

One-off and recurrent grants, to a usual maximum of £500, to aid and improve quality of life. This can include grants for electrical goods, medical and disability equipment, food and living costs and so on.

Annual grant total

In 2010/11 the trust had assets of £954,000 and an income of £39,000. Grants were made totalling £30,000, of which around £17,000 was given in grants to individuals.

Exclusions

No grants are given towards debts or where funds are available from public funds.

Applications

On a form available from the correspondent, to be submitted directly by the individual or through a social worker, Citizens Advice, other welfare agency or other third party. Applications must be supported by a doctor's certificate or similar. The trustee's may send a visitor to the applicant for the purpose of preparing a report to support the application.

Other information

Grants of £1,000 or more were made to nine organisations in the year.

Humberside Police Welfare and Benevolent Fund

£11,000

Correspondent: Humberside Police, Queens Gardens, Hull HU1 3DJ (0845 606 0222; email: webmail@humberside. pnn.police.uk; website: www.humberside. police.uk)

Trustees: David Collinson; Debra Kemp; Tracey Windas; Janet Jeffrey.

CC Number: 503762

Eligibility

Serving and retired officers of the Humberside Police and retired officers from other forces who live in Humberside, and their partners and dependents; and civilian employees of Humberside Police Authority, retired civilian employees and their partners and dependents.

Types of grants

One-off and recurrent grants of up to £500.

Annual grant total

In 2010 the fund had an income of £17,000 and a total expenditure of £12,000.

Applications

In writing to the correspondent at any time, either through the branch/ divisional representative or the headquarters.

The Nafferton Feoffee Charity Trust

£1,200

Correspondent: Margaret Buckton, South Cattleholmes, Wansford, Driffield, East Yorkshire YO25 8NW (01377 254293)

Trustees: Margaret Buckton; David Wigglesworth; Winifred Cooper; Jean Artley; Fiona Trewartha; Jean Towers; Andrew Oliver; Hugo Glover; Caroline Harrison.

CC Number: 232796

Eligibility

People in need who live in the parish of All Saints Nafferton with St Mary's Wansford.

Types of grants

One-off grants in the range of £100 to £250. Recent grants have been given for hospital travel costs, heating expenses and food vouchers. Bursaries are also available to local students.

Annual grant total

In 2011 the trust had assets of £1.5 million and an income of £48,000. Welfare grants to individuals totalled £1,200.

Exclusions

The trust stated that the parish only consists of 3,000 people and every household receives a copy of a leaflet outlining the trust's work. People from outside this area are not eligible to apply.

Applications

In writing to the correspondent at any time, directly by the individual.

Other information

Grants are also made to organisations and to individuals for welfare purposes.

Ethel Maude Townend Charity

£5,500

Correspondent: Stephen Walker, Gosschalks, 61 Queens Gardens, Hull HU1 3DZ (01482 324252; email: sw@ gosschalks.co.uk)

Trustees: Stephen Walker; John Victor Ayre; Bruce Wilkie.

CC Number: 225085

Eligibility

People in need who live in Hull and the East Riding of Yorkshire. Applicants should have been in the medical, nursing or legal professions or have been ministers of religion, accountants or architects, or members of other professions generally. Their widows can also be supported.

Types of grants

Usually weekly payments plus a Christmas bonus. Also one-off grants towards, for example, nursing registration fees; outstanding telephone bills; washing machines; roof and window repairs; medical equipment; and Tens machines.

Annual grant total

In 2010/11 the fund had an income of £5,400 and a total expenditure of £5,900.

Exclusions

There are no grants available for educational purposes.

Applications

On a form available from the correspondent following an advertisement. Applications can be submitted directly by the individual or through a social worker, Citizens Advice, doctor or other welfare agency. Applications can be made at any time of the year.

Robert Towries Charity

£3,000

Correspondent: Mrs Debbie Ulliot, The Cottage, Carlton Lane, Aldbrough, Hull HU11 4RA (01964 527255; email: roberttowerytrust@googlemail.com)

Trustees: Donald Fields; John Hart; John Clayton; Peter Greaves; Timothy Maltas; Geoffrey North; John Porter.

CC Number: 222568

Eligibility

People in need who live in Aldbrough and Burton Constable.

Types of grants

One-off and recurrent grants for food and fuel.

Annual grant total

In 2010/11 the charity had an income of £10,000 and a total expenditure of £6,000.

Applications

In writing to the correspondent directly by the individual.

Other information

Grants are also given for educational needs.

Aldbrough

Aldbrough Poor Fields

£450

Correspondent: Moira Allison, 260 Seaside Road, Aldbrough, Hull HU11 4SA (01964 529298; email: m. allison09@btinternet.com)

Trustees: Mr J. T. Handley; Mr K. Blackwell; Mr S. C. Turner; Mr T. Floater; Mr R. M. Robinson; Mr G. A. North.

CC Number: 222569

Eligibility

People aged over 65 and widows who are in need and live in Aldbrough village.

Types of grants

Grants are given towards food and fuel. Gifts in kind are also made.

Annual grant total

In 2010/11 the charity had an income of £7,400 and a total expenditure of £600. No further information was available.

Applications

In writing to the correspondent for consideration in November.

Barmby on the Marsh

The Garlthorpe Charity

£3,200

Correspondent: John Burman, c/o Hepstonstalls Solicitors, 7–15 Gladstone Terrace, Goole, North Humberside DN14 5AH (01405 765661)

Trustees: Dorothy Margaret Houlder; John Valentine Shaw; Peter Bassindale; Timothy John Harper; Stuart Bostock; David Giles; David Pridmore.

CC Number: 224927

Eligibility

People in need who live in the parish of Barmby on the Marsh.

Types of grants

One-off grants according to need.

Annual grant total

In 2010/11 the charity had an income of £9,700 and a total expenditure of £3,500.

Applications

In writing to the correspondent.

Bridlington

The Bridlington Charities

£46,500 (221 grants)

Correspondent: Andrew Mead, 118 St James Road, Bridlington, North Humberside YO15 3NJ (01262 403333)

CC Number: 224609

Eligibility

People in need who live in the parish of Bridlington and Bridlington Quay.

Types of grants

Grants of between £50 and £210 for the purchase of fuel (gas, coal, electricity). Payment is made direct to the suppliers. One-off grants towards school clothing can also be made.

Annual grant total

In 2010 the charities had assets of £165,000 and an income of £53,000. The charity paid £46,500 in fuel payment grants to 221 beneficiaries.

The charities also made grants totalling £3,000 to local organisations for poverty relief and educational purposes in the year.

Exclusions

No loans or grants for meals or paid help.

Applications

In writing to the correspondent, usually for consideration in February, May, August and November. Applications can be submitted through a social worker, Citizens Advice or other welfare agency. The charities' field officers visit the applicants and report to the trustees in writing.

Other information

Some money is made available for local organisations.

Kingston upon Hull

The Charity of Miss Eliza Clubley Middleton

£14,000

Correspondent: Trust Administrator, Rollits, Rowntree Wharf, Navigation Road, York YO1 9WE (01904 625790; fax: 01904 625807)

Trustees: Mary Clark; Anne Trynka; Linda Davey.

CC Number: 229134

Eligibility

Poor women of the Catholic faith who have lived in the Hull area for over ten years.

Types of grants

Grants are distributed twice a year, at Christmas and in the summer. The typical average value of any individual grant is less than £75.

Annual grant total

In 2010/11 the charity had an income of £9,600 and a total expenditure of £19,000.

Applications

A list of current beneficiaries is circulated to all local priests each year. They then recommend any additions or note changes in circumstances.

The 'Mother Humber' Memorial Fund

£18,000

Correspondent: Malcom Welford, Secretary, 5 Summerfield Close, Driffield, East Yorkshire YO25 5YS (01377 256212)

Trustees: John Rose; Leonard Maxwell Bird; Patricia May Ellis; John Harvey; Dr Michael Bott.

CC Number: 225082

Eligibility

People in need who live in the city of Kingston upon Hull.

Types of grants

One-off grants ranging from £50 to £500 for individuals

Annual grant total

In 2010/11 the fund had an income of £31,000 and made grants totalling £18,000.

Exclusions

No grants are made for: educational appeals and sponsorship e.g. of Duke of Edinburgh Award students; the payment of debts; and the payment of wages or administration expenses.

Applications

On a form available from the correspondent, submitted through a social worker, Citizens Advice or other welfare agency.

The Joseph Rank Benevolent Fund

£75,000

Correspondent: Mrs D Burman, Clerk to the Trustees, Artlink Centre, 87 Princes Avenue, Hull HU5 3QP (01482 225542)

Trustees: Colin Roderick Palmer; David Gray Simpson; Joseph Newton; Kevin Simon Webster; Rodney Stuart Johnson;

Malcolm Harold Lucas; Victoria Rixon Heuck.

CC Number: 225318

Eligibility

Men aged 65 or over and women aged 60 or over who are retired and have lived in Hull for at least ten of the last 15 years. If the applicant is married, their partner must also meet these age limits.

Types of grants

Recurrent grants of £30 per quarter to single people and £60 per quarter to married couples.

Annual grant total

In 2011 the fund had assets of £2.9 million which generated an income of £116,000. Grants were made to individuals totalling £75,000.

Applications

On a form available from the correspondent. Applications are considered throughout the year.

Other information

The fund also makes grants to local charities (£3,000 in 2009).

The Wilmington Trust

£3,800

Correspondent: Revd Carol Fisher-Bailey, 25 Church Street, Sutton, Hull HU7 4TL (01482 709699)

Trustees: Dennis Campion; Graham Wragg; Revd Carol Fisher-Bailey; Ann Pullen.

CC Number: 250765

Eligibility

People in need who live in Kingston upon Hull (east of the river Hull).

Types of grants

One-off grants ranging from £50 to £100 towards, for instance, clothing, holidays, emergencies, furniture, white goods and other household items.

Annual grant total

In 2011 the trust had an income of £5,100 and a total expenditure of £4,000.

Applications

On a form available from the correspondent. Applications must be made through Citizens Advice, social workers or members of the clergy. The trustees meet twice a year to consider grants, although decisions can be made between meetings.

Other information

The trust also makes grants to local organisations.

Newton on Derwent

Newton on Derwent Charity

£3,000

Correspondent: The Clerk to the Charity, FAO, Grays Solicitors, Duncombe Place, York YO1 7DY (01904 634771)

CC Number: 529830

Eligibility

People who are sick, older or in need who live in the parish of Newton on Derwent.

Types of grants

One-off grants according to need.

Annual grant total

Welfare grants usually total around £3,000 per annum.

Applications

In writing to the correspondent.

Other information

This charity has been given a dispensation by the Charity Commission from publishing the names of its trustees.

Ottringham

The Ottringham Church Lands Charity

£3,000

Correspondent: Luisa Hopkinson, Jasmine House, Station Road, Ottringham, East Yorkshire HU12 0BJ (01964 626323; email: luisahopkinson@btinternet.com)

Trustees: John Hinchciffe; Revd Ronald Howard; Mary Fairweather; Patricia Taylor; Sylvia Sugden; Ernie Oldfield; Cathryn Brown; Julia Billaney; Graham Houston.

CC Number: 237183

Eligibility

People in hardship and/or distress who live in the parish of Ottringham.

Types of grants

Normally one-off grants, but recurrent grants may be considered.

Annual grant total

About £6,000. Educational grants are also made.

Exclusions

No grants are given which would affect the applicant's state benefits.

Applications

In writing to the correspondent at any time. Applications can be submitted either directly by the individual, through a third party such as a social worker or teacher, or through an organisation such as Citizens Advice or a school.

North Yorkshire

Bedale Welfare Charity

£3,000

Correspondent: John Winkle, 25 Burrill Road, Bedale, North Yorkshire DL8 1ET (01677 424306; email: johnwinkle@awinkle.freeserve.co.uk)

Trustees: Robert Dunning; Robert Pocklington; Adrienne Reynolds; Denis O'Neil; Harry Lillystone; Herbert Smith; Malcolm Young; Mary Megson; Richard Vasey; Susan Nattrass; John Weighell; Mike Barningham; Alan Johnson; Brian Hall; Eileen Cockburn; John Thompson; Dr Stephen Wilkinson; Sue Inglis; Malcolm Gill; Trevor Johnson; Neil Pocklington; Jonathan Neale; Ian Watkins; Revd Simon Rudkin.

CC Number: 224035

Eligibility

Older people who are infirm and/or in need who live in Bedale and the immediate surrounding area.

Types of grants

One-off grants usually ranging from £40 to £500.

Annual grant total

In 2010/11 the trust had an income of £14,000 and a total expenditure of £7,000, most of which is distributed in relief-in-need grants and to organisations to a larger extent.

Applications

On a form available from the correspondent, to be submitted at any time either directly by the individual or through a third party such as a social worker or teacher.

The Gargrave Poor's Land Charity

£13,000

Correspondent: The Trustees, Kirk Syke, High Street, Gargrave, Skipton, North Yorkshire BD23 3RA

Trustees: Hugh Turner; Valerie Cutter; Geoffrey Gardner; Philip Ellis; Graham Thomson; Lynn Cuthbert.

CC Number: 225067

Eligibility

People in need who live in Gargrave, Banknewton, Coniston Cold, Flasby, Eshton or Winterburn.

Types of grants

One-off and recurrent grants for debt relief, travel to hospital, household equipment, furniture, respite care, electrical goods and essential repairs. Christmas gifts are also made each year to permanent residents who are poor, older, disadvantaged or disabled.

Annual grant total

In 2010/11 the charity had assets of £386,000 and an income of £42,000. Grants were made totalling £13,000 and were distributed as follows:

Christmas distribution	£9,100
Hardship relief	£4,300

Applications

On a form available from the correspondent. Applications can be submitted at any time.

The Goldsborough Poor's Charity

£1,500

Correspondent: J L Clarkson, 25 Princess Mead, Goldsborough, Knaresborough, North Yorkshire HG5 8NP (01423 865102)

Trustees: Betty Jobling; Len Clarkson; Alan Walgate.

CC Number: 502912

Eligibility

Older people who live in Goldsborough, Flaxby or Coneythorpe (or near Knaresborough). Most recipients tend to be widows or widowers.

Types of grants

Recurrent grants are given to supplement pensions or low incomes.

Annual grant total

Grants usually total around £1,500 a year.

Applications

In writing to the correspondent. Applications can be submitted either directly by the individual, through a third party or via a social worker, Citizens Advice or other welfare agency.

Reverend Matthew Hutchinson Trust (Gilling and Richmond)

£5,000

Correspondent: Mrs C Wiper Gentry, 3 Smithson Close, Moulton, Richmond,

North Yorkshire DL10 6QP (01325 377328)

Trustees: Gilling: Anthony Warton; Marian Lewis; Richard Watts; Shiona Robotham; Jennifer Ross; Revd Alan Gledhill; Revd Stan Haworth. Richmond: Jean Robertson; Revd Stan Haworth; Margaret Clayson; Alison Metcalf; Revd Alan Gledhill; Elisabeth Grant.

CC Number: 220870/220779

Eligibility

People who are in need and live in the parishes of Gilling and Richmond in North Yorkshire.

Types of grants

One-off grants according to need. Recent grants have been given towards medical care, telephone rental, a violin, running shoes and children's nursery fees.

Annual grant total

This charity has branches in both Gilling and Richmond, which are administered jointly, but have separate funding. In 2010 the combined income of the charities was £20,500 and their combined expenditure was £13,000. The combined grant total is usually about £10,000 a year.

Applications

In writing to the correspondent. Applications can be submitted directly by the individual or through a trustee, social worker, Citizens Advice or other welfare agency.

Other information

Grants are also made to local schools and hospitals.

The Purey Cust Trust

£2,500

Correspondent: Mrs Kathryn Hodges, 5 Grimston Park Mews, Grimston Park, Tadcaster LS24 9DB (01378 34730; email: pureycusttrust@btinternet.com or pureycusttrust@hotmail.com; website: www.pureycrusttrust.org.uk)

Trustees: Dr David Hesseltine; Maggie Browne; Anne Pugh; Barbara Scott; Nicholas Andrew McMahon Turner; Patricia Sessions.

CC Number: 516030

Eligibility

People with medical needs who live in York and the surrounding area.

Types of grants

One-off grants ranging between £100 and £1,500, for healthcare equipment, specialist medical equipment and medical education.

Annual grant total

In 2010/11 the trust had an income of £23,000 and a total expenditure of £5,900.

Applications

On a form which is available on the website. Applications may be emailed or posted. Applications must show evidence of the medical need and can be submitted directly by the individual or through a social worker, Citizens Advice, other welfare agency or third party. Applications are considered throughout the year.

Other information

Grants are also made to organisations.

The Rowlandson and Eggleston Relief-in-Need Charity

£1,000

Correspondent: Peter Vaux, Chair, Brettanby Manor, Barton, Richmond, North Yorkshire DL10 6HD (01325 377233; fax: 01325 377647)

Trustees: Allan Flowers; Colin Tennick; Gwendoline Cook; Peter Vaux; Dr Mark Hodgson; Patricia Walsh; Clifford Howe; Barry McQueen.

CC Number: 515647

Eligibility

People in the parishes of Barton and Newton Morrell who are in need.

Types of grants

One-off grants usually in the range of £100 to £500. Recent grants have been given towards funeral expenses, medical equipment, disability aids and lifeline telephone systems for older people.

Annual grant total

In 2010/11 the charity had an income of £3,600 and a total expenditure of £2,300.

Applications

In writing to the correspondent including details of circumstances and specific need(s). Applications may be submitted directly by the individual or through a social worker, Citizens Advice or other third party.

Other information

This charity also provides other facilities and make grants to individuals for educational purposes.

The York Dispensary Charitable Trust

£1,500

Correspondent: The Secretary, 1 St Saviourgate, York YO1 8ZQ (01904 558600)

Trustees: Carolyn Margaret Haynes; Dr Sarah Penelope Anderson; Dr Alan Scott; William Miers; James Anthony Player; David Peter Walkden; Paul Hobkinson; Gail Hardie Tams.

CC Number: 221277

Eligibility
People living in York and the surrounding districts who are experiencing poverty and ill health.

Types of grants
One-off grants for specific needs such as clothing, domestic equipment or holidays.

Annual grant total
In 2011 the fund had an income of £20,000 and a total expenditure of £22,000. Grants to individuals often make up a very small proportion of total expenditure, with most grants being made to local organisations.

Applications
In writing to the correspondent, preferably through social services or a similar welfare agency, although direct application is possible. Applications are considered regularly.

Carperby-cum-Thoresby

The Carperby Poor's Land Charity

£1,600

Correspondent: David Brampton, The Basta Hhouse, Carperby, Leyburn, North Yorkshire DL8 4DD

Trustees: Martin Beckett; Janice Peacock; David Brampton; Roger Dinsdale.

CC Number: 502524

Eligibility
People in need who live in the parish of Carperby-cum-Thoresby.

Types of grants
One-off and recurrent grants are given according to need.

Annual grant total
Grants average around £1,600 a year.

Applications
In writing to the correspondent, with details of the financial need. Applications can be submitted directly by the individual or through a social worker, Citizens Advice or other welfare agency. They are usually considered quarterly.

Craven

The Gertrude Beasley Charitable Trust

£0

Correspondent: J C Mewies, J P Mewies and Co. Solicitors, Clifford House, Keighley Road, Skipton, North Yorkshire BD23 2NB (01756 799000)

Trustees: Dr Raubitschek Raubitschek; John Christopher Mewies.

CC Number: 1074589

Eligibility
Children and young people who are disabled and live in Craven.

Types of grants
Grants given according to need.

Annual grant total
In 2010/11 the trust had an income of £4,000 and nil expenditure.

Applications
In writing to the correspondent.

Other information
Grants are also made to organisations.

Danby

The Joseph Ford's Trust

£1,200

Correspondent: Liz Sheard, Trustee, 28 West Lane, Danby, Whitby YO21 2LY (01287 660416)

Trustees: Colin Grout; David Tyreman; Pam Reeves; Revd Michael Hazelton; Revd Alan Coates; Mary Elizabeth Sheard; Joyce Champion.

CC Number: 514043

Eligibility
People who live within the original parish of Danby and are blind, aged or in poverty or misfortune.

Types of grants
One-off or recurrent grants according to need.

Annual grant total
Around £1,200.

Applications
In writing to the correspondent or any other trustee, at any time.

Knaresborough

The Knaresborough Relief-in-Need Charity

£16,000

Correspondent: Mike Dixon, Administrator, 9 Netheredge Drive, Knaresborough, North Yorkshire HG5 9DA (01423 863378; email: thedixongang@btinternet.com)

Trustees: Jean Dunn; Neil Willans; Beverley Hallam; Eileen Rita Ferguson; Eunice Althea Farmer; Revd Elizabeth Sewell; Christine Graham.

CC Number: 226743

Eligibility
People in need who live in the parish of Knaresborough, with a preference for people who have lived there for at least five years or twenty years for a pension.

Types of grants
Pensions of £30 a year and occasional one-off grants of up to £5,000.

Annual grant total
Grants total around £10,000 annually. Pensions are also paid with payments made to 200 individuals totalling £6,000 in 2010.

Applications
In writing to the correspondent.

Lothersdale

Raygill Trust

£4,000

Correspondent: Roger Armstrong, Armstrong Wood and Bridgman, 12–16 North Street, Keighley, West Yorkshire BD21 3SE (01535 613660; email: mail@awbclaw.co.uk)

Trustees: Patricia Wilson; Robert Davis; Jennifer Smith; Harry Liversedge; Revd Gill Hall; Geoffrey Carr.

CC Number: 249199

Eligibility
Older people who live in the ecclesiastical parish of Lothersdale.

Types of grants
One-off grants are available to assist with the cost of living.

Annual grant total
In 2010/11 the trust had an income of £11,000 and a total expenditure of £10,500.

Applications

In writing to the correspondent. Applications can be submitted directly by the individual or through a third party or welfare agency.

Northallerton

The Grace Gardner Trust

£1,000

Correspondent: The Secretary, c/o Town Hall, High Street, Northallerton, North Yorkshire DL7 8QR (01609 776718; email: enquiries@ northallertontowncouncil.gov.uk)

Trustees: David Maurice Blades; Jack Dobson; John Forrest.

CC Number: 511030

Eligibility

Older people, people with disabilities or those who are disadvantaged who live within the boundary of Northallerton parish.

Types of grants

One-off grants of up to £200 according to need including those for electric goods, home improvements, travel expenses, furniture and disability equipment.

Annual grant total

In 2010/11 the trust had an income of £5,300 and a total expenditure of £2,200.

Applications

In writing to the correspondent including details of age and place of residence. Applications can be submitted directly by the individual or through a recognised referral agency (such as social worker, Citizens Advice or doctor) at any time.

Other information

The trust also makes grants to local organisations for day trips.

Scarborough

The Scarborough Municipal Charities

£9,000

Correspondent: Elaine Greening, 42 Green Lane, Scarborough YO12 6HT (01723 371063; email: scar. municipalcharity@yahoo.co.uk)

Trustees: Ken Dale; Dorothy Clegg; Janette Wilby; D. C. Jeffels; Janet Jefferson; W. Chatt; Bernard Pearson; Eileen Vickers; Geoffrey Evans.

CC Number: 2177793

Eligibility

People in need who are of retirement age and live in Scarborough.

Types of grants

Grants are one-off and range between £250 and £1,500. Support is given towards livings costs and travel expenses.

Annual grant total

In 2011 the charity had assets of £1.6 million and an income of £160,000. Grants to individuals for welfare and education totalled £18,000.

Applications

In writing to the correspondent. Applications are considered quarterly.

St Margaret

Robert Winterscale's Charity

£1,100

Correspondent: Richard Watson, Crombie Wilkinson, 17–19 Clifford Street, York YO1 9RJ (01904 624185; email: r.watson@crombiewilkinson.co. uk)

Trustees: John Mawson; Revd David Porter; Michael Bulmer; Michael Lilley; Revd Jane Nattrass; Jose Linnane.

CC Number: 224230

Eligibility

People over 60 years of age who have lived in the ancient parishes of St Margaret's and St Denys for more than five years and are in need.

Types of grants

Biannual pensions totalling about £25 a year.

Annual grant total

Grants have averaged around £1,900 over the past five years.

Applications

On a form available from the correspondent. Applications can be submitted directly by the individual, through an organisation such as Citizens Advice or through a third party such as a social worker. Applications are considered on a regular basis.

West Witton

The Smorthwaite Charity

£5,000

Correspondent: Geoff Clarke, Pen Cottage, Main Street, West Witton, Leyburn, North Yorkshire DL8 4LX (01969 624393)

Trustees: Geoff Clarke; Sam James; Ruth Farrow.

CC Number: 247681

Eligibility

Older people in need who live in West Witton.

Types of grants

Annual grants of ranging from £100 to £150.

Annual grant total

In 2010/11 the charity had an income of £12,000 and a total expenditure of £19,000. Grants usually total about £5,000 each year.

Applications

The charity usually advertises in the local post-office. Most applications tend to be submitted by word of mouth and through conversations with the trustees rather than through a formal application process.

Other information

The charity also maintains five rental properties in the area.

York

The Micklegate Strays Charity

£100

Correspondent: Roger Lee, 29 Albemarle Road, York YO23 1EW (01904 653698)

Trustees: Roger Lee; Alec Stephenson; Beryl Stephenson; Geoffrey Barraclough; Gerald Downs.

CC Number: 237179

Eligibility

Freemen of the city of York and their dependents living in the Micklegate Strays ward. (This area is now defined as the whole of that part of the city of York to the west of the River Ouse.)

Types of grants

Pensions and medical grants of £30 a year.

Annual grant total

In 2010/11 the charity had an income of £300 and a total expenditure of £100. Grants are for educational and welfare purposes.

Applications

On a form available from the correspondent. Applications should include the date of the freeman's oath and are considered in November.

Other information

The trust was created by the 1907 Micklegate Strays Act. The city of York agreed to pay the freemen £1,000 a year in perpetuity for extinguishing their rights over Micklegate Stray. This sum has been reduced due to the forced divestment of the trust government stock, following the Charities Act of 1992.

The Charity of St Michael-le-Belfrey

£8,000

Correspondent: C C Goodway, Clerk, Grays Solicitors, Duncombe Place, York YO1 7DY (01904 634771)

Trustees: Peter Gibson; Alistair Duncan Haldane; Dorothy Joyce Cook.

CC Number: 222051

Eligibility

People in need who live in the parish of St Michael-le-Belfrey, York.

Types of grants

One-off and recurrent grants ranging from £50 to £500. Quarterly pensions are available to older people as well as one-off payments to relieve special needs.

Annual grant total

In 2011 the charity had an income of £7,700 and a total expenditure of £16,400.

Exclusions

No grants for the purposes of education.

Applications

On a form available from the correspondent. Evidence of financial circumstances will be required. Applications can be submitted directly by the individual or through a social worker, Citizens Advice, other welfare agency or other third party.

Other information

Grants are also given to organisations.

The Charity of Jane Wright

£7,800

Correspondent: Diane Grayson, Clerk, Harland and Co., 18 St Saviourgate, York YO1 8NS (01904 655555; email: post@harlandsolicitors.co.uk)

Trustees: Viola Jones; Michael Saville; Colin Michael Stroud; Anne Sains; Christopher William Birch; Rosalind Barbara; Jane Coleman; Quentin Nigel Smallpage; Dianne Suzanne Joyce Wood; Sue Cooke; Derek Mottram.

CC Number: 228961

Eligibility

People in need who live in the city of York.

Types of grants

One-off grants and vouchers according to need.

Annual grant total

In 2010/11 the charity held assets of £1.1 million and had an income of £56,000. Grants totalled £7,800, distributed as follows:

School uniforms	£4,400
Miscellaneous grants	£2,700
Residential grants	£700

Applications

Applications must be made directly or via recognised welfare agencies. They are considered at or between trustees' meetings.

Other information

The charity also maintains a number of flats as almshouses.

York Children's Trust

£38,000

Correspondent: Margaret Brien, 29 Whinney Lane, Harrogate, North Yorkshire HG2 9LS (01423 504765)

Trustees: Colin Stroud; Mark Sessions; Lenore Janet Hill; Keith Hayton; Peter Watson; William Miers; Lynn Wagstaff; Alan Derrick Ward; Dr Anne Kelly; Percy Roberts; Rosalind Fair Fitter; Julie Anne Simpson; Dawn Margaret Moores; Kathy Pickard; Kitty Lamb.

CC Number: 222279

Eligibility

Young people under the age of 25 living within a 20 mile radius of the city of York.

Types of grants

One-off grants according to need.

Annual grant total

During the year grants totalled £76,000 of which £39,000 was paid to individuals for relief in need purposes. Grants to individuals were broken down as follows:

Social and medical	£28,000
Travel and fostering talents	£11,000
Youth and playgroups	£500

Applications

On a form available from the correspondent. Trustees meet to consider applications four times a year. More urgent grants of up to £300 may be awarded between meetings.

Other information

The trust was established through the amalgamation of five existing charities: St Stephen's Orphanage, Blue Coat Boys' and Grey Coat Girls' Schools, The William Richard Beckwith Fund, The Charity of Reverend A.A.R. Gill and The Matthew Rymer Girls Education Fund.

Grants are also made to organisations and to individuals for educational purposes.

York City Charities

£500

Correspondent: M Richard Watson, Clerk, Crombie Wilkinson, 17–19 Clifford Street, York YO1 9RJ (01904 624185; email: r.watson@ crombiewilkinson.co.uk)

Trustees: Ian Carstairs; M. Browne; Anne Fraser Hamilton; Keith Lewis Scott; Elizabeth Fieldsend; G. Ball; Cllr Neil Barnes.

CC Number: 224227

Eligibility

People in need who live within the pre-1996 York city boundaries (the area within the city walls).

Types of grants

One-off grants of between £50 and £200. Recent grants have been given towards furniture and to people on probation to set up a new home.

Annual grant total

In 2011 the charities had assets of £1.1 million and an income of £226,000. Grants made to individuals totalled £1,000.

Applications

In writing to the correspondent, to be submitted by a doctor, occupational nurse, headteacher, social worker, Citizens Advice or other third party or welfare agency. Applications are considered throughout the year.

The York Fund for Women and Girls

£2,200

Correspondent: Carole Money, c/o York CVS, 15 Priory Street, York YO1 6ET (01904 621133)

Trustees: Elizabeth Anne Ellison; Judith Kay Ridge; Patricia Joan Sessions; Alison Mary Baldwin; Barbara Anne Cooke; Judith Margaret Stephenson; Peter Ronald Batty.

CC Number: 21690

Eligibility

Women and girls under the age of 50, who live in York and who are in need.

Types of grants

Generally one-off grants, between £50 and £100, to help with essential household items, fuel bills, furnishings, baby equipment and children's clothes.

Annual grant total

Grants usually average around £2,200 per year.

Exclusions

No grants for education or travel costs.

Applications

On a form available from the correspondent. Applications should be made through a recognised agency and include details of the individual's income. They are considered on an ongoing basis.

Other information

Grants may also be made to local organisations which operate with similar aims.

Northumber-land

The Henry Bell Trust

£0

Correspondent: A Sharp, Secretary, Land Factor, Market Place, Haltwhistle, Northumberland NE49 0BP (01434 320363; fax: 01434320675; email: info@ landfactor.co.uk)

Trustees: Revd Canon Graham Usher; Brian Wood Massey; John Clark; George Brogdon.

CC Number: 702166

Eligibility

People in need who live in the parish of Hexham or the Hexhamshire area.

Types of grants

One-off and recurrent grants ranging from £50 to £400. Grants to individuals are used to help individuals complete volunteer projects.

Annual grant total

In 2010/11 the trust held assets totalling £296,000 and had an income of £11,000. A total of £12,000 was made in grants to local organisations. No grants to individuals were made in the year.

Applications

In writing to the correspondent directly by the individual or family member. Applications are considered twice a year.

Giles Heron Trust

£2,000

Correspondent: George Benson, Trustee, Brunton House, Wall, Hexham, Northumberland NE46 4EJ (01434 681203)

Trustees: George Benson; Judith Weir; David Prest; Revd John Thompson; Nicholas Ridley; Veronica Allgood; Pierce Grant; Jane Keep.

CC Number: 224157

Eligibility

People in need who live in the ancient parish of Simonburn.

Types of grants

One-off grants ranging from £100 to £500.

Annual grant total

In 2010/11 the charity had both an income and a total expenditure of £12,000. Previously grants were made totalling around £8,000, of which about £4,000 was given in individual awards, with the rest being donated to local organisations.

Applications

In writing to the correspondent directly by the individual.

Other information

Individual grants are also made for educational purposes.

The Morpeth Dispensary

£3,000

Correspondent: Michael Gaunt, Trustee, 15 Bridge Street, Morpeth, Northumberland NE61 1NX (01670 512336)

Trustees: Michael Abbott Gaunt; Thomas Henry Horne; Mrs A. Rutherford.

CC Number: 222352

Eligibility

People who are sick and poor and live in or around Morpeth.

Types of grants

Grants are one-off and range from £40 to £300 including those for new washing machines, household bills, cookers, decorating costs, clothing, furniture and so on.

Annual grant total

Grants average around £2,500 per year.

Applications

In writing to the correspondent at any time through a third party such as a social worker, GP, Citizens Advice or other welfare agency. Applications must include detail of the applicant's age, whether a single parent, whether on benefits, their address and any details regarding health matters. Grants are made directly to the third party, not the applicant.

Other information

Grants are also made to organisations to provide additional help at Christmas, for instance a trip to the theatre at Christmas for those individuals meeting the eligibility criteria.

Berwick-upon-Tweed

The Berwick-upon-Tweed Nursing Amenities Fund

£650

Correspondent: Alan J Patterson, Greaves West and Ayre, 1–3 Sandgate, Berwick-upon-Tweed TD15 1EW (01289 306688; fax: 01289 307189; email: ap@ gwayre.co.uk)

Trustees: Isobel Elder; Alice Moore; Eva Sinclair.

CC Number: 230711

Eligibility

People who are sick, poor or in need and live in the borough of Berwick-upon-Tweed.

Types of grants

One-off grants up to £200.

Annual grant total

About £650.

Applications

In writing to the correspondent through a social worker, Citizens Advice or other welfare agency at any time.

South Yorkshire

The Aston Charities

£8,000

Correspondent: Jim Nuttall, Clerk, 3 Rosegarth Avenue, Aston, Sheffield S26 2DB (01142 876047)

Trustees: James Anthony Nuttall; Hilda Jack; Mildred Nuttall; Cllr Ossie Eyre; Terry Drury; Bob O'Keeffe; Revd Ian Jennings; Geoff Boulton; Bernadette Bartholemew.

CC Number: 225071

Eligibility

People in need who live in Aston, Aughton or Swallowness with a particular preference for older people.

Types of grants

One-off and recurrent grants according to need. Recent grants have been made towards the cost of holidays for a single parent family and an unemployed couple and their three children. Help has also been given towards installing a telephone for an older couple. The trust does not normally give cash grants instead it pays the supplier of the services.

Annual grant total

In 2011 the charity had an income of £21,000 and a total expenditure of £18,000.

Exclusions

The charity does not make loans or give to profit-making concerns.

Applications

In writing to the correspondent or any trustee, directly by the individual or through a social worker, Citizens Advice or other welfare agency. Applications are considered quarterly.

Other information

Grants are also made for educational purposes and to organisations catering for the elderly.

The Brampton Bierlow Welfare Trust

£9,000

Correspondent: Jill Leece, Newman and Bond, 35 Church Street, Barnsley S70 2AP (01226 213434)

Trustees: Frank Hodgkiss; Sid Bailey; Charles Wright; Gerald Dennis; Harry Edward Beaumont; Ken Sanderson; Walter Cutts; Ann Peace; Revd Peter Bold; Ronald Norman.

CC Number: 249838

Eligibility

People in need who live in Brampton Bierlow and West Melton, and those parts of Wentworth and Elscar within the ancient parish of Brampton Bierlow.

Types of grants

One-off grants from £100 to £250 for necessities and comforts. Christmas grocery vouchers are also distributed.

Annual grant total

In 2011 the trust had an income and total expenditure of £10,000.

Applications

Applications in writing to the correspondent can be submitted by the individual and are considered at any time.

Other information

The trust also makes grants to local organisations.

The Cantley Poor's Land Trust

£17,000 (147 grants)

Correspondent: Margaret Jackson, Clerk to the Trustees, 30 Selhurst Crescent, Bessacarr, Doncaster, South Yorkshire DN4 6EF (01302 530566)

Trustees: Roni Chapman; Sarah Rogerson; Gillian Warrender; Colin S. Kingston; Yvonne Butterworth; David Elvin; Susan Forbes.

CC Number: 224787

Eligibility

People in need who live in the ancient parish of Cantley with Branton.

Types of grants

One-off grants ranging from £50 to £500 including those towards electric goods, clothing, medical equipment, furniture and disabled equipment.

Annual grant total

In 2010/11 the trust held assets of £719,000 and had an income of £28,000. Grants totalled just over £21,000.

The average grant was £145.

Exclusions

Restrictions apply to the relief of rates, taxes and repeat grants.

Applications

On a form available from the correspondent, to be submitted directly by the individual or through a welfare agency. Applications are considered on a monthly basis.

The Fisher Trust

£1,000

Correspondent: Jennifer Laister, 77 Woodburn Drive, Chapeltown, Sheffield S35 1YT (01142 462293)

Trustees: Gavin Mason; Patricia Emmingham; William Henry Emmingham; Joseph Woodhouse; Kenneth Smith; David Shaw; Phillip Cooper; Diane Malaure; Marion Baker; Barbara Laycock; Stephen Attwood; Jennifer Laister; Patrick Smith.

CC Number: 226355

Eligibility

Unitarian and Roman Catholic widows and unmarried women in need who are over 45 and live in and around Sheffield.

Types of grants

Annual allowances of £100 to £150 to help supplement low incomes.

Annual grant total

Grants usually total about £1,000 each year.

Applications

On a form available from the correspondent, to be submitted via the applicant's minister. Applications are normally considered in April.

The George and Clara Ann Hall Charity

£5,500

Correspondent: Judith Harrison, c/o Voluntary Action Sheffield, The Circle, 33 Rockingham Lane, Sheffield S1 4FW (01142 536615; email: j.harrison@vas.org.uk)

Trustee: Voluntary Action Sheffield.

CC Number: 223026

Eligibility

Widows and unmarried women over 45 who have lived in the city of Sheffield or the township and chapelry of Bradfield for the past five years and are in receipt of benefits.

Types of grants

Annual grants of £600 are paid half yearly to a small number of beneficiaries.

Annual grant total

In 2010/11 the charity had an income of £3,900 and a total expenditure of £6,200.

Applications

In writing to the correspondent. However, the charity has only a limited amount of funds and wants to ensure that the annual grants it awards are a meaningful amount. As a result, new applicants are only considered when an existing beneficiary has died.

Rebecca Guest Robinson Charity

£1,500

Correspondent: John Armitage, 10 St Mary's Gardens, Worsbrough, Barnsley, South Yorkshire S70 5LU (01226 290179)

Trustees: Keith Burkinshaw; Martin Taylor; John Armitage; Douglas Stewart; Sheila Jackson; Kathleen Goldsby-West.

CC Number: 247266

Eligibility

People who live in the villages of Birdwell and Worsbrough, near Barnsley, and are in need. Preference is given to children, young people and older people.

Types of grants

One-off grants, usually ranging between £50 and £250, towards clothing, household equipment, disability equipment, holidays and childcare.

Annual grant total

This trust generally has an income of around £1,600 and a total expenditure of £1,000 to £2,000.

Applications

On a form available from the correspondent. Applications should be submitted directly by the individual or a family member.

Other information

Local organisations are also supported.

The Sheffield West Riding Charitable Society Trust

£2,500

Correspondent: Malcolm Fair, Diocesan Secretary, Diocesan Church House, 95–99 Effingham Street, Rotherham S65 1BL (01709 309100; email: malcolm.fair@sheffield.anglican.org; website: www.sheffield.anglican.org)

Trustee: Sheffield Diocesan Board of Finance.

CC Number: 1002026

Eligibility

Clergymen of the Church of England in the diocese of Sheffield who are in need. Also their widows, orphans or distressed families, and people keeping house, or who have kept house, for clergymen of the Church of England in the diocese or their families.

Types of grants

One-off and recurrent grants of £100 to £1,000.

Annual grant total

In 2010 the trust had an income of £11,000 and a total expenditure of £5,500. Around 20 grants are made each year.

Applications

On a form available from the correspondent.

Other information

Welfare grants are also made to the clergy, house-keepers and disadvantaged families in the diocese.

Armthorpe

Armthorpe Poors Estate Charity

£5,000

Correspondent: Frank Pratt, 32 Gurth Avenue, Edenthorpe, Doncaster DN3 2LW (01302 882806)

Trustees: Revd R. Landall; Mr F. A. Paling; J. Lowndes; Mrs B. Fox; Mrs P. Grant; L. George.

CC Number: 226123

Eligibility

People who are in need and live in Armthorpe.

Types of grants

One-off and recurrent grants of £50 to £500 towards items such as mobility aids, aids for people with visual difficulties, hospital visiting and care of older people.

Annual grant total

In 2010/11 the charity had an income of £10,000 and a total expenditure of £10,000.

Applications

Contact the clerk by telephone who will advise if a letter of application is needed. Applicants outside of Armthorpe will be declined.

Other information

The trust gives to both individuals and organisations.

Barnsley

The Barnsley Tradesmen's Benevolent Institution

£1,800

Correspondent: David Bishop Richards, 9 Kensington Road, Barnsley, South Yorkshire S75 2TX (01226 281929)

Trustees: Malcolm Bird; Sanders Gordon Ernest.

CC Number: 246313

Eligibility

Merchants and traders, their widows and unmarried daughters, who are in need and have lived in the old borough of Barnsley for at least seven years.

Types of grants

Recurrent grants are given towards general daily living expenses such as food, medical care and equipment and travel to and from hospital.

Annual grant total

Generally this trust gives grants totalling around £1,800 a year.

Applications

In writing to the correspondent, either directly by the individual or through a third party such as a Citizens Advice or other welfare agency. Applications are considered monthly.

The Fountain Nursing Trust

£1,400

Correspondent: The Trustees, Newman and Bond, 35 Church Street, Barnsley, South Yorkshire S70 2AP (01226 213434; fax: 01226 213435)

Trustees: Keith Roddam; Lorraine Acott; Sister Susan Mary Doran.

CC Number: 224507

Eligibility

People in need who are in poor health, convalescent or who have a disability and live in the urban district of Darton, Barnsley.

Types of grants

One-off and recurrent grants according to need. Recent grants have been given for medical equipment and expenses, nursing fees and help in the home.

Annual grant total

Grants average about £1,400 a year, though the actual grant figure tends to fluctuate quite widely.

Applications

In writing to the correspondent.

Beighton

Beighton Relief-in-Need Charity

£3,500

Correspondent: Diane Rodgers, 41 Collingbourne Avenue, Sothall, Sheffield S20 2QR (01142 692875; email: beigtonrelief@hotmail.co.uk)

Trustees: Ian Saunders; Sheila Dootson; Norman Dunn; Ruth Hodson; Mike Healey; Diane Rodgers.

CC Number: 225416

Eligibility

People in need who live in the former parish of Beighton.

Types of grants

One-off grants according to need. Recent grants have been given towards bath lifts and child care seats for people who are disabled. Winter fuel grants of £15 per household were also given to older people.

Annual grant total

Grants usually total around £7,000 per year.

Applications

In writing to the correspondent. Applications can be submitted directly by the individual or through a social worker, Citizens Advice, other welfare agency or a third party such as a relative, neighbour or trustee.

Other information
Grants are also made for educational purposes.

Bramley

The Bramley Poor's Allotment Trust

£1,500

Correspondent: Mrs Marian Houseman, 9 Horton Rise, Rodley, Leeds LS13 1PH (01132 360115)

Trustees: Margaret Charnley; John Stocks; Revd Ian Rodley; Jeffrey Houseman; Margaret Seaman.

CC Number: 224522

Eligibility
People in need who live in the ancient township of Bramley, especially people who are elderly, poor and sick.

Types of grants
One-off grants between £40 and £120.

Annual grant total
In 2010 the trust had both an income and total expenditure of £3,000.

Applications
In writing to the correspondent. The trust likes applications to be submitted through a recognised referral agency (social worker, Citizens Advice, doctor, headmaster or minister). They are considered monthly.

Doncaster

The John William Chapman Charitable Trust

£30,000

Correspondent: Rosemary Sharp, Jordans, 4 Priory Place, Doncaster DN1 1BP (01302 365374; email: info@ chapmantrust.org; website: chapmantrust.org/)

Trustees: Lady Catherine Anne Maria Neill; Victoria Rebecca Ferres; Michael George Gornall; Mark John Hunter; David Geoffrey Kirk.

CC Number: 223002

Eligibility
People in need who live in the metropolitan borough of Doncaster.

Types of grants
One-off grants in kind, not cash, up to the value of £500 towards fridges, cookers, washing machines, beds, cots, carpets and clothing.

Annual grant total
In 2010/11 the trust had assets of £3.7 million and an income of £189,000. Grants to individuals totalled £30,000.

Exclusions
No grants are given towards wardrobes, cupboards, drawers, living room suites, TV, Hi-Fi, video players, educational course fees, funeral expenses, external work to a property, payment of debts including rent bonds, decorating materials, toys, removal expenses, baby high chairs or gates.

Applications
Online or on a form available from the correspondent or to download from the website. Applications must be accompanied by a letter from a social worker, GP or welfare agency and are considered monthly. The trust visits all applicants.

Only one application can be accepted in any 12 month period, except in exceptional circumstances.

Other information
Grants to organisations amounted to £39,000.

Epworth

Epworth Charities

£300

Correspondent: Mrs Margaret Draper, 16 Fern Croft, Epworth, Doncaster, South Yorkshire DN9 1GE (01427 873234; email: margaret.draper1@tiscali. co.uk)

Trustees: John Lambert; Stephen Selby; Jayne Oliver; Susan Astle; Ian Walker; Eileen Tatton.

CC Number: 219744

Eligibility
People in need who live in Epworth.

Types of grants
One-off and recurrent grants in the range of £50 and £250.

Annual grant total
Grants usually total between £400 and £1,000 per year.

Applications
In writing to the correspondent to be submitted directly by the individual. Applications are considered on an ongoing basis.

Other information
Grants are also made for educational purposes.

Finningly

The Sir Stuart and Lady Florence Goodwin Charity

£13,000

Correspondent: Grants Administrator, Bassetlaw District Council, Finance Department, Queen's Buildings, Potter Street, Worksop, Nottinghamshire S80 2AH (01909 533296; email: democratic.services@bassetlaw.gov.uk)

Trustees: Revd Jonathan Smithurst; David Challinor; Shirley Isard; Jeffrey Briggs Rickells; Revd George Brigham; Hazel Magarete Brand; Patricia Douglas.

CC Number: 216902

Eligibility
People over 60 who are need and live in the former rural district of East Retford. Consideration may be given to younger applicants.

Types of grants
One-off grants to improve quality of life. Recent grants have been given for medical equipment such as nebulisers, access ramps, walk-in baths and mobility scooters.

Annual grant total
In 2010/11 the charity had an income of £9,900 and a total expenditure of £13,000.

Applications
In writing to the correspondent. Applications can be submitted directly by the individual or through a third party such as Age Concern or social services. Grants will only be made to the person raising the invoice, not the individual.

Rotherham

The Common Lands of Rotherham Charity

£5,000

Correspondent: W B Copley, Barn Cottage, 5 Crossland Gardens, Tickhill, Doncaster, South Yorkshire DN11 9QS (01302 743947)

Trustees: John Clark; Anthony Grice; John Bingham; Nigel Elmhirst; Peter Watson; Christopher Badger; Jane Collier.

CC Number: 223050

Eligibility
People in need who live in Rotherham. Preference is usually given to older people.

Types of grants

One-off and recurrent grants according to need.

Annual grant total

Grants usually total about £5,000 a year.

Applications

In writing to the correspondent following advertisement in September.

The Stoddart Samaritan Fund

£10,000

Correspondent: Peter Wright, 7 Melrose Grove, Rotherham, South Yorkshire S60 3NA (01709 376448)

Trustees: Dr Gavin Beattie Peckitt; Dr Malcolm Venables; Dr Naresh Ambalal Patel; Dr Robert Charles Adair Collinson; Dr Adrian John Cole; Dr Gail Crowley; Dr Catherine Anne Cooper.

CC Number: 242853

Eligibility

People in need who have medical problems and would benefit from financial assistance to help their recovery. Applicants must live in Rotherham and the surrounding area.

Types of grants

One-off grants to assist recovery.

Annual grant total

In 2010/11 the trust had an income £12,000 and a total expenditure of £10,400.

Applications

On a form available from the correspondent, to be submitted by the applicant's doctor. Applications are considered on a regular basis.

Sheffield

Sir George Franklin's Pension Charity

£5,000

Correspondent: Rick Plews, Clerk, 2nd Floor, Fountain Precinct, Balm Green, Sheffield S2 3QE (01142 767991)

CC Number: 224883

Eligibility

People in need aged 50 and over who live in the city of Sheffield.

Types of grants

Annual allowances of £350 paid half yearly in June and December.

Annual grant total

In 2010/11 the charity had an income of £4,900 and a total expenditure of £5,300.

Applications

On a form available from the correspondent. Vacancies arise infrequently and are publicised locally. Applications should only be made in response to this publicity. Speculative applications will not be successful.

Sir Samuel Osborn's Deed of Gift Relief Fund

£2,700

Correspondent: Sue Wragg, South Yorkshire Community Foundation, Unit 3 – G1 Building, 6 Leeds Road, Attercliffe, Sheffield S9 3TY (01142 424294; fax: 01142 424605; email: grants@sycf.org.uk; website: sycf.org.uk/)

Trustees: Alan Sheriff; Lady Ruby Sykes; Frank Carter; Galen Ives; Timothy Greenacre; Dr Robert John Giles Bloomer; Jonathan Hunt; Maureen Shah; Jane Marshall; Jane Kemp; Jackie Drayton; Allan Jackson; Sue Scholey; Timothy Henry Reed; Peter John Hollis; Charles William Hugh Warrack; Earl of Scarborough Richard Scarborough.

CC Number: 1140947

Eligibility

Residents of Sheffield, with some preference for those with a connection to the Samuel Osborn Company.

Types of grants

One-off grants for people with disabilities, affected by hardship or suffering from medical conditions. Grants can be for short breaks, medical equipment and 'any other comforts associated with poor health'.

Annual grant total

In 2010/11 grants totalled around £2,700.

Exclusions

Grants are not given for medical items available from the NHS.

Applications

On a form available to download from the website. The community foundation welcomes informal approaches about applications prior to submitting. Applicants with a connection to the Osborn company should include written evidence. Decisions should be made within 12 weeks.

Only one grant per applicant per year.

Other information

The fund is now administered by the South Yorkshire Community Foundation. Grants are also made for educational purposes.

Teesside

John T. Shuttleworth Ropner Memorial Fund

£33,000

Correspondent: Brenda Dye, Grants Manager, County Durham Community Foundation, Victoria House, St Johns Road, Meadowfield Industrial Estate, Durham DH7 8XL (01913 786340; fax: 01913 782409; email: brenda@cdcf.org.uk; website: www.cdcf.org.uk)

Trustee: County Durham Community Foundation.

CC Number: 1047625

Eligibility

Sick, elderly or disabled individuals and their carers in the Tees Valley area who are in need of respite care, or who need temporary support following hospitalisation, bereavement or because of dependency treatment. Applicants must live in Stockton, Thornaby on Tees, Redcar, Middlesbrough, Hartlepool or Darlington. Applicants must also have exhausted all statutory options before applying and must not have savings of more than £16,000. Priority will be given to first time applicants.

Types of grants

Grants of up to £1,000 for recuperative or respite care, home help assistance, bereavement related costs, travel and accommodation for individuals (and for their families) undergoing dependency treatment at a clinic or centre away from their place of residence.

Annual grant total

The fund can distribute around £33,000 per year.

Exclusions

Only one grant per family per financial year. Retrospective grants will not be made. No grants for medical equipment or treatment, or nursing care.

Applications

On an application form available to download from the Durham Community Foundation website. A reference and covering note on headed paper or a compliments slip must also be included from your GP, community nurse or social worker who is willing to discuss your request.

The Teesside Emergency Relief Fund

£13,000

Correspondent: Linda Leather, Client Case Officer, Tees Valley Community

Foundation, Wallace House, Falcon Court, Preston Farm Industrial Estate, Stockton-on-Tees TS18 3TX (01642 260860; email: info@teesvalleyfoundtion. org; website: www.teesvalletfoundation. org)

Trustees: Peter Rowley; Alan Kitching; Christopher Ian Hope; Pamela Ann Taylor; Rosemary Young; John Irwin; Marjory Houseman; Keith Robinson; Neil Kenley; Wendy Shepherd; Brian Beaumont; Tracey Stonehouse.

CC Number: 1111222–3

Eligibility

People in need who live in county borough of Teesside area including Hartlepool, Middlesbrough, Redcar and Cleveland and Stockton on Tees.

Types of grants

Grants of up to £250 for items needed to relieve immediate hardship although larger grants may be considered in exceptional circumstances. Grants are paid directly to the referring organisation to administer on the applicants behalf. Shop vouchers may also be provided.

Annual grant total

The fund has £16,000 to distribute up to 13 March 2013. For the 2013/14 year they expect to distribute £10,000.

Exclusions

No grants for non-essential items such as TVs, DVD players, stereos, etc. or for replacement mattresses soiled through bed wetting. No grants are paid to alleviate debts.

Applications

On a form available to download from the website. Applications should be supported by a social worker, health visitor, welfare officer, GP, probation officer, local tenancy office or other welfare agency representative. Proof of household income must also be attached – this includes benefit confirmation letters, benefit books or payslips. Applications are considered on a regular basis.

Hartlepool

The Furness Seamen's Pension Fund

£10,000

Correspondent: Heather O'Driscoll, Trust Administrator, Waltons Clark Whitehill, Oakland House, 38–42 Victoria Road, Hartlepool, Cleveland TS26 8DD (01429 234414; fax: 01429 231263; email: heather.odriscoll@ waltonscw.co.uk)

Trustees: John Furness; David Williams; Nigel Hogg; Cllr Mary Fleet; Michael Furness; Sir Stephen Roberts Furness; Gordon Rennie; Cllr Sheila Griffin; Alan Hodgson.

CC Number: 226655

Eligibility

Seamen in need who are 50 or over and live in the borough of Hartlepool or the former county borough of West Hartlepool, or who had their permanent residence there during their sea service. All applicants must have served as seamen for at least 15 years and with some part of the sea service in vessels registered in Hartlepool, West Hartlepool or the Port of Hartlepool, or vessels trading to/from any of these ports.

Types of grants

Quarterly pensions.

Annual grant total

In 2010/11 the fund had an income of £10,200 and total expenditure of £11,000.

Applications

On a form available from the correspondent. Advertisements are placed in the Hartlepool Mail when vacancies are available.

Middlesbrough

The Lady Crosthwaite Bequest

£60

Correspondent: Mark Taylor, Middlesbrough Council, PO Box 340, Middlesbrough, Cleveland TS1 2XP (01642 727337)

Trustee: Middlesbrough council.

CC Number: 234932

Eligibility

Pensioners in need who live in the former county borough of Middlesbrough.

Types of grants

Small grants at Christmas, and occasional day trips, via the social services and community councils, together with one-off lump sums to organisations.

Annual grant total

In 2010/11 the charity had an income of £2,000 and a total expenditure of £60.

Applications

In writing to the correspondent, through social services.

Middleton

Ralph Gowland Trust

£1,000

Correspondent: Joan Staley, 38 Hill Terrace, Middleton-in-Teesdale, Barnard Castle, County Durham DL12 0SL (01833 640542)

Trustees: Derek Stanley Carr; Joan Staley; John Anderson; Judith Tarn.

CC Number: 701019

Eligibility

People in need aged 60 or over who live in the parish of Middleton in Teesdale.

Types of grants

One-off and recurrent grants according to need.

Annual grant total

Grants average around £1,000 each year.

Applications

In writing to the correspondent.

Tyne and Wear

Charity of John McKie Elliott Deceased

£500

Correspondent: Robert Walker, 6 Manor House Road, Newcastle upon Tyne NE2 2LU (01912 814657; email: bobwalker9@aol.com)

Trustees: Ronald Eager; David Napier; Bob Walker.

CC Number: 235075

Eligibility

People who are blind in Gateshead or Newcastle upon Tyne.

Types of grants

One-off and recurrent grants according to need.

Annual grant total

Annual income usually ranges between £200 and £2,500.

Applications

In writing to the correspondent.

Other information

The trust gives educational grants and grants to individuals in need.

The Sunderland Guild of Help

£4,000

Correspondent: Norman Taylor, Chair, 4 Toward Road, Sunderland, Tyne and Wear SR1 2QG (01915 672895; email: info@guildofhelp.co.uk; website: www. guildofhelp.co.uk)

Trustees: Dr Norman Taylor; Brian Dodds; Eric Thursby; Mrs J. Dunn.

CC Number: 229656

Eligibility
People in need who live in Sunderland.

Types of grants
Support is given for the advancement of health and the relief of poverty.

Annual grant total
In 2010/11 the guild had an income of £13,000. Grants to individuals usually total around £4,000.

Exclusions
No grants for new goods or goods made to order.

Applications
Applications can only be considered if they are submitted through a social worker. They should include an income and expenditure statement and are considered throughout the year.

Other information
The guild administers the Sunderland Queen Victoria Memorial Fund 1901, the Sunderland Convalescent Fund and the Chest and Heart Fund. It also manages the trust funds connected with the tuberculosis care committee of the guild.

In addition, the guild acts as an enabling charity through its premises on Toward Road, Sunderland where other small charities are provided accommodation at rents that reflect their charitable status.

The Sunderland Orphanage and Educational Foundation

£11,000

Correspondent: Peter Taylor, McKenzie Bell, 19 John Street, Sunderland SR1 1JG (01915 674857)

Trustees: Denys Briggs; Mary Smith; Mrs W. Lundgren; John Mann; John Knight; Carole Pattison; Paul Madison; Michael Mordey.

CC Number: 527202

Eligibility
Young people under 25 who are resident in or around Sunderland who have a parent who is disabled or has died, or whose parents are divorced or legally separated.

Types of grants
Grants are given to children for clothing and living expenses. Grants are also made to students.

Annual grant total
In 2010/11 the trust had an income of £22,000 and a total expenditure of £25,000.

Applications
Applications should be made in writing to the correspondent. They are considered every other month.

The Thomas Thompson Poors Rate Gift

£4,500

Correspondent: Anthony Francis, Newcastle City Council, 5th Floor, Civic Centre, Barras Bridge, Newcastle NE99 1RD (01912 116919; email: anthony.francis@newcastle.gov.uk)

Trustees: George Allison; Anne Veronica Dunn.

CC Number: 253846

Eligibility
People in need who live in Byker.

Types of grants
One-off grants for items such as washing machines, furniture and cookers. Grants have also been given to replace Christmas presents and children's bikes which have been stolen.

Annual grant total
Grants average around £4,500 a year.

Applications
In writing to the correspondent, for consideration throughout the year. Grants to replace stolen property are usually submitted through Victim Support.

The Tyne Mariners' Benevolent Institution

£122,000 (192 grants)

Correspondent: Janet Littlefield, Hadaway and Hadaway, 58 Howard Street, North Shields, Tyne and Wear NE30 1AL (01912 570382; email: janetl@ hadaway.co.uk)

Trustees: Michael Bird; Revd Timothy Duff; Douglas Hamilton; Pat Wilson; Richard Souter; Bob McClean; Cap Mike Nicholson; Tom Rutter; Cap Anthony James Hogg; Mstr Raymond Douglas Nelson; Dianne Erskine; Revd Kirkwood; Cap Stephen Christopher Healy; Peter Anthony Dade; Lt Cdr Andrew Sheldon Collier.

CC Number: 229236

Eligibility
Former merchant seamen who live in Tyneside (about five miles either side of the River Tyne) and their widows. Applicants must be: (a) at least 55 years old and have served at least five years at sea; (b) under the age of 55, but unable to work owing to ill-health; or (c) the widows of such people.

Types of grants
Recurrent grants of about £40 per calendar month and two bonuses of varying value.

Annual grant total
In 2011 the trust had assets of £1.1 million and an income of £232,000. Grants and pensions were made to 192 individuals totalling £122,000

Applications
On a form available from the correspondent, to be submitted either directly by the individual or through a social worker, Citizens Advice or other welfare agency. Applications can be considered at any time.

Other information
The institution also administers The Master Mariners Homes in Tynemouth which provides 30 flats for its beneficiaries.

Gateshead

The Gateshead Relief-in-Sickness Fund

£1,000

Correspondent: Victoria Spark, Thomas Magnay and Co., 8 St Mary's Green, Whickham, Newcastle on Tyne NE16 4DN (01914 887459)

Trustees: Peter Magnay; Sidney Atkinson; Peter Moran; Walter Nigel Picken; Tom Steanson.

CC Number: 234970

Eligibility
People who are in poor health, convalescent or who have disabilities and live in the borough of Gateshead.

Types of grants
One-off grants towards providing or paying for items, services or facilities, which will alleviate need or assist with recovery, and are not readily available from other sources. Recent grants have been given to adapt a bathroom for a boy with learning and physical disabilities and for computers and talking typewriters for people who are registered blind.

Annual grant total

Grants are given to both individuals and organisations and total around £2,000 each year.

Applications

In writing to the correspondent. Applications can be submitted directly by the individual or through a social worker, Citizens Advice or other welfare agency.

Horton

Houghton-Le-Spring Relief in Need Charity

£3,500

Correspondent: Mr Brian Scott, 28 Finchale Close, Houghton Le Spring, Tyne and Wear DH4 5QU (01915 841608; email: rectorstmichaels@ btinternet.com)

Trustees: Cllr Allen Maddison; Brenda Telford; Revd Cannon Suzanne Pinnington; Susan Wardle; Angela Fitzroy Morris.

CC Number: 810025

Eligibility

People in need living in the Ancient Parish Of Houghton-Le-Spring.

Types of grants

One-off and recurrent according to need.

Annual grant total

In 2010/11 the charity had an income of £3,600 and a total expenditure of £4,000.

Applications

In writing to the correspondent.

Newcastle upon Tyne

The Non-Ecclesiastical Charity of William Moulton

£31,000

Correspondent: George Jackson, Clerk to the Trustees, 10 Sunlea Avenue, Cullercoats, Tyne and Wear NE30 3DS (01912 510971; email: jgeorgelvis@ blueyonder.co.uk)

Trustees: Christopher Dalliston; M. Mc Williams; M. Pearson; R. Allison; S. Pearson; D. S. Priestly; Bill Schardt.

CC Number: 216255

Eligibility

People in need who have lived within the boundaries of the city of Newcastle upon Tyne for at least the past 12 months.

Types of grants

Grants range between £50 and £200 towards general household/personal needs such as washing machines, cookers, furniture, clothing and so on.

Annual grant total

In 2011 the charity had assets of £1.1 million and an income of £52,000. Grants made to individuals totalled £31,000.

Exclusions

No grants are given for education, training or rent arrears.

Applications

On a form available from the correspondent. Applications should be submitted through a social worker, Citizens Advice or other welfare agency and are considered monthly.

The Town Moor Money Charity

£84,000 (344 grants)

Correspondent: Richard Grey, Moor Bank Lodge, Claremont Road, Newcastle upon Tyne NE2 4NL (01912 615970; email: admin@freemenofnewcastle.org; website: www.freemenofnewcastle.org)

Trustees: Keith Hall; John Norman Frizzell; William George Frizzle; David Mar Loraine; Philip M. Errington; David Hughes; Sherod William Duguid Walker.

CC Number: 248098

Eligibility

Freemen of Newcastle upon Tyne, Northumberland and Durham and their widows and children who are in need.

Types of grants

One-off and recurrent grants according to need. Grants are means-tested and paid in June and December.

Annual grant total

In 2010/11 the charity had assets of £242,000 and an income of £48,000. Grants were made to 344 beneficiaries totalling £84,000.

Applications

Application forms are available in April and October from the senior steward of the appropriate company. They are usually considered in May and November.

Sunderland

The George Hudson Charity

£19,000 (49 grants)

Correspondent: Peter Taylor-McKenzie Bell, 54 John Street, Sunderland SR1 1QH (01915 674857; fax: 01915 109347; email: enquires@mckenzie-bell. co.uk)

Trustees: John Brown; George Brown; P. Moodie; Dinah McKenzie; Gavin Spencer; J. E. Hedley; Gillian Walker; Peter Wood.

CC Number: 527204

Eligibility

People under the age of 18 whose father has died or is unable to work and are living in Sunderland, with preference to children of seafarers.

Types of grants

The trust gives pocket money of £12 a month to children up to the age of 14 and £14 a month to older children. Children can receive a grant towards clothing and footwear and Christmas bonuses are also given.

Annual grant total

In 2010/11 the charity had assets of £502,000 and an income of £35,000. £8,900 was given in monthly allowances to 49 children, £2,200 was given in Christmas bonuses and £8,000 was given in clothing and footwear grants totalling £19,000.

Applications

On a form available from the correspondent. Applications are considered every other month.

The Mayor's Fund for Necessitous Children

£500

Correspondent: Children's Services Financial Manager, Children's Services, Sandhill Centre, Grindon Lane, Sunderland SR3 4EN (01915 531826)

Trustees: I. W. Kay; Paul Maddison; Patricia Smith; J. Kelly.

CC Number: 229349

Eligibility

Children in need (under 16, occasionally under 19) who are in full-time education, live in the city of Sunderland and whose family are on a low income.

Types of grants

Grants of about £25 for the provision of school footwear, paid every six months

Annual grant total

About £500.

Exclusions

No grants are made to asylum seekers.

Applications

Applicants must visit the civic centre and fill in a form with a member of staff. The decision is then posted at a later date. Proof of low income is necessary.

Tynemouth

The Charlton Bequest and Dispensary Trust

£0

Correspondent: Roy King, Trustee, 50 The Broadway, North Shields NE30 2LQ (01912 575297)

Trustees: Dorothy Chilvers; Alan Galley; Peter Headley; William Stephenson; Hilda Annie Amos; James Henry Donnalley; Roy Hugh King; Kath Stewart.

CC Number: 1055160

Eligibility

People who are sick, poor, have disabilities or who are convalescent and live in the former county borough of Tynemouth, now part of North Tyneside County Borough. Preference is given to people resident at one of the trust's almshouses.

Types of grants

Grants to pay for items, services or facilities which are calculated to alleviate the suffering or assist the recovery of eligible people who do not have funds readily available to them from other sources.

Annual grant total

No grants were made in 2010/11 (£310 in 2008/9).

Applications

In writing to the correspondent.

Other information

This trust was formed from the North Shields and Tynemouth Dispensary and the County Borough of Tynemouth Nursing Association. It is primarily concerned with the provision of apartments for older people in poor health.

Wallsend

Wallsend Charitable Trust

£2,000

Correspondent: The Secretary, North Tyneside Council, 16 The Silverlink North, Newcastle upon Tyne NE27 0BY (01916 437006)

Trustees: Michael Joseph Huscroft; Cllr Mary Glindon; Margaret Anne Finlay; Mary Kelly; Susan Richardson.

CC Number: 215476

Eligibility

People over 60 who are on or just above state benefit income levels and live in the former borough of Wallsend.

Types of grants

One-off grants ranging between £10 to £500 to help meet extra requirements, for example, washing machines, fridge-freezers, carpets, home decoration, safety and security measures and medical equipment.

Annual grant total

In 2010 the trust held assets of £732,000 and had an income of £80,000. The majority of grants are usually given to organisations.

Exclusions

The trust will not help with continuing costs such as residential care or telephone rentals and will not help a person whose income is significantly above state benefit levels. Applicants must have exhausted all statutory avenues such as DWP, Social Fund, social services department and so on.

Applications

In writing to the correspondent either directly by the individual or through a social worker, Citizens Advice or other welfare agency or third party, such as a friend or relative. Applications are considered quarterly in April, July, September and December. They must include details of the purpose of the grant and an estimate of the cost.

Other information

Grants can be given to organisations provided that the majority of members meet the same criteria as apply to individuals.

West Yorkshire

Bradford and District Wool Association Benevolent Fund

£4,000

Correspondent: Sir James F Hill, Chair, Sir James (Wool) Ltd, Unit 2 Baildon Mills, Northgate, Baildon, Shipley, West Yorkshire BD17 6JX (01274 532200)

Trustees: Sir James Hill; John Wilde.

CC Number: 518439

Eligibility

Former workers in the wool trade in Bradford and district or their spouses, who are in need. Preference is given to those who are elderly or disabled.

Types of grants

Normally recurrent grants up to a maximum of £200 towards heating, electricity and telephone costs. Special cases (such as the need for mobility aids, for example) are considered.

Annual grant total

Grants total around £4,000 per year.

Applications

In writing to the correspondent either directly by the individual or through a relative or friend. Applications are considered at any time.

The Bradford Jewish Benevolent Fund

£1,800

Correspondent: Walter Behrend, 1 Fern Chase, Leeds LS14 3JL (01132 893274)

Trustees: Michael Levi; Albert Abraham Waxman.

CC Number: 227667

Eligibility

Older people in need who are Jewish and live in the city of Bradford and district.

Types of grants

One-off and recurrent grants according to need. Grants are to relieve poverty and sickness.

Annual grant total

Grants average around £1,800 a year.

Applications

In writing to the correspondent, directly by the individual or through a third party such as a social worker.

245

Mary Farrar's Benevolent Trust Fund

£8,500

Correspondent: Peter Haley, P Haley and Co., Poverty Hall, Lower Ellistones, Saddleworth Road Greetland, Halifax HX4 8NG (01422 376690)

Trustees: Barry Wright; Harry Brook; Vernon Fawkes; Alan Jowett.

CC Number: 223806

Eligibility
Women of limited means who are over 55 years of age and have lived in the parish of Halifax for more than five years.

Types of grants
Annual pensions are paid quarterly.

Annual grant total
In 2010/11 the fund had an income of £5,000 and a total expenditure of £9,000.

Exclusions
No more than six grants are given to married women and widows.

Applications
On a form available from the correspondent. Applications can be submitted by the individual, through a recognised referral agency (such as a social worker, Citizens Advice, or doctor) or another third party such as a relative, friend, minister of religion or trustee.

The Harrison and Potter Trust (incorporating Josias Jenkinson Relief-in-Need Charity)

£33,000

Correspondent: Ann Duchart, Clerk, Wrigleys Solicitors, 19 Cookridge Street, Leeds LS2 3AG (01132 446100)

Trustees: Peter Wooler; Hilary Vinall; George Whitehead; John Smith; Jean White; Alison Lowe; Ian Blomfield; Gill Cartwright; Nigel Wainman; Mike Andrews; Lord Mayor of Leeds; Rector of Leeds.

CC Number: 224941

Eligibility
People in need who live in Leeds.

Types of grants
One-off grants range from £100 to £200 with a monthly budget limit of £2,500. Grants are made primarily for household equipment, furniture, bedding and electrical goods, although help may also be given for gas and electricity bills.

Annual grant total
In 2011 the trust had assets of £4.3 million and an income of £369,000. Grants totalled £33,000, of which £30,000 was given in small individual grants and £3,600 was given in vouchers to almshouse residents.

Applications
On a form available from the correspondent and supported by a detailed breakdown of income and expenditure. Applicants should also indicate any other charities approached. Forms should be submitted through a Citizens Advice, social worker or other welfare agency and are considered at the end of each month.

Other information
The trust owns and operates two housing schemes for older people in Leeds. Eligible applicants must be in financial hardship and under the terms of the scheme preference must be given to women. Suitable applicants are eligible for grants to meet removal costs, furnishings and so on.

The trust also makes grants to groups which provide services or facilities to those in need.

Huddersfield and District Army Veterans' Association Benevolent Fund

£10,000

Correspondent: Mrs Sarah Lamont, 10 Belton Grove, Huddersfield HD3 3RF (01484 310193)

Trustees: Stephen Michael Armitage; Ian Fillan; John Edward James Wakely.

CC Number: 222286

Eligibility
Veterans of the army, navy and air force who are in need, aged over 60 years, and who were discharged from the forces 'with good character' and live in Huddersfield and part of Brighouse.

Types of grants
One-off and recurrent grants according to need.

Annual grant total
In 2010 the fund had an income of £24,000 and a total expenditure of £27,000. Grants to individuals usually total around £10,000.

Applications
In writing to the correspondent, or on a form published in the fund's applications leaflet. The leaflet is available from doctor's surgeries, local libraries and so on.

Other information
The fund also provides social activities and trips for members of the forces in the Huddersfield area.

The Lucy Lund Holiday Grants

£400

Correspondent: Ms Beverley Goldsmith, Teachers Assurance, Tringham House, Deansleigh Road, Bournemouth BH7 7DT

Trustees: Anne Moran; John Wallbridge; David George Morris; Jerry Glazier.

CC Number: 236779

Eligibility
Present and former teachers who need a recuperative holiday. Preference is given to female teachers and particularly those from the former West Riding of Yorkshire. No grants are given to dependents or students.

Types of grants
One-off grants for recuperative holidays.

Annual grant total
Grants average around £400 a year.

Applications
On a form available from the correspondent to be submitted by the individual.

Sir Titus Salt's Charity

£1,300

Correspondent: Dr Norman Roper, 6 Carlton Road, Shipley, West Yorkshire BD18 4NE (01274 599540)

Trustees: N. Roper; J. Carroll; Hawarun Hussein; John Briggs; Gwen Whelan; Martin Love; Carol Thirkill; Susan Hinchcliffe; Rizwan Malik; Richard Sowman; Mrs V. Carroll.

CC Number: 216357

Eligibility
People in need who are over the age of 75 and live in Shipley, Baildon, Saltaire, Nab Wood and Wrose of Bradford.

Types of grants
Food vouchers paid once a year, available from Shipley Information Centre. On average 300 grants of £5 each are made every year.

Annual grant total
Grants usually total about £1,500 each year.

Applications
Applications should be made through the Shipley Information Centre to be considered in November/December each year.

West Yorkshire Police (Employees) Benevolent Fund

£2,300

Correspondent: Pat Maknia, West Yorkshire Police Finance Department, PO Box 9, Wakefield WF1 3QP (01924 292841)

Trustees: Martin Stubbs; Claire Chapman; Mick Bubb; Sandra Berwick; John Parkinson; Jayne Wilkinson.

CC Number: 701817

Eligibility

Employees and ex-employees of the West Yorkshire Police Force or the West Yorkshire Metropolitan County Council under the direct control of the chief constable who are in need, and their widows, orphans and other dependents.

Types of grants

One-off and recurrent grants according to need.

Annual grant total

In 2010/11 the fund had an income of £3,300 and a total expenditure of £2,500.

Applications

In writing to the correspondent. Trustee meetings are held every three months, although urgent cases can be considered at any time.

Baildon

The Butterfield Trust

£1,000

Correspondent: Revd John Nowell, The Vicarage, Browgate, Baildon, West Yorkshire BD17 6NE (01274 594941)

Trustee: Revd John David Nowell.

CC Number: 216821

Eligibility

People in need who live in the parish of Baildon.

Types of grants

One-off grants for emergencies.

Annual grant total

Grants usually average around £2,500 a year.

Applications

In writing to the correspondent. Decisions can be made immediately.

Bingley

The Bingley Diamond Jubilee Relief-in-Sickness Charity

£900

Correspondent: John Daykin, Clerk, Weatherhead and Butcher, 120 Main Street, Bingley BD16 2JJ (01274 562322; email: info@wandb.uk.com)

Trustees: Dennis Child; Clifford Bryan Hobson; James Albert Hinchcliffe; Mary Seal; Robert Bell; Nicholas Hempel; Mr Baxter.

CC Number: 508248

Eligibility

People who live in the parish of Bingley (as constituted on 14 February 1898) who are sick, convalescent, have disabilities or are infirm.

Types of grants

Emergency payments or annual grants.

Annual grant total

Grants average around £900 a year.

Applications

In writing to the correspondent through a social worker, Citizens Advice, other welfare agency or a third party. For specific items, estimates of costs are required. The trustees meet in February and November. A subcommittee of trustees can deal promptly with emergency payments.

Other information

The charity also makes grants to local organisations.

The Samuel Sunderland Relief-in-Need Charity

£5,200

Correspondent: John Daykin, Clerk, Weatherhead and Butcher Solicitors, 120 Main Street, Bingley BD16 2JJ (01274 562322; email: info@wandb.uk.com)

Trustees: Dennis Child; Clifford Bryan Hobson; James Albert Hinchliffe; Mary Seal; Robert Bell; Nicholas Hempel; Mr Baxter.

CC Number: 225745

Eligibility

People who live in the former parish of Bingley (as constituted on 14 February 1898) and are in need, hardship or distress.

Types of grants

Emergency payments and annual grants averaging £500 each.

Annual grant total

In 2010 the charity had an income of £6,800 and a total expenditure of £5,400.

Applications

In writing to the correspondent through a social worker, Citizens Advice, other welfare agency or any other third party on behalf of the individual. When specific items are required estimates of the cost must be provided. Applications are considered in February and November.

Other information

Grants are also given to local organisations which serve a similar purpose.

Bradford

The Bradford and District Children's Charity Circle

£500

Correspondent: Julie Cadman, 14 Oakwood Drive, Bingley, West Yorkshire BD16 4AH (01274 561204)

Trustees: Isobel Dorothy Whitaker; Pamela Mary Cadman.

CC Number: 230279

Eligibility

Children in need under 16 who live in Bradford.

Types of grants

One-off grants usually of £100 towards disability equipment, holidays, bedding and clothing.

Annual grant total

Grants to individuals generally total around £500 a year. Grants are also made to organisations.

Exclusions

No grants are given towards domestic bills or electrical goods.

Applications

In writing to the correspondent through a social worker, Citizens Advice or other welfare agency. They are considered monthly. Individuals should not apply directly.

The Bradford Tradesmen's Homes

£6,900

Correspondent: Colin Askew, Trust Administrator, 44 Lily Croft, Heaton Road, Bradford BD8 8QY (01274 543022; email: admin.bth@btconnect.com)

Trustees: James Edward Barker; John Stephen Behrens; Margaret Glover; David Sutcliffe; Martin Sweeney; Mr P. Trevor Smith.

CC Number: 224389

Eligibility

Unmarried women over the age of 60 who have lived in Bradford metropolitan district for at least seven years who are not in employment and are in need.

Types of grants

Pensions of £65 per quarter, plus a Christmas grant of £80.

Annual grant total

In 2010/11 the trust made grants to individuals totalling £6,900. Annuities made to unmarried women amounted to £1,500 and Christmas gifts totalled £5,400.

Applications

On a form available from the correspondent. Applications can be submitted directly by the individual or through a social worker, Citizens Advice, other welfare agency, doctor, clergy or other third party. Applicants will be visited before an award is made and they must provide the names of two referees. Applications are considered throughout the year.

Other information

The trust also runs almshouses.

The Moser Benevolent Trust Fund

£3,500

Correspondent: D C Stokes, 33 Mossy Bank Close, Queensbury, Bradford, West Yorkshire BD13 1PX (01274 817414)

Trustees: Donald Stokes; Kath Kenningham; Michael Chappell; Liam O'Neill; Roger Teece.

CC Number: 222868

Eligibility

People in need who are 60 or over and have lived or worked in the former county borough of Bradford for at least three years.

Types of grants

On average around ten recipients receive pensions of £400 a year.

Annual grant total

In 2010/11 the trust had an income of £6,000 and a total expenditure of £3,900.

Applications

In writing at any time to: M Chappell, 56 Carr Lane, Shipley, West Yorkshire BD18 2LD. Applicants should include details of income and assets.

Joseph Nutter's Foundation

£14,000

Correspondent: Mr John Lambert, 2 The Mews, Gilstead Lane, Bingley BD16 3NP (01274 688666; email: john@ bradfordtextilesociety.org.uk)

Trustees: Sir James Hill; Robert James Barraclough; Cllr John Derek Godward; William Robert Pagan; John Watson; Cllr Malcolm Sykes; Cheryl Paul; Sajawal Hussain; Paul Burkinshaw.

CC Number: 507491

Eligibility

People aged 18 or under who live in the metropolitan district of Bradford and have suffered the loss of a parent.

Types of grants

One-off grants of around £100 to £200 are given towards clothing, bedding, beds and household equipment which specifically benefit the child, such as cookers, fires and washing machines. Other needs may occasionally be considered on an individual basis.

Annual grant total

In 2010/11 the foundation had an income of £14,000 and a total expenditure of £14,500.

Applications

In writing to the correspondent at any time. Applications can be submitted directly by the individual or family member.

Paul and Nancy Speak's Charity

£11,500

Correspondent: Michael Chappell, Secretary, 56 Carr Lane, Windhill, Shipley, North Yorkshire BD18 2LD (01274 585301)

Trustees: Brian Emmett; Denise Taylor; Michael Chappell; David John; Malcolm Dixon; Lorry Mann.

CC Number: 231339

Eligibility

Women in need who are over the age of 50 and live in Bradford.

Types of grants

Regular allowances of £500 a year, paid quarterly.

Annual grant total

In 2010 the charity had an income of £11,300 and expenditure of £12,500.

Applications

In writing to the correspondent.

Calderdale

The Community Foundation for Calderdale

£20,000

Correspondent: Grants Department, The 1855 Building (first floor), Discovery Road, Halifax, West Yorkshire HX1 2NG (01422 438738; fax: 01422 350017; email: grants@cffc.co.uk; website: www.cffc.co.uk)

Trustees: Leigh-Anne Stradeski; Rod Hodgson; Russell Earnshaw; John Beacroft-Mitchell; Juliet Chambers; Roger Moore; Claire Townley; Susannah Hammond; Wim Batist; Stuart Rumney; Andy Banks; Spencer Lord; Trevor Lodge; Nick Worsnop.

CC Number: 1002722

Eligibility

People in need who live in Calderdale.

Types of grants

One-off grants of up to £130 and occasionally small loans to meet urgent needs, such as household equipment, clothing and food which cannot be readily funded from other sources. People over 60 can apply for grants of up to £250 towards a short break away from home.

Annual grant total

£20,000 in 2010/11.

Applications

Individuals should apply through a referring agency, such as Citizens Advice, on an application form available from the website. Grants will only be awarded to individuals in the form of a cheque; cash is not given.

Other information

The foundation also gives to organisations and to individuals for educational purposes.

The Halifax Society for the Blind

£8,000

Correspondent: Eileen Holmes, 34 Clare Road, Halifax, West Yorkshire HX1 2HX (01422 352383; email: eholmes@ halifaxsocietyfortheblin.fsnet.co.uk; website: www.hxblindsoc.co.uk)

Trustees: James Bernard McAndrew; Peter Horsfall Benson.

CC Number: 224258

Eligibility

People in need who are registered blind or partially sighted and live in Calderdale.

Types of grants

One-off grants of cash or equipment according to need. Recent grants have been given towards beds, school equipment, televisions and decorating costs.

Annual grant total

In 2010/11 the society had an income of £77,000 and a total expenditure £109,000. Grants were made totalling £8,000.

Applications

On a form available from the correspondent, to be submitted through one of the visiting staff of the society. Applications are considered on a regular basis.

Other information

The society visits each of its 415 members 3–4 times a year and also provides six social centres, a resource centre, subsidised holidays and a mini bus service.

The Halifax Tradesmen's Benevolent Institution

£24,000

Correspondent: Anthony Wannan, West House, Kings Cross Road, Halifax HX1 1EB (01422 352517)

Trustees: Jonathan Peter Frank Dixon; John Richard Newbound; Peter Helliwell.

CC Number: 224056

Eligibility

People in need aged 60 or over who have been self-employed or a manager of a business for at least seven years and live in the parish of Halifax and the surrounding area. Applicants should have no other income than a pension and have only modest savings.

Types of grants

Pensions of about £550 a year.

Annual grant total

In 2010/11 the institution had an income of £15,000 and a total expenditure of £26,000.

Applications

In writing to the correspondent for consideration quarterly.

Dewsbury

Dewsbury and District Sick Poor Fund

£10,000

Correspondent: John Alan Winder, 130 Boothroyd Lane, Dewsbury, West Yorkshire WF13 2LW (01924 463308)

Trustees: Margaret Watson; Dolores Bernadette Mulrennan; David Keith Shaw; Stuart Brown; Valerie Archer.

CC Number: 234401

Eligibility

People who are sick and in need who live in the county borough of Dewsbury and the ecclesiastical parish of Hanging Heaton.

Types of grants

One-off grants according to need for essential household items, convalescence holidays, food, clothing and medical aids.

Annual grant total

In 2011 the fund had an income of £3,200 and a total expenditure of £12,000.

Applications

In writing to the correspondent including details of illness and residential qualifications. Applications can be submitted either directly by the individual, through a third party such as a social worker or through an organisation such as a Citizens Advice.

Halifax

The Goodall Trust

£3,200

Correspondent: Andrew Buck, 122 Skircoat Road, Halifax HX1 2RE (01422 255880; email: atbuck@tiscali.co.uk)

Trustees: Revd Martin Christopher Russell; Revd Hilary Barber; Revd Lees; Mr Appleyard; Thomas Rodney Barnett; Stuart David Finlay; Josephine Mary Hutchison.

CC Number: 221651

Eligibility

Widows and unmarried women who are in need and live in the present Calderdale ward of Skircoat or the parts of the parishes of St Jude and All Saints (Halifax) which are within the ancient township of Skircoat.

Types of grants

Recurrent grants are given according to need.

Annual grant total

Grants average around £2,800 each year.

Applications

On a form available from the correspondent. Applications should be submitted by mid-September either directly by the individual; by a relative, friend or neighbour; or through a welfare agency. They are considered in October.

Charity of Ann Holt

£10,000

Correspondent: G D Jacobs, Oak House, 9 Cross Street, Oakenshaw, Bradford, West Yorkshire BD12 7EA (01274 679835; email: oakey9uk@yahoo.co.uk)

Trustees: Mrs B. M. Birtwhistle; Miss S. E. Fox; Mr S. Holmes; Mrs W. M. Astin; Mr R. E. Begley; Mr G. Mitchell.

CC Number: 502391

Eligibility

Single women who are over the age of 55 and in need and have lived in Halifax for at least five years.

Types of grants

Pensions of around £200 a year, paid in quarterly instalments until the recipient dies, moves out of the area or moves into a residential home. About 75 grants are given each year.

Annual grant total

Grants to individuals usually total around £10,000 per year.

Applications

In writing to the correspondent, directly by the individual. Applicants will need to be prepared to provide two referees who are not relations, such as a vicar, ex-employer or someone else they have known for a number of years.

Horbury

St Leonards Hospital Charity

£2,500

Correspondent: Ian Whittell, 31 New Road, Horbury, Wakefield, West Yorkshire WF4 5LS (01924 272762)

Trustees: Mavis Walsh; Valerie Crowther; Father Brian Bell.

CC Number: 243977

Eligibility

People in need, hardship or distress who live in the former urban district of Horbury.

Types of grants

One-off grants usually ranging from £20 to £200. Recent grants have been given towards adaptations, convalescence, nursing, renovation and repairs to homes for disabled access and helping people who are homeless or experiencing marital problems.

Annual grant total

In 2011 the charity had an income of £3,300 and a total expenditure of £2,600.

Exclusions

No grants are made towards maintenance of equipment already paid for. No loans are made although recurrent grants are considered if necessary.

Applications

In writing to the correspondent. Applications can be submitted directly by the individual, through a social worker, Citizens Advice or other welfare agency or through a church member. They are considered at any time and the trustees can act quickly in urgent cases.

Other information

Grants may also be made to local organisations.

Horton

The John Ashton Charity (including the Gift of Hannah Shaw).

£2,000

Correspondent: Gordon Doble, Trustee, Upper Beck House, 22 Hammerton Drive, Hellifield, Skipton BD23 4LZ (01729 851329)

Trustees: Gordon Doble; Margaret Hilary Bradley; Ruth Margaret Richardson; Sheila Priestley.

CC Number: 233661

Eligibility

People in need who are over 65 and live alone in the Great Horton area of Bradford.

Types of grants

Small grants, according to need.

Annual grant total

Grants usually total about £2,000 per year.

Applications

On a form available from the correspondent to be submitted directly by the individual or through a family member for consideration in June and December.

Huddersfield

The Beaumont and Jessop Relief-in-Need Charity

£2,500

Correspondent: Leslie Chadwick, 35 Westcroft, Honley, Holmfirth HD9 6JP (01484 662880; email: lesbuk@gmail.com)

Trustees: Doreen Maude; Leslie Chadwick; Sylvia Hallas; Revd David Keith Barnes; John Muir; Betty Staniforth; Revd Charlotte Lorimer; Wendy Peach.

CC Number: 504141

Eligibility

People in need who are over 65 and live in the ancient township of Honley (near Huddersfield).

Types of grants

One-off grants ranging from £60 to £500 towards, for instance, Winged Fellowship holidays, heating grants (nominated by doctors), medical equipment, spectacles, transport to luncheon clubs and so on.

Annual grant total

In 2009/10 the trust had an income of £3,200 and a total expenditure of £2,700.

Applications

In writing to the correspondent, indicating the purpose of the grant. Applications can be submitted directly by the individual or through a social worker, Citizens Advice, other welfare agency or other third party (nurses or doctors). Applications are considered throughout the year.

The Charles Brook Convalescent Fund

£12,000

Correspondent: Carol Thompson, Mistal Barn, Lower Castle Hill, Almondbury, Huddersfield HD4 6TA (01484 532183)

Trustees: Malvern Goodall; Margaret Fearnley; Barbara Sykes; Kathleen Boothroyd; Cllr Linda Wilkinson; David Clayton.

CC Number: 229445

Eligibility

People in need who live within the old Huddersfield Health Authority catchment area.

Types of grants

One-off grants for medical comforts, items essential to live independently and convalescent holidays.

Annual grant total

In 2011/12 the fund had had an income of £14,000 and a total expenditure of £13,000.

Exclusions

No loans.

Applications

On a form available from the social work department at Royal Infirmary, Huddersfield and St Luke's Hospital, Huddersfield. Applications must be submitted through a social worker and include details of weekly income/expenditure and family situation. Applications sent directly to the correspondent cannot be considered.

The H. P. Dugdale Foundation

£71,000

Correspondent: T J Green, Clerk, Bank Chambers, Market Street, Huddersfield HD1 2EW (01484 648482)

Trustees: David Broadbent Simpson; Giles David Thomas Cliffe; John Anthony Thorpe; Robert Edward Christian Charnock; Roger Thornton Dugdale; Michael Christopher Baggs; Andrew Simon Wagstaff.

CC Number: 200538

Eligibility

People in need who live in the county borough of Huddersfield (comprising the urban districts of Colne Valley, Kirkburton, Meltham and Holmfirth). People who have previously lived in the area for a period of ten consecutive years are also eligible for assistance.

Types of grants

One-off and recurrent grants according to need.

Annual grant total

In 2010/11 the trust had assets of £1.3 million and an income of £65,000. Grants were made totalling £71,000, and were distributed as follows:

Regular payments	41	£55,000
Christmas gifts	-	£8,000
One-off payments	23	£7,600

Applications

Application forms are given to local organisations such as social services and churches. They are then submitted by or on behalf of the individual. The trustees meet twice a year to consider applications.

Keighley

The Beamsley Trust

£6,600

Correspondent: Lynn Leadbeatter, Administrator, Central Hall, Alice Street, Keighley, West Yorkshire BD21 3JD (01535 612509; website: www. craventrust.org.uk/grant_forms/guide_indi.html)

Trustees: Peter Marshall; George Fisher; Jeremy Mackrell; Nicola Chambers; Caroline Schwaller; Paul Slater; Mark Facer; Giles Bowring; Carole Nelson; Alison Kaye.

CC Number: 1045419

Eligibility

People resident within the Craven area who are in need, hardship or distress. The area of benefit includes Settle, Skipton and Bornoldswick and is bordered by Sedbergh to the north, Keighley to the east, Denholme and Hurst Green to the South and Ingleton to the west, see the map on the website for the exact area.

Types of grants

Grants of £100 to £1,000 for 'items, services or facilities which help to reduce their difficulties'.

Annual grant total

In 2010/11 the trust had assets of £319,000, an income of £17,000 and gave grants to individuals totalling £6,600.

Exclusions

No grants for students, foreign travel or taxes.

Applications

On a form available from the website, preferably to be submitted through a referral agency or a referee such as Citizens Advice, Social Services or a vicar or doctor. Applications are considered at trustee meetings which are held four times a year in January, April, July, October. Applications should be considered a month before the meeting, see the website for exact deadlines.

Bowcocks Trust Fund for Keighley

£1,000

Correspondent: Alistair Docherty, 17 Farndale Road, Wilsden, Bradford BD15 0LW (01535 272657)

Trustees: Mr R. A. Wilkinson; Mr S. V. Stell; Mr D. R. Binns; Mr R. F. Marriott;.

CC Number: 223290

Eligibility

People in need who live in the municipal borough of Keighley as constituted on 31 March 1974.

Types of grants

One-off grants according to need.

Annual grant total

In 2010/11 the trust had an income of £8,000 and a total expenditure of £6,000. Grants for education and welfare purposes totalled around £5,500. In previous years a majority of the grant total has gone towards educational grants.

Applications

Initial telephone calls are welcomed. Applications should be made in writing to the correspondent by a third party.

The William and Sarah Midgley Charity

£1,500

Correspondent: Eileen Proctor, 7 Lachman Road, Trawden, Colne, Lancashire BB8 8TA (01282 862757)

Trustees: Ronald Albert Humphreys; Jack Binns; John R. Calvert; Dorothy Scarff; Anne Arana; Revd Peter Wilson.

CC Number: 500095

Eligibility

People who are in need and live in Barcroft, Lees and Cross Roads in the former borough of Keighley, West Yorkshire.

Types of grants

Christmas hampers are normally given to older people in the area. Occasional one-off cash grants and grants in kind have also been made for electrical goods, clothing, food, travel expenses, medical and disability equipment and furniture.

Annual grant total

Around £1,500 on average.

Applications

In writing to the correspondent.

Leeds

The Bramhope Trust

£2,000

Correspondent: Bryan Bundey, 4 The Sycamores, Bramhope, Leeds LS16 9JR (01132 678534)

Trustees: Canon Alistaire Thompson; Anthony Hodgetts; Bryan Bundey; Muriel Drayton; Jane Rigby.

CC Number: 504190

Eligibility

People in need within the parish of Bramhope.

Types of grants

Gifts of varying amounts are given to organisations and individuals.

Annual grant total

In 2010/11 the trust had assets of £417,000 and an income of £31,000. Grants were given totalling £22,000 including one to an individual.

Applications

In writing to the correspondent directly by the individual or through a doctor. Applications are considered throughout the year.

The Chapel Allerton and Potternewton Relief-in-Need Charity (Leeds)

£1,500

Correspondent: Christopher Johnson, 6 Grosvenor Park, Leeds LS7 3QD (01132 680600)

Trustees: Gerald Robin Sanderson; Revd David Mark Robinson; Jennifer Laycock; Christopher Johnson.

CC Number: 245504

Eligibility

People who live in the parish boundaries of Chapel Allerton, Chapeltown and Potternewton, Leeds.

Types of grants

One-off grants of £5 to £150 mainly for white electrical goods. Grants can also be to assist with arrears of fuel bills, rent (where housing benefit is not available); telephone (where required by people who are sick or housebound); to replace cookers beyond repair; and to provide food in emergencies when social security is not available.

Annual grant total

Grants average around £1,500 per year.

Exclusions

No grants for furniture as there are two local furniture stores organised by churches.

Applications

Applications must be made through the Leeds or Chapeltown Citizens Advice, a social services department, probation officer, health visitor and so on. Trustees meet in March but applications can be dealt with at any time according to need.

The Community Shop Trust

£35,000

Correspondent: Lynn Higo, Administrator, Unit 4, Clayton Wood Bank, West Park Ring Road, Leeds LS16 6QZ (01132 745551; fax: 01132 783184; email: info@ leedscommunitytrust.org; website: www. leedscommunitytrust.org)

Trustees: Teresa Felton; John Felton; Marjory Stephens; Sheila Goodall; Norman Jones; John Crawley.

CC Number: 701375

Eligibility

People in need who live in the Leeds area. Families with children are usually given preference.

Types of grants

One-off grants for emergency assistance for electrical and kitchen appliances, beds, bedding, carpets, removals and so on. Christmas grants are issued as grocery vouchers 1–2 weeks before Christmas. Holiday grants to enable families to go on holiday together. 'Kosy Kids' grants for improving a child's bedroom. 'Keen Kids' grants for education, sport and music.

Annual grant total

In 2011 the trust made 417 grants to 351 families totalling £35,000, broken down as follows:

- 213 emergency grants – £22,000
- 183 Christmas grants – £8,300
- 17 holidays – £3,400
- 3 'Kosy Kids' grants – £250
- 1 'Keen Kids' grant – £100

Applications

In writing to the correspondent through a social worker, Citizens Advice or other welfare agency. Potential applicants are then sent an application form to complete. For this reason the initial letter must give details of the personal circumstances. Decisions on emergency grant applications are usually made within two days.

Other information

The trust is also known as the Leeds Community Trust. It runs two shops and distributes the profits to local charities, groups and individuals in need, particularly people in vulnerable situations.

Kirke Charity

£2,500

Correspondent: J A B Buchan, 8 St Helens Croft, Leeds LS16 8JY (01924 465860)

Trustees: John Hamilton; Selwyn Pennington; David Breton; Bruce Buchan; Norman Green; Ian White; Stuart Lewis.

CC Number: 246102

Eligibility

People in need who live in the ancient parishes of Adel, Arthington or Cookridge.

Types of grants

One-off grants, generally of around £100.

Annual grant total

In 2010/11 the charity had an income of £8,600 and an expenditure of £5,300. Grants usually total around £5,000 for education and welfare purposes.

Applications

Applications can be submitted directly by the individual or through a social worker, Citizens Advice or other welfare agency.

The Leeds Benevolent Society for Single Ladies

£56,000 (102 grants)

Correspondent: Elisabeth A Stephens, Chair, 5 Scarcroft Grange, Wetherby Road, Scarcroft, Leeds LS14 3HJ (01132 892482)

Trustees: Peter Wooler; David Simpson; Elisabeth Stephens; Jane Wainman; Janet Wenham; Jill Richardson; Kate Sleath; Margie Wooler; Freda Ellis; Gladys Morton; Jean Butler; Rita Cox; Yvonne Brownett; David Coates; Ann Coates; Nigel Winman; Julie Valerie Adams; Sally Johnson.

CC Number: 227343

Eligibility

Single ladies in need who are over 60 and have lived in the Leeds metropolitan area for seven years, although in special cases (but without creating a precedent) the Committee reserves the right to benefit candidates who do not conform to these criteria.

Types of grants

Mainly regular allowance of £10 a week paid quarterly. The society also pays telephone rental and television licence fees and helps with holiday payments.

Annual grant total

In 2010 the trust had assets of £3.5 million, an income of £260,000 and a total expenditure of £100,000. Grants were made totalling £46,000 with a further £10,000 paid towards holidays, outings and convalescence for individuals.

Applications

On a form available by telephoning the correspondent or writing to: Applications Secretary, 36 Holland Road, Kippax, Leeds LS25 7PP.

Applications can be submitted directly by the individual or through a social worker, Citizens Advice, other welfare agency or other third party. Applicants are visited to assess their needs.

The Leeds District Aid-in-Sickness Fund

£3,000

Correspondent: Valerie Kaye, Nidd View Cottage, 39 Kirkgate, Knaresborough, North Yorkshire HG5 8BZ (01423 797842; email: vjk@kaye-estates.co.uk)

Trustees: Elizabeth Ann Loach; Margaret Josephine Pullan; Valerie Joan Kaye; Brenda Edmondson; Ann Clark; Michael Edward Coles; June Valerie Adams; Revd David Anthony Kirby; Dr Aleck Michael Brownjohn; Colette Crossen.

CC Number: 221531

Eligibility

People who live in the city of Leeds and are in need through unexpected illness or accident ('city of Leeds' refers to the Leeds boundaries as they were prior to the re-organisation of 1974 and the establishment of the metropolitan district of Leeds).

Types of grants

One-off cash grants of £50 to £250 towards domestic appliances, furnishings, food, medical aid, travel, holidays, adapted computers and so on.

Annual grant total

Grants average around £2,000 a year. Grants are given to both individuals and organisations.

Exclusions

No recurrent grants or loans are given and there is no support for debts, rates or taxes.

Applications

On a form available from the correspondent, sent on behalf of the applicant by a social worker, welfare agency, doctor, teacher, clergyman or similar third party (personal applications will not be accepted). Application deadlines are March, June, September and December with decisions made quarterly.

NORTH EAST – WEST YORKSHIRE

The Leeds Tradesmen's Trust

£36,000

Correspondent: John C Suttenstall, Secretary, 17 Wayside Crescent, Scarcroft, Leeds LS14 3BD (01132 893346)

Trustees: P. Chadwick; K. Grainge; B. Bradbury; F. Thompson; C. Seller; J. Cairns; J. Schofield; N. Tolkin; R. South; P. Shaggouri; S. Moss; A. Miller.

CC Number: 222866

Eligibility

People over 50 who have carried on business, practised a profession or been a tradesperson for at least five years (either consecutively or in total) and who, during that time, lived in Leeds or whose business premises (rented or owned) were in the city of Leeds. Grants are also given to self-employed business/professional people who 'have fallen upon misfortune in business'; normally older people. Widows and unmarried daughters of the former are also eligible.

Types of grants

Quarterly pensions of £10 to £500 a year, plus Christmas grants and spring fuel grants only to those already receiving a pension.

Annual grant total

In 2011 the trust had assets of £790,000 and an income of £39,000. Grants were made totalling £36,000, the bulk of which was given as pensions with just £1,200 given in one-off grants.

Applications

In writing to the correspondent, including details of the business or professional addresses, length of time spent there and financial position. All applicants are visited by the assistant secretary.

The Metcalfe Smith Trust

£11,000 (28 grants)

Correspondent: Geoff Hill, Secretary, c/o Voluntary Action Leeds, Stringer House, 34 Lupton Street, Hunslet, Leeds LS10 2QW (email: secretary@metcalfesmithtrust.org; website: www.metcalfesmithtrust.org.uk)

Trustees: Barbara Siedlecki; Ashley Rowthorn; Carmel Kent; Emily Brown; Jason Slack; Vicky Witter; Dr J. L. Ramsay; Stacey Selby; Nicola Perrott; Laura Conrad.

CC Number: 228891

Eligibility

Adults and children who live in Leeds and have 'a physical disability, long-term illness or a mental health difficulty'.

Types of grants

One-off grants ranging from £250 to £2,500 towards items or services that will significantly improve quality of life. For example, disability equipment, computers, respite breaks, heating costs, small items of furniture and course fees.

Annual grant total

In 2010/11 the trust had an income of £21,000. There were 28 grants made to individuals totalling £11,000, including four emergency grants.

Exclusions

No support for individuals outside the area of benefit, general appeals, recurrent grants, fundraising initiatives or research costs.

Applications

Application forms are available on request by filling in the 'application request form' on the trust's website. Individual applications must be supported by a social worker or local welfare organisation. They are considered twice a year in May and November and should be submitted by April and October respectively. Emergency grants of up to £100 can be made at any time and applicants can use the online application form.

Other information

The trust also makes grants to organisations (£800 in 2010/11).

Radio Aire and Magic 828's Cash For Kids

£380,000

Correspondent: Katy Winterschladen, 51 Burley Road, Leeds LS1 3LR (01132 835555 or 5527; email: katy.winterschladen@radioaire.co.uk; website: www.radioaire.co.uk/charity)

Eligibility

Children under the age of 18 resident in Leeds and West Yorkshire.

Types of grants

One-off grants for children in need. A large part of the charity's activity is the provision of Christmas gifts to local children who might otherwise not receive anything. Grants have also been made for specialist medical equipment, surgery and therapy; mobility aids, beds and bedding; day trips and kitchen appliances.

Annual grant total

In 2011 the charity raised £669,000 for local children. This included a contribution of £335,000 towards the annual Christmas appeal which provided gifts to over 10,000 local children.

Applications

On an application form available from the correspondent or to download from the website. Applicants should attach payslips or other evidence of income and bank statements for the last three months. Details of application deadlines are posted on the website. Trustees meet four times a year to consider applications.

Other information

Grants are also made to local organisations with similar aims. Funds are not restricted but the charity has told us that in practice approximately 60% of funds raised are distributed to organisations and the remaining 40% distributed to individual appeals each year.

Sandal Magna

The Henry and Ada Chalker Trust

£1,000 (90 grants)

Correspondent: The Trustees, Beaumont Legal, Beaumont House, 1 Paragon Avenue, Wakefield, West Yorkshire WF1 2UF (0845 122 8100)

Trustees: Roy Cusworth; Daniel James Hilton.

CC Number: 224808

Eligibility

People in need who live in Sandal Magna, with a preference for elderly residents.

Types of grants

Recurrent grants of around £10 a year are distributed in the first week of December.

Annual grant total

Grants to individuals total around £1,000 each year. Approximately 90 grants are awarded.

Applications

On a form available from the correspondent. As this is a recurrent grant new applications are stockpiled until there is a vacancy on the current list.

The Sandal Magna Relief-in-Need Charity

£600

Correspondent: Martin J Perry, 50 Dukewood Road, Clayton West,

Huddersfield HD8 9HF (01484 860594; email: marpam@fsmail.net)

Trustees: Dr David Oughtibridge; Canon Ian Gaskell; Ian McCourt; Norman Hazell; Elizabeth Marshall; Sue Saville; Revd Rupert Martin; Colin Barker; Elizabeth Fairclough.

CC Number: 810052

Eligibility

People in need who live in the old parish of Sandal Magna (this includes Sandal, Walton, Crigglestone, Painthorpe and West Bretton).

Types of grants

One-off grants of about £50 to £300 are made each year to six to ten individuals. Recent grants have been used for the purchase of a second-hand washing machine, decorating materials, bedding for a child and a safety gate for the stairs.

Annual grant total

Grants usually total around £1,000 per year.

Applications

In writing to the correspondent. Applications can be sent directly by the individual or through a social worker, Citizens Advice or other welfare agency.

Todmorden

Todmorden War Memorial Fund

£1,000

Correspondent: Stephen Ormerod, Trustee, 2 Maitland Close, Todmorden, West Yorkshire OL14 7TG (07941 195488)

Trustees: Anne James; Freda Heywood; Margareta Holmstedt; Dorothy Jordan; Linda Ingham; Stephen Romero; Roy Gunton; Maureen Fielden; Ann Buglass.

CC Number: 219673

Eligibility

Veterans of the First and Second World Wars who are sick or in need and live in the former borough of Todmorden, and their dependents.

Types of grants

Grants are mostly one-off; recurrent grants are very occasionally given. TV licences are given to First and Second World War families. Food vouchers, medicine, medical comforts, bedding, fuel, domestic help and convalescence expenses are also given.

Annual grant total

Grants to individuals usually total about £1,000 a year.

Applications

In writing to: Mrs M Gunton, Case Secretary, 8 Walton Fold, Todmorden, Lancashire OL14 5TE. Applications must be through a welfare agency or similar organisation and they are considered monthly.

Other information

The fund also makes grants to organisations.

Wakefield

The Brotherton Charity Trust

£2,300

Correspondent: C Brotherton-Ratcliffe, PO Box 374, Harrogate HG1 4YW

CC Number: 221006

Eligibility

People in need who are over 60 years old and live in Wakefield.

Types of grants

Annual pensions.

Annual grant total

Grants usually total about £2,300 each year.

Applications

On a form available from the correspondent. When vacancies arise an advert is placed in the Wakefield Express and a waiting list is then drawn up. Applications can be made directly by the individual or family member.

North West

General

The Charity of Miss Ann Farrar Brideoake

£47,000

Correspondent: Alan Ware, Cowling Swift and Kitchin, 8 Blake Street, York YO1 8XJ (01904 625678; fax: 01904 620214)

Trustees: Arthur Haywood Hope; Richard William Rusby; David John Clarke; David Michael Gibson; Alan L. Ware.

CC Number: 213848

Eligibility

Communicant members of the Church of England living within the dioceses of York, Liverpool and Manchester, who are in need. This includes clergy and retired clergy.

Types of grants

Recurrent grants of £500 to £1,500 are given to help in 'making ends meet'. Support is given towards household outgoings, domestic equipment, holidays, children's entertainment and so on as well as special medical needs. One-off payments are made in special circumstances and debt relief can be supported in exceptional circumstances.

Annual grant total

In 2010/11 the charity had assets of £2 million and an income of £64,000. Grants totalled around £47,000.

Applications

On a form available from the correspondent, to be countersigned by the local vicar as confirmation of communicant status. Applications should be submitted in April or May for consideration in July/August.

Cockshot Foundation

£3,000

Correspondent: The Trustees, Belle Isle, Windermere, Cumbria LA23 1BG (01539 447087; email: cockshotfoundation@ belleisle.net)

Trustees: Peter Cassidy; Michelle Lefton; Roger Coleman.

CC Number: 1104085

Eligibility

People in need, hardship or distress resident in the counties of Cumbria, Lancashire and Greater Manchester.

Types of grants

On-off and recurrent grants according to need.

Annual grant total

In 2010/11 the foundation had an income of £2,000 and a total expenditure of £9,000.

Applications

In writing to the correspondent.

The Cotton Districts Convalescent Fund and the Barnes Samaritan Charity

£21,000

Correspondent: Nicholas Stockton, c/o Cassons Chartered Accountants, Rational House, 64 Bridge Street, Manchester M3 3BN (0845 337 9409; fax: 0845 337 9408; email: manchester@cassons.co.uk; website: www.cotton-districts.co.uk)

Trustees: David Wilson; James Walter Shaw; Winefride Mary Rossall; Revd Canon Peter Vowles; Paul Goddard; Dr Michael John Taylor; Bernadette Speakman; Sharman Birtles; Laura Nuttall.

CC Number: 224727

Eligibility

People in need who have a severe/long-term illness, are convalescent or who have a disability and live in Lancashire and Greater Manchester.

Types of grants

The fund makes grants to enable a subsidised convalescent holiday of one week to be taken at hotels in Blackpool and St Annes. Applicants are expected to pay approximately £80 towards the cost of a week's half board holiday with the fund paying the difference. Consideration will be given to making a grant towards the costs of a special needs holiday proposed by the applicant (for example where nursing or other care is required).

Monthly grants of £40 are also available towards living costs for those who are in poor health, convalescent or who have a disability.

Annual grant total

In 2010 the trust had assets of £922,000 and an income of £40,000. Grants from the convalescence fund totalled £2,000. A further £19,000 was awarded in a single lump grant of £645 and recurrent grants of £40 per month, although the number of beneficiaries changed throughout the year.

Applications

In writing to the secretary. Applications may be submitted directly by the individual or through a social worker, Citizens Advice or other welfare agency.

Note: the trust has stated that due to a lack of income, future grantmaking will be limited.

Other information

This trust was previously known as The Cotton Districts Convalescent Fund.

The Grant, Bagshaw, Rogers and Tidswell Fund

£12,000

Correspondent: Lawrence Downey, Ripley House, 56 Freshfield Road, Formby, Liverpool L37 3HW (fax: 01512 275010; email: lawrencedowney@ btconnect.com)

Trustees: Roger Watson; David Faragher; Muriel Proven; Bill Howarth; Neville Ward; Derek Craig; Jenny Hope.

CC Number: 216948

Eligibility

Older people in need who live, or were born in, Liverpool, the Wirral, Ellesmere Port or Chester.

Types of grants

Pensions, currently around £425 per annum, are paid half yearly. Occasional one-off grants may also be given.

Annual grant total

In 2010/11 the fund had an income of £10,500 and a total expenditure £13,000.

Applications

On a form available from the correspondent. Applications should be returned by 31 March and 30 October for consideration in April and November respectively. Applications should be submitted through a social worker, Citizens Advice or other welfare agency, although direct applications will also be considered.

The Gregson Memorial Annuities

£2,500

Correspondent: Geoffrey Miller, Trustee, Brabners Chaffe Street Solicitors, Horton House, Exchange Flags, Liverpool L2 3YL (01516 003000; fax: 01512 273185; email: alison.houghton@ brabnerscs.com)

Trustees: Geoffrey Robin Mitchell Miller; Andrew Manock Neville Scorah.

CC Number: 218096

Eligibility

Female domestic servants who have been in service for at least ten years in Liverpool, Southport, Malpas and the surrounding area and who cannot work now for health reasons.

Governesses and other 'gentlewomen', widows and unmarried daughters or sisters of professional men and merchants, who are over 50 years old and members of the Church of England, may also be eligible for assistance.

Types of grants

Annuities of about £300 a year, payable in two six-monthly instalments.

Annual grant total

Grants usually total about £2,500 each year.

Applications

Applications in writing to the correspondent are considered throughout the year.

The Lancashire Infirm Secular Clergy Fund

£118,000 (90 grants)

Correspondent: Revd Peter Stanley, St Josephs Presbytery, Harpers Lane, Chorley PR6 0HR (01257 262713)

Trustees: Revd Peter Birmingham; Canon Joseph Kelly; Revd Peter Stanley; Revd Joseph William Bootle.

CC Number: 222796

Eligibility

Catholic secular clergy of the dioceses of Liverpool, Salford and Lancaster who are unable, through age or infirmity, to attend to their duties of office and are in need.

Types of grants

Annual grants mostly of £1,300 each although smaller grants of around £600 are also available.

Annual grant total

In 2010/11 the fund had assets of £3.2 million and an income of £141,000. Grants to infirm clergy totalled £118,000. The average grant was for £1,320

Applications

On a form available from the correspondent, to be submitted directly by the individual.

North West Police Benevolent Fund

£131,000

Correspondent: Constable Jackie Smithies, Secretary, Progress House, Broadstone Hall Road South, Stockport SK5 7DE (01613 554420; fax: 01613 554410; email: jsmithies@gmpf.polfed. org; website: www.nwpbf.org)

Trustees: David Anderton; June Roby; Ian Leyland; Jacqueline Ann Smithies; Sandie Wilde; Ken Davies; Bernard Lawson; Michael Griffin; Karan Lee; Anthony Barton; Neil Shacklock; John Ainsworth; Rachael Baines; Mark Sweet; Philip Charleton; Andrew Cameron; Jackie Bowen; Mark Sutton; David Johnston; Robert Moore; Rachel Gallagher; Stuart Williams; Carl Kruegar; William Grancis; Andrew Marsden.

CC Number: 503045

Eligibility

Serving officers and pensioners of Cheshire County Constabulary, Lancashire Constabulary, Greater Manchester and Merseyside Police Forces and amalgamated forces of those areas and their dependents.

Types of grants

Recurrent grants and loans for convalescence and medical equipment (but not for private health care), financial help for cases of need arising from unforeseen circumstances. Orphaned children of police officers can receive a weekly allowance and a death grant of £5,000 is paid to the dependent family of an officer who dies.

Annual grant total

In 2011 the fund had assets of just under £5 million and an income of £1.9 million. Grants were made totalling £131,000.

Exclusions

No grants available for private health, education or legal fees.

Applications

On a form available from the correspondent. Applications are usually made through a force welfare officer or a member of the management committee. They are considered each month and should be submitted by the second Wednesday in January or by the first Wednesday in any other month.

Other information

The fund does not give grants to organisations but does contribute to other police funds and convalescent homes.

The SF Group Charity
See entry on page 42

United Utilities Trust Fund

£4.1 million

Correspondent: The Secretary (Auriga Services Ltd), FREEPOST RLYY-JHEJ-XCXS, Sutton Coldfield B72 1TJ (0845 179 1791; email: contact@uutf.org.uk; website: www.uutf.org.uk)

Trustees: Deborah Morton; Alastair Richards; Nick Pearson; Carl Smith; Allan Mackie; Simon Sewsnip; David Burdis.

CC Number: 1108296

Eligibility

People in need who live in the area supplied by United Utilities Water (predominantly the north west of England).

Types of grants

Payments for water and/or sewerage charges due to United Utilities Water. The trust states that it aims 'to help people out of immediate crisis and financial difficulty and wherever possible, to encourage future financial stability.' The trust can also help with water or sewerage charges which are collected by other companies or organisations on behalf of United Utilities Water. In certain cases, the trust can also consider giving some help to meet other essential bills, household needs or priority debts.

Annual grant total

In 2010/11 the trust had an income of £5 million which was paid from United Utilities Water plc. The sum of £4.1 million was given on behalf of individuals.

The applicant success rate was 61% with 5,186 of 8,470 applications being approved.

Exclusions

No grants for court fines, catalogue debts, credit cards, personal loans or other forms of borrowing; social fund loans/benefit overpayments/tax credit overpayments now being reclaimed; retrospective payments.

Applications

Application forms and full guidelines are available on the website. Money advisers and other referral agents may use the online application process. Applicants may be visited. All applications will be acknowledged and applicants will be issued with a reference number which they must use when making enquiries about the application. Successful applicants may not reapply for a period of two years, while unsuccessful applicants may apply again after six months.

Other information

Grants were also made to 14 debt counselling organisations in 2008/09 totalling £210,000.

Cheshire

The Charity of Letitia Beamont

£1,700

Correspondent: Norman Banner, Forshaws Davies Ridgway LLP, 21 Palmyra Square, Warrington WA1 1BW (01925 230000)

Trustee: Canon James Colling.

CC Number: 244655

Eligibility

People in need who were born or who have lived for some time in the borough of Warrington or the parish of Moore.

Types of grants

Annual pensions of approximately £160 per person, paid quarterly.

Annual grant total

About £1,700.

Applications

In writing to the correspondent.

The Cheshire Provincial Fund of Benevolence

£12,000

Correspondent: Peter Carroll, Ashcroft House, 36 Clay Lane, Timperley, Altrincham WA15 7AB (01619 806090; email: enquiries@cheshiremasons.co.uk)

Trustees: Alan Glazier; David Hinde; Gordon Viner; Ian Cranston; Eric McConnell; Michael J. McGarva; Roger Quayle.

CC Number: 219177

Eligibility

Freemasons of Cheshire, and their dependents, who are in need.

Types of grants

One-off and recurrent grants according to need.

Annual grant total

In 2010/11 the fund had assets of £3.6 million and an income of £332,000. Grants to individuals totalled around £12,000.

Grants to organisations totalled £84,000.

Applications

In writing to the correspondent.

Other information

Grants are also available for masons connected to the lodge through the grand charity fund.

John Holford Charity

£15,000

Correspondent: Kerris Owen, Friars, 20 White Friars, Chester CH1 1XS (01244 356789; email: kerris.owen@cullimoredutton.co.uk; website: www.johnholfordcharity.org)

Trustees: Edward Simon Tudor; Anita Luleen Lockett; Ven Ian Bishop; Rosamond Ann Mahon; Revd Canon David Taylor; Jane Shelmerdine; Revd Jonathan David Sharples.

CC Number: 223046

Eligibility

People in need who live in the parishes of Astbury, Clutton and Middlewich, and the borough of Congleton.

Types of grants

One-off and recurrent grants for a variety of needs, ranging from £100 to £2,500.

Annual grant total

In 2011 the charity had an income of £64,000 and made grants to individuals and organisations totalling £23,000.

Exclusions

No grants for education, or for medical treatment.

Applications

On the website via an online application form or on a form available from the correspondent or to download from the website. Applications should be submitted by a social worker, carer, Citizens Advice, other welfare agency or other third party such as a relative. They are considered at any time.

The Ursula Keyes Trust

£30,000 (36 grants)

Correspondent: Dot Lawless, Baker Tilly, The Steam Mill Business Centre, Steam Mill Street, Chester CH3 5AN (01244 505100; fax: 01244 505101; website: www.ursula-keyes-trust.org.uk)

Trustees: Dr A. E. Elliott; Mr J. F. Kane; Mr J. R. Leaman; Dr R. A. Owen; Harold Shaw; John Brimelow; Dr Guy Sissons.

CC Number: 517200

Eligibility

People in need, especially those with a medical condition, who live in the area administered by Chester District Council and in particular those within the boundaries of the former City of Chester and the adjoining parishes of Great Boughton and Upton.

Types of grants

One-off grants towards, for example, washing machines for families in need or computers for children with disabilities.

Annual grant total

In 2010 the trust had assets of £5.4 million and an income of £305,000. Grants were made to 36 individuals totalling £30,000.

Exclusions

No grants to repay debts or loans or to reimburse expenditure already incurred.

Applications

In writing to the correspondent, with details of applicant's income and expenditure. Applications must be supported by a social worker, a doctor (if relevant) or another professional or welfare agency. A summary form, which is available to download from the website, should also be included with the application.

Applications are considered at the end of January, April, July and October and should be received at least four weeks in advance to be certain of consideration at any particular meeting.

Other information

Grants were also paid to organisations totalling £108,000 in the year.

The Wilmslow Aid Trust

£830

Correspondent: Dr Iain Duncan, 41 Stanneylands Road, Wilmslow, Cheshire SK9 4ER (01625 533384)

Trustees: Adrian Henry Bradley; Hilary Anne Reeman; Hilary Spencer Burch; Iain Benson Duncan; Jim Crockatt; David Pincombe.

CC Number: 253340

Eligibility

People in need who live in Wilmslow and the surrounding neighbourhood.

Types of grants

One-off grants according to need for items such as replacement beds and bedding after a house fire, fridge/freezers for single parents, removal costs due to bankruptcy, heating system repairs, furniture, clothing and decorating materials.

Annual grant total

Grants have averaged around £1,500 in recent years.

Applications

In writing to the correspondent: to be submitted through a welfare agency, church, social worker or Citizens Advice. Applications should include the individual's address, income and a summary of what is needed and why.

Other information

The trust also gives grants to organisations.

The Wrenbury Consolidated Charities

£1,000

Correspondent: Helen Smith, Eagle Hall Cottage, Smeatonwood, Wrenbury, North Nantwich CW5 8HD (01270 780262)

Trustees: Bruce Edwards; George Bebbington; Helen Smith; Peter Bebbington; Roger Blake; Roger King; Ronald Benbow; Ruth Harrison; William Wright; Donald Mason; Paul Griffiths; Revd David Walton.

CC Number: 241778

Eligibility

People in need who live in the parishes of Chorley, Sound, Broomhall, Newhall, Wrenbury and Dodcott-cum-Wilkesley.

Types of grants

Payments on St Marks' (25 April) and St Thomas' (21 December) days to pensioners and students. Grants are also given for one-off necessities. Grants range from £120 to £130.

Annual grant total

About £1,000.

Applications

In writing to the correspondent either directly by the individual or through another third party on behalf of the individual. The Vicar of Wrenbury and the parish council can give details of the six nominated trustees who can help with applications. Applications are considered in December and March.

Other information

Grants are also given to churches, the village hall and for educational purposes.

Chester

Chester Municipal Charities

£40,000

Correspondent: Grants Administrator, PO Box 360, Tarporley CW6 6AZ (01829 759416; fax: 01829 759010; email: info@ chestermunicipalcharities.org)

Trustees: Jeanne Storrar; Elizabeth Bolton; Peter Catherall; Denis Ainsworth; Mark Fearnall; Peter Lowe; Peter Dutton; Philip Hebson; Kevin Hassett; Christine Russell; David Challen; John Ebo; Clive Pointon.

CC Number: 1077806

Eligibility

Residents of Chester, for the purpose of relieving, either generally or individually, persons who are in conditions of 'need, hardship or distress'. Some preference is given to freemen of the city and members of the city companies (or their widows).

Types of grants

Mainly one-off grants for relief-in-need.

Annual grant total

Grants for welfare purposes usually total around £40,000 each year.

Applications

On a form available from the correspondent.

The Chester Parochial Charity

£14,000

Correspondent: Kerris Owen, Cullimore Dutton, Friars, 20 White Friars, Chester

CH1 1XS (01244 356789; website: www. bclaw.co.uk)

Trustees: Elizabeth Bolton; Adrienne Elizabeth Elloy; Pamela Gertrude Joan Taylor; Pauline Hackett; Fr David Chesters; Margaret Bellis; Cllr Hilarie McNae.

CC Number: 1001314

Eligibility

People in need who live in the city of Chester.

Types of grants

One-off grants, usually ranging from £50 to £1,000, are given for furniture, washing machines, cookers, electrical items, clothing, carpets, and so on. A supermarket vouchers scheme is also available to help low-income families, mainly over the Christmas period.

Annual grant total

In 2010/11 the charity had an income of £40,000 and a total expenditure of £27,000. Grants were made totalling £14,000, with the remaining £13,000 paid in administration costs.

Applications

On a form available from the correspondent. Applications can be made directly by the individual, through a recognised referral agency or through a third party such as a family member. All applicants will be visited by a trustee who will then report back to the subcommittee for a final decision. Applications are considered at any time.

Other information

Grants are also made to organisations.

Congleton

The Congleton Town Trust

£15,000

Correspondent: Ms J Money, Clerk, c/o Congleton Town Hall, High Street, Congleton CW12 1BN (01260 291156; email: info@congletontowntrust.co.uk; website: www.congletontowntrust.co.uk)

Trustees: Gordon Baxendale; Louise Beard; Robert Boston; Alex Hurst; David Daniel; James Morris; Dennis Murphy; Douglas Parker; Arthur Smart; Jeanne Whitehurst; Margaret Williamson.

CC Number: 1051122

Eligibility

People in need who live in the town of Congleton (this does not include the other two towns which have constituted the borough of Congleton since 1975).

Types of grants

Grants in the range of £200 to £3,000 are given to individuals in need or to organisations that provide relief, services or facilities to those in need.

Annual grant total

In 2010 the trust had an income of £24,000 and a total expenditure of £20,000.

Applications

On a form available from the correspondent or downloaded from the trust's website, to be submitted directly by the individual or a family member. Applications are considered quarterly, on the second Monday in March, June, September and December.

Other information

The trust also administers several smaller trusts.

Frodsham

Frodsham Nursing Fund

£400

Correspondent: Miss J Pollen, 22 Fluin Lane, Frodsham WA6 7QH (01928 731043)

Trustees: Dr Andrew Gibson Faraday; Joan Pollen; Graham Redvers Ainsworth; Anita Backus; Wynford Andrews; Annabelle Thompson; Doreen Woods.

CC Number: 503246

Eligibility

People in need who are sick, convalescent or living with disabilities and are resident in the town of Frodsham.

Types of grants

One-off grants according to need. Recently grants have been given for items such as bedding, clothing, medical aids, heating and other domestic appliances. Temporary relief may also be provided to those caring for somebody who is sick or disabled.

Annual grant total

In 2010/11 the fund had an income of £2,700 and a total expenditure of £500.

Applications

In writing to the correspondent, either directly by the individual or on their behalf by a doctor, nurse or social worker. Applicants should briefly state their circumstances and what help is being sought.

Macclesfield

The Macclesfield Relief-in-Sickness Fund

£2,000

Correspondent: Lesley Bull or Margaret Southern, c/o Community and Voluntary Services Cheshire East, 81 Park Lane, Macclesfield, Cheshire SK11 6TX (01625 420530/01625 572418)

Trustees: Peter Womby; Margaret Southern; Betty McWhirk; Eileen Davies; Lesley Alison Bull.

CC Number: 501631

Eligibility

People in need who live in Macclesfield town and who have a chronic illness or a learning disability.

Types of grants

One-off grants only for necessary items such as washing machines, telephone installation, removals or specialist wheelchairs and especially for health-related items that would improve the quality of the applicant's situation.

Annual grant total

On average around £2,000.

Applications

Applications must be made through a local social services office, doctor's surgery or other welfare agencies and they should verify the need of the applicant.

Mottram St Andrew

The Mottram St Andrew United Charities

£3,000

Correspondent: Ronald Taylor, The Farmhouse, Moss Lane, Mottram St Andrew, Macclesfield, Cheshire SK10 4QZ (01625 585039)

Trustees: Mr G. Beard; Mr J. D. Carr; Mrs L. Rowbotham.

CC Number: 217145

Eligibility

People in need who live in the parish of Mottram St Andrew.

Types of grants

On average 35 one-off grants ranging from £35 to £250 reviewed annually; recurrent grants according to need. Recent grants have been given in cases of illness and death, for travel to and from hospital and Christmas bonuses to pensioners.

Annual grant total

Grants usually total around £3,000 a year.

Applications

In writing to the correspondent or to individual trustees. Applications can be submitted directly by the individual or through a social worker, Citizens Advice, other welfare agency or other third party. They are considered in November and should be received by early November.

Warrington

The Police-Aided Children's Relief-in-Need Fund

£0

Correspondent: Stephanie Saxon, Warrington Council For Voluntary Services, The Gateway, 89 Sankey St, Warrington WA1 1SR (01925 444263)

Trustees: Diana Terris; Brian Maher; Lynton Green.

CC Number: 223937

Eligibility

Children of pre-school or primary school age living in the borough of Warrington and whose families are in financial or physical need. Applications from students of secondary school age and over will be considered in exceptional circumstances.

Types of grants

Vouchers to help with the cost of clothing and footwear. Vouchers are only redeemable at selected retailers in the borough.

Annual grant total

No accounts have been submitted since 2008/09 when the fund had an income of £5,000 and an expenditure of £0.

Applications

The trust states that grantmaking is currently suspended whilst various structural issues are sorted out.

Widnes

The Knight's House Charity

£6,500

Correspondent: Wendy Jefferies, Halton Borough Council, Municipal Building, Kingsway, Widnes, Cheshire WA8 7QF (01514 242061; email: wendy.jefferies@ halton-borough.gov.uk)

Trustees: Jean Crawford Gravett; Mr B. Dodd.

CC Number: 218886

Eligibility

People in need who live in Widnes.

Types of grants

One-off grants for kitchen appliances, clothing, carpets, and decorating materials. Second-hand furniture and beds may also be provided through an informal partnership with a separate organisation, Justice and Peace.

Annual grant total

In 2010/11 the charity had an income of £10,000 and a total expenditure of £7,000.

Applications

On a form available from the correspondent.

Wilmslow

The Lindow Workhouse Trust

£2,500

Correspondent: Jacquie Bilsborough, 15 Westward Road, Wilmslow SK9 5JY

Trustees: Stanley Horner; William Warburton; Barbara Briggs; Pat Burrow; Grahame Harris; Pat Breen; Richard Briggs; Ken Mackay; James Montgomery; Jackie Watts; Richard Lowson; Magdalen Smith; Myra Clarke; Jenny Lloyd.

CC Number: 226023

Eligibility

People in need who live in the ancient parish of Wilmslow.

Types of grants

One-off grants to help with, for example, fuel bills, equipment repairs, property repairs. Any cases of real need are considered.

Annual grant total

About £5,000 for welfare and educational purposes.

Exclusions

No grants are made towards relief of rates, taxes or other public funds.

Applications

In writing to the correspondent at any time. Applications can be submitted either directly by the individual or a family member, through a third party such as a social worker or teacher, or through an organisation such as Citizens Advice or a school.

Wybunbury

The Wybunbury United Charities

£5,000

Correspondent: Barnabas Pettman, 12 Lyndhurst Grove, Stone, Staffordshire ST15 8TP (01785 819677; fax: 01785 819677)

Trustees: Frank Morton; Peter Yoxall; Michael Gear; John Gibbons Cornell; Andrew Brereton; Ronald Clarke; Neil Arnott; Rodney Walker; Keith Lawrence; Canon Helen Chantry; Shirley Brazier; Geoffrey Breffitt.

CC Number: 227387

Eligibility

People in need who live in the 18 townships of the ancient parish of Wybunbury as it was in the 1600s and 1700s. The townships are Basford, Batherton, Blakenhall, Bridgemere, Chorlton, Checkley-cum-Wrinehill, Doddington, Hatherton, Hough, Hunsterson, Lea, Rope, Shavington-cum-Gresty, Stapeley, Walgherton, Weston, Willaston and Wybunbury.

Types of grants

The three administering trustees for each township are responsible for distribution of grants. Some make annual payments to individuals in need but funds are also kept in most townships to cover emergency payments for accidents, bereavement or sudden distress.

Annual grant total

Grants usually total around £5,000 a year.

Applications

By direct application to one of three administering trustees.

Cumbria

Barrow Thornborrow Charity

£5,000

Correspondent: Fred Robinson, The Parrock, Stankelt Road, Silverdale, Carnforth LA5 0TW

Trustees: David Leonard Poole; Sydney Procter; Valerie Fisher; Allen Crossley; Fred Robinson.

CC Number: 222168

Eligibility

People who are disabled or sick and live, or were born in, the former county of Westmorland, the former county borough of Barrow, the former rural districts of Sedbergh and North Lonsdale, or the former urban districts of Dalton-in-Furness, Grange and Ulverston.

Types of grants

One-off grants towards items, services or facilities which are calculated to alleviate suffering and assist recovery and which are not available from other sources. In previous years grants have been given for household equipment, assistance with travelling expenses in case of hospitalisation, clothing, computer aids and assistance with essential property repairs.

Annual grant total

Grants normally average around £5,000 per year although at the time of writing (October 2012) the most recent financial figures available from the Charity Commission were for 2009.

Applications

In writing to the correspondent including details of the applicant's circumstances. Applications can be submitted through a social worker, Citizens Advice or other welfare agency.

Cumbria Community Foundation

£30,000

Correspondent: The Grants Team, Cumbria Community Foundation, Dovenby Hall, Cockermouth, Cumbria CA13 0PN (01900 825760; fax: 01900 826527; email: enquiries@ cumbriafoundation.org; website: www. cumbriafoundation.org)

Trustees: J. R. Carr; D. L. Brown; J. F. Whittle; I. W. Brown; Robin Burgess; S. F. Young; A. Naylor; J. Chapman; R. J. Cairns; C. A. Alexander; M. Casson; W. Slavin; S. E. Snyder; J. E. Humphries; J. B. Donnelly; C. Tomlinson; T. Foster; T. J. Knowles; C. A. Giel; T. Jones.

CC Number: 1075120

Eligibility

People resident in Cumbria. Other restrictions inlcuding geographical and age related pertain depending upon the fund being applied to.

Types of grants

One-off and recurrent grants for various welfare needs, equipment, fuel bills, household adaptations and independent living and homelessness.

Annual grant total

In 2010/11 the foundation made 1,070 grants to individuals totalling £735,000, including £671,000 from various flood recovery funds to relieve hardship arising from the floods of

November 2009. The figure of £30,000 given above is reflective of typical grantmaking, aside from the one-off funds for flood relief. £64,000 was given for both welfare and educational needs. Flood grab bags Distributed to households cost an additional £153,000.

Applications

The foundation administers numerous funds that give grants to individuals, they have differing eligibility criteria and application forms. Applicants should check the website for full details of each scheme, and how to apply.

The Cumbria Constabulary Benevolent Fund

£5,000

Correspondent: Federation Representative, Cumbria Constabulary Police Headquarters, 1 The Green, Carleton Hall, Penrith, Cumbria CA10 2AU (01768 217073; fax: 01708 217425)

Trustee: Mr S. Hyde.

CC Number: 505994

Eligibility

Members and former members of the Cumbria Constabulary in need, and their widows and dependents.

Types of grants

One-off cash grants ranging from £250 to £750, usually for the purchase of medical equipment.

Annual grant total

In 2011 the fund had an income of £23,000 and a total expenditure of £11,000. Grants are made to both organisations and individuals.

Applications

In writing to the correspondent directly by the individual or family member. Applications are considered within 14 days.

The Jane Fisher Trust

£4,500

Correspondent: Steven Marsden, Secretary, Livingstons Solicitors, 9 Benson Street, Ulverston, Cumbria LA12 7AU (01229 585555; fax: 01229 584950; email: s.paling@livingstons.co.uk)

Trustees: Anthony Edmondson; Geoffrey Bradbury; Simon Jeremy Hollis.

CC Number: 225401

Eligibility

People in need over 50, and people who are disabled, who have lived in the townships of Ulverston and Osmotherly or the parish of Pennington for at least 20 years.

Types of grants

Small monthly payments. No lump sum grants have been made for many years.

Annual grant total

Grants usually total around £4,500 a year.

Applications

On a form available from the correspondent. Applications are considered when they are received. They must include details of income, capital, age, disabilities, marital status and how long the applicant has lived in the area.

Lakeland Disability Support

£25,000

Correspondent: Brenda Robinson, Trust Secretary, 46 Victoria Road North, Windermere, Cumbria LA23 2DS (01539 442800)

Trustees: Ian Jones; Robert Gordon Smith; Eric Alan Jones; Carole Pouton; Brenda Robinson; Frederick Haworth Tattersall; Beryl Blasdale; Sheila Williams; Andrew James.

CC Number: 1102609

Eligibility

People with physical disabilities who live in South Lakeland, Cumbria.

Types of grants

Grants for respite care, day care, equipment and services that will enhance the life of people with disabilities and which the applicant or social services are unable to provide.

Annual grant total

In 2011 the trust had an income of £23,000 and a total expenditure of £33,000.

Exclusions

No grants for long-term care provision.

Applications

On a form available from the correspondent. Trustees meet quarterly in January, April, July and October. Applications must be received on or before the 15th of the preceding month.

Other information

This trust was established in 2004 following an announcement in October 2003 that Leonard Cheshire would vacate Holehird (a home for people with disabilities in South Lakeland) in two to three years' time. The trust aimed to raise sufficient funds to allow it to keep the home open for the benefit of present and future residents. However, in 2008 Leonard Cheshire surprisingly reversed its decision and announced its intention to remain at Holehird for the foreseeable future.

The trust has since reoriented its activities and now makes grants to individuals and local organisations.

Ambleside

The Ambleside Welfare Charity

£43,000

Correspondent: Michael Johnson, Clerk to the trustees, Lakes Parish Office, The Police Station, Rydal Road, Ambleside LA22 9AY (01539 431656; email: lakesparish@fsmail.net)

Trustees: Linda Dixon; Revd Tim Ball; Brian Elleray; Donald Cook; Ian Benson.

CC Number: 214759

Eligibility

People in need who live in the parish of Ambleside, especially those who are ill.

Types of grants

One-off and recurrent grants according to need. Help is also given to local relatives for hospital visits.

Annual grant total

In 2011 the charity had assets of £959,000 and an income of £44,000. Welfare grants came to £43,000 (£14,000 in 2010).

Applications

In writing to the correspondent.

Agnes Backhouse Annuity Fund

£14,000

Correspondent: James Hamilton, Temple Heelis Solicitors, Bridge Mills, Stramongate, Kendal LA9 4UB (01539 723757)

Trustees: Mr R. Brownson; Mr J. Hamilton.

CC Number: 224960

Eligibility

Unmarried women (including widows) aged over 50 who live in the parish of Ambleside.

Types of grants

Recurrent grants of £50.

Annual grant total

In 2010 the fund had an income of £19,000 and a total expenditure of £14,500.

Applications

In writing to the correspondent.

Other information
The trust states that people who currently fit the above criteria should be receiving a grant, whether rich or poor.

Carlisle

The Carlisle Sick Poor Fund

£4,000

Correspondent: Lynne Rowley, Atkinson Ritson Solicitors, 15 Fisher Street, Carlisle, Cumbria CA3 8RW (01228 674507)

Trustees: Marguerite Murray; Lily Reid; Margaret Paterson; Peter Yardley; Ronald Rangecroft; Sylvia Smith.

CC Number: 223124

Eligibility
People living in Carlisle who are in financial hardship due to ill health.

Types of grants
One-off grants of up to £200 towards bedding, food, fuel, medical aids and equipment, convalescence, holidays and home help.

Annual grant total
The fund has an average income of around £7,500 and expenditure of £4,800.

Applications
On a form available from the correspondent.

Cockermouth

The Cockermouth Relief-in-Need Charity

£400

Correspondent: Revd Wendy Sanders, Parish Administration, Christ Church Rooms, South Street, Cockermouth, Cumbria CA13 9RU (01900 829926)

Trustees: Revd Wendy Sanders; David Holt; Elizabeth Jackson.

CC Number: 221297

Eligibility
Older people in need who live in Cockermouth.

Types of grants
One-off grants in the range of £25 to £35.

Annual grant total
Grants average around £800 a year and are divided between individuals and local organisations.

Applications
In writing to the correspondent. Applications can be made directly by the individual or family member.

Crosby Ravensworth

The Crosby Ravensworth Relief-in-Need Charities

£2,200

Correspondent: G Bowness, Ravenseat, Crosby Ravensworth, Penrith, Cumbria CA10 3JB (01931 715382; email: gordonbowness@aol.com)

Trustees: George Bowness; John Hall; Frank Jackson; James Relph; Joyce Raine; Thomas Harris; Hazel Blenkinship; Betsy Bell; Jill Winder; Revd S. Fyfe.

CC Number: 232598

Eligibility
People in need who have lived in the ancient parish of Crosby Ravensworth for at least 12 months. Preference is given to older people.

Types of grants
One-off and recurrent grants. Grants include £30 coal vouchers to senior citizens and a basket of fruit (or other gift) to people who have been in hospital. Grants can also be given to local students entering university if they have been educated in the parish.

Annual grant total
In 2010 the trust had an income of £12,000 and a total expenditure of £3,400.

Applications
In writing to the correspondent submitted directly by the individual including details of the applicant's financial situation. Applications are considered in February, May and October.

Kirkby Lonsdale

The Kirkby Lonsdale Relief-in-Need Charity

£1,000

Correspondent: Mary Quinn, 19 Fairgarth Drive, Kirkby Lonsdale, Carnforth, Lancashire LA6 2DT (01524 271258)

Trustees: Alan Derwent Day; David Higson; Richard Snow; Ann Ward; Dr David Gareth Thomas; Mary Quinn.

CC Number: 224872

Eligibility
People in need who live in the parish of Kirkby Lonsdale.

Types of grants
One-off grants of £30, usually given just before Christmas.

Annual grant total
Grants usually total around £1,000.

Applications
In writing to the correspondent directly by the individual, or by a third party on his or her behalf. Applications are considered in early December.

Workington

The Bowness Trust

£2,000

Correspondent: Richard Atkinson, Milburns Solicitors, Oxford House, 19 Oxford Street, Workington, Cumbria CA14 2AW (01900 67363; fax: 01900 65552)

Trustees: Richard Atkinson; Colin Doorbar; Ian Goss Chambers; Andrew White.

CC Number: 502323

Eligibility
People in need who live in Workington and live at home (not in institutions).

Types of grants
One-off grants only.

Annual grant total
In 2010/11 the trust had an income of £28,000 and made grants totalling £2,000.

Applications
In writing to the correspondent.

Greater Manchester

J. T. Blair's Charity

£18,000

Correspondent: Anne Hosker, Gaddum Centre, Gaddum House, 6 Great Jackson Street, Manchester M15 4AX (01618 346069; fax: 01618 398573; website: www.gaddumcentre.co.uk)

Trustees: Anthony Murray; Jean Strogen; Donald A. Sutherland; Michael N. G. Evans.

CC Number: 221248

Eligibility
People over 65 who live in Manchester and Salford and who are in need.

Types of grants

Weekly pensions of up to £10, paid at four-weekly intervals.

Annual grant total

On average the charity normally gives around £17,000 every year.

Applications

On a form available from the correspondent, to be submitted by a social worker or other professional person. The trustees meet three or four times a year. Applicants should contact the charity for specific deadlines. Those in receipt of a pension are visited at least once a year.

The Lawrence Brownlow Charity

£1,400

Correspondent: R Hill, 24 Exford Drive, Bolton BL2 6TB (01204 524823; email: brownlow.trust@ntlworld.com)

Trustees: Edward Rae Hill; Elisabeth Mulliner; Reginald Parry; Helen Jones; Judith Heald; Craig Howard; Philip Heald.

CC Number: 223414

Eligibility

People (particularly children and older people) in need who live in the ancient townships of Tonge, Haulgh and Darcy Lever in Bolton.

Types of grants

One-off grants given for a variety of purposes including household bills, living costs and help in the home.

Annual grant total

Grants usually total around £1,400 a year.

Applications

In writing to the correspondent. Applications can be submitted either directly by the individual, through a social worker, a Citizens Advice or another welfare agency. Applications are considered in November.

The FED (Federation of Jewish Services)

£10,000

Correspondent: Heathlands Drive, Prestwich, Manchester M25 9SB (01617 724800; fax: 01617 724934; email: info@ thefed.org.uk; website: www.thefed.org. uk)

Trustees: Michael Ernest Sciama; Simon Albert Philip Jenkins; Herzl Eric Hamburger; Leslie Kay; Deborah Rachael Hamburger; Mark Isaac Addlestone; Bernard Yaffe.

CC Number: 1117126

Eligibility

Jewish people in need who live in Greater Manchester.

Types of grants

Small grants of up to £100 to people on low income or one-off help with utility bills, childcare support, respite care, essential household items and the additional food costs of Passover and other religious festivals. The federation also provides help for children's holidays and playschemes and help to re-establish within the community i.e. removal.

Annual grant total

We were not able to obtain a figure for grants made in recent years. However in the past a small grants programme has distributed around £10,000 per year.

Applications

On a form available from the correspondent, submitted directly by the individual or, with the applicant's permission, through a social worker, Citizens Advice, other welfare agency or other third party. Applications are considered throughout the year. A referral and advice officer is available each day from 9.30 to 12.30 to discuss requests for financial assistance (call 01617 950024 for North Manchester or 01619 414442 for South Manchester).

Other information

Other services are also provided, including a full social work service, a centre for people with mental health needs, respite support for parents of children with special needs, a carer's helpline, a luncheon club, a toy library and other help for people who are isolated or housebound.

Forever Manchester

£45,000

Correspondent: The Grants Team, 5th Floor, Speakers House, 39 Deansgate, Manchester M3 2BA (01612 140953 (Grants Hotline: 01612 140951); fax: 01612 140941; email: enquiries@ communityfoundation.co.uk; website: forevermanchester.com/)

Trustees: A. Burns; J. Farrell; C. Hurst; P. Hogben; Han-Son Lee; S. Lindsay; N. Qureshi; J. Sandford; S. Webber.

CC Number: 1017504

Eligibility

People in need who live in Greater Manchester.

Types of grants

Grants are usually one-off. Funds for individuals have included those from the Greater Manchester Sports Fund and the Joshua Short Foundation, for parents of

pre-schoolchildren who have autism and live in the borough of Stockport.

Annual grant total

£89,000 in 2010/11 to individuals for welfare and education.

Applications

Visit the foundation's website or contact the foundation for details of grant funds that are appropriate for individuals to apply for.

Other information

The Community Foundation for Greater Manchester manages a portfolio of grants for a variety of purposes which are mostly for organisations, but there are a select few which are for individuals. Funds tend to open and close throughout the year as well as new ones being added, and others being spent out. Check the website for information on current schemes.

The Manchester District Nursing Institution Fund

£10,000

Correspondent: Anne Hosker, Gaddum Centre, Gaddum House, 6 Great Jackson Street, Manchester M15 4AX (01618 346069; fax: 01618 398573; website: www.gaddumcentre.co.uk)

Trustees: Anthony Murray; Richard Connolly; Shirley Meri Adams; Sonia Alexander; Dr Lisa Kauffmann; Tim Hall; Jack Beresford; Peter James-Robinson; Deborah Evans; Jan O'Connor; William Edgerton.

CC Number: 235916

Eligibility

People with health related needs in the cities of Manchester and Salford and the borough of Trafford.

Types of grants

One-off grants. It is important that the request is directly related to the health issue of the applicant and is not related to a general condition of poverty.

Annual grant total

In 2010 the fund had an income of £21,000 and a total expenditure of £14,000. Grants totalled around £10,000.

Exclusions

No grants for funeral expenses, taxes, bills, debts or fines.

Applications

On a form available from the correspondent which must be completed by a sponsor from a recognised social and/or health agency. Trustees meet monthly and the deadline for any meeting is the first Wednesday of the month.

Other information

Grants are also made to organisations.

The Mellor Fund

£0

Correspondent: Peter James-Robinson, 95 Salisbury Road, Radcliffe, Manchester M26 4NQ (01617 235835)

Trustees: Gerrard Walsh; Gillian Critchley; Peter Melvin Hughes; Phillipa Norton Dodd; Peter James-Robinson.

CC Number: 230013

Eligibility

People who are sick or in need and live in Radcliffe, Whitefield and Unsworth.

Types of grants

One-off grants towards fuel, food and clothing, domestic necessities, medical needs, recuperative breaks and so on. Recurrent grants are generally not given.

Annual grant total

In both 2009 and 2010 the fund had no income or expenditure, though grants have averaged around £2,000 in previous years.

Applications

In writing to the correspondent. Applications can be submitted directly by the individual or through a social worker, Citizens Advice, other welfare agency or a relative, and should include brief details of need, resources, income and commitments. Applications are considered when received.

The Pratt Charity

£1,000

Correspondent: Anne Hosker, Gaddum Centre, Gaddum House, 6 Great Jackson Street, Manchester M15 4AX (01618 346069; email: info@gaddumcentre.co.uk)

Trustees: The Revd Canon Michael Arundel; John Miller; Janet Hennessey; Robert Payne; Barbara Schofield; Irene Walton; David Tattersall.

CC Number: 507162–1

Eligibility

Women over 60 who live in or near Manchester and have done so for a period of not less than five years.

Types of grants

Grants are given towards education, health and relief of poverty, distress and sickness.

Annual grant total

About £1,000 per year.

Applications

In writing to the correspondent via a social worker.

Other information

The charity is administered by the Gaddum Charity.

Bolton

The Bolton and District Nursing Association

£1,000

Correspondent: David Wrennall, Trustee, Bolton Guild of Help (Inc), Scott House, 27 Silverwell Street, Bolton BL1 1PP (01204 524858)

Trustees: David Lupton Wrennall; Frank Dewhurst Fielding; Geoffrey Dyson; Gregory Pelham; Janette Margaret Winstanley; Geoffrey Chadwick; Glennis Joyce Aston; Diane Wynne Leigh; Ruth Shaw; Mr R. G. Cumming; Diana Bradley; Linda Ball.

CC Number: 250153

Eligibility

People who are sick, convalescing, have disabilities or who are infirm and live in the area of Bolton Metropolitan Borough Council.

Types of grants

One-off grants for items and services, such as the provision of medical equipment, disability equipment and convalescence.

Annual grant total

This trust's income is around £3,000 a year. Expenditure recovered to some extent in 2010 (£1,000) but to this point had been declining with nil expenditure in 2008 and just £35 in 2009.

Applications

On a form available from the correspondent. Applications can be submitted directly by the individual or through a third party such as a social worker, health visitor or welfare agency. Initial telephone enquiries are encouraged to establish eligibility.

The Bolton Poor Protection Society

£1,000

Correspondent: The Trustees, Bolton Guild of Help, Scott House, 27 Silverwell Street, Bolton BL1 1PP (01204 524858)

Trustees: David Wrennall; Frank Fielding; Geoffrey Dyson; Gregory Pelham; Janette Winstanley; Geoffrey Chadwick; Diana Leigh; Glennis Aston;

Ruth Shaw; R. Cumming; Diana Brierley; Linda Ball.

CC Number: 223099

Eligibility

People in need who live in the former county borough of Bolton.

Types of grants

One-off grants for emergencies and all kinds of need, ranging from £25 to £50.

Annual grant total

The total annual expenditure for this charity averages around £1,000.

Applications

Initial telephone enquiries are encouraged to establish eligibility. Application forms are sent out thereafter.

The Louisa Alice Kay Fund

£48,000 (329 grants)

Correspondent: Tracey Wallace, Secretary, Bolton Guild of Help (Inc), Scott House, 27 Silverwell Street, Bolton BL1 1PP (01204 524858)

Trustees: David Lupton Wrennall; Frank Dewhurst Fielding; Geoffrey Dyson; Gregory Pelham; Janette Margaret Winstanley; Geoffrey Chadwick; Diana Wynne Leigh; Glennis Joyce Aston; Ruth Shaw; R. G. Cumming; Diana Brierley; Jane Ball.

CC Number: 224760–1

Eligibility

People in need who live in Bolton.

Types of grants

One-off grants for emergencies and relief-in-need, mostly for replacing household equipment and furniture.

Annual grant total

In 2011 grants were made to 329 (2009: 131) individuals totalling £48,000 and were distributed in the following areas:

Washing machines	£16,000
Cookers	£11,000
Other assistance	£10,000
Fridges/freezers	£7,300
Beds/furniture	£4,100

Applications

On a form available from the correspondent. Applications can be submitted either directly by the individual or a family member, through a third party such as a social worker, or through an organisation such as a Citizens Advice or other welfare agency. Applicants will sometimes be interviewed before a grant is awarded.

Other information

The fund is the main subsidiary of the Bolton Guild of Help Incorporated.

Bury

The Bury Relief-in-Sickness Fund

£3,000

Correspondent: Gill Warburton, The Royal Bank of Scotland plc, PO Box 26, 40 The Rock, Bury, Lancashire BL9 0NX (01617 978040)

Trustees: Gill Warburton; Elizabeth Scholfield; Francine Healey; Iona Worthington; Pamela Brown; Christa Findon; Diane Robinson; Royal Bank of Scotland.

CC Number: 256397

Eligibility

People living in the metropolitan borough of Bury who are in poor health, convalescent or who have disabilities.

Types of grants

One-off grants towards convalescence, medical equipment and necessities in the home which are not available from other sources.

Annual grant total

Grants usually total about £3,000 each year.

Applications

In writing to the correspondent.

Denton

The Denton Relief in Sickness Charity

£1,400

Correspondent: Mary Goodliffe, Apartment 44, Enfield Court, Garside Street, Hyde SK14 5GU (01613 660586)

Trustees: Ian McDonald; Mary Goodliffe; Frances Gertrude Taylor; Allan Arrowsmith.

CC Number: 223597

Eligibility

People in need who are sick, convalescent, disabled or infirm who live in the parish of Denton.

Types of grants

One-off grants ranging from £250 to £500. Grants are given to provide a medical need not available from the NHS.

Annual grant total

Grants usually total around £2,800 a year.

Applications

In writing to the correspondent. Applications can be submitted directly by the individual, by an organisation such as Citizens Advice or through a third party such as a social worker.

Other information

Grants are given to individuals and organisations.

Golborne

The Golborne Charities

£3,000

Correspondent: Paul Gleave, 56 Nook Lane, Golborne, Warrington WA3 3JQ (01942 727627)

Trustees: Alan Tootell; Jeanette Ashurst; Pauline Lawrence; Rita Williams; Sheila Ince; Linda Owen; Beryl O'Hare; John Reed; Julie Jameson.

CC Number: 221088

Eligibility

People in need who live in the parish of Golborne as it was in 1892.

Types of grants

One-off grants between £50 and £80 but occasionally up to £250. Grants are usually cash payments, but are occasionally in kind, for example for food, bedding, fireguards, clothing and shoes. Also help with hospital travel and necessary holidays.

Annual grant total

The charities have an average expenditure of £5,000 per year.

Exclusions

Loans or grants for the payments of rates are not made. Grants are not repeated in less than two years.

Applications

In writing to the correspondent through a third party such as a social worker or a teacher, or via a trustee. Applications are considered at three-monthly intervals. Grant recipients tend to be known by at least one trustee.

Other information

Grants are also given to charitable organisations in the area of benefit, and for educational purposes.

Manchester

The Crosland Fund

£5,200

Correspondent: John Atherden, Accountant, Manchester Cathedral, Victoria Street, Manchester M3 1SX (01618 332220)

Trustee: Revd Rogers Morgan Govender.

CC Number: 242838

Eligibility

People affected by hardship who live in central Manchester.

Types of grants

One-off grants, usually of £40 to £50, for basic necessities such as clothing, food, bedding, furniture, repairs and household materials. Children's Christmas presents may also be given.

Annual grant total

In 2010/11 the fund had an income of £6,800 and a total expenditure of £5,400.

Applications

In writing to the correspondent, through a social worker, Citizens Advice or other welfare agency. Applications are considered in February, May, August and November.

The Dr Garrett Memorial Trust

£9,500

Correspondent: Anne Hosker, Gaddum Centre, Gaddum House, 6 Great Jackson Street, Manchester M15 4AX (01618 346069; fax: 01618 398573; email: amh@gaddumcentre.co.uk; website: www.gaddumcentre.co.uk)

Trustees: Elsie Gilliland; Paddy McKenna; William Egerton; Debbie Morrison.

CC Number: 1010844

Eligibility

Families or groups in need who live in Manchester.

Types of grants

Grants are given towards the cost of convalescence or holidays for individual families and groups.

Annual grant total

In 2010/11 the trust had an income of £11,000 and a total expenditure of £10,000.

Exclusions

Applicants should not have had a funded holiday during the past three years.

Applications

On a form available from the correspondent which should be completed by a sponsor from a recognised social or health agency. Applications must be submitted by the end of April each year.

Other information

The trust also provides information and advice on a range of social and health care issues.

The Manchester Relief-in-Need Charity and Manchester Children's Relief-in-Need Charity

£35,000

Correspondent: Anne Hosker, Gaddum Centre, Gaddum House, 6 Great Jackson Street, Manchester M15 4AX (01618 346069; fax: 01618 398573; email: amh@gaddumcentre.co.uk; website: www.gaddumcentre.co.uk)

Trustees: Anthony Murray; Richard Connolly; Shirley Meri Adams; Sonia Alexander; Dr Lisa Kauffmann; William Egerton; Cllr H. Lyons; Cllr M. Hackett; Jan O'Connor; Juliet Eadie; Jack Beresford.

CC Number: 224271 and 249657

Eligibility

People in need who live in the city of Manchester and are over 25 (Relief-in-Need) or under 25 (Children's Relief-in-Need).

Types of grants

One-off grants for domestic appliances, furniture, clothing, heating and fuel bills and other general necessities. Cheques are made out to the supplier of the goods or services.

Annual grant total

In 2010/11 both charities had a combined income of £76,000. 110 Grants were made from the Children's charity totalling £7,700 while the Relief in Need charity made 240 grants totalling £27,000.

Exclusions

Debts are very rarely paid and council tax and rent debts are never met. Normally an individual may only receive one grant in any 12 month period.

Applications

On a form available from the correspondent which should be completed by a sponsor from a recognised social or health related agency. The trustees meet during the last week of every month. Applications must be received by the 15th of the month.

Other information

Both charities also make grants to organisations (£20,000 in 2010/11).

New Mills

John Mackie Memorial Ladies' Home

£3,800

Correspondent: Mrs Margaret Wood, 27 Low Leighton Road, New Mills, High Peak SK22 4PG (01663 743243; email: dhw111@hotmail.com)

Trustees: David Wellens; Frank Crosland; Margaret James; Margaret Wood; Vera Thorpe; Barbara Matthews; Revd John Baines.

CC Number: 215726

Eligibility

Widows or unmarried women, who are members of the Church of England, are over 50 and are in need.

Types of grants

Christmas gifts to about 80 individuals of £65 each. Applicants will not receive help if they re-marry.

Annual grant total

In 2010 the trust had an income of £2,300 and a total expenditure of £4,000.

Applications

In writing to the correspondent, with (i) evidence of the birth, marriage and death of the applicant's husband, (ii) references from three house owners, confirming her character, respectability and needy circumstances, (iii) proof that she has a small income and (iv) evidence that she is a member of the Church of England. Applications can be submitted either directly by the individual, through a third party such as a social worker, or through an organisation such as Citizens Advice or other welfare agency. Applications are considered throughout the year.

Oldham

The Sarah Lees Relief Trust

£4,000

Correspondent: Catherine Sykes, 10 Chew Brook Drive, Greenfield, Oldham OL3 7PD (01457 876606)

Trustees: Roger Gould; Catherine Sykes; Margaret Struthers; Richard Michael Eastwood; Jennifer Louise Sheehan.

CC Number: 514240

Eligibility

People living in Oldham who are sick, convalescent, disabled or infirm.

Types of grants

One-off grants and gifts in kind. Approximately 12 grants are made each year of up to £500 each.

Annual grant total

Grants average around £4,000 a year.

Exclusions

No grants for items, services or facilities that are readily available from other sources.

Applications

In writing to the correspondent through a social worker, Citizens Advice or other recognised welfare agency. Trustees meet three times a year, but urgent requests will be considered in between meetings.

The Oldham United Charities

£3,000

Correspondent: Mr P Higgins, Oldham MB Council, Level 14, Civic Centre, West Street, Oldham OL1 1UT (01617 703000)

Trustees: K. Knox; Fred Yates; Vernon Cressey; Derrick Joseph Mather; Doris Caroline Hadfield; Joan Capener; A. McInnes; Barbara Jackson; Kevin Anthony Dawson; Patricia Gray.

CC Number: 221095

Eligibility

People in need who live in the borough of Oldham.

Types of grants

One-off grants according to need. Recent grants have been mainly for medical needs, for example, wheelchairs and washing machines for people who are incontinent. Some grants are given to students towards educational expenses.

Annual grant total

About £3,000 is available each year for relief-in-need purposes.

Applications

In writing to the correspondent. Grants are usually considered quarterly.

Rochdale

The Norman Barnes Fund

£10,000

Correspondent: Mr R Ellis, Clerk to the Norman Barnes Fund, PO Box 15, Town Hall, Rochdale OL16 1AB (01706 647474 (ext: 4716); website: www.rochdale.gov.uk/benefits_and_grants/grants/charitable_trusts.aspx)

Trustees: Cllr Jane Gartside; James Edward Flynn; Cllr Barbara Todd; Cllr Peter Davidson; Cllr Pat Colclough.

CC Number: 511646

Eligibility

People over the age of 60 who live in Rochdale, Castleton, Norden or Bamford.

Types of grants

One-off grants according to need. There is no limit to the number of applications or the amount which can be applied for.

Annual grant total

In 2010/11 the trust had an income of £13,000 and a total expenditure of £14,000.

Exclusions

No payments for council tax, rates or other public debts.

Applications

On an application form available to download from the Rochdale council website or by contacting the correspondent. It is recommended that applicants include a supporting comment from a doctor, social worker, AgeUK representative or some other relevant professional.

Requests for items or services should include a written quotation(s). Standard items like fridges or cookers will be ordered directly by the trustees.

Other information

The fund may also make grants to local organisations which benefit the elderly in the area of benefit.

Heywood Relief-in-Need Trust Fund

£8,000

Correspondent: Roger Ellis, Clerk to the Heywood Relief in Need Trust, Committee Services Section, Legal and Democratic Services, Town Hall, Rochdale OL16 1AB (01706 924713; fax: 01706 924185; email: moira.whitehead@ rochdale.gov.uk; website: www.rochdale. gov.uk/benefits_and_grants/grants/ charitable_trusts.aspx)

Trustees: Brian Davies; Cllr Linda Robinson; Tony Ryan; James Crossley; Mrs Maureen-Housley; Cllr Jean Hornby; Brian Bennion; Terry Carpenter; Cllr Alan Godson.

CC Number: 517144

Eligibility

People in need who live in the former municipal borough of Heywood. In exceptional cases applications may be considered from those who are only temporarily located within the borough.

Types of grants

One-off grants usually ranging from £50 to £400. Recent grants have been given to help with fuel arrears, clothing and furniture.

Annual grant total

In 2010/11 the fund had an income of £6,600 and a total expenditure of £7,800.

Exclusions

No grants to pay council tax, public funds or other taxes. No repeat grants.

Applications

On a form available from the correspondent or to download from the Rochdale Borough Council website. Applications should be supported by a social worker, health visitor or similar professional.

The Middleton Relief-in-Need Charity

£1,600

Correspondent: Adelle Hart, Committee Services, Clerk to the Middleton Relief in Need Charity, PO Box 15, Town Hall, Rochdale OL16 1AB (01706 924717; email: adelle.hart@rochdale.gov.uk)

Trustees: John Robinson; Peter Burton; Cllr Lil Murphy; Cllr Maureen Rowbotham; Cllr Alan James Godson.

CC Number: 200079

Eligibility

People in need who live in the former borough of Middleton. In exceptional circumstances people who are only temporarily resident in the area may be considered.

Types of grants

One-off grants (typically £200) for emergencies, for example, travel expenses to visit people in hospital or similar institutions, fuel bills, television licence fees, arrears, holidays for disadvantaged families and general household necessities.

Annual grant total

About £1,600.

Exclusions

No grants for rates, taxes or other public funds. No repeat grants.

Applications

On an application form available to download from the Rochdale council website or by contacting the correspondent. Made by individual application or through social workers, health visitors, victim support schemes and Citizens Advice. All applications must include supporting information from, for example, a social worker, health visitor or other professional.

The Nurses' Benefit Fund

£600

Correspondent: Susan M Stoney, Clerk, The Old Parsonage, 2 St Mary's Gate, Rochdale OL16 1AP (01706 644187; email: law@jbhs.co.uk)

Trustees: Anthony Richard Shackleton; Lois Rigg; Edmund Travis Gartside; Hilary Elizabeth Collins; Malcolm Rigg; John Murray Porritt; Penelope Porritt; Anne Ripley; Nigel Adamson.

CC Number: 222651

Eligibility

Nurses or any other person formerly in the employment of Rochdale District Nursing Association and any retired or district nurse living in the borough of Rochdale.

Types of grants

Recurrent grants paid either once or twice a year.

Annual grant total

Grants average around £1,100 a year. Grants are given to both individuals and organisations.

Applications

In writing to the correspondent.

The Rochdale Fund for Relief-in-Sickness

£15,000

Correspondent: Susan Stoney, The Old Parsonage, 2 St Mary's Gate, Rochdale OL16 1AP (01706 644187; email: law@ jbhs.co.uk; website: www.rochdalefund. org.uk)

Trustees: Anthony Richard Shackleton; Lois Rigg; Edmund Travis Gartside; Hilary Elizabeth Collins; Malcolm Rigg; John Murray Porritt; Penelope Porritt; Anne Ripley; Nigel Adamson.

CC Number: 222652

Eligibility

People living in the borough of Rochdale (including Wardle, Littleborough, Middleton, Heywood, Norden, Birtle, Milnrow and Newhey) who are in poor health, convalescent or who have disabilities. Help may also be given to those whose physical or mental health is likely to be impaired by poverty, deprivation or other adversity.

Types of grants

One-off grants according to need. The trustees will consider any requests for items which will make life more comfortable or productive for the individual. For example, recent grants have been given towards wheelchairs, hoists, IT equipment, house adaptations, special leisure equipment, medical aids, washing machines, cookers, clothing, beds, bedding and respite breaks.

Annual grant total

In 2010/11 the fund had assets of £1.2 million and an income of £39,000. Grants were made totalling £25,000, of which £10,000 was awarded to organisations and £15,000 was given to specific families.

Exclusions

Grants are not given for the payment of debts, including utility bills, council tax and Inland Revenue payments or to help with hardship not directly related to, or caused as a result of, sickness.

Applications

On a form available from the correspondent or to download from the website. Applications can be made either directly by the individual (if no other route is available) or through a social worker, Citizens Advice, other welfare agency or other third party such as a doctor. Whether completed by the individual or a third party all applications must be supported by a letter from a recognised body such as Social Services, Doctor, etc.

Other information

The trust website states that it may also make grants to organisations, 'both statutory and voluntary, to assist them in providing equipment, services or facilities which may alleviate the suffering, or promote the recovery of, persons who qualify.'

Rochdale United Charity

£12,000

Correspondent: Adelle Hart, Clerk to the Rochdale United Charities, Committee Services Section, Legal and Democratic Services, PO Box 15, Town Hall, Rochdale, Lancashire OL16 1AB (01706 924717; email: adelle.hart@ rochdale.gov.uk; website: www.rochdale. gov.uk/benefits_and_grants/grants/ charitable_trusts.aspx)

Trustees: Cllr Brian Lord; Pat Swanston; Cllr Jane Gartside; Julie Warmisham; Yvonne Noble; James Edward Flynn; Cllr Alan Godson.

CC Number: 224461

Eligibility

People in need who live in the ancient parish of Rochdale (the former county borough of Rochdale, Castleton, Wardle, Whitworth, Littleborough, Todmorden and Saddleworth).

Types of grants

One-off grants ranging from £50 to £250. Grants have been given to help with washing machines, cookers, fridges/ freezers, bedding, clothing, recuperative holidays for people long deprived of such, special food, medical or other aids, and telephones, televisions or radios for people who live alone.

Annual grant total

In 2010/11 the charity had both an income and total expenditure of £14,500.

Exclusions

No grants for the relief of rates, taxes or other public funds.

Applications

On a form available from the correspondent or from the council website, to be submitted through a social worker, GP, health visitor, Citizens Advice or other welfare agency. Though, applications can be made directly by the individual if they include a supporting letter from any of those listed above. Applications are usually considered quarterly.

Salford
The Booth Charities

£3,200 (30 grants)

Correspondent: Jonathan Aldersley, Butcher and Barlow, 34 Railway Road, Leigh, Lancashire WN7 4AU (01942 674144)

Trustees: David John Tully; Philip Webb; Richard Peter Kershaw; Edward Simon Tudor Evans; Edward Wilson Hunt; Roger Jeremy Weston; William Thomas Whittle; Richard Fildes; Michael John Prior; John Chistensen Willis; Alan Graham Dewhurst.

CC Number: 221800

Eligibility

People who are retired, over 60, on a basic pension, live in the city of Salford and are in need.

Types of grants

Annual pensions of up to £113 and one-off grants towards TV licences and other needs.

Annual grant total

In 2010/11 the charities held assets of £29.9 million and generated an income of £901,000.

The charities' main area of activity is providing grants to organisations. In the year they had a total charitable expenditure of £395,000 of which £3,200 was paid in grants to individuals.

25 individuals received pensions in the year and five received assistance with TV licence fees.

Applications

On a form available from the correspondent. Applications for one-off grants must be made by social services, ministers of religion, doctors and so on. Distribution meetings are held regularly throughout the year.

Other information

The charities' main grantmaking activity is directed towards organisations.

The City of Salford Relief-in-Distress Fund

£750

Correspondent: Keith Darragh, c/o Salford City Council: Social Services, Crompton House, 100 Chorley Road, Swinton, Manchester M27 6BP (01617 278875)

Trustees: Bill Hinds; Eric Burgoyne; George Wilson; John Mullen.

CC Number: 251658

Eligibility

People in need who live in the city of Salford.

Types of grants

One-off grants to families and individuals of up to £250 (although grants over this amount may be considered). Applications will be considered for clothing, convalescence/ holidays, furniture, special equipment for those with special needs, bedding and so on. Previous grants have included funds for a memorial to a young person's father, a grant to enable a family to partially equip their home after a fire, and a holiday for a family where the mother had terminal cancer.

Annual grant total

About £1,000 each year.

Exclusions

Grants cannot be considered for local authority rent or council tax arrears.

Applications

On a form submitted by a city of Salford social worker, who must be prepared to attend a meeting with the trustees to present the case.

Stockport

Sir Ralph Pendlebury's Charity for Orphans

£1,700

Correspondent: S M Tattersall, Carlyle House, 107–109 Wellington Road South, Stockport SK1 3TL

Trustees: Nigel Neary; Philip Cuddy; Peter Robinson; Stephen Jones; David Kerr.

CC Number: 213927

Eligibility
People who have been orphaned and live, or whose parents lived, in the borough of Stockport for at least two years.

Types of grants
Grants can be for £5 or £6 a week and orphans can also receive a clothing allowance twice a year.

Annual grant total
About £1,700 a year for welfare purposes.

Applications
In writing to the correspondent.

Other information
Grants are also made for educational purposes.

Sir Ralph Pendlebury's Charity for the Aged

£7,000

Correspondent: Stephen Tattersall, c/o Lacy Watson and Co., Carlyle House, 107–109 Wellington Road South, Stockport, Cheshire SK1 3TL

Trustees: Peter Bryan Robinson; Stephen Howell Jones; David Kerr; Stephen Cuddy.

CC Number: 213928

Eligibility
Older people in need who have lived in the borough of Stockport for at least two years.

Types of grants
Small pensions to older people.

Annual grant total
In 2011 the charity had an income and total expenditure of £7,700.

Applications
In writing to the correspondent.

The Stockport Sick Poor Nursing Association

£2,000

Correspondent: Grants Team, Forever Manchester The Community Foundation for Greater Manchester, 2nd Floor, 8 Hewitt Street, Manchester M15 4GB (01612 140940)

Trustee: Forever Manchester The Greater Manchester Community Foundation.

CC Number: 226751

Eligibility
People in need who are sick, poor or infirm and who live in the old county borough of Stockport.

Types of grants
One-off grants up to £400 for household goods and appliances, carpets and other flooring, bedding, medical equipment and so on.

Annual grant total
Grants usually total around £2,000 a year.

Exclusions
Recurrent grants are not given.

Applications
In writing to the correspondent through social services or a welfare agency. Direct applications from individuals are not accepted. The trustees meet on the third Wednesday of every other month to discuss applications. If grants are approved, cheques are sent out straight away. Cheques are made payable to the agency that supports the application who will then buy the items for the applicant.

Tameside

The Mayor of Tameside's Distress Fund

£1,500

Correspondent: Scott Littlewood, Tameside M B C, Room 2.23, Wellington Road Offices, Ashton-under-Lyne, Tameside OL6 6DL (01613 422878)

Trustee: Cllr John Taylor.

CC Number: 519960

Eligibility
People in need who live in Tameside. Preference is generally given to older people and those who are, or have been, homeless.

Types of grants
One-off cash grants of up to about £200.

Annual grant total
Grants average about £1,500 each year.

Applications
On a form available from the correspondent: to be submitted through a social worker or similar third party. Applications should include details of personal income and expenditure, the amount requested, why it is needed and any other organisations approached.

Isle of Man

The Manx Marine Society

£5,000

Correspondent: Capt. R K Cringle, 10 Carrick Bay View, Ballagawne Road, Colby, Isle of Man IM9 4DD (01624 838233)

Eligibility
Seafarers, retired or disabled seafarers and their widows, children and dependents, who live on the Isle of Man. Young Manx people under 18 who wish to attend sea school or become a cadet are also eligible.

Types of grants
One-off and recurrent grants of up to £400 according to need.

Annual grant total
About £5,000.

Applications
On a form available from the correspondent. Applications are considered at any time and can be submitted either by the individual, or through a social worker, Citizens Advice or other welfare agency.

Lancashire

The Accrington and District Helping Hands Fund

£5,000

Correspondent: The Secretary, Tithe Cottage, 4 Grindleton Road, West Bradford, Clitheroe BB7 4TE (01200 422062)

Trustees: Jean Battle; Wendy B. Dwyer; Kenneth Flannagan; Patricia Jones; Patricia Omerod; Cllr Pamela Barton; Pat Matthews; Cllr June Harrison.

CC Number: 222241

Eligibility

People living in the former borough of Accrington, Clayton-Le-Moors and Altham, who are in poor health and are either supported by benefits or are on a low income.

Types of grants

One-off grants usually ranging from £100 to £300 towards the cost of: (i) special foods and medicines, medical comforts, extra bedding, fuel and medical and surgical appliances; (ii) provision of domestic help; (iii) convalescence (iv) provision of mobile physiotherapy service. Grants are usually made directly to the supplier.

Annual grant total

The trust usually has an income of around £11,00 and a grant expenditure of £6,000.

Applications

On a form available from the correspondent submitted either directly by the individual or through a social worker, Citizens Advice or other welfare agency. Applications should include evidence of income and state of health, as well as estimates of what is required.

The Baines Charity

£9,500

Correspondent: Duncan Waddilove, 2 The Chase, Normoss Road, Blackpool, Lancashire FY3 0BF (01253 893459)

Trustees: Graham Cocker; James Hargreaves; Capt. John Caley; Patricia Catlow; Julie Newsham; Lyne Bowen; David Bannister; Susan Hawley.

CC Number: 224135

Eligibility

People in need who live in the ancient townships of Carleton, Hardhorn-cum-Newton, Marton, Poulton and Thornton.

Types of grants

One-off grants ranging from £100 to £250. 'Each case is discussed in its merits.'

Annual grant total

In 2011 the charity had an income of £12,000 and a total expenditure of £20,000. Grants are made for both welfare and educational purposes.

Applications

On a form available from the correspondent, either directly by the individual, or through a social worker, Citizens Advice or other welfare agency. Applications are considered upon receipt.

The Blackpool, Fylde and Wyre Society for the Blind

£2,500

Correspondent: The Trustees, Princess Alexandra Home for the Blind, Bosworth Place, Blackpool FY4 1SH (01253 362688; email: kevin@nvision-nw.co.uk; website: www.nvision-nw.co.uk)

Trustees: Martin Edward Gunson; Joy Killip; Neville Preston; Margaret Gough; Rene Szweda; Gary Bradley Lowcock Bell; John Hodgkinson; Gillian Mary Mackenzie; Raymond James Cowburn; John Robert Morris.

CC Number: 1009955

Eligibility

People who are blind, or who suffer substantially from a visual impairment whether or not registered as blind or partially sighted, living in Blackpool, Fylde and Wyre districts of Lancashire.

Types of grants

One-off grants of between £10 and £250 to relieve difficulties arising from visual impairment.

Annual grant total

In 2010/11 the society had assets of £3.4 million and an income of £1.2 million. Charitable expenditure totalled £1.1 million, but only about £2,500 is available in grants each year.

Applications

On a form available from the correspondent to be submitted through a society welfare officer. Applications are considered throughout the year.

Other information

The society provides a range of services including a resource and rehabilitation centre, a talking newspaper service and a library with over 1,000 audio book titles.

James Bond/Henry Welch Trust

£7,500

Correspondent: Jane Glenton, The Clerk to the Trustees, c/o Democratic Services, Lancaster City Council, Town Hall, Dalton Square, Lancaster LA1 1PJ (01524 582068)

Trustees: Alan Robert Sandham; Veronica Anne Hayton; Pamela Gilbert; John Thomas Harrison; Sarah Taylor; Joyce Taylor; Cllr Niki Penney.

CC Number: 222791

Eligibility

People in need who live in the area covered by Lancaster City Council and have diseases of the chest/lung and early forms of phthisis. Children with disabilities and other special needs are also eligible.

Types of grants

One-off and recurrent grants ranging from £100 to £500 towards, for example, computer equipment, household essentials and holidays.

Annual grant total

In 2010/11 the trust had an income of £10,700 and expenditure of £12,800.

Applications

The trust's home visitor will visit the individual and complete the form. Applications can be submitted at any time.

Other information

This trust also gives to organisations.

Brentwood Charity

£2,500

Correspondent: Marion Bolton, Community Futures, 15 Victoria Road, Fulwood, Preston, Lancashire PR2 8PS (01772 717461; fax: 01772 900250; email: ccl@communityfutures.org.uk; website: www.communityfutures.org.uk)

Trustee: Community Council of Lancashire.

CC Number: 225249

Eligibility

Individuals in need who live in Lancashire (boundaries pre-1974).

Types of grants

One-off grants ranging from £50 to £150, towards such items as necessary household appliances, furnishings and special equipment.

Annual grant total

About £2,500 is available each year for grants to individuals.

Exclusions

No grants to pay for debts or rent bonds.

Applications

On a form available directly from the correspondent or to download from the website. Applications should be submitted through a social worker, Citizens Advice or other welfare agency. No response is made without an sae. Applications are considered quarterly, in January, April, July and October.

Daniel's and Houghton's Charity

£15,000

Correspondent: Miss H A Ryan, Brabners Chaffe Street LLP, 7–8 Chapel

Street, Preston PR1 8AN (01772 823921; fax: 01772 201918)

Trustees: Colin Ovenden; Patricia Frances Wilson; Josephine Booth; Revd Sidney Fox.

CC Number: 1074762

Eligibility

People in need who live in Lancashire with preference given to those living in Preston, Grimsargh, Broughton, Woodplumpton, Eaves, Catforth, Bartle, Alston and Elston.

Types of grants

One-off and recurrent grants according to need.

Annual grant total

In 2010/11 the charity held assets of £693,000 and had a total income of £26,000. Grants paid during the year totalled £15,000.

Exclusions

No grants are given for items or services where statutory funds are available.

Applications

In writing to the correspondent.

Other information

Grants are also made to organisations.

The Foxton Dispensary

£21,000

Correspondent: Robert Dunn, PO Box 227, Lytham St Annes FY8 9BJ (01253 722277; email: clerk@foxtoncharity.co. uk; website: www.foxtoncharity.co.uk)

Trustees: Jim Houldsworth; Anne Cecilia Taylor; Audrey Patricia McLennan; Ian Benson; Marie Cargan; Roy Layfield.

CC Number: 224312

Eligibility

People in need who are in poor health, convalescent or who have a disability and live in the urban district of Poulton-le-Fylde and the county borough of Blackpool.

Types of grants

One-off grants towards food and other necessities such as household equipment.

Annual grant total

In 2010 the dispensary held assets of £643,000 and had an income of £28,000. Grants were made totalling £21,000.

Applications

On a form available from the correspondent or through the website. Applications should be made via a doctor, healthcare professional or social services department. They are considered on an ongoing basis. All applicants are

visited by one of the trustees before a grant is made.

The Goosnargh and Whittingham United Charity

£3,200

Correspondent: John Bretherton, Trustee, Lower Stanalea Farm, Stanalea Lane, Goosnargh, Preston PR3 2EQ (01995 640224)

Trustees: Norman Coulthurst; Tom Kirby; Cllr Trevor J. Tomlinson; Bill Watson; Stan Hunter; John Bretherton; John Pearson; John Singleton.

CC Number: 233744

Eligibility

Older people in need who live in the parishes of Goosnargh, Whittingham and Barton.

Types of grants

One-off and recurrent grants are given according to need.

Annual grant total

In 2010 the charity had an income of £3,700 and a total expenditure of £3,300.

Applications

In writing to the correspondent: to be submitted directly by the individual or family member.

The Harris Charity

£3,800

Correspondent: P R Metcalf, Richard House, 9 Winckley Square, Preston PR1 3HP (01772 821021; fax: 01772 259441; email: harrischarity@ mooreandsmalley.co.uk; website: theharrischarity.co.uk/)

Trustees: W. Huck; E. Booth; B. Banks; T. Scott; S. Smith; S. Huck; R. Jolly; K. Mellalieu; A. Scott; N. Fielden.

CC Number: 526206

Eligibility

People in need under 25 who live in Lancashire, with a preference for the Preston district.

Types of grants

One-off grants of £100 to £5,000 for electrical goods, travel expenses and disability equipment.

Annual grant total

In 2010/11 the charity had assets of £3.1 million, an income of £97,000 and a total expenditure of £92,000, of which £7,400 was given in grants to individuals. Organisations received grants totalling £59,000.

Exclusions

No grants for course fees or to supplement living expenses.

Applications

On an application form downloaded from the website, where guidance and criteria can also be found. Applications are considered during the three months after 31 March and 30 September and must be submitted before these dates either directly by the individual or a third party on behalf of the individual (social worker, Citizens Advice and so on).

Other information

The charity also supports charitable institutions that benefit individuals, recreation and leisure and the training and education of individuals.

Lancashire County Nursing Trust

£9,000

Correspondent: Hadyn Gigg, Plumpton House, Great Plumpton, Preston PR4 2NJ (01772 673618; email: hadyngigg@yahoo.co.uk)

Trustees: Mrs B. Hilton; Graham Curwen; Hadyn Gigg; Shirley Gill; Janet Cross; Margaret Bradley; John Wainwright; Rosemary Russell.

CC Number: 224667

Eligibility

Retired nurses who are in need and have been employed in Lancashire, south Cumbria or Greater Manchester. Grants are also given to people who are in need in the area but it is important to note that most of the trust's income is for the benefit of nurses and only a relatively small amount is available for others.

Types of grants

One-off grants usually ranging from £100 to £300. Support for retired nurses can be for any purpose but funding for people who are sick and in need is generally focused on medical care, holidays and equipment.

Annual grant total

In 2010 the trust had an income of £11,800 and a total expenditure of £9,700.

Applications

In writing to the correspondent. Applications can be submitted directly by the individual or through a social worker, Citizens Advice, nursing authority or other welfare agency.

The Lancashire Football Association Benevolent Fund

£600

Correspondent: David Burgess, The County Ground, Thurston Road, Leyland, Preston, Lancashire PR25 2LF (01772 624000; fax: 01772 624700; email: info@lancashirefa.com; website: www. lancashirefa.com)

Trustees: Charles Gordon Howard; Derek James Lewin; David Presley Burgess.

CC Number: 247179

Eligibility

People in need who are members of clubs associated with Lancashire Football Association and players or officials injured during, or travelling to or from, matches organised by the association.

Types of grants

One-off grants ranging from £100 to £300 towards, for example, hospital expenses, living costs and household bills.

Annual grant total

Grants average around £600 a year.

Applications

On a form available from the correspondent. Applications can be submitted directly by the individual or through a personal representative or a friend.

Peter Lathom's Charity

£600 (2 grants)

Correspondent: Christine Aitken, 13 Mallard Close, Aughton, Ormskirk, Lancashire L39 5QJ (01515 202717)

Trustees: William Waterworth; Peter Godfrey; Lynda Tither; Anthony Lewis; Ellis Draper; Owen Taylor; Philip Scarisbrick; Robert Brunswick; John McKie; William Cropper; John Snape; Geoffrey Monk; Kenneth Mather; Kenneth Vincent; Hilary Rosbotham; James Halsall; Henry Butler; A. Owens; Christopher Byron; David Lawrenson; Jim Hill; John Stanley; Peter Harrison; Terence Aldridge; Terry Kershaw; Beatrice Fairclough; Eileen Doran; Elizabeth Sharrock; Jennifer Rushton; Edward Hey; Ian Tinsley; Sheila Braithwaite.

CC Number: 228828

Eligibility

People in need living in West Lancashire.

Types of grants

One-off grants in November/December.

Annual grant total

In 2011 the charity had assets of £1.2 million and and income of £40,000. Welfare grants to two individuals totalled £600.

Applications

On a form available from the correspondent.

Other information

Grants are also given for education.

The Shaw Charities

£1,000

Correspondent: Mrs E Woodrow, 99 Rawlinson Lane, Heath Charnock, Chorley, Lancashire PR7 4DE (01257 480515; email: woodrows@tinyworld.co. uk)

Trustees: Colin Nelson; Alison South; Harold Howard; Dr Frank Yates; James Ashworth; Prof. John Baldwin; Ann Tomlinson; Pamela Smith; Lynn Wilcox; Robert Davison; Lyn Berry; John Appleyard.

CC Number: 214318

Eligibility

People over 60 who are on low incomes and live in Rivington, Anglezarke, Heath Charnock and Anderton, Lancashire.

Types of grants

Recurrent grants at Easter and Christmas. Grants range from £15 to £20.

Annual grant total

In 2010/11 the charities had an income of £2,700 and a total expenditure of £2,200.

Applications

On a form available from the correspondent to be submitted by the individual for consideration in March and November.

Other information

Grants for the purchase of books by undergraduates are also given through the Shaw's Educational Endowment.

Blackpool

The Blackpool Ladies' Sick Poor Association

£28,000

Correspondent: Ronald A Shaw, 156 Highcross Road, Poulton-Le-Fylde, Lancashire FY6 8DA (01253 893188)

Trustees: Paul Anthony Olive; Isabel Janina Henshaw; Ronald Anthony Shaw; Simon Oliver Hargreave; Beverly Jean Lester; Chris Brown; Elaine Robinson.

CC Number: 220639

Eligibility

People in need who live in Blackpool.

Types of grants

Mainly food vouchers of £12 to £20 a month per family. Special relief grants can be made for immediate needs such as rent, second-hand cookers and washers, clothing, heaters, fireguards, stair gates and so on.

Annual grant total

In 2010/11 the association had assets of £371,000 and an income of £32,000. Grants were made totalling £28,000.

Applications

Applications must include proof of extreme hardship and must be in writing via health visitors, social workers, Citizens Advice or other welfare agencies such as Age Concern, Mind and so on. Health visitors and social workers can write to the association's treasurer directly, otherwise letters should be sent to the correspondent. Applications are considered all year round, excluding August.

Other information

The association occasionally makes grants to organisations.

The Swallowdale Children's Trust

£26,000

Correspondent: The Secretary, 23 Abingdon Street, Blackpool FY1 1DG (01253 712937)

Trustees: Dr D. Haworth; J. Leeson; J. Baggaley; Dr C. Taylor; N. Law; J. Barlow; S. Marshall; Dr H. Miller.

CC Number: 526205

Eligibility

People who live in the Blackpool area who are under the age of 25. Orphans are given preference.

Types of grants

One-off grants are given for a wide variety of needs, including hospital expenses, clothing, food, travel expenses, medical equipment, nursing fees, furniture, disabled equipment and help in the home.

Annual grant total

In 2010/11 the trust had assets of £968,000 and an income of £39,000. There were 193 relief-in-need grants made during the year totalling £26,000. No grants were made for educational purposes.

Applications

On a form available from the correspondent, with the financial details of the individual or family. Applications must be made through a social worker or teacher. They are considered every two months.

Caton-with-Littledale

The Cottam Charities

£25,000

Correspondent: Amanda Owen, Blackhurst Swainson Goodier Solicitors, 3 and 4 Aalborg Square, Lancaster LA1 1GG (01524 32471; email: ajo@ bsglaw.co.uk)

Trustees: Revd Graham Pollitt; Joyce Gregory; John Taylor.

CC Number: 223936 and 223935

Eligibility

People in need who are over 50 and have lived in the parish of Caton-with-Littledale for at least five years.

Types of grants

One-off grants ranging from about £100 to £140.

Annual grant total

Grants usually total around £25,000 each year.

Applications

In writing to the correspondent directly by the individual or family member by mid-November for consideration in November/December each year. Applicants must reapply each year.

Darwen

The W. M and B. W. Lloyd Trust

£10,000

Correspondent: John Jacklin, Trustee, Gorse Barn, Rock Lane, Tockholes, Darwen, Lancashire BB3 0LX (01254 771367)

Trustees: Mrs D. E. Parsons; Mr J. N. Jacklin; Mr D. G. Watson.

CC Number: 503384

Eligibility

People in need who live in the old borough of Darwen in Lancashire. Preference is given to single parents.

Types of grants

One-off and recurrent grants according to need. Educational grants are given priority over social or medical grants.

Annual grant total

In 2010/11 the trust had an income of £76,000 and made grants totalling £70,000 to organisations and individuals.

Applications

On a form available from the correspondent, only through a social worker, Citizens Advice, other welfare agency, doctor or health visitor. Applications are considered quarterly in March, June, September and December.

Lancaster

The Gibson, Simpson and Brockbank Annuities Trust

£5,200

Correspondent: Amanda Owen, Blackhurst Swainson Goodier Solicitors, 3 and 4 Allborg Square, Lancaster LA1 1GG (01524 32471; fax: 01524 386515; email: ajo@bsglaw.co.uk; website: www.bsglaw.co.uk)

Trustees: Mark Burrow; Shirley Sharples; Andrea Katherine Brown; David Robert Bennetts; Thomas Patrick O'Neill.

CC Number: 223595

Eligibility

Unmarried women or widows in need (with an income of less than £1,000 from sources other than their state pension), who are over 50 years old and have lived in Lancaster for the last three years.

Types of grants

Quarterly grants.

Annual grant total

In 2010 the trust had an income of £6,800 and a total expenditure of £5,400.

Applications

On a form available from the correspondent to be submitted directly by the individual. Applications are usually considered every three months.

The Lancaster Charity

£2,400

Correspondent: Philip Oglethorpe, William Penny's, Regent Street, Lancaster LA1 1SG (01524 842663; email: lancastercharity@btconnect.com)

Trustees: John Harrison; John Michael Gorrill; Cllr Keith William Budden; Roger James Sherlock; Cllr Susan Charles; Susan Elizabeth Hodgson; Veronica Anne Hayton; J. P. Ayrton; Roger W. Carradice; John R. Lodge; Cllr David Brookes; Revd Christopher Newlands; Cllr Sheila Denwood; Cllr Robert Redfern.

CC Number: 213461

Eligibility

People over 60 who are in need and have lived in the old city of Lancaster for at least three years. People under 60 may be considered if they are unable to work to maintain themselves due to age, accident or infirmity.

Types of grants

Top-up pensions according to need.

Annual grant total

In 2011 the charity had assets of £1.8 million and an income of £152,000. During the year, payments totalling £2,400 were made to pensioners. The majority of income is spent on maintaining the charity's almshouses.

Applications

On a form available from the correspondent. Applications are considered when vacancies occur.

Littleborough

The Littleborough Nursing Association

£500

Correspondent: Marilyn Aldred, 26 Hodder Avenue, Shore, Littleborough OL15 8EU (01706 370738)

Trustees: Marilyn Aldred; Kathleen Garlick; George Kelsall; Joan Wild; Monica Wild; Norman Joseph Angus; Eddie Holden; Sheila Wildman; Stuart Wildman.

CC Number: 222482

Eligibility

People in need who are sick, convalescent, disabled or infirm and live in the former urban district of Littleborough.

Types of grants

Recurrent grants according to need.

Annual grant total

Grants to individuals usually total around £500 each year.

Exclusions

Grants are not given for costs which are normally covered by the DWP or NHS.

Applications

In writing to the correspondent for consideration in October. Applications can be submitted directly by the individual or through a social worker, Citizens Advice, other welfare agency or other third party.

Lowton

The Lowton United Charity

£2,000

Correspondent: J Naughton, Secretary, 51 Kenilworth Road, Lowton, Warrington WA3 2AZ (01942 741583)

Trustees: Alan McLeod; Norman Holt; Alan Baldwin; Gillian Dickinson; Jeremy Dean; Joseph Newson; Pamela Hampson; Revd William Stalker; Avis Freeman; Linda Graham.

CC Number: 226569

Eligibility

People in need who live in the parishes of St Luke's and St Mary's in Lowton.

Types of grants

One-off grants at Christmas and emergency one-off grants at any time.

Annual grant total

Grants total about £4,000 a year. About half of grants are given at Christmas for relief-in-need purposes and the rest throughout the year. Educational grants are also made.

Applications

Usually through the rectors of the parishes or other trustees.

Lytham St Anne's

The Lytham St Anne's Relief-in-Sickness Charity

£0

Correspondent: Jill Walker, Fylde YMCA, Parry Way, Breck Road, Poulton-le-Fylde FY6 7PU (01253 893928)

Trustees: Elizabeth Anne Smith; Revd Peter Law Jones.

CC Number: 500498

Eligibility

People with a physical or mental disability or long-term illness who are in need and live in the borough of Fylde, mainly St Annes.

Types of grants

One-off grants of up to £500 towards, for example, fuel bills, washing machines, special beds/chairs, respite holidays and travel for medical treatment or to visit sick relatives.

Annual grant total

In 2010/11 the charity had an income of £1,400 and no expenditure.

Exclusions

No grants for court fees or funeral costs.

Applications

In writing to the correspondent with financial details and information about the illness or the reason for need. Applications can be submitted directly by the individual or through a social worker, Citizens Advice, other welfare agency or other third party.

Nelson

The Nelson District Nursing Association Fund

£2,000

Correspondent: Joanne Eccles, Democratic and Legal Services, Pendle Borough Council, Nelson Town Hall, Market Street, Nelson, Lancashire BB9 7LG (01282 661654; email: joanne. eccles@pendle.gov.uk)

Trustees: Geoff Yates; Kathleen Haydock; Christine Hartley; Julia Kelly; Denise Shuttleworth; Asjad Mahmood.

CC Number: 222530

Eligibility

Sick, poor people who live in Nelson, Lancashire.

Types of grants

One-off grants according to need, ranging from £50 to £500.

Annual grant total

In 2010/11 the fund had an income of £4,100 and a total expenditure of £2,100.

Applications

In writing to the correspondent. Applications can be submitted directly by the individual or through a social worker, Citizens Advice or other welfare agency. All applicants will be visited by the association's welfare officer as part of the assessment process.

Pendle

The Fort Foundation

£1,800

Correspondent: E S Fort, Trustee, Fort Vale Engineering Ltd, Calder Vale Park, Simonstone Lane, Simonstone, Burnley BB12 7ND (01282 440000)

Trustees: Edward Sagar Fort; Ian Wilson; Susan Friedlander.

CC Number: 1028639

Eligibility

Young people in Pendle Borough and district, especially those undertaking courses in engineering.

Types of grants

One-off grants of £50 to £1,000.

Annual grant total

In 2011/12 the foundation held assets of £306,000 and had an income of £153,000. Grants made for welfare purposes totalled £1,800.

Applications

In writing to the correspondent, directly by the individual. Applications are considered at any time.

Other information

Grants are primarily made to organisations.

Merseyside

Channel – Supporting Family Social Work in Liverpool

£6,000

Correspondent: Janet Corke, 294 Aigburth Road, Liverpool L17 9PW (01517 260443; fax: 01517 260443)

Trustees: Revd C. Critchley; J. Monaghan; Ms C. Morris; Ms D. Davies; Mrs R. Black; Mrs R. Stirrup; Mr R. Lovering.

CC Number: 257916

Eligibility

Children living in Merseyside who are in need, where the need cannot be met by statutory grants from the Social Services.

Types of grants

One-off grants up to £100 for clothing, food, furniture, kitchen equipment and childcare.

Annual grant total

In 2010/11 the trust had an income of £7,000 and a total expenditure of £6,000.

Applications

Applications can only be made through a social worker, health worker or voluntary agency, who should contact the correspondent for advice on funding, an application form and guidelines. Applications are considered on an ongoing basis.

The Girls' Welfare Fund

£4,500

Correspondent: S M O'Leary, West Hey, Dawstone Road, Heswall, Wirral

CH60 4RP (email: gwf_charity@hotmail.com)

Trustees: Mrs S. M. O'Leary; Mrs M. Von Zweighbergk; Mrs P. D. Milne.

CC Number: 220347

Eligibility

Girls and young women (usually aged 15 to 25) who are in need and were born, educated and live in Merseyside. Applications from other areas will not be acknowledged.

Types of grants

One-off and recurrent grants according to need. Grants range from £50 to £750.

Annual grant total

In 2011 the fund had an income of £9,400 and an expenditure of £9,300.

Exclusions

Grants are not made to charities that request funds to pass on and give to individuals.

Applications

By letter to the correspondent or via email (including full details of what is needed and for what purpose). Applications can be submitted directly by the individual or through a social worker, Citizens Advice or another welfare agency. Applications are considered quarterly in March, June, September and December.

Other information

The trust also gives grants to organisations benefiting girls and young women on Merseyside, and to eligible individuals for leisure, creative activities, sports, arts and education.

The Liverpool Caledonian Association

£14,000

Correspondent: I A Fisher, Secretary, 72 Cambridge Road, Crosby, Liverpool L23 7TZ (01519 243909)

CC Number: 250791

Eligibility

People of Scottish descent, or their immediate family, who are in need and who live within a 15-mile radius of Liverpool Town Hall. The association states: 'generally speaking we do not welcome applications from people who have fewer than one grandparent who was Scots born'.

Types of grants

Regular monthly payment of annuities, heating grants and a limited number of Christmas food parcels. The usual maximum grant is £50.

Annual grant total

In 2009 the association had an income of £9,700 and a total expenditure of £19,000. At the time of writing (winter 2012) more recent financial information was not available.

Exclusions

Holidays are generally excluded.

Applications

In writing to the correspondent either directly by the individual, through a social worker, Citizens Advice, or other welfare agency or through any other third party. Applications are considered at any time and applicants will be visited.

The Liverpool Ladies' Institution

£5,000

Correspondent: David Anderton, 15 Childwall Park Avenue, Childwall, Liverpool L16 0JE (01517 229823; email: d.anderton68@btinternet.com)

Trustees: Brian Gillbanks; Bill Merry; David Anderton; Gill Gargan; John Marsden; John Moore; Lindsey Cross; Rob Oliver; Michael Collins; Charles Paton; Helen Clarey.

CC Number: 209490

Eligibility

Single women in need who were either born in the city of Liverpool or live in Merseyside. Preference is given to such women who are members of the Church of England, and to older women.

Types of grants

Recurrent grants.

Annual grant total

In 2010 the trust had an income of £4,200 and a total expenditure of £5,200.

Applications

On a form available from the correspondent. Applications should be submitted, at any time, through a social worker, Citizens Advice or other welfare agency. The trust has stated that it receives a lot of inappropriate applications.

The Liverpool Merchants' Guild

£825,000 (335 grants)

Correspondent: Brian McGain, Moore Stephens, 110–114 Duke Street, Liverpool L1 5AG (01517 031080; fax: 01517 031085; email: info@liverpoolmerchantsguild.org.uk; website: www.liverpoolmerchantsguild.org.uk)

Trustees: Roy Morris; Robert John Carter; Sandy Timothy Chapple Gill; David Stern; Gillian Ferrigno; Susan Newton; Andrew Morris; Anthony Roberts; Lawrence Downey; Kenneth Head.

CC Number: 206454

Eligibility

Retired, professional, supervisory, clerical or self-employed people and their dependents who live on Merseyside (or who have lived there for a continuous period of at least 15 years), are aged over 50, and are in need or distress.

Types of grants

Annual pensions of £200 upwards, paid twice yearly. One-off grants of up to £5,000 for items of exceptional expenditure e.g. equipment or adaptations to support independent living.

Annual grant total

In 2011 the guild had assets of £29 million and an income of £1.1 million. Grants were made totalling £825,000. This included £717,000 given in pensions and £108,000 given in grants.

Applications

On a form available from the correspondent or to download from the website. Applications must be countersigned by two unrelated referees and include all relevant supporting documentation. They can be submitted at any time and are considered every three months.

Note: Applicants wishing to apply for a one-off grant will need to fill in the standard application form and a supplementary grants form (also available on the website).

The Liverpool Provision Trade Guild

£6,000

Correspondent: The Secretary, KBH Accountants Ltd, 255 Poulton Road, Wallasey, Wirral CH44 4BT (01516 388550)

Trustees: Clifford Maxwell Lawrenson; Thomas J. Granby.

CC Number: 224918

Eligibility

Members of the guild and their dependents who are in need. If funds permit, benefits can be extended to other members of the provision trade on Merseyside who are in need and their dependents.

Types of grants

Recurrent grants of £400 to £900 paid monthly, half-yearly or annually.

Annual grant total

In 2010/11 the trust had an income of £4,300 and a total expenditure of £6,200.

Applications

In writing to the correspondent, directly by the individual. Meetings are held in May and December to discuss applications.

The Liverpool Queen Victoria District Nursing Association

£28,000

Correspondent: Company Secretaries, Liverpool Charity and Voluntary Services, 151 Dale Street, Liverpool L2 2AH (01512 275177; fax: 01512 373998; email: info@lcvs.org.uk; website: www.lcvs.org.uk)

Trustees: William David Fulton; Charles Sheridan Feeny; Susan Newton; Roger Morris; Prof. Hilary Russell; Mark Francis Whitlock Blundell; Andrew Robert Lovelady; Christine Elizabeth Reeves; Heather Akehurst; Adeyinka Olushonde; Perminda Bal.

CC Number: 223485

Eligibility

People who are sick or disabled, live in Merseyside and are in need. No help is given where this should be provided by the 'public purse'.

Types of grants

One-off grants of between £10 and £200 to provide financial help towards food, appliances or other items to help alleviate suffering or assist the recovery of eligible people.

Annual grant total

Grants have previously totalled £28,000.

Exclusions

No grants for debts, holidays, pilgrimages or medical treatment.

Applications

On a form only available from the Community Nursing Services of Merseyside Health Districts (not from the correspondent) via district nurses, health visitors or through a social worker. An initial telephone call to the correspondent to discuss eligibility and needs is welcomed. Applications are considered all year round.

Other information

The fund is administered by Liverpool Charity and Voluntary Services (223485).

Merseyside Jewish Community Care

£14,000

Correspondent: Lisa Dolan, Chief Executive, Shifrin House, 433 Smithdown Road, Liverpool L15 3JL (01517 332292; email: info@mjccshifrin.co.uk; website: www.merseysidejewishcommunitycare.co.uk)

Trustees: Graham Anthony Rubin; Susan Livingstone; Lorna Baygot; Stuart Alan Tinger; Paulette Rubin; Walter Beilin; Julian Lionel Green; Edward Marks Mott-Cowan; Gordon Sherr Globe; Simon Richard Lewis.

CC Number: 1122902

Eligibility

People of Jewish faith who live in Merseyside and are in need due to poverty, illness, old age, social disadvantage, disability or mental health problems.

Types of grants

Small one-off grants and loans to help towards medical equipment, respite breaks and basic essentials such as food and clothing. Grants are only paid on the provision of receipts for the goods/services purchased or are simply made directly to the supplier.

Annual grant total

In 2010/11 the trust had assets of £1.8 million and an income of £274,000. 'Relief grants' were made totalling £14,000.

Applications

By letter or telephone to the correspondent, directly by the individual.

Other information

Merseyside Jewish Community Care provide a care and welfare service for Jewish people in Merseyside.

Billinge

John Eddleston's Charity

£500

Correspondent: Graham Bartlett, Parkinson Commercial Property Consultants, 10 Bridgeman Terrace, Wigan, Lancashire WN1 1SX (01942 740 180)

Trustees: James Heyes; Raymond Hutchinson; Cliff Stockley; William Tyrer; Charles Mather; William Bradbury; Gillian Sainsbury.

CC Number: 503695

Eligibility

People in need who live in the ecclesiastical parish of Billinge.

Types of grants

One-off and recurrent grants according to need.

Annual grant total

Grants to individuals usually total around £1,000 for education and welfare purposes.

Applications

In writing to the correspondent by the end of March. The annual meeting of the trustees takes place after the end of March.

Birkenhead

The Birkenhead Relief in Sickness Fund

£2,300

Correspondent: Viv Kenwright, Wirral CVS, 46 Hamilton Square, Birkenhead, Merseyside CH41 5AR (01516 475432; email: viv@wirralcvs.org.uk)

Trustee: Wirral Council for Voluntary Service.

CC Number: 217686

Eligibility

People in need through ill health who are on a low income and live in the old county borough of Birkenhead. Applicants should have tried to obtain a social fund loan before approaching the trust.

Types of grants

One-off grants to a usual maximum of £250. Grants are given for essential items such as clothing, electrical appliances, furniture (e.g. beds), travel costs and household items (e.g. bedding, towels).

Annual grant total

Grants average around £2,300 per year.

Applications

Applications can be submitted through a recognised referral agency (e.g. social worker, Citizens Advice or doctor) or other third party, and are considered throughout the year. A doctor's note will be needed to back up the claim if the applicant is not in receipt of Disability Living Allowance. An appointment will be made with the claimant, or a member of the family if they are unable to attend, to discuss the claim.

The Christ Church Fund for Children

£1,200

Correspondent: Robert Perry, 28 Beresford Road, Prenton CH43 1XG

Trustees: Nikki Eastwood; Robert Perry; Marie Szydlowska; Revd Andre James Haslam; Debbie Baldwin; Mary Kirby.

CC Number: 218545

Eligibility

Children in need up to the age of 17 whose parents are members of the Church of England and who live in the county borough of Birkenhead. Preference is given to children living in the ecclesiastical parish of Christ Church, Birkenhead.

Types of grants

Grants for any kind of need, but typically for bedding, furniture, clothing and trips.

Annual grant total

Total annual expenditure is around £1,500 on average.

Applications

In writing through a recognised referral agency (for example, a social worker or Citizens Advice) or other third party. Applications are usually considered quarterly (around January, April, September and December), but emergency applications can be considered at any time.

Higher Bebington

The Thomas Robinson Charity

£2,000

Correspondent: Charles F Van Ingen, 1 Blakeley Brow, Wirral, Merseyside CH63 0PS

Trustees: Canon Anne Samuels; Diane Shaw; David Evans.

CC Number: 233412

Eligibility

People in need who live in Higher Bebington.

Types of grants

One-off grants of £50 to £500. Grants can be made for educational purposes.

Annual grant total

About £2,000.

Applications

In writing to: The Vicar, Christ Church Vicarage, King's Road, Higher Bebington, Wirral CH43 8LX. Applications can be submitted directly by the individual or a family member, through a social worker, or a relevant third party such as Citizens Advice or a school. They are considered at any time.

Huyton with Roby

The Huyton with Roby Distress Fund

£0

Correspondent: The Trustees, Knowsley MBC, KMBC Finance, Po Box 23, Nutgrove Villa, Westmorland Road, Huyton, Liverpool L36 6GA (01514 433757; fax: 01514 433452)

Trustees: Cllr Robert Samuel Maguire; Cllr Tony Harvey; Cllr Christine Bannon.

CC Number: 231171

Eligibility

People in need who live in the former urban district of Huyton with Roby (in Knowsley).

Types of grants

One-off grants ranging from £100 to £350 towards the cost of items such as washing machines, carpets and beds.

Annual grant total

No accounts had been submitted for the 2010/11 year at the time of writing. The fund has an average expenditure of around £900 per year although this does tend to fluctuate.

Exclusions

No grants for debts or fuel costs or to buy non-essential items.

Applications

In writing to the correspondent through a social worker, Citizens Advice or other welfare agency. A social worker would usually assess the need and should inform the trust about the applicant's full circumstances and give details about the item required (e.g. the cost). Applications are considered on receipt.

Liverpool

The Charles Dixon Pension Fund

£6,500

Correspondent: Richard J Morris, Treasurer, The Society of Merchant Venturers, Merchants' Hall, The Promenade, Clifton Down, Bristol BS8 3NH (01179 738058; fax: 01179 735884; email: enquiries@ merchantventurers.com)

Trustees: Richard John Morris; David Marsh; Karen Morgan; Anthony Roger Ernest Brown; James John Dennis McArthur; Trevor Smallwood; Christopher John Curling; Charles Giles Clarke; Colin Skellett; Anthony Kenny; Andrew Temple Yates; Peter John Rilett; Colin Henry Green; Charles Griffiths; Peter John McCarthy; Tim Ross;.

CC Number: 202153

Eligibility

Merchants who are married men, widowers or bachelors of good character, who are practising members of the Church of England, and widows of pensioners who are in reduced circumstances. Applicants must live in Bristol, Liverpool or London and must be over 60 years.

Types of grants

Pensions of between £520 and £2,000 a year.

Annual grant total

In 2010/11 the fund had an income of £8,000 and a total expenditure of £6,800.

Applications

On a form available from the correspondent. Applications can be submitted directly by the individual or through a social worker, Citizens Advice, other welfare agency or a third party such as a clergyman. They are dealt with as received.

The Liverpool Corn Trade Guild

£10,500

Correspondent: Ian Garth Bridge, 1a St Johns Road, Southport PR8 4JP (01704 565596)

Trustees: Michael Groves; Anthony Joseph McGuinness; Ian Garth Bridge; Simon Nicholas Gooderham; Eric Stephen Thomas.

CC Number: 232414

Eligibility

Members of the guild and their dependents who are in need. If funds permit benefits can be extended to former members and their dependents. Membership is open to anyone employed by any firm engaged in the Liverpool Corn and Feed Trade.

Types of grants

One-off and recurrent grants according to need.

Annual grant total

Grants average around £11,000 a year.

Applications

In writing to the correspondent. Applications should be made directly by the individual.

The Liverpool Wholesale Fresh Produce Benevolent Fund

£3,000

Correspondent: Thomas J C Dobbin, Secretary, 207 Childwall Road, Liverpool L15 6UT (01517 220621)

Trustees: Austin David Molyneux; Martin James Halliwell.

CC Number: 1010236

Eligibility
People in need, who are or have been associated with the Liverpool fruit trade either as importers or wholesalers, and their families.

Types of grants
One-off and recurrent grants usually ranging from £50 to £80.

Annual grant total
In 2010/11 the trust had an income of £6,700 and a total expenditure of £11,100. The fund currently supports around five individuals involved with the trade on a recurrent basis.

Applications
In writing to the correspondent.

Other information
The fund has stated that it now predominantly makes grants to local charities in Merseyside due to a dwindling number of applications from individuals connected with the fresh produce trade.

The Ann Molyneux Charity

£16,000

Correspondent: John Wilson, Trustee, Liverpool Seafarers Centre, 20 Crosby Road South, Liverpool L22 1RQ (0300 8008085; email: john.wilson@ liverpoolseafarers.org.uk)

Trustees: Lord Mayor of Liverpool; Revd Steven Brookes; Pam Brown; Patricia E. Dixon; John P. Wilson.

CC Number: 229408

Eligibility
Seamen and their widows living in the city of Liverpool. Preference for men who sailed from the city for most of the last five years that they were at sea. Applicants must receive Income Support, housing benefit or council tax benefit.

Types of grants
Pensions of £200 a year (paid quarterly).

Annual grant total
In 2010/11 the charity had an income of £18,000 and a total expenditure of £20,000.

Applications
On a form available from Liverpool Parish Church and Our Lady and St Nicholas. Applications should be accompanied by seamen's books, details of income and a testimonial from a person of good standing in the community.

The Pritt Fund

£9,000

Correspondent: Liverpool Law Society, The Cotton Exchange Building, Second Floor, Edmund Street, Liverpool L3 9LQ (01512 366998)

Trustee: Liverpool Law Society.

CC Number: 226421

Eligibility
Solicitors who are in need and have practised in the city of Liverpool or within the area of Liverpool Law Society, and their dependents.

Types of grants
One-off and recurrent grants according to need.

Annual grant total
In 2010/11 the fund had an income of £15,000 and a total expenditure of £9,200.

Applications
On a form available from the correspondent.

Lydiate

John Goore's Charity

£1,300

Correspondent: E R Bostock, Stanley Building, 43 Hanover Street, Liverpool, Merseyside L1 3DN (01772 642387; email: info@cfmerseyside.org.uk; website: www.cfmerseyside.org.uk)

CC Number: 238355

Eligibility
People in need living in the parish of Lydiate only.

Types of grants
Grants of up to £500 to alleviate some of the difficulties faced by people with a physical or mental disability, for example, small home improvements, travel to community activities/facilities and specialist equipment. Grants of up to £250 are also available to local carers for respite breaks, travel expenses and additional costs of living incurred as a direct result of being a carer.

Annual grant total
In 2010/11 the charity had an income of £6,700 and a total expenditure of £9,700. The Community Foundation for Merseyside 2010/11 accounts record grants of £2,700 made by the trust.

Exclusions
No grants for payment of debts.

Applications
Applications should be made through the Community Foundation for Merseyside. Forms are available from the Foundation's website and can be filled out electronically and returned to applications@cfmerseyside.org.uk.

Applications should include a letter of support from the person being cared for (if appropriate). Applications for home improvements should include details of the service provider, the quote received and the amount requested.

Other information
The charity also makes grants to organisations and to individuals for educational purposes.

Sefton

Southport and Birkdale Provident Society

£13,000

Correspondent: Ian Jones, Treasurer, 12 Ascot Close, Southport, Merseyside PR8 2DD (01704 560095)

Trustees: Ian Paul Sherwood Glover Jones; Andrea Higham; Geoffrey Vernon Williams; Cathy Crook; Cnl Robert William Menary; Charles Dennis O'Hara.

CC Number: 224460

Eligibility
People in need who live in the metropolitan borough of Sefton.

Types of grants
One-off grants in kind only after social services have confirmed that all other benefits have been fully explored. Recent grants have been given towards clothing, bedding, cookers, washing machines and other basic household needs.

Annual grant total
In 2011 the society had assets of £519,000 and an income of £26,000. Grants were made to 105 individuals totalling £13,000.

Exclusions
No cash payments. Grants are not given for education, training experience, rental deposits, personal debt relief or hire

purchase. Medical services are not supported.

Applications

In writing to the correspondent with as much background information of family and reasons for request as possible. Applications should be submitted through social services. They are considered at any time.

Other information

Local charitable organisations are also supported (£6,900 in 2011).

Wirral

The Conroy Trust

£1,700

Correspondent: Tom Bates, 22 Waterford Road, Prenton, Wirral CH43 6UU (01516 522128)

Trustees: Beryl Lord; Lucy Millington; Elizabeth Cartwright; Maureen Preston; Revd Philip Venables.

CC Number: 210797

Eligibility

People in need who live in the parish of Bebington.

Types of grants

Bi-monthly payments to regular beneficiaries and one-off grants for special needs. Grants usually range from £50 to £300.

Annual grant total

About £3,500 a year. Grants are given to both individuals and local organisations.

Exclusions

No grants are made for educational purposes.

Applications

In writing to the correspondent directly by the individual.

The John Lloyd Corkhill Trust

£1,000

Correspondent: Michelle Jafrate, 5 Broadway, Greasby, Wirral, Merseyside CH49 2NG (01516 784428; email: jlct. wirral@tiscali.co.uk)

Trustees: Dr David Lawrence; Gavin Edward Price; Cllr Moira McLaughlin; Dr John Corless.

CC Number: 216371

Eligibility

People with lung conditions who live in the metropolitan borough of Wirral.

Types of grants

Mostly for equipment (e.g. nebulisers). Help is also given towards services and amenities, for example holidays and occasionally to buy domestic appliances such as fires, washing machines and so on.

Annual grant total

In 2009/10 the trust had an income of £3,800 and total expenditure of £1,000.

Applications

Clients are generally referred by their social worker or doctor and have a low income. Supporting medical evidence must be supplied. Applications are considered in June and December.

The Maud Beattie Murchie Charitable Trust

£13,000

Correspondent: Anthony Michael Bayliss, Duncan Sheard Glass, Castle Chambers, 43 Castle Street, Liverpool L2 9TL (01512 431209)

Trustees: Lynda Susan Mitchell; Jessica Innes Marvin; Francesca Innes Claire Murchie; Anthony Michael Bayliss.

CC Number: 265281

Eligibility

Retired members of Beattie stores who are in need and people in need who live on the Wirral.

Types of grants

One-off and recurrent grants according to need. Grants to organisations are mostly recurrent.

Annual grant total

In 2010/11 the trust had assets of £761,000 and an income of £27,000. Grants were made totalling £26,000 of which half was given to individuals and the remaining £13,000 to organisations.

Exclusions

No grants for educational purposes.

Applications

Applications should be made through Wirral Social Services. They are usually considered in June and December.

The West Kirby Charity

£13,500

Correspondent: Jane Boulton, 14 Surrey Drive, Wirral CH48 2HP (01516 254794)

Trustees: Dorothy Robinson; Cllr Geoffrey Christopher John Watt; Cllr David Elderton; Vicky Gawith; Revd Cheryl Joy Coverley; Alan Du Cros; Roger Bennett Brown; David Stevenson; Cllr Edwin Boult; Revd Buddy Owen.

CC Number: 218546

Eligibility

People in need who have lived in the old urban district of Hoylake (Caldy, Frankby, Greasby, Hoylake, Meols and West Kirby) for at least three years. Preference is given to older people and people who have a disability.

Types of grants

Pensions of about £20 a month. Christmas gifts and one-off grants are also made to non-elderly locals.

Annual grant total

In 2010 the trust had an income of £14,000 and a total expenditure of £15,500.

Applications

On a form available from the correspondent. Applications are usually considered quarterly.

Midlands

General

The Beacon Centre for the Blind

£10,000

Correspondent: Chief Executive, Beacon Centre for the Blind, Wolverhampton Road East, Wolverhampton WV4 6AZ (01902 886781; fax: 01902 886795; email: enquiries@beacon4blind.co.uk; website: www.beacon4blind.co.uk)

Trustees: Michael Beardsmore; Dr John Wright; George Bullock; Joan Quirke; Colin Banks; Richard Ennis; John Throneycroft; Simon Biggs; Sue Rawlings; Pauline Heffernan; Nick Price; Joe Ledwidge; James Fernihough.

CC Number: 216092

Eligibility

People who are registered blind or partially sighted and live in the metropolitan boroughs of Dudley (except Halesowen and Stourbridge), Sandwell and Wolverhampton, and part of the South Staffordshire District Council area.

Types of grants

One-off grants up to £250 towards socials and outings; holidays; and talking books and newspapers. Grants for specific items of equipment can be given to those who are visually impaired.

Annual grant total

In 2010/11 the charity had assets of £8.9 million, an income of £2.1 million and a total expenditure of £2.3 million. In previous years a small number of grants have been made to individuals.

Applications

In writing to the correspondent stating the degree of vision and age of the applicant, and their monthly income and expenditure. Applications can be submitted through a social worker or a school, and are considered throughout the year.

The Birmingham and Three Counties Trust for Nurses

£15,000

Correspondent: David Airston, 16 Haddon Croft, Halesowen B63 1JQ (01216 020389; email: ruthmadams_45@ msn.com)

Trustees: Ann Hirons; Clare Norton; Joy Hey; Joan McManus; Paul Hyde; Joan Smith; Joyce Mellors; Margaret Standly; Margaret Humpherson; Mary Nobles; Norah Warnaby; Margaret Emes; Jenny Edwards; Jeanette Griffiths.

CC Number: 217991

Eligibility

Nurses on any statutory register, who have practiced or practice in the city of Birmingham and the counties of Staffordshire, Warwickshire and Worcestershire.

Types of grants

One-off or recurrent grants according to need. Grants are given to meet the costs of heating, telephone bills, cordless phones for the infirm, household equipment, household repairs, car repairs, electric scooters, wheelchairs, medical equipment and personal expenses such as spectacles and clothing. Grants are also made for convalescent care, recuperative holidays and to clear debt.

Annual grant total

In 2010/11 the trust had an income of £8,000 and a total expenditure of £17,000.

Applications

On a form available from the correspondent. Applications can be submitted either directly by the individual or through a friend, relative or a social worker, Citizens Advice or other welfare agency. Details of financial status including income and expenditure, reasons for application, and health status where relevant should be included. Applications are considered throughout the year.

Applicants are visited by a trustee (where distance allows) for assessment. Supportive visiting continues where considered necessary.

The Charities of Susanna Cole and Others

£3,500

Correspondent: Peter Gallimore, Trustee, 19 Oak Tree House, 153 Oak Tree Lane, Bournville, Birmingham B30 1TU (01214 714064)

Trustees: Anne Ullathorne; Peter Gallimore; Michael Andrews; Stella Roberts; Betty Haglund; Tony Pegler; Elizabeth MacGregor; Anna Baker.

CC Number: 204531

Eligibility

Quakers in need who live in parts of Worcestershire and most of Warwickshire and are 'a member or attendee of one of the constituent meetings of the Warwickshire Monthly Meeting of the Society of Friends'. Preference is given to younger children, and retired people on an inadequate pension.

Types of grants

One-off and recurrent grants according to need. Help may be given with domestic running costs, rent or accommodation fees, convalescence, recreation and home help, and to those seeking education or re-training.

Annual grant total

In 2010 the charity had an income of £18,000 and a total expenditure of £7,000. Grants are made for welfare and educational purposes.

Applications

In writing to the correspondent via the overseer of the applicant's Quaker meeting. Applications should be received by early March and October for consideration later in the same months.

The J. I. Colvile Charitable Trust

£3,000

Correspondent: John Hankey, 4 Park Lane, Appleton, Abingdon, Oxfordshire OX13 5JT (01865 862668)

Trustees: Rosemary Pelham; Miss K. M. Colvile; Mr R. R. Colvile.

CC Number: 1067274

Eligibility

People in need who are resident in Gloucestershire, west Oxfordshire and south Warwickshire. Help is regularly given to ex-servicemen and their families via, for example, SSAFA.

Types of grants

One-off grants ranging from £250 to £500.

Annual grant total

Grants usually total around £3,000 per year.

Applications

In writing to the correspondent. Applications can be submitted directly by the individual or family member, or by an organisation such as Citizens Advice. They are considered as necessary.

Other information

Grants are also made to youth training projects.

Thomas Corbett's Charity

£500

Correspondent: Andrew G Duncan, Clerk, 16 The Tything, Worcester WR1 1HD (01905 731731)

Trustees: Richard Webb; Michael Brinton; Michael Thomas; Judith Anne Pearce; Richenda Rachel Wyatt.

CC Number: 202032

Eligibility

People in need who live in Worcestershire, Staffordshire and Birmingham.

Types of grants

One-off grants according to need.

Annual grant total

In 2010 the charity had assets of £621,000 and an income of £36,000. Grants by way of gift vouchers were given to residents totalling £520.

In addition two organisations were paid grants of £100 each.

Applications

In writing to the clerk directly by the individual.

Other information

The charity has stated that most of its income is used for the upkeep of the Wychbold almshouses and that, therefore, very few grants are made to individuals.

Baron Davenport's Charity

£408,000 (1,671 grants)

Correspondent: Marlene Keenan, Charity Administrator, Portman House, 5–7 Temple Row West, Birmingham B2 5NY (01212 368004; fax: 01212 332500; email: enquiries@ barondavenportscharity.org; website: www.barondavenportscharity.org)

Trustees: Rob Prichard; W. Colacicchi; Christopher Hordern; Sue Ayres; Philip Gough; Paul Dransfield.

CC Number: 217307

Eligibility

Widows, unmarried women and divorcees aged over 60 and in need; women and children abandoned by their partners; and people under 25 whose fathers are dead. Exceptions may be made for younger widows with limited income and school-age children living at home who are in financial need. Applicants must have lived in the West Midlands, Shropshire, Staffordshire, Warwickshire or Worcestershire area within a 60 mile radius of Birmingham town hall for at least five years. Applicants must have a net income of less than £170 per week and savings that do not exceed £10,000.

Types of grants

Recurrent grants, typically of £200 to £230, paid twice annually. In very special circumstances one-off grants of up to £250 are given for varying cases of need.

Annual grant total

In 2011 the charity had assets of over £27 million and an income of £1.1 million. Grants were made to 1,671 individuals totalling £408,000.

Exclusions

Applications will not be accepted from those in receipt of Low/High Rate Attendance Allowance; Middle/High rates of Disability Living Allowance or Mobility Allowance (or car allowance).

Applications

Except for emergency cases, applications should be made through local authority social services departments or recognised welfare agencies, although direct applications from individuals may also be considered.

Application forms are available from the secretary or may be downloaded from the website and should be submitted by 15 March or 15 September. Grants awarded are paid in June and November. Applications where prompt relief is needed should be addressed to the local Council of Voluntary Service, as listed under their separate entries.

Other information

The trust and CVS regard as fatherless those whose fathers are dead, and in some cases children abandoned by their fathers.

For emergency needs, see the separate entries in: Staffordshire, Warwickshire, Worcestershire, and West Midlands.

Grants are also made to organisations (£635,000 in 2011).

The W. E. Dunn Trust

£40,000 (263 grants)

Correspondent: Alan H Smith, Secretary, The Trust Office, 30 Bentley Heath Cottages, Tilehouse Green Lane, Knowle, Solihull B93 9EL (01564 773407)

Trustees: David Corney; C. P. King; Leita Smethurst; Jennifer Warbrick.

CC Number: 219418

Eligibility

People who are in need and live in the West Midlands, particularly Wolverhampton, Wednesbury, north Staffordshire and the surrounding area. Preference is given to people who are very old or very young, who the trust recognises as possibly being the least able to fund for themselves.

Types of grants

One-off grants ranging from £50 to £200.

Annual grant total

In 2010/11 the trust had assets of £4.2 million and an income of £137,000. Grants totalling £44,000 were distributed to individuals in the following areas:

Clothing and furniture	119	£16,000
Convalescence and holidays	14	£2,500
Domestic equipment	90	£15,000
Education	22	£4,000
Radio, TV and licences	15	£2,000
Social and welfare	25	£4,000

Exclusions

Grants are not made to settle or reduce debts already incurred.

Applications

Applications should be made in writing via a social worker, Citizens Advice or other welfare agency. The trustees meet on a regular basis to consider applications.

Other information

Grants are also made to organisations (£70,000 in 2010/11).

The Frimley Fuel Allotments Charity

£68,000 (219 grants)

Correspondent: Kim Murray, Hon. Secretary, St Martin's Church, 231 Upper College Ride, Camberley, Surrey GU15 4HE (01276 23958; email: ffa.office@googlemail.com; website: www.frimleyfuelallotments.org.uk)

Trustees: Revd Bruce Nicole; Bruce Mansell; Cllr Josephine Mary Hawkins; Mary Keys; Michael John Lyons; Cllr Paul Frederick Ilnicki; Bill Andrews; John Phillips; David Chesneau; Revd Scott Edwards; Craig Fennell; Frank Smithin; Stuart Parr; Revd Bob.

CC Number: 231036

Eligibility

People in need who live in the parish of Frimley. Priority is given to people who are older or who have a disability, and those who care for them.

Types of grants

One-off grants ranging from about £100 to £1,500 for a variety of needs.

Annual grant total

In 2011 the trust had assets of £1.7 million and an income of £130,000. Grants totalled £68,000 of which £47,000 was awarded as standard grants to individuals with a further £ £21,000 paid in heating grants.

Applications

On a form available from the secretary or a local Citizens Advice, Church or social services centre. Applications for the Christmas heating grants should be returned to the respective social service centre by mid-November and can be made directly by the individual. Applications for other grants can be made at any time and are considered on a regular basis. The charity has limited resources so accurate and complete data on the form is essential.

Other information

Grants are also made to local organisations (£30,000 in 2011).

The Fund for the Forgotten

See entry on page 469

Francis Butcher Gill's Charity

£13,500

Correspondent: Anna Chandler, Freeth Cartwright, Cumberland Court, 80 Mount Street, Nottingham NG1 6HH (01159 015562; fax: 01159 015500; email: anna.chandler@freethcartwright.co.uk)

Trustees: Jennifer Cursham; David Henderson Fice; Richard Bullock; Sir Andrew Buchanan; Peter David Courtney Allen; Brian R. Dunn; Richard A. Craven-Smith Milnes.

CC Number: 230722

Eligibility

Unmarried or widowed women aged over 50 in need, who are regular attendees of Protestant Christian worship, or who would be were they not prevented by bodily infirmity. Applicants must also be of good standing and live in Nottinghamshire, though those living in Derbyshire or Lincolnshire may also be considered.

Types of grants

Pensions of £350 per quarter are given to a fixed number of pensioners. One-off grants may also occasionally be available for items such as gas fires.

Annual grant total

In 2010/11 the charity had an income £16,000. Pensions totalled £13,500.

Applications

On a form available from the correspondent. Applications should be submitted either through a doctor or member of the clergy or directly by the individual supported by a reference from the one of the aforementioned. Applications can be submitted at any time for consideration in March and October, or at other times in emergency situations.

For pensions, applications will only be considered as a vacancy arises.

The Edmund Godson Charity

£6,000

Correspondent: Freya Villis, 30 Hemingford Road, Cambridge CB1 3BZ (email: fv221@cam.ac.uk)

Trustees: David John Ritchie; Revd John Lewis; Cllr Mary Mills; Carola Mary Barrington Morrison; Christopher Young; Freya Villis.

CC Number: 227463

Eligibility

People in need who wish to emigrate and who currently live in and around Woolwich, Shinfield and Spencers Wood near Reading, north east Herefordshire and Tenbury Wells in Worcestershire.

Types of grants

One-off grants according to need.

Annual grant total

In 2010/11 the charity had an income of £7,200 and a total expenditure of £9,300.

Applications

Directly by the individual on a form available from the correspondent. Details of the proposed destination, occupation, emigration eligibility and financial circumstances should be given.

Other information

The charity mainly makes grants to organisations.

Jordison and Hossell Animal Welfare Charity

£3,000

Correspondent: Sally Reid, 173 Tanworth Lane, Shirley, Solihull, West Midlands B90 4BZ (01217 454274)

Trustees: Lady Brook Susan; Drew Sumner; Irene Sumner; Sally Reid.

CC Number: 515352

Eligibility

People in the Midlands who are on low incomes and are in need of financial assistance in meeting vets' bills for their pets.

Types of grants

One-off grants of up to £500 towards vets' bills.

Annual grant total

In 2009/10 the charity had an income of £2,300 and a total expenditure of £3,200.

Exclusions

No grants for vets' bills for larger animals such as horses and farm animals.

Applications

In writing to the correspondent. Applications must be made by the vet in question or a third party such as Citizens Advice, rather than from the client. The charity does not deal with the client directly. Evidence that the beneficiary is on benefits is required.

Melton Mowbray Building Society Charitable Foundation

£5,000

Correspondent: Mr Martin John Reason, Leicester Road, Melton Mowbray LE13 0D3 (01664 414141; fax: 01664 414040; email: m.reason@mmbs.co.uk)

Trustees: Robert Anthony Brownlow; Kenrick Albert Saunders; Angela Wright; David Wood; Martin Reason; Karen Middleton; Keith Hallam.

CC Number: 1067348

Eligibility

Individuals in need who live within a 30 mile radius of Melton Mowbray.

Types of grants

One-off grants in the range of £100 and £250, for example to provide security and protection for older people.

Annual grant total

In 2010/11 the foundation had an income of £23,000 and total expenditure of £19,000.

Exclusions

No grants are made for circular appeals or for projects of a high capital nature.

Applications

In writing to the correspondent to be submitted either directly by the individual or a family member, through a third party such as a social worker or teacher, or through an organisation such as Citizens Advice or a school. Applications should include details of the cash value sought, the nature of the expense, the reason for application and the location of the applicant. Applications are considered at meetings held on a quarterly basis.

Other information

Grants may also be given to local organisations and community projects.

Thomas Monke's Charity

£750

Correspondent: C P Kitto, Steward, 5/7 Breadmarket Street, Lichfield, Staffordshire WS13 6LQ (01543 267995)

Trustees: Charles Wollaston; Dawn Roach; Josephine Beniston; Jean Angus; Sally Wollaston.

CC Number: 214783

Eligibility

Young individuals between the ages of 17 and 21 who live in Austrey in Warwickshire and Measham, Shenton and Whitwick in Leicestershire.

Types of grants

One-off and recurrent grants of £100 to £250 according to need.

Annual grant total

About £1,500 a year for educational and welfare purposes.

Exclusions

Expeditions and scholarships are not funded.

Applications

Application forms are available from the correspondent and should be submitted directly by the individual before the end of March, in time for the trustees' yearly meeting held in April.

The Newfield Charitable Trust

£25,000

Correspondent: D J Dumbleton, Clerk, Rotherham and Co. Solicitors, 8–9 The Quadrant, Coventry CV1 2EG (02476 227331; fax: 02476 221293; email: d.dumbleton@rotherham-solicitors.co.uk)

Trustees: E. Bresnen; R. Stanley; A. Parsons; Mrs H. Jones; Revd Canon J. Eardley; Mrs R. Bott; Mrs S. Walden.

CC Number: 221440

Eligibility

Girls and women (under 30) who are in need of care and assistance and live in Coventry or Leamington Spa.

Types of grants

'The relief of the physical, mental and moral needs of, and the promotion of the physical, social and educational training of' eligible people. Most grants are under £500 towards things such as clothing, electrical goods, holidays, travel expenses and furniture.

Annual grant total

In 2010/11 the trust had assets of £1.5 million and an income of £45,000. During the year, the trustees received a total of 155 applications, from which 154 applicants were awarded grants. Grants totalled just over £36,500 and were distributed as follows:

Educational	8	£3,200
Clothing	43	£8,000
General	103	£25,400

Exclusions

No grants for arrears or utility bills.

Applications

Write to the correspondent for an application form. Applications are accepted from individuals or third parties e.g. social services, Citizens Advice, school/college etc. A letter of support/reference from someone not a friend or relative of the applicant (i.e. school, social services etc.) is always required. Details of income/expenditure and personal circumstances should also be given.

Applications are considered eight times a year.

The Norton Foundation

£11,000

Correspondent: Clerk to the Trustees, PO Box 10282, Redditch, Worcestershire B97 9ZA (01527 544446; email: correspondent@nortonfoundation.org; website: www.nortonfoundation.org)

Trustees: Graham Suggett; Michael Bailey; Alan Bailey; Jane Gaynor; Parminder Singh Birdi; Richard Hurley; Sarah Henderson; Brian Lewis; Robert Meacham; Richard Perkins; Louise Sewell.

CC Number: 702638

Eligibility

Young people under 25 who live in Birmingham, Coventry or Warwickshire and are in need of care, rehabilitation or aid of any kind. Young people who have experienced abuse or neglect, or who are at risk of offending.

Types of grants

One-off grants of up to £500 are given towards clothing, household items and holidays.

Annual grant total

In 2010/11 the trust had assets of £4.2 million and an income of £137,000. Grants were made totalling £105,000, of which £14,000 was given in individual grants, £26,000 was awarded in discretionary grants and the remaining £65,000 was given to institutions. Grants to individuals were distributed as follows:

Clothing	15	£1,600
Education and training	25	£3,600
Household	72	£8,600

Applications

By a letter which should contain all the information required as detailed in the guidance notes for applicants. Guidance notes are available from the correspondent or the website. Applications must be submitted through a social worker, Citizens Advice, probation service, school or other welfare agency. They are considered quarterly.

The Pargeter and Wand Trust

£9,500

Correspondent: Marcus Fellows, BCOP, 40B Imperial Court, Kings Norton Business Centre, Pershore Road South, Birmingham B30 3ES (01214 597670; email: marcus.fellows@bcop.org.uk)

Trustees: Hazel Reynolds; Ruth Archer; David Mearman; Revd Simon Ramsay; Revd Dr Arthur Stewart; Marcus Fellows.

CC Number: 210725

Eligibility

Women who have never been married, are aged over 55 and live in their own homes. There is a preference for those living in the West Midlands area, but other areas of the country are considered.

Types of grants

Annuities of around £300 are paid quarterly and reviewed annually. One-off grants, usually in the range of £50 to £150, are also available.

Annual grant total

In 2010/11 the trust had an income of £13,000 and a total expenditure of £11,400. The trust usually has around £10,000 available each year for grants.

Applications

Applications should be made via Age UK.

The Pedmore Sporting Club Trust Fund

£12,000

Correspondent: The Secretary, Nicklin LLP, Church Court, Stourbridge Road, Halesowen B63 3TT (email: psclub@pedmorehouse.co.uk; website: www.pedmoresportingclub.co.uk)

Trustees: N. A. Hickman; R. Herman-Smith; J. M. Price; R. Williams; T. J. Hickman.

CC Number: 263907

Eligibility

People in need who live in the West Midlands.

Types of grants

One-off grants have included those for medical care equipment, travel to and from hospital, wheelchairs and IT equipment. Christmas and Easter parcels are also given.

Annual grant total

In 2011 the trust had assets of £299,000 and an income of £81,000. Grants were made totalling £12,000.

Applications

Applicants for the Easter food parcels should be recommended by a member of the sporting club. Other applications should be made in writing to the correspondent. The trustees meet four or five times a year.

Other information

Grants are also made to organisations (£51,000 in 2011).

The Persehouse Pensions Fund

£6,500

Correspondent: C S Wheatley, 12a Oakleigh Road, Stourbridge, West Midlands DY8 2JX (01384 379775)

Trustees: Catherine White; Thelma Justham; Mike Lloyd; Maryann Bettinson; Sally Mackison Purnell.

CC Number: 500660

Eligibility

Elderly or distressed people belonging to the upper or middle classes of society who were born in the counties of Staffordshire or Worcestershire, or people who have lived in either county for ten years or more.

Types of grants

Mainly pensions, but occasional one-off grants.

Annual grant total

In 2010/11 the trust had an income of £12,000 and a total expenditure of £7,200.

Applications

On a form available from the correspondent to be submitted directly by the individual.

The Roddam Charity

£1,800

Correspondent: Stuart Barber, Merewood, Springfields, Newport TF10 7EZ (01952 814628; email: bougheyroddamha@btinternet.com)

Trustees: Mrs S. Cleaves; Irene Evans; Jennifer Emery; Maj. J. Muir; Mrs S. Askin; Revd Steven Mitchell; Barry Pierce; Mrs E. C. Watson Todd; Caroline Worth.

CC Number: 213892

Eligibility

People in need who live in the TF10 postcode area who are sick, convalescent, disabled or infirm. The beneficial area includes the parishes of Newport, Chetwynd, Church Aston, Chetwynd Aston, Woodcote, Moreton, Sambrook, Tibberton, Edgmond and Lilleshall in Shropshire and Forton in Staffordshire.

Types of grants

One-off grants in the range of about £50 to £200. Grants are made to help with items, services or facilities that are not readily available from other sources and which will relieve the suffering or assist the recovery of individuals in poor health and people living with disabilities.

Annual grant total

Grants have averaged around £3,000 a year over the last number of years although the figure changes annually.

Exclusions

No grants for rates, taxes or other public funds.

Applications

On a form available from the correspondent to be submitted directly by the individual. Applications are usually considered quarterly.

The SF Group Charity
See entry on page 42

Richard Smedley's Charity

£5,000

Correspondent: M T E Ward Esq., Robinsons Solicitors Co., 21–22 Burns Street, Ilkeston, Derbyshire DE7 8AA (01159 324101; email: maurice.ward@robinsons-solicitors.co.uk)

Trustees: Joyce Brown; Stanley Wright; Brian Allsopp; Jack Geary; Paul Stephenson; John Wheatley; Thomas Hodson; Susan Clarke.

CC Number: 221211

Eligibility

People in need who live in the parishes of Breaston, Dale Abbey, Draycott with Church Wilne, Heanor, Hopwell, Ilkerton, Ockbrook and Risley (all in Derbyshire) and of Awsworth, Bilborough, Brinsley, Greasley and Strelley (all in Nottinghamshire).

Types of grants

One-off grants generally in the range of £50 to £350 are given towards items such as furniture, washing machines, mobility aids, clothing and carpets.

Annual grant total

Grants usually total about £5,000 a year.

Applications

On an application form available from the correspondent to be submitted either directly by the individual or through a social worker, Citizens Advice or other welfare agency. Applications can be submitted at any time and are usually considered quarterly.

Other information

Grants are also made to organisations.

The Snowball Trust

£15,000

Correspondent: Ian Smedley, The Barn, Wood End Lane, Fillongley, Coventry CV7 8DB (01676 542255)

Trustees: Elaine Hancox; Dr Alan Rhodes; Ian Smedley; Darren Parkin; Dominic Parker.

CC Number: 702860

Eligibility

Children and young people under 21 who are in poor health or who have a disability and live in Coventry and Warwickshire.

Types of grants

One-off grants mainly for medical equipment and disability aids. The charity's policy is, 'to grant sums of money for the provision of moveable equipment and other resources for qualifying individuals or organisations.'

Annual grant total

In 2010/11 the trust had an income of £14,500 and a total expenditure of £50,000. Previously, grants to individuals totalled £15,000.

Applications

On a form available from the correspondent: to be submitted either by the individual or through a third party such as a special school, social worker or other welfare agency. Applications should include a firm quote for the equipment to be supplied, a letter of support from the individual's school and/or a medical professional, and confirmation of the parents'/guardians' financial need.

Other information

The trust also makes grants to organisations.

The Edwin John Thompson Memorial Fund

£500

Correspondent: David Thompson, Trustee, Albrighton Hall, High Street, Albrighton, Wolverhampton WV7 3JQ (01902 372036)

Trustees: David Thompson; Mr C. E. Guinness; Henrietta Jane Greig; Peter Richard Swanson.

CC Number: 213690

Eligibility

People in need who live in the counties of Staffordshire, Worcestershire, Shropshire and Warwickshire.

Types of grants

One-off and recurrent grants according to need.

Annual grant total

Grants to individuals usually total around £500 a year.

Applications

In writing to the correspondent.

Other information

Grants are also made to organisations.

The Eric W. Vincent Trust Fund

£2,200 (25 grants)

Correspondent: Mrs Janet Stephen, Clerk, PO Box 6849, Stourbridge DY8 9EN (email: vttrust942@gmail.com)

Trustees: Dorothy Williams; Alan Richard Birch; Marianne Marta England; Stephen Canham; Tom Smith; John Claughton; Margaret John Harding; Marilyn Benjamin.

CC Number: 204843

Eligibility

People in need living within a 20 mile radius of Halesowen.

Types of grants

Grants of around £100 can be made for clothing, furniture, hospital travel expenses, equipment and holidays.

Annual grant total

In 2010/11 the trust had assets of £1.2 million and an income of £36,000. Grants were made to 25 individuals totalling £2,200.

Exclusions

The trust does not make loans or give grants for gap year projects, any educational purposes or to pay off debts.

Applications

Trustees normally meet bi-monthly. Applications should be in writing through a health professional, social worker, Citizens Advice or other welfare agency. Applications will not be considered if they are not made through a relevant third party. Details of financial circumstances must be included.

Other information

Small grants (£1,000 or less) are also made to organisations (£26,000 in 2010/11).

The Anthony and Gwendoline Wylde Memorial Charity

£2,000

Correspondent: D J Nightingale, Clerk, 3 Waterfront Business Park, Dudley Road, Brierley Hill, West Midlands DY5 1LX (0845 111 5050)

Trustees: Geoffrey Hill; Brian Edwards; Martyn Morgan; David Johnson; Dianna Jeffries; Olive Dukes; Ian Lowe; Patricia Gardener; Michael Evers.

CC Number: 700239

Eligibility

People in need with a preference for residents of Stourbridge (West Midlands) and Kinver (Staffordshire).

Types of grants

One-off grants in the range of £50 and £500.

Annual grant total

In 2010/11 the charity had assets of £882,000 and an income of £43,000. Grants were made totalling £37,500, of which £4,000 was given to individuals for educational and relief-in-need purposes. The remaining was given to organisations.

Exclusions

No grants are made towards bills or debts.

Applications

In writing to the correspondent. Applications can be submitted directly by the individual or a family member and are considered on an ongoing basis.

The Jonathan Young Memorial Trust

£15,000 (56 grants)

Correspondent: John Young, Trustee, 10 Huntingdon Drive, The Park, Nottingham NG7 1BW (01159 470493; email: info@jonathan-young-trust.co.uk; website: www.joanthan-young-trust.co.uk)

Trustees: Barbara Gregson; Margaret Willmot; Rod Beadles; Armorel Hilary Young; John Young.

CC Number: 1067619

Eligibility

People who are living with a disability and would benefit from access to computer technology. The trust operates primarily within the East Midlands (Nottinghamshire, Derbyshire, Leicestershire, Lincolnshire and South Yorkshire) but will occasionally consider applications from further afield. Grants are occasionally made to those who are disadvantaged by reasons other than disability.

Types of grants

Grants of £200 to £500 towards the cost of computer equipment.

Annual grant total

In 2011 the trust had an income of £11,000 and a total expenditure of £16,000. 56 grants were made totalling £15,000.

Exclusions

The trust does not make grants for general living expenses, course or college fees, disability aids such as wheelchairs or any non-electronic items.

Applications

In writing to the correspondent, either directly by the individual, carer or parent or through a welfare organisation such as social services or a Citizens Advice. Applications should include:

- Name, address, telephone number and age
- Background information
- The nature and extent of the disability
- Financial information – income/ expenditure and how much can be contributed towards the equipment
- Why a computer would be beneficial
- The specific equipment needed, including any software and a quotation if possible

For individuals applying directly, a supporting letter from a GP, social worker, teacher or similar should be included. Applications are considered in April and October.

Derbyshire

The Alfreton Welfare Trust

£1,500

Correspondent: Celia Johnson, Clerk, 30 South Street, Swanwick, Alfreton, Derbyshire DE55 1BZ (01773 609782)

Trustees: Colin Thornton; Agnes Burns; Revd Frank James C. Mercurio.

CC Number: 217114

Eligibility

People in need who live in the former urban district of Alfreton (i.e. the parishes of Alfreton, Ironville, Leabrooks, Somercotes and Swanwick).

Types of grants

Grants have included travel expenses to hospital; provision of necessary household items and installation costs; recuperative holidays; relief of sudden distress (such as theft of pension or purse, funeral costs, marital difficulties);

telephone installation; and outstanding bills. Support is also given to people who are disabled (including helping to buy wheelchairs and so on).

Annual grant total

The trust has an average income and expenditure of £2,000.

Exclusions

Grants are not given to organisations or for educational purposes.

Applications

In writing to the correspondent directly by the individual. Applications are considered throughout the year.

The Dronfield Relief-in-Need Charity

£1,000

Correspondent: Dr A N Bethell, Ramshaw Lodge, Crow Lane, Unstone, Dronfield, Derbyshire S18 4AL (01246 413276)

Trustees: Christine Smith; Frances Robinson; Dr Anthony Bethell; Jane Shute; Doug Oxspring; Sue O'Donnell; Angela Talford.

CC Number: 219888

Eligibility

People in need who live in the ecclesiastical parishes of Dronfield, Holmesfield, Unstone and West Handley.

Types of grants

One-off grants, up to a value of £100, towards household needs (such as washing machines), food, clothing, medical appliances (such as a nebulizer) and visitors' fares to and from hospital.

Annual grant total

This charity gives around £1,000 a year in grants for welfare purposes.

Exclusions

No support for rates, taxes and so on.

Applications

In writing to the correspondent though a social worker, doctor, member of the clergy of any denomination, a local councillor, Citizens Advice or other welfare agency. The applicants should ensure they are receiving all practical/ financial assistance they are entitled to from statutory sources.

Other information

Grants are also given to local organisations.

The Margaret Harrison Trust

£3,000

Correspondent: Alexandra Mastin, 5 The Avenue, Darley Dale, Matlock, Derbyshire DE4 2HT (01629 732931)

Trustees: Ian Duff; Revd Benedict Mark Crowther-Alwyn; Christopher David Gale; Alexandra Mastin; Revd Brian Smith.

CC Number: 234296

Eligibility

'Gentlewomen of good character' aged 50 or over who have lived within a 15-mile radius of St Giles Parish Church, Matlock for at least five years.

Types of grants

Small quarterly pensions.

Annual grant total

Grants usually total around £3,000 per year.

Applications

On a form available from the correspondent, although the trust is already spending all its income and will not be looking for applicants until interest rates rise.

The Sawley Charities

£2,300

Correspondent: Monica Boursnell, 35 Weston Crescent, Long Eaton, Nottingham NG10 3BS (01159 726727)

Trustees: William Camm; Keith Reedman; Graham Grammer; Monica Boursnell; Roland Hosker; Judith Kingscott.

CC Number: 241273

Eligibility

People over 60 years of age in need who have lived in the parishes of Sawley and Wilsthorpe in Derbyshire for at least six years. Normally only state pensioners are considered.

Types of grants

One-off cash grants, usually of around £15 each, towards heating costs.

Annual grant total

Grants usually total around £2,300 per year.

Applications

On an application form available from the correspondent. Applications can be submitted directly by the individual or family member and should be received by September for consideration in October/November.

Other information

Grants are also made to welfare organisations.

The Stanton Charitable Trust

£500

Correspondent: Clive Turner, Saint-Gobain PAM plc, Lows Lane, Stanton-by-Dale, Ilkeston DE7 4QU (01159 898012)

Trustees: Geoffrey Norton; Clive Turner; Phillip Burrows; Stewart Nicholas; George Bennett.

CC Number: 328727

Eligibility

People of any age or occupation who are in need, due for example to hardship, disability or sickness, and who live near Staveley Works in Chesterfield, Derbyshire, namely Staveley, Brimington, Barrowhill, Hollingwold and Inkersall.

Types of grants

One-off cash grants towards items, services or facilities.

Annual grant total

This trust has an annual income of around £2,000.

Applications

In writing either directly by the individual or a family member, or through an organisation such as Citizens Advice or a school. Applications should state the specific amount for a specific item.

Other information

Grants are also made to schools, churches, scouts, guides and local fundraising events.

Limited information is available as documents have never been filed with the Charity Commission.

The Wirksworth and District Trust Fund

£1,000

Correspondent: Dorothy Jill Hughes, Clerk, 8 Lady Flatts Road, Wirksworth, Matlock, Derbyshire DE4 4BQ (01629 822706)

Trustees: Albert Morley; Irene Ratcliff; Revd David Charles Truby; Jill Hughes; Elizabeth Bunting; Dick Parkin; Steve Maskrey; Stella Truby; Sue Mosley.

CC Number: 217842

Eligibility

People in need who live in the parishes of Alderwasley, Ashleyhay, Callow, Cromford, Hopton, Ible, Idridgehay and Alton, Middleton-by-Wirksworth and Wirksworth.

Types of grants

One-off cash grants of between £25 and £200.

Annual grant total

About £2,000 a year. Grants are given to both individuals and organisations.

Applications

In writing to the correspondent for consideration in March and November, although urgent needs can be considered at any time. Applications can be submitted either directly by the individual or through a social worker, Citizens Advice or other welfare agency.

Other information

The Wirksworth Charities are made up of 21 smaller charities, the funds from which are distributed as one sum.

The Woodthorpe Relief-in-Need Charity

£1,500

Correspondent: M Scott, Clerk, 8 Wigley Road, Inkersall, Chesterfield, Derbyshire S43 3ER (01246 474457)

Trustees: John Sedgwick; Keith Taylor Nobbs; Peter Norman; Tony Finley; Cllr Jim McManus; Cllr Dean Collins.

CC Number: 244192

Eligibility

People in need who live in the ancient parishes of Barlborough, Staveley and Unstone.

Types of grants

One-off grants, up to £750 for general purposes such as fuel, beds, washing machines, furnishings, mobility chairs and so on.

Annual grant total

The charity usually has an income of approximately £5,500 and gives around £1,500 in grants to individuals annually.

Applications

In writing to the correspondent.

Buxton

The Bingham Trust

£4,400

Correspondent: Roger Horne, Trustee, Blinder House, Flagg, Buxton, Derbyshire SK17 9QG (01298 83328; email: binghamtrust@aol.com; website: www.binghamtrust.org.uk)

Trustees: Dr Geoffrey Willis; Roger Horne; Alexandra Hurst.

CC Number: 287636

Eligibility

People in need, primarily those who live in Buxton. Most applicants from outside Buxton are rejected unless there is a Buxton connection.

Types of grants

One-off grants ranging from £200 to £1,500. Grants are made for a wide variety of needs, for example, to relieve poverty, to further education and for religious and community causes.

Annual grant total

In 2010/11 the trust had assets of £2.4 million and an income of £91,000. Grants to individuals for welfare and education totalled £8,800.

Exclusions

No grants are made for debts.

Applications

On a form available from the correspondent or to download from the website. Applications should include a supporting letter from a third party such as a social worker, Citizens Advice, doctor or minister. They are considered during the first two weeks of January, April, July and October and should be received before the end of the previous month.

Other information

The trust also makes grants to organisations (£79,000 in 2008/09).

Chesterfield

The Chesterfield General Charitable Fund

£6,000

Correspondent: Richard Lamb, Riversdale, Castle Street, Bakewell DE45 1DU (01246 221872; email: kpo12@talktalk.net)

Trustees: Michael A. Hadfield; Keith Pollard; Martin Thacker of Fetternear; John Brown; Richard Lamb; Revd Canon Michael Knight; David E. Windle; Linda Robbins; Simone Smith.

CC Number: 511375

Eligibility

People in need in the parliamentary constituency of Chesterfield.

Types of grants

One-off and recurrent grants ranging from £200 to £800.

Annual grant total

In 2010/11 the trust had an income of £11,000 and a total expenditure of £6,200.

Applications

In writing to the correspondent, directly by the individual. Applications are considered quarterly.

The Chesterfield Municipal Charities

£12,000

Correspondent: David Dolman, Shipton Halliwell and Co., 23 West Bars, Chesterfield, Derbyshire S40 1AB (01246 232140)

Trustees: Canon Michael Knight; Mr Falconer; Pat Maskrey.

CC Number: 217112

Eligibility

There are two charities, one for older and poor people who were born or live in Hasland; the other for respectable widows and older unmarried women who were born or live in Chesterfield.

Types of grants

One-off grants and regular payments of about £100 made twice a year.

Annual grant total

The Municipal Charities income has been gradually decreasing from around £19,000 in 2006 to just £2,500 in 2010, although total expenditure has held constant at around £14,000 per year.

Applications

In writing to the correspondent.

Other information

The existing beneficiaries have remained the same for a number of years, although the charity welcomes new applicants.

Clay Cross

The Eliza Ann Cresswell Memorial

£1,200

Correspondent: Dr Christine Fowler, Correspondent Trustee, Blue Dykes Surgery, Eldon Street, Clay Cross, Chesterfield, Derbyshire S45 9NR (01246 866771; fax: 01246 861058)

Trustees: Revd Charles Beresford; Dr Christine Fowler; Revd Jim Magee; Revd Jonathan Brook; Dr Tara George.

CC Number: 230282

Eligibility

People in any kind of need who live in the former urban district of Clay Cross (now the civil parish of Clay Cross), particularly needy families with young children.

Types of grants

Usually one-off grants in whole or part payment of a particular need for example heating costs, housing, debts, replacement of bedding and damaged furniture, removal costs, and holidays.

Annual grant total

The charity has an average annual expenditure of £1,500.

Exclusions

The trust does not give cash directly to applicants nor does it usually pay the full amount of a debt unless any repayment is beyond the individual's means.

Applications

In writing to the correspondent. A description of the person's financial position, the gaps in statutory provision, what contribution the applicant can make towards the need and what help can be given to prevent the need for future applications should be included. Applications are considered throughout the year. Grants are given on the recommendation of social workers, health visitors, probation officers, home nurses, doctors, clergy and welfare organisations (for example Citizens Advice), and are paid through these bodies.

Other information

The charity also makes grants to organisations.

Derby

The Derby City Charity

£500

Correspondent: Jacquelynne Dominiczak, Derby City Council, Constitutional Services, 5th Floor, Saxon House, Friary Street, Derby DE1 1AN (01332 643654)

Trustees: Finbar Sonny Richards; Michael Fuller; Raymond Baxter; Roy Webb; Martin Repton.

CC Number: 214902

Eligibility

People under 25 who live in the city of Derby and are in need.

Types of grants

One-off grants only according to need.

Annual grant total

In 2010/11 the charity had an income of £3,500 and an expenditure of £1,000. Grants are given for education and welfare.

Applications

On a form available from the correspondent on written request. Applications can be submitted either through a relevant third party such as a social worker, Citizens Advice or other welfare agency; or directly by the individual. The trustees meet at least twice a year to consider applications.

The Liversage Trust

£20,000

Correspondent: Yvonne Taylor, The Boardroom, 6b Liversage Almshouses, London Road, Derby DE1 2QW (01332 348155; fax: 01332 349674; email: yvonne.taylor@liversagetrust.org)

Trustee: Mrs S. Tarling.

CC Number: 216219

Eligibility

Older people in need who live in the city of Derby.

Types of grants

Cash grants for the relief of poverty, usually limited to a maximum of £150 although most grants are of between £30/£40 and £150. Grants can be made towards clothing, food or consumer durables.

Annual grant total

In 2010/11 the trust had assets of £14.9 million and an income of £1.7 million. Grants usually total around £20,000.

Applications

On a form available from the correspondent. Applications should be submitted through a recognised referral agency such as a social worker, Citizens Advice or doctor. They are considered throughout the year.

Other information

The trust's main concern is the management of almshouses and the care home, Liversage Court.

Glossop

The Mary Ellen Allen Charity

£6,000

Correspondent: Philip Sills, 1 Bowden Road, Glossop, Derbyshire SK13 7BD (01457 865685)

Trustees: Edward William Schofield; David Lomax; Jean Wharmy; Graham Oakley; John Dearn.

CC Number: 512661

Eligibility

People over 60 who are in need and live in the former borough of Glossop (as it was in 1947). There is a preference for those who have lived in the area for at least five years in total.

Types of grants

About 15 one-off grants a year in the range of £50 to £500.

Annual grant total

In 2010/11 the trust had an income of £5,000 and a total expenditure of £8,500.

Applications

In writing to the correspondent either through a social worker, Citizens Advice or other welfare agency, or directly by the individual. Applications can be submitted at any time for consideration in January, April, July and October.

Other information

The charity also makes grants to organisations.

Ilkeston

The Old Park Ward Old Age Pensioners Fund

£1,200

Correspondent: J Dack, 3 Knole Road, Nottingham NG8 2DB (01159 132118)

Trustees: Jean Thomas; Joan Ellson; Joan Ann Bagshaw; Violet Haupt; Alfred Baker; Malcolm Roughton.

CC Number: 201037

Eligibility

People over 65 who are in need and live in the Old Park ward of the former borough of Ilkeston.

Types of grants

One-off cash grants, usually at Christmas time.

Annual grant total

In 2010/11 the fund had an income of £17,000 and a total expenditure of £18,500. Grants were made totalling about £1,200.

Applications

In writing to the correspondent.

Other information

The majority of the fund's income is spent on providing recreational facilities and events such as dancing, bingo, a monthly Sunday lunch club and other outings.

Matlock

The Ernest Bailey Charity

£1,500

Correspondent: Brian Evans, Derbyshire Dales District Council, Town Hall, Bank Road, Matlock, Derbyshire DE4 3NN

(01629 761100; email: brian.evans@ derbyshiredales.gov.uk)

Trustee: Derbyshire Dales District Council.

CC Number: 518884

Eligibility

People who are sick, poor, elderly, in distress and in need and live in Matlock (this includes Bonsall, Darley Dale, South Darley, Tansley, Matlock Bath and Cromford).

Types of grants

Most applications have been from local groups, but individuals in need and those with educational needs are also supported. Each application is considered on its merits. Grants to individuals are one-off and usually to a maximum of £250.

Annual grant total

In 2009/10 the trust had an income of £16,000 and a total expenditure of £15,000. Around £1,500 is given in grants to individuals per year.

Applications

On a form available from the correspondent. Applications are considered in October and must be returned by the end of September. They can be submitted directly by the individual and/or can be supported by a relevant professional. Applications should include costings (total amount required, funds raised and funds promised). Previous beneficiaries may apply again, with account being taken of assistance given in the past.

Spondon

The Spondon Relief-in-Need Charity

£12,000

Correspondent: Richard J Pooles, Secretary and Treasurer, PO Box 5073, Spondon, Derby DE21 7ZJ (01332 669879; email: info@ spondonreliefinneedcharity.org; website: www.spondonreliefinneedcharity.org)

Trustees: Malcolm Stevens; Pauline Jennings; Peter Berry; Adrian Martin; Margaret Bools; Rosemary Archer; Susan Bown; Teresa Kokiet; Chris Poulter; Julian Hollywell; Catherine Leatherbarrow.

CC Number: 211317

Eligibility

People in need who live in the ancient township of Spondon.

Types of grants

One-off grants in kind up to the value of £500, including those towards electric

goods, white goods, clothing, furniture, disabled equipment, carpets, childcare and so on. Christmas goodwill gifts are also made.

Annual grant total

In 2011 welfare grants totalling £12,000 were made for the following purposes:

- Christmas goodwill: 39 grants totalling £2,300
- Furniture/bedding: four grants
- White goods: three grants
- Carpets: nine grants
- Others: nine grants

Exclusions

The charity does not contribute towards domestic debts and so on.

Applications

On a form available from the correspondent. Each form must be accompanied by a letter of support from a sponsor such as a doctor, health authority official, social worker, city councillor, clergyman, headteacher, school liaison officer, youth leader or probation officer. The sponsor must justify the applicant's need. The latter is particularly important. The applicant should provide as much information on the form as possible. It is better to ask for a visit by a trustee if possible.

The trustees meet four times a year and applications must be received by the end of January, April, July and October; grants are given one month later.

Other information

Grants are also made for educational purposes.

Hereford-shire

The Harley Charity (formerly The Honourable Miss Frances Harley Charity)

£4,000

Correspondent: Thomas Davies, Trustee, Elgar House, Holmer Road, Hereford HR4 9SF (01432 352222)

Trustees: Thomas Davies; Edward Harley; Susan Elizabeth Harley.

CC Number: 207072

Eligibility

(i) Church of England clergy and their widows/widowers who are in need and live primarily, but not exclusively, in the diocese of Hereford.
(ii) People who are blind, in need and are members of the Church of England.

Usually grants are given to those people living within the area defined above.

Types of grants

One-off grants, but individuals who receive a grant can reapply each year.

Annual grant total

In 2010/11 the trust had an income of £5,600 and a total expenditure of £4,700.

Applications

In writing to the correspondent.

Other information

When funds allow, the charity also supports Hereford Cathedral and other local churches and charities.

The Hereford Corn Exchange Fund

£1,000

Correspondent: E P Edwards, Secretary, 7 Yew Tree Gardens, Kings Acre, Hereford HR4 0TH (01432 263040)

Trustees: Sir John Cotterrell Bart; Jonathan Bengough; Sir Thomas Dunne.

CC Number: 218570

Eligibility

People in Herefordshire who have been employed at one farm for over 30 years.

Types of grants

Grants of between £100 and £500 for the advancement of agriculture in the county of Herefordshire.

Annual grant total

In 2010/11 the fund had an income of £3,800 and a total expenditure of £3,900. The fund gives about £1,000 to individuals and £1,000 to agricultural organisations each year.

Applications

In writing to the correspondent in March/April for consideration in May.

The Hereford Society for Aiding the Industrious

£1,000

Correspondent: Sally Robertson, Secretary, 18 Venns Close, Bath Street, Hereford HR1 2HH (01432 274014 – Thursdays only; email: hsaialms@ talktalkbusiness.net)

Trustees: C. George; G. Kent; M. Bricknell; Mrs J. O'Donnell; Mrs M. E. Phillips; M. Jones; R. Miller; R. Weston; T. Nellist.

CC Number: 212220

Eligibility

People in need who live in Herefordshire (particularly Hereford City) and are trying to better themselves by their own efforts.

The early history of the society involved aid to the 'industrious poor' and those who would not make an effort to help themselves were excluded. This is reflected today by priority being given to individuals who are trying to obtain training to get back to work, often as mature students.

Grants will be considered when a person is required to fund a gap between formal education and training for a career. The society also considers applications from girl guides and boy scouts for assistance with the cost of camp, but need must be proved in all cases.

Types of grants

Grants or interest free loans, of £50 to £1,000, according to need.

Annual grant total

In 2010/11 the trust had assets of £949,000 and an income of £96,000. Grants to individuals totalled £5,500. Previously £1,000 was spent on Christmas gifts for elderly residents.

Applications

On a form available from the correspondent. Applicants are then interviewed by the secretary. Trustees usually meet on the third Monday of every month.

Other information

Grants are also made to organisations.

The Herefordshire Community Foundation

£2,500

Correspondent: The Secretary, The Fred Bulmer Centre, Wall Street, Hereford, Herefordshire HR4 9HP (01432 272550; email: info@ herefordshirecommunityfoundation.org)

Trustees: Miiss S. Evans; Mrs C. Forrester; Ms W. Gilmour; Mr R. Hunter; Mr N. Hone; Mr W. Lindesay; Ms B. Parkinson.

CC Number: 1094935

Eligibility

People in need who live in Herefordshire.

Types of grants

One-off and recurrent grants according to need.

Annual grant total

In 2010/11 the foundation had assets of £1.2 million and an income of £334,000. Approximately £5,000 is given each year to individuals.

Applications

In writing to the correspondent including standard information such as contact details, what the grant is to be used for and why it is needed.

Other information

Grants are also made to organisations.

The Rathbone Moral Aid Charity

£5,000

Correspondent: Carol Thompson, Clerk, Herefordshire Community Council, PO Box 181, Hereford HR2 9YN (01981 250899)

Trustees: Donald Smith; Jackie Boys; Revd Michael Tavinor; Andrea Lewis; Bridget Ann Jones; Judith Ann Stevens.

CC Number: 222697

Eligibility

People who live in Herefordshire who are under 25 and in need of rehabilitation, due to experiencing addiction, abuse, neglect, sex work or offending.

Types of grants

One-off and recurrent grants according to need.

Annual grant total

In 2010 the trust had an income of £7,800 and a total expenditure of £6,900.

Exclusions

No grants are given for nursery fees.

Applications

In writing to the correspondent. Individual applications are considered throughout the year. All individual applications must be supported by a welfare agency or doctor, social worker, teacher or other professional.

Other information

Grants are also made to organisations.

Hereford

All Saints Relief-in-Need Charity

£4,000

Correspondent: Douglas Harding, Trustee, 6 St Ethelbert Street, Hereford HR1 2NR (01432 267821)

Trustees: Mrs R. Ford; Mr D. Harding; Mrs P. J. Morris; Mrs J. Whitcombe; Mrs A. Brown; Dr R. Richmond; Mrs P. Thomas.

CC Number: 244527

Eligibility

Individuals in need who live in the city of Hereford, with a preference for those resident in the ancient parish of All Saints.

Types of grants

In previous years the charity has preferred to provide items rather than giving cash grants. However, one-off grants are available to those in need.

Annual grant total

In 2010/11 the charity had an income of £6,700 and a total expenditure of £5,200. No further information was available.

Applications

On a form available from the correspondent.

The Hereford Municipal Charities

£14,000

Correspondent: The Trustees, 147 St Owen Street, Hereford HR1 2JR (01432 354002; email: herefordmunicipal@btconnect.com)

Trustees: Derek Duffett; Polly Andrews; Aubrey Oliver; Alan Blake; John Lewis-Davies; Kenneth Rayner; Elizabeth Evans; Jennifer Davies; Jennifer Holmes; Jim Kenyon.

CC Number: 218738

Eligibility

People in need who live in the city of Hereford.

Types of grants

One-off grants of amounts up to £200. Grants are given to help with household equipment, clothes, educational equipment, emergencies and so on.

Annual grant total

In 2011 the charity had assets of £3.7 million and an income of £257,000. Grants to individuals for welfare totalled £14,000.

Exclusions

No grants towards debts or nursery fees.

Applications

On a form available from the correspondent to be submitted directly by the individual or through a relevant third party. Applications are considered monthly.

Other information

Most of the charity's expenditure is allocated to the running costs of its almshouses.

Middleton-on-the-Hill

The Middleton-on-the-Hill Parish Charity

£1,000

Correspondent: Clare Halls, Secretary, Highlands, Leysters, Leominster, Herefordshire HR6 0HP (01568 750257; email: leystershalls@aol.com)

CC Number: 527146

Eligibility

People living in the parish of Middleton-on-the-Hill.

Types of grants

One-off and recurrent grants for both welfare and educational purposes.

Annual grant total

About £2,000 a year is given in grants.

Applications

In writing to the correspondent.

Norton Canon

The Norton Canon Parochial Charities

£5,000

Correspondent: Mary Gittins, Ivy Cottage, Norton Canon, Hereford HR4 7BQ (01544 318984)

Trustees: David Palliser; Howard Jones; Nigel Lewis; Robert Loxston; Mairion Jones; Robert King.

CC Number: 218560

Eligibility

People in need who live in the parish of Norton Canon.

Types of grants

One-off and recurrent grants according to need.

Annual grant total

Grants total around £10,000 a year and are given for educational and welfare purposes.

Applications

In writing to the correspondent at any time.

Leicestershire and Rutland

The Ashby-de-la-Zouch Relief-in-Sickness Fund

£600

Correspondent: Leanne Cooper, Crane and Walton, 30 South Street, Ashby-de-la-Zouch, Leicestershire LE65 1BT (01530 414111; fax: 01530 417022; email: leannecooper@craneandwalton.co.uk)

Trustees: John Martin Crane; Margaret Holdich-Monk; Dr John Martin Vaughan; Revd Graham Heath; Janet Onions.

CC Number: 508621

Eligibility

People in need who live in Ashby-de-la-Zouch and Blackfordby.

Types of grants

One-off grants in the range of £50 to £60 for things such as hospital expenses, electrical goods, convalescence, clothing, holidays, travel expenses, medical equipment, furniture, disabled equipment and help in the home.

Annual grant total

Grants total, on average, around £600 each year.

Applications

In writing to the correspondent at any time directly from the individual, or through a social worker, Citizens Advice or other welfare agency. Anybody who thinks they know someone who needs help is welcome to submit an application. It is useful to know whether any other source of help has been approached. Applications are considered at all times.

William Clayton Barnes Trust

£2,500

Correspondent: John Thornton, The Old Rectory, Main Road, Wyfordby, Melton Mowbray, Leicestershire LE14 4RY (01664 564437)

Trustees: John Thornton; Derek Stanley Cragg; Richard Winters; Neil Pidgeon.

CC Number: 500877

Eligibility

People in need who are sick and infirm and live in Melton Mowbray, Eye Kettleby or Great Dalby and have lived there for three years.

Types of grants

One-off grants for a range of needs, including wheelchairs, stairlifts (purchase and rental), household equipment for special needs, food and travel to hospital.

Annual grant total

The trust has an average grant expenditure of around £2,100.

Applications

The trust welcomes an initial telephone call. Applications should be in writing to the correspondent either directly by the individual or through a doctor, church leader, social worker, Citizens Advice or other welfare agency. They are considered all year round.

The John Heggs Bates' Charity for Convalescents

£6,500

Correspondent: Barbara Amos, 1 Mill Lane, Leicester LE2 7HU (01162 046620; email: barbara.amos@stwcharity.co.uk)

Trustees: Christopher Russell Hilton; Hugh Stevenson; John Maxwell Waite; Mary Elizabeth Bass; Mr M. G. Hearth; William James Howard; Christopher John Sturmey; Simon Peter Astill; Gordon Albert Upton Squires; David Alan Hope; James Robert Sellicks; Anthony Oliver Norman; Stephen John Riddington; David Crawford Howard; James Milton; Peter Jonathan Doleman; Bhiku Hindocha.

CC Number: 218060

Eligibility

'Necessitous convalescents' and their carers who reside in Leicester, Leicestershire and Rutland.

Types of grants

One-off grants of £100 to £600 for convalescence breaks.

Annual grant total

Typically around £10,000 a year, however, both income and total expenditure have fallen in the past number of years.

Applications

On a form available from: Leicester Charity Link, 20a Millstone Lane, Leicester LE1 5JN. Applications should be submitted through a social worker, Citizens Advice, doctor or church and are considered throughout the year.

The Brooke Charity

£3,000

Correspondent: Barbara J Clemence, Old Rectory Farm, Main Street, Brooke, Oakham, Leicestershire LE15 8DE (01572 770558)

Trustees: Barbara Jane Clemence; Robert Lionel Eayrs; Terence Michael Greer; Tracy Hull; Dr William Theodore Lamb; Derek Malcolm Harrington.

CC Number: 221729

Eligibility

People in need who live in the parishes of Brooke, Oakham, Braunston, Ridlington and Morcott with priority given to the sick, elderly and children.

Types of grants

One-off grants to relieve financial difficulty, usually in the range of £50 to £250.

Annual grant total

In 2010/11 the charity had an income of £5,600 and a total expenditure of £3,200.

Applications

In writing to the correspondent. Applications can be submitted directly by the individual or through a social worker, Citizens Advice or other welfare agency. They are considered at any time.

Other information

The charity also provides support to organisations.

The Elizabeth Clarke Relief-in-Need Fund and The Wigston Relief-in-Need Fund

£1,500

Correspondent: Debbie Watson, Oadby and Wigston Borough Council, Council Offices, Station Road, Wigston, Leicestershire LE18 2DR (01162 572680)

Trustees: Both: Helen Loydall; Barbara Dearing; Gillian Standley; Joy Lydia Heskins; Elizabeth Clarke only: Julie Slatford. Wigston only: Janice Broughton; Revd Layton Richard Curtis; Marion Kathleen Daetwyler; Shirley Anne Spence.

CC Number: 255015/217952

Eligibility

People in need who live in the urban district of Wigston.

Types of grants

One-off grants towards general relief-in-need, including clothing, safety alarms, special chairs, wheelchairs, orthopaedic footwear, travel costs for medical treatment, bedding, spectacles and so on.

Annual grant total

In 2011 the two funds gave approximately £3,100 in grants to individuals and organisations.

Applications

In writing to the correspondent, accompanied by a supporting letter from a social worker or other welfare agency if possible.

Other information

These two trusts work closely together, and often large grants are paid from both funds. However, grants from the Elizabeth Clarke Relief-in-Need Fund can only be given to those who live in the All Saints, Central, Westfield and Wolstan's wards of the urban district of Wigston.

Coalville and District Relief in Sickness Fund

£700

Correspondent: Sue Clarke, 6 Meadow Lane, Coalville, Leicestershire LE67 4DL (01530 834992)

Trustees: Nancy Baxter; Sue Clarke; Vera May Smith; Jeff Holmes; Mike Quinn; Stuart Johnson; Liza Webb; Robert Hickling; Anita Mullins.

CC Number: 512986

Eligibility

People in need of medical equipment not provided by the NHS who live in Coalville and district.

Types of grants

One-off grants in the range of £100 to £1,000 towards, for example, medical needs, special mattresses, gas fires, washing machines, reconditioned computers and home alterations.

Annual grant total

In 2010/11 the trust had an income of £1,700 and a total expenditure of £1,500.

Applications

In writing to the correspondent to be submitted directly by the individual. Applications are considered at quarterly intervals.

Other information

The trust gives grants to both individuals and organisations.

Leicester ARC (also known as Leicester and County Convalescent Homes Society)

£700 (2 grants)

Correspondent: J A S Pooley, 22 St George's Way, Leicester LE1 1SH

(01162 620617; fax: 01162 621323; email: enquiries@arcleicester.org; website: www.arcleicester.org)

Trustees: Sonia Bray; Mary Smith; Gillian Anne Aires; Jeffrey William Dean; Joan Pamela Archer; John Albert Sydney Pooley; Peter Saunders.

CC Number: 1016951

Eligibility

Existing contributors (see below) and people in need who are ill, disabled or receiving medical care and live in Leicester, Leicestershire and Rutland.

Types of grants

Generally small grants to assist with medical needs with the aim of achieving a better quality of life, whether it be the purchase or hire of a piece of equipment, or a period of 'quality' time away. Consideration will be given to both short and long-term medically-related needs.

Annual grant total

In 2010 two grants were made totalling £700 to cover medical requirements for individuals in need.

It is possible that this amount will increase in future years, as the 2010 accounts state: 'With the need for convalescence falling over recent years the Society is providing more grants to cover medical requirements for individuals in need…The charity, along with convalescence, is developing itself-as a grant providing charity both for contributors and for individuals in need.'

Applications

On a form available from the correspondent. Applications must be returned with supporting evidence from a doctor/occupational therapist. In the case of powered/manual wheelchairs or other medical equipment – no application is considered without an assessment from an occupational therapist or physiotherapist as to the best type of chair, make, model, price and adaptations (if any).

Other information

The organisation operates a scheme in which people contribute towards, via pay roll or annual subscription, the costs of any future convalescent needs that may be required. See the ARC website for further details.

The Leicester Charity Link

£348,000 (2,709 grants)

Correspondent: James Munton, Director of Operations, 20a Millstone Lane, Leicester, Leicestershire LE1 5JN (01162 222200; fax: 01162 222201; email: info@charity-link.org; website: www.charity-link.org)

Trustees: Caroline Wessel; Catherine Mary Boulton; Rodney John Hudson; Anthony Henry Jarvis; Clive Smith; Ruth Margaret Ingman; Veronica Tordimah.

CC Number: 1078271

Eligibility

People in need who live in the city of Leicester and the vicinity, which includes the whole of Leicestershire and Rutland.

Types of grants

One-off grants and occasionally recurrent grants or pensions. The society makes payments from its own funds, administers funds on behalf of other charities and puts potential beneficiaries into contact with funds and charities which may be able to help. A very wide range of grants are considered from small immediate payments, for example, for food, to larger payments of, for example, £6,500 for a special computer for a person with disabilities.

Goods and services are received by the charity and delivered directly to applicants.

Annual grant total

In 2010/11 the charity held assets of £407,000 and had an income of £663,000. Grants to individuals totalled £348,000.

In addition to grants paid directly from the charity's funds they secured a further £354,000 on behalf of individuals and organisations from various donors.

Applications

The charity's website notes: 'We use a network of local organisations that are in the community working with individuals and families in need. Using organisations already in place keeps our overheads to a minimum, increases the efficiency of our services and ensures that we get the help to those who need it when they need it most.'

Other information

The organisation also makes grants to organisations – £750 to Bostik Charitable Trust in 2010.

The Leicester Freemen's Estate

£8,700 (17 grants)

Correspondent: Mrs Lynda Bramley, Estate Office, 32 Freemen's Holt, Old Church Street, Aylestone, Leicester LE2 8NH (01162 834017; fax: 01162 834017; email: leicester.freemen@talktalkbusiness.net; website: www.leicester-freemen.com)

Trustees: Andrew Chawner; Maurice Freer; Maurice Hill; Michael Kellett; Paul Ross; Robert Staines; Roger John Porter; Wayne Manship; Peter Bates; Brian Mudford; William Stanley Hargrave; Susan Cave; Barry George Daniell; David Chettle; Jane Bell; Lynn Allyson Roffee; Jane Maria Wildbore.

CC Number: 244732

Eligibility

Needy freemen of Leicester and their widows who are elderly or infirm.

Types of grants

One-off cash grants, recurrent grants/pensions and loans are available.

Annual grant total

In 2011 the trust had assets of £4.8 million and an income of £210,000. Grants were made to four freemen and thirteen widows through monthly payments and a Christmas bonus which totalled £8,700.

Applications

On a form available from the correspondent and including proof of status as a freeman/widow of a freeman. Applications can be submitted directly by the individual and are considered monthly throughout the year.

Other information

The trust also provides accommodation for needy freemen and their widows. Applications should be made to the above address.

The Leicestershire Coal Industry Welfare Trust Fund

£7,000

Correspondent: Peter Smith, Trustee, Miners Offices Unit 12, Springboard Centre, 18 Mantle Lane, Coalville, Leicestershire LE67 3DW (01530 832085; email: leicesternum@ukinbox.com)

Trustees: Mr Howe; Peter Smith; Mrs Smith; George Dixon.

CC Number: 1006985

Eligibility

Miners and their dependents working in the British coal mining industry aged over 16, who have not taken up other full-time work.

Types of grants

Grants have been given towards holidays, special needs assistance, house repairs, house conversions and televisions.

Annual grant total

In 2011 the trust had assets of £365,000 and gave grants to individuals totalling £13,000.

Applications

In writing to the correspondent, including details of the individual's mining connection, proof of their residence in Leicestershire and dependence on the mineworker (in the case of children). Trustees hold meetings to discuss applications throughout the year.

Other information

Grants are also given to organisations.

The Leicestershire County Nursing Association

£2,200 (2 grants)

Correspondent: Edward Cufflin, Brewin Dolphin, Permanent House, 31 Horsefair Street, Leicester LE1 5BU (01162 420700)

Trustees: John Trevor Oakland; Caroline Wessel; Georgina Maltby; Jennifer Wood; Richard Henry Bloor; Jayne Beverley Peacock Pochin; David Wood; David Christopher Burrows; Sally Illesley; Sarah Creswell-Black.

CC Number: 216594

Eligibility

Retired district nurses and people who are sick and in need, who live in Leicestershire or Rutland (excluding the city of Leicester). Priority is given to retired district nurses.

Types of grants

One-off grants up to £3,000 for any need. Recent grants have been given towards hospital costs, bedding and convalescence.

Annual grant total

In 2010/11 the trust had assets of £1.3 million and an income of £51,000. Grants were made to retired nurses totalling £2,200.

Applications

In writing to the correspondent, directly by the individual in the case of retired district nurses or through Leicester Charity Link in other cases. Applications are considered in January and October.

Other information

The trust also makes grants to organisations (£43,000 in 2010/11).

The Loughborough Welfare Trusts

£21,000

Correspondent: Mrs Lesley Cutler, Bird Wilford and Sale Solicitors, 20 Churchgate, Loughborough

LE11 1UD (01509 232611; email: loughweltrsts@fsmail.net)

Trustees: Elizabeth Harrison; Mavis Mason; Cllr Jane Hunt; Cllr Albert Dodd; Ranjit Jalota; John Fox-Russell; Richard Minfie; Cllr Pauline Ranson; Dennis Jolley; Ivy Strachan; Cllr Joseph Tormey; Kathleen Jackson; Lindsey Henshall; Dermot Breen; Cllr Ron Jukes; Revd Hedley Cousin.

CC Number: 214654

Eligibility

People in need who live in Loughborough and Hathern.

Types of grants

One-off and recurrent grants are given to people on low income for decoration costs, second-hand fridges, holidays, cookers and so on. Grants are also made towards clothing for primary schoolchildren aged under 11.

Annual grant total

In 2011 the trust had assets of £581,000 and an income of £42,000. Grants were made totalling £17,000, which included £19,000 relief in need grants and £2,800 in relief in sickness grants.

Applications

In writing to the correspondent for consideration in January, March, May, July, September or November.

Other information

This trust administers Edgar Corah Charity, John Storer Education Foundation, The Reg Burton Fund, Loughborough Adult Schools, Herrick Charities, and The Loughborough Community Chest.

The Sir Andrew Martin Trust for Young People

£15,000

Correspondent: Trust Administrator, Walkers Charnwood Bakery, 200 Madeline Road, Beaumont Leys, Leicester LE4 1EX (001162 340033; website: www.sirandrewmartintrust.org)

Trustees: David Knowles; John Aldridge; Terry Higgins; Hon Lady Brooks; Robert Bruce Collins; Alec Jeffrey; David Smith; Liverpool Charity and Voluntary Services.

CC Number: 1042358

Eligibility

Young people in need living in the Leicestershire and Rutland areas.

Types of grants

One-off and recurrent.

Annual grant total

In 2011/12 the trust held assets of £690,000 and had an income of £43,000.

Grants totalled £26,000 of which £15,000 was paid in grants to individuals.

Applications

In writing to the correspondent.

Other information

Grants are also made to organisations.

The Rosehill Trust

£6,000

Correspondent: Jim Munton, c/o Leicester Charity Link, 20a Millstone Lane, Leicester LE1 5JN (01162 222200; email: info@charity-link.org; website: www.charity-link.org)

Trustees: Rod Hudson; Ann Brennan; Rosemary Joan Freer; Fergal O'Rorke; Dr Robert Kevin Andrew Feltham; Peter Charles Osborne; Barry Garner.

CC Number: 1000860

Eligibility

Young people and children 'who are delinquent, deprived, neglected or in need of care' in Leicestershire or Rutland.

Types of grants

One-off grants according to need. No more than one grant in any two year period, except in exceptional circumstances.

Annual grant total

In 2010/11 the trust had an income of £11,000 and total expenditure of £14,000.

Applications

On a form available from Leicester Charity Link website.

Other information

Leicester Charity Link, the administrator of this fund, provides a wide range of support and advice to people in need, for example through directing them to suitable funding bodies.

The Thomas Stanley Shipman Charitable Trust

£41,500

Correspondent: Andrew York, 6 Magnolia Close, Leicester LE2 8PS (01162 835345; email: andrew_york@sky.com)

Trustees: Mr E. Watts; Mrs J. Cartwright; Mr M. Newby; Mr H. Stevenson.

CC Number: 200789

Eligibility

People in need who live in the city and county of Leicester.

Types of grants

One-off and recurrent grants ranging from between £500 to £5,000 for living expenses, garden alterations and gifts at Christmas.

Annual grant total

In 2010/11 the charity had assets of £1.1 million and an income of £45,000. Grants were made totalling £45,000, of which £41,500 was given to individuals and £3,500 to organisations.

Applications

In writing to the correspondent either directly by the individual or via a relevant third party such as a social worker, Citizens Advice or other welfare agency, or through Leicester Charity Link. Applications should be submitted in mid-October and mid-April for consideration in November and June.

Other information

The trust does not usually provide educational grants due to lack of resources, and in light of its other objectives.

Barwell

Poor's Platt (Barwell)

£7,000

Correspondent: Jim Munton, Clerk to the trustees, 20A Millstone Lane, Leicester LE1 5JN (01162 222200; website: barwell.leicestershireparishcouncils.org/ parishcouncilgrantstoindividuals.html)

Trustees: Andre Wheeler; David Alan Stanborough; David Harry Bendell; Eileen Hemsley; Revd Philip Watson; Gillian Brown; Matthew Hulbert.

CC Number: 503580

Eligibility

People in need in the ancient parish of Barwell.

Types of grants

One-off grants of between £50 and £500 according to need.

Annual grant total

In 2011 the trust had an income of £22,000 and a total expenditure of £16,000. Grants are made to both individuals and organisations.

Applications

On an application available from the Barwell parish council website or from Leicester Charity link. Applications are considered quarterly in March, June, September and December with application deadlines being the 15th of the preceding month. Only one grant may be awarded in any 12 month period.

Cossington

Babington's Charity

£7,500

Correspondent: The Trustees, 14 Main Street, Cossington, Leicester, Leicestershire LE7 4UU (01509 812271)

Trustees: John Gregory; Helen McCague; Rachel Cutts; Gary Drew; Dean Hopkinson; Louise Turnbull.

CC Number: 220069

Eligibility

People in need in the parish of Cossington.

Types of grants

One-off and recurrent grants according to need.

Annual grant total

In 2010 the trust had assets of £452,000, an income of £34,000 and a total expenditure of £31,000. Grants totalled £19,000, of which £15,000 was given to students and individuals.

Applications

In writing to the correspondent.

Great Glen

Great Glen Relief in Need Charity

£1,000

Correspondent: Major Gerald Hincks, Trustee, 19 Naseby Way, Great Glen, Leicester LE8 9GS (01162 593155)

Trustees: Maj Gerald William Hincks; Mary Ireland; Alan Selway; Frazier Gilbert; Andrew Duerden.

CC Number: 231977

Eligibility

People in need (especially older people) who live in the parish of Great Glen and have been living there for a number of years.

Types of grants

One-off grants according to need. Older people receive grants in the form of vouchers at Christmas, at a rate of £15 per individual and £30 per couple.

Annual grant total

Grants usually total around £1,000.

Applications

In writing to the correspondent. Applications are considered twice a year, usually in November and April.

Other information

In recent years the charity has also made grants to a local church project and to young people in the parish undertaking voluntary work abroad.

Groby

Thomas Herbert Smith's Trust Fund

£1,000

Correspondent: A R York, 6 Magnolia Close, Leicester LE2 8PS (01162 835345; email: andrew_york@sky.com)

Trustees: Jamie Craig; Martyn Allison; Peter Griffin; Martin Cartwright; Ken Rushby.

CC Number: 701694

Eligibility

People who live in the parish of Groby in Leicestershire.

Types of grants

One-off and recurrent grants ranging from £100 to £500.

Annual grant total

In 2010/11 the fund had an income of £14,000 and a total expenditure of £28,000. Grants are made to organisations and individuals.

Applications

On a form available from the correspondent, for consideration throughout the year. Applications can be submitted either directly by the individual, or through a social worker, Citizens Advice or other third party.

Illston

Illston Town Land Charity

£6,000

Correspondent: J F Tillotson, Warwick House, 5 Barnards Way, Kibworth Harcourt, Leicester LE8 0RS (01162 792524)

Trustees: Mr M. J. Radcliffe; Mr R. C. G. Clowes; Mr M. J. Brankin-Frisby; Mr R. C. Hillar; Mrs S. J. Hercock; Kathleen Rose Moss.

CC Number: 246616

Eligibility

People in need who live in the town of Illston in Leicestershire.

Types of grants

Grants towards the costs of council tax charges.

Annual grant total

In 2010/11 the charity had an income of £6,200 and a total expenditure of £6,300.

Applications

In writing to the correspondent.

Keyham

Keyham Relief in Need Charity

£10,000

Correspondent: D B Witcomb, Tanglewood, Snows Lane, Leicester, Leicestershire LE7 9JS (01162 595663)

Trustees: Brian Atkin; John Letts; Richard Windle; David Brian Witcomb; Margaret Isobel Hughes; Carole Johnson.

CC Number: 215753

Eligibility

People who live in the parish of Keyham (Leicestershire) and are in need. Though, applications from people who do not live in the area but have strong connections to residents in Keyham have previously been considered.

Types of grants

One-off grants according to need.

Annual grant total

In 2010 the charity had an income of £13,800 and a total expenditure of £27,000. Grants usually total around £10,000 each year.

Applications

In writing to the correspondent, to be submitted directly by the individual. If the applicant does not live in Keyham, information about their connection with residents should be provided with the application.

Leicester

The Leicester Aid-in-Sickness Fund

£12,000

Correspondent: M K Dunkley, Clerk, Harvey Ingram Owston, 20 New Walk, Leicester LE1 6TX (01162 545454; email: mark.dunkley@harveyingram.com)

Trustees: Edward Guy Cufflin; Margaret Jane Stewart; Angela R. Stray; Des Cloake; Dr Rosemary S. Shannon; Edgar Watts; Simon Barrington William Edwards; Simon M. Gravett.

CC Number: 219785

Eligibility

People who are in poor health and financial need and live in the city of Leicester.

Types of grants

One-off grants, generally ranging from £20 to £125.

Annual grant total

Grants usually average around £12,000 each year.

Applications

In writing to the correspondent. Applications are usually considered quarterly.

The Leicester Indigent Old Age Society

£6,000

Correspondent: Jim Munton, 20a Millstone Lane, Leicester LE1 5JN (01162 222200; fax: 01162 222201; email: info@charity-link.org; website: www.charity-link.org/leicester-indigent-old-age)

Trustees: Caroline Mary Wessel; Rodney John Hudson; Clive Edmund Smith; Anthony Henry Jarvis; Ruth Margaret Ingman; Veronica Tordimah; Catherine Mary Boulton.

CC Number: 208476

Eligibility

People aged 65 or over who are in need and live in the city of Leicester. Note the following statement from the trust's website: 'Due to pressure on funds help is only given once every two years unless there are exceptional circumstances.'

Types of grants

Pensions of £80 a year paid in quarterly instalments.

Annual grant total

In 2010/11 the trust had an income of £5,600 and a total expenditure of £6,200.

Applications

Applications should be made though Leicester Charity Link using their application form which can be found on their website.

Other information

The trust also makes grants for coach trips and outings for older people living in Leicester.

The Parish Piece Charity

£7,000

Correspondent: Revd Canon Barry Naylor, St Martins House, 7 Peacock Lane, Leicester LE1 5PZ (email: stephen.franklin1946@btinternet.com)

Trustees: Revd Canon Barry Naylor; Janet Margaret Bass; Margaret Gillespie; Raymond Leslie Procter.

CC Number: 215775

Eligibility

People in need who live in the parish of St Margaret in Leicester. Priority is usually given to older people and people with disabilities.

Types of grants

One-off grants and small pensions. Recent grants have been given for heating and electrical appliances.

Annual grant total

Grants usually total around £7,000 a year.

Applications

In writing to the correspondent or via Leicester Charity Link using their standard application form, available from the website.

Other information

The charity also gives grants to organisations.

St Margaret's Charity

£3,500

Correspondent: Revd Canon Barry Naylor, St Martins House, 7 Peacock Lane, Leicester LE1 5PZ (email: stephen.franklin1946@btinternet.com)

Trustees: Revd Canon Barry Naylor; Janet Margaret Bass; Margaret Gillespie; Raymond Leslie Procter.

CC Number: 234626

Eligibility

People in need who live in the city of Leicester.

Types of grants

One-off grants, usually ranging from £25 to £100.

Annual grant total

In 2010/11 the charity had an income of £5,100 and a total expenditure of £7,300.

Applications

In writing to the correspondent or via the Leicester Charity Link website.

Other information

The charity also makes grants to local organisations.

Sir Edward Wood's Bequest Fund For Gentlewomen

£400

Correspondent: J A Norris, 63 Carisbrooke Road, Leicester LE2 3PF (01162 704223)

Trustee: James Andrew Norris.

CC Number: 220606

Eligibility

Women who are 55 years old or over, are either unmarried or widows, who have lived in the area administered by

Leicester City Council for at least ten years, and who are members of a Protestant Non-conformist church.

Types of grants
Pensions only of £400 a year, paid quarterly.

Annual grant total
In 2010/11 the fund had an income of £2,700 and a total expenditure of £400.

Applications
On a form available from the correspondent either directly by the individual or through a third party. A reference from a church minister is also needed. There are only a limited number of pensions available and applications can only be considered when a vacancy arises.

Market Harborough

Market Harborough and the Bowdens Charity

£41,000 (258 grants)

Correspondent: James G Jacobs, Steward, Godfrey Payton and Co., 149 St Mary's Road, Market Harborough, Leicester LE16 7DZ (01858 462467; fax: 01858 431898; email: admin@mhbcharity.co.uk; website: www. mhbcharity.co.uk)

Trustees: Janice Hefford; Ian Wells; Mark Stamp; Adrian Trotter; George Stamp; John Clare; Tim Banks; Joan Williams; Paul Edward Beardsmore; Alan Walker; Janet Roberts; David Battersby; Dr Julie Jones; Lennie Rhodes; Guy R. D. Hartopp.

CC Number: 1041958

Eligibility
People in need who have lived in the former urban council district area of Market Harborough for at least six months. 'The Charity prefers prevention to palliatives. It wishes to foster self-help and the participation of those intended to benefit; enable less advantaged people to be independent, gain useful skills and overcome handicaps; and encourage volunteer involvement.'

Only one application per household may be considered in a 12 month period.

Types of grants
Grants are one-off and typically under £1,000.

Annual grant total
In 2011 the charity had assets of £15 million and an income of £584,000. Grants were made to 85 individuals totalling £28,000. A further £13,000 was given in Christmas donations to 273 children.

Applications
On a form available from the correspondent or to download from the website. Applications can be submitted either directly by the individual or via a relevant third party such as a social worker, Citizens Advice or other welfare agency. If applications are not completed by a third party they should be supported by one. Potential applicants are welcome to contact the correspondent directly for further guidance.

Other information
Grants are also given to local organisations (£289,000 in 2011).

Market Overton

Market Overton Charity

£0

Correspondent: M Crowther, Trustee, 6 The Limes, Market Overton, Oakham LE15 7PX (01572 767779)

Trustees: Michael Crowther; Alan Lane.

CC Number: 242932

Eligibility
People in need who live in the parish of Market Overton.

Types of grants
One-off grants of up to £250 for those in need, typically for help towards replacement domestic appliances, but also help towards education needs e.g. school educational visits.

Annual grant total
In 2010 the charity had an income of about £400. Since 2008 the total expenditure has been zero.

Applications
In writing to the correspondent. Applications can be submitted directly by the individual or through a social worker, Citizens Advice, Church or other welfare agency. They are considered at any time.

Markfield

Jane Avery Charity – Markfield

£1,000

Correspondent: Revd Simon Nicholls, The Rectory, 3a The Nook, Markfield, Leicestershire LE67 9WE (01530 242844)

Trustees: Roy L. Browning; Mrs S. M. Browning; Dr Tom Hailstone; Revd Simon Nicholls; Jacqui Williams.

CC Number: 231958

Eligibility
People in need who live in the ancient parish of Markfield.

Types of grants
Normally one-off grants of £25 to £300. Grants have included those towards holiday costs, nursery school fees, a wheelchair and house repairs.

Annual grant total
In 2010 the trust had an income of £1,000 and a total expenditure of nearly £2,000.

Exclusions
There are no grants available for educational purposes.

Applications
In writing to the correspondent. Applications can be submitted directly by the individual or through a social worker, Citizens Advice, other welfare agency, or through a third party such as a doctor, minister, neighbour or relative. They can be considered at any time.

Mountsorrel

The Mountsorrel Relief-in-Need Charity

£67,000 (178 grants)

Correspondent: Paul Blakemore, Educational fund secretary, KDB Accountants and Consultants Ltd, 21 Hollytree Close, Hoton, Loughborough LE12 5SE (01509 889369; website: mountsorrelunitedcharities.co.uk)

CC Number: 217615

Eligibility
People in need who live in the parish of Mountsorrel.

Types of grants
One-off grants towards electrical household goods, garden maintenance, decorating costs, carpets/flooring, Charnwood Piper Lifelines, mobility equipment, child care expenses, hospital travel expenses and so on.

Annual grant total
In 2010 the charity considered 199 applications and made 181 grants. Grants to individuals totalled £67,000 with a further £37,000 paid in grants to three organisations.

Applications
To apply, contact Anni Reid, Benefit Secretary at 3 Heron Close, Mountsorrel, Loughborough LE12 7FH (Tel: 01162 375132 or 07534 604337), who will visit the applicant in their home and help them to complete the application form.

Other information

This charity is closely linked to the Mountsorrel United Charities (1027652).

Oadby

The Oadby Educational Foundation

£0

Correspondent: Rodney Waterfield, 2 Silverton Road, Oadby, Leicester LE2 4NN (01162 714507)

Trustees: Mrs Gore; Robert Borthwick; Gillian Austen; Kay Relf; Michael Rusk; Michael Thornton; Paul Webster; Donald Smith; Rodney Waterfield.

CC Number: 528000

Eligibility

People in need in the parish of Oadby only.

Types of grants

One-off and recurrent grants in the range of £50 and £200.

Annual grant total

In 2011 the foundation had assets of £1 million and an income of £46,000. £16,000 was given in educational grants and no grants for welfare were made during the year.

Applications

In writing to the correspondent, to be submitted either through a social worker, Citizens Advice or other welfare agency, or directly by the individual. They are considered in March, June and October.

Other information

Grants are also made to organisations.

Queniborough

Alex Neale Charity

£2,500

Correspondent: Maurice Kirk, 6 Ervin Way, Queniborough, Leicester LE7 3TT (01162 606851)

Trustee: D. Taylor.

CC Number: 260247

Eligibility

Older people in need who live in the parish of Queniborough.

Types of grants

Grants towards gas and electricity bills.

Annual grant total

Grants have averaged around £2,500 over the past three years.

Applications

The trustees publicise the grants, usually every two years, in The Queniborough Gazette. An application form is then available from the correspondent. The trust may ask for copies of fuel bills for the two years prior to application, and then a grant would be made towards the costs of these bills.

Quorn

The Quorn Town Lands Charity

£4,200

Correspondent: Geoffrey Gibson, Clerk, 2 Wallis Close, Thurcaston, Leicester LE7 7JS (01162 350946; fax: 01162 350946)

Trustees: John Hutchinson; Ian Newcombe; David Slater; Mrs C. Gilliver; Michael Bird; Paul Matthews; Mrs P. J. Kinch; Mr D. C. Cawdell.

CC Number: 216703

Eligibility

People in need who live in the parish of Quorn.

Types of grants

One-off and recurrent grants in the range of £50 to £250. Grants given include those for hospital expenses, convalescence, living costs, household bills, food, travel expenses and help in the home.

Annual grant total

In 2010/11 the trust had an income of £9,000 and a total expenditure of £4,600.

Applications

In writing to the correspondent. Applications should be submitted directly by the individual or through a relevant third party. They are considered quarterly.

Other information

This charity consists of three different funds: Quorn Town Lands Charity, Quorn Aid in Sickness Fund and Quorn Education Fund.

Rutland

The Rutland Dispensary

£2,000

Correspondent: Fred Bellingall, 8 Holyrood Close, Oakham, Leicestershire LE15 6SF (01572 723480; email: fredbellingall@aol.com)

Trustees: Angela Humphreys; Peter Light; Alfred Strickland; Revd Brian Nicholls; William Murray; Lindsay Henshaw-Dann.

CC Number: 230188

Eligibility

People who are poor, old or sick and live in Rutland.

Types of grants

One-off and recurrent grants ranging from £100 to £250.

Annual grant total

About £2,000.

Applications

In writing to the correspondent including details of any medical conditions and the general circumstances.

The Rutland Trust

£4,000

Correspondent: Richard Adams, Clerk, 35 Trent Road, Oakham, Rutland LE15 6HE (01572 756706; email: adams@apair.wanadoo.co.uk)

Trustees: Alistair Haywood; Frank Hinch; Elizabeth Bingley; Colonel James Weir.

CC Number: 517175

Eligibility

People who are disabled and live in Rutland and are in need.

Types of grants

One-off and recurrent grants ranging between £50 and £400, to buy equipment.

Annual grant total

In 2011 the trust had an income of £17,000 and a total expenditure of £14,000.

Applications

An initial telephone call is recommended.

Other information

Grants are also made for educational purposes and to organisations.

Smisby

The Smisby Parochial Charity

£1,000

Correspondent: Mrs S Heap, Clerk, Cedar Lawns, Forties Lane, Smisby, Ashby-De-La-Zouch, Leicestershire LE65 2SN (01530 414179)

Trustees: Barbara Ball; Jeffrey Barnes; Peter Heap; Andrew Parnham.

CC Number: 515251

Eligibility

People in need who live in Smisby.

Types of grants

Christmas hampers to older people.

Annual grant total

About £1,500, mostly for welfare purposes.

Applications

In writing to the correspondent. Applications can be submitted either directly by the individual or a relevant third party, or through a social worker, Citizens Advice or other welfare agency. They can be considered at any time.

Syston

The H. A. Taylor Fund

£7,000

Correspondent: James Munton, LCOS, 20a Millstone Lane, Leicester LE1 5JN (01162 222200; fax: 01162 222201; email: info@charity-link.org; website: www. charity-link.org)

SC Number: SC019308

Eligibility

People in need who have been in resident in the parish of Syston for at least one year.

Types of grants

One-off grants ranging from £50 to £1,000 towards, for example, travel costs, furniture, clothing, fuel, household repairs, medical treatment, books and course fees, mobility aids and telephone and television expenses.

Annual grant total

In 2010/11 the fund had an income of £24,000 and a total expenditure of £18,500. Previously grants to individuals have totalled around £7,000.

Exclusions

Repeat applications can only be made every two years unless there are exceptional circumstances.

Applications

Application forms are available from Syston and District Volunteer Centre, Syston Health Centre and Syston Library or can be downloaded from the website. They can be submitted at any time either through a third party or directly by the individual and are considered every two months.

Other information

Grants are also made to local organisations.

Wymeswold

The Wymeswold Parochial Charities

£4,000

Correspondent: The Trustees, 94 Brook Street, Wymeswold, Loughborough LE12 6TU (01509 880538)

Trustees: Sandra Brown; Nicholas Shaw; Mr C. Collington; Mr J. Mills.

CC Number: 213241

Eligibility

People in need who have lived in Wymeswold for the last two years.

Types of grants

Winter gifts to senior citizens, widows and widowers. One-off grants are also given to people who are ill.

Annual grant total

Grants total about £4,000 a year for educational and welfare purposes.

Applications

In writing to the correspondent at any time.

Lincolnshire

The Addlethorpe Parochial Charity

£3,000

Correspondent: Sara Marshall, Beck Cottage, Welton-Le-Marsh, Spilsby, Lincolnshire PE23 5TA (01754 890377; email: mrsh225@aol.com)

Trustees: Mrs B. Barker; Angela Ann Clift; Mrs D. L. Shrive; G. C. Wilson; J. G. Cragg; J. W. V. Leeman; Revd Malcolm France; Mr B. Short.

CC Number: 251412

Eligibility

People in need who live in the parish of Addlethorpe, or who previously lived in Addlethorpe and now live in an adjoining parish. Applicants must be either living on a low income, with limited savings or investments of less than £10,000, or have a disability or illness that renders them unable to work.

Types of grants

Most grants are in the form of solid fuel or electricity/gas cheques. One-off grants are given towards funeral expenses, household repairs and other necessities. Grants have also been given for hospital or doctor's visits. Grants of £60 are available, and may be given up to three times during the year.

Annual grant total

The trust usually has both and income and a total expenditure between £3,000 – £4,000, all of which is given in grants to individuals.

Applications

In writing to the correspondent to be submitted either directly by the individual or a family member, through a third party such as a social worker, or through an organisation such as Citizens Advice or other welfare agency. Applicants must state that they are living on a reduced income and that savings/investments are below £10,000. Applications are considered on an ongoing basis.

The Bishop of Lincoln's Discretionary Fund

£11,000

Correspondent: Revd Michael Silley, Bishop's House, Eastgate, Lincoln LN2 1QQ (01522 534701)

Trustee: Revd Michael Silley.

CC Number: 1022582

Eligibility

Ministers of the Church of England who live and work in the Diocese of Lincoln.

Types of grants

One-off grants of £25 to £450 according to need. Grants are usually to assist sick clergy and their families and for holiday grants.

Annual grant total

On average the fund makes grants totalling around £12,000 a year.

Applications

In writing by the individual or one of the other local bishops to the Bishop of Lincoln. Applications are considered throughout the year.

Boston and District Sick Poor Fund

£1,100

Correspondent: Susan M Ganley, Trustee, 65 Manor Gardens, Boston PE21 6JJ (01205 368977)

Trustees: Sue Kirk; Dr Richard Kime Allday; Mary Elizabeth Stanley; Eirwen Thompson; Susan Margaret Ganley; Ann Woods; John Scott Longton; Patricia Ann Lowther; Ray Sharpe.

CC Number: 500743

Eligibility

People in need through low income or sickness who live in Boston and the surrounding district.

Types of grants

One-off grants according to need.

Annual grant total

In 2011 the trust had an income of £2,400 and a total expenditure of £1,200.

Applications

In writing to the correspondent.

Michael Cornish Charitable Trust

£0

Correspondent: Richard L J Vigar, Trustee, 15 Newland, Lincoln LN1 1XG (01522 531341)

Trustees: Michael John Cornish; R. L. J. Vigar; Susan Margaret Cornish.

CC Number: 1107890

Eligibility

Children and young people who are in need with a preference those who live in Lincolnshire.

Types of grants

One-off and recurrent grants according to need.

Annual grant total

In 2011 the trust had assets of £13.2 million and an income of £145,000. No grants were made to individuals during the year.

Applications

In writing to the correspondent.

Other information

The trust predominantly makes grants to organisations but support for individuals is considered in exceptional circumstances.

The Charity of John Dawber

£13,000

Correspondent: Andrew and Co. Solicitors, St Swithins Square, 1 Flavian Road, Lincoln LN2 1HB (01522 512123; email: helen.newson@andrew-solicitors. co.uk)

Trustees: Tony Brogden; Denis Frank Clarke; John Barry Jackson; Peter Denby; Julia Welch.

CC Number: 216471

Eligibility

People in need who live in the city of Lincoln and the parish of Bracebridge.

Types of grants

Christmas grocery vouchers and quarterly payments.

Annual grant total

In 2010/11 the charity had assets of £1.3 million and an income of £40,000. During the year, charitable expenditure totalled £13,000, which went to 12 annuities and 883 recipients of Christmas vouchers, of which 613 were redeemed.

Applications

In writing to the correspondent. There are no deadlines for applications.

Other information

The trust also makes grants to organisations that benefit people living in the beneficial area.

The Farmers' Benevolent Institution

£3,000

Correspondent: J D Andrew, c/o Duncan and Toplis, 3 Castlegate, Grantham, Lincolnshire NG31 6SF (01476 591200; fax: 01476 591222; email: info@grantham.duntop.co.uk)

Trustees: John Thomas Lord; John Graham Kerr; Peter Hornbuckle; John Bennett Weston; Richard Eric Johnson; John Anthony Fisher; Richard Skelton; Graham Wade; James Knight; Jonathon William Ireland.

CC Number: 216042

Eligibility

People living within a 15-mile radius of Grantham who have 'been owners or occupiers of land, but who from losses or other untoward circumstances have become destitute'. Applicants must be over 60 if they have been a subscriber of the fund for ten years or more. Otherwise they should be over 65.

Types of grants

Annual payments of around £150 and a supplementary payment at Christmas.

Annual grant total

Grants usually total about £3,000 each year.

Applications

In writing to the correspondent.

The Gainsborough Dispensary Charity

£8,500

Correspondent: Bernard Stonehouse, Clerk, 15 Chestnut Avenue, Gainsborough, Lincolnshire DN21 1EX (01427 613067)

Trustees: Anne Sandall; Bernard Ernest Stonehouse; Jonathan David Swatton; Joan Howitt; Elizabeth Brockbank.

CC Number: 250376

Eligibility

People in need who live in Gainsborough and Morton.

Types of grants

One-off grants, usually up to about £300. Recent grants have been given for furniture, domestic appliances, holidays (where there is a medical need) and clothing.

Annual grant total

In 2010 the charity had an income of £8,200 and a total expenditure of £8,700.

Applications

In writing to the correspondent through a social worker, Citizens Advice or other welfare agency or through a third party such as a community nurse or a minister of religion.

Hunstone's Charity

£16,000

Correspondent: Tony Bradley, 58 Eastwood Road, Boston, Lincolnshire PE21 0PH (01205 364175)

Trustees: Charles Geoffrey Wright; Revd Kenneth Targett; William James Atkin; Samuel James Cooper.

CC Number: 214570

Eligibility

Gentlemen in need who live in Lincolnshire with preference for 'Decayed gentlemen of the family of Edward Hunstone or of the several families of the Gedneys or of Robert Smith or of the Woodliffes and decayed gentlemen living in the county of Lincoln'. Particular mention is also made of retired clergymen, members of HM Forces, farmers, farm labourers or anyone connected with land, and people with disabilities.

Types of grants

Recipients receive £250 per year, paid in two instalments of £125 in April and October. The assistance will be given as long as the trustees consider necessary or until the death of the recipient.

Annual grant total

In 2010 the charity had an income of £21,000 and a total expenditure of £18,000.

Exclusions

Grants are not given to women.

Applications

On a form available from the correspondent. Applications should be submitted either through a social worker, Citizens Advice or other welfare agency, or directly by the individual. They are considered in May each year and should be received by 30 April; urgent applications can be considered at other times. Two references are required with each application.

The Kitchings General Charity

£3,900

Correspondent: J Smith, Secretary, 42 Abbey Road, Bardney, Lincoln LN3 5XA (01526 398505)

Trustees: M. Sankey; Maurice Bellwood; Barry Percival; Geoffrey Pacey; Richard Muxlow; Robert Armstrong; Marjorie Cash; Elizabeth Franklin.

CC Number: 219957

Eligibility

People in need who live in the parish of Bardney (covers Stainfield, Apley, Tupholme and Bucknall).

Types of grants

One-off grants to relieve hardship or distress e.g. holidays/respite care for disabled people (mostly at a special home at Sandringham), specialised nursing equipment including wheelchairs, funeral expenses and household essential such as carpets, flooring and bedding. Grants are in the range of £200 and £500 but can be up to £2,000.

Annual grant total

In 2011 the trust had an income of £43,000. Widows pensions totalled £1,100 and four relief in need grants were also made totalling £2,800

Applications

In writing to the correspondent directly by the individual, only basic details are required. Applications are considered in May, October and January.

Other information

The charity also gives grants to local schools and organisations, and to individuals for education.

The Lincoln General Dispensary Fund

£7,000

Correspondent: M Bonass, Durrus, Scothern Lane, Dunholme, Lincoln LN2 3QP (01673 860660; fax: 01673 861701)

Trustees: Yvonne Bodger; Joyce Mary Walton; John Thomas; Pat Parker; Marigold Hodgkinson; Canon Edward Burnley Barlow; Alison Short; Les Smith;

Pat Middleton; Russell Pond; Victoria Cohen.

CC Number: 220159

Eligibility

People who are in poor health, convalescent or who have disabilities and live within the ten mile radius of the Stonebow (Lincoln).

Types of grants

One-off grants up to about £250 to alleviate suffering or aid recovery. Recent grants have been given for orthopaedic beds, alarm systems and recuperative holidays.

Annual grant total

In 2010 the fund had an income of £13,100 and a total expenditure of £15,400.

Exclusions

No grants are given for building adaptations, debts already incurred or anything that could be provided by public funds.

Applications

On a form available from the correspondent: to be submitted through a recognised social or medical agency. Applications are considered throughout the year.

Other information

Grants are also given to local organisations.

Lincolnshire Community Foundation

Correspondent: Sue Fortune, Grants Manager, 4 Mill House, Moneys Yard, Carre Street, Sleaford, Lincolnshire NG34 7TW (01529 305825; email: lincolnshirecf@btconnect.com; website: www.lincolnshirecf.co.uk)

Trustees: Charles Richard Ferens; Stephen Cousins; David Close; Jean Burton; Margaret Serna; Bernadette Jones, Dr Cheryl Berry; Jane Hiles; Paul Scott; Lizzie Milligan-Manby.

CC Number: 1092328

Eligibility

Generally, residents of Lincoln who are in need. However, different funds have different eligibility criteria attached. See types of grant section.

Types of grants

Health and Wellbeing Fund: grants of up to £500 for residents of Horncastle and surrounding district of East Lindsey who are sick, convalescent or disabled and in financial need.

Be aware that like other community foundations schemes can open and close at very short notice. Check the website before applying.

Annual grant total

No financial information was available on previous grantmaking, however, the Health and Wellbeing Fund is expected to distribute around £18,000 to individuals and community groups each year.

Applications

On an application form available to download from the website.

Lincolnshire Police Charitable Fund

£47,000

Correspondent: Mrs Cilla Smith, Lincolnshire Police Welfare Department, 19 Sixfield Close, Lincoln LN6 0EJ (01522 805757; email: charitable.fund@lincs.pnn.police.uk)

Trustees: Jennifer Ann Nicholson; Peter Thomas Justin Davies; Cilla Smith; Richard Crompton; Vanessa Mawer; Paul Joseph Diggins; Neil Rhodes; Stuart Hamilton; Judith Kent; Maria Staniland; Susan McEachran; Anthony Miller.

CC Number: 500682

Eligibility

People in need who are present or former employees of Lincolnshire Police Authority, and their dependents. Former employees of other Police Authorities who have retired and now live in Lincolnshire may also qualify for assistance.

Types of grants

One-off grants according to need.

Annual grant total

In 2010/11 the trust had assets of £160,000 and an income of £39,000. Grants were made totalling £47,000 and were distributed as follows:

Medical, travel and expenses	£24,000
General cases	£13,000
Death grants	£4,800
Loans converted to grants	£3,400
Christmas gifts	£1,200
Fruit, flowers and donations	£900
Comforts fund	£60

Applications

On a form available from the Welfare Officer. Applications can be submitted directly by the individual or through a social worker, Citizens Advice or other welfare agency.

Other information

The fund also makes grants to organisations (£1,000 in 2010/11).

The Tyler Charity for the Poor

£1,200

Correspondent: Mrs E M Bradley, 22 Market Place, Gainsborough, Lincolnshire DN21 2BZ (01427 010761)

Trustees: Peter John Blagg; Derrick Hill; Hilary Churchman; Matthew James Gleadell; Alan Clapham.

CC Number: 217594

Eligibility
People in need who live in the parishes of Morton and Thornock.

Types of grants
One-off and recurrent grants according to need.

Annual grant total
Grants totalled around £1,200.

Applications
In writing to the correspondent.

The Willingham and District Relief-in-Sickness Charity

£4,000

Correspondent: Mrs J C Spencer, Secretary, 4 Church Road, Upton, Gainsborough, Lincolnshire DN21 5NS (01427 838385)

Trustees: Marion Garner; Susan Rockall; Dr Kathryn Fickling; Rosemary Winter; Stewart Sleight.

CC Number: 512180

Eligibility
People in need who live in the parishes of Corringham, Heapham, Kexby, Springthorpe, Upton and Willingham.

Types of grants
One-off and recurrent grants according to need, such as for one-off items or respite care. Priority is usually given to help with bills.

Annual grant total
Grants usually average around £4,000 a year.

Applications
In writing to the correspondent by 1 April or 1 October for meetings at the end of those months.

Barrow-upon-Humber

The Beeton, Barrick and Beck Relief-in-Need Charity

£3,300

Correspondent: Mrs A Lawe, Barrow Wold Farm, Deepdale, Barton-upon-Humber, North Lincolnshire DN18 6ED (01469 531928)

Trustees: Alan Marritt; Revd Barrie Leah; John Cherry; John Thompson; Malcolm Bell; Pamela Green; Peter Clark; Susan Knapton; Kathleen Fraser.

CC Number: 234571

Eligibility
People in need who are over 60 and live in the parish of Barrow-upon-Humber.

Types of grants
Christmas vouchers and one-off grants for a variety of purposes, for example, travel costs to hospital.

Annual grant total
In 2010/11 the trust had both an income and a total expenditure of £3,600.

Applications
On a form available from the correspondent.

Barton-upon-Humber

The Barton-upon-Humber Relief-in-Sickness Fund

£2,000

Correspondent: H K Ready, Market Place, Barton-upon-Humber, North Lincolnshire DN18 5DD (01652 632215)

Trustees: John Oxley; Janet Smurthwaite; Margaret Searle; Dr Robert Mark Jaggs-Fowler; Cllr Wendy Witter.

CC Number: 504255

Eligibility
People in the parish of Barton-upon-Humber who are suffering from ill-health and their relatives/carers (in appropriate cases).

Types of grants
Discretionary grants are given for all kinds of need, but usually for medical aids and equipment.

Annual grant total
Grants usually total around £2,000 each year.

Applications
In writing to the correspondent. The trustees discuss cases which are known personally to them, although written applications are equally welcome and are considered when received.

Blue Coat Charity

£13,000

Correspondent: Keith Ready, Market Place, Barton-upon-Humber, North Lincolnshire DN18 5DD (01652 632215)

Trustees: Max Withrington; John Oxley; Sarah Louise Walker; Dr Timothy John Charles Birtwhistle; Keith Vickers.

CC Number: 237891

Eligibility
People in need who live in Barton-upon-Humber.

Types of grants
One-off grants, usually of around £25 to £30, towards footwear, clothing, bedding and other essential items.

Annual grant total
In 2010/11 the charity had an income of £15,400 and a total expenditure of £14,300.

Applications
In writing to the correspondent. Unless urgent, applications are considered each November.

Other information
The charity is also known as the Charity of John Tripp.

Billingborough

The Billingborough United Charities

£800

Correspondent: Neal Newnham, The Old Chapel, Barbridge Farmhouse, Low Grounds, Swineshead, Boston, Lincolnshire PE20 3PG (01205 820448)

Trustees: Revd Anna K. E. Sorensen; Neal Newnham.

CC Number: 217451

Eligibility
People in need who live in the civil parish of Billingborough.

Types of grants
One-off grants of £40 including those to people in need at Christmas.

Annual grant total
Grants average around £800 a year.

Exclusions

No payments are made towards statutory liabilities for example council tax, income tax or national insurance.

Applications

Applications should be submitted in writing either by the individual or on their behalf by a vicar, churchwarden, school master, doctor, district nurse, friend, family member, social worker, Citizens Advice or other welfare agency. They are considered at any time.

Deeping

The Deeping St James United Charities

£13,000

Correspondent: Julie Banks, Clerk, The Institute, 38 Church Street, Deeping St James, Lincolnshire PE6 8HD (01778 344707 (Tues/Thurs 9am-12pm); email: dsjunitedcharities@btconnect.com; website: www.dsjunitedcharities.org.uk)

Trustees: Kate Shinkins; Phil Dilks; Ray Auger; Revd Janet Donaldson; Carol Precey; Judy Stevens; Trevor Harwood; Peter Francis Ward; Graham Thompson; Les Bullock.

CC Number: 248848

Eligibility

People in need living in the parish of St James, Deeping. Grants are also paid to widows over 60 who have lived in the parish for three years or more.

Types of grants

One-off and recurrent grants according to need are given for a variety of purposes such as school uniforms, hospital travel expenses, household equipment and repairs. Interest free loans may also be made.

Annual grant total

In 2011 the charities had assets of £2.5 million and an income of £75,000. Relief in need and relief of sickness grants totalled £13,000.

Applications

In writing to the correspondent for consideration at the start of March, June, September and December. The trust welcomes telephone calls to discuss suggestions for grants with potential applicants.

Other information

This trust also gives grants to college and university students and local organisations.

Dorrington

Dorrington Welfare Charity

£500

Correspondent: Mrs Susan Tong, Penneshaw Farm, Sleaford Road, Dorrington, Lincoln LN4 3PU (01526 833395; email: susantong@btinternet.com)

Trustees: John Fox; Frank Cheffings; Ruth Blackbourn; Peter Eastwood; Susan Tong.

CC Number: 216927

Eligibility

People over the age of 18 who are in need and have lived in the village of Dorrington for at least the last year.

Types of grants

In the past one-off grants of up to £200 have been made along with Christmas payments to children of primary school age and to persons over 65.

Annual grant total

Grants usually total around £1,000 per year for educational and welfare purposes.

Applications

In writing to the correspondent, or a trustee, directly by the individual. Applications are considered at any time. Applications should include a general explanation of assistance required, an estimate of the expenses involved, details of any other assistance received or confirmation that no assistance has been or can be received from public funds.

Frampton

The Frampton Town Lands and United Charities

£8,500

Correspondent: Mark Hildred, Moore Thompson, Bank House, Broad Street, Spalding, Lincolnshire PE11 1TB (01775 711333; fax: 01775 711307)

Trustees: Wendy Cope; Peter James Udy; Myra Scott; Mr E. King; John Cooper; Colin Semmelroth.

CC Number: 216849

Eligibility

People in need who have lived in the ancient parish of Frampton for at least five years. Preference is usually given to older people (over 65) and recently bereaved widows.

Types of grants

One-off grants towards electricity bills, Christmas gifts for older people and so on.

Annual grant total

In 2010/11 the charities had both an income and expenditure of £8,600.

Applications

In writing to the correspondent. Applications are normally considered in October.

Friskney

The Friskney United Charities

£400

Correspondent: Jacquie Scott, Sigtoft Farm, Low Road South, Friskney, Boston PE22 8QH (01754 820554)

Trustees: George Henry Caudwell; Peter John Shaw; Robert Edward Lyon; Nicola Smith; Revd Fiona Cotton-Betteridge.

CC Number: 217282

Eligibility

Older people in need who live in Friskney, particularly those who have a connection with agricultural work.

Types of grants

Annual grants of 3cwt of coal and/or £10 each, classed as Christmas gifts.

Annual grant total

This trust's main purpose is the provision of housing for older people. Coal and charitable gifts given usually total around £400.

Applications

In writing to the correspondent. Applications are considered in November. A list of applicants is produced by the trustees based upon their local knowledge.

Grimsby

Sir Alec Black's Charity

£18,800

Correspondent: Stewart Wilson, Trustee, Wilson Sharpe and Co., 27 Osborne Street, Grimsby, North East Lincolnshire DN31 1NU (01472 348315; fax: 01472 251574; email: sc@wilsonsharpe.co.uk)

Trustees: Stewart Wilson; Dr Diana Frances Wilson; Michael Parker; Philip Arnold Mounfield; John Nicholas Harrison.

CC Number: 220295

Eligibility

Fishermen and dockworkers who are sick and poor, who live in the borough of Grimsby. Grants are also available to people employed by Sir Alec Black during his lifetime.

Types of grants

One-off and recurrent grants according to need.

Annual grant total

In 2010/11 the charity had an income of £82,000 (a £273,000 recorded income from sale of investments was not included by the trust as income in their summary submitted to the Charity Commission. This is likely due to the process of immediate reinvestment of the sale proceeds.)

Grants to fishermen and dockworkers totalled £1,800, former employees received £17,000 and grants to organisations totalled £50,000.

Applications

In writing to the correspondent. The trustees meet twice a year, in May and November, to consider applications.

Hacconby and Stainfield

Hacconby Poor's Money and Others

£4,600

Correspondent: Gillian Stoneman, 8 Church Street, Hacconby, Bourne, Lincolnshire PE10 0UJ (01778 570607; email: beamsend@tiscali.co.uk)

Trustees: Gillian Frances Stoneman; Ada Mary Atkinson; George William Tickler.

CC Number: 218589

Eligibility

People in need who live in the parish of Hacconby and Stainfield.

Types of grants

One-off and recurrent grants according to need. Recent grants have included Christmas grants to people aged over 60, help with home alterations for disabled people and grants towards funeral expenses and hospital travel costs.

Annual grant total

In 2010 the trust had an income of £3,200 and a total expenditure of £4,800.

Applications

In writing to the correspondent. Applications can be submitted directly by the individual or through a third party such as a social worker, Citizens Advice, welfare agency or neighbour.

Kesteven

The Kesteven Children in Need

£16,000

Correspondent: Mrs Alexandra Howard, Ram Farm, Bloxholm Lane, Nocton Heath, Lincoln LN4 2AH (01522 722701; email: enquiries@kcin.org; website: www.kcin.org)

Trustees: Lucy Lee; Sarah Robertson; Sue Knott; Tracey Bridges-Webb; Alexandra Howard; Erica Spurrier; Katherine Robertson; Stephanie Thorne.

CC Number: 700008

Eligibility

Children/young people up to the age of 16 who live in Kesteven.

Types of grants

One-off and recurrent grants of up to £500. Examples of grants include clothing, educational holidays, days out, prams/pushchairs, beds/sheets, fireguards, second-hand washing machines, educational toys and playschool fees.

Annual grant total

In 2010 the charity had an income of £21,000 and a total expenditure of £17,500. Previously the majority of grants were made for welfare purposes (about £19,000), with an additional £500 given for educational purposes.

Applications

Generally through local social workers, health visitors, teachers and education officers. Information should include the family situation, the age of the child and his/her special needs. Applications are considered throughout the year.

A. L. Padley Charity Fund

£600

Correspondent: William Cursham, Fraser Brown Solicitors, 84 Friar Lane, Nottingham NG1 6ED (01159 472541)

Trustees: Mr P. S. Gray; Mr W. E. C. Cursham.

CC Number: 1062216

Eligibility

People living in Kesteven who are: couples wishing to get married where the man is 24 years or older and the woman is 21 years or older; pensioners; or people who have been experiencing prolonged illness.

Types of grants

One-off and recurrent grants according to need.

Annual grant total

In 2010/11 the trust had both an income and total expenditure of £1,300.

Applications

The trust asks applicants to write a short initial letter to see if their interests match those of the trustees. Mark all correspondence with ref. WECC.

Other information

Grants are also made to organisations.

Lincoln

The Lincoln Municipal Relief-in-Need Charities

£25,000

Correspondent: M G Bonass, Clerk, Durrus, Scothern Lane, Dunholme, Lincoln LN2 3QP (01673 860660)

Trustees: Yvonne Bodger; Elizabeth May Denby; Tony Brogden; Joseph Roger Hansard; John Handley; Patrick Joseph Vaughan; Kim Kendall; Jane Clark; Sandra Gratrick.

CC Number: 213651

Eligibility

People in need who live in the city of Lincoln.

Types of grants

One-off grants up to £500 each, for all kinds of need except relief of rates, taxes or public funds; improvement to properties; or debts already incurred.

Annual grant total

In 2010/11 the trust had assets of £749,000 and an income of £39,000. Grants were made to individuals totalling £25,000, of which £4,500 was given in quarterly payments.

Applications

On a form available from the correspondent, to be submitted through a social worker, Citizens Advice or other welfare agency. Applications are considered at any time, although requests for more than £500 must be approved at a quarterly trustee meeting.

Other information

Grants are occasionally made to organisations.

The Herbert William Sollitt Memorial Trust

£750

Correspondent: Jacqueline Smith, Secretary, 24 Sunfield Crescent, Birchwood, Lincoln LN6 0LL (01522

885006; email: jacq.smith@ntlworld.com)

Trustees: Diane Garner; Denis Clarke; George Altoft; William Mundy.

CC Number: 1085018

Eligibility

Older people in need who are widows or widowers and live in the city of Lincoln.

Types of grants

One-off grants towards, for example, household items, life line alarms, decoration, convalescent holidays and telephone installation.

Annual grant total

About £1,500 a year. Grants are given to both individuals and organisations.

Exclusions

Grants are not given to married people or people who live outside the area of benefit.

Applications

On a form available from the correspondent to be submitted through a social worker, Citizens Advice or other welfare agency. Applications are considered on a regular basis.

Moulton

The Moulton Poor's Lands Charity

£8,000

Correspondent: Richard Lewis, Clerk, Maples and Son Solicitors, 23 New Road, Spalding, Lincolnshire PE11 1DH (01775 722261)

Trustees: John Grimwood; Tom Charlton; David Buck; Derek Thorpe; John Biggadike; Peter Dean; Robert Oldershaw; Pamela Pates; John Barnett.

CC Number: 216630

Eligibility

People in need, generally older people, who live in the civil parish of Moulton.

Types of grants

Grants can be paid in cash or in kind. Relief-in-need grants are generally paid following a severe accident, unexpected loss or misfortune.

Annual grant total

In 2011 the trust had an income of £24,000 and an expenditure of £31,000. Previously grants to individuals have totalled £9,000. Grants may also be given for educational needs.

Applications

In writing to the correspondent, usually through a trustee. Applications are considered in April and December.

Navenby

The Navenby Towns Farm Trust

£4,000

Correspondent: Mr Leonard Coffey, Secretary, 17 North Lane, Navenby, Lincoln LN5 0EH (01522 810273)

Trustees: Leonard Coffey; Jennifer Playford; Peter Welbourne; Brian Henderson; Ruth Sharp.

CC Number: 245233

Eligibility

People in need who live in the village of Navenby.

Types of grants

One-off grants according to need.

Annual grant total

About £11,000 to individuals and organisations.

Exclusions

No grants can be given outside the village.

Applications

On a form available from the correspondent, the village post-office, or Smith and Willows the newsagents. Applications are considered in September. Urgent applications may occasionally be considered at other times. Unsolicited applications are not responded to.

South Holland

The Spalding Relief-in-Need Charity

£18,000

Correspondent: R A Knipe, Clerk and Solicitor, Dembleby House, 12 Broad Street, Spalding, Lincolnshire PE11 1ES (01775 768774; email: patrick.skells@chattertons.com)

Trustees: S. R. Coltman; George Hastings; Angela Newton; Alexander Walton; Apt Sykes; George Alexander; Christopher Longstaff; John Lister; Petronella Keeling; John Bennet; Diane Clay; Elizabeth Sneath.

CC Number: 229268

Eligibility

People in need who live in the area covered by South Holland District Council with priority to residents of the parishes of Spalding, Cowbit, Deeping St Nicholas, Pinchbeck and Weston.

Types of grants

One-off grants in the range of £100 to £400 towards furniture and domestic appliances, rent arrears and other debts and children's clothing.

Annual grant total

In 2011 the charity had an income of £43,000 and gave grants totalling £31,000, broken down as follows:
- Individuals: £27,000
- Individuals TV licences: £2,400
- Individuals annual grants: £1,500

Applications

On a form available from the charity. Applications can be submitted directly by the individual or assisted if appropriate by a social worker, Citizens Advice, other welfare agency or third party. Grants are considered fortnightly.

Other information

Grants can also be made to organisations. Normally payments are made directly to suppliers.

Spilsby

The Spilsby Poorlands Charity

£2,300

Correspondent: Mrs J Tong, Clerk, Rosedale Lodge, Ashby Road, Spilsby, Lincolnshire PE23 5DW (01790 752885)

Trustees: Valerie Mowbray; Andrew Ellerby; Revd Canon Peter Coates; Peter Grant; Gordon Iremonger; Maurice Beecham; Arlene Cadman.

CC Number: 220613

Eligibility

People of retirement age in need who have lived in Spilsby for at least five years.

Types of grants

Grants of up to £25 are made twice a year in June and December.

Annual grant total

Grants average around £2,300.

Applications

On a form available from the correspondent. Applications must be submitted directly by the individual and are considered in June and December. Applicants must state how long they have lived in Spilsby.

Stamford

Winifrede Browne's Charity

£3,500

Correspondent: N P Fluck, Clerk to the trustees, Stapleton and Son, 1 Broad

Street, Stamford, Lincolnshire PE9 1PD (01780 751226; fax: 01780 766407)

Trustees: John Binder; Susan Elizabeth Macey; Catherine Louise Barlow; Revd Mark Warrick; Harold Martin Bluff; Nicholas Peter Fluck; Christine Norah Brough.

CC Number: 221587

Eligibility

People in need who are sick or elderly and live in Stamford.

Types of grants

Grants given include those for clothing, medical and disabled equipment, household bills, help in the home, travel to hospital and assistance with funeral expenses.

Annual grant total

About £3,500 a year. At the time of writing (winter 2012) no accounts had been submitted to the Commission since 2009, however, the trustees have informed us that the charity is still operational.

Exclusions

Grants are not given for 'relief of rates, taxes or other public funds.'

Applications

In writing to the correspondent, to be submitted either through a social worker, Citizens Advice or other welfare agency, or directly by the individual. They are considered quarterly unless urgent.

Stickford

The Stickford Relief-in-Need Charity

£7,500

Correspondent: Katherine Bunting, Clerk, The Old Vicarage, Church Road, Stickford, Boston, Lincolnshire PE22 8EP (01205 480455)

Trustees: Geoffrey Hattersley; Pamela Bryant; Michael Bursnell; Wendy Morely.

CC Number: 247423

Eligibility

People in need who live in the parish of Stickford.

Types of grants

One-off and recurrent grants for relief-in-need purposes, towards school uniforms, and a Christmas bonus. Further grants are given towards a bus service for older people, youth club outings and so on.

Annual grant total

About £15,000.

Applications

In writing to the correspondent. Applications should be submitted directly by the individual and are considered all year.

Surfleet

The Surfleet United Charities

£4,000

Correspondent: Leanne Barlow, Crimond, Hedgefield Hurn, Gosberton, Spalding, Lincolnshire PE11 4JE (01775 750183)

Trustees: Bryan Templeman; Simon Harrison; James Allen Dobney; M. Chapman; Glynn Waltham; Michael Garner.

CC Number: 215260

Eligibility

Retired people in need who have lived in the parish of Surfleet for over ten years (exceptions will be made on the age restriction in cases of extreme need).

Types of grants

Normally grants before Christmas each year of £15 (individuals) and £25 (couples). Other one-off grants according to need.

Annual grant total

In 2010 the charities held assets of £31,000 and had an income of £31,000 and a total expenditure of £27,000. Grants were made totalling £4,000.

Applications

In writing to the correspondent. Applications can be submitted directly by the individual and are considered in November.

Sutterton

The Sutterton Parochial Charity Trust

£6,000

Correspondent: Mrs D P McCumiskey, 6 Hillside Gardens, Wittering, Peterborough PE8 6DX (01780 782668)

Trustees: Cyril Baker; Rosamund Bowler; John Craft; Peter Leslie Cropley; Graham Truman; John White; Susan Ward; Christopher Stephenson; Edmund Sellars; John Thorpe; Rachel Hunn; Revd David De Verny.

CC Number: 234839

Eligibility

People in need who live in the parishes of Sutterton and Amber Hill.

Types of grants

One-off grants of about £50 are given at Christmas time.

Annual grant total

In 2010/11 the trust had an income of £14,000 and a total expenditure of £13,000.

Applications

On a form available from the correspondent which can be submitted directly by the individual or a family member. Applications should be received by the trust by the end of November for consideration in early December.

Other information

Grants are also made to organisations.

Sutton St James

The Sutton St James United Charities

£8,000

Correspondent: Keith Savage, Clerk, Lenton Lodge, 94 Wignals Gate, Holbeach, Spalding, Lincolnshire PE12 7HR (01406 490157; email: keithsavage@btinternet.com)

Trustees: Brian Sadd; Alison Campling; Elaine Harrison; Christopher Gaff; Mathew Ellis; John Garner; Philip Newton.

CC Number: 527757

Eligibility

People in need who live in the parish of Sutton St James.

Types of grants

One-off and recurrent grants according to need. Recent grants have been given for funeral expenses and to help people who have been evicted.

Annual grant total

In 2010/11 the charities had an income of £17,000 and a total expenditure of £16,000. Grants are made for educational and welfare purposes.

Applications

On a form available from the correspondent. Applications are only considered when all other available avenues have been explored.

Swineshead

The Swineshead Poor Charities

£25,000

Correspondent: Lynne Richardson, Hawthorn Farm, Station Road,

Swineshead, Boston, Lincolnshire
PE20 3NZ (01205 821628)

Trustees: Michael Welberry-Smith; Keith Harwood; Michael Brookes; Gavin Hutson; John Wright; Mark Leggott; Dr Peter Dawson.

CC Number: 216557

Eligibility
People in need who live in the parish of Swineshead.

Types of grants
One-off and recurrent grants and loans according to need.

Annual grant total
In 2010/11 the charities had an income of £13,000 and a total expenditure of £32,000.

Applications
In writing to the correspondent.

Other information
The charities also make grants to organisations.

Northamptonshire

Edmund Arnold's Charity (Poors Branch)

£1,050

Correspondent: Jane Forsyth, Clerk, 4 Grange Park Court, Roman Way, Grange Park, Northampton NN4 5EA (01604 876697)

Trustees: Peter Stuart White; Ann Slater; Margaret Hooper; Joanna Frances Dickson; Nicholas Hugh Adams; Joan Kirkbride; Adrian Michael Peter; John Stuart Gjers Gloag; Revd Ross Northing; Ian Brodie.

CC Number: 260589

Eligibility
People in need who live in the parish of Nether Heyford, Northamptonshire, the ancient parish of St Giles in Northampton and the parish of Stony Stratford, Buckinghamshire.

Types of grants
One-off cash grants of between £50 and £400 for 'extra comforts'.

Annual grant total
In 2010 grants to individuals totalled £1,050

Applications
On a form available on written request from the correspondent. Applications can be submitted either directly by the individual or through a third party such as a social worker, Citizens Advice or

another welfare agency. They are considered in March/April and September/October.

The Valentine Goodman Estate Charity

£2,800

Correspondent: John Stones, Adminstrator, Blaston Lodge, Blaston Road, Blaston, Market Harborough LE16 8DB (01858 555688)

Trustees: Laurie Smith; Roger Pocock; Albert Simkin; Valerie McKeggie; Ian Drummond; John Stones; Muriel Noble; Lindsay Blaaberg.

CC Number: 252108

Eligibility
People in need who live in the parishes of Blaston, Bringhurst, Drayton, East Magna, Hallaton and Medbourne.

Types of grants
One-off or recurrent grants according to need.

Annual grant total
In 2010 the charity had an income of £16,000 and made grants totalling £2,800.

Applications
In writing to the correspondent. Grants are distributed in February each year.

The Henry and Elizabeth Lineham Charity

£23,000

Correspondent: Angela Moon, Hewitson's LLP, 7 Spencer Parade, Northampton NN1 5AB (01604 233233; email: mail@hewitsons.com)

Trustees: Ulric Egerton Gravesande; Francis Helen Wire; Paul Frederick Morris; Francis Lilley; Garry Simmons; Trevor Bailey; Revd Canon David John Wiseman; Donald Edwards; Wendy Howes; John Nightingale; Philip Ager; Jean Bulteel; Jenny Conroy; Timothy John Hadland; Michael James O'Leary; Matthew Golby; Andrew Simpson; Janet March.

CC Number: 205975

Eligibility
Women in need who are at least 55 and live in the borough of Northampton.

Types of grants
Annuities are paid half yearly.

Annual grant total
In 2011 the trust had assets of £1.1 million, and an income of £47,000.

Grants were made to 67 individuals totalling £23,000.

Applications
In writing to the correspondent. Beneficiaries are usually nominated by one of the trustees, mostly councillors or ex-councillors.

The Page Fund

£4,200

Correspondent: Jane Forsyth, Wilson Browne Solicitors, 4 Grange Park Court, Roman Way, Northampton NN4 5EA (01604 876697; fax: 01604 768606; email: jforsyth@wsqblaw.com)

Trustees: Colin Andrew Stewart McAra; James Buckby; Keith Davidson; Ronald Gates.

CC Number: 241274

Eligibility
People in need who live in the borough of Northampton or within five miles of the Guild Hall and have done so for more than five years. Preference is given to older people, and to those with a sudden and unforeseen drop in income, for example widows following the death of a husband.

Types of grants
Pensions of up around £1,000 per year for people who have experienced a reduction in income due to widowhood or old age.

Annual grant total
In 2010/11 the fund had assets of £720,000 and an income of £29,000. Grants were made totalling £29,000, of which £4,200 was given to four individuals and the remaining £25,000 to 13 organisations.

Applications
On a form available from the correspondent. Applications can be submitted directly by the individual or through a social worker, Citizens Advice or other welfare agency. They are accepted at any time and are considered in May and November.

Saint Giles Charity Estate

£20,000

Correspondent: Grants Administrator, DFA Law, 2 Waterside Way, Northampton NN4 7XD (01604 609560)

Trustees: Anne Marrum; Bruce John Clayton; David Michael Orton Jones; Elizabeth Jane Berrill; Iain Manning Kennedy; Joan Randell; Simon George Schanschieff; Terence O'Connor; Jacqueline Phillips; Kenneth Ernest

Hammond; John Charles Bunyan; Thomas Oliver Matthew Starkie; Dr Thomas John Gill; Wendy Olgilve Lee.

CC Number: 202540

Eligibility
People in need who live within the borough of Northampton.

Types of grants
Grants of up £1,000 to individuals and families towards, for example, helping to fund individual household requirements such as carpets/washing machines and so on. Grants are always made for a specific purpose, not as a financial 'top up'.

Annual grant total
In 2011 the charity had assets of £3 million and an income of £613,000. 76 grants were made totalling £41,000 and were given to both individuals and organisations.

Exclusions
The charity does not normally make grants towards paying off debts, funeral expenses, tuition fees or for building projects.

Applications
On a form available from the correspondent. The charity prefers applications to be supported by a third party such as a social worker, or to come through an organisation such as Citizens Advice or another welfare agency. Applications should be submitted by the end of January, April, July and October for consideration in the next month.

All enquiries must be made by post.

Other information
The charity's main activity is the provision of almshouses and the support of Nicholas Rothwell House, a specially designed and purpose built complex dedicated to providing both short and long-term residential care.

Sir Thomas White's Northampton Charity

£88,000

Correspondent: Angela Moon, Hewitsons, 7 Spencer Parade, Northampton NN1 5AB (01604 233233; email: angelamoon@hewitsons.com)

Trustees: Tim Hadland; Ulric Gravesande; David Wiseman; Donald Edwards; Frank Lilley; Paul Morris; Wendy Howes; Frances Wire; Garry Simmons; Trevor Bailey; John Nightingale; Philip Ager; Jean Bulteel; Jenny Conroy; Michael O'Leary; Andrew Simpson; Matthew Golby; Janet March.

CC Number: 201486

Eligibility
People aged between 21 and 34 years of age who live in the extended borough of Northampton.

Types of grants
Nine-year interest-free loans for education, business start-ups and household essentials and grants for education.

Annual grant total
In 2011 the trust had assets of £3.2 million and an income of £247,000. 70 loans totalling £175,000 and £74,000 in student grants were made.

Applications
Apply in writing for a form in November, following a public notice advertising the grants.

Other information
Previously called Sir Thomas White's Loan Fund.

The Yelvertoft and District Relief-in-Sickness Fund

£8,000

Correspondent: Anne Drewett, Secretary and Trustee, 6 Monks Way, Crick, Northampton NN6 7XB (01788 823499)

Trustees: Anne Drewett; Richard Atterbury.

CC Number: 285771

Eligibility
People in need who live in the parishes of Yelvertoft, West Haddon, Crick, Winwick, Clay Coton and Elkington, who are sick, convalescent, disabled or infirm.

Types of grants
Small one-off grants.

Annual grant total
In 2010 the fund had an income of £7,800 and a total expenditure of £6,600.

Applications
In writing to the correspondent. Applications should be submitted directly by the individual, a relative or district nurse, and can be considered at any time.

Blakesley

The Blakesley Parochial Charities

£3,000

Correspondent: Derek Lucas, Bradworthy, Main Street, Woodend, Towcester NN12 8RX (01327 860517)

Trustees: B. Bird; John Hall; A. Bell; J. Weekley; N. Manners; P. Osborne; Christine Hill; Ian Spiby; Michael Adams.

CC Number: 202949

Eligibility
People in need who live in Blakesley.

Types of grants
One-off and recurrent grants according to need. Grants are given towards the fuel bills of older people and as pensions to widows.

Annual grant total
In 2011 the charity had both an income and expenditure of £6,500.

Applications
In writing to the correspondent. Applications are considered in December.

Other information
The charities also make grants for educational purposes.

Brackley

The Brackley United Feoffee Charity

£5,900

Correspondent: Rosemary Hedges, 7 Easthill Close, Brackley, Northamptonshire NN13 7BS (01280 702420; email: caryl.billingham@tesco.net)

Trustees: Caryl Billingham; Geoffrey Wilkins; George Britchfield; Keith Bunker; Nicholas Gandy; Philip Stevens; Trevor Gregory; Blake Stimpson; Peter Jeskins; Gwenllian Rhys.

CC Number: 238067

Eligibility
People in need who live in Brackley.

Types of grants
The trust gives funding to a wide range of causes, including the distribution of Christmas donations to around 60 elderly residents of Brackley. Previous grants have included: help towards the cost of aids for people with disabilities, temporary accommodation for a couple following a serious house fire, the purchase of a new washing machine for the young mother of a child with disabilities, help with childcare for parents deemed vulnerable and a contribution towards the repair of the headstone of a young child.

Annual grant total
In 2010/11 the trust had an income of £30,000 and made grants to individuals in need totalling £5,900.

Applications

In writing to the correspondent preferably by the individual or through a social worker, Citizens Advice or other welfare agency. Trustees meet every three to four months.

Braunston

The Braunston Town Lands Charity

£800

Correspondent: Sheila Rowley, 5 Danecourt, Church Road, Braunston, Daventry, Northamptonshire NN11 7HG (01788 890559)

Trustees: Janet McCarthy; Terry Waddleton; Sheila Rowley; Ben Berry; Revd Claire Rose-Casemore; Janita Cooper; Pauline Gurney; Wendy Wilson.

CC Number: 243109

Eligibility

People who live in Braunston and have to spend four nights or more in a hospital. Grants are given to patients and to their relatives. The size of grant depends on the distance that has to be travelled to the hospital and the amount of time spent at hospital. Residents in their nineties and the housebound may also receive grants or gifts at Christmas.

Types of grants

One-off grants in the form of cash donations for those over 90 years of age and Christmas gifts for people who are hospitalised or housebound. Grants generally range from £15 to £25.

Annual grant total

Grant giving to individuals generally totals around £800 a year.

Exclusions

No grants to individuals living outside the beneficial area.

Applications

In writing to the correspondent, directly by the individual.

Other information

Grants are also made to organisations.

Brington

The Chauntry Estate

£5,000

Correspondent: Rita Tank, Walnut Tree Cottage, Main Street, Great Brington, Northampton NN7 4JA (01604 770809)

Trustees: Robert Billingsby; Dr Elizabeth Gardner; John Lawrence; Martin Wright; Robert Spokes; Derek Bull; Jenny Cooch; Donna Ibbott; Revd Sue Kipling.

CC Number: 200795

Eligibility

Elderly people and other people in need who live in the parish of Brington. Applicants must have lived in the parish for at least five years.

Types of grants

One-off grants to relieve sudden distress or infirmity are made, for example, towards travel expenses for visits to hospital, food, fuel and heating appliances, and comforts or aids not provided by health authorities.

Annual grant total

In 2010/11 the trust had both an income and total expenditure of £10,000.

Applications

In writing to the correspondent.

Other information

Grants are also made to individuals for educational purposes.

Byfield

The Byfield Poors Allotment

£400

Correspondent: Ms Delith Jones, 15 Banbury Lane, Byfield, Daventry, Northamptonshire NN11 6UX (01327 261405)

Trustees: Angela Weller; Rosemary Johnson; Jean Hicks; Joyce Goddard; Mark Challice; Delith Jones; Christopher Buck; Chris Cross.

CC Number: 220321

Eligibility

People in need who live in the parish of Byfield.

Types of grants

One-off grants of £10 and £100, towards household bills, travel expenses, dental costs, spectacles and other 'minor medical items'. Grants, usually to older people, are also given for Christmas expenses.

Annual grant total

In 2010 the Allotment had both an income and total expenditure of £800.

Applications

On a form available from the correspondent. Applications can be made directly by the individual or a relevant third party. They can be submitted at any time for consideration in March, June, September and December.

Chipping Warden

Relief in Need Charity of Reverend William Smart

£1,500

Correspondent: Mr N J Galletly, 3 Allens Orchard, Chipping Warden, Banbury, Oxfordshire OX17 1LX (01295 660365)

Trustees: Revd Chris Whiteman; Mr N. J. Galletly; David Cross; Val Woodford.

CC Number: 239658

Eligibility

People in need who live in the parish of Chipping Warden, Northamptonshire. Preference is given to elderly people and young people in education.

Types of grants

One-off grants according to need.

Annual grant total

About £3,000 each year.

Applications

In writing to the correspondent either directly by the individual or by another third party such as a social worker. Applications are considered at any time.

Daventry

The Daventry Consolidated Charity

£5,000

Correspondent: Maggie Dowie, 15 Astbury Close, Daventry, Northamptonshire NN11 4RL

Trustees: Christopher Over; Pauline Smith; Gillian Rigby; Alfred Goodridge; Colin Morgan; Malcolm Adcock; Gloria Edwards-Davidson.

CC Number: 200657

Eligibility

People in need who live in the borough of Daventry.

Types of grants

One-off grants for a specific need such as a special chair for a child with cerebral palsy, travel to hospital 45 miles from home and help with the costs of adaptations to a motability vehicle.

Annual grant total

In 2010 the trust had an income of £10,000 and a total expenditure of £11,000.

Exclusions

There are no grants available towards debts or ongoing expenses.

Applications

In writing to the correspondent. Trustees meet three times a year in March, July and November. Applications must include financial circumstances and the specific purpose for the grant. Relevant information not included will be requested if required.

Other information

The charity also makes grants to organisations.

Desborough

The Desborough Town Welfare Committee

£6,000

Correspondent: Ann King, Honorary Secretary, 190 Dunkirk Avenue, Desborough, Kettering, Northamptonshire NN14 2PP (01536 763390)

Trustees: Michael Ginns; James Stanley.

CC Number: 235505

Eligibility

People who are older, sick or in need and living in Desborough.

Types of grants

One-off and recurrent grants, paid mainly at Christmas.

Annual grant total

Grants usually total around £5,500 a year.

Applications

In writing to the correspondent, for consideration within two to three months.

East Farndon

The United Charities of East Farndon

£1,500

Correspondent: C L Fraser, Linden Lea, Main Street, Market Harborough, Northamptonshire LE16 9SJ (01858 464218; email: fraser-cameron@hotmail.com)

Trustees: Cameron Fraser; Shirley Biggin; Nigel Haynes; Adrian Hill.

CC Number: 200778

Eligibility

Families in need who live in East Farndon.

Types of grants

One-off cash grants of up to £50 are provided for travel expenses to hospital, fuel grants towards electricity, disabled equipment, living costs and household bills.

Annual grant total

In 2011 the charity had an income of £6,300 and an expenditure of £3,400.

Applications

In writing to the correspondent directly by the individual or a family member for consideration as they are received.

Other information

Grants are also made for educational purposes.

Harpole

The Harpole Parochial Charities

£1,200

Correspondent: Nicholas Paul, 4 Mount Pleasant, Harpole, Northampton NN7 4DL (01604 830585)

Trustees: Jeremy Calderwood; Mary Burt; Richard Starmer.

CC Number: 202568

Eligibility

People in need who have lived in Harpole for more than seven years, with a preference for those over 65.

Types of grants

Recurrent grants ranging from £25 to £30.

Annual grant total

Grants usually average around £1,200 a year.

Applications

On a form available from the correspondent including details of financial status; benefits and income. Applications can be submitted either directly by the individual or through a relative. They are considered in December and should be submitted in November.

Kettering

The Broadway Cottages Trust

£500 (27 grants)

Correspondent: Peter Wilson, Chair, 35 Westhill Drive, Kettering, Northamptonshire NN15 7LG (01536 482017)

Trustees: Peter Wilson; Nina Kerr Wilson; Michael Anthony Purcell Jeans; Julie Mabel James; Nicholas James Drake-Lee; William Michael Drake-Lee.

CC Number: 203763

Eligibility

People in need who live or have lived in or near Kettering.

Types of grants

One-off and recurrent grants according to need.

Annual grant total

In 2010/11 the trust held assets totalling £1 million and had an income of £45,000. Total charitable expenditure came to £44,000, of which £500 was made in grants to 27 individuals.

Applications

In writing to the correspondent.

Other information

The trust also provides housing with affordable rent and makes grants to organisations.

The Kettering Charities (Fuel Grants)

£10,000

Correspondent: Anne Ireson, Kettering Borough Council, Council Offices, Bowling Green Road, Kettering NN15 7QX (01536 534398; email: anneireson@kettering.gov.uk)

Trustees: Ian Watts; Bryn Morgan; Shirley Lynch; Duncan Bain; Lloyd Bunday; Stephen Bellamy; Jennifer Henson; Cliff Moreton.

CC Number: 207698

Eligibility

Widows, widowers and single people over the age of 60 who live alone in Kettering or Baron Seagrave and who are in receipt of retirement pension.

Types of grants

Grants of £25 towards winter fuel bills.

Annual grant total

In 2009/10 the charities had an income of £14,000 and a total expenditure of £28,000.

Applications

On a form available from the correspondent which can be obtained after advertisements have been placed in local newspapers in November each year. Applications are considered in November. Applicants must include details of income, status, age and address.

Other information

The charities also make grants towards education expenses to people over 16 years old.

The Stockburn Memorial Trust Fund

£7,000

Correspondent: Mrs P M Reynolds, 70 Windermere Road, Kettering, Northamptonshire NN16 8UF (01536 524662)

Trustees: Edward Lamb; Sue Watts; Maurice Bayes; Angela Reynolds; Revd Peter Strong; Trish Dewar; Sushila Wright.

CC Number: 205120

Eligibility

People in need who live in the borough of Kettering.

Types of grants

One-off grants according to need.

Annual grant total

In 2011 the fund had an income of £8,500 and a total expenditure of £7,600.

Applications

In writing to the correspondent through a social worker, Citizens Advice or other welfare agency. Applicants should include details of age, address, telephone number, financial situation and health circumstances.

Litchborough

The Litchborough Parochial Charities

£5,000

Correspondent: Maureen Pickford, 18 Banbury Road, Litchborough, Towcester, Northamptonshire NN12 8JF (01327 830110)

Trustees: Anthony Harvey; Patricia Sykes; Mary Davies; Maureen Pickford; Margaret Ashby.

CC Number: 201062

Eligibility

People in need who live in Litchborough.

Types of grants

One-off grants and pensions.

Annual grant total

In 2010/111 the charities had an income of £5,600 and an expenditure of £5,300.

Applications

In writing to the correspondent.

Northampton

The Coles and Rice Charity

£11,000

Correspondent: Grants Officer, Wilson Browne, 4 Grange Park Court, Roman Way, Northampton NN4 5EA (01604 876697; fax: 01604 768606)

Trustees: Jill Vowden; Ronald Gates; Laurice Percival; Peter Newham; Dr Judith Robinson.

CC Number: 238375

Eligibility

Pensions are only available to people in need who are over 55 years old and have lived in Northampton for at least five years. However, the charity also makes one-off grants to younger people in need.

Types of grants

One-off grants of up to about £500. Most grants are annual pensions of around £200 paid in quarterly instalments.

Annual grant total

In 2010 the trust had both an income and expenditure of £12,000.

Applications

On a form available from the correspondent. Forms can be submitted either directly by the individual or through a social worker. Applications are usually considered in March and November.

The John and Mildred Law Fund

£8,900 (16 grants)

Correspondent: Jane Forsyth, Clerk to the trustees, Wilson Browne, 4 Grange Park Court, Roman Way, Grange Park, Northampton NN4 5EA (01604 876697; email: jforsyth@qswblaw.com)

Trustees: Colin McAra; James Buckby; Ronald Gates; Keith Davidson.

CC Number: 1121230

Eligibility

People in need who live in the Borough of Northampton although the trustees do have the discretion to give grants to those immediately outside the Borough.

Types of grants

One-off grants of up to £1,000 according to need.

Annual grant total

In 2010/11 the fund held assets of £802,000 and had an income of £34,000. Grants to 16 individuals totalled £8,900.

Applications

In writing to the correspondent. Trustees meet twice a year to consider applications in May and November.

Other information

Grants are also made to organisations (£23,000 in 2010/11).

The Northampton Municipal Church Charities

£52,000

Correspondent: Jane Forsyth, Wilson Browne Solicitors, 4 Grange Park Court, Roman Way, Grange Park, Northampton NN4 5EA (01604 876697; fax: 01604 768606; email: jforsyth@qswblaw.com)

Trustees: James Buckby; Keith Davidson; Ronald Gates; Paul Wain; Ruth Hampson; Brian May; Clive Fowler; Terrence O'Connor; Tony Sanderson.

CC Number: 259593

Eligibility

People in need who live in the borough of Northampton.

Types of grants

People aged over 55 are eligible for payments of £85 a quarter and a Christmas voucher of £45. People of any age can receive one-off grants of up to a maximum of £500.

Annual grant total

In 2010/11 the charities had assets of £4.3 million and an income of £243,000. Grants were made totalling £52,000, and were distributed as follows:

Pensioner grants	£39,000
Individual grants	£7,000
Christmas vouchers	£5,500

A further £59,000 was given to organisations.

Exclusions

The Charity is unable to assist with debt.

Applications

On a form available from the correspondent, including details of age, residence, income, assets and expenditure. Applications can be submitted either directly by the individual or through a third party such as a social worker, Citizens Advice or other welfare agency. They are considered on a regular basis.

Other information

The charity runs a sheltered housing scheme at St Thomas House in St Giles Street, Northampton. It is warden controlled and has 17 small flats for people over 55. The charities' income must firstly be used for maintaining St Thomas House, secondly for the benefit of residents, and thirdly for the relief-in-need of people who live in Northampton.

Pattishall

The Pattishall Parochial Charities

£6,000

Correspondent: Wendy Watts, 59 Leys Road, Pattishall, Towcester, Northamptonshire NN12 8JY (01327 830583)

Trustees: Mike Bayley; Jan Taylor; Jessie Susannah Townsend; Roger Clarke.

CC Number: 204106

Eligibility

People in need who have lived in the parish of Pattishall for at least three years. Preference is given to people who are over 65.

Types of grants

One-off grants of between £15 and £500 for a variety of needs, for example provision of a downstairs toilet and a contribution towards a child's playgroup fees. 15 widows and widowers receive monthly pensions of £15, and around 40 older people receive grants for fuel at Christmas (£40 to single people and £55 to couples).

Annual grant total

Grants usually total around £6,000 a year.

Applications

In writing to the correspondent. Applications are usually considered in November for fuel grants, July for pensions, and throughout the year for other grants. Applications can be submitted either directly by the individual or by anybody who hears of a need such as one of the trustees or the rector of the parish. Receipts (copies will do) should be included for the cost of travel for hospital visits and estimates for the purchases of large equipment, for example wheelchairs.

Ringstead

The Ringstead Gift

£500

Correspondent: Mrs D Pentelow, 20 Carlow Street, Ringstead, Kettering, Northamptonshire NN14 4DN (01933 626894)

Trustees: Andrew Sharman; Revd Shena Bell; Geoffrey Goodchild; Clifford Harris; Philip Surridge.

CC Number: 239517

Eligibility

People in need who live in the parish of Ringstead.

Types of grants

One-off grants in kind. 'The trustees would consider all applications.'

Annual grant total

About £1,000 a year for educational and welfare purposes.

Exclusions

No grants to cover the cost of rent or rates.

Applications

In writing to the correspondent, to be submitted either directly by the individual or a family member, through a third party such as a social worker or teacher or through an organisation such as Citizens Advice or a school. Applications are considered in June and November and should be submitted at least two weeks prior to this.

Roade

The Roade Feoffee and Chivall Charity

£9,000

Correspondent: Michael Dowden, 67 High Street, Roade, Northampton NN7 2NW

Trustees: Ian Calder; Revd Michael Burton; Michael Christopher Dowden; Christine Elizabeth Marshall; Graham John Frost.

CC Number: 202132

Eligibility

People in need who live in the ancient parish of Roade.

Types of grants

One-off grants usually ranging from £15 to £100. Recent grants have been given at Christmas time and for such things as travel expenses to visit relatives in hospital.

Annual grant total

In 2010 the charity had an income of £22,000 and a total expenditure of £9,100.

Applications

In writing to the correspondent, specifying the reason for the application.

Scaldwell

The Scaldwell Relief-in-Need Charity

£900

Correspondent: Mrs S K Dodds-Smith, The Old Barn, High Street, Scaldwell, Northampton NN6 9JS (01604 881950; email: d.doddssmith@btinternet.com)

Trustees: Dr Roger Morgan; Mr M. Monk; Mrs P. Long; Mrs J. Deacon; Mrs B. Vinton; Mrs S. Thorne.

CC Number: 205281

Eligibility

People in need who live in the parish of Scaldwell only.

Types of grants

One-off grants ranging from £50 to £250.

Annual grant total

Grants average around £1,000 a year.

Applications

In writing to the correspondent. Applications can be submitted directly by the individual or family member and are considered in November and February.

Towcester

The Sponne and Bickerstaffe Charity

£1,150

Correspondent: T Richardson, Clerk to the Trustees, Moorfield, Buckingham Way, Towcester, Northamptonshire NN12 6PE (01327 351206; email: sponneandbickerstaffe@btconnect.com)

Trustees: S. J. Burnley; Jacqueline Hart; Penelope Bennett; Peter Allen; Tony Bryer; E. Nunn; Dennis Dale; Carole Tyrrell; Brian Giggins; Julie Godwin; Karen Wheeler; Alan Maycock; James Rawbone; Dominique Yates.

CC Number: 204117

Eligibility

People in need who live in the civil parish of Towcester.

Types of grants

One-off grants of £50 to £250 towards household essentials, such as furniture, clothing and electrical goods.

Annual grant total

In 2012 the charity gave grants totalling £2,300 for welfare and educational purposes.

Applications

In writing to the correspondent, through a social worker, Citizens Advice or other welfare agency. Applications are considered monthly.

Wappenham

The Wappenham Poors Land Charity

£2,500

Correspondent: Mrs J E McNeil, Flat 1, Green Norton Park, Greens Norton, Towcester NN12 8DP (01327 350873)

Trustees: Daniel Barry Haycock; Frank Alan Osborne; Roger Francis Allibone; Michael Norman Sheppard.

CC Number: 205147

Eligibility

People in need who live in the ecclesiastical parish of Wappenham.

Types of grants

The trust gives a small standard grant to pensioners in need. Grants are also given to widows, widowers and people who are sick or disabled and are in need of specific items e.g. wheelchairs, orthopaedic beds, home improvements, shower installation, redecoration and so on.

Annual grant total

Grants have averaged around £2,500 in recent years.

Applications

In writing to the correspondent.

Welton

Welton Village Hall (formerly The Welton Town Lands Trust)

£1,300

Correspondent: Mr Gary Holmes, c/o Kingsford Solutions Ltd, 37 Churchill Road, Welton, Daventry NN11 2JH (01327 312055)

Trustees: Robert Somerville; Caroline Maxwell; Peter O'Mahoney; Carole Bertozzi; Michael Taylor; Clive Younger; Lee Henstridge; Gary Holmes; Revd Chris Tremththanmor.

CC Number: 304449

Eligibility

People in need, irrespective of age, who have lived in the village of Welton for at least two years.

Types of grants

One-off grants of around £50 per family. The amount varies according to the total number of applicants as it is divided in equal shares.

Annual grant total

In 2010/11 the charity had an income of £6,000 and a total expenditure of £5,500. Previously, grants were made to individuals totalling £2,000, of which £700 was given in educational grants and £1,300 was distributed in welfare awards.

Applications

On a form available from the correspondent. Applications are considered in November for distribution in December. The details of the trust are usually well publicised within the village.

Other information

The trust also makes grants to local schools and churches.

Nottingham-shire

The John and Nellie Brown Farnsfield Trust

£6,000

Correspondent: Alan Dodd, Roan House, Crabnook Lane, Farnsfield, Newark NG22 8JY

Trustees: Alan Dodd; Frank Reynolds; Dr Elisabeth Hiller; John Brown; Peter Teather; Heather Johnston; David Harvey.

CC Number: 1078367

Eligibility

People in need who live in the Farnsfield, Edingley Halam and Southwell areas of Nottinghamshire.

Types of grants

Grants given according to need.

Annual grant total

In 2010/11 the trust had an income of £5,300 and a total expenditure of £21,000.

Applications

In writing to the correspondent.

Other information

Grants are also made to organisations and for educational purposes.

The Lucy Derbyshire Annuity Fund

£1,600

Correspondent: Richard Minshall, Minshalls, 370–374 Nottingham Road, Newthorpe, Nottingham NG16 2ED (01773 538930; email: mco@minshall.co.uk; website: www.derbyshirehaven.org.uk/annuity-fund)

Trustees: Hester Bedell; Ronald Kenyon; Jean Margaret Fairclough; Shirley Patricia Keays; Brenda Kenyon; Geoff Parkinson.

CC Number: 215350

Eligibility

People of good character who are in reduced circumstances or of limited means and have lived in Nottinghamshire for at least five years preceding their application. The fund only offers grants to those over the age of 75.

Types of grants

Recurrent grants are given according to need.

Annual grant total

In 2009/10, the most recent year for which accounts were available from the Charity Commission, grants totalled £1,600.

Applications

In writing to the correspondent. Applications can be submitted directly by the individual or through a social worker, Citizens Advice or other welfare agency.

Other information

The fund also runs a small care home in Wollaton, Nottingham.

The Mary Dickinson Charity

£21,000 (30 grants)

Correspondent: Nigel Cullen, Freeth Cartwright LLP, Cumberland Court, 80 Mount Street, Nottingham NG1 6HH (01159 369369; fax: 01158 599600)

Trustees: Charles Foxon; Douglas Brian Adderley; Mary Stacey; David John Towers; John Howard Treece; Janet Baston; Christopher John Powell; Jane Dorothy Moore; Margaret Susan Ratcliffe; Revd Ian Wiseman.

CC Number: 213884

Eligibility

Older people in need who live in the city or county of Nottingham. Preference is given to Christians.

Types of grants

Pensions are given to a fixed number of older people. One-off grants may also be available for emergency items such as replacing gas fires and safety alarm and telephone systems.

Annual grant total

In 2010 the charity had assets of £1.2 million and an income of £27,000.

Pensions and grants to 30 people amounted to £21,000.

Applications

On a form available from the correspondent. Applications should be submitted through a doctor/member of the clergy or directly by the individual, supported by a reference from one of the aforementioned. Applications can be submitted all year round and are considered in March, June, September and December, although emergency cases can be considered at any time.

The Fifty Fund

£57,000 (74 grants)

Correspondent: The Trustees, 10 St Mary's Crescent, Ruddington, Nottinghamshire NG11 6FQ (01159 844819; email: marion.ff@btinternet. com)

Trustees: Edward Arthur Randall; E. W. Whiles; Revd Canon George Bryan Barrodale.

CC Number: 214422

Eligibility

People in need who live in Nottinghamshire.

Types of grants

Payments of about £130 a quarter and one-off grants and loans to help with debts, disability equipment and white goods. Loans may be made where trustees consider it appropriate.

Annual grant total

In 2010 the fund had assets of £6.8 million and an income of £256,000. 18 beneficiaries received regular support and a further 56 received one-off support. Grant expenditure can be broken down as follows:

Payments to beneficiaries	£48,000
Christmas gifts	£4,900
Summer gifts	£4,100

Exclusions

No grants are given for education, sponsorship or holidays.

Applications

Applications, in writing to the correspondent, can be submitted either by the individual or through a recognised referral agency (such as a social worker, Citizens Advice or doctor) or other third party. The trustees meet twice a year to consider applications.

Other information

Grants are also made to organisations (£137,000 in 2010).

The Charles Wright Gowthorpe Fund and Clergy Augmentation Fund

£9,000

Correspondent: Geoff Gleeson, Lloyds TSB Private Banking Ltd, UK Trust Centre, 22–26 Ock Street, Abingdon, Oxfordshire OX14 5SW (01235 232700)

Trustee: Lloyds TSB. Private Banking Ltd.

CC Number: 213852/213852

Eligibility

(i) The Gowthorpe Fund supports widows and other women in need who live within a 12-mile radius of the Market Square, Nottingham.

(ii) The Clergy Augmentation Fund generally supports clergymen within a 10-mile radius of St Peter's Church, Nottingham.

Types of grants

Grants usually of £100, paid once a year in December.

Annual grant total

In 2010/11 the Gowthorpe Fund had an income of £6,300 and a total expenditure of £7,300. In the same year, the Clergy Augmentation Fund had an income of £2,500 and a total expenditure of £2,300.

Applications

On a form available from local Church of England vicars, to be returned by the end of October. Do not write to the correspondent initially; only send the application form once it has been completed.

The John William Lamb Charity

£16,000 (30 grants)

Correspondent: The Trustees, Nottinghamshire Community Foundation, Cedar House, Ransom Wood Business Park, Southwell Road West, Mansfield, Nottinghamshire NG21 0HJ (01623 620202; fax: 01623 620204; email: enquiries@nottscf.org.uk; website: www.nottscf.org.uk)

Trustees: Alexander Nall; Amanda Margaret Farr; John David Pears.

CC Number: 221978

Eligibility

People in need who have been living for at least one year within the city of Nottingham, or within 20 miles of the Nottingham Exchange.

Types of grants

Annuities of around £130 a quarter.

Annual grant total

In 2010/11 the trust had assets of £853,000, which generated an income of £33,000. Annuities were made totalling £15,000 with a further £700 made in other grants to individuals.

Applications

In writing to the correspondent. Applicants will be visited by a member of the trust.

The New Appeals Organisation for the City and County of Nottingham

£39,000 (119 grants)

Correspondent: Phil Everett, Joint Chairman, 4 Rise Court, Hamilton Road, Nottingham NG5 1EU (01159 609644 (answering service); email: enquiries@ newappeals.org.uk; website: www. newappeals.org)

Trustees: Lou Levin; Phil Everett; Elaine Litman; Gareth Davis; Paula Elizabeth McLaren; Kevin Hyland; Christopher Bossart.

CC Number: 502196

Eligibility

People in need who live in the city and county of Nottingham.

Types of grants

One-off grants ranging from £50 to £2,000 to meet needs which cannot be met from any other source. For example, wheelchairs, white goods, flooring, beds and bedding, rise/recliner chairs, adapted vehicles, holidays, computers and other electrical goods. Much of the money is raised for specific projects or people.

Annual grant total

In 2010/11 the organisation had assets of £55,000 and an income of £56,000. There were 119 grants made to individuals totalling £39,000.

Exclusions

The trust does not usually help with debt arrears, building works, wages, educational costs, foreign travel for students or requests from outside Nottingham.

Applications

On a form available from the correspondent. Applications should ideally be made through a social worker, Citizens Advice, medical establishment or other welfare agency, although those submitted directly by the individual are considered. Applications are considered on the first Monday of each month.

Other information

The trust has a 'library of equipment' for adults and children including electric scooters, sports wheelchairs and computers.

Grants are also made to organisations, in particular, local schools (£11,600 in 2010/11).

The Nottingham Annuity Charity

£12,000

Correspondent: David A Simmons, c/o Nottingham Community Housing Association, Property Management Services, 12–14 Pelham Road, Sherwood Rise, Nottingham NG5 1AP (01158 443404; email: davids@ncha.org.uk)

Trustee: Nottingham Community Housing Association.

CC Number: 510023

Eligibility

People in need who live in Nottinghamshire. Preference is given to widows and unmarried women.

Types of grants

Regular yearly allowances of about £200 (paid in quarterly grants).

Annual grant total

In 2010/11 the charity had an income of £15,000 and a total expenditure of £14,000.

Applications

On a form available from the correspondent to be submitted either directly by the individual or via an appropriate third party such as a social worker, Citizens Advice or other welfare agency. Applications are usually considered quarterly.

The Nottingham Children's Welfare Fund

£2,400

Correspondent: Gwen Derry, 37 Main Road, Wilford, Nottingham NG11 7AP (01159 811830)

Trustees: Doris Elcock; Gwen Derry; Judith James; Revd Rachael Shock.

CC Number: 215445

Eligibility

Children under 18, with priority given to young children, who live in Nottinghamshire especially in Nottingham and especially those who have lost either or both of their parents.

Types of grants

One-off grants of around £50 to £75. Recent awards have been made for domestic appliances, furniture, furnishings, clothing, toys and contributions to school trips and family holidays.

Annual grant total

About £2,400.

Applications

On a form available from the correspondent: to be submitted by social services, the probation service or another welfare agency or third party such as a teacher. Applications are usually considered four times a year.

The Nottingham General Dispensary

£27,000 (55 grants)

Correspondent: Nigel Cullen, Cumberland Court, 80 Mount Street, Nottingham NG1 6HH (01159 015558; fax: 01159 015500; email: nigel.cullen@ freethcartwright.co.uk)

Trustees: Pauline Johnston; David Levell; Alan Hopwood; Dr Ian McLachlan; Roy Batterbury; Dr Stanley Harris; William John Bendall; Dr Angela Truman; Andy Roylance.

CC Number: 228149

Eligibility

People who are in poor health, convalescent or who have disabilities and live in the county of Nottinghamshire.

Types of grants

One-off grants ranging from £20 to £1,000 are given for a variety of needs including home adaptations, mobility equipment, medical aids, hospital travel costs, computer equipment, holidays and respite breaks.

Annual grant total

In 2010/11 the charity had assets of £1.2 million and an income of £37,000. Grants were made to over 55 individuals totalling £27,000.

Exclusions

No grants are given where funds are available from statutory sources. No recurrent grants are made.

Applications

In writing to the correspondent through a social worker, Citizens Advice, other welfare agency or a professional, for example a doctor or teacher. Individuals can apply directly, but they must include supportive medical evidence with their application. Applications are considered all year round though requests for grants exceeding £1,000 may take longer.

Other information

The charity also makes grants to local organisations (£29,000) and maintains a standing relationship with the Nottingham Self-Help Project Fund.

Nottingham Gordon Memorial Trust for Boys and Girls

£40,000

Correspondent: Anna Chandler, Cumberland Court, 80 Mount Street, Nottingham NG1 6HH (01159015562; fax: 01159 015500; email: anna. chandler@freethcartwright.co.uk)

Trustees: John Foxon; Nigel Solicitor; Paul Watts; Jean Ramsden; John Tordoff; Peter Hill; Anthony King; Ian Wiseman; Bill Hammond.

CC Number: 212536

Eligibility

Children and young people aged up to 25 who are in need and who live in Nottingham and the area immediately around the city.

Types of grants

One-off grants are made for needs such as clothing, bedding, electrical goods, basic equipment for people who are disabled, family holidays and educational courses.

Annual grant total

In 2011 the trust had assets of £1.1 million and an income of £46,000. Grants totalling £47,000 were awarded, including:

▶ Bed and bed linens – £7,200
▶ Educational grants – £6,600
▶ Electrical goods – £6,500
▶ Holidays/trips – £6,100
▶ Baby items and equipment – £3,500

Applications

On a form available from the correspondent to be submitted through the individual's school, college, educational welfare agency, health visitor, social worker or probation officer. Individuals, supported by a reference from their school/college, can also apply directly. Applications are considered all year round.

Other information

The trust also supports organisations in the Nottingham area.

The Nottinghamshire Miners' Welfare Trust Fund

£51,000

Correspondent: D A Brookes, CISWO, Welfare Offices, Berry Hill Lane, Mansfield, Nottinghamshire NG18 4JR (01623 625767)

Trustees: Michael Leslie Stevens; Jeffrey Edward Wood; Mr Longden; Michael Francis Ball.

CC Number: 1001272

Eligibility

Members of the mining community in Nottinghamshire who are in need, and their dependents.

Types of grants

One-off and recurrent grants are given to improve health and living conditions. Recent grants have been given for bathroom alterations, mortgage repayments, stair lifts, wheelchairs, scooters, beds and bedding, furniture and replacement boilers. Holiday grants of £100 to £250 are also available.

Annual grant total

In 2010 the fund had assets of £2.5 million and an income of £92,000. Grants were made totalling £51,000 and were distributed as follows:

Personal welfare and hardship grants	£40,000
Holiday grants	£11,000

Applications

On a form available from the correspondent, to be submitted directly by the individual or through a third party such as the Coal Industry Social Welfare Organisation (CISWO), a Citizens Advice, social worker or similar welfare organisation. Applications are considered regularly throughout the year.

Other information

Grants are also made to organisations (£37,000 in 2010).

The Perry Trust Gift Fund

£12,000

Correspondent: Anna Chandler, c/o Freeth Cartwright LLP, Cumberland Court, 80 Mount Street, Nottingham NG1 6HH (01159 015562)

Trustees: Maureen Allsopp; Mr A. Parker; Mr A. Mitchell; Revd J. Stapleton; Mr N. Williamson; Charles Nigel Cullen; Paula Bailey.

CC Number: 247809

Eligibility

In order of preference: (a) people in need who have lived in the city of Nottingham for at least five years; (b) people in need who have lived in Nottinghamshire for at least five years. Grants are mainly given to older people with low incomes but some help is also available to younger people in need.

Types of grants

One-off grants up to £200 towards, for example, electric bills, clothing, living costs, household bills, food, furniture, disabled equipment and help in the home.

Annual grant total

In 2010/11 the fund had an income and total expenditure of £14,000.

Applications

On a form available from the correspondent. Applications can be made through a third party such as a social worker, Citizens Advice or other welfare agency. They are considered in May and November.

The Puri Foundation

£10,000

Correspondent: Nathu Ram Puri, Environment House, 6 Union Road, Nottingham NG3 1FH (01159 013000)

Trustees: Nathu Ram Puri; Mary McGowan; Mr A. Puri.

CC Number: 327854

Eligibility

Individuals in need living in Nottinghamshire who are from India (particularly the towns of Mullan Pur near Chandigarh and Ambala). Employees/past employees of the Melton Medes Group Ltd, Blugilt Holdings or Melham Inc and their dependents, who are in need, are also eligible

The trust wants to support people who have exhausted state support and other avenues, in other words to be a 'last resort'.

Types of grants

One-off and recurrent grants according to need, for items such as furniture or clothes. The maximum donation is usually between £150 and £200.

Annual grant total

In 2010/11 the foundation had assets of £3.4 million and an income of £922,000. Grants mostly to organisations totalled approximately £526,000.

Applications

In writing to the correspondent, either directly by the individual or through a social worker.

The Skerritt Trust
See entry on page 27

The West Gate Benevolent Trust

£59,000

Correspondent: Stephen Carey, Secretary, 17 Storcroft Road, Retford, Nottinghamshire DN22 7EG (01234 567890)

Trustees: Dr John Tonge; Catherine Anne Richardson; Michael Brian Backhouse; Margaret Cox; Rodney William Duckworth.

CC Number: 503506

Eligibility

People in need who live in Nottinghamshire.

Types of grants

One-off grants ranging from about £50 to £5,000. For example, recent grants have been given for washing machines, holidays and travel to visit relations in hospital.

Annual grant total

In 2010/11 the trust had an income and grant expenditure of £59,000.

Applications

Applications cannot be made by individuals directly, but only through a third party such as a social worker or Citizens Advice.

Balderton

The Balderton Parochial Charity

£1,000

Correspondent: Mrs Louise Tetlaw, 1 Birch Road, New Balderton, Newark, Nottinghamshire NG24 3DB (07818 081490; email: bpc@jimandlou.com)

Trustees: Gordon Brooks; Christine Cox; Mary Holland; Pat Wood; Revd Tony Tucker.

CC Number: 217554

Eligibility

People in need who live in the parish of Balderton.

Types of grants

One-off grants according to need. Recent grants have been given for cookers, electric wheelchairs, cycle trailers and garden alterations.

Annual grant total

In 2010/11 the charity had an income of £3,000 and a total expenditure of £2,000. Grants are given to both individuals and organisations.

Exclusions

No donations for the relief of rates, taxes, fines or other public funds.

Applications

In writing to the correspondent either directly by the individual or through a social worker, Citizens Advice or other welfare agency. Applications are considered at any time.

Bingham

The Bingham Trust Scheme

£0

Correspondent: Gillian M Bailey, 20 Tithby Road, Bingham, Nottingham NG13 8GN (01949 838673)

Trustees: Joan Ward; Philip Bacon; Gillian Bailey; Janet Richie; Kathleen Quibell; Philip Jacques; Brian Richie; Rosemary Pigula; Mike Fish; Catherine Hobson; Ponniah Chandrakumar; Katherine Cox.

CC Number: 513436

Eligibility

People under the age of 21 living in Bingham.

Types of grants

Grants in the range of £50 and £150 to help with expenses incurred in the course of education, religious and physical welfare and so on. They are made in January and early July each year.

Annual grant total

In 2010/11 the scheme had an income of £162 and a total expenditure of £0.

Applications

Application forms are available from: Mrs R Pingula, 74 Nottingham Road, Bingham, Nottinghamshire NG13 8AW. They can be submitted directly by the individual or a family member by 30 April and 31 October each year.

Bingham United Charities

£1,500

Correspondent: Claire Pegg, 6 Park Road, Barnstone, Nottinghamshire NG13 9JG (01949 861181)

Trustees: Maureen Stockwood; Eric Sharp; Sally Abbey; Paul Durber.

CC Number: 213913

Eligibility

People in need who live in the parish of Bingham.

Types of grants

One-off grants in the range of £50 to £600. Grants given have included those towards: Christmas gifts for a struggling family; carpets for a recently rehabilitated man; respite care; and visiting expenses for local clergy members.

Annual grant total

In 2010/11 the trust had an income of £8,400 and a total expenditure of £3,600.

Exclusions

Grants are not given to the same person twice.

Applications

In writing to the correspondent, preferably directly by the individual; alternatively, they can be submitted through a social worker, Citizens Advice or other welfare agency. Applications are considered on the second Tuesday in alternate months, commencing in May. Details of the purpose of the grant and other grants being sought should be included.

Other information

Grants are also given to organisations and individuals for educational purposes.

Carlton in Lindrick

The Christopher Johnson and the Green Charity

£1,000

Correspondent: C E R Towle, Hon. Secretary and Treasurer, 135 Windsor Road, Carlton in Lindrick, Worksop, Nottinghamshire S81 9DH (01909 731069; email: 1cert@tiscali.co.uk)

Trustees: Alistair Williams; Robin Johnson; Christine Connelly; Robin Towle; Christopher Smith; Jeanette Hurcon; Yvonne Jones; Jim Halpin; Gordon Greenwood; Michael Mills.

CC Number: 219610

Eligibility

People in need who live in the village of Carlton in Lindrick.

Types of grants

One-off grants according to need.

Annual grant total

Grants usually total about £2,000 each year and are given for educational and welfare purposes.

Applications

In writing to the correspondent either directly by the individual, via a third party such as a social worker, doctor or district nurse or through a Citizens Advice or other welfare agency. Applications are considered throughout the year.

Coddington

The Coddington United Charities

£9,000

Correspondent: A Morrison, Clerk to the Trustees, Alasdair Morrison and Partners, 26 Kirkgate, Newark, Nottinghamshire NG24 1AB (01636 700888; fax: 01636 700885)

Trustees: Mike Clark; Isabel Allen; William John Bartley; Mary Molloson; Patricia Bartley; Mike Bache; Gill Southgate.

CC Number: 1046378

Eligibility

People in need who live in the parish of Coddington.

Types of grants

One-off grants for individuals resident in the charity's almshouses and general relief in need.

Annual grant total

In 2011 the charities had an income of £13,000 and a total expenditure of £11,000.

Applications

In writing to the correspondent. Applications can be submitted at any time, either through a third party such as a social worker or Citizens Advice or directly by the individual.

Farndon

The Farndon Relief-in-Need Charity

£600

Correspondent: L G Aslin, Trustee, 1 Village Close, Farndon, Newark, Nottinghamshire NG24 4SY (01636 705798)

Trustees: Mr L. G. Aslin; Christine Ruth Clark; Keith Helliwell; Michael Baker; Revd W. D. Milner.

CC Number: 215940

Eligibility

People in need who live in the parish of Farndon.

Types of grants

One-off grants, Christmas hampers and clothing vouchers.

Annual grant total

About £1,200 a year. Grants are given to both individuals and organisations.

Applications

In writing to the correspondent directly by the individual or through a third party such as Citizens Advice or a social worker. The trustees meet twice a year, usually in May and October. Emergency applications can be considered at other times.

Gotham

Doctor M. A. Gerrard's Gotham Old People's Benevolent Fund

£600

Correspondent: Ms J Raven, The Old Rectory, 33 Leake Road, Gotham, Nottingham NG11 0HW (01159 830863; email: gothamclerk@yahoo.co.uk)

Trustees: J. A. Raven; Rebecca Muir; Revd Richard Coleman; David Smith; Valerie Brown.

CC Number: 244908

Eligibility
Older people in need who live, or have lived, in the parish of Gotham.

Types of grants
One-off grants according to need. Gifts in kind are also available.

Annual grant total
Grants usually total around £600 per year.

Applications
In writing to the correspondent, submitted directly by the individual or via a third party such as a social worker.

Other information
The fund also makes grants to organisations.

Hucknall

The Hucknall Relief-in-Need Charity

£1,000

Correspondent: Kenneth Creed, 67 Glendon Drive, Hucknall, Nottingham NG15 6DF (01159 635929)

Trustees: Brian William Whitelocks; Revd George Knowles; John Frederick Deller; Alan Cooper; James Blagden; Harry S. Toseland.

CC Number: 215974

Eligibility
People in need who live in Hucknall, with a preference for 'poor householders'.

Types of grants
One-off and recurrent grants according to need.

Annual grant total
Income averages around £4,000 per year and expenditure around £2,300 per year.

Exclusions
No grants for the relief of rates, taxes or other public funds.

Applications
In writing to the correspondent at any time. Individuals should apply through a social worker, minister of religion or similar third party.

Other information
The charity also makes grants to organisations.

Long Bennington and Foston

Long Bennington Charities

£6,500

Correspondent: Mrs Nicola Brown, Trustee, 61 Main Road, Long Bennington, Newark, Nottinghamshire NG23 5DJ (01400 282458)

Trustees: Margaret Ogden; Gay Baggaley; Colin Edward Bates; Nicola Beverley Brown; Sandra Jane Pocock; Revd Michelle Massey; Paul Wood.

CC Number: 214893

Eligibility
People in need who live in the parish of Long Bennington.

Types of grants
One-off grants according to need. Recent grants have been given for garden maintenance and disability aids like wheelchairs and ramps.

Annual grant total
In 2010 the charity had an income of £5,400 and a total expenditure of £6,600.

Applications
In writing to the correspondent directly by the individual or through a third party.

Mansfield

The Brunts Charity

£14,000

Correspondent: K F Williams, Brunts Chambers, 2 Toothill Lane, Mansfield, Notts NG18 1NJ (01623 623055)

Trustees: Reg Strauther; Keith Frederick Williams; Chris Paul Winterton; Dawn Undy; John Maltby White; Cllr Barry Answer; Cllr Linda Wilkinson; Jim

Hawkins; Malcolm Sage; Jim Ellsey; Cllr Andrew Tristram.

CC Number: 213407

Eligibility
Older people over 60 who are in need and have lived in the former borough of Mansfield (as constituted in 1958) for at least five years.

Types of grants
Regular allowances in the form of small pensions. Christmas gifts are also available.

Annual grant total
In 2010/11 the charity had assets of £11.6 million and an income of £593,000. During the year £3,800 was given in pensions, £8,700 in Christmas gifts and £1,900 in other grants.

Applications
On a form available from the correspondent to be submitted directly by the individual. Applications are considered regularly.

Other information
The charity's main concern is the provision of almshouses for elderly residents in financial difficulty. It also makes grants to local organisations.

Newark

The Mary Elizabeth Siebel Trust

£66,000 (77 grants)

Correspondent: Frances Kelly, Tallents Solicitors, 3 Middlegate, Newark, Nottinghamshire NG24 1AQ (01636 671881; fax: 01636 700148; email: frances.kelly@tallents.co.uk)

Trustees: Jean Moore; David McKenny; Sarah Watson; Ann Austin; Peter Blatherwick; Rosemary White.

CC Number: 1001255

Eligibility
People over 60 years of age who are in poor health and live within a 12 mile radius of Newark Town Hall.

Types of grants
One-off grants ranging from £50 to £2,500. The trust aims to enable individual applicants to live in their own homes e.g. help with the cost of stairlifts, essential home repairs, aids for disabled people, care at home, relief for carers and so on.

Annual grant total
In 2010/11 the trust had assets of £2.5 million, an income of £131,000 and a total expenditure of £117,000. Grants were made to 77 individuals totalling £66,000.

Applications

On a form available from the correspondent. Applications can be submitted at any time but must be endorsed by a recognised third party such as a doctor or social worker. Individuals are usually visited by the charity's assessor who will then make a recommendation to the trustees. The trustees meet every two months to consider applications.

Other information

Grants are also made to organisations (£17,000 in 2010/11).

Nottingham

Bilby's and Cooper's Relief in Need Charity

£500 (3 grants)

Correspondent: The Trustees, Somersby Consulting Ltd, 100 Somersby Road, Woodthorpe, Nottingham NG5 4LT

Trustees: John Vernon Moore; Richard Nowell; Cllr Michael Edwards.

CC Number: 215185

Eligibility

People in need who live in the city of Nottingham.

Types of grants

One-off grants ranging from £50 to £200.

Annual grant total

About £500.

Applications

In writing to the correspondent either through a social worker, Citizens Advice or other welfare agency, or directly by the individual. Applications are considered at any time.

The Frank Hodson Foundation Ltd

£1,600

Correspondent: Mr John Ball, 23 Caroline Close, Alvaston, Derby DE24 0QX (email: john.ball@ jbprofessionalservices.co.uk)

Trustees: Sidney John Christophers; Gordon Melvyn Gill; Simon Perkins; John Ball; Ian Fisher; Nicola Suzanne Grant Pyatt; Paul John Tomkins; Michael James Price; Richard Harley Pascual.

CC Number: 213320

Eligibility

People who live in one of the trust's properties and are in need.

Types of grants

Small grants and other benefits to residents.

Annual grant total

In 2010/11 the trust had assets of £7.4 million and an income of £235,000. 'Gifts to residents' totalled £1,600.

Exclusions

The foundation does not provide grants for lifts nor for any nursing or warden-aided assistance.

Applications

On a form available from the correspondent, submitted directly by the individual. Applications should be sent to Mrs E Ellis, 9 Old Hall Drive, Mapperly Park, Nottingham NG3 5EZ.

Other information

The trust provides rent free accommodation for people over 60 years old.

The Nottingham Aged Person's Trust

£0

Correspondent: Vicky Richards, Nottingham City Council, Single Gateway Unit, Communities Courtyard, Wollaton Road, Nottingham NG8 2AD (01158 762179)

CC Number: 242499

Eligibility

People in need, over 60 years of age, who live in the city of Nottingham and are in receipt of, or eligible for, the state retirement pension.

Types of grants

One-off grants ranging from £15 to £200 towards, for example, travel expenses to visit sick or older relatives; help for victims of crime; medical items; household costs.

Annual grant total

There has been no expenditure by this fund since before 2007, although the administrators have informed us that it is still active and open to applications.

Exclusions

Only one award per year will be made to any individual who makes a successful application.

Applications

On a form available from the correspondent. Applications can be submitted directly by the individual or family member. There are no deadlines.

The Thorpe Trust

£18,000

Correspondent: Mrs Mandy Kelly, Actons Solicitors, 20 Regent Street, Nottingham NG1 5BQ (email: mandy. kelly@actons.co.uk)

Trustees: Richard Frank Leman; Margaret Alison Shaw; Joan Dunn.

CC Number: 214611

Eligibility

Widows and unmarried women in need who live within a mile radius of Nottingham city centre. The recipients must be the widows or fatherless daughters of clergymen, gentlemen or professional people or of people engaged (otherwise than in a menial capacity) in trade or agriculture.

Types of grants

Recurrent grants according to need.

Annual grant total

In 2010/11 the trust had an income of £16,000 and a total expenditure of £15,600.

Applications

On a form available from the correspondent. Applications can be submitted directly by the individual or through a social worker, Citizens Advice or other welfare agency. They are considered once during the summer and at Christmas.

Warsop

The Warsop United Charities

£2,500

Correspondent: Mrs J R Simmons, Newquay, Clumber Street, Warsop, Mansfield, Nottinghamshire NG20 0LX

Trustees: Peter Crawford; Alex Hague; Angela Price; Anthony Hague; Jean Simmonds; Joan Long.

CC Number: 224821

Eligibility

People in need who live in the urban district of Warsop (Warsop, Church Warsop, Warsop Vale, Meden Vale, Spion Kop and Skoonholme).

Types of grants

One-off grants for necessities and quarterly grants to about 60 individuals.

Annual grant total

Previously about £5,000.

Applications

In writing to the correspondent. Trustees meet three or four times a year.

Other information

Grants are also made for educational purposes.

Shropshire

The Atherton Trust

£900

Correspondent: Paul Adams, Whittingham Riddell LLP, Belmont House, Shrewsbury Business Park, Shrewsbury SY2 6LG (01743 273273; email: pa@whittinghamriddell.co.uk)

Trustees: Frederick Morris; George Hall; Rodney Scott; Neville Lewis; John Pope; Stella Bridgewater.

CC Number: 515220

Eligibility

People who are widowed, orphaned, sick, have disabilities or are otherwise in need and live in the parishes of Pontesbury and Hanwood and the villages of Annscroft and Hook-a-Gate in the county of Shropshire.

Types of grants

One-off and recurrent grants according to need.

Annual grant total

In 2010/11 the trust had an income of £4,000 and a total expenditure of £5,000. Generally the trust gives around £900 annually to individuals for welfare purposes.

Applications

On a form available from the correspondent, to be submitted directly by the individual. Applications are considered in February, May, August and November.

Other information

The trust also supports institutions that give support and services to people who need aid due to loss of sight, limb or health by accident or inevitable causes.

The Ellen Barnes Charitable Trust

£5,000

Correspondent: Mark Haddon Woodward, Crampton Pym and Lewis, 47 Willow Street, Oswestry, Shropshire SY11 1PR (01691 653301; fax: 01691 658699; email: info@crampton-pym-lewis.co.uk; website: www.crampton-pym-lewis.co.uk)

Trustees: David Herbert; Heather Hughes; John Bampfield; David Adams; Karen Ashton; Peter Bevington.

CC Number: 217344

Eligibility

People in need who live in Weston Rhyn and adjoining parishes.

Types of grants

Although the trust's income is mainly used to run six almshouses, one-off grants are considered.

Annual grant total

In 2010 the trust had an income of £20,000 and a total expenditure of £35,000. Grants were made totalling about £5,000.

Applications

In writing to the correspondent either directly by the individual or through a social worker, Citizens Advice, doctor or other welfare agency. Applications are considered throughout the year.

Other information

The trust's main activity is the provision of almshouses.

The Lady Forester Trust

£47,000 (89 grants)

Correspondent: Mrs Janet McGorman, The Administrator, Willey Park, Broseley, Shropshire TF12 5JJ (01952 884318; fax: 01952 883680; email: ladyforesttrust@willeyestates.co.uk)

Trustees: Catherine Lady Forester; Hon Alice Stoker; Libby Collinson; John Michael Dugdale; Henry Carpenter; Lord Forester; Lady Forester; Janette Stewart.

CC Number: 241187

Eligibility

Firstly, people who live in the ancient Borough of Wenlock and then to the inhabitants of the county of Shropshire who are sick, disabled, convalescent or infirm.

Types of grants

One-off grants for medical equipment, nursing care, travel to and from hospitals and other medical needs not otherwise available on the NHS.

Annual grant total

In 2011 the trust held assets of £4.3 million and had an income of £146,000. Grants to 89 individuals totalled £47,000.

Exclusions

No retrospective grants are made, nor are grants given for building repairs/alterations, home/garden improvements or household bills.

Applications

On a form available from the correspondent. Applications should be made through a doctor (or Social Services in exceptional circumstances) and are considered on a quarterly basis.

Other information

Grants are also made to local charitable organisations (£67,000 in 2011).

Dr Gardner's Charity for Sick Nurses

£1,000

Correspondent: Dr L F Hill, Radbrook Stables, Radbrook Road, Shrewsbury SY3 9BQ

Trustees: Revd Mark Thomas; Ian Davies; Judith Williams; June Whitaker; Dr Leonard Hill; Sheila Astbury; Dr Roger Thompson; Dr Jonathan Beach; Jackie Brennand; Emma Kidson; Jill L. Maltby; Peter J. Stewart; Cllr Peter Adams.

CC Number: 218202

Eligibility

Nurses in need who live in Shropshire.

Types of grants

One-off grants, usually of up to about £300, to help sick nurses to convalesce or to have further help to enable them to return to work. Grants are made to individuals and organisations.

Annual grant total

Grants average around £1,000 per year.

Applications

On a form available from the correspondent. Applications can be submitted at any time either through a social worker, Citizens Advice or other welfare agency, or directly by the individual or a relevant third party.

Gibbons Charity

£2,800

Correspondent: D G Woolford, The Swallows, Station Road, Admaston, Telford, Shropshire TF5 0AW (01952 243846; email: don.woolford@btinternet.com)

Trustees: Revd Stephen Lowe; Ven John Hall; The Bishop of Shrewsbury; Revd Alistair Magowan; Revd David Mawson; Mayor of Shrewsbury.

CC Number: 215171

Eligibility

Widows and widowers and children of Shropshire Church of England clergy and clergy who have retired and face hardship.

Types of grants

One-off and recurrent grants according to need.

Annual grant total

On average this charity has a total annual expenditure of around £1,500.

Applications

In writing to the correspondent.

The Basil Houghton Memorial Trust

£5,000

Correspondent: Julia Baron, c/o Community Council Building, The Creative Quarter, Shrewsbury Business Park, Shrewsbury SY2 6LG (01743 360641; email: houghton.trust@ shropshire-rcc.org.uk)

Trustees: Julia Baron; John Hollick; John Lionel Miles; Peter Smith; Moira Smith; Elizabeth Hayward; Denis Orme.

CC Number: 1101947

Eligibility

People with learning disabilities who are in need and live in Shropshire.

Types of grants

One-off grants usually of no more than £250. Grants should be additional to any services provided by statutory bodies.

Annual grant total

In 2010/11 the trust had an income of £11,000 and a total expenditure of £9,000.

Applications

On a form available from the correspondent.

Other information

Grants are also made to organisations.

The Oswestry Dispensary Fund

£400

Correspondent: Emyr Richard Lloyd, Brown and Lloyd, The Albany, 37–39 Willow Street, Oswestry, Shropshire SY11 1AQ (01691 659194)

Trustees: Betty Yvonne Gull; John Neave; Revd Simon Godfrey Thorburn; Owen Jones; Emma Humpherys; Peter Carkeet-James; William E. Bowen; Cynthia Hawksley; Judy Breeze; Revd Paul Trevor Darlington; Revd Russell Howes.

CC Number: 212212

Eligibility

People who are in poor health and financial difficulties and live in the borough of Oswestry and its surrounding district.

Types of grants

One-off grants, normally up to £300, for items such as medical equipment and care and second-hand television sets.

Annual grant total

Over the past number of years grants have averaged around £300 each year.

Applications

In writing to the correspondent either directly by the individual or via a relevant third party such as a social worker, Citizens Advice or other welfare agency.

The Shropshire Football Association Benevolent Fund

£500

Correspondent: Roy Waterfield, New Stadium, Oteley Road, Shrewsbury, Shropshire SY2 6ST (01743 362769; fax: 01743 270494; email: secretary@shropsfa. com)

Trustees: Graham Arrowsmith; David Ralphs; John Williams.

CC Number: 505509

Eligibility

People in need who live in Shropshire, who are: (i) amateur and professional footballers; (ii) apprentices; (iii) coaches; (iv) managers; (v) any other official or employee of any football team; (vi) referees and referees' assistants and widows and orphans of other persons dependent wholly or partially on any of the above people who may die or be disadvantaged.

Types of grants

One-off and recurrent grants according to need.

Annual grant total

About £500.

Applications

Applications can be submitted at any time and should include details of present income, occupation and any dependents along with any other information which may be helpful.

The Shropshire Welfare Trust

£800

Correspondent: Dr Len Hill, Hon. Secretary, Radbrook Stables, Radbrook Road, Shrewsbury SY3 9BQ (01743 236863; email: dr.lenhill@tiscali.co.uk; website: www.shropshirewelfaretrust.co. uk)

Trustees: Revd Mark Thomas; Ian Davies; Col John Garton-Jones; Judith Williams; June Whitaker; Dr Leonard Hill; Sheila Astbury; Dr Peter Boardman; Dr Roger Thompson; Dr Jonathan

Beach; Jackie Brennand; Emma Kidson; Jill Maltby; Peter Stewart; Peter Adams.

CC Number: 218216

Eligibility

Patients and members of staff in specified hospitals in Shropshire who are in need. People living in Shropshire with medically-related and disability-related expenses.

Types of grants

One-off grants generally in the range of £50 to £300. Previously grants have been given towards the cost of repairs to wheelchairs, washing machines and fridges and for hospital travel costs.

Annual grant total

Grants average about £1,500 per annum. However, the actual figure tends to fluctuate quite widely from year to year.

Applications

On a form available from the correspondent or to download from the website. Advice is also available. Applications can be submitted directly by the individual or through a social worker, Citizens Advice or similar third party.

Other information

Occasional grants are given to organisations with similar objects.

The St Chad's and St Alkmund's Charity

£1,000

Correspondent: L E Smith, Little Garth, 3 Roman Road, Shrewsbury SY3 9AZ (01743 353869; email: lawson-smith@ tiscali.co.uk)

Trustees: Revd Mark Thomas; John Curra Goldsworthy; Mary Thornton Marston; Hazel Sturges; John Holmwood; Joyce Allaway; Andrew Cross; Revd Murray McBride.

CC Number: 231383

Eligibility

People in need who have lived in the ecclesiastical districts of St Chad and St George, Shrewsbury, Astley, Kinnerley, Guildsfield, Great Ness, Annscroft, Oxon and Bicton for not less than five years immediately before their application.

Types of grants

One-off grants of up to £50 to help with the cost of clothes, linen, bedding, tools, medical or other aid in sickness, food or other articles in kind.

Annual grant total

About £1,000.

Applications
On a form available from the correspondent. Applications should be submitted directly by the individual and they are considered at any time.

Other information
The charity also gives support to religious work of the Church of England and to promote education for people under 25.

The Thompson Pritchard Trust

£11,000

Correspondent: Dr Len Hill, Radbrook Stables, Radbrook Road, Shrewsbury SY3 9BQ (01743 236863)

Trustees: Revd Mark Thomas; Ian Davies; Judith Williams; June Whitaker; Dr Leonard Hill; Sheila Astbury; Dr Roger Thompson; Dr Jonathan Beach; Jackie Brennand; Emma Kidson; Jill Maltby; Peter J. Stewart; Cllr Peter Adams.

CC Number: 234601

Eligibility
Individuals who live in Shropshire and have medically-related and disability-related expenses and problems. Preference is given to those who have recently been discharged from hospital.

Types of grants
One-off grants up to £300 are given towards: medical equipment (and repairs); convalescent treatment; domestic equipment which affects health such as washing machine or fridge repairs; expenses incurred during illness, including treatment; and travel and occasional accommodation for relatives during major operations.

Annual grant total
In 2011 the trust had an income of £18,000 and a total expenditure of £14,000.

Exclusions
No recurrent grants or grants towards purchasing, repairing or maintaining buildings or to pay off debts.

Applications
On a form available from the correspondent. Applications for small grants can be submitted at any time either directly by the individual or through a relevant third party such as a social worker, Citizens Advice or other welfare agency. Advice is available from the trust.

Alveley
The Alveley Charity

£11,000

Correspondent: The Trustees, MFG Solicitors, Carlton House, Worcester Street, Kidderminster DY10 1BA (01562 820181)

CC Number: 1026017

Eligibility
People in need who live in the parishes of Alveley and Romsley.

Types of grants
One-off grants according to need.

Annual grant total
In 2010/11 the charity had an income of £19,000 and a total expenditure of £12,000.

Applications
In writing to the correspondent either directly by the individual, or through a social worker, Citizens Advice or other welfare agency.

Bridgnorth
The Bridgnorth Parish Charity

£2,000

Correspondent: Elizabeth Smallman, Clerk, 37 Stourbridge Road, Bridgnorth WV15 5AZ (01746 764149; email: eeesmallman@aol.com)

Trustees: Revd Simon Cawdell; Revd Angela Rogers; Dr Simon Martin; Elizabeth Smallman; Constance Baines.

CC Number: 243890

Eligibility
People living in Bridgnorth parish, including Oldbury and Eardington, who are in need.

Types of grants
One-off grants according to need, including those towards playgroup fees, school visits, funeral expenses and heating costs.

Annual grant total
In 2010 the charity had both an income and total expenditure of £5,500.

Applications
In writing to the correspondent either directly by the individual or through a doctor, nurse, member of the local clergy, social worker, Citizens Advice or other welfare agency.

Other information
Grants are also made to organisations.

Hodnet
The Hodnet Consolidated Eleemosynary Charities

£1,000

Correspondent: Mrs S W France, 26 The Meadows, Hodnet, Market Drayton, Shropshire TF9 3QF (01630 685907)

Trustees: Janice Parker; Ann Taylor; John Powell; Gerald Mothershaw; Gillian Roberts; Dr James Mehta; David Morgan; Revd Charmian Beech.

CC Number: 218213

Eligibility
People in need who live in Hodnet parish.

Types of grants
Grants include Christmas parcels for people of pensionable age.

Annual grant total
In 2010 the charities had an income of £3,500 and a total expenditure of £2,500. Grants usually total around £2,000.

Applications
In writing to the correspondent for consideration throughout the year. Applications can be submitted directly by the individual or through a social worker, Citizens Advice or other welfare agency.

Other information
This is essentially a relief-in-need charity that also gives money to students for books.

Hopesay
Hopesay Parish Trust

£500

Correspondent: David Evans, Park Farm, The Fish, Hopesay, Craven Arms, Shropshire SY7 8HG (01588 660545)

Trustees: Anne Weller; Judith Clarke; Caroline Habershon; Albert Evans; Christine Perkins; David Evans.

CC Number: 1066894

Eligibility
People in need living in the parish of Hopesay. Priority is given to those under 25 years old.

Types of grants
One-off grants between £25 and £650 according to need.

Annual grant total
Grants usually total around £1,000 per year.

Exclusions

Grants are not made where the funding is the responsibility of central or local government, whether or not the individual has taken up such provision.

Applications

Preferably on an application form, available from the correspondent. The application form covers the essential information required, and the trustees will ask for further details if necessary. Applications can be made at any time, either directly by the individual, or by a third party on their behalf, such as parent/guardian, teacher or social worker, or through an organisation such as Citizens Advice or a school. They can be submitted at any time.

Other information

The trust gives priority to educational grants. At the trustees' discretion, any surplus income may be applied for other charitable purposes but only within the parish.

Lilleshall

The Charity of Edith Emily Todd

£7,000

Correspondent: Mary Heather Ayres, 4 Willmoor Lane, Lilleshall, Newport, Shropshire TF10 9EE (01952 606053)

Trustees: C. R. G. Ayres; Gillian Margaret Hornby; Revd Michael Christopher Jones; Edith Pamela Millard; Jean Rozzell.

CC Number: 215058

Eligibility

People over the age of 60 who are in need and who live in the ecclesiastical parish of Lilleshall.

Types of grants

Pensions of £15 a month with a bonus payment of around £30 at Christmas.

Annual grant total

In 2010/11 the charity had an income of £8,200 and a total expenditure of £7,300

Applications

In writing directly by the individual to the correspondent. Applications are considered on receipt.

Shrewsbury

The Gorsuch, Langley and Prynce Charity

£32,000 (242 grants)

Correspondent: Pamela Moseley, 116 Underdale Road, Shrewsbury SY2 5EF

Trustees: Ken Vine; Chris Huss; Revd Philip James Williams; Revd Paul Gregory Firmin; Tony Durnell; Diana Morgan; Jo Jones.

CC Number: 247223

Eligibility

People in need who live in the parishes of Holy Cross (the Abbey) and St Giles in Shrewsbury.

Types of grants

One-off and recurrent grants ranging from £50 to £500. Recent grants have been given towards furniture, carpets, washing machines, cookers, fridges, baby clothes and cots.

Annual grant total

In 2011 the charity had assets of £841,000 and an income of £37,000. Grants were made to 242 individuals and families totalling £32,000.

Applications

In writing to the correspondent through a social worker, healthcare professional, Citizens Advice or other welfare agency such as Homestart. Applications should include details of the full the amount required and why it is needed. They are considered on a regular basis.

Staffordshire

Albrighton Relief in Need Charity

£1,400

Correspondent: David Beechey, 34 Station Road, Albrighton, Wolverhampton WV7 3QG (01902 372779; email: dabeechey@blueyonder. co.uk)

CC Number: 240494

Eligibility

People in need who live in the parishes of Albrighton and Boningale.

Types of grants

One-off grants according to need. Recent grants have been made for clothing, electrical goods, food, holidays, travel expenses, specialised computers, furniture and medical and disability equipment. Christmas hampers are also distributed.

Annual grant total

Grants average around £1,500 a year, though the actual grant figure tends to fluctuate quite widely.

Applications

In writing to the correspondent either directly by the individual or through a third party such as a social worker, Citizens Advice, GP, district nurse or health visitor.

The Burton on Trent Nursing Endowment Fund

£3,000

Correspondent: Marilyn Arnold, East Staffordshire CVS, Voluntary Services Centre, Union Street, Burton-on-Trent DE14 1AA (01283 543414)

Trustees: Gwendoline Margaret Foster; Mary Angela Adams; Alison Mary Parker; Elizabeth Anne Timms; Susan Anne Rose; Valerie McCarthy; Alderman Marie Lorain Nash.

CC Number: 239185

Eligibility

People in need who live in the former county borough of Burton-on-Trent.

Types of grants

One-off grants towards, for example, chiropody treatment, bedding, removal costs, electric scooter batteries, fridges, freezers and childcare provision.

Annual grant total

Grants to individuals average around £3,000 per year.

Applications

On a form available from the correspondent. Applications can come directly via the individual or through a recognised referral agency (social worker, Citizens Advice, local GP and so on).

Other information

The fund also makes grants to organisations.

Consolidated Charity of Burton upon Trent

£37,000 (131 grants)

Correspondent: Thomas J Bramall, Clerk, Talbot and Co., 148 High Street, Burton upon Trent, Staffordshire DE14 1JY (01283 564716; fax: 01283 510861; email: clerk@ consolidatedcharityburton.org.uk; website: www.consolidatedcharityburton. org.uk)

Trustees: Valerie Burton; Gwendoline Foster; Patricia Hill; Tom Dawn; Beryl Toon; Alison Parker; Dinsdale Salter;

John Peach; Marie Nash; Peter Davies; Margaret Heather; Dennis Fletcher; Patricia Ackroyd; Gerald Hamilton; Elizabeth Staples; Ben Robinson; David Leese; Robert Styles; Leonard Milner.

CC Number: 239072

Eligibility

People in need who live in the former county of Burton upon Trent or the parishes of Branston, Stretton or Outwoods.

Types of grants

One-off grants of up to £500 (£250 for applicants who have been living in the area for less than two years) for essential items such as cookers, fridge-freezers, washing machines, carpets, furniture, bedding, mobility aids and children's clothing.

Annual grant total

In 2011 the trust had assets of £10.7 million and an income of £436,000. The trust gave £37,000 in 131 grants to individuals for relief-in-need purposes

Exclusions

Grants are not awarded for the relief of debt. Only one item per applicant.

Applications

On a form available to download from the website or from the correspondent, supported by evidence of income and outgoings, quotes from recommended suppliers and a letter of support from an appropriate support worker or welfare agency. Applications can be made at any time.

Other information

The trust also makes grants to local organisations and to individuals for educational purposes.

The Baron Davenport Emergency Grant (North Staffordshire)

£5,000

Correspondent: Information and Advice Service, c/o Age UK, 83–85 Trinity Street, Hanley, Stoke-on-Trent ST1 5NA (01782 286809)

Eligibility

Women (widows, singles and divorcees) who have lived in north Staffordshire for at least ten years and are over the age of 60. Applicants must live alone and have a low income and little or no savings.

Types of grants

One-off grants for emergencies only.

Annual grant total

Grants usually total about £5,000 a year.

Applications

On a form available from the correspondent. Applications are considered upon receipt.

Other information

For information on Baron Davenport's Charity Trust, see entry in the Midlands general section.

The Baron Davenport Emergency Grant (Staffordshire)

£2,400

Correspondent: Grants Administrator, Stafford District Voluntary Services, 131–141 North Walls, Stafford ST16 3AD (01785 606670; email: office@ sdvs.org.uk)

Eligibility

Widows, unmarried women, divorcees and women abandoned by their husbands, who are over 60 years old and have lived in Staffordshire for at least ten years. Help may be given to younger women in special circumstances.

Types of grants

One-off and recurrent grants of up to £250 towards electrical goods, clothing, living costs, household bills, food, medical equipment, furniture, disability equipment, help in the home and so on.

Annual grant total

In 2012 grants totalling £2,400 were distributed.

Applications

On a form to be submitted either directly by the individual or through an appropriate third party, such as a family member or welfare agency. Applications are usually considered upon receipt.

The Fred Linford Charitable Trust

£0

Correspondent: David Linford, Trustee, The Kennels, Stockings Lane, Upper Longdon, Rugeley, Staffordshire WS15 1QF (01543 491230)

Trustees: David Linford; Barbara Linford; Kenneth William Bedford.

CC Number: 1012203

Eligibility

People who live in the south Staffordshire area and are in need.

Types of grants

One-off and recurrent grants according to need.

Annual grant total

The income and expenditure of the trust fluctuates annually, with no income or expenditure in 2010/11 and 2008/9. In 2009/10 the trust had an income and expenditure of £9,000.

Applications

In writing to the correspondent.

Malam-Heath Fund

£2,000 (19 grants)

Correspondent: Grants team, Staffordshire Community Foundation, The Dudson Centre, Hope Street, Hanley, Stoke-on-Trent ST1 5DD (01782 683000; fax: 01782 683199; email: info@ staffsfoundation.org.uk)

Trustees: Mark Barnish; Neil Dawson; Jacqueline Farrell; Richard Haszard; Patricia Griffin; Dr Teeranlall Ramgopal; Ben Robinson; Prakash Samani; Jean Marjorie Gibson; Simon John Morris.

CC Number: 1091628

Eligibility

People in need, who live in Stoke-on-Trent, are in receipt of benefits and need a holiday as part of their convalescence.

Types of grants

One-off grants to contribute towards the cost of recuperative holidays. The award rates are as follows:
- Single person for one week (£100) or two weeks (£150)
- Couple for one week (£200) or two weeks (£250)

Annual grant total

In 2010/11 19 grants were made totalling £2,000.

Exclusions

No grants to pay for holidays already booked and paid for without the express permission of the grants panel.

Applications

On a form available from the website. The form may be returned by post-or completed electronically and emailed to the community foundation. The form includes a reference section to be completed by a doctor, health visitor, local councillor or similar.

Other information

The fund was formed in 2011 by the merger of the Edward Malam Convalescent Fund and the Heath Memorial Trust Fund. It is managed by the Staffordshire Community Foundation.

The North Staffordshire Coalfield Miners Relief Fund

£15,000

Correspondent: Susan Jackson, c/o Coal Industry Social Welfare Organisation, 142 Queens Road, Penkhull, Stoke-on-Trent, Staffordshire ST4 7LH (01782 744996; fax: 01782 749117)

Trustees: Joe Wills; Jim Dowling; John Lockett; Ken Hollingsworth.

CC Number: 209616

Eligibility

Mineworkers or retired mineworkers who worked in the North Staffordshire coalfield (including Cheadle), and their widows or dependents. The mineworker must have suffered an industrial accident or disease or died as a result of their duties.

Types of grants

One-off grants according to need.

Annual grant total

In 2010/11 the trust had an income of £2,900 and a total expenditure of £16,000.

Applications

In writing to the correspondent or by telephone either directly by the individual or via a third party such as a social worker, Citizens Advice or other welfare agency. Grants are given after a home visit. Applications are considered throughout the year.

Other information

Grants are also made to organisations.

The Strasser Foundation

£1,000

Correspondent: The Trustees, c/o Knights Solicitors, The Brampton, Newcastle-under-Lyme, Staffordshire ST5 0QW (01782 619225)

Trustees: Tony Bell; Alan Booth.

CC Number: 501703

Eligibility

Individuals in need in the local area, with a preference for North Staffordshire.

Types of grants

Usually one-off grants for a specific cause or need, to help with the relief of poverty.

Annual grant total

In 2010/11 the trust had an income of £16,000 and a total expenditure of £26,000. Previously grants were made totalling £24,000, of which about £2,000 was given to individuals for educational and welfare purposes. The remaining £22,000 was awarded to organisations.

Applications

In writing to the correspondent. The trustees meet quarterly. Applications are only acknowledged if an sae is sent.

Church Eaton

The Church Eaton Charities

£6,000

Correspondent: Stephen Rutherford, 5 Ashley Court, Church Eaton, Stafford ST20 0BJ (01785 823958)

Trustees: Stephen Henry Rutherford; Irene Bennett; David Rogers; Elizabeth Joyce Beard; Penelope Jane Taylor.

CC Number: 216179

Eligibility

People in need who live in the parish of Church Eaton.

Types of grants

Payment for, or provision of, items, services or facilities that would reduce the individual's need. Recent grants have been given for TV licences, winter fuel payments and lifeline telephones.

Annual grant total

In 2011 the charity had an income of £8,800 and a total expenditure of £6,800.

Applications

In writing to the correspondent. Applications are considered when received.

Enville

The Enville Village Trust

£2,400

Correspondent: J A Gloss, Walls Cottage, Kinver Road, Enville, Stourbridge DY7 5HE (01384 873691)

Trustees: Brian Edwards; John Redwood; Michael Scott-Bolton; Peter Williams; Dianna Williams; Richard Elliot Jones.

CC Number: 231563

Eligibility

People in need who live in the parish of Enville, with a preference for older people.

Types of grants

One-off grants ranging from £50 to £150. Grants may not always be given directly to individuals; sometimes they may be to provide a service to individuals, which they cannot themselves afford. Grants have been given for telephone installation/connection (including an emergency contact line), emergency medical help, optician bills for partially-sighted people, special dental treatment, travel to hospital, food parcels, clothing and fuel in winter.

Annual grant total

On average this trust has an income of around £2,400 and a total expenditure of between £1,500 and £2,500.

Applications

In writing to the correspondent. Applications can be submitted either directly by the individual or through a social worker, the vicar of the parish church or the village welfare group. They are considered at any time.

Leek

The Carr Trust

£20,000

Correspondent: Alison Carp, St Lukes Church of England, Fountain Street, Leek, Staffordshire ST13 6JS (01538 373306; fax: 01538 399180; email: stlukesleek@hotmail.co.uk)

Trustees: John Herbert Davis; Revd Roger Woods; Peter R. Stretch; John Edwin Belfield; Patricia Lockett; Leslie Scott; Maureen Belfield.

CC Number: 216764

Eligibility

People in need who live in Leek.

Types of grants

Primarily recurrent grants, usually of around £20 a month towards items, services and facilities that will help to reduce need or hardship. One-off grants are also available and most beneficiaries receive a Christmas bonus.

Annual grant total

In 2010 the trust had assets of £538,000 and an income of £27,000. Grants totalled £31,000 although no further breakdown was available.

Applications

In writing to the correspondent. An advert about the grants appears in a local paper in March each year. The trustees require details of the applicant's age, marital status, income, savings and details of any property owned.

Other information

The trust also makes grants to organisations.

Lichfield

The Lichfield Municipal Charities

£7,800 (21 grants)

Correspondent: Simon R James, Clerk, Ansons Solicitors, St Mary's Chambers, 5 Breadmarket Street, Lichfield, Staffordshire WS13 6LQ (01543 263456; fax: 01543 250942; email: sjames@ ansonsllp.com)

Trustees: John Norman Wilks; N. G. Sedgwick; John Russell; Cllr Mark Andrew Warfield; Doris English; Jeanette Allsopp; Barry Davis Diggle; Janet May Eagland; Valerie Ann Diggle; Carl Stokes; Lorna Benham; Catherine Pepper.

CC Number: 254299

Eligibility

Individuals in need who live in the city of Lichfield (as it was pre-1974).

Types of grants

One-off grants according to need.

Annual grant total

In 2011 the charity had assets of £1.9 million and an income of £69,000. Grants were made to 21 individuals totalling £7,800.

Applications

On a form available from the correspondent. Trustees meet four times a year in March, June, September and December.

Other information

Grants are also made to organisations (£3,800 in 2011).

Michael Lowe's and Associated Charities

£36,000 (207 grants)

Correspondent: C P Kitto, Ansons LLP, 5–7 Breadmarket Street, Lichfield, Staffordshire WS13 6LQ (01543 267995)

Trustees: John Norman Wilks; Peter Charles Boggis; N. G. Sedgwick; Tony Wilkins; Jeanette Allsopp; Barry Davis Diggle; Anthony Wilson; E. J. Ashley; Terry Finn; Gordon Hudson; Revd Ian Hayter.

CC Number: 214785

Eligibility

People in need who live in the city of Lichfield, particularly older people and those requiring help in an emergency.

Types of grants

One-off grants ranging from £50 to £600 for domestic items, special chairs, school uniforms, wheelchairs and so on. People who are over 70 and living on a low income can also apply for fuel grants. The trustees may require the recipient to make a contribution of 10% to the cost of any item provided.

Annual grant total

In 2010/11 the trust had assets of £1.6 million and an income of £94,000. Grants were made to 207 individuals totalling £36,000 and were distributed as follows:

Individual grants	88	£29,000
Fuel grants	119	£7,100

A further £17,000 was made in grants to organisations.

Applications

On a form available from the correspondent. Applications are considered on their own merits and individuals are usually interviewed before any grant is awarded. The trustees meet on average five times a year to consider grant applications, though special meetings may be called to deal with urgent requests.

Other information

The trust also operates a 'furniture transfer scheme' whereby families are recommended by local welfare agencies and, depending on their circumstances, invited to choose suitable items from the furniture warehouse. 71 families were helped in 2010/11.

Newcastle-under-Lyme

The Newcastle-under-Lyme United Charities

£4,000

Correspondent: Caroline Horne, Civic Offices, Merrial Street, Newcastle-under-Lyme, Staffordshire ST5 2AG (01782 742232; email: caroline.horne@ newcastle-staffs.gov.uk)

Trustees: Gill Williams; David Clarke; Betty Cox; Derek Huckfield; Yvonne Burke; Michael Foy; Betty Caddy; Sandra Simpson; Barry Critchlow; June Walklate.

CC Number: 217916

Eligibility

People in need who live in the borough of Newcastle-under-Lyme (as it was before 1974).

Types of grants

Christmas grants.

Annual grant total

In 2010/11 the trust had an income of £4,000 and a total expenditure of £4,300.

Exclusions

No grants are given to older people living in sheltered housing.

Applications

In writing to the correspondent. Applications should be submitted either directly by the individual or via a friend or family member. They are considered in October each year. The circumstances of beneficiaries are assessed on an annual basis by trustees.

Rugeley

Chetwynd Charity

£2,500

Correspondent: Mr Carl Bennett, Trustee, Sherwood, 17 East Butts Road, Rugeley WS15 2LU (01889 800727)

Trustees: Carl Bennett; Alan Derek Loweth; Annie May Walker; Gary Phillip Bennett; Patricia Tams; Irene Talbot; Paul Adams; Thomas Bryce Anderson; Geoffrey Martin; Michael Grocott.

CC Number: 234806

Eligibility

Inhabitants of the ancient parish of Rugeley, Staffordshire who are in need.

Types of grants

One-off grants according to need.

Annual grant total

In 2011 the trust had an income of £3,400 and a total expenditure of £2,700.

Applications

In writing to the correspondent.

Stoke-on-Trent

The Stoke-on-Trent Children's Holiday Trust Fund

£3,200

Correspondent: The Grants Officer, The Staffordshire Community Foundation, The Dudson Centre, Hope Street, Hanley, Stoke-on-Trent ST1 5DD (01782 683000; fax: 01782 683199; email: jean@ staffsfoundation.org.uk; website: www. staffsfoundation.org.uk)

CC Number: 217005

Eligibility

Children (4–17 years old) with health problems who live in Stoke-on-Trent and whose parents are in receipt of benefits or are on a low income.

Types of grants

One-off grants between £100 and £200 for children who suffer from ill health in Stoke on Trent, towards a recuperative holiday or day trip. Preference is given to educational holidays that are run through a school or college, although private and family holidays will be supported if the need can be demonstrated.

Annual grant total

In 2010/11 the fund assets were valued at £173,000. It had an income of £15,000 and a total expenditure of £4,000.

Exclusions

It is very rare that the trustees will give retrospective grants. Grants are not given to cover the costs of parents' or siblings' holidays.

Applications

On a form available from the website. Applications should be completed by the parent or guardian, although for educational holidays the trust will liaise directly with the school. Applications must also be endorsed by a third party such as the child's doctor, headteacher or social worker. It may help your application to include pricing quotes. Allow six weeks for your application to be processed.

Other information

The fund is now administered by the Staffordshire Community Foundation (1091628).

Tamworth

Beardsley's Relief-in-Need Charity

£8,000

Correspondent: Derek Tomkinson, 'Torview', 95 Main Road, Wigginton, Tamworth, Staffordshire B79 9DU (01543 255612)

Trustees: Mr D. Tomkinson; Mrs D. Templeman; Mr R. P. E. Cope; Mrs J. E. Cope; Mrs E. Coates.

CC Number: 214461

Eligibility

People in need who live in the borough of Tamworth.

Types of grants

One-off grants for health and welfare purposes.

Annual grant total

In 2010/11 the charity had an income of £12,000 and a total expenditure of £11,000.

Applications

In writing to the correspondent, either directly by the individual or through a social worker, Citizens Advice or other welfare agency.

Other information

This trust also makes grants to organisations.

The Rawlet Trust

£15,000

Correspondent: Christine Gilbert, 47 Hedging Lane, Wilnecote, Tamworth B77 5EX (01827 288614; email: christine.gilbert@mail.com)

Trustees: Revd Alan Barrett; Richard Hughes; Ian Perkins; David Milson; Vivian Khan; Jane Mallinson; Betty Bates; Kenneth Gant; Jeremy Oates; Michael Oates.

CC Number: 221732

Eligibility

People in need who live in the borough of Tamworth.

Types of grants

One-off and recurrent grants towards disability aids, bathroom adaptations, holidays, bibles for children and Home Link telephone expenses.

Annual grant total

In 2010/11 the trust had both an income and a total expenditure of £23,000. Previously, grants were made totalling £20,000, of which £4,600 was given in educational grants and £15,000 in non-educational grants.

Applications

On a form available from the correspondent, to be submitted either directly by the individual or through a third party such as a social worker or Citizens Advice. The clerk or one of the trustees will follow up applications if any further information is needed. The trustees meet in January, April, July and October to consider applications.

Other information

Grants are also made to organisations.

The Tamworth Municipal Charity

£2,600

Correspondent: Anthony Goodwin, Tamworth Borough Council, Marmion House, Lichfield Street, Tamworth, Staffordshire B79 7BZ (01827 709212)

Trustees: Revd Alan Barrett; Sheila Scott; Dorothy Munn; Cllr Evelyn Rowe; Cllr John Garner; Jeremy Oates; Anthony Goodwin; Cllr Richard McDermid.

CC Number: 216875

Eligibility

People in need who live in the borough of Tamworth.

Types of grants

One-off grants towards, for example, equipment, household items and hospital travel costs.

Annual grant total

Grants average around £2,600.

Applications

In writing to the correspondent: to be submitted either directly by the individual or through a social worker, Citizens Advice or other welfare agency. Applications should include details of the individual's financial circumstances.

Other information

Grants may also be given to organisations.

Trentham

The Lady Katherine and Sir Richard Leveson Charity

£500

Correspondent: Adam Bainbridge, 67 Jonathan Road, Stoke-on-Trent ST4 8LP (01782 643567)

Trustees: Neil Robinson; Revd Everton McLeod; Kevin Waters; Ross Irving; David Clarke; Adam Bainbridge.

CC Number: 1077372

Eligibility

People in need who live in the ancient parish of Trentham.

Types of grants

One-off and recurrent grants according to need.

Annual grant total

In 2010 the charity had an income of £2,000 and a total expenditure of £1,000.

Applications

In writing to the correspondent either directly by the individual or a relevant third party, or through a social worker, Citizens Advice or other welfare agency. Applications are usually considered in spring and autumn.

Other information

The charity also makes grants to organisations and to individuals for educational purposes.

The Todd Fund

£1,500

Correspondent: Adam Bainbridge, Clerk to the Trustees, 67 Jonathan Road, Trentham, Stoke-on-Trent ST4 8LP (01782 643567)

Trustees: Revd Everton McCleod; Paul Trevor; John Francis Massey.

CC Number: 209922

Eligibility

People in need who live in the ecclesiastical parish of St Mary and All Saints, Trentham.

Types of grants

Older people can receive a recurrent grant, which are reviewed twice a year. The trust can also make one-off grants.

Annual grant total

Grants total around £1,500 each year.

Applications

In writing to the correspondent at any time. Applications can be submitted either through a third party such as a social worker, Citizens Advice or other welfare agency, or directly by the individual.

Tutbury

The Tutbury General Charities

£2,500

Correspondent: Jeanne Minchin, 66 Redhill Lane, Tutbury, Burton-on-Trent, Staffordshire DE13 9JW (01283 813310)

Trustees: Glenys Shenton; Arthur Henry Tipper; David Alan Stephenson; Owen Dyke; Eileen Mason; Juliana Bentley; Frank Turner; Revd Alexandrina Elizabeth Mann; Francis Crossley; Janice Hamer; L. Evans.

CC Number: 215140

Eligibility

Only people in need who live in the parish of Tutbury.

Types of grants

One-off and recurrent grants according to need. All residents in the parish who are over 70 receive a birthday card. Vouchers for fuel or goods at a local store (usually under £20) are also given to about 200 people in need who live within the parish regardless of their age at Christmas.

Special cases are considered on their merits by the trustees but applicants must live in the parish of Tutbury.

Annual grant total

In 2010/11 the charities had an income of £8,000 and a total expenditure of £5,700. Grants are made for welfare and educational purposes.

Applications

The charities have application forms, available from the correspondent, which should be submitted for consideration in November for Christmas vouchers. Inclusion in the birthday voucher scheme can be done at any time (all that is needed is the name, address and date of birth of the person).

Other information

The clerk of the trust states that details of the trust are well publicised within the village.

Warwick-shire

Sir Edward Boughton Long Lawford Charity

£30,000 (125 grants)

Correspondent: Jean Taylor, 12 Millfields Avenue, Rugby, Warwickshire CV21 4HJ (01788 571140)

Trustees: Revd Paul Martin Wilkinson; Audrey Constance Badger; David Bernard Bragg; Elizabeth Barlow; Jacqueline Lewis; Keith Judge; Michael Roberts; Cynthia Langham; Neil Mackenzie.

CC Number: 237841

Eligibility

People in need who live in the parish of Long Lawford or Rugby. Applicants for pensions must have lived in the parish for the last five years.

Types of grants

Pensions of £10 a month and Christmas bonuses of £40. One-off grants are awarded for various welfare purposes, including disability aids, TV licences and stairlifts. Small awards have also been made for swimming classes.

Annual grant total

In 2010 the charity had assets of £1.6 million and an income of £120,000. Grants were made totalling £30,000, of which £17,000 was given in pensions to 113 individuals and £13,000 in 12 one-off grants.

Applications

On a form available from the correspondent, to be considered by the trustees every three months, usually February, May, August and November.

Other information

Grants are also made to local schools and organisations (£53,000 in 2010).

The Baron Davenport Emergency Grant (Leamington Spa, Kenilworth or Warwick)

£4,000 (23 grants)

Correspondent: Linda Price, Grants Administrator, c/o WCAVA – Warwick District, 4–6 Clemens, Leamington Spa, Warwickshire CV31 2DL (01926 477512; fax: 01926 315112; email: warwickinfo@ wcava.org.uk; website: www.wcava.org. uk)

Trustees: Catherine Ann Hayes; Joanne Audrey Shine; John Harris; Eva Robin Aldridge; Revd Mark Beach; Timothy John Jones; Stephen Nightingale; Kathleen Elizabeth Harper.

Eligibility

Widows, single women over 60, and occasionally, young single women who are in need. The children (aged under 25) of these individuals may also qualify for assistance. All beneficiaries must live alone apart from school-aged children and have resided in the Midlands for at least ten years. The applicant's household income should not be more than £165 a week and savings should amount to no more than £6,000.

Applicants who are in receipt of Attendance Allowance or Disability Living Allowance could be eligible for a twice yearly payment of £200–230.

Types of grants

One-off grants of up to £150 can be given for cookers, bath lifts, baby equipment, carpets, telephone extensions, showers, pushchairs and so on.

Annual grant total

In 2010/11 23 women received grants totalling £4,000.

Applications

Applications should be made by letter, including details of status, circumstances, financial situation and a supporting statement from a GP, social worker or similar professional. Grants will only be paid to individuals via the person supporting the applications. For the additional payment for those in receipt of Disability Living Allowance or Attendance Allowance there is a form to complete, available from the correspondent.

Applications should be marked confidential. Those from within the Warwick district should be sent to the correspondent. Other applicants should apply to their closest office of either the Nuneaton and Bedworth office: 72 High Street, Nuneaton, Warwickshire CV11 5DA or the Rugby office: 19 and

20 North Street, Rugby, Warwickshire
CV21 2AG.

Other information

For information on Baron Davenport's
Charity Trust, see entry in the Midlands
general section.

The Baron Davenport Emergency Grant (North Warwickshire)

£500

Correspondent: The Manager, c/o North
Warwickshire Citizens Advice, The
Parish Rooms, Welcome Street,
Atherstone, Warwickshire CV9 1DU
(0844 855 2322; fax: 01827 721944;
email: nwcab.advice@cabnet.org.uk;
website: www.nwcab.org.uk)

Eligibility

(i) Widows, unmarried women and
divorcees over 50 years old, and women
abandoned by their partners; and (ii)
children under the age of 25 whose
mothers are in the first category, in the
borough of North Warwickshire.
Applicants must have been resident in
the West Midlands for 10–15 years, be
living alone (except where school age
children are living with their mother)
and have a bank, building society or
Post-Office account.

The total income of the household
should be no more than about £141 a
week; this figure changes in line with
state benefits.

Types of grants

One-off grants of between £150 and £200
for house repairs, furniture, school
clothes, bedding, emergencies and so on.
Pensions are also given of either £110 or
£90 at each half-yearly distribution.

Annual grant total

Around £500.

Applications

On a form available from the
correspondent. Applications should be
submitted through a social worker or
welfare agency. They are considered
throughout the year.

Other information

For information on Baron Davenport's
Charity Trust, see entry in the Midlands
general section.

The Baron Davenport Emergency Grant (Warwickshire)

£1,000

Correspondent: Pauline Dye, Coventry
Carers Centre, 3 City Arcade, Coventry

CV1 3HX (0247632972; email:
contactus@coventrycarers.org.uk;
website: www.coventrycarers.org.uk)

Eligibility

Widows, unmarried women (over 18)
and children whose fathers are dead
(under 21) who are in need. Applicants
should not have savings over £1,000.
Applicants must have lived within the
old county boundaries of Warwickshire
for at least ten years (this includes
Coventry).

Types of grants

One-off grants for emergencies only,
particularly unexpected domestic
expenses, heavy funeral expenses or
similar instances where state benefit is
not available or undue delay would cause
hardship. Grants are normally between
£100 and £200.

Annual grant total

In 2011/12 grants totalled £500.

Applications

In writing to the correspondent.
Applications can be submitted through a
social worker, Citizens Advice or other
welfare agency; or directly by the
individual. They are considered at any
time.

Other information

For information on Baron Davenport's
Charity Trust, see entry in the Midlands
general section.

The Hatton Consolidated Charities

£4,000

Correspondent: M H Sparks, Clerk,
Weare Giffard, 32 Shrewley Common,
Shrewley, Warwick CV35 7AP (01926
842533)

Trustees: Catherine Eleanor Price;
Gillian Ward; Janet Lewis; Keith
Mobberley; Sheila Light; Richard Wood.

CC Number: 250572

Eligibility

People in need who live in the parishes
of Hatton, Beausale and Shrewley.
Applications from outside these areas
will not be considered.

Types of grants

One-off grants usually in the range of
£50 to £500.

Annual grant total

In 2010/11 the charity had an income of
£9,800 and an expenditure of £9,300.

Exclusions

Grants are not given to schoolchildren.

Applications

In writing to the trustees or the
correspondent.

Other information

Grants are also given to help students
and young people starting work to help
buy books and tools.

The South Warwick-shire Welfare Trust

£8,000

Correspondent: Mrs V Grimmer, Clerk,
62 Foxes Way, Warwick CV34 6AY
(01926 492226)

Trustees: Hilary Alexis Holland; David
Andrew Bullivant; Ian Peter Scott;
Margaret Estelle Shenkman; John Peter
Wood; Sarah Ann Strachan; Lucia Ann
Kander.

CC Number: 235967

Eligibility

People who are sick and in need and live
in Warwick district and the former rural
district of Southam.

Types of grants

One-off grants of £25 to £400 for items,
services or facilities to alleviate suffering
or assist recovery for people who are
sick, convalescent, disabled or infirm.
Recent grants have been given towards
household goods such as washing
machines, carpets, beds and fridges;
school uniforms; and towards larger
items such as central heating,
conditional upon the full amount being
raised elsewhere.

Annual grant total

In 2010 the trust had an income £7,800
and a total expenditure of £8,600.

Exclusions

Grants are not repeated and are not
given for relief of taxes or other public
funds.

Applications

On an application form available from
the correspondent to be submitted
through a social worker, Citizens Advice
or other welfare agency, or through a
doctor, church official or similar third
party. Applications are considered in
January, April, July and October and
should be submitted in the preceding
months. Details of income/expenditure
must be disclosed on the application
form.

Warwick Combined Charity

£11,000 (29 grants)

Correspondent: Christopher Houghton, c/o Moore and Tibbits Solicitors, 34 High Street, Warwick CV34 4BE (01926 491181; fax: 01926 402692; email: choughton@moore-tibbits.co.uk)

Trustees: Revd Arthur William John Fitzmaurice; Anne Henderson; Anthony Atkins; Janet Honnoraty; Revd Dr Vaughan Roberts; Sheila Brown; Cllr Peggy Bennett; Cllr Michael Kinson; Revd Linda Duckers; Cllr Anne Mellor.

CC Number: 256447

Eligibility

People in need who live in the town of Warwick.

Types of grants

One-off grants of up to £1,000 for washing machines, beds, mattresses, vacuum cleaners, carpets, holidays and so on.

Annual grant total

In 2011 the charity had assets of £3.1 million and an income of £132,000. Grants were made to 29 individuals totalling £11,000.

Applications

On a form available from the correspondent with a covering letter explaining the nature of the need. Applications are normally submitted through social services or a similar welfare organisation and considered at quarterly meetings.

Other information

Grants are also made to organisations (£77,000 in 2011).

Warwickshire Constabulary Benevolent Fund

£18,000

Correspondent: Grants Officer, PO Box 4, Leek Wootton, Warwick CV35 7QB (01926 415000)

Trustees: Suzanne Biddle; Adrian McGee.

CC Number: 504560

Eligibility

Police officers of the Warwickshire Constabulary who regularly subscribe to the fund, retired members who take on honorary membership, and their immediate dependents.

Types of grants

One-off and recurrent grants and loans of up to £5,000 for individuals in financial difficulty. Help is also given to members attending a police convalescence home to assist with their travel costs and other expenditure.

Annual grant total

In 2010, the most recent year for which accounts were available from the Charity Commission website, the fund held assets totalling £198,000 and had an income of £22,000. Grants to eight individuals totalled £18,000.

Applications

On a form available from the correspondent to be submitted either directly by the individual or through a work colleague, occupational health department or local NARPO secretary to the trustees or the force welfare department. Applications are considered on a regular basis.

The Warwickshire Miners' Welfare Fund

£12,000

Correspondent: David Thomas, CISWO, 142 Queens Road, Stoke-on-Trent ST4 7LH (01782 744996; email: david.thomas@ciswo.org.uk)

Trustees: Mr Gay; Mr Ellis; Paul Burke; Terence Hastelow.

CC Number: 519724

Eligibility

Mineworkers and former mineworkers who have worked within the coal industry in Warwickshire and their dependents.

Types of grants

One-off grants from £50 to £1,500 towards convalescent holidays, hospital visits to spouse (or applicant), electrical appliances such as cookers and vacuum cleaners, carpets, beds and other furniture, wheelchairs, stairlifts, scooters, and medical reports for industrial diseases.

Annual grant total

In 2010 the trust had an income of £16,000 and a total expenditure of £24,000. Grants are made to both individuals and organisations.

Exclusions

No death grants or grants to people who have received redundancy pay in the last ten years. Grants will not be given for any purpose for which the DWP will pay.

Applications

In writing to the correspondent. Applications can be submitted directly by the individual or through a social worker, Citizens Advice or other welfare agency or other third party. Applications should include weekly income and medical proof from a doctor (if applicable). They are considered at any time.

Atherstone

The Charity of Priscilla Gent and Others

£4,000

Correspondent: M L R Harris, Clerk, 42 King Street, Seagrave, Loughborough, Leicestershire LE12 7LY (01509 812366)

Trustees: Mr Norman; Revd Harris; Mrs Gilbert; Mr K. Wise; Mr K. Ford; Denise Clewes.

CC Number: 259461

Eligibility

People in need who live in Atherstone, Warwickshire.

Types of grants

One-off grants ranging from £50 to £250. Grants have included those to clear rent arrears and towards the cost of furniture and bedding, clothes, shoes (particularly for children), heaters and washing machines, travel expenses to hospital and short breaks for poor children and families.

Annual grant total

In 2010 the charity had an income of £5,400 and a total expenditure of £7,500. Grants are given to both individuals and organisations.

Applications

Applications can be submitted in writing by the individual or through a recognised referral agency (e.g. social worker, Citizens Advice or doctor). They are considered in May and November. Emergency applications can be considered at other times.

Barford

The Barford Relief-in-Need Charity

£4,000

Correspondent: Mr and Mrs T Offiler, 14 Dugard, Barford, Warwick CV35 8DX (01926 624153)

Trustees: Revd D. Jessett; Gerard Veness; Ian Webster; John Barrott; Philip Swallow; Philippa Mitchell; Lorraine Sayers.

CC Number: 256836

Eligibility

People in need who live in the parish of Barford.

Types of grants

One-off cash grants and gifts in kind are given towards 'any reasonable need', including hospital expenses, electric goods, convalescence, living costs, household bills, holidays, travel expenses, medical equipment, nursing fees, furniture, disabled equipment and help in the home.

Annual grant total

Around £8,000.

Exclusions

No loans are given.

Applications

In writing to the correspondent, directly by the individual or a family member. Applications are considered upon receipt. One of the trustees will visit to elicit all necessary information. Applications are usually considered in May and October.

Other information

Grants are also given to organisations.

Bedworth

The Henry Smith Charity (Bedworth)

£1,000

Correspondent: Pam Matthews, Democratic Support Services, Nuneaton and Bedworth Borough Council, Town Hall, Coton Road, Nuneaton, Warwickshire CV11 5AA (02476 376204)

Trustees: Jeffrey Hunt; John Haynes; William Hancox; Robert Copland.

CC Number: 248109

Eligibility

Older people in need who live in Bedworth.

Types of grants

Small Christmas food vouchers to be used at a local shop.

Annual grant total

Grants usually total about £1,000 each year.

Applications

In writing to the correspondent before September, for consideration in December.

Other information

This charity is also known as the 'Consolidated Charity of Hammersley, Smith and Orton'.

Bilton and New Bilton

The Bilton Poor's Land and Other Charities

£4,000

Correspondent: Robin Walls, Trustee, 6 Scotts Close, Rugby CV22 7QY (01788 810930)

Trustees: Michael Goode; Revd Tim Cockell; Ish Mistry; Ian Lowe; Robin Walls; David Wright; Graham Gare; Lisa Parker; William Shields.

CC Number: 215833

Eligibility

People in need who live in the ancient parish of Bilton (now part of Rugby). Preference is given to older people and those referred by social services.

Types of grants

One-off grants, generally of between £15 and £250.

Annual grant total

In 2010/11 the charity had assets of £498,000 and an income of £30,000. Grants to individuals and organisations totalled £6,700.

Applications

In writing to the correspondent, by the individual or through a third party such as a minister, although often applications are forwarded by social services. They are considered three times a year.

Coleshill

Relief in Need Charity of Simon Lord Digby and Others

£1,400

Correspondent: Juliet Bakker, The Vicarage Office, High Street, Coleshill, Birmingham B46 3BP (01675 462188)

Trustees: John Hoyle; Eileen Burton; Jean Johnson; John Wall; Peggy Childs; Bena Stuart; Revd Nick Parker.

CC Number: 237526

Eligibility

People in extreme hardship who live in the parish of Coleshill.

Types of grants

One-off grants according to need. Recent grants have been given to an individual with multiple sclerosis towards the cost of electric reclining/rising chair and to a family of an eight year old with leukaemia for help with extra expenses.

Annual grant total

Grants average around £1,400.

Applications

In writing to the correspondent. Applications are usually decided in March and November although decisions can be made more quickly in an emergency. They should be submitted directly by the individual or through a social worker, Citizens Advice or other welfare agency and should give as much detail as possible including information about applications to other organisations/trusts.

Grandborough

The Grandborough and Sutton Charities

£700

Correspondent: Mrs Joy Coling, Manor Farm, Grandborough Fields Road, Grandborough, Rugby, Warwickshire CV23 8DT (01788 813825)

Trustees: Kay Elizabeth Worrall; Revd Barbara Carol Clutton; Robin Joseph Coling; Revd Close; Tracy Pawsey.

CC Number: 260425

Eligibility

People in need who live in the parish of Grandborough.

Types of grants

Small one-off grants to help with optician's fees, hospital travel expenses and other general needs. Support is also available for older people at Christmas time.

Annual grant total

Around £700 in grants each year.

Exclusions

Grants are not given when the need is covered by the state.

Applications

In writing to the correspondent directly by the individual or family member. Applications are considered on an ongoing basis. Evidence of expenditure is required.

Other information

Grants may be given towards educational books for students.

Kenilworth

The Kenilworth Carnival Comforts Fund

£1,000

Correspondent: James A Evans, Treasurer, 7 Queens Road, Kenilworth, Warwickshire CV8 1JQ (01926 859161)

Trustees: James Evans; Marjorie Davies; Dawn Constable; Elizabeth Mable Meaton.

CC Number: 255027

Eligibility

People in need who live in Kenilworth.

Types of grants

Mainly one-off grants of £15 per person or £20 per couple, usually in the form of a grocery voucher redeemable at various shops in Kenilworth, hampers of food or bouquets of flowers. About 60 grants are given at Christmas, the rest are given throughout the year. Grants are not made to charities.

Annual grant total

About £1,000.

Applications

In writing to the correspondent. Applications can be submitted directly by the individual or through a social worker, Citizens Advice, other welfare agency or a third party, for example, a friend or relative. They are considered bi-monthly from February.

The Kenilworth United Charities

£5,000

Correspondent: Clerk to the trustees, Damian J Plant and Co., 29b Warwick Road, Kenilworth, Warwickshire CV8 1HN (01926 857741)

Trustees: John Hatfield; Revd Richard Awre; Revd Andrew Attwood; Ann Blacklock; Phillip Griffiths; Lynn Pollard; Madeleine Hamper.

CC Number: 215376

Eligibility

People in need who live in the ancient parish of Kenilworth.

Types of grants

Generally grocery vouchers given to one-parent families. One-off grants have also been made towards white goods.

Annual grant total

Grants have previously totalled around £5,000 a year.

Applications

On a form available from the correspondent. Applications are considered quarterly, although urgent cases will receive special consideration.

Other information

The charities also fund almshouses and the CAB office in Kenilworth.

Leamington Spa

The Leamington Relief-in-Sickness Fund

£2,000

Correspondent: Peter Byrd, Trustee, 2 Oakley Wood Cottages, Banbury Road, Bishops Tachbrook, Leamington Spa CV33 9QJ (01926 651789; email: peterandsuebyrd@hotmail.com)

Trustees: Hilary Alexis Holland; Mary Milton; Dr Peter Byrd; Dr John Holliday; Anthony J. Coltman; John E. Francis.

CC Number: 216781

Eligibility

People suffering from ill-health who live in the former borough of Leamington Spa and the neighbourhood and are in need. People with disabilities or mental health problems are especially welcomed.

Types of grants

One-off grants only from around £25, including help with fuel debts, television licences, baby necessities, food for special diets, fares for visiting hospitals or sick relatives, replacing locks after a burglary, children's clothing, and repairs to washing machines and so on.

Annual grant total

Around £2,000 in grants every year.

Exclusions

Applicants can only receive one grant each year.

Applications

In writing through a social worker, Citizens Advice, health visitor, doctor, probation service, Mind or other welfare agency. Applications submitted by individuals will not be acknowledged or considered. Applications are considered throughout the year.

Napton-on-the-Hill

The Napton Charities

£1,000 (17 grants)

Correspondent: Trevor Griffin, 1 Howcombe Lane, Napton-on-the-Hill, Southam, Warwickshire CV47 8NX (01926 812205)

Trustees: John Line; Alfred Fletcher; Barbara Jane Collett; Margaret Fox; Revd Michael Lawie Dickson Greig; Gordon Clarke.

CC Number: 244051

Eligibility

People in need who live in the parish of Napton-on-the-Hill only.

Types of grants

One-off grants ranging from £30 to £35 mainly towards heating for older people (e.g. gas, electricity, solid fuel) although other applications are considered, including clothing and living costs.

Annual grant total

Around £600 went towards helping 17 individuals with heating and transport costs in 2010/11.

Applications

On a form available from the correspondent. Applications can be submitted either directly by the individual or by a relative or friend with the consent of the individual. Proof of having lived in Napton for over a year is required.

Rugby

Rugby Relief in Need Charity

£1,300

Correspondent: Carol Patricia Davies, Clerk, 14 School Street, Long Lawford, Rugby, Warwickshire CV23 9AU (01788 544630)

Trustees: Cllr Christina Anne Avis; Maggie Telford; Revd Mark Beach; Cllr Patricia Wyatt; Marjorie Sims; David Edwards.

CC Number: 217987

Eligibility

People in need who live in the ancient parish of Rugby, which includes the parishes of St Andrew's and St Matthew's.

Types of grants

Christmas vouchers to the elderly of the parish. Some one-off grants may be made in cases of emergency.

Annual grant total

In 2010/11 the charity had an income of £1,600 and a total expenditure of £1,300.

Applications

In writing to the correspondent. Applications are generally considered three or four times a year, although urgent cases can be considered at any time.

Stratford upon Avon

The Baron Davenport Emergency Grant (Stratford upon Avon)

£1,500

Correspondent: Grazyna Hominiec-Meek, Voluntary Action Stratford, Suite 3 Arden Court, Arden Street, Stratford upon Avon CV37 6NT (01789 298115; email: enquiries@vasa.org.uk; website: www.vasa.org.uk)

Eligibility

Widows, unmarried women and divorced women who are over 60 years old. Applicants must:

- Live alone and have a total household income of no more than £165 per week and less than £5,000 in savings
- Not be in receipt of low/high rate Attendance Allowance, middle/high rates of Disability Living Allowance, or in receipt of Mobility Allowance
- Have lived in the Midlands area for at least five years

Types of grants

Small one-off grants of up to £150 for emergencies only.

Annual grant total

Grants usually total about £1,500 each year.

Applications

Applications can be made directly to the correspondent but must include supporting evidence from a third party, such as a health visitor, social worker, doctor or other professional.

Other information

For information on Baron Davenport's Charity, see entry in the Midlands general section.

The Mayor's Fund (Stratford upon Avon)

£3,000

Correspondent: Mrs R Dobson, Secretary, 155 Evesham Road, Stratford upon Avon, Warwickshire CV37 9BP (01789 293749; email: themayorsfund@ yahoo.com; website: www. themayorsfund.webs.com)

Trustees: Francess Rudd; Dr Geoffrey Lees; Sheila Price; Mick Love; Karen Symes; John Insoll; Gina Lodge; Steve Turner; Mayor of Stratford upon Avon.

CC Number: 220136

Eligibility

Older people in need who live in the former borough of Stratford upon Avon.

Types of grants

One-off and recurrent grants are usually given in the form of grocery vouchers.

Annual grant total

Grants usually total about £3,000 a year, paid to an average of 45 beneficiaries.

Applications

In writing to the correspondent. Applications can be submitted directly by the individual or through a social worker, Citizens Advice, other welfare agency or other third party such as a member of the clergy. They should include a general summary of income, other relief received (for example housing benefits) and financial commitments.

The Stratford upon Avon Municipal Charities – Relief in Need

£18,000

Correspondent: Ros Dobson, Clerk to the Trustees, 6 Guild Cottages, Church Street, Stratford upon Avon, Warwickshire CV37 6HD (01789 293749; email: municharities@btinternet.com; website: www.municipal-charities-stratforduponavon.org.uk)

Trustees: Mary Nicol; Mick Love; Charles Bates; Colin McDowall; Maureen Beckett; Norman Price; Bill Dowling; Jenny Howard; Carole Taylor; Shelagh Sandle; Joy Seaman; Timothy Hewson; Tessa Bates; Rob Fradley; Stratford upon Avon Town Council.

CC Number: 214958

Eligibility

People in need, generally older people, living in the town of Stratford upon Avon.

Types of grants

One-off and recurrent grants in the range of £100 and £500 towards essential items of furniture and household equipment (e.g. bed, support chair, cooker, microwave, fridge, freezer, washing machine), mobility aids and unexpected household bills. Educational grants are occasionally given.

Annual grant total

In 2011 the charity gave £18,000 in welfare grants.

Exclusions

No grants for: the repayment of debts; rent and council tax arrears; or, rental deposits.

Applications

On a form available from the correspondent, including details of the financial circumstances of the applicant and parent(s) if appropriate. When applying for financial assistance in connection with a specific health condition, applicants are asked to include a letter from a GP, occupational therapist, social worker or similar professional.

Sutton Cheney

Sir William Roberts Relief in Need Charity

£1,000

Correspondent: Miss D A Read, Secretary, Chatsmoth Cottage, Main Street, Sutton Cheney, Nuneaton, Warwickshire CV13 0AG (01455 291037)

Trustees: Philip Orton; Ann Read; Carole Ann Saunders; Mary Helen Yemm; Ruth Mary Evans; Peter Charles Bowman; D. T. Burgess.

CC Number: 242296

Eligibility

People who live in the village of Sutton Cheney and are in need.

Types of grants

One-off grants, usually in the range of £150 to £200, for basic necessities only.

Annual grant total

Grants to individuals generally total around £1,000 a year.

Applications

In writing to the correspondent, or any of the trustees. Applications may be submitted directly by the individual at any time.

Other information

Grants are also made to organisations based in Sutton Cheney.

Thurlaston

The King Henry VIII Endowed Trust – Warwick

£10,000

Correspondent: Jonathan Wassall, Clerk and Receiver, 12 High Street, Warwick CV34 4AP (01926 495533; email: jwassall@kinghenryviii.org.uk; website: www.kinghenryviii.org.uk)

CC Number: 232862

Eligibility

People who live in the old borough of Warwick (CV34 postal district).

Types of grants

One-off grants according to need. Grants to individuals in need are usually made only if a previous application to The Warwick Relief in Need Charity has been unsuccessful.

Annual grant total

In 2011 the trust had assets of £24 million and an income of £1.5 million. There were 21 grants to individuals for education and welfare totalling £20,000.

Applications

On an application form available from the correspondent or from the trust's website. Though deadline dates are listed in the guidelines found on the trust website, applications can be submitted at any time. These can be submitted directly by the individual, a relevant third party or through a social worker, Citizens Advice or educational welfare agency.

Other information

Grants are also made to organisations.

Thurlaston Poor's Plot Charity

£1,000

Correspondent: Mrs K Owen, Clerk, Congreaves, Main Street, Thurlaston, Rugby CV23 9JS (01788 817466)

Trustees: Jennifer Stokes; Roland Robinson; Colin Cook; Steven Watts; Claire Garside.

CC Number: 232356

Eligibility

People of pensionable age who are in need and live in Thurlaston.

Types of grants

The charity gives help with the payment of bills.

Annual grant total

About £2,000 a year.

Applications

In writing to the correspondent directly by the individual. Applications are considered in January, September and November.

Other information

Educational grants are also made to students.

Warwick

The Austin Edwards Charity

£3,500

Correspondent: Jackie Newton, 26 Mountford Close, Wellesbourne, Warwick CV35 9QQ (01789 840135; website: www.warwickcharities.org.uk)

Trustees: Neil Thurley; Dr John Henderson; Robin Ogg; Tony Atkins.

CC Number: 225859

Eligibility

People living in the old borough of Warwick.

Types of grants

Grants ranging from £250 to £500 for relief-in-need purposes.

Annual grant total

In 2010/11 the trust had an income of £8,000 and a total expenditure of £7,500.

Applications

In writing to the correspondent. Applications are considered throughout the year.

The Warwick Provident Dispensary

£1,500

Correspondent: Christopher Houghton, Moore and Tibbits, 34 High Street, Warwick CV34 4BE (01926 491181; email: choughton@moore-tibbits.co.uk)

Trustees: D. E. Hanson; Marion Haywood; Kenneth Freeburn; Sheila Rouse; Maureen Cooper; Martyn Ashford; Maureen Elizabeth Sutherland; Bob Dhillon.

CC Number: 253987

Eligibility

People in need who are in poor health, convalescent or who have a disability and live in the town of Warwick.

Types of grants

One-off and recurrent grants according to need.

Annual grant total

In 2010 the trust had an income of £19,000 and a total expenditure of £14,000 – the majority of which is given in grants to local organisations. Previously, around £1,500 has been given in grants to individuals.

Applications

In writing to the correspondent, directly by the individual or through a third party.

Other information

The trust also makes grants to organisations.

West Midlands

The Avon Trust

£7,500

Correspondent: Andrew Cashmore, Trehue, 8 Trenwith Place, St Ives TR26 1QD (01736 793369)

Trustees: Peter John Sverre Johansen; Andrew Robert Cashmore; Richard John Nixon; Peter Maurice Cashmore.

CC Number: 219050

Eligibility

Retired Methodist ministers and their dependents with some preference for those living in the West Midlands, and people in residential homes who live in the West Midlands.

Types of grants

One-off and recurrent grants according to need.

Annual grant total

In 2010/11 the trust had an income of £6,500 and a total expenditure of £7,600.

Applications

In writing to the correspondent. The trustees meet once a year in July but can consider applications at other times.

The Badley Memorial Trust

£23,000 (61 grants)

Correspondent: Christopher Williams, 16 Manderville Gardens, Kingswinford DY6 9QW (01384 294019)

Trustees: John David Davies; David John Stanley; Jeanette Clement; Michael Stuart Williams; Rachel Naomi Harris; William Ashworth; Gerald Wood; Michael Shaw; Lynda Coulter; Cllr Stephen James Waltho; Dr Rebecca Jayne Pickin.

CC Number: 222999

Eligibility

People in need who are in poor health, convalescent or who have disabilities and live in the former county borough of Dudley (as constituted in 1953). In certain cases the present metropolitan boroughs of Dudley and Sandwell may be included.

Types of grants

One-off grants have been made towards medical aids, clothing, beds/bedding, heating appliances, domestic appliances, televisions, radios, fuel, respite holidays, and adaptations for people with disabilities. Recurrent grants are only given in exceptional cases.

Payments are made directly via cheque to the providers of goods or services, no cash payments are made to applicants.

Annual grant total

In 2010/11 the trust had assets of £1.4 million and an income of £63,000. Grants were made to 61 individuals totalling £23,000.

Exclusions

Grants are not given to pay off debts or for educational fees.

Applications

On a form available from the correspondent to be submitted directly by the individual, or through a social worker, Citizens Advice, other welfare agency; or a third party, for example a relative, doctor or member of the clergy. Applications are considered quarterly.

Other information

The trust also made £1,000 of grants to organisations in the year.

Birmingham Jewish Community Care

£500

Correspondent: Grants Administrator, Bill Steiner Suite, 1 River Brook Drive, Birmingham B30 2SH (01214 593819; email: admin@bhamjcc.co.uk)

Trustees: Dr Barry Roseman; George Greenstone; Michael Leek; Michael Abrams; Sir Bernard Zissman; Richard Henry Jaffa.

CC Number: 209078

Eligibility

Jewish people in need living in the West Midlands.

Types of grants

Mainly one-off grants ranging from £10 to £250. Grants have been given to a small number of clients at Jewish festivals and for school clothing, music lessons for a gifted child, holidays for disadvantaged children and travel expenses for visiting distant cemeteries and occasionally to pay household or car bills. There is also a kosher meals-on-wheels service.

Regular payments are no longer made. Applicants must be prepared to update their circumstances before a second grant is made (other than in the case of

regular telephone rental payment in some cases).

Annual grant total

In 2010/11 grants totalled £500.

Exclusions

Grants are not made for setting up businesses.

Applications

In writing to the correspondent, including information on length of residence in the area, other applications made and whether or not the applicant is in receipt of income support or support from other charities. Applications are considered monthly and may be submitted directly by the individual or through a social worker, Citizens Advice or other welfare agency or third party such as a rabbi. No grant is ever made without personal contact with someone from the trust's social work department.

Other information

The trust also runs a residential and nursing home, Andrew Cohen House, at Stirchley in Birmingham.

Blakemore Foundation

£110,000

Correspondent: P F Blakemore, A F Blakemore and Sons Ltd, Longacre, Willenhall, West Midlands WV13 2JP (01902 366066)

Trustees: Gwendoline Mary Blakemore; Julian Matthew John Tonks; Peter Francis Blakemore.

CC Number: 1015938

Eligibility

People in need in the UK wide, with a preference for the West Midlands.

Types of grants

Grants are given according to need.

Annual grant total

In 2010/11 the foundation made grants totalling £142,000 to organisations and individuals.

Applications

Unsolicited applications are not accepted.

The Thomas Bromwich Trust

£16,000

Correspondent: Revd Dr Crispin Pailing, Vicarage, Church Road, Perry Barr, Birmingham B42 2LB (01213 567998; email: vicar@st-johns-perry-barr.org.uk)

Trustees: Revd Martin Charles Rutter; Barbara Lancelott; Revd Canon Brian Arthur Hall; David Gravell; David Stammers; Revd Dr Crispin Pailing; Betty Lear; William Horrell; Sylvia Smith.

CC Number: 214966

Eligibility

People in need living in Handsworth (that is, the ecclesiastical parishes of St Mary, St Andrew, St James, St Michael, St Peter and the Holy Trinity, Birdfield and St Paul, and Hanstead); Great Barr (that is, the ecclesiastical parish of St Margaret), and Perry Barr (that is, the ecclesiastical parishes of St John the Evangelist, Perry Barr, St Luke, Kingstanding, and St Matthews and Perry Beeches).

Types of grants

One-off grants towards electric goods, clothing, household bills, food and help in the home.

Annual grant total

In 2009/10 the charity had an income of £20,500 and a total expenditure of £15,800. Although expenditure was lower in the year the average amount distributed in grants to individuals comes to around £20,000 each year.

Applications

In writing to the correspondent either directly by the individual or through a social worker, Citizens Advice or other welfare agency. Applications are considered at any time.

The Chance Trust

£1,500

Correspondent: Revd Anthony Perry, Trustee, St Mary's Vicarage, 27 Poplar Avenue, Edgbaston, Birmingham B17 8EG (01214 292165)

Trustees: Hayward Osborne; James Woodall; Revd Anthony Perry; Revd Andrew Smith; Madeline Page.

CC Number: 702647

Eligibility

People in need in the rural deaneries of Warley and West Bromwich.

Types of grants

One-off grants ranging from £50 to £400.

Annual grant total

The trust makes grants of between £2,500 and £3,000 a year to individuals for both educational and relief-in-need purposes.

Applications

In writing to the correspondent, outlining the need and the amount required. Applications are considered in January and July.

The Coventry Freemen's Charity

£514,000 (2,605 grants)

Correspondent: David J Evans, Clerk, Abbey House, Manor Road, Coventry CV1 2FW (02476 257317; fax: 02476 552845; email: john@foxevans.co.uk; website: www.foxevans.co.uk)

Trustees: Jim McCranor; David Mason; Richard Smith; John Milne; Keith Talbot; Mr E. John Bolton Robert F. Hawkes; Ronald F. Taylor; Terrence D. McDonnell; Adrian T. Hall; Michael Taberner; James Parry; Michael Rawson; Frederick David Handford.

CC Number: 229237

Eligibility

Freemen and their dependents who are in need and live within seven miles of St Mary's Hall, Coventry.

Types of grants

Recurrent grants of £40 to £60 are paid quarterly to individuals who are 67 or over. Lump sum grants are given to other applicants.

Annual grant total

In 2010 the charity had assets of £12.2 million and an income of £680,000. Grants totalled £514,000 and were distributed to 2,605 beneficiaries as follows:

Freemen and women	£406,600
Freemen's widows	£104,700
Special cases	£3,300
Payments for relief and need	£400

Applications

On a form available from the correspondent directly by the individual, for consideration bi-monthly.

Friends of the Animals

£166,000 (3,014 grants)

Correspondent: Martin J Gomez, 408 Bearwood Road, Bearwood, Warley, West Midlands B66 4EX (01214 204201; email: friendsoftheanimals@btinternet. com; website: www.friendsoftheanimals. co.uk)

Trustees: Martin John Gomez; John George Williams; Madeliene Eggleton; Margaret Williams; David Guest.

CC Number: 1000249

Eligibility

People who live in the West Midlands, Dorset and Hampshire.

Types of grants

Subsidised veterinary treatment, such as spaying, neutering, microchipping, inoculations and treatment of accidents.

Annual grant total

In 2010/11 the charity had assets of £165,000 and an income of £374,000. Over 3,000 treatments were paid for or subsidised at a cost of £166,000.

Applications

Applications vary depending on the area in which the applicant resides. Applicants should contact their closest office for details:
- West Midlands: 01214 204201, Tuesday – Saturday 10:00am – 5:00pm
- Isle of Wight: 01983 522511
- Portsmouth and Southampton: 01983 522511, Monday – Friday 10:00am – 4:00pm, Saturday 10:00am – 2:00pm

Grantham Yorke Trust

£11,400 (28 grants)

Correspondent: Christine Norgrove, Martineau, 1 Colmore Square, Birmingham B4 6AA (0870 763 2000; email: christine.norgrove@sghmartineau. com)

Trustees: Ms B. Welford; Mr H. E. Belton; Mr P. M. Jones; Mr P. N. Smiglarski; Revd T. J. Clarke; Revd P. Ogilvie; F. Rattley; Mr S. Monaghan; Mrs P. Mannion.

CC Number: 228466

Eligibility

People under 25 who were born in the old West Midlands metropolitan county area (basically: Birmingham, Coventry, Dudley, Redditch, Sandwell, Solihull, Tamworth, Walsall or Wolverhampton).

Types of grants

One-off grants according to need.

Annual grant total

In 2010/11 the trust had assets of £5.9 million and an income of £195,000. Grants were made to 28 individuals totalling £11,400. A further £159,000 was made in grants to organisations.

Applications

On a form available from the correspondent. Applications should be submitted directly by the individual or via a relevant third party such as a social worker, Citizens Advice or other welfare agency, in February, May, August and November for consideration in the following month.

Other information

The trust also makes grants to organisations and to individuals for educational purposes.

The Harborne Parish Lands Charity

£77,000 (156 grants)

Correspondent: Lynda Bending, 109 Court Oak Road, Birmingham B17 9AA (01214 261600; fax: 01214 282267; email: theclerk@hplc.org.uk; website: www. harborneparishlandscharity.org.uk)

Trustees: Cllr Roger Horton; Michael Lloyd; Peter Hollingworth; Rachel Silber; Victor Paul Silvester; Frank G. Wayt; Andrew Lawrence; Nigel Thompson; Geoff Hewitt; Kerry Bolister; Buddhi Chetiyawardana.

CC Number: 219031

Eligibility

People in need who live in the ancient parish of Harborne, which includes parts of Harborne, Smethwick, Bearwood and Quinton. A map of the old parish is available to view on the website and individuals are advised to check that they reside in the area of benefit before making an application.

Types of grants

One-off grants ranging from £50 to £700. Grants cover a wide range of needs, including furniture, aids and adaptations, clothing, and assistance with transport.

Annual grant total

In 2010/11 the charity had assets of £14.4 million and an income of £1.2 million. Grants were made to individuals totalling £77,000. A further £178,000 was given in general grants to organisations and £611,000 was spent on the charity's almshouses.

Exclusions

Grants are not made for help with statutory bills, such as taxes.

Applications

A short application form is available from the correspondent. Applications can be made at any time and should be submitted through a local agency or organisation, such as social services or a Citizens Advice. All applicants are visited.

The CB and AB Holinsworth Fund of Help

£5,000

Correspondent: Dave Boardman, Room B41, The Council House, Victoria Square, Birmingham B1 1BB (01213 032020)

Trustees: Joe Egan; Hugh Carslake; Michael Sharpe; Shona Mary Cutler; Cllr Anne Underwood; Lord Mayor of Birmingham Len Gregory.

CC Number: 217792

Eligibility

People in need who live in or near to the city of Birmingham and are sick or convalescing.

Types of grants

One-off grants ranging from £50 to £300. Grants are given towards the cost of respite holidays, travelling expenses to and from hospital, clothing, beds and carpets.

Annual grant total

In 2010/11 the trust had an income of £3,800 and a total expenditure of £9,200.

Exclusions

Generally grants are not given for bills or debt.

Applications

On a form available from the correspondent. Applications are considered throughout the year and should be submitted through a social worker, Citizens Advice or other welfare agency. Confirmation of illness is needed, for example a letter from a doctor, consultant or nurse.

Other information

Grants are also given to organisations.

The James Frederick and Ethel Anne Measures Charity

£5,000

Correspondent: The Clerk to the Trustees, Harris Allday, 2nd Floor, 33 Great Charles Street, Birmingham B3 3JN

Trustees: Rodney Watkins; Martin Green; Jeremy Wagg; David Seccombe.

CC Number: 266054

Eligibility

The following criteria apply:
1. Applicants must usually originate in the West Midlands
2. Applicants must show evidence of self-help in their application
3. Trustees have a preference for disadvantaged people
4. Trustees have a dislike for applications from students who have a full local authority grant and want finance for a different course or study

5. Trustees favour grants towards the cost of equipment
6. Applications by individuals in cases of hardship will not usually be considered unless sponsored by a local authority, health professional or other welfare agency

Types of grants

One-off or recurrent grants, usually between £50 and £500.

Annual grant total

In 2010/11 the charity had assets of £842,000 and an income of £38,000. Grants were made totalling £286,000 (this included a donation of £250,000 to Royal National Lifeboat Institution). Grants are awarded to individuals and organisations.

Applications

In writing to the correspondent. No reply is given to unsuccessful applicants unless an sae is enclosed.

Other information

Grants were made to 51 organisations during the year.

The Newman Trust Homes

£13,600 (23 grants)

Correspondent: Judy Dyke, Tydallwoods Solicitors, 29 Woodbourne Road, Harborne, Birmingham B17 8BY (01216 932222; email: jdyke@tyndallwoods.co.uk)

Trustees: Patricia Mary Whitely; Diana Gauton; Patricia Rowley; Rosella Fox; Revd Edmund Newey; Sue Thomas.

CC Number: 501567

Eligibility

People who are in need, hardship or distress who live, or have formerly lived, in the City of Birmingham. Grants are primarily paid to benefit people who are older, people with housing difficulties and people living within the area of Handsworth and its immediate vicinity.

Types of grants

One-off and recurrent grants according to need.

Annual grant total

In 2010/11 the trust held assets totalling £746,000 and an income of £39,000. Grants were made to 23 individuals totalling £13,600.

Exclusions

No funding for funerals.

Applications

Application forms are available from the charity. Applicants are encouraged to detail any additional information they believe may assist the trustees in their decision.

The Samuel Smith Charity, Coventry

£19,000

Correspondent: J C B Leech, Fourwinds, 9 Highland Road, Kenilworth, Warwickshire CV8 2EU (01926 852846)

Trustees: Richard Kenyon; A. C. E. Gillitt; I. N. Smith; J. F. Blythe; J. C. B. Leech; J. S. F. Grindlay; R. J. Ballantine; R. G. W. Caldicott; R. V. Wiglesworth.

CC Number: 240936

Eligibility

People in need who live in Coventry and the ancient parish of Bedworth.

Types of grants

Pensions and one-off grants.

Annual grant total

In 2011 the charity had assets of £870,000 and an income of £30,000. Grants totalling £19,000 were distributed as follows:

Pensions	£15,000
Payments in lieu of coal	£1,900
Christmas gifts to pensioners	£1,200
May gifts	£750
Bibles	£270

Applications

Applications can be made in writing to the correspondent, but most beneficiaries are referred by the charity's almoner. Trustees meet three times a year to consider applications. There can be a waiting list for pensions to which eligible applicants may be added.

Birmingham

The Freda and Howard Ballance Trust

£2,500

Correspondent: Michael Stocks, Appeals Secretary and Trustee, Blackhams, Lancaster House, 67 Newhall Street, Birmingham B3 1NR (01212 330062; fax: 01212 339880; email: stocks87@blackhams.com)

Trustees: Michael Geoffrey Marland Stocks; Alan Keith Hawkins; Hansa Shah; Jokhim Meikle; Dorothy Pridham; Margaret Holland.

CC Number: 513109

Eligibility
People in need who live in Birmingham.

Types of grants
One-off grants usually ranging from £50 to £200. Recent grants have been given for clothing, furniture and disability aids. A small amount is also available for educational items.

Annual grant total
Grants average around £2,500 each year.

Applications
On a form available from the correspondent. A letter giving brief details of the application is required before an application form is sent out. Applications can be made either directly by the individual or via a third party such as a charity, social worker or Citizens Advice. They are usually considered quarterly.

The Richard and Samuel Banner Trust

£9,500

Correspondent: Anne Holmes, c/o Cobbetts Solicitors, 1 Colmore Square, Birmingham B4 6AJ (0845 404 2505)

Trustees: Mr R. E. Barley; Mrs S. McCabe; Mrs V. Arnold; Mr T. Wagg; Revd Mother Christine.

CC Number: 218649

Eligibility
Men and widows who are in need and live in the city of Birmingham.

Types of grants
Clothing grants up to £100.

Annual grant total
In 2009/10 the trust had an income of £9,000 and a total expenditure of £9,800.

Applications
Applicants must be nominated by a trustee, doctor or the Council for Old People. Applications are considered on 1 November and grants are distributed immediately after this date.

Other information
The trust can also give apprenticing grants to male students under 21, but this is done through certain colleges; applicants should not apply directly.

Friends of Home Nursing in Birmingham

£9,000

Correspondent: Mrs J Burns, Hon. Treasurer, 46 Underwood Road, Handsworth Wood, Birmingham B20 1JS (01216 865565)

Trustees: Norma Karindikar; Julie Breen; Jackie Charlton.

CC Number: 218182

Eligibility
Sick and older people who live in Birmingham city and who are patients nursed at home by the district nurse.

Types of grants
The trust provides goods, equipment and occasional monetary grants which are not available from other sources. In the past this has included digital thermometers, a dressing trolley, cameras and films for ulcer recordings, and part of the cost of holidays. Grants are usually one-off and range from £50 to £500.

No grants are made for double glazing or electrical work.

Annual grant total
In 2010 the trust had an income of £8,300 and a total expenditure of £9,500.

Applications
In writing, via a district nurse, to the correspondent. Applications can be submitted at any time, for consideration in the spring and autumn, 'but if a real case of need occurs we deal with it as soon as possible'.

The Charity of Jane Kate Gilbert

£1,900

Correspondent: Phil Wright, Committee Services, Room B43, Council House, Victoria Square, Birmingham B1 1BB (01213 032023)

Trustees: Timothy Cuthbertson; Sandra Jenkinson; Michael Sharpe; Mary Edwards; Anne Underwood.

CC Number: 216800

Eligibility
People in need who are over 60 years of age and have lived in Birmingham for at least two years.

Types of grants
Small quarterly pensions with a possible Christmas bonus. One-off hardship payments up to a maximum of £100 will also be considered.

Annual grant total
Grants average around £1,900 a year.

Applications
On a form available from the correspondent to be submitted through a social worker, Citizens Advice or other welfare agency. Applications are usually considered in March and November.

The Handsworth Charity

£8,000

Correspondent: Dipali Chandra, 109 Court Oak Road, Birmingham B17 9AA

Trustees: Reverend Brian Hall; Cllr Paulette Hamilton; Bernard Parry; Mrs D. Duggan; Edward Lear; Julie Stock; Pat Lawrence; Cllr Kim Kirpaljit Kaur Brom; Keith Hemmings; Cllr Hendrina Quinnen.

CC Number: 216603

Eligibility
People in need who live in the parish of Handsworth (now in Birmingham).

Types of grants
One-off grants of up to £500 according to need.

Annual grant total
In 2010 the charity had an income of £15,000 and a total expenditure of £7,000. Grants were made totalling around £8,000.

Applications
In writing to the correspondent: to be submitted directly by the individual or through a referral organisation.

Harriet Louisa Loxton Trust Fund

£0

Correspondent: Gloria Zachariou, Adults and Communities Finance Section, 67 Sutton New Road, Birmingham B23 6QT (01214 645325)

Trustee: Birmingham City Council.

CC Number: 702446

Eligibility
People in need who live in Birmingham, with a preference for older people.

Types of grants
One-off grants ranging from £100 to £2,000, though the average is generally around £400. Examples of grants given include £500 to an older person with disabilities for a washing machine and drier, £100 for a vacuum cleaner for an older woman who was ill, £1,700 for central heating for a woman who was blind and £500 towards an electric scooter for a man who was totally immobile.

Annual grant total
In 2010/11 the fund had assets of £1.5 million and an income of £33,000. No grants were made due to a suspension of all grantmaking from July 2009. As of 31 March 2011 the

suspension has been removed and it is expected that the trust will continue to make grants as previously (£11,000 in 2008/9).

Exclusions

There are no grants available to pay off debts, relieve public funds or towards the community charge and no grants to organisations.

Applications

On a form available from the correspondent. The trustees meet four times a year to consider applications. Applications may take some considerable time to process. Immediate decisions on applications cannot be given.

Other information

The fund was established from proceeds of the sale of Icknield, a property donated to the city by Harriet Louisa Loxton for use as a home for older people.

Sands Cox Relief in Sickness Charity

£6,000

Correspondent: Ann Andrew, Secretary, 12 Hayfield Gardens, Moseley, Birmingham B13 9LE

Trustees: Brian Pratt; Jayne Walker; John Douthwaite; Louise Tomlinson; Peter Combellack; Graham Harvey; Mr C. Eaves.

CC Number: 217468

Eligibility

People in need who live in Birmingham.

Types of grants

One-off grants of up to £200.

Annual grant total

About £6,000.

Applications

In writing to the correspondent, either directly by the individual or through a responsible person, e.g. a trustee, doctor or Social Services professional.

Other information

The charity also makes grants to local organisations.

The Yardley Great Trust

£22,000

Correspondent: Mrs K L Grice, Clerk to the Trustees, 31 Old Brookside, Yardley Fields Road, Stechford, Birmingham B33 8QL (01217 847889; fax: 01217 851386; email: enquiries@ygtrust.org.uk; website: www.yardley-great-trust.org.uk)

Trustees: Conrad James; Iris June Ann Aylin; Joy Olive Kathleen Holt; Cllr

Barbara Jackson; Keith Rollins; Robert Jones; Revd Andrew Timothy Bullock; Revd John George Richards; Revd John Mead Ray; Malcolm Cox; Jean Hayes; Revd William Sands; Andrew Veitch.

CC Number: 216082

Eligibility

People living in the ancient parish of Yardley in the city of Birmingham. This includes the wards of Yardley, Acocks Green, Fox Hollies, Billesley, Hall Green and part of the wards of Hodge Hill, Shard End, Sheldon, Small Heath, Sparkhill, Moseley, Sparkbrook and Brandwood. (A map is produced by the trust outlining the beneficial area.)

Types of grants

One-off grants towards washing machines, fridges, cookers, clothing, beds and bedding and household furniture.

Annual grant total

In 2011 the trust had assets of £7.6 million and an income of £2.7 million. Grants were made to individuals totalling £22,000.

The 2011 accounts note that 'as in 2010 people who benefited most from grants in 2011 were lone parent families headed by women living in council housing. A large proportion were unemployed and claiming income support.'

Exclusions

No grants are given for educational needs or for items that should be met by local authorities, health authorities or social services.

Applications

Application forms are available in hardcopy from the correspondent or can be completed online via the website. Applications should be made through a Council Neighbourhood Office, Citizens Advice or other welfare agency. They are considered monthly.

Other information

The trust also makes grants to organisations (£34,000 in 2011) and provides second hand furniture through a partner organisation, Ladywood Furniture Project.

Bushbury

The Bushbury United Charities

£5,000

Correspondent: Administrator, Dallow and Dallow, 23 Waterloo Road, Wolverhampton, West Midlands WV1 4TJ (01902 420208)

Trustees: Tony Prendergast; Julie Patricia Smallman; Cllr David John

Clifft; Michael J. Hotchkiss; Revd Philip Dobson.

CC Number: 242290

Eligibility

People in need living in the ancient parish of Bushbury.

Types of grants

Annual grants paid at Christmas.

Annual grant total

In 2010 the charity had an income of £6,200 and a total expenditure of £5,700.

Applications

In writing to the correspondent.

Castle Bromwich

The Mary Dame Bridgeman Charity Trust

£500

Correspondent: Mr Jeremy Dutton, 60 Whateley Crescent, Birmingham, West Midlands B36 0DP

Trustees: Janet Richards; Jeremy Dutton; The Earl of Bradford; Alison Haywood; Ian Wright; P. Allen; Mark Smith; Revd Stuart Carter.

CC Number: 701557

Eligibility

People in need living in the ecclesiastical parishes of St Mary and St Margaret, and St Clement, Castle Bromwich.

Types of grants

One-off grants have in the past been used to meet the cost of heating bills or respite care.

Annual grant total

About £1,000.

Exclusions

Grants are not given if they will affect any statutory benefits.

Applications

In writing to the correspondent, directly by the individual or through a social worker, welfare agency or other third party such as a parent, partner or relative. Applications should include the applicant's income and expenditure. The trustees meet twice a year in May and November.

Other information

This entry is an amalgamation of three separate charity funds which are administered as one.

Coventry

The Children's Boot Fund

£7,500

Correspondent: Janet McConkey, Trustee, 123A Birmingham Road, Coventry CV5 9GR (02476 402837; email: martin_harban@btconnect.com)

Trustees: James Chapman Janet McConkey; Martin Harban; Patricia Timmons; Peter Hancock; William Smith; Lucy Hancock.

CC Number: 214524

Eligibility
Schoolchildren in the city of Coventry, aged 4 to 16.

Types of grants
Grants for school footwear for children in need. No other type of help is given. Grants are made direct to footwear suppliers in the form of vouchers.

Annual grant total
In 2010/11 the fund had an income of £8,900 and an expenditure of £17,000.

Applications
Application forms are available from schools in the area and should be completed, verified and signed by the headteacher of the child's school. Applications are considered four times a year.

The General Charities of the City of Coventry

£139,000

Correspondent: V A Tosh, General Charities Office, Old Bablake, Hill Street, Coventry CV1 4AN (02476 222769; email: cov.genchar@virgin.net)

Trustees: Richard Smith; David Mason; Michael John Harris; Edna Eaves; Edward John Curtis; Margaret Lancaster; Mavis Weitzel; Terence David McDonnell; William Phillip Thomson; Cllr Nigel Lee; David John Evans; Cllr Johnson; Terry Proctor; Dr Caroline Rhodes; Cllr Gary Crookes; Cllr Marcus Lapsa; Vivian Kershaw; Cllr Catherine Miks.

CC Number: 216235

Eligibility
People in need living in the city of Coventry.

Types of grants
One-off grants in kind and recurrent grants, but not cash grants. Recurrent grants of around £45 a quarter can be given to a maximum of 650 pensioners over the age of 65.

Annual grant total
In 2011 the charities held assets of £8.3 million and had an income of £826,000. Welfare grants totalled £139,000 and can be broken down as follows:

Regular allowances	£93,000
One-off relief in need grants	£39,000
Trustees' annual vouchers	£7,200

Exclusions
Cash grants are not given.

Applications
Applications should be made through social workers, probation officers, Citizens Advice or other welfare agencies.

Other information
The charities receive income from Sir Thomas White's Charity including the allocation for the Sir Thomas White's Loan Fund in Coventry. Grants are also made to organisations.

John Moore's Bequest

£900

Correspondent: Ian Cox, Sarginsons, 10 The Quadrant, Coventry CV1 2EL (02476 553181)

Trustees: Dr George Greenwood; George Drake; Richard Thomas Blanchard; John Owen Dawson.

CC Number: 218805

Eligibility
People in need, generally older people, living in the city of Coventry.

Types of grants
Grants of up to £20 given in December.

Annual grant total
In 2010/11 the bequest had an income of £4,600 and a low total expenditure of £950 (£5,600 in 2010/11).

Applications
The charity's trustees each select around 25 recipients either directly or through local churches.

The Dr William MacDonald of Johannesburg Trust

£2,000

Correspondent: Jane Barlow, Lord Mayor's Office, Council House, Earl Street, Coventry CV1 5RR (02476 833047)

Trustees: Jane Barlow; John Victor Gazey.

CC Number: 225876

Eligibility
People in need who live in the city of Coventry.

Types of grants
One-off welfare grants, typically about £50, usual maximum £200.

Annual grant total
Grants usually total around £2,000 each year.

Exclusions
No grants for the relief of debt.

Applications
In writing to the correspondent. Applications can be submitted directly by the individual or through a third party such as a social worker.

Spencer's Charity

£19,000

Correspondent: G T W Foottit, Mander Hadley and Co. Solicitors, 1 The Quadrant, Coventry CV1 2DZ (02476 631212)

Trustees: Richard Henry Powles Spencer; Michael John Cotton; Elizabeth Ann Mander; Anthony Vincent Nowell Richards; Gerald Charles Davies Osborne; Robert Gordon Woodruff Caldicott; Norma Jennifer King; George Thomas Welch Foottit.

CC Number: 212935

Eligibility
Women in need who are over 65, still living in their own homes and able to prove that they have lived in the city of Coventry for at least seven years. The charity stipulates that they must not be in receipt of 'too many' other benefits.

Types of grants
Pensions amounting to £200 per year are paid in two annual instalments.

Annual grant total
In 2011 the charity had an income of £24,000 and a total expenditure of £27,000. In previous years pensions have totalled around £19,000.

Applications
Application forms are available from the clerk to the trustees, Mr G Foottit, at the above address.

The Tansley Charity Trust

£4,200

Correspondent: Lara M Knight, Governance Services, Room 59, Council House, Earl Street, Coventry CV1 5RR (02476 833237)

Trustees: Mavis Weitzel; Cllr Johnson; Mr Auluck; Jane Halliday; Frances Marion Armitage; Suzanna Dixon; Lord Mayor.

CC Number: 505364

Eligibility

Women over 50 years old who are in poor health and live in the city of Coventry.

Types of grants

One-off grants up to £200. Recent grants have been given towards the purchase of clothing, household items and the payment of bills.

Annual grant total

In 2010/11 the trust had an income of £6,300 and a total expenditure of £4,600.

Exclusions

No grants for council tax or Inland Revenue payments.

Applications

On a form available from the correspondent. Applications can be submitted by the individual or through a recognised referral agency (e.g. a social worker, Citizens Advice or doctor). Grants are considered twice a year.

The Tile Hill and Westwood Charities for the Needy Sick

£2,500

Correspondent: John Ruddick, Clerk, 4 Poundgate Lane, Coventry CV4 8HJ (02476 466917; email: john.ruddick@bttj.com)

Trustees: John Nisbet; Gary Crookes.

CC Number: 220898

Eligibility

People who are both sick and in need and live in the parish of Westwood and parts of the parish of Berkswell, Kenilworth and Stoneleigh and elsewhere within a three and a half mile radius of 93 Cromwell Lane, Coventry.

Types of grants

One-off grants according to need. The trust is often able to provide assistance where a potential beneficiary 'falls between the cracks' of other providers.

Annual grant total

In 2010 the trust had an income of £20,000 and a total expenditure of £2,600.

Applications

In writing to the correspondent.

The Harry Weston Memorial Fund

£2,000

Correspondent: The Secretary, 8 Eaton Road, Coventry CV1 2FF (02476 713942)

Trustees: Anthony William Parsons; Gerald Osborne; Joyce Mary Lilyan Osborne; A. J. Jones; Jackie Lee; John Hartley.

CC Number: 254183

Eligibility

Pensioners, aged 65–75, who are in financial difficulty (usually those on pension credit) and live in the city of Coventry.

Types of grants

One-off grants up to about £50, mainly towards the cost of television licences. The fund has also helped with the provision of reconditioned television sets and the cost of converting aerials for the digital tv switchover.

Annual grant total

Grants usually average around £2,000 each year.

Applications

In writing to the correspondent either directly by the individual or through a third party such as a social worker, Citizens Advice, other welfare agency or a relative or neighbour. Applications must include information on the applicant's age, circumstances and date of TV licence renewal if relevant.

Dudley

The Reginald Unwin Dudley Charity

£2,200

Correspondent: David Hughes, 53 The Broadway, Dudley, West Midlands DY1 4AP (01384 259277; email: rududley@hotmail.com)

Trustees: Gordon Stanton; Patrick John McGraghan; Peggy West; David Frank Hughes; Joseph Barry Clarke.

CC Number: 217516

Eligibility

People in need who live in Dudley.

Types of grants

One-off grants of up to about £200.

Annual grant total

In 2010/11 the charity had an income of £3,200 and a total expenditure of £2,400.

Applications

On a form available from the correspondent.

The Dudley Charity

£3,600

Correspondent: Dennis Jones, Secretary to the Trustees, 1 Drew Road, Stourbridge DY9 0UZ (01384 392704)

Trustees: David Hughes; Peggy West; John Abbis; Timothy Rowe; Cllr Bryan John Cotterill; Cllr Lesley Joan Faulkner.

CC Number: 254928

Eligibility

People in need who live in the town of Dudley (as constituted prior to 1 April 1966) and its immediate surroundings, including Netherton.

Types of grants

One-off grants in the range of £100 to £250.

Annual grant total

In 2010/11 the charity had an income of £5,900 and a total expenditure of £3,800.

Applications

On a form available from the correspondent. Applications can be submitted directly by the individual or through a third party such as a social worker. They are normally considered monthly.

Other information

The charity also makes grants to organisations.

King's Norton

The King's Norton United Charities

£2,500

Correspondent: Canon Rob Morris, The Rectory, 273 Pershore Road, Kings Norton, Birmingham B30 8EX (01214 590560)

Trustees: Annette Dickers; Geoffrey Sutton; Rob Morris; Alistair Dow; Roger Goodchild; Revd Jeremy Dussick; Revd David Warbrick; Revd Rebecca Clarke; Revd Catherine Grylls.

CC Number: 202225

Eligibility

People who live in the ancient parish of King's Norton in Birmingham and the West Midlands.

Types of grants

One-off and recurrent grants according to need.

Annual grant total

Grants usually total around £5,000.

Applications

Grants are made to named individuals only.

Meriden

Meriden United Charities

£500

Correspondent: Alan Barker, 163 Avon Street, Coventry CV2 3GQ (02476 453342)

Trustees: Alan Gabbitas; David Bell; Christine Copper; Deborah Edwards; Grace Tuckey; Jennifer Harrison; Robert Hurton; Valerie Cotterrell.

CC Number: 234452

Eligibility

People in need who have lived in the parish of Meriden for at least two years.

Types of grants

One-off grants are given for older people, children and young people, people with disabilities, or those experiencing a sudden illness, and for the prevention or relief of poverty.

Annual grant total

The charity has an income of about £1,500 a year. Grants are made for education and welfare purposes.

Applications

Applications can be submitted either directly by the individual or a family member or through a third party such as a social worker or teacher. The existence of the charities is made known by a notice in the Meriden magazine and by a notice in the library.

Sandwell

The Fordath Foundation

£5,000

Correspondent: John Sutcliffe, 33 Thornyfields Lane, Stafford ST17 9YS (01785 247035; email: fordath-foundation@ntlworld.com)

Trustees: Elizabeth Shields; Freda May Bisseker; Geoffrey William Westwood; John Robert Sutcliffe; Vivien Farrell; Ben Sutcliffe; Tom Sutcliffe.

CC Number: 501581

Eligibility

People who are in need and live in the Metropolitan Borough of Sandwell. Preference is given to older people and those in poor health.

Types of grants

One-off grants to meet a specific expense.

Annual grant total

Grants usually total about £5,000 each year.

Applications

Applications are usually made through Sandwell Social Services, Citizens Advice, Carers' Centre or a similar organisation and should include brief details of the individual's circumstances. They are considered throughout the year, funds permitting.

The George and Thomas Henry Salter Trust

£8,200

Correspondent: J S Styler, Clerk, Lombard House, Cronehills Linkway, West Bromwich, West Midlands B70 7PL (01215 533286)

Trustees: Ann Maybury; David Payne; Hilary Pugh; Diana Wills.

CC Number: 216503

Eligibility

People in need who live in the borough of Sandwell.

Types of grants

One-off grants usually in the range of £50 to £1,000 towards clothing, household equipment and so on.

Annual grant total

In 2011 the trust had assets of £1.3 million and an income of £30,000. Educational grants totalled £20,000 and relief in need totalled £8,200.

Applications

On a form available from the correspondent. Applications are considered on a regular basis.

Other information

Grants are also given to local organisations.

Stourbridge

The Palmer and Seabright Charity

£3,900

Correspondent: Susannah Griffiths, c/o Wall, James and Chappell, 15–23 Hagley Road, Stourbridge, West Midlands DY8 1QW (01384 371622)

Trustees: G. L. Partridge; David Rogers; Olive Calder; Robert Wilson; Suzanne Lowe.

CC Number: 200692

Eligibility

Elderly people in need living in the parish of Stourbridge.

Types of grants

One-off and recurrent grants according to need.

Annual grant total

The latest accounts available were for 2010 when the trust had assets of £230,000 and an income of £40,000. Grants for welfare and education totalled £7,800.

Applications

On a form available from the correspondent. Applications can be submitted either directly by the individual or a family member, through a third party such as a social worker or teacher, or through an organisation such as Citizens Advice or a school.

Chris Westwood Charity

£35,000 (36 grants)

Correspondent: Martyn Morgan, Talbots Solicitors, 63 Market Street, Stourbridge DY8 1AQ (01384 445850; email: martynmorgan@talbotssolicitors. co.uk; website: www. chriswestwoodcharity.co.uk)

Trustees: Martyn Peter Morgan; Chris Westwood; Graham Wood; Janine Barnes.

CC Number: 1101230

Eligibility

Children and young people under the age of 25 in Stourbridge, and the surrounding areas (typically within a 50 mile radius), with physical disabilities.

Types of grants

Typical examples of support have included: special exercise equipment to assist in regaining and maintaining mobility; wheelchairs, special mobility chairs and lifting equipment; and contributions towards the cost of home modifications, to improve access, or provide specialised facilities that may be required.

Annual grant total

In 2011 the charity had an income of £34,000 and a total expenditure of £35,000 on 36 grants. The charity had no administrative or governance costs.

Applications

In writing to the correspondent. Applications should detail: background information, the reason for the request, a detailed quotation prepared after an assessment by the supplier and details of the financial position of the family along with any funds already raised.

Applications should also be supported by a suitable professional person detailing the applicants medical condition and any advantages the proposed equipment purchase would bring. The charity aims to respond to requests within 48 hours. Grants are made by cheque paid directly to the supplier.

Sutton Coldfield

Sutton Coldfield Municipal Charities

£46,000 (36 grants)

Correspondent: Pauline John, Personal Assistant/Secretary, Lingard House, Fox Hollies Road, Sutton Coldfield, West Midlands B76 2RJ (01213 512262; fax: 01213 130651; email: pauline.john@ suttoncharities.org; website: www. suttoncoldfieldmunicipalcharities.com)

Trustees: David Roy; James Whorwood; John Gray; Susan Bailey; Jane Rothwell; Rodney Kettel; Michael Waltho; Freddie Gick; David Owen; Carole Hancox; Margaret Waddington; S. C. Martin; Malcolm Cornish; Neil Andrews; Linda Whitfield; Andrew Watson.

CC Number: 218627

Eligibility

People in need living in the Four Oaks, New Hall and Vesey wards of Sutton Coldfield.

Types of grants

One-off grants are given to individuals in the range of £100 and £1,500. Grants are given for special needs, for example, stair lifts, adapted bathrooms and mobility vehicles for people who are elderly or disabled, school clothing, building repairs and essential household equipment e.g. carpets, washing machine, cookers.

Annual grant total

In 2010/11 the charity had assets of £42 million and an income of £1.5 million. There were 33 grants to individuals in need, hardship or distress totalling £41,000, five grants for individual educational and personal needs totalling £10,000 and 340 school clothing grants totalling £13,000.

Exclusions

Grants are not given to people in receipt of benefits from other sources, for example social services, family, DWP and so on.

Applications

On a form available from the correspondent. Applications should be made directly by the individual or through a parent or carer. They are considered every month, except April,

August and December. Telephone enquiries are welcomed.

Other information

The principal objectives of the charities are the provision of almshouses, the distribution of funds and other measures for the alleviation of poverty and other needs for inhabitants and other organisations within the boundaries of the former borough of Sutton Coldfield.

Tettenhall

The Tettenhall Relief-in-Need and Educational Charity

£1,000

Correspondent: Andrew Graham, Clerk to the Trustees, 4 Mayswood Drive, Wolverhampton WV6 8EF (01902 762021)

Trustees: Christine Young; Mr P. Hughes; Mrs B. Gollings; Mr G. Hopkins; Revd Richard Reeve; Phil Deeming; Cyril Randles.

CC Number: 1002952

Eligibility

People in need who live in the parish of Tettenhall, as constituted on 22 June 1888.

Types of grants

Grants are given mainly for clothing and food and range from £25 to £50.

Annual grant total

About £1,000 is available each year for relief-in-need purposes.

Applications

In writing to the correspondent. Applications should be made through a social worker, Citizens Advice or other welfare agency, doctor or senior citizen's organisation. They should be submitted in October for consideration in November.

Walsall

W J. Croft Charity

£2,000

Correspondent: Matthew Underhill, Legal and Constitutional Services, Civic Centre, Darwall Street, Walsall WS1 1TP (01922 653550; email: charities@walsall. gov.uk; website: cms.walsall.gov.uk/ charities)

Trustees: Guy Svensson-Lockley; John Lea; Cllr Eileen Russell; Hilary Dunphy.

CC Number: 702795

Eligibility

Residents of the borough of Walsall.

Types of grants

The charity stresses that limited funds mean it can only offer small grants.

Annual grant total

The trust typically has a small income and expenditure, usually around £2,000 each year,

Exclusions

Property deposits, rent arrears, mortgage payments and utility bills.

Applications

On a form available to download from the Walsall council website or by telephoning the council to receive a copy by post.

Walsall Wood Allotment Charity

£28,000

Correspondent: Craig Goodall, Constitutional Services, Walsall Council, The Civic Centre, Darwall Street, Walsall WS1 1TP (01922 653317; email: goodallc@walsall.gov.uk; website: cms.walsall.gov.uk/charities)

Trustees: Cllr Alan Paul; Cllr Keith Sears; Rick Gamble; Lynn Gamble; Michael Flower; Cllr Mike Bird.

CC Number: 510627

Eligibility

Residents of the borough of Walsall.

Types of grants

The remit of the charity is wide, but typically awards are made for items like clothing, white goods and furniture.

Annual grant total

In 2010/11 the trust had an income of £23,000 and a total expenditure of £30,000.

Exclusions

Property deposits, rent arrears, mortgage payments and utility bills.

Applications

On a form available to download from the Walsall council website or by contacting the council by telephone to request a copy. The trust requests that (if applicable) you include three quotations from reputable suppliers/contractors for any work required; however, the charity has its own suppliers for household and electrical items.

The charity meets approximately six times a year.

The Blanch Woolaston Walsall Charity

£600

Correspondent: Mathew Underhill, Democratic Services, Walsall Council, Civic Centre, Darwall Street, Walsall WS1 1TP (01922 652087; email: underhillm@walsall.gov.uk)

Trustees: Geoffrey Barlow; Norman Mathews; Charles Underwood; Louise Harrison; Alan Paul.

CC Number: 216312

Eligibility

People in need living in the borough of Walsall. Educational grants will only be given to those under 21 years of age. There is no age limit for relief-in-need grants.

Types of grants

Around 20 one-off grants are made each year ranging from £50 to £300 for school uniforms and small household items. The trustees cannot undertake to repeat/renew any grants.

Annual grant total

Grants average around £1,200 a year, though the actual grant figure tends to fluctuate quite widely.

Exclusions

No grants are made for the payment of rates, taxes or other public funds (including gas, electricity and so on).

Applications

On a form available from the correspondent. Applications are considered four times a year.

West Bromwich

The Charity of Jane Patricia Eccles

£440

Correspondent: David Coles, 9 Highcroft Drive, Sutton Coldfield, West Midlands B74 4SX (01283 513065)

Trustees: David Coles; Helen Barlow; Iris Reynolds; Catherine Fellows; Hilary Veasey-Pugh; Jonathan Veasey-Pugh; Ann E. Nicholls; Graham Woodall; Rosa Wilding.

CC Number: 516953

Eligibility

Older women in need who live in Sandwell.

Types of grants

One-off grants in kind to meet specific needs, for example phone installation, showers and Braille reader machines for the blind.

Annual grant total

Grants average around £500 a year, though the actual grant figure tends to fluctuate quite widely.

Applications

In writing to the correspondent for consideration at any time. Applications can be submitted either directly by the individual or a family member, through a third party such as a social worker, or through an organisation such as Citizens Advice or other welfare agency. Applications must be made through, and include, a letter of support from a doctor, church minister or welfare agency.

Wolverhampton

The Power Pleas Trust

£7,000

Correspondent: Keith Berry, 80 York Avenue, Wolverhampton WV3 9BU (01902 655962; email: keithoberry@hotmail.com)

Trustees: Dr Deepak Surendra Kalra; Keith Berry; David Parry; Paula Davies.

CC Number: 519654

Eligibility

Mainly young people, under 18 years, with muscular dystrophy and similar diseases living in the Wolverhampton area.

Types of grants

Grants are given primarily towards the purchase and provision of outdoor electric powered wheelchairs and other aids.

Annual grant total

In 2010/11 the trust had an income of £4,900 and a total expenditure of £7,100.

Applications

In writing to the correspondent directly by the individual or family member.

Worcester-shire

The Astley and Areley Kings Sick Fund

£1,000

Correspondent: Mary Wood, Muldoon, Areley Common, Stourport-on-Severn, Worcestershire DY13 0NG (01299 823619)

Trustees: Mary Wood; Pauline Susan Wilkinson; Sheila Elizabeth Jakeman; Revd Mark Turner; Alan Thomas Stanyer; Irene Hoare.

CC Number: 230709

Eligibility

People who suffer from ill health or have disabilities and who live in the parishes of St Peter Astley, St Bartholomew Areley Kings, St Michael and All Angels Stourport-on-Severn and All Saints Wilden.

Types of grants

One-off grants are made towards specialist equipment for home-care, disabled facilities and additional home support.

Annual grant total

Grants to individuals average around £1,000 a year.

Applications

In writing to the correspondent. Applications can be submitted either directly by the individual, or through a social worker, Citizens Advice or another third party. Trustees meet regularly throughout the year.

Other information

The charity also supports organisations.

The Baron Davenport Emergency Fund (Worcestershire)

£800

Correspondent: The Administrator, Community Action Malvern District, 28–30 Belle Vue Terrace, Malvern, Worcestershire WR14 4PZ (01684 892381; fax: 01684 575155; email: info@communityaction.org.uk)

Trustees: Jen Boyer; Christopher Robin Hopes; Marcus John Gardiner; Christopher Hamilton Kirk; Brian Alexandre Regimbeau; Carola Elizabeth Benion; Julian David Roskams; Susan Mary Caffull; Andrea Kirsten Middlebrook.

CC Number: 501700

Eligibility

Divorcees over 55, young single women/women abandoned by their partners, fatherless children under 25 and widows. Applicants must have been resident in the West Midlands for at least ten years. Applicants are means-tested.

Types of grants

One-off grants ranging from £100 to £150 for emergencies only. Grants have been given towards telephone debt, removal expenses and electrical goods.

Annual grant total

Grants are generally around £800 a year.

Applications

On a form available from the correspondent. A personal income and expenditure breakdown must accompany all applications. Applications can be made through a social worker, Citizens Advice or other welfare agency, or directly by the individual or family member. They are considered on receipt.

John Martin's Charity

£152,000

Correspondent: The Clerk, 16 Queen's Road, Evesham, Worcester WR11 4JN (01386 765440; fax: 01386 765340; email: enquires@johnmartins.org.uk; website: www.johnmartins.org.uk)

Trustees: Nigel Lamb; Julia Westlake; Revd Mark Binney; Revd Barry Collins; Richard Emson; Catherine Evans; Gabrielle Falkiner; Diana Raphael; John Smith; Cyril Scorse; Joyce Turner; Revd Andrew Spurr; John Wilson.

CC Number: 527473

Eligibility

People resident in Evesham, Worcestershire. Applicants or a parent/guardian must have lived in the town for at least 12 months at the date of application.

Note: Applications may also be considered from residents in a number of designated villages close to Evesham if they are suffering from chronic ill health conditions.

Types of grants

'Grants are available for the benefit of children, single parent families, the disabled and people who have fallen on hard times for a variety of circumstances beyond their control. Applications are subject to income assessment and will be considered for a variety of reasons including help with clothing, essential household items, medical and mobility equipment.'

Annual Heating Allowance – an annual award is currently made to assist those aged 60 and over in meeting their energy bills.

Annual grant total

In 2010/11 the charity had assets of £18.6 million and an income of £766,000. Welfare grants were made to individuals totalling £152,000 and were broken down as follows:

Relief in need	£133,500
Health	£6,000
Religious support	£13,000

Exclusions

Support is not normally approved for the repayment of debts, rent or council tax arrears, nor are rental deposits provided. Grants are not considered unless all statutory benefits are being claimed.

Applications

On a form available from the correspondent or downloaded from the website, where criteria are also posted. Applications can be submitted directly by the individual or through a social worker, Citizens Advice or other welfare agency. They are considered twice monthly.

Other information

Grants are also made to organisations and to individuals for educational purposes. The charity has an informative website.

Pershore United Charity

£6,300

Correspondent: Christopher Parsons, Town Hall, 34 High Street, Pershore, Worcestershire WR10 1DS (01386 561561; fax: 01386 561996)

Trustees: Kenneth Newall; Kenneth Rowe; Marjorie Ludlow; Valerie Anne Wood; Charles Gordon John Tucker; Robert Anton Speight; Terence Rose.

CC Number: 200661

Eligibility

People in need who live in private or rented accommodation (not residential or nursing homes) in the parishes of Pershore and Pensham. Priority is given to older people and people in need who have lived in the town for several years.

Types of grants

Recurrent, and occasional one-off grants to help with heating costs at Christmas.

Annual grant total

The charity usually has both an income and a total expenditure of approximately £4,000, all of which is distributed in grants to individuals.

Applications

In writing to the correspondent. Applications are considered in October.

The Ancient Parish of Ripple Trust

£2,500

Correspondent: John Willis, Secretary, 7 Court Lea, Holly Green, Upton-upon-Severn, Worcestershire WR8 0PE (01684 594570; email: willis.courtlea@btopenworld.com)

Trustees: Jane Crowther; Dorothy Marchant; Lady Jean Huntington-Whitely; Clive Astin; Revd Geoffrey Moore; Nicola Inchbald; Revd Frances Wookey; Gillian Sutton.

CC Number: 1055986

Eligibility

People in need living in the parishes of Ripple, Holdfast, Queenhill and Bushley.

Types of grants

Small one-off cash grants are made. Ongoing Christmas grants can also be made to older people.

Annual grant total

In 2010/11 the trust had an income of £11,500 and a total expenditure £13,000.

Applications

In writing to the correspondent. Grants are considered at any time of year.

Other information

Grants are also made to registered charities that serve local people.

The Henry and James Willis Trust

£5,500

Correspondent: John Wagstaff, Clerk, The Laurels, 4 Norton Close, Worcester WR5 3EY (01905 355659)

Trustees: David John Spencer Hallmark; Barnaby Valentine Walwyn Price; Celia Ninette Willis; John Maclaine Bawden; Dr Robert James Stockley; Richard Underwood; Gillian Swindin; Meredith Debenham; Martin Cooper.

CC Number: 201941

Eligibility

People who are convalescing and live in the city of Worcester.

Types of grants

One-off grants to allow convalescents to spend six weeks at the seaside or other health resort. Travel costs and accommodation are included and in special cases the cost of a carer. Patients are usually asked for a small weekly contribution.

Annual grant total

In 2010/11 the trust had an income of £4,600 and a total expenditure of £5,800.

Applications

On a form available from the clerk. Applications can be submitted directly by the individual, or through a social worker, Citizens Advice or other welfare agency.

The Worcestershire Cancer Aid Committee

£15,000

Correspondent: Anthony T Atkinson, c/o Kennel Ground, Gilberts End, Hanley Castle, Worcestershire WR8 0AS (01684 310408)

Trustees: Joanna Constance Atkinson; Anthony Thomas Atkinson; Doreen Merrill; Heather Ellis; Mavis Hutton; Monica Jean Adlington; Pamela Wade; Sally Dimmick; Phyllis Robison; Celia Beck.

CC Number: 504647

Eligibility

People with cancer who live in the old county of Worcestershire.

Types of grants

One-off and recurrent grants and loans, including grants in kind to assist cancer patients in financial distress with home nursing, transport to hospital, specialist equipment and so on.

Annual grant total

In 2010/11 the committee had an income of £19,000 and a total expenditure of £20,000.

Applications

On a form to be submitted through a third party such as a social worker, doctor or nurse. Applications are considered within one week.

Other information

The committee also makes grants to organisations.

Cropthorpe

Randolph Meakins Patty's Farm and the Widows Lyes Charity

£1,500

Correspondent: Mrs J Ayliffe, Orchard House, Main Street, Cropthorne, Pershore, Worcestershire WR10 3LT (01386 860011)

Trustees: John Ayliffe; Garth Wood; Mary Blizard; Roger Hutchins; Sheila Smith.

CC Number: 5624

Eligibility

People in need who live in the village of Cropthorne (Worcestershire).

Types of grants

As well as general welfare grants, Christmas parcels are also given.

Annual grant total

Grants are given for educational and welfare purposes and usually total about £3,000 per year.

Applications

In writing to the correspondent.

Kidderminster

The Kidderminster Aid In Sickness Fund

£8,000

Correspondent: Peter Hill, M F G Solicitors, Carlton House, Marlborough Street, Kidderminster DY10 1BA (01562 820181; email: peter.hill@mfgsolicitors.com)

Trustees: Christopher James Adam; Dr John Marston Wilner; Francesca Fraser Anton.

CC Number: 210586

Eligibility

People who are in poor health and financial need, and live in the borough of Kidderminster.

Types of grants

One-off grants towards, for example, fuel expenses, equipment, furniture, beds and bedding.

Annual grant total

Grants average around £8,000 per year.

Applications

In writing to the correspondent. Applications can be considered at any time.

Other information

Grants are also made to organisations.

Worcester

Armchair

£100

Correspondent: Steve Hines, Grevis Cottage, Lower Dingle, Malvern WR14 4BQ (01905 456080; fax: 01905 456080; email: armchair@talktalkbusiness.net; website: www.armchairworcester.co.uk)

Trustees: Mr P. Griffith; Mrs M. Jones; Mr M. Saunders; Mr J. Churchill; Mrs L. Brown; S. Osborne; Ms M. Kirk; Mr A. Purchon; Mr D. George.

CC Number: 702078

Eligibility

People in need, who have no savings, who live within a ten-mile radius of Worcester City.

Types of grants

The charity provides good quality second hand furniture at low cost (£22 per item in 2011/12) to families and individuals, for example, beds, wardrobes, tables/chairs and so on.

Annual grant total

In 2011/12 the trust had an income of £18,000 and a total expenditure of £24,000, all of which was likely to have been spent on the overheads required for the distribution of second hand furniture – the trust's main activity.

Applications

Applications should be submitted through a social worker, Citizens Advice or other welfare agency. They are considered all year round.

The Mary Hill Trust

£2,200

Correspondent: Andrew G Duncan, Clerk, 16 The Tything, Worcester WR1 1HD (01905 731731)

Trustees: Pamela Clayton; Sister Joan Hudspeth; James Wheldon.

CC Number: 510978

Eligibility

People in need who live within the boundaries of the city of Worcester.

Types of grants

One-off grants ranging from £50 to £500.

Annual grant total

Grants usually total around £6,000 per year, although in 2010 the trust had a lower than usual total expenditure of £2,600.

Applications

In writing to the correspondent either through a third party such as a social worker, Citizens Advice or other welfare agency, or directly by the individual. Applications from individuals are considered upon receipt. Applicants should include as many financial details as possible, for example income and weekly outgoings.

Mayor's Fund, Worcester

£0

Correspondent: Stephen Taylor, Worcester City Council, Guildhall, Worcester WR1 2EY (01905 722005; email: claire.chaplin@worcester.gov.uk)

Trustees: Pamela Clayton; Margaret Clutterbuck; Michael Layland; Dr David Tibbutt.

CC Number: 203691

Eligibility

People in need who live within the Worcester city boundary.

Types of grants

Usually one-off grants of between £30 and £100 for things such as: school books and clothing, bedding, carpets, decorating materials, pushchairs and household appliances.

Annual grant total

Grants usually total around £1,000 each year, although this does tend to fluctuate. In 2010/11 the charity had an income of £2,200 and no expenditure.

Exclusions

No support for course fees for students.

Applications

On a form available from the correspondent. Applications can be submitted by the individual, or through a third party such as a social worker, Citizens Advice or other welfare agency. They are considered in March, June, September and December.

The United Charities of Saint Martin

£2,900

Correspondent: Michael Bunclark, 4 St Catherine's Hill, London Road, Worcester WR5 2EA (01905 355585)

Trustees: Josephine Hodges; Bill Simpson; Lucy Hodgson; Revd Kenneth Boyce; Stephen Hodgson; Keith Burton; Jim Wheldon; Jabba Riaz; Robert Rowden.

CC Number: 200733

Eligibility

People in need who live in the parish of St Martin, Worcester.

Types of grants

One-off grants and pensions, according to need. Grants are also given for education.

Annual grant total

In 2010 the charities had an income of £6,000 and a total expenditure of £5,800.

Applications

In application to the correspondent.

The Worcester Consolidated Municipal Charity

£40,000

Correspondent: The Clerk to the Trustees, HallmarkHulme Solicitors, 3- 5 Sansome Place, Worcester WR1 1UQ

(01905 726600; email: mary.barker@ hallmarkhulme.co.uk)

Trustees: Paul Griffith; D. A. Tibbutt; Brenda Sheridan; M. Jones; R. C. Peachy; M. Saunders; P. Denham; R. E. Berry; C. W. Lord; R. A. Kington; S. M. Osborne; S. G. Markwell; G. V. Hughes; C. M. Panter; A. J. Witcher; J. M. Whitehouse; Melanie Kirk; Jess Bird; Ron Rust.

CC Number: 205299

Eligibility

People in need who live in the city of Worcester or the parishes of Powick, Bransford, Rushwick and Leigh.

Types of grants

One-off grants of £20 to £1,000, principally towards electrical goods, carpets, household items, clothing and so on.

Annual grant total

In 2011 484 grants totalling £96,000 were made to individuals for welfare purposes.

Applications

Applications are usually through a social worker, Citizens Advice or other welfare agency. Statutory sources must have first been exhausted. Applications are submitted on a form available from the correspondent and are considered every month.

Other information

The charity also provides grants to organisations, and to individuals for welfare purposes, and maintains almshouses amongst other charitable activities in Worcester.

South West

General

Viscount Amory's Charitable Trust

£1,800

Correspondent: The Trust Secretary, The Island, Lowman Green, Tiverton, Devon EX16 4LA (01884 254899)

Trustees: Sir Ian Amory; Catherine Cavender.

CC Number: 204958

Eligibility
People in need in the south west of England, with a preference for Devon (due to limited funds).

Types of grants
One-off and recurrent grants according to need.

Annual grant total
In 2010/11 the trust had assets of £12 million and an income of £355,000. The trust made 13 grants to individuals totalling £9,000, mostly for educational purposes. A further £342,000 was given to organisations.

Applications
In writing to the correspondent, for consideration every month.

Avon and Somerset Constabulary Benevolent Fund

£25,000

Correspondent: Mr D J Hayler, Company Secretary, Police Headquarters, PO Box 37, Portishead, Bristol BS20 8QJ (01275 816507; email: dave.hayler@avonandsomerset.police.uk)

Trustees: Bryan Brice; Brian Carl McDowell; Dave Hayler; Kenneth John Jones; Wendy Thompson; Colin Port; Alexander James Duncan; Robert John Beckley; Liz Keogh; Tracey Clegg; Keith Hawkins; Alan Bell; Louisa Rolfe; Caroline Peters.

CC Number: 1085497

Eligibility
Mainly serving and retired members of the Avon and Somerset Constabulary who are in need. Their dependents may also be supported.

Types of grants
One-off grants, ranging from £500 to £2,000, for equipment and house repairs, travel costs for hospital visits and holidays in extreme cases; interest free loans to cover debts or other urgent needs.

Annual grant total
In 2011 the fund had assets of £899,000 and an income of £73,000. Grants to organisations and individuals totalled £61,000.

Exclusions
No grants for private medical treatment, legal representation or private education.

Applications
Applications must be submitted with a report and recommendation by a force welfare officer. They can be considered at any time.

Avon Local Medical Committee Benevolent Fund

£0

Correspondent: Dr J C D Rawlins, Acacia House, Chew Magna, Bristol BS40 8PW (01275 332344; fax: 01275 332344)

Trustees: Dr J. C. D. Rawlins; Dr G. Papworth; Mr S. C. Illingworth.

CC Number: 271576

Eligibility
Medical practitioners who are practicing or have practiced in the former county of Avon, and his or her dependents who are in need.

Types of grants
One-off and recurrent grants according to need.

Annual grant total
Each year the fund has a consistent income and total expenditure of around £10,000. Grants to individuals usually total around £5,000; however, in 2010/11 the trust had nil expenditure.

Applications
In writing to the correspondent.

Other information
Grants are also made to organisations.

The Beckly Trust

£3,500

Correspondent: Stephen Trahair, 10 South Hill, Stoke, Plymouth PL1 5RR (01752 675071)

Trustees: Dr David Edwin Beckly; Stephen James Trahair; Margaret Elizabeth Beckly; James William Beckly.

CC Number: 235763

Eligibility
Children under 18 who live in the city of Plymouth or district of Caradon, Cornwall and who are sick or disabled and in need.

Types of grants
One-off grants of £200 to £500.

Annual grant total
Grants usually total around £3,500 per year.

Applications
In writing to the correspondent giving brief details of income and outgoings of the applicant's parent/guardian and a description of the child's need. Applications should be made preferably through a social worker, Citizens Advice or other welfare agency but can also be made directly by the individual or through another third party. They are considered on an ongoing basis.

Other information
The fund occasionally gives to charities/organisations that support such children.

Gloucestershire Football Association Benevolent Fund

£10,000

Correspondent: Tony Stone, Gloucestershire Football Association Ltd, Oaklands Park Stadium, Gloucester Road, Almondsbury, Bristol BS32 4AG (01454 615888; email: secretary@ gloucestershirefa.com; website: www. gloucestershirefa.com)

Trustees: Tony Stone; Roger Burden; Roy Schafer.

CC Number: 249744

Eligibility

The fund website states that it will assist: 'players of Clubs affiliated to the Gloucestershire Football Association and in membership of the Fund, and players of Representative League and County Teams, who may be injured whilst playing football in a recognised match.' The fund also helps affiliated referees who are injured whilst officiating at sanctioned matches. Applicants must be unable to work normally for at least two weeks before they will be considered eligible for a grant.

Types of grants

One-off and recurrent grants according to the nature of the accident and the applicant's personal circumstances.

Annual grant total

Grants usually total around £10,000 per year.

Applications

Forms are available from the correspondent or can be downloaded from the website. Applications must be made within 28 days of the injury unless there are exceptional circumstances. All forms must also include a report by a member of council and a doctor's certificate.

The Douglas Martin Trust

£35,000

Correspondent: David Evans, 45 Burnards Field Road, Colyton, Devon EX24 6PE (01297 553007; email: d.d. evans@btinternet.com)

Trustees: David Edmund Evans; Jonathan Harold Evans; Richard John Bridgeman; Ann Elizabeth Carruthers.

CC Number: 267876

Eligibility

People in need who live in southern England but only in cases personally known to the trustees. Unsolicited applications cannot be responded to.

Types of grants

On average 400 one-off grants are made a year of up to £300 for items such as bedding, furniture, children's holidays, debt relief and educational grants.

Annual grant total

In 2010/11 the trust had assets of £588,000 and an income of £47,000. Grants to individuals totalled £35,000.

Exclusions

The trust can only support cases known to the trustees.

Applications

Applications will not be accepted unless applicants are known by the trustees or referred by an organisation known by the trustees. Organisations which have recently made successful referrals include various Citizens Advicex (Bath, East Devon, Maidenhead), SAFE, Exeter Disability Centre, Barnet Homes, Outreach Barnet, Chestnut Centre and Maidenhead Turning Point.

Other information

In the past the trust had not previously given grants to organisations, however, in line with the wishes of retiring trustees in 2010/11 a small number of grants to organisations were made totalling £252,000.

The Pirate Trust

£15,000

Correspondent: Nicholas Lake, Pirate FM Ltd, Carn Brea Studios, Barncoose Industrial Estate, Redruth, Cornwall TR15 3XX (01209 314400)

Trustees: Richard Mitchell; Nick Lake; Carol Metters; Bev Warne; Bob McCreadie; Traci Brookfield; Allison Burton.

CC Number: 1032096

Eligibility

People in need living within the Pirate FM 102 broadcast area (Cornwall, Plymouth and west Devon). Preference is given to people with disabilities.

Types of grants

One-off and recurrent grants mainly towards disability equipment.

Annual grant total

In 2010/11 the trust had an income of £22,000 and a total expenditure of £25,000. Grants are given to both individuals and organisations.

Applications

In writing to the correspondent at any time.

The Plymouth and Cornwall Cancer Fund

£7,000

Correspondent: P W Harker, Whiteford Crocker, 28 Outland Road, Plymouth PL2 3DE (01752 550711; email: annepccf@blueyonder.co.uk)

Trustees: Pat Stapleton; Miss A. N. O'Connor; Ms J. Willmott; Mr M. F. Webb; Mr R. J. Parsons; Ms S. J. Aspley; Mr P. W. Harker; Mrs S. Dennison; Dr M. Nugent; Dr Sarah Pascoe; Mr T. A. V. Chandler; Mr T. Bedford; Mrs M. E. Conbeer; Mr F. C. Oppong; Juliet Cole; Mrs S. H. Lamb; Jutta Widlake.

CC Number: 262587

Eligibility

People in need who have cancer, or who have a dependent or relative with cancer, and live in the county of Cornwall and within a radius of 40 miles of Plymouth Civic Centre in Devon. Also in-patients or out-patients of any hospital controlled by Plymouth Hospital NHS Trust.

Types of grants

One-off grants between £30 and £500 to relieve hardship which is caused by cancer, for example, towards the cost of travel to hospital for patients and visitors, additional clothing, bed linen, stairlifts and telephone installations and bills.

Annual grant total

In 2010/11 the fund had assets of £187,000 and an income of £48,000. Hardship grants to individuals were made totalling £7,000.

Applications

In writing to the correspondent at any time. Applicants should have exhausted all other potential sources of help before approaching the fund.

St Monica Trust Community Fund

£535,000 (1,083 grants)

Correspondent: Community Fund Manager, Cote Lane, Westbury-on-Trym, Bristol BS9 3UN (01179 494003; email: community.fund@stmonicatrust. org.uk; website: www.stmonicatrust.org. uk)

Trustees: Revd Ian Gobey; Trevor Smallwood; Stuart Anthony Burnett; Gillian Elizabeth Camm; Richard Wynn-Jones; Charles Hunter; Jane Edwards Cork; John Laycock; Dr Pippa Marsh; Peter John Rilett; Helen Elizabeth Moss; Dr Rebecca Mary Slinn; Lady Paula Katherine Wills; Michael Lea; Charles Griffiths.

CC Number: 202151

Eligibility

People who have a physical or sensory impairment or a long-term physical health problem and live in Bristol or the surrounding area (Gloucestershire, Somerset, Bath and Wiltshire). Applicants must have a low income, limited savings and be over 16 years old.

Help is available to people who are in recovery from substance misuse or alcoholism, provided they have been drug or alcohol free for at least six months and also have a physical disability or long-term physical health problem.

Types of grants

Gifts

One-off grants averaging around £300 but never exceeding £500 to help towards mobility aids, home/car adaptations, domestic appliances, furniture and flooring, bedding, clothing, health costs, driving lessons, communication aids, bills and debts.

Short-term grants

A period of monthly payments designed to help a person through a time of crisis. For example, help can be given for: debt relief; adjusting to a sudden loss of income; unexpected costs; and, the extra costs involved when undergoing chemotherapy, interferon or similar treatments. Usually up to £25 each week is paid for anywhere between a couple of months up to a maximum of three years. It is important to note that help will only be given if the fund believes that the grants it can offer will make a substantial difference in the long term.

Annual grant total

In 2010 the fund held assets of £205 million and had an income of £21 million. Charitable expenditure totalled £21 million. Grants were made to 1,083 individuals (of 1,831 applications received) totalling £535,000 and can be categorised as follows:

Gifts	753	£309,000
Short-term, recurrent grants	314	£205,000
Annuities	16	£21,000

2,621 people received services directly from the trust in 2010. Of this total 1,787 (68%) were supported financially either through direct grants (see above) or the trust's residential or LinkAge services.

Exclusions

No help is given to people with mental health problems or people with a learning disability unless they also have a physical disability or long-term physical health problem. Help is not generally given to people who have more than £3,000 in savings.

Help will not be given for holidays; gardening; bankruptcy fees; funeral expenses; decorating labour costs; respite care and care home fees.

Applications

On a form available to download from the trust's website or by contacting the fund. If possible, applications should be submitted via a social worker, advice worker or a similar professional, although individuals can apply themselves. Depending on the request, a letter may be needed from an occupational therapist confirming the need for a particular item and why it is not available from statutory funds. Individuals should contact the trust if they are having any difficulties in filling out the form, and if needed a home visit can be arranged to help complete the application. Applicants are usually contacted within two weeks of receipt.

The fund expects you to have applied for statutory funding first, for example community care grants and disabled facilities grants, before applying. It may refer you to a relevant trade or forces benevolent fund before considering your application where possible. The fund website also advises: 'If you own your own home and are asking for help with repairs or improvements, we would expect you to investigate equity release schemes and charitable interest free loans before you ask us for help.'

Other information

Grants are also made to organisations whose aim is to support a similar group of beneficiaries, with 14 organisations receiving a total of £139,000 in 2010. The fund also provides sheltered housing and retirement accommodation; support services; recreational and social facilities; and nursing and residential care.

Avon

The Anchor Society

£19,000

Correspondent: Annie Berry, Administrator, 29 Alma Vale Road, Clifton, Bristol BS8 2HL (01179 734161; email: annie@anchorsociety.co.uk or info@anchorsociety.co.uk; website: www.anchorsociety.co.uk)

Trustees: Dr John Cottrell; Alan Reed; William Howard Robert Durie; Dr Jo Gipps; Stewart Wright; Michael Bothamley; Richard Jarratt; Paul Rowe; Charles Hignett.

CC Number: 208756

Eligibility

Isolated people over the age of 55 who are in genuine immediate need and live in the Bristol and former Avon postcode area (BS).

Types of grants

One-off and regular grants as well as Christmas gifts, usually up to £500.

Annual grant total

In 2010/11 the society had assets of £3.9 million and an exceptionally high income of £1.4 million (2009/10: £130,000), thanks to the receipt of a large legacy. Grants were made totalling £90,000, of which around £19,000 was given to individuals. The society informed us that in 2011/12 £26,000 was distributed to individuals, although complete financial information was unavailable for this year at the time of writing.

Exclusions

No grants to organisations, for respite or holidays or for ongoing care costs. Grants are not given for general living expenses, except for cases of extreme long-term hardship. The society will also not make a grant where family members, particularly children, can reasonably be expected to help their relative, especially with requests for building repairs.

Applications

Applications may be made in writing or by email and should include the following applicant details: name, address, age, what the grant is for, details of any disabilities, residential status – does the applicant live alone or with family, and financial circumstances – including income, housing costs and any other significant outgoings. Applicants should also indicate whether they have applied to any other charities for help. The society aims to respond to all enquiries within a few days.

Other information

The society has also invested in the provision of a new form of day care for elderly people within the region called LinkAge and has close links with other welfare charities in the area. It has also invested in a number of housing projects the most recent one providing affordable housing for elderly people on a shared equity basis where necessary.

Backwell Foundation

£890

Correspondent: David James Pike, Sedalia, Brockley Hall, Brockley Lane, Brockley, Bristol BS48 3AZ (01275 463261)

Trustees: Mr E. S. Wood; Mr D. J. Pike; Mr R. Taylor; Mrs E. O. King; M. Campbell.

CC Number: 1086036

Eligibility

People in need who live in the civil parishes of Backwell and Brockley.

Types of grants

One-off and recurrent grants according to need.

Annual grant total

Grants usually average around £750 per year.

Applications

In writing to the correspondent. The trust does not respond to applications made outside its area of interest.

The Federation of Master Builders (Bristol Branch) Benevolent Fund

£3,000

Correspondent: Geoff White, 15 Ransford, Clevedon BS21 7YW (01275 870744)

Trustees: Ted Lloyd; Geoffrey David White; Richard William Finlay Holmes.

CC Number: 235673

Eligibility

Members of the building trade who live in, or have worked in, Bristol, and their dependents who are in need, usually through illness or infirmity. New entrants training in the construction industry in the Bristol area are also eligible.

Types of grants

One-off grants ranging from £200 to £300 for help with living costs, household bills and disabled equipment.

'The fund is not rich. It provides short-term help to cover difficult or crisis periods. It also gives grants to assist in funding larger items where there are other agencies involved.'

Annual grant total

The total annual expenditure of this charity varies from £300 to £3,300.

Applications

In writing to the correspondent. Applications can be submitted either directly by the individual, through a third party such as a social worker, or through a member of the federation and should include details of the applicant's social circumstances. Applications are considered three times a year.

The Grateful Society

£67,000

Correspondent: June Moody, Administrator, 17 St Augustines Parade,

Bristol BS1 4UL (01179 291929; fax: 01179 253824; email: g-s.moody@ btconnect.com; website: gratefulsociety.org)

Trustees: David Marsh; C. J. L. Moorsom; Robert Bernays; Peter McIlwraith; Timothy Ritchie Thom; William Nicholas Hood; Stuart Morrison Andrews; Simon Awdry; Charles Calcraft Wyld; George Lankester; Nigel Sommerville; Tom James Hood; Charles Humphrey Cridland Densham; Andrew Thornhill; Cullum McAlpine; John Charles Tolmie Harvey; Kenneth Tim Pearce; George Morey Tricks; John Moger Woolley; Peter Ryan Cridland Densham; Nicholas Gordon Knibb Hutchen; Jim Hood; David Cryer; Grant Watson; Dr John Newman; Sir Richard Gaskell; M. Henry' G. W. Stobart; Julian Telling; Prof. Hugh Coakham; Ross Ancell.

CC Number: 202349

Eligibility

Ladies over 50 who have lived in Bristol and the surrounding area for at least ten years and would benefit from financial assistance, typically to pursue an independent life in their own home.

Grants may occasionally be given to men in reduced circumstances.

Types of grants

Regular allowances of £100 to £200 a year. One-off grants can be paid towards, for example, electrical goods, clothing, household bills, food, holidays, travel expenses, heating repairs, medical equipment, furniture and disability equipment.

Annual grant total

In 2011 the society had an income of £106,000 and a total expenditure of £86,000. 60 annuities as well as gifts were made totalling £67,000.

Applications

In writing to the correspondent: to be submitted directly by the individual or through a third party.

Other information

Grants may also be made to organisations with similar aims (£12,000 in 2011).

The Peter Hervé Benevolent Institution

£80,000

Correspondent: June Moody, Hon Secretary and Treasurer, 17 St Augustine Parade, Bristol BS1 4UL (01179 291929; fax: 01179 253824; email: g-s.moody@ btconnect.com)

Trustees: Nicholas Parker; Brenda Lalonde; Jean Duval; John Parsons;

Michael Pascoe; Pam Williams; Nancy Mann; Derek Nolan.

CC Number: 202443

Eligibility

People aged 60 and over who live within a 25-mile radius of Bristol city centre, own their own homes and have fallen on hard times.

Types of grants

Recurrent grants, averaging £200 a quarter and one-off emergency grants of up to £300, for example, towards a new boiler.

Annual grant total

In 2011 the trust had assets of £1.9 million and an income of £100,000. Annuities to 47 individuals along with regular gifts totalled £51,000 and emergency grants totalled £29,000.

Applications

In writing to the correspondent, for consideration throughout the year.

Almondsbury

Almondsbury Charity

£2,500 (10 grants)

Correspondent: Alan Gaydon, Chair, Highbank, 7a The Scop, Almondsbury, Bristol BS32 4DU (01454 613424; email: peter.orford@gmail.com; website: www. almondsburycharity.org.uk)

Trustees: Alan Gaydon; Ivor Humphries; Lewis Gray; Alan Bamforth; Diane Wilson; Michael Kirby; Sheila Fulton; Jane Jones; Lucy Hamid; David Chandler; Roger Ducker.

CC Number: 202263

Eligibility

People in need in the old parish of Almondsbury.

Types of grants

One-off grants according to need, for instance for household appliances.

Annual grant total

In 2010/11 the charity had assets of £1.8 million and an income of £59,000. Grants were made to 20 individuals totalling £5,000 for welfare and education.

Exclusions

Grants are not given towards fuel bills.

Applications

On a form available from the correspondent or the website. Cash grants are never made directly to the individual; the grant is either paid via a third party such as social services, or the trust pays for the item directly and donates the item to the individual. Trustees meet six times a year usually in

January, March, May, July, September and November (exact dates available on the website) and applications should be submitted at least two weeks beforehand.

Other information

Grants are also made to schools and organisations.

Bath

The Mayor of Bath's Relief Fund

£10,000

Correspondent: James Money-Kyrle, c/o St John's Hospital, 4–5 Chapel Court, Bath BA1 1SQ (01225 486400; email: james.money-kyrle@stjohnsbath.org.uk)

Trustees: Group Capt. David Smith; Judith Ann Pepler; Robert Andrew Newman; Alan Thomas Gwynn; John Clifford Barnet; Ian Donald MacKenzie; Mary Eileen Hayward; Elizabeth Jane Brooks; Robert William Chapman; Sarah Davies; Harriet Bosnell; Rear Adm Peter Franklyn; Revd Nicholas Williams.

CC Number: 204649

Eligibility

People in need who live in Bath.

Types of grants

One-off grants ranging from £50 to £350 for carpets, second-hand furniture and appliances, school uniforms and bills. The trust states that its key aim is to ensure that children have 'clean clothes, hot food and a warm house.'

Annual grant total

In 2010/11 the trust had an income of £19,000 and a total expenditure of £11,000.

Exclusions

No grants are given for tuition fees or rent arrears.

Applications

On a form available from local health visitors, social services or Citizens Advice. Applications should be submitted through one of these organisations or a similar third party and are considered throughout the year. Note grants are only made as a last resort for those who have already exhausted all other funding channels such as Social Security, social services and other local charities.

The St John's Hospital, Bath

£224,000

Correspondent: James Money-Kyrle, Director of Support Services, St John's Hospital, 4–5 Chapel Court, Bath BA1 1SQ (01225 486400; email: info@stjohnsbath.org.uk; website: www.stjohnsbath.org.uk)

Trustees: Group Capt. David Smith; Judith Ann Pepler; Robert Andrew Newman; Alan Thomas Gwynn; John Clifford Barnet; Mary Eileen Hayward; Ian Donald Mackenzie; Elizabeth Jane Brooks; Robert William Chapman; Harriet Bosnell; Sarah Davies; Revd Nicholas Williams; Rear Adm Peter Franklyn.

CC Number: 201476

Eligibility

People in need living in Bath. There are no age restrictions.

Types of grants

Grants may be made up of several payments, but generally not for more than a total of £1,500 over three years. Help is given towards: food; clothing; TV licences; furniture; white goods; carpets (if there is a child in the family, there are medical reasons or there are any other exceptional circumstances); bankruptcy fees; rent arrears; utility bills; and counselling. Other requests may be considered.

Annual grant total

In 2011 relief-in-need grants to individuals totalled £224,000.

Exclusions

No grants for: DWP loans; funeral expenses; magistrates court fines; deposits or rent in advance for accommodation; washing machines (unless there is a child in the family or there are medical grounds, in which case medical confirmation must be supplied).

Only one grant per individual/family is considered in any twelve-month period. No family or individual shall receive more than three grants within five years or up to a limit set by the trustees.

Applications

On a form available from most local welfare agencies, such as Citizens Advice, Housing Advice Centre and Social Services. Applications must be completed by a recognised local statutory agency. Direct applications are not accepted.

Other information

The charity also provides almshouse accommodation and grants to local organisations.

Bath and North East Somerset

Combe Down Holiday Trust

£31,000 (257 grants)

Correspondent: The administrator, c/o Combe Down Surgery, The Avenue, Combe Down, Bath BA2 5EG (01225 837181; email: ro@cdht.org.uk; website: www.cdht.org.uk)

Trustees: John Richard Carter; Howard Burgess; Alan Patmore; Richard Arthur Edwards; Liz Wilson; Rodney Hodgman; Gabrielle Jean Harris; Karen Margaret Gough.

CC Number: 1022275

Eligibility

People who are disabled, their families and carers, who live in the Bath and North East Somerset area.

Types of grants

One-off grants averaging around £130 towards the cost of a holiday, short break or respite care.

Annual grant total

In 2010 the trust had assets of £877,000 and an income of £72,000. There were 257 welfare grants made totalling £31,000.

Applications

On a form available from the correspondent, to be submitted directly by the individual or through a social worker, Citizens Advice or other welfare agency.

Other information

Note, specialised accommodation is usually booked months in advance, so applicants are advised to apply as early as possible to avoid disappointment.

Batheaston

Henry Smith Charity (Longney)

£1,500

Correspondent: John B Irons, Spindle Berries, 48 Northend, Batheaston, Bath BA1 7ES (01225 852440)

Trustees: Janet Mary Jackson; Elizabeth June Kingsley; John Irons; Roger Eggleton.

CC Number: 204620

Eligibility

People in need, particularly widows, who live in Batheaston.

Types of grants
One-off grants for fuel costs.

Annual grant total
Income and expenditure usually average around £1,500.

Applications
In writing to the correspondent.

Bristol

Thomas Beames' Charity

£5,000

Correspondent: David Cross, 1 All Saints Court, Bristol BS1 1JN (01179 665739)

Trustees: Dr Martin J. Crossley Evans; William Martin; Roger Metcalfe; Revd Richard Dunstan Hoyal.

CC Number: 245822

Eligibility
People in need who live in the ancient parish of St George with St Augustine, Bristol or the parishes of Christchurch with St George, St Stephen with St James or St John the Baptist with St Michael, Bristol. In exceptional cases, the charity may help people who live outside this area and who produce sufficient good reason why they should be treated as being resident within the parish.

Types of grants
Grants are made at the discretion of the trustees, towards, for example, bedding, food and electrical cookers.

Annual grant total
In 2009/10 the charity had an income of £5,600 and a total expenditure of £5,000.

Applications
In writing to the correspondent including details of why help is needed. Applications are usually considered quarterly.

The Bristol Benevolent Institution

£328,000 (260 grants)

Correspondent: Maureen Nicholls, Secretary, 45 High Street, Nailsea, Bristol BS48 1AW (01275 810365; email: maureen.nicholls1@btinternet.com)

Trustees: Sir James Tidmarsh; Michael Grant; David Farra; Fiona Robertson; Jonathan Williams; Lise Seager; Matthew Laws; George Morey Tricks; B. S. Thatcher; Dr Mary Bishop; Christine Anne Radford; Sarah Morris.

CC Number: 204592

Eligibility
Older people living in their own homes with small fixed incomes and little or no capital. Applicants must be over 60 and have lived in Bristol for 15 years or more.

Types of grants
Mostly small recurrent grants paid quarterly in advance within the level disregarded by the DWP when calculating benefits. One-off grants may also be made. Also, for people aged 70 or over who own their own house, free of mortgage, interest free loans of £1,500 a year can be given against the security of their deeds. Loans to be repaid on death or the sale of property. There is no charge for redemption at any time.

Annual grant total
In 2011 the trust had assets of £11.4 million and an income of £411,000. Grants to individuals totalled £328,000.

Applications
On a form available from the correspondent. Applications can be submitted directly by the individual or by a third party such as a social worker or Citizens Advice. Applicants are asked to provide details of income and expenditure. All applicants are visited. The trustees meet quarterly in March, June, September and December to discuss applications.

Other information
The institution notes that although it gives financial assistance, 'we believe that the most valued assistance we give is friendship and advice, ably provided by our lady visitors.' The institution circulates regular newsletters which provide reminders of the help available.

Bristol Charities

£278,000

Correspondent: D W Jones, Chief Executive, 17 Augustines Parade, Bristol BS1 4UL (01179 300303; fax: 01179 253824; email: info@bristolcharities.org.uk; website: www.bristolcharities.org.uk)

Trustees: Alfred Morris; Vanessa H. Wingate Stevenson; David Watts; Susan Hampton; Dudley Lewis; Barry Raymond England; Revd Dr David Hoyle; Kamala Das; Andrew Hillman; Helen Elizabeth Moss; Laura Claydon; John Webster; Anthony Beauchamp Harris.

CC Number: 1109141

Eligibility
People in need who have lived in Bristol for more than two consecutive years.

Types of grants
Grants will normally be considered for bedding/beds, carpets, clothing for school age children, white goods, furniture, medical equipment, decorating materials and respite care.

The following items, purchased through the 'retained ownership scheme' will be considered: wheelchairs, electric wheelchairs, electric powered chairs/electric scooters, standard stair lifts, stair lifts with a manual platform and stair lifts with a powered platform.

Annual grant total
In 2010/11 grants to over 1400 individuals totalled £278,000.

Exclusions
No grants for debts or rent arrears. Only one grant is given per applicant per year and there is a limit of three grants per person.

Applications
On a form available from the Bristol Charities website. All applicants require the support of a sponsor who should be a healthcare professional. Applications are considered daily.

Other information
The charities also run a group of almshouses and provide services for older people.

The Lord Mayor of Bristol's Christmas Appeal for Children

£42,000

Correspondent: B N Simmonds, Hon. Treasurer, 3 Park Crescent, Frenchay, Bristol BS16 1PD

Trustees: B. N. Simmonds; David Powell.

CC Number: 288262

Eligibility
Children under 16 who are in need and who live in the city of Bristol.

Types of grants
One-off grants of around £20 in the form of vouchers for food, clothes and toys at Christmas.

Annual grant total
In 2010/11 the trust held assets of £112,000 and an income of £49,000. Grants were made totalling £42,000.

Applications
Through a social worker, Citizens Advice, welfare agency or other third party such as a parent or a person who can confirm the individual's needs.

The Dolphin Society

£42,000

Correspondent: June Moody, Administrator, 17 Augustines Parade, Bristol BS1 4UL (01179 299649; email: dolphinsociety@btconnect.com; website: dolphinsociety.org.uk)

Trustees: Keith Bonham; Mary Prior; Helen Moss; Jos Moule; Tim R. Ross; Stephen Parsons; Sandie Foxall-Smith.

CC Number: 203142

Eligibility

People in need and/or at risk through poor health, disability or financial difficulty and who live in Bristol. Preference is given to older people who need help in maintaining their independence and security in their own homes.

Types of grants

Help with telephone installations, smoke alarms, pendant alarms and security items such as external security boxes and door and window locks. Payments from the hardship fund can be used to help with home adaptations to enable people to continue to live in their homes while coping with increasing disability. One-off cash grants are given occasionally and can range from £10 to £1,000.

Annual grant total

In 2010/11 the society held assets of £103,000 and had an income of £83,000. Total charitable expenditure came to £42,000 and can be broken down as follows:

Pendant alarms/telephone installation	£26,000
Hardship funds	£11,000
Home security	£5,000

Exclusions

No grants to applicants living outside the area of benefit.

Applications

On a form available from the correspondent. Applications can be submitted directly by the individual or family member or by an appropriate third party. There are no deadlines and applications are considered throughout the year.

Other information

The society also makes grants to local self-help groups, community centres and day care centres.

The Redcliffe Parish Charity

£3,000

Correspondent: Paul Tracey, 18 Kingston Road, Nailsea, Bristol, North Somerset BS48 4RD (01275 854057)

Trustees: Angela Clayton; Andrew Clarke; Graham Briscoe; Alan Stevens; Paul Tracey; Susan Heller; Peter Cole; Bryan Anderson; Revd Dr Simon Taylor; Paul Jenking.

CC Number: 203916

Eligibility

People in need who live in the city of Bristol.

Types of grants

One-off grants usually of £25 to £50. 'The trustees generally limit grants to families or individuals who can usually manage, but who are overwhelmed by circumstances and are in particular financial stress rather than continuing need.' Grants are typically given for electric goods, clothing, living costs, food, holidays, furniture and disabled equipment.

Annual grant total

In 2010/11 the charity had an income of £9,000 and a total expenditure of £7,000.

Exclusions

No grants for bankruptcy fees, debts in respect of Council Tax, rent arrears or credit debts.

Applications

In writing to the correspondent. Applications should be submitted on the individual's behalf by a social worker, doctor, health visitor, Citizens Advice or appropriate third party, and will be considered early in each month. Ages of family members should be supplied in addition to financial circumstances and the reason for the request.

Other information

Grants to schoolchildren occur as part of the trust's wider welfare work.

The Unity Fund for the Elderly

£12,000

Correspondent: D H T Rowcliffe, Secretary, 5 Bishop Road, Emersons Green, Bristol BS16 7ET (01179 561289)

Trustees: Alan Feltham; Brian Miller; David Howard Thomas Rowcliffe; Megan Ruth Grace; Michael Alan Badman; Maggie Hill; Maureen Helen Rowcliffe Quarry.

CC Number: 1000421

Eligibility

People over 60 in need, hardship or distress in the Bristol area.

Types of grants

One-off grants towards repairs, clothing, electric goods, household bills, medical equipment, furniture, disability equipment and so on.

Annual grant total

In 2011 the fund had an income and total expenditure of £13,000.

Applications

In writing to the correspondent. Applications should be submitted through a social worker, Citizens Advice or other welfare agency. They are considered at any time.

Other information

Grants are also made to organisations.

Wraxall Parochial Charities

£7,000

Correspondent: Mrs A Sissons, Clerk to the Trustees, 2 Short Way, Failand, Bristol BS8 3UF (01275 392691)

Trustees: Anthony Tavener; Lorraine Marshfield; Raymond Llewellyn; Rosemary Hayes; Stephen Young; Rosey Lunn; Richard Smith.

CC Number: 230410

Eligibility

People living in the parish of Wraxall and Failand, Bristol who are in need due to hardship or disability.

Types of grants

One-off grants.

Annual grant total

In 2010 the charity had an income of £13,500 and a total expenditure of £14,500.

Applications

In writing to the correspondent, directly by the individual. Applications are considered in February, June, September and November.

Other information

Grants are also made for educational purposes.

Midsomer Norton

Ralph and Irma Sperring Charity

£25,000

Correspondent: The Secretary, Thatcher and Hallam Solicitors, Island House, Midsomer Norton, Bath BA3 2HJ (01761 414646)

Trustees: S. A. Blanning; N. M. Busby; Revd C. G. Chiplin; E. W. Hallam; Dr P. Haxell; K. W. Saunders.

CC Number: 1048101

Eligibility

People in need who live within a five-mile radius of the Church of St John the Baptist in Midsomer Norton, Bath.

Types of grants

One-off and recurrent grants according to need.

Annual grant total

In 2010/11 the charity had assets of £5.7 million, which generated an income of £201,000. Awards to local causes amounted to £114,000. Further details were not available, however the charity makes grants to both individuals and organisations.

Applications

In writing to the correspondent, to be considered quarterly.

North Somerset

Nailsea Community Trust Ltd

£2,000

Correspondent: Mrs Helen Owen, 42 Green Pastures Road, Wraxall, Bristol BS48 1ND (01275 856429)

Trustees: Robert Westlake; John Smithson; Karl Day; Nancy Elliott; Norman Baker; Patricia Robinson; Anthony Tavener; Philippa Taylor; Mary Jaggard; Alan Shaw; Dr Martin Elford.

CC Number: 900031

Eligibility

People of any age or occupation who are in need due, for example, to hardship, disability or sickness, and who live in the town of Nailsea and the immediate area in North Somerset.

Types of grants

One-off grants, usually up to £500, towards items, services or facilities.

Annual grant total

About £4,000 for educational and welfare purposes.

Applications

On a form available from the correspondent. Applications can be submitted either directly by the individual or via a relevant third party such as a school, social worker or Citizens Advice. Applications are considered at meetings held every three months.

Charles Graham Stone's Relief-in-Need Charity

£6,000

Correspondent: John Gravell, Easton Grey, Webbington Road, Cross, Axbridge BS26 2EL (01934 732266)

Trustees: Trevor Jones; John Hunt; Anthea Garley; Angela Walker; Ann Pursey; Peter Walker; Kenneth Young; Anthony Brown.

CC Number: 260044

Eligibility

People in need who live in the parishes of Churchill and Langford, North Somerset.

Types of grants

One-off grants of £50 to £150 towards travel expenses of visiting relatives in hospitals or nursing homes, help in the home, household bills or medical/disability equipment.

Annual grant total

In 2010 the charity had an income of £4,000 and an expenditure of £8,000.

Exclusions

No grants for payment of national or local taxes or rates.

Applications

In writing to the correspondent with a full explanation of the personal circumstances. Applications should be submitted by the end of February or August for consideration in the following month. Initial telephone calls are not welcomed.

Other information

Grants are also made to individuals for educational and vocational purposes.

Portishead

The Portishead Nautical Trust

£5,000

Correspondent: Mrs Liz Knight, 108 High Street, Portishead, Bristol BS20 6AJ (01275 847463; fax: 01275 818871)

Trustees: Sheila Belk; Tean Jessie Francis Kirby; Stephen Paul Gillingham; Mr M. R. Cruse; Mrs S. Haysom; Colin Crossman; Iris Perry; Dr Gerwyn Owen; Wendy Bryant; Peter Dingley-Brown.

CC Number: 228876

Eligibility

People in need, usually under 25, who live in Portishead. Preference is given to people who are: homeless; unemployed; experiencing problems related to drug or solvent abuse; being ill-treated; being neglected, in the areas of physical, moral and educational well-being; or 'people who have committed criminal acts, or are in danger of doing so'.

Types of grants

Small grants and bursaries, 'where such a grant will enable a young person to realise their full potential'.

Annual grant total

In 2010/11 the trust had an income of £77,000. Grants totalled £48,000, of which £5,000 was awarded to individuals. The remainder was awarded to local organisations.

Applications

On a form available from the correspondent. Applications must be supported by a sponsor, such as a welfare officer or health visitor. Trustees meet four times a year to consider applications.

South Gloucestershire

The Chipping Sodbury Town Lands

£9,900 (165 grants)

Correspondent: Nicola Gideon, Clerk, Town Hall, 57–59 Broad Street, Chipping Sodbury, South Gloucestershire BS37 6AD (01454 852223; email: nicola.gideon@ chippingsodburytownhall.co.uk)

Trustees: Colin Hatfield; David Shipp; Jim Elsworth; Bill Ainsley; Bryan Seymour; Michelle Cook; Paul Robins; Wendy Whittle; Paul Tily.

CC Number: 236364

Eligibility

People in need who live in Chipping Sodbury or Old Sodbury.

Types of grants

One-off and recurrent grants according to need.

Annual grant total

In 2011 the charity had assets of £7.9 million, an income of £349,000 and made grants totalling £9,900 to 165 households for 'winter expenses'.

Applications

In writing to the correspondent. Grant aid is advertised locally in schools, clubs, associations, churches and other religious orders, in the local press, and the Town Hall.

Stanton Prior

The Henry Smith Charity (Longnet Estate)

£1,000

Correspondent: Alistair Hardwick, Church Farm, Stanton Prior, Bath BA2 9HT (01761 479625)

Trustees: Alistair Hardwick; Revd Jan Knott; Ronald Hardwick.

CC Number: 240003

Eligibility

People in need who have lived in Stanton Prior for more than three years. Preference is usually given to those living in rented accommodation.

Types of grants

One-off cash grants and gift vouchers.

Annual grant total

Grants usually total around £1,000 each year.

Applications

In writing to the correspondent, directly by the individual, for consideration by the trustees in November and December.

Thornbury

Thornbury Consolidated Charities (administered by Thornbury Town Trust)

£29,000

Correspondent: Margaret Powell, 9 Elmdale Crescent, Thornbury, Bristol BS35 2JH (01454 281777; email: margaret.towntrust@googlemail.com)

Trustees: Margaret Woodford; Shirley Holloway; Tony Lines; Ron Clutterbuck; Clive Parkinson; Paul Morrish; Chris Clifford.

CC Number: 238273

Eligibility

People in need who live in the parish of Thornbury. Beneficiaries are often of pensionable age or disabled but anyone in the parish can apply.

Types of grants

One-off grants usually ranging from £80 to £120 to help with the extra expense of Christmas but they are also given at other times.

Annual grant total

In 2010 the charities had assets of £825,000 and an income of £42,000. Grants were made totalling £29,000.

Exclusions

No grants for educational purposes. Grants are not given where the need is covered by statutory authorities.

Applications

By letter to the correspondent. Applications can be submitted directly by the individual or through a social worker, Citizens Advice or other welfare agency and should include details of income. They are considered in November for Christmas but applications for special needs can be made at any time.

Other information

Grants are also given to organisations.

Cornwall

The Blanchminster Trust

£17,000 (42 grants)

Correspondent: Jane Bunning, Clerk to the Trustees, Blanchminster Building, 38 Lansdown Road, Bude, Cornwall EX23 8EE (01288 352851; fax: 01288 352851; email: office@blanchminster. plus.com; website: www.blanchminster. org.uk)

Trustees: Owen May; John Gardiner; Byron Rowlands; Gordon Rogers; Leonard Tozer; Julia Shepherd; Valerie Newman; Christine Bilsand; Christopher Cornish; Wilfred Keat; Chris Nichols; Ian Whitfield; Michael Worden.

CC Number: 202118

Eligibility

People who live in the parishes of Bude, Stratton and Poughill (the former urban district of Bude-Stratton).

Types of grants

Generally one-off grants up to a maximum of £25,000 for the relief of need, hardship or distress, for example for clothing, food, electrical goods, furniture, medical care and equipment, and travel to and from hospital.

Annual grant total

In 2011 the trust had assets of £10 million, an income of £476,000 and made 42 grants for welfare totalling £17,000.

Applications

On a form available from the correspondent. Applications are considered monthly and should be submitted directly by the individual. Where possible the application should include a request for a specific amount and be supported with quotes for the costs needed and/or written support

from a social worker or other welfare agency. Applications must include evidence of financial need.

Other information

Grants are also made to individuals for education and for community projects.

The Lizzie Brooke Charity

£11,000

Correspondent: Mrs Sheila Bates, 13 Church Close, Lelant, St Ives TR26 3JX (01736 752383; email: mail@ anthony-williams.co.uk)

Trustees: Revd John Dibb-Smith; Michael John Vickers; Peggy Harvey; Anne Vickers; Winifred Ann Stone.

CC Number: 254764

Eligibility

Older people, people who are sick and those in need who live in West Cornwall.

Types of grants

One-off grants ranging from £100 to £200 for the necessities of everyday living. Grants can be given towards electric goods, clothing, holidays, travel expenses, furniture and hospital expenses.

Annual grant total

In 2011 the charity had a higher than usual income of £10,000 (£300 in 2010) and a total expenditure of £12,500. Grants were made totalling around £11,000.

Exclusions

Grants are not made to people living in other parts of Cornwall or for students for fees.

Applications

On a form available from the correspondent and completed by a sponsor. Applications should be submitted through a social worker, Citizens Advice or other welfare agency. They are considered at any time.

Cornwall Community Foundation

£12,000

Correspondent: The Grants Team, Suite 1, Sheers Barton, Lawhitton, Launceston, Cornwall PL15 9NJ (01566 779333; email: grants@cornwallfoundation.com; website: www.cornwallfoundation.com)

Trustees: Tony Hogg; Oliver Baines; Hon Evelyn Boscawen; Lady Mary Holborow; Jane Margaret Hartley; James Williams; Margaret Bickford-Smith; Daphne Skinnard; Michael Miles; John Ede; Bishop Tim Thornton; Lady

George; Tim Smith; Elaine Hunt; Mark Mitchell; Thomas Varcoe; Charles Reynolds.

CC Number: 1099977

Eligibility

People in need living in Cornwall.

Types of grants

Usually one-off. Grants have been made to alleviate poverty, hardship and distress. A special fund has also been established to help people affected by flooding.

Annual grant total

In 2011 the foundation had assets of £2.2 million and an income of £478,000. Grants were made to individuals through four funds totalling £12,000.

Applications

Initial enquiries should be directed to the grants team to check what funds are available. Alternatively a list of open grant schemes is available on the foundation's website. Note that as with all community foundations schemes open and close regularly, so check before applying.

The Cornwall Retired Clergy, Widows of the Clergy and their Dependents Fund

£11,000

Correspondent: C M Kent, Truro Diocesan Board Of Finance, Diocesan House, Truro, Cornwall TR1 1JQ (01872 274351; email: accountant@truro. anglican.org)

Trustees: Ven. Roger Bush; Revd Royden Screech; Revd Timothy Martin Thornton; Revd Prebendary Alfred James Vincent; Jennie Godwin; Revd Owen Blatchly; Revd Gordon Cryer; John Sansom; Jill Atkinson.

CC Number: 289675

Eligibility

Widows, widowers and dependents of deceased members of the clergy who live in, or have worked in, the diocese of Truro. Retired Anglican clergy who are in need and have links with Truro are also eligible for support.

Types of grants

Grants are one-off and occasionally recurrent according to need. Recent grants have ranged from £50 to £500 and included funding for dentist's fees, spectacles, travel to hospital and assistance with equipment for people with disabilities.

Annual grant total

In 2011 the fund had an income of £13,900 and a total expenditure of £14,100.

Exclusions

No grants for assistance with school fees or university fees.

Applications

In writing to the correspondent. Applications can be submitted directly by the individual or through a relative or a carer. They are usually considered monthly.

The Duke of Cornwall's Benevolent Fund

£0

Correspondent: Robert G Mitchell, 10 Buckingham Gate, London SW1E 6LA (020 7834 7346)

Trustees: Bertie Ross; James Henry Leigh-Pemberton.

CC Number: 269183

Eligibility

People who are in need, though in practice funds are steered towards the West Country and areas related to Duchy lands, which are principally in Cornwall.

Types of grants

One-off and recurrent grants according to need.

Annual grant total

In 2010/11 the fund had assets of £3 million and an income of £135,000. Grants totalled £143,000. No grants were made to individuals in 2010/11 although in previous years around £1,000 – £2,000 has been paid to individuals.

Applications

In writing to the correspondent.

Other information

The fund's main focus is on awarding grants to charitable organisations.

The United Charities of Liskeard

£1,000

Correspondent: A J Ball, Tremellick, Pengover Road, Liskeard, Cornwall PL14 3EW (01579 343577)

Trustees: Barry Glasson; John Talbot Goldsworthy; Margaret Ball; Patricia Rowe; Paula Arthur; Sandra Preston; William Richard Runnalls Fursman; Anne Purdon; Mrs C. M. Whitty; Ron Bennett; Eleanor Hoskin.

CC Number: 215173

Eligibility

For the relief-in-need fund, people in need who live in the town of Liskeard (formerly the borough of Liskeard). For the relief-in-sickness fund, people in need who live in Liskeard, the parish of Dobwalls with Trewidland (formerly the parish of Liskeard) and the parishes of Menheniot and St Cleer.

Types of grants

One-off and recurrent grants according to need.

Annual grant total

Grants usually total around £1,000 each year.

Applications

In writing to the correspondent.

Gunwalloe

The Charity of Thomas Henwood

£6,200

Correspondent: Jennifer Moyle, Homeleigh, Gunwalloe, Helston, Cornwall TR12 7QG (01326 564806)

Trustees: Michael John Thornton Mills; Peter Courtney Hocking; Winifred May Pollard; Jennifer Moyle.

CC Number: 206765

Eligibility

People who are unemployed, sick and retired and live in the parish of Gunwalloe.

Types of grants

One-off or recurrent grants according to need, and grants for the provision of nurses and to assist people recovering from illness. All by periodic distribution. Grants range from £60 to £100. Income is also used to care for graves in the churchyard if no relatives are still alive.

Annual grant total

In 2010 the charity had an income of £9,800 and a total expenditure of £6,500.

Applications

In writing to the trustees. Applications are considered in March and December.

Gwennap

Charity of John Davey

£10,000

Correspondent: E T Pascoe, Tregenna Lodge, Crane, Camborne TR14 7QX (01209 718853)

Trustees: Revd Eddie Woon; Revd Simon Bone.

CC Number: 232127

Eligibility

Ex-miners over 70 years of age, or their widows, who live in the ancient parish of Gwennap, near Redruth in Cornwall and are in need.

Types of grants

Quarterly grants of £10 to £40 for general living expenses.

Annual grant total

Income and total expenditure usually average around £11,000.

Applications

Initial telephone calls to the correspondent are welcome and application forms are available on request. Applications can be submitted directly by the individual or family member.

Helston

The Helston Welfare Trust

£800

Correspondent: Chris Dawson, Guildhall, Helston, Cornwall TR13 8ST (01326 572063; email: townclerk@ helstontc.com)

Trustees: Donald James Eddy; Ron Williams; Revd D. Miller; Mrs P. Eddy; Sue Swift; Andrew Hill; Cllr Niall John Campbell Devenish.

CC Number: 1014972

Eligibility

People in need who live in the area administered by Helston Town Council.

Types of grants

One-off grants in kind. The trust will purchase essential electrical goods like cookers, refrigerators or furniture on behalf of the individual.

Annual grant total

This trust's income is generally in the region of £2,700 a year. Total expenditure averages around £1,000.

Applications

In writing to the correspondent. Applications can be submitted directly by the individual or through a third party such as a social worker or an organisation such as Citizens Advice. Details of need and the financial circumstances of the applicant should be included. Applications are considered as they are received.

Devon

The Barnstaple and North Devon Dispensary Fund

£18,000

Correspondent: Christina Ford, 17 Sloe Lane, Landkey, Barnstaple, Devon EX32 0UF (01271 831551; email: bandnddf@gmail.com)

Trustees: Jillian Thurstans Waldron; David William Reginald Burgess; Diana Piercy; Dr John Marston; Terence Stephen Ford; Michael Oerton; Roger Jacob; Faye Valda Webber; Maurice Andrew Simpson.

CC Number: 215805

Eligibility

People in need who live in the North Devon parishes.

Types of grants

One-off grants towards coal and heating bills, convalescence, medical equipment and other costs, bedding, clothing, travel expenses and food.

Annual grant total

In 2011 the fund had an income of £13,000 and a total expenditure of £21,000.

Applications

In writing to the correspondent, preferably through a doctor, health visitor, social worker or other third party.

Bideford Bridge Trust

£21,000

Correspondent: P R Sims, Steward, 24 Bridgeland Street, Bideford, Devon EX39 2QB (01237 473122)

Trustees: P. Christie; William Isaac; E. Junkison; E. Hubber; J. Baker; Oliver Chope; Angus Harper; Philip Pester; Trevor Johns; Brian Lacey; David Frics.

CC Number: 204536

Eligibility

People in need who live in Bideford and the immediate neighbourhood.

Types of grants

One-off grants ranging from £150 to £500.

Annual grant total

In 2011 the charity had assets of £13 million, an income of £723,000 and made welfare grants totalling £21,000.

Exclusions

Grants are not given for computers for personal use.

Applications

On a form available from the correspondent, to be submitted at any time during the year by the individual, although a sponsor is usually required.

Edward Blagdon's Charity

£3,400

Correspondent: Joan McCahon, Clerk to the Trustees, Gunshot Cottage, Lower Washfield, Tiverton, Devon EX16 9PD (01884 253468)

Trustees: Colin French; Revd David Mark Fletcher; Robert Robson; Revd Godfrey Bryan Bell.

CC Number: 244676

Eligibility

People in need who live in Tiverton and Washfield in Devon.

Types of grants

One-off grants only ranging from £10 to £500.

Annual grant total

In 2010/11 the trust had an income of £17,000 and a total expenditure of £3,400.

Applications

In writing to the correspondent directly by the individual or through a social worker, Citizens Advice or other welfare agency.

The Brownsdon and Tremayne Estate Charity (also known as the Nicholas Watts' Gift)

£9,000

Correspondent: Joan Stewart, 17 Chapel Street, Tavistock, Devon PL19 8DX

Trustees: Dennis Maurice Carr; John Greening; Stephen Henry Charles Carr; Austin Dennis Carr; Christopher Robin Start; Clarence Yelland; Cyril William Hodge; David Paul Howell; Dennis Edward Greening; Duncan John Bird; Ian Austin Carr; John Cowling Doidge; Robert Eric Gilbert; Roger David Archer Bird; Russell George Woolcock; Stuart Charles Doidge; Dr Thomas Frederick Maynard Roskilly; Walter Lake; Revd Michael Brierley; John Collacott.

CC Number: 203271

Eligibility

For the Brownsdon Fund, men in need who live in Devon, with a preference for Tavistock applicants, preferably owner/ occupiers. For the Tremayne Estate

Charity, people in need who live in Tavistock.

Types of grants

One-off grants averaging around £300 each. In addition to general relief-in-need, the trustees help towards the maintenance of homes owned by beneficiaries, for example, providing new carpets, grants towards the costs of roof repairs and occasionally supplying computers to people with disabilities.

Annual grant total

In 2010/11 the charity had an income of £19,000 and a total expenditure £11,000.

Exclusions

The trust does not assist with mortgage repayments.

Applications

On a form available from the correspondent. The trustees advertise for applications in July, to be considered in September, but at other times for emergencies. Applications can be submitted directly by the individual.

Cranbrook Charity

£5,000

Correspondent: Stephen Purser, Venn Farm, Bridford, Exeter EX6 7LF (01647 252328; email: purseratvenn@hotmail. com)

Trustee: S. Purser.

CC Number: 249074

Eligibility

People in need who live in the parishes of Dunsford, Doddiscombeleigh and 'that part of the parish of Holcombe Burnel as in 1982 constituted part of the parish of Dunsford'.

Types of grants

One-off and recurrent grants to those in need. Recently, grants of £80 have been given every six months for relief-in-need and educational purposes.

Annual grant total

In 2010/11 the charity had both an income and total expenditure of £9,000.

Applications

In writing to the correspondent.

Other information

Grants are also made for educational purposes and to organisations.

The David Gibbons Foundation

£20,000

Correspondent: Cathy Houghton, Administrator, 14 Fore Street, Budleigh

Salterton, Devon EX9 6NG (01395 445259; website: www.gibbonstrusts.org)

Trustees: Roger Dawe; Dr Miles Joyner; Dr John Frankish; Kerensa Pearson.

CC Number: 1134727

Eligibility

The elderly, sick, disabled and needy in Devon, with a preference for East Devon.

Types of grants

One-off grants according to need.

Annual grant total

In 2010/11 the trust held assets of £2.3 million and had an income of £2.5 million and made grants totalling £120,000, the majority of which were made to organisations.

The accounts for 2011/12 were not available at the time of writing. However, the trust is very proactive in the use of its website and notes that in 2011/12 71 applications were received and 47 grants were made to individuals and organisations. The average individual grant was £652.

Applications

On an application form which can be downloaded from the website and posted to the trust. Applications must be supported by at least one letter from a professional third party such as a social worker, teacher, doctor, etc. Applications without a letter of support will not be considered. Applicants requesting payment by BACS must enclose a paying-in slip or a copy of a bank statement. All applications will be acknowledged by letter or email. Decisions may take up to three months.

Trustees meet every three months, usually in January, April, July and October.

Other information

The foundation was established by the will of Mr David Gibbons of Exmouth who passed away in February 2008.

The Devon County Association for the Blind

£1,500

Correspondent: Martin Pallett, Station House, Holman Way, Topsham, Exeter EX3 0EN (01392 876666; fax: 01392 874442; email: enquiries@devoninsight. org.uk; website: www.devonblind.org.uk)

Trustees: Gwyn Dickinson; Rose Hewitt; Sandra Semmens; Marilyn Lant; Dr Alma Swan; Steve Muncer; Roger Ascough; Alun Gwernan-Jones; Rod Wilson.

CC Number: 203044

Eligibility

People who are blind or partially sighted who live in Devon (excluding the city of Exeter and Plymouth).

Types of grants

Grants of up to £250 to cover specific needs including holidays, travel expenses, medical equipment, furniture and disabled equipment.

Annual grant total

In 2010/11 the charity had assets of £1 million and an income of £336,000. Grants were made totalling £3,000.

Applications

On a form available from the correspondent. Or call 01392 878802. Applications are considered quarterly and should be submitted either directly by the individual or through a third party such as a social worker. Applicants need to be in receipt of a means tested benefit or have income and savings of less than £10,000.

Other information

Grants are also made to organisations and to individuals for education.

Devonian Fund

£7,200

Correspondent: Devon Community Foundation, The Factory, Leat Street, Tiverton EX16 5LL (01884235887; fax: 01884 243824; email: grants@devoncf. com; website: www.devoncf.com/apply-for-a-grant/devonian-fund)

Trustees: David Stevens; Katherine Gurney; Steve Hindley; Mike Bull; Mark Haskell; Arthur Ainslie; David Searle; Peter Keech; Caroline Marks; Nigel Arnold; John Sunderland; John Glasby.

CC Number: 1057923

Eligibility

People resident in Devon who are experiencing mobility or transport issues due to illness or disability.

Types of grants

Grants of £500 to £1,000 for items that relieve mobility problems such as specialised equipment or specialised transport such as accessible coaches or taxis.

Annual grant total

£7,200 in 2010/11.

Exclusions

Grants for IT and associated equipment can only be made for up to £400.

Applications

On a form available from the website which must be filled out and submitted by a health care professional such as an occupational therapist or community group working with the individual. Applications are considered three times a year in January, May and September.

Other information
This fund is administered by Devon Community Foundation which mainly gives grants to organisations.

The Dodbrooke Parish Charity

£10,000

Correspondent: Jane Balhatchet, Springfield House, Ashleigh Road, Kingsbridge, Devon TQ7 1HB (01548 854321)

Trustees: Margaret Hellen Morgan; Joan Beryl Washington; Christopher Pedley; Christopher Barry Lane; Janet Hilary Wingate; Kenneth Flewings Court; Raymond Lewis Barrington; Robert Charles Massie Freeman.

CC Number: 800214

Eligibility
People in need who live in the parishes of Dodbrooke and Kingsbridge.

Types of grants
One-off grants and pensions to older people.

Annual grant total
In 2010 the trust had an income of £22,000 and a total expenditure of £16,000.

Applications
In writing to the correspondent. Applications are considered in January, March, June and September.

Other information
The charity also makes grants to organisations.

The Exeter Relief-in-Need Charity

£6,500

Correspondent: Martin R King, Clerk, Exeter Municipal Charities, Chichester Mews, 22A Southernhay East, Exeter EX1 1QU (01392 201550; email: admin@ exetermunicipalcharities.org.uk; website: www.exetermunicipalcharities.org.uk)

Trustees: Edna Norton; Peter Wadham; Joan Blackmore; John Marshall; Norman Long; Christopher Blong; Jean Rush; Stephen Force; William Rowe; John Winterbottom; Richard Branston; Kate Caldwell; Richard Halstead; Roger Charles Panter.

CC Number: 1002152

Eligibility
People in need who live in the city of Exeter.

Types of grants
One-off grants of between £50 and £150; individuals can reapply in subsequent years. Grants are made towards household furniture and equipment, floor coverings, school uniforms, essential travelling expenses, heating costs and so on.

Annual grant total
In 2010 the charity had an income of £22,000 and a total expenditure of £7,000.

Exclusions
No grants for debt repayment, interest on loans, rent, mortgage, or council tax arrears.

Applications
On a form available from the correspondent, submitted directly by the individual, or through a social worker, Citizens Advice or other welfare agency. Applications should include details of the income, including benefits and outgoings of the applicant. Three references must normally be supplied. Awards are made following interviews of the applicants by trustees in February, May, August and November.

Other information
This charity is part of Exeter Municipal Charities.

The Heathcoat Trust

£335,000

Correspondent: Mrs C J Twose, Secretary, The Factory, Tiverton, Devon EX16 5LL

Trustees: Mark Drysdale; Sir Ian Heathcote-Amery; John Smith; Stephen Butt; Susan Westlake.

CC Number: 203367

Eligibility
People who are older, in poor health or financial need and live in Tiverton and the mid-Devon area. Applicants need to have a personal connection with either the John Heathcoat or the Lowman Companies.

Types of grants
One-off and recurrent grants according to need.

Annual grant total
In 2010/11 the trust had assets of £19.5 million and an income of £474,000. There were 4,501 grants made to individuals totalling £450,000 and distributed as follows:

In cases of hardship	£4,000
Chiropody	£18,000
Consolidated grant	£220,000
Educational bodies	£115,000
Hospital visiting	£25,000
Death grants	£26,000
Communication grant	£5,500
Opticians' charges	£21,000
Dentists' charges	£13,500
Employees sickness	£4,000

Applications
In writing to the correspondent.

Other information
Grants were also made to charitable organisations (£115,000 in 2010/11).

The Christopher Hill Charity

£600

Correspondent: Colin Bond, Trustee, Fortescue Crossing, Thorverton, Exeter EX5 5JN (01392 841512; email: colinbond008@btinternet.com)

Trustees: Barry Forest-Jones; Colin John Bond; Capt. John Hill; Judith Penny; Helen May.

CC Number: 203380

Eligibility
People in need who live in the former parish of Netherexe or in the surrounding parishes in Devon.

Types of grants
One-off grants according to need.

Annual grant total
Grants to individuals are in the region of £600 a year.

Applications
In writing to the correspondent. Applications can be submitted directly by the individual or through a third party such as Citizens Advice or a social worker. Applications are considered in December or any time in urgent cases.

Other information
Grants are also given to organisations.

The Maudlyn Lands Charity

£7,000

Correspondent: Anthony Peter Golding, Clerk to the Trustees, Blue Haze, Down Road, Tavistock, Devon PL19 9AG (01822 612983)

Trustees: Enid Hamlyn; Revd Frederick Denman; John Earl of Morley; Roger Bailey; Sylvia Barker; Slyvia Serpell; David Farley; David Tozer; Iris Willis; Revd Margaret Cameron; Maureen Rose Diffy.

CC Number: 202577

Eligibility

People who live in the Plympton St Mary and Sparkwell areas and are in financial need.

Types of grants

One-off or recurrent grants, usually ranging between £250 and £500.

Annual grant total

Grants total around £7,000 each year.

Applications

In writing to the correspondent. Applications are considered in November.

Other information

The charity also makes grants to local organisations.

Northcott Devon Foundation

£182,000 (921 grants)

Correspondent: G Folland, 1b Victoria Road, Exmouth, Devon EX8 1DL (01395 269204; fax: 01395 269204)

Trustees: George Richard Spensley Simey; Maj Gen John Grey; Michael Pentreath; Patricia Anne Lane.

CC Number: 201277

Eligibility

People living in Devon who are in need as the result of illness, injury, bereavement or exceptional disadvantages.

Types of grants

One-off and recurrent grants of around £200 or above can be given towards, for example, computers for children with physical disabilities, adaptations, repairs, holidays, clothing, furniture and wheelchairs.

Annual grant total

In 2010/11 the foundation had assets of £5.4 million and an income of £173,000. Grants were made to 921 individuals totalling £182,000.

Exclusions

No grants towards long-term educational needs, funeral expenses or to relieve debts.

Applications

On a form available from the correspondent. Applications can be submitted through a social worker, Citizens Advice, welfare agency or a third party such as a doctor, health visitor or SSAFA. Applications should include the individual's name and address, and details of income and expenditure, type of household, age and children. They are considered every month.

Other information

Grants are also made to organisations (£12,000 in 2010/11).

South West Peninsula Football League Benevolent Fund

£800

Correspondent: Mark Hayman, SCONICCA, 17 Nelson Place, Newton Abbot, Devon TQ12 2JH (01626 363376; website: www.swpleague.co.uk)

Trustees: Mr M. Scott; M. Hayman; Mr P. A. Hiscox; J. Mead; K. Mann; Mr I. Phillips; Mr D. Baskwill; Mr M. Pett; Mr R. Holmes; Mr P. Lowe; Mr N. Call.

CC Number: 1079397

Eligibility

People in need who live in the county of Devon who are or were involved with a club in the Devon County Football League, and referees in the league. Grants are given to people who have disabilities, have a serious illness, or who have experienced personal misfortune.

Types of grants

One-off and recurrent grants ranging from £50 to £250. A recent grant was made to a player with a depressed cheekbone fracture.

Annual grant total

Grants to individuals are generally around £800 a year.

Exclusions

There are no grants available to people with short-term injuries, or anyone not considered to be 'in need'.

Applications

In writing to the correspondent either directly by the individual, or through a social worker, Citizens Advice, or other third party such as the club secretary. The trustees meet to consider applications on the first Thursdays in January, March, May, September and November. Applications should include the individual's marital and employment status, number of children and length of incapacity.

Other information

Grants are also given to organisations.

The Tavistock, Whitchurch and District Nursing Association Trust Fund

£2,000

Correspondent: Brenda Mary Moyse, Beechwood Lodge, 7 Wheal Josiah

Cottages, Tavistock PL19 8NZ (01822 834358)

Trustees: Judith Ann Williams; Linda Julie Ruth Glover; Cllr Robin Tresize Pike; Marian Greenaway; George Raymond Meneer.

CC Number: 200782

Eligibility

People in poor health who are in need and live in Tavistock, Whitchurch, Brentor, Mary Tavy and Peter Tavy, Lamerton, Tavistock Hamlets and part of the parish of Lydford.

Types of grants

One-off grants of up to about £100 to help with heating and water bills, travel to medical appointments, stair lifts and alarm systems to help people stay in their own homes and to assist carers in caring for spouses. Grants can occasionally be recurrent.

Annual grant total

Grants usually total about £2,000 each year.

Applications

In writing to the correspondent: to be submitted either directly by the individual or through a social worker, Citizens Advice or similar third party.

Other information

The fund also gives to organisations.

The Christine Woodmancy Charitable Foundation

£500

Correspondent: Jill Hill, Thompson and Jackson, 4–5 Lawrence Road, Plymouth PL4 6HR (01752 665037; email: jill@ thompsonandjackson.co.uk)

Trustees: William Jones; Tony Daniel; Robert Embleton.

CC Number: 1012761

Eligibility

Children and young people under the age of 21 who live in the Plymouth area and are in need.

Types of grants

One-off grants to help maintain and educate young people in need.

Annual grant total

In 2010/11 the foundation had an income of £11,000 and a total expenditure of £7,500. However, in previous years grants have tended to be given mostly to organisations rather than individuals.

Applications

In writing to the correspondent, directly by the individual or via a social worker,

Citizens Advice or other welfare agency. Applications should include background information and provide evidence of financial need.

Barnstaple

The Barnstaple Municipal Charities (The Poor's Charity Section)

£0

Correspondent: M Steele, 29 Carrington Terrace, Yeo Vale, Barnstaple, Devon EX32 7AF (01271 346354; email: barnstaplemunicipalcharities@msn.com)

Trustees: Brian Burgess; Val Monk; Beryl Yeo; Richard Smith; Janet Carter; Eddy Dymond; Sue Haywood; Diane Pennyfield; Revd Terry Spencer.

CC Number: 204460

Eligibility

People in need who live in the parish of Barnstaple.

Types of grants

One-off grants available to people in need.

Annual grant total

In 2010/11 the poor's charities fund had an income of £606. Only one grant of £125 has been made from this fund in the last three financial years.

Applications

In writing to the correspondent. Applications are considered quarterly.

Other information

The charity also provides almshouses and can fund certain educational costs.

Bridge Trust

£3,000

Correspondent: C J Bartlett, Clerk to the Trustees, 7 Bridge Chambers, Barnstaple, Devon EX31 1HB (01271 343995)

Trustees: David Trueman; Graham Kenneth Lofthouse; James William Waldron; Stephen Paul Upcott; Denzil Clive Burgess; Arnold James Bradbury; Suzanne Gail Haywood; John Lynch; Diana Piercy; Ian Edward Albert Scott; Amanda Jane Isaac; Julie Hunt; Karen Trigger; Elizabeth Davies; Richard Knight; Ian Roome.

CC Number: 201288

Eligibility

People who live in the borough of Barnstaple, Devon, with a preference for people who have disabilities, older and young people.

Types of grants

Emergency grants of up to £100.

Annual grant total

About £3,000 a year is available for individuals.

Applications

In writing to the correspondent. Applications must be made via a social worker, Citizens Advice or other welfare agency or third party.

Other information

The trust's main priority is the maintenance of 24 properties in Barnstaple and making grants to local organisations.

Bratton Fleming

The Bratton Fleming Relief-in-Need Charity

£700

Correspondent: Terrence Squire, Haxlea, 2 Threeways, Bratton Fleming, Barnstaple, Devon EX31 4TG (01598 710526)

Trustees: Revd Leslie Austin; Terence Squire; Arthur Ridd-Jones; Michael Huxtable; Sylvia Sparkes.

CC Number: 279285

Eligibility

People in any kind of need living within the parish of Bratton Fleming.

Types of grants

One-off and recurrent grants towards, for example, extra expenses caused by children going to new schools, heating during the winter or medical expenses.

Annual grant total

Grants usually average around £700 a year.

Applications

In writing to the correspondent or by word of mouth by the individual or a third party on their behalf, to be considered in early June and early December.

Brixham

John Mitchelmore's Charity

£2,000

Correspondent: Russell Denny Postlethwaite, The Tern, 38 Station Hill, Brixham, Devon TQ5 8BN (01803 851036; email: russelldenny@onetel.com)

Trustees: Christopher Mark Sumner; Russell Denny Postlethwaite; Revd Tim Deacon.

CC Number: 235640

Eligibility

People who live in Brixham who are in need, for example due to hardship, disability or sickness.

Types of grants

One-off or recurrent grants according to need.

Annual grant total

Grants average around £2,000 a year, though the actual grant figure tends to fluctuate quite widely.

Applications

In writing to the correspondent.

Brixton

The Brixton Feoffee Trust

£2,000

Correspondent: Sally Axell, 15 Cherry Tree Drive, Brixton, Plymouth PL8 2DD (01752 880262; email: brixtonfeoffeetrust@googlemail.com; website: www.brixton-village.co.uk)

Trustees: Revd Prebendary David Arnott; Brenda Joan Huxtable; Hilary Frances Pearn; Ralph Sydney James; Liz Hitchins.

CC Number: 203604

Eligibility

People in need who live in the parish of Brixton, near Plymouth.

Types of grants

One-off and recurrent grants according to need. Recent grants have been given for disability aids, driving lessons, insurance costs on a motability vehicle, pre-school costs and an orthopaedic chair.

Annual grant total

In 2010/11 the trust had assets of £1.2 million and an income of £37,000. Grants were made totalling £25,000 of which £2,000 was given to individuals, £12,000 to St Mary's Church and £10,600 to local organisations and initiatives.

Exclusions

The charity cannot give grants where the funds can be obtained from state sources.

Applications

In writing to the correspondent including as much detail as possible. Applications can be submitted directly by the individual or through a social worker, Citizens Advice or other welfare agency or third party. They are considered throughout the year.

Other information

The trust's scheme states that its net income should be shared equally between people in need in the parish of Brixton and a local church, St Mary's in Brixton, for its upkeep and maintenance. If any of the allotted money is unspent at the end of the financial year it is transferred to a third fund which is distributed to charitable schemes that benefit Brixton parish as a whole.

Broadhempston

The Broadhempston Relief-in-Need Charity

£500

Correspondent: Mrs Rosalind H E Brown, Meadows, Broadhempston, Totnes, Devon TQ9 6BW (01803 813130)

Trustees: Revd Nicholas Pearkes; Daisy Cock; Keith Beer; Lot Sutcliffe; Thomas White.

CC Number: 272930

Eligibility

People in need who live in the parish of Broadhempston.

Types of grants

One-off or recurrent grants ranging from £40 to £100. Recent grants have included assistance with food and fuel for older people, residential school trips for special needs families and aids for older people and people with disabilities. Grants are also made towards children's educational trips and aids for educational purposes.

Annual grant total

Grants for both welfare and educational purposes generally total around £1,000 a year.

Applications

In writing to the correspondent directly by the individual to be considered in June and December.

Other information

The charity also gives grants for educational purposes.

Budleigh Salterton

The Budleigh Salterton Nursing Association

£1,500

Correspondent: Mrs B Tilbury, Hayes End, 1 Boucher Way, Budleigh Salterton, Devon EX9 6HQ (01395 442304)

Trustees: Mrs M. Evans; Mr J. Perriam; Mary Kathleen Trick; Mr R. Mitchell; Joyce Helen Smith.

CC Number: 204219

Eligibility

People living in the parish of Budleigh Salterton who are in poor health, convalescent or who have disabilities.

Types of grants

One-off grants according to need. Recent grants have been given for wheelchairs, raised beds, reclining chairs, stair lifts, telephone extensions and travel allowances.

Annual grant total

Grants usually total about £1,500 each year.

Applications

In writing to the correspondent. Applications can be submitted directly by the individual or through a social worker, Citizens Advice or other appropriate third party.

Fryer Welfare and Recreational Trusts

£0

Correspondent: W K H Coxe, 29 Fore Street, Budleigh Salterton, Devon EX9 6NP (01395 445945)

Trustees: Brenda Olive Taylor; John Clatworthy; James Leslie Milverton; Alan Jones.

CC Number: 200632

Eligibility

People in need living in the local authority boundary of Budleigh Salterton.

Types of grants

One-off grants of £200 to £500 for recreational and welfare purposes.

Annual grant total

In 2011/12 the trust had an income of £1,200. Although the trust has had no expenditure in the past two years, previously grants have averaged around £800.

Applications

In writing to the correspondent at any time. Applications can be submitted directly by the individual or through a social worker, Citizens Advice or other welfare agency.

Other information

Grants may also be made to local organisations.

Colyton

The Colyton Parish Lands Charity

£500

Correspondent: The Bailiff, Colyton Chamber of Feoffees, Town Hall, Market Place, Colyton, Devon EX24 6JR

Trustees: Mr A. R. Bishop; Dr M. F. Askew; Mr R. J. Broom; Mr K. A. Budden; Mr A. J. Carthy; Mr G. P. Clode; Mr R. L. Collier; Mr A. D. Hibberd; Mr D. E. Hurford; Mr B. W. Love; Mr C. E. Pady; Mr A. W. H. Parr; Mr W. E. Platts; Mr P. S. Richards; Mr M. J. Rowland; Mr A. J. Underdown.

CC Number: 243224

Eligibility

People in need in the ancient parish of Colyton.

Types of grants

One-off and recurrent grants towards electrical goods, convalescence, clothing, household bills, holidays, travel expenses, medical equipment, furniture and disability equipment.

Annual grant total

In 2010/11 the charity had an income of £32,000. Grants totalled £4,500 which included grants made to the local primary school, local individuals and organisations.

Applications

In writing to the correspondent to be submitted either directly by the individual or a family member, through a third party such as a social worker or teacher, or through a welfare agency such as a Citizens Advice. Applications are considered monthly.

Other information

Grants are made to both individuals and organisations.

Cornwood

Reverend Duke Yonge Charity

£5,000

Correspondent: Mrs J M Milligan, 8 Chipple Park, Lutton, Nr Cornwood, Ivybridge, Devon PL21 9TA

Trustees: Gavin Tollard; Barbara Thomas; Andrew Bawn; Richard Yonge; David Farnham; Kathryn Downing; Susan Jenkins; Terry Brown; Robert Cannon.

CC Number: 202835

Eligibility

People in need who live in the parish of Cornwood.

Types of grants

One-off and recurrent grants according to need. Recent grants have included help with playgroup attendance fees, a sit-in shower facility, a support chair and winter heating costs.

Annual grant total

In 2010 the charity had both an income and total expenditure of around £13,500. Grants for welfare purposes usually total about £5,000 a year.

Applications

In writing to the correspondent via the trustees, who are expected to make themselves aware of any need. Applications are considered at trustees' meetings.

Other information

Grants are also made for education purposes and to organisations.

Crediton

Crediton United Charities

£6,200 (27 grants)

Correspondent: Mike Armstrong, 5 Parr House, Lennard Road, Crediton EX17 2AP (01363 776529)

Trustees: Joyce Harris; Andrew White; Gill Ponsford; Margaret Parr; Andy Cole; Peregrine Leigh; Sarah Turner.

CC Number: 247038

Eligibility

People in need who have been resident in Crediton town and the parish of Crediton Hamlets for at least 12 months.

Types of grants

One-off grants of up to £300 towards, for example, nursery school costs, travel expenses, furniture, medical equipment, food, hospital expenses, electric goods, household bills and disability equipment. 'General benefit tickets' of £5 each to buy food in local shops are also available from local health visitors.

As much as possible the charity tries to provide goods or services for the applicant – money is not usually given directly.

Annual grant total

In 2010/11 the charity gave grants totalling £6,200.

Exclusions

Grants are not given towards house improvements or to repay existing debts.

Applications

On a form available from the correspondent. Applications can be submitted directly by the individual, or through a third party such as a social worker. Applications are considered early every month (except August) and should be submitted before the end of the month. 'A supplementary letter is always useful.'

Other information

Grants are also given to local organisations (£2,500 in 2010/11).

Culmstock

Culmstock Fuel Allotment Charity

£1,500

Correspondent: Mrs J M Sheppard, Rexmead, Culmstock, Cullompton, Devon EX15 3JX (01823 680516)

Trustees: Mrs L. Gunningham; Mrs M. Perkins; Mr S. Vincent; Mr S. Priddle; Mr I. Clark.

CC Number: 205327

Eligibility

People in need who live in the ancient parish of Culmstock.

Types of grants

Recurrent grants according to need. Recently, grants have ranged from £20 to £70 for electricity and solid fuel bills and gifts for the eight oldest applicants.

Annual grant total

Grants usually total around £1,500.

Applications

In writing to the correspondent, directly by the individual.

Other information

Grants are also made for educational purposes.

Dartmouth

The Saint Petrox Trust Lands

£1,000

Correspondent: Hilary Bastone, Clerk, 30 Rosemary Gardens, Paignton, Devon TQ3 3NP (01803 666322; fax: 01803 666322; email: hilarybastone@hotmail.co.uk)

Trustees: B. Langworthy; Mrs L. Hodge; Peter Norton; Iris Pritchard; David Gent; Nicholas Coward; Kate Ryder; Richard Webb.

CC Number: 230593

Eligibility

People in need who live in the parish of Dartmouth and particularly within the ancient parish of St Petrox.

Types of grants

One-off grants of £100 to £500, to people affected by hardship through illness, homelessness, hospitalisation and so on for items including electrical goods, hospital expenses, household bills, travel expenses, medical equipment and furniture.

Annual grant total

In 2010/11 the trust had assets of £646,000 and an income of £46,000. Grants totalled £1,000.

Exclusions

Recurring grants are not made.

Applications

In writing to the correspondent either directly by the individual or through a social worker, Citizens Advice, other welfare agency, or other third party on behalf of the individual. Applications should include details on the purpose of grant, proof of need and estimates of costs. They are considered in January, April, July and October.

Other information

The trustees recently stated that they would like to support more individuals in need. They have therefore widened the trust's beneficial area to cover the whole of the Parish of Dartmouth.

Grants are also given towards the upkeep of ancient buildings within the ancient parish of St Petrox.

Exeter

The Central Exeter Relief-in-Need Fund

£2,500

Correspondent: M J Richards, 32 Oakley Close, Exeter EX1 3SB (01392 468531)

Trustees: Prof. Robert Snowden; Phil Brock; Mr M. J. Richards; Catherine Mary Dobson.

CC Number: 1022288

Eligibility

People in need who live in the parish of Central Exeter.

Types of grants

One-off grants usually of £50 to £150 for basic needs such as furniture, assistance with heating bills, children's clothing and mobility aids.

Annual grant total

The trust makes grants of about £2,500 each year.

Exclusions

Grants are not made for educational and training needs.

Applications

In writing to the correspondent with the support of a social worker, health visitor or other welfare agency. Applications are considered in June and December.

Exeter Dispensary and Aid-in-Sickness Fund

£16,000 (93 grants)

Correspondent: Carol Cathcart, Hon. Secretary, Ridge Farm, Broadhembury, Exeter EX14 3LU (01404 841401)

Trustees: Jean Hickey; Dr Jane Richards; John Parkin; Prof. Sir Denis Pereira Gray; Alan Eveleigh; Steve Preston; James Michelmore; Dr Judith Telfer; Sally Parkin; Julia Charles; Stella Brock; Tyna Crow.

CC Number: 205611

Eligibility

Sick or disabled poor people who live in the city of Exeter.

Types of grants

One-off grants for day-to-day needs including convalescence breaks, help with fuel or telephone bills, cooking or heating appliances, clothing, food, medical care, bedding, travel to and from hospitals and so on. The average such grant is £100. Larger grants are made towards medical appliances and aids.

Annual grant total

In 2011 the fund had assets of £746,000 and an income of £35,000. There were 93 grants made to individuals totalling £16,000.

Exclusions

Grants are not given for items which are available from public funds or for structural alterations to property.

Applications

Applications should be made through Citizens Advice, other welfare agency, a social worker or other third party such as a doctor. They should include brief details of the medical condition, the financial circumstances and the specific need. Applications are considered throughout the year for day-to-day needs and in March and November for medical appliances and so on.

Other information

Grants are also given to other organisations with similar objectives.

The Exeter Nursing Association Trust

£3,500

Correspondent: Mrs Helen Margaret Hiscox, 1 Thompson Road, Exeter, Devon EX1 2UB (01392 211306)

Trustees: Anna Estella Jameson Evans; Elizabeth Mary Curzon Howe; Jane Crosse; Jean Hickey; Jennifer Ann St Johnstone; John Richard Coleman; Robert Mounce; Diana White; Helen Margaret Hiscox.

CC Number: 202314

Eligibility

People in need who are receiving, or in need of, medical/nursing care, or needy employees or ex-employees of the association and those who have been employed in nursing, who live in the city and county of Exeter.

Types of grants

Providing and supplementing nursing services of any kind. One-off grants are also made.

Annual grant total

In 2010/11 the trust had an income of £8,700 and a total expenditure of £7,000.

Applications

In writing to the correspondent. Patients should write via their attending health visitor or district nurse; nurses should write via a senior nurse at Community Nursing Services Exeter Localities.

Other information

Grants are also given to charities connected with nursing in the beneficial area.

Exminster

Exminster Feoffees

£800

Correspondent: R H Adams, 26 Exe View, Exminster, Exeter EX6 8AL (01392 833024; email: chris@chris-hodgson.co.uk)

Trustees: Christopher Hodgson; Revd John Williams; Michael Beckett; Raymond Henry Adams; Rosemary Sanders; Barbara Edmund; Carole Ann Smith; Gladys May Gush; Francis Jeffree.

CC Number: 212497

Eligibility

People in need living in the parish of Exminster.

Types of grants

One-off grants and loans usually of up to £200 each. Grants have previously included cash grants and goods in kind.

About four to five grants are made each year.

Annual grant total

Over five years, expenditure for this charity has averaged £800.

Applications

In writing to the correspondent. Applications can be submitted either directly by the individual, through a third party such as a social worker, or through an organisation such as a Citizens Advice or another welfare agency. They are dealt with within three weeks of receipt.

Other information

The trust gives to both individuals and organisations.

Exmouth

Exmouth Welfare Trust

£13,000

Correspondent: The Secretary, PO Box 16, Exmouth EX8 3YT

Trustees: Brenda Taylor; Eileen Wragg; Frank Anthony Oswin; Lynne Elson; Dr Clive Stubbings; Malcolm Elliott.

CC Number: 269382

Eligibility

People living in the former urban district of Exmouth, comprising the parishes of Withycombe Raleigh and Littleham-cum-Exmouth who are convalescent, disabled, infirm or in need. A fund is available for modest awards for those setting up home on a minimal budget.

Types of grants

One-off grants and gift vouchers, for example, towards dietary needs, childcare, respite costs, safety equipment, hospital expenses, electrical goods, convalescence, clothing, travel expenses, medical equipment, furniture, disability equipment and help in the home.

Cheques will be payable to charities, suppliers, service providers and official departments. Payments will not be made personally to individuals.

Annual grant total

In 2010 the charity had an income of £17,000 and a total expenditure of £14,000.

Exclusions

No grants for rents, rates, debts and outstanding liabilities.

Applications

On a form available from the correspondent, submitted through an independent third party (not a relative) such as a social worker, Citizens Advice, other welfare agency, or another professional or well experienced person with detailed knowledge. Applications are considered throughout the year.

Gittisham

Elizabeth Beaumont Charity

£4,000

Correspondent: Mrs Paula S Land, The Laurels, 46 New Street, Honiton, Devon EX14 1BY (01404 43431; email: paula.land@everys.co.uk)

Trustees: Mr Marker; Thomas James Eveleigh; Roy Christopher Abbott; Revd Sue Roberts.

CC Number: 202065

Eligibility

People in need who live in the parish of Gittisham.

Types of grants

Quarterly pensions and Christmas bonus paid to qualifying local pensioners.

Annual grant total

Grants usually total around £4,000 per year.

Applications

In writing to the correspondent at any time throughout the year. Applications can be submitted directly by the individual or through a third party such as a social worker and should include details of income and any savings.

Great Torrington

The Great Torrington Town Lands Poors Charities

£8,800

Correspondent: Ian Newman, Town Hall Office, High Street, Great Torrington, Devon EX38 8HN (01805 625738; email: greattorringtoncharities@btconnect.com)

Trustees: John Kelly; Harry Cramp; Richard Rumbold; Brian Davies; Elaine Norridge; Alan Stacey; Brian Nash; Steve Blake; Trevor Sutton; Elaine Weeks; Sharon Lambert; Geoffrey Lee; Toni Batty; Harold Martin; Lawrence MacLean.

CC Number: 202801

Eligibility

People in need who live in the former borough of Great Torrington.

Types of grants

Usually one-off grants according to need.

Annual grant total

In 2010/11 the charity had assets of £6.2 million, an income of £272,000 and gave welfare grants totalling £8,800.

Applications

In writing to the correspondent, with all relevant personal information.

Other information

Grants are also made to organisations and to individuals for educational purposes.

Highweek

Highweek Charities

£2,000

Correspondent: Mrs Lisa Hocking, 4 Castlewood Avenue, Highweek, Newton Abbot, Devon TQ12 1QL (email: highweekcharities@hotmail.co.uk)

Trustees: Phyllis Rosemary Deacon; Derek Hexter; Jack Fletcher; Peter Ball; Susan Ashworth; Elsie Diana Nicholls; Stuart Hocking; Revd Michael Thayer; Robert Bryant.

CC Number: 203004

Eligibility

People in need over the age of 65 who live in the ancient parish of Highweek.

Types of grants

One-off Christmas grants and other grants of around £50 to £60.

Annual grant total

In 2010 the charity had an income of £37,000 and a total expenditure of £23,000. Grants usually total around £2,000.

Applications

In writing to the correspondent, directly by the individual. Applications should be submitted in October, for consideration in November.

Other information

The charity's main priority is the management of almshouses in Highweek.

Holsworthy

The Peter Speccott Charity

£800

Correspondent: Denzil C Blackman, 8 Fore Street, Holsworthy, Devon EX22 6ED (01409 253262; email: denzilblackman@ppwhol.co.uk)

Trustees: Revd Richard Reynolds; Angela Blackman; Betty Wonnacott;

Elizabeth Curtis; James Rowland; Leslie Hobbs; Geoffrey Forster; Dawn Bewes.

CC Number: 203987

Eligibility

People in need who live in Holsworthy and Holsworthy Hamlet.

Types of grants

Grants and loans are given to provide temporary relief for people facing unexpected loss or sudden destitution.

Annual grant total

About £800.

Applications

In writing to the correspondent. The trust also advertises in local colleges, careers offices, social services and so on.

Honiton

Honiton United Charities

£6,000

Correspondent: Paula Land, The Laurels, 46 New Street, Honiton, Devon EX14 1BY (01404 43431; email: paula.land@everys.co.uk)

Trustees: Revd Susan Emma Roberts; Anne Davies; Dr Robin Stephen Kennedy Essame; Arthur John Dimond; Dr David Brian Penwarden; Cyril Henry George Pike; Cllr Vernon C. Whitlock; Cllr Vera Alice Howard; Cllr Ronald Anthony Farnham; Cllr Elizabeth Mary Tirard; Cllr John Zarcynski.

CC Number: 200900

Eligibility

People in need who live in the borough of Honiton.

Types of grants

One-off and recurrent grants ranging from £50 to £100. Pensions are paid quarterly.

Annual grant total

In 2010 the trust had an income of £10,000 and a total expenditure of £8,000.

Exclusions

No grants to people living outside the beneficial area or for funding a gap year.

Applications

In writing to the correspondent including details of income and savings. Applications can be submitted directly by the individual or through a social worker, Citizens Advice or other welfare agency, and are considered throughout the year.

Other information

Grants are also made to organisations.

Litton Cheney

The Litton Cheney Relief-in-Need Trust

£1,500

Correspondent: B P Prentice, Steddings, Chalk Pit Lane, Litton Cheney, Dorchester, Dorset DT2 9AN (01308 482535)

Trustees: Revd Bob Thorn; Brian Prentice; Margaret Thomas; Penelope Dewar; Freddie Spicer.

CC Number: 231388

Eligibility

People in need who live in the parish of Litton Cheney.

Types of grants

Grants ranging from £100 to £220 are distributed once a year at the beginning of December. One-off emergency grants can be made at any time, for example, where there is a serious illness in the family.

Annual grant total

About £3,000 for educational and welfare needs.

Applications

Applications, on a form available from the correspondent, should be submitted directly by the individual, and are considered throughout the year.

Ottery St Mary

The Non-Ecclesiastical Charity of Thomas Axe

£1,900

Correspondent: David Roberts, Eminence, Otter Close, Tipton St John, Sidmouth, Devon EX10 0JU (01404 813961; email: david.coral683844@btinternet.com)

Trustees: Arthur William Passey; William Geoffrey Parsons; Dr Graham Gordon Ward; Richard Coley.

CC Number: 202725

Eligibility

Older people living in Ottery St Mary (the old Ottery St Mary Urban District Council area).

Types of grants

One-off grants ranging from £25 to £200 in 'marriage portions', and aids for elderly and disabled people.

Annual grant total

Grants average about £1,900 a year.

Exclusions

Recurrent support cannot be given.

Applications

In writing to the correspondent directly by the individual. Applications are considered quarterly.

The Ottery Feoffee Charity

£500

Correspondent: John Akers, 7 Broad Street, Ottery St Mary, Devon EX11 1BS (01404 812228; email: osmlaw@gilbertstephens.co.uk)

Trustees: David Thomas Hemmings; Graham Hembury; John Michael Kennaway; Diane Veronica Passey; Dr Matthew King; Mark James Galpin Essame; June Glennie; Judy Davis; Anthony Charles Abbott; Wendy Cammack; Vesey Davoren.

CC Number: 202095

Eligibility

People in need who live in the ancient parish of Ottery St Mary. Priority is usually given to older people and people with disabilities.

Types of grants

One-off grants according to need.

Annual grant total

Grants to individuals usually total about £500 per year.

The vast majority of this charity's funds are spent on the provision of 22 flats for people in need. So while the charity has the ability to apply up to one half of its income in grants, in reality, the costs associated with property upkeep mean that only a small amount is usually available for welfare grants.

Applications

In writing to the correspondent.

Other information

The charity also runs a small day centre.

Paignton

Paignton Parish Charity

£5,000

Correspondent: Margaret A Palmer, Green Close, 12 Monastery Road, Paignton, Devon TQ3 3BU (01803 556680)

Trustees: Joseph John Cottam Dyet; Lee Fraklyn David Cochran; Mavis Louisa Hawkins; Ann Margaret Howard Churchwarden; Neil Edward Piper.

CC Number: 240509

Eligibility

Poor people who are long-term residents of Paignton.

Types of grants

Cash payments of £50 to £60 are given twice a year for use as the recipient wishes.

Annual grant total

In 2011/12 the charity had an income of £9,100 and a total expenditure of £8,100.

Exclusions

Payments are not made for living expenses.

Applications

On a form available from the correspondent. Applications are considered in May and November and should be submitted by the end of April and October respectively. They should include the applicant's age and length of residency in Paignton.

Other information

The trust also makes annual donations to surgery support groups.

Plymouth

The Joseph Jory's Charity

£11,000

Correspondent: Jennifer Rogers, c/o Wolferstans, 60–66 North Hill, Plymouth PL4 8EP (01752 292347)

Trustees: Leonard Charles Lovick; Mr Whittington; David Gabbittass; John Chapman.

CC Number: 235138

Eligibility

Widows over 50 who are in need and have lived in the city of Plymouth for the last seven years.

Types of grants

Small pensions, paid quarterly. Amounts vary according to available income.

Annual grant total

In 2010 the trust had both an income and expenditure of £11,000.

Applications

The trust advertises locally when funds are available; because ongoing grants are made funds only become available to new applicants when someone leaves the fund's list of beneficiaries. New applications made are, however, kept on file.

The Ladies' Aid Society and the Eyre Charity

£8,500

Correspondent: Mrs J M Stephens, Headland View, 14 Court Park, Thurlestone, Kingsbridge, Devon

TQ7 3LX (01548 560891; email: r_john_venngrove@hotmail.com)

Trustees: Paul Smith; Revd Karl Frederick Freeman; Revd Nicholas McKinnel; Revd Andrew Douglas Caldwell; Revd Paul Russell Bryce.

CC Number: 202137

Eligibility

Widows and unmarried women in need who live, or have lived, in Plymouth. Unfortunately, women who are divorced are not eligible for grants.

Types of grants

Annuities of around £100 are given quarterly to each recipient.

Annual grant total

In 2010 the trust had an income of £11,000 and a total expenditure of £9,200.

Applications

On a form available from the correspondent: to be submitted through a social worker, Citizens Advice, clergy, doctor, solicitor or similar third party. Before applying to the trust, the applicant should have obtained any statutory help they are entitled to.

Plymouth Charity Trust

£400

Correspondent: Susan Dale, Trust Manager, Charity Trust Office, 41 Heles Terrace, Prince Rock, Plymouth PL4 9LH (01752 663107; email: sdtm@charity-trust.demon.co.uk)

Trustees: Heather Binley; Derek Ackland; Andrew Lugger; Stephen Hole; Paul Northmore; Ronald Simmonds; John Lock; Fred Brimacombe; Christopher Robinson; Pauline Purnell.

CC Number: 1076364

Eligibility

People in need who live in the city of Plymouth.

Types of grants

Grants are one-off and can be towards the cost of clothes for children of families with very limited income and to relieve sudden distress, sickness or infirmity. Grants range between £50 and £100. The trust usually makes the donation in the form of vouchers or credit at a relevant shop. It prefers not to give payment directly to the applicant.

Annual grant total

In 2010/11 grants to individuals totalled around £700 for educational and welfare purposes.

Exclusions

No grants are given to other charities, to clear debts or for any need that can be met by Social Services.

Applications

On a form available from the correspondent, to be submitted directly by the individual or through a social worker, Citizens Advice or other third party. Applications are considered on the first Monday of every month.

Sandford

The Sandford Relief-in-Need Charity

£5,500

Correspondent: Mrs H D Edworthy, 7 Snows Estate, Sandford, Crediton, Devon EX17 4NJ (01363 772550)

Trustees: William Crooke; Christopher Theedom; David Nuthall; Jill Kinch; Joan Newstead; Catherine Carlyon; David Munday.

CC Number: 235981

Eligibility

Pensioners in need who live in Sandford parish.

Types of grants

One-off grants usually of £10 to £50 towards such things as repair of household utility items, bereavement expenses or recurrent grants of £12 a month (to about 30 households). Christmas vouchers of £25 are given to existing pensioners and other parishioners towards fuel bills to be exchanged at local suppliers.

Annual grant total

Grants usually total around £6,000 per year.

Applications

On a form available from the correspondent. Applications can be submitted either directly by the individual or through a social worker, Citizens Advice, or other welfare agency. They are usually considered in March, September and November, but they can also be considered outside of these times.

Sheepwash

The Bridgeland Charity

£1,300

Correspondent: Mrs D Tubby, Bramble Cottage, East Street, Sheepwash, Beaworthy, North Devon EX21 5NW (01409 231694)

Trustees: Charles Inniss; Brian Mayne; Graham Tidball; Jennifer Harris; John Newcombe; Michael Hearn; Tony Jones.

CC Number: 206377

Eligibility

Older people in need who live in the parish of Sheepwash.

Types of grants

One-off grants ranging from £50 to £500.

Annual grant total

In 2010/11 the trust had an income of £3,400 and a total expenditure of £2,700.

Applications

In writing to the correspondent through a third party such as a social worker for consideration throughout the year.

Other information

The trust also supports local schools and community projects.

Sidmouth

Sidmouth Consolidated Charities

£2,500

Correspondent: Ruth Rose, 22 Alexandria Road, Sidmouth, Devon EX10 9HB (01395 513079; email: ruth.rose@eclipse.co.uk)

Trustees: Penelope Beatty; David James; Elizabeth Atkinson; Ann Liverton; Anthony Reed; Simon Pollentine; Richard Eley; Heather Ludford; Maureen Bess.

CC Number: 207081

Eligibility

People in need who live in Sidmouth, Sidford, Sidbury or Salcombe Regis.

Types of grants

One-off grants of up to £1,000, towards, for example, new cookers, washing machines and stairlifts, and to help with travel expenses to visit someone in hospital.

Annual grant total

Grants usually total around £5,000 for both educational and welfare purposes.

Applications

In writing to the correspondent, either directly by the individual, or through a social worker, Citizens Advice or welfare agency. Applications are considered at monthly meetings.

Silverton

Silverton Parochial Charity

£4,500

Correspondent: Michelle Valance, Secretary to the Trustees, 3 St Anne's

Place, Silverton, Devon EX5 4NH (email: secretary@silvertonparochialtrust.co.uk)

Trustees: Alan MacDonald; Christine Walker; Arthur Williams; Jill Riggs; Robert Seward; Sue Tucker.

CC Number: 201255

Eligibility

People in need in the parish of Silverton.

Types of grants

One-off grants, with no minimum or maximum limit. Grants are towards anything that will help relieve hardship or need, such as alarms for people who are infirm, stair lifts, hospital travel costs, heating costs, medical equipment, children's clothing and wheelchairs.

Annual grant total

In 2010/11 the charity had an income of £28,000 and a total expenditure of £18,000. Grants to individuals for education and welfare purposes totalled £9,000.

Exclusions

No grants are made towards state or local authority taxes.

Applications

Application forms are available to download from the website. They can also be obtained from the Silverton Post-Office or the Community Hall, or prospective beneficiaries can write to the correspondent. Completed forms can be submitted to the correspondent by the individual or by a carer or welfare department, and so on. The trustees will need details of the applicant's financial situation. Applications are considered monthly.

Other information

Grants are also made to organisations providing assistance to people in need who live in the parish and for educational purposes.

The charity has an informative website.

South Brent
The South Brent Parish Lands Charity

£10,000

Correspondent: J I G Blackler, Luscombe Maye, 6 Fore Street, South Brent, Devon TQ10 9BQ (01364 646180)

Trustees: Anne Collier; David Winnington-Ingram; Philip French; Robert Savery; Roger Cockings; John Halliday; Colin Vallance; Greg Wall; Mary Andrew.

CC Number: 255283

Eligibility

People in need who live in the parish of South Brent.

Types of grants

One-off or recurrent grants and Christmas gifts. Grants can be £50 to £300 and can be for a variety of needs including hospital transport/travel costs and special treatment to adults and/or children where the family is desperately in need of help.

Annual grant total

In 2010/11 the charity had an income of £46,000 and gave around £10,000 in welfare grants.

Applications

On a form available from the correspondent which can be submitted at any time either directly by the individual or a family member, through a third party such as a social worker or teacher, or through an organisation such as Citizens Advice or a school.

Sowton
Sowton In Need Charity

£1,000

Correspondent: N Waine, Meadowsweet, Sowton, Exeter EX5 2AE (01392 368289; email: wn894@btinternet.com)

Trustees: Mr N. Waine; Michael Fernbank; Joanna O'Donnell.

CC Number: 204248

Eligibility

People in need who live in the parish of Sowton.

Types of grants

One-off grants for any specific educational or personal need. Grants have been given towards funeral expenses in the past.

Annual grant total

Grants total around £1,000 a year for individuals in need.

Applications

In writing to the correspondent, to be submitted either directly by the individual or through a social worker, Citizens Advice, other welfare agency or any third party.

Other information

Grants are also given to organisations and to individuals for educational purposes.

Teignbridge
The Special People Fund

£1,100

Correspondent: M Nosworthy, 5 Higher Drive, Dawlish EX7 0AS (01626 865221)

Trustees: M. Nosworthy; David Christopher George Cridge; Cindy Ann Morris.

CC Number: 1110652

Eligibility

'Children who live in Teignbridge who have learning difficulties, or a disability, or are suffering emotional trauma arising from the breakdown of marriage or family life, or bereavement or social circumstances.'

Types of grants

Grants are given according to need.

Annual grant total

In 2011/12 the fund had an income of £34 and a total expenditure of £2,400. Grants are made to organisations and individuals.

Applications

In writing to the correspondent.

Topsham
The Charity of John Shere and Others

£4,000

Correspondent: David John Tucker, 5 Elm Grove Gardens, Topsham, Exeter EX3 0EL (01392 873168; email: tucker-david@talktalk.net)

Trustees: Francis Luscombe; Myra Green; Mary Evans; Derek Whittingham; Michael Osborne; Richard Underhill; Richard Van Oppen; David Counter; John Elliott; William Nott; Margaret Butt; Sheila Harding; David Tucker.

CC Number: 220736

Eligibility

People in need who have lived in the parish of Topsham (as its boundaries were in 1966) for at least three years.

Types of grants

One-off and recurrent grants in the range of £350 to £400 are given where assistance cannot be obtained from any other means.

Annual grant total

In 2010 the charity had an income of £5,200 and a total expenditure of £4,300.

Applications

On a form available from the correspondent. Applications can be submitted at any time either directly by the individual or through a third party such as a social worker.

Torbay

Mrs E. L. Blakeley-Marillier Charitable Fund

See entry on page 223

The Leonora Carlow Trust Fund

£0

Correspondent: Michael Deeley, Administrative Officer, Disabilities Team Children's Services, Torbay Council, Oldway Mansion, Torquay Road, Paignton, Devon TQ3 2TE (01803 208227; email: michael.deeley@torbay.gov.uk)

Trustees: Richard Thorpe; Richard Williams; Dr Carol Tozer.

CC Number: 284681

Eligibility

Children up to 18 who have a physical or mental disability and live in Torbay.

Types of grants

One-off grants ranging up to £300 for computer equipment, holidays, furniture or disability equipment. Usually three or four grants are made each year.

Annual grant total

Grants typically average around £500, however, in 2010/11 the trust had an income of £1,100 but no expenditure.

Applications

On a form available from the correspondent, to be submitted directly by the individual or family member, or through a social worker, Citizens Advice or other welfare agency. Applications are considered throughout the year and should include details of help sought from any other source and the outcome and details of any previous assistance from the fund.

Torquay

The Annie Toll Bequest

£3,500

Correspondent: Alan Phare, Trustee, Wray Lodge, 63 Walnut Road, Torquay TQ2 6HU (01803 605767)

Trustees: Mr A. C. Phare; Mr K. Thompson; Mr M. Heitch; Revd A. Macey; Simon Brookman; Garry Phare.

CC Number: 201197

Eligibility

Older or sick women in need who live in Torquay.

Types of grants

Recurrent grants of £400 a year and one-off payments for special needs ranging from £100 to £300. Grants may be given towards the hire costs of equipment, for example a television.

Annual grant total

The trust usually has an income and a total expenditure of around £3,500.

Applications

In writing to the correspondent. Applications can be made directly by the individual or through a social worker, Citizens Advice, other welfare agency or other third party on behalf of the individual.

Dorset

Cole Anderson Charitable Foundation

£7,000

Correspondent: Martin Davies, Rawlins Davy, Rowlands House, Hinton Road, Bournemouth BH1 2EG (01202 558844; email: martin.davies@rawlinsdavy.com)

Trustees: Howard Alexander; Joyce Anderson.

CC Number: 1107619

Eligibility

People in need who live in Bournemouth and Poole.

Types of grants

Grants for providing or paying for services or facilities.

Annual grant total

About £14,000 for welfare and educational purposes.

Applications

In writing to the correspondent.

The Beaminster Charities

£3,000

Correspondent: John Groves, 24 Church Street, Beaminster, Dorset DT8 3BA (01308 862192)

Trustees: Janet Page; Audrey Bullock; Lynda Beazer; Margaret Harvey; Mike Beckett; Ralph Bugler; Richard Bugler; Sally Welsford; Robert Martin.

CC Number: 200685

Eligibility

People in need who live in Beaminster, Netherbury and Stoke Abbott.

Types of grants

One-off grants in the range of £50 and £1,000. The trustees will consider any application. About 50 grants are made each year.

Annual grant total

In 2010 the charities had an income of £8,500 and a total expenditure of £6,500.

Applications

Applications can be submitted in writing to the correspondent by the individual or through a recognised referral agency such as social worker, Citizens Advice or doctor. The trustees meet throughout the year.

The Boveridge Charity

£4,000

Correspondent: Mrs R D Hunt, Brinscombe House, Lower Blandford Road, Shaftesbury, Dorset SP7 0BG (01747 852511)

Trustees: Revd David Paskins; Anne Mackenzie; Thalia Anne Gordon-Watson; Michael Nurton; Viscount Robert E. Cranborne.

CC Number: 231340

Eligibility

Poor people who are in need and have lived in the ancient parish of Cranborne (which includes the present parishes of Cranborne-cum-Boveridge, Wimborne St Giles, Alderholt, Verwood, Ferndown, West Parley and Edmondsham) for at least two years.

People in need who live outside the beneficial area may also be supported in exceptional circumstances.

Types of grants

Pensions of £500 per annum. One-off grants ranging from £100 to £500.

Annual grant total

In 2010/11 the charity had an income of £4,700 and an expenditure of £4,300.

Applications

In writing to the correspondent, submitted directly by the individual, through a third party such as a social worker or through an organisation such as a Citizens Advice or other welfare agency. Applications are considered throughout the year and should contain details of the individual's annual income and capital, detail of need, age and occupation.

Other information

This charity also makes grants to organisations.

The MacDougall Trust

£17,000

Correspondent: Administrative Secretary, 96 Scarf Road, Poole, Dorset BH17 8QL (01202 730002; email: adminsecretary@macdougalltrust.com; website: www.macdougalltrust.com)

Trustees: Jacqueline Mary Claire Carlyle-Clarke; Andrea Valentine Lea; Richard John Carlyle-Clarke; Diana Hill Bucknall; Elizabeth Anne Kirby; Michal Alfred Palmer; Roger Ashton Gregory; Martin George Taylor; Jeffrey Russell.

CC Number: 209743

Eligibility

People in need who live in Dorset.

Types of grants

One-off grants of up to £250 for all kinds of personal need. Only in exceptional circumstances will more than £250 be awarded, though the trust can contribute towards larger projects which will be jointly funded.

Annual grant total

In 2010/11 the trust had an income of £17,000 and a total expenditure of £18,000.

Exclusions

Grants for education, sponsorship, childcare, debt, people living outside of Dorset or to organisations.

Applications

On a form available from the correspondent or to download from the trust's website. Applications should be supported by a recognised agency such as, Citizens Advice, local GP, social services or similar organisation. Forms should be returned to the administrative secretary. Applications are considered quarterly – usually in March, June, September and late November/early December – though urgent requests may be considered between meetings. For consideration at a quarterly meeting applications should be received the month before.

Note: if the application is being made on behalf of a minor, then details of the whole family will need to be included.

The Pitt-Rivers Charitable Trust

£0

Correspondent: George Pitt-Rivers, Hinton St Mary Estate Office,

Sturminster Newton, Dorset DT10 1NA (01258 472623)

Trustees: George Anthony Pitt-Rivers; Mrs Valerie Lane-Fox Pitt-Rivers.

CC Number: 283839

Eligibility

People who live in rural Dorset and North Dorset in particular who are in need, for example due to hardship, disability or sickness.

Types of grants

One-off grants, ranging from £100 to £1,000.

Annual grant total

In 2010/11 the trust had assets of £181,000 and an income of £46,000. No grants were made to individuals during the year. Grants to organisations totalled £54,000.

Applications

In writing to the correspondent. No email or telephone applications will be accepted. Applications can be submitted directly by the individual or family member and are considered at any time.

Other information

The trust stated that because of the geographical limitations of this trust, grants are only occasionally given to individuals.

St Martin's Trust

£4,500

Correspondent: The Revd David J Ayton, 201 Kinson Road, Bournemouth BH10 5HB (01202 547054; email: davidayton@btconnect.com; website: www.stmartinsbooks.co.uk)

Trustees: Anthony Harrington; Revd David James Ayton; Lynette Carol King; Robin Ergis.

CC Number: 1065584

Eligibility

People who are in need, people who are disabled and older people who live in Dorset.

Types of grants

One-off and recurrent grants according to need.

Annual grant total

In 2010/11 the trust had an income of £7,200 and a total expenditure of £7,400.

Applications

In writing to the correspondent.

Other information

Grants are also made to local organisations.

Tollard Trust

See entry on page 20

The William Williams Charity

£50,000

Correspondent: Ian Winsor, Steward, Stafford House, 10 Prince of Wales Road, Dorchester, Dorset DT1 1PW (01305 264573; email: enquires@ williamwilliams.org.uk; website: www. williamwilliams.org.uk)

Trustees: Robert Cowley; Ray Humphries; Leo Williams; Carole Sharp; Haydn White; Richard Gillam; Richard Prideaux-Brune; Joe Rose.

CC Number: 202188

Eligibility

People in need who live in the ancient parishes of Blandford, Shaftesbury or Sturminster Newton (DT11 7, DT10 1, DT10 2 and SP7 8).

Types of grants

One-off grants of £500 to £1,000 for furnishings, white goods and other relief in need.

Annual grant total

In 2011 the charity had assets of £7.9 million and an income of £292,000. Grants to 217 individuals totalled £146,000 with £50,000 given for welfare and £96,000 for education.

Applications

On a form available from the correspondent or the website along with guidelines.

Blandford Forum

Blandford Forum Charities

£3,500

Correspondent: Irene Prior, Barnes Homes, Salisbury Road, Blandford Forum, Dorset DT11 7HU (01258 451810)

Trustees: Heather Bracewell; Esme Butler; Lyn Lindsay; Carole Sharp; Haydn White; Jean Balmer; John Barnes Joseph Hickish; Stephen Hitchings; Sarah Loch; Colin Stevens; Rosemary Holmes.

CC Number: 230853

Eligibility

Residents of Blandford Forum who are in need.

Annual grant total

In 2010/11 the relief in need charity had an income of £9,000 and made grants totalling £3,500.

Applications

In writing to the correspondent.

Other information

The Blandford Forum Charities include the Relief in Need fund, the Blandford Forum Almshouse Charity, Blandford Forum Apprenticing and Educational Foundation Charity and George Ryves Apprenticing Charity.

Charmouth

The Almshouse Charity

£500

Correspondent: Mrs Anthea Gillings, Swansmead, Riverway, Charmouth, Bridport, Dorset DT6 6LS (01297 560465)

Trustees: Felicity Perkin; Mallory Hayter; Felicity Horton; Gillian Pile; Clare Perry; Richard Wyatt.

CC Number: 201885

Eligibility

People in need who, or whose immediate family, live in the parish of Charmouth.

Types of grants

One-off and recurrent grants, generally of £25 to £250. Grants have been given for hospital expenses, nursing fees, funeral expenses, special needs, health, sports and general living expenses. Grants can also be towards the total or part payment of the costs of equipment, such as electric chairs and cars, arthritic supports, shopping trolleys, washing machines and nebulisers. Annual grocery vouchers are given to selected people ranging from £40 to £60. The trust also makes interest-free loans.

Annual grant total

In 2010 the trust had an income of £3,000 and a total expenditure of £2,500.

Applications

In writing to the correspondent or other trustees. Applications can be submitted directly by the individual or through a third party such as a rector, doctor or trustee. They are usually considered at quarterly periods; emergencies can be considered at other times. Applications should include details of the purpose of the grant, the total costs involved, and an official letter or programme/itinerary.

Other information

Grants are also given to individuals for further and higher education and overseas voluntary work, and to youth clubs for specific purposes.

Christchurch

Legate's Charity

£8,500

Correspondent: Mrs M Parsa, Christchurch Borough Council, Civic Offices, Bridge Street, Christchurch, Dorset BH23 1AZ (01202 495050)

Trustees: Honorary Freeman Cllr John Lofts; Cllr Trish Jamieson; Cllr Tavis Fox; Cllr Myra Vivian Mawbey; Cllr Susan Spittle.

CC Number: 215712

Eligibility

People in need who live in the borough of Christchurch and the immediate surrounding area.

Types of grants

One-off grants for domestic items and clothes and small weekly allowances to help towards household bills.

Annual grant total

Grants average around £8,500 per year.

Applications

On a form available from the correspondent submitted either directly by the individual or through a friend, relative, social worker, Citizens Advice or other welfare agency.

Mayor's Goodwill Fund

£1,000

Correspondent: The Mayor's Secretary, Civic Offices, Bridge Street, Christchurch, Dorset BH23 1AZ (01202 495134; email: m.parsa@christchurch.gov.uk)

Trustees: John Lofts; David Fox; Norma Fox; Colin Reginald Bungley; Edward Coope; Cllr Josephine Spencer; Michael Hodges; Michael Pierce; Cllr Eric Spreadbury; Cllr Sally Derham-Wilkes; Mike Winfield; Eric Wood; Peggy Pardy; Sue Spittle; Cllr Nicholas Geary.

CC Number: 263342

Eligibility

People in need who live in the borough of Christchurch.

Types of grants

One-off grants for grocery parcels, potted plants, sweets and chocolates.

Annual grant total

About £1,000.

Applications

On a form available from the correspondent, to be submitted through a social worker, Citizens Advice, other welfare agency, friend, neighbour or clergy. Applications should include the applicant's name and address and details of their circumstances.

Other information

The fund also gives grants to local organisations.

Corfe Castle

Corfe Castle Charities

£8,600 (6 grants)

Correspondent: Mrs J Wilson, The Spinney, Springbrook Close, Corfe Castle, Wareham, Dorset BH20 5HS (01929 480873)

Trustees: Mr F. Spooner; Mr M. Bond; Mr C. Thompson; Mr J. Sabben-Clare; Mrs A. Lardner; Mrs D. Reynolds; Revd I. Jackson; Revd G. Clemts; Revd G. Burrett.

CC Number: 1055846

Eligibility

People in need who live in the parish of Corfe Castle.

Types of grants

One-off grants or interest free loans according to need. In recent years grants have been given to relieve sickness, infirmity or distress, such as rental of emergency lifelines, help with recuperative hospital costs and payment of travel expenses for patients and visiting relatives in hospital.

Annual grant total

In 2010/11 the charity had assets of £4.2 million and an income of £216,000. There were six relief-in-need grants made to individuals totalling £8,600.

Applications

On a form available from the correspondent, to be submitted directly by the individual. The trustees meet monthly, but emergency requests are dealt with as they arise.

Other information

Grants are also made to organisations.

Dorchester

Dorchester Relief-in-Need Charity

£1,000

Correspondent: R R E Potter, 8 Mithras Close, Dorchester, Dorset DT1 2RF (01305 262041)

Trustees: Derek Norris; Margaret Stephenson; Robert Potter; Revd Harold Stephens; Timothy Bullick; Mark Green.

CC Number: 286570

Eligibility

People in need who live in the ecclesiastical parish of Dorchester.

Types of grants

One-off grants according to need.

Annual grant total

Grants for welfare purposes usually total around £1,000 per year.

Applications

Application forms are available from the correspondent and can be submitted through a social worker, health visitor, Citizens Advice or social services.

Other information

This charity also gives educational grants.

Poole

The Poole Children's Fund

£250

Correspondent: Julia Palmer, 52 Hennings Park Road, Poole BH15 3QX (01202 261921)

Trustees: Joan Hart; Pauline Shuttle.

CC Number: 277300

Eligibility

Children up to 18 who are disadvantaged, disabled or otherwise in need and live in the borough of Poole. Preference is given to children with behavioural and social difficulties who have limited opportunities for leisure and recreational activities of a positive nature, for schoolchildren with serious family difficulties so the child has to be educated away from home and people with special educational needs.

Types of grants

One-off grants of £10 to £50 towards the cost of holidays, educational or recreational opportunities.

Annual grant total

About £500 for welfare and educational purposes.

Applications

On a form available from the correspondent completed by a third party such as a social worker, health visitor, minister or teacher. Applications are considered throughout the year. They should include details of family structure including: ages; reason for application; family income and any other sources of funding which have been tried; what agencies (if any) are involved in helping the family; and any statutory orders (for example, care orders) relating to the child or their family members.

Shaftesbury

John Foyle's Charity

£4,500

Correspondent: Simon Rutter, Cann Field House, Cann Common, Shaftesbury, Dorset SP7 8DQ (01747 851881)

Trustees: Trudie Stanley; Janet Lowe; Marion Purser; David Wheeler; Elaine Catherine Wynn-Mackenzie.

CC Number: 202959

Eligibility

People in need who live in the town of Shaftesbury.

Types of grants

One-off and recurrent grants and loans, including those for educational toys for people who are disabled, moving expenses, fuel, equipment, carpets and decoration. Around 15 grants a year are made ranging from £30 to £500.

Annual grant total

Grants usually total around £4,500 per year.

Exclusions

No grants for items/services that are the responsibility of the state.

Applications

In writing to the correspondent at any time. Applications can be submitted directly by the individual or through an appropriate third party and should show evidence of need, for example, benefit record, and proof of address. They can be submitted at any time, for consideration at the discretion of the trustees.

Wimborne Minster

Brown Habgood Hall and Higden Charity

£13,000

Correspondent: Mrs Hilary S Motson, Whiteoaks, Colehill Lane, Colehill, Wimborne, Dorset BH21 7AN (01202 886303; email: bhhh.charity@btinternet. com)

Trustees: Canon John Goodall; Michael John Evans; Susan Ward; Jill Laybourne; Dr Robin Sadler.

CC Number: 204101

Eligibility

Usually retired people on low income living in the ancient parish of Wimborne Minster, in Dorset.

Types of grants

One-off grants, but mainly quarterly payments. Grants are not usually for more than £200, and are mainly for smaller amounts. About 26 regular grants are given plus one-off grants.

Annual grant total

In 2011 the charity had an income of £17,000 and a total expenditure of £15,000.

Applications

In writing to the correspondent either directly by the individual, through a social worker, Citizens Advice, other welfare agency or through another third party such as a doctor, health visitor or clergy. The applicant's full name, address, age and employment should be included.

Gloucester-shire

The Barnwood Trust

£263,000 (735 grants)

Correspondent: Gail Rodway, Grants Manager, Ullenwood Manor Farm, Ullenwood, Cheltenham, Gloucestershire GL53 9QT (01452 611292; fax: 01452 634011; email: gail.rodway@ barnwoodtrust.org; website: www. barnwoodtrust.org)

Trustees: John Humphrey Colquhoun; James Davidson; Anne Cadbury; Richard Ashenden; David A. Acland; Clare De Haan; Sara Shipway; Roger H. Ker; Annabella Scott; Jonathan Carr; Revd John Horan.

CC Number: 218401

Eligibility

People in need in Gloucestershire who have a long-term disability that affects their quality of life, a low income and little or no savings.

Types of grants

The trust currently operates two funding schemes:

Wellbeing Fund

One-off grants ranging from £50 to £750 are given for household items, disability equipment, respite care breaks, holidays, clothes, selected bills and so on.

Opportunities Fund

One-off grants ranging from £200 to £2,000 to provide individuals with the opportunity to attempt something new that will enable them to move on to employment, volunteering or give them the ability to help others. It may also be used to fund training or equipment that will enhance their ability to pursue a current hobby. Detailed guidance notes have been produced for applicants to this fund and are available on the website.

Annual grant total

In 2011 the trust had assets of £69 million and an income of £2.6 million. Grants were made to 735 individuals totalling £263,000.

Exclusions

No grants for: funeral costs; medical equipment; private healthcare (e.g. assessment, treatment or medication); counselling or psychotherapy; top-up nursing home fees; private education or university tuition fees; council tax; court fines; house purchase, rent deposits, or rent in advance; regular payments to supplement income; the needs of non-disabled dependents or carers. No retrospective grants are given.

Applications

Application forms are available from the correspondent or to download from the website. All applications should be made through, or endorsed by, a social or healthcare professional, such as an occupational therapist, social worker, health visitor, district nurse or community psychiatric nurse. Wherever possible, the trust will visit applicants at home to discuss their needs in greater detail. The trust aims to provide an answer within ten working days of the home visit.

Other information

Small grants of up to £750 are also made to local organisations with similar aims.

Cheltenham Aid-in-Sickness and Nurses Welfare Fund (Gooding Fund)

£25,000

Correspondent: Mrs P Newman, Cheltenham Family Welfare Association, 21 Rodney Road, Cheltenham, Gloucestershire GL50 1HX (01242 522180; email: info@ cheltenhamfamilywelfare.co.uk; website: www.cheltenhamfamilywelfare.co.uk)

Trustees: Audrey Ann Turner; Judith Bull; Elizabeth Dobbin; Renate Young; Barbara Mears; Marion Jones.

CC Number: 205340

Eligibility

People in need who are engaged in domiciliary nursing in the Cheltenham area, or to retired nurses who were so engaged.

Types of grants

One-off and recurrent grants to those in need.

Annual grant total

In 2010/11 the fund had an income of £14,000 and a higher than usual expenditure of £34,000. No further information was available.

Applications

On a form available from the correspondent. Applications should be submitted through a third party, such as a health visitor, social worker or Citizens Advice.

The Fluck Convalescent Fund

£50,000 (210 grants)

Correspondent: Peter Francis Sanigar, c/o Whitemans Solicitors, Second Floor, 65 London Road, Gloucester GL1 3HT (01452 411601; fax: 01452 300922; email: info@whitemans.com)

Trustees: Nigel Halls; Ismail Ginwalla; Maggie Gorton; Nick Alexander; Peter Nesbitt; Revd Kathleen Irene Morgan; Dr Kenneth Watson.

CC Number: 205315

Eligibility

Women of all ages and children under 16 who live in the city of Gloucester and its surrounding area, and are in poor health or convalescing after illness or operative treatment.

Types of grants

One-off grants between £50 and £350 for recuperative holidays, clothing, bedding, furniture, fuel, food, household equipment, domestic help, respite care and medical or other aids.

Annual grant total

In 2011/12 the fund had assets of £916,000 and an income of £43,000. Grants were made to 210 individuals totalling £50,000.

Exclusions

No grants are made for the repayment of debts or for recurrent payments such as rent and rates.

Applications

In writing to the correspondent through a 'responsible person' such as a social worker, medical professional or welfare organisation. Applications are considered throughout the year.

Gloucestershire Bowling Association Benevolent Fund

£1,000

Correspondent: Derek Severs, 1 Wolfridge Ride, Alveston, Bristol BS35 3RA (01454 414179)

Trustees: Jack Crawford; Peter Bowles; Bryan Fox; Brian Clark.

CC Number: 257886

Eligibility

Bowlers, ex-bowlers and their immediate dependents, who are in need and are present or past members of the association.

Types of grants

One-off and recurrent grants towards, for example, hospital visits.

Annual grant total

About £1,000.

Applications

In writing to the correspondent.

Sylvanus Lyson's Charity

£22,000 (63 grants)

Correspondent: A Holloway, Morroway House, Station Road, Gloucester GL1 1DW (01452 301903)

Trustees: Bernard Day; Revd John Stewart Went; G. V. Doswell; Revd Anne Spargo; Robert Wilfred Springett (Archdeacon of Cheltenham).

CC Number: 202939

Eligibility

Widows and dependents of the clergy of the Church of England in or retired from the diocese of Gloucester who are in need.

Types of grants

One-off grants according to need.

Annual grant total

In 2010/11 the trust had assets of £8.4 million and an income of £303,000. Grants were made to 63 individuals totalling £22,000.

Applications

In writing to the correspondent, directly by the individual, for consideration in March, July, September and November.

The Prestbury Charity (also known as The Prestbury United Charities)

£12,000

Correspondent: Brian Wood, Clerk, 2 Honeysuckle Close, Prestbury, Cheltenham, Gloucestershire GL52 5LN (01242 515941; email: puc.clerk@ prestbury.net; website: www.prestbury. net/puc)

Trustees: Harry Derek Taylor; John Fogarty; Martin Ernest Kannreuther; Sheila Ann Beer; Pat Thornton; Liz Attwell; Revd Canon Michael Cozens; Nigel Woodcock; Jeneth Slater.

CC Number: 202655

Eligibility

People in need who live in the ecclesiastical parish of Prestbury and the adjoining parishes of Southam and Swindon village.

Types of grants

One-off grants according to need. Recent support has been given towards: heating costs for a person with disabilities; security lights for an elderly person; repairs and decorating costs; and, assistance for single parent families.

Annual grant total

In 2010 the charity had an income of £11,000 and a larger than usual total expenditure of £34,000.

Applications

In writing to the correspondent, either directly by the individual, or via a social worker, Citizens Advice or other welfare agency or third party. Applications should include the individual's home address, so that the trust can see that they live in the area of benefit.

Other information

Local organisations are also supported.

Bisley

The Ancient Charity of the Parish of Bisley

£6,500

Correspondent: Jane Bentley, The Old Post-Office, High Street, Bisley, Stroud GL6 7AA (01452 770756)

Trustees: Susie Bromley; Revd Simon Richards; Stephen Trinder; John Land; Ken Stevens.

CC Number: 237229

Eligibility

People in need who live in the ancient parish of Bisley.

Types of grants

One-off or recurrent grants according to need.

Annual grant total

In 2010/11 the charity had an income of £9,500 and a total expenditure of £6,700.

Applications

In writing to the correspondent.

Charlton Kings

Charlton Kings Relief in Need Charity

£1,250

Correspondent: Martin Fry, 7 Branch Hill Rise, Charlton Kings, Cheltenham GL53 9HN (01242 239903; email: martyn.fry@dsl.pipex.com)

Trustees: Peter Ginns; Dr Douglas Giraldi; Patricia Sherwell; Melanie Fletcher; Michael Palmer; Helena McCloskey; Duncan Smith.

CC Number: 204597

Eligibility

People in need who live in the parish of Charlton Kings or have a connection with the parish.

Types of grants

One-off grants of £50 to £1,000, according to need. In the past grants have been given towards travel expenses and medical equipment and can be used to help people to make a fresh start.

Annual grant total

Total expenditure averages around £2,500 a year. Grants are given to both individuals and organisations.

Applications

In writing to the correspondent.

Cirencester

The Smith's Cirencester Poor Charity

£3,500

Correspondent: Mrs Maria Ann Bell, 7 Dollar Street, Cirencester, Gloucestershire GL7 2AS (01285 650000)

Trustees: Peter Gillman; Jane Winstanley; Richard Mullings; Dawn Holland; Jeremy Clarke; Dr Adrienne Winter; Anthony Ferris.

CC Number: 232383

Eligibility

People in need who have lived in the parish of Cirencester for the last three years.

Types of grants

One-off and recurrent grants towards disability aids, domestic appliances, furniture, heating bills and living expenses.

Annual grant total

Grants average around £3,500 each year.

Applications

On a form available from the correspondent. Applications are usually considered quarterly.

Other information

Grants are also made to local organisations.

Gloucester

The United Charity of Palling Burgess

£2,000

Correspondent: Margaret Churchill, 30 Gambier Parry Gardens, Gloucester GL2 9RD (01452 421304)

Trustees: Hilary Paskins; Mary Gould; Canon Nikki Arthy; Eric Ede.

CC Number: 236440

Eligibility

People in need who live in the Gloucester city council administrative area, including people with disabilities, single parent families and people on a low income.

Types of grants

One-off cash grants and grants in kind up to a maximum value of £250.

Annual grant total

In 2010/11 the charity had an income of £1,900 and a total expenditure of £2,100.

Applications

In writing to the correspondent. Applications should be submitted through a social worker, nurse, health visitor, minister of religion or similar third party and are considered twice a year in March and October. Applications should be submitted by the end of February and September respectively.

Minchinhampton

Albert Edward Pash Charitable Trust Fund

£500

Correspondent: Diana Wall, Clerk, Minchinhampton Parish Council, The Trap House, West End, Minchinhampton, Gloucestershire GL6 9JA (01453 731186; fax: 01453

731186; email: minchparish@btconnect.com)

Trustee: Minchinhampton Parish Council.

CC Number: 278558

Eligibility
People who live in the civil parish of Minchinhampton, of any age or occupation, who are in need due to, for example, to hardship, disability or sickness.

Types of grants
One-off grants according to need.

Annual grant total
A minimum of 25% of the income must be given towards hospital research each year, with the rest donated to individuals. In 2010/11 the charity had an income and expenditure of £700.

Applications
In writing to the correspondent, directly by the individual or family member. Applications should be received by 31 March for consideration in April.

Tewkesbury
Gyles Geest Charity

£6,000

Correspondent: Mrs M Simmonds, 10 Troughton Place, Tewkesbury GL20 8EA (01684 850697)

Trustees: Anthony Brian Langley; Gordon Long; Peter Aldridge; Philip H. Workman.

CC Number: 239372

Eligibility
People in need who live in the borough of Tewkesbury.

Types of grants
Grants usually average about £30 per household and are given as vouchers for use in local shops.

Annual grant total
The charity usually spends between £6,000 and £7,000 on grants for welfare every year.

Applications
On a form available from the correspondent, to be submitted directly by the individual or through a third party.

Wotton-under-Edge
Edith Strain Nursing Charity

£600

Correspondent: Mrs Joan Deveney, 85 Shepherds Leaze, Wotton-under-Edge, Gloucestershire GL12 7LJ (01453 844370)

Trustees: John Grimes; Ruth Bushell; Revd Michael Chappell; Jean Terrett; Joan Heaven; Joan Barker; Susan Weeks.

CC Number: 204598

Eligibility
People who live in the town of Wotton-under-Edge and who are in need due to sickness or infirmity.

Types of grants
One-off and recurrent grants normally ranging between £50 and £100. Grants are not made where statutory money is available.

Annual grant total
Generally this charity has both an income and expenditure of around £2,500 with approximately £600 paid to individuals who are in need due to sickness or infirmity.

Applications
In writing to the correspondent, either directly by the individual, or via a social worker, Citizens Advice or other welfare agency. An sae is required. Applications are usually considered in May and November.

Other information
Grants are also made to local organisations which care for people who are sick.

Somerset

J. A. F. Luttrell Memorial Charity

£3,000

Correspondent: Agnes Auld, West Close, Church Road, Edington, Bridgwater, Somerset TA7 9JT (01278 722529)

Trustees: Dr Peter Simon Hayne; Catherine Ann Andrews; Anne Bassi; Revd Trish Ollive; Rosemary Jane Tucker.

CC Number: 201495

Eligibility
People in need who live in Edington, Catcott, Chilton Polden and Burtle.

Types of grants
On average 30 one-off grants are made a year ranging from £25 to £500.

Annual grant total
In 2010/11 the charity had an income of £4,200 and a total expenditure of £6,900.

Applications
In writing to the correspondent, directly by the individual or a family member. Applications are considered in March and October and should be received by February and September respectively.

Other information
Grants are also given to organisations supporting older people, environmental needs and cardiac rehabilitation.

The Nuttall Trust

£9,000

Correspondent: Nicholas Redding, 60 High Street, Burnham-on-Sea, Somerset TA8 1AG (01278 782371)

Trustees: Anthony John Hill; James Henry Counsell; Neil Corkish; Nicholas Redding.

CC Number: 1085196

Eligibility
People in need who live in the parishes of Brent Knoll, East Brent, Mark and Lympsham in Somerset.

Types of grants
One-off grants according to need.

Annual grant total
Grants generally average about £9,000, though this amount tends to fluctuate quite widely from year to year.

Applications
In writing to the correspondent. Applications can be submitted directly by the individual or via a third party.

Other information
The trust also makes grants to local organisations.

The Somerset Local Medical Benevolent Fund

£17,000

Correspondent: Dr J H Yoxall, Secretary to the Trustees, The Crown Medical Centre, Crown Industrial Estate, Venture Way, Taunton TA2 8QY (01823 331428; email: lmcoffice@somerset.nhs.uk)

Trustees: Dr Roger Bulley; Dr Susan Roberts; Dr S. Hanson; Dr Barry Moyse.

CC Number: 201777

Eligibility

General medical practitioners who are practising or have practised in Somerset and their dependents, who are in need.

Types of grants

One-off or recurrent grants according to need. Recent payments include: Contribution to the locum costs of a young GP undergoing a cardiac procedure and donation towards costs of a doctor absent from work to care for a sick relative. The trustees also make an automatic death in service payment of £4,000 to the dependents of any GP working in Somerset at the time.

Annual grant total

In 2010/11 the trust had an income of £24,000 and a total expenditure of £17,500.

Applications

In writing to the correspondent. Applications can be submitted directly by the individual or by any person on their behalf.

Axbridge

Axbridge Parochial Charities

£15,000

Correspondent: Julia Hill, Moonacre, Hillside, Axbridge, Somerset BS26 2AN (01934 732915)

Trustees: J. Lukins; Mr J. H. Chard; Mrs P. A. Chard; Revd T. D. Hawkings; Dr G. Miles.

CC Number: 233378

Eligibility

People in need who live in the town of Axbridge.

Types of grants

One-off grants according to need. Previously, the majority of funding has been given for Christmas gifts of about £25 to older people.

Annual grant total

In 2010/11 the charities had an income of almost £19,000 and a total expenditure of £17,000. Grants were made totalling around £17,000 although local organisations are also helped.

Applications

In writing to the correspondent.

Bridgwater

The Tamlin Charity

£800

Correspondent: Richard Young, Clerk, 5 Channel Court, Burnham-on-Sea, Somerset TA8 1NE (01278 789859)

Trustees: Kenneth Frederick Richards; Adrian John Moore; Graham John Granter.

CC Number: 228586

Eligibility

Older people, generally those over 65, who are in need and live in Bridgwater.

Types of grants

Small quarterly pensions.

Annual grant total

Grants average around £800 a year.

Applications

On a form available from a trustee or from the correspondent. Applications can be submitted directly by the individual or through a third party such as a social worker, Citizens Advice or other welfare agency.

Cannington

The Cannington Combined Charity

£3,000

Correspondent: Betty Edney, Clerk to the Trustees, Down Stream, 1 Mill Close, Cannington, Bridgwater, Somerset TA5 2JA (01278 653026)

Trustees: Revd Peter Martin; Colin Fitzpatrick; Edward Cubitt; Robin Child; Maureen Hudson; Alice Joan Greenslade; Janet Jenkins.

CC Number: 290789

Eligibility

People in need who live in the parish of Cannington. There is some preference for older people and those with disabilities.

Types of grants

Grants to meet regular or one-off bills where applicants cannot receive additional assistance from any other source. Other grants have been given towards a shower for a woman following major surgery, help with household expenses and travel expenses to a special school.

Annual grant total

Grants usually average around £3,000 per year.

Applications

On a form available from the correspondent. Applications can be submitted directly by the individual or through a social worker, family member, doctor or similar third party. Trustees meet quarterly in January, April, August and November.

Draycott

Charity of John and Joseph Card (also known as Draycott Charity)

£3,000

Correspondent: Helen Dance, Leighurst, The Street, Draycott, Cheddar, Somerset BS27 3TH (01934 742811)

Trustees: David Sheldon; Gerald Dally; Graham Brown; Trish Corrick; Sue Hewish; Di Ginger; Mike Sealey; Jeff Astle; Revd Sue Rose; Rachel Chard.

CC Number: 203827

Eligibility

People in need who live in the hamlet of Draycott, near Cheddar, with a preference for those who receive a pension from the charity.

Types of grants

Pensions usually range from £100 to £500 a year and are made to people of pensionable age on low incomes (i.e. basic pensions). One-off hardship payments range from £50 to £250 and can be made to people of all ages. One-off grants have recently been made for clothing and travel to and from hospital.

Annual grant total

In 2010/11 the charity had an income of £4,000 and a total expenditure of £5,000.

Exclusions

No grants to pay normal household bills.

Applications

For pensions apply on a form available from the correspondent and for hardship grants apply in writing. Applications for pensions are considered in November and hardship grants are considered at any time. Applications can be submitted directly by the individual or by a family member.

Other information

Grants are also made to organisations such as playgroups, churches and so on.

Ilchester

Ilchester Relief-in-Need and Educational Charity

£3,000

Correspondent: Wendy Scrivener, Milton House, Podimore, Yeovil, Somerset BA22 8JF (01935 840070)

Trustees: Philip Horsington; Alan Stephens; Greta Burke; Jonathan Coulson; Patricia Morley; Steven Marsh; Rachel Frampton.

CC Number: 235578

Eligibility

People in need who live in the parish of Ilchester only.

Types of grants

One-off grants according to need.

Annual grant total

In 2011 the charity had an income of £34,000 and made welfare grants to individuals totalling £3,000.

Applications

On a form available from the correspondent. Applications can be submitted directly by the individual or through a social worker, Citizens Advice or other welfare agency or third party.

Unsolicited applications are not responded to.

Other information

Grants are also given for education.

Pitminster

The Pitminster Charity

£5,500

Correspondent: Bryan Thomas, Greencrest, Sellicks Green, Taunton, Somerset TA3 7SD (01823 421616)

Trustees: Christine Mary Robinson; Michael John Sparks; Bryan Caleb Thomas; Pamela Noelle Alers Hankey; Toby Sebastian Kaye Snell.

CC Number: 281105

Eligibility

People who live or have recently lived in the parish of Pitminster and are in need.

Types of grants

One-off grants of at least £250 for items, services or facilities to reduce need.

Annual grant total

In 2010/11 the charity had an income of £5,600 and a total expenditure of £6,100.

Applications

In writing to the correspondent. Applications can be submitted at any time directly by the individual or family member. Enclose an sae.

Other information

The trust also supports the upkeep of a recreation ground in the parish.

Porlock

The Henry Rogers Charity (Porlock Branch)

£1,800

Correspondent: Mrs C M Corner, Tyrol, Villes Lane, Porlock, Minehead, Somerset TA24 8NQ (01643 862645)

Trustees: Dennis Corner; Keith Middleton; Vivian Perkins; John Sparks; Rosemary Cape; Lyn Purvis; Revd Bill Lemmey.

CC Number: 290787

Eligibility

Older people who live in Porlock.

Types of grants

One-off grants and small monthly payments.

Annual grant total

Over the past number of years grants have averaged around £1,800 a year.

Applications

On a form available from the correspondent, to be submitted directly by the individual.

Rimpton

The Rimpton Relief-in-Need Charities

£750

Correspondent: J N Spencer, Secretary, Field End House, Home Farm Lane, Rimpton, Yeovil, Somerset BA22 8AS (01935 850530)

Trustees: Daphne Coombs; Gordon Diment; John Spencer; Sheila Fewkes; Revd Dr Michael Hayes; Robert McCreight.

CC Number: 239816

Eligibility

People in need who live in the parish of Rimpton only. Preference is generally given to older people.

Types of grants

One-off or recurrent grants according to need.

Annual grant total

Grants usually total about £1,500 each year.

Applications

On a form available from the correspondent, to be submitted either by the individual, a family member or through a third party.

Street

The George Cox Charity

£2,000

Correspondent: Andrew Wride, 79 West End, Street, Somerset BA16 0LQ (01458 443990)

Trustees: Andrew Wride; Peter Andrews; Barbara Cowell; David Figures; Suzie Williams; Michael Bryan Bell; Valerie Appleby; Revd Sharon Anne Walker.

CC Number: 240491

Eligibility

People in need who live in the parish of Street.

Types of grants

One-off grants generally ranging from £50 to £100. Recent grants have been given for holidays; repair of domestic appliances such as washing machines and cookers; equipment for older people such as visual aids and Helping Hands; second hand furniture and carpets; and hospital travel costs. Grants are usually paid through the social services.

Annual grant total

In 2010 the charity had an income of £3,000 and a total expenditure of £4,200.

Applications

In writing to the correspondent. Applications are usually submitted through a social worker, Citizens Advice or other welfare agency, or through one of the trustees or someone known to the trustees.

Other information

Grants are made to both organisations and individuals.

Taunton

The Taunton Aid in Sickness Fund

£15,000 (43 grants)

Correspondent: Lynne Durman, Clerk, A C Moles and Sons, Stafford House, Blackbrook Park Avenue, Taunton, Somerset TA1 2PX (01823 624450)

Trustees: Dr Geoffrey Hayes; Trevor Hutchings; Jean Allgrove; Joan Martin; Annabel Martin; Christine Musgrave; Peter Deal; Ian Pinder; Maggie

Kinniburgh; Nan Williams; Kevin Davenport.

CC Number: 260716

Eligibility

People in poor health who are in need and live within a four mile radius of St Mary's Church, Taunton. Priority is given to those living in the former borough of Taunton and the parish of Trull.

Types of grants

One-off grants generally up to £200. Recent grants have been given towards holidays, travel costs, outings and entertainments, laundering, furniture, food for special diets, help with child care costs, and many other benefits for those in poor health.

Annual grant total

In 2010/11 the fund held assets of £154,000 and had an income of £33,000. Grants were made to 43 individuals totalling £15,000.

Exclusions

Grants cannot be used in place of public/ statutory funds, but can be used as a supplement to support those where need is proven. Grants cannot be made on a recurring basis.

Applications

On a form available from the correspondent. Applications should be completed and signed by a recognised referral agency such as social services or a local NHS trust. They should include details of any benefits received by the applicant and a summary of all applications made to other charities or other sources of help. Specific items of basic need should be costed and the actual amount required should be given. Applications can be made at any time.

Taunton Heritage Trust

£82,000

Correspondent: Clerk to the Trustees, Huish Homes, Magdalene Street, Taunton, Somerset TA1 1SG (01823 335348)

Trustees: John Ruff; Jean Allgrove; Beatrice Roberts; John Guy; John Richards; John Palmer; Richard Meikle; Michael Beer; Robert McKay; Alan Ladd; Mary Whitmarsh; Chris Cutting.

CC Number: 202120

Eligibility

People in need who live in the borough of Taunton Deane.

Types of grants

One-off grants for specific items such as, furniture, white goods, equipment for babies/children, household repairs/ decoration, flooring, holidays, clothing and disability aids.

Annual grant total

In 2011 the trust had assets of £5.1 million and an income of £518,000. Welfare grants to 266 individuals totalled £82,000.

Exclusions

Support is not given towards clearing debts.

Applications

On a form available from the website, for consideration throughout the year. Applications should be submitted through a third party, such as a social worker, Citizens Advice or other welfare agency and must be typed, not handwritten. The third party should verify that the applicant is in receipt of all statutory benefits to which they are entitled.

Other information

The prime role of the charity is to provide sheltered accommodation for older people. Grants are also made for educational purposes.

Previously called 'Taunton Town Charity'.

Wells

The Wells Clerical Charity

£3,800

Correspondent: Peter Thomas, The Rectory, Cat Street, Chiselborough, Stoke-Sub-Hamdon, Somerset TA14 6TT (01935 881202)

Trustees: Revd Colin Alsbury; Revd Peter Thomas; Revd Tony Perris; Ven Nicola Sullivan; Revd Christopher Hare; Revd Tim Hawkings; Revd Richard Taylor; Prebendary Rose Hoskins; Revd David John Lamont Macgeogh; Revd Prebendary Alexander Quintin Henry Wheeler.

CC Number: 248436

Eligibility

Clergy of the Church of England who have served in the historic archdeaconry of Wells and their dependents who are in need.

Types of grants

One-off grants according to need. Grants are also made for educational purposes.

Annual grant total

In 2011 the charity had an income of £8,500 and a total expenditure of £7,800.

Applications

In writing to the correspondent.

Wiltshire

Brave Hearts (formerly Children's Relief Fund Association)

£5,000

Correspondent: Ronald Bennett, 114 Launcelot Close, King Arthur's Way, Andover House, Hampshire SP10 4BZ (01264 394440; email: bravehearts@sky. com; website: braveheartscharity.webeden.co.uk/)

Trustees: Susan Elizabeth Bennett; Josephine Mary Hopgood; Kevin Michael Bennett; Ronald Nicholson Bennett.

CC Number: 1005070

Eligibility

'Children under 16 who are resident in Hampshire and Test Valley who need help due to distress, financial hardship, family crisis, physical or mental disability or infirmity.'

Types of grants

One-off grants towards special cycles, walking aids, body splints, wheelchairs, safety seats, special holidays, communication aids and so on. Help is also given to children in times of family crisis and to children with urgent special needs.

Annual grant total

In 2010/11 the trust had an income of £6,500 and a total expenditure of £5,100. Grants totalled around £5,000.

Applications

In writing to the correspondent either directly by the individual or through a social worker, Citizens Advice or other third party. Proposals should be a couple of paragraphs long and explain who the applicant is, what the grant is for, how much it will cost, and how much is required. Details of the child's name, age, and special needs should also be given. If possible, applicants are asked to provide a contact telephone number or email address.

Malmesbury Community Trust

£600

Correspondent: Phil Rice, The First, Milbourne Lane, Milbourne, Malmesbury, Wiltshire SN16 9JH (01666 824007; email: philrice@lineone.net)

Trustees: Cllr Carole Soden; Fredrick Moules; Cllr John Thomson; Philip James Rice; Jeff Penfold; Dr Kate

Badcock; Mrs D. Greenwood; Patrick Goldstone.

CC Number: 1018458

Eligibility

People in need who live in Malmesbury and the surrounding area, with priority given to older residents.

Types of grants

One-off grants according to need.

Annual grant total

In 2010/11 the trust had an income of £130 and a total expenditure of £1,300.

Applications

On an application form available from the correspondent.

Other information

The trust also makes grants to local organisations.

Salisbury City Almshouse and Welfare Charities

£13,000 (43 grants)

Correspondent: Clerk to the Trustees, Trinity Hospital, Trinity Street, Salisbury SP1 2BD (01722 325640; fax: 01722 325640; email: clerk@almshouses.demon. co.uk; website: www. salisburyalmshouses.co.uk)

Trustees: Lady Benson; Rodney Walter Shipsey; Trevor Austreng; Alan Corkill; Revd David Coulton; Gillian Ann Ellis; Peter Moss; Anna Taylor; Patricia Margaret Lush; Alastair James Brain; Fiona Green; Malcolm James Findlay.

CC Number: 202110

Eligibility

People in need who live in Salisbury and district.

Types of grants

One-off grants of between £100 and £300, to meet all kinds of emergency or other needs that cannot be met from public funds. Grants can be towards, for example, essential items such as reconditioned cookers, washing machines, refrigerators, school clothing, shoes, moving costs, beds/bedding, holidays and wheelchairs.

Annual grant total

In 2011 the charities had assets of £12.5 million and an income of £1.5 million. Welfare grants made to 43 individuals totalled £13,000. The charities usually have around £22,500 available for distribution each year.

Exclusions

No grants for debts. It is unusual for the trust to make more than one grant to an applicant in any one year.

Applications

Applications are considered in the second week of each month. Application forms should be submitted at least 15 days before and should be sponsored by a recognised professional who is fully aware of statutory entitlements and is capable of giving advice/supervision in budgeting and so on. Application forms, together with guidance notes, are available from to download from the website or by contacting the clerk.

Other information

The charities' main concern is the maintenance of almshouses.

Wiltshire Ambulance Service Benevolent Fund

£2,500

Correspondent: A C Newman, Treasurer, 82 Dunch Lane, Melksham, Wiltshire SN12 8DX (07966 534713)

Trustees: Andrew Charles Newman; Ryszard Orzechowski; Deborah Scammell.

CC Number: 280364

Eligibility

Serving and retired members of the Wiltshire Ambulance Service and their dependents.

Types of grants

One-off and recurrent grants according to need.

Annual grant total

In 2010/11 the trust had an income of £24,000 and a total expenditure of £20,000. Grants totalled around £2,000.

Applications

Applicants should contact their station benevolent fund representative, who will then contact the chair on their behalf.

Other information

The fund also owns and supports three properties that provide convalescence.

Aldbourne

Aldbourne Poor's Gorse Charity

£1,900

Correspondent: Terence Gilligan, Poors Allotment, 9 Cook Road, Aldbourne, Marlborough, Wiltshire SN8 2EG (01672 540205)

Trustees: William Brown; Brian Buckler; Christopher Humphries; Audrey Gilligan; Hugh Bland; Lindsey Keen.

CC Number: 202958

Eligibility

People in need who live in the parish of Aldbourne, with a preference for those over 65.

Types of grants

One-off grants towards fuel costs.

Annual grant total

Grants usually total around £1,900 each year.

Applications

In writing to the correspondent, directly by the individual, usually on the charity's invitation.

Ashton Keynes

The Ashton Keynes Charity

£9,000

Correspondent: Richard Smith, Trustee, Amberley, 4 Gosditch, Ashton Keynes, Swindon, Wiltshire SN6 6NZ (01285 861461)

Trustees: Ronald Thomas; Revd Judith Ashby; Michael Seymour; Richard Smith; David Wingrove.

CC Number: 205302

Eligibility

Older people in need who live in Ashton Keynes.

Types of grants

Grants to pensioners. In previous years around 180 individuals have benefited.

Annual grant total

In 2011 the trust had an income of £6,700 and a total expenditure of £14,000.

Applications

In writing to the correspondent.

Other information

Grants are also given to organisations.

Chippenham

Chippenham Borough Lands Charity

£10,000

Correspondent: Catherine Flynn, Jubilee Building, 32 Market Place, Chippenham, Wiltshire SN15 3HP (01249 658180; fax: 01249 446048; email: admin@cblc.org. uk; website: www.cblc.org.uk)

Trustees: Jenny Budgell; Jack Konyenburg; Chris Dawe; Peter Kemp; Margaret Harrison; Michael Braun; Mark Packard; Peter Hutton; Graham Bone; Desna Allen; Terry Burke; Mary Pile.

CC Number: 270062

Eligibility

People in need who are living within the parish of Chippenham at the date of application, and have been for a minimum of two years immediately prior to applying.

Types of grants

One-off, and occasionally recurrent, grants and loans are made according to need. Recent grants have included help with living costs, mobility aids, domestic appliances, debt relief, travel passes, food vouchers, furniture and childcare.

Annual grant total

In 2010/11 grants were given to 56 individuals totalling £21,000. Also, food vouchers with a total value of £6,600 were distributed as 'Christmas Hampers' to 73 nominated individuals or families who each received between £50 and £100.

Exclusions

Grants are not given in any circumstances where the charity considers the award to be a substitute for statutory provision. The charity will not consider an application if a grant has been received within the past two years (or one year for mobility aids) unless the circumstances are exceptional. The charity does not make awards for the provision of carpets or Council Tax arrears.

Applications

On a form available from the correspondent. Once received the application will be looked at in detail by a welfare officer. It is possible that the charity will visit, or ask applicants to call in at this stage. Applications are considered every month and can be submitted directly by the individual or through a third party such as a Citizens Advice, social worker or GP.

Other information

People applying for mobility equipment will be asked to attend the Independent Living Centre in order for them to assess which equipment would be most appropriate.

Grants are also given to organisations.

East Knoyle

The East Knoyle Welfare Trust

£800

Correspondent: Miss Sabrina Sully, Old Byre House, Millbrook Lane, East Knoyle, Salisbury SP3 6AW

Trustees: Michael Hull; Sabrina Sully; Cliff Sully; Andrew Burton; Helen Lever;

John Hacker; Margaret Browning; Revd S. Morgan; Sally-Anne Williams.

CC Number: 202028

Eligibility

People in need who live in the parish of East Knoyle.

Types of grants

One-off grants only, usually for heating bills.

Annual grant total

Grants usually total around £800.

Applications

Applications to the correspondent or any other trustee by the end of May to receive fuel payments for the next winter.

Other information

Grants are also made for educational purposes.

Salisbury

Charity of William Botley

£2,200 (6 grants)

Correspondent: Clerk to the Trustees, Trinity Hospital, Trinity Street, Salisbury, Wiltshire SP1 2BD (01722 325640; email: clerk@almshouses.demon. co.uk; website: www. salisburyalmshouses.co.uk)

Trustees: Lady Benson; Alison Hatton; Josephine B. A. Bailey; Rodney Walter Shipsey; Trevor Austreng; Alan Corkill; Revd David Coulton; Gillian Ann Ellis; Peter Moss; Anna Taylor; Patricia Margaret Lush; Alastair James Brain; Fiona Green.

CC Number: 268418

Eligibility

Women in need who live in the city of Salisbury.

Types of grants

One-off grants ranging from about £100 to £200, to meet all kinds of emergency and other needs which cannot be met from public funds. Recent grants have been made for second hand white goods, clothing for mothers and children, carpets and floor coverings and holiday costs.

Annual grant total

In 2011 the charity had an income of £8,700 and a total expenditure of £3,900. Grants were made to six individuals totalling £2,200. The charity usually has around £7,000 available for distribution each year.

Exclusions

No grants for the payment of debts.

Applications

Application forms are available from the Salisbury City Almshouse and Welfare charity website. Applications are considered during the second week of every month and should be received at least two weeks prior to this. They should be submitted through a recognised professional such as a social worker.

Swindon

Community Foundation for Wiltshire and Swindon

£79,000

Correspondent: The Grants Team, 48 New Park Street, Devizes SN10 1DS (01380 729284; fax: 01380 729772; email: info@wscf.org.uk; website: www.wscf. org.uk)

Trustees: Simon David Wright; Richard Gordon Handover; Timothy Edward Odoire; Helen Judith Birchenough; Sarah Rose Troughton; Christopher John Bertram Bromfield; David Holder; Ram Thiagarajah; Dame Elizabeth Louise Neville; Denise Angela Bentley; Angus Macpherson; Elizabeth Rosemary Webbe; John Paul Woodget; Alison Jane Radevsky; Andrew Cameron Kerr.

CC Number: 1123126

Eligibility

People in need living in Wiltshire and Swindon.

Types of grants

The Greenacres Fund

The Greenacres Fund supports the education and training of children and young people aged under 21 who live in Wiltshire or Swindon. Applicants will be, or will have been living in the care of Wiltshire County Council or the borough of Swindon, or will have long-term health needs or a disability. If an applicant is not currently living in care, they or their parents will need to be in receipt of means-tested benefits to be eligible for a grant from the fund.

The Shuker Educational Fund

The Shuker Educational Fund will be supporting young people from West Wiltshire District aged 17–24 who are studying for, or planning to study for, a Degree or Doctorate.

The aim of the fund is to help students from poorer backgrounds who are studying a practical subject at a well-established university.

See the flyer on the foundation's website for more information.

The Wiltshire Society

Founded in 1653 this fund transferred to the Community Foundation in 2010 and supports young people between the ages of 16 and 25 to pursue courses for which they are suited but from which they are likely to be precluded by lack of funds.

Note, as with all community foundations the open funds and eligibility criteria tend to change frequently so check the foundation's website or contact them before starting an application.

Annual grant total

In 2010/11 the foundation had assets of £8.5 million and an income of £1.6 million. Grants were made to individuals totalling £79,000.

Applications

Visit the website or contact the grants team for further information on grants available for individuals.

Other information

The foundation mainly makes grants to organisations.

Trowbridge

The Cecil Norman Wellesley Blair Charitable Trust

£6,000

Correspondent: Matthew Ridley, 6 Middle Lane, Trowbridge BA14 7LG (01225 752289)

Trustees: John Denby-Gardner; Nicholas Blakemore; Tony King; Doreen Thornton; Susan Bradbrooke.

CC Number: 202446

Eligibility

People in need who live in the civil parish of Trowbridge. Preference is given to those in receipt of income support, job seekers allowance or pension credit.

Types of grants

One-off grants only of around £12, mainly in the form of vouchers for food, fuel and clothing.

Annual grant total

In 2010/11 the trust had an income of £7,200 and a total expenditure of £6,100.

Applications

The trust advertises the date of distribution each year in the local press – usually the first Friday in December. It issues vouchers via two distribution points and beneficiaries must go to those points and present proof that they are in receipt of statutory benefits.

Other information

In very exceptional circumstances, when surplus money is available, the trust gives grants to local organisations.

Dr C. S. Kingston Fund

£5,500

Correspondent: Matthew Ridley, Castle House, 6 Middle Lane, Trowbridge, Wiltshire BA14 7LG (01225 752289)

Trustees: Sheila King; Tony King; Barbara Gage; Esther Cole; Geoffrey Holt; Bob Rogers; Rob Thomas.

CC Number: 265423

Eligibility

People in need who live in the urban district of Trowbridge.

Types of grants

One-off grants according to need. Recent grants have been given towards electrical goods (cookers, washing machines), school uniforms and school trips for families not otherwise able to afford them. Occasionally, financial grants (but NOT payable to individuals), help towards childcare and help towards holidays has been given.

Annual grant total

In 2010/11 the fund had an income of £4,500 and a total expenditure of £5,900.

Applications

On a form available from the correspondent. Applications can be submitted directly by the individual, but are generally made through a social worker, doctor, Citizens Advice or other welfare agency.

Westbury

The Henry Smith Charity (Westbury)

£1,000

Correspondent: W H White, Pinniger Finch and Co., Solicitors, 35–37 Church Street, Westbury, Wiltshire BA13 3BZ (01373 823791; email: info@ pinngerfinch.co.uk)

Trustees: Bill White; Evelyn Mead.

CC Number: 243888

Eligibility

People in need who live in Westbury and are aged over 40 years.

Types of grants

Grants of around £40 are given towards, for example, fuel, food and clothing.

Annual grant total

Grants usually total around £1,000 a year.

Applications

In writing to the correspondent.

South East

General

The Affinity Water Trust
See entry on page 467

Anglia Care Trust

£450

Correspondent: Jane Sharpe, 65 St Matthew's Street, Ipswich, Suffolk IP1 3EW (01473 213140; email: admin@ angliacaretrust.org.uk; website: www. angliacaretrust.org.uk)

Trustees: Ann Bryant; Chris Bally; Peter Heath; James Manning; Colin Reid; Gareth Roscoe; Colin Shiers; Alex Till; Mary Gibbons.

CC Number: 299049

Eligibility

People in need who live in East Anglia and are experiencing or have experienced a legal restriction on their liberty, and their families. Namely offenders, ex-offenders or people who are at risk of offending.

Types of grants

One-off grants towards rehabilitation and education. Grants usually range from £10 to £70. Sums of money are not usually paid direct, but itemised bills will be met directly. If items can be reclaimed from either housing benefit or returnable deposit, this must be considered.

Applicants will usually already be supported by, or are known to, ACT and should have exhausted all possible sources of statutory funds.

The areas that will be supported are:

- Education and/or training
- Basic equipment/tools
- Furniture
- Moving into new accommodation
- Clothing to enable people to seek employment/return to work
- Others on merit

Annual grant total

Grants usually total around £900.

Exclusions

Grants are not given towards payment of debts, fines, legal costs or hire purchases.

Applications

In writing to the correspondent. All applications must be supported by a probation officer or other professional person and are considered quarterly.

Other information

For this entry, the information relates to the money available from ACT. For more information on what is available throughout East Anglia, contact the correspondent.

The Argus Appeal

£21,000

Correspondent: Elsa Gillio, Argus House, Crowhurst Road, Hollingbury, Brighton BN1 8AR (01273 544465; email: elsa.gillio@theargus.co.uk; website: www.theargus.co.uk/ argusappeal)

Trustees: Elsa Gillio; David Goldin; Roger French; Julien Boast; Michael Beard; Sue Addis; Ian Hunter; Sue Meheux; Lee Gibbs.

CC Number: 1013647

Eligibility

People in need, particularly older people and underprivileged children, who live in the Sussex area.

Types of grants

One-off and recurrent grants according to need and food parcels for older people. Recently grants have been made to purchase computers for hospitalised children to enable them to continue with their school work and to purchase specially adapted trikes for four disabled children. More than 1,000 Christmas hampers and food vouchers were given to pensioners and low income families in 2010.

Annual grant total

In 2010 the trust held assets of £255,000 and had an income of £203,000. The charity had a total charitable expenditure of £68,000 of which £21,000 was made in grants to individuals.

Applications

In writing to the correspondent including details on who you are, what you do, how much is needed, how it will be spent and what has been done so far to raise the necessary funds.

Other information

The charity also makes grants to organisations. Generally it seems like quite a proactive charity, preferring to purchase items directly for organisations as well as individuals. This is also reflected in the provision of food hampers as opposed to finance for individuals in need.

The Berkshire Nurses and Relief-in-Sickness Trust

£48,000 (185 grants)

Correspondent: Mrs R Pottinger, Honorary Secretary, 26 Montrose Walk, Fords Farm, Calcot, Reading RG31 7YH (01189 010196; email: rosandken@aol. com)

Trustees: Eileen Pearson; Elizabeth Foster; Howard Slack; Robin Christian; Leslie Tester; Gill Silver; Lorna Catline; Margaret Walsh; Hazel Alexander; Margaret Winter.

CC Number: 205274

Eligibility

1. People in need through sickness or disability who live in the county of Berkshire and those areas of Oxfordshire formerly in Berkshire.

2. Nurses and midwives employed as district nurses in the county of Berkshire and those areas of Oxfordshire formerly in Berkshire and people employed before August 1980 as administrative and clerical staff by Berkshire County Nursing Association.

Types of grants

One-off grants only towards household accounts (excluding those below), holidays, some medical aids, special

385

diets, clothing, wheelchairs, electronic aids for people with disabilities, hospital travel costs, prescription season tickets and so on.

Annual grant total
In 2010/11 the trust had assets of £1.3 million, which generated an income of £61,000. Grants were made to 185 individuals totalling £48,000.

Exclusions
No grants for rent or mortgage payments, community charge, water rates, funeral bills, ongoing payments such as nursing home fees or any items thought to be the responsibility of statutory authorities.

Applications
On a form available from the correspondent. Applications should be made through a social worker, Citizens Advice or other welfare agency and supported by a member of the statutory authorities. They are considered as received. Applications are not accepted directly from members of the public.

Other information
Grants are also made to local caring organisations, when funds allow.

The Chownes Foundation

£28,000 (12 grants)

Correspondent: Sylvia J Spencer, Secretary, The Courtyard, Beeding Court, Steyning, West Sussex BN44 3TN (01903 816699)

Trustees: Revd Stephen Ortiger; Mrs U. Hazeel; Mr M. Wooley.

CC Number: 327451

Eligibility
Individuals and small charities primarily in Sussex, particularly Mid-Sussex, being the former home of the founder.

Types of grants
One-off and recurrent grants according to need.

Annual grant total
In 2010/11 the foundation had assets of £1.6 million and an income of £69,000. Grants were made to 12 individuals, ' for relief of hardship and other charitable purposes', totalling £28,000.

Applications
The trustees prefer a one page document and will request further information if they require it.

Other information
The majority of the charity's funds are committed to long-term support for poor and vulnerable beneficiaries, so only very few applications are successful.

The Derek and Eileen Dodgson Foundation

£74,000

Correspondent: Ian W Dodd, 8 Locks Hill, Portslade, Brighton and Hove BN41 2LB (01273 419802; email: ianwdodd@gmail.com)

Trustees: Peter Ernest Goldsmith; Ed Squires; Christopher Kempster Butler; Roy Prater; Natasha Glover; Georgina Reed.

CC Number: 1018776

Eligibility
People in need over 55, who live in East and West Sussex, with a strong preference for connections with Brighton and Hove.

Types of grants
On average 500 one-off grants or loans of up to £1,000 are made, mainly to older people. Most of the funds are given to local non-governmental organisations to pass on to individuals.

Annual grant total
In 2010/11 the foundation had assets of £2.1 million and an income of £113,000. Grants were made totalling £74,000.

Applications
On a form available from the correspondent. Applications can be submitted either directly by the individual or through a social worker, Citizens Advice or other third party.

East Sussex Farmers' Union Benevolent Fund

£10,000

Correspondent: c/o Gordon J Fowlie, Farthings, North Road, Ringmer, Lewes, West Sussex BN8 5JP (01273 812406)

Trustees: Gordon James Fowlie; Alan Catt; David Cornwell; John Thompson; John Henry Robinson.

CC Number: 271188

Eligibility
People in need who are farmers, farmworkers or their dependents, with priority for those who live in the county of East Sussex. When funds are available eligible people living in Kent, Surrey and West Sussex may also be supported.

Types of grants
One-off and recurrent grants according to need.

Annual grant total
In 2010/11 the fund had assets of nearly £1.2 million and an income of £31,000. Grants and donations to individuals

totalled £8,000, with costs for hampers amounting to £2,000.

Applications
In writing or by telephone to the correspondent.

The Hunstanton Convalescent Trust

£9,000

Correspondent: Mrs F Wilby, 66 Collingwood Road, Hunstanton, Norfolk PE36 5DY (01485 533788)

Trustees: David Hume; John Dawson; Jason Law; Cameron Green; Pat Stainby; Fay Wilby; Dr David Goose.

CC Number: 218979

Eligibility
People who are on a low income, physically or mentally unwell and in need of a convalescent or recuperative holiday, with a preference for those living in Norfolk, Cambridgeshire and Suffolk.

Types of grants
Grants ranging from £100 to £350 are given to provide or assist towards the expenses of recuperative holidays, including for carers. The trust can sometimes provide other items, services or facilities which will help the individual's recovery.

Annual grant total
In 2010/11 the trust had an income of £1,400 and a total expenditure of £9,200.

Applications
On a form available from the correspondent, through a social worker, doctor or other welfare workers. Applications should be submitted at least one month before the proposed holiday. The full board of trustees meet in January, June and September.

Jewish Care

£10,000

Correspondent: Grants Officer, Jewish Care, Amelie House, Maurice and Vivienne Wohl Campus, 221 Golders Green Road, London NW9 5AB (020 8922 2222; email: jcdirect@jcare.org; website: www.jewishcare.org)

Trustees: Howard Darryl Leigh; Steven David Lewis; Arnold Wagner; Dr Suzanne Lea Joels; Eli Shahmoon; Debra Fox; Stuart Roden; Anthony Grossman; Linda Bogod; Jonathan Zenios; Andrew Klein; Robert Suss.

CC Number: 802559

Eligibility

Members of the Jewish faith who are older, mentally ill, visually impaired or physically disabled, and their families, who live in London and the south east of England.

Types of grants

Jewish Care (includes the former Jewish Welfare Board, Jewish Blind Society and the Jewish Home and Hospital at Tottenham) is the largest Jewish social work agency, providing a range of services, both domiciliary and residential. Financial assistance is not a normal part of the trust's work, though some such expenditure is inevitably associated with its social work service.

Annual grant total

In 2010/11 the trust had assets of £99 million, an income of £62 million and a total expenditure of £46 million, the majority of which went on the provision and administration of Jewish social services. In the past direct financial help was provided in the form of grants, however, despite requests to the charity we were unable to determine the value of these awards.

Exclusions

No help with burial expenses or education fees.

Applications

Initial contact should be made in writing or by contacting the helpline on 020 8922 2222.

The Elaine and Angus Lloyd Charitable Trust

£0

Correspondent: Ross Badger, 3rd Floor, North Side, Dukes Court, 32 Duke Street, St James's, London SW1Y 6DF (020 7930 7797)

Trustees: Angus Selwyn Lloyd; John Strathearn Gordon; James Selwyn Lloyd; Philippa Juliet Satchwell Smith; Virginia Elaine Best; Christopher Robert Henry Lloyd; Sir Michael Craig-Cooper; Revd Richard Gary Lloyd.

CC Number: 237250

Eligibility

People 'whose circumstances are such they come within the legal conception of poverty'.

Types of grants

One-off and recurrent grants according to need.

Annual grant total

In 2010/11 the trust had assets of £2.5 million and an income of £77,000. £79,000 was paid in grants to organisations but no grants were made

to individuals this year (£5,100 in 2009/10).

Applications

In writing to the correspondent. The trustees meet regularly to consider grants.

Other information

The trust predominantly awards grants to organisations.

The B. V. MacAndrew Trust

£6,000

Correspondent: Roger Clow, 169 Preston Road, Brighton, East Sussex BN1 6AG (01273 562563)

Trustees: David John Eric Diplock; Christopher Ian Wellings; David Anthony Shaw; Roger Heber Clow; Christine Cohen Park.

CC Number: 206900

Eligibility

People in need who live in East and West Sussex.

Types of grants

One-off grants ranging from £50 to 1200 for a variety of needs including emergencies and household appliances.

Annual grant total

In 2010/11 the trust had an income of £6,600 and a total expenditure of £6,500.

Exclusions

The trust are unable to assist with bankruptcy fees or debts.

Applications

In writing to the correspondent at any time including the amount required and the name of the person the cheque is to be made out to. Applications can be made either through a third party such as a social worker or through an organisation such as Citizens Advice or other welfare agency. Applications are usually considered a month following receipt.

South East Water's Helping Hand

£100,000

Correspondent: Grants Team, Freepost-RSHE-ARTT-AAUE, South East Water's Helping Hand, PO BOX 42, Peterborough PE3 8XH (01733 421060; fax: 01733 421020; email: helpinghand@ southeastwater.co.uk; website: www. southeastwater.co.uk/helpinghand)

Eligibility

Domestic customers of South East Water who, through whatever difficulty, have

found themselves in debt and unable to pay their water/sewerage charges.

Types of grants

Grants are initially made on a provisional basis: following the receipt of a provisional award, an applicant needs to demonstrate their commitment and ability to improve their financial sustainability and their ability to pay current and future water charges. After this period, if the applicant is judged to have taken these steps, their award will be confirmed and their debt to the company at the time of the provisional award will be cleared.

Annual grant total

In the 2011/12 financial year the parent company of the fund contributed £120,000 to the fund.

Applications

Applicants may apply online on the fund's website. Applicants must attach the relevant supporting documents, otherwise the fund will contact you before the assessment of your application can begin. Such documents include: proof of income, relevant bills and evidence of any special circumstances such as disability. The application must be made in account holders name.

Applications may also be downloaded from the website or picked up from local advice centres such as Citizens Advice, and posted to the correspondent.

Successful applicants (and those who have also successfully applied to the EOS Foundation) may not apply again. Unsuccessful applicants may reapply after six months.

Other information

The fund was founded by South East Water upon the dissolution of the EOS Foundation in April 2010.

Sussex Police Welfare Fund

£29,000 (110 grants)

Correspondent: Barbara Castle, Sussex Police, Malling House, Church Lane, Lewes, East Sussex BN7 2DZ (0845 607 0999 (ext. 44137); email: spct@sussex. pnn.police.uk; website: www.sussex. police.uk/about-us/sussex-police-charitable-trust)

Trustees: Paul Allen; Graham Keenor; Lee Care; Ross Hollister; Diane Roskilly; Philip Taylor; Seve Biglands; Ahmed Ramiz; Mark White; Olivia Pinkney.

CC Number: 257564

Eligibility

Serving and retired Sussex police officers and their dependents.

Types of grants

One-off grants for convalescence, clothing, household bills, food, holidays, travel expenses, medical equipment, nursing fees, furniture, disability equipment, help in the home and short-term childcare. Grants are also given to facilitate mediation and initial legal advice.

Discretionary loans may be given to serving officers subscribing to the fund who are facing financial difficulties. Loans are repayable from salary at source per pay period. Any assistance agreed will usually be paid directly to the provider of a service requested by a member.

Annual grant total

In 2011 the fund had assets of £1 million, an income of £152,000. Grants were made to 110 individuals totalling £29,000. Four interest-free loans were also made during the year totalling £3,600.

Applications

By calling, emailing or writing to the fund. Your case will be dealt with by a trust adviser who will work with you to address your problems. If it is deemed appropriate they will prepare an anonymous application to the fund for financial assistance. The trust adviser then presents your application at a monthly meeting and advocates on behalf of the applicant. More urgent requests can be considered between the monthly meetings.

Other information

The fund employs two trust advisers who offer advice, information and practical support particularly to older members of the fund and those struggling with debt problems. The trust also owns a bungalow in Highcliffe, Christchurch, which is available to members in need of a recuperative break.

On 1 April 2012 the trust merged with the Sussex Police Staff Charitable Trust.

The Vokins Charitable Trust

£4,000

Correspondent: T W D Vokins, 56 Hove Park Road, Hove, East Sussex BN3 6LN (01273 556317)

Trustees: David Howard Vokins; Trevor William Derek Vokins; Mrs G. C. Vokins.

CC Number: 801487

Eligibility

People in Brighton and Hove and East and West Sussex.

Types of grants

One-off and recurrent grants according to need; scooters are also provided for the less able-bodied.

Annual grant total

In 2010 the trust had an income of £3,100 and a total expenditure of £4,400.

Applications

In writing to the correspondent.

Other information

Grants are also made to organisations.

The Wantage District Coronation Memorial and Nursing Amenities Fund

£4,400

Correspondent: Carol Clubb, 133 Stockham Park, Wantage, Oxfordshire OX12 9HJ (01235 767355)

Trustees: Terence Paul Ryland; Christine Divall; Chris Walters; John Edward Barlow; Penny Cox; Dr Paul Bryan; Veronica Roberts; Dr John Robinson; Dr Andrew Allen.

CC Number: 234384

Eligibility

People who are in poor health, convalescent or who have disabilities and live in the Wantage Oxfordshire area only.

Types of grants

One-off and recurrent grants ranging from about £20 to £100.

Annual grant total

In 2010/11 the fund had an income of £5,100 and a total expenditure of £4,700.

Exclusions

The income of the charity is not to be applied directly for the relief of taxes, rates or other public funds, but may be applied in supplementing relief or assistance provided out of public funds.

Applications

In writing to the correspondent.

Other information

Grants are also made to organisations.

Whitton's Wishes

£50,000

Correspondent: Kathryn Turner, 58 Addlestone Moor, Addlestone KT15 2QL (01932 566125; email: kathrynturnertrust@hotmail.co.uk)

Trustees: Kathryn Turner; Lucy Turner; Mark Richard Gwyther.

CC Number: 1111250

Eligibility

Children, young people, the elderly and people with disabilities/special needs in the area of the old county of Middlesex.

Types of grants

Grants towards the costs of equipment.

Annual grant total

In 2011 the trust had an income of £169,000 and a total expenditure of £164,000. Grants are made to organisations and individuals.

Applications

In writing to the correspondent.

Other information

The trust is also known as The Kathryn Turner Trust.

Bedfordshire

The Norah Mavis Campbell Trust

£0

Correspondent: David Baker, Committee Services Officer, Bedfordshire Borough Council, Borough Hall, Cauldwell Street, Bedford MK42 9AP (email: david.baker@bedford.gov.uk)

Trustees: Cllr Sylvia Gillard; Cllr Michael Headley; Cllr Roger Rigby.

CC Number: 1073047

Eligibility

People who are elderly and in need who reside in the area of Bedford Borough Council area.

Types of grants

Grants are given according to need.

Annual grant total

The income and total expenditure of the trust vary widely on an annual basis. Both income and total expenditure were at their lowest level in a number of years at £800 and £0 respectively.

Applications

In writing to the correspondent.

Other information

The trust also provides additional benefits for residents at the Puttenhoe Home in Bedford.

Mary Lockington Charity

£2,000

Correspondent: Yvonne E Beaumont, Grove House, 76 High Street North, Dunstable, Bedfordshire LU6 1NF (01582 660008; email: dunstablecharity@yahoo.com)

Trustees: Alan Trevor Hoose; Brenda Boatwright; Christina Margaret Scott; Trevor Owens; Revd Richard Andrews; Peter Francis Hatswell; John Bradley.

CC Number: 204766

Eligibility

Individuals living in the parishes of Dunstable, Leighton Buzzard and Hockliffe who are in need, for example due to hardship, disability or sickness.

Types of grants

One-off grants towards items, services or facilities.

Annual grant total

In 2010/11 the charity had an income of £10,600 and a total expenditure of £6,700.

Applications

In writing to the correspondent.

Other information

The charity also contributes to the upkeep of almshouses and makes grants to local organisations.

The Sandy Charities

£3,000

Correspondent: P J Mount, Clerk, Woodfines Solicitors, 6 Bedford Road, Sandy, Bedfordshire SG19 1EN (01767 680251; email: pmount@woodfines.co. uk)

Trustees: Christine Summerfield; Revd Derwyn Williams; William Bickerdike; Robert Browning; Barbara Arnold; David Stevinson; David Sharman; Jonathan Pym.

CC Number: 237145

Eligibility

People who live in Sandy and Beeston and are in need.

Types of grants

One-off grants only ranging from £100 to £1,000, towards, for instance, motorised wheelchairs, decorating costs and children's' clothing.

Annual grant total

In 2010/11 the charities had an income of £9,200 and a total expenditure of £8,200.

Applications

In writing to the correspondent who will supply a personal details form for completion. Applications can be considered in any month, depending on the urgency for the grant; they should be submitted either directly by the individual or via a social worker, Citizens Advice or other welfare agency.

Other information

Grants are also made to organisations and to individuals for educational purposes.

Bedford

Bedford Municipal Charities

£26,000

Correspondent: David Baker, Bedford Borough Council, Borough Hall, Cauldwell Street, Bedford MK42 9AP (01234 228788; email: david.baker@ bedford.gov.uk)

Trustees: Cllr Colleen Atkins; Graham Bates; Jane George; Mollie Foster; George Burton; Cllr Jim Brandon; Canon John Pedlar; Keith Lazenby; Shirley Groves; Roger Charles Whitbread; Dr Robert Main; Valerie Lane; Cllr Nigel Sparrow; Father Lawrence MacDonald.

CC Number: 2005566

Eligibility

People in need who live in the borough of Bedford.

Types of grants

Pensions; grants towards fuel bills and other necessities; occasional one-off grants for special purposes in the range of £25 to £700 and Christmas bonuses.

Annual grant total

In 2010/11 the trust held assets of £784,000 and had an income of £31,000. Charitable expenditure totalled £32,000 including grants of £26,000 which were distributed as follows:

Contingency grants	£16,300
Fuel grants	£4,800
Pensions	£3,900
Christmas distribution	£900
Church distribution	£300

Applications

In writing to the correspondent. Applications can be submitted directly by the individual or through an appropriate third party. Individual applicants may be visited to assess the degree of need.

Clophill

Clophill United Charities

£3,000

Correspondent: Gillian Hill, 10 The Causeway, Clophill, Bedford MK45 4BA (01525 860539)

Trustees: Ray Sharp; Julie Benson; Revd Dean Henley; Andrew Hicks; Richard Pearson.

CC Number: 200034

Eligibility

People who live in the parish of Clophill and are in need.

Types of grants

One-off and recurrent grants according to need.

Annual grant total

Grants usually total around £3,000 per year.

Exclusions

No grants where statutory funds are available.

Applications

On a form available from the correspondent.

Other information

Grants are also given to organisations.

Dunstable

The Dunstable Poor's Land Charity

£3,000

Correspondent: Yvonne E Beaumont, Grove House, 76 High Street North, Dunstable, Bedfordshire LU6 1NF (01582 660008; email: dunstablecharity@ yahoo.com)

Trustees: Brenda Boatwright; Christina Margaret Scott; Lawrence Vivien Lee; Cllr Ratan Rustomji Anklesaria; Patricia Russell; Pat Staples.

CC Number: 236805

Eligibility

People, usually pensioners, who live in the parish of Dunstable.

Types of grants

Grants of around £20 each are made annually on Maundy Thursday mostly to older people on Income Support or other benefits.

Annual grant total

Grants usually total about £3,000 each year.

Applications

By personal application to the trustees. Applicants must provide evidence of their income.

The Dunstable Welfare Trust

£200

Correspondent: Revd Richard Andrews, The Rectory, 8 Furness Avenue, Dunstable LU6 3BN (01582 703271)

Trustees: Ann Hathaway; Hilary Jackson; Revd Richard Andrews; Jackie Prince.

CC Number: 251859

Eligibility

People in need who live in the borough of Dunstable or in exceptional cases 'immediately' outside Dunstable. Preference is given to people who attend Church of England services.

Types of grants

One-off grants ranging from £50 to £100 for those in need.

Annual grant total

Grants average around £300 to £400 a year.

Exclusions

Grants are not given for relief of rates, taxes or other public funds. The trust may also give donations to organisations that provide services.

Applications

In writing to the correspondent through a social worker, Citizens Advice or other welfare agency or clergy. Applications are considered regularly.

Flitwick

The Flitwick Town Lands Charity

£4,000

Correspondent: David Empson, Trustee, 28 Orchard Way, Flitwick, Bedford MK45 1LF (01525 718145; email: Deflitwick8145@aol.com)

Trustees: Ann Lutley; David Empson; Revd Michael Bradley.

CC Number: 233258

Eligibility

People in need who live in the parish of Flitwick.

Types of grants

Usually one-off grants.

Annual grant total

In 2010/11 the charity had both an income and total expenditure of £8,800. Grants are given for education and welfare purposes.

Applications

On a form available from the correspondent.

Husborne Crawley

The Husborne Crawley Charities of the Poor

£2,000

Correspondent: Rita Chidley, 40 Leighton Street, Woburn, Milton Keynes, Bedford MK17 9PH (01525 290802)

Trustees: Rita Chidley; Revd Graham Bradshaw; Douglas Neale; Lindsey Styles; Sue Isaacs; Richard Lyman.

CC Number: 248497

Eligibility

People in need who live in the ancient parish of Husborne Crawley.

Types of grants

One-off grants according to need.

Annual grant total

In 2011 the charity had an income of £3,500 and a total expenditure of £4,800.

Applications

In writing to the correspondent either directly by the individual or via a third party. Applications are considered throughout the year.

Other information

Grants are also made to the local Church.

Kempston

The Kempston Charities

£1,000

Correspondent: Mrs Christine Stewart, 15 Loveridge Avenue, Kempston, Bedford MK42 8SF (01234 302323)

Trustees: Susan Oliver; Revd Stephen Huckle; Lance Blacklock; Philip Catteril; Richard Hyde; Kay Burley; Adrien Beardmore; George Lambert; Fiorentino Manocchio.

CC Number: 200064

Eligibility

People in need who live in Kempston (including Kempston rural).

Types of grants

One-off grants according to need.

Annual grant total

Grants average around £3,000 a year.

Exclusions

No recurrent grants are made.

Applications

In writing to the correspondent. Applications should be made either directly by the individual or through a social worker, Citizens Advice or other welfare agency. They are considered in March, July and November.

Other information

Grants are also given to local schools and other local institutions.

Potton

The Potton Consolidated Charities

£1,100

Correspondent: Christine Hall, 1a Potton Road, Everton, Sandy, Bedfordshire SG19 2LD (01767 680663; email: pot.concha@tiscali.co.uk)

Trustees: Mrs J. M. Norton; Mr F. W. Jakes; Mrs J. M. Way; Mr M. Horgan; Mr M. Ansell; Mrs R. Burmo; Mr C. Belcher; Revd Mrs G. Smith.

CC Number: 201073

Eligibility

People in need who live in the parish of Potton.

Types of grants

Grants given according to need.

Annual grant total

In 2010/11 grants to individuals for welfare purposes totalled £1,100.

Applications

Directly by the individual on a form available from the correspondent. Applications are considered in November and should be received by 31 October.

Ravensden

The Ravensden Town and Poor Estate

£3,000

Correspondent: Michael Day, Fairfield, Church End, Ravensden, Bedford MK44 2RP (email: mike.day@ cleverpelican.net)

Trustees: Revd Sheila Morton; Helena Walker; Michael Christopher Rock; Paul Woodcraft; Michael Day.

CC Number: 200164

Eligibility

Older people who are in need and live in the parish of Ravensden.

Types of grants

One-off and recurrent grants according to need.

Annual grant total

Grants usually total about £3,000 each year.

Applications

In writing to the correspondent. Applications can be submitted directly by the individual. They are usually considered in November, although urgent cases can be responded to at any time.

Other information

This charity also gives grants to a local school.

Shefford

The Charity of Robert Lucas for the Poor and for Public Purposes

£1,000

Correspondent: Keith Bland, 47 Lucas Way, Shefford, Bedfordshire SG17 5DX (01462 812870)

Trustees: John Ford; Jean Mack; John Donovan; Mary Faircloth; Jennifer Harrison; Colin Smith; Lorna McGregor.

CC Number: 204345

Eligibility

People in need who live in the ancient township of Shefford.

Types of grants

One-off or recurrent grants for needs which cannot be met by statutory sources.

Annual grant total

About £1,000 to individuals.

Applications

In writing to the correspondent. Applications should be submitted directly by the individual and are considered every two months.

Other information

The charity primarily makes grants to organisations.

Berkshire

The Earley Charity

£12,000 (56 grants)

Correspondent: Jane Wittig, The Liberty of Earley House, Strand Way, Earley, Reading RG6 4EA (01189 755663; fax: 01189 752263; email: enquiries@ earleycharity.org.uk; website: www. earleycharity.org.uk)

Trustees: Robert Edward Ames; Dr David Christopher Sutton; Dr Deborah

Gwendoline Jenkins; Miryam Eastwell; Philip Reginald Hooper; Lesley Owen; Bobbie Richardson; Richard Rodway.

CC Number: 244823

Eligibility

People in need who have lived in Earley and the surrounding neighbourhood for at least six months. Applicants must be living in permanent accommodation and have UK citizenship or have been granted indefinite leave to remain in the UK.

Types of grants

One-off grants according to need. Recent grants have been given for stairlifts, gardening tools; specialist computer software, laptop computer, counselling sessions, white goods and beds/mattresses.

Annual grant total

In 2011 the trust had assets of £12 million and an income of £1.1 million. Grants to 56 individuals totalled £12,000.

Exclusions

No grants can be made to those who are planning to move out of the area of benefit, have been awarded a grant within the last two years or have received three grants in the past.

Applications

On a form available from the correspondent to be submitted either directly by the individual or through a social worker, Citizens Advice or other welfare agency. Applications are considered eight times a year, though requests for grants of less than £500 may be dealt with more quickly. Meeting and deadline dates are published on the website.

Other information

Grants are also made to organisations (£466,000 in 2011).

The Finchampstead and Barkham Relief-in-Sickness Fund

£1,900

Correspondent: Dr John Dewhurst, Fourwinds, The Ridges, Finchampstead, Wokingham, Berkshire RG40 3SY (01189 732783; email: john.dewhurst1@tiscali. co.uk)

Trustees: Peter Sinclair Frederick Jourdan; Dr John Kesteven Dewhurst; Wally Chapman; Julie Anne Riddell; Dr Gaynor Popplestone.

CC Number: 259206

Eligibility

People in need who are sick, convalescent, who have mental or

physical disabilities, or who are infirm and who live in the parish of Finchampstead and Barkham.

Types of grants

One-off grants ranging from £100 to £1,000 towards the cost of, for example, electric goods, convalescence, clothing, living costs, household bills, food, holidays, travel expenses, medical equipment, nursing fees, furniture, equipment, help in the home and respite care.

Annual grant total

Grants average around £2,000 a year.

Exclusions

No grants for relief of rates or taxes. Grants cannot be repeated or renewed.

Applications

In writing to the correspondent including confirmation of eligibility. Applications can be made directly by the individual, through a social worker, Citizens Advice or other welfare agency or through a third party on behalf of the individual. Applications can be submitted throughout the year.

The Polehampton Charity

£2,200

Correspondent: Miss E Treadwell, Assistant Clerk, 114 Victoria Road, Wargrave, Berkshire RG10 8AE (website: www.thepolehamptoncharity.co.uk)

Trustees: Douglas Norris; James Weaver; Richard Fort; Janet Potter; Rosemary Pratt; David Turner; Robert Collett; William Treadwell; Simon Howard; Nic Downes; Rosie Chapman.

CC Number: 1072631

Eligibility

People in need who live in Twyford and Ruscombe.

Types of grants

One-off grants of £100 to £250 for items such as clothing, domestic appliances, holidays, medical equipment, furniture and equipment for people who are disabled.

Annual grant total

In 2011 the charity had assets of £2.3 million and an income of £97,000. Grants to individuals for education totalled £2,500 and for other purposes totalled £2,200.

Applications

Applications should be submitted either directly by the individual or a family member, through a third party such as a social worker or teacher, or through and organisation such as Citizens Advice or a school. Applications can be made at any time and are considered at trustee meetings.

Other information

Grants are also made to local schools and organisations.

Reading Dispensary Trust

£24,000

Correspondent: Walter Gilbert, Clerk, 16 Wokingham Road, Reading RG6 1JQ (01189 265698; email: admin@rdt. btconnect.com)

Trustees: Ian Hammond; Jim Durlin; Jean Horrocks; Norman Ross; A. Hendry; Jean Turton; Barbara Hirst; Denis Jones; Erina Titcomb; Judy Warwick; Geoff Chivers; Tom Lynch; Janet Wignall; Francis Read.

CC Number: 203943

Eligibility

People in need who are in poor health, convalescent or who have a physical or mental disability or illness and live in Reading and the surrounding area (roughly within a seven-mile radius of the centre of Reading).

Types of grants

One-off grants of on average around £200, for a wide range of needs including beds and bedding, counselling, clothing and footwear, computer equipment and software, cooking equipment, course fees, food vouchers, furniture and carpets, glasses, instruments, holidays, travel, respite care, house and garden adaptations, repairs and redecoration, theraputic assessments, play schemes, white goods and equipment, removals, baby and child equipment, disability and access equipment, play equipment and wheelchairs and scooters.

Annual grant total

In 2011 the trust had assets of £1.1 million and an income of £46,000. There were 163 grants to individuals totalling £25,000 with the majority being given for welfare purposes, and some for education.

Applications

On a form available from the correspondent. Applications should be submitted directly by the individual or through a social worker, Citizens Advice or other third party. They are considered on a monthly basis.

Other information

Grants are also made to organisations although the trust focuses on grants to individuals.

The Slough and District Community Fund

£5,000

Correspondent: John Brooks, 14 Shaggy Calf Lane, Slough SL2 5HJ (01753 530101)

Trustees: Gillian Brooks; Maureen Callaway; John Brooks; Sue Hann; Marilyn Fisher; David Nicks.

CC Number: 201598

Eligibility

People who are in need and live in Slough, New Windsor and Eton.

Types of grants

One-off grants according to need. Recent grants have been given towards household items, clothing, food and fuel costs, child and baby expenses and so on.

Annual grant total

In 2010 the fund had an income of £4,000 and a total expenditure of £6,000.

Applications

On a form available from the correspondent.

Other information

This trust was formed by the amalgamation of 'All Good Causes' and 'The Slough Nursing Fund'.

The Wokingham United Charities

£5,000

Correspondent: P Robinson, Clerk, 66 Upper Broadmoor Road, Crowthorne, Berkshire RG45 7DF (01344 351207; email: peter.westende@btinternet.com)

Trustees: Mr G. Cockroft; Mr R. Wyatt; Mr J. Tobin; Mr G. Brown; Mr D. Auger; Mrs P. Cox; Mr J. Ellis; Mr D. Eyriey; Mr M. Hall; Dr C. Gallagher; Mr A. King; Mrs G. Hewetson; Mr G. Veitch.

CC Number: 1107171

Eligibility

People in need who live in the civil parishes of Wokingham, Wokingham Without, St Nicholas, Hurst, Ruscombe and that part of Finchampstead known as Finchampstead North.

Types of grants

One-off grants between £25 and £150. Grants have been given towards household items, utility arrears and clothing.

Annual grant total

Grants usually total around £10,000 a year.

Applications

On a form available from the correspondent. Applications are considered each month (except August) and can be submitted directly by the individual, or through a social worker, school liaison officer or similar third party.

Binfield

The Muir Family Charitable Trust

£6,000

Correspondent: The Trustees, SG Hambros Trust Company Ltd, Norfolk House, 31 St James's Square, London SW1Y 4JR (020 7597 3060)

Trustees: Lady Rosemary Muir; Alexander Muir; Simon Muir; SG. Hambros Trust Co. Ltd.

CC Number: 255372

Eligibility

Older people who are in need.

Types of grants

One-off and recurrent grants ranging from £300 to £1,500.

Annual grant total

In 2010/11 the trust had an income of £8,000 and a total expenditure of £12,000. Grants are made to both organisations and individuals.

Applications

In writing to the correspondent.

Other information

The trust is also known by its registered name 'The Fritillary Trust' though it uses 'The Muir Family Charitable Trust' as its working name.

Datchet

The Datchet United Charities

£3,200

Correspondent: Gwenna Mary Howard, 59 London Road, Datchet, Slough SL3 9JY (01753 541883; email: gwennahoward@btinternet.com)

Trustees: Ivy Barbara Richards; Jean Marion Pinkerton; Timothy Anthony Joseph O'Flynn; Revd Peter Ward; Helen Sonia Dalton.

CC Number: 235891

Eligibility

People in need who live in the ancient parish of Datchet.

Types of grants

Grants of £15 to £1,500 are given for clothing, fuel bills, living costs, food, holidays, travel expenses and household bills. Christmas vouchers are also distributed.

Annual grant total

In 2010/11 the charities had assets of £642,000 and an income of £26,000. Grants were made to individuals totalling £3,200. A further £12,000 was given to organisations.

Applications

In writing to the correspondent either directly by the individual or through a social worker, Citizens Advice or other welfare agency. All applicants will be visited by the charities' social worker.

Other information

The trust also owns a day centre which local groups are able to use for free, loans medical equipment from its emergency centre and supports a 'people to places' car scheme.

Hedgerley
The Tracy Trust

£17,000

Correspondent: Jim Cannon, 21 Ingleglen, Farnham Common, Slough, Bucks SL2 3QA (01753 643930)

Trustees: Dr John Arthur Lunn; Jim Cannon; Chris Woodwark.

CC Number: 803103

Eligibility

People of a pensionable age who are in need and live in the parish of Hedgerley.

Types of grants

One-off grants towards medical and welfare needs such as, spectacles, chiropody, hospital travel costs, aid alarms, TV licences, stairlifts and so on.

Annual grant total

In 2010/11 the trust had an income of £22,000 and a total expenditure of £19,000.

Applications

In writing to the correspondent.

Newbury
Newbury and Thatcham Welfare Trust

£2,000

Correspondent: Jacqui Letsome, Volunteer Centre West Berkshire, 1 Bolton Place, Northbrook Street, Newbury, Berkshire RG14 1AJ (07917 414376; email: ntwt@hotmail.com)

Trustees: Alan Vince; Clifford Willis; Elizabeth Leigh; Garry Poulson; Philip Williams; Peter Gildersleeves; Sue Kitchener; Dr Geoffrey Shillam.

CC Number: 235077

Eligibility

People in need who are sick, disabled, convalescent or infirm and live in the former borough of Newbury as constituted on 31 March 1974 and the parishes of Greenham, Enborne, Hampstead, Marshall, Shaw-cum-Donnington, Speen and Thatcham.

Types of grants

One-off grants up to £250. Grants given include those for medical aids, food, holidays, respite care, travel, special equipment, TV licences, furniture and appliances.

Annual grant total

In 2010 the trust had an income of £2,800 and a total expenditure of £2,300.

Exclusions

Grants are not given towards housing or rent costs and debts.

Applications

By application form submitted either through a social worker, Citizens Advice or other welfare agency or through a third party on behalf of an individual such as a doctor, health visitor or other health professional. They can be considered at any time.

Reading
St Laurence Relief in Need Trust

£1,400 (7 grants)

Correspondent: C Hubbard, Clerk, c/o Vale and West, Victoria House, 26 Queen Victoria Street, Reading RG1 1TG (01189 573238)

Trustees: Patricia Thomas; Canon Brian Shenton; Cllr Rosemary Phyllis Williams; Revd Christopher Ian Russell; Lorraine Claire Joslin; Stewart Hotston; Nicholas Charles Burrows.

CC Number: 205043

Eligibility

People in need who live in the ancient parish of St Laurence in Reading. Surplus money can be given to people living in the county borough of Reading.

Types of grants

One-off and annual grants are awarded according to need. The minimum grant is £100.

Annual grant total

In 2011 the trust held assets of £129,000 and an income of £56,000. Grants to seven individuals totalled £1,400.

Exclusions

Grants are not made to students for training, research grants or to people not resident in the area of benefit.

Applications

In writing to the correspondent including details of requirements and place of residence. Applications can be made directly by the individual or by a third party such as a social worker or Citizens Advice. They are generally considered in April and November.

Other information

The trust also gives predominantly to organisations (£58,000 in 2011).

Sunninghill
Sunninghill Fuel Allotment Trust

£4,400 (14 grants)

Correspondent: Richard J Dugdale, 101 Victoria Road, Ascot, Berkshire SL5 9DS (01344 620614; email: r723@btinternet.com)

Trustees: Gary Alan Morris; Nigel Henry Green; Roger Goodwin Bailey; Ruth Louise Fettes; Revd Stephen Ashley Johnson.

CC Number: 240061

Eligibility

People in need who live in the parish of Sunninghill.

Types of grants

One-off grants ranging from about £100 to £1,000. Recent awards have been made to relieve sudden distress, to purchase essential equipment or household appliances and to cover utility bills.

Annual grant total

In 2010/11 the trust had assets of £2.6 million and an income of £79,000. Grants to 14 individuals totalled £4,400.

Applications

In writing to the correspondent either directly by the individual or through a third party such as a social worker, Citizens Advice or similar welfare agency. The trustees meet four times a year to consider applications, though urgent cases may be dealt with between meetings. Applicants should be prepared to provide documentary evidence of their difficulties and circumstances.

Other information

The majority of the trust's charitable giving is to organisations (£48,000 in 2010/11).

Buckingham-shire

1067 Trust Fund

£1,000

Correspondent: David Tracey, Uplands, New Road, Bourne End, Buckinghamshire SL8 5BY (01628 528699; email: tracey@brantridge.net)

Trustees: Mr D. J. Watts; Douglas Fergusson; Mr P. Yeeles; Mr B. Spires; Mr D. E. Tracey.

CC Number: 294975

Eligibility

People in need who live in the parishes of Wooburn, Little Marlow, Flackwell Heath, Hedsor, Bourn End and Loudwater (south of the A40).

Types of grants

One-off grants in the approximate range of £30 to £500 for utilities, rent, household essentials, medical costs and so on.

Annual grant total

Grants were around £1,000.

Applications

In writing to the correspondent. Applications should be made either through a social worker, Citizens Advice or other welfare agency or directly by the individual or a third party on behalf on an individual. Applications can be submitted at any time for consideration in March, June, September or December. Emergency applications can be considered at any time.

The Amersham United Charities

£0

Correspondent: C Atkinson, 25 Milton Lawns, Amersham, Buckinghamshire HP6 6BJ (01494 723416)

Trustees: Miss P. A. Appleby; Mrs G. Bungey; Mr E. Newhouse; Miss B. Webber; Revd T. Harper; Mrs L. Hollett; Mr S. Partridge; Mr P. Gray.

CC Number: 205033

Eligibility

Persons who are in need of financial assistance and are resident in the parishes of Amersham and Coleshill, Buckinghamshire.

Types of grants

One-off grants to relieve persons who are in need, hardship or distress.

Annual grant total

Although no grants have been made in recent years, the correspondent has stated that the charity is open to applications from individuals for relief in need and education.

Applications

In writing to the correspondent.

Other information

The main work of the charity is the administration and management of 13 almshouses.

The Iver Heath Sick Poor Fund

£1,300

Correspondent: John Shepherd, Loch Luichart, Bangors Road North, Iver SL0 0BN (01753 651398)

Trustees: Martin Jonathan Southgate Sands; Jean Pearson-Hall; Madeleine Mayling; Margaret Green; John A shepherd.

CC Number: 231111

Eligibility

People who are sick, convalescing, physically or mentally disabled or infirm and who live in the Iver Heath ward of the parish of Iver and part of the parish of Wexham.

Types of grants

Usually one-off grants for clothing, medical needs, home help, fuel, lighting, chiropody and other necessities, although recurrent grants will be considered.

Annual grant total

Income averages just over £3,000 while total expenditure averages around £1,700 each year.

Applications

In writing to the correspondent. Applications are considered twice a year in spring and autumn, although in emergencies they can be considered at other times.

The Salford Town Lands

£4,000

Correspondent: Julian Barrett, South Cottage, 18 Broughton Road, Salford, Milton Keynes MK17 8BH (01908 583494)

Trustees: Julian Barrett; Revd Hugh; Kathleen Draycott; Christopher Hall; Kevin Burke; Robert Harrison.

CC Number: 256465

Eligibility

People in need who live in the parish of Hulcote and Salford.

Types of grants

Grants are made for social purposes and to individuals for the relief of need, hardship and distress. Donations are usually one-off ranging from £60 to £200, including those for older people at Christmas and children's Christmas tokens.

Annual grant total

Previously about £5,000.

Applications

In writing to the correspondent. Applications can be submitted directly by the individual or through any other parishioner.

Other information

Grants are also made to organisations supporting the community.

The Stoke Mandeville and Other Parishes Charity

£10,000

Correspondent: Caroline Dobson, 17 Elham Way, Aylesbury HP21 9XN (01296 431859)

Trustees: Angela Norris; Barbara Ezra; David Brown; Peter Pugh; Robin Hunt; Stuart Allen; Paul Walter.

CC Number: 296174

Eligibility

People in need who live in the parishes of Stoke Mandeville, Great and Little Hampden and Great Missenden.

Types of grants

Annual Christmas grants to people over 70 and one-off grants to people who are disabled for specific needs such as wheelchairs or stairlifts.

Annual grant total

In 2011 the charity had assets of £1.8 million and an income of £85,000. Welfare grants totalled £10,000 comprising £8,900 in Christmas grants and £1,100 for senior railcards.

Applications

On a form available from the correspondent, considered in January, April, July and October.

Other information

The charity also gives grants to organisations and to individuals for education.

Tyringham Pension Fund for the Blind

£1,500

Correspondent: Vanessa Jones, Trustee, 6 St Faiths Close, Newton Longville, Milton Keynes MK17 0BA (01908 643816)

Trustees: Marianne Harding; Janet Rowe; Vanessa Jones; Diana Fitchett.

CC Number: 210332

Eligibility

People in need who are blind or partially sighted and live in Newton Pagnell and Wolverton.

Types of grants

Pensions of around £100 per year.

Annual grant total

Grants usually total about £1,500 each year.

Applications

Applications should not be made directly to the trust. Individuals should contact Buckinghamshire Association for the Blind (Tel. 01296 487556), who will approach the trust on their behalf.

Wooburn, Bourne End and District Relief-in-Sickness Charity

£16,000

Correspondent: Dorothea Heyes, 11 Telston Close, Bourne End, Buckingham SL8 5TY (01628 523498)

Trustees: Revd Ann Trew; Dr Elizabeth Bailey; Jean Eileen Elizabeth Peasley; Revd Martin Wallington; Mike Woolliams; Dr Sarah Buxton; Dr Janet Hopewell; Margaret Marshall.

CC Number: 210596

Eligibility

People who live in the parishes of Wooburn, Bourne End, Hedsor or parts of Little Marlow who are sick, convalescent, physically or mentally disabled or infirm.

Types of grants

One-off grants and gift vouchers in the range of £50 to £400 for telephone installation, help with nursing costs, convalescence, holidays, home help and other necessities. All items for which a grant is requested must have a direct connection with the applicant's illness.

Annual grant total

In 2010 the charity had an income of £14,000 and a total expenditure of £18,000.

Exclusions

No recurrent grants are given.

Applications

In writing to the correspondent through a doctor, health visitor, priest or other third party. Applications are considered throughout the year and should contain details of the nature of illness or disability.

Aylesbury
Elizabeth Eman Trust

£51,000

Correspondent: Neil Freeman, Horwood and James, 7 Temple Square, Aylesbury, Buckinghamshire HP20 2QB (01296 487361; email: enquiries@horwoodjames.co.uk; website: www.emans.co.uk)

Trustees: Jenny Puddefoot; Alan Sherwell; Tony Bayes; Leonora Pike; Lt Col John Williams.

CC Number: 215511

Eligibility

Due to the expansion of the trust both men and women living in Aylesbury Vale are eligible, however, priority is still given to people born in Aylesbury.

Types of grants

Allowances of £111 per quarter. Grants are for life.

Annual grant total

In 2010 the charity had assets of £621,000 and an income of £61,000. Annuities to pensioners totalled £51,000.

Applications

Applications can be made online through the trust's website. Alternatively, potential applicants can contact the correspondent or call 01296 487361 and ask for Mrs S Batchelor. Original birth, marriage and husband's death certificates should be included as appropriate.

Thomas Hickman's Charity

£28,000

Correspondent: John Leggett, Parrott and Coales, 14–16 Bourbon Street, Aylesbury, Buckinghamshire HP20 2RS (01296 318500; email: doudjag@pandclip.co.uk)

Trustees: Graham Aylett; Tim Voss; Shane Wood; Elizabeth Mossford; Roger Harwood.

CC Number: 202973

Eligibility

People in need who live in Aylesbury town.

Types of grants

One-off grants according to need.

Annual grant total

In 2011 the charity had assets of £16 million and an income of £601,000. Grants were made to 144 individuals totalling £53,000.

Applications

On a form available from the correspondent. Applications should be submitted either directly by the individual or a family member, through a third party such as social worker or school, or through an organisation such as Citizens Advice or a school. Trustees meet on a regular basis and applications are considered as they arise.

Other information

The charity also provides almshouses and gives grants to individuals for education.

Bletchley
The Poor's Allotments Charity

£1,500

Correspondent: Mrs E A Cumberland, 9 Katrine Place, Bletchley, Milton Keynes MK2 3DW (01908 642713)

Trustees: Jan Lloyd; Eileen Mary Bourne; Elizabeth Alice Cumberland; Reginald William Edwards.

CC Number: 240164

Eligibility

People in need who live in the MK3 area of Bletchley. Beneficiaries tend mainly to be older people.

Types of grants

Christmas grants of around £30 per family.

Annual grant total

Grants usually total about £1,300 each year.

Applications

In writing to the correspondent to be submitted either directly by the individual or through a third party such as a social worker. Applications are normally considered in November and should be received by the end of October.

Calverton

Calverton Apprenticing Charity

£1,000

Correspondent: Karen Phillips, 78 London Road, Stony Stratford, Milton Keynes MK11 1JH (01908 563350; email: karen.phillips20@yahoo.co.uk)

Trustees: Revd R. Northing; Mr C. H. Sherwood; Mr M. J. Luckett; Mrs D. L. West; Mrs J. Hildreth; J. Hayter.

CC Number: 239246

Eligibility

People in need who have lived in the parish of All Saints, Calverton for at least five years. Preference is given to widows and those over 65.

Types of grants

Grants in the range of £100 to £150 are awarded for items such as clothing, medical equipment, nursing fees, furniture, heating and so on.

Annual grant total

Grants for welfare purposes usually total around £1,000 each year.

Applications

On a form available from the correspondent, to be submitted either directly by the individual or a family member.

Other information

The charity also makes grants to organisations and to individuals for educational purposes.

Cheddington

Cheddington Town Lands Charity

£4,000

Correspondent: Stuart Minall, 10 Hillside, Cheddington, Leighton Buzzard LU7 0SP (01296 661987)

Trustees: Patricia Bannister; Stephen Fox; Stuart Minall; Revd Robert Wright.

CC Number: 235076

Eligibility

People in need who live in Cheddington.

Types of grants

One-off and recurrent grants according to need.

Annual grant total

Grants usually total around £4,000.

Applications

In writing to the correspondent, directly by the individual or a family member.

Emberton

Emberton United Charity

£1,500

Correspondent: Jeremy Howson, Trustee, 14 Gravel Walk, Emberton, Olney MK46 5JA (01234 712042)

Trustees: Jeremy Howson; W. Clarke; Gerald Mann; Susan Soul; Judith Taylor.

CC Number: 204221

Eligibility

Older people in need who live in the parish of Emberton.

Types of grants

One-off and recurrent grants, usually of up to £350.

Annual grant total

In 2011 the charity had an income of £22,000 and an expenditure of £11,000. Previously welfare grants have totalled around £1,500.

Applications

In writing to the correspondent, directly by the individual.

Other information

Grants are also given for educational purposes.

Great Linford

Great Linford Relief in Need Charity

£500

Correspondent: Michael Williamson, 2 Lodge Gate, Great Linford, Milton Keynes MK14 5EW (01908 605664)

Trustees: David Enticknap; Joan Wilson; Sandie Jenner; Edward Pawley; Michael Williamson; Revd Peter Ballantine.

CC Number: 237373

Eligibility

People in need who live in the parish of Great Linford.

Types of grants

One-off grants of up to £200. Grants have been given towards educational activities and to assist with the cost of sheltered housing.

Annual grant total

Grants usually total about £500 each year.

Applications

On a form available from the charity. Applications can be submitted either directly by the individual or through a social worker, Citizens Advice, other welfare agency or a third party such as a relative, teacher or carer. Applications are usually considered in January, June and September.

High Wycombe

The High Wycombe Central Aid Society

£4,400

Correspondent: Clyde Perkins, Secretary, West Richardson Street, High Wycombe, Buckinghamshire HP11 2SB (01494 535890; fax: 01494 538256; email: office@central-aid.org.uk; website: www.central-aid.org.uk)

Trustees: Margaret Stagg; Eric Hardy; Bill Reid; Patricia Mary Brown; Len Monk; Rosemary Vere; Michael Wood; Geoffrey Pearson; Christine Porter.

CC Number: 201445

Eligibility

People in need, usually older people and those in receipt of benefits, who live in the old borough of High Wycombe. The society will also help ex-service personnel and their dependents.

Types of grants

Mainly one-off grants in kind and gift vouchers to a maximum of £100. Recent grants have been given for food, clothing and furniture.

Annual grant total

In 2009/10 the society had assets of £409,000 and an income of £103,000. Grants were made totalling £4,400, the majority of which (£3,700) was made through the furniture warehouse operated by the society.

Exclusions

No grants towards council tax.

Applications

In writing to the correspondent including details of income, savings, family situation and a quote for the goods needed along with any relevant supporting documents. Applications can be submitted through a social worker, Citizens Advice or other welfare agency and are considered on a monthly basis.

Other information

The society also runs a Pensioners Pop-In for people over 50 twice a week and facilitates a division of SSAFA Forces help.

The society also has a second-hand furniture warehouse and clothes and soft furnishings store (Tel: 01494 443459 email: furniture@central-aid.org.uk).

Hitcham

Hitcham Poor Lands Charity

£7,000

Correspondent: Donald Cecil Lindskog, Little Orchard, Poyle Lane, Burnham, Slough SL1 8JZ (01628 605652)

Trustees: Donald Cecil Lindskog; Hilary Pauline Evans; Judith Foster; Margaret Jean Horwood; Nicola Jane Allen.

CC Number: 203447

Eligibility

People in need who live in the parishes of Hitcham, Burnham and Cippenham.

Types of grants

Grants in kind including furniture, white goods and so on. Around 300 Christmas parcels are also distributed each year.

Annual grant total

In 2010/11 the trust had both an income and expenditure of £8,000.

Applications

In writing to the correspondent. Applications can be submitted directly by the individual or through a third party such as Citizens Advice or a social worker. There are no deadlines for applications and they are considered frequently.

Other information

The charity also makes grants to organisations that support people in Burnham such as the Burnham Righthouse Project and Thames Hospice Care.

Radnage

Radnage Charity

£5,000

Correspondent: I K Blaylock, Clerk to the Trustees, Hilltop, Green End Road, Radnage, High Wycombe, Buckinghamshire HP14 4BY (01494 483346)

Trustees: Revd Nigel Lacey; Caroline Strange; Lindsay Wilcox; Richard Wheeler; Bill Guidery; Rosemary Oliphant; Linsay Welham.

CC Number: 201762

Eligibility

People in need who live in the parish of Radnage.

Types of grants

One-off and recurrent grants of around £50 to £200. Recent grants have been given towards hospital visits and food.

Annual grant total

In 2011 the trust had both an income and expenditure of £10,000. Grants usually total about £5,000 per year.

Applications

In writing to the correspondent either directly by the individual or through a social worker, Citizens Advice or other third party.

Other information

The trust also contributes to the upkeep of the twelfth-century parish church.

Stoke Poges

Stoke Poges United Charities

£2,000

Correspondent: Anthony Levings, Clerk, The Cedars, Stratford Drive, Wooburn Green, High Wycombe HP10 0QH (01628 524342)

Trustees: Trevor Egleton; Susan Lynch; Michael Dier; Chris Morris; Raymond Aldridge; Henry Latham; Hemantha Kumar.

CC Number: 205289

Eligibility

People in need who live in the parish of Stoke Poges, including parts of the parish of Slough Borough – Stoke wards. Preference is given to widows and people who are sick.

Types of grants

Grants of £30 to £1,500 can be given for clothing, food, household necessities, medical care and equipment.

Annual grant total

In 2011 the charity had assets of £431,000 and an income of £29,000. Grants to six individuals for welfare and education totalled £3,500.

Applications

In writing to the correspondent, to be submitted either directly by the individual or through a social worker, Citizens Advice, other welfare agency or any third party.

Stony Stratford

The Ancell Trust

£5,500

Correspondent: Karen Phillips, Secretary, 78 London Road, Stony Stratford, Milton Keynes MK11 1JH (01908 563350; email: karen.phillips20@yahoo.co.uk)

Trustees: Rosemary Dytham; Susan Starr; Michael Benham; Patricia Eales; Brian Faulkner; Lawrence Francis; Robert Ayers; Sheila Brazell; Wendy Cowley; Barbara Bird; Dr Kenneth Chambers.

CC Number: 233824

Eligibility

People in need in the town of Stony Stratford.

Types of grants

Grants are given to students for books and are occasionally made to individuals for welfare purposes and to organisations.

Annual grant total

In 2010/11 the trust had an income of £8,200 and a total expenditure of £11,000.

Applications

In writing to the correspondent at any time.

Water Eaton

Fuel Allotment

£1,500

Correspondent: Mrs E A Cumberland, 9 Katrine Place, Bletchley, Milton Keynes MK2 3DW

Trustees: Jan Lloyd; Eileen Mary Bourne; Elizabeth Alice Cumberland; Reginald William Edwards.

CC Number: 251127

Eligibility

People of pensionable age who live in Water Eaton.

Types of grants

Pensions of between £10 and £12.

Annual grant total

Grants usually total around £1,200 per year.

Applications

In writing to the correspondent for consideration in November.

Wolverton

The Catherine Featherstone Charity

£3,000

Correspondent: Miss K Phillips, Secretary, 78 London Road, Stony Stratford, Milton Keynes, Buckinghamshire MK11 1JH (01908

563350; email: karen.phillips20@yahoo.co.uk)

Trustees: Eric John Mayo; Jean Atter; Kenneth William Dunckley.

CC Number: 242620

Eligibility

People in need who live in the ancient parish of Wolverton.

Types of grants

One-off and recurrent grants ranging from £150 to £500. Recent grants have been given for household bills, food, medical and disability equipment, electrical goods, living costs and home help.

Annual grant total

In 2011 the charity had an income of £8,400 and a total expenditure of £3,400.

Applications

On a form available from the correspondent, to be submitted either directly by the individual or through a social worker, Citizens Advice or other welfare agency. Applications are considered in March, July and October.

Cambridge-shire

Cambridgeshire Children's Fund

Correspondent: Cambridgeshire Community Foundation, Administrator, The Quorum, Barnwell Road, Cambridge C85 8RE (01223 410535; email: info@cambscf.org.uk; website: www.cambscf.org.uk/cambridgeshire-childrens-fund.html)

Trustees: John Bridge; Nigel Atkinson; Allyson Broadhurst; Anthony Clay; Jerry Turner; William Dastur; Richard Barnwell; Anne Ridgeon; Peter Gutteridge; Sam Weller; Mick Leggett; Neil McKittrick; Christopher Belcher.

CC Number: 1103314

Eligibility

Families on low incomes with disadvantaged children in Cambridgeshire. Families must be experiencing additional difficulties such as domestic violence, mental health issues or addiction.

Types of grants

Grants of £100 to £150 for essential items for children such as clothing, disability equipment, baby items and bedding.

Annual grant total

A grants total was not available.

Exclusions

No support is given for rent/mortgage payments, catalogue debts, credit card debts, loan repayments or court costs and fines.

Applications

On a form available to download from the Cambridge Community foundation website, which must be submitted via a sponsoring organisation working with families in Cambridgeshire, such as Sure Start, a housing association or social services, and cheques will be made to the sponsoring organisation. Only one grant request can be made from each family per year. Applicants will hear of a decision by email within two to three weeks.

Other information

This fund is administered by Cambridgeshire Community Foundation, which also gives grants to organisations.

The Farthing Trust

£10,600

Correspondent: Heber Martin, PO Box 277, Cambridge CB7 9DE

Trustees: E. Martin; C. H. Martin; A. White; J. Martin.

CC Number: 268066

Eligibility

People in need, with a priority given to those either personally known to the trustees or recommended by those personally known to the trustees.

Types of grants

One-off and recurrent grants are given to meet 'charitable causes' in the UK and overseas.

Annual grant total

In 2010/11 the trust had assets of £3 million and an income of £116,000. Grants were made totalling £181,000, of which £10,600 was given to individuals in both the UK and abroad. The remaining £170,000 was awarded to organisations in the UK and overseas.

Applications

In writing to the correspondent. Applications can be submitted directly by the individual or through a social worker, Citizens Advice or other welfare agency. They are considered quarterly. Note applicants will only be notified of a refusal if an sae is enclosed.

Other information

The trusts states that it receives around ten letters a week and is able to help about 1 in 100. Therefore success is unlikely unless a personal contact with a trustee is established.

The Leverington Town Lands Charity

£9,000

Correspondent: Mrs R J Gagen, 78 High Road, Gorefield, Wisbech, Cambridgeshire PE13 4NB (01945 870454; email: levfeoffees@aol.com)

Trustees: David Henry Newling; John Rawson Maxey; Kitty Hall; Mervyn Ronald Baker; Robert Littlechild; Susan Robb; Mr B. T. Hunt; Mrs Lenton; Mr R. W. Gent; Michael John Humphrey; Mr S. W. Fisher; Mr E. Newling; Angela Kett; Jennifer Everall.

CC Number: 232526

Eligibility

People in need who live in the parishes of Leverington, Gorefield and Newton.

Types of grants

One-off grants towards, for example, glasses, new teeth or household appliances.

Annual grant total

In 2010/11 the charity held assets totalling £967,000 and an income of £42,000. Grants were made totalling £9,000.

Applications

On a form available from the correspondent. Applications are considered in May and November.

The Upwell (Cambridgeshire) Consolidated Charities

£3,500

Correspondent: Ronald Stannard, Riverside Farm, Birchfield Road, Nordelph, Downham Market, Norfolk PE38 0BP (01366 324217; email: ronstannard@waitrose.com)

Trustees: Roland Singleterry; Revd Alan Jesson; Christopher Crofts; Hazel Medlock; Jill Bliss; John Sparrow; Malcolm Hicks.

CC Number: 203558

Eligibility

People in need who are over 65 (unless widowed) and live in the parish of Upwell (on the Isle of Ely) and have done so for at least five years.

Types of grants

Christmas grants in the range of £10 to £40.

Annual grant total

The trust has an average annual income of around £4,600 and a total expenditure of around £3,500.

Applications

In writing to the correspondent. Applications should be submitted directly by the individual and are considered in November.

Cambridge

The Cambridge Community Nursing Trust

£5,000

Correspondent: Mrs M Hoskins, 11 Rutherford Road, Cambridge CB2 8HH (01223 840259)

Trustees: Margaret Hoskins; Jan Young; Revd Peter Page; Sue Roe; Ida Ghelli; Carol Spelzini; Hiltrude Hall.

CC Number: 204933

Eligibility

People in need who live in the boundaries of the city of Cambridge.

Types of grants

Grants of up to around £300 are given to provide extra care, comforts and special aids which are not available from any other source.

Annual grant total

In 2010 the trust had an income of £6,000 and a total expenditure of £5,100.

Applications

In writing to the correspondent. Applications are considered as received. The correspondent is happy to speak to potential applicants over the telephone before an application is submitted.

Chatteris

The Chatteris Feoffee Charity

£3,000

Correspondent: Brian Hawden, Brian Hawden and Co. Solicitors, The Coach House, Beechwood Gardens, London Road, Chatteris, Cambridgeshire PE16 6PX (01354 692133; email: hawden.co@talktalkbusiness.net)

Trustees: Mr G. Setchfield; Miss L. Brooks; John Childs; Florence Newell; Richard John Angood; Mrs A. Moody; Irene Parish; June Manion Rickwood; Mrs M. Billimore; Stephen Glenn Mandley; Linda Jane Cox.

CC Number: 202150

Eligibility

People who are 'poor and needy' and have lived in Chatteris for at least ten years.

Types of grants

Grants of around £25 given annually in January.

Annual grant total

In 2010/11 the charity had an income of £4,200 and a total expenditure of £3,500.

Applications

In writing to the correspondent, or upon recommendation of a trustee.

Downham

The Downham Feoffee Charity

£1,000

Correspondent: Jo Howard, 35 Fieldside, Ely, Cambridgeshire CB6 3AT (01353 665774; email: downhamfeoffees@hotmail.co.uk)

Trustees: Philip Laver; Carole Hall; Helen May Last; Bruce Smith; Caroline Frankland; Pat Golding; Debbie Adams Payne; Owen Winters; Revd Margaret Talbot; Marlyn Oldfield; Nathaniel Missin.

CC Number: 237233

Eligibility

People in need who live in the ancient parish of Downham.

Types of grants

One-off and recurrent grants according to need.

Annual grant total

In 2010/11 the charity had assets of £3.8 million and an income of £74,000. Grants to individuals totalled around £1,000.

Applications

In writing to the correspondent.

Other information

The charity's main focus is the provision of housing and allotments. It also gives grants to local schools and organisations.

Elsworth

The Samuel Franklin Fund

£11,000

Correspondent: Helen Oborne, Low Farm, 45 Brook Street, Elsworth, Cambridge CB23 4HX (01954 267197; email: helenobornesft@googlemail.com)

Trustees: Ian Maddison; Annie Howell; Sue Taylor; Fiona Windsor; John Hicks; Lorna Knight.

CC Number: 228775

Eligibility

Children, young people, older people and families, who are in need and who live in the parish of Elsworth. Preference is given to older people, those who are facing financial difficulties and people affected by hardship who are disabled.

Types of grants

One-off or recurrent grants of £10 to £1,000 according to need towards hospital expenses, convalescence, household bills, medical equipment, nursing fees, disability equipment and home help. Christmas grants are also given.

Annual grant total

In 2011 the trust had an income of £32,000 and gave grants to 31 individuals totalling £12,000, most of which was given in welfare grants.

Applications

In writing to the correspondent including brief details of requirements.

Ely

Thomas Parson's Charity

£4,300

Correspondent: Secretary, Hall Ennion and Young, 8 High Street, Ely, Cambridgeshire CB7 4JY (01353 662918; fax: 01353 662747; email: john@heysolicitors.co.uk)

Trustees: Walter Bebbington; R. B. Bamford; Richard Oliver Setchell; Bishop Anthony; Revd Dr Michael John Chandler, Dean of Ely; David Joseph Brand; Anthony Morbey; John Michael Smith; John Anthony Webster; Archdeacon of Huntingdon and Wisbech Hugh Kyle McCurdy; Richard Hobbs.

CC Number: 202634

Eligibility

People in need who live in the city of Ely.

Types of grants

One-off and occasionally recurrent grants and loans, ranging from £1,000 to £4,000.

Annual grant total

In 2010/11 the charity had assets of £6 million and an income of £216,000. Grants were made totalling £4,300.

Applications

In writing to the correspondent, for consideration on the first Friday in each month. Applications can be submitted either directly by the individual, or through a social worker, Citizens Advice or other welfare agency.

Other information

The charity is primarily concerned with the management and maintenance of its almshouses.

Grantchester

The Grantchester Relief in Need Charity

£5,000

Correspondent: Allen Wheelwright, 67 Coton Road, Grantchester, Cambridge CB3 9NT

Trustees: Dr Jonathan Peter Graffy; Dorothy Mary Pauley; Allen Peter Wheelwright; Ian Campbell Steen; June Muriel Loosely.

CC Number: 202175

Eligibility

People in need who live in the ancient parish of Grantchester.

Types of grants

One-off grants according to need.

Annual grant total

In 2011 the charity had an income of £4,000 and a total expenditure of £11,300. While income has been relatively stable over the past number of years (around £5,000) expenditure has varied widely with no expenditure in 2009.

Applications

In writing to the correspondent.

Other information

The charity also makes grants to local organisations.

Hilton

Hilton Town Charity

£1,500

Correspondent: Mr Stephen Sheppard, 20 Chequers Croft, Hilton, Huntingdon PE28 9PD

Trustees: Ralph Slater; Joanne Turner; B. Ward; Revd David Busk; Elizabeth Bush.

CC Number: 209423

Eligibility

People who live in the village of Hilton, Cambridgeshire, of any age or occupation, who may have unforeseen needs, due to for example hardship, disability or sickness.

Types of grants

One-off grants according to need.

Annual grant total

In 2010 the charity had an income of £5,000 and a total expenditure of £7,500. On average about £3,000 is available in grants.

Applications

In writing to the correspondent.

Other information

Grants in the main are directed towards organisations that serve the direct needs of the village.

Ickleton

The Ickleton United Charities (Relief-in-Need Branch)

£4,500

Correspondent: John Statham, 35 Abbey Street, Ickleton, Saffron Walden, Essex CB10 1SS (01799 530258)

Trustees: Jocelyn Ann Flitton; Lewis Duke; Derek James Rule; Mary Wombwell; David Lilley.

CC Number: 202467

Eligibility

People in need who live in the parish of Ickleton, Cambridgeshire.

Types of grants

One-off grants of around £40 towards fuel costs and necessities, and gift vouchers at Christmas.

Annual grant total

In 2010 the trust had an income of £8,500 and a total expenditure of £4,800.

Applications

In writing to the correspondent to be submitted directly by the individual.

Landbeach

Rev Robert Masters Charity for Widows

£600

Correspondent: Brian Marshall, Trustee, Flat 2 Cootes Court, Cootes Lane, Fen Drayton, Cambridge CB24 4YP

Trustees: Dr Ray Gambell; Margaret Patricia Patterson; Brian Marshall; Revd Lucy Cleland; Neville Diver.

CC Number: 265254

Eligibility

People in need who live in the parish of Landbeach, with a preference for widows.

Types of grants

One-off and recurrent grants according to need.

Annual grant total

Grants total around £600 each year.

Applications

In writing to the correspondent.

Little Wilbraham

The Johnson Bede and Lane Charitable Trust

£1,500

Correspondent: Mrs J Collins, The Gate House, Church Road, Little Wilbraham, Cambridge CB21 5LE (01223 811465)

Trustees: Mrs J. Collins; Gillian Clifford; Monica Wells; Prudence Addecott; Madhu Davies; Linda Stead.

CC Number: 284444

Eligibility

People in need who live in the civil parish of Little Wilbraham.

Types of grants

One-off grants usually between £50 and £150 for a wide range of welfare needs.

Annual grant total

In 2010/11 the trust had an income of £4,400 and a total expenditure of £4,000. Grants to individuals usually total around £3,000.

Applications

In writing to the correspondent directly by the individual or by a third party such as a social worker, Citizens Advice or neighbour. Applications are considered on an ongoing basis.

Other information

Grants are also made to organisations.

Pampisford

Pampisford Relief-in-Need Charity

£3,000

Correspondent: Dennis Beaumont, Clerk, 4 Hammond Close, Pampisford, Cambridge CB22 3EP (01223 833653)

Trustees: Geoffrey Charles Peel; Mary Hunt; Mary Russen; Mary Christine Molton; Timothy Nixon; Revd Ruth Whitehead; Roger Turnbull.

CC Number: 275661

Eligibility

People in need who live in the parish of Pampisford.

Types of grants

People who are older or disabled may receive Christmas gifts or individual grants of up to £250. Contributions are also made for the improvement of village amenities, which can then be enjoyed by people who are older or disabled.

Annual grant total

Grants are mostly made to organisations, but about £3,000 is available each year for individuals.

Applications

In writing to the correspondent directly by the individual. Applications can be considered at any time.

Other information

Half of the charity's income goes to the Pampisford Ecclesiastical Charity.

Peterborough

The Florence Saunders Relief-in-Sickness Charity

£6,000

Correspondent: Paula Lawson, Stephenson House, 15 Church Walk, Peterborough PE1 2TP (01733 343275; email: paula.lawson@stephensonsmart. com)

Trustees: Barbara Howitt; Judy Sharman; Dr Keith Sampson; Margaret Osker; Sheila Marshall.

CC Number: 239177

Eligibility

People in need who are in poor health, convalescent, or who have disabilities and live in the former city of Peterborough.

Types of grants

One-off grants between £100 and £500 for hospital expenses, convalescence, holidays, travel expenses, electrical goods, medical equipment, furniture, disability equipment and help in the home.

Annual grant total

In 2010/11 the charity had both an income and expenditure of £6,400.

Exclusions

No grants are given for the repayment of debts.

Applications

In writing to the correspondent to be submitted either directly by the individual or through a third party such as a family member, social worker or other welfare agency. Applications are considered at trustees' meetings, usually held three times per year.

Other information

Grants are also made to organisations.

Sawston

John Huntingdon's Charity

£18,000 (140 grants)

Correspondent: Revd Mary Irish, Charity Manager, John Huntingdon House, Tannery Road, Sawston, Cambridge CB2 4UW (01223 492492; email: office@johnhuntingdon.org.uk)

Trustees: Thomas Butler; Susan Reynolds; Reg Cullum; Christine Ingham; Eugene Murray; Eleanor Clapp; Catherine Gilmore; Alan Partridge; David Baslington; Eileen Wheatley.

CC Number: 1118574

Eligibility

People in need who live in the parish of Sawston in Cambridgeshire.

Types of grants

One-off grants, usually ranging from £25 to £250. Grants can be given for essential household items such as cookers, beds or fridges, TV licences, holidays, household bills, food, clothing, travel expenses, medical equipment, debts, transport costs, and nursery/playgroup fees.

Annual grant total

In 2011 the charity had assets of £7.3 million, an income of £329,000 and gave grants to 140 individuals totalling £18,000.

Applications

On an application form available from Sawston Support Services at the address above or by telephone. Office opening hours are 9am to 2pm Monday to Friday.

Other information

Grants are also made to organisations and to individuals for education.

Soham

Soham United Charities

£5,000

Correspondent: Elizabeth Stevenson, Ivy House, 33 Pratt Street, Soham, Ely, Cambridgeshire CB7 5BH (01353 722884)

Trustees: Richard Gowing; Geoff Fisher; Revd Tim Jones; Anne Tuite; Philip Lane; Christopher Palmer; Clem Tompsett; Peter Taylor; Rosemary Aitchison.

CC Number: 202479

Eligibility

People in need of all ages who live in the parish of Soham.

Types of grants

One-off grants can be made for items and services such as furniture, bedding, clothing, food, tools, books, holidays, house decorating, insulation and repairs, laundering, meals on wheels, child-minding and so on.

Annual grant total

Grants to individuals total around £5,000 each year.

Exclusions

No grants towards education.

Applications

In writing to the correspondent directly by the individual. Applicants should include a financial statement giving details of assets and liabilities, and reasons in support of the application. They are usually considered in November and February. There is also an emergency committee which can meet during the rest of the year. The trustees will discuss and investigate in detail the circumstances arising for the grant to be requested before making any award.

Other information

Grants are also made to organisations.

Stetchworth

The Stetchworth Relief-in-Need Charity

£1,600

Correspondent: Judith Mahoney, 26 High Street, Stetchworth, Newmarket, Suffolk CB8 9TJ (01638 508336)

Trustees: Diana Taylor; Lily Pamela Whymer; Paula Jayne Wiseman; Sarah Shaw-Smith.

CC Number: 245790

Eligibility

People in need who live in the parish of Stetchworth and have done so for at least two years.

Types of grants

One-off grants according to need. Grants have been given towards, for example, electricity bills, fuel, groceries (through an account at the local community shop), transport to hospital and educational needs.

Annual grant total

In 2010/11 the charity had an income of £2,400 and a total expenditure of £1,600.

Applications

On a form available from the correspondent or the Ellesmere Centre, Stetchworth which should include details of income, expenditure and any other applications for help, rebates or discounts. Applications are considered at any time. The charity says: 'we welcome information from anyone who knows someone in need'.

Other information

Grants are available at any time of the year, although many of the elderly applicants tend to apply for a Christmas bonus in December. Whilst it is not the policy of the charity to give Christmas bonuses, it is happy to be used in this way.

Swaffham Bulbeck

The Swaffham Bulbeck Relief-in-Need Charity

£2,500

Correspondent: Cheryl Ling, 43 High Street, Swaffham Bulbeck, Cambridge CB25 0HP (01223 811733)

Trustees: David Turner; Gilian Rushworth; Adam Rayner; Geoffrey Welton; John Lewin; Brian Ambrose; Bert Collins.

CC Number: 238177

Eligibility

People in need who are over 65 and live in the parish of Swaffham Bulbeck.

Types of grants

One-off and annual grants (in kind or in cash). Grants do not usually amount to more than £20 each.

Annual grant total

In 2010 the charity had an income of £7,500 and a total expenditure of £6,400. Grants are given to individuals and to local clubs, schools and churches.

Applications

In writing to the correspondent.

Swavesey

Thomas Galon's Charity

£3,000

Correspondent: Linda Miller, Clerk, 21 Thistle Green, Swavesey, Cambridge CB24 4RJ (01954 202982; email: thomasgaloncharity@swavesey.org.uk; website: www.swavesey.org.uk/thomas_galon_charity)

Trustees: Arthur Richard Parish; Revd Dr John David Yule; John Shepperson; Austin Day; James Ernest Dodson; Dudley Morgan; Tim Parish; Will Wright; Benjamin Baker.

CC Number: 202515

Eligibility

People in need who live in the parish of Swavesey. Preference is given to those who are over 70, single or widowed; married couples when one partner reaches 70; and widows and widowers with dependent children up to 18 years old.

Types of grants

An annual gift, to be agreed in November, for people in need. One-off grants for hospital travel expenses, fuel costs and other needs. Grants of at least £35 are generally made.

Annual grant total

Income and expenditure average around £5,500 each year. Grants are given to both individuals and organisations.

Exclusions

No grants for capital projects such as buildings.

Applications

In writing to the correspondent for consideration in November. Grants will be delivered in December.

Walsoken

The United Walsoken and Baxter Charities

£5,000

Correspondent: Derek Mews, Clerk, 7 Pickards Way, Wisbech, Cambridgeshire PE13 1SD (01945 587982)

Trustees: Francis David Leach; John William Anker; Peter Goodale; Alexander Gardiner Henderson.

CC Number: 205494

Eligibility

Older people in need who have lived in the parish of Walsoken for at least two years.

Types of grants

Small one-off grants and gifts in kind.

Annual grant total

In 2010 the charities had an income of £3,600 and a higher than usual total expenditure of £5,100.

Applications

In writing to the correspondent, directly by the individual.

Whittlesey

The Whittlesey Charity

£1,200

Correspondent: P S Gray, 33 Bellamy Road, Oundle, Peterborough PE8 4NE (01832 273085)

Trustees: Gordon Ryall; Ralph Butcher; Pearl Beeby; David Green; David Wright; Geoffrey Oldfield; Andrew Whitehouse; Philip Oldfield; Gill Lawrence; Claire Smith.

CC Number: 1005069

Eligibility

People in need who live in the ancient parishes of Whittlesey Urban and Whittlesey Rural only.

Types of grants

Small annual cash grants, plus the occasional one-off grant.

Annual grant total

In 2011 welfare grants totalled £1,200.

Applications

In writing to the correspondent. Applications are considered in February, May and September, but urgent applications can be dealt with at fairly short notice. Note, the trust will not respond to ineligible applicants.

Other information

The charity makes grants to organisations and individuals, for relief in need, educational purposes, public purposes and it also makes grants to churches.

Whittlesford

The Charities of Nicholas Swallow and Others

£4,000

Correspondent: Nicholas Tufton, Clerk, 11 High Street, Barkway, Royston, Hertfordshire SG8 8EA (01763 848888)

Trustees: June Bater; Carol Abson; Chris McSweeney; David Toop; John Jennings; Kenneth Winterbottom; Tim Teversham; Karen Wright; Martyn Postle; Robert Cassels; Llandre Pickup.

CC Number: 203222

Eligibility

People in need who live in the parish of Whittlesford (near Cambridge) and adjacent area.

Types of grants

One-off cash grants at Christmas; help can also be given towards hospital travel and educational costs.

Annual grant total

In 2010/11 the charities had assets of £603,000 and an income of £46,000. Welfare grants totalled around £4,000.

Applications

In writing to the correspondent directly by the individual.

Other information

The principal activity of this charity is as a housing association managing bungalows and garages.

Wisbech

Elizabeth Wright's Charity

£3,000

Correspondent: Sylvia Palmer, Beechcroft, 124 Fridaybridge Road, Elm, Wisbech PE14 0AT (01945 861312; email: wisbchar@aol.com)

Trustees: Richard Symond Gyles Barnwell; Dr Iain Mason; Jean Bowser; Janet Stevens; Keith Aplin; Father Paul John West.

CC Number: 203896

Eligibility

Residents of the parishes of Saints Peter and Paul and Saint Augustine only.

Types of grants

One-off grants for essential items to offset hardship or cope with long-term illness.

Annual grant total

In 2010, the most recent year for which accounts were available, the charity held assets totalling £951,000 and an income of £38,000. Grants totalled £14,000 of which no more than £3,000 was made in relief grants to individuals.

Applications

On a form available from the correspondent. The form may be completed by the applicant or by a third party on their behalf. Trustees usually meet quarterly.

Other information

Grants are also given for educational purposes and to local organisations.

East Sussex

The Catharine House Trust

£33,000 (129 grants)

Correspondent: Richard Palim, Ridge Cottage, New Cut, Westfield, Hastings, East Sussex TN35 4RL

Trustees: Susan Patricia Bobbins; Jenny Ridd; Peter Wood; Angela Reid; Paul Coop.

CC Number: 801656

Eligibility

Older individuals and people in poor health who live in the borough of Hastings.

Types of grants

One-off grants of up to £400. Funding is available for medical equipment and treatment; household goods when they are essential for maintaining health (but not general furniture); respite breaks for the client or carer; and relevant courses for instruction.

Annual grant total

In 2010/11 the trust held assets of £335,000 and had an income of £33,000. Grants were made totalling £33,000.

Exclusions

Usually only one application is accepted per person.

Applications

In writing to the correspondent, supported by a written statement from a medical professional or social worker. Most applications are made through NHS trusts, local authority social services departments and other charities.

Hart Charitable Trust

£18,000 (203 grants)

Correspondent: M R Bugden, Gaby Hardwicke, 2 Eversley Road, Bexhill-on-Sea, East Sussex TN40 1EY (01424 730945)

Trustees: Mr J. French; Mr M. B. Glynn; Mr M. R. Bugden; Mr R. J. Ostle.

CC Number: 801126

Eligibility

People in need who live in East Sussex.

Types of grants

One-off grants, usually of around £75, are given towards clothing, bedding, travel and most other needs. Small amounts are also given to meet immediate needs.

Annual grant total

In 2010/11 the trust had assets of £654,000 and an income of £26,000. Grants were made to 203 individuals totalling £18,000.

Applications

On a form available from the correspondent, to be submitted through a third party such as a social worker, Citizens Advice or other welfare agency.

Other information

The trust also makes grants to organisations (£3,600 in 2010/11).

The Hastings Area Community Trust

£22,000

Correspondent: Anthony Bonds, Bolton Tomson House, 49 Cambridge Gardens, Hastings, East Sussex TN34 1EN (01424 718880)

Trustees: Peter Carcas; Cllr Paul Smith; M. B. Glynn; Duncan Keir; Helen Viki Barraclough; Diane Elizabeth Chartrey; Jean Fletcher.

CC Number: 1002470

Eligibility

People in need who are under 60 and live in Hastings and St Leonards-on-Sea who are on a very low income and have children, or who have medical reasons for not working.

Types of grants

One-off grants of £80 to £100 mainly in the form of payments to suppliers for essential furniture and household items, including cookers, washing machines, beds and baby items.

Annual grant total

In 2009/10, the most recent year for which accounts were available at the time of writing (winter 2012), the trust had assets of £525,000 and an income of £46,000. Grants were made totalling £22,000.

Exclusions

No grants for carpets, curtains or televisions.

Applications

On a form available from the correspondent. Applications can only be accepted from a recognised referral agency (e.g. social worker, Citizens Advice or recognised advice agency) and are considered throughout the year. The trust encourages applicants who wish to telephone to leave a message on the answer phone if there is no reply as messages are listened to daily.

The Mrs A. Lacy Tate Trust

£8,000

Correspondent: The Trustees, Heringtons Solicitors, 39 Gildredge Road, Eastbourne, East Sussex BN21 4RY (01323 411020)

Trustees: Mr I. Stewart; Mrs L. Macey; Mrs J. Roberts; Mrs L. Burgess.

CC Number: 803596

Eligibility

People in need who live in East Sussex.

403

Types of grants
One-off and recurrent grants according to need.

Annual grant total
In 2010/11 the trust made 159 grants to individuals for both welfare and educational purposes totalling £16,000.

Applications
In writing to the correspondent.

Other information
Grants are also made to organisations.

Battle

The Battle Charities

£2,000

Correspondent: Timothy P Roberts, 1 Upper Lake, Battle, East Sussex TN33 0AN (01424 772401; email: troberts@heringtons.net)

Trustees: Derek Newton Bishop; Edith Joan Winchester; Susan Jennifer Winchester; Robert Anthony Emeleus; Revd Dr John J. W. Edmondson; Paula Fisher; Shelagh Eve Franks; Thelma Patricia Farr; Patricia Roberts; Jennifer Bickley; Paul Lewis.

CC Number: 206591

Eligibility
People in need who live in Battle and Netherfield, East Sussex.

Types of grants
Grants are usually made towards fuel and children's' clothing, and range from £50 to £200.

Annual grant total
Grants usually total about £2,000 each year.

Applications
In writing to the correspondent. Applications can be sent directly by the individual or family member, through an organisation such as a Citizens Advice or through a third party such as a social worker. Full details of the applicant's circumstances are required.

Brighton and Hove

The Brighton District Nursing Association Trust

£4,400

Correspondent: Anthony Druce, Hon. Secretary, Fitzhugh Gates, 3 Pavilion Parade, Brighton BN2 1RY (01273 686811; fax: 01273 676837; email: anthonyd@fitzhugh.co.uk)

Trustees: Joyce Watts; Jill Mary Krolick; Peter John Field; Revd Philip Anthony Pannett; Angela Diana Page.

CC Number: 213851

Eligibility
People in need who are in poor health, convalescent or who have a disability and live in the county borough of Brighton and Hove.

Types of grants
One-off grants of up to £250 for items in respect of medical treatment and for convalescence; some limited allowances for nurses may also be available.

Annual grant total
In 2010 the trust had assets of £2.1 million and an income of £53,000. Grants to individuals totalled £4,400. A further £49,000 was given in grants to organisations. Income and expenditure for 2011 remained at broadly similar levels, however, accounts were not available from the Charity Commission at the time of writing (January 2013).

Applications
In writing to the correspondent: preferably supported by a doctor or health visitor. Applications are considered quarterly, though emergency grants may be awarded between meetings in urgent cases.

The Brighton Fund

£11,000

Correspondent: The Secretary, Brighton and Hove Council, Democratic Services, Room 121, Kings House, Grand Avenue, Hove BN3 2LS (01273 291077; email: steven.clare@brighton-hove.gov.uk; website: www.brighton-hove.gov.uk)

Trustees: Cllr Anne Meadows; Cllr Geoffrey Bowden; Cllr Jeane Lepper; Cllr Anne Norman; Cllr Stephanie Powell.

CC Number: 1011724

Eligibility
Usually people over 60 who are in need who live in Brighton and Hove administrative boundary.

Types of grants
One-off cash grants according to need including those for household items, medical equipment and subsistence.

Christmas gifts of £20 in the form of gift vouchers.

Annual grant total
In 2010/11 the fund had assets of £1.1 million and an income of £43,000. Grants totalled £14,000 and were distributed between: individuals in need over 60 (£7,000); individuals in need under 60 (£3,000); and exception awards (£4,000).

Applications
On a form, available from the correspondent or the website, to be submitted either through an organisation such as Citizens Advice or a school or through a third party such as a social worker or teacher. Applications are considered upon receipt.

The Mayor of Brighton and Hove's Welfare Charity

£4,200

Correspondent: Michael Hill, Selborne Centre, 5 Selborne Place, Hove, East Sussex BH3 3ET (01273 779432; email: hill.michael4@sky.com)

Trustees: Geraldine Des Moulins; Audrey Buttimer; Betty Davis; Christine Mason; Judith Cousin; Andrew John Wealls; David Turner.

CC Number: 224012

Eligibility
Individuals in need living in the old borough of Hove and Portslade.

Types of grants
One-off grants up to a maximum of £250. The committee will only consider one grant for each applicant and successful applicants should not reapply.

Annual grant total
In 2010/11 the trust had an income of £2,900 and total expenditure of £4,700.

Exclusions
No retrospective grants are made.

Applications
On a form available from the correspondent along with full guidelines. Applications should be submitted directly by the individual or a relevant third party, for example, a friend, carer or professional (social worker, health visitor). Grants are considered bi-monthly, in January, March, May, July, September and November. No money is given directly to the applicant, but rather directly to settle invoices.

Eastbourne

The Mayor's Poor Fund, Eastbourne

£750

Correspondent: The Mayor's Secretary, The Town Hall, Grove Road, Eastbourne, East Sussex BN21 4UG (01323 415002)

Trustees: Chief Executive Eastbourne Borough Council; Carolyn Heaps.

CC Number: 210664

Eligibility

People living in the borough of Eastbourne who are in need of temporary financial assistance.

Types of grants

One-off grants, generally ranging between £25 and £100.

Annual grant total

Grants average around £750 a year.

Applications

In writing to the correspondent, including all relevant information. Applications are usually submitted through a social worker or health visitor but individuals can apply directly if they wish.

The Doctor Merry Memorial Fund

£3,100

Correspondent: Ronald Pringle, Friston Corner, 3 Mill Close, East Dean, Eastbourne, East Sussex BN20 0EG (01323 423319; email: ronpringle@ hotmail.com)

Trustees: Diana Norman Blake-Dyke; Dorothy Eileen Barr; Jeremy Hugh Sogno; Dr Michael James Mynott.

CC Number: 213449

Eligibility

People who are ill and who live in the Eastbourne Health Authority area.

Types of grants

One-off grants for nursing home care, help with Lifeline rentals and medical equipment.

Annual grant total

In 2010/11 the fund had an income of £6,700 and a total expenditure of £3,400.

Applications

Individuals should apply via their doctor on a form available from the correspondent. Applications are considered throughout the year.

Other information

This charity was founded in 1922 as a memorial to Dr Merry who died of exhaustion after caring for the people of Eastbourne in the 'flu epidemic of that time'.

Hastings

William Shadwell Charity

£2,500

Correspondent: C R Morris, 4 Barley Lane, Hastings, East Sussex TN35 5NX (01424 433586)

Trustees: Keith Veness; Brian Brazier; Ian Steel; Norman Salmon; Susan Phillips; Susan Brazier.

CC Number: 207366

Eligibility

People in need who are sick and live in the borough of Hastings.

Types of grants

One-off and recurrent grants.

Annual grant total

Grants usually total around £2,500 each year.

Exclusions

No grants are given for the payment of debt, taxes and so on.

Applications

In writing to the correspondent to be submitted in March and September for consideration in April and October, but urgent cases can be considered at any time. Applications can be submitted directly by the individual or through a third party.

Mayfield

The Mayfield Charity

£2,000

Correspondent: Brenda Hopkin, Appletrees, Alexandra Road, Mayfield, East Sussex TN20 6UD (01435 873279)

Trustees: Ann Adam; Fiona Bickerton; John Logan; Mary Pennington; Father Nigel Prior.

CC Number: 212996

Eligibility

People in need who live in the ancient parish of Mayfield.

Types of grants

One-off grants of £50 to £500 according to need. Grants have been given towards hospital travel, clothing, equipment for people who are disabled, purchase of aids and Christmas gifts for older people.

Annual grant total

Grants are made for relief-in-need and educational purposes and total about £2,000 each year

Exclusions

Grants are not made for religious or political causes.

Applications

In writing to the correspondent at any time either directly by the individual or a family member, through a third party such as a social worker or teacher, or through an organisation such as Citizens Advice or a school. Proof of need should be included where possible.

Newick

The Newick Distress Trust

£1,500

Correspondent: Geoffrey Clinton, Dolphin Cottage, 3 High Hurst Close, Newick, East Sussex BN8 4NJ (01825 722512)

Trustees: Geoffrey Lionel Clinton; Ian Gerald Benson Reekie; Rosina Grace Ellen Hallett; Karen Rita Fordham.

CC Number: 291954

Eligibility

People in need who live in the village of Newick. Preference is given to those who have experienced a drastically reduced income due to bereavement, ill-health, unemployment and broken marriages.

Types of grants

One-off or recurrent grants towards, for example, heating bills in very cold weather, school uniforms required due to a change of school and other basic living costs.

Annual grant total

Grants usually total about £1,500 a year, but it depends on the number of requests.

Applications

In writing to the correspondent or one of the trustees.

Rotherfield

Henry Smith (Rotherfield Share)

£2,800

Correspondent: Trevor Thorpe, Trustee, 82 Fermor Way, Crowborough TN6 3BJ (01892 664245; email: rotherfieldpc@ yahoo.co.uk; website: www. rotherfieldparishcouncil.co.uk)

Trustees: Philippa Hewes; Philip Fermor; Jean Harris; Trevor Thorpe.

CC Number: 235516

Eligibility

People in need who live in the ancient parish of Rotherfield (Rotherfield and Crowborough civil parishes).

Types of grants

One-off and recurrent grants according to need.

Annual grant total

In 2011 the charities had an income of £1,600. Grants totalled £2,800.

Applications

In writing to the correspondent to be submitted either directly by the individual, through a third party such as a social worker, or through an organisation such as a Citizens Advice or other welfare agency. Applications are considered upon receipt.

Rye

Rye Relief In Need Charity

£1,000

Correspondent: The Secretary, Rye Town Council, Town Hall, Market Street, Rye, East Sussex TN31 7LA (01797 223902; fax: 01797 227706; email: townhall@ryetowncouncil.gov.uk; website: www.ryetowncouncil.gov.uk)

Trustee: Rye Town Council.

CC Number: 1075806

Eligibility

People who live in Rye who are in need.

Types of grants

One-off grants according to need. Recent grants have been given for removal costs and debt relief.

Annual grant total

About £1,000.

Applications

On a form available from the correspondent or to download from the website. Applications may be made at any time and are generally considered within two months of submission.

St Leonards-on-Sea

The Sarah Brisco Charity

£0

Correspondent: Steven Sleight, Chichester Diocesan Fund and Board, Church House, 211 New Church Road, Hove BN3 4ED

Trustees: Lorraine Watkins; Nigel Brian Lowe.

CC Number: 211554

Eligibility

People in need who live in the parish of St Peter and St Paul, St Leonards-on-Sea.

Types of grants

One-off cash grants between £25 and £100 and gifts in kind (such as £100 at Christmas, £25 vouchers and so on).

Annual grant total

The trust has had an average income of around £7,700 and an average total expenditure of around £5,000 in the last number of years; however, in 2010 the trust had no expenditure.

Applications

In writing to the correspondent. Applications should be submitted directly by the individual and are considered at any time.

Other information

The trust donates to other local charities when funds allow.

Warbleton

Warbleton Charity

£500

Correspondent: John Leeves, 4 Berners Court Yard, Berners Hill, Flimwell, Wadhurst, East Sussex TN5 7NE (01580 879248)

Trustees: Christopher Wells; Richard Reading; Lionel Daw; Caroline Rees; Revd Marc Lloyd.

CC Number: 208130

Eligibility

People in need who live in the parish of Warbleton. Preference is usually given to older people.

Types of grants

One-off grants according to need. Recent awards have been made for fuel and Christmas hampers.

Annual grant total

Grants usually total about £1,000 each year.

Applications

In writing to the correspondent either directly by the individual or through a third party. Applications are considered on a regular basis.

Other information

Grants are also made for educational purposes.

Essex

Colchester Blind Society

£5,500

Correspondent: Marilyn Theresa Peck, Kestrels, Harwich Road, Beaumont, Clacton-on-Sea, Essex CO16 0AU (01255 862062)

Trustees: Marilyn Theresa Peck; Elizabeth Ann Lee; Raymond Leonard Hardisty; Andrew Millar; Gill Kearsley.

CC Number: 207361

Eligibility

People who are blind or sight impaired and live in the borough of Colchester.

Types of grants

One-off or recurrent grants according to need.

Annual grant total

In 2011/12 the society had an income of £5,400 and a total expenditure of £5,700.

Applications

In writing to the correspondent.

The Colchester Catalyst Charity

£228,000 (177 grants)

Correspondent: Stephanie Grant, Administrator, Catalyst House, Newcomen Way, Colchester, Essex CO4 9YR (01206 752545; fax: 01206 842259; email: info@colchestercatalyst. co.uk; website: www.colchestercatalyst. co.uk)

Trustees: Peter Wilfrid Edgar Fitt; Christine Hayward; Adrian William Livesley; Mark Ferens Pertwee; Dr Thilaka Prakash Rudra; Dr Max Peter Hickman; Dr Naomi Joan Busfield.

CC Number: 228352

Eligibility

People in north east Essex who are living with a disability or sickness.

Types of grants

One-off and recurrent grants for respite care and specialist therapy. Funding is also given for special equipment. Items can include wheelchairs, mobility scooters and other mobility aids, special beds, pressure relieving mattresses and cushions, computers for specific needs and communication aids.

Annual grant total

In 2010/11 the charity had assets of £7.8 million and an income of £284,000. Grant to individuals totalled £228,000 and were distributed as follows:

Respite care	£142,000
Special individual needs	£77,000
Equipment pools	£9,100

During the year there were 223 special individual needs applications with 177 grants made.

Exclusions

Funding will not be given for items already purchased or where there is an obligation for provision by a statutory authority. The charity states that it does not take responsibility for the insurance, maintenance and repairs of any items funded.

Applications
On a form available directly from the correspondent or on the charity's website. Applications should include supporting statements, professional assessments by an appropriate professional practitioner (GP, occupational therapist, district nurse) and any quotes or estimates. Applications for respite care and counselling are administered through the charity's partners, a full list of which is available on the website. Grants towards replacement vehicles will only be considered where evidence of a replacement fund is available.

Other information
The charity also gives grants to organisations (£121,000 in 2010/11) and will consider making loans to individuals when a grant is not suitable.

Essex Police Support Staff Benevolent Fund

£2,500

Correspondent: B G Faber, Essex Police Headquarters, PO Box 2, Chelmsford, Essex CM2 6DA (01245 452597)

Trustees: Barry Faber; Brenda Wilmot.

CC Number: 269890

Eligibility
People in need who work or worked full-time or part-time for Essex Police Authority, and their dependents.

Types of grants
One-off grants or loans for essential needs such as travel expenses for hospital visits and unforeseen bills such as car repairs.

Annual grant total
In 2010/11 the fund had an income of £20,000 and a total expenditure of £2,800.

Exclusions
No grants towards medical treatment.

Applications
Individuals should apply via the benevolent fund representative of their division or subdivision of Essex Police Authority. Applications are considered quarterly, although this can be sooner in emergencies.

Help-in-Need Association (HINA)

£4,000

Correspondent: The Trustees, Barts and the London Students Union, Stepney Way, London E1 2JJ (email: applications@blhina.org; website: blhina.org/)

Trustees: Dr Jane May McNeill; Aamenah Hawash.

CC Number: 285585

Eligibility
Individuals in need living in Tower Hamlets, the City of London, Hackney, Newham, Waltham Forest, Redbridge, Barking and Dagenham, Havering or Essex.

Types of grants
One-off grants of up to £175 each for a specified purpose.

Annual grant total
In 2010/11 around £4,000 was distributed in grants.

Applications
Online application form on the fund's website. Applications must be submitted via a third party such as a social worker, GP, support worker, etc, who should also include a supporting letter and any relevant supporting documentation. Additional documents may be uploaded along with the application form.

The Kay Jenkins Trust

£2,000

Correspondent: Diana Tritton, Hole Farmhouse, Great Leighs, Chelmsford, Essex CM3 1QR (01245 361204; email: dstritton@yahoo.com)

Trustees: Alan Scott; Diana Tritton; Terry Ringer; William Seabrook.

CC Number: 241344

Eligibility
People in need, especially older or disabled people, who live in Great and Little Leighs.

Types of grants
One-off, mainly small, grants to help with household expenditure, medical aids and equipment. Occasionally up to £1,000 is given for a large item. No loans are made.

Annual grant total
Grants average around £2,000 a year.

Applications
In writing to the correspondent directly by the individual or through a relative. Grants are considered throughout the year.

Braintree
The Braintree United Charities

£1,500

Correspondent: Sue Carlile, Smith Law Partnership, Gordon House, 22 Rayne Road, Braintree CM7 2QW (01376 321311; fax: 01376 559239; email: suecarlile@slpsolicitors.co.uk)

Trustees: Ian Macnee; David Bowtell; Revd Charles Mason; David Mann; Eric Lynch; Graham Savill; Trevor McArdle.

CC Number: 212131

Eligibility
People in need who live in the parishes of St Michael's and St Paul's, Braintree; usually those in receipt of an old age pension.

Types of grants
One-off and recurrent grants ranging from £50 to £100. Annual grants are given at Christmas to people in need who are registered with the charity.

Annual grant total
In 2010/11 the charities had an income of £3,700 and a total expenditure of £2,700.

Exclusions
Loans are not made.

Applications
On a form available from the correspondent. Applications should be submitted through a social worker, Citizens Advice, other welfare agency or other third party, or directly by the individual. They are considered in May and October and should be received by April and September respectively.

Other information
The charities also make grants to organisations.

Broomfield
Broomfield United Charities

£8,000

Correspondent: Brian H Worboys, 5 Butlers Close, Chelmsford CM1 7BE (01245 440540; email: brian@ theworboys.freeserve.co.uk)

Trustees: Dennis Patient; Barbara Thomas; Joyce Ashford; Sue Browning; Brian Worboys; Geoffrey William Garwood.

CC Number: 225563

Eligibility

People in need who live in the civil parish of Broomfield.

Types of grants

One-off grants according to need and vouchers at Christmas.

Annual grant total

In 2010/11 the charities had an income and expenditure of just over £5,000.

Applications

In writing to the correspondent directly by the individual for consideration at any time.

Chigwell and Chigwell Row

The George and Alfred Lewis (of Chigwell) Memorial Fund

£2,400

Correspondent: Miss Enid Smart, 16 Forest Terrace, High Road, Chigwell, Essex IG7 5BW (020 8504 9408)

Trustees: John Roger Redfern; Elizabeth Enid Smart; Winifred Ann Freeman.

CC Number: 297802

Eligibility

People in need and widows of those who served in HM Forces or the Merchant Service during the Second World War and were living in the parishes of Chigwell and Chigwell Row at the time of their enlistment.

Types of grants

One-off grants to help people who are in need due to family illness, old age, domestic emergencies and so on.

Annual grant total

In 2010 the trust had an income of £1,800 and a total expenditure of £2,500.

Applications

In writing to the correspondent. Applications can be made either directly by the individual or through a third party on behalf of the individual, such as a spouse or child, and should include as much detail of personal circumstances as is deemed appropriate. Applications are considered at any time.

Dovercourt

The Henry Smith Charity (Dovercourt)

£1,500

Correspondent: Anthony Peake, 2 Kings Court, Kings Road, Dovercourt, Harwich, Essex CO12 4DT (01255 502209)

Trustees: Revd Peter Mann; Anthony Peake; David Parsons; Kenneth Wheeler; John Gillett.

CC Number: 246792

Eligibility

People in need who live in the ancient parish of All Saints, Dovercourt.

Types of grants

The trust prefers to contribute towards the total cost of items and services rather than cash grants i.e. the purchase of a buggy for a disabled person, TV licence costs, food, and washing machine purchase and fitting. One-off cash donations up to a maximum of £100.

Annual grant total

In 2010/11 the trust had an income of £1,500 and a total expenditure of £1,600.

Applications

In writing to the correspondent for consideration at any time. Applications should be submitted through Citizens Advice or other welfare agency or through a third party such as a priest who can recommend the applicant. After receiving a letter, the trustees usually visit the applicant. Applications should contain family details and are considered throughout the year.

East Bergholt

The East Bergholt United Charities

£500

Correspondent: Greta Abbs, 31 Fiddlers Lane, East Bergholt, Colchester CO7 6SJ (01206 299822)

Trustees: Mr Dodgson; George Harris; Rodney James Moss; Mervyn Austin; Revd Stephne Van Der Toorn; Susan Templer Kramers.

CC Number: 208194

Eligibility

People in need who live in East Bergholt.

Types of grants

One-off grants according to need. If no cases of hardship are brought to the attention of the trustees, they usually give £20 each at Christmas to 10 to 20 older people who are known to have small incomes. These are not given to the same person two years running, although additional help can be given if needed.

Annual grant total

The main purpose of this charity is the provision and maintenance of almshouses. Grants to individuals are usually under £500. The 2010/11 accounts note that just one Christmas grant was made to a family with serious health problems.

Applications

In writing to the correspondent, although most cases are brought to the attention of the trustees. Applications can be submitted directly by the individual or by a relative at any time. Proof of the financial situation of the applicant is required.

East Tilbury

East Tilbury Relief-in-Need Charity

£4,000

Correspondent: Reginald F Fowler, Treasurer, 27 Ward Avenue, Grays, Essex RM17 5RE (01375 372304)

Trustees: Reginald Frederick Fowler; Robert Folkard; John Blackbond; Raymond Louis Osborne; Mark Raymond Osborne.

CC Number: 212335

Eligibility

People in need who live in the parish of East Tilbury.

Types of grants

One-off and recurrent grants have been given towards hospital visits and children in need.

Annual grant total

In 2011 the charity had an income of £6,700 and a total expenditure of £4,000.

Applications

In writing to the correspondent, to be considered in November.

Other information

Grants may also be made to organisations.

Halstead

Helena Sant's Residuary Trust Fund

£6,600

Correspondent: M R R Willis, Trustee, Greenway, Church Street, Gestingthorpe, Halstead, Essex CO9 3AX (01787 469920)

Trustees: Revd John Blore; Malcolm Willis; David Lorkin; Brian Vidler.

CC Number: 269570

Eligibility

People in need who live in the parish of St Andrew with Holy Trinity, Halstead who have at any time been a member of the Church of England.

Types of grants

One-off cash grants according to need.

Annual grant total

In 2010 the trust had an income of £4,000 and a total expenditure of £7,000.

Exclusions

Grants are not given to pay rates, taxes or public funds.

Applications

In writing to the correspondent directly by the individual, through an organisation such as Citizens Advice or through a third party such as a social worker. Applications are considered at any time.

Harlow

The Harlow Community Chest

£10,500

Correspondent: Connie Freeman, PO Box 11175, Harlow, Essex CM20 9JU (email: conniefre@hotmail.com)

Trustees: Glenford Watson; Janet Cable; Connie Freeman; Lee Parker-Brand; David Parker-Brand; Kevin Pitt; Mike Hayter; Philip Hill; Christine Brown; Malcolm McFarlane; Erica Bromage.

CC Number: 252764

Eligibility

Individuals and families in financial need, particularly where a small financial contribution will help to arrest the spiral of debt. Applicants must live in Harlow.

Types of grants

One-off grants up to £250. Recent grants have been made for: payment of outstanding utility bills for people with special needs; clothing (for example for unemployed young people going for a job interview); household items; funeral expenses; removal costs; lodging deposits; and nursery fees. Small emergency grants are also available.

Annual grant total

In 2010/11 the trust had both an income and expenditure of £11,000.

Exclusions

No grants for housing rents or rates. Only one main grant to an individual/family can be made in any one year.

Applications

On a form available from the correspondent: to be submitted through a recognised referral agency (for example a social worker, welfare organisation or doctor). Applications are considered on a monthly basis. Emergency payments can be made between meetings.

Hutton

Ecclesiastical Charity of George White

£7,000

Correspondent: Reverend Robert Wallace, c/o St Peter's Parish Office, Claughton Way, Hutton, Brentwood, Essex CM13 1JS (01277 262864; email: dawn_shaxon@btconnect.com; website: www.huttonchurch.org.uk)

Trustees: Alan Braid; Mary Kenyon; Kathleen Button; The Rector Robert Wallace; Cllr Claire Denise Cornell.

CC Number: 208601

Eligibility

People in need who live in the parish of All Saints with St Peter, Hutton. Particular favour is given to children, young adults and older people. The usual length of residency is seven years.

Types of grants

Pensions and one-off grants usually in the range of £100 and £400 towards necessary living expenses.

Annual grant total

Grants usually total around £7,000 per year.

Applications

In writing to the correspondent at any time. Applications can be submitted either directly by the individual, through a third party such as a social worker, or through an organisation such as Citizens Advice or other welfare agency. They are considered at any time.

Other information

The charity also makes grants towards the repair of the church fabric in the two local parish churches.

Saffron Walden

The Saffron Walden United Charities

£28,000

Correspondent: Jim Ketteridge, c/o Crossroads Care, Uttlesford, Barnards Yard, Saffron Walden, Essex CB11 4EB (01799 526122)

Trustees: Jack Golding; Daphne Cornell; Maj Carol Evans; Marion Barker; Gillian Mummery; John Noakes; Barbara Brouet; Meg Reed; Doug Perry; Revd David Tomlinson.

CC Number: 210662

Eligibility

People in need who live in Saffron Walden including the hamlets of Little Walden and Sewards End.

Types of grants

One-off grants in kind and gift vouchers. A range of help is considered including, for example, electrical goods, convalescence, clothing, household bills, food, holidays, travel expenses, furniture, disability equipment and nursery fees.

Annual grant total

In 2011 the charities had assets of £913,000 and an income of £37,000. Grants were made totalling £28,000.

Exclusions

No grants for credit card debt.

Applications

In writing to the correspondent either directly by the individual, through a third party such as a social worker, or through an organisation such as a Citizens Advice or other welfare agency. Applications are considered as they arrive.

Springfield

The Springfield United Charities

£1,000

Correspondent: Nick Eveleigh, Civic Centre, Duke Street, Chelmsford, Essex CM1 2YJ (01245 606606)

Trustees: Cllr R. Fishwick; Revd R. Brown; Cllr Robin Stevens; Cllr Neil Gulliver; Graham McGhie; Cllr John Styles.

CC Number: 214530

Eligibility

Individuals in need living in the parish of Springfield.

Types of grants

One-off grants according to need.

Annual grant total

In 2010/11 the charities had an income of £4,900 and a total expenditure of £1,000.

Applications

In writing to the correspondent.

Thaxed

Lord Maynard's Charity

£1,500

Correspondent: Michael Chapman, Wade and Davies Solicitors, 28 High Street, Great Dunmow, Essex CM6 1AH (01371 872816)

Trustees: Peter King; Daniel Fox; Lord Braybrooke.

CC Number: 278579

Eligibility

People who live in the parish of Thaxted.

Types of grants

One-off and recurrent grants of £50 to £100 for general relief-in-need.

Annual grant total

About £2,500 for education and welfare.

Applications

In writing to the correspondent. Applicants traditionally queue in the local church on the 1st Saturday in August for the money to be handed out, but postal applications prior to this are accepted.

Other information

Although records at the Charity Commission are very overdue, the correspondent has confirmed that the trust is active.

The Thaxted Relief-in-Need Charities

£2,000

Correspondent: M B Hughes, Secretary, Yardley Farm, Walden Road, Thaxted, Essex CM6 2RQ (01371 830642)

Trustees: Gerald Peter Lowe; Philip George Leeder; Adrian Peter Lowe; Fred Knight; Susan Lydia Freeman; David Robert Barnard; Richard Peter Hingston; Mrs Deviben; Khunti; Robert Draper Caton; Andrew Clark McKernan.

CC Number: 243782

Eligibility

People in need who live in the parish of Thaxted.

Types of grants

One-off and recurrent grants according to need.

Annual grant total

In 2010 the charities had an income of £24,000 and a total expenditure of £17,000. Around £2,000 a year is given in grants to individuals.

Applications

In writing to the correspondent.

Other information

The main priority for the charities is to maintain its almshouses. A small number of grants are also made to local organisations.

Hampshire

The Alverstoke Trust

£500

Correspondent: Mrs Jane Hodgman, 5 Constable Close, Gosport, Hampshire PO12 2UF (02392 589822)

Trustees: Aleck Hayward; Julia Grant; Timothy Hall.

CC Number: 239303

Eligibility

People in need who live in Alverstoke or nearby.

Types of grants

One-off grants, usually of amounts up to £200.

Annual grant total

In 2010 the trust had an income of £1,500 and a total expenditure of £1,100.

Exclusions

The trust does not make recurring awards.

Applications

In writing to the correspondent, either directly or through a third party such as a Citizens Advice, social worker, welfare agency or other third party. Applications are considered at any time.

The Bordon and Liphook Charity

£40,000

Correspondent: Robert Monteath, Room 29, The Forest Centre, Pinehill Road, Bordon, Hampshire GU35 0TN (01420 477787; fax: 01420 477787; email: bordoncharity@aol.com; website: www. bordonandliphookcharity.co.uk)

Trustees: Toni Shaw; Gerard Alexander; Jennifer Ann Vernon-Smith; Michael Gallagher; Mandy Batten.

CC Number: 1032428

Eligibility

People in need who live in North-East Hampshire and South-West Surrey.

Types of grants

One-off grants of between £50 and £3,000 can be awarded. The trustees consider a wide range of applications including heating and rent arrears.

Annual grant total

In 2011 grants totalled £52,000, of which around £40,000 was distributed to individuals.

Applications

On a form available from the correspondent or to download from the website. Applications can be made either directly by the individual or through a social worker, Citizens Advice, other welfare agency, health visitor or district nurse. Applications are considered monthly and the trust reserves the right to commission a case worker's report.

Other information

The charity raises money though its three charity shops – Bordon Care, Haslemere Care and Liphook Care.

Dibden Allotments Charity

£139,000 (1,609 grants)

Correspondent: Harvey Mansfield, 7 Drummond Court, Prospect Place, Hythe, Southampton SO45 6HD (02380 841305; email: dibdenallotments@ btconnect.com; website: daf-hythe.org.uk)

Trustees: Judith Saxby; Malcolm Fidler; Mrs M. McLean; Mike Harvey; Pat Hedges; Peter Parrott; Chris Harrison; Rosemary Dash; Jill Tomlin.

CC Number: 255778

Eligibility

People in need who live in the parishes of Hythe, Dibden, Marshwood and Fawley.

Types of grants

One-off grants according to need, for the relief of hardship or distress. Recent grants were made towards items and services such as the provision of household goods to families, hospital travel costs, assistance with gardening for older people, and childcare costs for full-time students.

Annual grant total

In 2010/11 the fund had assets of £8.1 million and an income of £328,000. There were 1609 grants given to individuals totalling £139,000. These included 685 grants totalling £17,000 for the Shoe Vouchers Scheme and 172 grants totalling £24,000 for the Garden Support Scheme.

Applications

On a form available from the fund's website, where the fund's criteria, guidelines and application process are also posted.

Other information

Grants are also made to charitable and voluntary organisations.

The Farnborough (Hampshire) Welfare Trust

£2,400

Correspondent: M R Evans, Bowmarsh, 45 Church Avenue, Farnborough, Hampshire GU14 7AP (01252 542726)

Trustees: Cllr Alan Ferrier; Revd David Willey; Gwen Griffin; Revd Ian Hedges; Cllr Neville Dewey; Rosemary Posse; Terence Bridgeman; Revd Rachel Bennetts; Nigel Harris.

CC Number: 236889

Eligibility

People in need who live in the urban district of Farnborough, Hampshire.

Types of grants

One-off and recurrent grants mainly to older people at Christmas. Grants are generally between £20 and £50.

Annual grant total

Grants usually average around £3,000 each year.

Applications

In writing to the correspondent: to be submitted either directly by the individual or by a third party. Applications are usually considered in early December.

Hampshire Ambulance Service Benevolent Fund

£6,200

Correspondent: Terence Forgham, Trustee, 8 Ashley Gardens, Chandler's Ford, Eastleigh, Hampshire SO53 2JH (02380 269600)

Trustees: Terence Forgham; Derek Barney; Colin Walker-White; David Reginald Watts; Philip M. Pimlott; Marilyn Mary Oliver; Simone Eileen Bowler.

CC Number: 1041811

Eligibility

Serving and retired members of Hampshire Ambulance Service/South Central Ambulance Service NHS Trust and their dependents.

Types of grants

One-off grants according to need.

Annual grant total

In 2010/11 the trust had an income of £8,600 and a total expenditure of £6,600.

Applications

In writing to the correspondent.

The Hampshire Constabulary Welfare Fund

£85,000

Correspondent: Ian Trueman, Hampshire Constabulary, West Hill, Romsey Road, Winchester SO22 5DB (01962 814795; email: hampshire@polfed.org)

Trustees: Derek Lacey; Kathleen Grace Symonds; Quita Walker; Alex Maeshall; Gary Steward; Ian Ogilvy; Andy Marsh; Paul Robertson; John Happel.

CC Number: 291061

Eligibility

Members, pensioners and civilian employees of the Hampshire Constabulary and their dependents. Assistance may also be available to special constables injured during police duty.

Types of grants

One-off and recurrent grants or loans to help support people experiencing family crisis or recovering from injury or illness. Recent grants have been given towards stair-lifts, bath-lifts, wheelchairs, respite holidays and general living costs.

Annual grant total

In 2010/11 the trust had assets of £579,000 and an income of £276,000. Grants totalled £85,000 and were distributed as follows:

Assistance and grants for individuals	£47,000
Widows and children's Christmas gifts	£29,000
Gifts to sick members, wreaths and donations to late members	£9,000

Applications

Applications should be made through a local police welfare officer. They are considered on a regular basis.

Other information

The trust also makes grants to other charitable trusts and organisations which support police officers.

Hampshire Football Association Benevolent Fund

£8,000

Correspondent: Robin Osborne, Winklebury Football Complex, Winklebury Way, Basingstoke, Hampshire RG23 8BF (01256 853000; email: See website for regional contacts.; website: www.hampshirefa.com/Governance/Benevolent+Fund)

Trustees: Martin Oliver; Robin Osborne; John Ward; Ian Walkom; James Pearson; Peter Butler; Simon Nethercott; Thura Win; Vanessa Raynbird; Neil Cassar; Nicholas Taplin.

CC Number: 232359

Eligibility

People in need who have been injured whilst playing football, and others who have 'done service' to the game of football. Applicants must be playing for a team affiliated with Hampshire Football Association.

Types of grants

One-off and recurrent grants, usually ranging from £50 to £1,000 according to need.

Annual grant total

In 2010 the trust had an income of £6,400 and a total expenditure of £8,800.

Applications

The club secretary must apply to Hampshire Football Association or the Area Benevolent Officer (contact details on the trust's website) for an application form on behalf of the applicant. The application should be completed by the applicant and endorsed for the secretary of the club.

A doctor's certificate clearly stating the nature of the injury and probable period of incapacitation must accompany each application. Completed application forms should be returned to the county office or the Area Benevolent Officer.

Hampshire Golfers' Benevolent Fund

£2,000

Correspondent: M J Dyer, Verisona, 64 West Street, Havant, Hampshire PO9 1PA (02392 380112; email: hampshirepga@yahoo.co.uk; website: www.hampshire-pga.co.uk)

Trustees: Michael John Dyer; David John Harrison; Malcolm Roy Scott.

CC Number: 255462

Eligibility

Priority is given to people who are members of Hampshire Professional Golfers' Association and their dependents. When funds are available the trust may also fund other people who have been employed as professional golfers and their dependents.

Types of grants

One-off and recurrent grants according to need.

Annual grant total

Around £2,000.

Applications

In writing to the correspondent.

The Kingsclere Welfare Charities

£1,000

Correspondent: Roy Forth, PO Box 7721, Kingsclere RG20 5WQ (07796423108; email: kclerecharities@ aol.co.uk)

Trustees: Mr G. Swait; Mr D. Chamings; Jean Turner; Penny Stewart; Rachel Theaker; Revd Lucy Thirtle; Patrick Dring; Marie Gundry; Irene Powers.

CC Number: 237218

Eligibility

People in need who live in the parishes of Ashford Hill, Headley and Kingsclere.

Types of grants

The provision or payment for items, services or facilities such as medical equipment, expenses for travel to hospital and grants to relieve hardship. Grants are mostly one-off, but recurrent grants can be considered. They range from around £100 to £2,500.

Annual grant total

In 2010 the trust had an income of £4,800 and a total expenditure of £1,100.

Applications

In writing to the correspondent. Applications are considered in February, April, June, September and November.

Open Sight

£2,000

Correspondent: Stacey Allen, 25 Church Road, Eastleigh, Hampshire SO50 6BL (02380 646378; email: info@opensight. org.uk; website: www.opensight.org.uk)

Trustees: Timothy Rogerson; Lynda Joyce Phear; Stephen Gosling; David Gaines; Derek Froud; Dean White.

CC Number: 1055498

Eligibility

People who are visually impaired, in need and live in Hampshire, excluding the cities of Portsmouth and Southampton.

Types of grants

One-off grants of up to £500 each to aid independent living for eligible people, e.g. towards special equipment, aids to daily living, holiday costs and costs incurred when moving into independent living.

Annual grant total

In 2010/11 the trust had assets of £822,000 and an income of £371,000. We were unable to obtain a grant figure, but in the past grants have totalled around £2,000.

Exclusions

No grants are given for educational purposes or to groups.

Applications

On a form available from the correspondent. Applications can be made directly by the individual or through a third party (as long as it is signed by the individual). The trust encourages a supporting statement from the individual. Applications are usually processed within five weeks.

Other information

The trust also administers the Scale Trust (see separate entry for further information).

The Portsmouth Victoria Nursing Association

£13,000

Correspondent: Susan Resouly, Secretary, Southlands, Prinsted Lane, Prinsted, Emsworth, Hampshire PO10 8HS (01243 373900; email: portsmouth.victoria.nursing@gmail.com)

Trustees: Jenny Golden; Nancy Mead; Dr Roger Knight; Suzane Hibbert; Sue Eardley-Stiff; Tony Knapman; Babs Gray; Dr Peter Alexander Beasley.

CC Number: 203311

Eligibility

People in need who are sick and live in the areas covered by the Portsmouth City Primary Care Trust, the Fareham and Gosport Primary Care Trust and the East Hampshire Primary Care Trust.

Types of grants

One-off grants of up to £750 towards medical equipment, household essentials, special clothing and respite care.

Annual grant total

In 2011 grants were made to individuals amounting to just under £13,000, for patients welfare (£12,400) and to assist nurses in need (£130).

Exclusions

Items that should be provided by the NHS.

Applications

All applications must be made through the community nursing staff and help is confined to those on whom the nurses are in attendance. Referrals are made by the district nurses on a form which is considered by the committee at monthly meetings.

Other information

Assistance is also given to the community nurses of the area to improve the care they give to their patients.

The Scale Charitable Trust Fund

£7,000

Correspondent: Local Democracy Manager, Portsmouth City Council, Civic Offices, Guildhall Square, Portsmouth PO1 2AL (02392 834057; email: joanne.wildsmith@portsmouthcc. gov.uk)

Trustees: Jason Fazackarley; Margaret Foster; David Horne; Frank Jonas; April Windebank.

CC Number: 202587

Eligibility

People over 30 who are blind and in need. Applicants must have been born or have lived in Hampshire for at least five years.

Types of grants

Grants to aid independent living for eligible people, for example, towards equipment, course fees or transport costs.

Annual grant total

In 2010/11 the fund had an income of £3,400 and a total expenditure of £7,500.

Applications

Portsmouth City Council still administer the trust, however, people living in Hampshire, excluding those living in Portsmouth, should apply in writing directly to: Stacey Allen, Open Sight, 25 Church Road, Bishopstoke, Eastleigh, Hampshire SO50 6BL (02380 641244).

People living in Portsmouth should apply in writing directly to: Jim Tolley, Portsmouth Association for the Blind, 48 Stubbington Avenue, Portsmouth PO2 0HY (02392 661717).

The Earl of Southampton Trust

£24,000 (94 grants)

Correspondent: Mrs S C Boden, Clerk to the Trustees, 24 The Square, Titchfield, Hampshire PO14 4RU (01329 513294; email: earlstrust@yahoo.co.uk; website: eost.org.uk/)

Trustees: Sally Loretto Hopton; Dennis Arthur Hignell; Constance Hockley; Frances Charlotte Knight; David Nation; Paul Vincent Cousins; Ann Hammond; John Stewart Peterkin.

CC Number: 238549

Eligibility

People in need who live in the ancient parish of Titchfield (now subdivided into the parishes of Titchfield, Sarisbury, Locks Heath, Warsash, Stubbington and Lee-on-the-Solent). Groups catering for people in need are sometimes considered.

Types of grants
One-off grants in the range of £25 and £1,000 towards motorised wheelchairs, stairlifts, specialist furniture for people who are disabled, respite care, household equipment, redecoration, home help, childminding, holiday activities, legal fees, respite holidays and so on.

Annual grant total
In 2010/11 the trust had assets of £1.5 million and an income of £85,000. There were 97 grants made totalling £25,000 for welfare and educational purposes.

Exclusions
The trust will not supply items or services which should be provided for by the state.

Applications
In writing to the correspondent through a social worker, Citizens Advice, other welfare agency or third party (for example, doctor, district nurse, clergy or councillor). Applications must include details of medical/financial status. Applications are considered on the last Tuesday of every month, although in the event of extreme urgency requests can be fast tracked between meetings. Forms are available to download from the website.

Other information
The trust runs almshouses and a day centre for old people.

The Sway Welfare Aid Group

£13,000

Correspondent: J R Stevens, Driftway, Mead End Road, Sway, Lymington, Hampshire SO41 6EH (01590 682843; email: info@swaghants.org.uk; website: www.swaghants.org.uk)

Trustees: Mr J. R. Stevens; Raymond Champion; Laura Ellen Simpkins; Dick Bugg.

CC Number: 261220

Eligibility
Individuals and families in need who live in the parish of Sway and its immediate neighbourhood.

Types of grants
One-off grants towards: household equipment; rent (to avoid eviction); bereavement costs; hospital travel costs; heating bills; essential decorating costs and home repairs; insulation; reasonable recreational equipment; and, disability

aids. Help may also be given towards training courses and school trips.

Annual grant total
In 2010/11 the group held assets of £151,000 and had an income of £14,000. Grants to individuals totalled £13,000, including 26 heating grants of £280.

Applications
In writing to the correspondent or by personal introduction.

Other information
The group runs a lunch club for people living on their own. It also has a team of volunteer drivers that can help local residents who have difficulty in getting to, for example, hospital appointments.

The Three Parishes Fund

£4,000

Correspondent: George Wilson, Fremont, 23 Taylor's Lane, Lindford, Bordon, Hampshire GU35 0SW (01420 472899; email: ttpf@gofast.co.uk)

Trustees: Carole Irene Wilson; Wanda Catherine Rix; Revd Marion Isobella Enid Warren; Rosemary Anne Wightman; Faith Elaine Thomas; Dennis Albert Preddy; Janice Christine Gale.

CC Number: 262563

Eligibility
People in need who live in the parishes of Headley, Grayshott and Lindford and the town of Whitehill/Bordon.

Types of grants
One-off grants.

Annual grant total
In 2011 the trust had an income of £3,900 and a total expenditure of £4,300.

Applications
In writing or by application form available from the correspondent. Applications are considered at any time and can be submitted directly by the individual, or by a social worker, doctor, clergy or similar third party.

Twyford and District Nursing Association

£3,200

Correspondent: Giselle Letchworth, Sunnyside, High Street, Twyford, Winchester SO21 1RG (01962 712158; email: giselleletchworth@btinternet.com)

Trustees: Jennifer Gray; Lesley Barrow; Angela Margaret Forder-Stent; Jean Millar; Martin Locke; Giselle Letchworth; Sandra Ellen Dunford.

CC Number: 800876

Eligibility
People who are in need and live in the parishes of Twyford, Compton and Shawford, Colden Common and Owslebury, in the county of Hampshire.

Types of grants
One-off grants according to need. Recent awards have been given for electric goods, convalescence, clothing, travel expenses, medical equipment, nursing fees, furniture, disability equipment and help in the home.

Annual grant total
In 2010 the association had an income of £6,800 and a total expenditure of £3,400.

Exclusions
The association cannot offer long-term care.

Applications
On a form available from the correspondent. Applications are usually made through the medical practices in the area (mainly the Twyford Practice) and people can also apply through the social services, a doctor or community nurse, or if they do not have a direct medical contact, directly to the correspondent or through a relevant third party.

The Winchester Rural District Welfare Trust

£3,000

Correspondent: Sue Lane, Witts Cottage, Oxford Road, Sutton Scotney, Winchester, Hampshire SO21 3JG (01962 760858)

Trustees: Barbara Jean Holyome; Michael Gilbert Lupton; Rosemary Sign; Susan Kathleen Lane; Gail Johnson; Susan Alexander; Maj Peter Barron; Alistair Lang; Penny Russell; Jan Hallam; Joe Winchester; John Hart.

CC Number: 246512

Eligibility
People in need who live in the former Winchester Rural District. This includes the parishes of Bighton, Bramdean, Compton, Headbourne Worthy and Abbot's Barton, Hursley, Itchen Valley, King's Worthy, Micheldever, Old Alresford, Owslebury, Sparsholt, Twyford, Wonston, Beauworth, Bishop's Sutton, Cheriton, Chilcomb, Crawley, Itchen Stoke and Ovington, Kilmeston, Littleton, New Alresford, Northington, Oliver's Battery and Tichborne. It does not include the city of Winchester.

Types of grants
One-off grants towards, for example, bedding, clothing, special food, fuel and heating appliances, telephone, nursing requirements, house repairs, hospital

413

travel costs and convalescent care. Support may also be given to students seeking employment and other educational needs.

Annual grant total
Grants have averaged around £3,000 in recent years.

Applications
In writing to the correspondent, to be submitted through a social worker, Citizens Advice or other welfare agency.

Other information
This trust was formed by merging the endowments of 26 charities in 25 parishes in the Winchester Rural District.

The Winchester Welfare Charities

£100

Correspondent: D Shaw, Hon. Clerk, Winchester Council, City Offices, Colebrook Street, Winchester, Hampshire SO23 9LJ (01962 848221; email: dshaw@winchester.gov.uk)

Trustees: John Higgins; Allan Mitchell; Jenny Meadows; Robert Foster Young.

CC Number: 810159

Eligibility
People who are in need or distress, or who are sick, convalescing, disabled or infirm and live in Winchester and its immediate surroundings.

Types of grants
The trust gives winter fuel payments in December and emergency grants throughout the year. These one-off grants (typically £25 to £50) have been towards repairs to an electric wheelchair, special shoes for people with disabilities, repairs to a washing machine and so on. Help can also be given for furniture, bedding, clothing, food, fuel and nursing requirements.

Annual grant total
Over recent years grants have averaged £1,000 although the charity only had a total expenditure of £100 in 2010/11.

Applications
Recipients of Christmas vouchers are nominated by the trustees and local agencies. Applications for emergency payments should be made through a social worker, Citizens Advice or similar third party.

Other information
A leaflet is available from the correspondent.

Brockenhurst
The Groome Trust

£2,000

Correspondent: Patricia Dunkinson, Belmont, Burford Lane, Brockenhurst SO42 7TN (01590 622303)

Trustees: Clare Coates; Elizabeth Tindall; Jacqui Fiorentini; Mary Richardson; Maureen Cooke; Terence Wingate; Alan Bartlett.

CC Number: 204829

Eligibility
People in need who live in the parish of Brockenhurst.

Types of grants
One-off grants towards talking books for the blind, lifelines for people living alone, Christmas gifts to nursing home residents and food vouchers for older people at Christmas.

Annual grant total
In 2010 the trust had an income of £6,400 and a total expenditure of £6,000.

Applications
In writing to the correspondent, although often the applicant is known to the trustees. Applications are considered as received.

Other information
The trust mainly makes grants to local organisations.

Fareham
The Fareham Welfare Trust

£9,000

Correspondent: Anne Butcher, Clerk, 44 Old Turnpike, Fareham, Hampshire PO16 7HA (01329 235186)

Trustees: Slyvia Coghlan; John Bryant; Delia Anne Yule; Valerie Thelma Miller; Mary Nadolski; Revd Christopher James Woodman; Revd Sally Elizabeth Davenport.

CC Number: 236738

Eligibility
People in need who live in the ecclesiastical parishes of St Peter and Paul, St John and Holy Trinity, all in Fareham. Preference is given to widows in need.

Types of grants
One-off and recurrent grants up to a maximum of about £250 a year. Recent grants have been given for clothing, furniture, food, cookers, washing

machines and other essential electrical items.

Annual grant total
In 2010/11 the trust had an income of £11,500 and a total expenditure of £9,000.

Applications
Applications should be submitted through a recognised referral agency (e.g. social worker, health visitor, Citizens Advice or doctor) or trustee. They are considered throughout the year. Details of the individual's income and circumstances must be included.

Gosport
Thorngate Relief-in-Need and General Charity

£3,000

Correspondent: Kay Brent, 16 Peakfield, Waterlooville PO7 6YP (02392 264400; email: kay@brentco.co.uk)

Trustees: Roy Dyer; Alexander Burns; John Eager.

CC Number: 210946

Eligibility
People in need who live in Gosport.

Types of grants
One-off grants mostly between £100 and £500.

Annual grant total
In 2010/11 the charity had an income of £9,000 and a total expenditure of £14,000. Grants are made for welfare and educational purposes.

Exclusions
No grants are made towards legal expenses.

Applications
On a form available from the correspondent. Applications can be made either directly by the individual or through a social worker, Citizens Advice, Probation Service or other welfare agency.

Other information
Grants are also given to organisations.

Hawley
The Hawley Almshouse and Relief-in-Need Charity

£1,300

Correspondent: The Secretary, Trustees' Office, Ratcliffe House, Hawley Road,

Blackwater, Camberley, Surrey GU17 9DD (01276 33515; email: frmartyn@aol.com; website: www. blackwaterandhawleytowncouncil.gov. uk/28/charities)

Trustees: Anne Leppard; Ann Thain; Revd Martyn Neale; Mary Kenny; John Housden; Stephen Twinn; Arthur Leonard Rose.

CC Number: 204684

Eligibility

People in need who live in the area covered by Hart District Council and Rushmoor Borough Council. Beneficiaries are generally women aged 60 or over and men aged 65 or over.

Types of grants

Generally one-off grants for needs that cannot be met from any other source. Recent grants have been given for very high heating bills during cold weather and the installation of equipment such as chairlifts.

Annual grant total

In 2010/11 the charity had assets of £1.6 million and an income of £96,000. Grants were made totalling £1,300.

Applications

Applications can be submitted directly by the individual or by an appropriate third party such as a social worker or close family member. They are normally considered quarterly, but small emergency grants can be made between meetings.

Other information

The trust also provides warden-operated individual accommodation for elderly people in the area.

Hordle

The Hordle District Nursing Association

£0

Correspondent: Mrs A Hill, 7 Firmount Close, Everton, Lymington, Hampshire SO41 0JN (01590 642272)

Trustees: Audrey Hill; Judith Rice; Ruth Lambe.

CC Number: 201328

Eligibility

People in need who live in the parish of Hordle (New Forest).

Types of grants

Grants are given to help with the costs incurred by illness. They are usually one-off.

Annual grant total

The association has had no expenditure in the last two years. Previously, however, grants averaged around £1,500.

Applications

In writing to the correspondent. Applications can be made either directly by the individual or by anyone with knowledge of the applicant's need. They are considered at any time throughout the year.

Isle of Wight

The Broadlands Home Trust

£8,500

Correspondent: Mrs M Groves, 2 Winchester Close, Newport, Isle of Wight PO30 1DR (01983 525630; email: broadlandstrust@btinternet.com)

Trustees: June Cox; Hilary Spurgeon; Caroline Baston; Revd Graham Morris; Revd Michael Weaver.

CC Number: 201433

Eligibility

Widows of pensionable age who are in need and live on the Isle of Wight.

Types of grants

Pensions of around £450 a year and Christmas boxes of between £50 and £100. General relief-in-need grants may occasionally be given.

Annual grant total

In 2010/11 the trust had an income of £11,500. Grants were made totalling £10,500 and were distributed as follows:

Pensions	£7,500
Advancement of life grants	£2,000
Christmas boxes to pensioners	£800

Exclusions

No grants for married women or graduates.

Applications

On a form available from the correspondent, to be submitted either directly by the individual or a family member. Applications are considered quarterly in January, April, July and October.

The Mary Pittis Charity for Widows

£5,500

Correspondent: Anthony Holmes, 62–66 Lugley Street, Newport, Isle of Wight PO30 5EU (01983 524431)

Trustee: Revd Graham Akers.

CC Number: 262018

Eligibility

Widows who are aged 60 and over, who live on the Isle of Wight and express Christian (Protestant only) beliefs. Applicants must be known to the minister and have some connection with the church detailed on the application form.

Types of grants

One-off grants ranging from £50 to £200 towards essential kitchen equipment, semi-medical items such as easy-lift armchairs, alarm systems and so on.

Annual grant total

Grants average around £4,000 a year.

Applications

On a form available from the correspondent, giving details of the church attended and the minister. Applications can be made directly, through a welfare agency or a minister of religion. They are considered at any time.

Lyndhurst

The Lyndhurst Welfare Charity

£1,000

Correspondent: A G Herbert, Trustee, 59 The Meadows, Lyndhurst, Hampshire SO43 7EJ (02380 283895)

Trustees: Mr A. G. Herbert; Mr T. M. Abbott; Mrs P. A. Wyeth; Mr B. J. Austin; Mrs A. V. Brooks; Dr Sarah Chinn; Mrs C. Gilbert; Miss C. Wickens.

CC Number: 206647

Eligibility

People in need who live in the parish of Lyndhurst.

Types of grants

Grants are normally one-off and are made towards items, services or facilities, e.g. household items, respite care and counselling. Grants usually range between £50 and £500.

Annual grant total

In 2010/11 the trust had a total income and expenditure of £4,000. Grants to individuals usually total around £1,000 per year.

Applications

Applicants should telephone or write to the correspondent, either directly themselves, or through a social worker, Citizens Advice or other welfare agency. Applications are usually considered in April and October, but emergency applications can be considered in between those times.

Other information
Grants are also made to organisations.

New Forest
The New Forest Keepers Widows Fund

£13,000

Correspondent: Richard Mihalop, 17 Ferndale Road, Marchwood, Southampton SO40 4XR (02380 861136)

Trustees: Michael Seddon; Derek Allan Gurney; Rachel Pearson.

CC Number: 1016362

Eligibility
Retired keepers or widows and children of deceased keepers who are in need and live in the New Forest.

Types of grants
One-off and recurrent grants ranging from £50 to £2,500.

Annual grant total
In 2010/11 the fund had an income of £13,000 and a total expenditure of £14,000.

Applications
In writing to the correspondent directly by the individual or family member. Applications can be submitted at any time.

Portsmouth
The Isaac and Annie Fogelman Relief Trust

£11,000

Correspondent: S J Forman, Torrington House, 47 Holywell Hill, St Albans, Hertfordshire AL1 1HD (01727 885560)

Trustees: Lawerence Justin Guyer; Stephen Forman.

CC Number: 202285

Eligibility
People of the Jewish faith aged 40 and over who live in Portsmouth and worship at the Portsmouth Jewish Synagogue.

Types of grants
One-off and recurrent grants according to need.

Annual grant total
In 2010/11 the trust had an income of £4,700 and a total expenditure of £12,000.

Applications
In writing to: The Secretary, Portsmouth and Southsea Hebrew Congregation, The Thicket, Elm Grove, Southsea PO5 2AA. Applications are considered quarterly.

Thomas King Trust

£1,500

Correspondent: Mrs Joanne Wildsmith, Local Democracy Manager, Portsmouth City Council, Civic Offices, Guildhall Square, Portsmouth PO1 2AL (02392 834057; email: joanne.wildsmith@ portsmouthcc.gov.uk)

Trustees: Keith Crabbe; David Stephen Butler; Christopher Trevellick; Cllr Margaret Adair.

CC Number: 202585

Eligibility
People in need who have lived in Portsmouth for ten years.

Types of grants
Mainly one-off grants according to need ranging from £20 to £50.

Annual grant total
In 2010/11 the trust had an income of £2,800 and a total expenditure of £1,600.

Applications
Application forms are available from the correspondent in October for decisions in December. They can be submitted either directly by the individual, or through a social worker, Citizens Advice or other third party.

Other information
The John Wallace Peck Trust and three other local charities were amalgamated with this trust in 1999.

The Montagu Neville Durnford and Saint Leo Cawthan Memorial Trust

£17,000

Correspondent: Local Democracy Manager, Portsmouth City Council, Civic Offices, Guildhall Square, Portsmouth PO1 2QR (02392 834052)

Trustees: Cmmdr Richard Lovett; Cllr Mike Park; Margaret Foster; Leo Madden.

CC Number: 264782

Eligibility
People over 60 who are in need and who live in the city of Portsmouth. Preference is given to ex-naval personnel and their dependents/widows.

Types of grants
Annual grants of £50 given by the Royal Naval Benevolent Trust (RNBT) and to those recommended by Age UK.

Annual grant total
In 2010/11 the trust had an income of £14,000 and a total expenditure of £19,000.

Applications
Application forms are available from the correspondent. Grants are made to the RNBT and Age UK in November, for redistribution.

The Lord Mayor of Portsmouth's Charity

£22,000

Correspondent: Local Democracy Manager, Portsmouth City Council, Civic Offices, Guildhall Square, Portsmouth, Hampshire PO1 2QR (02392 834052)

Trustees: Cllr Robert Gerald Vernon-Jackson; Cllr Jason Fazackarley; Cllr Simon Bosher.

CC Number: 258109

Eligibility
Individuals in need who live in the City of Portsmouth, or former residents who now live in Havant, Waterlooville, Fareham or Droxford.

Types of grants
One-off grants with average grants of around £200.

Annual grant total
In 2010/11 the trust had an income of £15,000. Grants to individuals totalled £22,000. Generally the charity aims to distribute all of its annual income.

Exclusions
Educational fees, scholarships, travel costs or arrears/debts are not funded.

Applications
In writing to the correspondent either directly or through a friend, family member or welfare organisation. Unsuccessful applicants will be informed.

Other information
Grants are also made to local organisations (£600 in 2010/11).

The E. C. Roberts Charitable Trust

£0

Correspondent: Revd Wendy Kennedy, First Floor, Peninsular House, Wharf Road, Portsmouth PO2 8HB (02392 899668; email: wendy.kennedy@ portsmouth.anglican.org)

Trustee: Bishop Christopher.

CC Number: 1001055

Eligibility

Children in need who live in the city of Portsmouth, with a preference for those living with blindness or disability.

Types of grants

One-off or recurrent grants according to need.

Annual grant total

Expenditure from the trust varies widely. In 2010 there was no expenditure, but in 2009 it was £36,000.

Applications

In writing to the correspondent. Applications can be submitted either directly by the individual, through a third party such as a social worker, or through an organisation such as a Citizens Advice or other welfare agency. Applications are considered upon receipt.

Ryde

The Ryde Sick Poor Fund (also known as Greater Ryde Benevolent Trust)

£6,500

Correspondent: Rachel McKernan, Secretary, 29 John Street, Ryde PO33 2PZ (01983 812552; email: rachel.mckernan@btinternet.com)

Trustees: Janet Bell; John Smith; Paul Ferguson; Claire Gale; Adrian Searle; John Barnes.

CC Number: 249832

Eligibility

Sick people in need who live in the former borough of Ryde.

Types of grants

Small, one-off grants only. The trust is unable to give recurrent grants.

Annual grant total

In 2010 the trust had an income of £6,500 and a total expenditure of £7,000.

Applications

In writing to the correspondent.

Southampton

The Southampton (City Centre) Relief-in-Need Charity

£7,000

Correspondent: Valerie Warren, 4 Morley Close, Burton, Christchurch BH23 7LA (01202 481984)

Trustees: Valerie Warren; Ann Marie McCarthy; Vilma Scott; Jean Richardson; Pat Hawkins; Hazel Cargill; Carole Adams; Revd Dr Julian Davis.

CC Number: 255617

Eligibility

People in need who live in the ecclesiastical parish of Southampton (in practice, the city centre).

Types of grants

One-off grants ranging from £50 to £100 for a wide range of needs such as travel to hospital, convalescence, heating, medical equipment, holidays, special food or equipment, book recordings and chiropody.

Annual grant total

In 2010 the charity had an income of £11,000 and a total expenditure of £8,000.

Exclusions

No grants towards rent, debts or council tax.

Applications

In writing to the correspondent submitted through a social worker, Citizens Advice, health visitor or other welfare agency. Applications are considered quarterly in March, June, September and December; those made directly by the individual will not be considered.

Southampton Charitable Trust

£10,000

Correspondent: Katy Norris, c/o BDO llp, Arcadia House, Maritime Walk, Southampton SO14 3TL (email: katy.norris@bdo.co.uk)

Trustees: Robert Oliver West; Stephen George Prince; Crispin Denys Chauncy Jameson; David Waldron; David William Chun; John Richard Parkhouse; Angela Scouller; Trevor Bell; David Hobbs.

CC Number: 201603

Eligibility

People who are sick and poor and live in Southampton and the immediate surrounding area. Grants and certificates are also awarded to people for saving or attempting to save someone from drowning or other dangers.

Types of grants

One-off grants usually ranging from £50 to £250 for bedding, food, fuel and specialist equipment to alleviate an existing condition or to assist with day-to-day living.

Annual grant total

In 2011 the society had an income of £11,000 and a total expenditure of £12,000.

Applications

In writing to the correspondent. Applications should preferably be submitted through a social worker, Citizens Advice or other welfare agency. The trustees usually meet twice a year, but applications can be dealt with outside these meetings. Applicants must clearly demonstrate that they are both sick and poor (such as evidence of Income Support or other state benefits).

Hertfordshire

The Bowley Charity for Deprived Children

£11,000

Correspondent: Kay Rees, 175 Cassiobury Drive, Watford WD17 3AL (01923 226710; email: kayrees@hotmail.com)

Trustees: Virginia Cates; Kay Rees; Jan Sherlock; Barbara Summers.

CC Number: 212187

Eligibility

Disadvantaged children up to 16 years (or 18 if in full-time education) who live in South West Hertfordshire.

Types of grants

Small one-off grants of between £50 and £500 (the upper limit is for larger families), for items such as cookers, beds, bedding, prams, cots and other essential household items. Grants are also given for essential items of clothing for children.

Annual grant total

In 2010/11 the charity had an income of £11,300 and a total expenditure of £11,400.

Exclusions

No grants for school uniforms.

Applications

On a form available from the correspondent. Applications should be made through a social worker, Citizens Advice or other welfare agency. Trustees meet quarterly to consider grants.

The Hertfordshire Charity for Deprived Children

£7,500

Correspondent: Ralph Paddock, 86 Ware Road, Hertford SG13 7HN (01992 551128; email: ralphiegerry@ btopenworld.com)

Trustees: Mrs B. Lerner; Mr C. Handford; Pat Read; Diane Hanlon.

CC Number: 200327

Eligibility

Disadvantaged children up to the age of 17 living in Hertfordshire (excluding the Watford area).

Types of grants

One-off grants generally for holidays (not overseas), clothing (such as school or cub uniforms or general clothing), and household items (such as cookers or washing machines, where this would improve the quality of life for the child). Grants usually range between £30 and £300.

Annual grant total

In 2010/11 the charity had an income and expenditure of £8,000.

Applications

On a form available from the correspondent. Applications should be made through a health visitor, social worker, probation officer or similar third party. Trustees normally meet in May and November, but applications can be considered between meetings and can be approved on the agreement of two trustees.

Hertfordshire Community Foundation

£21,000 (93 grants)

Correspondent: Christine Mills, Grants Manager, Foundation House, 2–4 Forum Place, Fiddlebridge Lane, Hatfield, Hertfordshire AL10 0RN (01707 251351; email: christine.mills@hertscf.org.uk; website: www.hertscf.org.uk)

Trustees: John Peters; Stuart Lewis; Katie Belinis; Patricia Garrard; Caroline McCaffrey; David Fryer; Michael Master; Gerald Corbett; Penny Williams; Brig John Palmer; Cllr Christopher Hayward; Jo Connell.

CC Number: 299438

Eligibility

People up to 18 years of age who live in Hertfordshire and are disabled, disadvantaged or who have been in care.

Types of grants

One-off grants of up to £300. Recent grants include the purchase of beds and bedding for two families living in one house with four children between them; a tumble drier and an ironing board for a mother and her two young children fleeing domestic violence; a cooker for a young woman living with her 12 year old sibling whose mother has recently died; a wardrobe and changing unit for a single parent with a new baby who has special needs.

Annual grant total

Grants to individuals totalled £21,000 in 2010/11.

Exclusions

Grants are not given for holidays, school trips, debt payment, rent arrears or one-off events.

Applications

On a form available from the correspondent. Applications can be made at any time through a recognised professional such as a social worker or health visitor. Evidence of income and expenditure should be provided. Note: grants are only payable to third parties, such as a shop, in order to purchase a much needed item.

Other information

The foundation mainly supports organisations.

The Hertfordshire Convalescent Trust

£19,000

Correspondent: Janet Bird, Administrator, 140 North Road, Hertford SG14 2BZ (01992 587544; fax: 01992 582595; email: janet_l_bird@ hotmail.com)

Trustees: Richard Norman Taylor; Graham Field.

CC Number: 212423

Eligibility

People in need who are convalescing following an operation or period of ill health, chronically sick, terminally ill or children with special needs and their carers. Families suffering from domestic violence or relationship breakdown may also be eligible for assistance. Applicants must live in Hertfordshire.

Types of grants

One-off grants in the range of £300 to £450 for traditional convalescence in a nursing home or for respite breaks and recuperative holidays in hotels and caravans.

Annual grant total

In 2010 the trust had a total income and expenditure of £31,000. Grants totalled £19,000

Exclusions

There are no grants available for equipment or transport costs.

Applications

On a form available from the correspondent. Applications should be sponsored by a health professional, social worker or member of the clergy. They are considered throughout the year.

The Ware Charities

£12,500

Correspondent: Mrs S Newman, 3 Scotts Road, Ware, Hertfordshire SG12 9JG (01920 461629; email: suedogs@hotmail. com)

Trustees: Alan Wiffen; Kathleen Sanders; Jacqueline Harrison; Terence Milner; Colin Millett; David Perman; Ann Hammond; Alan Mills; Peter Rolfe.

CC Number: 225443

Eligibility

People in need who live in the area of Ware Town Council, the Parish of Wareside and the parish of Thundridge.

Types of grants

Grants are made towards items or services not readily available from any other source.

Annual grant total

In 2010/11 the charities had assets of £1.1 million and an income of £57,000. There were 47 grants made to individuals for welfare and education totalling £25,000.

Applications

In writing to the correspondent at any time, to be submitted directly by the individual or a family member. Applications must include brief details of the applicant's income and savings and be supported and signed by a headteacher, doctor, nurse or social worker.

Other information

Grants are also made to local organisations.

Buntingford

The Buntingford Relief in Need Charity

£15,000

Correspondent: Eunice Woods, 38 Hare Street Road, Buntingford, Hertfordshire SG9 9HW (01763 271974)

Trustees: Cyril Berry; Alan Smith; Dennis Goodeve; Eunice Woods; Stanley Bull; Veronica Easley; Srjit Singh Basra; Jonathan Geoffrey Ling; Revd Ian Hill.

CC Number: 262264

Eligibility
Older people on state registered pensions who live in Buntingford and have lived there for ten years.

Types of grants
£20 per household given in early December towards fuel.

Annual grant total
In 2010 the charity had an income of £16,500 and a total expenditure of £25,500. Grants were made totalling around £15,000.

Applications
In writing to the correspondent.

Dacorum

The Dacorum Community Trust

£15,000

Correspondent: The Grants and Finance Officer, Cementaprise Centre, Paradise, Hemel Hempstead HP2 4TF (01442 231396; email: admin@dctrust.org.uk; website: www.dctrust.org.uk)

Trustees: Tony Williams; Brian Ivory; Mike Edis; John Carlton-Ashton; Gill Chapman; Jill Clarke; David Furnell; Sue Pesch; Mog Phillips; Stuart Wesley.

CC Number: 272759

Eligibility
People in need who live in the borough of Dacorum.

Types of grants
Generally one-off grants up to £500 towards domestic equipment; disability equipment; clothes and shoes; funeral expenses; respite breaks and holidays for families; debt relief; and the costs involved in making homes habitable and safe for young and old.

Annual grant total
In 2010/11 the trust had assets of £192,000 and received an income of £61,000. Grants totalling £39,000 were given to organisations and individuals for welfare and education purposes.

Exclusions
Grants are not normally given for the costs of further or mainstream education and only in exceptional circumstances for gap-year travel.

Applications
On a form available from the correspondent or to download from the website. Applications can be submitted by the individual, through a recognised referral agency (such as Social Services or Citizens Advice) or through an MP, doctor or school. Applications are considered in March, June, September and December. The trust asks for details of family finances. A preliminary telephone call is always welcome.

Harpenden

The Harpenden Trust

£44,000

Correspondent: Dennis Andrews, The Trust Centre, 90 Southdown Road, Harpenden AL5 1PS (01582 460457; email: admin@theharpendentrust.org.uk; website: www.theharpendentrust.org.uk)

Trustees: Dennis Andrews; Roy Brimblecombe; Jan Seager; Geoff Kelly; Teresa Heritage; John Goodson; Rodger Livesey; Sue Coad.

CC Number: 1118870

Eligibility
People in need who live in the 'AL5' postal district of Harpenden, with a preference for younger and older people.

Types of grants
One-off grants for up to £200 are made, for example, for large unexpected bills, essential household items and children's food and clothing. Grants towards the cost of utility bills are available to pensioners on a low income. Educational grants may also be made.

Annual grant total
In 2010/11 the trust had assets of £3.5 million and an income of £197,000. Grants were made to 845 individuals totalling £56,000 and were distributed as follows:

Grants	511	£29,000
Utilities Grants	76	£14,000
Christmas Parcels	187	£1,500
Youth Grants	71	£12,000

A further £32,000 was given to local organisations.

Exclusions
Grants are not given to individuals living outside of Harpenden.

Applications
In writing to the correspondent, either directly by the individual or through a third party such as a social worker or Citizens Advice.

Other information
The trust runs its own centres in Southdown Road and at the High Street Methodist Church. There is a weekly coffee morning and summer coach trips are often organised. The trust also delivers a Christmas dinner to housebound residents on Christmas day.

The trust has an informative website.

Hatfield

Hatfield Broad Oak Non-Ecclesiastical Charities

£7,500

Correspondent: Martin Gandy, Carters Barn, Cage End, Hatfield Broad Oak, Bishop's Stortford, Hertfordshire CM22 7HL (01279 718316)

Trustees: Wendy Brandham; Fiona Jane Cattermole; Martin Broad; Mr R. Simons.

CC Number: 206467

Eligibility
People in need who live in Hatfield Broad Oak.

Types of grants
One-off and recurrent grants ranging from £20 to £25.

Annual grant total
In 2010 the trust had an income of £6,000 and a total expenditure of £8,000.

Applications
In writing to the correspondent directly by the individual or family member.

Wellfield Trust

£11,000

Correspondent: Mrs Jeanette Bayford, Birchwood Leisure Centre, Longmead, Hatfield, Hertfordshire AL10 0AN (01707 251018; email: wellfieldtrust@aol.com; website: www.wellfieldtrust.co.uk)

Trustees: Adrian Ashby; Maggie Haynes; Howard Morgan; Bernard Prestion; John Dean; Margaret White; Mick Clark; Anthony Bailey; Sheila Jones.

CC Number: 296205

Eligibility
People in need who are on a low income and who have lived in the parish of Hatfield for six months.

Types of grants

One-off grants of £100 to £500 towards a range of welfare needs. The trust also loans motorised scooters.

Annual grant total

In 2010/11 grants to individuals totalled £14,000, with a further £7,400 given towards projects.

The majority of grants are given for welfare purposes.

Exclusions

Grants are not made for council tax arrears, rent or funeral costs.

Applications

On a form available from the correspondent or to download from the website, only via a third party such as social services or Citizens Advice. Most of the local appropriate third parties also have the application form. Applications are considered monthly and should be received by the first Monday of every month.

Other information

The trust has an informative website.

Letchworth Garden City

The Letchworth Civic Trust

£2,300

Correspondent: Sally Jenkins, Broadway Chambers, Letchworth Garden City SG63 AD (07785 104357; email: letchworthct@gmail.com; website: letchworthct.org.uk/)

Trustees: Jenny Green; Keith Emsall; Mary Deary; William Armitage; Neville Brammer; Patricia Walker; Lynda Needham; Ian Cotterill; Monica Bloxham; Sally Jenkins.

CC Number: 273336

Eligibility

People who are in need, sick or require accommodation and live in Letchworth Garden City, and have lived there for two years or more.

Types of grants

One-off grants and occasionally loans in the range of £50 to £500. Grants aim to make a 'significant difference', for example to purchase a wheelchair, tools for an ex-prisoner or 'key money' for a homeless person finding accommodation.

Annual grant total

In 2010/11 the trust had assets of £583,000 and an income of £69,000. Grants to individuals totalled £48,000

including nine grants for 'educational or medical support' totalling £4,500.

Applications

On forms available from the website. Applications are considered in January, March, June, September, October and December and can be submitted by the individual or a third party such as a headteacher, social worker, probation officer or police officer.

Other information

Grants are also made to schoolchildren and students, and to groups and societies, but not religious or political groups.

Watford

The Watford Health Trust

£18,000

Correspondent: Ian Scleater, Allways, 23 Shepherds Road WD18 7HU (01923 222745; email: ian@scleater.co.uk)

Trustees: Ian Scleater; Jean Maire Spivey; Paul Stroud; Valerie Cecilia Wigman.

CC Number: 214160

Eligibility

People in need who are in poor health, convalescent or who have a disability and live in the borough of Watford and the surrounding neighbourhood.

Types of grants

One-off and recurrent grants to assist recovery or improve quality of life.

Annual grant total

In 2010/11 the trust had an income of £23,000 and a total expenditure of £21,000.

Applications

In writing to the correspondent. Grants are generally made through official bodies or practices familiar with the applicant's needs.

Other information

Grants are also made to local organisations.

Wormley

The Wormley Parochial Charity

£3,000

Correspondent: Mrs C Proctor, 5 Lammasmead, Broxbourne, Hertfordshire EN10 6PF

Trustees: Peter Lardi; Prof. Stanley Earles; Carol Procter; Barbara Burgess; Iris Banerjee; Christopher House.

CC Number: 218463

Eligibility

People in need who live in the parish of Wormley as it was defined before 31 March 1935, particularly those who are elderly, sick or newly bereaved.

Types of grants

Grants towards (i) transport to or from hospital, either as a patient or visitor; (ii) Christmas vouchers to spent locally for food and other necessities for people who are in need, sick, frail, elderly, bereaved and so on; (iii) one-off grants for people with special needs.

Annual grant total

About £6,000.

Exclusions

The trust does not give loans.

Applications

In writing to the charity, either directly by the individual, or through a social worker, Citizens Advice, welfare agency or a third party such as a friend who is aware of the situation. Applications are considered in April and October.

Kent

The Appleton Trust (Canterbury)

£5,400 (6 grants)

Correspondent: J Hills, Diocesan House, Lady Wootton's Green, Canterbury, Kent CT1 1NQ (01227 459401)

Trustees: Ray Harris; Julian Hills; Christopher Parish.

CC Number: 250271

Eligibility

People in need connected with the Church of England in the diocese of Canterbury.

Types of grants

One-off grants ranging between £100 and £500. Recent grants include those made to youth workers and wives of the clergy. The trust also makes loans to member of the clergy, local parishes and widows of clergymen for items such as cars, computer equipment and equity loans.

Annual grant total

In 2010 the trust had assets of £754,000 and an income of £33,000. Grants were made to six individuals totalling £5,400.

Exclusions

Grants are not given for further education.

Applications

In writing to the correspondent. Applications should be submitted directly by the individual or a church organisation and are considered every two months.

Other information

Organisations connected to the Church of England in Canterbury Diocese are also supported.

The Coleman Trust

£47,000 (89 grants)

Correspondent: Peter Sherred, Clerk, Bradleys, 15–21 Castle Street, Dover, Kent CT16 1PU (01304 204080)

Trustees: Beryl Evelyne Harrison; Margaret Mary Rosaleen Pain; Brian Lawrence; Mary Kathleen Mee; Pamela Mary Brivo; Dr Michael John Parks.

CC Number: 237708

Eligibility

People who live in Dover and the immediate neighbourhood and are sick, convalescing, or living with a mental or physical disability.

Types of grants

One-off grants according to need. Recent grants have been given for periods in residential care and nursing homes, disability aids, telephone facilities and convalescent holiday breaks.

Annual grant total

In 2011 the trust held assets of £1.5 million and had an income of £58,000. Grants to 89 individuals totalled £47,000.

Exclusions

No grants for furniture, home repairs or debts.

Applications

Applications should be made through a social worker, Citizens Advice, welfare agency, doctor or consultant and sent to Mrs Barbara Godfrey, Welfare Officer, 41 The Ridgeway, River, Dover, Kent CT16 1RT.

Cornwallis Memorial Fund

£15,000

Correspondent: Richard Bushrod, Honorary Secretary, Dundurn House, St Fillans, Crieff PH6 2NH (email: secretary@cornwallisfunds.org.uk; website: www.cornwallisfunds.org.uk)

Trustees: Lord Cornwallis; Jeremy Leigh Pemberton; Allan Willett; Hon Chris Cowdrey; Matthew Fleming; Charles Philipson; Hon Charlotte Cornwallis; Michael Firmin.

CC Number: 220391

Eligibility

People in need who live in Kent. Only those who were born in, or have lived in Kent for some time will be considered.

Types of grants

One-off grants of £50 to £300.

Annual grant total

The trust has an average total annual expenditure of around £16,500.

Applications

On a form available from the correspondent, on receipt of an sae. Applications can be made either directly by the individual, or through a social worker, Citizens Advice or other third party. Applicants should provide as much detail as possible, including extra information sheets with the application as relevant.

Headley-Pitt Charitable Trust

£10,500

Correspondent: Thelma Pitt, Old Mill Cottage, Ulley Road, Kennington, Ashford, Kent TN24 9HX (01233 626189; email: thelma.pitt@headley.co.uk)

Trustees: H. C. Pitt; J. R. Pitt; R. W. Pitt; Mrs S. D. Pitt.

CC Number: 252023

Eligibility

Individuals in need who live in Kent with a preference for Ashford. There is also a preference for older people.

Types of grants

One-off grants, usually in the range of £100 to £300.

Annual grant total

In 2010/11 the trust had assets of £2.5 million and an income of £64,000. Grants made to individuals totalled £21,000.

Applications

In writing to the correspondent, either directly by the individual or through a third party.

Other information

Grants are also made to organisations and to individuals for educational purposes.

Kent Community Foundation

£20,000

Correspondent: Administrator, Office 23, Evegate Park Barn, Evegate, Ashford, Kent TN25 6SX (01303 814500; email: admin@kentcf.org.uk; website: www.kentcf.org.uk)

Trustees: Arthur Gulland; Bella Colgrain; Ann West; Peter Lake; Tim Bull; Vicki Jessel.

CC Number: 1084361

Eligibility

Children and young people affected by disability or life threatening conditions and adult carers in Kent. Young carers seeking support in the Borough of Gravesham and Medway.

Types of grants

Grants for respite, equipment, short breaks, holidays, pamper days and days out.

Annual grant total

Around £20,000 in 2010/11.

Applications

Contact the foundation in the first instance to discuss an application and obtain an application form. Nominations for other individuals can also be made.

Other information

The Kent Community Foundation administers a number of funding schemes for both organisations and individuals.

The Kent County Football Association Benevolent Fund

£1,800

Correspondent: Keith Masters, Chief Executive, Invicta House, Cobdown House, London Road, Ditton, Aylesford, Kent ME20 6DQ (01622 791850; email: info@kentfa.com; website: www.kentfa.com)

Trustees: Barry Bright; Colin Ian Boswell; Peter Maurice Enright; Paul Dolan.

CC Number: 273118

Eligibility

Players and others directly connected with affiliated bodies or within the jurisdiction of the association who may be injured whilst playing football or who may be incapacitated through illness definitely attributable to participation in the game.

Types of grants

One-off grants according to need.

Annual grant total

In 2010 the fund had an income of £2,300 and a total expenditure of £2,000

Applications

On a form available from the correspondent.

The Kent Fund for Children

£10,000

Correspondent: Mike Ballard, Customer Relationship Team, Customer Services, Invicta House, County Hall, Maidstone, Kent ME14 1XX (01622 694845; fax: 01622 694911; email: mike.ballard@kent.gov.uk; website: www.kenttrustweb.org.uk)

Eligibility

Children and young people up to the age of 21, who are in need and live in Kent County Council area.

The trust is keen to support children and young people who have not had the opportunities that most children and young people enjoy, either because they have physical or learning disabilities, a sensory impairment, or difficult social circumstances.

Types of grants

One-off grants usually up to £500. Grants must be of direct benefit to the child or young person. The trust is particularly keen to enable children and young people to pursue activities, hobbies and interests which cannot be financed through usual sources, i.e. local authorities, schools and community groups and where applicants show self-help through fundraising. Grants may be for equipment for personal development, or to allow the opportunity to learn new skills, or being involved in an expedition or outing.

Annual grant total

Grants usually total around £10,000 per year.

Applications

In writing to the correspondent. Applications must be made on behalf of individuals by a charity, an organised group, society or professional. This includes schools, youth, and community groups and so on.

Other information

Formerly known as The Kent Children's Trust.

Kent Nursing Institution

£3,300

Correspondent: Canon R B Stevenson, The Vicarage, 138 High Street, West

Malling ME19 6NE (01732 842245; email: woolystevenson@yahoo.co.uk)

Trustees: Revd Canon Brian Stevenson; Revd Noel McConachie; Catherine Gore; David Nevill; Elizabeth English; John Noble.

CC Number: 211227

Eligibility

People in need who are sick, convalescent, disabled or infirm and live in west Kent.

Types of grants

One-off grants ranging between £200 and £500. Recent grants have been given in cases of known hardship caused by family illness (to help cover the costs of hospital visits etc.) and to assist in buying specialist equipment to relieve discomfort (special beds, ultrasound matching etc.).

Annual grant total

In 2010 the trust had an income of £4,300 and a total expenditure of £3,500.

Exclusions

The trust does not assist with debt or bankruptcy fees.

Applications

In writing to the correspondent either directly by the individual or through a social worker, doctor, priest, Citizens Advice or other welfare agency. Applications are usually considered in March and October.

Other information

The trust also makes grants to organisations.

Littledown Trust

£9,100

Correspondent: P G Brown, Littledown Farmhouse, Lamberhurst Down, Lamberhurst, Tunbridge Wells TN3 8HD (01892 890867)

Trustees: Jessica I. Brown; Michelle K. Brown; Clare Joanna Brown; Richard Gregorius Brown; Paul G. Brown.

CC Number: 1064291

Eligibility

People in need with a preference for those who live in Kent.

Types of grants

One-off and recurrent grants according to need.

Annual grant total

In 2010/11 the trust had an unusually high income of £22,000 and a total expenditure of £9,600.

Applications

In writing to the correspondent.

The Lord Mayor of Canterbury's Christmas Gift Fund

£17,000

Correspondent: Jennifer Sherwood, Larkings Chartered Accountants, 31 St George's Place, Canterbury, Kent CT1 1XD (01227 464991)

Trustees: Timothy William Brett; John Wiltshier; Sheila Mary Warwick Cragg.

CC Number: 278803

Eligibility

People in need who live in Canterbury and the surrounding area comprised in the former district of Bridge Blean. Preference is generally given to older residents.

Types of grants

Food parcels and toy vouchers are distributed at Christmas time.

Annual grant total

In 2010/11 the fund had an income of £16,000 and a total expenditure of £17,400.

Applications

A list is compiled over the year from local doctors, clergy, Age UK, direct applications and other sources. Direct applications should be made in writing to the correspondent.

The Dorothy Parrott Trust Fund

£3,000

Correspondent: Gina Short, 10 The Landway, Kemsing, Sevenoaks TN15 6TG (01732 760263)

Trustees: Revd Angus MaCleay; Joy Alice May Pennells; John Frederick London; Avril Doreen Hunter; Norman Francis Oldale.

CC Number: 278904

Eligibility

People in need who live in the area administered by Sevenoaks Town Council and adjoining parishes. Young children and older people are given preference.

Types of grants

Usually one-off grants ranging from £25 to £100 according to need. Recent grants have been given towards a fridge, a school outing for the child of a single parent, house decoration, boots, ballet shoes, a mattress for twins and project trips such as Operation Raleigh.

Annual grant total

Grants average around £2,400 per year.

Applications

Either direct to the correspondent or through a social worker, Citizens Advice or similar third party, including a general history of the family. Applications are considered on the last Monday of January, April, July and October.

Other information

Grants may also be made to local organisations.

Sir Thomas Smythe's Charity

£23,000

Correspondent: Charities Administrator, The Skinners' Company, Skinners' Hall, 8 Dowgate Hill, London EC4R 2SP (020 7213 0562; fax: 020 7236 6590; email: charitiesadmin@skinners.org.uk; website: www.skinnershall.co.uk)

Trustee: Worshipful Company of Skinners.

CC Number: 210775

Eligibility

People of pensionable age who are in need and live within the 26 parishes of Tonbridge and Tunbridge Wells.

Types of grants

Pensions are distributed in quarterly payments of £130. One-off crisis grants are typically made for items not covered by benefits, for example, unexpected household repairs or the replacement of domestic appliances.

Annual grant total

In 2010/11 the charity had assets of £1.1 million and an income of £32,000. Pension payments totalled £23,000. No grants were made.

Exclusions

Grants are not made to people in residential care and cannot be given to cover funeral costs or debt repayments.

Applications

Applications are only recommended via local trustees. For contact details of your Local Trustee, contact the Charities Administrator.

Other information

The charity has an informative website.

Borden

The William Barrow's Charity

£11,000 (22 grants)

Correspondent: Stuart Mair, George Webb Finn, 43 Park Road, Sittingbourne, Kent ME10 1DY (01795 470556; email: stuart@georgewebbfinn.com)

Trustees: Denis Arthur Jarrett; Donald Jordan; Edmund Garth Doubleday; Peter Mair; Jeremy James Jefferiss; Pauline Emily Cole; Janet Marian Scott; Father John Lewis; Stephen Charles Batt; Christine Ford.

CC Number: 307574

Eligibility

People in need who live in the ancient ecclesiastical parish of Borden or have lived in the parish and now live nearby. There is a preference for people of 60 years or over and disabled people.

Types of grants

One-off grants and twice-yearly allowances may be given for pensions, disability and medical equipment, travel expenses, convalescence and living costs. Grants typically range from £350 to £500.

Annual grant total

In 2011 the foundation had assets of £5.9 million and an income of £190,000. Grants made to pensioners totalled £10,000 and disability grants totalled £1,300.

Applications

On a form available from the correspondent. Applications are considered in January, April, July and October.

Other information

The charity works in close cooperation with Age UK.

Canterbury

The Canterbury United Municipal Charities

£3,000

Correspondent: Aaron Spencer, Furley Page, 39–40 St Margaret's Street, Canterbury, Kent CT1 2TX (01227 863140; email: aas@furleypage.co.uk)

Trustees: Marjorie Lyle; Ann Burgess; Mercia Powell; Canon Michael Bunce; Clive Bowley; Catherine Hellman; Joan Pritchard; Gina Langford-Allen; Gill Prett; Revd Iain Taylor; Fred Powell; Susan Dawkins.

CC Number: 210992

Eligibility

People in need who have lived within the boundaries of what was the old city of Canterbury for at least two years.

Types of grants

One-off and recurrent grants and pensions. Annual pensions of £100 are given to about 20 needy older people.

Also at Christmas, vouchers/tokens of £25 are given for: clothing for children aged 6 to 16 (30 children); and people who are elderly and in need (120 adults).

Annual grant total

In 2010 the charities had an income of £8,500 and a total expenditure of £6,000. Approximately £3,000 was given towards welfare needs.

Applications

In writing to the correspondent through the individual's school/college/educational welfare agency or directly by the individual. Applications are considered on an ongoing basis and should include a brief statement of circumstances and proof of residence in the area.

Other information

Grants are also given for educational purposes and to organisations with similar objects.

Streynsham's Charity

£23,000

Correspondent: The Clerk to the Trustees, PO Box 970, Canterbury, Kent CT1 9DJ (0845 094 4769)

Trustees: Alicia Pentin; Alasdair Hogarth; David Bentley; James Lees; Philippa Trewby; William Mearns; Anne Ovenden; Jacqui Webber. Mark Ball; Gavin Kennett; Jeanie Armstrong; Leonore Edwards.

CC Number: 214436

Eligibility

People who live in the ancient parish of St Dunstan's.

Types of grants

One-off grants, up to a maximum of about £300.

Annual grant total

In 2011 the trust made grants for welfare totalling £23,000.

Applications

In writing to the correspondent. Applications should be made directly by the individual. They are usually considered in March and October but can be made at any time and should include an sae and telephone number if applicable.

Chatham

Chatham District Masonic Trust

£0

Correspondent: John Knight, 42 The Everglades, Hempstead, Gillingham ME7 3PY (01634 300755)

Trustees: Mr K. Mitten; Bernard Arlington; Alan Joseph Gillespie; Geoffrey Scutt; Jeffrey Peter Prestage.

CC Number: 1040230

Eligibility

Freemasons and their widows and children, living in Chatham.

Types of grants

One-off and recurrent grants according to need.

Annual grant total

In 2010/11 the trust had an income of £25,000 and a total expenditure of £28,000. No further information was available. The trust has not made any grants to individuals in recent years.

Applications

In writing to the correspondent.

Other information

The principal activity of the trust is the running of the Masonic Centre at Manor Road, Chatham.

Dover

The Casselden Trust

£1,000

Correspondent: Leslie Alton, 26 The Shrubbery, Walmer, Deal, Kent CT14 7PZ (01304 375499)

Trustees: John Morgan; Martin Husk.

CC Number: 281970

Eligibility

People in need who live in the Dover Town Council area.

Types of grants

One-off and recurrent grants, up to a maximum of £250.

Annual grant total

Grants usually total around £2,000 each year.

Applications

In writing to the correspondent.

Folkstone

Folkestone Municipal Charities

£68,000

Correspondent: Michael A Cox, Romney House, Cliff Road, Hythe CT21 5XA (01303 260144; email: gillyjc@btinternet.com)

Trustees: John Bonomy; Alec Perry; Betty Heppenstall; David Dunks; Philip Rimington Bean; Sarah Thorne; Ann Berry; Charles Medlicott; Peter Gane; Rosemary Braid; Cllr Martin Salmon; Molly Hunter.

CC Number: 211528

Eligibility

People in need who live in the borough of Folkestone and have done so for at least five years. Preference is usually given to older people and single parent families.

Types of grants

One-off and recurrent grants ranging from about £200 to £400 for a variety of needs. Previously grants have been given for telephone installation, help after a burglary, loss of a purse/wallet, shoes for disadvantaged children, gas/electricity bills, beds/bedding, prams, clothing and household repairs.

Annual grant total

In 2010/11 the trust had assets of £2.6 million and an income of £107,000. Pensions totalled £42,000 while a further £26,000 was distributed in relief in need grants.

Applications

On a form available from the correspondent. Applications should be submitted through a third party such as a social worker, Citizens Advice or similar welfare agency. They are considered on a monthly basis, though urgent requests can be dealt with between meetings.

Fordwich

The Fordwich United Charities

£5,000

Correspondent: Aaron Spencer, Furley Page Solicitors, 39 St Margaret's Street, Canterbury CT1 2TX (01227 863140; fax: 01227 863220)

Trustees: Roger Green; Peter Cornish; David Keegan; June Hardcastle; Elizabeth Lewis; Sylvia McNally.

CC Number: 208258

Eligibility

People in need or with disabilities living in Fordwich.

Types of grants

One-off grants mostly given towards household bills.

Annual grant total

In 2010 the charity had an income of £19,000 and an expenditure of £11,000.

Applications

In writing to: M R Clayton, Ladywell House, Fordwich, Canterbury CT2 0DL. The deadline for applications is 1 September and a decision will be made within a month.

Gillingham

Dobson Trust

£2,200

Correspondent: Mrs Margaret Taylor, Resources, Medway Council, Gun Wharf, Dock Road, Chatham, Kent ME4 4TR (01634 332144; email: margaret.taylor@medway.gov.uk)

Trustees: Rodney Chambers; Robert Russell; Carol Ann Harries; Wendy Purdy; Jonathan Baynes.

CC Number: 283158

Eligibility

People in receipt of a state pension or over the age of 60 who are in financial need and live in the former borough of Gillingham.

Types of grants

One-off grants according to need. Recent grants ranged from £70 for audio books to £2,500 for a replacement boiler. Grants are generally given to help cover exceptional outgoings or unexpected bills, such as to repair or replace an essential domestic appliance or piece of furniture; specialist equipment associated with disability or impairment; or the costs associated with the death of a partner (excluding funeral costs).

Annual grant total

In 2010/11 the trust had an income of £2,200 and a total expenditure of £2,400.

Applications

On a form available from the correspondent. Applications can be submitted at any time and the trustees meet about four times a year.

Other information

Local organisations are also supported.

Godmersham

Godmersham Relief in Need Charity

£3,000

Correspondent: David T Swan, Feleberge, Canterbury Road, Bilting, Ashford, Kent TN25 4HE (01233 812125)

Trustees: Christine Luckhurst; Gregory Ellis; Patricia Fletcher; Revd Ian Campbell; David Jones.

CC Number: 206278

Eligibility

People in need who live in the ancient parish of Godmersham.

Types of grants

One-off grants according to need, towards items, services or facilities.

Annual grant total

In 2010 the charity had both an income and total expenditure of £6,000. Grants are given for both educational and relief-in-need purposes.

Applications

In writing to the correspondent, either directly by the individual or through a third party.

Gravesham

William Frank Pinn Charitable Trust

£170,000 (1,923 grants)

Correspondent: Trust Officer, HSBC Trust Company (UK) Ltd, 10th Floor Norwich House, Nelson Gate, Commercial Road, Southampton, Hampshire SO15 1GX (02380 722224)

Trustee: HSBC. Trust Company (UK) Ltd.

CC Number: 287772

Eligibility

People of pensionable age who live in the borough of Gravesham. Priority is given to those on lower incomes.

Types of grants

One-off grants averaging £90 are made for specific purposes only, such as clothing, furniture, holidays and fuel.

Annual grant total

In 2010/11 the trust had assets of £6.2 million and an income of £234,000. There were 1,932 grants made totalling £170,000. Trustee management costs were relatively high at £62,000.

Exclusions

No more than two grants may be made to any household per calendar year.

Applications

On a form available from the correspondent. Applications should be submitted directly by the individual and are considered monthly.

Hayes

Hayes (Kent) Trust

£4,100

Correspondent: Richard Marlin, 43 Eastry Avenue, Hayes, Bromley, Kent BR2 7PE (020 8462 1363; email: hayes.kent.trust@btinternet.com)

Trustees: Revd David Graham; Carol Truelove; Alison Naish; Susan Rogers; Brian Lightoller; Richard Marlin.

CC Number: 221098

Eligibility

People in need who live in the parish of Hayes.

Types of grants

One-off grants in the region of £75 to £1,500 are given according to need.

Annual grant total

In 2010/11 the trust had assets of £890,000 and an income of £44,000. Grants totalling £4,100 were given to individuals for welfare needs.

Applications

In writing to the correspondent. Applications should include the full name of the applicant, postal address in Hayes (Kent), telephone number and date of birth. Applications can be made either directly by the individual, or through a third party such as a social worker, Citizens Advice or other welfare agency.

Other information

The trust also makes grants to organisations and to individuals for educational purposes.

Herne Bay

The Herne Bay Parochial Charity

£1,200

Correspondent: Susan Emily Record, 39 William Street, Herne Bay, Kent CT6 5NR (01227 367355)

Trustees: Peter John Lee; Stanley Kenneth Ranger; Douglas Rupert Gomm; Priscilla Cox; Ann Taylor; Dr Keith Arthur Frank Record; Revd Elaine Richardson.

CC Number: 1069542

Eligibility

People in need who live in Herne Bay. Applicants preferably should be on income support or in receipt of similar financial assistance.

Types of grants

Both one-off and regular grants during the year and at Christmas. The usual grant to individuals consists of:
(i) a monthly voucher of around £6 which can be exchanged at certain shops or the local council office
(ii) a cash grant of £20 at Christmas
(iii) a cash grant of £10 in February towards fuel
(iv) a cash grant of £10 in November towards fuel.

The charities make a £10 Christmas grant to several other individuals. Examples of other grants are to purchase a particular necessary item such as providing a telephone or to clear a debt, for example.

Annual grant total

Grants average around £1,500 a year.

Applications

In writing to the correspondent through a social worker, Citizens Advice or other welfare agency or directly by the individual or some relevant third party. Applications are normally considered in April and October and ideally should be received in the preceding month. The charities have to be satisfied that the applicant is financially in need, such as by providing supporting evidence of low income through wages slips or a benefit award letter. Particulars of what the grant is required for should be included.

Other information

Grants are also made to organisations helping people in need.

Hildenborough

Helen Georgie Hills Charity

£900

Correspondent: David E Williams, 19 Elm Grove, Hildenborough, Tonbridge, Kent TN11 9HF (01732 833540)

Trustees: David Edward Williams; Janet Richardson.

CC Number: 238999

Eligibility

People who are sick and in need and live in the village of Hildenborough.

Types of grants

One-off grants according to need including those for convalescence,

425

medical equipment, nursing fees and disability equipment.

Annual grant total

Grants average around £900 a year.

Exclusions

Grants are not given to replace statutory responsibilities.

Applications

In writing to the correspondent. Applications can be submitted directly by the individual, or through a social worker, Citizens Advice or other welfare agency or another third party. They are considered at any time.

Other information

The trust also supports local organisations.

Hothfield

The Thanet Charities

£3,400

Correspondent: Mrs Pat Guy, Garden House, Bethersden Road, Hothfield, Ashford, Kent TN26 1EP (01233 612449)

Trustees: George Sainsbury; John Richard Eimer Coles; Alan Peter Guy; Anna Rawlins.

CC Number: 213093

Eligibility

People in need who live in the parish of Hothfield.

Types of grants

Small monthly payments to elderly residents of Hothfield village as well as a limited number of hardship payments to individuals in need.

Annual grant total

Grants average around £3,400 a year.

Applications

In writing to the correspondent.

Hythe

Anne Peirson Charitable Trust

£5,000

Correspondent: Mrs Ina Tomkinson, Trustee/Secretary, Tyrol House, Cannongate Road, Hythe, Kent CT21 5PX (01303 260779)

Trustees: Ina Tomkinson; Kenneth Crowe; Revd Tony Windross; Richard Carroll; Capt. Karen Layton.

CC Number: 800093

Eligibility

People who live the parish of Hythe and are in need, due for example to

hardship, disability or sickness. Support is primarily given for educational needs but grants for emergency needs will be made if financial hardship is demonstrated.

Types of grants

One-off grants ranging from £100 to £600. Recent grants were made towards nursery school fees, special needs for people with children who have disabilities, household goods and so on.

Annual grant total

In 2010 the trust had an income of £11,000 and a total expenditure of £10,000. Further information was not available.

Exclusions

No grants are made where statutory support is available.

Applications

In writing to the correspondent via either Citizens Advice, a social worker, health visitor, school headteacher or other third party. Grants are considered on an ongoing basis.

Other information

Grants are also made to organisations.

Leigh

The Leigh United Charities

£40,000

Correspondent: Sally Bresnahan, 3 Oak Cottages, High Street, Leigh, Tonbridge, Kent TN11 8RW (01732 838544; email: sally@bresnahan.co.uk)

Trustees: John Edwin Knock; Revd Lionel Kevis; Brian Frank Ball.

CC Number: 233988

Eligibility

People in need who live in the ancient parish of Leigh.

Types of grants

One-off grants according to need.

Annual grant total

In 2010/11 the trust had an income of £47,000 and a total charitable expenditure of £40,000. Of this, total grants amounting to £33,000 were committed to Leigh and £7,000 to Hildenborough. No further information was available.

Exclusions

No payment for rates.

Applications

In writing to the correspondent directly by the individual. Applications are considered throughout the year.

Maidstone

The Edmett and Fisher Charity

£7,500

Correspondent: R P Rogers, 72 King Street, Maidstone, Kent ME14 1BL (01622 698000)

Trustees: Dr Anne Carolyn McVittie; Revd Canon Christopher Morgan Jones; Jean Barbara Barrett; Joan Margaret Callaghan; Lorretta Rogers; Betty MacFarlane.

CC Number: 241823

Eligibility

People in need who are aged over 60 and live in the former borough of Maidstone (as it was before April 1974).

Types of grants

One-off and recurrent grants according to need. Christmas gifts have also been given in previous years.

Annual grant total

In 2010/11 the charity had an income of £8,800 and a total expenditure of £8,000.

Applications

On a form available from the correspondent to be submitted directly by the individual. Applications are usually considered twice a year.

The Maidstone Relief-in-Need Charities

£1,700

Correspondent: Debbie Snook, Maidstone Borough Council, Maidstone House, King Street, Maidstone ME15 6JQ (01622 602030)

Trustees: Cllr Dan Daley; Cllr Peter Parvin; Cllr Daphne Parvin; Mike Evans; Cllr Jenni Paterson; Phillip Dodd; Cllr Alistair Black; Cllr Brian Mortimer.

CC Number: 210539

Eligibility

People in need, hardship or distress who live in the former borough of Maidstone.

Types of grants

One-off grants of up to around £300. Grants given include those for hospital expenses, electrical goods, convalescence, clothing, household bills, food, travel expenses, medical equipment, nursing fees, furniture, disability equipment and help in the home.

Annual grant total

In 2010/11 the trust had an income of £4,000 and a total expenditure of £3,800. Grants are given to both individuals and organisations.

Applications

Applications must be made through a social worker, health visitor, doctor or similar third party on a form available from the correspondent.

Margate

Margate and Dr Peete's Charity

£4,800

Correspondent: Dorothy Collins, 31 Avenue Gardens, Cliftonville, Margate, Kent CT9 3AZ (01843 226173)

Trustees: Shirley Tomlinson; Deanna Elizabeth Balchin; Revd Brian Sharp; Iris Johnston; Barbara Anne Kemp; Christine Harper; Geoffrey Kirkpatrick.

CC Number: 212503

Eligibility

People in need who live in the former borough of Margate (as constituted before 1974).

Types of grants

One-off and recurrent grants generally in the range of £50 to £250.

Annual grant total

In 2010/11 the charity had an income of £8,000 and a total expenditure of £4,900.

Applications

On a form available from the correspondent, to be submitted either directly by the individual or through a social worker, Citizens Advice or other welfare agency.

Rochester

Cliffe at Hoo Parochial Charity

£2,300

Correspondent: Paul Kingman, Clerk, 52 Reed Street, Cliffe, Rochester, Kent ME3 7UL (01634 220422; email: paul.kingman@btopenworld.com)

Trustees: Marie Vyse; Diane Forman; Revd Edward Wright; Christopher Fribbins; Kenneth Kentell; Linda Jones; Yvonne Kingman; Doreen Ellis; Lynne Bush.

CC Number: 220855

Eligibility

People in need who live in the ancient parish of Cliffe-at-Hoo.

Types of grants

One-off grants according to need. For example, grants towards household bills and nursing fees.

Annual grant total

In 2010/11 the charity had an income of £3,600 and a total expenditure of £4,600. Around £2,300 was given for welfare purposes.

Applications

In writing to the correspondent, to be submitted directly by the individual or a family member, or through a third party such as a social worker or Citizens Advice.

The William Mantle Trust

£10,000

Correspondent: Barbara Emery, Clerk, Administrative Offices, Watt's Almshouses, Maidstone Road, Rochester, Kent ME1 1SE (01634 842194; email: wattscharity@btconnect.com)

Trustees: Roger Hill; Juliet Wright; David John Bradley; Donald Alexander Gordon Troup; Ian Rex Robinson; Michael Robin Bailey; Daphne Isabel MacDonald; Eunice Madeline Tiber; Jean Elsie Lingham; Ronald Vernon Kettle; Roger Kenneth Hawkes; Hilary Mary Moore; Terence James Burton; Anthony William Clayton; Brian Peter Cox; Hilary Harwood.

CC Number: 248661

Eligibility

People in need who are over 60 and were either born in that part of Rochester which lies to the south and east of the River Medway, or have at any time lived in that part of the city for a continuous period of at least 15 years.

Types of grants

Recurrent grants of about £65 per person, per month.

Annual grant total

In 2010/11 the trust had an income of £9,100 and a total expenditure of £10,800.

Applications

On a form available from the correspondent. Applications should be submitted directly by the individual or through a third party on their behalf. They are considered on a regular basis.

Richard Watts and The City of Rochester Almshouse Charities

£18,000

Correspondent: Jane Rose, Clerk, Watts Almshouses, Maidstone Road, Rochester, Kent ME1 1SE (01634 842194; email: admin@richardwatts.org.uk; website: www.richardwatts.org.uk)

Trustees: Roger Hill; Juliet Wright; David Bradley; Donald Troup; Ian Robinson; Michael Bailey; Daphne MacDonald; Eunice Tober; Jean Lingham; Ronald Kettle; Roger Hawkes; Hilary Moore; Terence Burton; Anthony Clayton; Brian Cox; Hilary Harwood.

CC Number: 212828

Eligibility

People in need who live in the city of Rochester.

Types of grants

Pensions for retired people and one-off grants towards a wide variety of needs, including clothing, electrical goods, travel expenses, medical equipment, furniture, disabled equipment and help in the home. In kind grants are also made. Grants are usually in excess of £50.

Annual grant total

In 2011 the trust had assets of £19 million and an income of £1.7 million. £37,000 was given in grants to individuals, broken down into the following categories:
- Helpline: 12 grants totalling £1,800
- Education: 13 grants totalling £19,000
- Children and family: 39 grants totalling £9,600
- Elderly: four grants totalling £2,600
- Others: seven grants totalling £1,000

Additionally, pensions were provided to 91 individuals.

Applications

On a form available from the correspondent. Applications can be submitted at any time and are considered on a monthly basis.

Other information

Grants are also given to organisations which benefit the local community. The charity also runs an almshouse.

Sevenoaks

The Kate Drummond Trust

£1,000

Correspondent: David Batchelor, The Beeches, Packhorse Road, Sevenoaks, Kent TN13 2QP (01732 451584)

Trustees: David Batchelor; Revd Angus MacLeay; Carlton Andrews; Janet Batchelor.

CC Number: 246830

Eligibility

People in need who live in Sevenoaks, preference is given to young people.

Types of grants

The majority of grants are one-off.

Annual grant total

Grants tend to total around £2,000 each year.

Applications

In writing to the correspondent, with an sae if a reply is required.

Tunbridge Wells

Miss Ethel Mary Fletcher's Charitable Bequest

£20,000

Correspondent: Mrs S Currie, Thomson, Snell and Passmore, Ref 1295, 3 Lonsdale Gardens, Tunbridge Wells, Kent TN1 1NU (01892 510000)

Trustees: Simon Brown; Dr Anthony Brian Hugo.

CC Number: 219850

Eligibility

Older people in need who live in the Tunbridge Wells area.

Types of grants

One-off and recurrent grants according to need.

Annual grant total

In 2010/11 the charity had an income of £9,500 and a total expenditure of £21,000.

Applications

In writing to the correspondent, through a social worker, Citizens Advice or other welfare agency. The charity has recently stated: 'funds are fully committed, although consideration will be given to extreme applications'.

Other information

Occasional grants are made to organisations with similar objectives.

Wilmington

The Wilmington Parochial Charity

£8,500

Correspondent: Derek Maidment, 23 The Close, Dartford DA2 7ES (01322 224829)

Trustees: Ann Allen; Chris Settle; Michael Iveson; Richard Arding; Shelagh Longstaff; Tom Maddison; Jenny Rickwood.

CC Number: 1011708

Eligibility

People in need, living in the parish of Wilmington, who are receiving a statutory means-tested benefit, such as Income Support, Housing Benefit or help towards their council tax.

Types of grants

Recurrent grants are available as follows: grocery vouchers of £30, cash grants of £10 at Christmas and heating grants of £60 at Easter.

Annual grant total

Welfare grants to individuals total about £8,500 a year.

Applications

Applications should be submitted by the individual, or through a social worker, Citizens Advice or other welfare agency. The trustees meet in February and November. Urgent applications can be considered between meetings in exceptional circumstances.

Other information

Grants are also given to local schools at Christmas and to individuals for education.

Norfolk

The Blakeney Twelve

£11,000

Correspondent: Christopher Scargill, 24 Kingsway, Blakeney, Holt, Norfolk NR25 7PL (01263 741020)

Trustees: Anthony Warde Faulkner; Christopher Samson Scargill; Darren Paul Bishop; David James Buckey; Malcolm Josiah Reed; Michael Robert John Welch; Morris Charles Arthur; Dr Peter Franklin; Trevor Preston; Steven William Hall; Willie Weston; Sam Blakeney Curtis.

CC Number: 276758

Eligibility

Individuals who are older, infirm or disabled and who live in the parish of Blakeney, Morston and surrounding district.

Types of grants

One-off and recurrent grants, donations of coal and the payment of insurance.

Annual grant total

In 2010/11 the trust had an income of £12,600 and a total expenditure of £12,700.

Applications

In writing to the correspondent.

The Calibut's Estate and the Hillington Charities

£4,000

Correspondent: William J Tawn, Trustee/Chair, 2 Wheatfields, Hillington, King's Lynn, Norfolk PE31 6BH (01485 600641)

Trustees: Edward Dawnay; Revd Jonathan Riviere; Janet Rose Nunn; William Tawn; Mary Freeman.

CC Number: 243510/243511

Eligibility

People in need, usually over 65, who live in Hillington and East Walton.

Types of grants

One-off and recurrent grants, generally ranging from £25 to £100.

Annual grant total

In 2011 the charities had a combined income of £4,500 and a total expenditure of £4,100.

Exclusions

Owner occupiers are not eligible for support.

Applications

In writing to the correspondent to be submitted directly by the individual. Applications are considered in November.

The Anne French Memorial Trust

£65,000

Correspondent: Christopher H Dicker, Trustee Training and Support Ltd, Hill House, Ranworth, Norwich NR13 6AB (01603 270356; email: cdicker@hotmail.co.uk)

Trustee: Revd the Lord Bishop of Norwich.

CC Number: 254567

Eligibility

Members of the Anglican clergy in the diocese of Norwich.

Types of grants

Holiday and other relief-in-need grants as well as training costs for clergy and young people.

Annual grant total

In 2010/11 the trust had assets of £6.3 million and an income of £208,000. Grants to individuals totalled around £65,000 and were broken down as follows:

Gifts to clergy	£44,000
Youth and training	£16,000
Training of the clergy	£5,000

Applications

In writing to the correspondent.

Other information

The charity has a close association with the Bishop of Norwich Fabric Fund Trust and the Norwich Diocesan Board of Finance Ltd.

The King's Lynn and West Norfolk Borough Charity

£6,000

Correspondent: Veronica Stiles, Secretary to the Trustees, 54 Park Road, Hunstanton, Norfolk PE36 5DL (01485 533352)

Trustees: Allan Croose; Cllr Roy Groom; Derek Stiles; Katherine Ann Beale; Mike Hadfield; Will Wright; Cllr Stephanie Margaret Smeaton.

CC Number: 243864

Eligibility

People in need who live in the borough of King's Lynn and West Norfolk.

Types of grants

One-off grants up to £300 towards furniture (such as beds), washing machines, carpets, bedding, cookers, electric scooters and so on.

Annual grant total

Grants usually total around £8,000 a year.

Exclusions

Grants are not given to relieve public funds.

Applications

On a form available from the correspondent. Applications should be submitted through a social worker, Citizens Advice or other welfare agency. They are usually considered in March, June, September and December and should be received in the preceding month.

The Saham Toney Fuel Allotment and Perkins Charity

£4,000

Correspondent: Jill Glenn, Orchard House, 1 Cressingham Road, Ashill, Thetford, Norfolk IP25 7DG (01760 441738; email: jill@glenn8530.freeserve.co.uk)

Trustees: Roger Harrold; Leslie Cator; Roger Baldwin; Roger Cooper; Marlene Grapes.

CC Number: 211852

Eligibility

People in need who have lived in Saham Toney, Saham Hills or Saham Waite for at least two years.

Types of grants

Recurrent grants of between £40 and £120, to help with the cost of fuel.

Annual grant total

In 2010 the charity had an income of £5,000 and a total expenditure of £4,000.

Applications

On a form available from the correspondent, submitted directly by the individual, giving details of dependents and income. Applications should be submitted in May for consideration in June.

The Shelroy Trust

£14,000

Correspondent: Roger Wiltshire, 4 Brandon Court, Brundall, Norwich NR13 5NW (01603 715605)

Trustees: A. Calff; P. Calff; R. C. Snelling; D. Carding; Dr D. A. Varvel; D. Clark; R. Wiltshire; R. D. Kinsley.

CC Number: 327776

Eligibility

Residents of East Norfolk and Norwich, with a preference for Christians, older people and people with disabilities.

Types of grants

One-off grants, ranging from £200 to £500 to cover a specific need.

Annual grant total

In 2010/11 the trust had both an income and total expenditure of £32,000. Grants to individuals for relief-in-need totalled around £14,000.

Exclusions

The trust does not assist with bankruptcy costs.

Applications

In writing to the correspondent at any time. Individuals applying for grants must provide full information and two referees are required. Applications can be made directly by the individual or through a social worker, Citizens Advice or other third party. They are considered at the trustees' quarterly meetings in March, June, September and December. The trust is not able to reply to unsuccessful applicants unless an sae is provided.

Other information

Grants are also made to organisations.

The Southery, Feltwell and Methwold Relief in Need Charity

£1,000

Correspondent: Mrs J K Hodson, 36a Lynn Road, Southery, Downham Market, Norfolk PE38 0HU (01366 377303)

Trustees: Mr B. J. Holman; Mrs M. Lewis; Mrs M. W. Yaxley; Maureen Sharman; Mr D. J. Everitt.

CC Number: 268856

Eligibility

People in need who live in the parishes of Southery, Feltwell and Methwold.

Types of grants

One-off grants in the range of £25 to £100. Grants are often given towards the costs of travel to and from hospital.

Annual grant total

About £1,000.

Applications

In writing to the correspondent. Applications are to be submitted by a third party such as a parishioner or committee member, and must be received by the application deadline of 31 March.

Witton Charity

£200

Correspondent: Beryl Lodge, Trustee, The Old Chapel, Chapel Road, Witton, North Walsham NR28 9UA (01692 650546)

Trustees: Beryl Lodge; John Michael Sings; William Donald.

CC Number: 1009959

Eligibility

Pensioners and other people in need who live in Witton and Ridlington.

Types of grants

Grants of coal twice a year and food parcels at Christmas.

Annual grant total

Over the past six years the charity had an average income of £2,000 and expenditure of £250.

Applications

In writing to the correspondent.

Banham

The Banham Parochial Charities

£9,000

Correspondent: Martin Baglin, Murrfield, Church Road, Carleton Rode, Norwich NR16 1RW (01953 788696)

Trustees: John F. Ninham; Brian William Harper; David Andrew Hicks; Revd David Royston Hills.

CC Number: 213891

Eligibility

People in need who live in the parish of Banham.

Types of grants

One-off grants according to need. Grants have been given towards such things as heating bills, fuel, clothing and funeral expenses.

Annual grant total

In 2010 the trust had an income of £9,500 and a total expenditure of £10,000.

Applications

In writing to the correspondent. Applications can be considered at any time.

Barton Bendish

The Barton Bendish Poor's Charity

£1,000

Correspondent: Freda Rumball, Clerk, 45 Church Road, Barton Bendish, King's Lynn, Norfolk PE33 9GF (01366 347324)

Trustees: Jack Richardson; Philip A. J. Carter; Trevor English; Bill Chapman.

CC Number: 211638

Eligibility

Widows and people in need who live in Barton Bendish, including Eastmoor.

Types of grants

One-off grants of about £40 to help with fuel expenses during the winter and towards travel to hospitals and funeral expenses.

Annual grant total

Grants usually total around £1,000 a year.

Applications

In writing to the correspondent at any time throughout the year.

Beeston

The Beeston Fuel Charity (Fuel Allotment)

£1,000

Correspondent: Bryan Leigh, Riverside Cottage, River Lane, East Bilney, Norfolk NR20 4HS (01362 861112)

Trustee: Beeston with Bittering Parish Council.

CC Number: 213779

Eligibility

People over 65 years old who are in need and have lived in the parish of Beeston for at least five years.

Types of grants

Fuel grants of between £20 and £25 given at Christmas.

Annual grant total

Grants usually total about £1,000 each year.

Applications

In writing to the correspondent for consideration in December. Application deadlines are in November.

Burnham Market

The Harold Moorhouse Charity

£7,500

Correspondent: Christine Harrison, 30 Winmer Avenue, Winterton-on-Sea, Great Yarmouth, Norfolk NR29 4BA (01493 393975; email: haroldmoorhousecharity@yahoo.co.uk)

Trustees: Peter Groom; Reginald Utting; David Greenwood; Christine Harrison; Tanya Harrison; Daniel Harrison; Jennie Worship.

CC Number: 287278

Eligibility

Individuals in need who live in Burnham Market in Norfolk only.

Types of grants

One-off grants are made ranging from £50 to £200 for heating, medical care and equipment, travel to and from hospital, education equipment and school educational trips.

Annual grant total

About £15,000 for educational and welfare purposes.

Applications

In writing to the correspondent. Applications should be submitted directly by the individual in any month.

Buxton with Lammas

Picto Buxton Charity

£1,000

Correspondent: Stephen Pipe, Clerk, The Beeches, Coltishall Road, Buxton, Norwich NR10 5JD (01603 279771)

Trustees: Ronald Colman; Maureen Wickham; Kay Blythe; Molly Walter; Matt Morely.

CC Number: 208896

Eligibility

People in need who live in the parish of Buxton with Lamas.

Types of grants

One-off and recurrent grants of £100 to £200 towards household bills, food, living expenses and so on.

Annual grant total

In 2010/11 the trust made charitable donations totalling £22,000. Grants totalling £2,000 were given to individuals.

Applications

In writing to the correspondent directly by the individual or a family member, or through a third party such as a social worker or teacher. Applications are considered at any time.

Other information

Educational help for needy families is also available. Grants are also made to organisations or groups within the parish boundary.

Diss

The Diss Parochial Charities Poors Branch

£1,500

Correspondent: Cyril Grace, 2 The Causeway, Victoria Road, Diss, Norfolk IP22 4AW (01379 650630; email: cj.grace@btinternet.com)

Trustees: John Maskell; Adrian Kitchen; Tony Billett; Graham Elliott; Barbara Roberts; Terence Gilbert; Trevor Wenman.

CC Number: 210154

Eligibility

People in need who live in the town and parish of Diss.

Types of grants

One-off grants ranging between £30 and £200 are made for a range of welfare purposes, including bereavement and funeral expenses.

Annual grant total

In 2011 the charity had assets of £678,000 and an income of £29,000. Grants to individuals totalled £2,000. Previously the majority of grants have been welfare-related, with a couple of awards made for educational purposes.

Applications

In writing through DWP, Citizens Advice, Diss Health Centre, Diss Town Hall or directly to the correspondent. Applications are considered upon receipt.

Other information

The charity also supports local organisations.

Downham Market and Downham West

Downham Aid in Sickness

£500

Correspondent: Philip Reynolds, Clerk, 39 Bexwell Road, Downham Market PE38 9LH (01366 383385; email: p. reynolds@fsbdial.co.uk)

Trustees: Mrs J. Reed; Mr P. Reynolds; Mrs D. Scott; Mrs S. Hitchens; Mr C. Hartley.

CC Number: 258153

Eligibility

People who are sick, convalescent or infirm and live in the district of Downham Market or the parish of Downham West.

Types of grants

One-off and recurrent grants according to need.

Annual grant total

Income and expenditure for the charity is around £1,000 per year. It gives grants to both individuals and organisations.

Applications

In writing to the correspondent for consideration in May and November. Applications can be submitted directly by the individual or through a social worker, Citizens Advice or other welfare agency.

The Hundred Acre Charity – Dolcoal

£6,000

Correspondent: R W Stannard, Riverside Farm, Birchfield Road, Nordelph, Downham Market, Norfolk PE38 0BP (01366 324217)

Trustees: Malcolm John Burton; Mr P. Allen; Mr P. Walker; Mr R. Cranwell; Mr T. M. Brown; Mr B. Bowman; Mrs D. Burton; Ian Massingham; Colin Sampson; Judith Day; Raymond Hudson.

CC Number: 208301

Eligibility

People in need who live in Downham Market, Downham West, Stow Bardolph and Wimbotsham.

Types of grants

Fuel and food vouchers of around £15.

Annual grant total

In 2010 the charity had an income of £7,100 and a total expenditure of £6,200.

Applications

In writing to the correspondent, after local advertisements are placed in shops in the village. Applications can be submitted directly by the individual and are usually considered at the end of November.

East Dereham

The East Dereham Relief-in-Need Charity

£5,200

Correspondent: Derek Edwards, Lansdown House, 3 Breton Close, Dereham, Norfolk NR19 1JH (01362 695835)

Trustees: Valerie Woodhall; Ann Patricia Johnston; Josephine Elizabeth Matthews; Michael Fanthorpe; Robin Frederick Goreham; Revd Canon Sally Theakston; John Everett.

CC Number: 211142

Eligibility

People in need who live in East Dereham.

Types of grants

One-off and recurrent grants ranging from £35 to £100 including payments of coal and clothing vouchers.

Annual grant total

In 2010/11 the charities had an income of £42,000 and a total expenditure of £11,000. Grants to individuals through the Christmas voucher scheme totalled £5,200.

Applications

On a form available from the correspondent, submitted either directly by the individual or through a social worker, Citizens Advice or other welfare agency. Applications are considered in December.

Other information

One-off grants are also made to organisations helping people in the community.

East Tuddenham

The East Tuddenham Charities

£1,000

Correspondent: Janet Guy, 7 Mattishall Road, East Tuddenham, Dereham, Norfolk NR20 3LP (01603 880523)

Trustees: Colin Cram; Leslie Anderson; Maurice Marchant; Tilly Taylor; Audrey Ratcliffe; Binnie Lenihan.

CC Number: 210333

Eligibility

People in need who live in East Tuddenham.

Types of grants

Christmas grants for fuel and occasional one-off grants.

Annual grant total

Grants are usually awarded totalling £1,800 a year, mostly for welfare purposes.

Applications

In writing to the correspondent.

Feltwell

The Edmund Atmere Charity

£2,000

Correspondent: Mr P Garland, 16 Falcon Road, Feltwell, Thetford, Norfolk IP26 4AJ (01842 827029)

Trustees: Edmund Lambert; Eileen Gillians; P. Garland; C. Parker.

CC Number: 270226

Eligibility

People, generally aged over 70 or who have a disability, (except in special cases of dire need) who have lived in Feltwell for at least ten years. Grants have been made to people with multiple sclerosis or a similar condition and children who are sick.

Types of grants

One-off grants in the range of £10 to £250.

Annual grant total

Grants usually total around £2,000 a year.

Applications

In writing to the correspondent. Applications can be submitted between

1 October and 1 November either directly by the individual or through a relevant third party. Applications are considered in November.

Sir Edmund Moundeford's Educational Foundation

£8,800

Correspondent: Barry Hawkins, The Estate Office, 15 Lynn Road, Downham Market, Norfolk PE38 9NL (01366 387180)

Trustees: Edmund Lambert; P. Garland; Tim Fox; Martin Storey; Josephine Leveridge; Leslie Ward; Christopher Cock.

CC Number: 1075097

Eligibility
Individuals in need who live in Feltwell.

Types of grants
Fuel grants.

Annual grant total
In 2011 the charity had assets of £3.8 million and an income of £123,000. Christmas fuel payments totalled £8,800.

Applications
In writing to the correspondent.

Foulden

The Foulden Parochial Charities

£1,000

Correspondent: Robin Orrow, Foulden Watermill, Foulden, Thetford, Norfolk IP26 5AG (01366 328001)

Trustees: Revd David Hanwell; Andy Marrs; Robin Orrow; Luc D'iorio; Shelia Stancombe.

CC Number: 213885

Eligibility
People in need who live in Foulden.

Types of grants
One-off and recurrent grants according to need.

Annual grant total
Grants usually total around £1,000 a year.

Applications
In writing to the correspondent, directly by the individual or through a welfare agency. Applications are considered when necessary.

Garboldisham

The Garboldisham Parish Charities

£1,000

Correspondent: P Girling, Treasurer, Sandale, Smallworth Common, Garboldisham, Diss, Norfolk IP22 2QW (01953 681646)

Trustees: Mr P. Girling; Revd D. Sheppard; Mr T. Lambert; Revd M. Bull; Mr D. Atkins; Mrs B. Sears; David Hance.

CC Number: 210250

Eligibility
People in need who live in the parish of Garboldisham. Generally, this is covered by the Relief-in-Need Fund, although widows and those over 65 who have lived in the parish of Garboldisham for over two years may qualify for allowances given by the Fuel Allotment Charity.

Types of grants
One-off and recurrent grants in the range of £30 to £600. Grants in kind are also made.

Annual grant total
Welfare grants usually total around £1,000 per year.

Applications
Applications can be submitted directly by the individual, including specific details of what the grant is required for. They are usually considered in July and December.

Gayton

The Gayton Fuel Allotments

£1,500

Correspondent: Annmarie Parker, Journeys End, Wormegay Road, Blackborough End, King's Lynn, Norfolk PE32 1SG (01553 841464; email: annmarieparker@pcoffice.freeserve.co.uk)

Trustees: Herbert John Haggas; Stanley Raymond Watkinson; Penny Andrews; Tracey Haggas; Revd Jane Margaret Holmes.

CC Number: 243082

Eligibility
People in need or distress who live in the administrative parish of Gayton, which includes the village of Gayton Thorpe.

Types of grants
One-off and recurrent grants from £25 according to need.

Annual grant total
Grants usually total around £1,500 a year.

Applications
In writing to the correspondent. Applications should be submitted directly by the individual or a family member.

The Gayton Relief-in-Need Charity

£750

Correspondent: Barry Steer, 12 St Marys Court, Gayton, Northampton NN7 3HP (01604 858886)

Trustees: Barry Steer; Christine Carter; Deryck Blunt; Irene Dundas; Joan Adams; John Edmund Metcalfe; Manja Ronne.

CC Number: 201685

Eligibility
People in need who live in the parish of Gayton.

Types of grants
One-off grants usually ranging from £10 to £100.

Annual grant total
On average around £3,000 a year. Grants are given to both individuals and organisations.

Applications
In writing to the correspondent, or through the vicar of Gayton Church.

Gaywood

The Gaywood Poor's Fuel Allotment Trust

£4,000

Correspondent: Mrs M Lillie, 'Edelweiss', Station Road, Hillington, King's Lynn, Norfolk PE31 6DE (01485 600615)

Trustees: Mrs M. Lillie; Mr P. G. Elwin; Cllr. C. L. Walters; B. Daws; Cllr. Laurence A. J. Scott; Revd B. J. Wood.

CC Number: 209364

Eligibility
Older people who are in need and live in the parish of Gaywood.

Types of grants
Grants to help with fuel costs.

Annual grant total

Grants usually total about £4,000 each year.

Applications

In writing to the correspondent through social services.

Harling

Harling Fuel Allotment Trust

£800

Correspondent: David Gee, Clerk, Hanworth House, Market Street, East Harling, Norwich NR16 2AD (01953 717652; email: gee@harlingpc.org.uk)

Trustees: Dorothy Jubb; David John Barrie Galliford; Patricia Evelyn Harbour; Valerie Sheldrake; Revd Sarah Oakland.

CC Number: 211117

Eligibility

People in need living in Harling. (In exceptional cases, grants may be made to people resident immediately outside the parish).

Types of grants

One-off grants to assist with the purchase of fuel.

Annual grant total

Grants average around £800 a year.

Applications

On a form available from the correspondent at any time from any source; a brief financial statement will also be required.

Hilgay

The Hilgay Feoffee Charity

£500

Correspondent: P Golds, 1 St James Drive, Downham Market, Norfolk PE38 9SZ (01306 388496)

Trustees: Peter Bates; David Evans; Alistair Dent; Brian Charlesworth; Colin Wills; Derrick Gordon; Gerald Veal; Graham Carter; Raymond Houghton; Michael Starling.

CC Number: 208898

Eligibility

People in need who live in the parish of Hilgay.

Types of grants

One-off and recurrent grants according to need, including fuel vouchers and

help towards costs of apprenticeship or training.

Annual grant total

In 2011 the charity had an income of £21,000 and an expenditure of £18,000. Grants to individuals generally total around £2,000 with 75% for education, training and apprenticeships and the remainder for general grants.

Applications

In writing to the correspondent, directly by the individual. Applications are considered in June each year.

Other information

The charity also makes grants to local schools.

Horstead with Stanninghall

The Horstead Poor's Land

£1,500

Correspondent: W B Lloyd, Watermeadows, 7 Church Close, Horstead, Norwich NR12 7ET (01603 737632; email: chadlloyd@btopenworld. com)

Trustees: Charles Thacker; Gillian Bunn; John Neville; Margot Miller; Michael Blackburn; William Lloyd; Gordon Boulter.

CC Number: 264730

Eligibility

People in need who live in Horstead with Stanninghall.

Types of grants

One-off and recurrent grants for amounts up to a maximum of £2,000.

Annual grant total

The latest figures available were for 2009/10 when the trust had an income of £7,800 and an expenditure of £7,200. Grants are given for both welfare and educational purposes, and to local organisations.

Applications

Applications, in writing to the correspondent, can be submitted directly by the individual, through a recognised referral agency (such as a social worker, doctor or Citizens Advice) or other third party, and are considered throughout the year.

Little Dunham

The Little Dunham Relief-in-Need Charities

£2,500

Correspondent: Mrs Susan Nally, Beech Cottage, Burrows Hole Lane, King's Lynn, Norfolk PE32 2DP (01760 336864)

Trustees: David Walker; Alban Brian Coughlin; Beverley Keeble; Revd Michael James Thompson; Richard Simon James.

CC Number: 241875

Eligibility

People in need who live in Little Dunham.

Types of grants

One-off grants according to need.

Annual grant total

Grants usually total around £2,500 per year.

Applications

The trustees usually depend on their local knowledge, but also consider direct approaches from village residents.

Other information

Grants may be given to the local primary school, church and community organisations.

Lyng

The Lyng Heath Charity

£500

Correspondent: P L Dilloway, Woodstock, Etling Green, Dereham, Norfolk NR20 3EY (01362 691243)

Trustees: Peter Dilloway; Revd David Head; Mrs G. Lambley; Mrs M. Keeler; Irene Speakman.

CC Number: 206756

Eligibility

People in need who have lived in the parish of Lyng for at least one year.

Types of grants

One-off and recurrent grants between £30 and £40, primarily for fuel.

Annual grant total

Grants usually total around £500 per year.

Applications

On a form available from the correspondent or any member of the committee at any time. Applications can be submitted directly by the individual and are considered in November.

Other information

Grants are occasionally made to village organisations.

Marham Village

The Marham Poor's Allotment

£23,000

Correspondent: Wendy Steeles, Jungfrau, The Street, Marham, Kings Lynn, Norfolk PE33 9JQ (01760 337286)

Trustees: Barry Caley; Barry John Howard; David Eric Watson; Elizabeth Ann Nudd; Peter Edward Aves; Wendy Patricia Steeles; John White; Ben Eves; Jodie Caley.

CC Number: 236402

Eligibility

People of a pensionable age who are in need and live in Marham Village.

Types of grants

One-off vouchers of £35 for food and fuel, to be spent in local shops.

Annual grant total

In 2010/11 the allotment had an income of £33,000. Grants were made totalling around £23,000.

Applications

In writing to the correspondent. Applications are considered in October.

Northwold

The Northwold Combined Charities and Edmund Atmere Charity

£4,500

Correspondent: Helaine Wyett, Pangle Cottage, Church Road, Wretton, King's Lynn PE33 9QR (01366 500165)

Trustees: Jennifer Mary Langley; Christine Collins; James Michael Ayres; Rosemary Crisp; Verity Lynch; Michael Howarth; David Lavender.

CC Number: 270227

Eligibility

People in need who live in the parish of Northwold.

Types of grants

One-off grants according to need. Aids for disabled people are also loaned by the charity.

Annual grant total

In 2011 the charity had an income of £6,000 and a total expenditure of £4,600.

Applications

In writing to the correspondent directly by the individual.

Norwich

Benevolent Association for the Relief of Decayed Tradesmen, their Widows and Orphans

£4,000

Correspondent: Nicholas Saffell, c/o Brown and Co., The Atrium, St George's Street, Norwich, Norfolk NR3 1AB (01603 629871; fax: 01603 760756; email: nick.saffell@brown-co.com)

Trustees: Geoffrey Loades; Barbara Elizabeth Miller; Revd Peter Warwick Nokes; Richard Elliot Jarrold; William George Myall; Zara Hammond.

CC Number: 209861

Eligibility

People who are in need and live in Norwich or the parishes of Costessey, Earlham, Hellesdon, Catton, Sprowston, Thorpe St Andrew, Trowse with Newton and Cringleford. Preference is given to those who have carried on a trade in the area of benefit and their dependents.

Types of grants

One-off and recurrent grants according to need.

Annual grant total

In 2010/11 the trust had an income of £5,000 and a total expenditure of £4,400.

Exclusions

The trust does not assist with bankruptcy fees.

Applications

In writing to the correspondent.

Norwich Consolidated Charities

£281,000 (367 grants)

Correspondent: The Clerk, 1 Woolgate Court, St Benedicts Street, Norwich NR2 4AP (01603 621023; email: david. walker@norwichcharitabletrusts.org.uk)

Trustees: David Fullman; Brenda Ferris; Geoffrey Loades; Pamela Scutter; Philip Blanchflower; Dr Iain Brooksby; Roy Blower; Jeanne Southgate; Brenda Arthur; Heather Tyrrell; Peter Shields; Jeremy Hooke; Amy Stammers.

CC Number: 1094602

Eligibility

People on low incomes who are permanent residents of the city of Norwich. Grants are generally only made to those with dependents, unless the application is supported by a social worker. Applicants, if eligible, must have evidence that they have applied, and been rejected, for a Social Fund loan.

Types of grants

One-off grants for welfare in the range of £50 to £500. Grants given include those for carpets, cookers, beds, washing machines, bankruptcy fees and debt relief orders, as well as childcare costs for low income, single parents. Some assistance is given towards medical items if supported by a doctor and social worker and all other avenues of help have been explored.

The charity is developing a more holistic grant programme including the provision of free legal advice and targeting grants at debt prevention and relief.

Annual grant total

In 2011 the charity had assets of £25 million and an income of £1.6 million. Grants were made totalling £168,000, with an additional £113,000 given to residents of the charities almshouses, predominantly for care charges.

Applications

On a form available from the correspondent either through a social worker, Citizens Advice or other welfare agency or directly by the individual. Ring or write to the office to confirm eligibility. Applications are considered by the trustees at five committee meetings each year.

Generally applicants will be asked to attend for an interview or they will be visited.

Other information

The main activity of the charity is the provision of almshouses. Grants are also made to charitable organisations within Norwich for welfare purposes (£109,000 in 2011) and runs a collaborative project with the local Age UK branch to which it contributed £50,000 in the year.

Norwich Town Close Estate Charity

£113,000

Correspondent: David Walker, Clerk to the Trustees, 1 Woolgate Court, St Benedicts Street, Norwich NR2 4AP (01603 621023; email: david.walker@ norwichcharitabletrusts.org.uk)

Trustees: Nigel Back; Eddie Burton; Anthony Hansell; Richard Gurney;

Michael Quinton; Michael G. Quinton; Robert Self; John Rushmer; John Symonds; Brenda Arthur; Philip Blanchflower; David Fullman; Brenda Ferris; Pamela Scutter; Geoffrey Loades; Heather Tyrrell; Jeanne Southgate.

CC Number: 235678

Eligibility

Freemen of Norwich and their families who are in need.

Types of grants

One-off grants, for example towards decorating costs, house repairs, carpets, spectacles and dental work. Grants are occasionally given for holiday costs. Small regular pensions have also been made to older people.

Annual grant total

In 2010/11 the charity made grants to individuals totalling £178,000, these were broken down as follows:

- Pension: £104,000
- Educational: £65,000
- TV licence: £3,600
- Relief in need: £5,500

Applications

On a form available from the correspondent. Applications are considered throughout the year. Applicants living locally will usually be required to attend for interview.

Old Buckenham

The Old Buckenham United Eleemosynary Charity

£2,000

Correspondent: Joan Jenkins, Priest Hill House, 49 Fen Street, Old Buckenham, Attleborough NR17 1SR (01953 452716; fax: 01953 452716; email: add.j@linelone. net)

Trustees: Dr Lindner; Bridget Mary Burton; Colin Michael Arksey; Eileen Margaret Oliver; Jean Pearl Norton; John Charles Frost; John E. Smith; Revd Alistair Monkhouse; Mr Cracknell; Adrian Joel.

CC Number: 206795

Eligibility

People in need who live in Old Buckenham, Norfolk. Preference for pensioners (over 65) but others are considered.

Types of grants

Normally recurrent grants in coal or cash in lieu for those without coal fires. Grants are currently £50 or equivalent and distributed yearly in early December. Cases considered to be of exceptional need may be given more.

Annual grant total

Grants usually total about £2,000 each year.

Applications

New applicants should write to the correspondent following posted notices around the parish each autumn. Applications are usually considered in early November and can be submitted either directly by the individual, or through another third party such as any of the ten trustees. Any relevant evidence of need is helpful, but not essential.

Pentney

The Pentney Charity

£7,500

Correspondent: Emma Greeno, 19 Westfields, Narborough, King's Lynn, Norfolk PE32 1SX (email: emmagreeno@ aol.com)

Trustees: Canon Stuart Nairn; Marian Elizabeth Storey; Richard Timothy Edwards; Yvonne Olive Sizeland; Michael John Parker.

CC Number: 212367

Eligibility

People over 65 who have lived in the parish of Pentney for the last two years are eligible for fuel grants. Other people in need may also apply for help.

Types of grants

One-off grants of £50 to £150 for fuel costs, travel to and from hospital, funeral expenses, medical expenses, disability equipment, clothing and household bills.

Annual grant total

In 2010/11 the charity had an income of £12,000 and a total expenditure of £10,000.

Exclusions

No grants are given where help is available from the social services.

Applications

In writing to the correspondent either directly by the individual; through a social worker, Citizens Advice or other welfare agency; or by a third party on behalf of the individual, for example a neighbour or relative. Applications are usually considered twice a year.

Other information

Grants are also made to organisations in the local area.

Saham Toney

The Ella Roberts Memorial Charity for Saham Toney

£500

Correspondent: Rosemary Benton, Treasurer, 36 Richmond Road, Saham Toney, Thetford, Norfolk IP25 7ER (01953 881844)

Trustees: Barbara Harrold; Rosemary Benton; Jill Glenn; Kathleen Bowman; Marian Dolphin; Pamela Grigg; Ronald Wheeler; Sandra Spillman; Timothy Gibbs.

CC Number: 1025909

Eligibility

People in need who are older, sick or who have disabilities and live in Saham Toney.

Types of grants

One-off cash grants to cover half the cost of dentures, glasses, physiotherapy or dental treatment, up to a maximum of £100 per application.

Annual grant total

About £500.

Applications

On a form available from the correspondent, to be submitted directly by the individual or a family member. Applications are considered on receipt.

Saxlingham

The Saxlingham Relief in Sickness Fund

£4,000

Correspondent: Mrs Jane Helen Turner, 4 Pitts Hill Close, Saxlingham, Nethergate, Norwich NR15 1AZ (01508 499623)

Trustees: Linda Durrant; Corrine Douglas; David Moore.

CC Number: 254689

Eligibility

People who have medical needs who live in Saxlingham Nethergate and Saxlingham Thorpe.

Types of grants

One-off grants are given to eligible applicants for medical and other needs, including grants towards fuel at Christmas.

Annual grant total

In 2010/11 the fund had an income of £8,200 and a total expenditure of £4,000.

Applications

In writing to the correspondent, to be considered as they arrive.

The Saxlingham United Charities

£2,000

Correspondent: Mrs Jane Turner, 4 Pitts Hill Close, Saxlingham, Nethergate NR15 1AZ (01508 499623)

Trustees: Anthony Hook; Linda Durrant; David Moore.

CC Number: 244713

Eligibility

People in need aged 70 or over who have lived in the village of Saxlingham Nethergate for five or more years.

Types of grants

Recurrent grants for coal and electricity of £50 to £100 and one-off grants for widows and widowers.

Annual grant total

In 2010/11 the charities had an income of £4,200 and a total expenditure of £4,000. Grants are made for welfare and educational purposes.

Applications

In writing to the correspondent. Applications can be submitted directly by the individual and are usually considered in October.

Shipdham

The Shipdham Parochial and Fuel Allotment

£13,000

Correspondent: Helen Crane, Meadow Bank, Carbrooke Lane, Shipdham, Thetford, Norfolk IP25 7RP (01362 821440; email: hscmeadowbank@yahoo.co.uk)

Trustees: Carol Playford; Susan Dewing; Helen Crane; Steve Parfitt; Revd Louise Alder.

CC Number: 206339

Eligibility

People in need who live in Shipdham.

Types of grants

One-off grants generally ranging from £50 to £350.

Annual grant total

In 2010/11 the trust had an income of £16,000 and a total expenditure of £14,000. Grants were made totalling about £13,000.

Applications

On an application form available from the correspondent. Applications are usually considered quarterly.

Other information

The trust also makes grants to organisations.

South Creake

The South Creake Charities

£2,000

Correspondent: Miss Sarah Harvey, The Vicarage, 18 Front Street, South Creake, Fakenham, Norfolk NR21 9PE (01328 823234)

Trustees: Barbara Allen; Christopher Gardner; Rodney Wakeman; Sara Freakley.

CC Number: 210090

Eligibility

People in need who live in South Creake.

Types of grants

Mostly recurrent annual grants towards fuel of between £35 and £100 per year. No grants are given to people in work.

Annual grant total

In 2010/11 the charities had an income of £4,700 and a total expenditure of £4,300.

Applications

In writing to the correspondent. Applications should be submitted directly by the individual and are considered in November; they should be received before the end of October.

Other information

Grants can also be given to schools and playgroups.

Swaffham

Swaffham Relief In Need Charity

£5,000

Correspondent: Richard Bishop, The Town Hall, Swaffham, Norfolk PE37 7DQ (01760 722922; email: reliefinneed@swaffhamtowncouncil.gov.uk)

Trustees: Ian Sherwood; Shirley Mathews; David Harman; Pamela Buxton; David Butters; David Cannon; Paul Ison; Anne Greaves; Terry Jennison; Paul Darby.

CC Number: 1072912

Eligibility

People in need who live in Swaffham.

Types of grants

Grants have been given for a number of reasons, for example for school uniforms, to provide disabled access facilities or mobility scooters, towards the installation of central heating, to relieve long-term debt and to provide basic home start-up facilities such as washing machines, fridges, cookers and so on.

Annual grant total

In 2010/11 the charity had an income of £12,000 and a total expenditure of £8,000.

Applications

In writing to the correspondent.

Other information

Grants are also made to organisations.

Swanton Morley

Thomas Barrett's Charity

£2,000

Correspondent: Nicholas Saffell, Brown and Co., The Atrium, St George's Street, Norwich NR3 1AB (01603 629871)

Trustees: Denise Janes; Roger Atterwill; John Carrick; Rodney Arthur Fearnley; Rosemary Northall; Revd Sally Theakston; Bernie Marsham; Pat Mayer; Maureen Horstead; Gerry Palmer.

CC Number: 207494

Eligibility

Older people in need who live in Swanton Morley.

Types of grants

One-off and recurrent grants according to need.

Annual grant total

Grants usually total around £2,000 a year.

Applications

In writing to the correspondent directly by the individual. Applications are considered in June and December.

Walpole

The Walpole St Peter Poor's Estate

£750

Correspondent: Edward Otter, 1 Sutton Meadows, Leverington, Wisbech, Cambridgeshire PE13 5ED (01945 665018)

Trustees: Gerard Fletcher; Revd Michael Chesher; Clive Melton; George Baty; John Bliss; Jack Bowers; Kenneth Horspole; William Brooks.

CC Number: 233207

Eligibility

Older people over 65 who are in need and live in the old parishes of Walpole St Peter, Walpole Highway and Walpole Marsh.

Types of grants

Annual Christmas grants of £10 to individuals over the age of 65, limited to one per household.

Annual grant total

The trust distributes about £1,500 a year in grants.

Applications

In writing to the correspondent. Applications should be submitted directly by the individual and are considered in November.

Other information

Grants are also made to college or university students for books.

Watton

The Watton Relief-in-Need Charity

£2,500

Correspondent: Derek I Smith, 39 Dereham Road, Watton, Norfolk IP25 6ER (01953 884044; email: derek@frenzymail.co.uk)

Trustees: Oliver Adcock; John Brannan; Peter John Sharman; Roy William Rudling; Lorraine Kay McCarthy; Geoff Garrett; Margaret Holmes.

CC Number: 239041

Eligibility

People in need who live in Watton.

Types of grants

One-off grants according to need. Recent grants have been given towards medical equipment, funeral expenses, clothing, carpets, kitchen and household expenses and to older people at Christmas time.

Annual grant total

Grants usually total about £2,500 each year.

Applications

In writing to the correspondent either directly by the individual or via a social worker, Citizens Advice, welfare agency or through a friend or neighbour. Applications are usually considered quarterly.

Other information

Grants are also made to organisations with similar objects.

Welney

The Bishop's Land Charity

£800

Correspondent: Mrs P Copeman, 1 Chestnut Avenue, Welney, Wisbech, Cambridgeshire PE14 9RG (01354 610226; email: g8sww@aol.com)

Trustees: David Rowlett; Ken Goodger; Charlotte Cox; Dennis Markham; Douglas Carter; Grant Tomkins.

CC Number: 200801

Eligibility

People in need (men over 65 years and women over 60 years) who live in the parish of Welney.

Types of grants

Grants of around £12 per person each year.

Annual grant total

This charity has an annual total expenditure of around £1,000.

Applications

Applications should be made by personal attendance or a signed note, to St Mary's Church – Welney on the second Saturday of December.

Other information

The charity owns approximately 12 acres of land which is let, and the income is used to make a payout to the elderly residents of the village at Christmas.

Marshall's Charity

£9,200

Correspondent: Lynda Clarke-Jones, The Barn, Main Street, Littleport, Cambridgeshire CB6 1PH (01353 860449; email: littleportpc@btconnect.com)

Trustees: Ken Goodger; Douglas Carter; John Gilbert; Alec Singleterry; John Frost; John Scott; Susan Dobson; Kevin Fitzgibbon; Graham Rainbird; Sean Booth; Bishop of Ely.

CC Number: 202211

Eligibility

Widows in need who live in the parish of Welney.

Types of grants

Grants of £120 paid quarterly.

Annual grant total

In 2011 the charity had assets of £2 million and an income of £51,000. Quarterly payments to widows totalled £9,200.

Applications

In writing to the correspondent. The list of recipients is reviewed quarterly.

Other information

The local church receives an annual grant out of the net income from land rents.

West Walton

Poor's Estate (The West Walton Poor's Charity)

£3,000

Correspondent: Mrs J E Johnson, Clerk, 1–3 York Row, Wisbech, Cambridgeshire PE13 1EA (01945 468700)

Trustees: Edward Thompson; Elizabeth Anne Elsegood; Mabel Ethel Christine Gray; Cllr Roy Groom; Pamela Bottom.

CC Number: 206424

Eligibility

Older people in need who live in the parish of West Walton.

Types of grants

One-off grants are usually given at Christmas time.

Annual grant total

Grants average around £3,000 a year.

Applications

The grants are advertised locally every year, giving a closing date for applications.

Wiveton

The Charities of Ralph Greenway

£1,000

Correspondent: Mr Robert Harris, East Barn, Hall Lane, Wiveton, Holt, Norfolk NR25 7TG (01263 740090)

Trustees: Mr J. Woodhouse; Dinah Comins; Hazel Clift; Janet Harcourt; Philippa Stancomb; Revd Neil Batcock; Margaret Bennett.

CC Number: 207605

Eligibility

People in need who are over 60 and have lived in the village of Wiveton for at least three years. Preference is given to widows. Consideration is also given to other villagers who are in need and have lived in the parish for three years.

Types of grants

Small weekly pensions and one-off fuel grants. Other needs can also be considered.

Annual grant total

In 2010/11 the charities had an income of £2,700 and a total expenditure of £3,300. In previous years grants for welfare purposes have totalled around £1,000.

Applications

Applications, on a form available from the correspondent, should be submitted directly by the individual and are considered twice a year. However, if a need arises, a special meeting can be convened.

Other information

Educational grants are also available from a subsidiary charity, for young people up to university age, including young people who are starting work.

Woodton

Woodton United Charities

£1,500

Correspondent: P B Moore, 6 Triple Plea Road, Woodton, Bungay, Suffolk NR35 2NS (01508 482375)

Trustees: Jane Bond; Christine Taylor; Peter Moore; Michael Beckett; Liz Billett.

CC Number: 207531

Eligibility

People in need who live in the parish of Woodton.

Types of grants

One-off and recurrent grants of £20 to £300 according to need. Annual grants are made to older people and people who are disabled. Contributions are also made towards funeral expenses.

Annual grant total

In 2010/11 the charities had an income of £4,000 and a total expenditure of £3,400. Grants are made for educational and welfare purposes.

Applications

In writing to the correspondent directly by the individual, including details of the nature of the need. Applications can be submitted at any time.

Wretton

The Jane Forby Charity

£3,000

Correspondent: Sarah Jane Scarrott, Warren House, Brandon Road, Methwold, Thetford IP26 4RL (01366 728238; email: jamescarrott@btinternet.com)

Trustees: Barry Ernest Tiffin Glover; Leslie Alfred Peake; Michael John Peake; Syd Briston.

CC Number: 208899

Eligibility

People in need who live in the parish of Wretton.

Types of grants

One-off and recurrent grants according to need.

Annual grant total

Grants usually total around £3,000 per year.

Applications

In writing to the correspondent, directly by the individual or by a third party aware of the circumstances. Applications are considered in November.

Oxfordshire

The Appleton Trust (Abingdon)

£4,000

Correspondent: David J Dymock, 73 Eaton Road, Appleton, Abingdon, Oxfordshire OX13 5JJ (01865 863709; email: appleton.trust@yahoo.co.uk)

Trustees: June Edgington; Revd Lyn Sapwell; Margaret Caroline Reading; Mary Blake; Andrew Salmon.

CC Number: 201552

Eligibility

People in need who live in Appleton or Eaton.

Types of grants

One-off and recurrent grants in the range of £50 to £100, towards needs such as fuel and bereavement costs.

Annual grant total

The trust usually has an average income and total expenditure of around £5,500.

Applications

In writing to the correspondent, either directly by the individual or through an appropriate third party.

Other information

Grants are also given to local organisations and for educational purposes to former pupils of Appleton Primary School.

The Bampton Welfare Trust

£7,000

Correspondent: David Pullman, Mill Green Cottage, Bampton, Oxon OX18 2HF (01993 850589; email: david@dpullman.plus.com)

Trustees: Revd David John Lloyd; Rosemary Pelham; Anne Graham Grinsell; Colin Rouse; Gerald Arthur Mills; Janet Gwladys Newman; Joan Barnes Haslam; Dr Matthew Giles Perry; Diana O'Brien.

CC Number: 202735

Eligibility

People who live in the parishes of Bampton, Aston, Lew and Shifford, of any occupation, who are in need. Preference is given to children, young people and older people.

Types of grants

One-off grants which can be repeated in subsequent years at the discretion of the trustees. Grants given include food vouchers for a family awaiting benefit payment, heating allowance for older people in need and assistance in purchasing a washing machine for a single parent with multiple sclerosis.

Annual grant total

In 2010 the trust had an income of £7,700 and a total expenditure of £7,400.

Applications

Applicants are advised to initially discuss their circumstances with the correspondent, who will advise the applicant on what steps to take. This initial contact can be made directly by the individual, or by any third party, at any time.

The Banbury Charities

£60,000 (428 grants)

Correspondent: Anthony Andrews, 36 West Bar, Banbury, Oxfordshire OX16 9RU (01295 251234)

Trustees: Craig Brodey; Janet Justice; Fred Blackwell; Judy May; Julia Colegrave; Angela Heritage; Nigel Morris; Helen Madeiros; Colin Clarke; Martin Humphris; Jamie Briggs; Kieron Mallon.

CC Number: 201418

Eligibility

People in need who live within the former Borough of Banbury.

Types of grants

One-off and recurrent grants towards living costs, household essentials, medical and surgical needs and appliances, bedding, fuel and domestic help.

Annual grant total

In 2010 the charities had assets of £4.4 million and an income of £374,000. Grants were made to 428 individuals for both education and welfare purposes at an average of £279 per grant, totalling £119,000.

Applications

In writing to the correspondent. Applicants are encouraged to obtain a letter of support from their social worker, carer or other person in authority to give credence to their application. If this is not available, the trust will often arrange to visit the applicant.

Other information

The Banbury Charities contains six constituent charities: Bridge Estate Charity, Countess of Arran's Charity, Banbury Almshouse Charity, Banbury Sick Poor Fund, Banbury Arts and Educational Charity and Banbury Welfare Trust.

The charities give to organisations as well as individuals and also maintain almshouse accommodation for six people.

The Bartlett Taylor Charitable Trust

£5,500 (22 grants)

Correspondent: Gareth Alty, c/o John Welch and Stammers, 24 Church Green, Witney, Oxfordshire OX28 4AT (01993 703941; email: galty@ johnwelchandstammers.co.uk)

Trustees: Brenda Cook; James WIlliam Dingle; Richard Bartlett; Rosemary Warner; Gareth Alty; Mrs K. Bradley; Mrs S. Boyd.

CC Number: 285249

Eligibility

People in need who live in Oxfordshire.

Types of grants

Grants ranging from £200 to £800.

Annual grant total

In 2010/11 the trust had assets of £1.8 million and an income of £71,000. Grants were made to 22 individuals totalling £5,500.

Applications

In writing to the correspondent.

Other information

Grants are also made to organisations and international charities (£39,000 in 2010/11).

The Burford Relief-in-Need Charity

£10,000

Correspondent: Mrs R M Reavley, 124 High Street, Burford OX18 4QR (01993 823957)

Trustees: Revd Richard Coombs; Brig Clendon Daukes; John Walter Hannah; Carol Hemming; John Marks; John Kimberley; Michael Brown; Pat Matthews; Penny Barraclough; Charles Greville Williams; James Arthur Middleton; Jane Tunnell-Westmacott.

CC Number: 1036378

Eligibility

People in need who live within seven miles of the Tolsey, Burford.

Types of grants

One-off grants towards hospital expenses, electrical goods, travel costs, convalescence, medical equipment and disability aids.

Annual grant total

In 2011 the trust had an income of £13,000 and a total expenditure of £11,000.

Applications

In writing to the correspondent either directly by the individual or through a social worker, Citizens Advice or other welfare agency. Applications should include the individual's full name, address, age, and the number of years they have lived in Burford or their connection with Burford. Receipts are required for grants towards the cost of equipment. Applications are usually considered on a quarterly basis but urgent cases can be dealt with quickly.

Other information

Grants may also be given for educational purposes.

Cozens Bequest

£1,500

Correspondent: Mr A Martin, 26 Marsh End, Tetsworth, Thame, Oxfordshire OX9 7AU (01844 281202)

Trustees: Mr M. Paul; Mr A. Martin; Dr C. Carr; Mr S. P. Thorpe; Revd G. P. Waterson.

CC Number: 204368

Eligibility

People need who live in the parishes of Tetsworth, Thame, Great Haseley, Stoke Talmage, Wheatfield, Adwell, South Weston, Lewknor and Aston Rowant.

Types of grants

One-off grants according to need.

Annual grant total

In 2009/10 the trust had an income of £2,000 and a total expenditure of £3,000. Grants usually total around £1,500 per year.

Applications

In writing to the correspondent.

Other information

Grants are also made to organisations.

Ducklington and Hardwick with Yelford Charity

£2,000

Correspondent: Mrs Joyce Parry, 16 Feilden Close, Ducklington, Witney, Oxfordshire OX29 7XB (01993 705121)

Trustees: Diana Scott; Edmund Strainge; Philip Rogers; Revd Bob Edy; Glyn Rees.

CC Number: 237343

Eligibility

People in need or hardship who live in the villages of Ducklington, Hardwick and Yelford.

Types of grants

One-off grants in the range of £75 to £200. Grants given include those towards heating for older people, assistance with playgroup fees, furniture, funeral expenses, conversion of rooms for people who are older or disabled, provision of telephones, spectacles, school holiday assistance and assistance with rent arrears.

Annual grant total

Welfare grants usually total around £2,000 per year.

Applications

In writing to the correspondent. Applications are considered in March and November, but emergency cases can be dealt with at any time.

Other information

Grants are also made to organisations such as clubs, schools and so on.

The Faringdon United Charities

£6,000

Correspondent: Vivienne Checkley, Bunting and Co., 7 Market Place,

Faringdon, Oxfordshire SN7 7HL (01367 243789; fax: 01367 243789)

Trustees: B. Barber; J. Carter; D. Keeling; David McKay; Peter Eyre-Brook; Revd Charles Draper; Alan Hickmore; Jill Woodward; Julie Farmer.

CC Number: 237040

Eligibility

People in need who live in the parishes of Faringdon, Littleworth, Great and Little Coxwell, all in Oxfordshire.

Types of grants

One-off grants towards clergy expenses for visiting the sick, domestic appliances, holidays, travel expenses, medical and disability equipment, furniture and food and so on.

Annual grant total

In 2010/11 the trust had both an income and total expenditure of £13,500.

Exclusions

Grants cannot be given for nursing/retirement home fees or the supply of equipment that the state is obliged to provide.

Applications

In writing to the correspondent throughout the year. Applications can be submitted either through Citizens Advice, a social worker or other third party, directly by the individual or by a third party on their behalf for example a neighbour, parent or child.

Other information

Grants are also made for educational purposes and to organisations helping people in need.

The Lockinge and Ardington Relief-in-Need Charity

£5,000

Correspondent: Mrs A Ackland, c/o Lockinge Estate Office, Ardington, Wantage, Oxfordshire OX12 8PP (01235 833200)

Trustees: Thomas Christopher Loyd; Dr Clive Knights; Colin Stutt; Ron East; Terence Welch; Vernon Gaylard; Revd Elizabeth Birch.

CC Number: 204770

Eligibility

People in need who live in the parish of Lockinge and Ardington.

Types of grants

One-off and recurrent grants between £30 and £60.

Annual grant total

Grants usually total around £5,000 a year.

Applications

In writing to the correspondent by the individual. Applications are considered in March, July and November although urgent cases can be considered at any time.

Ellen Rebe Spalding Memorial Fund

£2,000

Correspondent: Tessa Rodgers, Secretary, PO Box 85, Wetherden, Stowmarket, Suffolk IP14 3NY (website: www.spaldingtrust.org.uk)

Trustees: Dr Kevin Ward; Dr Anne Spalding; Prof. Oliver Davies; Prof. Edmund Bosworth; Revd Prof. John Emerton; Prof. Julius Lipner; Dr Michael Loewe.

CC Number: 209066

Eligibility

To help disadvantaged women and children to adjust more easily to the pressure of modern life, and to promote those conditions of society that will enable people of different cultures and faiths to understand and appreciate one another.

Types of grants

Grants are at the discretion of trustees and are administered monthly throughout the year. Grants are only distributed to those who intend to further the objectives of the trust.

Annual grant total

In 2010 grants to individuals for welfare purposes totalled £2,000.

Applications

Applications should be made through Oxfordshire Social Services.

Other information

The Ellen Rebe Spalding Memorial Fund is part of the larger Spalding Trusts. While a small amount is given in welfare grants through the Ellen Rebe fund, the majority of the Spalding Trusts' funds are spent on educational grants.

The Thame Welfare Trust

£12,000

Correspondent: J Gadd, 2 Cromwell Avenue, Thame, Oxfordshire OX9 3TD (01844 212564)

Trustees: Ann Midwinter; Cecil Wiggs; David Youens; David Dodds; Jane Hussey; Helen Fickling; Dr Patricia Markus; Rosalie Gibson; Dr Timothy Mitchell; Karen Vear; Alan Garratt; Mrs J. Mander.

CC Number: 241914

Eligibility

People in need who live in Thame and immediately adjoining villages.

Types of grants

One-off grants of amounts up to £1,000, where help cannot be received from statutory organisations. Recent grants have been given towards a single parent's mortgage repayments and a wheelchair for a person who is disabled.

Annual grant total

In 2010/11 the trust had an income of £20,500 and a total expenditure of £77,000. Grants are made to organisations and individuals for relief-in-need and education.

Applications

In writing to the correspondent mainly through social workers, probation officers, teachers, or a similar third party but also directly by the applicant.

The Peter Ward Charitable Trust

£2,000

Correspondent: M D Stanford-Tuck, Trustee, A J Carter and Co., 22b High Street, Witney, Oxfordshire OX28 6RB (01993 703414; fax: 01993 778052)

Trustees: Rt Hon James Edward Daventry; Michael David Stanford-Tuck.

CC Number: 258403

Eligibility

People in need who live in Oxfordshire.

Types of grants

One-off and recurrent grants according to need.

Annual grant total

In 2010/11 the trust had an income of £6,700 and a total expenditure of £38,000 the majority of which was made in grants to organisations known to the trustees.

Applications

In writing to the correspondent although unsolicited applications are not encouraged.

Other information

Grants are also made to organisations (£81,000 in 2008/09). The trust has stated that 'grants to individuals are not normally considered, and unsolicited applications are not encouraged'.

Bletchington

The Bletchington Charity

£5,000

Correspondent: Sue Green, Causeway Cottage, Weston Road, Bletchington, Kidlington, Oxon OX5 3DH (01869 350895)

Trustees: Revd Derek Walker; John Smith; Ian Gelding; Julie Fenn; Ronald Gamage; Sue Lane; Julian Howe.

CC Number: 201584

Eligibility

People in need who live in the parish of Bletchington, in particular people who are elderly or infirm.

Types of grants

Grants to people who are elderly and infirm at Christmas and Easter towards fuel bills and other needs. Help is given for travel, chiropody and television licences. Otherwise one-off grants for social welfare, education and relief-in-sickness according to need.

Annual grant total

In 2010 the charity had an income of £11,000 and a total expenditure of £12,000.

Applications

Generally as the trustees see a need, but applications can be made in writing to the correspondent by the individual or by a social worker, doctor or welfare agency.

Other information

The charity also seeks to support any educational, medical and social needs that will benefit the village community as a whole.

Eynsham

The Eynsham Consolidated Charity

£800

Correspondent: Robin Mitchell, 20 High Street, Eynsham, Witney, Oxfordshire OX29 4HB (01865 880665)

Trustees: Andrew Mosson; Dr Max Peterson; Raymond Clarke; Leslie Gerrans; Ann Kershaw; Stephen Burke; Revd Morey Andrews; Revd David Tyler; Donald Richards.

CC Number: 200977

Eligibility

People in need who live in the ancient parish of Eynsham (which covers Eynsham and part of Freeland).

Types of grants

One-off grants ranging from £50 to £200.

Annual grant total

Grants to individuals generally total around £800 a year.

Applications

In writing to the correspondent including details of what the grant is for, the personal circumstances of the applicant and the cost involved. Applications can be submitted through a social worker, Citizens Advice or other welfare agency; or by the individual. They are considered quarterly, usually in January, April, August and October.

Other information

This charity also gives grants to organisations.

Great Rollright

The Great Rollright Charities

£11,000

Correspondent: Paul Dingle, Tyte End Cottage, Tyte End, Great Rollright, Chipping Norton, Oxfordshire OX7 5RU (01608 737676)

Trustees: Revd John Acreman; David John Portman; Edward Deakin; Gordon Moss; Christopher Glasson.

CC Number: 242146

Eligibility

People who are in need and live in the ancient parish of Great Rollright.

Types of grants

One-off grants towards, for example, fuel payments and to older people at Christmas.

Annual grant total

In 2010/11 the charities had an income of £13,000 and a total expenditure of £11,000.

Exclusions

No grants are given for the relief of rates, taxes or other public funds.

Applications

In writing to the correspondent.

Other information

The charities also give to local organisations and for educational purposes.

Henley-on-Thames

The John Hodges Charitable Trust

£6,500

Correspondent: Miss Julie Griffin, 3 Berkshire Road, Henley-on-Thames RG9 1ND (01491 572621)

Trustees: Stuart Crippen; Carol Devonald Brook-Partridge; Richard Fletcher; Fr Martyn Griffiths; Brian Martin Whittaker; Martin Rasch.

CC Number: 304313

Eligibility

People in need living in the Parish of St Mary the Virgin, Henley-on-Thames and the surrounding area.

Types of grants

One-off and recurrent grants towards, for example, white goods, carpets and flooring, clothing, mobility aids, bankruptcy fees and heating bills.

Annual grant total

In 2010/11 the trust had an income of £11,800 and total expenditure of £8,500.

Applications

In writing to the correspondent.

Over Norton

The Over Norton Welfare Trust

£3,000

Correspondent: Cannon Stephen Weston, The Vicarage, Church Street, Chipping Norton, Oxfordshire OX7 5NT

Trustees: Denise Macrae; Glen Pashley; Emma Kettlewell; Kate Kilbane; Revd Stephen Weston; Chris Sole.

CC Number: 237881

Eligibility

People in need who live in the parish of Over Norton.

Types of grants

One-off grants for electricity stamps or coal vouchers to the value of £45 to £60.

Annual grant total

Grants usually total about £3,000 each year.

Applications

In writing to the correspondent.

Oxford

The City of Oxford Charities

£65,000

Correspondent: The Administrator, 11 Davenant Road, Oxford OX2 8BT (01865 247161; email: enquiries@ oxfordcitycharities.fsnet.co.uk; website: www.oxfordcitycharities.org)

Trustees: Judith Iredale; Robin Birch; Diana Pope; Dorothy Tonge; Tony Woodward; John Gould; Verena Brink; Jean Fooks; Jason Tomes; Richard Whittington; Michael Lancashire; Ben Lloyd-Shogbesan; Roger SMith; Susan Bright; Alan Armitage; Ivan Coulter; Gillian Sanders.

CC Number: 239151

Eligibility

People in need who have lived in the city of Oxford for at least three years and who have a low income. Priority is given to children and people who are elderly, disabled or have a medical condition.

Types of grants

One-off grants of up to £600. Grants have been awarded for furniture to people moving home; washing machines; recuperation holidays for people with disabilities or medical problems and/or their carers; baby equipment; wheelchairs and mobility scooters and bankruptcy fees.

Annual grant total

In 2011 the charity made relief in need and sickness grants to 263 individuals totalling £62,000, plus 30 grants for bankruptcy fees totalling £3,400.

Applications

Application forms are available from the correspondent or can be downloaded from the website. They can be submitted through a social worker, Citizens Advice or other welfare agency, or from from individuals. Applications are considered at meetings of the trustees which are held every six weeks. Applications should specify exactly what the money is for and the cost, as applications without exact costings will be delayed.

Other information

Grants are also made to organisations and to individuals for educational purposes.

The Stanton Ballard Charitable Trust

£35,000

Correspondent: The Secretary, PO Box 81, Oxford OX4 4ZA

Trustees: Mary Joan Tate; Tony Woodward; John William Martin; Keith Pawson; Martin Alan Slade; Rosamund Clare Nicholson; Howard Minns; Dianna Marsh.

CC Number: 294688

Eligibility

Individuals in need who live in the city of Oxford and the immediate area.

Types of grants

Small one-off grants according to need.

Annual grant total

In 2010/11 the trust had assets of £2.6 million and an income of £109,000. Grants to individuals average around £35,000 per year.

Applications

On an application form available from the correspondent on receipt of an sae. Applications should be made through social services, probation officers or other bodies and are considered five times a year.

Sibford Gower

The Town Estate Charity

£2,000

Correspondent: Mrs Jean White, Whitts End, Sibford Gower, Banbury, Oxfordshire OX15 5RT (01295 780529)

Trustees: Dr Oswyn Murray; Dr David Spackman; Frederick Inns; Graham Wealsby; Jean White; Joanna Gilkes; Bill Sabin; William Wealsby; Michael Lewis.

CC Number: 253440

Eligibility

People in need who live in the civil parish of Sibford Gower.

Types of grants

One-off and recurrent grants. The trust also provides free home chiropody treatment.

Annual grant total

In 2010 the charity made grants totalling £2,000 for relief in need purposes.

Applications

In writing to the correspondent, to be considered at the twice-yearly trustees meeting.

Other information

Grants are also given to organisations.

Souldern

The Souldern United Charities

£8,000

Correspondent: Mrs C Couzens, 2 Cotswold Court, Souldern, Bicester, Oxfordshire OX27 7LQ (01869 346694)

Trustees: Revd Paul Hunt; Thomas Jordan; Carol Couzens; Christopher Rothero; Karen Smith; Jan Martin.

CC Number: 1002942

Eligibility

People in need who live in the parish of Souldern.

Types of grants

One-off and recurrent grants according to need.

Annual grant total

In 2010/11 the trust had an income of £8,000 and a total expenditure of £9,000.

Applications

In writing to the correspondent.

Steventon

The Steventon Allotments and Relief-in-Need Charity

£2,000 (8 grants)

Correspondent: Patrina Effer, 19 Lime Grove, Southmoor, Abingdon, Oxfordshire OX13 5DN (01865 821055; email: sarinc@patrina.co.uk)

Trustees: Anne Veronica Shrimpton; Philip Michael Brew; Steven Arthur Frederick Ward; Dr Diana Ruth Bowder; Bill Temple; Robin Wilkinson; Kevin Paul Curley.

CC Number: 203331

Eligibility

People in need who live in Steventon.

Types of grants

One-off grants for the provision of food, fuel and personal items such as clothing, repair or replacement of faulty domestic equipment or furniture, loans of electric wheelchairs, provision of special equipment to chronically sick people and grants or loans for unforeseen difficulties. Priority is given to assist young people in obtaining independent housing, to set up home within the community in which they were raised. Large loans will need to be secured as a percentage of a second mortgage.

Annual grant total

In 2011 the charity made grants to eight individuals totalling £2,000.

Applications

In writing to the correspondent. The trust advertises regularly in the local parish magazine. Applications should include full details of income and expenditure, and will be treated in strictest confidence.

Other information

Educational grants are also made.

Wallingford

The Wallingford Municipal and Relief-in-Need Charities

£6,000

Correspondent: A Rogers, Town Clerk, 9 St Martin's Street, Wallingford, Oxfordshire OX10 0AL (01491 835373; email: wallingfordtc@btconnect.com)

Trustees: Patricia Granados; David Kershaw; Jacqueline Payne; Elizabeth Atkins; Elizabeth Lee; Chris Tyndall; Elizabeth Vaisey; Rose Owen; Mrs J. Castle; Mrs A. Willis; Pat Hayton; Revd David Rice; Theresa Jordan.

CC Number: 292000

Eligibility

People in need who live in the former borough of Wallingford.

Types of grants

One-off grants for necessities including the payment of bills, shoes, cookers, fridges and so on. Payments are made to local suppliers, cash grants are not made directly to the individual.

Annual grant total

Grants total approximately £8,000 a year.

Applications

On a form available from the correspondent, submitted either directly by the individual or through a local organisation. Trustees meet about every three months, although emergency cases can be considered. Urgent cases may require a visit by a trustee.

Wheatley

The Wheatley Charities

£3,400

Correspondent: R F Minty, 24 Old London Road, Wheatley, Oxford OX33 1YW (01865 874676)

Trustees: P. J. Targett; D. A. S. John; R. F. Minty; G. J. Colverson.

CC Number: 203535

Eligibility

Residents of Wheatley, Oxford who are in need.

Types of grants

One-off and recurrent grants according to need.

Annual grant total

In 2011 the charities had an income of £4,200 and a total expenditure of £6,900.

Applications

In writing to the correspondent.

Other information

Educational grants are also made.

Suffolk

The Cranfield Charitable Trust

£6,000

Correspondent: Mrs S Price, Trustee, 22 Lucas Lane, Ashwell, Hertfordshire SG7 5LN (01462 748386)

Trustees: Virginia Cranfield; Sarah Anne Louise Price; Judith Rosemary Banham; Lynn Cranfield; Edward Cranfield.

CC Number: 263518

Eligibility

People who live in Suffolk and are in need.

Types of grants

One-off grants ranging from £100 to £1,500.

Annual grant total

In 2011/12 the trust had an income of £14,000 and a total expenditure of £12,000.

Applications

In writing to the correspondent.

Other information

The charity also gives grants to organisations.

The Martineau Trust

£16,000

Correspondent: Roger Lay, Clerk, 5 Princethorpe Road, Ipswich, Suffolk IP3 8NY (01473 724951; email: clerk@ martineautrust.org.uk; website: www. martineautrust.org.uk)

Trustees: Richard Makepeace Martineau; Margaret Anne Kember; Selwyn Pryor; Dr Bryant Maitland; Agnes Hallander.

CC Number: 206884

Eligibility

'Deserving people living in Suffolk who suffer directly or indirectly from an illness or disability and are in need.'

Types of grants

One-off grants up to £200 towards: clothing, including wigs, required following illness or surgery; bedding, including protective covers and special mattresses; travel for hospital appointments or visits; domestic appliances where the need arises through illness; mobility aids, scooters and 'riser chairs' not provided by the PCT or local authority; respite breaks for the sick and their carers; and, heating costs where the need arises specifically from illness.

Annual grant total

The trust has an annual grant budget of around £20,000, although this is not always entirely distributed: in 2010/11 the trust had a total expenditure of £17,000.

Exclusions

No grants for: holidays and breaks for families; child care; alternative treatment therapies e.g. acupuncture; normal household running expenses; recurring grants; applications not relating to an illness or disability; and, equipment that should be provided by the PCT or local authority.

Applications

On a form available from the correspondent or to download from the website. Applications must be completed by a suitable third party, such as a social worker, health visitor, nurse or charity welfare officer.

The Mills Charity

£1,600

Correspondent: Chairman of the Trustees, PO Box 1703, Framlingham, Suffolk IP13 9WW (01728 638038; email: info@themillscharity.co.uk; website: www.themillscharity.co.uk)

Trustees: Howard Wright; Kenneth William Musgrave; Mr Kelleway; Dr C. Wright; Mrs P. C. Booth; Revd Vipond; Kate Hunt; Nick Corke.

CC Number: 207259

Eligibility

Individuals in need who live in Framlingham or are very closely associated with the town.

Types of grants

One-off grants towards hospital expenses, electrical goods, living costs, household bills, travel expenses, medical equipment, furniture and disability equipment.

Annual grant total

In 2010/11 the charity had assets of £7.3 million and an income of £159,000. Grants to individuals totalled £1,600.

Applications

In writing to the correspondent. Applications should outline the need and why it has arisen and preferably include a supporting letter from a professional or other suitable referee. They are considered every two months.

Other information

Grants were also made to four organisations amounting to £34,000. The charity's main activity is the maintenance of its almshouses.

Aldeburgh

Aldeburgh United Charities

£1,500

Correspondent: Lindsay Lee, Administrator, Moot Hall, Market Cross Place, Aldeburgh IP15 5DS (01728 452158; email: aldeburghtc@moothall1.fsnet.co.uk)

Trustees: Dotsie Wardley; Sarah Duerr; Revd Nigel Hartley; Andrew Harris; Felicity Bissett; Kevin Webster; Cllr Mayor Gary Davis.

CC Number: 235840

Eligibility

People in need who live in the town of Aldeburgh. The trust describes its current constituency of beneficiaries as including, 'senior citizens, people in specific sensitive situations, young and young minded people, and people in the development stage of life's experience'.

Types of grants

One-off and recurrent grants according to need.

Annual grant total

Grants are approximately £1,500 each year.

Applications

In writing to the correspondent.

Other information

The charity is a combination of various charities in Aldeburgh, some hundreds of years old.

Brockley

The Brockley Town and Poor Estate (Brockley Charities)

£650

Correspondent: Jane Forster, Brooklands, Chapel Lane, Brockley, Bury St Edmunds IP29 4AS (01284 830558)

Trustees: Ian Robertson; Peter Miller; Geoffrey Baber; Sue Parker; Jane Forster.

CC Number: 236989

Eligibility

People in need who live in Brockley village.

Types of grants

In previous years recurrent grants of £65–£70 have been given, usually as rebates on electricity bills paid directly to the suppliers.

Annual grant total

In 2010 the trust had an income of £1,700 and a total expenditure of £1,300. Grants are made for educational and welfare purposes.

Applications

In writing to the correspondent, to be submitted directly by the individual or through relatives or family friends.

Bungay

Bungay Charities

£1,500

Correspondent: Peter Morrow, 11 Wharton Street, Bungay, Suffolk NR35 1EL (01986 893148)

Trustees: Arthur Fisher; Martin Evans; John Victor Palin; Roma Went; Revd Ian Byrne; Alan Eric Jones.

CC Number: 210362

Eligibility

People in need who live in the parish of Bungay.

Types of grants

One-off grants averaging £200, to meet a wide range of needs. Older people, for example, can receive help with the costs of telephone installation, heating costs or travel to hospital, children from needy families can receive grants to pay for school trips or clothing and single parents can be given grants to help pay for furniture, washing machines and so on.

Annual grant total

About £1,500 a year.

Applications

In writing to the correspondent.

Carlton and Calton Colville

The Carlton Colville Fuel and Poor's Allotment Charity

£12,000

Correspondent: Keith Vincent, 23 Wannock Close, Carlton Colville, Lowestoft, Suffolk NR33 8DW (01493 852411)

Trustees: Keith Richard Vincent; Michael Solomon; Peter Frederick Dyer; Sheila Hundleby.

CC Number: 242083

Eligibility

People in need who live in the ancient parish of Carlton Colville, with a preference for older people who only receive the basic state pension and have limited savings.

Types of grants

Recurrent grants for fuel and heating costs.

Annual grant total

In 2010 the charity had an income of £10,000 and a total expenditure of £13,000.

Applications

On a form available from the correspondent. Applications can be submitted directly by the individual or through a social worker, Citizens Advice or other welfare agency.

Chediston

The Chediston United Charities, Town and Poor's Branch

£2,000

Correspondent: David Mantell, Rosecroft Farm, Chediston Green, Chediston, Halesworth, Suffolk IP19 0BB (01986 785440; email: dpmantell@gmail.com; website: www.onesuffolk.co.uk)

Trustees: Gilbert Burroughes; Pat Gregory; Janet Mantell; Wendy Burroughes.

CC Number: 206742

Eligibility

People in need who live in the civil parish of Chediston.

Types of grants

One-off and recurrent grants according to need ranging from £5 to £100. Grants are given for alarm systems for older people, hospital transport and as Christmas gifts to all pensioners and children in full-time education.

Annual grant total

About £4,000.

Applications

In writing to the correspondent. Applications are considered throughout the year, although mainly in November. The trust has no formal application procedure as requests are usually made personally to the trustees.

Chelsworth

The Chelsworth Parochial Charity

£1,000

Correspondent: Alison Russell, Tudor Cottage, 70–72 The Street, Chelsworth, Ipswich, Suffolk IP7 7HU (01449 740438)

Trustees: Alison Russell; Revd Canon Brian James; David Sugden; Sarah Cullen; Jane Wincer; Sarah Buckeridge; Angela Ellis.

CC Number: 210224

Eligibility

People in need who live in the parish of Chelsworth.

Types of grants

One-off grants or payment for items, services and facilities that will reduce the person's need, hardship or distress.

Annual grant total

About £1,000.

Applications

In writing to the correspondent. The charity stated in 2006 that it is 'solely for residents' and it will not accept any unsolicited applications.

Corton

Corton Poor's Land Trust

£3,000

Correspondent: Claire Boyne, 48 Fallowfields, Lowestoft NR32 4XN (01502 733978)

Trustees: Frederick Leonard Taylor; Michael James Spencer Edwards; Wendy Sheila Rodgers; Revd Roger Astley Key; Mary Rudd; Heather Habbin; Robin Jones.

CC Number: 206067

Eligibility

People in need who live in the ancient parish of Corton.

Types of grants

Recent grants have included Christmas gifts for older people, funding for chiropody treatment, taxi fares to hospital and payment for home alarm installation and rent.

Annual grant total

In 2010/11 the trust had an income of £17,000 and a total expenditure of £15,000. Much of the expenditure is committed to maintaining the almshouses owned by the trust.

Applications

In writing to the correspondent. Applications can be submitted at any time directly by the individual or by an appropriate third party.

Other information

Grants are also made to organisations which carry out the charity's aims within the area of benefit.

Dennington

The Dennington Consolidated Charities

£3,000

Correspondent: Dr W Blakeley, Clerk, Thorn House, Saxtead Road, Dennington, Woodbridge, Suffolk IP13 8AP (01728 638031)

Trustees: Robert Rous; Elizabeth Hickson; Revd Jonathan Olanczu; Robert Wardley; Mandy Sayer; Adrian Neill; Keir Wyatt.

CC Number: 207451

Eligibility

People in need who live in the village of Dennington.

Types of grants

One-off and recurrent grants according to need including travel expenses for hospital visiting of relatives, telephone installation for emergency help calls for people who are elderly and infirm, and Christmas grants to older people. Grants range from £50 to £250.

Annual grant total

In 2010 the charities had an income of £13,000 and a total expenditure of £10,000. The charities give approximately £500 each year for educational purposes and £3,000 for welfare.

Exclusions

The trust does not make loans, nor does it make grants where public funds are available unless they are considered inadequate.

Applications

In writing to the correspondent. Applications are considered throughout the year and a simple means test questionnaire may be required by the applicant.

Grants are only made to people resident in Dennington (a small village with 500 inhabitants). The charities do not respond to applications made outside this specific geographical area.

Dunwich

The Dunwich Town Trust

£12,000

Correspondent: John Cary, Black Pig Studio, Dunwich, Saxmundham, Suffolk IP17 3DR (01728 648927)

Trustees: John Salusbury; Veronica Donovan; Nick Mayo; David Cook; Angela Abell; Linda Prior; Keith Maunder; Crispin Clay.

CC Number: 206294

Eligibility

People in need who live in the parish of Dunwich.

Annual grant total

In 2011 grants to individuals for welfare totalled £12,000.

Applications

Write to the correspondent requesting an application form.

Earl Stonham

Earl Stonham Trust

£2,000

Correspondent: San Wilson, College Farm, Forward Green, Stowmarket, Suffolk IP14 5EH (01449 711497; email: sam_wilson@talk21.com)

Trustees: Sam Wilson; Jennifer Griffiths; Cynthia Collins; Barry Rice; Colin Woods; Phil Hurt.

CC Number: 213006

Eligibility

People in need who live in the parish of Earl Stonham.

Types of grants

One-off grants up to a maximum of £200.

Annual grant total

In 2010/11 the trust had an income of £6,800 and an expenditure of £4,200.

Grants are made for both educational and welfare purposes.

Applications

In writing to the correspondent, to be submitted either by the individual or through a social worker, Citizens Advice or other third party. Applications are considered in March, June, September and December.

Framlingham

The Florence Pryke Charity

£600

Correspondent: Sally Butcher, 90 Station Road, Framlingham, Woodbridge IP13 9EE (01728 723365)

Trustees: Diana Howard; Eileen Coe; Victor Stanbrook; Graham Owen; Carl Moore; Sally Butcher.

CC Number: 262319

Eligibility

People in need who live in the ecclesiastical parish of Framlingham.

Types of grants

One-off grants ranging from £30 to £50 towards, for example, hospital travel costs and medical care.

Annual grant total

Grants total around £600 a year.

Applications

In writing to the correspondent either directly by the individual or through a relevant third person. Applications are considered monthly.

Other information

The charity also gives grants to organisations.

Gisleham

The Gisleham Relief in Need Charity

£2,300

Correspondent: Elizabeth Rivett, 2 Mill Villas, Black Street, Gisleham, Lowestoft, Suffolk NR33 8EJ (01502 743189; email: elizabethrivett@hotmail.co.uk)

Trustees: Elizabeth Rivett; Pamela Cole Podd; Sylvia Gilbert; Lyndy Domoney; Brian Soloman; John Ford.

CC Number: 244853

Eligibility

People in need who live in the parish of Gisleham.

Types of grants

One-off and recurrent grants according to need, but usually averaging about £50. Recent grants have been given for household bills, travel expenses and disability aids.

Annual grant total

In 2010/11 the charity had an income of £600 and a total expenditure of £2,500.

Applications

In writing to the correspondent: to be submitted directly by the individual. Applications are considered at any time.

Other information

A luncheon club for older people is held at the local school once a month during term time. Those that are deemed not able to pay are paid for by the trust.

Gislingham

The Gislingham United Charity

£5,000

Correspondent: Robert Moyes, 37 Broadfields Road, Gislingham, Eye, Suffolk IP23 8HX (01379 788105; email: r.moyes1926@btinternet.com)

Trustees: Jane Franklin; Andrew Dickson; Betty Cunningham; Geoffrey Laurence; Pamela Shorten; Ron Pye; Alan Harding; Geoff Mason; Peter Neale; Christopher Wells.

CC Number: 208340

Eligibility

People in need who live in Gislingham.

Types of grants

Usually one-off grants according to need. For example, the cost of hospital travel for older people, playgroup fees or specific items or equipment.

Annual grant total

In 2011 the charity had an income of £21,000 and an expenditure of £23,000.

Applications

In writing to the correspondent directly by the individual or verbally via a trustee.

Other information

The charity also gives educational grants and supports village organisations and ecclesiastical causes.

Halesworth

The Halesworth United Charities

£1,000

Correspondent: Janet Staveley-Dick, Clerk, Hill Farm, Primes Lane, Blyford, Halesworth, Suffolk IP19 9JT (01986 872340)

Trustees: Edward Hyde-Clarke; Joan Lee; Janet Wright; Annette Dunning; Anne Wilkinson; Mary Hussey; Paul Widdowson.

CC Number: 214509

Eligibility

People in need who live in the ancient parish of Halesworth.

Types of grants

One-off grants according to need. Recent examples include travel abroad for educational purposes, medical equipment or tools needed for a trade.

Annual grant total

Grants usually total between £2,000 and £3,000.

Applications

In writing to the correspondent, directly by the individual or through a social worker, Citizens Advice or other welfare agency. Applications can be submitted at any time for consideration in January, July and December, or any other time if urgent.

Other information

Grants are also made to individuals for educational purposes.

Ipswich

The John Dorkin Charity

£13,000

Correspondent: G R Sutton, Kerseys Solicitors, 32 Lloyds Avenue, Ipswich, Suffolk IP1 3HD (01473 213311)

Trustees: Mr J. Andreasen; Mr G. W. Leverett; Revd Canon Lionel Simpkins; Mrs M. R. Kirby; William Knowles; Revd Michael J. A. Tillett.

CC Number: 209635

Eligibility

People in need who live in the ancient parish of St Clement's, Ipswich (broadly speaking the south-eastern sector of Ipswich bounded by Back Hamlet/Foxhall Road and the River Orwell). Preference for the widows and children of seamen.

Types of grants

One-off cash grants of about £200 towards electrical goods, clothes, holidays, furniture and disability equipment.

Annual grant total

In 2010 the trust had an income of £12,000 and a total expenditure of £16,500.

Exclusions

No grants to applicants resident outside the beneficial area.

Applications

In writing to the correspondent at any time, giving details of financial circumstances. Applications can be submitted through a third party such as a social worker, or through an organisation such as Citizens Advice or other welfare agency, and are considered twice a year.

Mrs L. D. Rope's Third Charitable Settlement

£331,000 (1,358 grants)

Correspondent: Grants administrator, Crag Farm, Boyton, Woodbridge, Suffolk IP12 3LH (01473 333288)

Trustees: Crispin Rope; Jeremy Philip Winteringham Heal; Ellen Jolly; Paul Jolly; Catherine Scott.

CC Number: 290533

Eligibility

People who are on a low income and live in the Ipswich area.

Types of grants

One-off grants according to need. Grants given include those for food, clothing and furnishings/furniture.

Annual grant total

In 2011/12 the settlement held assets of £52 million and had an income of £1.3 million. Grants were made to 1,358 individuals totalling £331,000.

Exclusions

Grants are not given for individuals working overseas, debt relief, health/palliative care or educational fees.

Applications

In writing to the correspondent preferably through a social worker, Citizens Advice or other welfare agency. Apply in a concise letter, saying what is needed and how the trust may be able to help. It helps to include details of household income (including benefits) and expenses, and a daytime telephone number.

Other information

Grants are also made to local organisations.

Kirkley

Kirkley Poor's Land Estate

£15,000

Correspondent: Lucy Walker, 4 Station Road, Lowestoft, Suffolk NR32 4QF (01502 514964)

Trustees: Jennifer Pelt; Andrew Shepherd; Michael Cook; Ralph Castleton; Elaine High; Rose Hudson; Revd Andrew White.

CC Number: 210177

Eligibility

Individuals in need who live in the parish of Kirkley.

Types of grants

One-off grants ranging from £50 to £300. Vouchers of £20 are also available to pensioners each winter to help towards the cost of groceries.

Annual grant total

In 2010/11 the charity had assets of £1.9 million and an income of £84,000. Grants were made totalling £39,000 and were distributed as follows:

Grants to individuals (education)	£1,700
Grocery voucher scheme	£15,000
Grants to organisations	£22,000

Applications

In writing to the correspondent.

Lakenheath

The Charities of George Goward and John Evans

£7,000

Correspondent: Laura Williams, 8 Woodcutters Way, Lakenheath, Brandon, Suffolk IP27 9JQ

Trustees: Horace Parsons; John Gentle; Mrs Shipp; Robert Rolph; Kevin Wickham; Steve Hills.

CC Number: 253727

Eligibility

People in need who live in the parish of Lakenheath in Suffolk.

Types of grants

One-off grants of £25 to £300 according to need.

Annual grant total

In 2010 the charity had both an income and total expenditure of £15,000.

Exclusions

No help is given for the relief of public funds.

Applications

In writing to the correspondent. Applications can be submitted either directly by the individual or a family member, through a third party such as a social worker or teacher, or through an organisation such as Citizens Advice. They should be received by February and August for consideration in March and September respectively. Applications should include a brief financial situation and receipts are required for book grants.

Other information

Grants are also made to organisations and to individuals for welfare purposes.

Lowestoft

The Lowestoft Church and Town Relief in Need Charity

£3,500

Correspondent: John M Loftus, Clerk, Lowestoft Charity Board, 148 London Road North, Lowestoft, Suffolk NR32 1HF (01502 718700; fax: 01502 718709)

Trustees: John Allen; Jill Collins; June Chapman; Edith Sybil Mary McClean; Elizabeth Anne Hudd; Gerda Patricia Buckley; Myrtle Wigg; Mary Rudd; Sandra Keller; Roy Stebbings; Cllr Ian Graham; John Parle; Revd Michael Asquith.

CC Number: 1015039

Eligibility

People in need who have lived in the area of the old borough of Lowestoft for at least three years.

Types of grants

On average ten one-off grants are made each year ranging from £50 to £500 for items and services such as furniture, clothing, childcare costs, help for disabled people, debt relief, help with funeral costs and so on.

Annual grant total

In 2010/11 the charity had an income of £8,800 and a total expenditure of £3,600.

Applications

In writing to the correspondent, directly by the individual. Applications are considered monthly.

Other information

The charity also makes grants to local organisations.

The Lowestoft Fishermen's and Seafarers' Benevolent Society

£36,000

Correspondent: H G Sims, Secretary, 10 Waveney Road, Lowestoft, Suffolk NR32 1BN

Eligibility

Widows, children and dependents of fishermen and seamen lost at sea from Lowestoft vessels, who are in need.

Types of grants

Monthly payments and one-off grants. Recent one-off grants have been made for funeral costs, mobility aids and household adaptations.

Annual grant total

In 2011 grants totalled £36,000. 13 widows received regular monthly payments and a number of one-off grants were also made.

Applications

In writing to the correspondent.

The Lowestoft Maternity and District Nursing Association

£1,500

Correspondent: Mrs Barbara Knights, Trustee, Pinecroft, 48 Lowestoft Road, Worlingham, Beccles NR33 8HP (01502 711708)

Trustees: Andrew Craig Shepherd; Jennifer Grint; Dawn Rhodes; Pam Chatters.

CC Number: 235309

Eligibility

People in a nursing or caring profession and retired nurses/carers who live/work in the borough of Lowestoft and either: (a) are retired and on a low income; (b) have a long-term disability; or (c) are experiencing short-term hardship, usually through illness.

Types of grants

On average 30 one-off and recurrent grants are made a year according to need, ranging from £25 to £250.

Annual grant total

Grants average around £1,500 a year.

Applications

In writing to the correspondent through community nurses or carers. Applications are usually considered in October.

Melton
The Melton Trust

£3,000

Correspondent: Revd Michael Hatchett, Melton Rectory, Station Road, Melton, Woodbridge IP12 1PX (01394 380279; email: meltontrust.suffolk@googlemail. com)

Trustees: Revd Michael Hatchett; Marion Davis; Jean King; Christopher Wilson; Anthony Thompson; Mary Addington Hall.

CC Number: 212286

Eligibility

People living in Melton who are in need, hardship or distress.

Types of grants

One-off and recurrent grants according to need. All pensioners in the parish can receive Christmas grants.

Annual grant total

Around £3,000.

Applications

Previous research suggested that the trust does not want people to apply, but it does 'try to give to everyone' (who is eligible).

Other information

Grants are also made to organisations.

Mendlesham
Mendlesham Town Estate Charity

£4,000

Correspondent: Mrs S C Furze, Beggars Roost, Church Road, Mendlesham, Stowmarket, Suffolk IP14 5SF (01449 767770)

Trustees: Hugh Cutting; Eric Roy Bauly; James Bristow Baker; Revd Philip Gray; Richard Hails; Stuart John Clark; Peter John Cole; Raymond Miles Fenning; John Downie; David Lambert; Peter Fredrick Freeman.

CC Number: 207592

Eligibility

People who are in need and live in the parish of Mendlesham, Suffolk.

Types of grants

One-off grants towards, for example, heating, hospital visiting and associated special needs, including bereavement.

Annual grant total

Grants to individuals usually total around £4,000 each year.

Applications

In writing to the correspondent. Applications can be submitted directly by the individual or through a third party such as a social worker or Citizens Advice.

Other information

Grants are also made to the Church Estate Charity for the upkeep of St Mary's Church.

Mildenhall
The Mildenhall Parish Charities

£13,000

Correspondent: Vincent Coomber, Clerk, 22 Lark Road, Mildenhall, Bury St Edmunds IP28 7LA (01638 718079)

Trustees: John Barker; Adrian Frederick John Peachey; Brian Sulman; Gerald Harry Taylor-Balls; Jennifer Reeve; Teresa Gooch-Taylor-Balls; Kay Sallis.

CC Number: 208196

Eligibility

Pensioners, widowers and widows in need who live in the parishes of Mildenhall and Beckrow.

Types of grants

The majority of the trust's giving is achieved through annual payments of £10 per person. One-off cash grants up to £500 towards travelling expenses to hospital, assistance to persons preparing to enter into a trade or profession and subscriptions to homes or hostels for infirm or homeless persons are also available.

Annual grant total

In 2010 the trust had an income of £14,000 and total expenditure of £15,500.

Applications

In writing to the correspondent either directly by the individual or through a recognised third party. Applications are considered three times a year.

Pakenham
The Pakenham Charities for the Poor

£5,000

Correspondent: Christine Cohen, Clerk, 5 St Mary's View, Pakenham, Bury St Edmunds, Suffolk IP31 2ND (01359 232965)

Trustees: Marion Sargent; Derek Dorling; John Wyeth Culley; Michael Bryant; Revd Katherine Valentine.

CC Number: 213314

Eligibility

People in need who live in Pakenham.

Types of grants

One-off and recurrent grants of £20 to £1,250. Grants given include those for fuel, alarms for people who are elderly, disability equipment, medical equipment, hospital expenses, clothing and travel expenses.

Annual grant total

Grants usually average around £5,000 per year.

Applications

In writing to the correspondent either directly by the individual, through a third party such as a social worker, or through an organisation such as Citizens Advice or other welfare agency. Applications are considered in early December and should be received by 30 November.

Other information

Grants are also made to organisations which benefit the elderly, the sick or the poor of the parish.

Reydon

The Reydon Trust

£12,000

Correspondent: H C A Freeman, 22 Kingfisher Crescent, Reydon, Southwold, Suffolk IP18 6XL (01502 723746)

Trustees: Ronald Stanley Leach; Archer Robert Ginn; Phyllis Lily Martin; Susan Elizabeth Moore; Revd Richard Henderson.

CC Number: 206873

Eligibility

People in need who live in the parish of Reydon.

Types of grants

One-off grants towards hospital expenses, clothing, food, travel costs and disability equipment. Vouchers are also given out at Christmas time.

Annual grant total

In 2010/11 the trust had assets of £627,000 and an income of £27,000. Grants were made totalling £12,000.

Applications

In writing to the correspondent. Applications can be submitted either directly by the individual, through a third party such as a social worker or via a doctor or health centre. They are considered upon receipt.

Risby

The Risby Fuel Allotment

£3,000

Correspondent: Penelope Wallis, 3 Woodland Close, Risby, Bury St Edmunds, Suffolk IP28 6QN (01284 81064)

Trustees: Bernard Abrey; Penelope Wallis; Heather Wagner; Eric Tennant.

CC Number: 212260

Eligibility

People in need who live in the parish of Risby.

Types of grants

Annual grants, primarily to buy winter fuel, although also for other needs.

Annual grant total

In 2010/11 the charity had an income of £5,700 and an expenditure of £4,600. Grants are given primarily for relief-in-need purposes and fuel costs.

Applications

In writing to the correspondent. Applications made outside the specific area of interest (the parish of Risby) are not acknowledged.

Rushbrooke

Lord Jermyn's Charity

£2,500

Correspondent: Mrs W Cooper, Estate Office, Rushbrooke, Bury St Edmonds, Suffolk IP30 0EP (01284 386276)

Trustees: Anita Patience Wigan; David Watts; Revd Nicholas Cutler; Mrs W. Cooper.

CC Number: 240282

Eligibility

People in need who are over 60 and live in the parish of Rushbrooke.

Types of grants

One-off grants according to need. Recent grants have been given for electricity, coal or other fuel, chiropody treatment, taxis for shopping and Christmas hampers.

Annual grant total

In 2010/11 the charity had an income of £2,700 and a total expenditure of £2,900.

Applications

In writing to the correspondent, either directly by the individual or through a third party.

Stanton

The Stanton Poor's Estate Charity

£3,200

Correspondent: Susan Buss, Treasurer, 3 Shepherds Grove Park, Stanton, Bury St Edmunds, Suffolk IP31 2AY (01359 250388)

Trustees: John William Lawrence Mann; Susan Buss; Rita Baker; Bryan Walter Cooper; David Atherton; Angela Burrows.

CC Number: 235649

Eligibility

People in need who live in the parish of Stanton and are in receipt of means-tested benefits. Grants can be made in special cases of need or hardship outside these criteria at the trustees' discretion.

Types of grants

Grants generally range between £40 and £90, although larger applications may be considered.

Annual grant total

In 2010/11 the charity had an income of £4,100 and a total expenditure of £3,500.

Applications

In writing to the correspondent, for consideration in November.

Stowmarket

The Stowmarket Relief Trust

£39,000

Correspondent: C Hawkins, Kiln House, 21 The Brickfields, Stowmarket, Suffolk IP14 1RZ (01449 674412; email: colinhawkins08@aol.com)

Trustees: David Henry Hopgood; Raymond Arthur Taylor; William Patrick Smith; Hazel Burl; Ron Snell; Lesley Maureen Mayes; Revd Michael Eden; Kathleen Butt; Kate Riddleston; Keith Edward.

CC Number: 802572

Eligibility

People in need who live in the town of Stowmarket and its adjoining parishes including the parish of Old Newton with Dagworth.

Applicants must have approached all sources of statutory benefit. People on Income Support will normally qualify. People in full-time paid employment will not normally qualify for assistance, but there are possible exceptions. People with substantial capital funds are also ineligible.

Types of grants

Normally one-off, but recurrent grants have been given in special circumstances. Recent grants have been made for the purchase and repair of white goods; payment of modest arrears (rent, council tax, electricity, gas, water and telephone charges); payment of bankruptcy fees and debt relief orders; repayments resulting from the overpayment of state benefits; carpets and floor coverings; beds, bedding and household furniture; electric wheelchairs and riser/recliner chairs; living/household expenses; car repairs; medical aids; and, clothing and footwear. Grants generally range from about £15 to £700, although in exceptional circumstances awards may exceed £1,000.

Annual grant total

In 2010/11 the trust had assets of £1.1 million and an income of £68,000. Grants were made to 153 individuals totalling £39,000 (£58,000 in 2009/10). A further £600 (£25,000 in 2009/10) was distributed to two institutions.

Applications

On a form available from the correspondent. Applications should be submitted through a third party such as a social worker, probation officer, Citizens Advice or doctor. Applications are considered at trustee meetings held three times a year, though urgent cases can be dealt with between meetings.

Stutton

The Charity of Joseph Catt

£6,000

Correspondent: Keith R Bales, 34 Cattsfield, Stutton, Ipswich, Suffolk IP9 2SP (01473 328179)

Trustees: Revd Geoffrey Clement; Dr Jane Pavitt; Keith Bales; Karl Baxter.

CC Number: 213013

Eligibility

People in need who live in the parish of Sutton only.

Types of grants

One-off grants and loans to help with fuel, hospital travel expenses, convalescent holidays, household goods and clothing.

Annual grant total

In 2010 the trust had an income of £9,000 and a total expenditure of £10,000.

Applications

Applications can be submitted by the individual, or through a recognised referral agency (e.g. social worker,

Citizens Advice or doctor) and are considered monthly. They can be submitted to the correspondent, or any of the trustees at any time, for consideration in May and November.

Other information

The charity also supports local almshouses.

Sudbury

The Sudbury Municipal Charities

£3,000

Correspondent: Adrian Walters, Clerk, Longstop Cottage, The Street, Lawshall, Bury St Edmunds IP29 4QA (01284 828219; email: a.walters@sclc.entadsl.com)

Trustees: Geoffrey Challacombe; Elizabeth May Wiles; Mary Atkins; Michael Raymond Hills; Peter Whiteley; Peter Francis Goodchild; Philip Richardson; Revd Richard Titford; May Onca Catharina Berkouwer; Mark James Geddes; Keith Robins; Ross Bentley.

CC Number: 213516

Eligibility

Older people (generally those over 70) who are in need and live in the borough of Sudbury.

Types of grants

Ascension Day and Christmas gifts, usually in the range of £10 to £30. Grants for special cases of hardship are also available.

Annual grant total

Grants usually total about £3,000 each year.

Applications

Grants are usually advertised in the local newspaper when they are available.

Other information

The charities also make grants to local organisations.

Walberswick

The Walberswick Common Lands

£6,000

Correspondent: Jayne Tibbles, Lima Cottage, Walberswick, Southwold, Suffolk IP18 6TN (01502 724448; website: walberswick.onesuffolk.net/walberswick-common-lands-charity/)

Trustees: Nigel Hunt; Kate Goodchild; Brian Fisher; James Darkins; Clive brynley-Jones; Madeline Dabbs; Keith Graham Webb.

CC Number: 206095

Eligibility

People in need who live in Walberswick.

Types of grants

Grants include quarterly payments to individuals and grants of £35 to £1,200 towards gardening, telephone rental and television licence payments, household items, access adaptations, travel expenses and Christmas cash and vouchers. Personal loans are also available.

Annual grant total

In 2011 grants for welfare totalled £3,600. A further £5,800 was given in personal loans.

Applications

In writing to the correspondent through a social worker, Citizens Advice or other welfare agency, or directly by the individual or through a relative or neighbour. Applications are considered in February, April, June, August, October and December.

Other information

Grants are also made to individuals for educational purposes and to organisations.

Surrey

The Banstead United Charities

£1,500

Correspondent: Michael Taylor, 6 Garratts Lane, Banstead SM7 2DZ (01737 355827)

Trustees: Anthony Thomas Gannon; Revd Maria Pallis; Richard Mantle; Muriel Stronach; Joy Teunion; Revd Garth Barber.

CC Number: 233339

Eligibility

People in need who live in the ancient parish of Banstead and Kingswood.

Types of grants

One-off grants, usually up to £500. Grants have been given towards funeral expenses, equipment for people who are disabled, travel for hospital treatment and rehabilitation, children's clothing and a small number of educational grants.

Annual grant total

In 2010 the charities had an income of £70 and a total expenditure of £1,200.

Applications

In writing to the correspondent. Applications can be submitted directly by the individual or through a social worker, Citizens Advice or other welfare agency. They are considered throughout the year.

John Beane's Eleemosynary Charity (Guildford)

£22,000 (124 grants)

Correspondent: B W France, 4 Henderson Avenue, Guildford GU2 9LP (01483 504180)

Trustees: Margaret Hicks; Keith Childs; Nick Brougham; Colin Edward Fullagar; Diana Elizabeth Ferguson; Pamela Hosegood.

CC Number: 242309

Eligibility

People in need living in the administrative county of Surrey.

Types of grants

One-off or recurrent grants according to need. In the year grants were made for furniture, bedding, clothing, removal expenses and electrical appliances.

Annual grant total

In 2010/11 the charity made grants to 124 individuals totalling £22,000.

Applications

On a form available from the correspondent, submitted through a social worker, health visitor, Citizens Advice or other welfare agency.

The Bookhams, Fetcham and Effingham Nursing Association Trust

£4,000

Correspondent: Margaret Blow, Secretary, 1a Howard Road, Great Bookham, Leatherhead, Surrey KT23 4PW (01372 452054)

Trustees: Carol Acres; Fran Reece; Jane Bourne; Jenny Peers; Margaret Elizabeth Blow; Phyllis Noel-Finch; Patricia Ann Bird.

CC Number: 265962

Eligibility

People in need who are sick, convalescent, disabled or infirm who live in Great Bookham, Little Bookham, Fetcham and Effingham.

Types of grants

Grants of between £100 and £1,500 for items, services or facilities which will alleviate the discomfort or assist the recovery of such people, where these facilities are not available from any other sources.

Annual grant total

In 2010/11 the trust had an income of £7,500 and a total expenditure of £8,900. Grants to individuals and local organisations totalled around £8,000.

Applications

Applications should be referred through medical or social services, not directly from the public.

Other information

This trust also gives grants to organisations.

Lady Noel Byron's Nursing Association

£1,000

Correspondent: J R Miles, Postboys, Cranmore Lane, West Horsley, Leatherhead, Surrey KT24 6BX (01483 284141; email: maganddave@tiscali.co.uk)

Trustees: David Donald Morgan; Heather Mary Lickley; Jeremy Robin Miles.

CC Number: 237970

Eligibility

People in need of medical or welfare assistance who live in the parishes of East and West Horsley.

Types of grants

One-off or recurrent grants according to need for medical or welfare related purposes only. This has included grants towards holidays, equipment and such like.

Annual grant total

Grants total around £1,000 to individuals each year.

Applications

In writing to the correspondent. Applications can be made directly by the individual or through a social worker, other welfare agency or third party. They are considered at any time.

Other information

Grants are also made to organisations.

The Churt Welfare Trust

£8,000 (34 grants)

Correspondent: Mrs E Kilpatrick, Hearn Lodge, Spats Lane, Headley Down, Bordon, Hampshire GU35 8SU (01428 712238)

Trustees: John Brain; Michael Blagden; Sheila Leaning; Pauline Buchanan; Sally Ann Fraser; Revd Richard Bodle; Eileen Kilpatrick; Maureen Trotter.

CC Number: 210076

Eligibility

People in need who live in the parish of Churt and its neighbourhood.

Types of grants

One-off grants usually in the range of £10–£1,000.

Annual grant total

In 2010/11 the trust had an income of £35,000 and a total expenditure of £20,000. Grants to organisations and individuals were made totalling £16,500.

Exclusions

The trust cannot commit to repeat or renew grants.

Applications

In writing to the correspondent.

Other information

Grants are also given to organisations (seven grants in 2010/11).

The Cranleigh and District Nursing Association

£2,000

Correspondent: Gill Bowles, 8 Mower Place, Cranleigh GU6 7DE (01483 276213)

Trustees: Revd Canon Nigel Nicholson; Pauline Hazel Gallagher; Roger Bracking; Judith Joyce Wynne Wedderspoon.

CC Number: 200649

Eligibility

People in need who are sick and poor and live in the parishes of Cranleigh and Ewhurst.

Types of grants

One-off grants ranging from £25 to £500. Recent grants have been made towards carpets, phone rental, MedicAlert bracelets, chiropody, hospital visits and pavement vehicles.

Annual grant total

Total expenditure is around £2,000 a year.

Applications

In writing to the correspondent through a social worker, Citizens Advice or other welfare agency.

The Dempster Trust

£8,000

Correspondent: Peter Jeans, Trustee, 21 Broomleaf Road, Farnham GU9 8DG (01252 721075)

Trustees: Jack Arthur Mayhew; Peter Jeans; Dr Genny Lane; George Francis Onslow Alford; Paul Whitlock.

CC Number: 200107

Eligibility

People in need, hardship or distress who live in Farnham and the general neighbourhood.

Types of grants

One-off grants or help for limited periods only. Grants have in the past been given towards nursing requisites, to relieve sudden distress, travelling expenses, fuel, television and telephone bills, clothing, washing machines, televisions, radios, alarm systems and so on. Grants range from £50 to £500.

Annual grant total

In 2010/11 the trust had an income and total expenditure of £9,000.

Exclusions

Help is not given towards rent, rates or house improvements.

Applications

On a form available from the correspondent to be submitted through a doctor, social worker, hospital, Citizens Advice or another welfare agency. Applications can be considered at any time.

The Ewell Parochial Trusts

£27,000

Correspondent: Miriam Massey, 19 Cheam Road, Ewell, Epsom, Surrey KT17 1ST (020 8394 0453; email: mirimas@globalnet.co.uk)

Trustees: Geoffrey Berry; Mildred Evelyn Jarrett.

CC Number: 201623

Eligibility

People in need who live, work or are being educated in the ancient ecclesiastical parish of Ewell and the domain of Kingswood.

Types of grants

One-off or recurrent grants according to need.

Annual grant total

In 2011 the trusts had an income of £41,000 and a total expenditure of £38,000 although no breakdown was offered.

Applications

In writing to the correspondent. Applications which do not meet the eligibility criteria will not be acknowledged.

The Godstone United Charities

£6,500

Correspondent: Mrs P Bamforth, Bassett Villa, Oxted Road, Godstone, Surrey RH9 8AD (01883 742625; website: www.godstonepc.org.uk)

Trustees: Valerie Faulkner; Jo Clarke; Mrs D. I. Jackson-Grose; Terry Tomlinson; Paula Quincy; Mrs S. Rouse.

CC Number: 200055

Eligibility

People in need who live in the old parish of Godstone (Blindley Heath, South Godstone and Godstone Village).

Types of grants

Food vouchers are usually given in December and March. One-off grants are also available.

Annual grant total

In 2010/11 the charities had an income of £8,800 and a total expenditure of £7,300.

Applications

In writing to the correspondent: either directly by the individual, through a relevant third party or via a social worker, Citizens Advice or other welfare agency. Applications should include relevant details of income, outgoings, household composition and reason for request. All grants are paid directly to the supplier.

Other information

The charities also make grants to local organisations.

The Henry Smith Charity (Ash and Normandy)

£3,000

Correspondent: Michael Ratcliffe, 84 Shawfield Road, Ash, Aldershot GU12 6RB (01252 656711)

Trustees: Lesley Cole; Rosemary Hall; Revd Pauline Godfrey; Nigel Manning; Revd Keith Bristow; Roger Shapley; Lionel Covey.

CC Number: 240485

Eligibility

People in need who live in Ash and Normandy.

Types of grants

One-off or recurrent grants according to need.

Annual grant total

Grants usually total about £3,000 each year.

Applications

In writing to the correspondent, either directly by the individual or through a social worker, Citizens Advice or other welfare agency. Applications are normally considered as they arrive.

Other information

The charity also makes grants to organisations.

The Henry Smith Charity (Eastbrook Estate)

£2,100

Correspondent: Ron Howard, Trustee, 4 Cholmley Terrace, Portsmouth Road, Thames Ditton, Surrey KT7 0XX (email: ron_286@yahoo.co.uk)

Trustees: Ron Howard; Torq Stewart; Alan Dean.

CC Number: 200123

Eligibility

Widows or people over 60 who are in need, of good character and have lived in the parishes of Long Ditton and Tolworth for the past five years.

Types of grants

Grants to be spent on heating fuel, clothing and electricity bills at named retailers.

Annual grant total

Grants usually total around £2,100 a year.

Applications

In writing to the correspondent. Applications are considered in December and January and must include details of the applicant's age and length of residence in the parish.

The Henry Smith Charity (Frimley)

£200

Correspondent: Derek McManus, Surrey Heath Borough Council, Surrey Heath House, Knoll Road, Camberley, Surrey GU15 3HD (01276 707302; email: derek.mcmanus@surreyheath.gov.uk)

Trustees: Ian Sams; Bruce Mansell; David Hamilton.

CC Number: 236367

Eligibility

People in need who live in the former parish of Frimley (Frimley, Frimley Green, Camberley and Mytchett).

Types of grants

One-off grants ranging from £100 to £200 towards clothing, bedding, furniture, disability equipment and electrical goods.

Annual grant total

Grants usually average around £600 a year. However, in 2010/11 the charity had a total expenditure of £200.

Applications

In writing to the correspondent through a social worker, Citizens Advice or other welfare agency.

The Henry Smith Charity (I. Wood Estate)

£18,000

Correspondent: Bernard Fleckney, c/o Committee Section, Civic Offices, Runnymede Borough Council, Station Road, Addlestone, Surrey KT15 2AH (01932 425620)

Trustees: Ann Edwards; Inga Tuley; John Edwards; Christopher Knight; Shan Hughes; Diana Cotty.

CC Number: 233531

Eligibility

People over 60 who are in need and live in Chertsey, Addlestone, New Haw and Lyne, Surrey.

Types of grants

Recurrent fuel vouchers of £40, which can be used as part-payment of fuel bills.

Annual grant total

In 2010/11 the charity had an income of £21,000 and a total expenditure of £19,000.

Applications

In writing to the correspondent either through a social worker, Citizens Advice or other third party or directly by the individual. Applications can be considered at any time during the year.

The Henry Smith Charity (Puttenham and Wanborough)

£2,000

Correspondent: David Knapp, Crossways, Lascombe Lane, Puttenham, Surrey GU3 1BA (01483 887772; fax: 01483 887757; email: dsk@hartbrown.co.uk)

Eligibility

People in need who live in Puttenham and Wanborough parishes.

Types of grants

One-off grants for needy people who do not have an income other than pensions.

Annual grant total

The charity receives around £2,000 a year, allocated by Henry Smith's (General Estate) Charity.

Exclusions

Grants are not given to people who are working or who own their house.

Applications

In writing to the correspondent, submitted in October for consideration in November.

Other information

Grants are also given for the benefit of the parish as a whole.

The Henry Smith Charity (Richmond)

£2,000

Correspondent: Catherine Rumsey, The Richmond Charities, 8 The Green, Richmond, Surrey TW9 1PL (020 8948 4188; fax: 020 8948 6224; email: richmondcharities@richmondcharities. org.uk)

Trustees: Serge Lourie; Frances Bouchier; Pauline Gore; Jean Love; Gillian Mathers; Colin Craib; Peter Marr; Canon Robert Titley; Steven Weddle; Susan John; Emma Davies.

CC Number: 200431

Eligibility

People experiencing hardship or distress who live in Richmond, Ham, Petersham and Kew.

Types of grants

One-off grants ranging up to £250. Recently the greatest number of grants have been made to unemployed single parents, towards children's clothing and fuel bills.

Annual grant total

Grants usually total around £2,000 per year.

Applications

In writing to the correspondent, from referring bodies such as social services, health authority or a Citizens Advice. Applications are considered at trustees' meetings in February, March, May, June, September, November and December.

The Henry Smith Charity (Send and Ripley)

£4,500

Correspondent: Geoffrey A Richardson, Emali, 2 Rose Lane, Ripley, Surrey GU23 6NE (01483 225322)

Trustees: Geoffrey Richardson; David Conisbee.

CC Number: 200496

Eligibility

People in need who live in Send and Ripley, and have done so for five years.

Types of grants

One-off annual grants of £30 a year to around 50 or 60 people in Send and a similar number in Ripley. Other grants are available from any remaining funds, and have included money towards a wheelchair for a disabled student.

Annual grant total

The annual income is about £4,500, all of which is available in grants.

Applications

In writing to the correspondent. Applications can be submitted directly by the individual, through a social worker, Citizens Advice or any other welfare agency or third party on behalf of the individual. Applications are considered as they arrive.

The Surrey Association for Visual Impairment

£3,100

Correspondent: Lance Clarke, Chief Executive, Rentwood, School Lane, Fetcham, Leatherhead, Surrey KT22 9JX (01372 377701; fax: 01372 360767; email: info@sa-vi.org.uk; website: www. surreywebsight.org.uk)

Trustees: Sue Joslin; Alan Howell; Edmund Gowler; Nina Aberdein; Stephen Cleveland Caswell; Colin Mills; Cecilia Power; Clare Black; Geoffrey Pierson; Elle Mohan; Tony Madison; Aidan Kiely.

CC Number: 1121949

Eligibility

People who are blind or partially-sighted and who live in the administrative county of Surrey.

Types of grants

Small one-off grants are given when absolutely necessary. Grants are usually to help pay for equipment required to overcome a sight problem or a sudden domestic need.

Annual grant total

In 2010/11 the association had assets of £1.2 million and an income of £1.6 million. A budget of £5,000 is allocated for grants to individuals and to local clubs/classes. During the year £3,100 of this was distributed to individuals.

Applications

On a form available from the correspondent. Applications can be submitted at any time by the individual or through a social worker, welfare agency, club or any recognised organisation for blind or partially-sighted people.

Other information

The association's main focus is the provision of services, advice and information for visually impaired people. It runs a resource centre equipped with a wide range of aids, equipment and media, some of which are provided free of charge. It also provides guidance on benefit claims and advice and support to young people and parents.

The Windlesham United and Poors Allotment Charities

£3,900 (63 grants)

Correspondent: Mrs D V Christie, Clerk to the Trustees, 4 James Butler Almshouses, Meade Court, Bagshot, Surrey GU19 5NH

Trustees: June Elizabeth Janet Green; Leslie Edward Coombs; Peter Malcolm Colegrove; Raymond James Christie; Samuel Keith Hand; Jill Ward.

CC Number: 200224

Eligibility

Mainly elderly people and people with disabilities, who are in need and live in the parishes of Bagshot, Lightwater and Windlesham.

Types of grants

One-off grants mainly in the form of small heating grants.

Annual grant total

The most recent set of accounts available were for 2010, when the trust made grants totalling £3,900.

Applications

In writing to the correspondent at any time.

The Witley Charitable Trust

£1,300

Correspondent: Daphne O'Hanlon, Triados, Waggoners Way, Grayshott, Hindhead, Surrey GU26 6DX (01428 604679)

Trustees: Daphne O'Hanlon; Pamela Pile; Peter Herring; John Withers; John Cable; Dr David Pollard.

CC Number: 200338

Eligibility

Children and young people aged under 20 and older people aged over 60 who

are in need and who live in the parishes of Witley and Milford.

Types of grants

One-off grants of £25 to £300, towards, for example, telephone, electricity and gas debts (up to about £150) usually paid via social services, and medical appliances not available through the Health Service. At Christmas about 40 food hampers are given.

Annual grant total

Around £3,000 each year for welfare and educational needs.

Exclusions

The trust does not give loans or for items which should be provided by statutory services.

Applications

In writing to the correspondent, to be submitted through nurses, doctors, social workers, the clergy, Citizens Advice and so on but not directly by the individual. Applications are usually considered in early February and September, although emergency applications can be considered throughout the year.

The Wonersh Charities

£3,200

Correspondent: Molly Howard, Pen Pell, Barnett Lane, Wonersh, Guildford GU5 0RZ (01483 893857)

Trustees: Louise Elizabeth Hamilton Healy; Michael Harding; Sally Davies; Deborah Mary Sellin; Nicky Cooke; Diane Savage; Sue King; Anne Powell-Evans; Karen Munday; Penny Kirkwood.

CC Number: 200086

Eligibility

Older people and people with a disability who live in the parishes of Wonersh, Shamley Green and Blackheath.

Types of grants

Cash grants are given at Christmas. One-off grants are also available.

Annual grant total

In 2010/11 the trust had an income of £5,200 and a total expenditure of £3,400.

Applications

In writing to the correspondent preferably through a third party such as a Citizens Advice, trustee of the charity, local clergy or other organisation. Applications are usually considered in early July and early December.

Abinger

The Abinger Consolidated Charities

£4,000

Correspondent: Caroline Sack, The Rectory, Abinger Lane, Abinger Common, Dorking, Surrey RH5 6HZ (01306 737160)

Trustees: Revd Anthony Berry; Sally McCance; Belinda Crabbe; Diana Prideaux; Helen Clear; Ann Ing,.

CC Number: 200124

Eligibility

People in need who live in the ancient parish of Abinger.

Types of grants

One-off or recurrent grants according to need.

Annual grant total

In 2010/11 the charity had an income of £10,000 and a total expenditure of £8,500. Grants are given to both individuals and local organisations.

Applications

In writing to the correspondent.

Ashford

Ashford Relief in Need Charities

£3,000

Correspondent: Peter G Harding, 8 Portland Road, Ashford TW15 3BT (01784 241257; email: pjlr_2000@yahoo.co.uk)

Trustees: Mrs B. Bartlett; Mrs M. C. Haarer; Mrs C. A. Beasley; Mrs F. Forsbrey; Mrs P. Kyle; Mrs C. Coleman.

CC Number: 231441

Eligibility

People in need who live in the ancient parishes of Ashford and Laleham.

Types of grants

One-off grants according to need.

Annual grant total

In 2010/11 the charities had an income of £9,500 and a total expenditure of £3,000. Grants to individuals usually total around £3,000.

Applications

In writing to the correspondent. Applications can be made either directly by the individual, or through a third party such as a social worker, Citizens Advice or relative.

Other information

Grants are also made to organisations.

Betchworth

Betchworth United Charities

£14,000

Correspondent: Mrs Sally Drayson, Hambledon, Blackbrook Road, Dorking, Surrey RH5 4DT (01306 888727)

Trustees: Revd Jonathan Willans; Roger Hammond; Heather Knight; Janet Powell; Jean Ann Hurman; Joanna Louis Ellis.

CC Number: 200299

Eligibility

People in need who live in the ancient parish of Betchworth.

Types of grants

One-off grants usually ranging from £60 to £250. The majority of funding is given for welfare purposes but a small amount is also available for educational needs under the Margaret Fenwick fund.

Annual grant total

Grants usually total around £9,000 per year.

Applications

In writing to the correspondent to be submitted by a third party, such as, a doctor, minister or social worker. Applications are considered at trustee meetings.

Bisley

The Henry Smith Charity (Bisley)

£1,000

Correspondent: Mrs Alexandra Gunn, 213 Guildford Road, Bisley, Woking, Surrey GU24 9DL (email: sandy213@ntlworld.com)

Trustees: Jim Evans; Joan Cheeseman; Andy Armitt; Alexandra Gunn; Gaynor Moore.

CC Number: 200157

Eligibility

People in need who live in Bisley.

Types of grants

Grants to assist with food costs are distributed twice a year.

Annual grant total

Grants total around £1,000 each year.

Applications

On a form available from the correspondent to be submitted directly by the individual.

Bletchingley

The Bletchingley United Charities

£4,000

Correspondent: Mrs C A Bolshaw, Cleves, Castle Street, Bletchingley, Surrey RH1 4QA (01883 743000; email: chrisbolshaw@hotmail.co.uk)

Trustees: Angela Price; David Martin; Dr Colin Howard; Revd Peter Moseling; Ronald Napper; Wendy Mason; Lisa Carolyn Thurston.

CC Number: 236747

Eligibility

People in need, hardship or distress who live in the parish of Bletchingley.

Types of grants

One-off and recurrent grants in the range of £20 to £200 towards medical items, welfare support, gas and electricity and equipment such as cookers, fridges, freezers and so on.

Annual grant total

The trust has an average annual income and expenditure of £10,000.

Exclusions

Grants are not given for rates, taxes or other public funds.

Applications

In writing to the correspondent or to David Martin (94 High Street, Bletchingley, Surrey). Applications can be submitted either directly by the individual, through a third party such as a social worker, or through an organisation such as a Citizens Advice or other welfare agency. They are considered throughout the year.

Other information

Care organisations working locally are also considered.

Bramley

The Henry Smith Charity (Bramley)

£3,000

Correspondent: Kathy Victor, Bramley Village Hall, Hall Road, Bramley, Guildford GU5 0AX (01483 894138; email: bramleyparish@gmail.com; website: www.bramleyparish.co.uk)

Trustees: John Compton; Maurice Byham; Richard Gates; Peter Wadham; Sue O'Connell; Patrick Molineux; Roy Harrall; Tony Allenby; Francesca Stern.

CC Number: 200128

Eligibility

People in need who live in the parish of Bramley, Surrey.

Types of grants

One-off grants according to need.

Annual grant total

Grants usually total about £3,000 each year.

Applications

In writing to the correspondent; there are no application forms. The letter should contain as much information as possible about why support is required.

Other information

This charity is also known as the 'Smiths Charity'.

Byfleet

The Byfleet United Charities

£271,000

Correspondent: Mrs C M Heath, Administrator, 10 Stoop Court, Leisure Lane, West Byfleet, Surrey KT14 6HF (01932 340943)

Trustees: Revd Alan Bernard Elkins; Joan Patricia Mackintosh; Kenneth Roy Mears; Robert Martin Barker; Anne Daly; Tony James Thompson; Revd John Hamilton McCabe; Patrick Land.

CC Number: 200344

Eligibility

People in need who have lived in the ancient parish of Byfleet for at least a year.

Types of grants

Monthly pensions. One-off grants can also be given for items such as cookers, heaters, vacuum cleaners and nursery schools fees.

Annual grant total

In 2010 the charity had assets of £6 million and an income of £474,000. Grants were made to 96 individuals totalling £46,000 and a further £225,000 was paid in pensions.

Applications

By writing to, or telephoning, the correspondent. Applications can be made directly by the individual or through a third party such as a social worker, Citizens Advice, local GP or church. Applicants are usually visited and assessed.

Other information

The charity gives money to local organisations who work in a similar field (£4,000 in 2010). It also operates a sheltered housing complex of 24 flats, which are available to those in real need.

This charity is an amalgamation of smaller trusts, including the Byfleet Pensions Fund.

Capel

The Henry Smith Charity (Capel)

£2,000

Correspondent: Mrs J Richards, Old School House, Coldharbour, Dorking, Surrey RH5 6HF (01306 711885)

Eligibility

People in need who have lived in Beare Green, Capel and Coldharbour, usually for at least five years.

Types of grants

Mostly Christmas vouchers for older people redeemable at several local stores. The vouchers are £20 for couples and £15 for single people.

Annual grant total

Grants usually total about £2,000 each year.

Applications

In writing to the correspondent directly by the individual or a family member. Applications should be received by 1 November and are considered in December.

Charlwood

John Bristow and Thomas Mason Trust

£300

Correspondent: Marie Singleton, Trust Secretary, 3 Grayrigg Road, Maidenbower, Crawley RH10 7AB (01293 883950; email: trust.secretary@ jbtmt.org.uk; website: www.jbtmt.org.uk)

Trustees: R. Parker; William Campen; Martin James; Feargal Hogan; Howard Pearson; Alison Martin; J. King; C. Jordan.

CC Number: 1075971

Eligibility

People who are in need who live in the parish of Charlwood as constituted on 17 February 1926, including Hookwood and Lowfield Heath.

Types of grants

One-off and recurrent grants and loans are given according to the need. Support for illness and disability and recreation and leisure.

Annual grant total

In 2011 the trust had assets of £2.3 million, an income of £76,000 and made grants totalling £66,000, of which £300 went to individuals for welfare purposes.

Applications

On a form available from the correspondent or to download from the website. Applications can be submitted directly by the individual or through a third party. They will normally be considered within two weeks but can be dealt with more quickly in urgent cases.

Other information

Grants are also available for educational purposes.

Smith and Earles Charity

£4,000

Correspondent: Robin Pacey, Ivy Cottage, Russ Hill Road, Charlwood, Horley, Surrey RH6 0EJ (01293 863933)

Trustees: Ivor Gillespie; Christa Longhurst; David Parsons; Eileen Lanzer; Colin Gates.

CC Number: 200043

Eligibility

People with disabilities or those over 65 and in need who have lived in the old parish of Charlwood for at least five years.

Types of grants

One-off and recurrent grants of up to £80.

Annual grant total

In 2010 the charities had an income and total expenditure of £6,200. Grants to individuals for welfare purposes have previously totalled around £4,000.

Applications

On a form available from the correspondent. Applications for one-off (usually larger) grants should be submitted through a recognised referral agency (such as a social worker, Citizens Advice or other welfare agency). Applications for recurrent grants can be submitted directly by the individual. They are considered in November. Details of any disability or special need should be given.

Other information

Help is also given towards the hiring of halls for meetings for older people, hospices and school requirements.

Cheam

Cheam Consolidated Charities

£1,800

Correspondent: Darren Miller, Trustee, The Rectory, 33 Mickleham Gardens, Sutton SM3 8QJ (020 8641 4664)

Trustees: Fr Darren Miller; Brian Stevens; Margaret Sheppard; Nola Freeman; Chris Chambers.

CC Number: 238392

Eligibility

People in need who live in Cheam. Preference is given to older people.

Types of grants

One-off and recurrent grants, of £50 to £200.

Annual grant total

Grants average around £3,600 a year. They are given to both individuals and organisations.

Applications

In writing to the correspondent, for consideration at the start of May and November. Applications can be made either directly by the individual, or via a social worker, Citizens Advice or other welfare agency.

Chertsey

The Chertsey Combined Charity

£1,250

Correspondent: M R O Sullivan, Secretary, PO Box 89, Weybridge, Surrey KT13 8HY

Trustees: Malcolm Loveday; Christopher Norman; David Harding; John Gooderham; Judith Norman; Michael Everett; Peter Austin; Richard Fleming; Revd Timothy Hillier; Claire Gant; Derek Cotty; David Frith; John Leach.

CC Number: 200186

Eligibility

People in need who live in the electoral divisions of the former urban district of Chertsey.

Types of grants

Grants are given in the form of fuel vouchers, Christmas grants and one-off grants.

Annual grant total

In 2010/11 the charity had an income of £62,000 and a total expenditure of £68,000. Grants to individuals were made totalling £2,500.

Applications

On a form available from the correspondent.

Other information

The charity also makes grants to organisations (£45,000 in 2010/11).

Chessington

Chessington Charities

£2,000

Correspondent: Mrs L Roberts, St Mary's Centre, Church Lane, Chessington, Surrey KT9 2DR

Trustees: Revd Peter Jenner; Jackie Bone; Michael Brook; Revd Sara Oakland; Marjorie Redding; Joy Fogg.

CC Number: 209241

Eligibility

People in need who live in the parish of St Mary the Virgin, Chessington. Applicants must have lived in the parish for at least one year.

Types of grants

Grants are usually one-off in the range of £30 to £250. Donations include those given to older people (with low income) at Christmas and for items such as special food, furniture, medical equipment, electrical goods and clothing.

Annual grant total

In 2010 the charities had both an income and total expenditure of £5,400.

Exclusions

Grants are not given 'as a dole' or to pay debts. Applicants must live in the Parish of St Mary the Virgin, which excludes those who live in the rest of the Chessington postal area.

Applications

On a form available from the correspondent to be submitted either directly by the individual or through a social worker, Citizens Advice or other agency. Other applications are considered throughout the year. A home visit will be made by a trustee to ascertain details of income and expenditure and to look at the need. Applications for Christmas grants for older people must be received by 1 November and are distributed in this month.

Other information

Grants are also given to local organisations which help older people or people with disabilities such as Chessington Voluntary Care and Arthritis Care. Educational grants are also available for individuals.

Chobham

The Chobham Poor Allotment Charity

£9,600 (123 grants)

Correspondent: Mrs Elizabeth Thody, 46 Chertsey Road, Windlesham GU20 6EP

Trustees: David John Elliott; Violet May Elizabeth Tedder; Winifred Mary Patterson; Jennifer Stratford; Anthony Astall; Sue Bush; Edward Bentall.

CC Number: 200154

Eligibility

People in need who live in the ancient parish of Chobham, which includes the civil parishes of Chobham and West End.

Types of grants

The majority of grants are given in the form of vouchers, valuing between £30 and £50, as payment towards goods in local shops. Awards were also made towards stair lifts, electric scooters and school trips and uniforms.

Annual grant total

In 2010/11 the charity had assets of £424,000 and an income of £49,000. Grants were made through a voucher system to 123 individuals totalling £9,600.

Applications

On a form available from the correspondent. Applications should be submitted directly by the individual for consideration at any time.

Other information

The trust also makes grants to organisations which benefit the local community (£5,500 in 2010/11) and manages an area of allotment land and almshouses.

Henry Smith Charity (Chobham)

£6,000

Correspondent: Mrs Elizabeth Thody, 46 Chertsey Road, Windlesham, Surrey GU20 6EP

Trustees: Violet Tedder; David Elliott; Simon Lowe; Diane Beach.

CC Number: 200155

Eligibility

People in need who live in the ancient parish of Chobham (roughly the current civil parishes of Chobham and West End) in Surrey.

Types of grants

One-off grants, usually in the form of vouchers worth £20 to £30, to be used to purchase goods from local shops.

Annual grant total

In 2010/11 the charity had both an income and total expenditure of £6,800.

Applications

On a form available from the correspondent.

Crowhurst

Crowhurst Relief-in-Need Charities

£1,600

Correspondent: Mrs Edwards, 1 Lankester Square, Oxted, Surrey RH8 0LJ (01883 712874)

Trustees: Mrs P. Edwards; Mr R. Nuttall; Revd S. Gendall; Mr V. Din; Mr G. Jackson.

CC Number: 200315

Eligibility

People in need who live in Crowhurst, Surrey.

Types of grants

One-off grants according to need. Recent grants of £100 to £250 have been given to help with fuel bills and travel to or from hospital.

Annual grant total

In 2010/11 the trust had a total income of £2,400 and an expenditure of £1,900.

Applications

On a form available from the correspondent.

Dunsfold

The Henry Smith Charity (Dunsfold)

£2,000

Correspondent: Celeste Lawrence, Dunsfold Parish Clerk, Council Office, Unit 4, The Orchard, Chiddingfold Road, Dunsfold GU8 4PB (01483 200980; email: dunsfoldparishclerk@ btconnect.com)

Eligibility

People in need who live in Dunsfold and who have done so for the past five years.

Types of grants

Grocery vouchers for about £40 to £50, exchangeable in the village store.

Annual grant total

Around £2,000.

Applications

In writing to the correspondent. Applications are considered in December.

East Horsley

Henry Smith Charity (East Horsley)

£250

Correspondent: Mr R Deighton, East Horsley Parish Council Office, Kingston Avenue, East Horsley, Surrey KT24 6QT (01483 281148; email: henrysmithcharity@easthorsley.net)

Trustees: Olive Ridler; Stephen Skinner; Roy Proctor; Revd Elisabeth Bussmann.

CC Number: 200796

Eligibility

People in need who have lived in East Horsley for at least two years and are disabled or in need.

Types of grants

One-off or recurrent grants according to need.

Annual grant total

Each year the trust receives about £1,000, allocated by Henry Smith's (General Estate) Charity which is divided according to need between welfare and educational grants.

Applications

In writing to the correspondent through a third party such as a social worker, teacher or vicar. Applications are considered in December.

Effingham

The Henry Smith Charity (Effingham)

£2,000

Correspondent: The Clerk, Effingham Parish Council, The Parish Room, 3 Home Barn Court, The Street, Effingham, Surrey KT24 5LG (01372 454911; email: clerk2009@ effinghamparishcouncil.gov.uk)

Trustee: Effingham Parish Council.

CC Number: 237703

Eligibility

People in need who live in Effingham.

Types of grants

One-off grants and gift vouchers, generally of £50 to £100; many grants are given at Christmas.

Annual grant total

In 2010/11 the charity had an income of £3,600 and a total expenditure of £2,100.

Applications

In writing to the correspondent. Applications are considered monthly.

Egham

The Egham United Charity

£12,000

Correspondent: Max Walker, 33 Runnemede Road, Egham, Surrey TW20 9BE (01784 472742; email: eghamunicharity@aol.com; website: www.eghamunitedcharity.org)

Trustees: Betty Florence Wheeler; Jill Reynolds; John Robert Ashmore; Yvonna Pia Lay; Christine Mary Searle; Diana Margaret Brickell.

CC Number: 205885

Eligibility

People in need who have lived in Egham, Englefield Green (West and East), Hythe or Virginia Water for at least five years.

Types of grants

One-off grants according to need.

Annual grant total

In 2011 the trust had an income of £14,000 and a total expenditure of £16,000.

Exclusions

No recurrent grants or loans.

Applications

On a form available to download from the website. Applications should be submitted through an appropriate third party such as a Citizens Advice or a social worker. Ideally applications should include quotations for goods or services required. Applications should be received 10–14 days before trustee meetings which are held every six weeks. Applicants may occasionally be visited.

Other information

Grants are also given for educational purposes.

Epsom

Epsom Parochial Charities

£750

Correspondent: Patricia Vanstone-Walker, 42 Canons Lane, Tadworth, Surrey KT20 6DP (01737 361243; email: vanstonewalker@ntlworld.com)

Trustees: Robert Leach; Gillian Heym; John Steward; Joan Harridge; A. R. M. Watson; Christine Long; Simon Talbott; David Eggett; Colin Bird; Neil Dallen.

CC Number: 200571

Eligibility

People in need who live in the ancient parish of Epsom.

Types of grants

One-off grants ranging from £100 to £500 according to need. Grants given include those for clothing, food, medical care and equipment and household appliances.

Annual grant total

£750 in 2010.

Applications

On a form available from the correspondent. Applications can be submitted by the individual or through a social worker, Citizens Advice or other welfare agency. They are usually considered in March, June, September and December but should be submitted in the preceding month.

Other information

Grants are also made for education.

The Henry Smith Charity (Ewell)

£12,000

Correspondent: The Administrator, 19 Cheam Road, Ewell, Epsom, Surrey KT17 1ST

Eligibility

People in need who live, work or are being educated in the ancient ecclesiastical parish of Ewell and the liberty of Kingswood.

Types of grants

One-off or recurrent grants according to need.

Annual grant total

The trust receives about £12,000 each year, allocated by Henry Smith's (General Estate) Charity.

Applications

In writing to the correspondent. Applications which do not meet the criteria will not be acknowledged.

Esher

The Henry Smith Charity (Esher)

£2,000

Correspondent: Mrs G B Barnett, Clerk, 24 Pelhams Walk, Esher KT10 8QD (01372 465755; email: gill@gillmikebarnett.plus.com)

Eligibility

People in need who live in the ancient parish of Esher.

Types of grants

Annual grants to a number of elderly/low income families to help with winter expenses; and emergency grants for furniture, white goods and so on. Grants are only to cover expenses not met by statutory authorities.

Annual grant total

The trust has an income of about £2,000, allocated by Henry Smith's (General Estate) Charity, all of which is given in grants.

Applications

In writing to the correspondent through a social worker, Citizens Advice or other third party. Details of the applicant's financial circumstances should be included. Annual grants are considered in December, emergency grants at any time.

Guildford

The Guildford Poyle Charities

£36,000 (285 grants)

Correspondent: Janice Bennett, 208 High Street, Guildford GU1 3JB (01483 303678; fax: 01483 303678; email: admin@guildfordpoylecharities.org; website: www.guildfordpoylecharities.org)

Trustees: Jonathan Jessup; Joan O'Byrne; Sarah Creedy; Gordon Reid; Tamsy Baker; Carol Dunnett; Colin Wright; Peter Farrell; Michael Owen; Brian Green; Christopher Dean; Dr John Nichols; Bryan Templeman.

CC Number: 1078131

Eligibility

People in need who live in the borough of Guildford as constituted prior to 1 April 1974 and part of the ancient parish of Merrow. A map showing the beneficial area can be viewed on the website.

Types of grants

Mainly one-off grants ranging between £100 and £300 for furniture, domestic appliances, decorating materials, children's clothing and so on. Christmas food vouchers are also available to families. Grants for carpets are only considered in special circumstances. You must get a quote from Carpetright on Ladymead, mentioning the Poyle charities, and enclose it with the application form.

Annual grant total

In 2011 the charities had assets of £3.6 million, an income of £145,000 and a total expenditure of £164,000. Grants were made to 285 individuals totalling £36,000.

Exclusions

Grants are usually not made to pay for basic items such as food, rent and utility bills. No help towards debt.

Applications

On a form available from the correspondent or to download from the website. Applications can be submitted at any time either directly by the individual or through a social worker, Citizens Advice or other welfare agency. They are considered every two to three weeks and decisions are confirmed in writing.

Other information

The charities are also known as the Henry Smith's or The Poyle Charity. Grants are also made to organisations (£72,000 in 2011).

The Mayor of Guildford's Christmas and Local Distress Fund

£7,000

Correspondent: Kate Foxton, Guildford Borough Council, Millmead House, Millmead, Guildford, Surrey GU2 4BB (01483 444031)

Trustees: David Hill; Sue Sturgeon; Cllr Terence Dickson Patrick.

CC Number: 258388

Eligibility

People in need who live in the borough of Guildford.

Types of grants

One-off grants of up to £150. There are no specific restrictions on what can be applied for and the purpose of the grant is defined in the application form. Grants are also made for Christmas events.

Annual grant total

In 2010/11 the trust had an income of £2,800 and a total expenditure of £7,400.

Applications

On a form available from the correspondent, to be submitted through a social worker, Citizens Advice, local GP or other relevant third party. Applications are usually considered in January, April, July and October.

Hascombe

The Henry Smith Charity (Hascombe)

£2,000 (30 grants)

Correspondent: Beverley Weddell, Hascombe Parish Clerk, Lock House Lodge, Knightons Lane, Dunsfold GU8 4NU (01483 200314; email: clerk@hascombeparishcouncil.co.uk)

Eligibility

People in need, generally older people who live in Hascombe. The trustees will consider giving grants to other residents of Hascombe in cases of real need or emergency whatever their age and not necessarily only at Christmas.

Types of grants

Generally grants are given at Christmas of £60–70 each.

Annual grant total

In 2011 the charity had £2,200 available for distribution. 29 grants of £65 were made and one grant of £100.

Applications

In writing to the correspondent.

Headley

The Henry Smith Charity

£5,000

Correspondent: Anthony Vine-Lott, Broom Cottage, Crabtree Lane, Headley, Epsom KT18 6PS (01372 374728; email: tony.vinelott@btinternet.com)

Eligibility

People in need who live in the parish of Headley.

Types of grants

One-off and recurrent grants are available to help with, for example, groceries and hospital travel.

Annual grant total

Grants usually total about £5,000 each year.

Applications

In writing to the correspondent or any trustee, giving the reasons for the application.

Horne

The Henry Smith Charity (Horne)

£5,000

Correspondent: Mrs Pam Bean, Hon. Secretary, Yew Tree Cottage, Smallfield Road, Horne, Horley, Surrey RH6 9JP (01342 843173)

Trustees: Pamela Anne Bentley Bean; Colin Buckley; Barbara Prentice; Cherry Caddy; Debby Pickering; Sally Charman.

CC Number: 201988

Eligibility

Older people and people in need who live in the ancient parish of Horne.

Types of grants

One-off grants are the norm, although recurrent grants can be considered.

Annual grant total

Grants usually average about £4,500 each year.

Exclusions

Group applications are not accepted.

Applications

On a form available from the correspondent. Applications can be submitted either directly by the individual or through a social worker and should include details of the applicant's level of income. They are normally considered twice a year (notices are posted around the parish).

Kingston upon Thames

The Charities of Ann Savage

£600

Correspondent: Christopher Ault, Trustee, 18 Woodbines Avenue, Kingston upon Thames KT1 2AY (020 8546 8155)

Trustees: Joy Campbell; Revd Jonathan Wilkes; Rosemary Gout; Chris Ault.

CC Number: 237108

Eligibility

People in need who live in the borough of Kingston upon Thames.

Types of grants

Mainly recurrent grants.

Annual grant total

Grants to individuals are generally around £1,000 a year. When funds allow, the trust donates half of its income to their local church.

Applications

The trustees usually support individuals known via their contacts at All Saints Parish Church in Kingston upon Thames. It is unlikely that grants would be available to support unsolicited applications.

Leatherhead

The Leatherhead United Charities

£10,000

Correspondent: David Matanle, Homefield, Fortyfoot Road, Leatherhead, Surrey KT22 8RP (01372 370073; email: luchar@btinternet.com)

Trustees: John Buchanan Henderson; Bridget Lewis-Carr; Alan Wright; Graham Osborne; Michael Ward; David Sharland.

CC Number: 200183

Eligibility

People in need who live in the area of the former Leatherhead urban district council.

Types of grants

One-off grants in the range of £100 to £750 are given for the relief of need generally. Pensions are also given.

Annual grant total

In 2011 the charity gave 54 grants to individuals. No grants total was available but in previous years grants to individuals have totalled around £20,000, for welfare and educational purposes.

Applications

On a form available from the correspondent and submitted through a recognised referral agency (e.g. social worker, Citizens Advice or doctor) giving details of income and the names of two referees. Applications are considered throughout the year.

Other information

The charity also makes grants to organisations.

Leigh

The Henry Smith Charity (Leigh)

£4,500

Correspondent: Mrs J Sturt, 12 Knoll Road, Dorking RH4 3EW (01306 881547)

Trustees: Derek Harrington; Laurie Aplin; John Worsfold.

CC Number: 237335

Eligibility

People in need who live in Leigh, Surrey.

Types of grants

The trust has a list of all people over 65; each receives support at Christmas in the form of food vouchers, or help with household bills. Gifts may also be given at Easter in the years when the trust receives more income.

Annual grant total

In 2010 the trust had an income of £4,800 and a total expenditure of £4,900.

Applications

In writing or by telephone to the correspondent, or through a third party.

Newdigate

The Henry Smith Charity (Newdigate)

£5,000

Correspondent: Diana Salisbury, 'Langholm', Village Street, Newdigate, Dorking, Surrey RH5 5DH (website: newdigate.atspace.com/benefact.htm)

Eligibility

People in need who live in the parish of Newdigate.

Types of grants

One-off grants for a variety of needs. Grants are typically made to help residents with bereavement, health needs and special educational requirements.

Annual grant total

Grants usually total around £5,000 per year.

Applications

In writing to the correspondent to be submitted directly by the individual.

Nutfield

Smith's Charity-Parish of Nutfield

£4,000

Correspondent: Kenneth Rolaston, 7 Morris Road, South Nutfield, Redhill RH1 5SB (01737 823348; email: smithsnutfield@aol.com)

Trustees: Kenneth Rolaston; John Burnett; Sylvia Gammon; Eric Putland; Keith Richardson.

CC Number: 255839

Eligibility

People in need who live in the parish of Nutfield.

Types of grants

One-off and recurrent grants ranging from £35 to £45. Vouchers for local shops are given. The charity also makes some grants to village organisations.

Annual grant total

In 2010/11 the charity had an income of £4,800 and a total expenditure of £4,300.

Applications

In writing to the correspondent. Applications can be submitted either directly by the individual or by any of the four trustees and are considered in December.

Ockley

Ockley United Charities (Henry Smith Charity)

£9,000

Correspondent: Timothy Pryke, Danesfield, Stane Street, Ockley, Dorking, Surrey RH5 5SY (01306 711511)

Trustees: David Christopher Ansell; Gordon Lee Steere; Sally Noel Calvert; Tim Pryke; Richard Curties; Deborah Herbert.

CC Number: 200556

Eligibility

People in need who live in Ockley (primarily older people living in sheltered accommodation provided by Ockley Housing Association or rented housing).

Types of grants

Recurrent annual cash gifts of £110. Assistance is also given to local families for nursery fees.

Annual grant total

In 2010/11 the charities had both an income and expenditure of £9,400.

Applications

In writing to the correspondent. Applications should include details of income, housing and need. They are considered on a regular basis.

Other information

Local organisations are also supported.

Oxted

The Oxted United Charities

£5,500

Correspondent: C J Berry, Trustee, Robinslade, Wilderness Road, Oxted, Surrey RH8 9HS (01883 714553)

Trustees: Christopher John Berry; Mrs B. Harling; Mrs V. Lea; Gill Fairs; Revd Prof. Mary Joan Seller; Mrs A. Pullar-Strecker.

CC Number: 200056

Eligibility

People in need who live in the parish of Oxted.

Types of grants

One-off grants, generally in the range of £20 to £500. Recent grants have been given for clothing, food, education, utility bills, television licences, furniture and floor covering.

Annual grant total

In 2010/11 the charity had an income of £5,000 and a total expenditure of £5,800.

Applications

In writing to the correspondent. Applications are considered at any time and should be submitted directly by the individual or through a social worker, Citizens Advice or other welfare agency.

Pirbright

The Pirbright Relief-in-Need Charity

£2,000

Correspondent: Philip Lawson, Stanemore, Rowe Lane, Pirbright, Surrey GU24 0LX (01483 472842)

Trustees: Dr Euan George Mackintosh Cameron; Joy Valerie Underwood; Revd Christine Musser.

CC Number: 238494

Eligibility

People in need, hardship or distress who live in the parish of Pirbright.

Types of grants

One-off grants for a variety of items, services or facilities that will reduce the need, hardship or distress of the individual, including buying or renting medical equipment to use at home.

Annual grant total

Grants total around £2,000 per year.

Exclusions

Grants will not be given for taxes, rates or any other public funds. The trustees must not commit themselves to repeating or renewing any grant.

Applications

In writing to the correspondent or any of the trustees.

Shalford

Smith's Charity

£3,000

Correspondent: Nuala Livesey, Shalford Parish Council, Thursley House, 53 Station Road, Shalford, Guildford GU4 8HA (01483 459108; email: shalfordpc@tiscali.co.uk)

Trustees: Anna Souster; Mike Parsons; Norah Morden; Zoe Figueiredo.

CC Number: 240135

Eligibility

People in need who live in Shalford parish.

Types of grants

One-off and recurrent cash grants of £100, to relieve financial problems.

Annual grant total

Grants usually total around £3,000 a year.

Applications

In writing to the correspondent, either directly by the individual or through a social worker, Citizens Advice or other welfare agency or directly by the individual or a relevant third party. Applications are considered in March, after the grants are advertised locally.

Shottermill

Shottermill United Charities (Henry Smith and Others)

£1,000

Correspondent: Hilary Bicknell, 7 Underwood Road, Haslemere, Surrey GU27 1JQ (01428 651276)

Trustees: Jackie Keen; Maura Howard; Rita Bicknell; Vanessa Kemp; Revd Daniel Wignall; Pat Blades.

CC Number: 200394

Eligibility

People in need who live in the parish of Shottermill, Surrey.

Types of grants

Grants usually ranging from £40 to £50 according to need. The charity distributes grocery vouchers at Christmas.

Annual grant total

About £1,000.

Applications

In writing to the correspondent. Applications can be submitted directly by the individual or through a social worker, Citizens Advice or other welfare agency or third party. They are considered at any time, but particularly at Christmas.

Other information

The charities also give grants to organisations.

Staines

The Staines Parochial Charity

£4,000

Correspondent: Carol Davies, Honorary Clerk to the Trustees, 191 Feltham Hill Road, Ashford, Middlesex TW15 1HJ (01784 255432)

Trustees: Peter Pattinson; Alice Deere; John O'Hara; Father Rod Cosh; Denise Saliagopoulos; Alex Forrester; Christine Bannister; Elizabeth Mackendar-Moore.

CC Number: 211653

Eligibility

Older people over the age of 60 who live in the parish of Staines; people who are unable to work; people caring for a person with disabilities and occasionally other people in need who live in the area of the former urban district of Staines.

Types of grants

One-off grants according to need for payment of gas or electricity bills. Grants usually range from £80 to £100.

Annual grant total

In 2010/11 the charity had an income of £5,000 and a total expenditure of £4,200.

Exclusions

No grants to individuals living outside the beneficial area.

Applications

On a form available from the correspondent including evidence of need, hardship or distress. Applications can be submitted either directly by the individual, through a social worker, Citizens Advice, welfare agency or other third party. The application must be sent via a trustee who must countersign the application. Applications are normally considered in September.

Other information

Eligibility for Housing Benefit or Income Support is taken as an indication of need.

Stoke D'Abernon

The Stoke D'Abernon Charities

£1,500

Correspondent: Mr Ron Stewart, Old Timbers, Manor Way, Oxshott, Leatherhead, Surrey KT22 0HU (07785 272590; email: ronandjackie@tecres.net)

Trustees: Revd Robert Jenkins; Ronald Stewart; Jennifer Mary Mathieson; Mary Pomery; Rosemary Elizabeth Nelson.

CC Number: 200187

Eligibility

People in need who live in the ancient parish of Stoke D'Abernon (which includes part of Oxshott).

Types of grants

One-off and recurrent grants according to need. Grants are made at Christmas and on average are around £50. Occasionally smaller distributions are made in the summer.

Annual grant total

Income and grant expenditure average around £1,500 a year.

Applications

Applications may be made formally in writing, however, many applications are made informally by word of mouth given the small size and catchment area of the charity. If a formal application is to be made the trustees prefer email where possible.

Thorpe

The Thorpe Parochial Charities

£1,000

Correspondent: Mrs D Jones, 9 Rosefield Gardens, Ottershaw, Chertsey, Surrey KT16 0JH (01932 872245)

Trustees: Diana Andrews; Brian Relph; Doris Mackie; Jane Nadin; Margaret Harnden; Susan Knight.

CC Number: 205888

Eligibility

People in need who live in the ancient parish of Thorpe, especially those over 60 years of age.

Types of grants

Grants of solid fuel or contributions to gas or electricity accounts and 'aids to the sick'. Grants range between £35 and £50. Educational grants are also available.

Annual grant total

About £2,000.

Applications

In writing to the correspondent by the end of October. Applications are usually considered in November.

Thursley

The Thursley Charities

£2,300

Correspondent: The Trustees, Yew Cottage, Dye House Lane, Thursley, Godalming GU8 6QA (01252 702360; email: peter.muir@thursleychurch.org.uk)

Trustees: Drusilla Pye; Maurice Redbond; Hon Marion O'Brien; Revd Peter Muir; Revd John Page.

CC Number: 239259

Eligibility

People in need, including older people, single parents, those with disabilities and bereaved young people, who live in the parish of Thursley in Surrey.

Types of grants

One-off and recurrent grants according to need ranging from £100 to £300.

Annual grant total

Grants usually total around £2,300 a year.

Applications

In writing to the correspondent. Applications can be submitted directly by the individual or through an organisation such as Citizens Advice, or through a third party such as a social worker. Applications are considered in November each year.

Other information

The charities are the Charities of Anthony Smith and Henry Smith.

West Clandon

The Henry Smith Charity (West Clandon)

£2,500

Correspondent: Stephen Meredith, 11 Bennett Way, West Clandon, Guildford GU4 7TN

Trustees: Revd Barry Preece; Jean Fawley; Stephen Meredith; Robert Wood.

CC Number: 200165

Eligibility

People in need, mainly older people, who have lived in the parish of West Clandon for at least five years.

Types of grants

One-off cash grants of £45 to £100.

Annual grant total

Grants usually total about £2,500 a year.

Applications

In writing to the correspondent. The deadline for applications is 31 October. Grants are usually distributed during December.

West Horsley

The Henry Smith Charity (West Horsley)

£200

Correspondent: Mollie Lewendon, Trustee, Lansdowne, Silkmore Lane, West Horsley, Surrey KT24 6JB (01483 284167)

Trustees: Mollie Lewendon; Doreen Stark; Ruth Isaac.

CC Number: 249496

Eligibility

People in need who live in West Horsley.

Types of grants

One-off or recurrent grants according to need.

Annual grant total

Grants usually total about £1,000 a year. However, in 2010/11 the total expenditure was £200.

Applications

In writing to the correspondent. Note, the charity has previously stated that resources are fully committed.

West Molesey

The Henry Smith Charity (West Molesey)

£1,600

Correspondent: Revd Peter Tailby, 518 Walton Road, West Molesey, Surrey KT8 2QF (020 8979 3846)

Eligibility

People in need who live in West Molesey.

Types of grants

Small one-off grants, usually under £50.

Annual grant total

About £1,600.

Applications

In writing to the correspondent. Applications can be submitted directly by the individual or through a social worker, Citizens Advice or other welfare agency.

Weybridge

Weybridge Land Charity

£43,000 (286 grants)

Correspondent: Howard Turner, Little Knowle, Woodlands, Send, Surrey GU23 7LD (01483 211728)

Trustees: Geoff Banks; Graham Winton; Mr Wolstenholme; Cllr Harman; Cllr Dearlove; Peter Vey; Dee Stone; Ivan Pratt; Cllr Gordon Macleod.

CC Number: 200270

Eligibility

People in need who live in Weybridge.

Types of grants

- Emergency grants – individuals needing immediate help can receive supermarket vouchers or payments are made directly to suppliers of household essentials
- Christmas grants (including fuel payments) – grants generally in the range of £100 to £280

Annual grant total

In 2011 the charity had assets of £1.4 million and an income of £96,000. Grants to 286 individuals totalled £43,000. Of this total 265 individuals (of 320 applications) received Christmas grants totalling £35,000 and 21 received emergency grants paid through a number of intermediary referral agencies.

The trustees have planned to increase grant aid by £50,000 over the period 2011–15.

Exclusions

No funding towards debt relief.

Applications

Application forms for the emergency grants are available from Citizens Advice at Walton-on-Thames, the local GP surgery and from health and social workers throughout the area. Application forms for Christmas grants are available during September and October at the Weybridge Day Centre and Library and should be returned before 31 October for payments in first week in December.

Other information

Grants are also made to organisations (£8,200 to eight organisations in 2011).

Woking

The Henry Smith Charity (Woking)

£5,500

Correspondent: David Bittleston, Pin Mill, Heathfield Road, Woking, Surrey GU22 7JJ (01483 828621)

Trustees: Revd Barry Grimster; David Bittleston; Revd Giles Williams; Graham Cundy; Revd Nick Grew; Revd Dr Peter Harwood; Revd Richard Cook; Mrs M. Tuckey; Ian Johnson; Simon Bellord.

CC Number: 232281

Eligibility

People in need who live in the ancient parish of Woking.

Types of grants

One-off grants only.

Annual grant total

In 2010/11 the trust had both an income and a total expenditure of £5,800.

Exclusions

Grants are not given for the relief of rates, taxes and other public funds.

Applications

In writing to the vicar of the parish, either directly by the individual or through a social worker, Citizens Advice or other welfare agency.

Worplesdon

Worplesdon Parish Charities (including the Henry Smith Charity)

£2,000

Correspondent: Eric S Morgan, 21 St Michael's Avenue, Fairlands,

Guildford, Surrey GU3 3LY (01483 233344)

Trustees: Alastair Buchan; Eric Sidney Morgan; Eric Marks-Oldham.

CC Number: 200382

Eligibility

People in need who live in the parish of Worplesdon.

Types of grants

Grants of around £60 to buy coal, clothing or groceries at Christmas.

Annual grant total

Grants usually total around £2,000 per year.

Applications

Apply when the distribution is advertised within the parish (normally in October/ November each year). Emergency grants can be considered at any time.

Wotton

The Henry Smith Charity (Wotton)

£5,000

Correspondent: Rosemary Wakeford, Secretary, 2 Brickyard Cottages, Hollow Lane, Wotton, Dorking, Surrey RH5 6QE (01306 730856)

Trustees: Patrick Evelyn; Audrey Bradley; Barbara Rowling; Revd Pam Robson; Sue Gibbs; Tony Gibbons.

CC Number: 240634

Eligibility

People in need who live in the ancient parish of Wotton.

Types of grants

One-off grants ranging from £100 to £500. Grants have in the past been given to older people of the parish towards fuel and lighting bills and holidays, young people taking part in schemes such as The Duke of Edinburgh Award which will enhance their job prospects, and help towards the cost of independent projects or travel costs.

Annual grant total

Grants usually total around £5,000 each year.

Applications

In writing to the correspondent. Applications are considered in March and September. They can be submitted directly by the individual or through a third party.

West Sussex

Ashington, Wiston, Warminghurst Sick Poor Fund

£7,200

Correspondent: Rod Shepherd, Sheen Stickland, 7 East Pallant, Chichester, West Sussex PO19 1TR

Trustees: John Wyatt; Rod Shepherd; Basil Boxall; Val Edwards.

CC Number: 234625

Eligibility

People in need – typically those who are ill – who live, firstly in the villages of Ashington, Wiston and Warminghurst, and secondly in West Sussex.

Types of grants

One-off grants according to need. Grants are given to provide or pay for items or services which will alleviate the need or assist the recovery of beneficiaries where assistance is not readily available from any other source.

Annual grant total

In 2011 the fund had an income of £900 and a total expenditure of £7,600. The average grant was around £400.

Applications

On a form available from the correspondent. Applications can be submitted directly by the individual or a relevant third party.

Sussex County Football Association Benevolent Fund

£4,200

Correspondent: Nigel Williams, 3 Oak Tree Lane, Woodgate, Chichester, West Sussex PO20 3GU (01243 543177; website: www.sussexfa.com)

Trustees: Douglas Arthur Austen-Jones; Paul Edward Hartman; Stanley Williams; Paul Beard; Mike Brown; Nigel Williams.

CC Number: 217496

Eligibility

Members of Sussex county FA clubs and their relatives or dependents.

Types of grants

Grants to support those who players and officials affiliated to Sussex County FA who have suffered a football-related injury and, as a result, find themselves in financial hardship.

Grants may be one-off or recurrent.

Annual grant total

In 2010/11 the trust had an income of £12,000 and total expenditure of £4,400.

Applications

On forms available from the correspondent. Requests for applications must be received by the secretary within 14 days of the injury and then completed and returned within a further 28 days.

A medical certificate or its equivalent must accompany each application.

The West Sussex County Nursing Benevolent Fund

£4,500

Correspondent: Rod Shepherd, Sheen Stickland, 7 East Pallant, Chichester, West Sussex PO19 1TR (01243 781255)

Trustees: John Wyatt; Rod Shepherd; Basil Boxall; Val Edwards.

CC Number: 234210

Eligibility

Nurses who are or have been engaged in community nursing in West Sussex and are in need. Beneficiaries must also be in poor health, convalescent or have disabilities as well as being in financial need.

Types of grants

One-off and recurrent grants according to need. Recent grants include those towards wheelchairs, tricycles for children with disabilities and a respite holiday for a child with severe mental disabilities. Christmas gifts are also given.

Annual grant total

Around £4,500.

Applications

On a form available from the correspondent. Applications can be submitted directly by the individual, or through a third party such as a social worker, Citizens Advice or other welfare agency.

Crawley

Crawley and Ifield Relief in Sickness Fund

£2,000

Correspondent: Roger Gibson, 7 Priestcroft Close, Crawley RH11 8RL (01293 520752; email: roger.gibson7@ talktalk.net)

Trustees: Jean Winter; David Hawkins; Roger Gibson; Ann Buck.

CC Number: 254779

Eligibility

People in need who live within a three mile radius of the church of St John Crawley who are sick, disabled, convalescent or infirm.

Types of grants

One-off grants according to need.

Annual grant total

In 2011 the fund had an income of £2,400 and a total expenditure of £2,100.

Applications

In writing to the correspondent.

Horsham

The Innes Memorial Fund

£3,000

Correspondent: Mr James Richard Innes, Campfield Lodge, Leith Hill, Dorking RH13 6DH (01306 713192)

Trustees: James Richard Innes; Ian Alexander Innes; Dr Jonathan Patrick Heatley; Peter Christopher Freeman; Sterling Byrd Innes Lacy; Andrew Innes.

CC Number: 21936

Eligibility

People who are poor, sick and in need and who live in Horsham.

Types of grants

One-off grants given towards wheelchairs, cookers, alarms, domestic help, school uniforms, holidays, disability equipment, travel expenses and chiropody costs. On average ten grants are made a year ranging between £100 and £250.

Annual grant total

In 2010/11 the trust had an income of £15,500 and total expenditure of £17,000. Expenditure on grants tends to be quite low as the fund also supports the Roffey Institute and other local charities.

Applications

In writing to the correspondent, to be submitted through a doctor or social worker.

Midhurst

The Midhurst Pest House Charity

£750 (4 grants)

Correspondent: Tim Rudwick, Clerk, 31 Pretoria Avenue, Midhurst, West Sussex GU29 9PP (01730 812489; email: timrudwick@yahoo.co.uk)

Trustees: Anthony Beck; Edward Stanley Dummer; Winifred Passmore; David Michael Tunks; John Alan Backshall; Dr Trevor Guthrie; Carol Lintott.

CC Number: 227479

Eligibility

People in need who live in the parish of Midhurst.

Types of grants

One-off grants in the range of £60 to £500. Recent awards have been given towards transport and holiday costs.

Annual grant total

In 2010 the charity had an income of £18,000 and a total expenditure of £13,000, the majority of which was used to maintain trust properties. Grants to four individuals totalled £750.

Applications

In writing to the correspondent either directly by the individual or through a social worker, Citizens Advice or other welfare agency. Applications are considered in April and October and should be received in the preceding month.

Other information

Grants are also occasionally made to a local school.

Wisborough Green

The Elliott Charity

£500

Correspondent: Dr Graham Parr, The Brambles, Balchins Close, Wilsborough Green, West Sussex RH14 0DW (01403 700793)

Trustees: Revd Peter Dixon; Dr Graham Parr.

CC Number: 216197

Eligibility

People who are older or who have disabilities, live in the parish Wisborough Green and are in need.

Types of grants

One-off or recurrent grants according to need, usually ranging between £200 and £500.

Annual grant total

Grants to individuals usually total around £500 a year.

Applications

In writing to the correspondent. Applications can be submitted directly by the individual or through a social worker, Citizens Advice or other welfare agency.

Other information

Grants are also made to community causes, including an annual donation to the Village Minibus Association.

London

General

The Affinity Water Trust

£415,000 (1,068 grants)

Correspondent: Grants team, Freepost-RSHH-JKZA-HAUY, PO Box 42, Peterborough PE3 8XH (01733 421020; fax: 01733 421020; email: awt@ charisgrants.com; website: www. veoliawatertrust.org.uk)

Trustees: Keith Taylor; Peter William Darby; David Hewitt; David Butcher.

CC Number: 1128398

Eligibility
Account holders may apply for help with water, sewerage, gas or electricity debts. A condition of the grant is that an applicant must be financially stable going forward and prepared to keep up to date with payments in the future. Anyone in need, poverty, hardship or other distress may apply to clear other priority debts and provide essential household items.

Types of grants
Payments can be made to help vulnerable people clear domestic water and sewerage debt. Further assistance payments are also made to clear other priority debts and to purchase essential household items.

Annual grant total
In 2011/12 the trust held assets of £323,000 and had an income of £572,000. Grants to individuals totalled £415,000. Of this £303,000 was paid in respect of assistance with water and sewerage debts and £113,000 was paid in further assistance payments. Overall, there was an increase in the value of grants of 86% on 2010/11.

In 2011/12 1,989 applications were received and 1,068 awards were made to individuals and families: 777 to clear water and sewerage debts and 291 further assistance payments. The average grant value was £388.

Exclusions
No help with bills already paid or items already purchased. No help with fines or criminal penalties; overpayment of benefits; education or training costs; business debts; tax and national insurance debts; catalogue, credit card or other non-secured lending debts; medical equipment, aids or adaptations; deposits to secure accommodation; holidays or debts to Thames Water.

Applications
Applications can be completed online. Supporting documentation should be scanned and attached to the form. Alternatively forms may be downloaded from the website or by calling the application request line: 01733 421060. Applications must be completed by, or on behalf of, the relevant account holder. If completed by a third party the account holder must still sign the form. Applications will be acknowledged by email or post.

Note that the trust operates a shared programme of giving with other utility trusts operated by Charis grants, including: Anglian Water Assistance Fund, British Gas Energy Trust, EDF Energy Trust, nPower Energy Fund and Southeast Water's Helping Hand. An applicant only has to complete one form to be considered for help by any of these trusts.

Other information
Grants are also made to organisations (£79,000 in 2011/12). The trust funds debt counselling and money advice via grants to Citizens Advice.

In October 2012 Veolia Water was bought and renamed Affinity Water.

The Arsenal Foundation

£6,900 (9 grants)

Trustees: David Miles; Alan Sefton; Kenneth Friar; Ivan Gazidis; Svenja Geissmar.

CC Number: 1008024

Eligibility
People in need including those injured whilst playing sport, or their dependents who live in Greater London, with a preference for Islington and Hackney. The charity also supports the provision of recreational activities to those in need.

Types of grants
Grants and loans according to need.

Annual grant total
In 2010/11 the foundation had assets of £1.2 million and an income of £276,000. Grants were made to nine individuals totalling £6,900.

Applications
In writing to the correspondent.

Other information
Grants are also made to local organisations and charities working in Israel and Sri Lanka (£83,000 in 2010/11).

Benevolent of Strangers' Friend Society

£800

Correspondent: Chris Linford, Room 403, 1 Central Buildings, Westminster, London SW1H 9NH (020 7222 8010; fax: 020 7799 1452; email: chris.linford@ methodistlondon.org.uk)

Trustees: Mr C. Linford; Mr G. T. Slater.

CC Number: 239385

Eligibility
People in need, particularly 'strangers not entitled to parochial relief', that is people who have exhausted all other possible sources of funding. Beneficiaries must live in London, mainly inner London.

Types of grants
One-off and recurrent grants in the range of £50 and £150.

Annual grant total
Grants usually total about £1,000 a year, but in 2009/10 total expenditure totalled

just £900. No further information was available

Applications

Applications should not be made to the society since it does not make grants directly to individuals. It allocates funds to certain Methodist ministers living in most areas of inner London and some areas of outer London, who in turn distribute the funds to individuals in need of whom they become aware.

BlindAid

£31,000 (86 grants)

Correspondent: Sue O'Hara, Chief Executive, Lantern House, 102 Bermondsey Street, London SE1 3UB (020 7403 6184; fax: 020 7234 0708; email: enquiries@blindaid.org.uk; website: www.blindaid.org.uk)

Trustees: John Pattie Bennet Bryce; Peter Welsby Holland; Andrew Blessley; Douglas Leonard Osborne; Keith David Felton; Valerie Joan Scarr; Charles Goodall; Jean Conway.

CC Number: 262119

Eligibility

Blind and partially sighted people who live on a permanent basis in one of the 12 central London boroughs or the City of London and who are in receipt of means tested benefits, with a preference for those registered blind/partially sighted.

Types of grants

One-off grants up to £500 towards computer equipment; electronic text-magnification equipment; holidays and family visits; and domestic equipment such as a talking microwave, fridges and other furniture.

Annual grant total

In 2011 the trust had assets of £4.3 million and an income of £511,000. Grants to 86 individuals totalled £31,000 and were broken down as follows:

General purpose	£22,000
Small grants	£6,700
Holiday grants	£2,500

Exclusions

Awards are not normally made for the following: payment of outstanding debts, bankruptcy/insolvency costs, house deposits, home modifications, funeral expenses, removal expenses, motor vehicle costs, gardening costs, medical treatment or remedial therapies; holidays outside the UK (although help with associated costs could be considered); payment of council tax/rent arrears; educational grants (although help with associated costs may be considered); installation of a telephone service where

the applicant is in short-term or temporary accommodation.

Applications

Online application process; or on a form available to download or from the correspondent. Applications should be made through a third party such as a social worker or through an organisation such as Citizens Advice or other welfare agency. A supporting letter may be attached to explain the background to the case, although it is not mandatory. Decisions are usually made within 28 days.

Only one application per person/ household can be considered in any two year period.

Other information

BlindAid's core service is a Home Visiting service to provide company and conversation and lessen isolation in the community, on which it spends almost half its income; it also offers telephone support for those who choose not to have a visit, as well as advice, information and links to other appropriate organisations. The Charity also supports small local organisations helping visually impaired people such as social clubs.

Formerly known as The Metropolitan Society for the Blind.

Brentford and Chiswick Relief in Need and Sick Poor Persons Fund

£430

Correspondent: Julie Cadman, St Paul's Church Office, St Paul's Road, Brentford, Middlesex TW8 0PN (020 8568 7442; email: clerk@ brentfordchiswick.org.uk; website: www. brentfordchiswickmc.org.uk)

Trustees: Revd Derek Simpson; Mel Collins; Peter Thomas Williams; Cllr Matt Harmer; Cllr Andrew Dakers; Cllr Steve Curran.

CC Number: 21186/209811

Eligibility

People in need who live in Brentford and Chiswick.

Types of grants

One-off grants ranging from £50 to £200, which have recently been given towards a specialised computer, a special buggy for a child with disabilities, debts and a holiday for a person with disabilities.

Annual grant total

The fund had a small income of £1,300. Grants to individuals totalled £430 between the two funds.

Exclusions

No grants for items which should be provided by a statutory authority.

Applications

On an application form available through the funds' website. The form must be signed by a professional person such as a vicar, social worker, teacher or doctor.

Other information

The fund also makes grants to organisations.

The Charity of Sir Richard Whittington

£240,000 (206 grants)

Correspondent: Rebecca Farrell, Worshipful Company of Mercers, Mercers Hall, Ironmonger Lane, London EC2V 8HE (020 7776 7235; email: rebeccaf@mercers.co.uk; website: www. mercers.co.uk/grants-elderly-individuals)

Trustee: The Mercers' Company.

CC Number: 1087167

Eligibility

Elderly London residents on a low income. Applicants must be over the age of 60, although priority will be given to older and more frail applicants.

Types of grants

Regular grants of around £1,140, paid quarterly.

Annual grant total

In 2011 the charity held assets of £67 million and had an income of £3.7 million. Grants to 206 individuals totalled £240,000.

Applications

Application forms may be requested by contacting the correspondent. The application must also include the details of a referee such as a GP, social worker, member of the clergy, etc.

Other information

The charity also operates a number of almshouses. Grants are also made to organisations with similar aims (£159,000 in 2010/11).

Cripplegate Foundation

£51,000

Correspondent: Chris Robbs, 76 Central Street, London EC1V 8AG (020 7566 3135; fax: 020 7566 3139; email: chris. hobbs@cripplegate.org.uk; website: www. cripplegate.org)

Trustees: John Tomlinson; Barbara Helen Riddell; Paula Kahn; Judith Moran; Revd Katharine Rumens; John Gilbert; Lucy Watt; David Sulkin;

Heather Lamont; Rob Hull; Mark Yeadon; Anne-Marie Ellis; Rob Abercrombie; Frances Elizabeth Carter; Cllr Barry Edwards; David Graves; Cripplegate Foundation Ltd.

CC Number: 207499

Eligibility

People in need who have lived or worked for more than 12 months in the ancient parish of St Giles, Cripplegate, the former parish of St Luke's, Old Street and the London borough of Islington. Asylum seekers and those who were previously homeless do not have to meet the one year residential qualification and can apply as soon as they move into the area. Applications are considered from people on a low income, with priority being given to those who are also coping with, for instance, illness, disability, debt, or family break-up.

Types of grants

One-off grants of up to £500 for household items, white goods, disability aids, respite breaks and adaptations and start-up packages for newly housed homeless people. With the exception of white goods applicants should attach a written quotation for the items requested. Direct cash grants are not made, goods will be ordered from a supplier.

Annual grant total

In 2011 the foundation had assets of £29 million and an income of £2.4 million. Cripplegate foundation grants made to individuals totalled £51,000.

Exclusions

No grants are given towards debts, items already purchased, money that has been stolen, computers, rental of privately owned caravans, childcare costs, education or student expenses and wheelchairs. No repeat applications are considered within three years of the last approved grant award or within 12 months of the last unsuccessful grant application. This applies to applications to the cripplegate foundation grants programme and the other grant programmes administered by the foundation – St Sepulchre United Charities and Richard Cloudesley's Charity. This rule will only be waived in exceptional circumstances.

Applications

On a form available from the correspondent or on the website. Decisions are usually made within four weeks of receipt of the completed form. People who are unsure of whether they live in the beneficial area should telephone the trust before making an application.

Other information

Grants are also made to organisations.

The Edmonton Aid-in-Sickness and Nursing Fund

£5,000

Correspondent: David M Firth, Hon. Secretary, 9 Crossway, Bush Hill Park, Enfield, Middlesex EN1 2LA (020 8127 1949)

Trustees: Ruth Davis; Brian Howard; David M. Firth; Geoffrey James; Maurice Levit; Ruth Firth.

CC Number: 210623

Eligibility

People in need who are in poor health and live in the old borough of Edmonton (mainly N9 and N18).

Types of grants

One-off grants usually up to £300. Recent grants have been made for clothing, furniture, household necessities, convalescence, household bills and debts and medical equipment not covered by NHS provision.

Annual grant total

The trust has an average annual income and total expenditure of £5,600.

Exclusions

The trust will not subsidise public funds, therefore applicants should have sought help from all public sources before approaching the trust.

Applications

In writing to the correspondent either directly by the individual or through social services, Citizens Advice or other welfare agency. Applications can be received at any time.

The Emanuel Hospital Charity

£54,000 (59 grants)

Correspondent: Clerk to the Trustees, Town Clerk's Office, Corporation of London, PO Box 270, Guildhall, London EC2P 2EJ (020 7332 1408; email: jacky.compton@cityoflondon.gov.uk; website: www.cityoflondon.gov.uk)

Trustees: Cllr Paul Judge; Sir Michael Savory; Cllr Ian Luder; Alderman David Hugh Wootton; Sir David Howard; Cllr Simon Walsh; Sir Robert Finch; Roger Gifford; Dr Andrew Parmley; Cllr John Stuttard; Cllr Alison Gowman; Rober Hall; Cllr Michael David Bear; Sir David Lewis; Cllr Nicholas Anstee; John Garbutt; Gordon Haines; Lord Levene of Portsoken; Cllr Fiona Woolf; Cllr Alan

Yarrow; Cllr Jeffrey Evans; Cllr John White; Cllr David Graves; Cllr Neil Redcliffe; Philip Remnant.

CC Number: 206952

Eligibility

Needy persons of 60 years of age or older who have lived in the London boroughs of Kensington and Chelsea, Hillingdon or Westminster for at least two years.

Types of grants

Pensions of £1,020 a year are paid in monthly instalments along with a Christmas 'bonus' of £85 per person. One-off grants are also available for essential household items.

Annual grant total

In 2010/11 the charity had assets of £1.9 million and an income of £75,000. Grants were made totalling £54,000, of which £52,600 was given in pensions to 56 beneficiaries and £1,600 in one-off grants to three individuals.

Applications

Application forms can be obtained from the City of London website and should be returned along with evidence of income such as benefit award notices, a copy of your birth certificate and two written testimonials confirming your eligibility and need for assistance, at least one of which must be from someone other than a friend or relative. Applications should be submitted directly by the individual.

Other information

The charity publicises its activities and details of pension vacancies in local papers, through welfare agencies and churches within the beneficial areas.

The Fund for the Forgotten

£1,000 (2 grants)

Trustees: Peter Beattie; Paul Beattie; Trevor Beattie.

CC Number: 1142892

Eligibility

People facing social injustice and inequality in the Midlands and London.

Types of grants

One-off grants of £500 – £1,000 'will be awarded to individuals facing injustice or inequality against their dignity, freedom or sanctuary.' Grants may help with everyday living costs and purchasing essential household items, for example.

Annual grant total

In 2011/12, the launch year of the fund, two grants of £500 were made. It is anticipated that there will be up to around 20 grants made per year.

Applications

Initial applications are made by sending a proposal, via email, summarising your situation, the injustice/inequality you face and how it is aligned to the foundation's objectives and values. You should also explain how support from the foundation can help you.

If your proposal is successful you will be invited to submit an application form, which can be downloaded from the website. Applications must be accompanied by two references and identity documentation.

Other information

The fund is part of the larger Jack and Ada Beattie Foundation.

The Ronnie Gubbay Memorial Fund

£6,800

Correspondent: The Secretary, 2 Ashworth Road, London W9 1JY (020 7289 2573)

Trustees: Susan Kendal; Dr Stuart Morganstein; Sabah Zubaida; Sylvia Graham; Philip Magnus; Natalie Leon-Gonn.

CC Number: 231315

Eligibility

Jewish women of Spanish and Portuguese origin who are in need. Preference is generally given to those living in the Greater London area.

Types of grants

One-off and recurrent grants according to need.

Annual grant total

In 2010/11 the fund had an income of £11,200 and a total expenditure of £7,000.

Applications

In writing to the correspondent.

Other information

This fund is one of the several trusts administered by the Spanish and Portuguese Jews Congregation and was established in 1944.

The Hampton Fuel Allotment Charity

£779,000 (2,152 grants)

Correspondent: David White, Clerk to the trustees, 15 High Street, Hampton, Middlesex TW12 2SA (020 8941 7866; fax: 020 8979 5555; website: www.hfac.co.uk)

Trustees: Revd Derek Winterburn; Jamie Mortimer; Revd Geoffrey Clarkson; David Parish; Dr Jane Young; Stuart Leamy; Jonathan Cardy; David Cornwell; Paula Williams; Richard Montgomery.

CC Number: 211756T

Eligibility

People who are in poor health or financial need and live in the ancient parish of Hampton. Priority is given to applicants from Hampton but grants may also be made to those living in the remainder of the former borough of Twickenham.

Types of grants

One-off grants are given for heating costs (average £390), lifeline alarm systems and other essentials such as fridges, cookers, washing machines, wheelchairs and special medical equipment.

Annual grant total

In 2010/11 the charity had assets of £48 million and an income of £1.8 million. Grants were made to over 2,100 individuals totalling £779,000 and were distributed as follows:

Fuel grants	1,778	£683,000
Essential equipment and furniture	357	£58,000
'Careline' telephone equipment	17	£18,000
Miscellaneous other welfare support – children with disabilities		£20,000

Exclusions

The charity is unlikely to support: private and further education; building adaptations; holidays, unless there is severe medical need; decorating costs, carpeting or central heating; anything which will replace statutory funds.

Applications

On a form available to download from the website or St Mary's, All Saints and St James's vicarages, the Greenwood Centre and the Citizens Advicex. Applications should be submitted by post-either directly by the individual or through a third party. They are considered every two months, although decisions can be made more quickly in urgent cases.

Other information

Grants are also given to organisations which support people in need or provide community benefits in line with the charity's objects (£842,000 in 2010/11).

The Hornsey Parochial Charities

£26,000

Correspondent: Lorraine Fincham, Clerk to the Trustees, PO Box 22985, London N10 3XB (020 8352 1601; fax: 020 8352 1601; email: hornseypc@blueyonder.co.uk)

Trustees: Peter Kenyon; Ann Jones; Barbara Simon; Eddie Griffith; John Hudson; Lorraine Marshall; Patrick Henderson; Vivienne Manheim; Ann Gillespie; Carol O'Brien; Katy Jones; Paula Lanning.

CC Number: 229410

Eligibility

People in need who live in the ancient parish of Hornsey in Haringey and Hackney, which comprises N8 and parts of N2, N4, N6 N10 and N16.

Types of grants

One-off grants of £120 to £1,000 for all kinds of need provided funding is not available from statutory or other sources, such as clothing, bedding or essential items and the costs of heating and lighting.

Annual grant total

In 2011 the charity made 124 grants to individual and organisations for welfare. Grants to individuals averaged £400.

Applications

Individuals can write requesting an application form which, on being returned, can usually be dealt with within a month.

Other information

Grants are also made for educational purposes.

Mary Minet Trust

£18,000

Correspondent: The Trustees, PO Box 53673, London SE24 4AF (07906 145199; email: admin@maryminettrust.org.uk)

Trustees: David Martin; Gillian Easty; Russell Baird; Millicent Stoney; Dr Barbara Wesby; Bridget Beilby; Temple Sambo; Roland Lam; Peter John Frost.

CC Number: 212483

Eligibility

People who are living with a disability, sickness or infirmity and reside in the boroughs of Southwark or Lambeth.

Types of grants

One-off grants towards convalescence holidays, disability aids, medical equipment and household items such as washing machines, fridges, cookers, essential furniture, carpets, clothing, beds and bedding.

Annual grant total

In 2010/11 the trust had an income of £23,000 and a total expenditure of £19,000.

Applications

Applications for individuals are invited from sponsoring organisations, social workers, housing officers and other involved professionals. Applications should be made on the trust's application form, available by contacting the trust by email or telephone. Payments are made to the sponsoring organisation to ensure that the money is spent appropriately, and are paid by BACS transfer. Applications from families and friends, interested persons or the individual in need will be considered only in exceptional circumstances and supporting information will be needed.

Arthur and Rosa Oppenheimer Fund

£3,000

Correspondent: A Oppenheimer, Trustee, 27 Hove Park Villas, Hobve BN3 6HH (01273 770094)

Trustees: Arthur Oppenheimer; Carolyn Kornbluth; Naomi Taub.

CC Number: 239367

Eligibility

Jewish people who are sick or disabled and live in London. Preference is given to older people.

Types of grants

One-off grants to those in need and recurrent grants over a longer period to cover nursing care for patients in their own homes. The charity also provides support for the provision of kosher food and other amenities.

Annual grant total

Grants usually total around £3,000 per year.

Applications

In writing to the correspondent, either directly by the individual, or via a social worker, Citizens Advice or other third party.

Other information

Organisations are also supported.

Port of London Authority Police Charity Fund

£8,000

Correspondent: Andrew Masson, Chief Officer, Police Headquarters, Tilbury Freeport, Tilbury, Essex RM18 7DU (01375 846781; email: andrew.masson@ potll.com)

Trustees: George Wright; Jim Wilson; Paul Alexander Scotcher; Robin Albert Aylward; Roy Charles Mansfield; Anthony John William Harding; Andy Masson.

CC Number: 265569

Eligibility

Former officers who have served in the port authority's police force, and their dependents.

Types of grants

One-off grants are given to help with unforeseen bills, household items, holidays and so on.

Annual grant total

In 2010/11 the fund had an income of £2,000 and a total expenditure of £8,000.

Applications

In writing to the correspondent, clearly stating the need for financial assistance. Applications are considered at quarterly meetings, or sooner if the need is urgent.

Positive East

£3,000

Correspondent: Alastair Thomson, Finance Director, The Stepney Centre, 159 Mile End Road, London E1 4AQ (020 7791 2855; email: info@positiveeast. org.uk; website: www.positiveeast.org.uk)

Trustees: Anne Peters; Florence Labwo; Paul Fleming; Graham Stoner; Marigold Chirisa; Mike Reardon; Peter McDonnell; Ravi Ravindran; Rebecca Wilkins; Katie Coulson Elizabeth; Nena Foster; Simon Killick.

CC Number: 1001582

Eligibility

People affected by HIV who live and/or receive treatment in East London and are in need of short-term financial assistance to cover basic needs.

Types of grants

Grants of up to £25 each, up to a maximum of £50 in a year, with six months between each application. Each individual has a 'lifetime limit' of £150, after which access to the fund will be closed to them. Grants are given for one-off, HIV related expenses, child expenses such as school uniforms or medical treatment, utility bills, the cost of travel to an essential appointment and basic necessities such as food or clothing.

Annual grant total

Around £3,000 is allocated each year for emergency hardship grants.

Exclusions

Grants are not given for:
- Legal costs
- Non-essential travel or travel outside of London
- Funeral costs
- Ongoing non-HIV related treatment
- Household goods
- Credit card or other debts

Applications

On a form available from the correspondent. Applications can only be made through Positive East staff and are only available to registered members of the trust (new service users will need to fill in a registration form). Forms can be submitted at any time but applicants should note that the fund is a limited resource and will not be topped up again until the end of the financial year.

Before any grant is awarded proof will be required that the individual is not eligible for any other financial assistance. Equally, if the person has been the victim of a crime, a crime reference number should be included in the application.

Other information

Positive East is a charity formed from the merger between the London East AIDS Network (LEAN) and the Globe Centre in 2005. The trust provides specialist advice on housing, welfare benefit and immigration issues. It also runs a range of support services including one-to-one counselling and training courses.

The Saint George Dragon Trust

£5,000

Correspondent: Alison Barraball, 68 Chaucer Road, London SE24 0NU (email: sgdt@barraball.com)

Trustees: Nicholas Fogg; Dudley Savill; Arthur Lennox; David Crawford; Russell Prescott; Steffan Thomas; James MacDonald; Sir Michael Wilmot Bart; Jerry Witts; Maj Nicholas Cann; Tessa Radcliffe; Alison Barraball; Emma Stranack.

CC Number: 275674

Eligibility

People in need who live in Greater London and are moving, or have recently moved, from supported housing into independent accommodation.

Types of grants

One-off grants ranging from £100 to £400 for buying essential household equipment and furniture. Small grants of £50 to £100 are also available for the purchase of essential items following move-on. Applicants should not be eligible for a Community Care grant or support from the Social Fund and have only minimal resources. (A rare exception may be where a very low Community Care grant has been awarded – see Applications section.)

Annual grant total

In 2010/11 the trust had an income of £8,400 and a total expenditure of £5,200.

Exclusions

Grants are not made to students or to 'able young people'.

Applications

In writing, through a social, housing or welfare worker. Applications should be typed wherever possible and should be made on the headed notepaper of the organisation through which the application is being made.

The application should include: the name, age and sex of the applicant; the address of the applicant and time spent there; the address of new accommodation and date of move-on; the social history including history of homelessness and Case Plan; financial circumstances of the applicant detailing income sources and amounts, together with amounts of present outgoings plus those of the future as far as is possible; the applicant's eligibility for a Community Care Grant in relation to current need, and if a Community Care Grant was refused, the reason why, and whether the appeal process has been finalised; where a very low Community Care Grant has been awarded applications should include details of the amount granted, the purpose of the grant and how it has been spent; the amount requested from the trust and its purpose; help that has been obtained from other sources and details of other organisations approached; has the applying agency any funds of its own to make grants and if so, what grant is it making to the applicant or if it is not, why not; how long the referring worker has personally known the applicant and the worker's appraisal of this application; the name of the organisation to which any grant should be made payable; the signature of the applicant; and the signature of the referring worker and the work telephone number and address if different to that shown on the headed notepaper of the organisation.

It is the aim of the trustees to respond with the outcome together with the grant if applicable, within fifteen working days, or with the reason for and timescale of a deferment.

The Sheriffs' and Recorders' Fund

£113,000

Correspondent: The Chair, c/o Central Criminal Court, Old Bailey, Warwick Square, London EC4M 7BS (020 7248 3277; email: secretary@srfund.net; website: www.srfund.org.uk)

Trustees: Christopher Thomas; David Biddle; Lady Prue Davies; James Harman.

CC Number: 221927

Eligibility

People on discharge from prison, and families of people imprisoned. Applicants must live in the Greater Metropolitan area of London.

Types of grants

One-off grants towards clothing, household items, furnishings, beds and bedding, white goods, carpets, baby needs and so on. In 2010/11 the average grant was £124.

Annual grant total

In 2010/11 the fund had assets of £973,000 and an income of £179,000. Grants were made to 1040 individuals totalling £130,000, around £113,000 of which was given in welfare grants.

Applications

On a form available from the correspondent, submitted through probation officers or social workers. They are considered throughout the year.

Other information

Grants are also made for educational purposes and for special projects.

The Society for the Relief of Distress

£15,000

Correspondent: Caroline Armstrong, Trustee, 57 Bowerdean Street, London SW6 3TN

Trustees: Caroline Armstrong; Charles Petri; Ian McCulloch; Susan Kumelben; Laura Bains; James Petri.

CC Number: 207585

Eligibility

People in need who live in the boroughs of Camden, Greenwich, Hackney, Hammersmith and Fulham, Islington, Kensington and Chelsea, Lambeth, Lewisham, Southwark, Tower Hamlets, Wandsworth, Westminster and the City of London.

Types of grants

One-off grants, usually of £25 to £100, for 'any cases of sufficient hardship or distress, whether mental or physical'. Grants may be given towards essential household items and clothing.

Annual grant total

In 2010 the society had both an income and total expenditure of £17,000.

Exclusions

Grants are very rarely given towards holidays, funeral expenses or debts.

Applications

Through a social worker, Citizens Advice, registered charity or church organisation only. Applications submitted by individuals will not be considered.

The South London Relief-in-Sickness Fund

£10,000

Correspondent: Ozu Okere, Room 111, Wandsworth Town Hall, Wandsworth High Street, London SW18 2PU (020 8871 6035; fax: 020 8871 6036; email: ookere@wandsworth.gov.uk)

Trustees: Shirley Cosgrave; Hazel Elam; Tamara Flanagan; Val Johnson; Hippolyte Grigg; Jackie Wenham; Elizabeth Stokes; Nick Davies.

CC Number: 210939

Eligibility

People in need through sickness, disability or infirmity who live in the boroughs of Lambeth and Wandsworth.

Types of grants

One-off grants up to £200, towards, for example, furniture, furnishings, clothing, holidays and medical equipment.

Annual grant total

In 2011 the fund had an income of £12,000 and a total expenditure of £11,000.

Exclusions

No grants towards taxes or debts.

Applications

In writing to the correspondent through a social worker, Citizens Advice or other welfare agency. Applications are considered quarterly (normally March, June, September and December). They should include details of the applicant's name, address, age, family composition, disability/illness, source of income and benefits, purpose of the grant, whether any other funding has been applied for and whether any applications have been made to the fund before.

The Spanish Welfare Fund

£5,000

Correspondent: Robert Rouse, 9 Bridle Close, Surbiton Road, Kingston upon Thames, Surrey KT1 2JW (020 8546 1817)

Trustees: Alonso Caro; Mercedes Licudi; Mercedes Sutherland; Miguel Dols.

CC Number: 273177

Eligibility

People of Spanish nationality and their dependents in need who live in the UK.

Types of grants

One-off and recurrent grants according to need.

Annual grant total

In 2010 the fund had an income of £6,400 and a total expenditure of £5,200.

Applications

In writing to the correspondent.

St John Southworth Fund

£20,000 (16 grants)

Correspondent: Mary Gandy, Grants Administrator, Department of Pastoral Affairs, Vaughan House, 46 Francis Street, London SW1P 1QN (020 7798 9063; fax: 020 7798 9077; email: sjsfadmin@rcdow.org.uk; website: www.rcdow.org.uk/stjohnsouthworth)

Trustee: Westminster Roman Catholic Diocese Trustee.

CC Number: 233699

Eligibility

Generally: individuals in need within the thirty-three London boroughs. Eligibility is restricted to young people up to 18 years of age and those over 65 in the dioceses of Southwark and Brentwood.

More specifically, the panel administers six linked funds under the St John Southworth Fund banner. Guidance notes available on the website detail the exact criteria for each fund and applicants should ensure that they meet the criteria for at least one of these funds.

Types of grants

One-off grants of around £500 to assist those in poverty, in danger of homelessness, with disabilities, and so on.

Annual grant total

Around £20,000 a year is available, however, usually only one or two small grants of around £500 are made to individuals with the rest given to groups and organisations.

Applications

On a form available from the correspondent or to download from the website. Applications need to include details of two referees. Applications can be made at any time and the grants panel meets quarterly each year. Applications need to be received at least three weeks before the panel meeting. Meeting and deadline dates are available on the website. Emergency grants of up to £250 may be given between meetings.

Note the following statement from the fund: 'In the case of applications from individuals, the panel is particularly interested in applications which are supported by third party organisations and where the referee is someone willing to act in the role of third party for any grant awarded.'

Other information

Grants are also made to organisations.

Barnet

The Mayor of Barnet's Benevolent Fund

£1,000

Correspondent: The Grants Unit, London Borough of Barnet, North London Business Park, Oakleigh Road South, London N11 1NP (020 8359 2020; fax: 020 8359 2685; email: ken.argent@barnet.gov.uk)

Trustees: Brian Coleman; Andrew Travers; Jeffrey Lustig.

CC Number: 1014273

Eligibility

People who are on an income-related benefit and who live in the London borough of Barnet and have done so for at least six months.

Types of grants

One-off grants of up to £100 towards school uniforms and other children's clothing, essential household items, such as cookers, furniture and small one-off debts such as telephone bills.

Annual grant total

In 2009/10 the trust had an income of £3,000 and a total expenditure of £2,000.

Applications

Applications should preferably be submitted directly by the individual, but may also be made directly by a supporting agency. All requests should include a quotation for the items required.

Other information

Grants are also made for educational purposes.

The Finchley Charities

£0

Correspondent: Jean Field, Manager, 41A Wilmot Close, East Finchley, London N2 8HP (020 8346 9464; fax: 020 8346 9466; email: info@thefinchleycharities.org; website: www.thefinchleycharities.org)

Trustees: Cllr Colin Rogers; Ian Anderson; Michael Piercy; Revd Dr Desmond Gordon; Revd Philip Davison; Cllr Brian Coleman; Andrew Galatopolous; John Huckstep; Leslie Sussman; Martin O'Donnell; Peter Hart; Cllr Daniel Thomas; Elizabeth Davies; Michael Nolan; Roger Chapman; Dr Marion Witton.

CC Number: 206621

Eligibility

People in need who live in the former borough of Finchley.

Types of grants

One-off grants only.

Annual grant total

In 2011 the charities had assets of £6.4 million, an income of £1.1 million. No grants were made to individuals in the year.

Exclusions

No educational grants are made.

Applications

In writing to the correspondent either directly by the individual or through a social worker, Citizens Advice or welfare agency. Applications must include details of the amount being asked for and the reason for the application.

Other information

The trust's main concern is the provision of 156 flats for people in Finchley aged 60 and over, who have insufficient funds to purchase their own property.

The Hyde Foundation

£3,000

Correspondent: Robin Marson, 1 Hillside, Codicote, Hitchin SG4 8XZ (020 8449 3032; email: marson36@homecall.co.uk)

Trustees: Barbara Taylor; Nigel Baker; Revd Canon Hall Speers; Averill Lovatt; Ann Evans; Jennifer Smith; Judy Burstow; Bob Burstow; Sarah Lloyd-Winder; Katherine Grace Morris; Tim Bennett.

CC Number: 302918

Eligibility

People in need in the ancient parishes of Chipping Barnet and Monken Hadley.

Types of grants

One-off grants to those in need.

Annual grant total

In 2011 the trust had assets of £648,000 and an income of £42,000. Grants made to 19 individuals totalled £11,000, to assist them in further education and cultural activities.

Applications

In writing to the correspondent, who will forward an application form. Trustees meet quarterly in January, April, July and October to consider applications. Applications should be received by the end of December, March, June and September respectively.

Other information

Grants are also given to local schools and organisations (£11,000 in 2011).

Jesus Hospital Charity

£8,000

Correspondent: Mr Simon Smith, Ravenscroft Lodge, 37 Union Street, Barnet EN5 4HY (020 8440 4374; email: info@jesushospitalcharity.org.uk; website: www.jesushospitalcharity.org.uk)

Trustees: Michael Andrew Holford; Janet Hulme; Neil Anthony Kobish; Brenda Sandford; Mr P. J. Mellows; William David Carrington; Ian Lawless; Revd Canon Hall Speers; Catherine Cavanagh; Stephen Payne; Maureen Violet Relfe; Dr Ian Johnston; Malcolm Bye.

CC Number: 1075889

Eligibility

People in need who live in the former district of Barnet, East Barnet and Friern Barnet.

Types of grants

One-off grants between £100 and £1,000 towards, for example, lifeline rentals, winter clothing, shoes, food vouchers, fridges/freezers, beds, gas cookers and utensils for single parent families and couples living on low incomes; and holidays for people with disabilities.

Annual grant total

In 2010 the charity held assets of £9.2 million and had an income of £505,000. Grants to individuals – both residents and non-residents of the almshouses – totalled £8,200.

Applications

On a form which can be downloaded from the charity's website. Applications are considered by trustees who meet every other month. Applicants may be visited by the clerk.

Other information

The charity maintains 54 almshouses in the Chipping Barnet and Monken Hadley area and also makes grants to local organisations (£4,000 in 2010).

Eleanor Palmer Trust

£29,000

Correspondent: Fred Park, The Clerk to the Trustees, 106b Wood Street, Barnet, Hertfordshire EN5 4BY (020 8441 3222; fax: 020 8364 8279; email: info@eleanorpalmertrust.org.uk; website: www.eleanorpalmertrust.org.uk)

Trustees: Mr A. Grimwade; Revd Canon Hall Speers; Tony Alderman; Mrs H. Davis; Stephen Lane; Wendy Prentice; David Tait; Christopher Dallison.

CC Number: 220857

Eligibility

People in need who live in the former urban districts of Chipping Barnet and East Barnet, This includes those living within the postal codes of EN4, EN5 N11 and N14. Applicants must have lived within the area for at least two years prior to the submission of your application.

Types of grants

One-off grants up to £1,000 towards, for example, carpets, furniture and clothing. Items or services are purchased directly, no cash grants are made.

Annual grant total

In 2010/11 the trust held assets of £4 million, had an income of £1.3 million and made grants totalling £29,000. These consisted of:
- Grants for relief in need – £20,000
- Amenities and grants to residents – £6,900
- Lunch club for residents – £2,500

Exclusions

No grants available towards educational purposes, bankruptcy fees, medical costs, taxes or debts.

Applications

On an application form available from the trust website. Applications are considered every two months. They should include the names of any other charities to which applications have been made. The clerk visits most applicants in order to assess need.

Other information

The trust concentrates on running its own almshouses and a residential home for older people.

The Valentine Poole Charity

£30,000

Correspondent: Victor Russell, Clerk, The Forum Room, Ewen Hall, Wood Street, Barnet, Hertfordshire EN5 4BW (020 8441 6893; email: vpoole@btconnect.com)

Trustees: Hall Speers; Tony Alderman; Stephen Lane; Helena Davis; Brenda Sandford; I. Butcher; June Hughes; M. Jamieson; Susan McKenzie; Brian Salinger.

CC Number: 220856

Eligibility

People in need who live in the former urban districts of Barnet and East Barnet (approximately the postal districts of EN4 and EN5).

Types of grants

One-off grants are given towards essential items such as household goods, children's clothing, travel and food. Pensions of £80 to £100 a month are also made to older people.

Annual grant total

In 2011 the trust had assets of £508,000 and an income of £66,000. Grants to individuals included £9,600 for essential household equipment and travel costs, 20 Christmas grants totalling £1,900 and pensions totalling £18,000.

Applications

On a form available from the correspondent for consideration in March, July and November. Applications should be submitted by a social worker, Citizens Advice or other third party or welfare agency, not directly by the individual.

Other information

Grants are also made to local organisations.

Bexley

The Bexley Mayor's Benevolent Fund

£1,000

Correspondent: Dave Easton, Mayors Office, London Borough of Bexley, Civic Offices, Broadway, Bexleyheath, Kent DA6 7LB (020 3045 3678)

Eligibility

People in need who live in the borough of Bexley.

Types of grants

Grants, usually in the range of £50 to £100, for a variety of needs (for example towards an electric wheelchair for an individual with disabilities and to buy new clothes for an older person whose home had been damaged in a fire). There can be an immediate response in emergency cases.

Annual grant total

A grant total figure was not available; however, the figure does tend to fluctuate depending on funds available but is never usually more than a few thousand pounds.

Applications

In writing to the correspondent. In practice, many applications are referred by the council's social services department who also vet all applications from individuals. Applications can be submitted at any time.

The Samuel Edward Cook Charity for the Poor

£800

Correspondent: The administrator, Barclays Bank Trust Company Ltd, Osborne Court, Gadbrook Park, Rudheath, Northwich CW9 7UE (01606 313195)

CC Number: 220274

Eligibility

People in need who live in Bexleyheath.

Types of grants

One-off grants to individuals and families ranging from £50 to £300 for household essentials, holidays and so on.

Annual grant total

Total expenditure averages around £800 each year.

Applications

In writing to the correspondent, directly by the individual. Allocation of the funds is at the discretion of the Minister of Trinity Baptist Church.

The John Payne Charity

£1,600

Correspondent: Bill Price, Clerk, Foster's Primary School, Westbrooke Road, Welling, Kent DA16 1PN (020 8317 8142)

Trustees: Bill Price; Ken Scottow; Cllr Ronald Horace French; Bruce Fletcher; Cllr Nigel Betts; Cllr Katie Perrior.

CC Number: 210999

Eligibility

Older people who live in the ancient parish of East Wickham.

Types of grants

One-off grants of up to £100, mostly towards gas, electricity and water bills.

Annual grant total

Grants average around £2,000 each year, though the actual grant figure tends to fluctuate quite widely.

Applications

In writing to the correspondent, to be submitted through a social worker,

Citizens Advice, Age UK or a similar agency. They are considered in March and October. Financial details such as sources of income, rent and other bills are required.

Other information

Grants are also made to the British Polio Fellowship to be given as grants for holiday relief for carers.

Brent

The Kingsbury Charity

£1,000

Correspondent: Mrs Philomena Hughes, 29 Bowater Close, London NW9 0XD (020 8205 9712)

Trustees: Gwendolen Tookey; Julia Day; Revd Clive Frederick Morton; Rose Peacock; Valerie Pope; Terence Hopkins.

CC Number: 205797

Eligibility

People in need who live in the ancient parish of Kingsbury.

Types of grants

One-off grants according to need. Most of the charity's expenditure is on almshouses. Grants to individuals have previously included £100 towards the cost of a trip to Lourdes for a terminally-ill woman, and £100 to help a family with a six-year-old child with leukaemia.

Annual grant total

Grants to individuals usually total around £1,000.

Applications

In writing to the correspondent, either directly by the individual or through a social worker, Citizens Advice, other welfare agency or other third party. They are considered every six weeks.

Other information

The charity's main area of activity is the maintenance of almshouses, it also makes grants to organisations.

The Wembley Samaritan Fund

£2,000

Correspondent: Jack Taylor, c/o Sudbury Neighbourhood Centre, 809 Harrow Road, Wembley, Middlesex HA0 2LP (020 8908 1220)

Trustees: Mary Steele; Ron Dawson; Gill Barrons; Kath Barrett; Betty Harvel; Jean Hows; Mona Gregory; Anne Lake; Janet Bartlett.

CC Number: 211887

Eligibility

People in need who live in the electoral wards of Wembley (Tokyngton, Alperton, Sudbury, Sudbury Court and Wembley Central). The charity is particularly aimed at children.

Types of grants

One-off grants mostly for school uniforms, warm clothing, nursery equipment and the costs of school outings.

Annual grant total

About £4,000 for education and welfare.

Applications

By telephone or in writing to the correspondent.

Bromley

The Bromley Relief-in-Need Charity

£2,000

Correspondent: M Cox, Clerk, Lavender House, 11 Alexandra Crescent, Bromley, Kent BR1 4ET (020 8460 5242)

Trustees: Mr M. Cox; Joyce Sutton; Jane Carolyn Farrer; Peter Ayres; Rhoda Mackenzie; Revd Michael Maurice Camp; Dr Keith Ernest; Mark Andrew Gill; Heather Dancy; Beryl Maureen Ross Martyn.

CC Number: 262591

Eligibility

People in need who live in the ancient borough of Bromley, though there is some discretion to make grants within the wider area of the modern borough of Bromley.

Types of grants

One-off grants of up to £150. Twice-yearly seasonal grants are also available.

Annual grant total

Grants generally total around £2,000 a year.

Applications

Only through social services or a similar welfare agency or a Citizens Advice, doctor, health worker, headteacher and so on.

Camden

Hampstead Wells and Campden Trust

£224,000

Correspondent: Sheila Taylor, Director and Clerk, 62 Rosslyn Hill, London

NW3 1ND (020 7435 1570; email: grant@hwct.co.uk; website: www.hwct.org.uk)

Trustees: Ms Chung; Jocelyne Tobin; Diana Dick; Ian Harrison; Geoffrey Berridge; Gaynor Bassey; Alistair Voaden; Christina Williams; Dennis Finning; Francoise Findlay; Gaynor Humphreys; Ted Webster; Mike Bieber; Stephen Tucker; Alistair Jacks; Charles Perrin; Ilan Jacobs; Michael Katz.

CC Number: 1094611

Eligibility

People who are sick, convalescent, disabled, infirm or in conditions of need, hardship or distress and who live in the former metropolitan borough of Hampstead.

Types of grants

In addition to pensions, grants are given for a range of purposes including holidays, clothing, help with debts, removals and transport, furniture, gas, electric, fuel, TV and telephone bills and medical purposes. Kitchen starter packs and birthday and Christmas hampers are also given.

Annual grant total

In 2010/11 the trust had assets of £15 million, an income of £611,000 and gave grants to 3,642 individuals totalling £224,000. 95 pensions totalling £74,000 were also awarded.

Applications

Applications should normally be sponsored by a statutory or voluntary organisation, or by a person familiar with the circumstances of the case e.g. a social worker, doctor or clergyman. Applications for pensions are made on a form available from the correspondent. Applications for one-off grants can be made in writing and should include the client's name, date of birth, occupation, address and telephone number, details of other household members, other agencies and charities applied to, result of any application to the Social Fund, household income, and details of any savings and why these savings cannot be used. Decisions are usually made within two weeks.

Other information

The trust also assists organisations or institutions providing services and facilities for the relief of need or distress. Grants are also made to individuals for educational purposes although this only makes up a small proportion of funding.

St Andrew Holborn Charities

£113,000

Correspondent: The Grants Officer, 5 St Andrew Street, London EC4A 3AB (020 7583 7394; email: info@standrewholborn.org.uk; website: www.standrewholborn.org.uk)

Trustees: Lyle Dennen; John Booth; Edward Lord; Nasim Ali; Brian Hanson; Jeremy Simons; Janie Spring; Jane Cruse; Ian Wilson; Tom Deidun; Abdul Hai.

CC Number: 1095045

Eligibility

People in need resident in a defined area of Holburn (applicants should call or check the website for confirmation of the beneficial area).

Types of grants

One-off grants up to £500 towards household appliances, furnishing and clothing and so on. Annual awards of £650 a year are available for the long-term sick, older retired people, widows or widowers with children and people living with disabilities.

Annual grant total

In 2011 the charity had assets of £7.8 million and an income of £209,000. There were 91 grants totalling £37,000 and 121 annual awardees, totalling £76,000. Altogether funding for individuals totalled £113,000.

Exclusions

No grants for holidays unless in exceptional circumstances.

Applications

On a form available from the correspondent or to download from the trust's website. Once received, a home visit may be arranged and supporting documentary evidence will be requested. Most applications take about 21 days.

Other information

This charity is the result of an amalgamation of three trusts: The City Foundation, The Isaac Duckett Charity and The William Williams Charity. Grants are also given to organisations.

The St Pancras Welfare Trust

£46,000

Correspondent: John Knights, Secretary to the Trustees, PO Box 51764, London NW1 1EA (020 7267 8428; fax: 020 7267 8428; email: thesecretary@spwt.org.uk; website: www.spwt.org.uk)

Trustees: Joyce Morton; Clive Leverton; Eleanor Sturdy; Jocelyne Tobin; Jill Fraser; Mayor of Camden.

CC Number: 261261

Eligibility

People in need or who are sick, convalescent, disabled or infirm who live in the old Metropolitan Borough of St Pancras (postal districts NW5, most of NW1, parts of N6, N19 NW3 and WC1). If you are unsure of whether you live in a qualifying area the trust website has a street directory on their website. Applicants must have the support of a sponsoring agency. The trust does not accept direct applications.

Types of grants

One-off grants, usually between £100 and £300, for a wide range of needs. Grants may be cash or vouchers.

Annual grant total

In 2010/11 the trust made 234 grants totalling £46,000. Grants are made primarily to individuals but some small (£1,000 or less) grants are also made to organisations with similar objects. Four organisations were helped in the year.

192 applications were received on behalf of individuals, of which 156 were offered support. Food vouchers were also distributed to 78 families at Christmas.

Exclusions

No grants are made for educational purposes, computers, utility bills, statutory payments or rent arrears.

Applications

On an application form available from the trust website, with an accompanying cover letter. The trustees will only consider applications made through statutory bodies such as social services or community organisations like Citizens Advice. Applications are considered in March, June, September and December and should be received two weeks prior to the meeting.

The Stafford Charity

£71,000 (141 grants)

Correspondent: Charlotte Maizels, Grants Officer, St Andrew's Holborn, 5 St Andrew Street, London EC4A 3AB (020 7583 7394; fax: 020 7583 3488; email: charities@standrewholborn.org.uk; website: www.standrewholborn.org.uk/charities)

Trustees: Dr Lyle Dennen; Mary Lamorna Wallis; Dr Brian John Taylor Hanson; Janet Agostini; Revd John Harvey Valentine; Jeremy Simons; Jane Cruse; Edwin Tarry; Revd Christopher Smith.

CC Number: 206770

Eligibility

People in need who have lived in the Holborn locality, centred on the ancient parish of St Andrew Holborn now comprising of the guild church of St Andrew Holborn and the parishes of St George the Martyr, Queen Square and St Alban the Martyr Holborn for at least three years.

Annual payments are made to the long-term sick and those with a chronic illness on a low income: less than £75 (single person/£120 (couple) per week.

Types of grants

Pensions of £600 per year for people in financial need who suffer from chronic medical problems and who are sick and disabled. One-off grants of up to £500 are also available to people on a low income for kitchen appliances, furnishings, carpets, medical equipment, clothing, redecoration costs and so on.

Annual grant total

In 2010 the charity had assets of £4.2 million and an income of £143,000. Annual awards to 96 people totalled £56,000 and 45 grants to individuals totalled £15,000.

Applications

On a form available to download from the website or from the correspondent, to be submitted either directly by the individual or through a social worker, Citizens Advice or other welfare agency. Applications must include photocopies of income eg. pay slips or benefit books; as well as copies of recent utility bills. Applications can be submitted at any time. All applicants are visited by the grants officer.

Other information

Grants are also made to organisations (£13,000 in 2010).

City of London

The Aldgate Freedom Foundation

£5,400

Correspondent: Michael A Sonn, 140 Hall Lane, Upminster, London RM14 1AL (01708 222482)

Trustees: Stephen James Borton; Michael David Bear; Henry Jones; Inhwa Priest; Gary Caughey; Revd Laura Burgess; Cathy Jones; Mr C. Knowles.

CC Number: 207046

Eligibility

People over 65 who are in need who live in the parish of St Botolph's, Aldgate.

Types of grants

One-off and recurrent grants of £200 a year plus a £30 Christmas gift.

Annual grant total

In 2010 the charity gave grants totalling £5,400 to pensioners.

Applications

On a form available from the correspondent, directly by the individual, through a social worker, Citizens Advice or through a councillor or an alderman. Details of income/capital/expenditure and length of residence in the parish must be included. Applications are considered at any time.

Other information

Grants are also given to hospitals within the city and St Botolph's church project.

The Hyde Park Place Estate Charity (Civil Trustees)

£4,500

Correspondent: Shirley Vaughan, Clerk, St George's Hanover Square Church, The Vestry, 2a Mill Street, London W1S 1FX (020 7629 0874)

Trustees: Revd Roderick Leece; Mark Hewitt; Michael Beckett; Mrs R. Botting; Lady Rees-Mogg; Lady Clare Howes; Mrs J. Prendergast; Mrs H. Acton.

CC Number: 212439

Eligibility

People in need who are residents of the borough of Westminster.

Types of grants

One-off grants in the range of £50 and £500 to individuals and families for all kinds of need, including educational.

Annual grant total

In 2010/11 the civil trustees had an income of £458,000 and made grants totalling £107,000 for the relief of hardship, the relief of sickness and the advancement of education, of which £98,000 went to organisations and £9,000 to 106 individuals.

Exclusions

Refugees and asylum seekers are not eligible.

Applications

All applications should be made through a recognised third party/organisation and include a case history and the name, address and date of birth of the applicant. Applications are considered on an ongoing basis.

The Mitchell City of London Charity

£15,000 (30 grants)

Correspondent: Mrs Lucy Jordan, Ash View, High Street, Orston, Nottingham NG13 9NU (01949 835632; email: mitchellcityoflondon@gmail.com)

Trustees: Charles Richard Stephen Link; Billy Dove; Dennis Cotgrove; David Levin; Derek Balls; Eleanor Stanier; John Barker; Michael Robin Castle Sherlock; Michael Chesterton; Peter Borrowdale; Rodney East; Cllr John Leslie Marshall; Diana Charlotte Vernon; Donald Payne.

CC Number: 207342

Eligibility

Men over 65 and women over 60 who are in need and who live or work, or have lived or worked, in the City of London for at least five years. Widows of men so qualified may also apply.

Types of grants

Pensions of £300 a year, paid quarterly. One-off grants are also given at Christmas (£125) and on the Queen's birthday (£75).

Annual grant total

In 2010/11 the foundation held assets of £1.7 million and had an income of £7,000. Pensions to 30 people totalled £15,000.

Applications

On a form available from the correspondent including details of the applicant's income and expenditure. Applications can be submitted directly by the individual or through an organisation such as Citizens Advice. They are considered in March, June, September and November.

Other information

One grant was made to an organisation in the year totalling £1,500.

Croydon

Croydon Relief in Need Charities

£4,500 (2 grants)

Correspondent: Mr W B Rymer, Clerk to the Trustees, Elis David Almshouses, Duppas Hill Terrace, Croydon CR40 4BT (020 8774 9382; website: www.croydonalmshousecharities.org.uk)

Trustees: Christopher Clementi; Revd Canon Colin J. L. Boswell; Alan Galer; Beryl Cripps; Mrs C. D. A. Trower; Derek Cripps; Lynda Talbot; Noel P. Hepworth; Marlene Bourne; Diana Hemmings; Diana M. Harries; John

M. Tough; Caroline Melrose; Cllr Margaret Mead; Gail Winter; Cllr Donald Speakman; Patricia Galer.

CC Number: 810114

Eligibility

Residents of the London Borough of Croydon who are in conditions of need, hardship or distress (including ill health).

Types of grants

One-off grants according to need.

Annual grant total

In 2010 the charities had an income of £160,000 and paid grants totalling £185,000. Of this total £4,500 was paid to individuals and the remainder to organisations.

Applications

In writing to the correspondent.

Other information

This trust mainly makes grants to organisations.

Ealing

Acton (Middlesex) Charities

£1,500

Correspondent: Revd David Brammer, The Rectory, 14 Cumberland Park, London W3 6SX (020 8992 8876; email: acton.charities@virgin.net; website: www. actoncharities.co.uk)

Trustees: Mr J. S. Gallagher; Miss L. Dodd; Revd D. Brammer; Mrs D. Young; Mrs L. Robinson; Dr M. Kenny; Mr D. Crawford; Cllr A. Said; Mr B. Dennehey; Mr N. Sumner.

CC Number: 312312

Eligibility

People in need between the ages of 18 and 25 who have lived in the former ancient parish of Acton for at least five years.

Types of grants

One-off grants for the purchase of domestic items or other needs. Payments are made directly to suppliers.

Annual grant total

In 2010 the trust had an income of £9,000 and a total expenditure of £2,800. No further information was available.

Applications

On a form available from the correspondent, by referral from clergy, doctors, health visitors or other professional people.

Other information

The trust also gives grants towards education and the arts, supporting individuals and local schools and carnivals.

The Ealing Aid-in-Sickness Trust

£1,200

Correspondent: Caroline Lumb, c/o William Hobbayne Community Centre, St Dunstans Road, London W7 2HB (020 8810 0277; email: hobbaynecharity@btinternet.com)

Trustees: Dr Nicholas Robinson; Allison Rockley; Angela Wallis; John Sawyer; Mark Cosstick; Revd Matthew Grayshon; Roy Price; Robert Coomber; David Muir.

CC Number: 212826

Eligibility

People in need, who live in the old metropolitan borough of Ealing (this includes Hanwell, Ealing, Greenford, Perivale and Northolt but not Southall or Acton), who are incurring extra expense due to long or short-term illness.

Types of grants

One-off grants according to need.

Annual grant total

Grants average around £1,200 a year.

Applications

On a form available from the correspondent. Applications should be made through a third party such as a social worker or an organisation such as Citizens Advice.

The Eleemosynary Charity of William Hobbayne

£3,400 (14 grants)

Correspondent: Mrs Caroline Lumb, Clerk, The William Hobbayne Centre, St Dunstan's Road, London W7 2HB (020 8810 0277; email: hobbaynecharity@btinternet.com)

Trustees: Dr Nicholas Robinson; Allison Rockley; Angela Wallis; John Sawyer; Mark Cosstick; Revd Matthew Grayshon; Roy Price; Robert Coomber; David Muir.

CC Number: 211547

Eligibility

People in need who live in the civil parish of Hanwell. Only in exceptional circumstances will grants be made to people who live outside of this area.

Types of grants

One-off grants, usually ranging between £50 and £600, for clothing, furniture and domestic appliances. Grants are paid directly to the sponsors or suppliers.

Annual grant total

In 2010/11 the charity held assets of £2.7 million and had an income of £177,000. Grants were made to 14 individuals totalling £3,400. A further £17,000 was distributed to local organisations.

Applications

On a form available from the correspondent: to be submitted through a sponsoring organisation such as a local health centre, church, outreach organisation or social services. Applications are considered on a monthly basis, though urgent cases can be dealt with more quickly.

Enfield

The Old Enfield Charitable Trust

£90,000

Correspondent: The Trust Administrator, The Old Vestry Office, 22 The Town, Enfield, Middlesex EN2 6LT (020 8367 8941; email: enquiries@toect.org.uk; website: www. toect.org.uk)

Trustees: Gordon Smith; Colin Griffiths; Audrey Thacker; Clive Parker; Horace Brown; Jim Eustance; Michael Braithwaite; Nicholas Taylor; Dr Patrick O'Mahony; Phyllis Oborn; Richard Cross; Susan Attwood; Chris Bond; Sam Bell; Bob Sander.

CC Number: 207840

Eligibility

People in need, hardship or distress who live in the ancient parish of Enfield.

Types of grants

One-off grants can include help with unexpected expenses, help with clothing, replacing/providing household goods, beds, furniture and carpets, the special needs of people who are disabled or chronically ill, and exceptionally help with bills and debts and so on. Around 50 regular quarterly grants are also made to people on a low income in financial need.

Annual grant total

In 2010/11 the trust had an income of £547,000. A total of £141,000 was given in grants to 292 individuals, of which £90,000 was given for welfare purposes. A further £1,000 was donated to organisations.

Exclusions

No grants to people who are homeless or for items which the local or central government should provide.

Applications

On a form available on request from the correspondent. Applications can be made either directly by the individual or through social services, probation service, hospitals, clinics or clergy. Applicants who write directly are visited and assessed. Grants are distributed either directly to individuals or through a welfare agency or suitable third party. Applications are considered on a monthly basis.

Greenwich

The Greenwich Charity

£6,000

Correspondent: Raymond Crudington, Grant Saw Solicitors, Norman House, 110–114 Norman Road, London SE10 9EH (020 8858 6971)

Trustees: Francis Edward Smith; John Robert Miles; John Mallalieu Stanley; Revd Chris Moody; Daphne Barnett; Elizabeth Clark; Robert Ridyard; Susan Rendall.

CC Number: 1074816

Eligibility

People in need who live in Greenwich.

Types of grants

One-off and recurrent grants according to need.

Annual grant total

In 2010/11 the trust had an income of £7,200 and a total expenditure of £6,500.

Applications

In writing to the correspondent.

Other information

The charity also makes grants to organisations.

The Woolwich and Plumstead Relief-in-Sickness Fund

£8,000

Correspondent: Dave Lucas, Royal Borough of Greenwich, The Woolwich Centre, 35 Wellington Street, Woolwich, London SE18 6HQ (email: dave.lucas@ greenwich.gov.uk)

Trustees: Margaret Elizabeth Stenhouse; Linda Sanders; Esther Ifinnwa; Adrian Dassrath; Revd Jesse Van Der Valk; Susan Green; Cllr Donald Austen; Mary Vale.

CC Number: 212482

Eligibility

People in need who have a physical illness or disability and live in the parishes of Woolwich and Plumstead. When funds allow, applications may be accepted from people living in the borough of Greenwich.

Types of grants

On average 20 one-off grants are made a year ranging between £50 and £500 towards meeting a specific need or a contribution towards the total cost. Support for recurring items is not usually provided.

Annual grant total

In 2011/12 the trust had an income of £10,500 and a total expenditure of £9,200.

Exclusions

No grants to help with debts, utility bills, recurrent expenditure, structural works or rent.

Applications

On a form available from the correspondent either directly by the individual or through a health visitor, district nurse, social services or other welfare agency. The application should include the applicant's income and expenditure; a supporting letter from a health professional confirming the diagnosis and the resulting problems; and the reason why a grant is needed. Applications can be dealt with as and when received.

Hackney

Mr John Baker's Trust

£5,000

Correspondent: Diane Coyne, Brewers' Hall, Aldermanbury Square, London EC2V 7HR (020 7600 1801)

Trustee: The Brewers Company.

CC Number: 215541

Eligibility

Widows and unmarried women in need who are over 50 and have lived for at least five years in the parish of Christchurch, Spitalfields in the borough of Tower Hamlets.

Types of grants

Pensions normally amounting to about £90 per quarter.

Annual grant total

Grants usually total about £5,000 each year.

Exclusions

People under 50 years of age are not eligible for support.

Applications

An application form is available from the correspondent. The trust requires information regarding details of income, age and residency. Note that the trust can only accept new beneficiaries when a vacancy occurs.

Hackney Benevolent Pension Society

£5,300

Correspondent: Janet Cassell, Larch Corner, Coopers Lane, Crowborough, East Sussex TN6 1SN (01892 667416)

Trustees: Frances Broadway; Jenny Brailsford; Rachel Timson.

CC Number: 212731

Eligibility

People who are older and in need, and who have lived in Hackney for at least seven years.

Types of grants

Gifts of around £30 are given to pensioners at Christmas, on their birthday and at the society's annual general meeting in November.

Annual grant total

In 2010/11 the society had an income of £2,600 and a total expenditure of £5,600.

Applications

In writing to the correspondent.

The Hackney Parochial Charities

£24,000

Correspondent: Robin Sorrell, Clerk to the Trustees, c/o Sorrells Solicitors, 157 High Street, Chipping Ongar, Essex CM5 9JD (01277 365532; email: rsorrell@sorrells.org.uk)

Trustees: Fr R. Wickham; Mrs M. Cannon; G. Taylor; C. Kennedy; Ms N. Baboneau; Ms V. Belfon; Mr D. Horder; Mr P. Cofie.

CC Number: 219876

Eligibility

People in need who live in the former metropolitan borough of Hackney (as it was before 1970).

Types of grants

The charities state that grants to individuals are usually made for the purchase of clothing and essential household equipment, although grants can be given for many other welfare purposes, such as bedding, furniture and medical and travel expenses for hospital visits. Grants have also been given for holidays for widows with small children and single parent families and for gifts at Christmas for children in need.

Grants are one-off, generally of £100 to £250, although individuals can apply annually.

Annual grant total

In 2010/11 the charities had assets of £4.9 million and an income of £185,000, of which £136,000 was distributed in grants mainly to organisations.

Exclusions

No grants for statutory charges, rent, rates, gas, electricity or telephone charges.

Applications

In writing to the correspondent. The trustees meet in March, June, September and November and as grants cannot be made between meetings it is advisable to make early contact with the correspondent.

Other information

In 2008 the Charities took over the administration of Hackney District Nursing Association. In 2010/11 the Trustees made no grants out of the Hackney District Nursing Association's funds.

Hammersmith and Fulham

Dr Edwards' and Bishop King's Fulham Charity

£125,000 (264 grants)

Correspondent: The Clerk to the Trustees, Percy Barton House, 33–35 Dawes Road, London SW6 7DT (020 7385 9387; fax: 020 7610 2856; email: clerk@debk.org.uk; website: www. debk.org.uk)

Trustees: Mr M. C. JP; Mr C. Treloggan; Mr A. R. Smith; Mr R. Lawrence; Mr M. Waymouth; Mrs S. M. O'Neill; Mrs C. Bailey; Mrs L. Brock; Cllr Mrs A. Alford; Mrs PVR. Richards; Revd M. W. Osborne.

CC Number: 1113490

Eligibility

People in need who are on low incomes and live in the old Metropolitan borough of Fulham. This constitutes all of the SW6 postal area and parts of W14 and W6.

Types of grants

One-off grants according to need are made towards essential items of daily living including kitchen appliances, beds, furniture and clothing (including school uniforms). Grants for other things such as, floor coverings, decorating materials, baby items, and disability aids are also considered.

Annual grant total

In 2010/11 grants to individuals totalled £125,000 with 264 grants given for relief in need and five for education or training.

Exclusions

Grants are not normally given to people who are homeowners. Arrears on utility bills are not paid, nor are grants given retrospectively. The trust will only give cash grants if they are to be administered by an agency.

Applications

Application forms are available from the correspondent or on the charity's website. Applications must be submitted in hard copy either directly by the individual or through a third party. Though, it is important to note that individuals applying directly for a grant will be visited at home by the grants administrator.

The committee which considers relief-in-need applications, including educational grant applications, meets ten times a year, roughly every 4–5 weeks. The charity suggests that applications be submitted around two to three weeks before the next meeting.

Other information

In April 2006 the activities, assets and liabilities of the Dr Edwards' and Bishop King's Fulham Charity (No. 247630) were transferred to the charitable company, of which it became a subsidiary and was renamed the Dr Edwards and Bishop King's Fulham Endowment Fund (No. 1113490 – 1). The fund continues to give money to both individuals and organisations, with its main responsibility being towards the relief of poverty rather than assisting students.

Fulham Benevolent Society

£9,000

Correspondent: Angela Rogers, 4 Maltings Place, London SW6 2BT (020 7736 6128)

Trustees: Heather Pearman; Joan Harsent; Angela Theresa Rogers; Keith Whitehouse; Jill Mary Palmer; Kathleen Margaret Ashman.

CC Number: 207938

Eligibility

People in need living in the metropolitan borough of Fulham in need of temporary financial assistance.

Types of grants

One-off and recurrent grants according to need.

Annual grant total

In 2010/11 the society had an income of £5,000 and a total expenditure of £9,600.

Applications

In writing to the correspondent. Applications should be submitted through a third party such as, social services, Citizens Advice, general practitioner or minister of religion.

The Mayor of Hammersmith and Fulham's Appeal Fund

£10,000

Correspondent: I Hartzenberg, Mayor's Office, Room 201, Hammersmith Town Hall, London W6 9JU (020 8753 2013)

Trustees: Mayor Adronie Alford; Mayor Alex Karmel.

CC Number: 1023401

Eligibility

People in need who live in the borough of Hammersmith and Fulham.

Types of grants

Grants vary and are given for general relief-in-need.

Annual grant total

In 2010/11 the fund had an income of £10,600 and a total expenditure of £10,200.

Applications

In writing to the correspondent either through a social worker, Citizens Advice or other third party.

Haringey

The Tottenham District Charity

£83,000

Correspondent: Carolyn Banks, Hon. Clerk, 7th Floor, River Park House, 225 High Road, London N22 8HQ (020 8489 2965)

Trustees: Kaushika Amin; Robert Edmonds; Sheila Peacock; L. W. Stritter; P. Jones; S. Whittle; Tasmin Piper; Revd Bunmi Fagbemi; Cllr David Browne; Nora Mulready; Eugene Akwasi Ayisi.

CC Number: 207490

Eligibility

People in need, especially the elderly, who have lived in the urban district of Tottenham (as constituted on 28 February 1896, which is largely the postal districts of N15 and N17) for at least three years prior to applying.

Types of grants

One-off grants to people who are poor, elderly, sick or who have a disability to reduce need, hardship or distress. Grants are to help with clothes, carpets and essential household items and range from £50 to £500. Pensions of £260 per annum are paid twice a year in April and October to elderly people.

The charity can offer pensions to a maximum of 300 people per year.

Annual grant total

In 2010/11 the charity had assets of £2.3 million and an income of £100,000. Grants (£32,000) and pensions (£51,000) were made totalling £83,000.

Exclusions

No grants for education or debts.

Applications

On a form available from the correspondent, which can be submitted directly by the individual or through social services, Citizens Advice, other welfare agency or any other third party. Applications are considered on an ad hoc basis.

The Wood Green (Urban District) Charity

£1,250

Correspondent: Mrs Carolyn Banks, Clerk, PO Box 365, Laughton, Essex IG10 9EY (07758 730078; email: charities@virginmedia.com)

Trustees: Sylvia Acott; John Broadhurst; Cheery McAskill; Khaled Moyeed; John Hawting; Pauline Gibson; Hannah Essex.

CC Number: 206736

Eligibility

People in need who have lived in the urban district of Wood Green (as constituted in 1896, roughly the present N22 postal area) for at least three years.

Types of grants

Pensions and small one-off grants ranging from, on average, £50 to £300. Grants have in the past been given towards household items such as beds, fridges and clothes.

Annual grant total

About £2,500 for welfare and educational purposes.

Applications

On a form available from the correspondent, to be submitted directly by the individual or via a social worker, Citizens Advice or other welfare agency or third party. Applications are considered all year round.

Harrow

The Mayor of Harrow's Charity Fund

£2,000

Correspondent: Hasina Shah, London Borough of Harrow, Finance Department, PO Box 21, Harrow, Middlesex HA1 2UJ (020 8424 1573)

Trustees: Owen W. N. Cock; Brenda Diana Cripps; Renee Feakins; Cllr Christine Bednell; Mrinal Choudhury; Gaye Branch; Myfanwy Barrett; Hugh Peart.

Eligibility

People in need who live in the borough of Harrow.

Types of grants

One-off grants usually up to a maximum of £150 are given for basic items such as beds, food, heating appliances, cookers, clothing and so on.

Annual grant total

In 2010/11 the fund had an income of £5,200 and a total expenditure of £4,600.

Applications

On a form available from the correspondent. Most applications come through a social worker, Citizens Advice or other welfare agency, although this does not preclude individuals from applying directly. Applications are considered at any time. Applicants must demonstrate that the individual/family is experiencing financial hardship and that the grant will alleviate ill health or poverty or improve essential living conditions. Grants are paid directly to the supplier or through a third party.

Other information

Grants are also given to local organisations and to schools for school trips.

Hillingdon

The Harefield Parochial Charities

£3,100

Correspondent: John Ross, Chair, 3 Coppermill Lock, Harefield, Middlesex UB9 6JA (01895 823058; fax: 01895 823644; email: hpc@harefieldcharities.co.uk; website: www.harefieldcharities.co.uk)

Trustees: John Ross; Paul Mander; Paul Davis; Claudine Elaine O'Connor; Wendy Ann Rice-Morley; Revd Martin Davies.

CC Number: 210145

Eligibility

People in need who live in the ancient parish of Harefield, especially those who are older or in poor health.

Types of grants

Mainly small grants at Christmas time. Support may also be given for clothing, food, furniture, convalescence, home help, educational costs, hospital travel expenses, medical equipment and disability aids.

Annual grant total

In 2011 the charities had assets of £1.5 million, an income of £122,000. Grants were made totalling £3,100.

Applications

In writing to the correspondent either directly by the individual or through a social worker, Citizens Advice or other welfare agency.

Other information

The charities also provide alms accommodation for older women and families in need.

The Hillingdon Partnership Trust

£10,000

Correspondent: John Matthews, Chief Executive, Room 22–25, Building 219, Epsom Square, London Heathrow Airport, Hillingdon, Middlesex TW6 2BW (020 8897 3611; fax: 020 8897 3613; email: john@hillingdonpartnershiptrust.org.uk; website: www.hillingdonpartnershiptrust.org.uk)

Trustees: Albert Kanjee; Prof. Heinz Wolff; James Crowe; John Randall; Michael Wisdom; Nicholas Smith; Air Commodore Paul Thomas; John Watts; Cllr David Routledge; Nicholas Hurd; Peter O'Reilly; Robert Brightwell;

Miranda Clark; Prof. Ian Campbell; Tony Woodbridge.

CC Number: 284668

Eligibility

People in need who live in the borough of Hillingdon.

Types of grants

Occasional one-off grants or gifts of equipment, furniture, clothes and toys. The 2010/11 accounts note: 'Hillingdon Partnership Trust was not established to be a grantmaking body. It does not own or have access to resources for such a role... As in previous years, we may occasionally meet a need by arranging the purchase of necessary items and arranging delivery direct to an applicant, using funds held in reserve or generated through a number of fundraising activities.'

Annual grant total

In 2010/11 the trust had an income of £311,000 and made contributions in cash or in kind worth £294,000, the majority of which was given to local organisations. However, the accounts do note that the trust 'generated toys, games and food hampers with a cumulative value in excess of £10,000 for distribution through qualified authorities and groups to children and families in need, the elderly and to the homeless at Christmas.'

Applications

On a form available from the correspondent.

Other information

The trust is a formal grouping of businesses and people in business who have come together as volunteers, either as representatives of local companies or as individuals. Essentially the trust acts as a broker between business and the community and tries to match projects in need of funding with a company wishing to sponsor a local activity. As such, grantmaking to individuals is only a small part of the trust's overall activities.

Uxbridge United Welfare Trusts

£46,000 (118 grants)

Correspondent: David W Routledge, Chair, Trustee Room, Woodbridge House, New Windsor Street, Uxbridge UB8 2TY (01895 232976; email: enquires@uuwt.org; website: www.uuwt.org)

Trustees: Cheryl Evans; John Childs; Pauline Crawley; David Routledge; Peter Ryerson; Gerda Driver; Duncan Struthers; Alan Morris; Ray Graham; Michael Cater; Susan James.

CC Number: 217066

Eligibility

People in need who are physically or mentally disabled and people on low incomes (such as families with young children or people who are elderly) who live in the Uxbridge area (bordered by Harefield in the north, Ickenham in the east, Uxbridge in the west and Cowley/Colham Green in the south).

Types of grants

One-off grants either in cash or for services or specific items such as furniture, equipment, clothing, baby equipment and help with fuel bills.

Annual grant total

In 2011 the trust had assets of £6.7 million and an income of £462,000. Grants for 'hardship' were given to 118 individuals totalling £46,000

Exclusions

No grants are given for rent or rates.

Applications

On a form available from the correspondent. Applications can be submitted directly by the individual or through a social worker, Citizens Advice or other welfare agency. They are considered each month. A trained member of staff may visit applicants to assist them in the application.

Other information

Grants are also given for educational purposes.

Hounslow

The John Fielder Haden (Isleworth) Relief in Sickness Charity

£2,000

Correspondent: Juliet Ames-Lewis, Executive Clerk's Office, 9 Sermon's Amshouses, Twickenham Road, Isleworth, Middlesex TW7 6DJ (020 8569 9200; fax: 020 8847 5514; email: info@iahcharity.org.uk; website: www.iahcharity.org.uk)

Trustees: Cllr Felicity Barwood; Anthony Lake Ladden; Desmond Begley; Revd Anna Brooker; Peter George Dodkins; Roy Alan Heaps; Ann Turner; Paul Andrew Turner; Caroline Jane Andrews; Alan John Cooke; Angela Carroll; Geraldine Horwood; Cllr Edward Owen Mayne; Ronald John Bartholomew; Cllr Mindu Bains; Nisar Malik; Revd Thomas Alan Gillum; Anthony Charles McKendry.

CC Number: 267271

Eligibility

People in need who have been resident in the London borough of Hounslow for at least two years.

Types of grants

One-off grants according to need.

Annual grant total

Grants total around £2,000 each year.

Exclusions

No grants for educational or religious purposes or for funding animals or pets. Grants cannot be awarded for items which should be provided out of statutory funds. No repeat grants are made.

Applications

Application and accompanying referral forms (to be completed by the referral agency) are available from the correspondent or to download from the website. Applications should be made through a recognised referral agency such as social services, Citizens Advice or other welfare organisation. Applications are considered six times a year. Upcoming deadline dates can be found on the website.

Other information

Grants are also made to organisations.

Islington

Richard Cloudesley's Charity

£181,000

Correspondent: Chris Hobbs, c/o Cripplegate Foundation, 76 Central Street, London EC1V 8AG (020 7566 3135; email: chris.hobbs@cripplegate.org.uk; website: www.cripplegate.org/richard-cloudesley)

Trustee: Richard Cloudesley Trustee Ltd.

CC Number: 205959

Eligibility

People in need who are sick or disabled and live in the ancient parish of St Mary's Islington (roughly the modern borough, excluding the area south of the Pentonville and City Roads). A map of the area of benefit is available on the Cripplegate website.

Types of grants

One-off grants, typically up to £500, to help with cases of sickness or disability. No breakdown of grants was given in recent accounts but in previous years welfare expenditure was spread across household items, holidays and respite care, personal equipment and therapy. Cash grants are not made, payment is made directly to the supplier.

Annual grant total

In 2010/11 the charity had assets of £23 million and an income of £987,000. Grants to individuals totalled £181,000.

Exclusions

No help for debts, education, computers, childcare, funeral expenses or for money that has been stolen.

Applications

Applications may be made online on the Cripplegate website. Alternatively contact the correspondent to receive an application pack. Applications should be made through social services, a doctor, Citizens Advice or similar agency. Applicants who do not apply through a third party will be visited for an assessment. Applications are normally assessed within four weeks. Only one grant per applicant in a three year period in normal circumstances. If your application is unsuccessful you may not reapply for one year.

Lady Gould's Charity

£35,000 (87 grants)

Correspondent: G A Couch, Bircham Dyson Bell, 50 Broadway, Westminster, London SW1H 0BL (020 7783 3769; email: andycouch@bdb-law.co.uk; website: www.ladygouldscharity.org)

Trustees: Revd Dr Jonathan David Trigg; Margaret Elsie Short; J. K. Russell.

CC Number: 234978

Eligibility

People in need who live in Highgate (i.e. the N6 postal district and part of the N2, N8 N10 and N19 districts). This includes the temporary occupants of Beacon House and asylum seekers who can be said to be resident in the area. A reference map and street index is available on the website. Most grantees are in receipt of income support and housing benefit, though the charity will also consider applications from people earning under £10,000 a year.

Types of grants

One-off grants generally ranging from £200 to £400, though more is available in exceptional circumstances. Grants are given for clothing, furniture, furnishings, baby necessities and white goods. Grants to help towards debts and holidays are available but will only be given in very needy cases. It is possible that more than one grant will be awarded during the accounting year.

Annual grant total

In 2011 the charity had assets of £237,000 and an income of £57,000. Grants were made to 87 individuals totalling £35,000.

Exclusions

Grants are rarely made for educational or recreational purposes or for debt.

Applications

On a form available to download from the website. Applications should be accompanied by a supporting statement from a social worker, GP or other recognised body. If this is not possible attach evidence of your entitlement to benefits, such as a housing benefit letter. Applications can be submitted directly by the individual or through a third party such as a social worker, Citizens Advice or other welfare agency. They are considered at any time.

Dame Alice Owen's Eleemosynary Charities

£1,750

Correspondent: The Clerk, The Worshipful Company of Brewers, Brewers' Hall, Aldermanbury Square, London EC2V 7HR (020 7600 1801)

Trustee: The Worshipful Company of Brewers.

CC Number: 215543

Eligibility

Widows in need who are over 50 and have lived in the parishes of St Mary, Islington and St James, Clerkenwell for at least seven years.

Types of grants

Recurrent grants including pensions.

Annual grant total

Grants are usually made totalling around £2,000 per year.

Applications

In writing to the correspondent.

The St Sepulchre (Finsbury) United Charities

£37,000

Correspondent: Elias Poli, Smithfield Accontants LLP, 117 Charterhouse Street, London EC1M 6AA (020 7253 3757)

Trustees: Edward Price; David Anthony Sandell; Cllr Joseph Russell Trotter; Cllr Gary Doolan.

CC Number: 213312

Eligibility

People over 45 who are in need who live in the old London Borough of Finsbury.

Types of grants

Pensions and one-off grants ranging from around £100 to £300.

Annual grant total

In 2010/11 the charities held assets totalling £1.9 million and had an income of £69,000. Grants totalled £14,000 and quarterly pensions totalled £23,000.

Applications

Grants are administered by the Cripplegate Foundation, apply using the Cripplegate grants for residents application form available on the website.

Other information

Grants are also given to organisations (£10,000 in 2010/11). The charities are now collaborating with the Cripplegate Foundation to make grants to qualifying individuals.

Kensington and Chelsea

The Campden Charities

£958,000 (985 grants)

Correspondent: Christopher Stannard, Clerk, 27a Pembridge Villas, London W11 3EP (020 7243 0551, Grants officer: 020 7313 3797; website: www.cctrustee.org.uk)

Trustees: Revd Gillean Craig; David Banks; Susan Valerie Lockhart; Dr Kit Davis; Cllr Richard Walker-Arnott; Terry Myers; Elisabeth Brockmann; Tim Martin; Sam Berwick; Dr Christopher Calman; Ben Pilling; Marta Rodkina; Michael Finney.

CC Number: 1104616

Eligibility

Individuals applying for funding must:

- Be living in the former parish of Kensington
- Have been living continuously in Kensington for two years or more,
- Are a British or European citizen or have indefinite leave to remain in Britain
- Be renting their home

Working age members of the family must also be in receipt of an out-of-work benefit (e.g. Income Support, Jobseeker's Allowance, Pension Credit Guarantee or Incapacity Benefit) or on a very low income.

Types of grants

The charity considers funding to all ages of applicant; however it divides its funding into three basic categories:

- Young people (16–24)
- People of working age
- People of retirement age

The charity will give grants for:

- The costs associated with education or training courses that have a strong likelihood of leading to work
- The costs associated with moving from benefits to paid employment
- The costs associated with engaging in volunteer work or work experience that has a strong likelihood of leading to work
- Goods or services that are related to education or work goals

Annual grant total

In 2010/11 welfare grants totalled £958,000, the majority of which was given to 791 pension age individuals totalling £844,000, with the remaining £114,000 given to 194 individuals and families of working age for child-care, fares, goods and services to assist them towards financial independence.

Exclusions

The charity will not give funding for:

- Direct payment of council tax or rent
- Debt repayments
- Fines or court orders
- Foreign travel or holidays
- Career changes
- Personal development courses
- Postgraduate studies
- Computers
- Individuals whose immediate goal is self-employment
- Goods and services catered for by central government

Applications

Preliminary telephone enquiries are welcomed. Specific application forms are available for social work organisations seeking pensions or charitable relief for individuals in the parish. Applications are considered by the case committee, the education committee or the board of trustees as appropriate. Each of these meets monthly (except during August).

Applicants should also be willing for a grants officer to visit them at home.

Other information

The charities also makes grants to organisations and individuals for educational purposes.

The Kensington and Chelsea District Nursing Trust

£38,000 (120 grants)

Correspondent: Margaret Rhodes, 13b Hewer Street, London W10 6DU (020 8969 8117; email: kcdnt@tiscali.co.uk)

Trustees: Richard Baker; Peter Alfred Kraus; Dr Angela Ida Hamilton; Celia Rosamund Duncan; Cherry David; Susan Maisie Kaye; Gila Ann Falkus.

CC Number: 210931

Eligibility

People who are older and frail and people who are physically or mentally ill who are in need and have lived for at least two years in the borough of Kensington and Chelsea.

Types of grants

One-off grants up to £1,000 for domestic appliances, medical and nursing aids and equipment, beds, bedding and other furniture and clothing. Up to 60 heating allowances of £100 are also made.

Annual grant total

In 2010/11 the trust had assets of £1.6 million, which generated an income of £63,000. Grants totalled £38,000, £37,000 of which was given to 120 individuals and £550 was given in Christmas gifts.

Exclusions

Grants are not given for payment of salaries, rents, court orders or fines.

Applications

On a form available from the correspondent. Applications must be submitted through a social worker, Citizens Advice or other welfare agency and are considered each month.

Other information

During the year there were four grants made to organisations totalling £10,500.

Kingston upon Thames

The Hampton Wick United Charity

£10,000

Correspondent: Roger Avins, Hunters Lodge, Home Farm, Redhill Road, Cobham, Surrey KT11 1EF (01932 596748)

Trustees: Miss M. Kearn; A. Arbour; Mr M. McDougall; Dr P. Butterworth; Revd P. Warner.

CC Number: 1010147

Eligibility

People in need who live in Hampton Wick and most of South Teddington, within the parishes of St John the Baptist, Hampton Wick and St Mark, South Teddington.

Types of grants

One-off grants (with the possibility of future reapplication).

Annual grant total

Previously over £20,000 a year in educational and welfare grants. Recent information was not available.

Applications

In writing to the correspondent. The trustees normally meet three times a year to consider applications.

The Kingston upon Thames Association for the Blind

£3,300

Correspondent: Della Murphy, Kingston Association for the Blind, Adams House, Dickerage Lane, New Malden, Surrey KT3 3SF (020 8605 0060; email: kingstonassoc@btconnect.com; website: www.kingstonassociationforblind.org)

Trustees: John Howard; Jonathan Cooper; David Fraser; Phil Margree; Brian Gaff; John Paine; Ruth Walmsley; Adrian Munt; Diana Goodhew; Jake Van Es; David Charles Broughton; Sheila Austin; George Phillips; Carol Barnshaw.

CC Number: 249295

Eligibility

Blind and partially sighted people who live in the royal borough of Kingston upon Thames.

Types of grants

One-off grants of £50 to £2,000 have been given to help towards the cost of holidays, travel expenses, white goods, furniture, household repairs, computers and aids like 'Easy Reader'.

Annual grant total

In 2010/11 the association held assets of £197,000 and had an income of £72,000. Charitable expenditure totalled £71,000 but we could not obtain a figure for grants. In previous years grants were made totalling around £3,300.

Applications

On a form available to download from the website or from the office. If the applicant is not in receipt of income support, housing benefit, or family credit they will need to provide detailed financial circumstances. Applications are considered every other month from January onwards.

Other information

The association runs a home visiting scheme. Support is also given to satellite clubs for the blind and to talking newspapers.

Lambeth

The Clapham Relief Fund

£15,000

Correspondent: Shirley Cosgrave, Clerk to the Trustees, PO Box 37978, London SW4 8WX (020 7627 0306; email: enquires@claphamrelieffund.org; website: claphamrelieffund.org/)

Trustees: Canon David Isherwood; Euan Stewart Kennedy; Francis St John Brown; Sheila Eileen Jones; Revd Susan Peake; Girda Sandra Tamara Niles; Dr Carole Glasson; Christopher John Woolls; Claire Alexandra Whittle.

CC Number: 1074562

Eligibility

People in need who live in Clapham. A map of the area of benefit is available on the website.

Types of grants

One-off grants of up to £300 towards domestic appliances, beds and bedding, redecoration, clothing, convalescent holidays and so on. Recurrent grants can be made for a limited period to meet a particular need.

Annual grant total

In 2011 the fund had an income of £25,000 and a total expenditure of £24,000. Grants were made totalling around £15,000.

Exclusions

No grants will be given where sufficient help is available from public sources. Support will only be given to permanent residents of Clapham. Grants are not usually given for debts and living expenses.

Applications

On a form available to download from the website, including details of monthly income and outgoings and verification by a sponsor. Applications can be submitted either directly by the individual, through a welfare agency or by a third party such as a district nurse, charitable agency worker, parish priest or doctor. They are considered at trustee meetings held four times a year, in March, June, September and December. Application forms should be submitted during the last week of the month before meetings. Emergency grants of up to £300 can be awarded between meetings.

Other information

Grants are also made to local organisations with similar objectives.

Lewisham

The Deptford Pension Society

£7,000

Correspondent: Mike Baker, 144 Farnaby Road, Shortlands, Bromley BR1 4BW (020 8402 0775; email: mjpbaker@hotmail.co.uk)

Trustees: Desmond Pye; Ernest William Groeger; Peter Macdonald; Donald Henry White; Eileen Crichton; Patricia Anne Gillard; Peter George Baker; Francis Ernest Smith; Alison Claremont-Davies.

CC Number: 219232

Eligibility

Retired people in receipt of supplementary benefits who have lived in the former London borough of Deptford for at least seven years.

Types of grants

Pensions of £15 a month (£30 in December) to about 30 individuals.

Annual grant total

Grants usually total around £7,000 per year.

Applications

On a form available from the correspondent, for consideration bi-monthly. Applications can be submitted either directly by the individual or a family member, through a third party such as a social worker, or through an organisation such as a Citizens Advice or other welfare agency. The application form must be signed by the individual.

Sir John Evelyn's Charity

£15,000

Correspondent: Colette Saunders, Clerk's Office, Armada Court Hall, 21 McMillan Street, Deptford, London SE8 3EZ (020 8694 8953)

Trustees: Kay Ingledew; Bridget Mary Perry; Revd Jack Kenneth Lucas; Janet Miller; Jasmine Viola Barnett; Cllr Maureen O'Mara; Margaret Bernadette Mythen.

CC Number: 225707

Eligibility

People in need who are in receipt of state benefits and live in the ancient parish of St Nicholas, Deptford and St Luke, Deptford.

Types of grants

Grants for welfare purposes such as domestic equipment, holidays, outings and pensions.

Annual grant total

In 2010 the charity had assets of £2.7 million and an income of £57,000. Grants to individuals totalled £15,000, and were broken down as follows:

Payment to pensioners	£8,600
Pensioner outings and holidays	£5,800
Miscellaneous grants to individuals	£365

Applications

On a form available from the correspondent. Applications are considered every two months.

The Lee Charity of William Hatcliffe

£19,000 (55 grants)

Correspondent: Gordon Hillier, Oakroyd, Bowers Place, Crawley Down, Crawley, West Sussex RH10 4HY (01342 713153; email: gandbhillier@tiscali.co.uk)

Trustees: Revd Alan Race; Christopher Rowland Jeal; Ray Brookes; Roger Thomas; Doreen Dorothy Brooker; Kathryn Charlotte Donnelly; Anne Smith.

CC Number: 208053

Eligibility

People in need, particularly people who are elderly or disabled, who have lived in the ancient parish of Lee in Lewisham for at least five years.

Types of grants

Regular allowances.

Annual grant total

In 2010 the trust had assets of £143,000 and an income of £31,000. Grants were made to 55 individuals totalling £19,000.

Applications

In writing to the correspondent.

Other information

Grants are also made to organisations. During the year grants totalled £46,000 to 13 organisations.

Lewisham Relief in Need Charity

£1,100 (10 grants)

Correspondent: Emily Roberts, Clerk's Office, Lloyd Court, Slagrove Place, London SE13 7LP (020 8690 8145)

Trustees: Alan Till; Gloria Phillips; Veronica Shirfield; Omega Ferilia Jackson; Julia Ann Pring; Julian Watson; Cllr Stella Janet Jeffrey; Norma Dixon.

CC Number: 1025779

Eligibility

People in need, including those who are who are older, disadvantaged or who have disabilities and who live in the ancient parish of Lewisham, which does not include Deptford or Lee.

Types of grants

Small one-off grants for specific purposes rather than general need, including those for clothing, household bills, travel expenses, furniture, disabled equipment and legal fees. Christmas grants of £25 are also made to older people.

Annual grant total

Around £1,000 a year is given in grants to individuals. During 2011/12 three people received grants and seven also received Christmas gifts.

Exclusions

No grants are made where statutory assistance is available.

Applications

In writing to the correspondent either directly by the individual, through a third party such as a social worker, or through an organisation such as Citizens Advice or other welfare agency. Applications should include as much supporting information as possible to enable the trustees to make informed decisions about why the individual is in need. Applications are considered throughout the year.

Other information

The charity is primarily engaged in providing sheltered accommodation for the elderly at its almshouse, Lloyd Court. It also makes grants to small organisations aiding the people of Lewisham.

Merton

Wimbledon Guild of Social Welfare (Incorporated)

£19,000

Correspondent: Sheila Dunman, Welfare Committee Chair, 30–32 Worple Road, Wimbledon, London SW19 4EF (020 8946 0735; fax: 020 8296 0042; email: info@wimbledonguild.co.uk; website: www.wimbledonguild.co.uk)

Trustees: Charles Lucas; Amir Siddiqui; Eileen Marian Grace; John Strover; Richard Andrew Steele; Susan Cooke; Simon Leathes; Peter Mitchell; Clive Handford.

CC Number: 200424

Eligibility

Individuals in need who live primarily in Wimbledon but also in the borough of Merton, with some preference for older people.

Types of grants

Small one-off grants according to need towards kitchen equipment, children's clothing, household bills and so on. The guild also distributes gifts in kind, including furniture, food and Christmas toys. Grants will not normally be given to anyone who has been a recipient in the previous year.

Annual grant total

In 2010/11 the guild had assets of £6.5 million and an income of £3.1 million. Grants were made to individuals totalling £19,000.

Applications

On a form available from the correspondent or to download from the website. Applications are considered every other month. Upcoming meeting dates can be found on the website. Applications must be received a week before the date of each meeting, except when applying for an emergency food grant.

Other information

The guild also runs clubs, classes and a furniture recycling service; manages a care home and provides a counselling service.

Newham

The Mary Curtis' Maternity Charity

£3,000

Correspondent: Geoffrey Wheeler, Durning Hall, Earlham Grove, Forest Gate, London E7 9AB (020 8536 3812; email: geoffrey.wheeler@aston-mansfield.org.uk)

Trustees: Sharon Alexandra Higgins; Revd Canon Ann Rosemarie Easter; Geoffrey Wheeler; Pat Mossop.

CC Number: 235036

Eligibility

Pregnant women or mothers with children under one. Applicants must live in Newham and can be asylum seekers or pregnant underage.

Types of grants

One-off grants ranging from £150 to £100 towards, for instance, cots, pushchairs and baby clothes.

Annual grant total

The charity has an average expenditure of around £3,000.

Applications

In writing to the correspondent, through a doctor, vicar, teacher, midwife or social worker. Applications are considered every month and should include details about the area in which the individual lives and how many children she is responsible for.

Redbridge

The Ethel Baker Bequest

£4,700

Correspondent: Revd Charles Neil Spencer, 18 Chestnut Walk, Woodford Green IG8 0TE (020 8530 4916)

Trustees: Revd Charles Neil Spencer; Keith Raymond Hawkins.

CC Number: 270274

Eligibility

People in need who live in the parish of Woodford Baptist Church in the London borough of Redbridge.

Types of grants

One-off and recurrent grants according to need.

Annual grant total

In 2010/11 the bequest had an income of £1,700 and a total expenditure of £4,700.

Applications

In writing to the correspondent, although the trust states that its funds are already allocated.

Other information

Grants are also made to organisations.

Richmond upon Thames

The Barnes Workhouse Fund

£21,000

Correspondent: Miranda Ibbetson, PO Box 665, Richmond, Surrey TW10 6YL (020 8241 3994; email: mibbetson@barnesworkhousefund.org.uk; website: www.barnesworkhousefund.org.uk)

Trustees: Nicolas Phillips; Peter Siddall; Wendy Kyrle-Pope; Philip Conrath; John Brocklebank; K. Pengelley; Timothy Besley; Lucy Hine; Paul Hodgins.

CC Number: 200103

Eligibility

People in need who live in the ancient parish of Barnes (in practice SW13).

Types of grants

Grants of up to £350, for example to provide items such as carpets, domestic appliances, furniture, children's clothing and school trips and assistance with the costs of medical needs not available from the National Health Service. Grants are also made for bills and bankruptcy orders

Annual grant total

In 2011 the fund had assets of £11 million and an income of £603,000. There were 62 grants made to individuals totalling £17,000 plus £4,200 given through the furniture scheme.

Exclusions

Grants are not generally made to people who are homeless, as the scheme requires applicants to be resident in Barnes.

Applications

Applications can be submitted through a recognised referral agency (such as social worker, health visitor, housing association, Citizens Advice or doctor) on a form available from the correspondent. Applications are considered upon receipt.

Other information

Grants are also made to organisations.

The Hampton and Hampton Hill Philanthropic Society

£2,000

Correspondent: Joan Barnett, Waverley, Old Farm Road, Hampton, Middlesex TW12 3RL (020 8979 0395)

Trustees: Joan Barnett; Roger Barnett; Marie Martin; Ken Mace; Patricia Barnett.

CC Number: 208992

Eligibility

People in need in St Mary's and All Saints', Hampton and St James, Hampton Hill.

Types of grants

Grants of about £200 each are made to people who have suddenly come into financial need.

Annual grant total

Grants average around £2,000 a year. Priority is given to making grants to individuals, with any surplus funds left over donated to local organisations.

Applications

In writing to the correspondent.

The Petersham United Charities

£2,500

Correspondent: The Clerk, The Vicarage, Bute Avenue, Richmond TW10 7AX (020 8940 8435)

Trustees: Richard Robinson; Arthur Carter; Ivy Faulks; Charles Archer; James Kimble; Revd Timothy Marwood.

CC Number: 200433

Eligibility

People in need who live in the ecclesiastical parish of Petersham, Surrey.

Types of grants

Pensions and grants of £75 to £500, including Christmas and birthday gifts and grants towards heating and disability equipment.

Annual grant total

In 2010 the trust had an income of £4,000 and a total expenditure of £6,000.

Applications

In writing to the correspondent. Applications are considered in January, April, July and October and can be submitted either directly by the individual or through a social worker, Citizens Advice or other welfare agency.

Other information

Grants are also given for educational purposes and to organisations.

The Richmond Aid-in-Sickness Fund

£7,500

Correspondent: Catherine Rumsey, 8 The Green, Richmond, Surrey TW9 1PL (020 8948 4188; email: richmondcharities@richmondcharities. org.uk; website: www. therichmondcharities.co.uk)

Trustees: Frances Bouchier; Pauline Gore; Serge Lourie; Jean Love; Colin Craib; Gillian Elisabeth Mathers; Peter Marr; Canon Robert Titley; Steven Weddle; Susan John; Emma Davis.

CC Number: 200434

Eligibility

People in need who live in the borough of Richmond.

Types of grants

One-off grants ranging from £25 to £250 for bedding, fuel bills, recuperative holidays and other small cash grants for the relief of those in poor health.

Annual grant total

In 2011 the trust had an income of £5,000 and a total expenditure of £7,700.

Applications

Applications should be submitted through a social worker, Citizens Advice or other welfare agency. They are considered on the first Wednesday of February, March, May, June, September, November and December.

The Richmond Parish Lands Charity

£110,000

Correspondent: The Clerk to the Education Committee, The Vestry House, 21 Paradise Road, Richmond, Surrey TW9 1SA (020 8948 5701; fax: 020 8332 6792; website: www.rplc.org. uk)

Trustees: Rita Biddulph; Ashley Casson; Colin Craib; Clare Head; Jeffery Harris; Kate Ellis; Lisa Blakemore; Paul Coles; Niall Cairns; Ros Sweeting; Rosie Dalzell; Sue Jones; Susan Goddard; Dr Vivienne Press; Tim Sketchley.

CC Number: 200069

Eligibility

People who are in need and have lived in the TW9 TW10 or SW14 areas of Richmond for at least six months prior to application and have no other possible sources of help. Older people must be in receipt of a means tested benefit to qualify for a winter heating grant.

Types of grants

Crisis grants of up to £250, mostly for household goods, bills, debts, food and clothing. Grants of £60 towards heating bills are available to older people.

Annual grant total

In 2010/11 the charity made grants to over 1,000 individuals totalling £220,000. Crisis grants and Winter Fuel grants were given to 900 individuals and totalled £110,000.

Applications

On a form available from the Clerk to the Education Committee, to be submitted directly by the individual. This includes details of current employment, income and expenditure, details of the course/expenses applied for and a statement in support of the application. Two references are required and applicants are usually asked to attend an interview. Applications should be based on financial need and parental income is taken into account up to the age of 25 years. There are two trusts which are also administered by the Richmond Parish Lands Charity:

The Barnes Relief in Need Charity (BRINC) – CC no. 200318
BRINC small grant forms are available for existing RPLC small grants referral

agencies. In addition some Mortlake based organisations will be invited to become referral agencies for individuals in need. Application forms for organisational and individual grants are available from the correspondent.

The Bailey and Bates Trust – CC no. 312249

Grants are made for relief in need purposes for individuals living in the postcode area SW14. Contact the correspondent for further details of how to apply. However, note that charitable expenditure for this trust has been particularly low since 2005.

Other information

Grants are also made to organisations. The charity has an informative website.

The Richmond Philanthropic Society

£6,500

Correspondent: Mrs Catherine Rumsey, 8 The Green, Richmond, Surrey TW9 1PL (020 8948 4188; email: richmondcharities@richmondcharities. org.uk)

Trustees: Margaret Marshall; Jean Love; Gillian Mathers; Susan John; Emma Davis; Colin Craib; Peter Marr; Steven Weddle; Canon Robert Titley; Pauline Gore; Cllr Frances Bouchier; Serge Lourie.

CC Number: 212941

Eligibility

People in need who live in the borough of Richmond, including Kew, Petersham and Ham (post-codes TW9 and TW10).

Types of grants

Small one-off grants up to a maximum of £250 including those for washing machines, cookers and fridges, prams, beds and bedding, TV licences, rent arrears and utility bills.

Annual grant total

In 2011 the society had an income of £15,000 and a total expenditure of £6,700.

Exclusions

No grants are given for educational purposes or for the payment of council tax. There are no cash grants available.

Applications

Preferably through Citizens Advice, social services, district nurses, health visitors or other established third parties.

Other information

This charity no longer exists as a single entity and now falls under the Richmond Charities. It is also known as The Phil.

Southwark

The Camberwell Consolidated Charities

£42,000

Correspondent: Mrs J McDonald, London Borough of Southwark, Level 2 Hub 5, PO Box 64529, London SE1P 5LX (020 7525 7511)

Trustees: Cllr Michael Mitchell; Al-Haj Hussain Malik; Dawn Marie Martin; Evelyne Jarrett; John Palmer; Joyce May Somerville; Veronica Anne Hunt; Patricia Cox; Festus James Fairweather; Gloria Brown; John Edward Major; Barry Noon.

CC Number: 208441

Eligibility

Primarily older people in need who have lived in the former parish of Camberwell for at least two years. Priority is given to those whose income is on or around the minimum state pension.

Types of grants

Annual pensions of £375 per person or £565 per couple. Hardship grants are also available for emergency items.

Annual grant total

In 2010/11 the charities had an income of £52,000. Pensions amounted to £42,000 while a single one-off grant of £80 was also paid.

The accounts also note that, 'after conducting a survey of beneficiaries' preferences the Trustees reflected the wish of the majority by making higher cash payments rather than sending beneficiaries a Christmas hamper.'

Applications

On a form available from the correspondent. Vacancies are advertised in the local press and by social services, Age UK and so on.

The Peckham and Kent Road Pension Society

£1,100

Correspondent: Tim Reith, The Peckham Settlement, Goldsmith Road, London SE15 5TF (020 7639 1823)

Trustees: Spencer McGuire; Jeff Burnige; Chris Hutchins; Tim Reith.

CC Number: 210210

Eligibility

People who have lived in Peckham, SE15, for at least five years, receive Income Support and are over 60 (women) or 65 (men).

Types of grants

Monthly pensions.

Annual grant total

The most recent accounts available were for 2009/10 when the trust had an income of £5,700 and a total expenditure of £1,200.

Applications

In writing to the correspondent.

Rotherhithe Consolidated Charities

£79,000

Correspondent: B D Claxton, Amwell House, 19 Amwell Street, Hoddesdon, Hertfordshire EN11 8TS (01992 444466; fax: 01992 447476; email: brian@ hbaccountants.co.uk)

Trustees: Bill Griffiths; Coral Newell; John Edwards; Kay Lovett; John Phillips; Father Graham Preston; Victoria Ellen Green; Father Mark Nicholls; Phillip Mock; Barry Noon; Sian Bunclarke; David Paine; Alan White; Jeff Hook; Wilma Nelson.

CC Number: 211980

Eligibility

Recurrent grants are made primarily to widows who are in need and have lived in the ancient parish of Rotherhithe for at least ten years. Help is also given for the general benefit of those in need who live in the parish.

Types of grants

The trust pays an annual pension to widows in need. It also gives one-off grants and provides holidays.

Annual grant total

In 2010 the charity had assets of £4.2 million and an income of £95,000. Grants were made to 731 individuals totalling £79,000, and were distributed as follows:

Stipend Grants	£35,000
Christmas Donations	£1,400
Holidays	£43,000

Applications

In writing to the correspondent. Applications can be submitted directly by the individual or through a third party, and are considered at any time.

Other information

Grants are also made to organisations (£4,600 in 2010).

Southwark Charities

£45,000

Correspondent: Patrick McSorley, Secretary, Charities Office, Municipal Office, 151–153 Walworth Road, London

SE17 1RY (020 7525 2128; email: charities@almshouse-southwark.org)

Trustees: Charles Cherrill; Robert Percival Brice; Gerald Walter Denny; Capt. Guy Philip Brocklebank; William Joseph Pearsall; Cllr Lorraine Lauder; Stephen James Graham; Patrick Edward McSorley; Malcolm John Bresman; Caroline Charlotte Croft; Revd Alan James Wild.

CC Number: 1137760

Eligibility

Older people in need who have lived in the former metropolitan borough of Southwark for at least five years.

Types of grants

Quarterly pensions and one-off grants towards the cost of holidays.

Annual grant total

In 2011 the charity held assets of £19 million and had an income of £551,000. Grants were made totalling £45,000 and were distributed as follows:

Pensions	£31,000
Summer holiday grants	£9,000
Christmas parties and gifts	£5,400

Applications

In writing to the correspondent, either directly by the individual, via a third party or through a social worker, Citizens Advice or other welfare agency.

Other information

The charity also maintains a number of almshouses for the benefit of older people over the age of 60 who are in financial difficulties, with preference given to single women.

The Mayor of Southwark's Common Good Trust (The Mayor's Charity)

£6,200 (35 grants)

Correspondent: Eric John Bassett, 90 Sunnywood Drive, Haywards Heath RH16 4PB (01444 412812; email: eric.bassett@btinternet.com)

Trustees: Ian Ritchie; John Wallington; William Skelly; Vicky Naish; John Clark; Cllr Jeffrey Hook; David Payne; Dussell Charlambous; Patrick Wentworth.

CC Number: 280011

Eligibility

People in need who live in the borough of Southwark and the immediate surrounding area.

Types of grants

One-off grants, averaging about £175 each, for essential kitchen items, medical equipment, clothing, furniture and household items.

Annual grant total

In 2010/11 the trust had assets of £103,000 and an income of £31,000. Grants were made totalling £6,200.

Applications

In writing to the correspondent. Applications can be made either directly by the individual or through a social worker, Citizens Advice or other third party such as, a family member, MP or doctor. Applications should include full details of family/financial/health background and details of other sources of funds, including whether a previous application has been made to this trust. Applicants may be visited to assess need.

Other information

The trust also makes grants to local community groups who provide services to the young and elderly, particularly at Christmas.

The United Charities of St George the Martyr

£167,000

Correspondent: Mrs S Harding, Clerk to the Trustees, Marshall House, 66 Newcomen Street, London SE1 1YT (020 7407 2994; email: stgeorge@marshalls.org.uk)

Trustees: Pat Notton; Ken Hayes; Duncan Field; Revd Ray Andrews; William Griffiths; Andrew Starte; Ian Duncan; Samantha Louise Fennell.

CC Number: 208732

Eligibility

Older people in need in the parish of St George the Martyr (in north Southwark SE1).

Types of grants

Pensions and Christmas parcels mainly. One-off grants according to need, usually of up to £300, towards buying items such as kitchen equipment, furnishing and flooring, mobility aids, accompanied transport to medical and dental treatments, easy-fitting slippers and shoes and illuminated magnifying lenses.

Annual grant total

In 2011 the charity had assets of £6.3 million and an income of £442,000. Grants to individuals totalled £167,000, and were broken down as follows:

Pensioner holiday costs	£84,000
Pensions	£36,000
Pensioner day trips and outings	£28,000
Christmas parcels and parties	£15,000
Amenities for pensioners	£4,800

Applications

In writing to the correspondent. The charity has previously stated that its grants and pensions are fully committed but that any new applications will be kept on file.

St Olave's United Charity, incorporating the St Thomas and St John Charities

£199,000

Correspondent: Angela O'Shaughnessy, 6–8 Druid Street, off Tooley Street, London SE1 2EU (020 7407 2530; email: st.olavescharity@btconnect.com)

Trustees: F. Colley; J. Lynch; P. John; J. Donovan; D. Brasier; C. Bennett; G. Johnson; S. Broughton; L. Rowe; D. Hams; D. Trescher; B. Albin-Dyer.

CC Number: 211763

Eligibility

People in need who live in Bermondsey (part SE1 and all SE16).

Types of grants

Individuals over the age of 70 can receive a birthday gift of £100 a year and a further grant towards holidays once every year or every two years. Depending on additional income, other one-off grants can be made for a wide variety of needs, including clothes, musical instruments and holidays.

Annual grant total

In 2010/11 the charity had assets of £12.1 million and an income of £304,000. Relief in need grants totalled £127,000 with a further £72,000 given for holidays.

Applications

Applications should be made in writing to the correspondent and are considered four times a year.

Other information

Grants are also made to organisations and to individuals for education purposes.

The Emily Temple West Trust

£700

Correspondent: The Administrator, Christ Church, 27 Blackfriars Road, London SE1 8NY (020 7928 4707; fax: 020 7928 1148; email: admin@christchurchsouthwark.org.uk)

Trustees: Janet Amery; Jean Vigar; Terry McLeman; Revd Timothy Scott.

CC Number: 210077

Eligibility

People under 19, or their parents, who are in need and live in the metropolitan borough of Southwark.

Types of grants

One-off cash grants ranging from £150 to £500 towards, for example, clothing, food and toys.

Annual grant total

About £1,400 a year. Grants are given to both individuals and organisations.

Applications

On a form available from the correspondent. This can be completed by the individual or the individual's parents or through a third party such as a church, social services, advice centre and so on. Applications are considered in May and November.

Sutton

The Sutton Nursing Association

£3,500

Correspondent: John Helps, 28 Southway, Carshalton SM5 4HW (020 8770 1095; email: sna@skingle.co.uk)

Trustees: Dr Peter Heywood; Tony Stacey; Marilyn Gordon-Jones; Dr Frank Assinder; Reginald Baldwin Whellock; Pamela Norton; R. Hobbs; F. Owen; J. Alexander; J. Herrington; Betsy Graham.

CC Number: 203686

Eligibility

People who are in poor health and in need and live in the London borough of Sutton and the surrounding area.

Types of grants

One-off grants generally up to £500 for domestic items, furniture, respite care, carpets, disability aids and so on.

Annual grant total

In 2010 the association had an income of £18,000 and a total expenditure of £29,000. Grants to individuals totalled around £3,500.

Exclusions

Recurrent grants and matters relating to ongoing liabilities are not considered.

Applications

Applications are usually made through a social worker, Citizens Advice or other welfare agency. They are considered bi-monthly and must include as much information as possible, such as the costs involved, funds available from other sources and the ability of the individual to contribute.

Other information

The association also makes grants to the community nursing services, hospitals and local organisations.

Tower Hamlets

Bishopsgate Foundation

£41,000 (55 grants)

Correspondent: Geoff Wilson, Director of Finance and Administration, 230 Bishopsgate, London EC2M 4QH (020 7392 9200; fax: 020 7392 9250; email: enquiries@bishopsgate.org.uk; website: www.bishopsgate.org.uk)

Trustees: May Kunle Dare; Michael Brooke Maunsell; Max Weaver; Helen Antonia Byatt; Ruth Lesirge; Revd Dr Alan McCormack; Abigail Pogson; Alderman Neil Redcliffe; Marc Jordan; Nigel J. W. Brockmann; Christopher P. Eason Cook; Graham Bulpitt.

CC Number: 1090923

Eligibility

Pensioners over the age of 60 who live and work, or have lived or worked, in the parishes of St Botolph's without Bishopsgate; Christchurch, Spitalfields; and St Leonard's, Shoreditch – all within the borough of Tower Hamlets.

Types of grants

Recurrent grants of around £180 per quarter plus a Christmas bonus.

Annual grant total

In 2010/11 the foundation had assets of £20 million and an income of £2.3 million. Pensions were distributed to 55 people totalling £41,000. Grants to local organisations totalled £35,000.

Applications

On a form available from the correspondent. Applications can be submitted either directly by the individual or through a social worker, Citizens Advice or other welfare agency. There are no deadlines and applications are considered as and when a vacancy arises.

Other information

The foundation's principal activity is the running of the Bishopsgate Institute and library. As well as making top-up pension grants to individuals it also makes grants to organisations.

The Henderson Charity

£22,000

Correspondent: Jonathan Woodbridge, 8 Masters Lodge, Johnson Street, London E1 0BE (020 7790 1793)

Trustees: Oliver Wagstaff; Sylvia Cashman; Revd Peter McGeary; Allan

Ramanoop; Michael Ainsworth; Alexandra Nelson.

CC Number: 1012208

Eligibility

Older people who live in the hamlet of Ratcliff and the parish of St George's-in-the-East, Stepney. Applicants must be longstanding residents of the beneficial area and there is a maximum income requirement.

Types of grants

Small pensions of around £20 a month.

Annual grant total

In 2011/12 the charity had an income of £19,000 and a total expenditure of £25,000.

Applications

Vacancies are normally advertised locally through social services and appropriate welfare agencies. When a pension is available, application forms can be obtained from social services or the correspondent.

The Trevor Huddleston Fund for Children

£500

Correspondent: David Longbottom, 87 Saunders Ness Road, London E14 3EB (020 7515 5388; email: huddlestonfund@aol.com)

Trustees: Mary Martinson; Amanda Elsie Boutwood; David Michael Longbottom; Penny Harris; Revd Tom Pyke; Glenda Higgins.

CC Number: 277361

Eligibility

Children in need who live on the Isle of Dogs.

Types of grants

A number of one-off grants towards basic needs, particularly winter clothes and shoes.

Annual grant total

In 2010/11 the trust had an income of £6,200 and a total expenditure of £7,900.

Applications

In writing to the correspondent on behalf of the individual child by schools, social services, churches or other community agencies for consideration at any time. Applications made by individuals or their families are not considered.

Other information

Grants are given mainly to organisations.

The Ratcliff Pension Charity

£10,000 (19 grants)

Correspondent: Adrian Carroll, Clerk, Cooper's Hall, 13 Devonshire Square, London EC2M 4TH (020 7247 9577; fax: 020 7377 8061; email: clerk@coopers-hall.co.uk; website: www.coopers-hall.co.uk)

Trustees: Mr P. J. Timms; John Hughesdon; Keith Brown; Michael Andre Zuckerman; Judge Brian John Barker; George Andrew Prescott; Graham Sutton; John Anthony Newton; John Wildred Spencer Clark; Richard Edmonde Miles Philippe Sibley; Thomas Paul Hicks Godfrey; Vivian Bairstow; Bryan Scott Pickering; Dr Ian James Macaulay Frood; Alderman Luder; Roy Edward Campbell; Anthony William Behrens; Richard Robin Wilmington; Julian Michael Day; Pergrine Anthony Guy Bousfield.

CC Number: 234613

Eligibility

Older people in financial need who live in the London borough of Tower Hamlets, with a preference for the Stepney area.

Types of grants

One-off and recurrent grants according to need.

Annual grant total

In 2010/11 the trust had assets of £490,000 and an income of £37,000. Grants were made to 19 individuals totalling £10,000.

Applications

In writing to the correspondent.

Other information

Grants are also made to organisations operating locally (£25,000 in 2010/11).

Stepney Relief-in-Need Charity

£10,000

Correspondent: Mrs J Partleton, Clerk to the Trustees, Rectory Cottage, 5 White Horse Lane, Stepney, London E1 3NE (020 7790 3598)

Trustees: Ms V. Jenkins; Mrs C. Horlor; The Revd C. Burke; Mrs V. Hullyer; Capt. N. Coke; Mrs B. Harris; Mrs J. Yeatman.

CC Number: 250130

Eligibility

People in need who live within the old Metropolitan Borough of Stepney.

Types of grants

One-off grants of £100 to £500 will be considered for a variety of needs, including household items, clothing, holidays where individuals will benefit from a short break, convalescence costs following discharge from hospital, hospital travel, mobility aids and so on.

Annual grant total

In 2010/11 the charity had an income of £36,000 and a total expenditure of £34,000. Grants totalled £13,000 and are made for relief-in-need and educational purposes.

Exclusions

No grants are made towards the repayment of loans, rent, council tax or utility bills.

Applications

An application form is available from the correspondent and may be submitted either directly by the individual or through a relative, social worker or other welfare agency. The trustees usually meet four times a year, but some applications can be considered between meetings at the chair's discretion.

Miss Vaughan's Spitalfields Charity

£1,200

Correspondent: Philip Whitehead, 45 Quilter Street, Bethnal Green, London E2 7BS (020 7729 2790)

Trustees: Revd Andrew Rider; Revd Kevin Scully; Revd Paul Robert Turp.

CC Number: 262480

Eligibility

People in need who live in the ecclesiastical parishes of Christchurch with All Saints in Spitalfields, St Matthew in Bethnal Green and St Leonard, Shoreditch.

Types of grants

Originally clothing and support was given to poor mechanics and weavers in Spitalfields who were unable to work. Now grants are given to individuals and families who are convalescing, unemployed or disabled and also to large families on a low income.

Annual grant total

Total annual expenditure for this charity is around £1,200.

Applications

In writing to a member of the clergy from any of the eligible parishes.

Wandsworth

The Peace Memorial Fund

£500

Correspondent: Gareth Jones, Town Hall, Room 153, Wandsworth High Street, London SW18 2PU (020 8871 7520; email: garethjones@wandsworth.gov.uk)

Trustee: Gordon Passmore.

CC Number: 213167

Eligibility

Children aged 16 or under who live in the borough of Wandsworth.

Types of grants

Grants of £40 to £75 towards holidays and school trips.

Annual grant total

About £1,000 for welfare and education purposes

Applications

Through a welfare agency on a form available from the correspondent. Applications should be submitted in February/March and May/June.

The Wandsworth Combined Charity

£13,000

Correspondent: R J Cooles, 179 Upper Richmond Road West, East Sheen, London SW14 8DU (020 8876 4478; fax: 020 8878 5686)

Trustees: Beryl Jeffery; William James Haddock; Tessa Strickland; Cllr Charles McNaught Davis; Revd Gregory Stephen Prior; Jennifer Nickels; Rosemary Torrington; Robert White; Karen Ashworth.

CC Number: 210269

Eligibility

Older people in need who have lived in the London borough of Wandsworth for at least three years.

Types of grants

Monthly pensions of about £20 and a small bonus payment at Christmas time. One-off grants are occasionally made but only when there is an exceptional need.

Annual grant total

In 2010/11 the charity had an income of £11,000 and a total expenditure of £13,000.

Applications

In writing to the correspondent, to be submitted either directly by the individual or through a social worker,

491

local church, Age Concern or similar third party.

Other information

Grants may also be made to organisations working in the local area.

Westminster

The Charity of A. J G. Cross

£6,000

Correspondent: Michael Horsley, 4 Chester Square, London SW1W 9HH (020 7730 8889)

Trustees: Revd Charles Marnham; Andy Greenacre; Georgina Hunter Gordon; Sally Breeden; Janet Cynthia Whiting.

CC Number: 210466

Eligibility

People who are sick and in need and live in South Westminster (i.e. south of Oxford Street).

Types of grants

One-off grants to a maximum of £150 including those towards heating costs, clothing, holidays and furnishings.

Annual grant total

In 2010/11 it had an income of £8,000 and a total expenditure of £6,500.

Exclusions

No grants are given towards arrears.

Applications

On a form available from the correspondent to be submitted through a third party such as a social worker. The charity does not deal directly with the individual.

St Giles-in-the-Fields and Bloomsbury United Charity

£2,700

Correspondent: Pam Nicholls, Clerk to the Trustees, The Rectory, 15a Gower Street, London WC1E 6HW (020 7323 1992; email: pam.nicholls@london. anglican.org; website: www. stgilescharities.org.uk)

Trustees: Bill Jacob, Archdeacon of Charing; Jill Hutchings; Peter David; Julian Sharpe; Nduka Agada; Revd Thomas Peebles; Peter Bloxham.

CC Number: 1111908

Eligibility

People in need, with a preferences for those who are sick or infirm, who live in the ancient parishes of St Giles in the Fields, St Martin in the Fields and St Paul, Covent Garden. A map of the area of benefit is available on the website.

Types of grants

One-off grants, usually up to £500, towards the purchase of white goods, furniture, bedding, clothing, medical equipment and to cover the costs of restorative holidays.

Annual grant total

In 2011 the charity had assets of £1.7 million, an income of £76,000 and made grants to individuals totalling £2,700.

Exclusions

No grants to students or for education.

Applications

On a form available to download from the website. Applications are considered at trustees' meetings, which take place four times a year, normally in January, April, July and October. Applications should ideally be received least two weeks in advance of the meeting. Meeting dates are published on the website. In urgent cases, grants may be considered between meetings.

The St Marylebone Health Society

£2,000

Correspondent: David Dunbar, 31 Llanvanor Road, London NW2 2AR (020 8455 9612; email: dgldunbar@aol. com)

Trustees: June Patricia Eva Savage; David James Dunbar; Nicholas Roach; Margaret Pollock; Anne Scher; Janet Brook; Phillida Inman.

CC Number: 248984

Eligibility

Families with children of school age and under who live in the former borough of St Marylebone in the city of Westminster i.e. east of Edgware Road and north of Oxford Street in NW8 NW1 or W1.

Types of grants

One-off grants for beds, bedding, household equipment, children's equipment, clothing and so on. Grants average between £300 and £400. Christmas grants are made in the form of grocery vouchers.

Holidays and outings for parents and their children are also supported. The applicant should have lived in the beneficial area for two years.

Annual grant total

In 2010 the society had a lower than usual income of £7,400 (£14,000 in 2009) and a total expenditure of £2,000 (£11,000 in 2009).

Exclusions

Overseas holidays and families without children cannot be funded. Grants are not given to adults not caring for children, to assist older people or to students. Cash grants are rarely given.

Applications

Through a social worker, educational welfare officer or health visitor using the application form available from the correspondent. Holiday applications should be made by February if possible; other applications at any time.

Strand Parishes Trust

£46,000 (181 grants)

Correspondent: Frank Brenchley-Brown, 169 Strand, London WC2R 2LS (020 7836 3205; fax: 020 7836 9850; email: sptwestminster@aol.com)

Trustees: Peter Maplestone; Jane Marian Ker-Reid; Margery Diana Roberts; Stephen Paul Harrow; Katharine Mary Lewis; John D'Auvergne Maycock; Jean Valerie Rymer; Peter David Symmons.

CC Number: 1121754

Eligibility

People who live and/or work in the London borough of the City of Westminster, with preference for the parish of St Clement Danes and St Mary le Strand.

Types of grants

One-off grants and pensions.

Annual grant total

In 2010 the charity had assets of £5.3 million and an income of £176,000. Pensions were made to 70 individuals totalling £27,500 and a further £18,000 was given in grants to 111 individuals.

Exclusions

No grants for expeditions, electives, non-residents of Westminster or asylum seekers.

Applications

On a form available from the correspondent. Applications must be made through a sponsoring organisation i.e. social services or Citizens Advice.

Other information

The Isaac Duckett's Charity, St Mary le Strand Charity and St Clement Danes Parochial Charities were amalgamated with other charities to form the Strand Parishes Trust.

Grants are also made to organisations (£78,000 in 2010).

The United Charities of St Paul's, Covent Garden

£4,000

Correspondent: Maggie Rae, Flat 9, 19 Henrietta Street, London WC2E 8QH (020 7379 6080; email: mrae@clintons.co.uk)

Trustees: Revd S. Grigg; David Alexander; Noel Tobin; Tim Bienias.

CC Number: 209568

Eligibility

People in need who live in the city of Westminster.

Types of grants

One-off grants ranging from £50 to £120. Monthly payments are also made to several people. Grants can be paid directly or through hospitals, health authorities, family service units or an early intervention service.

Annual grant total

In 2010/11 the charities had an income of £4,100 and a total expenditure of £5,400. Approximately £4,000 is given annually in grants to individuals.

Exclusions

Tuition fees and holidays are not funded.

Applications

In writing to the correspondent.

The Waterloo Parish Charity for the Poor

£900

Correspondent: Parish Administrator, c/o St John's Vicarage, 2 Secker Street, London SE1 8UF (020 7450 4601; email: adminstjohnswaterloo@hotmail.co.uk)

Trustees: Rosa Louisa Wright; Eileen Hamilton; Holly Adenle; Revd David Pape; Revd Giles William Goddard.

CC Number: 251594

Eligibility

People in need who live in the parish of Waterloo, St John with St Andrew.

Types of grants

Small grants ranging from £25 to £100 for living expenses and domestic items.

Annual grant total

Grants average around £900 a year.

Applications

On a form available from the correspondent. Applications can be submitted either by the individual or through a social worker, Citizens Advice or similar third party. They are considered quarterly.

The Westminster Almhouses Foundation

£113,000

Correspondent: Cristina O'Halloran, Clerk to the Trustees, 42 Rochester Row, London SW1P 1BU (020 7828 3131; fax: 020 7828 3138; email: clerk@westminsteralmshouses.com; website: www.westminsteralmshouses.com)

Trustees: Regina Kibel; Lady Joanna Knatchbull; Dr Cyril Nemeth; Ian Steers; Revd Philip Welsh; Polly Williams; Virginia Lady Crowe; Laurence Martin Soden; Cllr Rachael Robathan.

CC Number: 226936

Eligibility

People in need who live in the London Borough of Westminster. Limited support is available to those living elsewhere in Greater London and to women living elsewhere in the UK.

Types of grants

One-off grants averaging around £250 for a variety of needs, for example, helping a previously homeless person set up home through the provision of white goods or basic furniture. Recurrent grants are also made.

Annual grant total

In 2011 the foundation had assets of £21 million and an income of £697,000. Pensions and over 300 welfare grants were made totalling £113,000.

Applications

In writing to the correspondent through a third party (i.e. social worker, GP or Citizens Advice worker) who can verify the circumstances.

Other information

The foundation also makes educational grants.

The Westminster Amalgamated Charity

£46,000 (357 grants)

Correspondent: Mrs Julia Moorcroft, Grants Administrator, School House, Drury Lane, London WC2B 5SU (020 7395 9460; fax: 020 7395 9479; email: wac@3chars.org.uk; website: www.w-a-c.org.uk)

Trustees: Alexander Nicoll; Mark Edgar Walter Studer; Jenny Bianco; Dr Cyril Nemeth; Paul Gardner; Eileen Terry; Jean Rymer; Linda McHugh; Graham Mordue; Simon Carruth; David Cavaye.

CC Number: 207964

Eligibility

People in need who live, work or study in the old City of Westminster (the former Metropolitan Borough of Westminster) or those who have previously lived or worked in the area for a total of five years or more.

Note: the old City of Westminster is that area covered by Westminster Council which is situated south of Oxford Street.

Types of grants

One-off grants ranging from £100 to £350 towards: clothing; essential household items (furniture, white goods, kitchen equipment); holidays for individuals aged 60 and over (taken in the UK only); and decorating and flooring costs. Payments will be made to the sponsor or a designated retailer.

Annual grant total

In 2010 the charity had assets of £6.5 million and an income of £224,000. Grants to 357 individuals (360 applications considered) totalled £46,000 and were distributed as follows:

Discretionary	£18,800
Household	£16,000
Clothing	£9,000
Holidays and fares	£2,700
Other	£20

As of May 2012 there remained £35,000 for distribution to individuals during the year. The charity regularly publishes and updates the amount of money available for distribution on its website.

Exclusions

No grants for: TVs; CD/DVD players; mobile phones; computers/software; educational needs; holidays abroad; debt repayment or fees. No retrospective grants.

Applications

On a form available from the correspondent or to download from the website. Applications must be submitted through a recognised referral agency such as Social Services, Citizens Advice, hostel worker etc; and be accompanied by a supporting statement. The supporting statement should include all of the details which explain the individual's need, for example: family circumstances; medical, domestic or behavioural issues; the extent of your agency's involvement with the applicant and why assistance is sought. Applications will usually take four to six weeks to process.

Other information

The charity also makes grants to organisations (£150,000 in 2010).

Advice organisations

The following section lists the names and contact details of voluntary organisations that offer advice and support to individuals in need. The list is split into two sections: 'Welfare' and 'Illness and disability'. Each section begins with an index before listing the organisations by category.

The listings are a useful reference guide to organisations that individuals can contact to discuss their situation and receive advice and support. These organisations will have experience in tackling the sorts of problems that other individuals have faced, and will know the most effective and efficient ways of dealing with them. They may also be able to arrange for people to meet others in a similar situation. As well as providing advice and support, many of the organisations will be happy to help individuals submit applications to the trusts included in this guide. They may also know of other sources of funding available.

Some organisations included in this list have their own financial resources available to individuals. We have marked these with an asterisk (*). This list should not be used as a quick way of identifying potential funding – the organisations will have criteria and policies that may mean they are unable to support all the needs under that category and the guide will include many more potential sources of funding than there are organisations here.

Some organisations have local branches, which are better placed to have a personal contact with the individual and have a greater local knowledge of the need. We have only included the headquarters of such organisations, which will be happy to provide details for the relevant branches.

It is helpful for the organisations listed if any request for information includes an sae.

This list is by no means comprehensive and should only be used as a starting point. It only contains organisations that have a national remit and does not include organisations that provide general advice and support solely to members of a particular religion, country or ethnic group. For further details of groups, look for charitable and voluntary organisations in your local phone book, or contact your local council for voluntary service (CVS) (sometimes called Voluntary Action) which should be listed in the phone book.

The following general welfare section includes 'Benefit and grants information' and 'Debt and financial advice', which may be of particular relevance during these difficult economic times.

There is also a separate section 'Service and regimental funds' (see page 148), which details where support and advice for ex-service men and women and their families in need can be sought.

Welfare

General

Advice NI, 1 Rushfield Avenue, Belfast BT7 3FP (tel: 02890 645919; email: info@adviceni.net; website: www.adviceni.net). For information on sources of advice and support in Northern Ireland.

National Association of Citizens Advice Bureaux (NACAB), Myddelton House, 115–123 Pentonville Road, London N1 9LZ (tel: 020 7833 2181 [admin only]; email: info@nacab.org.uk; website: www.nacab.org.uk). For details of your local Citizens Advice office please see the website. Online advice is also available on a range of topics from the Citizens Adviceguide website: www.adviceguide.org.uk.

The Salvation Army, Territorial Headquarters, 101 Newington Causeway, London SE1 6BN (tel: 020 7367 4500; email: info@ salvationarmy.org.uk; website: www. salvationarmy.org.uk)

Samaritans, The Upper Mill, Kingston Road, Ewell KT17 2AF (tel: 020 8394 8300; 24-hour helpline: 0845 790 9090; see phone book for local number; email: admin@samaritans. org (general) jo@samaritans.org (helpline); website: www.samaritans. org)

Benefit and grants information

The Association of Charity Officers (ACO), Central House, 14 Upper Woburn Place, London WC1H 0NN (tel: 020 7255 4480; email: info@aco. uk.net; website: www.aco.uk.net)

Benevolence Today, (website: www. benevolencetoday.org)

Child Benefit, PO Box 1, Newcastle upon Tyne NE88 1AA (helpline: 0845 302 1444 [8am–8pm Monday to Friday and until 4pm Saturday]; textphone: 0845 302 1474; website: www.hmrc.gov.uk/childbenefit)

Child Maintenance Options, (tel: 0800 988 0988 [Mon–Fri, 8am–8pm and Sat 9am–4pm]; textphone: 0800 988 9888; website: www.cmoptions. org). Contact can also be made through an online live chat feature.

Child Trust Fund, Child Trust Fund Office, Waterview Park, Mandarin Way, Washington NE38 8QG (helpline: 0845 302 1470 [Mon–Fri, 9am–5.30pm]; textphone: 0845 366 7870; website: www.gov.uk/child-trust-funds)

Gov.uk, general information on money, tax and benefits (website: www.gov.uk)

Disability Benefits Helpline, Warbreck House, Warbreck Hill, Blackpool, Lancashire FY2 0YE (tel: 0845 712 3456 [Mon–Fri, 8am–6pm]; textphone: 0845 722 4433; email: DCPU.Customer-Services@dwp.gsi. gov.uk; website: www.gov.uk/browse/ benefits/disability)

Jobseekers (Benefit claim line: 0800 055 6688 [Mon–Fri, 8am–6pm]; textphone: 0800 023 4888; website: www.gov.uk/jobseekers-allowance/ overview). You may also make a claim online.

Pension Credit Claim Line, (tel: 0800 991 234 [Mon–Fri, 8am–6pm]; textphone: 0800 169 0133; website: www.gov.uk/pension-credit/overview) See the website for information on local offices.

Tax Credits helpline, Tax Credit Office, Preston PR1 4AT (tel: 0345 300 3900 [8am–8pm Monday-Friday, 8am – 4pm Saturday]; textphone 0345300 3909; website: www.hmrc. gov.uk/taxcredits)

Veterans Agency, SPVA, Norcross, Thornton Cleveleys, Lancashire FY5 3WP (Veterans helpline: 0800 169 2277 [Mon–Thurs, 8.15am–5.15pm and Fri 8.15am–4.30pm]; textphone: 0800 169 2277; email: veterans.help@spva. gsi.gov.uk; website: www.veterans-uk. info)

Winter Fuel Payments Winter Fuel Payment Team, Department for Work and Pensions, PO Box 10142, Annesley, Nottingham NG15 5WY (helpline: 0845 915 1515 [Mon–Fri, 8.30am–4.30pm]; textphone: 0845 601 5613; website: www.gov.uk/ winter-fuel-payment.

Bereavement

Cruse Bereavement Care, PO Box 800, Richmond upon Thames, Surrey TW9 1RG (tel: 020 8939 9530; helpline: 0844 477 9400; email: info@ cruse.org.uk or helpline@cruse.org.uk; website: www. crusebereavementcare.org.uk)

Natural Death Centre, In The Hill House, Watley Lane, Twyford, Winchester SO21 1QX (tel: 01962 712690; email: contact@naturaldeath. org.uk; website: www.naturaldeath. org.uk)

Survivors of Bereavement by Suicide (SOBS), The Flamsteed Centre, Albert Street, Ilkeston, Derbyshire DE7 5GU(tel: 01159 441117; helpline: 0844 561 6855 [9am–9pm daily]; minicom: 01925826204; Typetalk: 18002–01925 826204; email: sobs. admin@care4free.net; website: www. uk-sobs.org.uk)

Children

Child Bereavement UK, Clare Charity Centre, Wycombe Road, Saunderton, Buckinghamshire HP14 4BF (tel: 01494 568900; email: support@ childbereavement.org.uk; website: www.childbereavement.org.uk)

Winston's Wish, 3rd Floor, Cheltenham House, Clarence Street, Cheltenham, Gloucestershire GL50 3JR; (tel: 01242 515157; helpline: 0845 203 0405 [Mon–Fri,9am–5pm, and Wed evening 7pm–9.30pm]; email: info@ winstonswish.org.uk; website: www. winstonswish.org.uk)

Parents

Child Death helpline, York House, 37 Queen Square, London WC1N 3BH; (tel: 020 7813 8416 [admin]; helpline: 0800 282 986 or from mobiles 0808 800 6019 [Mon, Thurs and Fri, 10am–1pm; Tues–Wed, 10am–4pm; and every evening 7pm–10pm]; email: contact@ childdeathhelpline.org; website: www. childdeathhelpline.org.uk)

The Compassionate Friends, 53 North Street, Bristol BS3 1EN (tel: 0845 120 3785; helpline: 0845 123 2304 [10am–4pm and 7pm–10pm daily]; Northern Ireland helpline: 02887 788016 [10am–4pm and 7pm–9.30pm daily]; email: info@tcf.org.uk or helpline@tcf.org.uk; website: www.tcf. org.uk)

Foundation for the Study of Infant Deaths, 11 Belgrave Road, London SW1V 1RB (tel: 020 7802 3200; helpline: 0808 802 6868; email: office@fsid.org.uk or helpline@fsid.org.uk; website: www. fsid.org.uk)

Stillbirth and Neonatal Death Society (SANDS), 28 Portland Place, London W1B 1LY (tel: 020 7436 7940; helpline: 020 7436 5881 [Mon–Fri, 9.30am–5.30pm and Tues and Thurs, 6pm–10pm]; email: support@uk-sands.org [general information] or helpline@uk-sands.org; website: www. uk-sands.org)

Carers

Carers UK, 20 Great Dover Street, London SE1 4LX; (tel: 020 7378 4999; CarersLine: 0808 808 7777 [Wed–Thurs, 10am–12pm and 2pm–4pm]; email: Online contact form; website: www.carersuk.org)

Leonard Cheshire Disability, 66 South Lambeth Road, London SW8 1RL; (tel: 020 3242 0200; email: info@ LCDisability.org; website: www. lcdisability.org). Contact can also be made by completing an online enquiry form.

Children and young people

Action for Children, 3 The Boulevard, Ascot Road, Watford WD18 8AG (tel: 01923 361500; email: ask.us@ actionforchildren.org.uk; website: www.actionforchildren.org.uk)

Catch 22, 27 Pear Tree Street, London EC1V 3AG (tel: 020 7336 4800; email: information@catch-22.org.uk; website: www.catch-22.org.uk)

ChildLine, 42 Curtain Road, London EC2A 3NH (tel: 020 7825 2500; 24-hour advice helpline: 08001111; website: www.childline.org.uk). A personal inbox can be set up on the site which will allow you to send emails to Childline and save replies in similar way to a normal email service. Alternatively, send a message without signing in through the 'send Sam a message' function. You can also chat online with a ChildLine counsellor.

Coram Children's Legal Centre, University of Essex, Wivenhoe Park, Colchester, Essex, CO4 3SQ (tel: 01206 877910 [general]; helpline: 0808 802 0008) email: clc@essex.ac. uk; website: www.childrenslegalcentre. com)

The Children's Society, Edward Rudolf House, Margery Street, London WC1X 0JL (tel: 020 7841 4400; email: supportercare@ childrenssociety.org.uk; website: www.childrenssociety.org.uk)

Get Connected, PO Box 51719, London NW1 5UH. (tel: 020 7009 2500; helpline: 0808 808 4994 [1pm–11pm daily]; text: 80849; email: admin@getconnected.org.uk [general enquiries]; website: www. getconnected.org.uk). The helpline can be contacted through an online enquiry form. There is also a Webchat service available between 1pm and 11pm every day accessible through the website.

National Youth Advocacy Service, Egerton House, Tower Road, Birkenhead, Wirral CH41 1FN (tel: 01516 498700; helpline: 0300 330 3131 Mon–Fri 9am–8pm, Sat 10am–4pm; email: main@nyas.net or help@nyas.net; website: www.nyas. net)

NSPCC, Weston House, 42 Curtain Road, London EC2A 3NH (tel: 020 7825 2500; helpline: 0808 800 5000; email: help@nspcc.org.uk; website: www.nspcc.org.uk)

Save the Children UK, 1 St John's Lane, London EC1M 4AR (tel: 020 7012 6400; email: supporter.care@ savethechildren.org.uk; website: www. savethechildren.org.uk)

The Who Cares? Trust, Kemp House, 152–160 City Road, London EC1V 2NP (tel: 020 7251 3117; email: mailbox@thewhocarestrust.org.uk; website: www.thewhocarestrust.org. uk)

Youth Access, 1–2 Taylors Yard, 67 Alderbrook Road, London SW12 8AD (tel: 020 8772 9900; email: admin@youthaccess.org.uk; website: www.youthaccess.org.uk; for an online directory of information, advice and support services for young people)

Bullying

The Anti-bullying Alliance, National Children's Bureau, 8 Wakely Street, London EC1V 7QE (email: aba@ncb. org.uk; website: www.anti-bullyingalliance.org; details of the regional offices are available on the website)

Kidscape, 2 Grosvenor Gardens, London SW1W 0DH (tel: 020 7730 3300; helpline: 0845 120 5204 [please note the helpline is only for parents, guardians or friends who are concerned about a child being bullied]; email: webinfo@kidscape.

org.uk; website: www.kidscape.org. uk)

Young people leaving care National Leaving Care Advisory Service (NLCAS), Catch 22, 27 Pear Tree Street, London EC1V 3AG(tel: 020 7336 4824; email: ncas@catch-22.org. uk; website: www.leavingcare.org)

Debt and financial advice

Age UK Money Matters, provides a range of advice on topics such as pensions, tax, financial management, consumer issues and benefits (website: www.ageuk.org.uk/money-matters; Age UK Advice: 0800 169 6565)

Business Debtline, (tel: 0800 197 6026 [Mon–Fri, 9am–5pm]; website: www. bdl.org.uk). The debtline does not provide advice by letter or email.

Citizens Advice: Adviceguide, for online advice on a range of topics, including debt (website: www. adviceguide.org.uk). Details of your local Citizens Advice office can be found on the website.

StepChange Debt Charity, Wade House, Merrion Centre, Leeds LS2 8NG (helpline: 0800 138 1111 [8am–8pm Mon–Fri, 9am–3pm Sun]; website: www.stepchange.org). Contact can also be made by completing an online enquiry form.

Gamblers Anonymous (GANON), c/o CVS Building, 5 Trafford Court, off Trafford Way, Doncaster DN1 1PN (helplines vary according to the day and time of the week, please check the website for details; website: www. gamblersanonymous.org.uk)

The Money Advice Service, Holborn Centre, 120 Holborn, London EC1N 2TD (tel: 0300 500 5000; typetalk: 18001 0300 500 5000 [Mon–Fri, 8am–8pm, Sat 9am–1pm]; email: enquiries@moneyadviceservice. org.uk; website: www.moneyadvice. org.uk; an online chat facility is also available.)

National Debtline, Tricorn House, 51–53 Hagley Road, Edgbaston, Birmingham B16 8TP (helpline: 0808 808 4000 [Mon–Fri, 9am–9pm and Sat 9.30am–1pm]; website: www. nationaldebtline.co.uk). Contact can also be made by completing an online enquiry form.

TaxAid, 304 Linton House, 164–180 Union Street, London SE1 0LH (tel: 020 7803 4950 [advice agencies only]; helpline: 0345 120 3779; website: www.taxaid.org.uk). Contact can also be made by completing an online enquiry form.

TPAS (Pensions Advisory Service), 11 Belgrave Road, London SW1V 1RB (tel: 020 7630 2250; pensions advice: 0845 601 2923; helpline for women: 0845 600 0806; helpline for self-employed: 0845 602 7021; email: enquiries@pensionsadvisoryservice. org.uk; website: www. pensionsadvisoryservice.org.uk)

Families

Home-Start UK, Home-Start Centre, 8–10 West Walk, Leicester LE1 7NA (tel: 01162 587900; freephone: 0800 068 6368 Mon–Fri, 8am–8pm, Sat 9am–12pm; email: info@home-start. org.uk; website: www.home-start.org. uk)

Housing

Shelter, 88 Old Street, London EC1V 9HU (tel: 0300 330 1234; helpline: 0808 800 4444; email: info@ shelter.org.uk; website: www.shelter. org.uk)

Homes and Communities Agency, Arpley House, 110 Birchwood Boulevard, Birchwood, Warrington WA3 7QH (tel: 0300 1234 500; email: mail@homesandcommunities.co.uk; website: www.homesandcommunities. co.uk)

Legal

Advice Services Alliance (ASA), The Foundry (Room 303), 156 Blackfriars Road, London SE1 8EN (tel: 020 7398 1470; email: admin@asauk.org.uk; website: www.asauk.org.uk)

Bar Pro Bono Unit, 48 Chancery Lane, London WC2A 1JF (tel: 020 7092 3960 Mon, Wed and Fri 10am–4pm; email: enquiries@ barprobono.org.uk; website: www. barprobono.org.uk)

Community Legal Advice, (tel: 0800 085 6643; helpline: 0845 345 4345 [Mon–Fri, 9am–8pm and Sat 9am–12.30pm]). An online chat facility for legal advice is also available.

Law Centres Network, 64 Great Eastern Street London EC2A 3QR

(tel: 020 7749 9120; an online enquiry form is also available; website: www. lawcentres.org.uk). See the website for information on your local law centre.

LGBT

The Lesbian and Gay Foundation (LGF), 5 Richmond Street, Manchester M1 3HF (helpline: 0845 330 3030 [6pm–10pm daily]; email: info@lgf.org.uk; website: www.lgf.org. uk)

Stonewall, Tower Building, York Road, London SE1 7NX (Office (admin): 020 7593 1850; Info Line: 0800 050 2020 [Mon–Fri, 9.30am–5.30pm]; email: info@ stonewall.org.uk; website: www. stonewall.org.uk)

Men's Rights

Mankind, Flook House, Belvedere Road, Taunton, Somerset TA1 1BT (tel: 01823334244; helpline: 01823 334244 [Mon–Fri, 10am–4pm and 7pm–9pm]; email: admin@mankind. org.uk; website: www.mankind.org. uk)

Missing people

Missing People, 284 Upper Richmond Road West, London SW14 7JE; (tel: 020 8392 4590; helpline: 116 000; email: info@missingpeople.org.uk [general]; or report@missingpeople. org.uk [to report a missing person])

Offenders and ex-offenders

APEX Trust, Unit 1, Ruskin Leisure Ltd, Ruskin Drive, St Helens, Merseyside WA10 6RP (tel: 01744 612898; email: sthelens@apextrust. com)

National Association for the Care and Rehabilitation of Offenders (NACRO), Park Place, 10–12 Lawn Lane, London SW8 1UD (tel: 020 7840 7200; Resettlement Advice Service: 020 7840 1212; email: helpline@nacro.org.uk; website: www. nacro.org.uk)

Prisoners Abroad, 89–93 Fonthill Road, Finsbury Park, London N4 3JH (tel: 020 7561 6820; helpline: 0808 172 0098; email: info@ prisonersabroad.org.uk; website: www.prisonersabroad.org.uk)

UNLOCK, the National Association of Reformed Offenders, 35a High Street, Snodland, Kent ME6 5AG (tel:

01634 247350; helpline open Tues and Thurs 9am–5pm; email: advice@unlock.org.uk; website: www.unlock.org.uk)

Families of offenders

Offenders' Families helpline, (tel: 0808 808 2003 [Mon–Fri, 9am–5pm and Sat 10am–3pm]; email: info@offendersfamilieshelpline.org.uk. Information sheets are available on request by post or can be downloaded from the website: www.offendersfamilieshelpline.org.uk)

Partners of Prisoners and Families Support Group (POPS), Valentine House, 1079 Rochdale Road, Blackley, Manchester M9 8AJ (tel: 01617 021000; email: mail@partnersofprisoners.co.uk; website: www.partnersofprisoners.co.uk)

Prisoners' Families and Friends Service, 20 Trinity Street, London SE1 1DB (tel: 020 7403 4091; helpline: 0808 808 3444; email: info@pffs.org.uk; website: www.pffs.org.uk)

Women offenders and ex-offenders

Creative and Supportive Trust (CAST), Unit 1 Lysander Mews, Lysander Grove, Upper Holloway, London N19 3QP (tel: 020 7281 9928)

Older people

Friends of the Elderly, 40–42 Ebury Street, London SW1W 0LZ (tel: 020 7730 8263; email: enquiries@fote.org.uk; website: www.fote.org.uk)

Age UK, Tavis House, 1–6 Tavistock Square, London WC1H 9NA (helpline: 0800 169 6565 [Mon–Fri, 9am–4pm]; email: contact@ageuk.org.uk; website: www.ageuk.org.uk)

The Age and Employment Network, Tavis House, 1–6 Tavistock Square, London WC1H 9NA (tel: 020 3033 1507; email: info@taen.org.uk; website: www.taen.org.uk)

Parenting

Home-Start UK, Home-Start Centre, 8–10 West Walk, Leicester LE1 7NA (tel: 01162 587900; freephone: 0800 068 6368 Mon–Fri, 8am–8pm, Sat 9am–12pm; email: info@home-start.org.uk; website: www.home-start.org.uk)

Family Lives, CAN Mezzanine, 49–51 East Road, London N1 6AH (tel: 020 7553 3094; 24-hour helpline: 0808 800 2222; website: www.parentlineplus.org.uk). Contact can also be made by using the online support service.

Twins and Multiple Births Association (TAMBA), Lower Ground Floor and The Studio, Hitherbury House, 97 Portsmouth Road, Guilford, Surrey GU2 4YF (tel: 01483 304442; helpline: 0800 138 0509 [10am–1pm and 7pm–10pm daily]; email: asktwinline@tamba.org.uk; website: www.tamba.org.uk)

Abduction

Reunite (National Council for Abducted Children), P.O Box 7124, Leicester LE1 7XX (tel: 01162 555345; Advice line: 01162 556234; email: reunite@dircon.co.uk; website: www.reunite.org)

Adoption and fostering

British Association for Adoption and Fostering (BAAF), Saffron House, 6–10Kirby Street, London EC1N 8TS (tel: 020 7421 2600; email: mail@baaf.org.uk; website: www.baaf.org.uk)

Adoption UK, Linden House, 55 The Green, South Bar Street, Banbury OX19 9AB (tel: 01295 752240; helpline: 0844 848 7900 [Mon–Fri, 10am–4pm]; online contact form also available; website: www.adoptionuk.org.uk)

After Adoption, Unit 5 Citygate, 5 Blantyre Street, Manchester M15 4JJ (tel: 01618 394932; Action Line: 0800 056 8578; email: information@afteradoption.org.uk; website: www.afteradoption.org.uk)

Fostering Network, 87 Blackfriars Road, London SE1 8HA (tel: 020 7620 6400; Fosterline: England – 0800 040 7675, Wales – 0800 316 7664, Scotland – 01412 041400, Northern Ireland 02890 705056 email: fosterline@fostering.net; website: www.fostering.net)

National Association of Child Contact Centres, 1 Heritage Mews, High Pavement, Nottingham NG1 1HN (tel: 0845 450 0280 or 01159 484557 from mobiles [call for information on nearest centre]; email: contact@naccc.org.uk; website: www.naccc.org.uk)

Post-Adoption Centre, 5 Torriano Mews, Torriano Avenue, London NW5 2RZ (tel: 020 7284 0555; Advice line: 020 7284 5879 [Mon–Fri, 10am–1pm and Wed–Thurs 5.30pm–7.30pm]; email: advice@postadoptioncentre.org.uk; website: www.postadoptioncentre.org.uk)

Childcare

Daycare Trust (National Childcare Campaign), 2nd Floor, 81 Southwark Bridge Road, London SE1 0NQ (tel: 020 7940 7510; tel: 0845 872 6260 or 020 7940 7510; email: info@daycaretrust.org.uk; website: www.daycaretrust.org.uk)

Family Rights Group, The Print House, 18 Ashwin Street, London E8 3DL (tel: 020 7923 2628; advice line: 0808 801 0366 [Mon–Fri, 9.30am–3:30pm]; email: advice@frg.org.uk; website: www.frg.org.uk)

Divorce

Both Parents Forever, 39 Cloonmore Avenue, Orpington, Kent BR6 9LE (helpline: 01689 854343 [8am–9pm daily])

Families Need Fathers, 134 Curtain Road, London EC2A 3AR (helpline: 0300 0300 110 [Mon–Fri, 6pm–10pm]; email: fnf@fnf.org.uk; website: www.fnf.org.uk)

National Family Mediation, Margaret Jackson Centre, 4 Barnfield Hill, Exeter, Devon EX1 1SR (tel: 0300 4000 636; email: general@nfm.org.uk; website: www.nfm.org.uk)

NCDSW (National Council for the Divorced and Separated and Widowed), 68 Parkes Hall Road, Woodsetton, Dudley DY1 3SR (tel: 07041 478120; email: secretary@ncdsw.org.uk; website: www.ncdsw.org.uk)

CAFCASS (Children and Family Court Advisory and Support Service), 6th Floor, Sanctuary Buildings, Great Smith Street, London SW1P 3BT (tel: 0844 353 3350; email: webenquiries@cafcass.gsi.gov.uk; website: www.cafcass.gov.uk)

Pregnancy

ARC (Antenatal Results and Choices), 345 City Road, London EC1V 1LR (tel: 020 7713 7356; helpline: 0845 077 2290 [Mon–Fri, 10am–5.30pm]; email: info@arc-uk.org; website: www.arc-uk.org)

British Pregnancy Advisory Service (BPAS), 20 Timothys Bridge Road, Stratford Enterprise Park, Stratford upon-Avon, Warwickshire CV37 9BF

(tel: 0845 365 5050; Advice line: 0845 730 4030 or 01789 508211 from mobiles; email: info@bpas.org; website: www.bpas.org)

Brook, 50 Featherstone Street, London EC1Y 8RT (tel: 020 7284 6040; helpline [for people under 25]: 0808 802 1234 [Mon–Fri, 9am–6pm]; email: admin@brook.org.uk; website: www.brook.org.uk). You may also use the Ask Brook facility to ask questions via email or text.

Disability Pregnancy and Parenthood International (DPPI), 336 Brixton Road, London SW9 7AA (tel: 020 7263 3088; helpline: 0800 018 4730 [Mon and Thurs 10.30am–3pm; email: info@dppi.org.uk; website: www.dppi.org.uk)

National Childbirth Trust, Alexandra House, Oldham Terrace, London W3 6NH (tel: 0300 330 0700 website: www.nct.org.uk; email: ceo@nct.org.uk). Contact can also be made by completing an online enquiry form.

Grandparents

Grandparents Association, Moot House, The Stow, Harlow, Essex CM20 3AG (tel: 01279 428040; helpline: 0845 434 9585 [Mon–Fri, 10am–4pm]; email: advice@grandparents-association.org.uk; website: www.grandparents-association.org.uk)

Mothers

Mothers Apart from their Children (MATCH), BM Box No. 6334, London WC1N 3XX (email: enquiries@matchmothers.org; website: www.matchmothers.org)

Mumsnet, (email: contactus@mumsnet.com; website: www.mumsnet.com)

Single parents

Gingerbread, 520 Highgate Studios, 53–79 Highgate Road London NW5 1TL (tel: 020 7428 5420; helpline: 0808 802 0925 [Mon, 10am–6pm, Tues, Thurs and Fri 10am–4pm and Wed 10am–1pm and 5pm–7pm]; website: www.gingerbread.org.uk). Contact can also be made by completing an online enquiry form.

One Space, for information, advice and links to online support groups (website: www.onespace.org.uk)

Poverty

Care International, 9th Floor, 89 Albert Embankment, London SE1 7TP (tel: 020 7091 6000; website: www.careinternational.org.uk). Contact can also be made by completing an online enquiry form.

Counselling, 5 Pear Tree Walk, Wakefield, West Yorkshire WF2 0HW (website: www.counselling.ltd.uk)

Family Action 501–505 Kingsland Road, London E8 4AU (tel: 020 7254 6251; grants service: 020 7241 7459 [Tues, Wed and Thurs 2pm–4pm]; website: www.family-action.org.uk). Contact can also be made by completing an online enquiry form.

Law Centres Network, 64 Great Eastern Street London EC2A 3QR (tel: 020 7749 9120; an online enquiry form is also available; website: www.lawcentres.org.uk). See the website for information on your local law centre.

The Trussell Trust, Unit 9 Ashfield Trading Estate, Ashfield Road, Salisbury SP2 7HL (tel: 01722 580180; email: enquiries@trusselltrust.org; website: www.trusselltrust.org). You can also use the sites search facility to find your nearest foodbank.

Refugees and asylum seekers

Asylum Aid, Club UnionHouse, 253–254 Upper Street, London N1 1RY (tel: 020 7354 9631; advice line: 020 7354 9264 [Mon 1pm–4pm and Thurs 10am–12:30pm]; email: info@asylumaid.org.uk; website: www.asylumaid.org.uk)

Migrant helpline, Charlton House, Dour Street, Dover, Kent CT16 1AT (tel: 01304 203977; helpline: 020 8683 4767; website: www.migranthelpline.org.uk; an online contact form is also available)

Refugee Action, Victoria Charity Centre, 11 Belgrave Road, London SW1V 1RB (tel: 020 7952 1511; email: info@refugee-action.org.uk [for agency-wide matters only]; website: www.refugee-action.org.uk). See the website for a list of local offices.

Refugee Council, PO Box 68614, London E15 9DQ; (tel: 020 7346 6700; advice line: 0808 808 2255 [Mon, Tues, Thurs and Fri 9.30am–1pm and 2pm–4.30pm and Wed 2pm–5pm]; Children's Panel: 0808 808 0500 [Mon–Fri, 9.30am–5.30pm]; website: www.refugeecouncil.org.uk)

Refugee Support Centre, 47 South Lambeth Road, London SW8 1RH (tel: 020 7820 3606). Relationships Albany Trust Counselling, 239a Balham High Road, London SW17 7BE (tel: 020 8767 1827; email: info@albanytrust.org; website: www.albanytrust.org.uk)

Family Planning Association, 50 Featherstone Street, London EC1Y 8QU (tel: 020 7608 5240; helpline: 0845 122 8690 [Mon–Fri 9am–5pm]; email: general@fpa.org.uk; website: www.fpa.org.uk)

Relate (National Marriage Guidance) Premier House, Carolina Court, Lakeside, Doncaster DN4 5RA (tel: 0300 100 1234; email: enquiries@relate.org.uk; website: www.relate.org.uk)

Social isolation

Rural Stress helpline, Arthur Rank Centre, Stoneleigh Park, Kenilworth, Warwickshire CV8 2LG (helpline: 0845 094 8286 [9am–5pm weekdays]; email: help@ruralstresshelpline.co.uk website: www.ruralstresshelpline.co.uk)

The Single Concern Group, P.O. Box 40, Minehead TA24 5YS (tel: 01643 708008; helpline: 01643 708008 [Office Hours])

Squatters

Advisory Service for Squatters (ASS), Angel Alley, 84b, Whitechapel High Street, London E1 7QX (tel: 020 3216 0098; email: advice@squatter.org.uk; website: www.squatter.org.uk)

Victims of accidents and crimes

Abuse

NSPCC, Weston House, 42 Curtain Road, London EC2A 3NH (tel: 020 7825 2500; helpline: 0808 800 5000; email: help@nspcc.org.uk; website: www.nspcc.org.uk)

Action on Elder Abuse (AEA), PO Box 60001, Streatham SW16 9BY (tel: 020 8835 9280; helpline: 0808 808 8141; email: enquires@elderabuse.org.uk; website: www.elderabuse.org.uk)

The Clinic for Boundaries, 49–51 East Road, London N1 6AH (tel: 020 3468 4194; email: info@

professionalboundaries.org.uk website: www.professionalboundaries. org.uk)

Crime

Victim Support, Octavia House, 50 Banner Street, London EC1Y 8ST (tel: 020 7336 1730; Supportline: 0845 303 0900 [weekdays 9am–9pm and Sat–Sun, 9am–7pm]; email: supportline@victimsupport.org.uk; website: www.victimsupport.org). For details on the regional offices please see the website.

Voice UK, Kelvin House, RTC Business Centre, London Road, Derby DE24 8UP (tel: 01332291042; helpline: 0808 802 8686; textphone: 07797 800642; email: voice@voiceuk. org.uk or helpline@voiceuk.org.uk; website: www.voiceuk.org.uk)

Disasters

Disaster Action, No.4, 71 Upper Berkeley Street, London W1H 7DB (tel: 01483 799066; email: pameladix@disasteraction.org.uk; website: www.disasteraction.org.uk)

Domestic violence

Broken Rainbow (tel: 0845 260 5560; helpline: 0300 999 5428 [Mon and Thurs 10am–8pm, Tues and Wed 10am–5pm]; email: mail@broken-rainbow.org.uk or help@brokenrainbow.org.uk; website: www.brokenrainbow.org.uk)

Men's Advice Line and Enquiries (MALE), (helpline: 0808 801 0327 [Mon–Fri, 10am–1pm and 2pm–5pm]; email: info@ mensadviceline.org.uk; website: www. mensadviceline.org.uk)

National Centre for Domestic Violence, 5 Riverview, Walnut Tree Close, Guildford GU1 4UX (24-hour helpline: 0844 804 4999; minicom: 18001 08009702070; text: 'NCDV' to 60777; email: office@ncdv.org.uk; website: www.ncdv.org.uk)

Women's Aid Federation, Head Office, PO BOX 391, Bristol BS99 7WS (tel: 01179 444411; national 24-hour helpline: 0808 200 0247; email: info@womensaid.org.uk or helpline@womensaid.org.uk; website: www.womensaid.org.uk). For details on the regional offices please see the website.

Medical accidents

Action for Victims of Medical Accidents (AVMA), 44 High Street, Croydon, London CR0 1YB (tel: 020 8688 9555 [admin only]; helpline: 0845 123 2352; email: advice@avma. org.uk; website: www.avma.org.uk)

Rape

Rape Crisis Centre, BCM Box 4444, London WC1N 3XX (helpline: 0808 802 9999 [12pm–2.30pm and 7pm–9.30pmdaily); email: info@ rapecrisis.org.uk; website: www. rapecrisis.co.uk). See website for contact information on local rape crisis centres.

Women Against Rape (WAR) and Black Women's Rape Action Project, Crossroads Women's Centre,25 Wolsey Mews NW5 2DX (tel: 020 7482 2496 [Mon–Fri, 1.30pm–4pm]; email: war@womenagainstrape.net orbwrap@dircon.co.uk; website: www. womenagainstrape.net)

Road accidents

RoadPeace, Shakespeare Business Centre, 245a Cold Harbour Lane, Brixton, London SW9 8RR (tel: 020 7733 1603; helpline: 0845 450 0355; email: info@roadpeace.org; website: www.roadpeace.org)

Widows

National Association of Widows, 48 Queens Road, Coventry CV1 3EH (tel: 02476 634848; website: www. widows.uk.net)

Work issues

Employment Tribunals Enquiry Line, 3rd Floor, Alexandra House, 14–22, The Parsonage, Manchester M3 2JA (Public Enquiry Line: 0845 795 9775; minicom: 0845 757 3722; gsi.gov.uk; website: www.justice.gov.uk/tribunals/ employment). See website for the contact details of local employment tribunals.

Public Concern at Work, 3rd Floor, Bank Chambers, 6–10 Borough High Street, London SE1 9QQ (tel: 020 7404 6609; email: helpline@pcaw.co. uk; website: www.pcaw.co.uk)

Women

Refuge, Fourth Floor, International House, 1 St Katharine's Way, London E1W 1UN (tel: 020 7395 7700 (general); 24-hour helpline: 0808 200 0247; email: info@refuge.org.uk; website: www.refuge.org.uk)

Women and Girls Network, PO Box 13095, London W14 0FE (tel: 020 7610 4678; helpline: 020 7610 4345 [Mon 10am–1pm, Tues and Wed 6.30pm–9.30pm, Fri and Sat 10am–1pm]; email: website: www. wgn.org.uk; an online contact facility is also available)

Women's Health Concern, 4–6 Eton Place, Marlow, Buckinghamshire SL7 2QA (tel: 01628 890199; helpline: 0845 123 2319; email and telephone advice is available for a small fee; website: www.womens-healthconcern. org)

Illness and disability

Disability (general)

Action Medical Research, Vincent House, North Parade, Horsham, West Sussex RH12 2DP (tel: 01403 210406; email: info@action.org.uk; website: www.action.org.uk)

Contact a Family, 209–211 City Road, London EC1V 1JN (tel: 020 7608 8700; helpline: 0808 808 3555; textphone 0808 808 3556; email: info@cafamily.org.uk; website: www.cafamily.org.uk)

Disabled Living Foundation (DLF), 380–384 Harrow Road, London W9 2HU (tel: 020 7289 6111; helpline: 0845 130 9177 [Mon–Fri, 10am–4pm]; email: helpline@dlf.org.uk; website: www.dlf.org.uk)

Disabled Parents' Network, Poynters House, Poynters Road, Dunstable LU5 4TP (helpline and general enquiries: 0300 3300 639; website: www.disabledparentsnetwork.org.uk; online contact facility also available)

Disabilities Trust, First Floor, 32 Market Place, Burgess Hill, West Sussex RH15 9NP (tel: 01444 239123; email: info@thedtgroup.org; website: www.disabilities-trust.org.uk)

Disability Rights, 12 City Forum, 250 City Road, London EC1V 8AF (tel: 020 7250 3222; there are a number of different advice lines for different issues, please see the website for more information, Independent Living Advice Line: 0845 026 4748; email: enquiries@disabilityrightsuk.org or independentliving@disabilityrightsuk.org; website: www.disabilityrightsuk.org)

Disability Law Service (DLS), 39–45 Cavell Street, London E1 2BP (tel: 020 7791 9800; minicom: 020 7791 9801; email: advice@dls.org.uk; website: www.dls.org.uk)

Disability Pregnancy and Parenthood International (DPPI), 336 Brixton Road, London SW9 7AA (tel: 020 7263 3088; helpline: 0800 018 4730 [Mon and Thurs 10.30am–3pm; email: info@dppi.org.uk; website: www.dppi.org.uk)

I CAN's, 8 Wakley Street, London EC1V 7QE (tel: 0845 225 4073; email: info@ican.org.uk; website: www.ican.org.uk)

* Jewish Care, Amélie House, Maurice and Vivienne Wohl Campus, 221 Golders Green Road, London NW11 9DQ (tel: 020 8922 2000; helpline: 020 8922 2222 [Mon–Thurs, 8am–7pm and Fri 8am–2pm]; email: jcdirect@jcare.org; website: www.jewishcare.org)

Kids, National Office, 49 Mecklenburgh Square, London WC1N 2NY (tel: 020 7520 0405; email: enquiries@kids.org.uk; website: www.kids.org.uk)

PHAB England, PHAB Centre, Summit House, 50 Wandle Road, Croydon CR0 1DF (tel: 020 8667 9443; email: info@phab.org.uk; website: www.phab.org.uk)

Queen Elizabeth's Foundation (QEFD), Leatherhead Court, Woodlands Road, Leatherhead, Surrey KT22 0BN (tel: 01372 841100; online contact form also available; website: www.qefd.org.uk)

RESPOND, 3rd Floor, 24–32 Stephenson Way, London NW1 2HD (tel: 020 7383 0700; helpline: 0808 808 0700; email: admin@respond.org.uk; website: www.respond.org.uk)

Addiction

Addaction, 67–69 Cowcross Street, London EC1M 6PU (tel: 020 7251 5860; email: info@addaction.org.uk; website: www.addaction.org.uk)

Tacade (Advisory Council on Alcohol and Drug Education), Old Exchange Building, 6 St Ann's Passage, King Street, Manchester M2 6AD (tel: 0844 963 2427; email: lifeskillsmandy@tacade.co.uk; website: www.tacade.com)

Ageing

Age UK, Tavis House, 1–6 Tavistock Square, London WC1H 9NA (helpline: 0800 169 6565 [Mon–Fri, 9am–4pm]; email: contact@ageuk.org.uk; website: www.ageuk.org.uk)

* Independent Age, 6 Avonmore Road, London W14 8RL, (tel: 020 7605 4200; advice line: 0845 262 1863; email: charity@independentage.org)

AIDS/HIV

National Aids Trust, New City Cloisters, 196 Old Street, London EC1V 9FR (tel: 020 7814 6767; email: info@nat.org.uk; website: www.nat.org.uk)

ADVICE ORGANISATIONS

Terrence Higgins Trust,
314–320 Grays Inn Road, London
WC1X 8DP (tel: 020 7812 1600;
advice and support: 0808 802 1221
[Mon–Fri, 10am–8pm]; email: info@
tht.org.uk; website: www.tht.org.uk)

Alcohol

Al-Anon Family Groups UK and Eire
(AFG), 61 Great Dover Street,
London SE1 4YF (helpline: 020 7403
0888 [10am–10pm]; email:
enquiries@al-anonuk.org.uk; website:
www.al-anonuk.org.uk)

Alcohol Concern, Suite B5, West
Wing, New City Cloisters, 196 Old
Street, London EC1V 9FR (tel: 020
7566 9800; website: www.
alcoholconcern.org.uk; online contact
form available)

Alcoholics Anonymous (AA), General
Service Office, PO Box 1, 10 Toft
Green, York YO1 7NJ (tel: 01904
644026; helpline: 0845 769 7555;
email: help@alcoholics-anonymous.
org.uk; website: www.alcoholics-
anonymous.org.uk)

Drinkline, helpline: 0800 917 8282
[Mon–Fri, 9am–8pm, Sat-Sun, 11am
– 4pm].

Foundation 66, 7 Holyrood Street,
London SE1 2EL (tel: 020 7234 9940;
email: info@foundation66.org.uk;
website: www.foundation66.org.uk)

Turning Point, Standon House,
21 Mansell Street, London E1 8AA
(tel: 020 7481 7600; email: info@
turningpoint.co.uk; website: www.
turning-point.co.uk)

Allergy

Action Against Allergy, PO Box 278,
Twickenham TW1 4QQ (tel: 020 8892
4949; helpline: 020 8892 2711; email:
AAA@actionagainstallergy.freeserve.
co.uk; website: www.
actionagainstallergy.co.uk)

Allergy UK, Planwell House, LEFA
Business Park, Edgington Way
Sidcup, Kent DA14 5BH (helpline:
01322 619898; email: info@allergyuk.
org; website: www.allergyuk.org)

Alopecia areata and alopecia androgenetica

Alopecia UK, 5 Titchwell Road,
London SW18 3LW (tel: 020 8333
1661; email: please see website for
details; website: www.alopeciaonline.
org.uk)

Alzheimer's disease

* Alzheimer's Society, Devon House,
58 St Katharine's Way, London
E1W 1JX (tel: 020 7264 5980;
helpline: 0300 222 1122 [Mon–Fri,
9am–5pm; Sat-Sun, 10am–4pm];
website: www.alzheimers.org.uk;
online contact form available)

Angelmann syndrome

ASSERT (Angelman Syndrome
Support Education and Research), PO
Box 4962, Nuneaton CV11 9FD (tel:
0300 999 0102; email: assert@
angelmanuk.org; website: www.
angelmanuk.org)

Ankylosing spondylitis

National Ankylosing Spondylitis
Society (NASS), Unit 0.2, One
Victoria Villas, Richmond, Surrey
TW9 2GW (tel: 020 8948 9117; email:
admin@nass.co.uk; website: www.
nass.co.uk)

Arthritis/rheumatic diseases

Arthritis Care, Floor 4, Linen Court,
10 East Road, London N1 6AD (tel:
020 7380 6500; helpline: 0808 800
4050 [Mon–Fri, 10am–4pm]; email:
info@arthritiscare.org.uk or
helplines@arthritiscare.org.uk;
website: www.arthritiscare.org.uk)

Arthritis Research UK, Copeman
House, St Mary's Gate, Chesterfield
S41 7TD (tel: 0300 790 0400; email:
enquiries@arthritisresearchuk.org;
website: www.arthritisresearchuk.org)

Arthrogryposis

Arthrogryposis Group (TAG), PO
Box1199, Spalding, Lincolnshire
PE11 9EY (tel: 0800 028 4447; email:
info@taguk.org.uk; website: www.
tagonline.org.uk)

Asthma

Asthma UK, Summit House,
70 Wilson Street, London EC2A 2DB
(tel: 0800 121 6255; Advice line: 0800
121 6244; email: info@asthma.org.uk;
website: www.asthma.org.uk)

Ataxia

* Ataxia UK, Lincoln House,
Kennington Park, 1–3 Brixton Road,
London SW9 6DE (tel: 020 7582
1444; helpline: 0845 644 0606
[Mon–Thurs, 10.30am–3.30pm and
Fri 10am–1pm]; email: enquiries@
ataxia.org.uk or

helpline@ataxia.org.uk; website: www.
ataxia.org.uk)

Autism

National Autistic Society (NAS),
393 City Road, London EC1V 1NG
(tel: 020 7833 2299; helpline: 0808
800 4104; email: nas@nas.org.uk;
website: www.autism.org.uk)

Back pain

Back Care, 16 Elmtree Road,
Teddington, Middlesex TW11 8ST
(tel: 020 8977 5474; helpline: 0845
130 2704; website: www.backcare.org.
uk). Contact can also be made by
completing a helpline enquiry form.

Behçet's syndrome

Behçet's Syndrome Society, 8 Abbey
Gardens, Evesham, Worcester
WR11 4SP (tel: 0845 130 7328;
helpline: 0845 130 7329; email: info@
behcetsdisease.org.uk; website: www.
behcets.org.uk)

Blind/Partially sighted

CALIBRE (Cassette Library of
Recorded Books), Aylesbury,
Buckinghamshire HP22 5XQ (tel:
01296 432339; website: www.calibre.
org.uk). Contact can also be made by
completing an online enquiry form.

International Glaucoma Association
(IGA), Woodcote House,
15 Highpoint Business Village,
Henwood, Ashford, Kent TN24 8DH
(tel: 01233 648164; helpline: 01233
648170; email: info@iga.org.uk;
website: www.iga.org.uk)

Listening Books, 12 Lant Street,
London SE1 1QH (tel: 020 7407 9417;
email: info@listening-books.org.uk;
website: www.listening-books.org.uk)

National Federation of the Blind of
the UK, Sir John Wilson House,
215 Kirkgate, Wakefield WF1 1JG
(tel: 01924 291313; email: nfbuk@
nufbk.org; website: www.nfbuk.org)

Partially Sighted Society,
7–9 Bennetthorpe, Doncaster
DN2 6AA (tel: 0844 477 4966; email:
info@partsight.org.uk; website: www.
partsight.org.uk)

* Royal National Institute for the
Blind (RNIB), 105 Judd Street,
London WC1H 9NE (helpline: 0303
123 9999; email: helpline@rnib.org.
uk; website: www.rnib.org.uk)

RP Fighting Blindness, PO Box 350, Buckingham MK18 5GZ (tel: 01280 821334; helpline: 0845 123 2354; email: info@rpfightingblindness.org.uk or helpline@rpfightingblindness.org.uk; website: www.rpfightingblindness.org.uk)

Voluntary Transcribers' Group, 8 Segbourne Road, Rubery, Birmingham B45 9SX (tel: 01214 534268; email: braillist@btinternet.com)

Bone marrow

Anthony Nolan Trust, 2 Heathgate Place, 75–87 Agincourt Road, London NW3 2NU (tel: 0303 303 0303; email: info@anthonynolan.org; website: www.anthonynolan.org.uk)

Bowel disorders

National Advisory Service for Parents of Children with a Stoma (NASPCS), 51 Anderson Drive, Darvel, Ayrshire KA17 0DE (tel: 01560 322024)

Children with Crohn's and Colitis (CICRA) Parkgate House, 356 West Barnes Lane, Motspur Park, Surrey KT3 6NB (tel: 020 8949 6209; email: support@cicra.org; website: www.cicra.org)

National Association for Colitis and Crohn's Disease (NACC), 4 Beaumont House, Sutton Road, St Albans, Hertfordshire AL1 5HH (tel: 01727 830038; helpline: 0845 130 2233 [Mon–Fri, 10am–1pm] and 0845 130 3344 [Mon–Fri 1–3pm and 6.30–9pm]; email: info@CrohnsAndColitis.org.uk; website: www.nacc.org.uk)

Brain injury

British Institute for Brain-Injured Children (BIBIC), Knowle Hall, Bridgwater, Somerset TA7 8PJ (tel: 01278684060; email: info@bibic.org.uk; website: www.bibic.org.uk)

Brittle bones

* Brittle Bone Society, Grant-Paterson House, 30 Guthrie Street, Dundee DD1 5BS (tel: 01382 204446; helpline: 0800 028 2459; email: contact@brittlebone.org; website: www.brittlebone.org)

Burns

British Burn Association, Royal College of Surgeons, 35–43 Lincoln's Inn Fields, London WC2A 3PE (tel: 020 7869 6923; email: info@britishburnassociation.org; website: www.britishburnassociation.org)

Children's Burns Trust, 38 Buckingham Palace Road, London SW1W 0RE (tel: 020 7233 8333; email: info@cbtrust.org.uk; website: www.cbtrust.org.uk)

Cancer and leukaemia

Action Cancer, 1 Marlborough Park South, Belfast BT9 6XS (tel: 02890 803344; email: info@actioncancer.org; website: www.actioncancer.org)

* CLIC Sargent Cancer Care for Children, Griffin House, 161 Hammersmith Road, London W6 8SG (tel: 0300 330 0803; website: www.clicsargent.org.uk; online enquiry form also available)

* Leukaemia Care Society, One Birch Court, Blackpole East, Worcester WR3 8SG (tel: 01905 755977; helpline: 0808 801 0444; email: care@leukaemiacare.org.uk; website: www.leukaemiacare.org.uk; online chat facility also available)

* Macmillan Cancer Relief, 89 Albert Embankment, London SE1 7UQ (tel: 020 7840 7840; helpline: 0808 808 0000; website: www.macmillan.org.uk). Contact can also be made by completing an online enquiry form.

Marie Curie Foundation, 89 Albert Embankment, London SE1 7TP (tel: 0800 716 146; email: info@mariecurie.org.uk; website: www.mariecurie.org.uk)

Tak Tent Cancer Support www.taktent.org.

Tenovous Cancer Information Centre, 9th Floor, Gleider House, Ty Glas Road, Llanishen, Cardiff CF14 5BD (tel: 02920 768850; helpline: 0808 808 1010; email: post@tenovus.com; website: www.tenovus.org.uk)

Cerebral palsy

SCOPE, 6 Market Road, London N7 9PW (tel: 020 7619 7100; helpline: 0808 800 3333; email: response@scope.org.uk; website: www.scope.org.uk)

Chest/lungs

British Lung Foundation, 73–75 Goswell Road, London EC1V 7ER (tel: 020 7688 5555; helpline: 0845 850 5020; website: www.blf.org.uk; online contact form also available)

Child growth

Child Growth Foundation, 21 Malvern Drive, Sutton Coldfield B76 1PZ (tel: 020 8995 0257; email: info@childgrowthfoundation.org; website: www.childgrowthfoundation.org)

Cleft lip/palate disorder

Cleft Lip and Palate Association (CLAPA), 1st Floor, Green Man Tower, 332B Goswell Road, London EC1V 7LQ (tel: 020 7833 4883; email: info@clapa.com; website: www.clapa.com)

Charcot-Marie-Tooth disease

CMT International United Kingdom, 98 Broadway, Southbourne, Bournemouth BH6 4EH (tel: 0800 652 6316; email: info@cmtuk.org.uk; website: www.cmt.org.uk)

Coeliac disease

Coeliac UK, 3rd Floor, Apollo Centre, Desborough Road, High Wycombe HP11 2QW (tel: 01494 437278; helpline: 0845 305 2060; website: www.coeliac.org.uk). Contact can also be made by completing an online enquiry form.

Colostomy

Colostomy Association (CA), 2 London Court, East Street, Reading RG1 4QL (tel: 01189 391537; 24hr helpline: 0800 328 4257; email: cass@colostomyassociation.org.uk; website: www.colostomyassociation.org.uk)

Cot death

Compassionate Friends, 14 New King Street, Deptford, London SE8 3HS (helpline: 0845 123 2304; or 02887 788016 in Northern Ireland; email: helpline@tcf.org.uk; website: www.tcf.org.uk)

Foundation for the Study of Infant Deaths, 11 Belgrave Road, London SW1V 1RB (tel: 020 7802 3200; helpline: 0808 802 6868; email: office@fsid.org.uk or helpline@fsid.org.uk; website: www.fsid.org.uk)

Counselling

British Association for Counselling and Psychotherapy, 15 St John's Business Park, Lutterworth LE17 4HB, (tel: 01455 883300; email: bacp@bacp.co.uk; website: www.bacp.co.uk)

Samaritans, The Upper Mill, Kingston Road, Ewell KT17 2AF (tel: 020 8394 8300; 24-hour helpline: 0845 790 9090; see phone book for local number; email: admin@samaritans.org (general) jo@samaritans.org (helpline); website: www.samaritans.org)

SupportLine, PO Box 2860, Romford, Essex RM7 1JA (tel: 01708 765222; helpline: 01708 765200; email: info@supportline.org.uk; website: www.supportline.org.uk)

Craniosynostosis orcraniostenosis

Headlines Craniofacial Support, 8 Footes Lane, Frampton, Cottrell, Bristol BS36 2JQ (tel: 01454 850557; email: info@headlines.org.uk; website: www.headlines.org.uk)

Crohn's disease

Children with Crohn's and Colitis (CICRA) Parkgate House, 356 West Barnes Lane, Motspur Park, Surrey KT3 6NB (tel: 020 8949 6209; email: support@cicra.org; website: www.cicra.org)

National Association for Colitis and Crohn's Disease (NACC), 4 Beaumont House, Sutton Road, St Albans, Hertfordshire AL1 5HH (tel: 01727 830038; helpline: 0845 130 2233 [Mon–Fri, 10am–1pm] and 0845 130 3344 [Mon–Fri 1–3pm and 6.30–9pm]; email: info@CrohnsAndColitis.org.uk; website: www.nacc.org.uk)

Crying/restless babies

The CRY-SIS Helpline, BM CRY-SIS, London WC1N 3XX (sae required); (helpline: 0845 122 8669 [9am–10pm daily]; website: www.cry-sis.org.uk)

Cystic fibrosis

Butterfly Trust, Swanston Steading, 109/3B Swanston Road, Edinburgh EH10 7DS (tel: 01314 455590; email: info@butterflytrust.org.uk; website: www.butterflytrust.org.uk)

* Cystic Fibrosis Trust, 11 London Road, Bromley, Kent BR1 1BY (tel: 020 8464 7211; support helpline: 0300 373 1000; email: enquiries@cftrust.org.uk; website: www.cftrust.org.uk)

Deafblind

Deafblind UK, National Centre for Deafblindness, John and Lucille Van Geest Place, Cygnet Road, Hampton, Peterborough PE7 8FD (tel: 01733358100; helpline: 0800 132 320; textphone: 0800 132 320; email: info@deafblind.org.uk; website: www.deafblind.org.uk)

* Sense, 101 Pentonville Road, London N1 9LG (tel: 0845 127 0060; textphone: 0845 127 0062; email: info@sense.org.uk; website: www.sense.org.uk)

Deafness/hearing Difficulties

Action on Hearing Loss 19–23 Featherstone Street, London EC1Y 8SL (tel: 020 7296 8000; text: 020 7296 8001; information line: 0808 808 0123 [voice] 0808 808 9000 [text]; email: informationonline@hearingloss.org.uk; website: www.actionhearingloss.org.uk)

British Deaf Association (BDA), 18 Leather Lane, London EC1N 7SU (tel: 020 7405 0090; email: bda@bda.org.uk; website: www.bda.org.uk)

Guide Dogs for the Blind Association, Burghfield Common, Reading RG7 3YG (tel: 01189 835555; email: guidedogs@guidedogs.org.uk; website: www.gdba.org.uk)

Hearing Dogs for Deaf People, The Grange, Wycombe Road, Saunderton, Buckinghamshire HP27 9NS (tel and minicom: 01844 348100; email: info@hearingdogs.org.uk; website: www.hearingdogs.org.uk)

* National Deaf Children's Society, 15 Dufferin Street, London EC1Y 8UR (tel: 020 7490 8656; minicom: 020 7490 8656; helpline: 0808 800 8880; email: ndcs@ndcs.org.uk or helpline@ndcs.org.uk; website: www.ndcs.org.uk)

Royal Association for Deaf People (RAD), Century House South, Riverside Office Centre, North Station Road, Colchester, Essex CO1 1RE (tel: 0845 688 2525; minicom: 0845 688 2527; email: info@royaldeaf.org.uk; website: www.royaldeaf.org.uk)

Dental health

British Dental Association, 64 Wimpole Street, London W1G 8YS (tel: 020 7935 0875; email: enquiries@bda.org website: www.bda.org)

British Dental Health Foundation (BDHF), Smile House, 2 East Union Street, Rugby, Warwickshire CV22 6AJ (tel: 01788 546365; helpline: 0845 063 1188; website: www.dentalhealth.org.uk). Contact can also be made by completing an online enquiry form.

Depression

Befrienders Worldwide, c/o The Samaritans, Upper Mill, Kingston Road, Ewell, Surrey KT17 2AF (tel: 08457909090; minicom: 0845 790 9192; website: www.befrienders.org)

Depression Alliance, 20 Great Dover Street, London SE1 4LX (tel: 0845 123 2320; email: information@depressionalliance.org; website: www.depressionalliance.org)

Depression UK, c/o Self Help Nottingham, Ormiston House, 32–36 Pelham Street, Nottingham NG1 2EG (tel: 01912 399630; email: info@depressionuk.org; website: www.depressionuk.org)

Bipolar UK, 11 Belgrave Road, London SW1V 1RB (tel: 020 7391 6480; email: mdf@mdf.org.uk; website: www.mdf.org.uk)

Samaritans, The Upper Mill, Kingston Road, Ewell, Surrey KT17 2AF (tel: 020 8394 8300; 24-hour helpline: 0845 790 9090; see phone book for local number; email: admin@samaritans.org [general] jo@samaritans.org [helpline]; website: www.samaritans.org)

Diabetes

Diabetes Foundation, Macleod House, 10 Parkway, London NW1 7AA (tel: 020 7424 1000; website: www.diabetesfoundation.org.uk)

Diabetes UK, 10 Parkway, London NW1 7AA (tel: 020 7424 1000; helpline: 0845 120 2960; email: info@diabetes.org.uk or careline@diabetes.org.uk; website: www.diabetes.org.uk)

Disfigurement

Disfigurement Guidance Centre, PO Box 7, Cupar, Fife KY15 4PF (tel: 01337 870281)

Let's Face It, 72 Victoria Avenue, Westgate-on-Sea, Kent CT8 8BH (tel: 01843 833724; email: chrisletsfaceit@ aol.com; website: www.lets-face-it. org.uk)

Down's syndrome

Down's Syndrome Association, The Langdon Down Centre, 2a Langdon Park, Teddington TW11 9PS (helpline: 0333 1212 300; email: info@downs-syndrome.org.uk; website: www.downs-syndrome.org. uk)

Drugs

ADFAM National, 25 Corsham Street, London N1 6DR (tel: 020 7553 7640; email: admin@adfam.org.uk; website: www.adfam.org.uk)

Cocaine Anonymous UK, Talbot House, 204–226 Imperial Way, Rayners Lane, Harrow HA2 7HH (helpline: 0800 612 0225 [10am–10pm daily]; email: info@ cauk.org.uk or WTF@cauk.org.uk; website: www.cauk.org.uk)

DrugScope, Prince Consort House, 4th Floor, Asra House, 1 Long Lane, London SE1 4PG (tel: 020 7234 9730; email: info@drugscope.org.uk; website: www.drugscope.org.uk)

Early Break, 7–11 Bury Road, Radcliffe M26 2UG (Bury and Rochdale: 01617 233880; East Lancashire: 01282 604022; email: info@earlybreak.co.uk; website: www. earlybreak.co.uk)

Families Anonymous, Doddington and Rollo Community Association, Charlotte Despard Avenue, Battersea, London SW11 5HD (helpline: 0845 120 0660; website: www.famanon.org. uk)

FRANK (National Drugs Helpline), (24-hour helpline: 0800 776 600; text: 82111; website: www.talktofrank. com). Contact can also be made via an online chat facility.

Narcotics Anonymous (NA), 202 City Road, London EC1V 2PH (tel: 020 7251 4007; helpline: 0300 999 1212; website: www.ukna.org)

Turning Point, Standon House, 21 Mansell Street, London E1 8AA (tel: 020 7481 7600; email: info@ turning-point.co.uk; website: www. turning-point.co.uk)

Dyslexia

British Dyslexia Association, Unit 8, Bracknell Beeches, Old Bracknell Lane, Bracknell RG12 7BW (tel: 0845 251 9003; helpline: 0845 251 9002 [Mon–Fri, 10am–4pm and Tues–Wed, 5pm–7pm]; email: helpline@bdadyslexia.org.uk; website: www.bdadyslexia.org.uk)

Dyslexia Action, Egham Centre, Park House, Wick Road, Egham, Surrey TW20 0HH (tel: 01784 222300; email: info@dyslexiaaction. org.uk; website: www.dyslexiaaction. org.uk)

Dyspraxia

Dyspraxia Foundation, Administrator, 8 West Alley, Hitchin, Hertforshire SG5 1EG (tel: 01462 455016; helpline: 01462 454986 [Mon–Fri, 10am–1pm]; email: dyspraxia@dyspraxiafoundation.org. uk; website: www. dyspraxiafoundation.org.uk)

Dystonia

Dystonia Society, Second Floor, 89 Albert Embankment, London SE1 7TP (tel: 0845 458 6211; helpline: 0845 458 6322; email: info@dystonia. org.uk; website: www.dystonia.org. uk)

Eating disorders

Eating Disorders Association (Beat), 103 Prince of Wales Road, Norwich NR1 1DW (tel: 0300 123 3355; helpline: 0845 634 1414 [Mon– Fri, 10.30am–8.30pm and Sat 1.00pm–4.30pm]; Youth helpline: 0845 634 7650 [Mon–Fri, 4.30pm–8.30pm and Sat 1.00pm–4.30pm]; email: help@b-eat. co.uk or fyp@b-eat.co.uk (youth); website: www.b-eat.co.uk)

Eczema

National Eczema Society, Hill House, Highgate Hill, London N19 5NA (tel: 020 7281 3553; helpline: 0800 089 1122; email: info@eczema.org or helpline@eczema.org; website: www. eczema.org)

Endometriosis

National Endometriosis Society, 1&2 Manchester Street, London W1U 7LS (tel: 020 7222 2781; Crisis helpline: 0808 808 2227 [opening times vary depending on volunteer availability, see website for details]; email: admin@endometriosisuk.org; website: www.endometriosis-uk.org.uk)

Epidermolysis bullosa

Dystrophic Epidermolysis Bullosa Research Association (DEBRA), Debra House, 13 Wellington Business Park, Dukes Ride, Crowthorne, Berkshire RG45 6LS (tel: 01344 771961; specialist helplines – Clinical Specialist Team Leader: Jackie Denyer 020 7829 7808; Adult Nurse Consultant: Liz Pillay 07833 401111; EB Nurse Specialists in Scotland: Pippa Millican 01698 477777; email: debra@debra.org.uk; website: www. debra.org.uk)

Epilepsy

Epilepsy Action, New Anstey House, Gateway Drive, Yeadon, Leeds LS19 7XY (tel: 01132 108800; helpline: 0808 800 5050 [Mon–Thurs, 9am–4.30pm; Fri 9am–4pm]; email: epilepsy@epilepsy.org.uk orhelpline@epilepsy.org.uk; website: www.epilepsy.org.uk)

The National Society for Epilepsy, Chesham Lane, Chalfont St Peter, Buckinghamshire SL9 0RJ (tel: 01494601300; helpline: 01494 601400 [Mon–Fri, 10am–4pm]; website: www.epilepsysociety.org.uk)

Feet

Sole-Mates, 46 Gordon Road, London E4 6BU (tel: 020 8524 2423 [Mon, Tues, Thurs and Fri, 10am–3pm]. Send an sae for further information about sharing the cost of shoes for amputees and people with different sized feet.

Gambling

Gamblers Anonymous (GANON), c/o CVS Building, 5 Trafford Court, off Trafford Way, Doncaster DN1 1PN (helplines vary according to the day and time of the week, please check the website for details; website: www. gamblersanonymous.org.uk)

GamCare, 2nd Floor, 7–11 St John's Hill, London SW11 1TR (tel: 020 7801 7000; helpline: 0808 802 0133

[8am–12am daily]; email: info@gamcare.org.uk; website: www.gamcare.org.uk)

Growth problems

Child Growth Foundation, 21 Malvern Drive, Sutton Coldfield B76 1PZ (tel: 020 8912 0722; helpline: 020 8995 0257; email: info@childgrowthfoundation.org; website: www.childgrowthfoundation.org)

Restricted Growth Association (RGA), PO Box 15755, Solihull B93 3FY (tel: 0300 111 1970; email: office@restrictedgrowth.co.uk; website: www.restrictedgrowth.co.uk)

Guillain Barré syndrome

Guillain Barré Syndrome Support Group(GBS), Ground Floor, Woodholme House, Heckington Business Park, Station Road, Heckington, Sleaford NG34 9J (tel: 01529 469910; helpline: 0800 374 803; email: admin@gbs.org.uk; website: www.gbs.org.uk)

Haemophilia

* Haemophilia Society, First Floor, Petersham House, 57a Hatton Garden, London EC1N 8JG (tel: 020 7831 1020; helpline: 0800 018 6068; email: info@haemophelia.org.uk; website: www.haemophilia.org.uk)

Head injury

Headway – National Head Injuries Association Ltd, Bradbury House, 190 Bagnall Road, Old Basford, Nottingham, Nottinghamshire NG6 8SF (tel: 01159 240800; helpline: 0808 800 2244; email: enquiries@headway.org.uk or helpline@headway.org.uk; website: www.headway.org.uk)

Heart attacks/heart disease

British Heart Foundation, Greater London House, 180 Hampstead Road, London NW1 7AW (tel: 020 7554 0000; helpline: 0300 330 3311; website: www.bhf.org.uk). Contact can also be made by completing an online enquiry form.

HeartLine Association, 32 Little Heath, London SE7 8HU (tel: 03300224466; email: admin@heartline.org.uk; website: www.heartline.org.uk)

Hemiplegia

Hemi-Help, 6 Market Road, London N7 9PW (tel: 0845 120 3713, helpline: 0845 123 2372 [Mon–Fri, 10am–1pm during term time]; email: support@hemihelp.org.uk or helpline@hemihelp.org.uk; website: www.hemihelp.org.uk)

Herpes

Herpes Viruses Association (SPHERE), 41 North Road, London N7 9DP (helpline: 0845 123 2305; email: info@herpes.org.uk; website: www.herpes.org.uk)

Hodgkin's disease

Lymphoma Association, PO Box 386, Aylesbury, Buckinghamshire HP20 2GA (helpline: 0808 808 5555 [Mon–Thurs, 9am–6pm and Fri 9am–5pm]; email: information@lymphomas.org.uk; website: www.lymphoma.org.uk). Contact can also be made by completing an online enquiry form.

Huntington's disease

* Huntington's Disease Association, Suite 24, Liverpool Science Park ic1, 131 Mount Pleasant Liverpool L3 5TF (tel: 01513 315444; email: info@hda.org.uk; website: www.hda.org.uk)

Hyperactive children

Hyperactive Children's Support Group, 71 Whyke Lane, Chichester, West Sussex PO19 7PD (tel: 01243 539966 Mon–Fri, 2.30–4.30pm; email: hacsg@hacsg.org.uk; website: www.hacsg.org.uk). If writing, the Group requests that you enclose a large sae.

Hypertension

Coronary Artery Disease Research Association (CORDA), Chelsea Square, London SW3 6NP (tel: 020 7349 8686; email: info@corda.org.uk; website: www.corda.org.uk). Contact can also be made by completing an online enquiry form.

Hypogammaglobulinaemia

Primary Immunodeficiency Association: the charity is now closed but an archive of their information is available on www.ukpin.org.uk

Incontinence

Association for Continence Advice (ACA), Drumcross Hall, Bathgate, West Lothian EH48 4JT (tel: 01506 811077; email: aca@fitwise.co.uk; website: www.aca.uk.com)

Industrial diseases

Mesothelioma UK, Glenfield Hospital, Groby Road, Leicester LE3 9QP (helpline: 0800 169 2409; email: mesothelioma.uk@uhl-tr.nhs.uk; website: www.mesothelioma.uk.com)

Repetitive Strain Injury Association (RSIA), c/o Keytools Ltd, 2 Swangate, Charnham Park, Hungerford, Berkshire RG17 0YX (tel: 02380 294500; email: rsia@rsi.org.uk; website: www.rsi.org.uk)

Infantile hypercalcaemia

Williams Syndrome Foundation, 161 High Street, Tonbridge, Kent TN9 1BX (tel: 01732 365152; website: www.williams-syndrome.org.uk)

Infertility

Infertility Network UK, Charter House, 43 St Leonards Road, Bexhill-on-Sea, East Sussex TN40 1JA (Advice line: 0800 008 7464; email: admin@infertilitynetworkuk.com; website: www.infertilitynetworkuk.com)

Irritable bowel syndrome

The IBS Network 5, Unit 1.12 SOAR Works, 14 Knutton Road, Sheffield S5 9NU (tel: 01142 723253; email: info@ttheibsnetwork.org; website: www.theibsnetwork.org)

Kidney disease

* British Kidney Patient Association (BKPA), 3 The Windmills, St Mary's Close, Turk Street, Alton GU34 1EF (tel: 01420 541424; helpline: 01420 541424; email: info@britishkidney-pa.co.uk; website: www.britishkidney-pa.co.uk)

National Kidney Federation, The Point, Coach Road, Shireoaks, Worksop, Notts S81 8BW (tel: 01909 544999; helpline: 0845 601 0209; email: nkf@kidney.org.uk; website: www.kidney.org.uk)

Learning disability

Mencap, Mencap National Centre, 123 Golden Lane, London EC1Y 0RT (tel: 020 7454 0454; helpline: 0808

808 1111; email: help@mencap.org.
uk; website: www.mencap.org.uk)

Limb disorder

*British Limbless Ex-Servicemen's
Association (BLESMA),
185–187 High Road, Chadwell Heath,
Romford RM6 6NA (tel: 020 8590
1124; email: headquarters@blesma.
org; website: www.blesma.org)

Limbless Association, Unit 16,
Waterhouse Business Centre,
2 Cromar Way, Chelmsford
CM1 2QE (tel: 01245 216670/1/2;
email: enquiries@limbless-association.
org; website: www.limbless-
association.org)

Reach – The Association for Children
with Hand or Arm Deficiency, PO
Box54, Helston, Cornwall TR13 8WD
(tel: 0845 130 6225; email: reach@
reach.org.uk; website: www.reach.org.
uk)

STEPS (A National Association for
Families of Children with Congenital
Abnormalities), Wright House,
Crouchley Lane, Lymm, Cheshire
WA13 0AS (helpline: 01925 750271;
email: info@steps-charity.org.uk;
website: www.steps-charity.org.uk)

Literacy/learning difficulties

National Institute of Adult
Continuing Education (NIACE),
Chetwynd Street, Leicester LE1 7GE
(tel: 01162 044200; email: enquiries@
niace.org.uk; website: www.niace.org.
uk)

Liver disease

British Liver Trust, 2 Southampton
Road, Ringwood BH24 1HY (tel:
01425 481320; helpline: 0800 652
7330; email: info@britishlivertrust.
org.uk; website: www.britishlivertrust.
org.uk)

Lowe Syndrome Trust (UK Contact
Group) (LSA) 77 West Heath Road,
London NW3 7TH (tel: 020 7794
8858; email: lowetrust@gmail.com;
website: www.lowetrust.com)

Lupus

Lupus UK, St James House, Eastern
Road, Romford RM1 3NH (tel: 01708
731251; email: headoffice@lupusuk.
org.uk; website: www.lupusuk.com)

Raynaud's and Scleroderma
Association, 112 Crewe Road, Alsager,
Cheshire ST7 2JA (tel: 01270 872776;

freephone: 0800 917 2494; email:
info@raynauds.org.uk; website: www.
raynauds.org.uk)

Marfan syndrome

Marfan Association UK, Rochester
House, 5 Aldershot Road, Fleet,
Hampshire GU51 3NG (tel:
01252810472; email: contactus@
marfan-association.org.uk; website:
www.marfan-association.org.uk)

Mastectomy

Breast Cancer Care (BCC),
5–13 Great Suffolk Street, London
SE1 0NS (tel: 0845 092 0800; helpline:
0808 800 6000 [Mon–Fri, 9am–5pm
and Sat 10am–2pm]; email: info@
breastcancercare.org.uk; website:
www.breastcancercare.org.uk)

Ménière's disease

Ménière's Society, The Rookery,
Surrey Hills Business Park, Wotton,
Dorking, Surrey RH5 6QT (tel: 01306
876883; helpline: 0845 120 2975;
email: info@menieres.org.uk; website:
www.menieres.org.uk)

Meningitis

Meningitis Trust, Fern House, Bath
Road, Stroud, Gloucestershire
GL5 3TJ (tel: 01453 768000; 24-hour
helpline: 0808 801 0388; email: info@
meningitis-trust.org or
helpline@meningitis-trust.org;
website: www.meningitis-trust.org)

Menopause

The Daisy Network Premature
Menopause Support Group, PO Box
183, Rossendale, Lancashire BB4 6WZ
(email: daisy@daisynetwork.org.uk;
website: www.daisynetwork.org.uk)

Mental health

CARE (Self Unlimited), 13 & 14
Nursery Court, Kibworth Business
Park, Harborough Road, Leicester
LE8 0EX (tel: 01162 793225; email:
info@selfunlimited.co.uk; website:
www.selfunlimited.co.uk; online
contact form also available)

Mental Health Foundation,
Colechurch House, 1 London Bridge
Walk, London SE1 2SX (tel: 020 7803
1100; email: mhf@mhf.org.uk;
website: www.mentalhealth.org.uk)

Mind (National Association for
Mental Health), 15–19 Broadway,
Stratford, London E15 4BQ (tel: 020

8519 2122; Mind information line:
0300 123 3393; email: info@mind.org.
uk; website: www.mind.org.uk)

SANE (The Mental Health Charity),
1st Floor, Cityside House, 40 Adler
Street, London E1 1EE (tel: 020 7375
1002; helpline: 0845 767 8000; email:
info@sane.org.uk; website: www.sane.
org.uk; an online contact support
service is also available)

Metabolic disorders

CLIMB (Research Trust for Metabolic
Diseases in Children), Climb
Building, 176 Nantwich Road, Crewe
CW2 6BG (tel: 0845 241 2173 or 0800
652 3181; email: info.svcs@climb.org.
uk; website: www.climb.org.uk)

Migraine

Migraine Action Association
(formerly British Migraine
Association), Fourth Floor, 27 East
Street, Leicester LE1 6NB (tel: 01162
758317; website: www.migraine.org.
uk). Contact can also be made by
completing an online enquiry form.

Migraine Trust, 52–53 Russell Square,
London WC1B 4HP (tel: 020 7631
6970; email: info@migrainetrust.org;
website: www.migrainetrust.org)

Miscarriage

The Miscarriage Association,
17 Wentworth Terrace, Wakefield,
West Yorkshire WF1 3QW (tel: 01924
200795; helpline: 01924 200799
[Mon–Fri, 9am–4pm]; email: info@
miscarriageassociation.org.uk;
website: www.miscarriageassociation.
org.uk)

Tommy's, Nicholas House,
3 Laurence Pountney Hill, London
EC4R 0BB (tel: 020 7398 3400; Advice
line: 0800 014 7800; email: mailbox@
tommys.org; website: www.tommys.
org)

Motor neurone disease

* Motor Neurone Disease Association
(MND), PO Box 246, Northampton
NN1 2PR (tel: 01604 250505;
helpline: 0845 762 6262; email:
enquiries@mndassociation.org or
mndconnect@mndassociation.org;
website: www.mndassociation.org)

Multiple sclerosis

* Multiple Sclerosis Society, MS
National Centre, 372 Edgware Road,

London NW2 6ND (tel: 020 8438 0700; helpline: 0808 800 8000 [Mon–Fri, 9am–9pm]; email: info@ mssociety.org.uk orhelpline@mssociety.org.uk; website: www.mssociety.org.uk)

Muscular dystrophy

Muscular Dystrophy Campaign, 61 Southwark Street, London SE1 0HL (tel: 020 7803 4800; helpline: 0800 652 6352; email: info@ muscular-dystrophy.org; website: www.muscular-dystrophy.org)

Myasthenia gravis

Myasthenia Gravis Association, The College Business Centre, Uttoxeter New Road, Derby DE22 3WZ (tel: 01332290219; helpline: 0800 919 922; email: info@mga-charity.org; website: www.mgauk.org.uk)

Myotonic dystrophy

Myotonic Dystrophy Support Group, 19–21 Main Road, Gedling, Nottingham NG4 3HQ (tel: 01159 875869; helpline: 01159 870080; email: contact@mdsguk.org; website: www.mdsguk.org)

Narcolepsy

Narcolepsy Association (UK), PO Box 13842, Penicuik EH26 8WX (tel: 0845 450 0394; email: info@narcolepsy.org. uk; website: www.narcolepsy.org.uk)

Neurofibromatosis

The Neurofibromatosis Association, Quayside House, 38 High Street, Kingston on Thames, Surrey KT1 1HL (tel: 020 8439 1234; minicom: 020 8481 0492; email: info@nfauk.org; website: www.nfauk. org)

Organ donors

British Organ Donor Society (BODY), Balsham, Cambridge CB21 4DL (tel: 01223 893636; email: body@argonet.co.uk; website: body.orpheusweb.co.uk)

Osteoporosis

National Osteoporosis Society, Camerton, Bath BA2 0PJ (tel: 01761471771; helpline: 0845 130 3076; email: info@nos.org.uk; website: www.nos.org.uk). Contact can also be made by completing an online helpline enquiry form.

Paget's disease

National Association for the Relief of Paget's Disease, 323 Manchester Road, Walkden, Worsley, Manchester, M28 3HH (tel: 01617 994646; nurse helpline: 07713 568197; email: sue@paget.org.uk; website: www.paget.org.uk)

Parkinson's disease

* Parkinson's Disease Society of the United Kingdom, 215 Vauxhall Bridge Road, London SW1V 1EJ (tel: 020 7931 8080; helpline: 0808 800 0303 weekdays [9am–8pm and Saturdays 10am–2pm]; email: hello@ parkinsons.org.uk; website: www. parkinsons.org.uk)

Perthes' disease

Perthes Association, PO Box 773, Guildford GU1 1XN (tel: 01483 447122; helpline: 01483 306637; email: admin@perthes.org.uk; website: www.perthes.org.uk). Contact can also be made by completing an online enquiry form.

Phobias

Anxiety UK (National Phobics Society), Zion Community Resource Centre, 339 Stretford Road, Hulme, Manchester M15 4ZY (tel: 01612 267727: helpline: 0844 477 5774; email: info@anxietyuk.org.uk; website: www.anxietyuk.org.uk)

Pituitary disorders

Pituitary Foundation, 86 Colston Street, Bristol BS1 5BB (tel: 0845 450 0376; support line: 0845 450 0375; Endocrine Nurse helpline: 0845 450 0377 [Mondays 6pm–9pm and Thursdays 9am–1pm]; website: www. pituitary.org.uk). Contact can also be made by completing an online enquiry form.

Poliomyelitis

British Polio Fellowship, Eagle Office Centre, The Runway, South Ruislip, Middlesex HA4 6SE (tel: 0800 018 0586; email: info@britishpolio.org.uk; website: www.britishpolio.org.uk)

Post-natal

Association for Post-Natal Illness, 145 Dawes Road, Fulham, London SW6 7EB (tel: 020 7386 0868 [Mon–Fri, 10am–2pm]; email: info@ apni.org; website: www.apni.org)

Prader-Willi syndrome

Prader-Willi Syndrome 23 Boscobel Road, St Leonards on Sea, East Sussex TN38 0LX (tel: 01424 421684 email: admin@newdirections.gb.com; website: www.praderwillisyndrome. org.uk)

Pre-eclampsia

Pre-Eclampsia Society, c/o Dawn James, Rhianfa, Carmel, Caernarfon LL54 7RL (tel: 01286 882685; email: dawnjames@clara.co.uk; website: www.pre-eclampsiasociety.org.uk)

Psoriasis

Psoriasis Association, Dick Coles House, 2 Queensbridge, Northampton NN4 7BF (tel: 01604 251620; helpline: 0845 676 0076; email: mail@psoriasis-association.org. uk; website: www.psoriasisassociation. org.uk)

Raynaud's and Scleroderma Association, 112 Crewe Road, Alsager, Cheshire ST7 2JA (tel: 01270 872776; freephone: 0800 917 2494; email: info@raynauds.org.uk; website: www. raynauds.org.uk)

Retinitis pigmentosa

RP Fighting Blindness, PO Box 350, Buckingham MK18 5GZ (tel: 01280 821334; helpline: 0845 123 2354; email: info@rpfightingblindness.org. uk or helpline@rpfightingblindness.org.uk; website: www.rpfightingblindness.org. uk)

Rett syndrome

Rett Syndrome Association UK, Langham House West, Mill Street, Luton LU1 2NA (tel: 01582 798910; helpline: 01582 798911; email: info@ rettuk.org or support@rettuk.org; website: www.rettsyndrome.org.uk)

Reye's syndrome

National Reye's Syndrome Foundation of the UK (NRSF), 15 Nicholas Gardens, Pyrford, Woking, Surrey GU22 8SD (tel: 01932 346843; email: gordon@ reyessyndrome.co.uk; website: www. reyessyndrome.co.uk)

Sacoidosis

SILA (Sacoidosis and Interstitial Lung Association), c/o Department of Respiratory Medicine, 1st Floor,

Cheyne Wing, King's College Hospital, Denmark Hill SE5 9RS (tel: 020 7237 5912; email: info@sila.org.uk; website: www.sila.org.uk)

Schizophrenia

Rethink, 15th Floor, 89 Albert Embankment, London SE1 7TP (tel: 0300 5000 927; email; website: www.rethink.org; an online contact form is also available)

Scoliosis

Scoliosis Association (UK) (SAUK), 4 Ivebury Court, 325 Latimer Road, London W10 6RA (tel: 020 8964 5343; helpline: 020 8964 1166; email: info@sauk.org.uk; website: www.sauk.org.uk)

Seasonal affective disorder

SAD Association (SADA), PO Box 989, Steyning, West Sussex BN44 3HG (email: contact@sada.org.uk; website: www.sada.org.uk). If writing, the Association asks that you include an sae.

Sickle cell disease

Sickle Cell Society (SCS), 54 Station Road, London NW10 4UA (tel: 020 8961 7795; email: info@sicklecellsociety.org; website: www.sicklecellsociety.org). Contact can also be made by completing an online enquiry form.

Sjögren's syndrome

British Sjögren's Syndrome Association (BSSA), PO Box 15040, Birmingham B31 3DP (tel: 01214 780222; helpline: 01214 781133 [Mon–Fri, 9.30am–4pm]; website: www.bssa.uk.net)

Sleep disorders

British Snoring and Sleep Apnoea Association (BSSAA), Chapter House, 33 London Road, Reigate RH2 9HZ (tel: 01737 245638; email: info@britishsnoring.co.uk; website: www.britishsnoring.co.uk)

Smoking

Fag Ends (Roy Castle Lung Cancer Foundation), The Roy Castle Centre, 4–6 Enterprise Way, Wavertree Tech Park, Liverpool, Merseyside L13 1FB (helpline: 0800 195 2131 [Mon–Fri, 9.30am–8pm]; specialist pregnancy helpline: 0800 169 9169 [daily:

12.00pm–9.00pm]; website: www.stopsmoking.org.uk). Other language helplines are available; please see the website for details. Contact can also be made by completing an online enquiry form.

QUIT (National Society of Non-Smokers), 20–22 Curtain Road, London EC2A 3NF (tel: 020 7539 1700; helpline: 0800 002 200; email: counselling: stopsmoking@quit.org.uk; website: www.quit.org.uk). Bengali, Urdu, Punjabi, Gujarati, Hindi, Turkish and Kurdish speaking counsellors are also available – please see the website for the individual helpline numbers and times.

Solvent abuse

Re-Solv, 30a High Street, Stone, Staffordshire ST15 8AW (tel: 01785817885; email: information@re-solv.org; website: www.re-solv.org)

Speech and language difficulties

Association for All Speech-Impaired Children (AFASIC), 1st Floor, 20 Bowling Green Lane, London EC1R 0BD (tel: 020 7490 9410; helpline: 0845 355 5577; email: info@afasic.org.uk; website: www.afasic.org.uk). You can also contact the helpline by completing an online enquiry form.

British Stammering, 15 Old Ford Road, London E2 9PJ (tel: 020 8983 1003; helpline: 020 8880 6590; email: mail@stammering.org or info@stammering.org (helpline); website: www.stammering.org)

Royal Association for Deaf People (RAD), Century House South, Riverside Office Centre, North Station Road, Colchester, Essex CO1 1RE (tel: 0845 688 2525; minicom: 0845 688 2527; email: info@royaldeaf.org.uk; website: www.royaldeaf.org.uk)

Speakability, 1 Royal Street, London SE1 7LL (tel: 020 7261 9572; helpline: 0808 808 9572 [Mon–Fri, 10am–4pm]; email: speakability@speakability.org.uk; website: www.speakability.org.uk)

Spina bifida

SHINE, 42 Park Road, Peterborough PE1 2UQ (tel: 01733 555988; email:

helpline@asbah.org; website: www.shinecharity.org)

Spinal injuries

Spinal Injuries Association, SIA House, 2 Trueman Place, Oldbrook, Milton Keynes MK6 2HH (tel: 0845 678 6633; counselling: 0800 980 0501 [Mon–Fri, 9.30am–4.30pm]; email: sia@spinal.co.uk; website: www.spinal.co.uk)

Stress

The Coronary Artery Disease Research Association (CORDA), Chelsea Square, London SW3 6NP (tel: 020 7349 8686; email: info@corda.org.uk; website: www.corda.org.uk)

Stroke

Stroke Association, Stroke House, 240 City Road, London EC1V 2PR (tel: 020 7566 0300; helpline: 0303 303 3100; textphone: 020 7251 9096; email: info@stroke.org.uk website: www.stroke.org.uk)

Thalassaemia

United Kingdom Thalassaemia Society (UKTS), 19 The Broadway, Southgate Circus, London N14 6PH (tel: 020 8882 0011; email: office@ukts.org; website: www.ukts.org)

Thrombocytopenia with absent radii

TAR Syndrome Support Group, for further information please contact SusyEdwards (email: SusyEdwards@hotmail.co.uk; website: www.ivh.se/TAR)

Tinnitus

British Tinnitus Association (BTA), Ground Floor, Unit 5, Acorn Business Park, Woodseats Close, Sheffield S8 0TB (tel: 01142 509922; freephone: 0800 018 0527; minicom: 01142 585694; email: info@tinnitus.org.uk; website: www.tinnitus.org.uk)

Action on Hearing Loss 19–23 Featherstone Street, London EC1Y 8SL (tel: 020 7296 8000; text: 020 7296 8001; information line: 0808 808 0123 [voice] 0808 808 9000 [text]; email: informationonline@hearingloss.org.uk; website: www.actionhearingloss.org.uk)

Tourettes syndrome

Tourettes Action, Kings Court, 91–93 High Street, Camberley, Surrey GU15 3RN (tel: 01276 482903; helpline: 0300 777 8427; email: admin@tourettes-action.org.uk; website: www.tourettes-action.org.uk)

Tracheo-oesophagealfistula

Aid for Children with Tracheotomies (ACT), Lammas Cottage, Stathe, Bridgwater, Somerset TA7 0JL. For further information please contact the secretary Amanda Saunders (tel: 01823 698398; email: support@ actfortrachykids.com; website: www. actfortrachykids.com)

Tracheo-Oesophageal Fistula Support Group (TOFS), St George's Centre, 91 Victoria Road, Netherfield, Nottingham NG4 2NN (tel: 01159 613092; email: info@tofs.org.uk; website: www.tofs.org.uk)

Tranquillizers

Tasha Foundation, 112 High Street, Brentford, Middlesex TW8 8AT (tel: 020 8560 4583; email: enquiries@ tasha-foundation.org.uk; website: www.tasha-foundation.org.uk)

Tuberous sclerosis

Tuberous Sclerosis Association, Toad Hall, White Rose Lane, Woking, Surrey GU22 7LB (tel: 01214 456970; website: www.tuberous-sclerosis.org)

Turner syndrome

Turner Syndrome Support Society, 12 Simpson Court, 11 South Avenue, Clydebank Business Park, Clydebank G81 2NR (tel: 01419 528006; helpline: 0300 111 7520; website: www.tss.org. uk)

Urostomy

Urostomy Association, 4 Demontfort Way, Uttoxeter ST14 8XY (tel: 01889563191; email: secretary.ua@ classmail.co.uk; website: www. urostomyassociation.org.uk)

Williams syndrome

Williams Syndrome Foundation, 161 High Street, Tonbridge, Kent TN9 1BX (tel: 01732 365152; website: www.williams-syndrome.org.uk)

Index